ISBN 0–679–02693–2

Fodor's Australia & New Zealand

Editors: Chelsea Mauldin and Marcy Pritchard
Contributors: Bob Blake, Sharon Cohen, Terry Durack, Betty Forrest, Peter Forestal, Echo Garrett, Michael Gebicki, Walter Glaser, Lorraine Ironside, Chips Mackinolty, David McGonigal, Bevin McLaughlin, Jacki Passmore, Tracy Patruno, Mary Ellen Schultz, Joan Storey, Ross Terrill, Nancy Van Itallie, Jacqueline van Santen
Creative Director: Fabrizio La Rocca
Cartographer: David Lindroth
Illustrator: Karl Tanner
Cover Photograph: Paul Steel/Stock Market

Design: Vignelli Associates

Special Sales

Fodor's Travel Publications are available at special discounts for bulk purchases for sales promotions or premiums. Special editions, including personalized covers, excerpts of existing guides, and corporate imprints, can be created in large quantities for special needs. For more information contact your local bookseller or write to Special Markets, Fodor's Travel Publications, 201 East 50th St., New York, NY 10022. Inquiries from Canada should be directed to your local Canadian bookseller or sent to Marketing Dept., Random House of Canada, Ltd., 1265 Aerowood Dr., Mississauga, ON L4W 1B9. Inquiries from the United Kingdom should be sent to Fodor's Travel Publications, 20 Vauxhall Bridge Rd., London, England SW1V2SA.

MANUFACTURED IN THE UNITED STATES OF AMERICA
10 9 8 7 6 5 4 3 2 1

Contents

Foreword	*vii*
Highlights '95	*xi*
Fodor's Choice	*xiv*
Introduction to Australia	*xxiv*
Introduction to New Zealand	*xxix*

1 Essential Information   *1*

Before You Go *2*

Australian Government Tourist Offices *2*
New Zealand Government Tourist Offices *2*
U.S. Government Travel Briefings *2*
Tour Groups *3*
Package Tours for Independent Travelers *5*
When to Go *6*
Festivals and Seasonal Events *9*
What to Pack *11*
Taking Money Abroad *12*
Getting Money from Home *13*
Currency *13*
What Australia Will Cost *14*
What New Zealand Will Cost *14*
Passports and Visas *15*
Customs and Duties *16*
Traveling with Cameras, Camcorders, and Laptops *18*
Language *18*
Staying Healthy *19*
Insurance *19*
Car Rentals *21*
Rail Passes *23*
Bus Passes *24*
Student and Youth Travel *24*
Traveling with Children *26*
Hints for Travelers with Disabilities *27*
Hints for Older Travelers *29*
Hints for Gay and Lesbian Travelers *30*
Contacts *30*
Further Reading: Australia *31*
Further Reading: New Zealand *32*

Arriving and Departing *32*

From North America by Plane *32*
From the United Kingdom by Plane *35*

Staying in Australia *35*

Geography *35*
Getting Around Australia *36*
Telephones *38*
Mail *39*
Tipping *40*
Opening and Closing Times *40*
Shopping *40*
Sports and the Outdoors *41*
Beaches *43*
Dining *43*
Lodging *45*

Staying in New Zealand *46*

Geography *46*
Getting Around New Zealand *47*
Telephones *48*
Mail *48*
Tipping *48*
Opening and Closing Times *48*
Shopping *48*
Sports and the Outdoors *49*
Beaches *52*
Dining *53*
Lodging *53*
Credit Cards *54*

Great Itineraries *54*

Highlights of Australia and New Zealand *54*
Australia's Main Cities *55*
Wine-Tasting Odyssey *55*
Reef and Rock *56*
Flora and Fauna Around Australia *57*
Highlights of New Zealand's North and South Islands *58*
Experiencing New Zealand *58*
South Island Adventure Tour *59*

2 **Sydney**   60

3 **New South Wales**   118

4 **Canberra**   155

5 **Melbourne and Victoria**   174

6 **Tasmania**   240

7 **Queensland**   268

8 **The Great Barrier Reef**   327

9 **Adelaide and South Australia**   352

Fodor's 95
Australia &
New Zealand

PRAISE FOR FODOR'S GUIDES

"Fodor's guides . . . are an admirable blend of the cultural and the practical."

—The Washington Post

"Researched by people chosen because they lived or have lived in the country, well-written, and with good historical sections . . . Obligatory reading for millions of tourists."

—The Independent, *London*

"Usable, sophisticated restaurant coverage, with an emphasis on good value."

—Andy Birsh, Gourmet restaurant columnist, quoted by Gannett News Service

"Packed with dependable information."

—Atlanta Journal Constitution

"Fodor's always delivers high quality . . . thoughtfully presented . . . thorough."

—Houston Post

"Valuable because of their comprehensiveness."

—Minneapolis Star-Tribune

Fodor's Travel Publications, Inc.
New York • Toronto • London • Sydney • Auckland

10 The Red Centre *389*

11 Darwin, the Top End, and the Kimberley *409*

12 Perth and Western Australia *436*

13 Auckland and the North *472*

14 Rotorua to Wellington *504*

15 The South Island *531*

16 Adventure Vacations *563*

Index *581*

Maps

Australia *xviii–xix*
New Zealand *xx*
Distances and Flying Times *xxi*
World Time Zones *xxii–xxiii*
Sydney Harbour *69*
Central Sydney *72–73*
Sydney Beaches *95*
Central Sydney Dining and Lodging *100–101*
Sydney Area Dining *102*
New South Wales *120–121*
The Blue Mountains *124*
The North Coast *140*
Canberra *160*
Canberra Dining and Lodging *166*
Downtown Melbourne *181*
Downtown Melbourne Dining and Lodging *192*
Metropolitan Melbourne Dining and Lodging *193*
Melbourne Environs *206*
Victoria *212–213*
Tasmania *242–243*
Downtown Hobart *246*
Queensland *270–271*
Brisbane *275*
Brisbane Dining and Lodging *281*
The Sunshine Coast *297*
North Queensland Coast *316*
Great Barrier Reef *329*
South Australia *354*
Adelaide *357*
Adelaide Dining and Lodging *364*
Barossa Valley *378*
The Red Centre *391*
Alice Springs *394*

The Top End and the Kimberley *412–413*
Darwin *415*
Western Australia *438*
Perth *442*
Perth Dining and Lodging *448*
Auckland *477*
Auckland Dining and Lodging *484*
Northland and the Bay of Islands *492*
The Coromandel Peninsula *500*
Central North Island *508*
Napier *519*
Wellington *525*
Marlborough, Nelson, and the West Coast *535*
Christchurch *544*
Canterbury *548*
Southland, Otago, and Stewart Island *554*

Foreword

While every care has been taken to ensure the accuracy of the information in this guide, the passage of time will always bring change, and, consequently, the publisher cannot accept responsibility for errors that may occur.

All prices and opening times quoted here are based on information supplied to us at press time. Hours and admission fees may change, however, and the prudent traveler will avoid inconvenience by calling ahead.

Fodor's wants to hear about your travel experiences, both pleasant and unpleasant. When a hotel or restaurant fails to live up to its billing, let us know and we will investigate the complaint and revise our entries where the facts warrant it.

Send your letters to the editors of Fodor's Travel Publications, 201 East 50th Street, New York, NY 10022.

Highlights'95 and Fodor's Choice

Highlights '95

Australia The Australian economy is recovering from recession but despite the increasing numbers of visitors from overseas, there are few other major developments to report in the tourism industry. The Sydney and Melbourne hotel markets remain oversupplied so there are significant discounts available on four- and five-star rooms, especially on weekends.

Since the 1992 absorption of Australian Airlines by Qantas Airways, Australia's major international carrier has become a complete international and domestic carrier. Although Australian Airlines has disappeared, some of its regional subsidiary airlines retain their names. The other major domestic carrier, Ansett Australia, began international service in September 1993 with weekly flights to Bali. Ansett's service to Osaka begins in September 1994, and the airline will be operating flights to Singapore, Hong Kong, and South Korea by the end of 1994.

Northern Australia is becoming more and more popular as a point of entry. Recent statistics show that Cairns is attracting more international arrivals, primarily at the expense of Melbourne, while the number of visitors arriving at Sydney and Brisbane is growing slowly.

The **Northern Territory Tourist Commission** has privatized its operations and now works through a series of specialized tour companies designated Northern Territory Travel Stations. General inquiries and reservations can still be made through the commission's head office in Alice Springs (tel. 1-800/80–3833).

The **Kakadu National Park Visitors Information Centre** opened mid-1994 and houses state-of-the-art audiovisual displays and other exhibits on the park, which has the world's largest variety of birdlife and diverse ecosystems. A special feature will be interpretive information provided by the Aboriginal traditional owners of Kakadu.

Ayers Rock Resort has a new central reservations line for all five of its accommodation areas (tel. 089/56–2737). The resort has also introduced several new tours that broaden its coverage of the desert experience: Camp out under the desert stars while still enjoying breakfast in bed and aperitifs with dinner, hike the remote Petermann ranges, or go on a seven-day trip into Pitjantjatjara land to learn about Aboriginal life and culture.

Sydney is now the home port of the Cunard Line's 530-passenger *Crown Monarch,* the first four-star vessel to be permanently based in Australia. Contact **Cunard** (146 Arthur St., North Sydney, NSW 2060, tel. 02/956–7777, fax 02/956–6229, or 555 Fifth Ave., New York, NY 10017-2453) for information on cruises up the east coast and through the Great Barrier Reef.

Dreamworld, the excellent amusement park on Queensland's Gold Coast, recently introduced a new ride called Wipeout. The only attraction of its kind in the Southern Hemisphere, the ride pays homage to Australia's surf culture by subjecting passengers to 2.5 g's of force as they twist and tumble through an experience some have described as "riding a tidal wave while strapped to an armchair."

Tasmania's newest resort, **Freycinet Lodge,** is set on the east coast's Freycinet Peninsula. The lodge's 38 cabins offer guests access to a remarkable range of outdoor activities including hiking, climbing, scuba diving, and fishing.

Rivaling the spectacle of the world-famous wild dolphins of Monkey Mia, Western Australia's North West Cape offers a year-round show for marine enthusiasts. In mid-winter, huge manta rays migrate through the narrow lagoons north of Exmouth Gulf. Spring sees the migration of humpback whales, and in summer the loggerhead and hawksbill turtles begin nesting. From March to May, following the coral spawning, the giant whale sharks that gather off the coast form the world's largest such population. This abundance of wildlife provides an unforgettable spectacle for those who snorkel, scuba, or take a light aircraft charter over the Indian Ocean waters of **Ningaloo Marine Park,** 4,000 square kilometers (10,360 square miles) of some of Australia's most pristine reef.

The local Western Australian airline **Skywest** (tel. 09/334–2288) has inaugurated a thrice-weekly flight to the new $1-million **Shark Bay Airport,** which serves the Monkey Mia world heritage area. Using 18-seater Jetstream 31 aircraft, the two-hour flight is a timesaving alternative to the 805-kilometer (500-mile) road journey from Perth. The air service provides easy access to the dolphin area and the rare stromatolites at Hamelin Pool.

About 25 kilometers (15.5 miles) north of Perth, a multimillion-dollar hotel, condominium, golf course, and clubhouse development at Joondalup, one of the state's fastest-growing coastal suburbs, is due for completion in 1995. The **Joondalup Resort** will offer a 27-hole golf course, a 140-bed luxury hotel with gym and sauna, a clubhouse, and condominiums.

The spirit of the Dreamtime has quietly descended on Subiaco, a suburb of Perth. **Indigenart** (115 Hay St., tel. 09/381–1705, fax 09/381–1708) is a unique gallery and Aboriginal cultural center where visitors can view the works of more than 100 artists from 15 Aboriginal communities in Western Australia, South Australia, and the Northern Territory, as well as talk with Aboriginal artists about their work, hear Aboriginal music played, and learn to play the didgeridoo.

New Zealand The number of international arrivals in New Zealand continues to grow in a world increasingly aware of the benefits of fresh air and sparkling water. Despite a low overall inflation rate, prices in the tourism industry—especially for hotels and guided tours—have jumped by around 10%. However, the declining value of the New Zealand dollar means that a holiday in New Zealand is no more expensive this year.

New Zealand is to get its first casino: The $30-million **Christchurch Casino,** on Victoria Street opposite the Parkroyal Hotel, should bring new life to the heart of the garden city when it opens at the end of 1994.

Fodor's Choice

No two people will agree on what makes a perfect vacation, but it's fun and helpful to know what others think. We hope you'll have the chance to experience some of Fodor's Choices yourself while visiting Australia and New Zealand. For detailed information about each entry, refer to the appropriate chapter in the guidebook.

Beach Resorts

Great Barrier Reef	Heron Island Resort (*$$$–$$$$*)
	Hayman Island Resort (*$$*)
	Lady Elliot Island (*$–$$*)
NSW	Aanuka Beach Resort, Coffs Harbour (*$$$*)
Queensland	Sheraton Mirage, Southport (*$$$$*)
	Hyatt Regency Resort, Coolum Beach (*$$$*)
Top End	Cable Beach Club, Broome (*$$$$*)
Western Australia	Radisson Observation City Resort Hotel, Perth (*$$$$*)

Dining

Adelaide	Blake's (*$$$$*)
Brisbane	Pier 9 (*$$–$$$*)
Canberra	Fringe Benefits (*$$$$*)
Darwin	Hanuman (*$$–$$$*)
Hobart	Dear Friends (*$$$$*)
Melbourne	Paul Bocuse Restaurant (*$$$$*)
	Marchetti's Latin (*$$$*)
Perth	San Lorenzo (*$$$*)
	Iguana (*$$*)
Sydney	Kamogawa (*$$$$*)
	Rockpool (*$$$$*)
	Bayswater Brasserie (*$$*)
Auckland	The French Café (*$$$*)
	Cin Cin on Quay (*$$*)
Christchurch	Sign of the Takahe (*$$$$*)
	Espresso 124 (*$$*)

Wellington Le Petit Lyon (*$$$$*)

Brasserie Flipp (*$$$*)

City Lodging

Adelaide Hyatt Regency Adelaide (*$$$$*)

Brisbane Beaufort Heritage (*$$$$*)

Darwin Beaufort Hotel (*$$$$*)

Hobart Sheraton Hobart Hotel (*$$$$*)

Lenna of Hobart (*$$$*)

Melbourne The Regent (*$$$$*)

Windsor Hotel (*$$$$*)

Perth Parmelia Hilton (*$$$$*)

Sydney Park Hyatt (*$$$$*)

The Regent (*$$$$*)

Auckland The Regent (*$$$$*)

Devonport Villa (*$$*)

Christchurch Parkroyal Christchurch (*$$$$*)

Riverview Lodge (*$$*)

Wellington Parkroyal Wellington (*$$$$*)

Country Lodging

New South Wales Cleopatra, Blue Mountains (*$$$$*)

Taylors, North Coast (*$$$*)

Jemby Rinjah Lodge, Blue Mountains (*$$*)

Reynella, Snowy Mountains (*$$*)

Wollombi House, Hunter Valley (*$$*)

Northern Territory and the Kimberley Sails in the Desert, Uluru National Park (*$$$$*)

Seven Spirit Bay, Cobourg Peninsula (*$$$$*)

El Questro Cattle Station (*$$–$$$$*)

Queensland Silky Oaks Lodge, Mossman Gorge (*$$$$*)

South Australia The Lodge, Barossa Valley (*$$$$*)

Mount Lofty Country House, Adelaide Hills (*$$$$*)

Apple Tree Cottage and Gum Tree Cottage, Adelaide Hills (*$$*)

Collingrove, Barossa Valley (*$$*)

Victoria Quamby Homestead, West Coast (*$$*)

Western Australia	Cape Lodge, Margaret River (*$$$*)
	The Esplanade Hotel, Albany (*$$$*)
New Zealand	Huka Lodge, Lake Taupo, North Island (*$$$$*)
	Lake Brunner Sporting Lodge, Mitchells, near Greymouth, South Island (*$$$$*)
	Puka Park Lodge, Coromandel Peninsula, North Island (*$$$$*)
	Millbrook Resort, near Queenstown, South Island (*$$$$*)
	California Guest House, Nelson, South Island (*$$$*)
	Lake Moeraki Wilderness Lodge, South Island (*$$$*)

National Park Attractions

The Forests of Washpool National Park, New South Wales

The Three Sisters formation in Blue Mountains National Park, New South Wales

Rain forest in Bellenden Ker National Park, Queensland

Ayers Rock and the Olgas in Uluru National Park, Red Centre

Jim Jim and Twin falls in Kakadu National Park, Top End

Tiger-striped, beehive-shaped sandstone hills in Purnululu National Park, The Kimberley, Western Australia

Twelve Apostles formation in Port Cambell National Park, Victoria

Lake Waikaremoana, Urewera National Park, North Island, New Zealand

The Milford Track, Mitre Peak, and Milford Sound, Fiordland National Park, South Island, New Zealand

Mount Cook and Tasman Glacier, Mount Cook National Park, South Island, New Zealand

Special Moments

Adelaide and S. Australia	Afternoon tea in the Adelaide Hills
	The drive into Seppeltsfield, Barossa Valley
Victoria	Coffee at an open-air café in Lygon Street, Carlton, on the bohemian fringe of inner-city Melbourne
	Watching the whales at Warrnambool
New South Wales	Mount Wilson in autumn, Blue Mountains
	Riding the Zig Zag Railway, Blue Mountains
	The view from Wentworth Falls, Blue Mountains
Queensland	The train ride through mountains and rain forest from Cairns to Kuranda
	The coastal drive from Cairns to Port Douglas

The first view of Heron Island by helicopter

Red Centre Sunrise/sunset over Ayers Rock

Walking through King's Canyon

Sydney Bondi Beach on a warm summer evening

Ferry ride to Manly

Tasmania Saturday morning at Salamanca Market, Hobart

A late-afternoon walk through Allendale Gardens (near Smithton)

Top End Studying the Aboriginal rock art at Nourlangie Rock, Kakadu National Park

A sunset cruise on Yellow Water, Kakadu National Park

Western Australia Spring wildflowers in King's Park, Perth

Twilight yacht races on the Swan River, Perth

Wine tasting at the vineyards of Margaret River

New Zealand The Maori choir, St. Faith's Church, Rotorua

Kayaking with the dolphins off Abel Tasman National Park, South Island

Sampling smoked snapper at Nature Smoke, Mapua, South Island

Wildlife Attractions

S. Australia Walking among the sea lions, Seal Bay, Kangaroo Island

N.S.W. Taronga Park Zoo, Sydney

Top End Crocodile-spotting on the Yellow Waters cruise, Kakadu

Queensland Cuddling a koala at Lone Pine Koala Sanctuary, Brisbane

Hand-feeding giant potato cod at Cod Hole off Lizard Island, Great Barrier Reef

Watching the marine mammals perform at the Gold Coast's Seaworld at the Spit, Southport

Victoria Petting the wild kangaroos at Zumstein in the Grampians

Tasmania Watching Tasmanian devils feed at Cradle Mountain Lodge

Western Australia Hand-feeding wild dolphins at Monkey Mia

Swimming with whale sharks at Exmouth

New Zealand The gannet colony, Cape Kidnappers, North Island

Cruising with sperm whales off Kaikoura, South Island

The royal albatrosses, Taiaroa Head, South Island

Australia

INDONESIA   Timor

Timor Sea

Darwin ✪ ✈

Katherine

INDIAN OCEAN

Kununurra

KIMBERLEY REGION

Broome Derby *Great Northern Hwy.* Halls Creek

NORTHERN TE

TANAMI DESERT WILDLIFE SANCTUARY

Port Hedland

GREAT SANDY DESERT

Dampier

RUDALL RIVER NATIONAL PARK

Exmouth

Newman

Tropic of Capricorn

Yulara (Ayers Rock)

WESTERN AUSTRALIA

BROWNE RANGE NATURE RESERVE

Carnarvon

North West Coastal Hwy.

Meekatharra

GREAT VICTORIA DESERT

GREAT VICTORIA DESERT NATURE RESERVE

Coober Pedy

Geraldton

Kalgoorlie

NULLARBOR PLAIN

Ce

Perth ✈ ✪

Merredin

Eyre Hwy.

Fremantle

Bunbury

Narrogin

Busselton

Esperance

Great Australian Bight

Albany

N

SOUTHERN OCEAN

0 _____ 400 miles
0 _____ 600 km

Bass Strait

King Island

Burnie

Launceston

St. Marys

Strahan TASMANIA

Hobart ✈ ✪

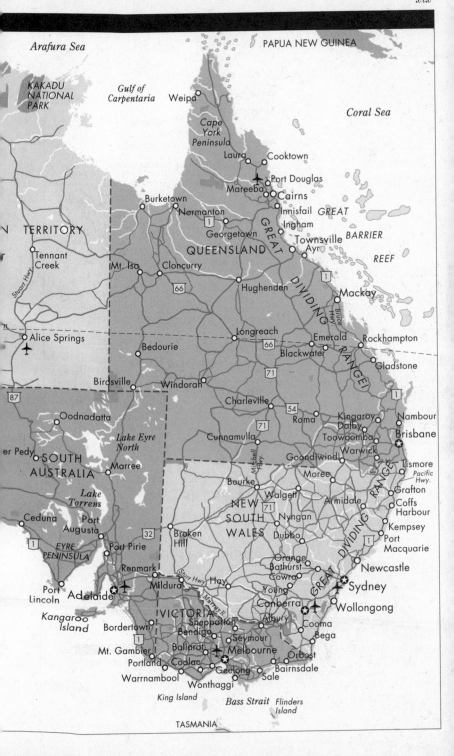

New Zealand

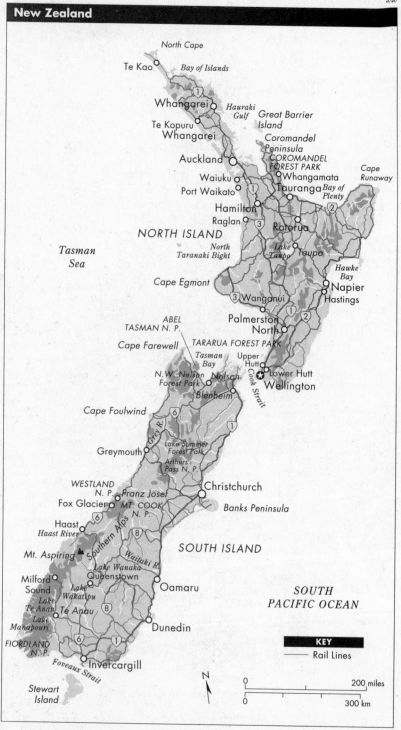

North Cape
Te Kao
Bay of Islands
Whangarei
Hauraki
Gulf
Great Barrier
Island
Te Kopuru
Whangarei
Coromandel
Peninsula
COROMANDEL
FOREST PARK
Auckland
Waiuku
Whangamata
Port Waikato
Tauranga
Bay of
Plenty
Cape
Runaway
Hamilton
Raglan
Rotorua
NORTH ISLAND
Tasman
Sea
North
Taranaki Bight
Lake
Taupo
Taupo
Hawke
Bay
Cape Egmont
Wanganui
Napier
Hastings
Palmerston
North
ABEL
TASMAN N. P.
TARARUA FOREST PARK
Cape Farewell
Tasman
Bay
Upper
Hutt
N.W. Nelson
Forest Park
Nelson
Lower Hutt
Wellington
Blenheim
Cook
Strait
Cape Foulwind
Grey R.
Lake Summer
Forest Park
Greymouth
Arthurs
Pass N. P.
Christchurch
WESTLAND
N. P.
Franz Josef
Fox Glacier
MT. COOK
N. P.
Banks Peninsula
Haast
Haast River
Southern Alps
Mt. Aspiring
Waitaki R.
SOUTH ISLAND
Lake Wanaka
Queenstown
Oamaru
SOUTH
PACIFIC OCEAN
Milford
Sound
Lake
Wakatipu
Lake
Te Anau
Te Anau
Dunedin
Lake
Manapouri
FIORDLAND
N. P.
Invercargill
Foveaux Strait
Stewart
Island

N

0   200 miles

0   300 km

KEY
—— Rail Lines

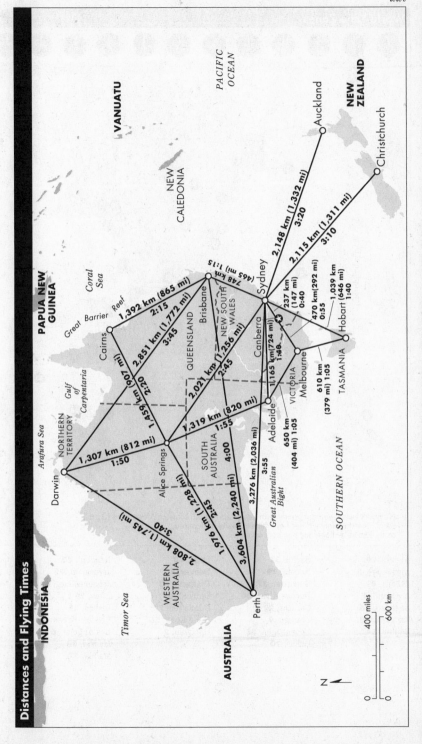

Distances and Flying Times

INDONESIA

Timor Sea

Arafura Sea

PAPUA NEW GUINEA

Coral Sea

PACIFIC OCEAN

VANUATU

NEW CALEDONIA

NEW ZEALAND

Auckland

Christchurch

2,148 km (1,332 mi) 3:20

2,115 km (1,311 mi) 3:10

Great Barrier Reef

Cairns

1,459 km (907 mi) 2:20

1,392 km (865 mi) 2:15

2,851 km (1,772 mi) 3:45

Brisbane

QUEENSLAND

NEW SOUTH WALES

748 km (465 mi) 1:15

Sydney

237 km (147 mi) 0:40

470 km (292 mi) 0:55

1,039 km (646 mi) 1:40

Hobart

TASMANIA

Canberra

1,165 km (724 mi) 1:40

610 km (379 mi) 1:05

Melbourne

VICTORIA

Gulf of Carpentaria

Darwin

NORTHERN TERRITORY

1,307 km (812 mi) 1:50

Alice Springs

1,319 km (820 mi) 1:55

2,021 km (1,256 mi) 2:45

650 km (404 mi) 1:05

Adelaide

SOUTH AUSTRALIA

Great Australian Bight

1,976 km (1,228 mi) 2:45

2,808 km (1,745 mi) 3:40

3,604 km (2,240 mi) 3:55

3,276 km (2,036 mi) 4:00

WESTERN AUSTRALIA

Perth

AUSTRALIA

SOUTHERN OCEAN

N

0   400 miles

0   600 km

World Time Zones

MONDAY
SUNDAY

International Date Line

+12 +13

-9

❸ 3

-10

-11

-10

❷ 2

+11

+12

❶ 1

+11 +12 - -11 -10 -9 -8 -7 -6 -5 -4 -3 -2

-4

-3

0

-1

㉕ 25 0

-5 -4

❼ 7

-7

⑭ 14 ⑮ 15

❹ 4

⑬ 13

-3:30

❺ 5 -8

❽ 8

❾ 9

⑰ 17 ⑯ 16

❻ 6

-6

⑩ 10

⑪ 11

⑱ 18

❿ 12

-4

⑲ 19

㉒ 22

⑳ 20

-5

-4

-3

㉓ 23

-3

㉑ 21

㉔ 24

Numbers below vertical bands relate each zone to Greenwich Mean Time (0 hrs.).
Local times frequently differ from these general indications,
as indicated by light-face numbers on map.

Algiers, **29**	Berlin, **34**	Delhi, **48**	Istanbul, **40**
Anchorage, **3**	Bogotá, **19**	Denver, **8**	Jerusalem, **42**
Athens, **41**	Budapest, **37**	Djakarta, **53**	Johannesburg, **44**
Auckland, **1**	Buenos Aires, **24**	Dublin, **26**	Lima, **20**
Baghdad, **46**	Caracas, **22**	Edmonton, **7**	Lisbon, **28**
Bangkok, **50**	Chicago, **9**	Hong Kong, **56**	London (Greenwich), **27**
Beijing, **54**	Copenhagen, **33**	Honolulu, **2**	Los Angeles, **6**
	Dallas, **10**		Madrid, **38**
			Manila, **57**

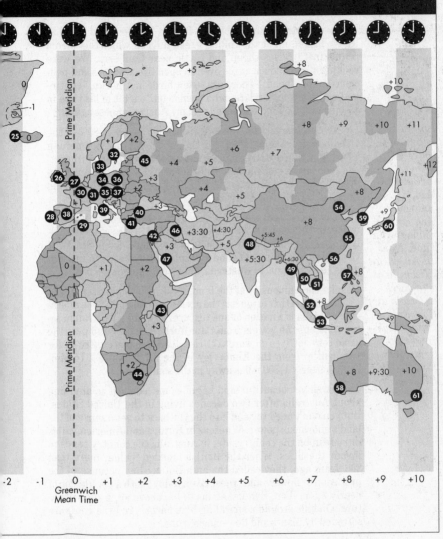

Mecca, **47**

Mexico City, **12**

Miami, **18**

Montréal, **15**

Moscow, **45**

Nairobi, **43**

New Orleans, **11**

New York City, **16**

Ottawa, **14**

Paris, **30**

Perth, **58**

Reykjavík, **25**

Rio de Janeiro, **23**

Rome, **39**

Saigon (Ho Chi Minh City), **51**

San Francisco, **5**

Santiago, **21**

Seoul, **59**

Shanghai, **55**

Singapore, **52**

Stockholm, **32**

Sydney, **61**

Tokyo, **60**

Toronto, **13**

Vancouver, **4**

Vienna, **35**

Warsaw, **36**

Washington, D.C., **17**

Yangon, **49**

Zürich, **31**

Introduction to Australia

By Ross Terrill

Australian-born Ross Terrill is the author of The Australians *and many books on China, including* Mao, Madame Mao, *and* China in Our Time. *Now an American citizen, he is a research associate at Harvard University's Fairbanks Center for East Asian Research.*

I love Australia for the birds," Rupert Murdoch said to me as we looked up at the rolling green hills on which this media magnate raises sheep and cattle near Canberra. We were cooking steak and sausages over an open fire as swans and pelicans flew overhead. "There are so few birds in America," continued my fellow expatriate, who spends quite a bit of his time in New York. "Coming out here I feel my Australianness again."

For all their cherished "bushman" legend, however, 80% of the 16 million Australians cluster in the suburbs of the "Boomerang Coast"—a thin arc stretching 1,000 miles around the southeastern seaboard from Adelaide to Brisbane. Few Australians have visited much of their huge, empty land, yet their souls dwell in the dusty, Technicolor Outback.

To realize the sparseness of the sixth-largest country in the world, imagine a land the size of the United States with virtually no people for the first 2,000 miles inland from the West Coast—as if nothing but sand and spinifex lay between Los Angeles and Chicago. In Australia, sheep outnumber people.

Despite the immensity of the land, local variations in style, and a sectionalism that often has the six states snarling at one another, Australia is a nation of one texture. The same Australian accent flattens the vowels from Cape York to Hobart and puts the same cozy suffixes on words ("Brissy" for Brisbane, "Fre-o" for Fremantle) from the Kimberley in the far northwest to Melbourne nearly 1,800 miles away in the southeast.

The harsh yet beautiful land beguiles me as much as anything about Australia after two decades living in the United States. But you don't need to head into the Outback to get a sense of the land's enormous power. Whereas in Europe and America, cities intrude upon the countryside, in Australia the country tends to invade the cities. When the British founded Sydney more than 200 years ago, they called the area Botany Bay because of the profusion of flowers and trees. Even today, with a population of nearly 3.5 million, Sydney seems to be, above all, a slice of nature. On hills around a sparkling blue harbor, red-tile roofs are softened by plants and flowering shrubs.

In the large, stately city of Melbourne you find a high, vast sky whose light overwhelms, and a silence that allows you to hear the rustle of a gum (eucalyptus) tree as you exit from the airport terminal. With its gray-green acacias and purple-flowering jacarandas, much of Brisbane looks like a horticultural exhibit, and one can become lost in dreams strolling through King's Park in Perth, where a riot of boronia, orchid, and kangaroo paw spreads beneath magnificent gums.

For tens of thousands of years the Aborigines and nature shared this continent together. The Aborigines arrived during the Ice Age, before sea levels rose and isolated Australia from the rest of Asia. Because European ships were better than Asian, the long isolation of the Aborigines was ended by white, not yellow, arrivals. As London sought a site for a prison colony, the British sea captain James Cook reached the east coast in the 1770s and claimed Australia for the modern world.

The British took Australia in casual stages, without ever dealing fully with the fact that it had already been occupied by the Aborigines. Some 300,000 Aborigines existed when Captain Cook arrived. As whites caught fish and the new settlements drove away kangaroos and other animals, the blacks lost their sources of food. And while the blacks welcomed some of the accoutrements of the white lifestyle, they could not cope with alcohol, and many thousands died from smallpox, venereal disease, and other infections. The Aborigine was pushed aside and Aboriginal life declined.

The days when Australia was a penal colony are not so far distant. All four of my grandparents were alive in Victoria when the last convict ships reached Western Australia in 1868. Australia's unique origin as a place of crime and punishment haunted Australians for a century and a half. It was only after World War II that most people could bring themselves to talk about their criminal ancestry. Today, it is fashionable to boast of it.

I see a legacy of the convict era in some Australian attitudes. This is a society that looks to the government for solutions to its problems. In part, geographic necessity dictates the posture—private enterprise won't build an unprofitable railroad in the sparse north, for example—but it also stems from the nation's origins as a government camp.

Paradoxically, Australians also have an antiauthoritarian streak that seems to echo the contempt of the convict for his keepers and "betters." This attitude, too, has been perpetuated by geographic realities. The farmer in the tough Outback was not inclined—and still isn't—to respect the city bureaucrat who does not know how to mend a fence or cook a meal in the desert. Thus, in one and the same Australian you find both the government-dependent mind-set and the antiauthoritarian rhetoric. It is appropriate that the historical figure who stands out most clearly as an Australian hero is Ned Kelly, a bushranger (highwayman) who killed policemen.

Possibly as a result of Australia's past and nature's influence, Australians are casual and easygoing. A businessman can sound as folksy as a worker, and an academic can look like a worker as he boozes and barracks at a football game. Some of the rich parade their wealth, but none can parade their status in a land that began as a prison colony. It is still an insult to a cab driver for any man traveling alone to ride in the back seat.

The nation's spirit dwells somewhere within a triangle, the points of which are diffidence, innocence, and skepticism. Aussies can neither be easily fooled nor easily enthused—they like to believe others will be reasonable, but at arm's length many a proposed scheme will seem flawed or not worth the bother. Despite such cynicism, there is a seductive softness to Aussie life.

People still say "sorry" if they bump into you on the street, and the word for thank you, "ta," is uttered even after you yourself have said thank you in a shop or restaurant. And whether the topic is the weather, the stupidity of politicians, or the way the world is going to pot, Australians tend to want your agreement.

This desire for affirmation may be due, in part, to the fact that Australians lived in the shadow of Great Britain for so long, during which time they developed something of an inferiority complex. Not so long ago, "a pie and tea" or "fish-and-chips" were a staple that, in an unspoken way, were defiantly asserted to be adequate "tucker" for any "real Australian." Today it is different, thanks largely to immigration. Although bare-armed and wearing sandals, diners in Melbourne and Sydney will peer lengthily at wine lists, fuss over the right sauce for the duckling, and dispute the most appropriate seasoning for the lamb.

The emergence of an Australian culinary tradition is part of a growing nationalism in which Australia can be seen to be moving away from Great Britain and forging an identity of its own. Movies of international repute, Aboriginal art, a quality wine industry, and a vibrant theater have given Australians new cultural confidence in themselves.

The most Australian thing you can do is lie on a clean, wide, beautiful beach. The beach possesses the Australian soul because it is an undeniably Australian asset for a people that until recently were dismissed—even by themselves—as mere derivatives from cold and distant Europe.

It takes time to establish an identity rooted in one's own geographic and climatic experience, however, and Australia can seem quite British at times and somewhat American at others. Political, legal, and educational institutions derive from Britain. Each state capital is named after a colonial politician (Perth, Brisbane, Sydney, Hobart, Melbourne) or a British royal figure (Adelaide). Dry and witheringly hot towns bear names from England's green and pleasant land. Each day in the leading newspapers a "Vice Regal" column lists the activities and visitors at the state and national government houses, where the representative of the English queen is the formal head of the governmental structure. Only since 1984 has it been required that a civil servant in Australia be an Australian—previously it was sufficient to be British.

American influence comes in culture (especially entertainment), technology, defense arrangements, and business. Television channels are well stocked with American programs, and American popular music and clothing styles attract youth in Sydney and Melbourne, as they do in much of the world. Books from the United States have made a major advance in Australian intellectual circles since the 1960s. American ideas of management and problem-solving are sweeping away many cobwebs as the presence of multilateral corporations grows and the public service sheds its British tradition of amateurism.

Aussie-born, eh?" said the immigration officer at Sydney airport as he flipped through my American passport when I arrived for a recent visit. "Yeah," I grunted in my best Australian accent. "Good—there's not many of us left," said the middle-aged officer with a smile.

The changes wrought by immigration impress a returning native son. Nearly half of Australia's population was either born outside Australia or has at least one parent who was. So far, only some 5% of the population is Asian (under 2% are Aborigines), but more than half the immigrants who have arrived in recent years are Asian.

The approach of a Eurasian Australia has been made possible by some basic changes in Australian policy and behavior. A massive European migration following World War II accustomed Australians to new arrivals who brought different foods, languages, and values. The long-standing British flavor of Australia became diluted as Greeks, Italians, and Yugoslavs settled in the big cities. Tourist travel by Australians to Southeast Asia and Japan liberalized Australian racial attitudes, as did the presence of thousands of Asian students who have graduated from Australian universities in recent decades. In the 1970s, as the arrival of Vietnamese refugees began an era of Asian immigration, both Labour and conservative (Liberal-National) governments put forward the doctrine of multiculturalism to express a new ethnic pluralism. Having tried to ward off Asia for so many years, Australia has finally begun to accept its geographic location in the world and is realigning itself accordingly. Today, Indonesia (as a defense worry) and Japan (as an economic partner) outweigh in priority any European country in Australia's foreign policy.

Australian urban life has become more cosmopolitan, with Chinese restaurants, Italian coffee lounges, and Vietnamese and Lebanese grocery stores in virtually every suburb. Greeks and Yugoslavs teach school classes that are half Vietnamese and Chinese—yesterday's students teaching today's—with gum trees outside the window and cricket played during the sports hour.

Eventually, Australia will complete the transformation from British outpost to Eurasian melting pot. When I was at college in Melbourne more than 30 years ago, some feared that Southeast-Asian countries might fail to resist the Communist threat, turning Australia into the "last domino." Today, some fear that the capitalist economies of Hong Kong, Singapore, Korea, and Taiwan might succeed so well that Australia will be left behind as a backwater in a dynamic "yellow sea." In some respects the "lucky country," as Australia is sometimes called, seems out of luck. The farmers are in debt, and industry labors under the disadvantages of a small internal market and high costs. The country's foreign debt is so huge that nearly a quarter of yearly export income goes to pay interest on it; and although the inflation rate has been cut to less than 1%, that has been at the cost of economic growth and of an unemployment rate that has soared to more than 11%.

Australia's economic problems have put severe pressure on a social unity that had been taken for granted. Unemployed youth do not like to see Asian immigrants take jobs they feel should be theirs. Special favors for Aborigines, however justified by history and by need, are less widely supported now than during the healthier economic years of the 1970s. Meanwhile, this ancient people's life expectancy is 20 years less than the Australian average, and Aboriginal infant mortality is three times that of non-Aborigines. In many ways, Australia's ancient past and its beckoning multicultural future tug in sharply different directions.

Australia has been kept pleasant and peaceable by a practical, if sometimes hit-or-miss approach to issues, a lack of compelling ideologies, an agreeable climate, and a beautiful landscape. Some Australians wonder if all this will be enough for tomorrow's challenges. Government ministers have suggested that Australia should forget about being the "lucky country" and strive to be a "clever country"—competing in Asia through high-tech development, ingenuity, and flexibility.

In the meantime, a young nation with few glorious moments in its past is still crystallizing its identity. An exciting maturation has been occurring as diverse immigration, artistic excellence, and the pleasures of a comfortable, safe, and healthy life all bring a new pride and sophistication to the country.

Introduction to New Zealand

*By Michael
Gebicki*

I first laid eyes on New Zealand in 1967, near the end of an ocean voyage from Los Angeles to Australia. For a long morning, we skirted the New Zealand coastline north of Auckland, slipping past a land of impossibly green hills that seemed to be populated entirely by sheep. When the ship berthed in Auckland, I saw parked along the quay a museum-quality collection of vintage British automobiles, the newest of which was probably 15 years old. The explanation was simple enough: All cars were imported, and imports were taxed at an enormous rate. But to a teenager fresh from the U.S.A., it seemed as though we had entered a time warp. When we took a day tour into the hills, the bus driver kept stopping for chats with other drivers; in those days it seemed possible to know everyone in New Zealand.

Since then, Auckland has caught up with the rest of the world. Its cars, its cellular-phone-toting execs, its waterfront restaurants with sushi and French mineral water all exist, unmistakably, in the modern world. Yet rural New Zealand still belongs to a greener, cleaner, friendlier time. Nostalgia remains a strong suit in New Zealand's deck—second, of course, to the country's splendid scenery. If you travel in search of glamorous shopping, sophisticated nightlife, and gourmet pleasures, it's probably not the place for you. You can find these garnishes, in a minor way, in the cities, but New Zealand's cities are strictly sideshows on the world stage. Gracious, calm, and welcoming they may be, but Auckland, Christchurch, and Wellington are never going to be mistaken for Paris or New York.

New Zealand was a late arrival on the world scene. Its first settlers were Polynesians who reached its shores about AD 850, followed by a second wave of Polynesian migrants in the 14th century. These were not carefree, grass-skirted islanders living in a palmy utopia, but a fierce, martial people who made their homes in hilltop fortresses, where they engaged in an almost continual state of warfare with neighboring tribes. It wasn't until the 1840s that European settlers, primarily from England, arrived in any numbers. Compared with such other immigrant societies as the United States and Australia, New Zealand is overwhelmingly British—in its love of gardens, its architecture, its political system, its food. The Maoris remain an assertive minority of 9%, a dignified, robust people whose art bears witness to a rich culture of legends and dreams. That culture comes dramatically to life in performances of traditional songs and dances, including the *haka*, or war dance, which was calculated to intimidate and demoralize the enemy; little wonder that the national rugby team performs a haka as a prelude to its games.

The New Zealand land mass is divided into two main islands. Most of the country's 3.42 million people live on the North Island, while the South Island has the lion's share of the national parks. (More than one-tenth of the country's total land area has been set aside as parks.) In a country about the size of Colorado—or just slightly larger than Great Britain—nature has assembled active volcanoes, subtropical rain forests, geysers, trout streams (some of the finest on earth), fjords, beaches, glaciers, and some two dozen peaks that soar to more than 3,000 meters (10,000 feet). The country has scenic spectaculars from top to bottom, but while the North Island often resembles a pristine golf course, the South Island is wild, majestic, and exhilarating.

Experiencing these wonders is painless. New Zealand has a well-developed infrastructure of hotels, motels, and tour operators—but the best the country has to offer can't be seen through the windows of a tour bus. A trip here is a hands-on experience: hike, boat, fish, hunt, cycle, raft, and breathe some of the freshest air on earth. And if these adventures sound a little too intrepid for you, the sheer beauty of the landscape and the clarity of the air will give you muscles you never knew you had.

1 Essential Information

Before You Go

Australian Government Tourist Offices

*By Joan
Storey
(Australia)
and Michael
Gebicki (New
Zealand)*

*An
Australian
who has lived
in the United
States for
many years,
Joan Storey
is a travel
writer
specializing
in Asia and
the Pacific.
She is
currently an
associate
editor at* Asia
Pacific Travel
magazine.

For information about traveling to and within Australia, contact the nearest office of the **Australian Tourist Commission** (ATC).

In the U.S.: 2121 Ave. of the Stars, Suite 1200, Los Angeles, CA 90067, tel. 310/552–1988, fax 310/552–1215; 100 Park Ave., 25th Floor, New York, NY 10017, tel. 212/687–6300, fax 212/661–3340.

In the U.K.: Gemini House, 10–18 Putney Hill, Putney, London SW15 6AA, tel. 081/780–2227, fax 081/780–1424.

In New Zealand: Level 13, 44–48 Emily Pl., Box 1666, Auckland 1, tel. 09/79–9594.

In addition to its information-packed booklet *Destination Austral-ia*, available free by calling 800/333–0262, ATC offers the **Aussie Help Line** (tel. 708/296–4900), which operates from 8 AM to 7 PM, Central Standard Time. Consumers calling this number can request information and brochures on subjects as diverse as home and farm stays, diving tours, Outback safaris, and shopping, as well as referrals to Aussie-specialist travel agents. ATC has also joined **Partnership Australia,** a collective effort between the Australian states and territories to promote tourism to their areas.

At press time (summer 1994), only three regions have representatives in the United States. Only one of these offices is run directly by the state: **Queensland Tourist & Travel Corporation** (tel. 310/788–0997, fax 310/788–0128; tel. 800/333–6050 in the U.S. for brochures only). The South Australian Tourist Commission is represented in the United States by **Australian Travel Headquarters** (tel. 800/546–2155, fax 714/852–2277), and information on the Northern Territory is available from **Australia's Northern Territory** (5855 Green Valley Circle, Suite 204, Culver City, CA 90230, tel. 310/645–9875, fax 310/645–9876).

New Zealand Government Tourist Offices

For information about travel to and within New Zealand, contact the nearest **New Zealand Tourism Board.**

In the U.S.: 501 Santa Monica Blvd., Los Angeles, CA 90401, tel. 800/388–5494.

In Canada: 888 Dansmuir St., Suite 1200, Vancouver, BC V6C 3K4, tel. 800/888–5494.

In the U.K.: New Zealand House, Haymarket, London SW1Y 4TQ, tel. 71/973–0360.

In Australia: Level 8, 35 Pitt St., Sydney 2000, tel. 02/247–3111.

U.S. Government Travel Briefings

The U.S. Department of State's **Overseas Citizens Emergency Center** (Room 4811, Washington, DC 20520; enclose a stamped, self-addressed envelope) issues Consular Information Sheets that detail crime, security, political climate, and health risks, as well as embassy locations, entry requirements, currency regulations, and other routine matters. For the latest information, stop in at any U.S. passport office, consulate, or embassy; call the interactive hot line (tel.

202/647–5225, fax 202/647–3000); or, with your PC's modem, tap into the Bureau of Consular Affairs' computer bulletin board (tel. 202/647–9225).

Tour Groups

Australia is the size of the continental United States, and New Zealand is as big as Colorado, so visitors wanting to sample a broad range of destinations may find it easier and more economical to go on a package tour. Fortunately, most tours are very flexible. You can join an escorted group tour, create your own itinerary by stringing together mini hotel packages in various cities, follow a prearranged itinerary independently, stay put at a resort, or whip up a unique combination of all of the above.

When considering a tour, be sure to find out (1) exactly what expenses are included, particularly tips, taxes, side trips, meals, and entertainment; (2) the ratings of all hotels on the itinerary and the facilities they offer; (3) the additional cost of single, rather than double, accommodations if you are traveling alone; and (4) the number of travelers in your group. Note whether the tour operator reserves the right to change hotels, routes, or even prices after you've booked, and check out the operator's policy regarding cancellations, complaints, and trip-interruption insurance. Many tour operators request that packages be booked through a travel agent; there is generally no additional charge for doing so.

Listed below is a sampling of operators and packages to give you an idea of what is available. For additional resources, contact your travel agent or the Australian Tourist Commission.

General-Interest Tours
U.S.-based Operators

Abercrombie & Kent International (1520 Kensington Rd., Suite 212, Oak Brook, IL 60521, tel. 708/954–2944 or 800/323–7308) offers 13- and 21-day tours of Australia with optional eight-day extensions to New Zealand, as well as a 20-day introduction to both. The 20-day "Natural Wonders" explores Australia's Outback, wildlife, and Aboriginal culture.

Australian Pacific Tours (512 S. Verdugo Dr., Suite 200, Burbank, CA 91502, tel. 818/840–9122 or 800/290–8687) offers motorcoach tours and safaris.

Gadabout Tours (700 E. Tahquitz Canyon Way, Palm Springs, CA 92262, tel. 619/325–5556 or 800/952–5068) offers a 14-day tour of New Zealand and Australia, hitting the major cities.

Globus & Cosmos Tourama (5301 S. Federal Circle, Littleton, CO 80123, tel. 800/851–0728, fax 303/798–5441) offers escorted tours of various lengths, several of which combine Australia and New Zealand with Fiji and Tahiti. Globus tours are first-class, and Cosmos tours are budget.

Islands in the Sun (760 W. 16th St., Suite L, Costa Mesa, CA 92627; tel. 800/TC–TOURS or 714/645–8300, fax 714/548–1654) offers individual and escorted group tours to Australia and New Zealand, some in combination with Tahiti and Fiji.

J & O Holidays (3131 Camino del Rio N, Suite 1080, San Diego, CA 92108, tel. 800/377–1080, fax 619/283–3131) has 17- and 21-day tours of Australia and New Zealand featuring home-hosted dinners.

Jetabout Qantas Vacations (300 N. Continental Blvd., Suite 610, El Segundo, CA 90245, tel. 800/641–8772, fax 310/535–1057) offers escorted tours to Australia and New Zealand as well as a host of options for extending and personalizing your trip.

Maupintour (Box 807, Lawrence, KS 66044, tel. 800/255–4266, fax 913/843–8351) offers a 26-day escorted tour to Australia, featuring Tasmania, and a 20-day jaunt that includes New Zealand and Fiji.

Olson Travelworld (970 W. 190th St., Suite 425, Torrance, CA 90502, tel. 800/421–2255, fax 310/768–0050) offers tours of Australia and New Zealand—together, separately, or in combination with South Sea islands.

Sunbeam Tours (1631 W. Sunflower Ave., Suite C36, Santa Ana, CA 92704, tel. 800/955–1818, fax 714/434–8009) takes in the best of the two countries in 21 days.

Tauck Tours (Box 5027, Westport, CT 06881, tel. 800/468–2825, fax 203/221–6828) presents 15- and 21-day tours combining Australia and New Zealand, with optional three-day extensions to Fiji.

Travcoa (Box 2630, Newport Beach, CA 92658, tel. 800/992–2003, fax 714/476–2538) offers escorted tours of Australia and New Zealand, some of which also include Fiji, Tahiti, or Papua New Guinea.

U.K.-based Operators
British Airways Holidays (Atlantic House, Hazelwick Ave., Three Bridges, Crawley, W. Sussex RH10 1NP, tel. 0293/51–8022) features a large number of Australian vacations, including escorted tours, independent travel, and car and camper-van holidays, and a Barrier Reef cruise; and a similar range of options in New Zealand.

Kuoni (Kuoni House, Dorking, Surrey RH5 4AZ, tel. 0306/74–0500) offers a flexible "Outback and Reef Experience" tour that visits Sydney, Ayers Rock, Alice Springs, Cairns, and Brisbane, with stopovers in Singapore and Bangkok. The new Australia brochure features independent and escorted tours, city stays, beach holidays, and tailormade arrangements.

Trailfinders (42–50 Earls Court Rd., London W8 7RG, tel. 071/938–3366; 58 Deansgate, Manchester M3 2FF, tel. 061/839–3636) has many options, ranging from deluxe Great Barrier Reef vacations to camper-van tours in both countries.

Special-Interest Tours
Special-interest tours have proliferated over recent years in Australia and New Zealand. Whatever your particular interest—food or wine, fishing, skiing, art, Aboriginal or Maori culture, trekking, golf, or shopping—there are tours available. Many of these last only three or four days, so it's possible to fit in a tour even on a vacation as short as two weeks.

Through 1995, tours commemorating the 50th anniversary of World War II are drawing veterans and military history buffs. For details, contact the Australian Tourist Commission (*see* Australian Government Tourist Offices, *above*).

Operators are too numerous to list in their entirety here; request the names of companies offering special-interest tours from the ATC. For additional information on adventure vacations, *see* Chapter 16. Some of the more popular tours are offered by the following companies:

Adventure/ Safaris
Tours including bicycling, canoeing, fishing, river rafting, sea kayaking, skiing, trekking, and nature and wildlife expeditions are offered by **Abercrombie & Kent** (*see* General-Interest Tour, *above*); **Adventure Center** (1311 63rd St., Suite 200, Emeryville, CA 94608, tel. 510/654–1879 or 800/227–8747, fax 510/654–4200); **American Wilderness Experience** (Box 1486, Boulder, CO 80306, tel. 800/

444–0099); **Beach's Motorcycle Adventures** (2763 W. River Pkwy., Grand Island, NY 14072, tel. 716/773–4960); **Mountain Travel/Sobek** (6420 Fairmount Ave., El Cerrito, CA 94530, tel. 800/227–2384, fax 510/525–7710); **Backroads Bicycle Touring** (1516 5th St., Berkeley, CA 94710, tel. 800/462–2848, fax 510/527–1444); **Journeys International** (4011 Jackson, Ann Arbor, MI 48103, tel. 800/255–8735, fax 313/665–2945); **Nature Expeditions International** (474 Willamette, Box 11496, Eugene, OR 97440, tel. 800/869–0639), and **Wilderness Travel** (801 Allston Way, Berkeley, CA 94710, tel. 800/368–2794).

Fishing **Rod & Reel Adventures** (3507 Tully Rd., Suite 5, Modesto, CA 95356, tel. 800/423–9731, fax 209/524–1220) and **The Best of New Zealand Fly Fishing** (2817 Wilshire Blvd., Santa Monica, CA 90403, tel. 800/528–6129).

Golf **ITC Golf Tours** (4134 Atlantic Ave., Suite 205, Long Beach, CA 90807, tel. 800/257–4981, fax 310/424–6683); **Golf International** (275 Madison Ave., New York, NY 10016, tel. 800/833–1389); and **New Zealand Golf Excursions** (2041 Rosencrans Ave., No. 103, El Segundo, CA 90245, tel. 800/622–6606).

Horseback Riding **FITS Equestrian** (685 Lateen Rd., Solvang, CA 93463, tel. 800/666–3487).

Scuba Diving **See & Sea Travel Service, Inc.** (50 Francisco St., Suite 205, San Francisco, CA 94133, tel. 800/348–9778, fax 415/434–3409); **Aqua Trek** (110 Sutter St., Suite 811, San Francisco, CA 94104, tel. 800/541–4334, fax 415/398–0479); and **Tropical Adventures** (111 Second Ave. N, Seattle, WA 98109, tel. 800/247–3483).

Tennis **Steve Furgal's International Tennis Tours** (11828 Rancho Bernardo Rd., San Diego, CA 92128, tel. 800/258–3664).

Wildlife **Biological Journeys** (1696 Ocean Dr., McKinleyville, CA 95521, tel. 800/548–7555, fax 707/839–4656); **Earthwatch** (680 Mount Auburn St., Watertown, MA 02272, tel. 617/926–8000); **Lindblad's Special Expeditions** (720 Fifth Ave., New York, NY 10019, tel. 800/762–0003); **National Audubon Society** (700 Broadway, New York, NY 10003, tel. 212/979–3000); and **Smithsonian Institution Study Tours and Seminars** (1100 Jefferson Dr. SW, Room 3045, Washington, DC 20560, tel. 202/357–4700).

Wineries **Austravel, Inc.** (51 E. 42nd St., Suite 616, New York, NY 10017, tel. 800/633–3404) and **World Travelers, Inc.** (2819 First Ave., Suite 280, Seattle, WA 98121, tel. 800/426–3610, fax 206/441–8862).

Package Tours for Independent Travelers

Abercrombie & Kent International (*see* General-Interest Tours, *above*) will arrange individual itineraries around such specific interests or activities as art, architecture, history, wildlife, sports, antiques, and gardens.

Austravel (51 E. 42nd St., Suite 616, New York, NY 10017, tel. 212/972–6880 or 800/633–3404) and **Swain Australia Tours** (6 W. Lancaster Ave., Ardmore, PA 19003, tel. 800/227–9246, fax 215/896–9592) are veritable supermarkets of customized packages, offering everything from hotel vouchers and rental cars to motorcoach tours and river cruises.

Destination World (28441 Highbridge, Suite 510, Rolling Hills Estates, CA 90274, tel. 800/426–3644, fax 310/544–9387), offers unusual customized and package tours, from driving itineraries with farm stays to a genuine country pub crawl on horseback.

Globus & Cosmos Tourama (*see* General-Interest Tours, *above*) offers a variety of "hosted" tours to Australia and New Zealand, combining the flexibility of independent travel with sightseeing excursions.

Islands in the Sun (*see* General-Interest Tours) offers fly-drive vacations and "add-on" modules to create personalized independent vacations in both countries.

J & O Holidays (*see* General-Interest Tours) offers a 14-day independent tour of Australia as well as fly/drive packages and more than a dozen short-stay itineraries.

Sunbeam Tours (*see* General-Interest Tours) will design custom itineraries to Australia and New Zealand, including transportation throughout the South Pacific.

United Vacations (tel. 800/351–4200) has packages to many destinations in the two countries, priced from moderate to deluxe. Prebook your entire itinerary or plan as you go.

Also check **Australian Pacific Tours** (*see* General-Interest Tours), **SO/PAC** (tel. 800/551–2012, fax 213/871–0811), and **Guthreys Pacific** (tel. 800/227–5317, fax 714/960–4678) for city packages in Australia and New Zealand.

When to Go

Australia is almost the same size as the continental United States, with a similar diversity of weather. Because Australia is in the Southern Hemisphere, the seasons are reversed, so it's winter in Australia during the American and European summer. The climate ranges from temperate in southern states, such as Victoria and Tasmania, to tropical in the far north. Good months for travel in the southern region are from the end of October to December (the Australian spring), or from February through April (late summer–autumn). These months are generally sunny and warm with only occasional rain in Sydney, Melbourne, and Adelaide. Perth is at its finest in springtime, when wildflowers blanket the land.

The ideal time to visit the north, particularly the Northern Territory's Kakadu National Park, is early in the dry season (around May). Bird life remains profuse on the drying floodplains, and the waterfalls are still spectacular and accessible. The Dry (April–October) is also a good time to visit northern Queensland's beaches and rain forests. You can swim without fear of the dangerous stinging box jellyfish, which infests ocean waters after November. In the rain forests, the heat and humidity are not as high as later in the year, and crocodile viewing is at its prime, because the creatures tend to bask on riverbanks rather than submerging in the colder water.

During school holidays, Australians take to the roads in droves. Accommodations and attractions are crowded and surcharges are often added to car rentals and hotel tariffs. The worst period is mid-December to the end of January, which is the equivalent of the U.S. and British summer break. The dates of other school vacations vary from state to state, but generally fall around Easter, mid-June to July, and from late September to mid-October.

New Zealand's climate varies from subtropical in the north to temperate in the south. Its seasons, like Australia's, are the reverse of those in North America and Europe. Summers (December–March) are generally warm, with an average of seven to eight hours of sunshine per day throughout the country. Winters (June–September) are mild at lower altitudes on the North Island, but heavy snowfalls are common on the South Island, particularly on the peaks of the Southern Alps. Rain can pour at any time of the year. (Some areas on the west coast of the South Island receive an annual rainfall of more than 100 inches.)

The ideal months for comfortable all-round travel are October–November and February–April, especially for anyone who wants to participate in adventure activities. Avoid the school holidays, when highways may be congested and accommodation is likely to be scarce and more expensive. The summer school holidays (the busiest) fall between mid-December and the end of January; other holiday periods are mid-May to the end of May, early July to mid-July, and late August to mid-September.

Climate The following are average daily maximum and minimum temperatures for some major cities in Australia and New Zealand.

Sydney	**Jan.**	79F	26C	**May**	67F	19C	**Sept.**	67F	17C
		65	18		52	11		52	11
	Feb.	79F	26C	**June**	61F	16C	**Oct.**	72F	22C
		65	18		49	9		56	13
	Mar.	76F	24C	**July**	61F	16C	**Nov.**	74F	23C
		63	17		49	9		61	16
	Apr.	72F	22C	**Aug.**	63F	17C	**Dec.**	77F	25C
		58	14		49	9		63	17

Darwin	**Jan.**	90F	32C	**May**	92F	33C	**Sept.**	92F	33C
		77	25		74	23		74	23
	Feb.	90F	32C	**June**	88F	31C	**Oct.**	94F	34C
		77	25		70	21		77	25
	Mar.	92F	33C	**July**	88F	31C	**Nov.**	94F	34C
		77	25		67	19		79	26
	Apr.	92F	33C	**Aug.**	90F	32C	**Dec.**	92F	33C
		76	24		70	21		79	26

Alice Springs	**Jan.**	97F	36C	**May**	74F	23C	**Sept.**	81F	27C
		70	21		47	8		49	9
	Feb.	95F	35C	**June**	67F	19C	**Oct.**	88F	31C
		70	21		41	5		58	14
	Mar.	90F	32C	**July**	67F	19C	**Nov.**	94F	34C
		63	17		40	4		65	18
	Apr.	81F	27C	**Aug.**	74F	23C	**Dec.**	97F	36C
		54	12		43	6		68	20

Cairns	Jan.	90F	32C	May	81F	27C	Sept.	83F	28C
		74	23		67	19		65	18
	Feb.	90F	32C	June	79F	26C	Oct.	86F	30C
		74	23		65	18		68	20
	Mar.	88F	31C	July	79F	26C	Nov.	88F	31C
		74	23		61	16		70	21
	Apr.	85F	29C	Aug.	81F	27C	Dec.	90F	32C
		70	21		63	17		74	23

Hobart	Jan.	72F	22C	May	58F	14C	Sept.	59F	15C
		54	12		45	7		43	6
	Feb.	72F	22C	June	54F	12C	Oct.	63F	17C
		54	12		41	5		47	8
	Mar.	68F	20C	July	52F	11C	Nov.	67F	19C
		52	11		40	4		49	9
	Apr.	63F	17C	Aug.	56F	13C	Dec.	70F	21C
		49	9		41	5		52	11

Melbourne	Jan.	79F	26C	May	63F	17C	Sept.	63F	17C
		58	14		47	8		47	8
	Feb.	79F	26C	June	58F	14C	Oct.	67F	19C
		58	14		45	7		49	9
	Mar.	76F	24C	July	56F	13C	Nov.	72F	22C
		56	13		43	6		52	11
	Apr.	68F	20C	Aug.	59F	15C	Dec.	76F	24C
		52	11		43	6		54	12

Auckland	Jan.	74F	23C	May	63F	17C	Sept.	61F	16C
		61	16		52	11		49	9
	Feb.	74F	23C	June	58F	14C	Oct.	63F	17C
		61	16		49	9		52	11
	Mar.	72F	22C	July	56F	13C	Nov.	67F	19C
		59	15		47	8		54	12
	Apr.	67F	19C	Aug.	58F	14C	Dec.	70F	21C
		56	13		47	8		58	14

Christchurch	Jan.	70F	21C	May	56F	13C	Sept.	58F	14C
		54	12		40	4		40	4
	Feb.	70F	21C	June	52F	11C	Oct.	63F	17C
		54	12		36	2		45	7
	Mar.	67F	19C	July	50F	10C	Nov.	67F	19C
		50	10		36	2		47	8
	Apr.	63F	17C	Aug.	52F	11C	Dec.	70F	21C
		45	7		36	2		52	11

Queenstown	Jan.	72F	22C	May	52F	11C	Sept.	56F	13C
		49	9		36	2		38	3
	Feb.	70F	21C	June	47F	8C	Oct.	61F	16C
		50	10		34	1		41	5
	Mar.	67F	19C	July	46F	8C	Nov.	65F	18C
		47	8		34	− 1		45	7
	Apr.	61F	16C	Aug.	50F	10C	Dec.	70F	21C
		43	6		34	1		49	9

Information   For current weather conditions for cities in the United States and
Sources   abroad, plus the local time and helpful travel tips, call the **Weather
Channel Connection** (tel. 900/WEATHER or 932–8437; 95¢ per min-
ute) from a touch-tone phone.

Festivals and Seasonal Events

Australian events range from international cultural festivals and
sporting matches to uniquely Australian celebrations with a distinctly tongue-in-cheek flavor. With the recent opening of performing arts centers in most capital cities in recent years, arts festivals
have become major features on the Australian events calendar. The
dates of some of these festivals may change, so call ahead to check.

Australia   **Jan. 1: New Year's Day** is observed as a holiday nationwide.
Jan.: Festival of Sydney inaugurates the year with several events, including free concerts in the parks, art exhibitions, a Mardi Gras parade through the city, and the Sydney Harbour Ferrython, a
procession of ferries followed by a ferry race. Information: Festival
of Sydney Committee, Suite 3, 12th floor, Stockland House, 175
Castlereagh Street, Sydney, NSW 2000, tel. 02/267–2311, fax 02/
261–3014.
Jan. 26: Australia Day, is a country-wide holiday that celebrates the
founding of the nation.
Feb. 3–Mar. 4: Sydney Gay Mardi Gras is a celebration of lesbian and
gay life that includes art and photography exhibitions and features a
grand parade. Information: Box 1064, Darlinghurst, NSW 2010, tel.
02/332–4088, fax 02/332–2969.
Mar. 10–19: Moomba turns out usually staid Melburnians for one of
the country's more ebullient festivals, beginning early in the month
with fireworks over the Yarra River, and culminating with a grand
pageant on the riverbank. Information: Peter Hudson, 117 Sturt
Street, South Melbourne, VIC 3205, tel. 03/699–4022, fax 03/699–
9877.
Apr. 14–17: The **Easter** holiday is observed from Good Friday
through Easter Monday (through Easter Tuesday in Victoria).
Apr. 17–23: The **Barossa Valley Vintage Festival,** the best known of
the wine-region celebrations, features a full week of entertainment
bearing the stamp of the valley's Germanic heritage, plus sheep-
shearing demonstrations, displays of vintage cars, and, of course,
wine tastings. Information: 66 Murray Street, Nuriootpa, SA 5355,
tel. 085/62–1866.
Apr. 25: Anzac Day is observed as a solemn holiday to honor the soldiers who died at Gallipoli in World War I.
Second Monday in June: The Queen's Birthday is a holiday in every
state but Western Australia (which celebrates it in October).
June or July: The Beer Can Regatta in Darwin is an event that shows
a fine sensitivity to recycling—the sailing craft are constructed
from used beer cans! It takes place during the Bougainvillea Festival celebrating the coming of the dry season.
Late Sept.: Warana Festival celebrates Brisbane in spring blossom
with a series of gala happenings, including a festive parade.
Late Sept.: Henley-On-Todd Regatta in Alice Springs is a boat race
with a difference—it's held on a dry riverbed. Crews "wear" the
boats, and leg power replaces rowing.
Oct. 19–Nov. 4: Melbourne International Festival of the Arts, formerly known as the Spoleto Festival, features Australia's top performers, along with outstanding international productions, at the
Performing Arts Centre and venues around Melbourne. Weekend

ticket packages are available. Information: 35 City Road, South Melbourne, VIC 3205, tel. 03/686–4484, fax 03/686–4168.

Mid-Oct.: Fun in the Sun Festival in Cairns highlights the city's tropical setting. A grand parade with floats climaxes a week of entertainment, exhibitions, a yacht race, and a fun run.

Dec. 25–26: Christmas Day, when almost everything is closed nationwide, and **Boxing Day,** observed as a holiday in all states except South Australia. (The latter stems from the era when English squires "boxed" the remains of their Christmas dinners for their tenants.)

New Zealand Not surprisingly, sport features heavily in New Zealand's festival calendar. Horse and boat races, triathlons, and fishing competitions are far more prominent than celebrations of the arts. Just about every town holds a yearly agricultural and pastoral ("A&P") show, and these proud displays of local crafts, produce, livestock, and woodchopping and sheep-shearing prowess provide a memorable look at rural New Zealand. An annual calendar of *New Zealand Special Events* is available from government tourist offices.

Jan. 1: New Year's Day is a nationwide holiday.

Feb. 1: For the **Auckland Anniversary Day Regatta,** Auckland's birthday party, the "City of Sails" takes to the water.

Feb. 6: Waitangi Day, New Zealand's national day, commemorates the signing of the Treaty of Waitangi between whites and Maoris in 1840. The focus of the nationwide celebration is, naturally enough, the town of Waitangi in the Bay of Islands.

Feb. 11–12: Speights Coast to Coast is the ultimate iron-man challenge—a two-day, 238-kilometer (148-mile) marathon of cycling, running, and kayaking that spans the South Island from west to east. Information: Canterbury Information Centre, corner Worcester Street and Oxford Terrace, tel. 03/79–9629.

Late Feb.–mid-Mar.: New Zealand International Festival of the Arts, a biennial event held in even-numbered years, is the country's premier performing-arts festival, during which many international performers can be seen in Wellington. Information: Wellington City Information Centre, corner Wakefield and Victoria streets, tel. 04/ 499–4444.

Mar. 2–4: Golden Shears International Shearing Championship is a three-day event that pits men armed with shears against fleecy sheep in the town of Masterton, just north of Wellington. Information: Masterton Visitor Information Centre, 5 Dixon Street, tel. 06/ 378–7373.

Apr. 2–10: Bluff Oyster Festival celebrates the beginning of the oyster season at this tiny seaport on the southern tip of the South Island. Information: Invercargill Information Centre, 82 Dee Street, tel. 03/218–6091.

Apr. 14–17: The **Easter** holiday weekend lasts from Good Friday through Easter Monday.

Apr. 25: Anzac Day honors the soldiers who fought and died in World War I.

First Monday in June: the Queen's Birthday is celebrated nationwide.

Oct. 23: Labour Day is observed throughout the country.

2nd Week in Nov.: Canterbury Agricultural and Pastoral Show spotlights the farmers and graziers of the rich countryside surrounding Christchurch. Information: Canterbury Information Centre, corner Worcester Street and Oxford Terrace, tel. 03/79–9629.

Dec. 25–26: On **Christmas Day** and **Boxing Day** the country virtually closes down.

What to Pack

If you need to pack for both the tropical north and the cooler south, try to put the woolen clothes in one suitcase and lighter clothes in another, so you don't have to delve into both at each stop. Valuables, such as jewelry, should always be packed in your carry-on luggage. It is also important to pack prescription medicines, as well as any allergy medication you may need, in hand luggage.

Clothing   The wisest approach to dressing in Australia is the use of layered outfits. Frequently, particularly at the change of season, the weather turns suddenly, so you'll appreciate being able to remove or put on a jacket. A light raincoat and umbrella are worthwhile accessories, but remember that plastic raincoats and nonbreathing polyester are uncomfortable in the tropics. Don't wear lotions or perfume in the tropics either, since they attract mosquitoes and other bugs. Consider carrying insect repellent. Bring a hat with a brim to provide protection from the strong sunlight (*see* Staying Healthy, *below*). In New Zealand, be prepared for a varied climate. Wet-weather gear and comfortable, sturdy shoes are essential.

Dress is fairly casual in most cities, though top resorts and restaurants may require a jacket and tie. In Melbourne and Sydney, the younger set tends to be trendy; women might want to take along a cocktail dress for evening dining. A light sweater or jacket will suffice for evenings in the coastal cities in the autumn, but winter demands a heavier coat—a raincoat with a zip-out wool lining is ideal. Comfortable walking shoes are a must. You should have a pair of running shoes or the equivalent if you're planning to trek, and rubber-sole sandals or canvas shoes are needed for walking on reef coral.

Miscellaneous   An extra pair of glasses, contact lenses, or prescription sunglasses is always a good idea. Stores carry the same cosmetic products as back home, so you don't need to carry extra supplies. If you have a health problem that may require you to purchase a prescription drug, take enough to last the duration of the trip. And don't forget to pack a list of the addresses of offices that supply refunds for lost or stolen traveler's checks.

Electricity   The electrical current in Australia and New Zealand is 230 volts, 50 cycles alternating current (AC); the United States runs on 110-volt, 60-cycle AC current. Unlike wall outlets in the United States, which accept plugs with two flat prongs, outlets in Australia and New Zealand take a slanted three-prong plug.

Adapters,   To use U.S.-made electric appliances abroad, you'll need an adapter
Converters,   plug. Unless the appliance is dual-voltage and made for travel, you'll
Transformers   also need a converter. Hotels sometimes have 110-volt outlets marked "For Shavers Only" near the sink; don't use them for a high-wattage appliance like a blow-dryer. If you're traveling with an older laptop computer, carry a transformer. New laptop computers are autosensing, operating equally well on 110 or 220 volts, so you need only the appropriate adapter plug. For a copy of the free brochure "Foreign Electricity is No Deep Dark Secret," send a stamped, self-addressed envelope to adapter-converter manufacturer **Franzus Company** (Customer Service, Dept. B50, Murtha Industrial Park, Box 142, Beacon Falls, CT 06403, tel. 203/723–6664).

Luggage   Free airline baggage allowances depend on the airline, the route,
Regulations   and the class of your ticket. In general, on domestic flights and on international flights between the United States and foreign destinations, you are entitled to check two bags—neither exceeding 62

inches, or 158 centimeters (length + width + height), or weighing more than 70 pounds (32 kilograms). A third piece may be brought aboard as a carryon; its total dimensions are generally limited to less than 45 inches (114 centimeters), so it will fit easily under the seat in front of you or in the overhead compartment. In the United States, the Federal Aviation Administration (FAA) gives airlines broad latitude for carry-on allowances and tailors limits to different aircraft and operational conditions. Charges for excess, oversize, or over-weight pieces will therefore vary.

If you are flying between two foreign destinations, note that bag-gage allowances may be determined not by number of pieces, but by weight; you'll generally be allowed 88 pounds (40 kilograms) of lug-gage in first class, 66 pounds (30 kilograms) in business class, and 44 pounds (20 kilograms) in economy. If your flight between two cities abroad *connects* with your transatlantic or transpacific flight, the piece method still applies. International passengers flying within Australia can check two pieces of luggage (you may be asked to show your international ticket); otherwise you are allowed up to 44 pounds of luggage in both countries.

Safeguarding Your Luggage Before leaving home, itemize your bags' contents and their worth so you'll be prepared if they somehow go astray. To minimize that risk, tag them inside and out with your name, address, and phone num-ber. (If you use your home address, cover it so that potential thieves can't see it.) At check-in, make sure that the tag attached by bag-gage handlers bears the correct three-letter code for your destina-tion. If your bags do not arrive with you, or if you detect damage, do not leave the airport until you've filed a written report with the air-line.

Taking Money Abroad

Traveler's Checks Traveler's checks are preferable in metropolitan centers, although you'll need cash in rural areas and small towns. The most widely rec-ognized are **American Express, Citicorp, Diners Club, Thomas Cook,** and **Visa.** Both American Express and Thomas Cook issue checks that can be countersigned and used by you or your traveling com-panion. Typically the issuing company or the bank at which you make your purchase charges 1% to 3% of the checks' face value as a fee. Some foreign banks charge as much as 20% of the face value as the fee for cashing traveler's checks in a foreign currency. Buy a few checks in small denominations to cash toward the end of your trip, so you won't be left with excess foreign currency. Record the numbers of checks as you spend them, and keep this list separate from the checks.

You can also buy traveler's checks in Australian or New Zealand dol-lars—a good idea if the U.S. dollar is falling and you want to lock in the current rate.

Currency Exchange Banks offer the most favorable exchange rates. If you use currency exchange booths at airports, rail and bus stations, hotels, stores, and privately run exchange firms, you'll typically get less favorable rates, but you may find the hours more convenient.

You can get good rates and avoid long lines at airport currency-ex-change booths by getting a small amount of currency at **Thomas Cook Currency Services** (630 Fifth Ave., New York, NY 10111, tel. 212/757–6915 or 800/223–7373 for locations in major metropolitan areas throughout the U.S.) or **Ruesch International** (tel. 800/424–2923 for locations) before you depart. Check with your travel agent to be sure that the currency of the country you will be visiting can be imported.

Getting Money from Home

Cash Machines Many automated-teller machines (ATMs) are tied to such international networks as **Cirrus** and **Plus.** You can use your bank card at ATMs away from home to withdraw money from an account and get cash advances on a credit-card account if your card has been programmed with a personal identification number, or PIN. Check in advance on limits on withdrawals and cash advances within specified periods. Ask whether your bank-card or credit-card PIN number will need to be reprogrammed for use in the area you'll be visiting, because only four-digit numbers are commonly used overseas. Note that on cash advances, interest is charged from the day that the money is withdrawn, without the usual grace period. Although transaction fees for ATM withdrawals abroad will probably be higher than fees for withdrawals at home, Cirrus and Plus exchange rates tend to be good. At press time, Cirrus was coming online in Australia and New Zealand; Discover cards, however, are still accepted only in the United States.

Wiring Money You don't have to be a cardholder to send or receive a **MoneyGram from American Express** for up to $10,000. Go to a MoneyGram agent in retail and convenience stores and American Express travel offices, and pay up to $1,000 with a credit card and anything over that in cash. You are allowed a free long-distance call to give the transaction code to your intended recipient, who needs only present identification and the reference number to the nearest MoneyGram agent to pick up the cash. MoneyGram agents are in more than 70 countries (call 800/926–9400 for locations). Fees range from 3% to 10%, depending on the amount and method of payment.

You can also use **Western Union.** To wire money, take either cash or a cashier's check to the nearest office or call and use your MasterCard or Visa. Money sent from the United States or Canada will be available for pickup at agent locations in Australia and New Zealand within minutes. Once the money is in the system, it can be picked up at any of 22,000 locations (call 800/325–6000 for the one nearest you).

Currency

Australia's currency operates on the decimal system, with the dollar (A$) as the basic unit and 100 cents (¢) equaling $1. Bills are in $100, $50, $20, $10 and $5 denominations; each denomination is a different color for easier identification. Coins are minted in $2, $1, 50¢, 20¢, 10¢, and 5¢ denominations.

Australia continues to struggle with high inflation and a stagnant ecomony. The weakening American dollar translates into increased buying power for visitors' currencies. At press time, the exchange rate was about A$1.40 to the U.S. dollar, $1.02 to the Canadian dollar, $2.10 to the pound sterling, and 80¢ to the New Zealand dollar. Prices quoted throughout the Australian chapters are in Australian dollars.

New Zealand's unit of currency is also the dollar, again divided into 100 cents. Bills are in $100, $50, $10, and $5 denominations. Coins are $2, $1, 50¢, 20¢, 10¢, and 5¢. At press time, the rate of exchange was NZ$1.85 to the U.S. dollar, NZ$1.41 to the Canadian dollar, NZ$2.78 to the pound sterling, and NZ$1.25 to the Australian dollar. Prices quoted throughout the New Zealand section are in New Zealand dollars.

What Australia Will Cost

It is difficult to be specific about costs in 1995 because at press time most companies had not set their tariffs. Also there is a certain amount of volatility in prices. Still, the ones given in these pages may be used as an approximate guide, since the variation should rarely exceed 10%.

Despite the growing perception in North America that Australia is an expensive destination it has become more price competitive. Although tariffs remain high at Sydney's five-star hotels, there are plenty of cheaper dining and lodging alternatives. Medium-priced hotels and hotel-apartments abound in the city centers and the inner suburbs. For example, double-occupancy rates at the luxury Regent of Sydney start at $210 a night, whereas the tariff at the Kendall, a bed-and-breakfast hotel classified as a landmark by the National Trust, is in the region of $120, including breakfast. Melbourne and Sydney tend to be more expensive than other cities.

Fares on international flights are usually lower between June and September, and many hotels offer lower tariffs in their off-peak season: April–September in the south, November–March in the Top End. Another way to save money is to buy passes, available for everything from hotels and interstate transportation (*see* Staying in Australia, *below*) to local bus and train services.

Taxes States do not levy hotel taxes, with the exception of the Northern Territory, which adds a 2.5% room tax. No value-added tax (VAT) is charged either—you pay exactly what is shown on the price tag.

Sample Costs Cup of coffee: $2–$3.50
Glass of beer in a bar: $2
Take-out ham sandwich or meat pie: $2.50–$4
Hamburger in a café: $4–$9
Room-service sandwich in a hotel: $12–$15
A 2-kilometer (1¼-mile) taxi ride: $5.30

What New Zealand Will Cost

For most travelers, New Zealand is not an expensive destination. The cost of meals, accommodation, and travel is slightly higher than in the United States but considerably less than in Western Europe. At about $1 per liter—equal to about US$2.10 per gallon—premium-grade gasoline is expensive by North American standards, but not by European ones.

Inflation, which reached a peak of almost 20% in the late 1980s, has now been reduced to less than 5%. Prices are expected to remain stable as the government pursues strict monetarist policies and continues to allow free market forces to determine costs.

Taxes A goods and services tax (GST) of 12.5% is levied throughout New Zealand. It's usually incorporated into the cost of an item, but in hotels and some restaurants it is added to the bill.

Visitors exiting the country must pay a departure tax of $20.

Sample Costs Cup of coffee: $2.50
Glass of beer in a bar: $2.50–$4
Take-out ham sandwich or meat pie: $2.50
Hamburger in a café: $4

Room-service sandwich in a hotel: $12
A 2-kilometer (1¼-mile) taxi ride: $5

Passports and Visas

If your passport is lost or stolen abroad, report it immediately to the nearest embassy or consulate and to the local police. If you can provide the information contained in the passport, the consular officer will usually be able to issue you a new passport. For this reason, it is a good idea to keep a photocopy of the data page of your passport separate from your money and traveler's checks. Also leave a photocopy with a relative or friend at home.

U.S. Citizens All U.S. citizens, even infants, need a valid passport to enter Australia or New Zealand for stays of up to 90 days. A visa is also required to enter Australia. You can pick up new and renewal application forms at any of the 13 U.S. Passport Agency offices and at some post offices and courthouses. Although passports are usually mailed within four weeks of your application's receipt, allow five weeks or more from April through summer. Call the Department of State Office of Passport Services' information line (tel. 202/647–0518) for fees, documentation requirements, and other details.

U.S. travelers require a visa to visit Australia. **Qantas** passengers may obtain an Australian visa from that airline; otherwise, application forms are available from one of the offices listed below (children traveling on a parent's passport do not need a separate application form, but should be included under Item 16 on the form). The completed form must be sent or brought in person to an issuing office, together with a recent passport-type photograph signed on the back (machine photographs are *not* acceptable), and your passport. Visitors planning to stay more than three months must pay a fee. Check with the Consulate-General (*see below*) to ascertain how much, since the cost varies with the volatile exchange rate. At press time, a visa was $21. If you travel on an under-three-month visa and decide to extend it while in Australia, the fee rises; currently it's $200. If applying by mail, enclose a 12½″ × 9½″, stamped, self-addressed envelope and allow 21 days for processing.

Contact the nearest Australian Consulate-General for visa application forms: **Honolulu** (1000 Bishop St., Penthouse, Honolulu, HI 96813–9998, tel. 808/524–5050, fax 808/523–1906); **Houston** (1990 Post Oak Blvd., Suite 800, Houston, TX 77056-9998, tel. 713/629–9131, fax 713/622–6924); **Los Angeles** (611 N. Larchmont Blvd., Los Angeles, CA 90004, tel. 213/469–4300, fax 213/469–9176); **New York** (International Bldg., 636 Fifth Ave., New York, NY 10111-0050, tel. 212/245–4000, fax 212/265–4917); **San Francisco** (1 Bush St., San Francisco, CA 94104, tel. 415/362–6160, fax 415/986–5440); **Washington** (Australian Embassy, 1601 Massachusetts Ave. NW, Washington, DC 20036-4673, tel. 202/797–3222, fax 202/797–3168).

Canadian Citizens Canadian citizens need a valid passport to enter Australia or New Zealand for stays of up to 90 days. In addition, a visa is required to enter Australia. Application forms are available at 23 regional passport offices as well as post offices and travel agencies. You must appear in person whether you're applying for a first-time or a subsequent passport. Children under 16 may be included on a parent's passport but must have their own passport if they will be traveling alone. Passports are valid for five years and are usually mailed within two weeks of an application's receipt. For fees, documentation requirements, and other information in English or French, call the passport office (tel. 514/283–2152 or 800/567–6868).

Australian visa requirements for Canadians are the same as for Americans. Visitors planning to stay more than three months must pay a $30 processing fee. (If you travel on an under-three-month visa and decide to extend it while there, the fee rises to about $150.) Contact the nearest Australian Consulate General for visa application forms: **Ottawa** (Australian High Commission, 50 O'Connor St., Suite 710, Ottawa, Ont. K1P 6L2, tel. 613/236–0841); **Toronto** (175 Bloor St. E, Suite 314, Toronto, Ont. M4W 3R8, tel. 416/323–1155); **Vancouver** (World Trade Center Office Complex, 999 Canada Pl., Suite 602, Vancouver, B.C. V6C 3E1, tel. 604/684–1177).

U.K. Citizens Citizens of the United Kingdom need a valid passport to enter Australia or New Zealand. A visa is also required to enter Australia. Applications for new and renewal passports are available from main post offices as well as at the six passport offices, located in Belfast, Glasgow, Liverpool, London, Newport, and Peterborough. You may apply in person at all passport offices or by mail to all except the London office. Children under 16 may travel on an accompanying parent's passport. All passports are valid for 10 years. Allow a month for processing.

Australian visa application forms are available from most travel agents and in the Australian Tourist Commission's brochure, "Australia, A Traveller's Guide." You may also apply in person at the **Australian High Commission** (Australia House, Strand, London WC2B 4LA, tel. 071/379–4334) or at the Australian consulates in Manchester and Edinburgh. Visitors planning to stay more than three months must pay a £15 processing fee. (If you travel on an under-three-month visa and decide to extend it while there, the fee rises to about £45.) Apply at least two weeks in advance if making your application by mail.

Customs and Duties

On Arrival Australia has strict laws prohibiting or restricting the import of
Australia weapons and firearms. Animals and certain foodstuffs are subject to quarantine. Anti-drug laws are strictly enforced, and penalties are severe. Nonresidents over 18 years of age may bring in 200 cigarettes, or 250 grams of cigars or tobacco, and 1 liter of liquor, provided this is carried with them. Other taxable goods to the value of $400 for adults and $200 for children may be included in personal baggage duty-free.

New Zealand New Zealand has stringent regulations governing the import of weapons, foodstuffs, and certain plant and animal material. Anti-drug laws are strict and penalties severe. In addition to personal effects, nonresidents over 17 years of age may bring in, duty-free, 200 cigarettes or 250 grams of tobacco or 50 cigars, 4.5 liters of wine, one bottle containing not more than 1,125 milliliters of spirits or liqueur, and personal purchases and gifts up to the value of US $380 (NZ$700).

Returning Provided you've been out of the country for at least 48 hours and
Home haven't already used the exemption, or any part of it, in the past 30
U.S. Customs days, you may bring home $400 worth of foreign goods duty-free. So can each member of your family, regardless of age; and your exemptions may be pooled, so one of you can bring in more if another brings in less. A flat 10% duty applies to the next $1,000 of goods; above $1,400, the rate varies with the merchandise. (If the 48-hour or 30-day limits apply, your duty-free allowance drops to $25, which may not be pooled.) Please note that these are the *general* rules, applicable to most countries, including Australia and New Zealand.

Travelers 21 or older may bring back 1 liter of alcohol duty-free, provided the beverage laws of the state through which they reenter the United States allow it. In addition, 100 non-Cuban cigars and 200 cigarettes are allowed, regardless of your age. Antiques and works of art more than 100 years old are duty-free.

Gifts valued at less than $50 may be mailed to the United States duty-free, with a limit of one package per day per addressee (do not send alcohol or tobacco products, nor perfume valued at more than $5); mark the package "Unsolicited Gift" and include the nature of the gift and its retail value on the outside of the package.

For a copy of "Know Before You Go," a free brochure detailing what you may and may not bring back to the United States, rates of duty, and other pointers, contact the **U.S. Customs Service** (Box 7407, Washington, DC 20044, tel. 202/927–6724).

Canadian Customs Once per calendar year, when you've been out of Canada for at least seven days, you may bring in C$300 worth of goods duty-free. If you've been away less than seven days but more than 48 hours, the duty-free exemption drops to C$100 but can be claimed any number of times (as can a C$20 duty-free exemption for absences of 24 hours or more). You cannot combine the yearly and 48-hour exemptions, use the C$300 exemption only partially (to save the balance for a later trip), or pool exemptions with family members. Goods claimed under the C$300 exemption may follow you by mail; those claimed under the lesser exemptions must accompany you on your return.

Alcohol and tobacco products may be included in the yearly and 48-hour exemptions but not in the 24-hour exemption. If you meet the age requirements of the province through which you reenter Canada, you may bring in, duty-free, 1.14 liters (40 imperial ounces) of wine or liquor *or* two dozen 12-ounce cans or bottles of beer or ale. If you are 16 or older, you may bring in, duty-free, 200 cigarettes, 50 cigars or cigarillos, and 400 tobacco sticks or 400 grams of manufactured tobacco. Alcohol and tobacco must accompany you on your return.

An unlimited number of gifts valued up to C$60 each may be mailed to Canada duty-free. These do not count as part of your exemption. Label the package "Unsolicited Gift—Value under $60." Alcohol and tobacco are excluded.

For more information, including details of duties on items that exceed your duty-free limit, ask the **Revenue Canada Customs and Excise Department** (Connaught Bldg., MacKenzie Ave., Ottawa, Ont., K1A OL5, tel. 613/957–0275) for a copy of the free brochure "I Declare/Je Déclare."

U.K. Customs From countries outside the EU such as Australia and New Zealand, you may import duty-free 200 cigarettes, 100 cigarillos, 50 cigars or 250 grams of tobacco; 1 liter of spirits or 2 liters of fortified or sparkling wine; 2 liters of still table wine; 60 milliliters of perfume; 250 milliliters of toilet water; plus £36 worth of other goods, including gifts and souvenirs.

For further information or a copy of "A Guide for Travellers," which details standard customs procedures as well as what you may bring into the United Kingdom from abroad, contact **HM Customs and Excise** (Dorset House, Stamford St., London SE1 9PY, tel. 071/928–3344).

Traveling with Cameras, Camcorders, and Laptops

About Film and Cameras If your camera is new or if you haven't used it for a while, shoot and develop a few rolls of film before leaving home. Store film in a cool, dry place—never in the car's glove compartment or on the shelf under the rear window.

Airport security X-rays generally aren't harmful to film with ISO below 400. To protect your film, carry it with you in a clear plastic bag and ask for a hand inspection. Such requests are honored at U.S. airports but are at the discretion of the inspector abroad. Don't depend on a lead-lined bag to protect film in checked luggage—the airline may increase the radiation to see what's inside. Call the **Kodak Information Center** (tel. 800/242–2424) for details.

About Camcorders Before your trip, put camcorders through their paces: shoot some practice tape, invest in a skylight filter to protect the lens, and check the batteries. Most newer camcorders are equipped with batteries that can be recharged with a universal or worldwide AC adapter charger (or multivoltage converter) usable whether the voltage is 110 or 220. All that's needed is the appropriate plug.

About Videotape Videotape is not damaged by X-rays, but it may be harmed by the magnetic field of a walk-through metal detector, so ask for a hand-check. Airport security personnel may ask you to turn on your camcorder to prove that it's not an explosive device, so make sure the battery is charged. Note that rather than the National Television System Committee video standard (NTSC) used in the United States and Canada, Australia and New Zealand use PAL technology. You will not be able to view North American tapes on TV sets down under, nor view movies bought there with your home VCR. Blank tapes bought in Australia or New Zealand can be used for NTSC camcorder taping, but they are pricey.

About Laptops Security X-rays do not harm hard-disk or floppy-disk storage, but you may request a hand-check, at which point you may be asked to turn on the computer to prove that it is indeed what it appears to be. (Check your battery before departure.) Most airlines allow you to use your laptop aloft except during takeoff and landing (so as not to interfere with navigation equipment). For international travel, register your foreign-made laptop with U.S. Customs as you leave the country. If your laptop is U.S.-made, call the consulate of the country you'll be visiting to find out whether it should be registered with customs upon arrival. Before departure, find out about repair facilities at your destination, and don't forget any transformer or adapter plug you may need (*see* Electricity, *above*).

Language

To an outsider's ear, Australian English can be mystifying. Not only is the accent thick and slightly slurred, but Australians have developed a vibrant vernacular quite distinct from that of any other English-speaking country. You can soon learn the idiom and how to speak "Strine"—as residents of Down Under pronounce "Australian"—with a copy of Danielle Martin's *Australians Say G'Day*, which comes with a cassette tape recording to help you interpret the book's dialogues. The *Ridgy Didge Guidebook to Australia*, by K. J. Condren, is a handy pocket guide to the intricacies of Australian terminology.

The Maori language is still spoken by many New Zealanders of Polynesian descent, but English is the everyday language for all races. A number of Maori words have found their way into common usage, most noticeably in place-names, which often refer to peculiar features of the local geography or food supply. The Maori word for New Zealand, *Aotearoa*, means "land of the long white cloud." The South Island town of Kaikoura is famous for its crayfish—and the word means "to eat crayfish." *Whangapiro*, the Maori name for the Government Gardens in Rotorua, means "an evil-smelling place"; if you visit the town, you'll find out why. A Polynesian noun you'll sometimes come across in Maori churches is *tapu*—"sacred"—which has entered the English language as *taboo*. Another Maori word you will frequently encounter is *pakeha*, which means you, the non-Maori. The Maori greeting is *kia ora*, which can also mean "goodbye," "good health," or "good luck."

A Personal Kiwi-Yankee Dictionary, by Louis S. Leland, Jr., is an amusing and informative guide to New Zealand idioms.

Staying Healthy

Hygiene standards in **Australia** are high and well monitored, and you can drink the water and eat fresh produce without concern. The major health hazard is sunburn or sunstroke: Australians suffer one of the world's highest incidences of skin cancer from overdoses of sun. Even people who are not normally bothered by strong sun should cover up with a long-sleeve shirt, a hat, and long pants or a beach wrap. Carry some sunscreen for nose, ears, and other sensitive areas such as eyelids and ankles, and be sure to drink plenty of fluids. Above all, limit the amount of time you spend in the sun for the first few days until you are acclimatized, and always try to avoid sunbathing in the middle of the day. You may take four weeks' supply of prescribed medication into Australia (more with a doctor's certificate).

Nutrition and general health standards in **New Zealand** are just as high, and it would be hard to find a more pristine natural environment. There are no venomous snakes, and the only poisonous spider, the katipo, is a rarity. One surprising health hazard is the water. While the country's alpine lakes might look like backdrops for mineral-water ads, some on the South Island harbor a tiny organism that can cause "duck itch," a temporary but intense skin irritation. The organism is found only on the shallow lake margins, so the chances of infection are greatly reduced if you stick to deeper water. Some streams are infected by giardia, a water-borne protozoal parasite that can cause gastrointestinal disorders, including acute diarrhea. Giardia is most likely to occur when streams pass through an area inhabited by mammals (such as cattle or possums). There is no risk of infection if you drink from streams above the tree line.

One New Zealander you will come to loathe is the tiny black sandfly, common to the western half of the South Island, which inflicts a painful bite that can itch for several days. Insect repellents are readily available throughout New Zealand.

Insurance

Every visitor to New Zealand is covered by the government's Accident Compensation scheme. Under this scheme, anyone who is injured in an accident is entitled to claim compensation, irrespective of fault. Benefits include most medical and hospital expenses and lump-sum payments for physical disability, but not loss of earnings outside New Zealand. (New Zealand law prohibits any injured party from bringing legal action for damages in New Zealand courts.)

For U.S. Residents	Most tour operators, travel agents, and insurance agents sell specialized health-and-accident, flight, trip-cancellation, and luggage insurance as well as comprehensive policies with some or all of these features. But before you make any purchase, review your existing health and homeowner policies to find out whether they cover expenses incurred while traveling.

Health-and-Accident Insurance Specific policy provisions of supplemental health-and-accident insurance for travelers include reimbursement of $1,000 to $150,000 worth of medical and/or dental expenses caused by an accident or illness during a trip. The personal-accident, or death-and-dismemberment, provision pays a lump sum to your beneficiaries if you die or to you if you lose one or both limbs or your eyesight; the lump sum awarded can range from $15,000 to $500,000. The medical-assistance provision may reimburse you for the cost of referrals, evacuation, or repatriation and other services, or it may automatically enroll you as a member of a particular medical-assistance company.

Flight Insurance Often bought on a last-minute impulse at the airport, flight insurance pays a lump sum when a plane crashes either to a beneficiary if the insured dies, or sometimes to a surviving passenger who loses eyesight or a limb. Like most impulse buys, flight insurance is expensive and basically unnecessary. It supplements the airlines' coverage described in the limits-of-liability paragraphs on your ticket. Charging an airline ticket to a major credit card often automatically entitles you to coverage and may also cover travel by bus, train, and ship.

Baggage Insurance In the event of loss, damage, or theft on international flights, airlines limit their liability to $20 per kilogram for checked baggage (roughly about $640 per 70-pound bag) and $400 per passenger for unchecked baggage. On domestic flights, the ceiling is $1,250 per passenger. Excess-valuation insurance can be bought directly from the airline at check-in for about $10 per $1,000 worth of coverage. However, you cannot buy it at any price for the rather extensive list of excluded items shown on your airline ticket.

Trip Insurance **Trip-cancellation-and-interruption insurance** protects you in the event you are unable to undertake or finish your trip, especially if your airline ticket, cruise, or package tour does not allow changes or cancellations. The amount of coverage you purchase should equal the amount of your travel costs that you'd be liable for if you, a traveling companion, or a family member fell ill and were forced to stay home; also include the nondiscounted, one-way airline ticket you would need to buy if you had to return home early. Read the fine print carefully, especially sections defining "family member" and "preexisting medical conditions." **Default** or **bankruptcy insurance** protects you against a supplier's failure to deliver. Such policies often do not cover default by a travel agency, tour operator, airline, or cruise line if you bought your tour and the coverage directly from the firm in question. Tours packaged by one of the 33 members of the **United States Tour Operators Association** (USTOA, 211 E. 51st St., Suite 12B, New York, NY 10022; tel. 212/750–7371), which requires members to maintain $1 million each in an account to reimburse clients in case of default, are likely to present the fewest difficulties. Even better, pay for travel arrangements with a major credit card, so that you can refuse to pay the bill if services have not been rendered—and let the card company fight your battles.

Comprehensive Policies Companies supplying comprehensive policies with some or all of the above features include **Access America, Inc.,** (Box 90315, Richmond, VA 23230, tel. 800/284–8300); **Carefree Travel Insurance,** (Box 310,

120 Mineola Blvd., Mineola, NY 11501, tel. 516/294–0220 or 800/323–3149); **Tele-Trip** (Mutual of Omaha Plaza, Box 31762, Omaha, NE 68131, tel. 800/228–9792); **The Travelers Companies** (1 Tower Sq., Hartford, CT 06183, tel. 203/277–0111 or 800/243–3174); **Travel Guard International** (1145 Clark St., Stevens Point, WI 54481, tel. 715/345–0505 or 800/782–5151); and **Wallach and Company, Inc.** (107 W. Federal St., Box 480, Middleburg, VA 22117, tel. 703/687–3166 or 800/237–6615).

U.K.
Residents
Most tour operators, travel agents, and insurance agents sell specialized policies covering accident, medical expenses, personal liability, trip cancellation, and loss or theft of personal property. Some policies include coverage for delayed departure and legal expenses, winter-sports, accidents, or motoring abroad. You can also purchase an annual travel-insurance policy valid for every trip you make during the year in which it's purchased (usually only trips of less than 90 days). Before you leave, make sure you will be covered if you have a preexisting medical condition or are pregnant; your insurers may not pay for routine or continuing treatment, or may require a note from your doctor certifying your fitness to travel.

For advice by phone or a free booklet, "Holiday Insurance," that sets out what to expect from a holiday-insurance policy and gives price guidelines, contact the **Association of British Insurers** (51 Gresham St., London EC2V 7HQ, tel. 071/600–3333; 30 Gordon St., Glasgow G1 3PU, tel. 041/226–3905; Scottish Provincial Bldg., Donegall Sq. W, Belfast BT1 6JE, tel. 0232/249176; call for other locations).

Car Rentals

All the major car rental car companies are represented in both countries, including **Alamo** (tel. 800/327–9633); **Avis** (tel. 800/331–1212); **Budget** (tel. 800/527–0700); **Eurodollar Rent a Car, Ltd.** (tel. 800/800–4000); **Hertz** (tel. 800/654–3131, 800/263-0600 in Canada); **National** (tel. 800/227–7368); and **Thrifty** (tel. 800/367–2277). **Koala Tours** (tel. 800/535–0316) also handles car rentals, but these must be made through travel agents. Visitors are advised to make a reservation in advance.

Requirements
Usually, you must be over 21 to rent a car (some rental companies require a driver to be 25) and some restrictions may apply to drivers over 60 years of age. Most companies will accept your driver's license from home, but some may require an International Driver's Permit, available from the American Automobile Association (AAA) and the Canadian Automobile Association (CAA).

Australia
In metropolitan areas rates range from $58 plus tax per day for an economy car to as high as $166 plus tax for a large car, with unlimited free mileage. Costs may be higher if you rent in the country. One-way rentals can be arranged, although they usually involve a drop-off charge. Two- or three-berth campers and four- to six-berth motor homes can also be rented, with a minimum one-week rental period usual. Four-wheel-drive vehicles are widely available.

New Zealand
The cost (including compulsory insurance) for a small vehicle such as a Toyota Corolla is about $75 per day with unlimited mileage; for a Ford Fairmont, $95 per day. Local operators will rent to you for about one-third less, but you have to return the car to the pick-up point, and the minimum hire period is usually four days.

The cost of a two-berth camper van varies from $100 to $185 per day, depending on the season; a six-berth camper runs $140 to $240 per day. The minimum hire period is usually six days. There are more than 400 motor camps, with communal bathroom and laundry facilities, grocery stores, and power sites, scattered the length and breadth of New Zealand; a van site at one of these goes for $6–$12 per night.

Extra Charges Picking up the car in one city and leaving it in another may entail substantial drop-off charges or one-way service fees. The cost of a collision or loss damage waiver (*see below*) can be high, also. Automatic transmissions and air-conditioning are not universally available abroad; ask for them when you book if you want them, and check the cost before you commit yourself to the rental. Fill the tank just before you turn in the vehicle to avoid being charged for refueling at what you'll swear is the most expensive pump in town.

Cutting Costs Major international companies have programs that discount their standard rates by 15%–30% if you make the reservation before departure (anywhere from 24 hours to 14 days), rent for a minimum number of days (typically three or four), and prepay the rental. Ask about these advance-purchase plans when you call for information. More economical rentals may come as part of fly/drive or other packages, including bare-bones deals that combine only the rental plus an airline ticket (*see* Package Tours for Independent Travelers, *above*). In Australia, Koala Tours' **Aussie Car Pass** offers discount rental rates. The Australian automobile clubs give international AAA members a nationwide car-rental rate affording discounts for a one- to three-day reservation up to a monthly rate.

Several companies operate as wholesalers—they don't own their own fleets but they rent in bulk from those that do and offer advantageous rates to their customers. Rentals through such companies must be arranged and paid for before you leave the United States. Among them are **Auto Europe** (Box 1097, Camden, ME 04843, tel. 207/236–8235 or 800/223–5555, 800/458–9503 in Canada), which rents cars in the United States, Europe, Australia, New Zealand, and other regions, and **Foremost Euro-Car** (5430 Van Nuys Blvd., Suite 306, Van Nuys, CA 91401, tel. 818/786–1960 or 800/272–3299), which rents in Europe as well as Australia and New Zealand. You won't see these wholesalers' deals advertised; they're even better in summer, when business travel is down. Always ask whether the prices are guaranteed in U.S. dollars or foreign currency and if unlimited mileage is available. Find out about any required deposits, cancellation penalties, and drop-off charges, and confirm the cost of the collision damage waiver.

Insurance and Collision Damage Waiver Until recently, standard rental contracts included liability coverage (for damage to public property, injury to pedestrians, and so on) and coverage for the car against fire, theft, and collision damage with a deductible. Due to law changes in some states and rising liability costs, several car rental agencies have reduced the type of coverage they offer. Before you rent a car, find out exactly what coverage, if any, is provided by your personal auto insurer. Don't assume that you are covered. If you do want insurance from the rental company, secondary coverage may be the only type offered. You may already have secondary coverage if you charge the rental to a credit card. Only Diners Club (tel. 800/234–6377) provides primary coverage in the United States and worldwide. In Australia, compulsory third-party insurance and collision damage waiver often are included in car rentals.

Rail Passes

Australia An inexpensive way to see Australia is by rail, although the huge distances between cities result in long journeys. For example, the *Indian-Pacific* from Sydney to Perth takes 65 hours, and the *XPT* from Sydney to Brisbane takes 16 hours.

The best value is an **Austrailpass,** available for unlimited first- or economy-class travel on all of Australia's government railways—interstate, intrastate, city, and suburban—as well as certain railroad-operated bus services. At press time, Austrailpasses were available for 14, 21, 30, 60, or 90 consecutive days at prices ranging from $435 to $1,125 for an economy-class seat and from $725 to $1,765 for a first-class seat. The passes don't cover sleeping berths or meals, which are extra. Economy-class sleeping berths are not available on all routes.

The **Austrail Flexipass** allows more flexibility for stopovers. The Flexipass allows unlimited economy-class or first-class rail travel for any 8, 15, 22, or 29 days within a period of six months. Prices start at $340 for the eight-day economy-class pass, which cannot be used for travel to Perth or on the *Ghan* to Alice Springs.

Another option is the **Kangaroo Road 'n Rail Pass,** which provides unlimited travel on government-owned rail services and Australian Coachline buses throughout the country within a 14-, 21-, or 28-day period, at costs ranging from $655 to $1,150 for economy class, and from $1,040 to $1,530 for first class. The Austrailpass, Austrail Flexipass, and the Kangaroo Road 'n Rail Pass should be purchased either before departure for Australia, or on arrival with presentation of your passport. You must begin use of your pass within 12 months of its issue. **Caper Fares,** which afford a 30% discount between some major cities on an advance purchase basis, are better bought before departure for Australia, as they tend to be booked up far in advance. It is advisable to make all rail reservations well in advance, particularly during peak tourist seasons. Contact your travel agent or the appropriate Rail Australia office: **U.S.** (tel. 800/423–2880; ATS Tours, tel. 818/841–1030; Austravel Inc., tel. 800/633–3404); **Canada** (Goway Travel, tel. 800/387–8850); **U.K.** (tel. 071/828–4111).

New Zealand Travelers can purchase an **InterCity Travelpass** good for unlimited travel on trains, buses, and InterIsland ferries. The pass allows 8 days of travel within a 21-day period ($425), 15 days of travel within 36 days ($530), or 22 days of travel within 56 days ($650). Children aged 4 to 14 pay 67% of the adult fare. The **4 in 1 New Zealand Travelpass,** which is available for purchase outside New Zealand only, includes one flight sector on Ansett New Zealand between assigned city pairs. The flight may be at any time after the date of issue of the Travelpass and up to seven days after expiry of the Travelpass. The pass entitles the visitor to 8 days of travel in 21 days ($616), 15 days of travel in 35 days ($721), or 22 days of travel in 56 days ($841). Children aged 4 to 14 travel at 67% of the adult fare. An additional two flight sectors may be purchased at $191 per sector. For Youth Hostel Association members, the **InterCity Youth Hostel Travel Card** ($75 for 14 days, $99 for 28 days) gives a 50% discount on most train services, all InterCity coach services, and on the InterIsland ferries. Students with an International Student Identity Card (ISIC) get a 20% discount (*see* Student and Youth Travel, *below*). Contact InterCity Travel Centres (tel. 09/358–4085 in Auckland, 03/379–9020 in Christchurch, 04/472–5111 in Wellington) for ticket information. In the United States, contact ATS Tours (tel. 818/841–1030) or Austravel Inc. (tel. 800/633–3404).

Bus Passes

Australian Coachlines, operators of the express bus companies with national networks—Greyhound, Pioneer, and Bus Australia—offers passes that can be used interchangeably on each of the companies' routes, resulting in considerable savings, especially when purchased overseas. Most can be bought on arrival in Australia, but at a 10%–15% higher price.

The **Aussie Pass** offers unlimited travel over the entire Australian Coachlines network, for periods ranging from 7 to 90 consecutive days, with a one- to six-month validity, at costs of $350 to $2,150 for adults, $275 to $1,680 for children. The pass, which includes discounts for certain accommodations, car rentals, and sightseeing, is available through Greyhound USA (tel. 800/64-COACH) and Goway Travel in Canada (*see* Rail Passes, *above*).

Valid for travel in both Australia and New Zealand, the **Down Under Pass** is offered by Australian Coachlines and Mt. Cook Line. The passes range from 9 to 45 days, to be used within prescribed time allotments that allow for a 10-day break in travel between the two countries. The passes are priced from $467 to $1,475.

For New Zealand's **InterCity Travelpass,** good for unlimited travel on trains, buses, and inter-island ferries, *see* Rail Passes, *above*.

Student and Youth Travel

In addition to the International Youth Hostels (*see below*), a network of low-cost, independent backpacker hostels operates in both Australia and New Zealand. They can be found in nearly every city and tourist spot, and they offer clean, twin- and small-dormitory–style accommodations and self-catering kitchens, similar to those of the Youth Hostel Association (or YHA, the Australian version of IYH), with no membership required. For a free guide to backpacker hostels in Australia, contact **Backpackers Resorts of Australia Pty. Ltd.** (Box 1000, Byron Bay, NSW 2481, tel. 018/666–888, fax 066/847–100); enclose US$3 for postage and handling. A **V.I.P. Backpacker** card, available for $20, entitles you to discounts at all Australian backpacker hostels and on Greyhound, Pioneer, and several other bus lines. The card and guide can be purchased at **Backpackers Travel Centre** (Imperial Arcade, Pitt St. Mall Level, Sydney, tel. 02/232–5166). To find out about backpacker hostels in New Zealand, contact **Budget Backpackers Hostels NZ, Ltd.** (Rainbow Lodge, 99 Titiraupenga St., Taupo, tel. 074/8–5754 or Downtown Backpackers, 208 Kilgore St., Christchurch, tel. 03/366–9720).

Backpackers Discounts is a pass specifically designed for young budget travelers. Applicable with either the Aussie Pass or regional Explorer Passes, it allows unlimited stopovers on all Australian Coachlines routes within the valid duration of the pass; travel need not be on consecutive days. Pass discounts are available to YHA members and V.I.P. Backpacker Card holders, and discounted bus pass/accommodation vouchers can be used at YHA hostels and Backpackers Resorts of Australia. For example, the seven-day Hostel Pass, with seven days' travel on Australian Coachlines plus five nights' YHA accommodation vouchers, costs $361. Contact SO/PAC (tel. 800/551–2012) for information and reservations.

Victoria Street in Sydney's Kings Cross, near the rear entrance to the Kings Cross subway station, is a gathering spot for international backpackers. There you can sometimes find drivers looking for a rider to share car expenses while exploring the country, or someone heading home who is selling a car.

Travel Agencies **Council Travel Services (CTS),** a subsidiary of the nonprofit Council on International Educational Exchange (CIEE) specializes in low-cost travel arrangements abroad for students and is the exclusive U.S. agent for several discount cards. Also newly available from CTS are domestic air passes for bargain travel within the United States. CIEE's twice-yearly *Student Travels* magazine is available at the CTS office at CIEE headquarters (205 E. 42nd St., 16th Floor, New York, NY 10017, tel. 212/661–1450); in Boston (tel. 617/266–1926), Miami (tel. 305/670–9261), and Los Angeles (tel. 310/208–3551); and at 43 branches in college towns nationwide (free in person, $1 by mail). **Campus Connections** (1100 E. Marlton Pike, Cherry Hill, NJ 08034, tel. 800/428–3235) specializes in discounted accommodations and airline fares for students. The **Educational Travel Centre** (438 N. Frances St., Madison, WI 53703, tel. 608/256–5551) offers low-cost domestic and international airline tickets, mostly for flights departing from Chicago, as well as rail passes. Other travel agencies catering to students include **TMI Student Travel** (1146 Pleasant St., Watertown, MA 02172, tel. 800/245–3672) and **Travel Cuts** (187 College St., Toronto, Ont. M5T 1P7, tel. 416/979–2406).

Discount Cards For discounts on transportation and on museum and attractions admissions, buy the **International Student Identity Card** (ISIC) if you're a bona fide student, or the **International Youth Card** (IYC) if you're under 26. In the United States the ISIC and IYC cards cost $15 each and include basic travel accident and sickness coverage. Apply to **CIEE** (*see* address *above*, tel. 212/661–1414; the application is in *Student Travels*). In Canada the cards are available for $15 each from **Travel Cuts** (*see above*). In the United Kingdom they cost £5 and £4 respectively at student unions and student travel companies, including Council Travel's London office (28A Poland St., London W1V 3DB, tel. 071/437–7767).

Hosteling A **Hostelling International** (HI) membership card is the key to more than 6,000 hostels in 70 countries; the sex-segregated, dormitory-style sleeping quarters, including some for families, go for $7 to $20 a night per person. Membership is available in the United States through **Hostelling International American Youth Hostels** (HIAYH, 733 15th St. NW, Washington, DC 20005, tel. 202/783–6161), the American link in the worldwide chain, and costs $25 for adults 18–54, $10 for those under 18, $15 for those 55 and over, and $35 for families. Volume 2 of the two-volume *Guide to Budget Accommodation*, which can be purchased from HIAYH and the other HI member organizations, lists hostels in Asia, Australia, and New Zealand as well as in Canada and the United States ($13.95 including postage). HI membership is available in Canada through **Hostelling International–Canada** (205 Catherine St., Suite 400, Ottawa, Ont. K2P 1C3, tel. 613/748–5638) for $26.75, and in the United Kingdom through the **Youth Hostel Association of England and Wales** (Trevelyan House, 8 St. Stephen's Hill, St. Albans, Herts. AL1 2DY, tel. 0727/55215) for £9.

Traveling with Children

Publications *Family Travel Times,* published 10 times a year by **Travel With Your**
Newsletter **Children** (TWYCH, 45 W. 18th St., 7th Floor Tower, New York, NY
10011, tel. 212/206–0688; annual subscription $55), covers destina-
tions, types of vacations, and modes of travel.

Books *Traveling with Children—And Enjoying It,* by Arlene K. Butler
($11.95 plus $3 shipping; Globe Pequot Press, Box 833, Old
Saybrook, CT 06475, tel. 800/243–0495, or 800/962–0973 in CT)
helps you plan your trip with children, from toddlers to teens.

Tour **Grandtravel** (6900 Wisconsin Ave., Suite 706, Chevy Chase, MD
Operators 20815, tel. 800/247–7651) offers tours for people traveling with their
grandchildren. The catalogue, as charmingly written and illus-
trated as a children's book, positively invites armchair traveling
with lap-sitters aboard. **Rascals in Paradise** (650 5th St., Suite 505,
San Francisco, CA 94107, tel. 800/872–7225) specializes in adventurous, exotic, and fun-filled vacations for families to carefully
screened resorts and hotels around the world.

Getting There On international flights, the fare for infants under two not occupy-
Air Fares ing a seat is generally 10% of the accompanying adult's fare; children
ages 2 to 11 usually pay half to two-thirds of the adult fare. On domestic flights, children under two not occupying a seat travel free,
and older children currently travel on the "lowest applicable" adult
fare.

Baggage In general, infants paying 10% of the adult fare are allowed one carry-on bag, not to exceed 70 pounds or 45 inches (length + width +
height), and a collapsible stroller; check with the airline before departure because you may be allowed less if the flight is full. The
adult baggage allowance applies for children paying half or more of
the adult fare.

Safety Seats The FAA recommends the use of safety seats aloft and details approved models in the free leaflet **"Child/Infant Safety Seats Recommended for Use in Aircraft"** (available from the Federal Aviation
Administration, APA–200, 800 Independence Ave. SW, Washington, DC 20591, tel. 202/267–3479). Airline policy varies. U.S. carriers allow FAA-approved models bearing a sticker declaring their
FAA approval. Because these seats are strapped into a regular passenger seat, they may require that parents buy a ticket even for an
infant under two who would otherwise ride free. Foreign carriers
may not allow infant seats, may charge the child's rather than the
infant's fare for their use, or may require you to hold your baby during takeoff and landing, thus defeating the seat's purpose.

Facilities Aloft Some airlines provide other facilities and services for children, such
as children's meals and freestanding bassinets (to those with seats
at the bulkhead, where there's enough legroom). Make your request
when reserving. The annual February/March issue of *Family Travel
Times* gives details of the children's services of dozens of airlines
(*see above*). "Kids and Teens in Flight" (free from the U.S. Department of Transportation, tel. 202/366–2220) offers tips for children
flying alone.

Dining In Australia, eating out with children is no problem in family restaurants, which cater to children with high chairs, booster seats,
and, frequently, child's menus. This type of restaurant is usually
found in the suburbs rather than city centers; look for the occasional
Sizzler, Sizzler-style Keg Steak and Seafood, and Smorgy's restaurants. For more casual eating, coffee shops, delis, bistros, and fast-

food eateries, both international chains and Aussie versions such as Hungry Jack's, are usually child friendly.

New Zealanders are genuinely fond of and considerate toward children, and their own children are included in most of their parents' social activities. Children are welcome in all restaurants throughout the country. However, they are rarely seen in those restaurants that appear in Fodor's very expensive ($$$$) and expensive ($$$) price categories. These restaurants may not have high chairs, nor might they be prepared to make special children's meals. Major cities and important tourist centers have McDonald's and Kentucky Fried Chicken outlets.

Lodging In hotels in Australia and New Zealand, roll-away beds are usually free, and children under 12 sharing a hotel room with adults either stay free or receive a discount rate. The **Hyatt** hotels (tel. 800/233-1234) located in Sydney, Sanctuary Cove, Coolum Beach, Perth, Melbourne, Canberra, and Adelaide, Australia and in Auckland, New Zealand, allow children under 18 to stay free when sharing a room with parents. The **Hyatt Regency Sanctuary Cove** and **Hyatt Regency Coolum Beach** both have a Camp Hyatt program for children. Few hotels have separate facilities for children. Exceptions include some of the Great Barrier Reef resorts: **Club Med** on **Lindeman Island** has a Kid's Club and Mini-Club; **Hayman Island** features a Kidz Club for children age 5 to 15; and **Great Keppel** offers family units plus special dining hours and activities for children. The **Sheraton Mirage Port Douglas** has a day-care center for children over 18 months.

In Australia and New Zealand, home hosting provides an ideal opportunity for visitors to stay with a local family, either in town or on a working farm. For information on home and farm stays, *see* Lodging in Staying in Australia and Staying in New Zealand, *below*. Also see those sections for information on home exchange and apartment rentals.

Baby-sitting Most hotels and resorts have baby-sitters available through the con-
Services cierge or front desk, at a charge of around $10 to $15 per hour. Baby-sitting services are also listed in the yellow pages of city telephone directories.

In New Zealand, strollers and bassinets can be rented from the **Royal New Zealand Plunket Society** (472 George St., Dunedin North, tel. 03/477-0110). Most car-rental agencies provide "cocoons" for newborns as well as child safety seats.

Baby Supplies Department stores and drug stores (called chemists locally) in Australia carry a wide range of baby products such as disposable diapers (ask for napkins or nappies), formula, and baby food. In New Zealand, these products can be found in chemist's shops. They are less expensive in supermarkets, but these are scarce outside the major cities.

Hints for Travelers with Disabilities

Both Australia and New Zealand are at the forefront in providing facilities for the disabled. The **Australian Council for Rehabilitation of the Disabled** (ACROD, 33 Thesiger Ct. Deakin, ACT 2605, tel. 062/82-4333) is one source of information on facilities, including the "Accessibility Guide for Disabled Travellers to Tourist Attractions in Australia." Since provisions vary from state to state, for additional information contact the ACROD offices in the states you plan to visit: Australian Capital Territory, tel. 062/82–4333; New South Wales, tel. 02/809–4488; Northern Territory, tel. 089/470–6811; Queensland, tel. 07/250–1511; South Australia, tel. 08/223–3335; Tasmania, tel. 002/23–6086; Victoria, tel. 03/597–0157; Western Australia, tel. 09/222–2961. In New Zealand, contact the **Royal New Zealand Plunket Society** (472 George St., Dunedin North, tel. 03/477–0110).

Lodging   The major hotel chains (such as Regent, Sheraton, InterContinental, Ramada, Hilton, Holiday Inn, and Hyatt) provide three or four rooms with disabled facilities in most of their properties. The **National Roads and Motorists Association** (151 Clarence St., Sydney, NSW 2000, tel. 02/260–9222) publishes the $10 *Accommodation Directory*, indicating which properties have independent access for wheelchairs and which ones provide wheelchair access with assistance. Another source of information is the "Disabled Travellers Guide to Australia, Accessible Motels and Hotels" from the **Council of Disabled Motorists** (2A Station St., Coburg, VIC 3058, tel. 03/386–0413). In New Zealand, all accommodations are required by law to provide at least one room with facilities for the disabled. The **New Zealand Tourism Board** publishes *Access: A Guide for the Less Mobile Traveller*, listing accommodations, attractions, restaurants, and thermal pools with special facilities.

Getting   In addition to making arrangements for wheelchair-using passen-
Around   gers, both Qantas and Ansett Airlines accommodate trained dogs
By Air   accompanying sight- and hearing-impaired passengers. On Air New Zealand, wheelchairs for in-flight mobility are standard equipment; seat-belt extensions, quadriplegic harnesses, and padded leg rests are also available. Ask for the company's brochure "Air Travel for People with Disabilities."

By Train   Passengers on mainline passenger trains in both Australia and New Zealand can request collapsible wheelchairs to negotiate the narrow interior corridors. However, compact toilet areas and platform access problems make long-distance train travel difficult. Both New South Wales State Rail and V/Line, the Victorian state rail company, issue brochures detailing assistance available on metropolitan and country trains. To request these, call 02/131–500 in Sydney or 03/610–7482 in Melbourne.

By Taxi   In Australia, wheelchair-accessible taxis are available in all state capitals except Hobart and Darwin: **Adelaide** (tel. 08/371–0033), **Brisbane** (tel. 07/229–5344, 07/391–0191, or 07/831–3000), **Melbourne** (tel. 03/819–1911, 03/345–4555, 03/480–2222, or 03/417–1111), **Perth** (tel. 09/322–0111), **Sydney** (tel. 02/339–0200). Companies in New Zealand have recently introduced vans equipped with hoists and floor clamps, but these should be booked several hours in advance if possible; contact the Plunket Society (*see above*) for more information.

Car Rental Only **Budget** (tel. 800/527–0700 in the U.S. and Canada) offers cars fitted with hand controls, but these are limited. **Hertz** (tel. 800/654–3131 in the U.S., and 800/263–0600 Canada) will fit hand-held controls onto standard cars in some cities.

Organizations Several organizations provide travel information for people with disabilities, usually for a membership fee, and some publish newsletters and bulletins. Among them are the **Information Center for Individuals with Disabilities** (Fort Point Pl., 27–43 Wormwood St., Boston, MA 02210, tel. 617/727–5540 or 800/462–5015 in MA between 11 and 4, or leave message; TTY tel. 617/345–9743); **Mobility International USA** (Box 10767, Eugene, OR 97440, tel. and TTY 503/

343–1284, fax 503/343–6812), the U.S. branch of an international organization based in Britain (*see below*) and present in 30 countries; **MossRehab Hospital Travel Information Service** (tel. 215/456–9603, TDD tel. 215/456–9602); the **Travel Industry and Disabled Exchange** (TIDE, 5435 Donna Ave., Tarzana, CA 91356, tel. 818/368–5648); and **Travelin' Talk** (Box 3534, Clarksville, TN 37043, tel. 615/552–6670, fax 615/552–1182).

In the United Kingdom Main sources include the **Royal Association for Disability and Rehabilitation** (RADAR, 25 Mortimer St., London W1N 8AB, tel. 071/637–5400), which publishes travel information for the disabled in Britain, and **Mobility International** (228 Borough High St., London SE1 1JX, tel. 071/403–5688), the headquarters of an international membership organization that serves as a clearinghouse of travel information for people with disabilities.

Travel Agencies and Tour Operators **Destination World** (*see* Package Tours for Independent Travelers, *above*) offers "I Can" tours to Australia for physically challenged and vision- or hearing-impaired travelers. **Flying Wheels Travel** (143 W. Bridge St., Box 382, Owatonna, MN 55060, tel. 507/451–5005 or 800/535–6790) is a travel agency specializing in domestic and worldwide cruises, tours, and independent travel itineraries for people with mobility impairments. Adventurers should contact **Wilderness Inquiry** (1313 Fifth St. SE, Minneapolis, MN 55414, tel. and TTY 612/379–3838), which orchestrates action-packed trips with whitewater rafting, sea kayaking, or dog sledding for those challenged with disabilities. Tours are designed to bring together people who are physically challenged with those who aren't.

Publications Several free publications are available from the Consumer Information Center (Pueblo, CO 81009): "New Horizons for the Air Traveler with a Disability," a U.S. Department of Transportation booklet describing changes resulting from the 1986 Air Carrier Access Act and those still to come from the 1990 Americans with Disabilities Act (include Department 608Y in the address), and the Airport Operators Council's *Access Travel: Airports* (Dept. 5804), which describes facilities and services for the disabled at more than 500 airports worldwide.

Travelin' Talk Directory (*see* Organizations, *above*) was published in 1993. This 500-page resource book ($35) is packed with information for travelers with disabilities. **Twin Peaks Press** (Box 129, Vancouver, WA 98666, tel. 206/694–2462 or 800/637–2256) publishes the *Directory of Travel Agencies for the Disabled* ($19.95), listing more than 370 agencies worldwide and *Wheelchair Vagabond* ($14.95), a collection of personal travel tips. Add $2 per book for shipping.

Hints for Older Travelers

Few, if any, of the discounts that Australian senior citizens enjoy are available to visitors, because an Australian "pensioner's card" is usually required as proof of age. In New Zealand, some senior citizen discounts are available.

Organizations The **American Association of Retired Persons** (AARP, 601 E St. NW, Washington, DC 20049, tel. 202/434–2277) provides independent travelers who are members of AARP (open to those age 50 or older; $8 per person or couple annually) with the Purchase Privilege Program. This program offers discounts on lodging, car rentals, and sightseeing and arranges group tours, cruises, and apartment living through **AARP Travel Experience from American Express** (400

Pinnacle Way, Suite 450, Norcross, GA 30071, tel. 800/927–0111 or 800/745–4567).

Two other organizations offer discounts on lodgings, car rentals, and other travel products, along with such nontravel perks as magazines and newsletters: the **National Council of Senior Citizens** (1331 F St. NW, Washington, DC 20004, tel. 202/347–8800, $12 annual membership fee) and **Mature Outlook** (6001 N. Clark St., Chicago, IL 60660, tel. 800/336–6330, $9.95 annually).

For reduced rates, mention your senior-citizen identification card when booking your accommodations, not when checking out. At restaurants, show your card before you're seated; discounts may be limited to certain menus, days, or hours. If you are renting a car, ask about promotional rates that might improve on your senior-citizen discount.

Educational Travel The nonprofit **Elderhostel** (75 Federal St., 3rd Floor, Boston, MA 02110, tel. 617/426–7788) has offered inexpensive study programs for people age 60 and older since 1975. Held at more than 1,800 educational institutions, courses cover everything from marine science to Greek myths to cowboy poetry. Participants usually attend lectures in the morning, then spend the afternoon sightseeing or on field trips; they live in dorms on the host campuses. Fees for two- to three-week international trips—including room, board, and transportation from the United States—range from $1,800 to $4,500.

Tour Operators **Saga International Holidays** (222 Berkeley St., Boston, MA 02116, tel. 800/343–0273), which specializes in group travel for people over 60, offers a selection of variously priced tours and cruises covering five continents. If you want to take your grandchildren, look into Grandtravel (*see* Traveling with Children, *above*).

Hints for Gay and Lesbian Travelers

Organizations The **International Gay Travel Association** (Box 4974, Key West, FL 33041, tel. 800/999–7925 or 800/448–8550), which has 700 members, provides names of travel agents and tour operators who specialize in gay travel. The **Gay & Lesbian Visitors Center of New York Inc.** (135 W. 20th St., 3rd Floor, New York, NY 10011, tel. 800/395–2315; $100 annually) mails a monthly newsletter, valuable coupons, and more to its members.

Tour Operators and Travel Agencies The dominant travel agency in the market is **Above and Beyond** (3568 Sacramento St., San Francisco, CA 94118, tel. 800/397–2681). Tour operator **Olympus Vacations** (8424 Santa Monica Blvd., Suite 721, West Hollywood, CA 90069, tel. 310/657–2220) offers all-gay-or-lesbian resort holidays. **Skylink Women's Travel** (746 Ashland Ave., Santa Monica, CA 90405, tel. 800/225–5759) handles individual travel for lesbians all over the world and conducts two international and five domestic group trips annually.

Publications The premier international travel magazine for gays and lesbians is **Our World** (1104 N. Nova Rd., Suite 251, Daytona Beach, FL 32117, tel. 904/441–5367; $35 for 10 issues). **Out & About** (tel. 800/929–2268; $49 for 10 issues) is a 16-page monthly newsletter with extensive information on resorts, hotels, and airlines that are gay-friendly.

Contacts

A nonprofit group called **Friends Overseas—Australia** puts North American visitors in touch with Australians who share their interests. Membership is $25. For information, contact them at 68–01 Dartmouth St., Forest Hills, NY 11375, tel. 718/261–0534.

Further Reading: Australia

Most of the following books are available in bookstores in the United States or Australia. If they prove hard to find, however, an excellent solution is **The Australian Book Source** (1309 Redwood La., Davis, CA 95616, tel. 916/753–1519, fax 916/753–6491). Owner Susan Curry issues an annual catalog of books in stock, and she will endeavor to fill special orders for those not immediately available.

History Australia's convict origins are placed in context with clarity and vigor by Robert Hughes in *The Fatal Shore*. In a scholarly yet readable way, the book traces the birth of the nation from the arrival of the First Fleet in 1788 through the end of convict transportation in 1868. Marcus Clarke's classic, *For the Term of His Natural Life*, was written in 1870 and brings to life the grim conditions endured by convicts in his tale of Rufus Dawes, condemned for a crime he did not commit. Subsequent events in the nation's past are detailed in historian Manning Clark's *A Short History of Australia*, an abbreviated version of his epic five-volume series, *A History of Australia*.

If you are particularly curious about the history of the Outback, *Frontier Country: Australia's Outback Heritage* is acclaimed as a definitive work. Written in two volumes by more than 50 authors, it encompasses the continent's 40,000 years of evolution and chronicles the people and events that have shaped the mystique of the Outback. *We of the Never Never*, written in 1908 by Mrs. Aeneas Gunn, describes her life as the wife of a pioneering homesteader in the Northern Territory's Roper River area at the turn of the century. A more recent book, *The Road from Coorain* by Jill Ker Conway, grippingly traces the author's path from childhood on an isolated sheep station through her education in Sydney to her departure for America, where in 1975 she became president of Smith College. A. B. Facey's award-winning autobiography, *A Fortunate Life*, published when the author was 87 years old, recounts his extraordinary, itinerant life, starting with his childhood hardships in the Outback.

Aboriginal In the acclaimed *Australian Dreaming: 40,000 Years of Aboriginal Culture History*, author Jennifer Isaacs has compiled the first Aboriginal history. Beautifully illustrated with color photographs, it tells the saga of the original Australians and explores their spiritual relationship with the land through their myths and legends as told by Aboriginal storytellers.

Australian authors have often examined the Aborigines' place in society in novels. Two classics still in print are Katharine Susannah Pritchard's 1929 *Coonardoo*, about the love between a white cattleman and an Aboriginal woman, and Xavier Herbert's 1938 *Capricornia*, an epic saga of the prejudices and brutality encountered by half-castes in northern Australia. *Burnum Burnum's Aboriginal Australia*, a stunning 1988 coffee-table book, guides you through the land, detailing scenes of historical events and tribal lore.

Society Several tomes focus on Australian characteristics, both individually and collectively as a society. Ross Terrill's *The Australians* (*see* the Introduction) offers a penetrating look at the social fabric of today's Australia from the perspective of an Australian-born naturalized American. The debate about Australians and their future was triggered back in 1964 by Donald Horne's *The Lucky Country*, which even today provides relevant insights about contemporary Australian attitudes. Another book that affected Australian attitudes in the early 1960s was *They're a Weird Mob* by Nino Culotta (a nom de plume for John O'Grady). It made Aussies laugh at their own disgruntlement about immigrants and began the process of reconciliation between old and new Australians.

Further Reading: New Zealand

History *The Oxford Illustrated History of New Zealand*, edited by Keith Sinclair, provides a comprehensive but highly readable account of the country's social, political, cultural, and economic evolution from the earliest days of settlement to 1989. *The Colonial New Zealand Wars*, by Tim Ryan and Bill Parham, is a vivid history of the Maori-British battles. Lavishly illustrated with photographs of colonial infantry and drawings of Maori hill forts, flags, and weapons, the book makes far more compelling reading than the dry military history suggested by the title. J. C. Beaglehole's *The Discovery of New Zealand* is an authoritative and scholarly analysis of the voyages of discovery, from the first Polynesians to the Europeans of the late-18th century.

Fiction New Zealand's best-known novelist is Katherine Mansfield (1888–1923), whose early stories were set in and around the city of Wellington, her birthplace. The most celebrated work of fiction to come from New Zealand in recent years is Keri Hulme's *The Bone People*, winner of the Booker McConnell Prize in 1985. Set on the isolated west coast of the South Island, this challenging, vital novel weaves Polynesian myth with Christian symbolism and the powerful sense of place that characterizes modern Maori writing. Another important contemporary writer is Janet Frame, who made an impact on the literary scene with the publication of *The Carpathians* in 1985.

Specialized Guidebooks Strictly for wine buffs, *The Wines and Vineyards of New Zealand*, by Michael Cooper, is an exhaustive evaluation in words and pictures of every vineyard in the country. For travelers who plan to make hiking a major component of their vacations, *Tramping in New Zealand*, published by Lonely Planet, is an invaluable guide.

Illustrated Books *Salute to New Zealand*, edited by Sandra Coney, is a coffee-table book that intersperses lavish photographs with chapters by some of the country's finest contemporary writers. *Wild New Zealand*, published by Reader's Digest, is a pictorial account of the country's landscape, flora, and fauna, supplemented by an informative text with such a wealth of detail that it turns the sensory experience of the landscape into a cerebral one.

Arriving and Departing

From North America by Plane

Flights are either nonstop, direct, or connecting. A **nonstop** flight requires no change of plane and makes no stops. A **direct** flight stops at least once and can involve a change of plane, although the flight number remains the same; if the first leg is late, the second waits. This is not the case with a **connecting** flight, which involves a different plane and a different flight number.

Airlines and Airports Currently, the following airlines serve Australia and New Zealand from the United States and Canada: Australia's national airline, **Qantas** (tel. 800/227-4500 in the U.S. and in Canada); **Air New Zea-**

land (tel. 800/262–1234 in the U.S., 800/663–5494 in Canada); **United** (tel. 800/538–2929 in the U.S.); **Canadian Air International** (tel. 800/665–1177 in Canada, 800/426–7000 in the U.S.); and **Northwest** (tel. 800/447–4747 in the U.S. and Canada).

Flights leave from Los Angeles, San Francisco, Honolulu, New York, Toronto, and Vancouver. Australia has 14 international airports, although most North Americans fly into Sydney, Melbourne, Brisbane, or Cairns. Depending on your airline and route, you can elect to stop over at Honolulu, Fiji, Tahiti, or Auckland. Nonstop service is available to Sydney from Los Angeles or San Francisco. Air New Zealand is the only carrier with direct flights from North America to Christchurch as well as Auckland.

Flying Times   Flying times from New York to Sydney (via Los Angeles) are about 21 hours; from Los Angeles or San Francisco to Sydney (nonstop) about 15 hours; from Los Angeles to Melbourne (via Auckland) around 16 hours. From New York to Auckland (via Los Angeles) is about 19 hours; from Los Angeles or San Francisco to Auckland (nonstop), about 13 hours. These are all actual air hours and do not include ground time.

Cutting   The Sunday travel section of most newspapers is a good source of
Flight Costs   deals. When booking, particularly through an unfamiliar company, call the Better Business Bureau or Consumer Protection Bureau to find out whether any complaints have been registered against the company, pay with a credit card if you can, and consider trip-cancellation and default insurance (*see* Insurance, *above*).

Promotional   Less expensive fares, called promotional or discount fares, are
Airfares   round-trip and involve restrictions, which vary according to the route and season. You must usually buy the ticket—commonly called an APEX (advance purchase excursion) when it's for international travel—in advance (7, 14, or 21 days are usual), although some of the major airlines have added no-frills, cheap flights to compete with new bargain airlines on certain routes.

With the major airlines the cheaper fares generally require minimum and maximum stays (for instance, over a Saturday night or at least seven and no more than 30 days). Airlines generally allow some return date changes for a $25 to $50 fee, but most low-fare tickets are nonrefundable. Only a death in the family would prompt the airline to return any of your money if you cancel a nonrefundable ticket. However, you can apply an unused nonrefundable ticket toward a new ticket, again with a small fee. The lowest fare is subject to availability, and only a small percentage of the plane's total seats will be sold at that price. Contact the U.S. Department of Transportation's **Office of Consumer Affairs** (I–25, Washington, DC 20590, tel. 202/366–2220) for a copy of "Fly-Rights: A Guide to Air Travel in the U.S." Randy Petersen's *Official Frequent Flyer Guidebook* ($14.99 plus $3 shipping; 4715-C Town Center Dr., Colorado Springs, CO 80916, tel. 800/487–8893) yields valuable hints on getting the most for your air travel dollars.

Consolidators   Consolidators or bulk-fare operators—"bucket shops"—buy blocks of seats on scheduled flights that airlines anticipate they won't be able to sell. They pay wholesale prices, add a markup, and resell the seats to travel agents or directly to the public at prices that still undercut the airline's promotional or discount fares. Their prices are higher than a charter ticket but lower than an APEX ticket and usually are without the advance-purchase restriction. Moreover, some consolidators will sometimes allow you to return your ticket; carefully read the fine print detailing penalties for changes and cancellations. If you doubt the reliability of a company, call the airline once you've made your booking and confirm that you do, indeed, have a reservation on the flight.

Charter Flights   Charters usually have the lowest fares and the most restrictions. Departures are limited and seldom on time, and you can lose all or most of your money if you cancel. (The closer to departure you cancel, the more you lose, although sometimes you will be charged only a small fee if you supply a substitute passenger.) The charterer may legally cancel the flight for any reason up to 10 days before departure; within 10 days of departure, the flight may be canceled only if it is physically impossible to operate it. The charterer may also revise the itinerary or increase the price after you have bought the ticket, but if the new arrangement constitutes a "major change," you have the right to a refund. Before buying a charter ticket, read the fine print for the company's refund policy and details on major changes. Money for charter flights is usually paid into a bank escrow account, the name of which should be on the contract. If you don't pay by credit card, make your check payable to the escrow account (unless you're dealing with a travel agent, in which case, the agent's check should be payable to the escrow account). The U.S. Department of Transportation's **Office of Consumer Affairs** (I–25, Washington, DC 20590, tel. 202/366–2220) can answer questions on charters and send you its "Plane Talk: Public Charter Flights" information sheet.

Charter operators may offer flights alone or with ground arrangements that constitute a charter package. Typically you must book charters through your travel agent. One good source is **Charterlink** (988 Sing Sing Rd., Horseheads, NY 14845, tel. 800/221–1802), a no-fee charter broker that operates 24 hours a day.

Discount   Travel clubs offer members unsold space on airplanes, cruise ships,
Travel Clubs   and package tours for as much as 50% below regular prices. Membership may include a regular bulletin or access to a toll-free hot line giving details of available trips departing from three or four days to several months in the future. Most also offer 50% discounts off hotel rack rates, but double-check with the hotel to make sure it isn't offering a better promotional rate independent of the club. Clubs include **Discount Travel International** (114 Forrest Ave., Suite 203, Narberth, PA 19072, tel. 215/668–7184; $45 annually, single or family), **Entertainment Travel Editions** (Box 1014 Trumbull, CT 06611, tel. 800/445–4137; $28–$48 annually), **Great American Traveler** (Box 27965, Salt Lake City, UT 84127, tel. 800/548–2812; $29.95 annually), **Moment's Notice Discount Travel Club** (425 Madison Ave., New York, NY 10017, tel. 212/486–0503; $45 annually, single or family), **Privilege Card** (3391 Peachtree Rd. NE, Suite 110, Atlanta, GA 30326, tel. 800/236–9732; annually $49.95 domestic, $74.95 international), **Travelers Advantage** (CUC Travel Service, 49 Music Sq. W, Nashville, TN 37203, tel. 800/548–1116; $49 annually, single or family), and **Worldwide Discount Travel Club** (1674 Meridian Ave., Miami Beach, FL 33139, tel. 305/534–2082; annually $50 family, $40 single).

Publications   The newsletter *Travel Smart* (40 Beechdale Rd., Dobbs Ferry, NY 10522, tel. 800/327–3633; $44 annually) has a wealth of travel deals in each monthly issue.

Enjoying   Fly at night if you're able to sleep on a plane. Because the air aloft is
the Flight   dry, drink plenty of beverages while on board; remember that drinking alcohol contributes to jet lag, as do heavy meals. Sleepers usually prefer window seats to curl up against; restless passengers

ask to be on the aisle. Bulkhead seats, in the front row of each cabin, have more legroom, but since there's no seat ahead, trays attach awkwardly to the arms of your seat, and you must stow all possessions overhead. Bulkhead seats are usually reserved for the disabled, the elderly, and people traveling with babies.

Smoking Smoking is banned on all Australian domestic flights. The ban also applies to domestic segments of international flights aboard U.S. and foreign carriers. On U.S. carriers flying to Australia and New Zealand and other destinations abroad, a seat in a no-smoking section must be provided for every passenger who requests one, and the section must be enlarged to accommodate such passengers if necessary as long as they have complied with the airline's deadline for check-in and seat assignment. If smoking bothers you, request a seat far from the smoking section.

Foreign airlines are exempt from these rules but do provide no-smoking sections, and some nations, including Canada as well as Australia, have gone as far as to ban smoking on all domestic flights; other countries may ban smoking on flights of less than a specified duration. The International Civil Aviation Organization has set July 1, 1996, as the date to ban smoking aboard airlines worldwide, but the body has no power to enforce its decisions.

From the United Kingdom by Plane

Australia **British Airways** (tel. 081/897–4000) and **Qantas** (tel. 081/846–0466) are the major airlines flying to Australia from Britain, although **Air New Zealand** (tel. 071/930–3434), **Cathay Pacific** (tel. 071/930–7878), and **Japan Airlines** (JAL) (tel. 071/408–1000) also operate scheduled flights. Qantas has the greatest number of flights, with service to nine Australian cities, including 12 flights a week to Sydney and nine to Perth. The flight to Sydney takes nearly 21 hours with a stopover in either Bangkok or Singapore.

New Zealand **British Airways, Cathay Pacific, Japan Airlines (JAL), Qantas,** and **Singapore Airlines** (tel. 081/747–0007) operate between London and Auckland via Asia. **Air New Zealand** and **United** (tel. 081/990–9900) operate between London and Auckland via the United States. The flying time from London to Auckland is about 24 hours via either route.

Cutting Flight Costs A round-trip ticket from London to Sydney or Auckland can cost more than £3,000. Fortunately, a number of specialist travel companies, such as **Trailfinders** (tel. 071/938–3366) and **Travel Cuts** (tel. 071/255–2082), offer significant reductions on scheduled fares, plus advice on stopovers and additional services, especially from Trailfinders, which specializes in discounted round-the-world airfares. Book several months in advance, especially for peak periods. Check the advertisements in *Time Out* magazine for further information.

Staying in Australia

Geography

Visitors to Australia are inevitably surprised by its vastness. The phrase "the tyranny of distance" entered Australian parlance almost at the very beginning of settlement. Although Australia occupies almost the same land mass as the continental United States, its population is strikingly less: 17 million Australians compared with 251 million Americans.

Australia is an ancient land. Over millions of years it has been weathered flat—the country's highest peak, Mt. Kosciusko, is only 2,230 meters (7,317 feet)—and huge stretches are desert. The eastern seaboard is backed by the Great Dividing Range, which parallels the coastline from Cape York in northern Queensland all the way south into western Victoria. Watered by swift rivers, this littoral is endowed with rolling pasturelands and lush rain forests. Off Queensland's coast, running from Cape York 2,000 kilometers (1,250 miles) southward, are the banks of coral reef known collectively as the Great Barrier Reef. Inland, beyond the Great Dividing Range, semiarid plains cover much of Queensland, New South Wales, Victoria, and South Australia. This is grazing land, drawing its moisture from the 3,719-kilometer (2,310-mile) system formed by the Murray River—Australia's Mississippi—and its tributaries, the Darling and the Murrumbidgee. Deserts occupy a large portion of Western Australia and the lower Northern Territory, known as the Red Centre.

When planning your itinerary, it's vital to bear in mind the huge distances involved. By road Brisbane is 1,031 kilometers (640 miles) from Sydney, 1,718 kilometers (1,067 miles) from Melbourne, and almost the same distance from Cairns in its own state. The journey from Sydney to Alice Springs, the gateway to Ayers Rock, is 2½ hours by jet and 52 hours by bus.

Getting Around Australia

By Plane Deregulation came to Australian skies in late 1990, and the change is still affecting domestic airlines. Traditionally there were two major domestic carriers—**Ansett Australia** and **Australian Airlines.** However, in mid-1992 **Qantas** acquired Australian Airlines, which now has been absorbed under the Qantas banner, with aircrafts repainted to carry the Qantas livery and logo. Consequently, North American passengers now can travel to and within Australia on a single Qantas ticket.

Ansett has entered an agreement with United Airlines whereby passengers arriving in Sydney on United flights can continue to six major cities on connecting Ansett flights. **Air New Zealand** may be granted rights to fly domestic routes within Australia, and Ansett entered the international market in 1993 with flights to Bali. By 1995, it may add additional Asian destinations.

Both Qantas and Ansett are affiliated with smaller carriers. Ansett's parent group controls commuter airlines Kendell Airlines, Skywest, and Aeropelican. Under the Qantas umbrella are Australian Airlink, Eastern Australia, Southern Australian, Sunstate, and Australian Regional Airlines. (At press time, Qantas has retained the names of these former Australian Airlines subsidiaries, but this may change.)

The frequency of flights on some routes is not as high as might be expected in a developed nation, and you need to take this into account when planning your itinerary. The long distances traditionally have made domestic airfares expensive, but competition since deregulation is bringing them down. Children fly free up to age two, and are then discounted 33% up to age 11.

The airlines offer international visitors various reductions in adult fares. At press time, Qantas has a **Discover Australia** fare, which gives a 45%–50% discount off the normal full economy fare on their domestic routes. Passengers flying to Australia on Qantas may purchase the **Australian Explorer Pass,** special fare coupons valid for economy-class flights between specified Australian cities and to some Great Barrier Reef islands on Qantas. Coupons are valid for travel only by nonresidents of Australia and must be purchased prior to arrival in Australia. The minimum purchase is four coupons for $700 and the maximum number of coupons allowed is eight, with each additional pair costing $160. There is a surcharge for travel to Perth, and the Pass is not combinable with any other fares.

Ansett's **Visit Australia Pass** allows international visitors to choose four to eight flights between selected cities and the Great Barrier Reef's Hamilton and Hayman islands. The initial four coupons, which are available only to nonresidents of Australia and must be purchased before departure, cost $640 (with a supplement for travel to Perth). Ansett's **Special See Australia Fare** cuts up to 40% off normal economy-class fares without restrictions; it must be purchased before you leave home or within 30 days of your arrival. Ansett's **Explore Australia Airpass** offers discounts of from 30% off economy-class fare for a minimum of three sectors, to 40% off for a minimum of eight sectors.

Given the current volatility of the airlines in Australia, the discounted fare structures described above could be modified or discontinued, so check with your travel agent for the latest information.

Smoking No smoking is allowed on any flight within Australia.

By Train Australia has a network of interstate, country, and urban trains offering first- and economy-class service. The major interstate trains are the ***Indian-Pacific*** from Sydney to Perth via Adelaide (26 hours Sydney–Adelaide, 41 hours Adelaide–Perth); ***Trans Australian*** from Adelaide to Perth (41 hours); the ***Ghan*** from Adelaide to Alice Springs (21 hours—*see* Chapter 10); the ***Overland*** and ***Daylink*** from Melbourne to Adelaide (10¼ hours); and the ***XPT*** (Express Passenger Train) from Sydney to Brisbane (14¼ hours). Service between Melbourne and Sydney is on the overnight *XPT* (10½ hours). The current decrease in air fares is occasioning cutbacks in service, as well as slashed rail fares, so there may be variations in what has been listed. Check in advance, and book early whenever possible, especially for the *Indian-Pacific* and the *Ghan* during peak times (August–October and Christmas holidays).

For more information or to make reservations, contact **Rail Australia** (tel. 800/423–2880), **Goway Travel** in Canada (tel. 800/387–8850; 071/828–4111 in the U.K.).

By Bus Most Australian towns are well served by bus. Route networks of the larger express companies cover the nation's major highways and link up with regional operators providing service to smaller communities. Buses are usually air-conditioned, with toilets and, on some routes, hostesses. Drivers run videos from time to time on an overhead monitor. One advantage of bus touring is that bus drivers also act as guides. They share their considerable knowledge of the countryside with passengers, blending illuminating descriptions of the areas you traverse with anecdotes about local characters.

In addition to the national bus passes on sale overseas (*see* Before You Go, *above*), there are regional passes that can be bought only in Australia: Australian Coachlines' **Explorer Pass,** covering travel in a single direction with unlimited stopovers, is a good bet for budget travelers with a little extra time. Tasmania's Redline Coaches has a

Tassie Pass, valid for 7-, 15-, 20-, or 31-day periods. Costs range from $111 to $177 for adults, with discounted fares for students, backpackers, HIYHA members, and children.

Following are some travel times and approximate costs at press time: Sydney–Adelaide (24 hours, $90); Sydney–Brisbane (17 hours, $69); Brisbane–Cairns (27 hours, $135); Melbourne–Adelaide (10 hours, $52); Adelaide–Perth, (36½ hours, $180); Adelaide–Alice Springs (24 hours, $135); Alice Springs–Ayers Rock (6 hours, $73).

By Car Driving is not difficult in Australia, once you adjust to traveling on the left. Except for some expressways in and around the major cities, the majority of highways are two-lane roads with frequent passing lanes. Roads are usually paved and well maintained, though traffic lanes are narrower than in the United States. Always take precautions if you are planning to drive through the Outback, however. Many of the roads are unpaved, traffic is very light, and the temperatures can be extreme. Carry plenty of water and always tell someone your itinerary and schedule. Flash flooding can occur on low-lying roads.

Service stations, both full- and self-service, are plentiful. The cost of gasoline (or "petrol") varies around the country from about 65¢ a liter in Sydney to about 90¢ a liter in the Outback. Speed limits are 60 kilometers per hour (kph) in populated areas, and 100–110 kph on open roads—the equivalent of 37 and 62–68 mph, respectively. Surveillance of speeders and "drink-driving" (the legal limit is a tough .05% blood alcohol level) is thorough and penalties are high. Seat belts are mandatory nationwide for drivers and all passengers.

Road regulations differ from state to state and even city to city. In Victoria, for instance, a driver turning left must yield to oncoming traffic turning right. At designated intersections in Melbourne's Golden Mile (the central business district), you must get into the left lane to make a right-hand turn—watch for the sign RIGHT HAND TURN FROM LEFT LANE ONLY. Traffic circles are widely used at intersections throughout Australia; cars that already have entered the circle have the right-of-way. It's wise to pick up a copy of the Highway Code of any state or territory in which you plan to drive from the local automobile club. The **Australian Automobile Association** has a branch in each state, known as the National Roads and Motorists' Association (NRMA) in New South Wales and Canberra, the Automobile Association in the Northern Territory (AANT), and the Royal Automobile Club (RAC) in all other states. It is affiliated with AAA worldwide and offers reciprocal services to American, Canadian, and British members, including emergency road service and discounts on car rental, accommodations, and other services. Reservations must be made through an NRMA or RAC office.

Telephones

Local Calls Pay phones accept either coins (40¢ for a local call in Sydney and Melbourne) or locally purchased Phone Cards (silver phones). Long-distance calls can be dialed directly using the city code or area code: Sydney is 02, for example, and Melbourne is 03. Rates are in three time periods: day (Mon.–Sat. 8–6), night (weekdays 6–10), and economy (Sat. 6 PM–Mon. 8 AM and daily 10 PM–8 AM). A $2.80 service fee is charged for operator-connected calls when direct dialing is possible. Rates, area codes, and dialing instructions are all listed in the white pages of the local telephone directory.

A note on phone numbers: You'll notice that phone numbers in this book are of variable lengths. Commonly, metropolitan areas have two-digit area codes and seven-digit numbers, while rural areas have three-digit area codes and six-digit numbers. Some exchanges, however, may use only four or five digits, and certain six-digit numbers that have the prefix 13 are country-wide and thus carry no area code at all. Finally, Australia's toll-free prefix, 008, may soon be changed to a 1-800 format similar to that in the United States; rumors abound that this is only the first step in a total reorganization of the Australian phone system. Check the white pages for the most current information.

International Calls You can dial direct overseas by using the 011 international access code followed by the country code, the area code, and the number. The country code for the United States and Canada is 1, the code for Australia is 61, and the code for New Zealand is 64. When dialing Australia from another country, drop the first zero from the area code; for example, to call a number in Sydney from the United States, you would dial 011–61–2/555–5555.

Calls to the United States and Canada cost about $1.50 per minute in off-peak hours. Operator-assisted calls can be made from any phone with IDD (International Direct Dialing) access—check the local telephone directory for the correct number of the international operator. A $6 fee is charged on person-to-person calls, an $8 fee on collect calls, known in Australia as "reverse charges." Remember that hotels frequently add a hefty surcharge for telephone calls from your room. Many hotels, particularly those catering to a business clientele, have fax and telex facilities.

AT&T, MCI, and Sprint each have operator services to make calling home or the office more affordable and convenient when you're on the road. To avoid pricey hotel surcharges, place your calling-card or collect calls by dialing the Australian access number for one of the following: **AT&T USADirect** (tel. 001–4881–011); **MCI Call USA** (tel. 008–5511–11 or 1800–881–100); or **Sprint Express** (tel. 022–903–014).

Mail

Postage Rates Mail service in Australia is normally efficient unless a union action slows down deliveries. Postage rates are 45¢ for a domestic letter, $1.05 per 20-gram (28.35 grams = 1 ounce) airmail letter, and 95¢ for an airmail postcard to North America; the same service costs $1.20 and $1 to the United Kingdom. Overseas fax service costs up to $12 for the first page plus $6 for each additional page. You can send printed material by Economy Air, which travels via surface mail within Australia but by airmail across the Pacific, at a cost of $19 for up to a kilogram (a little more than 2 pounds).

Receiving Mail You can receive mail care of General Delivery at the General Post Office or any branch post office; the service is free and mail is held one month. It is advisable to know the correct zip code, obtainable by telephoning the nearest Australian Consulate General: **Honolulu** (tel. 808/524–5050); **Houston** (tel. 713/629–9131); **Los Angeles** (tel. 213/469–4300); **New York** (tel. 212/245–4000); **San Francisco** (tel. 415/362–6160); **Washington** (tel. 202/797–3222); **Ottawa** (tel. 613/236–0841); **Toronto** (tel. 416/323–1155); **Vancouver** (tel. 604/684–1177).

Alternatively, **American Express** offers free mail collection at its main city offices. For a list of addresses, call 800/528–4800 (in the New York metropolitan area, tel. 212/477–5700).

Tipping

Tipping has never been the custom in Australia, and many are loath to have it start. Hotels and restaurants do not add service charges, but it is a widely accepted practice to tip a waiter 10%–12% for good service, although many Australians consider it sufficient to leave only $3 or $4. It is not necessary to tip a hotel doorman for carrying suitcases into the lobby, but porters could be given $1 a bag. Room service and housemaids are not tipped except for special service. Taxi drivers do not expect a tip, but you may want to leave any small change. Guides, tour bus drivers, and chauffeurs don't expect tips either, though they are grateful if someone in the group takes up a collection for them. No tipping is necessary in beauty salons or for theater ushers.

Opening and Closing Times

As a general rule, business hours in Australia are weekdays 9–5; this applies to post offices as well. Banks are open Monday–Thursday 9:30–4, Friday 9:30–5. In some states a few banks are open on Saturday mornings. Shops are normally open weekdays 8:30–5:30, with one late closing at 9 PM. On Saturday shops are open from 8:30 to between noon and 4. Some stores, particularly those in tourist areas, may be open a few hours on Sunday.

Shopping

Bargains are hard to come by in Australia. Prices are high, although quality is good, particularly in such clothing as hand-knitted wool sweaters, wool suits, and designer dresses and sportswear. Bargain-hunters are better advised to join one of the shopping tours in Melbourne and Sydney, which visit one or two factory outlets. Check with your hotel concierge or the state tourist office for information about these tours. Best buys are woolen goods, fashionable leather clothing, sheepskin rugs and car-seat covers, arts and crafts, Aboriginal art, and gemstones—particularly opals, diamonds, and pearls. Fine gems can be found in reputable jewelers throughout Australia, but consider going to the source. For opals, visit South Australia's Coober Pedy for "milky" stones, or New South Wales' Lightning Ridge, where the coveted black opals are found. Western Australia is the place for the rare "pink" diamonds (from the Kimberley's Argyle Diamond Mine), gold, and pearls produced in the waters off Broome in the north. Sapphires and other gemstones are mined in Queensland's ranges. Darwin, Alice Springs, and Kununurra in the Kimberley region are good places to look for Aboriginal art and artifacts.

There is no sales tax added to purchases in Australia but an excise tax is levied on some luxury goods. Many department stores and specialty shops, such as those selling opals, will deduct this tax—allowing you substantial savings—upon presentation of your passport and airline ticket. You can also avoid paying excise tax by shopping in one of the many duty-free stores scattered through the main cities. In Sydney, you don't even have to go to the store—you can order goods through the duty-free hotline (tel. 02/319–2233), and your purchases will be delivered to the airport for your departure. For more information, ask for the booklet **"Your Shopping Guide to Australia"** from the nearest Australian Tourist Commission office (*see* Before You Go, *above*).

Sports and the Outdoors

Probably in no other country is sport as pervasive a part of life as it is in Australia. The Australian zeal for competition has shown itself in the number of world champions it has produced in different sports, despite its small population. Amateur sports are a vital element of the country's active, outdoor lifestyle, and for visitors there are plenty of "soft" and "hard" adventure tours embracing virtually every sport (*see* Chapter 16, Adventure Vacations).

Bicycling Australia's flat terrain is perfect for long-distance bicycling, although it's equally enjoyable to rent a bike and take a spin through the city parks, most of which have bicycle trails. A network of rural trails for cyclists is being developed, and several books, such as *A Guide to Cycle Touring in the Southern Highlands and Adjacent Coastal Area of N.S.W.*, by Richard D. Kenderdine, can help guide you. For more information on bicycle touring, contact **Bicycle Institute of Australia** (Box 272, Sydney, NSW 2001, tel. 02/212–5628, fax 02/211–1867).

Boating and Sailing Australians are passionate sailors: Close to a million families own some sort of craft, and sailing charters on either bare-boat or crewed yachts abound, particularly in the Whitsunday Islands on the Great Barrier Reef (*see* Chapter 8, The Great Barrier Reef). If you're looking for a day on the water, contact the **Australian Yachting Federation, Inc.** (33 Peel St., Milsons Point, NSW 2061, tel. 02/922–4333, fax 02/923–2883).

Camping You should think twice before camping outside designated campgrounds particularly in the Outback, where such unexpected hazards as flash flooding can catch campers by surprise. Obviously, a four-wheel-drive vehicle is a necessity for any safari into the bush, and once there it is equally important to know what to look for. The **National Roads and Motorists' Association** (151 Clarence St., Sydney, NSW 2000) puts out the booklet "Outback Motoring." Another NRMA publication, "Caravaning and Camping Directory," lists campgrounds; it's free to members, $10 for nonmembers.

Canoeing and White-Water Rafting Favored areas for white-water canoeing or rafting are Tasmania's wild Franklin River and the Nymboida and Gwydir rivers in northern New South Wales. The Snowy River in Victoria's High Country, and Kosciusko National Park streams in nearby southern New South Wales, are also popular choices, as are the North Johnstone, Tulley, and Barron rivers in Queensland's Far North. You can experience sea-kayaking off Tasmania's rugged coast or in the calmer waters around the Great Barrier Reef. *See* Chapter 16 for more information, or contact the appropriate state tourism office.

Fishing Records for marlin are frequently broken off the east coast, and the region around Cairns and Lizard Island has won world acclaim for giant black marlin. Fighting fish, including black and blue marlin, mackerel, tuna, barracuda, and sailfish, are found all the way down the east coast. Gamefishing for marlin, tuna, and sharks is particularly good at Bermagui in southern New South Wales, and is less expensive than at Cairns. September through November is the best time for catching marlin off Cairns; off Bermagui, the end of November to June.

Barramundi, jacks, tarpon, and mackerel attract anglers to the fresh and sea waters of the Northern Territory's Top End, around Darwin and Bathurst Island. The barramundi run from June to November. Rainbow and brown trout thrive in the lake-fed streams of Tasmania, the rivers of the Australian Alps in both Victoria and

New South Wales, and in the Onkaparinga River on the outskirts of Adelaide. Fishing seasons vary according to the area but are generally December–May.

For information and brochures about fishing, including charters and vacations, contact **The Fishing Connection** (68 Mulgoa Rd., Mulgoa, NSW 2750, tel. 047/73–8824).

Golf Australia boasts more than 1,400 golf courses. Some private clubs extend reciprocal rights to overseas club members on proof of membership; check whether your club maintains reciprocal membership rights with any Australian clubs. You can always arrange a round on a municipal course, although you may have to contend with a kangaroo or two watching your form from the rough. Clubs can be rented, but you'll need your own shoes. Among U.S. operators offering golf packages are **Classic Australian Golf Tours** (tel. 800/426–3610); **ITC Golf Tours** (tel. 800/257–4981); **Swain Australian Tours** (tel. 800/227–9246).

Hiking With so much bird life, flora, and fauna to admire, hiking, or "bushwalking," as it's known in Australia, is a pleasurable and popular pastime. Every weekend thousands of Australians leave the city for the tranquility of national parks in nearby ranges. These parks are laced with trails that hikers can follow by themselves or with members of one of the many bushwalking clubs. Many of the country's major national parks are within easy reach of the cities. Despite the "national," the parks are operated by the individual states in which they are located. For information, contact the National Parks and Wildlife Service in the capital of the state in which you are interested (*see* National Parks at the end of the individual state chapters). Organized hiking tours can be arranged through the bushwalking clubs listed in the telephone directory of each capital city.

Skiing You can ski in Australia from late June through September. The ski resorts may not be as sophisticated as in the United States and Europe, but they retain an appealing natural bushland character. The major ski areas are Kosciusko National Park in New South Wales and Victoria's High Country. Both feature downhill and cross-country skiing; the latter tends to be especially rewarding because of the vast size of the snowfields and the unusual flora and fauna.

Kosciusko National Park contains the resorts of Thredbo, Perisher-Smiggins, Guthega, Mt. Blue Cow, and Mt. Selwyn. Mt. Blue Cow, the newest and highest ski area, has some of the most challenging runs for advanced skiers. Victoria's major mountains for downhill are Mt. Buller (three hours by car from Melbourne), Falls Creek (known for its lively après-ski scene), and Mt. Hotham. For cross-country, the alpine route between Kosciusko and Kiandra is recommended in New South Wales, as are the trails in Victoria around The Bluff near Mansfield, where the movie *The Man from Snowy River* was filmed.

Tennis Tennis courts, both municipal and private, are everywhere, and most resorts have courts as well. Call the nearest tennis club to arrange a game. Rackets can usually be rented, but you must bring your own shoes. Tennis legend Tony Roche has opened the four-star Roche Racquet Resort (tel. 049/841–111, fax 049/841–222) at Salamander Bay, 210 kilometers (130 miles) north of Sydney.

Water Sports With 36,735 kilometers (22,827 miles) of coast bordering two oceans and four seas, Australians spend a good deal of their time in and on the water. Opportunities are abundant for scuba diving, snorkeling, surfing, water-skiing, and windsurfing. The best known area for scuba and snorkeling, of course, is the Great Barrier Reef. The prime diving season there is September–December, though the diving is still good until late April. Western Australia's Ningaloo, 2,400 kilometers (1,500 miles) of Indian Ocean coral reefs off the central coast near Exmouth, is quickly gaining a reputation among international divers. Unlike the Great Barrier Reef, these reefs lie only a few hundred yards offshore. For an unusual diving experience, visit Western Australia's Rowley Shoals, 14 hours by boat from Broome, where you can "fly" with the tides through canyons formed by mountains close to the surface. If time is short, however, look no further than the metropolitan areas. Good diving is to be found right in Sydney Harbour at North Head, and off-shore at Port Hacking and Broken Bay. Shipwrecks are the lure in Melbourne's Port Phillip Bay, particularly near the bay's entrance. Close to Adelaide is Port Noarlunga Reef, a marine reserve popular with local divers. Rottnest Island, off Perth's port of Fremantle, is a major diving attraction for both marine life and wrecks.

For more information about scuba diving and all underwater sports, contact the **Australian Underwater Federation** (Box 1006, Civic Sq., Canberra, ACT 2608, tel. 06/247–5554, fax 06/257–3018). Check other city telephone directories in Australia for branches.

Beaches

Australia is renowned for its beaches. Along its coastline are miles and miles of pristine sand where you can sunbathe in solitary splendor. It is advisable, however, to swim only at designated areas where lifeguards are on duty. The surf is often rough, and many beaches have a treacherous undertow. Volunteer lifesavers monitor almost all the metropolitan and town beaches. Sydney has 34 ocean beaches, with such well-known names as Bondi, Manly, Coogee, Bronte, and Maroubra. Daily reports are given on the state of the ocean in metropolitan newspapers and on the radio. Queensland's Gold Coast boasts a 32-kilometer (20-mile) stretch of clean beach, washed by warm, moderate surf. This area does not have the box jellyfish that plague beaches farther north (except on Great Barrier Reef islands) from November to April. Perth's ocean beaches are excellent, too. From South Fremantle north, there are 19 beaches along the Indian Ocean with wide swathes of sand and good surf. On most Australian beaches, women sunbathe topless; some beaches, like Sydney's Lady Jane and Perth's Swanbourne, are for those who prefer their sunning and swimming au naturel.

Dining

Dining out in Australia was not always a pleasurable experience. For much of its history, Australian cuisine labored under the worst traditions of bland English fare. Fortunately, post–World War II migration changed all that. First European migrants brought Continental, Slavic, and Mediterranean cooking, and then Middle Eastern and Asian immigrants introduced a whole new spicy repertoire. Today every conceivable type of cuisine is available in the capitals, and often in regional towns, too.

Some restaurants offer a fixed-price dinner, but the majority are à la carte. It's wise to make a reservation and enquire whether the restaurant is licensed (meaning that it serves alcohol) or "BYOB" (Bring Your Own Bottle). In Australia, entrée means appetizer and main course means entrée. You'll also encounter the term "silver service," which indicates upscale dining. "Bistro" generally refers to a relatively inexpensive place, where you often order your meal at the counter and then wait at a table to be served. French fries are chips; if you want ketchup, ask for tomato sauce. Breakfast is usually served between 7 and 10, lunch 11:30–2:30, and dinner service begins around 5:30. Outside these times it may be hard to find anything but snacks, particularly in the country. And despite the vast array of restaurants in the cities—the Melbourne metropolitan area alone boasts some 1,500—it's sometimes difficult in business districts to locate a restaurant where you can sit at a table for lunch, since Australian workers tend to eat fast food or get their food to go. Look in the shopping areas instead, where arcade tearooms and cafés serve lunch and afternoon tea. Don't be surprised if someone joins you at your table in the more humble cafés. You also might try a counter lunch in a pub bar; the food is similar to that in England, including pies and pasties, sausage and mash (potatoes), and a ploughman's lunch of bread, cheese, and pickles. You can eat similar fare in the many wine bars that have sprung up, accompanied by a glass of one of Australia's excellent wines.

Native Australian cuisine usually relies on fresh ingredients, such as seasonal vegetables and fish. Each state boasts its own specialties, particularly seafood. In the Northern Territory, for instance, grilled barramundi fish is prized as a delicacy. Yabbies, or "Moreton Bay bugs," a crayfishlike crustacean, are also highly regarded. Australia molds its own distinct cuisine, so some rather unusual dishes—including kangaroo, camel, crocodile, and buffalo—have begun appearing on restaurant menus. Wichetty grubs—1-inch moth larvae that were originally part of the Aboriginal diet—are now served in some of Australia's finest restaurants, but the flavor is strong and unlikely to appeal to the mainstream diner. Reminders of Australia's pioneer days are evoked in two bush staples: damper (an unleavened bread cooked over a fire) and billy tea (brewed in an open pot). More traditional fare includes carpetbagger steak, a juicy piece of beef stuffed with oysters; tasty sausages made from pork, beef, or veal; and meat pies—minced meat and gravy inside flaky pastry. Australians are big meat-eaters; they like their roasts (beef, lamb, pork, and veal), breaded meats, and heavy sauces. You may wish to ask for sauces to be served on the side. Chicken (sometimes called "chook") is becoming more popular as health consciousness grows. Thus far, cholesterol concern has not occupied Australian thinking: It is difficult to find substitute eggs in a restaurant, though they are available in stores, and requests for margarine and nonfat milk (known as slim milk or skim milk) meet with varying success.

Australian wine and beer are now both known worldwide. The beer is strong, somewhat similar to Danish and German beers. Each state produces its own brews and each is very partisan about the superiority of its product. Locals prefer draught beer from the tap, served ice-cold with little head. Nowadays wine is eroding beer's popularity. South Australia is still regarded as the country's premier wine-growing state. The Barossa Valley, to the east of Adelaide, is considered by many to be the leading region for wine production, both red and white. McLaren Vale, to the south of the city, is also famous for both. The Coonawarra region, southeast of Adelaide, is renowned for its reds, and a bottle with this label is always a safe bet on an unfamiliar wine list. Other quality producers include Victoria's Yarra Valley and Rutherglen area. Chardonnay remains the most popular white; the trend has been away from the pronounced oak flavors of the past. No wine is more distinctively Australian than shiraz (also called hermitage), a ruby-colored red that at its best is well-balanced and soft. If you're looking for an after-dinner sweetener, the ports and tokays from the Rutherglen region can be outstanding. Western Australia's Swan Valley and Margaret River are also coming to the fore as wine producers.

Lodging

Generally, hotel and motel rooms have private bathrooms with a combined shower/tub, although some bed-and-breakfast hotels and hostels require guests to share bathrooms. Tea and coffee makers are a fixture in almost every type of accommodation, and refrigerators and stocked minibars are found in deluxe hotels. You can expect a swimming pool, a health club, tennis courts, and spas in many resort hotels, some of which also boast their own golf courses. Motel chains, such as Flag International, are usually reliable and much less expensive than hotels. You often can check into a motel without booking ahead, but reservations are required for weekends and holidays.

Vacation apartments, known as self-catering apartments, are a popular alternative in Australia. Professionally managed, with a reception area and staff, these apartments are equipped with linens, dishes, cutlery, cookwear, and kitchen appliances. Some are serviced daily, others every three days or weekly.

Except for designated bed-and-breakfasts and farm stays, the majority of prices listed by hotels are for room only, although resorts in remote areas may offer American Plan (three meals included) or Modified American Plan (two meals). Surcharges sometimes apply on weekends, long weekends, and during holiday seasons. No service charge or tax is levied for accommodations, except in the Northern Territory where there is a 2.5% room tax.

Most of the major international hotel chains are represented in Australia. Reservations in Australia can be made with the following chains: Best Western International (tel. 800/528–1234); Conrad International Hotels and Hilton International (tel. 800/445–8667); Holiday Inns (tel. 800/HOLIDAY); Hyatt Hotels (tel. 800/233–1234); Inter-Continental Hotels (tel. 800/327–0200); Marriott Hotels (tel. 800/228–9290); Quality Inns International (tel. 800/228–5151); Radisson Hotels (tel. 800/333–3333); Ramada International and Renaissance Hotels and Resorts (tel. 800/228–9898); Regent International (tel. 800/545–4000); Ritz-Carlton Hotels (tel. 800/241–3333 in the U.S., 800/341–8565 in Canada); Sheraton Corporation (tel. 800/325–3535); Federal Hotels & Resorts and P & O Resorts (tel. 800/225–9849); Flag International Hotels & Resorts (tel. 800/624–3524); Pan Pacific Hotels Corporation (tel. 800/937–1515); Southern Pacific Hotel Corporation (tel. 800/835–7742). Reservations for many of the Great Barrier Reef and beach resorts can be made in the United States through such groups as Utell International (tel. 800/44–UTELL) and SO/PAC Marketing (tel. 800/551–2012).

Home and Farm Stays Home and farm stays, which are very popular with visitors, offer not only comfortable accommodations but a chance to learn more about Australian life from the hosts. Most operate on a bed-and-breakfast basis, though some also offer an evening meal. Farm accommodations vary from modest shearers' cabins to elegant homesteads. Guests can join in farm activities or explore the countryside. Some hosts offer day trips, as well as horseback riding, hiking, and fishing. For information and reservations in the United States contact: **Australian Home Accommodation,** represented by ATS/Sprint (tel.

800/423–2880); **Australian Farm Host and Farm Holidays,** represented by ATS/Sprint, SO/PAC (tel. 800/551–2012), and Pacific Destination Center (tel. 800/227–5317); **Victoria Host Farms** and **Bed & Breakfast Australia,** represented by SO/PAC. Pacific Destination Center also represents **Grand Country Estates** and **Houseguest,** offering B&B accomodations in private homes.

A number of Queensland sheep and cattle stations offering farm and country vacations have banded together as the **Queensland Host and Farm Association.** For information and reservations, contact the Royal Automobile Club of Queensland (RACQ) Travel Service (Box 1403, Brisbane 4001, tel. 07/361–2390, fax 07/257–1504).

Home Exchange You can find a house, apartment, or other vacation property to exchange for your own by becoming a member of a home-exchange organization, which then sends you its annual directories listing available exchanges and includes your own listing in at least one of them. Arrangements for the actual exchange are made by the two parties to it, not by the organization. For more information contact the **International Home Exchange Association** (IHEA, 41 Sutter St., Suite 1090, San Francisco, CA 94104, tel. 800/788–2489). Another principal clearinghouse is **HomeLink International** (Box 650, Key West, FL 33041, tel. 800/638–3841), which has thousands of foreign and domestic listings and publishes four annual directories plus updates; the $50 membership includes your listing in one book. **Intervac International Home Exchange** (Box 590504, San Francisco, CA 94159, tel. 415/435–3497) is the oldest organization, with thousands of foreign and domestic homes for exchange in its three annual directories; membership is $62, or $72 if you want to receive the directories but remain unlisted. **Loan-a-Home** (2 Park La., Apt. 6E, Mount Vernon, NY 10552, tel. 914/664–7640) specializes in long-term exchanges; there is no charge to list your home, but the directories cost $35 or $45 depending on the number you receive.

Apartment and Villa Rentals If you want a home base that's roomy enough for a family and comes with cooking facilities, a furnished rental may be the solution. It's generally cost-wise, too, although not always—some rentals are luxury properties (economical only when your party is large). Home-exchange directories do list rentals—often second homes owned by prospective house swappers—and there are services that can not only look for a house or apartment for you (even a castle if that's your fancy) but also handle the paperwork. Some send an illustrated catalogue and others send photographs of specific properties, sometimes at a charge; up-front registration fees may apply.

Among the companies are **Europa-Let** (92 N. Main St., Ashland, OR 97520, tel. 800/462–4486), **Property Rentals International** (1 Park West Circle, Suite 108, Midlothian, VA 23113, tel. 800/220–3332), **Rent a Home International** (7200 34th Ave. NW, Seattle, WA 98117, tel. 206/789–9377 or 800/488–7368), and **Villas International** (605 Market St., Suite 510, San Francisco, CA 94105, tel. 415/281–0910 or 800/221–2260).

Staying in New Zealand

Geography

New Zealand consists of three main islands: North Island (44,197 square miles), South Island (58,170 square miles), and Stewart Island (676 square miles). If it were stretched out along the west coast of the United States, the country would extend from Los Angeles to

Seattle. No point is more than 70 miles from the sea, and owing to the hilly nature of the country, rivers tend to be short, swift, and broad. More than 70% of the total population of 3.36 million lives on the North Island, where industry and government are concentrated. The South Island is dominated by the Southern Alps, a spine of mountains running almost two-thirds the length of the island close to the west coast.

Getting Around New Zealand

By Plane The major domestic airlines are **Air New Zealand** (tel. 09/379–3510) and **Ansett New Zealand** (tel. 09/37–6950). Both compete on intercity trunk routes, while a third carrier, **Mount Cook Airline** (tel. toll-free 0800/800–737) services the country's resort areas. Economy-price air travel is expensive compared with the cost of bus or train travel; however, multi-trip tickets offer a substantial saving. Ansett New Zealand has a **New Zealand Airpass** entitling you to fly between three and eight sectors (i.e., point-to-point flights) at an adult fare that runs from $435 for a three-sector pass to $1,100 for an eight-sector pass. Children under 12 pay two-thirds the adult fare. The pass is valid for the duration of your stay in New Zealand and should be purchased prior to arrival to avoid New Zealand sales tax. You can fly one sector on Ansett New Zealand between designated city pairs as part of the 4 in 1 InterCity New Zealand Travelpass (*see* Rail Passes, *above*) and can add up to two sectors for an additional fare. Air New Zealand and Mount Cook offer similar discount tickets, available through travel agents.

Smoking Smoking is not allowed on any flight within New Zealand.

By Train New Zealand's railroad system operates under the **InterCity** (tel. 09/358–4085) banner. Trains usually cost the same as buses and are marginally quicker, but they run far less frequently. The country's most notable rail journey is the **TranzAlpine Express,** a scenic spectacular across the mountainous spine of the South Island between Greymouth and Christchurch (*see* Arriving and Departing by Train for Marlborough, Nelson, and the West Coast in Chapter 15).

By Bus New Zealand is served by an extensive bus network and for many travelers, buses offer the optimal combination of cost and convenience. The main bus line is **InterCity** (tel. 09/358–4085), which also operates the railroad system. The other major operator on the North Island is **Newmans** (tel. 09/309–9738), and on the South Island **Mount Cook Landline** (tel. 03/379–0690 in Christchurch or toll-free 0800/800–737). The **InterCity Travelpass** allows unlimited travel on all InterCity buses and trains and on the InterIslander ferries that link the North and South Islands (*see* Rail Passes, *above*).

By Car A valid American, Canadian, or British license allows you to drive in New Zealand, and nothing beats the freedom and mobility of a car for exploring. Even for those nervous about traveling on the "wrong" side of the road, driving here is relatively easy. Roads are well maintained and generally uncrowded, though signposting, even on major highways, is often poor. The speed limit is 100 kilometers per hour (62 mph) on the open road and 50 kph (31 mph) in towns and cities. A circular sign with the letters "LSZ" (Limited Speed Zone) means there is no speed limit—speed should be governed by prevailing road conditions.

If you drive in rural New Zealand, you will encounter one-lane bridges. These must be crossed with caution. A yellow sign on the left will usually warn that you are approaching a one-lane bridge, and another sign will tell you whether you have the right-of-way. A rectangular blue sign means you have the right-of-way; a circular sign with a red border means you must pull over to the left and wait to cross until oncoming traffic has passed. Even when you have the right-of-way, slow down and take care. Some one-lane bridges on the South Island are used by trains as well as cars; trains always have the right-of-way.

Telephones

Most pay phones now accept **PhoneCards** rather than coins. These plastic cards, available in denominations of $5, $10, $20, or $50, are sold at shops displaying the green PhoneCard symbol. To use a PhoneCard, lift the receiver, put the card in the slot in the front of the phone, and dial. The cost of the call is automatically deducted from your card; the display on the telephone tells you how much credit you have left at the end of the call.

Local Calls A local call from a public phone costs 20¢ per minute.

International Calls International calls may be dialed direct. The country code for the United States and Canada is 1, the code for Australia is 61, and the code for New Zealand is 64. For international directory assistance, dial 0172. For the international operator, dial 0170. AT&T, MCI, and Sprint each have services that allow you to contact an operator in the United States directly, thus circumventing some pricey hotel surcharges. Place your calling-card or collect calls by dialing the New Zealand access number for one of the following: **AT&T USADirect** (tel. 000–911), **MCI Call USA** (tel. 000–912), or **Sprint Express** (tel. 000–999). Similar toll-free numbers exist for other countries: UK, tel. 000–944; Canada, tel. 000–919; Australia, tel. 000–961.

Mail

Postage Rates Post offices are open weekdays 9–5. The cost of mailing a letter within New Zealand is 45¢ standard post, 80¢ fast post. Sending a standard-size letter by air mail costs $1.50 to North America, $1.80 to Europe, and $1 to Australia. Aerogrammes and postcards are $1 to any overseas destination.

Receiving Mail Mail will be held for collection for one month at the central post office in any town or city if it is addressed to you "c/o Poste Restante, CPO," followed by the name of the town. This service is free.

Tipping

Tipping is not widely practiced in New Zealand. Only in the better city restaurants will you be expected to show your appreciation for good service with a 10% tip.

Opening and Closing Times

Banks are open weekdays 9–4:30, but trading in foreign currencies ceases at 3. Shops are generally open Monday–Thursday 9–5:30, Friday 9–9, and Saturday 9–noon.

Shopping

New Zealand produces several unique souvenirs, but don't expect to find many bargains. Sheepskins and quality woolens are widely available. Bowls hewn from native timbers and polished to a lustrous finish are distinctive souvenirs, but a fine example will cost several hundred dollars. Greenstone, a type of jade once prized by the Maoris, is now used for ornaments and jewelry—especially the figurine known as a *tiki*, which is often worn as a pendant. The two major areas for crafts are the Coromandel Peninsula, close to Auckland, and the environs of Nelson, at the northern tip of the South Island. The Parnell area of Auckland and the Galleria in Christchurch Arts Centre are the places to shop for souvenirs. In Nelson, Craft Habitat brings together some of the finest local arts and crafts under one roof.

Sports and the Outdoors

Bicycling Despite its precipitous topography, New Zealand offers superb biking. A temperate climate, excellent roads with relatively little traffic, and scenic variety make cycling a delight for anyone who is reasonably fit and has the time to travel slowly. The most common problem for cyclists is buckled wheel rims: Narrow, lightweight alloy rims won't stand up long to the rigors of the road. A wide-rimmed hybrid or a mountain bike with road tires is a better bet for extensive touring.

If two-wheel touring sounds appealing but pedaling a heavily laden bicycle doesn't, consider a guided cycle tour. The tours last from two to 18 days; bikes are supplied, and your gear is loaded on a bus or trailer that follows the riders. (You have the option of busing in the "sag wagon" when your legs give out.) Contact **New Zealand Pedaltours** (Box 49–039, Auckland, tel. 09/302–0968) or **Unravel Tours** (Square Edge Bldg., Palmerston North, tel. 06/356–5500).

Boating and Sailing The country's premier cruising regions are the Bay of Islands and Marlborough Sounds, near the northern tips of the North and South Islands respectively. Both areas offer sheltered waters, marvelous scenery, and secluded beaches. Of the two, the Bay of Islands enjoys warmer summer temperatures, while Marlborough Sounds has a wild, untamed quality. Both are well supplied with operators offering either bare-boat or skippered charters, and a range of vessels from small motor cruisers to sleek Beneteau yachts. For more information, contact **Rainbow Yacht Charters** (Box 8327, Symonds St., Auckland, tel. 09/78–0719) or **Charterlink** (Box 246, Picton, tel. 03/573–6591).

Fishing Considering that they were introduced from California little more than a hundred years ago, the explosion in New Zealand's **trout** population has been phenomenal. The average summer rainbow trout taken from Lake Tarawera, near Rotorua, weighs 5 pounds, and 8- to 10-pound fish are not unusual. In the lakes of the North Island, fingerlings often reach a weight of 4 pounds nine months after they are released. Trout do not reach maturity until they grow to 14 inches, and in fact all trout below that length must be returned to the water.

Trout fishing has a distinctly different flavor on the two islands. In the Rotorua-Taupo region of the North Island, the main quarry is rainbow trout, which are usually taken from the lakes with a wet fly or spinners. Trolling is also popular and productive. On the South Island, where brown trout predominate, the streams offer outstanding dry-fly fishing. It's best in the Nelson region and in the Southern Lakes district, at the top and bottom end of the South Island respectively. On both islands, anglers who can afford to indulge their passion are well catered to. Several specialist lodges provide guides and transport to wilderness streams that are sometimes accessible only by helicopter. The trout season lasts from October through April in most areas, though Lakes Taupo and Rotorua are open all year.

Salmon are found in the rivers that drain the eastern slopes of the Southern Alps, especially those that reach the sea between Christchurch and Dunedin. Anglers are usually transported by jetboat up these shallow rivers to the pools where the salmon rest on their spawning run. The salmon season, which runs from October to April, is at its peak from January to March.

Fishing licenses are available from fishing-tackle and sports shops on a daily, weekly, monthly, or seasonal basis. The cost ranges from $10.50 for a single day to $53 for the season, and each is valid for the entire country, with the exception of Lake Taupo, for which a separate license is required. For anyone who plans to fish extensively, the best buy is a tourist fishing license—available from Visitor Information Centres in all the major cities—which, for $56.26, permits fishing anywhere in New Zealand for one month.

The seas off the east coast of the North Island are among the world's finest **big-game fishing** waters. The quarry is mako, hammerhead, tiger shark, and marlin—especially striped marlin, which average around 250 pounds. For light tackle fishing, bonito and skipjack tuna and kahawai (sea trout) offer excellent sport. Many anglers maintain that kahawai are better fighters, pound for pound, than freshwater trout. The bases for big-game fishing are the towns of Pahia and Russell, which have a number of established charter operators. The season runs from January to April, although smaller game fishing is good all year. No fishing license is required for big-game fishing.

Wherever they fish, and whatever they fish for, anglers will profit immensely from the services of a local guide. On Lake Taupo or Rotorua, a boat with a guide plus all equipment will cost around $130 for two hours. On the South Island, a top fishing guide who can supply all equipment and a four-wheel drive vehicle will charge about $400 per day for two people. In the Bay of Islands region, an evening fishing trip aboard a small boat can cost as little as $35. For a big-game fishing boat, expect to pay between $600 and $1,000 per day.

For more information and brochures on fishing in New Zealand, contact **Simon Dickie Adventures** (Box 682, Taupo, tel. 07/378–9680); **Lake Brunner Lodge** (Mitchells, RD1 Kumara 7871, Westlands, tel. 03/738–0163); or **Bay of Islands Sportfishing Ltd.** (Box 48, Russell, tel. 09/403–7008).

Golf   Golf is played all year; winter is the major season. Most of New Zealand's 400 courses welcome visitors. Greens fees range from $5 at country courses to $40 at the exclusive city courses. Many have clubs for hire, and the better urban courses offer resident professionals and golf carts for hire. For more information, contact the Executive Director, **NZ Golf Association,** Box 11–842, Wellington.

Hiking   If you want to see the very best the country has to offer, put on a pair of walking boots and head for the hills. Range upon range of mountains; deep, ice-carved valleys; wilderness areas that have never been farmed, logged, or grazed; and a first-class network of marked trails and tramping huts are just some of the reasons that hiking is a national addiction.

The traditional way to hike in New Zealand is freedom walking. Freedom walkers carry their own provisions, sleeping bags, food, and cooking gear, and sleep in basic huts. A more refined alternative—usually available only on the more popular trails—is the guided walk, on which you trek with just a light day pack, guides do the cooking, and you sleep in heated lodges. If you prefer your wilderness served with hot showers and an eiderdown on your bed, the guided walk is for you.

There are almost 900 **back country huts** in New Zealand; they provide basic shelter but few frills. Huts are usually placed about four hours apart, although in isolated areas it can take a full day to get from one hut to the next. They are graded 1 to 4, and the cost varies from nothing to $14 per person per night. Category 1 huts (the $14 ones) have cooking equipment and fuel, bunks or sleeping platforms with mattresses, toilets, washing facilities, and a supply of water. At the other end of the scale, Category 4 huts (the free ones) are simple shelters without bunks or other facilities. Payment is by coupons, available in books from Department of Conservation offices. If you plan to make extensive use of huts, an annual pass giving access to all Category 2 and 3 huts for one year is available for $58.

The most popular walks are located in the Southern Alps, where the postcard views of mountains, wild rivers, mossy beech forests, and fjords issue a challenge to the legs that is hard to resist. The trekking season in the mountains usually lasts from October to mid-April. The best-known of all New Zealand's trails is the **Milford Track,** a four-day walk through breathtaking scenery to the edge of Milford Sound. Its main drawback is its popularity. This is the only track in New Zealand on which numbers are controlled: You are required to obtain a permit and to begin walking on the day specified (to ensure that the overnight huts along the track don't become impossibly crowded). If you plan to walk the Milford in December or January, book at least six months in advance; at other times, three months is usually sufficient. (If you arrive without a booking, there are sometimes last-minute cancellations, and parties of one or two can often be accommodated.) The Milford Track is closed from the end of April to early September. Bookings, either as a freedom walker or on a guided walk, can be made by contacting the THC Milford Track Office, THC Te Anau Resort Hotel, Box 185, Te Anau, tel. 03/249–7411.

While the Milford gets the lion's share of publicity, many other walks offer a similar—some would say better—combination of scenery and exercise. The **Routeburn Track** is a three-day walk that rises through beech forests, traverses a mountain face across a high pass, and descends through a glacial valley. The **Kepler** and the **Hollyford** are both exceptional, and the **Abel Tasman,** at the northern end of the South Island, is a spectacular three-to-four-day coastal track that can be walked year-round.

Clothing and footwear are major considerations. Even at the height of summer the weather can change quickly, and hikers must be prepared—especially for the rainstorms that regularly drench the Southern Alps. (The Milford Sound region, with its average annual rainfall of 160 inches, is one of the wettest places on earth.) The most cost-effective rain gear you can buy is the U.S. Army poncho. For more information, contact Routeburn Walk Ltd. (Box 185, Te Anau, tel. 03/249–7411) or Abel Tasman National Park Enterprises (Old Cedarman House, Main Rd., Riwaka, Motueka RD3, tel. 03/528–7801).

Hunting New Zealand offers superb hunting. Faced with an abundance of food and a complete lack of predators, wild animals such as the deer that were introduced last century have multiplied to such numbers that they're considered pests, and an open season applies to many species. Sika stag are found in the beech forests of the North Island, and red stag are common to the forests of both islands. Higher altitudes of the Southern Alps are inhabited by the prized tahr and chamois.

Hunters can choose between "fair chase" hunts, for which they pay a minimum daily fee for a minimum number of days, and "ranch" hunts, in which the owner controls the game and the fee is charged per trophy. Ammunition is widely available for all common calibers. If you plan to bring a firearm into the country, you must present it on arrival to the police, who will issue you a license. March and April are the prime months for hunting most deer, May and June for tahr and chamois.

Except for national parks, forest parks, scenic reserves, and conservation areas, no hunting permit is necessary for deer; however, special conditions apply in some areas. When required, a permit can be obtained from Department of Conservation offices and from the visitor centers located in all national parks. A hunting guide is essential, not only for success but also for safety. For more information, contact **New Zealand Hunting and Fishing Consultants** (210–212 Lake Terr., Taupo. tel. 07/378–7070); **Mid Southern Tracks** (Box 2, Lake Tekapo, tel. 03/680–6774); or **Wildsouth** (Box 199, Mosgiel, tel. 03/489–7322).

Skiing New Zealand has 27 peaks that top the 10,000-foot mark, and the June–October ski season is the reason many skiers head "down under" when the snow melts in the northern hemisphere. On the South Island, the site of most of the country's 13 commercial skifields, the outstanding areas are **Treble Cone and Cardrona,** served by the town of Wanaka, and **Coronet Peak and the Remarkables,** close to Queenstown. The North Island has only two commercial skifields, **Whakapapa and Turoa,** both near Lake Taupo on the slopes of Mount Ruapehu. Lift prices average about $40 per day.

What the New Zealand skifields lack is sophistication. By international standards they are comparatively small, and the slopes lack the extensive interlocking lift systems that are a feature of European skiing. There is no such thing as snowfield accommodations: Skiers must stay in one of the nearby subalpine towns.

Heliskiing is very popular. Harris Mountains Heliski, the second largest heliski operation in the world, gives access from the town of Wanaka to more than 200 runs on more than 100 peaks accessible to skiers by no other means. The ultimate heliski adventure is the 13-kilometer (8½-mile) run down the Tasman Glacier, available from Glentanner Park, near Mount Cook Village.

Beaches

The list of great New Zealand beaches is almost endless. There are no private beaches, no risks from pollution; the greatest danger is sunburn. Most New Zealanders prefer the beaches along the east coast of the North Island, where the combination of gentle seas and balmy summers is a powerful attraction in the January holidays. During the summer months, popular beaches close to the cities and in major holiday areas are patrolled by lifeguards. Swim with caution on unpatrolled beaches.

Dining

Auckland, Wellington, and Christchurch offer cosmopolitan dining, but, apart from a few expensive sporting lodges, most country cooking still gets its recipes from the meat-and-two-veg school of English cuisine. The country's greatest culinary asset is its raw materials. The lamb and the New Zealand crayfish, often known as spiny or rock lobster, are delicious, and the succulent, white-shelled Bluff oysters, available from March to about July, are rated highly by gourmets. Watch for orange roughy, a delicate white-fleshed fish that is at its best with a light sauce. Venison is widely available, and many chefs are preparing exciting dishes based on cervena, a leaner, lighter style of farmed venison.

A New Zealand specialty is the *hangi*, the Maori feast of steamed meat and vegetables. Several hotels in Rotorua offer a hangi, usually combined with an evening of Maori song and dance. (These days it's unlikely that the food will be cooked by steaming it in the traditional hot earth oven.)

The difference in price between a reasonable meal and a very good one is often not great. Even bistro-style restaurants charge $12–$16 for a dish of pasta, and a main course at the French Café in Auckland—one of the country's finest restaurants—costs about $25. For cheap lunches, the standard take-aways are meat pies and fish and chips. Most country pubs serve inexpensive cooked lunches and sometimes a selection of salads. In season, stock up on fruit from the roadside stalls that are scattered throughout the country's fruit-growing areas.

New Zealand wines can be excellent, but there are few bargains. Hawke's Bay and Marlborough are the premier winegrowing regions. Some restaurants are not licensed to serve alcohol, but diners are welcome to bring their own; check when reserving a table.

Lodging

The New Zealand Tourism Board (*see* New Zealand Government Tourist Offices, *above*) publishes an annual *Where to Stay* directory listing more 1,000 properties.

Motels Motels are by far the most common accommodations, and most offer comfortable rooms for $60–$90 per night. Some motels have two-bedroom suites for families. All motel rooms come equipped with tea- and coffee-making facilities, many have toasters or electric frying pans, and full kitchen facilities are not uncommon.

Home and Farm Stays If you want more than just a bed for the night, farm stays and home stays are a great way to get to know the land and its people. Farm-stay guests can generally expect to share meals with the family and share in the farmwork if they feel inclined. For two people, the average cost is $90–$150 per night, including all meals. Home stays, the urban equivalent of farm stays, are less expensive. For a list, contact **New Zealand Farm Holidays Ltd.** (Box 256, Silverdale, Auckland, tel. 09/307–2024) or **Homestay Ltd. Farmstay Ltd.** (Box 25–115, Auckland, tel. 09/55–5980). For information on home exchange, *see* Lodging in Staying in Australia, *above*.

Tourist Cabins and Flats The least expensive accommodations are the tourist cabins and flats in most of New Zealand's 400 motor camps. Tourist cabins offer basic accommodation and shared cooking, laundry, and bathroom facilities. Bedding and towels are not provided. A notch higher up the comfort scale, tourist flats usually provide bedding, fully equipped kitchens, and private bathrooms. Overnight tariffs run about $6–$20 for cabins and $25–$70 for flats.

Sporting Lodges At the other end of the price scale, a number of luxury sporting lodges offer the best of country life plus fine dining and superb accommodations. Fishing is a specialty at most, but there is usually a range of outdoor activities for nonanglers. Tariffs run about $350–$800 per day for two people; meals are generally included.

Credit Cards

The following credit card abbreviations are used: AE, American Express; DC, Diner's Club; MC, MasterCard; V, Visa.

Great Itineraries

Highlights of Australia and New Zealand

This tour is a study in contrasts. It takes in the mountains, beach forests, glaciers, and thermal wonders of New Zealand's North and South islands, then crosses the Tasman Sea for a look at the deserts, wildlife, coral reefs, and steamy tropical forests of the sunburnt country of Australia. This itinerary, however, is not for the fainthearted! The tour has been designed to pack the best of both nations into the shortest possible time. Those who want a more in-depth experience rather than an overview should plan a more leisurely trip.

Length 20 days

The Main Route **Day 1:** Arive in Auckland. Explore the city on a half-day tour, then make an evening ferry trip across the harbor to Devonport.

Day 2: Drive south to Waitomo Caves, take a tour of the caves, then continue to Rotorua. Spend the evening at a Maori hangi.

Day 3: Tour Rotorua and its surroundings on the Waimangu Round Trip day tour and finish off with a soak in the Polynesian Pools.

Day 4: Fly from Rotorua to Mount Cook and take an afternoon hike along the Hooker Valley trail.

Day 5: Take an early morning flight over the Southern Alps or, if the weather is unsuitable, save this experience for the return journey via the west coast. Fly to Queenstown and take a dinner cruise aboard the T.S.S. *Earnslaw.*

Day 6: In the morning take a jet-boat ride along the Dart River, returning to Queenstown and exploring Arrowtown in the afternoon. In the evening, ride the Skyline Gondola to Bob's Peak.

Day 7: Join a one-day bus and boat tour to Milford Sound.

Day 8: Depart Queenstown and drive along the west coast to Lake Moeraki Wilderness Lodge. Spend the afternoon canoeing, walking, or wildlife watching on the beach.

Day 9: Continue to Franz Josef and hike on the glaciers, or take a late afternoon flight to see the sunset over the Southern Alps.

Day 10: Catch the alpine reflections in Lake Matheson, then drive to Greymouth and board the TranzAlpine Express at midday for the trip across the mountains to Christchurch. Take an evening flight to Sydney.

Day 11: Explore Sydney's waterfront area, take a ferry tour of the harbor, and spend the evening in the Royal Botanic Gardens.

Day 12: Take a day trip to the Blue Mountains.

Day 13: Fly to Ayers Rock via Alice Springs. Take an evening trip out to "sunset strip" to watch the rock change color at dusk.

Day 14: Take an early morning Uluru Experience tour. Travel to The Olgas in mid-afternoon for a hike and evening barbecue.

Day 15: Fly to Darwin and drive to Kakadu National Park. Spend the night at Jabiru or Cooinda.

Day 16: Take an early morning cruise on Yellow Water, then tour Kakadu's Aboriginal rock art sites.

Day 17: Return to Darwin and fly to Cairns.

Day 18: Take a cruise to the outer reef and spend the day snorkelling, diving, or coral viewing from a semisubmersible craft.

Day 19: Join a daytour that combines a wildlife-watching cruise along the Daintree River, with a four-wheel-drive safari into the Daintree rain forest.

Day 20: Board the train for Kuranda. Explore the town and see the Tjapukai Aboriginal theater troupe in action. Fly home from Cairns.

Information *See* Chapters 2, 7, 8, 10, 11, 13, and 14.

Australia's Main Cities

Sydney is Australia's window onto the world—a bright cosmopolitan city with a quick pace and a sassy look. Melbourne is Sydney's antithesis, its green trams and wide, tree-lined avenues symbols of an old-fashioned way of life. Despite a reputation for stuffiness, Melbourne is the nation's cultural, financial, and intellectual capital. Melbourne's fierce rivalry with Sydney was the driving force behind the creation of the federal capital compromise, Canberra, built on farmland between the two cities. Canberra is a totally planned city, with none of the vivacity and character of other Australian cities. It is the seat of government, however, and many of its monuments and buildings reflect its central role in Australian life.

Length 7 days

The Main Route **Days 1–2:** Explore Sydney. Spend an evening at the Sydney Opera House on a dinner/show package.

Day 3: Take a day tour to the Blue Mountains for an introduction to the bush, or to the Hunter Valley wine district.

Day 4: Fly to Canberra for the day. Tour the federal capital and lunch at a sheep station. Spend the night in Canberra.

Day 5: Fly to Melbourne in the early morning. Tour the city.

Day 6: Join a day-long excursion to the Dandenong Ranges, then watch the parade of fairy penguins at Phillip Island.

Day 7: Tour the Victorian Arts Centre and explore some of the nearby gardens. Fly back to Sydney.

Information *See* Chapters 2, 3, 4, and 5.

Wine-Tasting Odyssey

Like Californian wines, Australian wines were long shunned as inferior to the established European vintages. Such Eurocentrism has finally dissipated. Many of the best wines never leave Australian shores, however, making a wine tour of the country's vineyards a remarkably rewarding experience. The best wines come from the Barossa Valley in South Australia, a delightful region with a distinctly Germanic flavor created by the area's Silesian immigrants. The Hunter Valley in New South Wales and the wine districts of Victoria are also producing good wines. And don't overlook the wines from the boutique wineries, whose savory products never reach the international market. Almost all wineries have tasting rooms.

Length 8–11 days

The Main Route
Day 1: Drive north to the Hunter Valley wine country.
Day 2: Visit the Lower and Upper Hunter Valley wineries.
Day 3: Drive south on the Hume Highway. Make an optional detour to Canberra, then continue to Albury on the Murray River, which forms the New South Wales/Victoria border. Cross to Rutherglen, one of the main Victorian winery centers.
Day 4: Continue touring wineries. Follow Murray River Highway westward, stopping to view the historic port of Echuca and Swan Hill's Pioneer Village. Spend the night at Mildura.
Day 5: Cross into South Australia and head to the Barossa Valley wine area.
Day 6: Enjoy wine tasting through the Barossa Valley, then drive on to Adelaide.
Day 7: Tour the Adelaide Hills and the nearby wineries.
Day 8: Explore Adelaide before taking an early evening flight back to Sydney.

Information *See* Chapters 3, 4, 5, and 9.

Reef and Rock

The Great Barrier Reef and Ayers Rock, Australia's two most famous landmarks, give visitors completely different views of Australia. Running parallel to the tropical coast of Queensland, the Great Barrier Reef is the largest living organism in the world and home to thousands of multihued fish and corals. Diving and snorkeling in the crystal waters of the Reef cannot be rivalled. The coast is equally fascinating, covered in dense rain forest and laced with rivers populated with crocodiles. Ayers Rock, on the other hand, is smack in the middle of thousands of miles of red, waterless desert. The largest monolith in the world, Ayers Rock is the essence of the Outback and gives visitors a feel for the enormity of Australia's Red Centre.

Length 9–10 days

The Main Route
Day 1: Arrive in Cairns. Check into one of the resorts in the city or along the Marlin Coast. Explore Cairns.
Day 2: Take a cruise for a day on the Outer Great Barrier Reef.
Day 3: Enjoy narrated train ride up to Kuranda; attend the Tjapukai Aboriginal theater and tour Atherton Tablelands.
Day 4: Join a Daintree rain forest full-day tour, including an Aborigine-guided walk through the jungle on the Kuku Yulanji Dreamtime Trail, and a Daintree river cruise.
Day 5: Take a morning flight to Dunk Island. Swim and sun, or go butterfly-viewing in the bush.
Day 6: Spend another day enjoying island activities.
Day 7: Fly back to Cairns to connect with a flight to Alice Springs in the Red Centre.
Day 8: Explore the Alice and its environs.
Day 9: Fly to Ayers Rock Resort. Join a late-afternoon excursion to view the Olgas and sunset at Ayers Rock.
Day 10: Take an early morning tour to Ayers Rock. Climb to the top, if you wish. Board an afternoon flight to Sydney.

Information *See* Chapters 7, 8, and 10.

Flora and Fauna Around Australia

This tour circles the continent, offering visitors a first-hand look at the diversity and beauty of Australia's wildlife and terrain. From the marine wonders of the Great Barrier Reef to the rain forests of Queensland and the Top End, Australia remains one of the planet's final frontiers. Travel to Bungle Bungle in the Kimberley, a vast area of strangely shaped rock formations discovered in 1983; explore the waterfalls and swimming holes in Kakadu National Park, the site of the movie *Crocodile Dundee*, and watch flocks of birds gather at the drying water holes as they await the Wet. And no tour of Australia's wilderness region would be complete without a four-wheel-drive bush safari, complete with barbecue, damper, and billy tea.

Length 19–22 days

The Main Route
Day 1: Arrive in Cairns and transfer to the hotel in the city or on the Marlin Coast, between Cairns and Port Douglas.

Day 2: Relax with a day of sunning and snorkeling on a catamaran excursion (optional) to the Outer Great Barrier Reef.

Day 3: Take the narrated tour on the train to the mountain village of Kuranda. Attend a performance of the Tjapukai Aboriginal theater and tour Atherton Tablelands (optional).

Day 4: Join a Daintree rain forest tour, including an Aborigine-guided walk through the jungle on the Kuku Yulanji Dreamtime Trail and a Daintree River cruise, observing bird life, butterflies, and crocodiles.

Day 5: Fly to Darwin in the Northern Territory's Top End.

Day 6: Drive to Kakadu National Park. Check into a hotel at Jabiru or nearby.

Day 7: Enjoy a cruise on Yellow Water, viewing exotic bird life. Tour Aboriginal rock paintings at Ubirr or Nourlangie.

Day 8: Weather permitting, take a four-wheel-drive tour to view Jim Jim Falls. If possible, join a guided float tour (paddling upriver on an inflated air mattress) to picnic and swim in the awe-inspiring setting below Twin Falls.

Day 9: Return to Darwin. Explore the city.

Day 10: Take an early morning flight to Kununurra, gateway to Western Australia's Kimberley region. See Hidden Valley and the Waringarri Aboriginal Arts Centre.

Day 11: Take an aerial tour over the bizarrely shaped Bungle Bungle Range, then land to visit the Argyle Diamond Mine.

Day 12: Fly to Broome and explore this coastal pearling town.

Day 13: Take a daylong four-wheel-drive safari along the cliff-rimmed northern beaches, viewing mangrove swamps, rain forests, and bird life.

Day 14: Fly to Perth. Stroll alongside the Swan River and enjoy a panoramic overview of the city from Kings Park.

Day 15: Explore Perth and the port of Fremantle.

Day 16: Tour the southwest, including the Margaret River area's vineyards and caves.

Day 17: Spend the day at one of Perth's beaches. If it's spring, head for the Darling Ranges to admire the wildflowers.

Day 18: Fly to Sydney. Dine by candlelight on a harbor cruise.

Day 19: Explore Sydney, including the Taronga Park Zoo.

Day 20: Make a daylong excursion to the Blue Mountains.

Day 21: Finish your trip on a full-day Australiana tour: Enjoy a barbecue and sheep-shearing and boomerang-throwing demonstrations at a historic homestead and winery.

Day 22: Do some shopping before your departure for home.

Information *See* Chapters 2, 3, 7, 8, and 11.

Highlights of New Zealand's North and South Islands

New Zealand is an experience to be savored, not rushed, but if a one-week visit is all you can manage, this itinerary will introduce you to the main attractions of both islands.

Length 7 days

The Main Route **Day 1:** Arrive in Auckland and explore the city. Take an evening ferry ride across the harbor to Devonport.

Day 2: Travel to the Waitomo Caves; tour the Glow-worm Cave and hike the Waitomo Walkway, then continue to Rotorua.

Day 3: Take the Waimangu Round Trip day tour, finish off with a soak in the Polynesian Pools, then take in a Maori hangi.

Day 4: Catch the morning flight to Mount Cook. Hike along the Hooker Valley and watch the sun set over the Southern Alps.

Day 5: Take an early morning scenic flight around the Southern Alps with a glacier landing; then travel to Queenstown. Explore Arrowtown.

Day 6: Join a day tour to Milford Sound with a midday cruise, returning to Queenstown in the evening.

Day 7: Fly to Christchurch and explore the city center. Spend your last afternoon shopping for souvenirs in the Galleria.

Information *See* Chapters 13, 14, and 15.

Experiencing New Zealand

For anyone who wants to hike, canoe, fish, and explore some of the less well-known attractions, 10 days on each island is a practical minimum. This tour includes the main cities as well as the country's natural splendors, with emphasis on wildlife.

Length 20 days

The Main Route **Day 1:** Arrive in and explore Auckland. Take an evening ferry to Devonport and dine on the waterfront.

Day 2: Travel north to the Bay of Islands. Explore the Treaty House, and cross by ferry to spend the night in Russell.

Day 3: Explore Russell and take a catmaran trip out to Cape Brett, followed by an evening fishing trip.

Day 4: Travel to the Coromandel Peninsula via Auckland.

Day 5: Explore the seascapes and wilderness of the Coromandel Peninsula, preferably on a half-day tour with Doug Johansen. Travel to Rotorua in the late afternoon.

Day 6: Take the Waimangu Round Trip day tour. End with a mineral bath, and spend the evening at a Maori hangi.

Day 7: Travel to Taupo and view the thermal infernos along the way. Spend the evening on a sightseeing cruise of the lake, or trawling in champion trout territory.

Day 8: Travel to Napier and explore the city's art deco architecture and the surrounding wineries.

Day 9: Travel to Wellington and explore the national capital.

Day 10: Cross to the South Island by ferry, then travel to Nelson along the edge of the Marlborough Sounds.

Day 11: Join a one-day guided cruise along the coastline of the Abel Tasman National Park, with a flight back at the end.

Day 12: Travel to the west coast glacier country and spend the night at Franz Josef.

Day 13: Take an early scenic flight across the glaciers and Mount Cook, the highest peak in the country, or join a glacier-walking party. Travel on to Lake Moeraki Lodge and spend the evening canoeing on the lake.

Day 14: Join a beach tour from Lake Moeraki Lodge to see the penguins and seals; travel to Queenstown in the afternoon.

Day 15: Explore Queenstown and Arrowtown, go bungy jumping or trail riding, or take the Dart River jetboat safari.

Day 16: Join a one-day tour to Milford Sound, traveling through the spectacular wilderness of Fiordland National Park, followed by a cruise on the sound.

Day 17: Drive to Dunedin and visit the royal albatross colony at Taiaroa Head.

Day 18: Travel to Christchurch and spend the afternoon on a walking tour of the city.

Day 19: Travel to Kaikoura and join a whale-watching expedition. Return to Christchurch in the evening.

Day 20: Explore Akaroa and return to Christchurch for souvenir and duty-free shopping.

Information *See* Chapters 13, 14, and 15.

South Island Adventure Tour

This action-packed tour takes place against some of the finest natural backdrops in the country. It begins with a biking tour across the Southern Alps to the rugged west coast, travels south to Fiordland National Park for a hike on the Milford Track, and ends with a kayaking and camping trip along the edge of Abel Tasman National Park. While this might sound demanding, both the biking and the Milford Track are guided tours requiring only a moderate level of fitness.

Length 21 days

The Main Route **Day 1:** Arrive at Christchurch. Take a walking tour of the city and stock up on any necessary provisions.

Days 2–10: Join a nine-day Pedaltours Southern Comfort cycling tour, traveling to Queenstown via Arthur's Pass and the west coast glaciers. This tour concludes with a scenic flight to Milford Sound and a cruise.

Day 11: Travel to Te Anau and spend the afternoon preparing for the Milford Track, "the finest walk in the world."

Days 12–15: Walk the Milford Track.

Day 16: Return to Queenstown and spend the rest of the day exploring the surroundings—or bungee jumping, jet boating, or trying any of the other heart-stopping thrills in the area.

Day 17: Take the early morning flight to Mount Cook. Walk the Hooker Valley and watch the sun set.

Day 18: Fly to Nelson and spend the night in the town.

Days 19–21: Travel to Marahau, hire a kayak, and spend two days along the coastline of the Abel Tasman National Park.

Information *See* Chapter 15.

2 Sydney

By Michael Gebicki

A Sydney resident since 1979, Michael Gebicki writes and photographs for several Australian and international publications.

Take a taxi from Sydney airport and the chances are that the driver will not say "G'day" with the broad accent you might expect. Probe a little further and you will probably discover that he was not born in Australia. Like the United States, Australia is a society of immigrants—and Sydney has been a major destination for many of these new arrivals. Over the past half century, the city's original Anglo-Irish population has been enriched by successive waves of Italians, Greeks, Yugoslavs, Turks, Lebanese, and, more recently, Southeast Asians. This intermingling has given the city a cultural vibrancy and energy that was missing only a generation ago.

Today, Sydney is a city in a hurry. The traffic is fast and impatient and, for most drivers, the instinctive reaction to a yellow light is to accelerate! This city of 3.5 million people works hard and plays harder—moderation is something practiced by people from Melbourne. Sydney has the tallest buildings, the most expensive real estate, the finest beaches, and the seediest nightlife of any Australian city. Most Australians regard its loud, brash ways with a mixture of fear and fascination, although Sydneysiders prefer to think of their city as virile rather than vulgar.

The British writer Lawrence Durrell once lamented that Americans seem to live out of sync with their natural surroundings. The same could be said of Sydney, which seems determined to ignore its position on the cusp of a barren, unforgiving continent. In many ways, Sydney seems to have turned its cosmopolitan back on the heartland and established itself as a separate entity altogether. For the average Sydneysider, life unfolds in one of the red-roofed suburbs that sprawl around the city, and the suburban streets are the true terrain of Australia—bush talk is reserved for the pubs and foreigners.

Sydney may have forsaken the hinterland, but it has embraced its harbor with a passion. And who can blame it? The harbor is a shining gem, studded with small bays and inlets, and crowned by the billowing sails of the Opera House. The harbor makes Sydney beautiful despite dreary suburbs and haphazard high-rise construction that have left the city scarred and congested. None of that seems to matter, however, when you catch a glimpse of the harbor.

When he first set eyes on this harbor on January 26, 1788, Captain Arthur Phillip, commander of the First Fleet, wrote: "We had the satisfaction of finding the finest harbor in the world, in which a thousand ships of the line may ride in the most perfect security." It was not an easy beginning, however. The passengers on board the 11 ships of the First Fleet were not the "huddled masses yearning to breathe free" that migrated to the United States, but wretched inmates flushed from overcrowded jails in England and sent halfway around the globe. It says much of those early days that when the women prisoners came ashore two weeks after the men, an orgy ensued.

Sydney has long since outgrown the stigma of its convict origins, but the passage of time has not tamed its spirit. Other Australian cities can claim the title of the nation's cultural capital with more justification, but Sydney's panache and appetite for life are unchallenged. A walk among the scantily clad bathers at Bondi Beach or through the raucous nightlife district of Kings Cross provides evidence enough.

A visit to Sydney is an essential part of the Australian experience, but Sydney is not Australia any more than New York is the United States. Sydney has joined the ranks of the great cosmopolitan cities whose characters are essentially international. For visitors from

European or North American cities, Sydney's architecture, customs, and cuisine will be no more than a variation on a familiar theme.

Essential Information

Arriving and Departing by Plane

Airport and Airlines Among international airlines serving Sydney are **Ansett Australia, British Airways, Canadian Airlines International, Cathay Pacific, Hawaiian Airlines, Japan Airlines, Northwest, Qantas, Singapore Airlines,** and **United Airlines.**

Domestic flights into Sydney include **Ansett Australia** (tel. 13–1300), **Ansett Express** (tel. 13–1300), **Qantas** (tel. 13–1313), and **Hazelton Airlines** (tel. 02/235–1411).

Sydney's main airport is Kingsford-Smith, located 8 kilometers (5 miles) south of the city. Trolleys are available in the baggage area of the international terminal. Travelers can convert their money to Australian currency at the **Westpac Bank,** located on both floors of the international terminal. The bank is open from 5:30 AM until approximately 11:30 PM. At the other end of the arrivals hall from the bank, the **Travellers Information Service** provides free maps and brochures as well as an accommodations booking service. It's open from about 5:15 AM until 11 PM.

The domestic and international terminals are 3 kilometers (2 miles) apart. To get from one terminal to the other, either take a taxi for about $6 or use the **Airport Express bus,** which departs approximately every 20 minutes between 6 AM and 11 PM and costs $2.50 for adults and $1.50 for children under 16. Qantas and Australian Airlines have merged to become Qantas Airways. Qantas flights with numbers from QF1 to QF399 depart from the international terminal; QF400 and higher depart from the domestic terminal.

Between Sydney Airport and Center City
By Bus The **Airport Express bus** provides a fast, comfortable link between the airport terminals and the city and Kings Cross, and for those traveling with fewer than four people, the cost compares favorably with a taxi. The bus stops at Central Station and then makes five stops along George Street before terminating at Circular Quay. *Alternate buses depart to the city (Rte. 300) and Kings Cross (Rte. 350) weekdays every 20 min 6 AM–5:45 PM, every 30 min 5:45–10:55 PM; weekends every 30 min 6 AM–10:55 PM. Cost: $5 adults, $3 children under 16.*

By Taxi Taxis are available from the ranks outside the terminal buildings. The fare to the city hotels is about $16, about $14 to Kings Cross.

By Limousine A chauffeured limousine to the city hotels costs about $60. Waiting time is charged at the rate of $50 per hour. Operators include **Premier Limousines** (tel. 02/519–2388) and **Astra Hire Cars** (tel. 02/699–2233).

Arriving and Departing by Train, Bus, and Ship

By Train The main terminal for long-distance and intercity trains is **Central Station** (Eddy Ave., City, tel. 02/219–8888), about 2 kilometers (1 mile) south of the city center. Daily service between Sydney and Melbourne is available on the evening *Melbourne Express;* the trip takes about 13 hours. Morning and evening trains make the 4½-hour trip to Canberra daily. The *Indian-Pacific* leaves Sydney on Thursday around midday for Adelaide (28 hours) and Perth (66 hours). The overnight *Brisbane XPT* makes the 16-hour Sydney–Brisbane journey every day. Call 02/217–8812 between 6:30 AM and 10 PM for information about fares and timetables.

Central Station is also the hub of the suburban train network. For information about schedules and fares, contact the **State Transit** information line (tel. 13–1500) between 6 AM and 10 PM. Tickets for long-distance train travel can be purchased from **Countrylink Travel Centres** at Central Station, Circular Quay (1 Alfred St.), 11–31 York Street, and on the lower level of the Queen Victoria Building (George and Park Sts.).

By Bus   Bus service is available to all major cities from Sydney. Tickets for long-distance buses can be purchased from travel agents, by telephone with a credit card, or at the bus terminal. The terminal for **Greyhound** (tel. 13–1238) and **Pioneer Coachline** (tel. 13–2030) is located on the ground floor of the **Oxford Koala Hotel** (Oxford and Riley Sts., Darlinghurst), about 2 kilometers (1 mile) east of the city center. Lockers are available in the terminal. **Murrays** (Overseas Shipping Terminal, Circular Quay West, tel. 02/319–1266) is the other major intercity bus operator.

By Ship   Cruise ships call frequently at Sydney as part of their South Pacific itineraries. Passenger ships generally berth at the **Sydney Cove Passenger Terminal** (tel. 02/251–1510) at Circular Quay. The terminal is located in the shadow of the Harbour Bridge, close to many of the city's major attractions as well as to the bus, ferry, and train networks. Otherwise, passenger ships berth at **Pyrmont** (tel. 02/660–3516), from which it makes sense to take a $5 taxi ride into the city, since the walk is long and fairly uninteresting.

Getting Around

Driving a car around Sydney is not advisable. Many of the main roads are poorly marked, and the harbor inlets and hilly terrain result in few straight streets. Parking space is limited, furthermore, and the salient characteristics of Sydney drivers are speed and intolerance.

Despite its vast size, most of Sydney's main attractions are packed into a fairly small area, and places such as The Rocks, Darling Harbour, and the Opera House are best explored on foot. Getting to and from these areas is not difficult on Sydney's buses, ferries, and trains—except during the rush hours. Most travelers will find public transport an efficient, economical way to see the city.

The smart, cost-effective way to see the city is with the **Sydney Pass**. The three-day pass, which costs $50 for adults, $40 for children under 16, and $140 for families, allows unlimited travel on any public bus or harbor ferry, the Airport Express bus, the Sydney Explorer bus, and the three sightseeing cruises operated by the State Transit Authority. Five- and seven-day passes are also available. Passes can be purchased from the Travellers Information counter on the ground floor of the international airport terminal and from the **New South Wales Travel Centre**, *19 Castlereagh St., tel. 02/231–4444. Open weekdays 9–5.*

A **Travelpass** is another money-saver that entitles the bearer to unlimited travel on public transport within a designated area for a week or more. The most useful is probably the Blue Travelpass, which allows unlimited travel for one week aboard buses throughout the city and eastern suburbs and aboard inner-harbor ferries. The cost is $15.60 for adults, $7.80 for children under 16. Travelpasses are available from railway stations and from most news agents on bus routes. For all information on Sydney's buses, ferries, and trains, call the **State Transit Infoline** (tel. 13–1500). Travelers who plan to make extensive use of the city's bus and ferry systems should buy the **Bus & Ferry Travel Guide,** available for $2.45 from the New South Wales Travel Centre (*see above*).

By Bus On Sydney's well-developed bus system, journeys are measured in sections, and the fare depends on the number of sections traveled. The minimum bus fare, $1.20 for adults and 60¢ for children 4–16, applies to trips throughout the inner-city area. You would pay the minimum fare, for example, for a ride from Circular Quay to Kings Cross, or from Park Street to Oxford Street in Paddington. Tickets may be purchased from the driver.

By Ferry No finer introduction to the city is to be found than aboard one of the commuter ferries that ply Sydney Harbour. The hub of the ferry system is **Circular Quay,** and the ferries operate the length and breadth of the harbor between about 6 AM and 11:30 PM. One of the most popular sightseeing trips is aboard the Manly ferry, a 35-minute journey from Circular Quay that offers glimpses of harborside mansions and the sandstone cliffs and bushland along the north shore. The one-way fare is $3.60 for adults and $1.80 for children 4–16. On the return journey from Manly, consider taking the *Jetcat*, which skims the waves in an exhilarating 15-minute trip back to the city. The fare is $4.

By Train For journeys in excess of 6½ kilometers (4 miles), Sydney's trains are considerably faster than buses. However, the rail network has been designed primarily for rapid transit between outlying suburbs and the city. Apart from the city loop line and the spur line to Kings Cross and Bondi Junction, it does not serve areas of particular interest to visitors. Travelers who do use the trains should remember the following axioms: All trains pass through Central Station; Town Hall is the "shoppers" station; the bus, ferry, and train systems converge at Circular Quay. As an example of fare prices, a one-way ticket from Town Hall Station to Bondi Junction costs $1.60 for adults and 80¢ for children 4–16.

By Monorail The monorail is one of the most relaxing forms of public transport, but its use is limited to travel between the mid-city region and Darling Harbour. *Fare: $2, children under 5 free.*

By Taxi Taxis are a relatively economical way to cover short to medium distances in Sydney. A 3.2-kilometer (2-mile) trip from Circular Quay to the eastern suburbs costs about $7.50. Drivers are entitled to charge more than the metered fare if the passenger's baggage exceeds 55 pounds, if the taxi has been booked by telephone, or if the passenger crosses the Harbour Bridge, where a toll is levied. Taxis are licensed to carry four passengers. Many drivers accept payment by American Express or Diners Club cards. Taxis can be hailed on the street, hired from a rank, or booked by phone. Taxi ranks can be found outside most bus and railway stations as well as the larger hotels. On the south side of the harbor, the most efficient telephone booking service is provided by **Taxis Combined Services** (tel. 02/332–8888). North of the bridge, try **ABC Taxis** (tel. 02/897–4000).

By Limousine Chauffeur-driven limousines are available for trips around Sydney and, if requested, the driver will give a commentary on the major sights. Limousines can be rented for approximately $65 per hour. Operators include **Premier Limousines** (tel. 02/519–2388) and **Astra Hire Cars** (tel. 02/699–2233).

By Rental Car All the major rental companies, as well as a number of smaller operators, are represented in Sydney. Generally, the larger companies charge higher prices but offer unrestricted mileage and a greater number of pickup and dropoff facilities. Expect to pay about $85 per day for a medium-size automatic and about $75 for a compact standard model. Small local operators often restrict travel to within a 48-kilometer (30-mile) radius of the city center. Nevertheless, some real bargains are to be found, and an old model can cost as little as $30 per day. For rentals of one month or more with unrestricted travel, the rate on a new, medium-size sedan is about $50 per day. Major car hire operators include **Avis** (tel. 02/902–9292), **Budget** (tel. 13–2727), **Hertz** (tel. 02/360–6621), and **Thrifty** (tel. 02/380–5399). Smaller companies include **Dollar** (tel. 02/223–1444) and **Reliable** (tel. 02/358–6011).

Important Addresses and Numbers

Tourist Information The **Backpacker's Travel Centre** specializes in tours, accommodation, and information for the budget traveler. *Shop 33, Imperial Arcade (off Pitt St. near Market St.), tel. 02/232–5166.*

The **New South Wales Travel Centre** is the major source of information, brochures, and maps for travelers. Center staff will assist with inquiries and make all hotel, travel, and tour bookings. *19 Castlereagh St., a 10-min walk from Circular Quay, tel. 02/231–4444. Open weekdays 9–5.*

The **Tourist Information Service** is a free phone-in facility that provides information on accommodations, tours, shopping, and what to see and do in Sydney. *Tel. 02/669–5111. Open daily 8–6.*

Consulates **U.S. Consulate General.** *19–29 Martin Pl., tel. 02/234–9200. Open weekdays 8:30–11 AM.*

British Consulate General. *Gateway Plaza, 1 Macquarie Pl., tel. 02/247–9731. Open weekdays 10–3.*

Canadian Consulate General. *111 Harrington St., tel. 02/364–3050. Open weekdays 8:30–11:30 AM.*

New Zealand Consulate General, *1 Alfred St., Circular Quay, tel. 02/247–1999. Open weekdays 10–4.*

Emergencies Dial 000 for **fire, police,** or **ambulance** services.

Doctors **Camperdown Children's Hospital,** 4 kilometers (2½ miles) southwest of the city center, is a specialist pediatric hospital. *Pyrmont Bridge Rd., Camperdown, tel. 02/519–0466. Open 24 hrs.*

Royal North Shore Hospital is located 6.4 kilometers (4 miles) northwest of city center. *Pacific Hwy., St. Leonards, tel. 02/438–7111. Open 24 hrs.*

St. Vincent's Hospital is situated 2.4 kilometers (1½ miles) east of city center. *Victoria and Burton Sts., Darlinghurst, tel. 02/339–1111. Open 24 hrs.*

Dentist The **Dental Emergency Information Service** (tel. 02/962–7454) is a 24-hour referral service.

Travel Agencies Scarcely a shopping plaza or main street in Sydney lacks a travel agency. Both **American Express Travel Service** (345 George St., tel. 02/262–3666) and **Thomas Cook Travel** (175 Pitt St., tel. 02/229–6611) are located in the heart of the city, as well as in a number of suburbs.

Guided Tours

Orientation The only guided bus tour of the inner city is the red **Sydney Explorer** bus. The bus makes a 35-kilometer (22-mile) circuit of all the major attractions in the city, The Rocks, Kings Cross, Darling Harbour, and Chinatown. The ticket is valid for one day, and ticket holders can board or leave the bus at any of the 26 stops along the route and catch any following Explorer bus. The bright red buses follow each other every 20 minutes, and the service operates 9–7. Tickets can be purchased on board the bus or from the N.S.W. Travel Centre. *19 Castlereagh St., tel. 02/231–4444. Fare: $20 adults, $15 children under 16, $45 family.*

The **Bondi and Bay Explorer Bus** runs a guided bus tour of the eastern suburbs. The blue bus begins its 35-kilometer (22-mile) journey at Circular Quay and travels through Kings Cross, Double Bay, Vaucluse, and Watson's Bay to the Gap, then returns to the city via Bondi Beach, Centennial Park, and Oxford Street. Passengers can leave the bus at any of its 20 stops and catch a following bus. Buses follow one another at 30-minute intervals between 9 and 6. Prices are the same as those for the red Explorer bus.

Boat Tours A replica of Captain Bligh's HMS *Bounty* is alive and afloat on Sydney Harbour, and **Bounty Cruises** offers various harbor cruises aboard this famous vessel. A two-hour coffee cruise departs weekdays and travels east along the harbor. Subject to wind and weather, most of the voyage is made under sail and, in the best nautical tradition, all on board are encouraged to take a turn with the ropes and the wheel. A commentary is provided, and the cruise focuses as much on square-rigger sailing and the *Bounty*'s history as on the sights of Sydney Harbour. For photographers, the evening dinner cruise offers spectacular possibilities. Cruises depart from Campbell's Cove, in front of the Park Hyatt Hotel. *Tel. 02/247–1789. Coffee cruise: $25 adults, $12.50 children 5–12. Dinner cruise: $45. Coffee cruises: weekdays 1 PM. Dinner cruises: daily 7 PM.*

Captain Cook Cruises offers a two-hour guided tour of Fort Denison, a fortified harbor island that offers spectacular views of the Opera House and the Harbour Bridge. *Pier 6, Circular Quay terminal, tel. 02/251–5007. Reservations advised. Tickets: $8.50 adults, $6 children 4–16. Tues.–Sun. 10, 12:15, 2.*

The State Transit Authority operates the following three cruises aboard the harbor ferries, and the cost compares favorably with the privately operated cruises. Light refreshments are available on board.

The **River Cruise** focuses on the early days of the colony during a trip around five of the harbor islands that lie east and west of the city. *No. 4 Wharf, Circular Quay term., tel. 13–1500. Tickets: $16 adults, $12 children under 16, $44 family. Departs daily at 10 AM.*

The **Harbour Cruise** (*see* Tour 1, *below*) is a leisurely tour that takes in the scenic eastern suburbs and Middle Harbour, home to many of Sydney's wealthiest residents. *No. 4 Wharf, Circular Quay term., tel. 13–1500. Tickets: $16 adults, $12 children under 16, $44 family. Weekdays 1 PM, weekends and holidays 1:30.*

The 1½-hour **Harbour Lights Cruise** takes passengers into Darling Harbour for a nighttime view of the city from the west and then past the Garden Island naval base to view the Opera House and Kings Cross. *No. 5 Wharf, Circular Quay term., tel. 13–1500. Tickets: $14 adults, $10 children under 16, $38 family. Mon.–Sat. 8 PM.*

Walking Tours **Maureen Fry's Walking Tours** (tel. 02/660–7157) are an excellent introduction to Sydney, but are more of a stroll than a walk. Standard tours, costing $15, include the colonial buildings along Macquarie Street, a ramble through the historic waterside suburbs of Glebe and Balmain, and tours of Circular Quay and The Rocks area. Specialized theme tours include art galleries, shops, Sydney's farm and fish markets, and a fascinating tour of the Opera Centre, where operas are rehearsed before they move to the Sydney Opera House.

The Rocks Walking Tours offers an introduction to The Rocks (the site of Sydney's original settlement) with the emphasis on the buildings and personalities of the convict period. The tour, which lasts a little over an hour, travels at a gentle pace and involves little climbing. *106 George St., The Rocks, tel. 02/247–6678. Tickets: $9 adults, $5.50 children 10–17 (under 10 free). Weekdays 10:30, 12:30, and 2:30, weekends and holidays 11:30 and 2.*

Exploring Sydney

Orientation

Sydney is a giant city, stretching almost 97 kilometers (60 miles) from north to south and about 56 kilometers (35 miles) across. The city is divided into north and south by its harbor, and the areas of greatest interest are on the southern shore. The area bounded by Chinatown in the south, Harbour Bridge in the north, Darling Harbour to the west, and Kings Cross to the east has plenty to occupy any visitor for several days. On the northern side of the Harbour Bridge are the important commercial center of North Sydney and the pleasant, leafy suburbs of the north shore. Apart from the ocean beaches and Taronga Park Zoo, however, there is little reason to venture north of the harbor.

Any visit to Sydney should begin with a harbor cruise. The harbor is Sydney's crowning glory, and a few hours on the water will leave an indelible impression of the city. Next, explore the harborside highlights, including The Rocks, the Opera House, and the Royal Botanic Gardens. Running south from the harbor is Macquarie Street, a living reminder of Sydney's colonial history; to the west is Darling Harbour, a futuristic complex of shops, museums, and nightclubs. A longer stay might include a trip to the eastern suburbs of Paddington and Woolahra and a visit to Bondi—Australia's most famous beach.

We have divided Sydney into five exploring tours, whose themes range from the city's earliest convict days, through the colonial era, to the construction of the Sydney Opera House—the symbol of modern, cosmopolitan Australia. All of these tours start at Circular Quay, a central point in Sydney as well as the docking area for the harbor ferries. Tour One is a ferry tour and Tour Four requires some bus travel, but the others can be done easily on foot. Additional sights not covered in the tours are listed in the Sightseeing Checklist, *below.*

Outside Sydney are some areas of spectacular scenic beauty, but the city's sheer size and woeful road system do not encourage escape. It is possible to make day trips to areas such as the Blue Mountains or the vineyards of the Hunter Valley, and several coach companies offer such tours, but passengers face a long and tedious shuffle through suburban Sydney. If you want more than a fleeting glimpse of these places—and the Blue Mountains in particular deserve more—you would do far better to plan an overnight stop. (For more information about excursions from Sydney, *see* Chapter 3, New South Wales).

Tour 1: Sydney Harbour

Numbers in the margin of Tour 1 correspond to points of interest on the Sydney Harbour map.

Sydney's star attraction is her harbor. Governor Arthur Phillip, the first European to sail into these waters, called it ". . . in extent and security, very superior to any other that I have ever seen—containing a considerable number of coves, formed by narrow necks of land, mostly rocks, covered with timber." Although his account lacks poetry, few would dispute that Sydney Harbour is one of nature's extraordinary creations.

The harbor—officially titled Port Jackson—is actually a river valley that was carved by the Parramatta and Lane Cove rivers and the many creeks that flow from the north, and was then submerged as the sea level rose at the end of the last Ice Age. In the earliest days of the colony, the military laid claim to much of the harbor's 248 kilometers (150 miles) of waterfront, and it is for this reason that so much of the foreshore has survived in its natural splendor.

This tour is based on the route followed by the State Transit Authority ferries on their daily Harbour Cruise (*see* Boat Tours, *above*), although other harbor cruises follow a similar course. The tour takes in the eastern half of the harbor, from the city to the Heads and Middle Harbour. Although this is the glamour side of the harbor, the western shore also includes many areas of historic and natural distinction, including Homebush Bay, the main site for the Olympic Summer Games in 2000. Passengers should begin the voyage on the right side of the vessel. Refreshments are available on the lower deck during the 2½-hour cruise.

❶ The tour begins as the vessel leaves the ferry wharves at Circular Quay and crosses **Sydney Cove,** which was named after Lord Sydney, the British Home Secretary at the time the colony was founded. The settlement itself was to be known as New Albion, but the name never caught on and instead, the city took its name from this tiny bay.

❷ After rounding Bennelong Point, the site of the Sydney Opera House, the boat turns east and crosses **Farm Cove,** where the first attempts were made to establish gardens to feed the convict settlers. The tall, gothic chimneys that are just visible above the trees belong to Government House, the official residence of the state governor.

❸ Easily identifiable by its squadrons of sleek, gray warships is **Garden Island,** the country's largest naval dockyard. Visiting ships of the U.S. Navy's Pacific fleet can often be seen tied up here. During the 1941–45 War of the Pacific, Garden Island was a frontline base for allied ships. On the night of May 31, 1942, this battle fleet was the target of three Japanese midget submarines that were launched from a mother submarine at sea. One of the three penetrated the antisubmarine net that had been laid across the harbor and sank the HMAS *Kuttabul*, a ferry that was being used as a naval depot ship, with a loss of 21 lives. In the chaos that followed, one midget submarine escaped, but the other two were sunk.

Admiralty House
and Kirribilli
House, **14**
Castlecrag, **10**
Chowder Bay, **12**
Farm Cove, **2**
Fort Denison, **13**
Garden Island, **3**
Middle
Harbour, **9**
Middle Head, **11**
Rose Bay, **5**
Point Piper, **4**
Sydney Cove, **1**
Quarantine
Station, **8**
Vaucluse, **6**
Watsons Bay, **7**

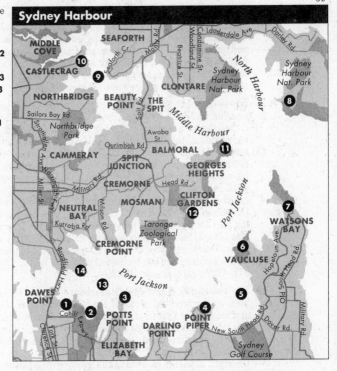

Sydney Harbour

The next headland, Darling Point, which is dominated by several tall apartment blocks, marks the beginning of Sydney's socially desirable eastern suburbs. Across Double Bay is **Point Piper,** famous as the ritziest address in the country. At the height of the real estate boom in the late 1980s, several waterfront mansions changed hands for close to $20 million.

The big expanse of water to the east of Point Piper is **Rose Bay.** The bay was a base for the Qantas flying boats that once provided the only passenger air service between Australia and America and Europe. The last flying boat departed Rose Bay only 20 years ago, and the "airstrip" is still used by floatplanes that connect Sydney with the Hawkesbury River and the Central Coast.

Beyond Rose Bay is **Vaucluse,** another suburb that conveys social stature. Vaucluse is named after Vaucluse House, the sandstone mansion built by 19th-century explorer, publisher, and politician William Wentworth. His Gothic-revival mansion is located at the rear of the horseshoe curve of Vaucluse Bay, although the lush gardens screen it from view. Much more visible are the Grecian columns of Strickland House, which was used as a convalescent home until a few years ago. The beach to the east is Shark Bay, part of Nielsen Park and one of the most popular of the harbor bathing beaches.

Watson's Bay, a former fishing village, is the most easterly of the southern shore's suburbs. Its beach, Camp Cove, is of some historical importance: It was intended that the convicts who were to be Australia's first settlers would establish a community at Botany Bay, which had been explored by Captain Cook in 1770. However, as Captain Phillip found when he arrived 18 years later, the unprotected nature of that site and lack of fresh water made settlement difficult; after a few days, he set off to explore Port Jackson, which had been named but not visited by Cook. Phillip rounded the heads and landed on a beach that he named Camp Cove, and, to his delight, found a far more pleasing site for settlement. Past Watson's Bay, the last beach inside the harbor on the southern shore is Lady Jane, the only Sydney beach where nude bathing is allowed.

The entrance to Sydney Harbor is protected by two giant sandstone headlands, North Head and South Head, and passengers will usually feel the vessel pitch in the big Pacific rollers as it crosses to the north side of the harbor. Just inside the jaws of the harbor, in the shadow of North Head, is the **Quarantine Station**—a remnant of a fascinating chapter in Australia's history. It was here that ships and passengers who arrived with contagious diseases were consigned until they were pronounced free of illness. Among the last to be quartered here were the victims of Cyclone Tracy, which devastated Darwin in 1974. Ten years later, after it was used briefly as a staging post for a group of Vietnamese orphans, the Quarantine Station was closed, its grim purpose brought to an end by modern medicines. Today, visitors can take a 90-minute guided tour of the station with a ranger from the National Parks and Wildlife Service (tel. 02/ 977–6229), caretakers of the site.

The vessel now enters **Middle Harbour**—formed by creeks that are born on the forested peaks of Ku-Ring-Gai Chase National Park— and sails under Spit Bridge. Note that the houses here on the northern side of the harbor are set back from the waterline behind bushland; by the time these were built, planning authorities no longer allowed direct water frontage. Except for the buzz of Jet Skis and the sight of yachts moored in the sandy coves, the upper reaches of Middle Harbour are exactly as they were when the first Europeans set eyes on Port Jackson, just over 200 years ago.

On the return journey to Spit Bridge, you'll pass the suburb of **Castlecrag,** which was founded by Walter Burley Griffin, the American architect responsible for the layout of Canberra. In 1924, after working on the national capital and in Melbourne, Griffin moved to Sydney and built a number of houses that are notable for their sympathy to the surrounding bushland—a radical departure from the domestic architecture of the time. About eight of his houses survive, although none is visible from the harbor.

Despite its benign appearance now, Sydney Harbour once bristled with armaments. In the middle of the last century, faced with expansionist European powers hungry for new colonies, artillery positions were erected on the headlands that guard the approaches to the harbor. At **Middle Head** you can still see the rectangular gun emplacements set into the cliff face. During this same period, Sydney Harbor became a regular port of call for American whaling ships. **Chowder Bay,** on army land to the west of Middle Head (identifiable by a cluster of wooden buildings at the water's edge and twin oil storage tanks), was named by those seamen for the stew they made from oysters and other shellfish collected from these rocks. Sydney's most prominent fortification is **Fort Denison,** which occupies a prime position just off the Opera House. The tiny island was fortified during the Crimean War, when it was feared the Russians might invade.

On the north side of the harbor, almost opposite the Opera House, are two colonial-style homes. The larger of the two is **Admiralty House,** the Sydney residence of the governor-general. The other is

Kirribilli House, and if the Australian flag is flying from the mast, it means that the prime minister is staying at his official Sydney home.

From the north side of the harbor, the vessel crosses to back to Circular Quay where the tour ends.

Tour 2: The Rocks

Numbers in the margins of Tours 2–5 correspond to points of interest on the Central Sydney map.

The Rocks is the birthplace not just of Sydney but of modern Australia. It was here that the 11 ships of the First Fleet dropped anchor in 1788, and this stubby peninsula that encloses the western side of the cove became known simply as "The Rocks."

The first crude wood huts erected by the convicts were followed by simple houses made from mud bricks cemented together by a mixture of sheep's wool and mud. The rain soon washed this crude mortar away, and no buildings in The Rocks survive from the earliest period of convict settlement. Most of the architecture dates from the Victorian era, by which time Sydney had become a thriving port. The warehouses that lined the waterfront were backed by a row of tradesmen's shops, banks, and taverns, and above them rose a tangled mass of alleyways lined with the cottages of seamen and wharf laborers. By the late 1800s, all who could afford to had moved out of the area, and it was widely regarded as a rough, tough, squalid part of town. As late as 1900 bubonic plague swept through The Rocks, prompting the government to offer a bounty for dead rats to exterminate their disease-carrying fleas. The character of The Rocks changed considerably when the Harbour Bridge was built in the 1930s, cutting a swath right through the area.

It is only in the last few years that The Rocks has become appreciated for its historical significance. Here you can see the evolution of a society almost from its inception to the present day, yet The Rocks is anything but a stuffy tutorial. Instead, history comes packaged in the form of shops, outdoor cafés, and a couple of great little museums. Combined with a harbor cruise or a visit to the nearby Opera House, a tour of The Rocks provides a very full day.

Begin at **Circular Quay,** where Sydney's ferry, bus, and train systems converge. Follow the quay toward the Harbour Bridge and, as you round the curve, turn left and walk about 20 paces. The map on the platform in front of you depicts the colony as it appeared in 1808. The **Tank Stream** entered Sydney Cove at this very spot. This tiny stream was the colony's fresh-water supply, and it was this that determined the location of the first European settlement in Australia.

Return to the waterfront and walk past the **Museum of Contemporary Art,** which is devoted to paintings, sculpture, film, video, and kinetic art produced during the past 20 years (*see* Museums and Galleries in the Sightseeing Checklist, *below*). When you reach the fig trees in the circular bed, look to your left. The bronze statue beneath the trees is the famous figure of **William Bligh** of HMS *Bounty*, whose crew mutinied and cast him adrift on a lifeboat. Bligh became governor of New South Wales in 1806, and two years later he faced the second mutiny of his life. Bligh had made himself unpopular with the soldiers of the New South Wales Corps, popularly known as the Rum Corps, who were the real power in the colony. When he threatened to end their monopoly of the lucrative liquor trade, he was imprisoned in an incident known as the Rum Rebellion. He spent the next two years as a captive until his successor,

Argyle Cut, **13**

Argyle Stores, **14**

Art Gallery of New South Wales, **31**

Arthur McElhone Reserve, **37**

Atherden Street, **5**

Boomerang, **38**

Cadman's Cottage, **2**

Campbell's Storehouse, **4**

Colonial House Museum, **8**

Conservatorium, **20**

Customs House, **17**

Elizabeth Bay House, **36**

Fort Denison, **7**

Hero of Waterloo, **9**

History House, **21**

Holy Trinity Church, **11**

Hyde Park Barracks, **28**

Juniper Hall, **42**

The Lands Department, **19**

The Lord Nelson, **12**

Macquarie Place, **18**

Mint Museum, **27**

Mrs. Macquarie's Chair, **35**

Mrs. Macquarie's Point, **34**

Nurses Walk, **16**

Observatory Hill, **10**

Palace Gates, **22**

The Rocks Heritage and Information Centre, **3**

Royal Australasian College of Physicians, **23**

Royal Botanic Gardens, **33**

Royal Hotel, **41**

Shadforth Street, **40**

State Library, **24**

State Parliament House, **25**

St. James Church, **29**

St. Mary's, **30**

Suez Canal, **15**

Sydney Harbour Bridge, **6**

Sydney Hospital, **26**

Sydney Opera House, **32**

Victoria Barracks, **39**

William Bligh's Statue, **1**

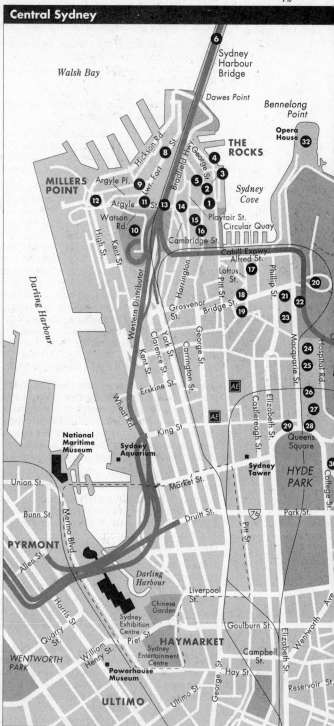

Central Sydney

Walsh Bay

Sydney Harbour Bridge

Dawes Point

Bennelong Point

Opera House

THE ROCKS

MILLERS POINT

Argyle Pl.

Argyle St.

Watson Rd.

Sydney Cove

Playfair St.

Circular Quay

Cambridge St.

High St.

Kent St.

Darling Harbour

Western Distributor

Cahill Expwy

Alfred St.

Loftus St.

Harrington St.

Grosvenor St.

Bridge St.

Phillip St.

Macquarie St.

Hospital Rd.

Pitt St.

Clarence St.

York St.

Erskine St.

Carrington St.

George St.

King St.

National Maritime Museum

Sydney Aquarium

Union St.

Bunn St.

Wheat Rd.

Merino Blvd.

Market St.

Druitt St.

Castlereagh St.

Elizabeth St.

Sydney Tower

HYDE PARK

College St.

Queens Square

PYRMONT

Allen St.

Harris St.

Quarry St.

William Henry St.

Darling Harbour

Chinese Garden

Liverpool St.

Park St.

Pitt St.

Sydney Exhibition Centre

Pier St.

Sydney Entertainment Centre

HAYMARKET

Goulburn St.

Campbell St.

Wentworth Ave.

Elizabeth St.

WENTWORTH PARK

Powerhouse Museum

Hay St.

George St.

Ultimo St.

Reservoir St.

ULTIMO

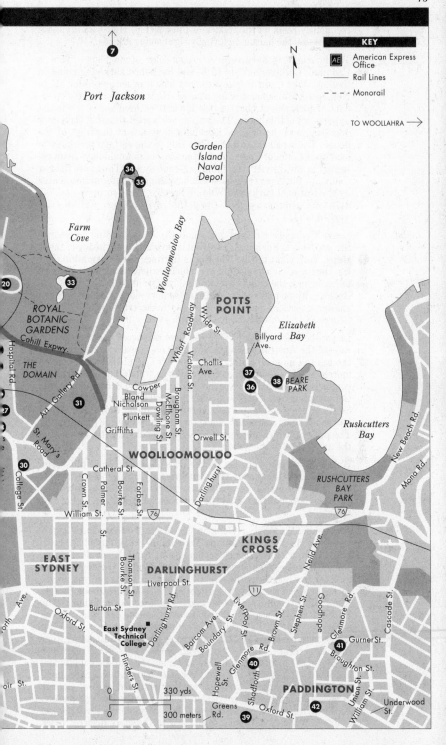

KEY

AE American Express Office

— Rail Lines

- - - Monorail

Port Jackson

TO WOOLLAHRA →

Garden Island Naval Depot

7

Farm Cove

34
35

Woolloomooloo Bay

POTTS POINT

Wylde St.

Elizabeth Bay

Billyard Ave.

33

20

ROYAL BOTANIC GARDENS

Cahill Expwy.

Art Gallery Rd.

THE DOMAIN

Hospital Rd.

St. Mary's Road

Kowper St.

Victoria St.

Challis Ave.

37

36

38

BEARE PARK

31

Cowper

Bland

Nicholson

Plunkett

Griffiths

Brougham St.

McElhone St.

Dowling St.

Orwell St.

Rushcutters Bay

27

WOOLLOOMOOLOO

Darlinghurst

30

Catheral St.

Crown St.

Palmer St.

Bourke St.

Forbes St.

RUSHCUTTERS BAY PARK

New Beach Rd.

Mona Rd.

College St.

William St.

76

76

KINGS CROSS

EAST SYDNEY

Thomson St.

Bourke St.

DARLINGHURST

Liverpool St.

Neild Ave.

Oxford St.

Burton St.

Darlinghurst Rd.

11

Liverpool St.

Brown St.

Stephen St.

Goodhope

Glenmore Rd.

Cascade St.

North Ave.

East Sydney Technical College

Barcom Ave.

Boundary St.

Glenmore Rd.

Shadforth St.

Brown St.

41

Gurner St.

Broughton St.

Union St.

William St.

Flinders St.

40

PADDINGTON

Underwood St.

0   330 yds

0   300 meters

Hopewell St.

Greens Rd.

39

Oxford St.

42

oir St.

Lachlan Macquarie, arrived. In historical irony, the statue's gaze frequently rests on the replica of Bligh's ship, HMS *Bounty*, as it sails around the harbor on its daily sightseeing cruises.

To the right is a two-story, cream-color stone house. This is **Cadman's Cottage,** built in 1816, and the oldest surviving house in Sydney. John Cadman was a convict who was sentenced for life to New South Wales for stealing a horse. He later became superintendent of government boats, a position that entitled him to live in the upper story of this house. The water once lapped almost at Cadman's doorstep, and the original seawall still stands at the front of the house. The small extension on the side of the cottage was built to lock up the oars of Cadman's boats, since oars would have been essential to any convict attemping to escape by sea. The upper floor of Cadman's Cottage is now used as a bookshop and information center by the National Parks and Wildlife Service. *110 George St., tel. 02/ 247–8861. Admission free. Open Mon. 10–3, Tues.–Fri. 9–4:30, weekends 11–4.*

Leave Cadman's Cottage and climb the stairs leading to George Street. Note the original gas street lamp burning at the top of these steps. Turn right toward **The Rocks Heritage and Information Centre.** Once a sailor's home that provided inexpensive accommodations for mariners, the building now offers insight into the history of The Rocks, with displays of artifacts and a short video. Center staff can answer questions about the area and make travel bookings. *106 George St., tel. 02/255–1788. Open daily 9–5.*

Leave the Information Centre and turn right past the redbrick facade of the Australian Steam Navigation Company; continue down the hill to **Campbell's Storehouse.** Robert Campbell was a Scottish merchant who is sometimes referred to as "the father of Australian commerce." Campbell broke the stranglehold the British East India Company exercised over seal and whale products, which were New South Wales's only exports in those early days. Built in 1838, his storehouse now serves as a home for several waterside restaurants. The pulleys, which were used to hoist cargoes, can still be seen on the upper level of the warehouses.

Walk back up the steps beside the warehouse and cross to George Street. Across the road is **Atherden Street,** Sydney's shortest street. Note the poinsettias, geraniums, and staghorn ferns that have been painstakingly cultivated on the tiny rock ledges at the end of this street.

Just behind the Westpac Bank on the corner of George and Playfair streets is the **Westpac Banking Museum** (6–8 Playfair St., tel. 02/ 251–1419), with its modest collection of early Australian coins. Climb George Street toward the Harbour Bridge, passing a row of pink terrace houses on the left. Go another 50 yards and you are directly beneath the massive girders of the **Sydney Harbour Bridge.** Known affectionately by Sydneysiders as "the old coat hanger," the Harbour Bridge was a monumental engineering feat when it was completed in 1932. The roadway is supported by the arch above, not by the massive stone pylons, which were added for aesthetic rather than structural reasons. Paul Hogan worked for several years as a rigger on the bridge, long before he tamed the world's wildlife and lowlifes as the star of the film *Crocodile Dundee.* Note the small green iron cubicle that stands on the landward side of George Street. This is a gentlemen's toilet, modeled on the Parisian pissoir. At the turn of the century these were fairly common on the streets of Sydney, but they have since lost favor to the more discreet brick constructions (a modern toilet stands at the rear of this sole survivor).

Walk along the path that runs directly beneath the bridge, and out in the harbor you will see a small island, **Fort Denison,** which appears to be just off the Opera House. In colonial times, convicts who committed petty offenses in the colony were kept on the island on a diet of bread and water; hence its earlier name—Pinchgut. The island was fortified during the Crimean War, when it was feared that the Russians might invade. Today, the firing of a cannon on Fort Denison does not signal an imminent invasion but merely the hour—one o'clock. The path ends at the southern pylon of the Harbour Bridge, once the site of a fortification known as Dawes Battery. The cannons on the hillside pointing toward the Opera House came from the ships of the First Fleet.

Turn your back on the harbor and follow Lower Fort Street, which runs to the right of the Harbour View Hotel. At one time the handsome Georgian houses along this street were among the best addresses in Sydney. Note the elaborate wrought-iron lacework that still graces many of the facades. Ring the bell of the **Colonial House Museum** and you will probably be ushered inside by Mrs. Shirley Ball, director of the museum as well as the occupant of the house above. Shirley Ball is one of the many remarkable characters of the area, a longtime resident and one of the most vocal campaigners in the fight to preserve the area. The museum is her personal indulgence, a vast and mostly unlabeled collection that includes a penny-farthing bicycle, documents from the convict era, cigarette cards from World War I, old bottles, carpet beaters, ships in bottles, and even a bowl of plastic fruit. Some of the most interesting exhibits are the photographs of The Rocks taken before the Harbour Bridge was built, when its character was changed forever. Essentially a haphazard social history of early Australian life, this museum adds flesh and blood to any tour of the area. *53 Lower Fort St., tel. 02/247–6008. Admission: $1 adults, 40¢ children under 15, $2.50 family. Open daily 10–5.*

Continue along Lower Fort Street. On the corner of Windmill Street is **The Hero of Waterloo,** one of the oldest pubs in the city as well as one of the most colorful. Gold fever struck the colony in the middle of the 19th century, and it was not uncommon for an entire ship's crew to desert and head for the goldfields as soon as the ship reached Sydney. Captains often resorted to skulduggery to recruit a new crew, and legend has it that many a lad who drank with a generous sea captain in the Hero would awake the next morning on a heaving deck, already out of sight of land. *81 Lower Fort St., tel. 02/252–4553. Open daily 11 AM–11 PM.*

As you approach the end of Lower Fort Street, look up at the hill ahead. This is **Observatory Hill,** known originally as Windmill Hill because the first windmill in the colony once stood here—but not for long. Soon after it was built, the canvas sails were stolen, the machinery was damaged in a storm, and the foundations cracked. Before it was 10 years old, the mill was useless. Several other windmills were erected in the area, however, and this part of The Rocks is still known as Millers Point.

In 1848, the signal station at the top of the hill was built. This later became an astronomical observatory, and Windmill Hill changed its name to Observatory Hill. Until 1982, the metal ball on the tower of the observatory was cranked up the mast and dropped at precisely 1 PM so ship captains could set their chronometers.

Lower Fort Street ends at **Argyle Place,** which was built by Governor Macquarie and named after his home county in Scotland. Argyle Place has all the traditional requirements of an English green—a pub at one end, a church at the other, and grass in between. The church is **Holy Trinity,** which dates from the middle of the last century. Every morning the redcoats would march here from Dawes Point Battery, so it became commonly known as Garrison Church. As the regimental plaques and colors around the walls testify, the church still retains a close association with the military. The tattered ensign on the left wall was carried into battle by Australian troops during the Boer War.

If you have the energy to climb the steps that lead to Observatory Hill, you will be rewarded with a quiet park shaded by giant Moreton Bay fig trees, one of the finest views in Sydney, and a memorable little museum. The observatory is no longer used for serious sky-gazing, because few stars can be seen through the glow of Sydney's lights. Instead, it has become a museum that features a number of hands-on displays, including constellation charts, talking computers, and games designed to illustrate principles of astronomy. During evening shows, visitors are offered a close-up view of such wonders as the rings of Saturn, the moons of Jupiter, distant galaxies, and the enormous, multicolored clouds of gas known as nebulae. Shows cost $5 per adult, $2 per student, and $12 per family. *The Sydney Observatory, Watson Rd., Millers Point, tel. 02/217–0485. Open weekdays 2–5, weekends 10–5. Shows Oct. 14–Mar. 31, Thurs.–Tues. 8:30; Apr. 1–Oct. 13, Thurs.–Tues. 6:15 and 8:15. Reservations required.*

Time Out If climbing has given you a thirst, consider the liquid temptations of **The Lord Nelson** at the far end of Argyle Place, one of the oldest and finest pubs in Sydney. The pub has its own brewery on the premises, and one of its specialties is Quayle Ale, named after the U.S. vice president who "sank a schooner" here during his 1989 visit to Australia. *19 Kent St., tel. 02/251–4044. Open 11 AM–11 PM.*

Leave Argyle Place and walk down the hill into the dark tunnel of the **Argyle Cut.** In the days before the cut was made, this sandstone ridge was a major barrier to traffic crossing between Circular Quay and Millers Point. In 1843, convict work gangs hacked at the sandstone with hand tools for 2½ years before the project was abandoned due to lack of progress. Work restarted in 1857, when drills, explosives, and paid labor completed the job.

On the lower side of the cut, the **Argyle Steps** lead up through an archway. Don't take these steps unless you are in good physical condition. This part of the walk leads up onto the Harbour Bridge and into the southeastern pylon for a dizzying view of the Opera House and the city. To get there from the top of the Argyle Steps, cross the road and walk left for 20 yards, then follow the signs to the **Harbour Bridge Pylon.** There are 200 steps inside the pylon itself, and you should allow at least 1½ hours for the trip to the pylon and back. *Admission: $1 adults, 50¢ students. Open Sat.–Tues. and daily during school holidays 10–5.*

The walk resumes at the foot of the steps on Argyle Street. Continue down the street and turn left under the archway inscribed with the words **Argyle Stores.** The old warehouses around this courtyard are in the process of being converted into shops and galleries that will showcase Australia's finest arts and crafts. Leave the Argyle Stores and cross into Harrington Street.

Time Out About 20 paces along the left side of Harrington Street is **The Gumnut Tea Garden,** the second-oldest building in The Rocks, where you can combine a painless history lesson with a delicious lunch. Originally the residence of a blacksmith, William Reynolds, the restaurant tucked away in this sandstone cottage is renowned for its salads, pies, and cakes. The best tables are at the back in the shady garden. The Gumnut has a devoted clientele, and reservations are necessary at lunchtime. If you're staying in the area, breakfast in the courtyard is a great start to the day. Prices are moderate. *28 Harrington St., The Rocks, tel. 02/247-9591. Open daily 8–5.*

⑮ Ten yards beyond the Gumnut Tea Garden is the **Suez Canal,** which runs down the incline toward George Street. The street got its name before drains were installed, when rainwater would pour down its funnellike passageway and gush across George Street.

⑯ Turn right at **Nurses Walk.** The colony's first hospital was established in this area. Of the 736 convicts who survived the voyage from Portsmouth aboard the 11 ships of the First Fleet, many were suffering from dysentery, smallpox, scurvy, and typhoid. A few days after he landed at Sydney Cove, Governor Phillip established a tent hospital to care for the worst cases. Only 40 convicts of the 776 who left England had died on board Phillip's ships, a mortality rate that was considered a triumph at the time. In comparison, by the time the Second Fleet dropped anchor in Sydney Cove in 1790, a quarter of its convicts had died and a great many more were critically ill. Luckily, one of the ships in the Second Fleet carried a prefabricated hospital, which was erected and filled almost immediately.

Turn left into Surgeons Court and left again into George Street. On the left is the handsome sandstone facade of the former **Rocks police station,** now a crafts gallery. Note the police truncheon thrust into the lion's mouth above the doorway, an architectural motif that appears on at least one other of Sydney's Victorian police stations. From this point, Circular Quay is only a short walk away.

Tour 3: Macquarie Street

This tour will introduce you to two of the most remarkable figures in Australian history—Governor Lachlan Macquarie and his government architect, Francis Greenway. Descended from Scottish clan chieftains, Macquarie was an accomplished soldier and a man of vision—the first governor to foresee a role for New South Wales as a free society rather than an open prison. Macquarie laid the foundations for that society by establishing a plan for the city, constructing imposing public buildings, and advocating that reformed convicts be readmitted to society. Francis Greenway was himself such a former prisoner. Macquarie's policies may seem perfectly reasonable today, but in the early 19th century they marked him as a radical. His vision of a free society threatened to blur the distinctions between soldiers, free settlers, and convicts, so Macquarie was forced to resign in 1821. He was buried on his Scottish estate three years later, and his gravestone is inscribed with the words "The Father of Australia."

The tour roughly follows the outline of the Royal Botanic Gardens and The Domain, and a shady park bench is never far away.

Begin at Circular Quay. Turn your back on the harbor and cross Alfred Street, which runs parallel to the waterfront. The only building
⑰ of any historic distinction along this street is the **Customs House.**

When it was built in the late 1880s, this sandstone building was surrounded by warehouses that stored the fleeces that were the colony's main source of prosperity. The building may soon become an Aboriginal cultural center. Walk up Loftus Street, which runs to the right of the Customs House, and in the lane at the rear you can still see a pulley that was used to lower the wool bales to the dockyard from the top floor of Hinchcliff's Wool Stores.

⑱ Follow Loftus Street to the small triangular park, **Macquarie Place.** The park contains a number of monuments, including the obelisk once used as the point from which all distances from Sydney were measured. On a stone plinth at the bottom of the park is the anchor of HMS *Sirius*, flagship of the First Fleet, which struck a reef and sank off Norfolk Island in 1790. The **bronze statue** of the gentleman with his hands on his hips is of Thomas Mort, who more than a century ago became the first person to ship a refrigerated cargo. The implications of this shipment were enormous. Mutton suddenly became a valuable export commodity, and for most of the next century the Australian economy rode on sheep's back.

The southern side of the park is bordered by busy Bridge Street, named for the bridge that once crossed the Tank Stream at the bottom of this V-shape street. On the other side of Bridge Street is **The**
⑲ **Lands Department,** one of the finest examples of Victorian public architecture in Sydney. The figures standing in the niches at the corners of this building are early Australian explorers and politicians.

Walk up Bridge Street, past the facade of the Education Department. The next sandstone building on the left is the old **Treasury Building,** now the Inter-Continental Hotel. Opposite it is the **Colonial Secretary's Office,** which was built by James Barnet, the same architect who designed the Lands Department. Note how similar the design is, right down to the figures in the corner niches.

Pause for a moment at the corner of Macquarie Street. The figure on horseback about to gallop down Bridge Street is Edward VII, successor to Queen Victoria. The castellated building behind him is the
⑳ **Conservatorium,** originally built in 1819 as stables for Government House (closed to the public), which is screened by the trees near the Opera House. The cost of building these stables caused a storm among Governor Macquarie's superiors in London and eventually helped bring about the downfall of both Macquarie and his architect, Francis Greenway.

㉑ Turn right onto Macquarie Street. On the right is **History House,** headquarters of the Royal Australian Historical Society. Visitors are welcome, and the society offers its considerable resources to anyone who wishes to delve into Australian history. *133 Macquarie St., City, tel. 02/247–8001. Open weekdays 9–5.*

㉒ On the opposite side of Macquarie Street are the **Palace Gates,** elegant wrought-iron gates leading to the Royal Botanic Gardens (*see* Tour 4, *below*). This is all that remains of the Garden Palace, a massive glass pavilion that was erected for the Sydney International Exhibition of 1879 and destroyed by fire three years later. The gates show the dome of the palace, and the stone pillars on either side are engraved with Australian wildflowers.

㉓ A little farther along Macquarie Street is the **Royal Australasian College of Physicians.** The patrician facade of this building gives some idea of the way Macquarie Street looked in the 1840s, when it was lined with the homes of the colonial elite. Today it is home to a different elite—the city's most eminent physicians, many of whom have their surgeries here.

㉔ The ponderous brown building ahead and to your left is the **State Library.** Cross the road toward this building, passing the **Light Horse Monument.** Australian cavalrymen fought with distinction in several Middle Eastern campaigns during World War I, and this statue is dedicated to their horses—which were not allowed to return due to Australian quarantine regulations.

Climb the steps to the portico of the library and enter through the heavy glass doors. You are now standing on one of the earliest maps of Australia. This marble mosaic is a copy of a map made by Abel Tasman, the Dutch navigator. Tasman was not the first European to set eyes on the Australian coastline, but his voyages established that Australia was not the fabled Great South Land for which the Dutch had been searching, believing that it possessed great riches. On his first voyage to Australia in 1642–43, Tasman sailed along the southern coast of Australia and discovered Tasmania, which he named Van Dieman's Land in honor of his patron, the governor of the Dutch East Indies. On his next voyage in 1644, Tasman explored much of the north coast of Australia. On the mosaic map, the two ships of the first voyage are shown off the south coast in the Great Australian Bight; the ships of the second voyage are shown off the northwest coast. The marble for the map came from Wombeyan, about 100 miles southwest of Sydney. The vast reading room that is visible through the glass doors is the Mitchell Library, but you need a reader's ticket to enter. *Macquarie St., tel. 02/230–1414. Open weekdays 9–9, Sat. 9–5, Sun. 11–5.*

Climb the marble staircase on the far side of the foyer, and on the floor above you will see the entrance to the Mitchell Gallery. Pass through this room to the **Dixson Gallery,** which holds changing exhibitions with historical and cultural themes.

㉕ Back on Macquarie Street, turn left and walk toward the gates of **State Parliament House,** a building with an intriguing history. This is the northern wing of Rum Hospital, which was built with profits from the rum trade. In a stroke of political genius, Macquarie persuaded two merchants to build a hospital for convicts in return for a three-year monopoly on the importation of rum. From 1829, two rooms of this hospital were used for meetings of the executive and legislative councils, which had been set up to advise the governor. The functions of these advisory bodies grew until New South Wales became self-governing in the 1840s, at which time parliament occupied the entire building. On weekdays between 9:30 and 4, visitors are welcome in public areas of the parliament building, which contain a number of portraits and paintings. The Legislative Council Chamber—the upper house of the parliament, identifiable by its red color scheme—is a cast-iron, prefabricated structure that was originally intended to be a church on the goldfields of Victoria.

State Parliament sits between mid-February and late May, and again between mid-September and late November. The New South Wales Parliament has a reputation as one of the rowdiest and toughest legislatures in the world, and visitors are welcome to the public gallery to watch the Westminster system of democracy in action. *Macquarie St., tel. 02/230–2111. Open Tues.–Thurs. 9:30–4:30. Reservations advised.*

㉖ The next building on the left is **Sydney Hospital,** constructed in 1894 to replace the central section of Rum Hospital, which had begun to fall apart almost as soon as it was completed. By all accounts, admission to Rum Hospital was only slightly preferable to death itself. The convict nurses stole the patients' food, and the abler patients stole from the weaker; the kitchen sometimes doubled as a mortuary, and the kitchen table was occasionally used to perform operations.

Walk along the front of the hospital to the bronze statue of the boar. This is *Il Porcellino,* a copy of a statue that stands in Florence, Italy. According to the inscription, if you make a donation in the coin box and rub the boar's nose, "you will be endowed with good luck." Perhaps the citizens of Sydney are a superstitious bunch, for the boar's nose is very shiny indeed!

27 Beyond the hospital is the **Mint Museum,** originally the southern wing of Rum Hospital. The building now serves as a museum of decorative and fine arts, with displays of stamps, coins, and some excellent examples of 19th-century silverwork. Much of the museum's collection of Victorian furniture is decorated with Australian motifs. *Queen's Sq., Macquarie St., tel. 02/217–0122. Admission: $5 adults, $3 children 5–15. Combined admission to the Mint and Hyde Park Barracks: $7 adults, $4 children 5–15. Open Thurs.- Tues. 10–5, Wed. noon–5.*

28 Next door is the **Hyde Park Barracks.** Before Macquarie arrived, the convicts were left to roam freely at night, and there was little regard for the sanctity of life or property on the streets of Sydney after dark. As the new governor, Macquarie was determined to establish law and order, and he commissioned Greenway to design this building to house the prisoners. The barracks is considered Greenway's architectural masterpiece, yet it is essentially a very simple building. Note the restrained, classical lines—the hallmark of the Georgian era. The clock on the tower is the oldest functioning public timepiece in New South Wales.

Today the Hyde Park Barracks houses a collection of artifacts from the convict era and from later years, when it was used as an asylum for Irish orphans and "unprotected women." A surprising number of relics from this period were preserved by rats, which carried away scraps of clothing for their nests beneath the floorboards—a fascinating and gruesome detail that is graphically illustrated in the foyer. A room on the top floor is strung with hammocks, exactly as it was when the building housed convicts. (Try one for size.) *Queen's Sq., Macquarie St., tel. 02/223–8922. Admission: $5 adults, $3 children 5–15. Open daily 10–5.*

Time Out   On a sunny day, the courtyard tables of the **Hyde Park Barracks Café** provide one of the finest places in the city to enjoy an outdoor lunch. The café serves a selection of light, imaginative meals, salads, and open sandwiches. The wine list includes several fine Australian wines, and the prices are moderate. *Queen's Sq., Macquarie St., City, tel. 02/223–1155. Open daily 10–4.*

Cross to the other side of the street, where the figure of Queen Victoria presides over Macquarie Street. To Victoria's left is another
29 Greenway building, **St. James Church.** Greenway had originally designed it as a court of law, and the building was half completed when Commissioner Bigge, who had been sent from England to investigate Macquarie's administration, ordered that the building be converted into a church.

Macquarie's grand plans for the construction of Sydney might have come to nothing but for Francis Greenway. The governor had been continually frustrated by his masters in the Colonial Office in London, who saw no need for an architect in a penal colony. Then, in 1814, fate delivered Greenway into his hands. Greenway, who had trained as an architect in England, was convicted of forgery and sentenced to 14 years in New South Wales. Macquarie seized this opportunity, gave Greenway a ticket of leave that allowed him to work outside the convict system, and set him to work transforming Sydney. For all his brilliance as an architect, however, he was a difficult and temperamental man. When his patron Macquarie returned to England in 1822, Greenway quickly fell from favor and retired to his farm north of Sydney. Some years later, he was charged with misappropriating this property but was able to produce a deed giving him title to the land. It is now believed that the signature on the title deed is a forgery.

Greenway was depicted on one side of the old $10 notes until they went out of circulation early in the 1990s. Only in Australia would a convicted forger be depicted on the currency.

Enter St. James Church through the door in the Doric portico. The interior walls of the church are covered with plaques commemorating some of the early Australian explorers and administrators. The inscriptions on the plaques testify to the hardships of those early days, when death either at sea or at the hands of the Aborigines seems to have been a common fate. *Queen's Sq., Macquarie St., tel. 02/232–3022. Open daily 9–5.*

③ Return to the barracks side of Macquarie Street and head to **St. Mary's,** Sydney's Roman Catholic cathedral. The design of this neo-Gothic church is based on Lincoln Cathedral in England. As you walk along the side of the cathedral, note the pointed arches above the doors and the flying buttresses—the tall arches that extend from the side of the cathedral—both characteristic of the Gothic style. Work began on the cathedral more than a century ago, but it has never been completed. Due to a shortage of funds, the spires that were planned for the towers in front have never been built.

Walk to the front of the cathedral and climb the steps, passing between the **statues of Cardinal Moran and Archbishop Kelly,** two Irishmen who were prominent in the Roman Catholic Church in Australia. Due to the high proportion of Irish men and women in the convict population, the Roman Catholic Church was often the voice of the oppressed in 19th-century Sydney, where anti-Catholic feeling ran high among the Protestant rulers. Australia's first cardinal, Patrick Moran, was a powerful exponent of Catholic education and a diplomat who did much to heal the rift between the two faiths. By contrast, Michael Kelly, his successor as head of the church in Sydney, was excessively pious and politically inept; Kelly and Moran remained at odds until Moran's death in 1911. The cathedral's large rose window inside came from England, and the Stations of the Cross were painted by the French artist Crovet. *College St., tel. 02/232–3788. Open weekdays 6:30 AM–6:30 PM, Sat. 8 AM–7:30 PM, Sun. 6:30 AM–7:30 PM.*

At the rear of the cathedral, cross St. Mary's Road to Art Gallery Road. Continue past the **statue of Robert Burns,** the Scottish writer. The big trees on the left with the enormous roots and the drooping limbs are Moreton Bay figs, which bear an inedible fruit.

③ Directly ahead is the **Art Gallery of New South Wales,** the largest in the state. The gallery contains permanent displays of Aboriginal, Asian, and European art, as well as the work of some of the best-known Australian artists. Note the evolution of an Australian style, from the early painters who saw the country through European eyes to such painters as Russell Drysdale, whose strident colors and earthy realism give a very different impression of the Australian landscape. Twentieth-century art is displayed on the ground floor of the gallery, where the big windows frame their own spectacular view of the harbor. If you want a change from the usual postcards of kookaburras, kangaroos, and koalas, the bookshop on the ground floor has an offbeat collection. *Art Gallery Rd., The Domain, tel. 02/225–1700. Open Mon.–Sat. 10–5, Sun. noon–5.*

This is where the tour ends. From the Art Gallery, you can return to Macquarie Street by crossing the parklands of the Domain or by wandering for a half mile through the Royal Botanic Gardens. If you have an Explorer bus pass, you can catch the bus back to the city from the front of the gallery.

Tour 4: The Opera House and the Royal Botanic Gardens

From Circular Quay, walk around Sydney Cove and onto the promontory on which the Opera House stands. With its distinctive white sails and prominent position jutting into the harbor, the **Sydney Opera House** is the most widely recognized landmark of urban Australia. Within Australia itself, it has also been a source of enormous controversy and debate. It has been compared to "a bunch of mussels stuck in the mud," called "the building of the century," and labeled the "greatest political public relations stunt since the pyramids." Whatever its merits, the Opera House leaves no visitor unmoved, and a tour of the building and the surrounding Royal Botanic Gardens can easily be accomplished in a few hours.

Considering everything that transpired during its construction, it's something of a miracle that the Opera House exists at all. In 1954, the state premier appointed a committee to advise the government on the building of an opera house. The site chosen was Bennelong Point—until that time, the site of a tram depot. The premier's committee launched a competition to find a suitable plan, and eventually 233 submissions were received from architects from all over the world, one of whom was a young Dane named Joern Utzon.

His plan was brilliant, but it had all the makings of a monumental disaster. The proposed building was so narrow that the stages had virtually no wings; the soaring "sails" that formed the walls and roof could not be built by existing technology.

Yet Utzon's dazzling, dramatic concept caught the imagination of the judges, and construction of the giant podium began in 1958. From the very beginning, the contractors faced a cost blowout—a problem that was to plague the Opera House throughout its construction. The building that was projected to cost $7 million and take four years to erect would eventually cost $102 million and take 15 years. The cost to the taxpayer was virtually nil, however, since the construction of the Opera House was funded by a state-run lottery.

Initially it was thought that the concrete exterior of the building would have to be cast in position, which would have meant building an enormous bird cage of scaffolding at huge cost. Then, when he was peeling an orange one day, Utzon had a flash of inspiration. Why not construct the shells from segments of a single sphere? The concrete ribs forming the skeleton of the building could be prefabricated in just a few molds, hoisted into position, and joined together.

These concrete ribs are clearly visible inside the Opera House, especially in the foyers and staircases of the Concert Hall.

In 1966, Utzon resigned as Opera House architect and left Australia, embittered by his dealings with the unions and the government (he has never returned to see his masterpiece). A team of young Australian architects carried on, completing the exterior one year later. Until that time, however, nobody had given much thought to the *interior*. The shells created awkward interior spaces, and conventional performance areas were simply not feasible. It is a tribute to the architectural team's ingenuity that the exterior of the building is matched by the aesthetically pleasing and acoustically sound theaters inside.

In September 1973 the Australian Opera performed *War and Peace* in the Opera Theatre; a month later, Queen Elizabeth II officially opened the building in a ceremony capped by an unforgettable fireworks display. Nowadays, the controversies that raged around the building seem inconceivable. Poised majestically on its peninsula, with Circular Quay and the Harbour Bridge on one side and the Royal Botanic Gardens on the other, it has become a much loved part of the city as well as a potent national symbol.

The building is actually far more versatile than its name implies. In reality, it is an entertainment complex hosting a wide range of performances and activities: dance, drama, films, opera, jazz bands in the forecourt, five restaurants and cafés, and six bars. *Guided 1-hr tours of the Opera House depart at frequent intervals from the tour office, lower forecourt level, 9:15–4. Tickets: $8.50 adults, $5.50 students. Except during rehearsal times, 90-min backstage tours are also available Sun. mornings from about 9. Cost: $13. No children. Tel. 02/250–7111.*

㉝ Adjoining the Sydney Opera House are the **Royal Botanic Gardens.** These gardens join with the rolling parkland of **The Domain** to form the eastern border of the city. Groves of palm trees, duck ponds, a cactus garden, a greenhouse, a restaurant, and acres of lawns coalesce around one of the finest walks in Sydney, along a path that follows the horseshoe curve of Farm Cove, where the convicts of the First Fleet established gardens. Their early attempts at agriculture were disastrous, and for the first couple of years the prisoners and their guards were close to starvation.

㉞ The path leads to a peninsula, **Mrs. Macquarie's Point,** named after the governor's wife, who planned the road through the gardens. The lawns at the water's edge are a popular place for picnics, especially on warm summer evenings when the sunset makes a spectacular backdrop to the Opera House and the Harbour Bridge. As you round the peninsula and turn toward the naval dockyard at Garden Island, notice the small bench carved into the rock with an inscription iden-
㉟ tifying it as **Mrs. Macquarie's Chair.** *Open 8 AM–sunset. Guided tours from the Visitor Centre, near Art Gallery of New South Wales, tel. 02/ 231–8125, Wed. and Fri. 10, Sun. 1.*

Tour 5: Kings Cross and Paddington

This is a bus and walking tour that looks at the people's Sydney—from the mansions of the colonial aristocracy to the humble laborers' cottages of the same period to the modernized terrace houses of Paddington (one of Sydney's most charming suburbs). Elderly travelers may have difficulty negotiating the steep steps of Paddington.

This tour begins at the bus stop on Alfred Street just behind Circular Quay. Catch Bus 311, which leaves from the stop at the Harbour Bridge end of the street. This bus carries the sign RAILWAY VIA KINGS CROSS or RAILWAY VIA ELIZABETH BAY. Ask the driver to drop you off at Elizabeth Bay House, and sit on the left side of the bus. Winding through the city streets to Macquarie Street, past the State Library, the New South Wales Parliament, Hyde Park Barracks, and St. Mary's Cathedral, this bus then follows the curve of Wooloomooloo Bay, where it passes beneath the bows of the naval vessels at the Garden Island Dockyard, the main base for the Australian navy. Visiting ships from other Pacific Ocean navies can often be seen along this wharf.

36 Just before the Garden Island gates, the bus turns right and climbs through the shady streets of Potts Point to **Elizabeth Bay House,** an aristocratic Regency-style mansion. Built some 150 years ago by Alexander Macleay, the colonial secretary, Elizabeth Bay House is one of Australia's finest colonial homes. Very little of the original furniture remains, but the rooms have been restored in the style of the period. The house's most striking feature is the oval-shape salon, which is lit by glass panels in a domed roof. Macleay lived here for only six years before suffering crippling losses in the colonial depression of the 1840s. In return for settling his father's debts, his son William took possession of the house and most of its contents and promptly evicted his father. *7 Onslow Ave., Elizabeth Bay, tel. 02/ 358-2344. Admission: $5 adults, $3 children under 16, $12 family. Open Tues.–Sun. 10–4:30.*

37 Leave Elizabeth Bay House and cross to the **Arthur McElhone Reserve.** Cross the stone bridge spanning the carp pond and pause for a breather in this delightful little park, with its tree ferns, gushing stream, and harbor views. The wrought-iron balconies and French doors on some of the older apartment blocks give this part of Elizabeth Bay a Mediterranean feel. During the 1920s and 1930s, this was a fashionably bohemian quarter of the city.

38 Take the stone steps leading down from the park to Billyard Avenue. Near the lower end of this street is a walled garden with cypress trees and banana palms visible over the top. Through the black iron gates of the driveway, you can catch a glimpse of **Boomerang**—a sprawling, Spanish-style villa built by the manufacturer of the harmonica of the same name. Just beyond the house, turn left to **Beare Park,** overlooking the yachts in Elizabeth Bay.

Return to Billyard Avenue. Wait at the bus stop opposite the first gate of Boomerang for Bus 311, but make sure that you catch one marked RAILWAY, not CIRCULAR QUAY. Ask the driver to deposit you at the end of Darlinghurst Road, near the courthouse. This bus threads its way through the streets of Kings Cross, Sydney's nightlife district. During the day The Cross is only half awake, although the doormen of the various strip clubs are never too sleepy to lure passersby inside to watch the nonstop video shows. From Kings Cross, the bus follows the high sandstone wall of the East Sydney Technical College, formerly a prison, before it reaches your stop.

39 When you leave the bus, turn left onto busy Oxford Street. About 300 yards farther on your right is another sandstone wall—the perimeter of **Victoria Barracks.** These barracks were built in the middle of the last century to house the British regiments stationed in the colony. The troops were withdrawn in 1870 and replaced by Australian troops. Most of the area within the walls is taken up by a parade ground, and an army band parades here from 9:30 AM every Thursday. Dress uniforms have been abolished in the Australian army, so the soldiers wear their parade-ground dress, which includes the famous slouch hat: The brim is cocked on the left side, allowing the soldiers to carry their rifles across their shoulders without knocking off their hats. On the far side of the parade ground, in the former military prison, is the **Army Museum.** The exhibits cover Australia's military history from the days of the Rum Corps to the Malayan conflict of the 1950s. The museum suffers from a shortage of funds, but its volunteer staff is knowledgeable and enthusiastic, and students of military history will not be disappointed. *Oxford St., tel. 02/339–3000. Museum open Thurs. 10–12, Sun. 1:30–4:30. Barracks closed to public early Dec.–early Feb.*

Almost opposite the main entrance to the barracks is the start of ❹⓿ **Shadforth Street.** Built at about the same time as Elizabeth Bay House, the tiny stone houses on this street are some of the oldest in Paddington. Constructed to house the workers who built and serviced the barracks, their design was copied directly from the simple laborers' cottages of England. At the first intersection, Shadforth Street changes its name to Liverpool Street and the terrace houses begin. These elegant two-story houses were built during the 1880s, when the population and affluence of the colony boomed during the gold rushes. The decorative wrought iron on the balcony, sometimes known as "Paddington lace," was initially imported from England and later made in Australian foundries. If you look closely at the patterns, you may be able to distinguish between the rose-and-thistle design that came from England and the flannel flower, fern, and lyre-bird feather designs that were made in Australia.

During the depression of the 1890s, Paddington's boom came to an abrupt end. The advent of the automobile and motorized public transport just a few years later meant that people could now live in the suburbs surrounded by gardens and trees, and inner-city areas such as Paddington became unfashionable. The area declined further during the depression of the 1930s, when many terrace houses were converted into low-rent accommodations, and most of the wrought-iron balconies were boarded up to make an extra room.

In the late 1960s, inner-city living suddenly became desirable again, and many young couples bought these dilapidated but quaint houses at bargain prices. Renovated and repainted, these now-stylish Paddington terrace houses give the area its characteristic village charm. Today, you can expect to pay at least $300,000 for a small terrace house.

Continue downhill on Liverpool Street and turn right at the intersection with Glenmore Road, where the terrace houses are even more elaborate. Follow this road past the intersection with Brown Street to the colorful collection of shops known as Five Ways. The ❹❶ **Royal Hotel** on the far corner offers a fine example of a pub, restored to its former Victorian glory with the help of newly furnished leather couches and stained-glass windows. On the floor above is a balconied restaurant that is especially popular on sunny afternoons.

Walk up Broughton Street to the right of the Royal Hotel. Turn right at Union Street, left onto Underwood, and right at William Street. You are now back among the boutique shops of Paddington. On the right is **Sweet William** (4 William St., Paddington, tel. 02/ 331–5468), a shop for chocolate connoisseurs.

Time Out On Oxford Street near the corner of William Street is the **New Edition Tea Rooms,** a bright lunchtime restaurant serving croissants, salads, and crusty French loaves filled with ham or smoked salmon, as well as cakes, herbal teas, and the biggest cappuccinos in town. The best tables are near the windows at the front, and the restaurant has a good selection of international magazines and newspapers. The prices are moderate. *328 Oxford St. (entry is through the New Edition Bookshop), Paddington, tel. 02/361–0744. Open weekdays 10–4, weekends 10–5.*

Continue along Oxford Street to another restored colonial mansion, **42 Juniper Hall.** This house was built by a gin distiller, Robert Cooper, who named it after the juniper berries used to make the drink. Cooper did everything on a grand scale—and that included raising and housing his family. He built Juniper Hall for his third wife, Sarah, whom he married when he was 46, and who bore 14 of his 24 children. The house later became an orphanage. Renovated at considerable public expense and opened as a museum during the 1980s, the house is presently closed to the public due to a lack of funds. *248 Oxford St., Paddington, tel. 02/332–1988.*

Juniper Hall marks the end of this tour. There are buses back to the city from the other side of Oxford Street. But if the sun is shining, consider heading out to Bondi Beach, a mere 15-minute ride on the number 380 bus.

Sydney for Free

Much of Sydney can be experienced for nothing. Indeed, Sydney's finest attractions—its harbor views and its beaches—are to be enjoyed for the taking. A visit to Bondi Beach or a sunset walk along the harbor's edge in the Royal Botanic Gardens is literally priceless. In addition, many museums, galleries, and historic sites charge no admission fee, and it is possible to complete the exploring tours described in this chapter for a few dollars at most.

Music On Wednesday at 1:10 between mid-February and mid-December, students at the **Conservatorium of Music** give free lunchtime concerts. A number of free recitals are also held on various evenings throughout the year: Check the *Sydney Morning Herald* for details. *Macquarie St., opposite the InterContinental Hotel, tel. 02/230–1222.*

Oratory Every Sunday, a varied assortment of soapbox orators can be seen, heard, and argued with at **Speakers' Corner** in The Domain. *Opposite the Art Gallery of N.S.W., Sun. 11–3.*

What to See and Do with Children

At **Koala Park Sanctuary,** a private park on the northern outskirts of the city, you can cuddle, feed, and photograph a koala. The sanctuary also houses dingoes, kangaroos, emus, and wallaroos. Feeding times are 10:20, 11:45, 2, and 3. *84 Castle Hill Rd., W. Pennant Hills, tel. 02/484–3141. Admission: $8 adults, $4 children 4–14. Open daily 9–5.*

Part of the Darling Harbour development, the **Sydney Aquarium** contains a fascinating display of marine life, from saltwater crocodiles to giant sea turtles and delicate, multicolored reef fish. The highlights of the aquarium are two transparent tunnels submerged in an oceanarium, complete with moving footpaths taking you safely through the water while sharks and stingrays glide overhead. The aquarium is often crowded on weekends. *Wheat Rd., Pier 26, Darling Harbour, tel. 02/262-2300. Admission: $13.50 adults, $6.50 children 3-15, $33.50 family. Open daily 9:30-9.*

Occupying a natural bush setting on the northern shore of the harbor, the **Taronga Park Zoo** has an especially extensive collection of Australian fauna, including everybody's favorite marsupial—the koala. Over the past few years, the zoo has made great progress in creating spacious enclosures that closely simulate the animals' natural habitats. The zoo is set on a hillside, and a complete tour can be tiring (although a free map that outlines a less strenuous route is available at the entrance gate). Children's strollers are provided free of charge. The easiest way to get to the zoo from the city is by ferry. At the Taronga Park Wharf, a bus will take you up the hill to the zoo entrance. Combined ferry/zoo tickets are available at Circular Quay. *Bradleys Head Rd., Mosman, tel. 02/969-2777. Admission: $13.50 adults, $6 children 4-15, $33 family. Open daily 9-5.*

Off the Beaten Track

The attraction of **Harry's Café de Wheels,** a dockyard nighttime food stall, is not so much the pies and coffee that Harry dispenses as the clientele. Harry's is an institution, and famous opera singers, actors, and international rock and roll stars have been spotted here rubbing shoulders with shift workers and taxi drivers. *1 Cowper Wharf Rd., Wooloomooloo. Open daily 8:30 PM-3 AM.*

A masterpiece of Victorian extravagance, the **Marble Bar** was once a hotel bar much favored by gentlemen of the racing fraternity. Threatened with demolition, the whole bar was moved—complete with its marble arches, colored glass ceiling, elaborately carved woodwork, and paintings of voluptuous nudes—to its present site beneath the Sydney Hilton. By night, the baroque splendor of this bar becomes the rather unlikely backdrop for high-decibel rock and roll. *Basement, Hilton Hotel, George St., tel. 02/266-0610. Open Mon. 4-11 PM, Tues.-Thurs. 4 PM-midnight, Fri. 4 PM-2 AM, Sat. 5 PM-2 AM.*

The Harold Park Hotel is a fairly ordinary pub about 2 kilometers (1 mile) from the city, but on Tuesday evening it becomes a venue for **Writers in the Park,** when artists and writers read and discuss their works with the audience. An invitation to read carries some prestige, and most Australian literary luminaries, as well as a number of well-known overseas authors, have appeared. *Harold Park Hotel, 115 Wigram Rd., Glebe, tel. 02/692-0564. Admission: $7, $5 students. Open Tues. 7:30-11 PM.*

Sightseeing Checklist

Historic Buildings and Sights	Argyle Cut (*see* Tour 2: The Rocks)
	Argyle Place (*see* Tour 2: The Rocks)
	Cadman's Cottage (*see* Tour 2: The Rocks)
	Campbell's Storehouse (*see* Tour 2: The Rocks)
	Conservatorium of Music (*see* Tour 3: Macquarie Street)
	Customs House (*see* Tour 3: Macquarie Street)
	Elizabeth Bay House (*see* Tour 5: Kings Cross and Paddington)
	Fort Denison (*see* Tour 1: Sydney Harbour)
	Garden Island (*see* Tour 1: Sydney Harbour)
	Hero of Waterloo Pub (*see* Tour 2: The Rocks)
	Juniper Hall (*see* Tour 5: Kings Cross and Paddington)
	Lands Department (*see* Tour 3: Macquarie Street)

Macquarie Place (*see* Tour 3: Macquarie Street)
Middle Harbour (*see* Tour 1: Sydney Harbour)
Mrs. Macquarie's Chair (*see* Tour 4: The Opera House and the Royal Botanic Gardens)
Nurses Walk (*see* Tour 2: The Rocks)
Observatory Hill (*see* Tour 2: The Rocks)
Old Treasury Building (*see* Tour 3: Macquarie Street)
Quarantine Station (*see* Tour 1: Sydney Harbour)
Rocks Police Station (*see* Tour 2: The Rocks)
Rum Hospital (*see* Tour 3: Macquarie Street)
State Parliament House (*see* Tour 3: Macquarie Street)
Suez Canal (*see* Tour 2: The Rocks)
Sydney Harbour Bridge (*see* Tour 2: The Rocks)
Sydney Hospital (*see* Tour 3: Macquarie Street)
Sydney Opera House (*see* Tour 4: The Opera House and the Royal Botanic Gardens)
Vaucluse (*see* Tour 1: Sydney Harbour)
Victoria Barracks (*see* Tour 5: Kings Cross and Paddington)

Museums and Galleries

Army Museum (*see* Tour 5: Kings Cross and Paddington)
Art Gallery of New South Wales (*see* Tour 3: Macquarie Street)
The Australian Maritime Museum. Part of the Darling Harbour complex, this soaring, futuristic white building is divided into six galleries that tell the story of Australia and the sea. In addition to figureheads, model ships, and the brassy apparatus of nautical enterprise, there are antique racing yachts, a World War II destroyer, and the jet-powered *Spirit of Australia*, current holder of the water speed record. Many displays are interactive. The most spectacular exhibit is the fully rigged *Australia II*, the famous 12-meter yacht with winged keel that finally broke the New York Yacht Club's hold on the America's Cup in 1983. *Darling Harbour, tel. 02/552–7777. Admission: $7 adults, $3.50 children 4–16, $17.50 family. Open daily 10–5.*
The Australian Museum: Although the first exhibit to greet you here is the skeleton of a sperm whale suspended from the ceiling, this museum of natural history is better known for its cultural exhibitions. The Aboriginal section of the museum is particularly rewarding, especially its treatment of the impact of white European society on the first Australians. Australian fauna and the tribal cultures of Papua New Guinea are also well represented. *William and College Sts., City, tel. 02/339–8111. Open daily 10–5.*
Colonial House Museum (*see* Tour 2: The Rocks)
The Earth Exchange. Subtitled "the Geological and Mining Museum," this is a stimulating experience even for those who used geology classes to catch up on sleep. Displays of mining, minerals, and such marvels as an earthquake simulator are used to pose challenging questions about the past, present, and possible future of Planet Earth. *18 Hickson Rd., The Rocks, tel. 02/251–2422. Admission: $7 adults, $5 children 4–16. Open daily 10–5.*
History House (*see* Tour 3: Macquarie Street)
Hyde Park Barracks (*see* Tour 3: Macquarie Street)
Mint Museum (*see* Tour 3: Macquarie Street)
Museum of Contemporary Art: Andy Warhol, Roy Lichtenstein, Cindy Sherman, and local artists Juan Devila, Maria Kozic, and Imants Tillers are just some of the well-known names whose works hang in this ponderous art deco building on the western side of Circular Quay. However, the exhibitions rarely challenge or inspire. The museum's café, with outdoor seating beside the harbor, is a pleasant, inexpensive option for breakfast and lunch. *Circular*

Quay, The Rocks, tel. 02/252–4033. Admission: $8 adults, $4 children 5–15. Open daily 11–6.

Powerhouse Museum: A striking example of high-tech architecture, this extraordinary museum of applied arts and sciences is housed in the electricity station that once powered Sydney's trams. Exhibits include a whole floor of working steam engines, a pub, an old movie theater auditorium, airplanes suspended from the ceiling, space modules, and state-of-the-art computer gadgetry. The Powerhouse uses hands-on displays to encourage visitor participation. For recorded information on current attractions, call the Powerhouse Hotline (tel. 02/217–0444). *500 Harris St., Ultimo (near Darling Harbour), tel. 02/217–0111. Admission: $5 adults, $2 children under 12, $12 family. Open daily 10–5.*

State Library (*see* Tour 3: Macquarie Street)
The Sydney Observatory (*see* Tour 2: The Rocks)
Westpac Banking Museum (*see* Tour 2: The Rocks)

Churches   **Holy Trinity** (*see* Tour 2: The Rocks)
St. James Church (*see* Tour 3: Macquarie Street)
St. Mary's Cathedral (*see* Tour 3: Macquarie Street)

Parks and   **The Domain** (*see* Tour 4: The Opera House and the Royal Botanic
Gardens   Gardens)
Koala Park Sanctuary (*see* What to See and Do with Children)
Royal Botanic Gardens (*see* Tour 4: The Opera House and the Royal Botanic Gardens)
Taronga Park Zoo (*see* What to See and Do with Children)

Statues and   **Archbishop Kelly, St. Mary's** (*see* Tour 3: Macquarie Street)
Monuments   **Cardinal Moran, St. Mary's** (*see* Tour 3: Macquarie Street)
Edward VII Statue (*see* Tour 3: Macquarie Street)
Il Porcellino Statue (*see* Tour 3: Macquarie Street)
Light Horse Monument (*see* Tour 3: Macquarie Street)
Robert Burns Statue (*see* Tour 3: Macquarie Street)
Thomas Mort Statue (*see* Tour 3: Macquarie Street)
William Bligh Statue (*see* Tour 2: The Rocks)

Other Places   **Boomerang Villa** (*see* Tour 5: Kings Cross and Paddington)
of Interest   **Darling Harbour:** Until the mid-1980s, this horseshoe-shape bay on the western edge of the city center was a wasteland of disused docks and railway yards. Then, in an explosive burst of activity, the whole area was redeveloped and opened in time for Australia's bicentennial in 1988. Today the Darling Harbour complex includes a Chinese garden, the National Maritime Museum, the Harbourside Festival Marketplace, the Sydney Aquarium, and a gleaming Exhibition Centre whose masts and spars recall the square riggers that once berthed here. Immediately to the south are Chinatown and the State Entertainment Centre, and to the west is the Powerhouse Museum. At the harbor's center is a large park shaded by palm trees, and the complex is laced together by a series of waterways and fountains. The best time to visit is in the evening, when the tall city buildings reflect the sunset and cast magical images on the water. Later, the pubs, cafés, and nightclubs turn on the lights and the music for a party that lasts until well past midnight.

Harbour Bridge Pylon (*see* Tour 2: The Rocks)
Sydney Aquarium (*see* What to See and Do with Children)
Sydney Opera House (*see* Tour 4: The Opera House and the Royal Botanic Gardens)
Sydney Tower: This 1,000-foot spike with its golden minaret is the tallest building in the city. If you come here on a smog-free day, the views from its observation deck will encompass the entire Sydney metropolitan area of more than 600 square miles. *Market St. bet.*

*Pitt and Castlereagh Sts., tel. 02/229-7444. Admission: $6 adults,
$2.50 children 5-16. Open Sun.-Fri. 9:30-9:30, Sat. 9:30 AM-11:30
PM.*

Shopping

Unless you come from New Zealand, it is not likely that shopping is
your primary reason for visiting Australia. Clothing is generally
more expensive than in Europe and North America, and very few
bargains are to be found. Some of the finest souvenirs are in the Aboriginal art galleries, opal shops, crafts galleries, or even the Saturday flea markets. If you're concerned about buying genuine
Australian products, look carefully at the labels: Stuffed koalas and
kangaroos made in Taiwan have become a standing joke in Australia. In the city, shops are open on weekdays between 9 and 5:30. On
Thursday night, most shops stay open until 7, some until 9. On Saturday, shopping hours are 9 to 4. Department stores in the city and
shops in The Rocks and Darling Harbour are open Sunday. The most
widely accepted credit cards are American Express, MasterCard,
and Visa.

**Shopping
Centers and
Arcades**
The Harbourside Festival Marketplace is the shopping area of the
Darling Harbour complex. This glass pavilion contains more than
200 clothing, jewelry, and souvenir shops. However, its attraction as
a shopping area is due not so much to the shops themselves as to its
striking architecture and spectacular waterside location. The shopping center includes a number of cafés that overlook the harbor.

The Pitt Street Mall, located between King and Market streets, is a
pedestrian plaza in the heart of Sydney's shopping area. Running off
the mall are the Mid-City Centre, Centrepoint Arcade, Imperial Arcade, Skygarden, and Strand Arcade—five multilevel shopping plazas crammed with more than 450 shops, most of which sell clothing.

The **Queen Victoria Building** is a sprawling example of Victorian architecture in the middle of the city (on George Street near Town
Hall) and contains more than 200 boutiques, cafés, and antiques
shops. Even if you have no intention of shopping, the building itself
is worth a tour. Originally the city's produce market, the sandstone
building had become a maze of shabby offices by the time it disappeared under scaffolding in 1981. When the wraps came off five
years later, the building featured sweeping staircases, enormous
stained-glass windows, and the 1-ton Royal Clock, which is suspended from the glass roof. The building is open 24 hours a day, although the shops trade at the usual hours.

**Department
Stores**
David Jones, or "Dee Jays," is the largest department store in the
city, with a reputation for excellent service and high-quality goods.
Clothing by many of Australia's finest designers is on display here,
and the store also markets its own fashion label at reasonable prices.
The basement level of the men's store is a food hall with a range of
gourmet treats from all over the world. *Elizabeth and Market Sts.
(women's store) and Castlereagh and Market Sts. (men's), tel. 02/
266-5544. Open Mon.-Wed. 9-5:30, Thurs. 9-9, Fri. 9-7, weekends
9-5.*

Grace Bros. is located near the Queen Victoria Building and features
moderately priced merchandise. The store also includes an opti-
cian's shop and a Ticketek theater-booking agency. *George and
Market Sts., City, tel. 02/238-9111. Open Mon.-Wed., Fri., and
weekends 8:30-5:30, Thurs. 8:30 AM-9 PM.*

Flea Markets   **Balmain Market** is set in a leafy churchyard less than 5 kilometers (3 miles) from the city. This Saturday market has a rustic appeal that is a relaxing change from city-center shopping. The 100 or so stalls display some unusual and high-quality bric-a-brac, craftwork, and jewelry. Inside the church hall you can buy a truly international range of gourmet snacks, from Indian samosas to Indonesian satays to Australian meat pies. *St. Mary's Church, Darling St., Balmain. Open Sat. 9–4.*

Paddington Village Bazaar, popularly known as Paddington Market, is where Sydney's New Age people come to buy their crystals and chunky tribal jewelry and have their tarot cards read. More than 250 stalls are located in this busy churchyard bazaar, offering finely made arts and crafts, clothing, and unusual souvenirs at bargain prices. The market is also a major outlet for a number of avant-garde but unknown dress designers, whose clothing is still affordable. Even if you are not interested in shopping, the market is a lively, entertaining environment that acts as a magnet for some of the flamboyant characters of the area. *St. John's Church, Oxford St., Paddington. Open Sat. 10–4.*

The Rocks Market is the biggest and best organized of Sydney's street markets. This weekend covered bazaar transforms the upper end of George Street into a cultural collage of music, food, arts, crafts, and entertainment. *Upper George St., near Argyle St., The Rocks. Open weekends 10–5.*

Duty-Free Shops   Overseas visitors can take advantage of great bargains on electrical goods, cameras, perfumes, and liquor at the duty-free shops scattered throughout the city. In fact, most of the prices in Sydney's duty-free shops are comparable with those in the duty-free bargain centers of Singapore and Hong Kong. Although goods may be purchased at any time with the display of a ticket to leave Australia and a passport, they can be collected from the shop only 48 hours before departure. The goods, sealed in plastic carrier bags, must not be opened until the passenger has cleared immigration formalities at the airport and must be carried onto the plane as hand luggage. In a survey of Sydney's duty-free shops published in the *Sydney Morning Herald*, Downtown duty-free shops (*see below*) offered the best prices, but only by a small margin on most goods. Downtown also operates the airside duty-free shop at Sydney's international airport, where the prices are identical to their city shops. The airport shop sells a good range of perfumes, liquor, and electrical and electronic items.

Angus and Coote are Sydney's specialist jewelers, offering a wide selection of duty-free watches and gemstones. *496 George St. (beneath Hilton Hotel), Sydney, tel. 02/267–1363. Open Mon.–Sat. 10–6:30, Sun. 11–6:30.*

Downtown Duty Free is popular among airline flight crews, who are generally a reliable indicator of the best prices. The store has several city outlets. *Strand Arcade, tel. 02/233–3166; 84 Pitt St., tel. 02/221–4444; 2nd floor, Queen Victoria Bldg., George St., tel. 02/267–7944. Open weekdays 8:45–5:30, Sat. 8:45–5.*

Specialty Stores
Aboriginal Art   Aboriginal art includes functional items, such as boomerangs and spears, as well as paintings and ceremonial implements that testify to a rich culture of legends and dreams. Although much of this artwork remains strongly traditional in character, the tools and colors used in Western art have fired the imaginations of many Aboriginal artists. The two outstanding sources of Aboriginal art are Arnhem Land and the Central Desert Region, which are close to Darwin and

Alice Springs, respectively. While there is no shortage of Aboriginal artwork in either place, much of the best artwork finds its way into the galleries of Sydney and Melbourne.

Aboriginal Art Centre has a shop that sells a variety of Aboriginal art, from large sculptures to bark paintings and such small collectibles as carved emu eggs. The museum shop also sells tribal art from Papua New Guinea. *117 George St., The Rocks, tel. 02/247-9625. Open daily 10-5.*

Aboriginal Art and Craft Museum, inside the Hogarth Gallery, displays superb bark paintings, wood carvings, and limited-edition prints that are suitable for the serious collector who can afford the best in contemporary Aboriginal art. *7 Walker La., Paddington, tel. 02/360-6839. Open Tues.-Sat. 11-5.*

Coo-Ee Aboriginal Art has a wide selection of "wearable" Aboriginal artwork, including jewelry and T-shirts painted with abstract designs, at moderate prices. *98 Oxford St., Paddington, tel. 02/332-1544. Open Mon.-Sat. 10:30-6.*

Books **Ariel Bookshop** is a browser's delight. This large, bright bookshop at the lower end of Paddington is the place to go for anything new or avant-garde. The shop also has the best collection of art books in Sydney. *42 Oxford St., Paddington, tel. 02/332-4581. Open daily 10 AM-midnight.*

The Travel Bookshop has Sydney's most extensive range of maps, guides, armchair travel books, and histories. *20 Bridge St., tel. 02/241-3554. Open Mon.-Sat. 9-5, Sun. 11-4.*

Bush Apparel **R. M. Williams** is the place where every stockman buys his Akubra hat, Drizabone riding coat, plaited kangaroo-skin belt, and moleskin trousers. *389 George St., tel. 02/262-2228. Open Mon.-Wed. and Fri. 9-5:30, Thurs. 9-9, Sat. 9-4.*

Crafts **Australian Craftworks** has a varied selection of superb woodwork, ceramics, knitwear, and glassware, as well as small souvenirs made by leading Australian crafts workers. Many of the wares are displayed in the cells of this former police station. *127 George St., The Rocks, tel. 02/247-7156. Open Mon.-Sat. 9-7, Sun. 10-7.*

Knitwear **Dorian Scott** sells a wide range of all-Australian knitwear for men, women, and children. The merchandise includes bright, bold high-fashion garments as well as sweaters and scarves in natural colors. *105 George St., The Rocks, tel. 02/247-4090. Open daily 9:30-6.*

Jenny Kee is the shop as well as the designer, who is best known for her eye-catching knitwear featuring Australian flora and fauna. Each garment is hand knitted and expensive. *2nd Floor, Strand Arcade, tel. 02/231-3027. Open Mon.-Wed. and Fri. 10-5:30, Thurs. 10-9, Sat. 10-5.*

Opals Australia has a virtual monopoly on the world's supply of this fiery gemstone, and nowhere else is there such a huge range from which to choose. The least expensive stones are doublets, which consist of a thin shaving of opal mounted on a plastic base. Sometimes the opal is covered by a quartz crown, in which case it becomes a triplet. The most expensive stones are the solid opals, which cost anything from a few hundred dollars to a few thousand. Opals are sold at souvenir shops all over the city, but anyone who intends to buy a valuable stone should go to an opal specialist.

Flame Opals sells nothing but solid opals, set in either sterling silver or 18-carat gold. The shop has a wide selection of black, white, and

Queensland boulder opals, which have a distinctive depth and luster. The sales staff is very helpful. *119 George St., The Rocks, tel. 02/247–3446. Open weekdays 9–7, Sat. 10–5, Sun. 11:30–5.*

Van Brugge House is a duty-free store that offers a wide range of souvenirs in addition to its stunning ground-floor showroom displaying the world's largest retail supply of opals. Customers can observe as artisans cut and polish the stones or watch a video of the miners at work. *37 Pitt St., Sydney, tel. 02/251–2833. Open Mon.–Sat. 10–6, Sun. 1–6.*

Records **Folkways** has an especially impressive range of Australian bush, folk, and Aboriginal records. *282 Oxford St., Paddington, tel. 02/361–3980. Open weekdays 9–9, Sat. 9–6, Sun. 11–6.*

T-Shirts and Towels **Ken Done,** a painter and former advertising man, catches the sunny side of Sydney with vivid, vibrant colors and bold brush strokes. His shop sells a variety of practical products that display his distinctive designs, including bed linens, sunglasses, beach towels, and T-shirts. *123 George St., The Rocks, tel. 02/251–6099. Open weekdays 9–6, Sat. 9–5, Sun. 10–4.*

Sports and the Outdoors

Participant Sports

Golf More than 80 golf courses lie within a 40-kilometer (25-mile) radius of the Sydney Harbour Bridge, 35 of them public courses where visitors are welcome. Golf clubs and electric carts are usually available for hire, but caddies are not.

Bondi Golf Club is a nine-hole public course offering challenging play on the cliffs overlooking famous Bondi Beach. *5 Military Rd., N. Bondi, tel. 02/30–1981. Visitors welcome every day. Greens fees $8.*

Moore Park Golf Club is a gently undulating course located barely 2 kilometers (1 mile) from the city center. *Cleveland St. and Anzac Parade, Moore Park, tel. 02/663–3960. Visitors welcome every day by arrangement with club pro Max Forrest. Greens fees: $12 weekdays, $20 weekends.*

A 90-minute drive northwest of Sydney, **Riverside Oaks PGA National Golf Club** offers spectacular golf in a classic bush setting on the banks of the Hawkesbury River. *O'Brien's Rd., Cattai, tel. 045/72–8477. Visitors welcome every day. Greens fees: $38 weekdays, $75 weekends (weekend fee includes golf cart and lunch).*

Jogging One of the finest jogging tracks in the city is the route from the Opera House along the edge of the harbor through the Royal Botanic Gardens to Mrs. Macquarie's Chair. At lunchtime on weekdays, this track is crowded with corporate joggers. In the eastern suburbs, an official jogging track runs south along the cliffs from Bondi Beach; it is marked by distance indicators and includes a number of exercise stations.

Tennis **Cooper Park Tennis Courts** is a complex of eight synthetic grass courts situated in a park surrounded by bush about 5 kilometers (3 miles) east of the city center. *Off Suttie Rd., Cooper Pk., Double Bay, tel. 02/389–9259. Cost: weekdays $14 per hr 8 AM–4 PM, $15 per hr after 5 PM, $17 per hr under floodlights to 10 PM; weekends add $1 for each time period.*

Situated in a park close to Central Station, **Jensen's Tennis Centre** consists of four synthetic grass courts. *Prince Alfred Pk., Surry Hills, tel. 02/698–9451. Cost: weekdays $11 per hr 7 AM–4 PM, $14 per hr 5–6 PM, $16 per hr 7–10 PM; weekends $15 per hr.*

Moore Park Tennis Courts have 10 courts set in a shady park approximately 2½ kilometers (1½ miles) from the city center. *Lang Rd. and Anzac Parade, Paddington, tel. 02/313–8000. Cost: $15 per hr 7 AM–5 PM, $17 per hr 6 PM–10 PM and weekends.*

Windsurfing The bays and inlets of Sydney Harbour offer great windsurfing opportunities, and **Rose Bay Windsurfer School** rents Windsurfers and gives individual lessons for $35 per hour. *1 Vickery Ave., Rose Bay, tel. 02/371–7036. Cost: $12 per hr, $15 for high-performance boards. Open daily Oct.–Mar., 9–6 (weather permitting).*

Spectator Sports

Cricket So leisurely is the pace of this game that to the uninitiated it looks more like an esoteric religious ritual than a sport. Despite the gentlemanly white garb and the tea breaks, however, this is a game of power and torrid passions. For Australians, the pinnacle of excitement is The Ashes, when they take to the field against their age-old rivals and forebears—the English. It happens every other summer (December–January), and the two nations take turns hosting it. The Australians have it in '94–'95 and '96–'97. *The Sydney Cricket Ground, Moore Pk., Paddington, tel. 02/360–6601. Season runs Oct.–Mar.*

Football Rugby league, known locally as "footie," is Sydney's winter addiction. This is a fast, gutsy, physical game that bears some similarities to North American football, although the action is more constant and the ball cannot be passed forward. *Sydney Football Stadium, Moore Pk., Paddington, tel. 02/360–6601. Season runs Apr.–Sept.*

Surfing Several international surfing competitions are held on Sydney's beaches, including the Coca-Cola Classic in April, the O'Neill Pro at Bondi Beach in March, and the Mambo Pro in December, also at Bondi Beach. For dates of international and local events, see the entertainment pages of the *Sydney Morning Herald*.

Beaches

The boom of the surf could well be Sydney's summer theme song: Forty beaches lie within the Sydney metropolitan area. With their fine, golden sand, average water temperature of 68° and surf ranging from sheltered harbor waters to crushing breakers, it's little wonder these beaches have Sydneysiders addicted to the pleasures of sun, sea, and sand.

If your hotel is located on the city side of the harbor, the logical choice for a day at the beach is to go to the southern ocean beaches between Bondi and Maroubra. On the north side of the harbor, Manly is easily accessible by ferry, but beaches farther north involve a long trip by car or public transport.

Lifeguards are on duty at most of Sydney's ocean beaches, and the patrolled areas are indicated by flags. "Swim between the flags" is an adage that is drummed into every Australian child, with very good reason: The undertow and sidewash can be very dangerous. Topless sunbathing is common at all Sydney beaches, but nudity is

Balmoral, **10**
Bondi, **14**
Botany Bay, **20**
Bronte, **16**
Bungan Beach, **3**
Camp Cove, **12**
Clovelly, **17**
Collaroy/Narrabeen, **5**
Coogee, **18**
Cronulla, **21**
Dee Why/Long Reef, **6**
Freshwater, **7**
Lady Jane Beach, **11**
Manly, **8**
Maroubra, **19**
Newport, **2**
Nielsen Park, **13**
Palm Beach, **1**
Shelly, **9**
Tamarama, **15**
Warriewood, **4**

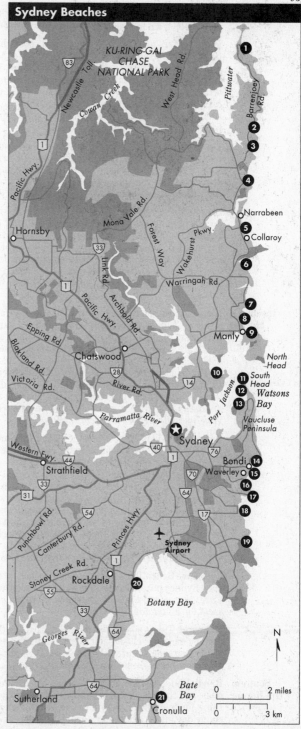

Sydney Beaches

permitted at only two, Lady Jane, on the south side of the harbor, and Obelisk, a north-side harbor beach with difficult access.

Many visitors to Sydney are concerned about sharks. While there is no shortage of sharks both inside and outside the harbor, most Sydney beaches are protected by nets, and the last shark attack in Sydney waters occurred more than 30 years ago. A more common hazard is the jellyfish, known locally as the bluebottle, which inflicts a painful sting. Fortunately, this danger is confined to the later part of the summer, and only rarely do the wind and currents send these jellyfish onto the beaches in any numbers.

The water pollution problem that made bathing off Sydney's beaches a health risk in 1990 has now been largely overcome. The sewage hasn't gone away—it's simply being pumped farther out to sea; however, even this stopgap solution has made it safe to go into the water again.

Another beach-related problem is the risk of skin cancer, caused by excessive exposure to sunlight. As a result of their addiction to a powerful sun, Australians suffer from this form of cancer more than any other people on earth, and the depletion of the ozone layer has increased the risk. The precautions are simple and should be followed by every visitor: Wear a hat to the beach, sit in the shade between 11 AM and 3 PM, and protect your skin with sun block at all times.

Inside the Harbor

Nielsen Park. This beach at the end of the Vaucluse Peninsula is small by Sydney standards, but behind the sand is a large, shady park that is ideal for picnics. The headlands at either end of the beach are especially popular for their magnificent views across the harbor. Despite the crowds, it is always possible to find a quiet spot on the grass. The beach is protected by a semicircular net, and swimmers should not be deterred by the correct name of this beach—Shark Bay. The shop behind the beach sells a limited range of snacks. Parking is often difficult on weekends. *Vaucluse Rd., Vaucluse. Bus 325 from Circular Quay.*

Camp Cove. This crescent-shape beach just inside South Head is where Sydney's fashionable crowd comes to see and be seen. The gentle slope of the beach and the relatively calm water make this a safe playground for young children. The shop at the northern end of the beach sells a variety of salad rolls and fresh fruit juices, as well as the usual snacks. The grassy knoll at the southern end of the beach has a plaque to commemorate the spot where Captain Arthur Phillip, the commander of the First Fleet, first set foot inside Sydney Harbour. Parking is limited, and anyone arriving by car after 10 AM on weekends will usually have a long walk to the beach. *Cliff St., Watsons Bay. Bus 324 or 325 from Circular Quay.*

Lady Jane Beach. This small, secluded beach is the only easily accessible Sydney beach where nude bathing is allowed. *Access via Camp Cove, then along the path above the shop and a short, difficult descent by ladder down the cliff face.*

Balmoral. This is a long, peaceful beach backed by parkland in one of Sydney's most exclusive northern suburbs. The Esplanade, which runs along the back of the beach, has several snack bars. *Raglan St., Mosman. Ferry from Circular Quay to Taronga Zoo, then Bus 238.*

South of the Harbor

Bondi. Wide, wonderful Bondi (pronounced *bond-eye*) is the most famous and the most crowded of all Sydney beaches. Bondi has something for just about everyone, and the droves who flock here on a sunny day give it a bustling, carnival atmosphere unmatched by any other Sydney beach. Facilities at Bondi include toilets and showers, and many cafés, ice-cream stands, and restaurants are located on Campbell Parade, which runs behind the beach. Family groups tend to prefer the more sheltered northern end of the beach. To the south, a path winds along the sea-sculpted cliffs to Tamarama. *Campbell Parade, Bondi. Bus 380 from Circular Quay via Elizabeth and Oxford Sts.*

Tamarama. This small, fashionable beach is one of Sydney's prettiest, but the rocky headlands that squeeze close to the beach on either side make it less than ideal for swimming. The café at the back of the beach sells open sandwiches, fresh fruit juices, and fruit whips. Surfing is not allowed. *Tamarama Marine Dr., Waverley. Bus 391 from Bondi Junction or a 10-min walk along the cliffs from south end of Bondi Beach.*

Bronte. If you want an ocean beach close to the city and with good facilities, a choice of sand or parkland, and a terrific setting, this one is hard to beat. The beach is surrounded by a wooded park of palm trees and Norfolk Island pines. The park includes a playground and sheltered picnic tables, and several snack bars lie in the immediate area. The breakers can be fierce here, but the sea pool at the southern end of the beach offers safe swimming at any time. *Bronte Rd., Waverley. Bus 378 from Central Station.*

Clovelly. This tiny beach sits at the end of a long, keyhole-shaped inlet where swimming is safe even on the roughest day. There are toilet facilities but no snack bars or shops in the immediate area. *Clovelly Rd. Bus 339 from Argyle St., Millers Point (The Rocks); Bus 329 from Bondi Junction; Bus 341 from Central Station.*

Coogee. This lively beach is protected by a reef that offers calmer swimming conditions than those found at its neighbors. The grassy headland to the north offers marvelous views but scarcely any shade. The beach is located near a major shopping area, but the local take-out shops offer little more than fried fish and chips. *Coogee Bay Rd. Bus 373 from Circular Quay or Bus 372 from Central Station.*

Maroubra. This expansive beach is very popular with surfers, although anyone looking for more than waves will probably be unimpressed by the rather scrappy surroundings and the lackluster shopping area. *Marine Parade. Bus 395 from Central Station or Bus 396 from Circular Quay.*

Botany Bay. Lady Robinson's Beach stretches for several miles along this wide bay, but the bleak, featureless view and nearby heavy traffic make it one of the least attractive of all Sydney beaches. *Grand Parade, Brighton-le-Sands. Bus 303 from Circular Quay.*

Cronulla. This is the southernmost and largest beach in the metropolitan area, and even on the hottest day you can escape the crowds here. A good surf is usually running at this beach, and the sand is backed by parkland. Cronulla is a long way from the city, however, and its attractions do not justify a long trip for anyone not staying in the area. *Kingsway, Cronulla. Train from the city.*

North of the Harbor   **Shelly.** This delightful little beach is protected by a headland rising behind it to form a green, shady park. It is well endowed, food-wise. The snack shop on the beach sells light refreshments, and the Fairy Bower Teahouse, which serves delicious lunches and Sunday breakfasts at tables along the waterfront, is within easy walking distance. The beach is crowded on weekends, and parking in the area is nearly impossible. *Marine Parade, Manly. Ferry from Circular Quay to Manly and a 1-km (½-mi) walk.*

Manly. This is the Bondi Beach of the north shore—a large, popular beach that caters to everyone except those who want to get away from it all. The beach itself is well equipped with changing and toilet facilities, and the nearby shopping area, The Corso, is lined with cafés, souvenir shops, and ice-cream parlors. For anyone coming from the city, the ferry ride makes a day at Manly more a holiday than just an excursion to the beach. *N. Steyne. Ferry from Circular Quay, then a short walk.*

Freshwater. This small beach is protected by sprawling headlands on either side, making it a popular beach for families. The surf club on the beach has good facilities as well as a small shop that sells light refreshments. *The Esplanade, Harbord. Bus 139 from Manly.*

Dee Why/Long Reef. These two beaches are separated by a narrow channel running between the ocean and Dee Why Lagoon. Long Reef Beach is remoter and much quieter than its southern neighbor, but Dee Why has better surfing conditions, a big sea pool, and several take-out shops. *The Strand, Dee Why. Bus 136 from Manly.*

Collaroy/Narrabeen. This is actually a single beach that passes through two suburbs. Its main attractions are its size—it's almost 3½ kilometers (2 miles) long—and the fact that it's always possible to escape the crowds here. The shops are concentrated at the southern end of the beach. *Pittwater Rd. Bus 155 or 157 from Manly; Bus 182 or 190 from the city (Wynyard).*

Warriewood. This enticing, petite cove at the bottom of looming cliffs has excellent conditions for surfers and windsurfers. For swimmers and sunbathers, however, the beach does not justify the difficult journey down the steep cliffs. Anyone traveling by public transport faces a long walk from the nearest bus stop. Basic toilet facilities are available on the beach, but there are no shops nearby. *Narrabeen Park Parade. Bus 184 or 190 from the city (Wynyard); Bus 155 from Manly.*

Bungan Beach. If you *really* want to get away from it all, this is the beach for you. Very few Sydneysiders have discovered Bungan, and those who have would like to keep it to themselves. As well as being relatively empty, this wide, attractive beach is one of the cleanest due to the prevailing currents. Access to the beach involves a difficult hike down a wood staircase, and there are no facilities. *Beach Rd., off Barrenjoey Rd., Mona Vale. Bus 190 from the city (Wynyard).*

Newport. With its backdrop of hills and Norfolk Island pines, this broad sweep of sand is one of the finest of the northern beaches. Within easy walking distance is a shopping center offering one of the best selections of cafés and take-out shops of any Sydney beach. Newport is known for its body surfing, and the atmosphere is fairly relaxed. *Barrenjoey Rd. Bus 190 from the city (Wynyard).*

Palm Beach. The wide, golden sands of Palm Beach mark the northern end of Sydney's beaches—a fitting finale that saves much of the best until last. The beach runs along one side of a long peninsula that separates Pittwater from the Pacific Ocean. Bathers can easily cross from the ocean side to the calm waters and sailing boats on the Pittwater side. The view from the lighthouse at the northern end of the beach is well worth the walk; on a windy day, the southern end of the beach affords some protection. Nearby shops sell light snacks. The suburb of Palm Beach is a favorite with successful filmmakers and with Sydney's wealthy elite, many of whom own weekend homes in the area. *Ocean Rd., Palm Beach. Bus 190 from the city (Wynyard).*

Dining

Given Sydney's ethnic makeup and climate, it should come as no surprise that its most popular cooking styles are Mediterranean and Southeast Asian. Nothing illustrates this point more than the seafood that is served in Sydney's restaurants. "Seafood"—once fish and chips with tartare sauce on the side—today might arrive at your table either spiced with a piquant lemongrass sauce, grilled with sweet red peppers and moistened with olive oil, carved into paper-thin sashimi, made fiery with a coconut and chili paste dressing, or simply panfried with lemon and butter.

The most recent trend to sweep the Sydney dining scene is casual outdoor eating. The sidewalk café, for many years frowned upon by municipal planning authorities, has taken firm root and transformed areas such as East Sydney, The Rocks, Leichardt, and the back-streets of Kings Cross. For anyone traveling on a budget, these relaxed, inexpensive café-bistros are the way to go.

Less expensive cafés and restaurants are usually not licensed to sell liquor, but alcohol can be consumed on the premises with a meal. Such restaurants are known as "bring your own"—"BYO" in common parlance. Bottles of wine can usually be obtained from the nearest pub.

Tipping is not compulsory, but it is customary to add 10% to the bill for good service. Credit cards are accepted in all but the smallest restaurants and cafés. Some establishments may charge a small surcharge on weekends and holidays.

Highly recommended restaurants are indicated by a star ★.

Category	Cost*
$$$$	over $50
$$$	$35–$50
$$	$20–$35
$	under $20

per person, excluding drinks and service

American **Hard Rock Cafe.** Loud music and flashy neon decor make this branch
$ of the international chain a favorite with the younger set—and that means there's always a wait. A fabulous collection of rock-and-roll memorabilia adorns the walls, and a Cadillac is suspended from the ceiling. The fare is simple, but servings are large and enjoyable: enormous hamburgers, chicken wings, onion rings, ribs, fish, and great salads. For dessert, don't miss the sumptuous strawberry shortcake; at the cocktail bar, try the Hurricane and hold on! The service is fast and friendly. *121–129 Crown St., Darlinghurst, tel. 02/331–1116. No reservations. Dress: casual. AE, MC, V.*

Australian **Bennelong.** Patrons at the Opera House's fine dining room are pay-
$$$$ ing a premium for the view—but what a view! This regal, airy restaurant is set against the glittering backdrop of the harbor and the bridge, and the pretheater dinner is a perfect prelude to a big night out in one of the concert halls. The à la carte menu has a few tradi-

Dining

Atlas Bistro
and Bar, **31**

Bar Paradiso, **13**

Bayswater
Brasserie, **27**

Bennelong, **5**

Beppi's, **36**

Bilson's, **4**

Brooklyn Thai, **12**

Buon Ricordo, **32**

Captain Torres, **37**

Chinatown Centre, **38**

Chinatown Gardens
Restaurant, **38**

Choy's Jin Jiang, **17**

Dov, **33**

Doyle's at the Quay, **3**

The Edge, **30**

Gastronomia
Chianti, **41**

Hard Rock Café, **29**

Imperial Peking
Harbourside, **2**

Jordon's, **19**

Kables, **11**

Kamogawa, **18**

The Last Aussie
Fishcaf, **26**

L'Aubbergarde, **43**

Malaya, **39**

MCA Café, **9**

Mohr Fish, **42**

Rockpool, **8**

Skydining, **16**

Taylors, **34**

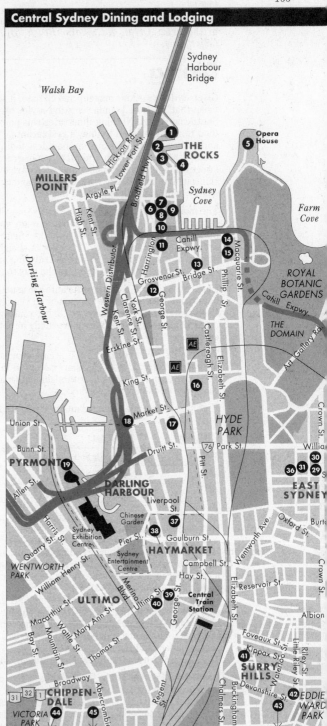

Central Sydney Dining and Lodging

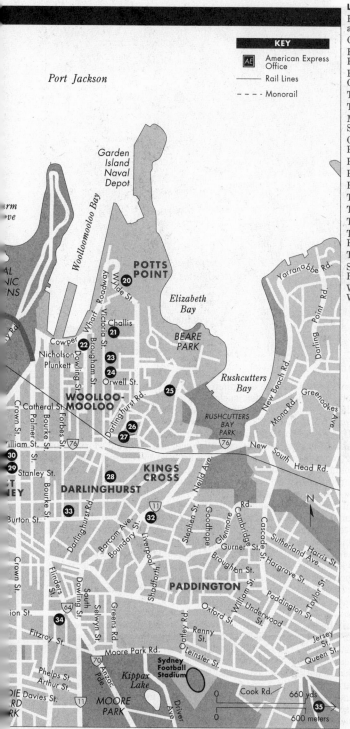

Port Jackson

KEY

AE American Express Office
—— Rail Lines
– – – Monorail

Garden Island Naval Depot

POTTS POINT

Elizabeth Bay

BEARE PARK

Rushcutters Bay

RUSHCUTTERS BAY PARK

WOOLLOO-MOOLOO

New South Head Rd.

KINGS CROSS

DARLINGHURST

PADDINGTON

Sydney Football Stadium

Kippax Lake

MOORE PARK

Lodging
Brooklyn [...] and Breakfas[...]
Challis Lodge, [...]
Harbour Rocks Hotel, **7**
Hotel Inter-Continental, **14**
The Jackson Hotel, **23**
The Kendall, **24**
Morgan's of Sydney, **28**
Oakford, Potts Point, **20**
Park Hyatt, **1**
Pensione Sydney, **45**
Ravesi's, **35**
The Regent, **11**
The Ritz-Carlton, **15**
The Russell, **10**
The Sebel Town House, **25**
The Stafford, **6**
Sydney Travellers Rest Hotel, **40**
Woolloomooloo Waters, **22**

0 660 yds
0 600 meters

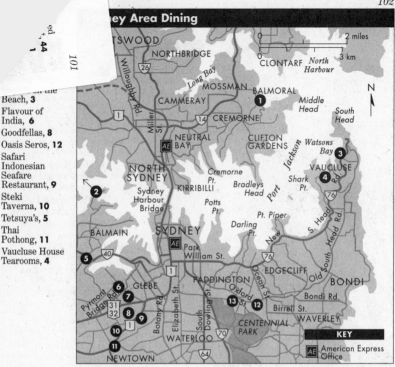

101

Beach, **3**

Flavour of
India, **6**

Goodfellas, **8**

Oasis Seros, **12**

Safari
Indonesian
Seafare
Restaurant, **9**

Steki
Taverna, **10**

Tetsuya's, **5**

Thai
Pothong, **11**

Vaucluse House
Tearooms, **4**

tional favorites, such as grilled lamb, chicken, and beef, as well as more fashionable dishes, such as Tasmanian scallops and Atlantic salmon cutlets. *Sydney Opera House, Bennelong Point, Circular Quay, tel. 02/250–7578. Reservations required. Dress: casual. AE, DC, MC, V. Closed Sun., holidays, 2 wks during Christmas.*

$$$$ **Kables.** Serge Dansereau, executive chef at the Regent's formal din-
★ ing room, is at the vanguard of a crusade to redefine Australian cooking by the innovative use of regional produce. Dishes such as seared Queensland scallops with roasted radicchio and a leek-and-red-wine sauce; roast milk-fed Ilabo lamb with rosemary, potato, and red onion fondue; and chartreuse of game duck with morels, pumpkin gnocchi, and white asparagus are a tribute to his persist-ence in obtaining supplies from small, distinctive producers of fish, fruit, cheese, and game. The wine list matches the originality of the menu, with bottles from some of the country's most notable small wine makers. The dinner menu is expensive but the fixed-price lunch offers exceptional dining at a reasonable price. *The Regent of Sydney, 199 George St., tel. 02/238–0000. Reservations required. Jacket and tie required. AE, DC, MC, V. No lunch Sat., closed Sun., no dinner Mon.*

$$$$ **Oasis Seros.** Food is taken very seriously indeed at this fashionably
★ stark restaurant, which has become hallowed ground for Sydney's gastronomes. Chef Philip Searle relies on bold combinations of in-gredients and recipes from the cuisines of France and Thailand to create exciting new taste sensations. Seared fillet of kangaroo with marinated beetroot and roast duck with ginger buns are recom-mended selections from the small, seasonal menu. For dessert, the checkerboard of star-anise ice cream is highly recommended. The fixed-price lunch menu offers a wide selection. *495 Oxford St., Pad-*

dington, tel. 02/361–3377. Reservations required. Jacket and tie recommended. AE, DC, MC, V. Lunch Fri. Closed Sun., Mon., Dec. 25–mid-Jan.*

$$$ **Bathers Pavilion.** Views of one of the city's prettiest harbor beaches and fabulous food make this chic restaurant decorated all in white one of the very best in Sydney. A Southeast Asian accent is manifest in such dishes as mint-flavored prawn spring rolls and grilled spatchcock marinated in chili paste and served with a snake bean salad. Celebrity spotters will find names worth dropping among the lunchtime crowd, and the Sunday breakfasts from 9 to 11 are well worth the 15-minute drive from the city. *4 The Esplanade, Balmoral, tel. 02/968–1133. Reservations advised. Dress: casual. AE, DC, MC, V.*

$$$ **Darling Mills.** Located in a neighborhood well known for its dining, Darling Mills serves modern Australian food cooked with flair and imagination. Bare brick walls, a stone-tile floor, stained Gothic windows, and columns of light filtered through greenery create an atmosphere that is somewhere between a Bavarian beer cellar and a church. Start with a warm seafood salad of prawns and Balmain bugs with curry butter. King Island beef fillet with roasted thyme potatoes and grilled field mushrooms, lamb loin stuffed with spinach and couscous, and grilled yellowfin tuna with braised fennel and roasted sweet red peppers are featured on the Italian-influenced menu. Vegetables come fresh from the restaurateur's farm. For dessert, try the sambuca soufflé with star-anise ice cream. *134 Glebe Point Rd. (opposite Post Office), Glebe, tel. 02/660–5666. Reservations advised. Dress: casual but neat. AE, DC, MC, V. Closed Sun., no lunch Sat. or Mon.*

$$ **Centennial Park Café.** Surrounded by parklands about 3 kilometers (2 miles) from the city center, this fashionable café has a fresh, interesting menu that is perfect for breakfast, lunch, or afternoon tea. The breakfast menu features muesli, pastries, fruit bread, homemade preserves, and porridge, and in the winter, sausages, beans, and kippers. For lunch, try either the barbecued fish with roasted red peppers, lemon butter, and potatoes or the roast kangaroo rump with tomato jam and polenta. If you find the buttermilk pudding hard to resist, there are acres of greenery all around where you can walk it off afterwards. You might combine the café with a trip to Paddington Markets on Saturday morning. Be prepared to wait for a table at Sunday lunch. *Grand and Parks Drs., Centennial Pk., tel. 02/360–3355. No reservations. Dress: casual but neat. AE, MC, V. No dinner.*

$$ **The Edge.** Buried in Sydney's gourmet gulch, midway between the city and Kings Cross, this bistro-style restaurant combines fashionably minimalist decor and food with a Mediterranean touch. Main courses include deep-fried perch with chili and lime, as well as grilled Italian sausage with garlic, mashed potatoes, and lemon. Pizzas from the wood-fired oven are some of the best in town, and they make a less expensive alternative to other main course dishes. Toppings include scampi, scallops, prawns, mushrooms with fresh herbs and fennel, and roast tomato and pancetta. The buttermilk pudding with summer berries is heavenly. *60 Riley St., East Sydney, tel. 02/360–1372. No reservations. Dress: casual. AE, MC, V. No dinner Sun.*

$$ **Goodfellas.** Prices at this city-fringe newcomer would be considerably higher were the restaurant located at the more fashionable eastern edge of town. The simple, uncluttered decor complements food that is unfussy and superbly presented. Standout main courses on the enticing menu include seared kangaroo with sweet-potato gnocchi and beetroot, an herb-crusted roast chicken breast with

sweet corn and carrots, and panfried rare beef with mushroom ravioli and parsley purée. The wine list is first-class. *111 King St., Newtown, tel. 02/557–1175. Reservations advised weekends. Dress: casual. AE, MC, V. No lunch.*

$$ **Vaucluse House Tearooms.** Set in the grounds of a colonial mansion, this pretty sandstone pavilion is one of the best places in Sydney for a leisurely lunch. The summer menu includes a superb Caesar salad, soups, braised tuna, and goat cheese wrapped in grape leaves. The baguettes are excellent value, and the trays of hot scones that emerge from the oven at mid-afternoon are practically irresistible. On weekdays, the serenity of the setting makes it well worth the 15-minute drive from the city, but avoid Sunday lunch. The courtyard tables, shaded by a giant Moreton Bay fig, are the place to sit in warm weather. *Vaucluse House, Wentworth Ave., Vaucluse, tel. 02/337–5027. No reservations. Dress: casual but neat. MC, V. No dinner; closed Mon.*

$ **Atlas Bistro and Bar.** This barnlike restaurant above a garage has cafeteria decor, but the menu offers dining with a dash of style at bargain prices, so there's a surprisingly hip crowd. Main courses include grilled spatchcock with chili, duck with green curry, spinach-and-ricotta ravioli, and corned beef with mashed potatoes and parsley sauce. The wine list shows a discerning palate, but the markup is steep. *95 Riley St., East Sydney, tel. 02/360–3811. No reservations. Dress: casual but neat. MC, V. No lunch Sat.–Tues.*

$ **MCA Café.** Great value, an imaginative menu, and a stunning location on the western side of Circular Quay—what more could you ask for than this chic café on the ground floor of the Museum of Contemporary Art? You can choose from a selection of salads, pasta, and fish dishes, from light snacks to substantial meals. Desserts include meringue filled with berries and mascarpone (Italian cream cheese), and peaches poached in champagne and served with vanilla ice cream. The café operates under the direction of Neil Perry, the chef behind the highly regarded—and far more expensive—Rockpool. On sunny days, eat outside on the terrace and watch the world go by. *Museum of Contemporary Art, West Circular Quay, The Rocks, tel. 02/241–4253. No reservations. Dress: casual. AE, MC, V. No dinner.*

Chinese **Imperial Peking Harbourside.** Several Sydney restaurants wear the
$$$$ Imperial Peking tag, but this glamorous restaurant set in the shadow of the Harbour Bridge is the taipan of the family. The nighttime views alone make this a standout establishment, but, in spite of bouts of mediocrity, it is also one of Sydney's finest Chinese restaurants. Northern Chinese dishes are the specialty of this restaurant, including the favored Peking duck and beggar's chicken. Fresh crabs and lobsters are cooked in a variety of ways here, and you can request a demonstration of the art of noodle making. *15 Circular Quay W, The Rocks, tel. 02/247–7073. Reservations required. Dress: casual but neat. AE, DC, MC, V.*

$$$ **Choy's Jin Jiang.** Located upstairs in the prestigious Queen Victoria building, elegant Jin Jiang is the showpiece of Dominic Choy's five Chinese restaurants. The rosewood and turquoise decor, exquisite antiques, and tasteful furnishings enhance the pleasure of such dishes as drunken duck and seaweed with shallots, or duck smoked over camphor wood. The dumplings and lantern prawns sautéed with shallots, chili, and ginger are sublime. The service is formal but restrained, like the decor. *2nd Level, Queen Victoria Bldg., George St., tel. 02/261–3388. Reservations required. Jacket required. AE, DC, MC, V.*

$ **Chinatown Centre.** This cafeteria-style hall at the heart of the Chinatown district has about 20 food outlets offering a feast of Asian delicacies, from spicy Malaysian *laksa* to Thai *tom yum* soup to Chinese noodles. It's bustling and bright and there is no inducement to linger after your meal, but the price is a real attraction: It would be almost impossible to spend more than $10 per person. At most stalls, the menu is displayed in the form of photographs and the food is cooked to order, usually in a couple of minutes. Stalls are open for both lunch and dinner. *25 Dixon St. (corner Goulburn St.), tel. 02/212–3335. No reservations. Dress: casual. No credit cards.*

$ **Chinatown Gardens Restaurant.** The forte of this vast restaurant is *yum cha* (also known as *dim sum*), an inexpensive lunch that consists of a number of hors d'oeuvre–size servings of Chinese food. Just select your dishes from the baskets or trolleys that are ferried around the room by an army of waitresses. Dishes might include tiny dumplings filled with prawns, spring rolls, pork buns, or duck in yam batter. The restaurant is often packed at lunchtime but waiting time is seldom more than five minutes. It's open for dinner, too. *Levels 4 and 5, Chinatown Centre, 25 Dixon St., tel. 02/212–2511. No reservations. Dress: casual but neat. AE, DC, MC, V.*

French **Berowra Waters Inn.** Surrounded by bushland and water, this is the
$$$$ benchmark by which Australia's haute cuisine restaurants are
★ judged—a position it has maintained consistently since the early 1980s. The service is superb, and the atmosphere pleasant and relaxed, but Gay Bilson's creative cooking is what makes this spot so popular. New dishes are constantly added to a menu that includes such inventive offerings as a terrine of pigs' trotters and pickled pork cooked in wine, ginger, and spices, or gefilte fish served on a bed of horseradish cream with cucumber. Other favorites include tripe lyonnaise, roasted pigeon with muscatel grapes, and grilled tuna with sorrel leaves, black olives, lemon rind, and virgin olive oil. Crème brûlée is standard on the dessert menu, although new sweets are introduced regularly. *Berowra Waters Rd., Berowra Waters, tel. 02/456–1027. Reservations required. Dress: casual but neat. AE, DC, MC, V. No dinner Sun. Closed Mon.–Thurs.*

$$$$ **Bilson's.** If your budget will stretch to just one expensive meal in
★ Sydney, this glamorous waterfront restaurant is the place for it. Located on the upper level of the international passenger terminal, Bilson's uses the best local ingredients to create such dishes as boned spatchcock (a small chicken) with watercress sauce and baked ham hocks with braised endive and mustard. Other main courses include roast tuna steak with mescalam salad, and medallions of veal with green-pepper sauce. The menu changes every eight weeks, the service is impeccable, and the wine list is one of the best in town. *Upper Level, International Passenger Terminal, Circular Quay W, tel. 02/251–5600. Reservations required. Jacket required. AE, DC, MC, V. No lunch Sat.*

$$ **L'Aubbergarde.** This is one of the few French restaurants in Sydney that is actually owned and run by a Frenchman. Gerard Pasquet has successfully operated L'Aubbergarde in its inner-city location for close to three decades. Like the menu, the decor in this petite two-room restaurant is 1960s Left Bank classic. Dishes include snails, frogs' legs, pepper steak, and rabbit casserole with mushrooms and an apple brandy cream sauce. Try the crêpes suzette for dessert. The service is personable and friendly. *353 Cleveland St., Surry Hills, tel. 02/319–5929. Reservations required. Dress: casual. AE, DC, MC, V. No lunch Sat. Closed Sun. and Dec. 25.*

Greek
$$

Steki Taverna. So evocative is the atmosphere of Greece here—from the bazouki music that spills out onto the dingy back street to the sizable and often voluble Greek clientele—that you'll wonder if you shouldn't be paying in drachmas instead of dollars. Start with the mixed platter for two, proceed to the moussaka, souvlaki, or one of the barbecued lamb dishes, and be prepared to join in the dancing. *2 O'Connell St., Newtown, tel. 02/516-2191. Reservations advised weekends. Dress: casual. MC, V. No lunch. Closed Mon., Tues.*

Indian
$$
★

Flavour of India. Fine northern Indian food served against a smart backdrop have made this city-fringe restaurant a popular choice for spice lovers. For a wide-ranging selection of taste sensations, start with the mixed entrée for two. For the main course, lamb in spinach sauce, beef *vindaloo* (a fiery-hot, mustard-laced curry dish), *malai kofta* (ground meat kabobs in butter-and-cream-enriched tomato sauce), and anything from the tandoor oven are recommended. *142 Glebe Point Rd., Glebe, tel. 02/692-0662. Reservations advised weekends. Dress: casual. AE, DC, MC, V. No lunch Sat.–Tues.*

Indonesian
$

Malaya. The Malaya has been in business for 20 years and has a loyal clientele at its city and North Shore locations. There is nothing even vaguely Eastern about the plain white walls and modern decor, but the strong points are consistency and low price. *Laksa* (rice and noodles in spicy coconut-milk soup) is the big favorite and is available with vegetables, chicken, king prawns, or seafood. Other dishes include chicken, beef, or fish curry, spring rolls, and noodles. *86 Walker St., N. Sydney, tel. 02/955-4306; 761 George St., (Central railway end), tel. 02/211-4659. Reservations advised Sat. Dress: casual. AE, DC, MC, V. Walker St. No lunch Sat. Closed Sun.*

$

Safari Indonesian Seafare Restaurant. This is the most popular Indonesian restaurant in Sydney, with large crowds drawn nightly to its inexpensive, authentic cooking. The restaurant extends through three rooms and is decorated with colored ceremonial umbrellas and masks. For starters try *lumpia* (spring rolls) or traditional Sumatran beef soup. Excellent vegetable dishes include *gado gado* (steamed vegetables with peanut sauce), jackfruit *gulai* (cooked in coconut and chili), and bean curd with soybeans. Also noteworthy are the seafood platter, whole fried fish served with ginger and sweet-and-sour sauce, and stuffed squid in coconut and chili sauce. Desserts consist of exotic fruits with ice cream or Indonesian black-rice pudding. Try the delicious nonalcoholic drink "Ice Campur," served with rosewater and Indonesian fruits. *22–26 King St., Newtown, tel. 02/51-4458. Reservations advised. Dress: casual. AE, DC, MC, V. BYOB. No lunch Sat.–Mon.*

International
$$
★

Bayswater Brasserie. One of the first to open in the brasserie boom of the early 1980s, this smart restaurant on the fringe of Kings Cross has remained the leader through a combination of flair, outstanding service, and a fresh and exciting menu. In true brasserie style, meals vary from Thai-style chicken to baby spinach salad with egg, bacon, and pine nuts to cotechino sausage with beetroot and mashed potato. The conservatory-style dining areas are delightful, but the lack of softening touches in the black-and-white interior creates a brisk atmosphere that may be more suitable for lunch than a romantic dinner. *32 Bayswater Rd., Kings Cross, tel. 02/357-2177. No reservations. Dress: casual but neat. DC, MC, V.*

$

Skydining. If you're looking for an inexpensive lunch in stylish surroundings in the heart of the city, this futuristic dining area on the top floor of the magnificent Skygarden shopping complex is just the place. Four food bars operate beneath the big domed roof, offering a choice of seafood, Italian pasta and pizzas, well-stuffed French-bread rolls, burgers, fruit juices, and pies. On weekdays, time your meal to avoid the 12:30 lunchtime crush of office workers. *Pitt St. bet. King and Market, opposite The Strand Arcade, tel. 02/231–1811. No reservations. Dress: casual. No credit cards. No dinner Fri.–Wed.; closed Sun.*

Italian
$$$$
Beppi's. Operated by the same dedicated owner for more than three decades, this city-fringe restaurant is a favorite among Sydney-siders who appreciate opulent surroundings, robust food, and superlative service. Tables are laid with white damask tablecloths and silver cutlery, and the walls are lined with wine bottles. Popular dishes include spaghetti with fresh crab sauce and saffron and carpaccio, whitebait fritters, and spaghetti in squid ink. Also recommended are the veal with eggplant and wine sauce and the sliced beef with rosemary, fresh cream, brandy, and mustard sauce. For dessert, sample the fresh fruit topped with brandy and ricotta cheese, or the peaches Bellini. *Yurong and Stanley Sts., E. Sydney, tel. 02/360–4391. Reservations required. Jacket required. AE, DC, MC, V. No lunch Sat. Closed Sun. and 3 wks following Dec. 24.*

$$$$
Taylors. The colonial sandstone facade may hark back to the earliest days of colonial Australia, but the surroundings and the menu at this stylish restaurant are flawlessly modern. One of Sydney's top restaurants, Taylors has a relaxed atmosphere and a menu that combines traditional Italian dishes with contemporary, light cuisine. Selections include a warm pasta salad with prawns, baked tomatoes, basil, and avocado, as well as pan-roasted veal in vermouth sauce with potatoes and artichokes. In summer, request a table in the conservatory; in winter, beside the open fire. *203–205 Albion St., Surry Hills, tel. 02/361–5100. Reservations required weekends. Dress: casual but neat. AE, DC, MC, V. No lunch. Closed Sun.*

$$$
Buon Ricordo. The northern Italian fare at this upscale restaurant maintains a reputation for invention teamed with consistency and is a longtime favorite with Sydney's gourmands. Served by a bright, friendly staff, the antipasto is always fresh and innovative, as are the menu's other delights, including carpaccio of salmon and grilled spatchcock basted with lemon and spices. The pasta and fresh fish are excellent, and the mascarpone soufflé is not to be missed for dessert. If you visit at the end of summer, the fresh figs wrapped in prosciutto and baked in gorgonzola and cream are highly recommended. *108 Boundary St., Paddington, tel. 02/360–6729. Reservations advised. Dress: casual but neat. AE, MC, V. No lunch Tues.–Thurs. Closed Sun.–Mon.*

$
Bar Paradiso. This slick bar/café transforms this shady square at the historic heart of the city into a southern European piazza. Meals can be ordered at the counter or from your table. The menu is tailored to produce fast, tasty meals for the office staff who descend on the place at lunchtime; focaccias, crusty rolls, salads, and pasta appear in many combinations. Save room for a superstrength espresso and cake. *7 Macquarie Pl., tel. 02/241–2141. No reservations. Dress: informal. No credit cards. No dinner.*

$
Gastronomia Chianti. Behind the big glass shopfront is a bustling food emporium that combines a bar, deli, coffee shop, and restaurant. Practically every Italian edible is available, from fresh *bocconcini* (small, soft balls of mozzarellalike cheese) to slices of warm suckling pig to fruity Siena cakes. The lunch menu is designed for the eat-and-run office workers who are the main clientele, and focaccia and well-stuffed rolls are favorites. The antipasto plate is excellent value. The evening menu relies heavily on pasta dishes. *444 Elizabeth St., Surry Hills, tel. 02/319–4748. Dinner reserva-*

tions advised. Dress: casual. MC, V. No dinner Mon.–Thurs. Closed Sun.

Japanese
$$$$
★

Kamogawa. At the foot of the giant Nikko Hotel, this restaurant attracted rave reviews and set a new standard in Sydney's Japanese cuisine when it opened in 1992. Diners can choose from three dining styles: either a *teppan* bar, sitting on mats in an individual tatami room, or a regular restaurant table. At the teppan bar, the buttery chicken, scallops, and melt-in-your-mouth steak are sliced and served with surgical knifework and theatrical flourishes. The formal service in the tatami rooms has been elevated to an art form, but the bill will probably be as memorable as the presentation. *Corn Exchange Building, Sussex and Market Sts., Darling Harbour, tel. 02/ 299–5533. Reservations advised. Jacket and tie required. AE, DC, MC, V. No lunch weekends.*

$$$$
★

Tetsuya's. The fusion of Oriental and Western flavors at this spacious, refined, inner-west restaurant has created probably the most exciting of Sydney's many Japanese dining experiences. Roasted and boned squab served with a white stock and smoky-flavored mushrooms; grilled prawns seasoned with tea and served with tomato, coriander, and olive oil sauce; and a mousse of lobster and sea urchin with pumpkin purée and shellfish jelly are typical examples from a menu that delights connoisseurs looking for something different. *729 Darling St., Rozelle, tel. 02/555–1017. Reservations required. Jacket and tie required. MC, V. BYOB. No lunch Tues. Closed Sun., Mon.*

Mixed Menu
$

Dov. This popular hangout for students across the road from East Sydney Technical College (Sydney's academy of all things avant-garde) offers casual, bistro dining, starkly chic decor, and a value-packed menu. The food is simple and robust and served with coarse Italian bread. The menu has a wide selection of inexpensive cold dishes, including chopped liver, grilled mushroom salad, onion tart, eggs mayonnaise, and grilled sweet peppers—all served with crusty rolls. Hot dishes include crumbed chicken and boiled beef with horseradish. The breakfasts are outstanding. *Forbes and Burton Sts., Darlinghurst, tel. 02/360–9594. No reservations. Dress: casual. No credit cards. Closed Sun.*

Seafood
$$$$
★

Rockpool. Winner of *Gourmet Traveller* magazine's 1992 award for Australia's best restaurant, this supertrendy restaurant is a showcase for one of Australia's most talented chefs. The five modern, plush dining areas include an oyster bar and a conservatory. Chef Neil Perry has plundered the culinary world to create such dishes as a salad of mudcrab with pork and lime-and-peanut sauce, smoked oysters with ginger and garlic, and prawns with polenta, mushrooms, and blackened onions. Nonfish dishes also appear on the menu. The fresh date tart is a longstanding favorite on the dessert menu. Though it's easy to spend well over $100 on a dinner for two, you can also dine extremely well for half that. The upstairs Oyster Bar is a less opulent and less expensive alternative to the restaurant. *109 George St., The Rocks (a few minutes' walk from the Regent Hotel and the heart of the city), tel. 02/252–1888. Reservations advised. Dress: casual but neat. AE, DC, MC, V. No lunch Sat. Closed Sun.*

$$$

Doyle's on the Beach. On a sunny day, a very Sydney thing to do is to eat fish-and-chips at this waterside restaurant. With sailing boats bobbing just a few feet away, the atmosphere is bustling, noisy, and informal, and the views of the city are unmatched. The dining room has been refurbished but still retains an old-fashioned Australian style in its woodgrain paneling, awnings, original ceiling, and wooden rafters. Doyle's has been serving seafood for more than five generations, and its specialties include John Dory, jewfish, snapper, and lobster cooked to order. Water taxis to Doyle's leave from the Commissioner's Steps at Circular Quay every half hour from 11:30 to 1:45 for lunch; the last return taxi leaves at 3:30. A second branch, **Doyle's at the Quay,** operates at the Overseas Terminal at Circular Quay, near the Opera House and Harbour Bridge. *11 Marine Parade, Watsons Bay, tel. 02/337–2007; Doyle's at the Quay, Overseas Terminal, tel. 02/252–3400. Reservations required. Dress: casual. DC, MC, V. Closed Dec. 25.*

$$$ **Jordon's.** Located in a delightful spot by the water at Darling Harbour, Jordon's has a large outdoor dining area that is far preferable to the noisy indoor restaurant. But even if you are inside, you can't miss the views of the courtyard and harbor, just a few steps away beyond the room's giant glass windows. Grilled swordfish, barramundi, jewfish, tuna, John Dory, and snapper are recommended here. Several meat entrées are available, as are such Japanese dishes as sashimi and fish or vegetable tempura. The atmosphere is lively, and the service is friendly though slow. Live music is featured in the evening. *197 Festival Market Pl., Darling Harbour, tel. 02/281–3711. Reservations advised weekends. Dress: casual but neat. AE, DC, MC, V.*

$$ **The Last Aussie Fishcaf.** Situated in a 1930s-style building, this restaurant is lively, noisy, informal, and a favorite with those who prefer live cabaret to culinary excellence. An enormous jukebox plays music from the '50s, while rock-and-roll dancers—who double as the wait staff—and the more enthusiastic customers strut their stuff. Fish-and-chips wrapped in paper is a recommended house specialty, and oyster lovers are in for a real treat. The menu is a fusion of flavors from Southeast Asia, Italy, and Cajun country. *24 Bayswater Rd., Kings Cross, tel. 02/356–2911. Reservations required. Dress: casual. AE, DC, MC, V. No lunch.*

$$ **Mohr Fish.** Great seafood, low prices, and a brisk, casual atmosphere mean that the tables at this tiny café are nearly always full. Collect a bottle of wine from the pub down the road, and choose from a wide variety of fresh fish—either grilled or deep-fried—accompanied by french fries or salad. Some French-inspired soups, such as bouillabaisse or *moules marinières* (mussel soup), are usually available. The fresh tarts are recommended. *202 Devonshire St., Surry Hills, tel. 02/318–1326. No reservations. Dress: casual. No credit cards. BYOB.*

Spanish   **Capitán Torres.** The old wood bar, stucco walls, and tile floor help
$$ capture the flavor of Spain in this restaurant where the aroma of garlic hangs heavy in the air. Start with *tapas* (hors d'oeuvres) and Spanish wine or sangria. Then select something from the large display of fresh seafood, including trout, bream, sardines, whiting, and leather jacket. Otherwise, consider the huge paella, a mélange of simmered fish, shellfish, chicken, and saffron rice. Suckling pig can be ordered for groups, and a banquet room is available upstairs. *73 Liverpool St., tel. 02/264– 5574. Reservations required weekends. Dress: casual. AE, DC, MC, V.*

Thai   **Brooklyn Thai.** The latest venture by wizard chef Prasit Prateep-
$$ prasen, this superb restaurant brings the sublime aromas of Thai cooking to a restored Victorian pub close to Circular Quay. Main courses include chicken curry with sweet potato, turmeric, and coconut milk; a medium-hot duck curry with coconut milk, lychees, pineapple, and cherry tomatoes; and a selection of superb stir-fry dishes with the emphasis on seafood. The *tom yum* soup is highly

recommended, as is the mango with sticky rice. The wine list offers an astute selection at moderate prices. Bare wood floors and the big bar create a boisterous atmosphere, and the restaurant is probably more suitable for lunch than a relaxing dinner. *Cnr. George and Grosvenor Sts., tel. 02/247–6744. Reservations advised. Dress: casual but neat. AE, DC, MC, V. No lunch Sat.; no dinner Mon.–Tues; closed Sun.*

$$ **Thai Pothong.** Thai cuisine is a favorite in this student quarter of Newtown, but despite its many competitors, this bright, cheerful restaurant remains a strong favorite. Service is snappy, and the sculptural flower arrangements create an atmosphere far more elegant than the price range would suggest. Recommended main courses are the clay pot of prawns, chicken, fish, and lemongrass in broth, and the sliced grilled beef with chili and lemon juice, accompanied by salad. *298 King St., Newtown, tel. 02/550–6277. Reservations advised weekends. Dress: casual. AE, DC, MC, V. No lunch weekends.*

Lodging

The price of accommodations in Sydney, which seemed to be heading toward the stratosphere for many years, tumbled in the early 1990s. Most city hotels have slashed their prices as they struggle for survival in a very competitive market. Discounts of around 30% on the published "rack" rate on hotel rooms are freely available, and it is now possible to find a modestly luxurious double room in a convenient location for between $80 and $150 per night.

The most expensive accommodations are in the five-star hotels close to the harbor, where even a discounted room will cost at least $225 per night. Yet there are a number of smaller hotels in the vicinity, concentrated in the historic Rocks area, that offer comfortable, atmospheric accommodation at about half the price of their glamorous neighbors.

If you arrive in Sydney without a hotel reservation, the best place to start looking is the **Travellers Information Service** (at the international airport) or the **New South Wales Travel Centre** (*see* Essential Information, *above*). Both act as clearinghouses for hotel rooms, and they can give you a significant saving on published room rates.

Highly recommended lodgings are indicated by a star ★ .

Category	Cost*
$$$$	over $275
$$$	$175–$275
$$	$85–$175
$	under $85

All prices are for a standard double room.

$$$$ **Hotel Inter-Continental.** The heart of this hotel is the Treasury Building, which dates from 1851. By incorporating the honey-color sandstone structure into the hotel's public areas, the architects have instilled a feeling of warmth and tradition in this sleek, sophisticated international hotel. Opened in 1985, it is near the harbor and within easy walking distance of Circular Quay, the Opera House, and the central business district. Australian motifs have been used extensively in the stylish rooms. The best views are from

the rooms facing north, which overlook the Sydney Harbour Bridge,
or from the rooms on the eastern side of the hotel, which have unobstructed views of the Royal Botanic Gardens and the harbor. Three
executive floors offer valet service, and complimentary breakfast
and evening cocktails are served in the private lounges. *117 Macquarie St., 2000, tel. 02/230–0200, fax 02/240–1240. 502 rooms with
bath. Facilities: heated indoor pool, gym, saunas, business center, 3
executive floors with private lounges, 2 nonsmoking floors, 3 restaurants, snack bar, bistro, cocktail lounge, delicatessen. AE, DC,
MC, V.*

$$$$ **Park Hyatt.** Moored in the shadow of the Harbour Bridge on the
★ western side of Circular Quay, the Park Hyatt has the finest location
of any hotel in Sydney. Its character is luxurious, cosmopolitan, and
distinguished by the extra dash of sophistication (such as butler
service) that is the hallmark of Park Hyatts. The color scheme is
dominated by sandstone and earth tones, and the decor combines re-
productions of classical statuary with bronzes and contemporary
Australian artwork. Most rooms in the four-story hotel overlook
Circular Quay and the Opera House, and most have balconies. All
rooms have a walk-in wardrobe and compact disc and videotape
players, and the white and honey-color marble bathrooms are among
the biggest and best in town. *7 Hickson Rd., The Rocks, 2000, tel.
02/256–1234, fax 02/256–1555. 159 rooms with bath. Facilities:
heated outdoor pool, gym, sauna, spa, 2 restaurants, bar. AE, DC,
MC, V.*

$$$$ **The Regent.** Completed in 1983 and extensively renovated since, this
★ glossy, glamorous harborfront hotel skirting Circular Quay and The
Rocks is a favorite with corporate clients and well-heeled vacationers. Each floor has its own steward who unpacks guests' luggage,
handles laundry, and arranges all tour, entertainment, and restaurant bookings. Rooms are luxuriously equipped and decorated with
light wood and a cocoa-and-gray color scheme. About half the rooms
have unobstructed views of the Opera House and the Harbour
Bridge. However, those rooms on the lower floors on the city side of
the hotel have unexceptional views. For the traveler who can afford
a room in the $500-per-night bracket, the junior suites are the best
in town. The hotel features one of Sydney's best restaurants, Kables
(*see* Dining, *above*). *199 George St., 2000, tel. 02/238–0000, fax 02/
251–2851. 520 rooms with bath. Facilities: heated outdoor pool,
gym, sauna, business center, 2 bars, 3 restaurants, beauty salon,
shops. AE, DC, MC, V.*

$$$$ **The Ritz-Carlton.** Opened in 1990, this is the aristocrat of the city's
★ deluxe elite hotels. It is located in a prime position close to the Opera
House, Circular Quay, the Botanic Gardens, and the business district. Decor throughout is a mixture of marble, antiques, warm-
toned fabrics, and soft lighting—an intimate, opulent blend that
evokes the European hotel tradition, and one that some guests
might find overwhelming. Service is polished, professional, and
friendly. Rooms are large and luxurious, and most have French
doors leading to a small balcony. For a view of the Botanic Gardens
and the Opera House, request a room on the eastern side of the hotel. *93 Macquarie St., 2000, tel. 02/252–4600, fax 02/252–4286. 106
rooms with bath. Facilities: heated outdoor pool, gym, sauna, restaurant, bar. AE, DC, MC, V.*

$$$$ **The Sebel Town House.** Situated close to the center of Sydney's
nightlife in Kings Cross, this hotel can boast as its greatest strength
its clubby atmosphere, which makes it a favorite with visiting rock
stars and senior executives alike. Bedrooms on the western side of
the hotel offer glimpses of the city, while those on the east overlook
the yacht basin in Rushcutters Bay. All rooms below the seventh

floor have restricted views, however. Rooms are spacious and well equipped, and the solid wood furnishings and heavy fabrics used throughout set a comfortable, conservative yet modern tone. The column-studded rooftop pool area is a charmer. *23 Elizabeth Bay Rd., Elizabeth Bay, 2011, tel. 02/358-3244 or toll-free 008/22-2266, fax 02/357-1926. 168 rooms with bath. Facilities: heated outdoor pool, sauna, gym, beauty salon, business center, restaurant, bar. AE, DC, MC, V.*

$$$ **The Stafford.** Opened in 1989, this sleek hotel in a peaceful corner of The Rocks offers a reasonable value and well-equipped rooms. The lower floor consists of two-story terrace units, with a kitchen and lounge on the lower floor and a bedroom and bathroom above. At the rear is a block of spacious studios and apartments with full kitchen facilities. The rooms and the apartments have a clean-cut Scandinavian feel that is both elegant and uncluttered. Rooms on the fourth through sixth floors have views across Circular Quay to the Opera House. *75 Harrington St., 2000, tel. 02/251-6711, fax 02/251-3458. 54 apartments, 7 terrace houses. Facilities: outdoor pool, sauna, gym, laundry facilities. AE, DC, MC, V.*

$$ **Harbour Rocks Hotel.** Created from a 150-year-old stone wool store, this friendly, intimate hotel offers good value and a central location at the heart of The Rocks. Rooms come in two grades—either "Superior," with en suite bathrooms, or "Standard," with shared bathrooms. Rooms in both categories are similar in size, furnishings, and facilities; the price difference is approximately $60. Top-floor rooms on the eastern side of the four-story building offer glimpses of Circular Quay and the Opera House. Room 119, a "Superior" on the lower floor, is spacious and particularly suitable for a family, but it has only street views. Bathrooms are small, but all the rooms—they are decorated in a muted pink-and-blue color scheme—are neat and well kept. In order to preserve the character of the building, the hotel has no air-conditioning and no elevators. *34-52 Harrington St., The Rocks, tel. 02/251-8944, fax 02/251-8900. 55 rooms, 30 with bath. Facilities: restaurant, bar. AE, DC, MC, V.*

$$ **The Jackson Hotel.** Totally renovated in 1989, the rooms in this century-old terrace house are neat, trim, and reasonably priced, although rather small. Breakfast is served in a pleasant conservatory. The hotel is situated on a tree-lined street within a five-minute walk of Kings Cross. *94 Victoria St., Potts Point, 2011, tel. 02/358-5144, fax 02/357-4935. 17 rooms, 8 with bath. Continental breakfast. AE, DC, MC, V.*

$$ **The Kendall.** Set on a leafy street near Kings Cross, this small, smart hotel offers many of the facilities of a luxurious accommodation at a fraction of the cost. The hand-painted tiles and etched-glass doors recall its Victorian ancestry, yet the rooms come with the modern blessings of en suite bathrooms and comfortable beds. *122 Victoria St., Potts Point, 2011, tel. 02/357-3200, fax 02/357-7606. 22 rooms with shower. Continental breakfast. Facilities: spa. AE, DC, MC, V.*

$$ **Morgans of Sydney.** Set within easy walking distance of the nightlife and restaurant area of Kings Cross, this boutique hotel offers an exceptional combination of location, facilities, comfort, and value. Rooms come in two categories: studio apartments and slightly more expensive one-bedroom apartments, which can sleep up to four. The largest rooms are the one-bedroom apartments at the rear of the building. All rooms are pleasant and modestly luxurious and offer such refinements as a fully equipped kitchen and a sophisticated video security system. Most have their own balcony or a bay window. Bathrooms are fairly small, although each has a bath as well as a shower. *304 Victoria St., Darlinghurst, 2010, tel. 02/360-7955, fax*

02/360–9217. 26 rooms, most with bath. Continental breakfast. Facilities: restaurant, rooftop garden. AE, DC, MC, V.

$$ Oakford Potts Point. Situated at the harbor end of Kings Cross, this apartment hotel has self-catering facilities in every room, views that any city hotel would be hard-pressed to match, and bargain prices. Decor consists of an understated gray, blue, and white color scheme accented with gray leather lounges and gold-framed prints. Rooms are scrupulously maintained throughout. Each room has a white-tile kitchen and big picture windows with a sensational view across the navy ships at Woolloomooloo Bay to the green finger of Mrs. Macquarie's Point, with the Opera House and the Harbour Bridge in the background. The smallest apartments are the studio units, while the two-bedroom units—just $15 more per night—sleep four in comfort. Request a room above the second floor. *10 Wylde St., Potts Point, tel. 02/358–4544, fax 02/357–1162. 37 apartments, 18 with shower, 19 with bath. Facilities: spa, outdoor pool, laundry. AE, DC, MC, V.*

$$ Pensione Sydney.
★ Located on a quiet, tree-lined street 4.8 kilometers (3 miles) from the city center, this is one of the most luxurious boutique hotels in Sydney. Two large Victorian town houses were completely renovated to create the hotel, which is extensively decorated and furnished in the style of that period. Highly recommended is the McDiarmid Room, which has a bathroom with French doors opening onto a balcony above the garden. On the same floor, the Windsor Room has its own wide balcony, equipped with cane furniture, overlooking the street. A small, walled garden shaded by palm trees can be found in back of the house. The hotel is close to King Street, Newtown, one of the main bus routes to the city, which also has a wide choice of restaurants. *25–27 Georgina St., Newtown, 2042, tel. 02/550–1700, fax 02/550–1021. 14 rooms with bath. Continental breakfast and airport pick-up/drop-off. Facilities: restaurant. AE, DC, MC, V.*

$$ Ravesi's. Overlooking Australia's most famous beach, this newly renovated boutique hotel is the smartest addition to Bondi's beachfront in a long time. Least expensive are the basic doubles without air-conditioning. All rooms are spacious, well kept, and uncluttered, and decorated in a stylish sand and blue color scheme enhanced by art deco touches, in keeping with the building's origins. The oceanfront rooms have the best views, in particular room 16. For family-size space, split-level suite number 13, which has a large terrace, is recommended. The second-floor restaurant is popular and noisy; request a room on the top floor for peace and privacy. There is frequent bus service for the 25-minute trip to the city. *Campbell Parade and Hall St., Bondi Beach, tel. 02/365–4422, fax 02/365–4483. 16 rooms with bath. Full breakfast. Facilities: bar, restaurant. AE, DC, MC, V.*

$$ The Russell. For charm, character, and central location, it would be hard to beat this small, century-old hotel on the edge of The Rocks. No two of its rooms are quite the same, and the tariff varies considerably depending on room size and facilities. The spacious double rooms at the front have views of Circular Quay but are subject to road noise. Request one of the quieter, standard-size double rooms overlooking Nurses Walk or room 19 or 20, both of which open onto an internal courtyard. Five rooms classified as small doubles are the least expensive, but they are tiny and guests must share bathrooms. The decor is a blend of Laura Ashley floral print fabrics and scrubbed pine furniture. In keeping with the Victorian character of the hotel, rooms are not air-conditioned and some do not have televisions. *143A George St., Circular Quay, 2000, tel. 02/241–3543, fax*

02/252–1652. 30 rooms, 3 with bath, 16 with shower. Facilities: roof-top garden, restaurant. AE, DC, MC, V.

$$ Woolloomooloo Waters. Guest suites in this modern, apartment-style hotel are spacious and attractively priced, although the hotel itself is not in a prime location; it's about a 10-minute walk from the city, and the immediate surroundings have little to offer in the way of restaurants, nightlife, or charm. Apartments come in four styles, from "Superior" to two-bedroom suites, and each has a well-equipped kitchen. Rooms are decorated in muted pastels with a gray-fleck carpet, and all but the standard suites have a clothes washer and dryer in the bathroom. *48–74 Dowling St., Woolloo-mooloo, 2011, tel. 02/358–3100, fax 02/356–4839. 94 rooms with bath. Facilities: indoor pool, spa, sauna, restaurant, bar. AE, DC, MC, V.*

$ Brooklyn Bed and Breakfast. Tucked away in an inner-west suburb, this patrician, late-Victorian guest house offers accommodations with character and exceptional value. Bedrooms are located on the upper level, and except for the single room at the rear, all are large and comfortable and equipped to sleep three. The front room with the balcony is especially recommended. Viewers of Australian ABC television will recognize the facade from the opening credits of the "GP" series. The house is located close to Petersham station, a 15-minute train journey from the city. The cafés and restaurants of Norton Street, Sydney's "little Italy," are within a 10-minute walk. Angela Finnigan, the owner, is convivial and helpful. *25 Railway St., Petersham, 2049, tel. 02/564–2312. 5 rooms share 1 bath, 1 shower. Breakfast. No credit cards.*

$ Challis Lodge. Rooms in this huge pink Victorian mansion are simply furnished, but they offer good value to the budget traveler. Each spotlessly clean room has a toaster, electric kettle, small sink, and refrigerator. If you stay for a week, the price is only four times the daily room rate. *21–23 Challis Ave., Potts Point, 2011, tel. 02/358–5422. 62 rooms, 12 with bath. MC, V.*

$ Sydney Travellers Rest Hotel. Rooms in this friendly, medium-size hotel are exceptional value, although the street noise makes it unlikely that the traveler will get much rest during the daylight hours. Guest accommodations come in several categories, from dormitory rooms with shared facilities to double and family-size rooms. The best room in the house is the Executive Apartment, which has a kitchen, a separate double bedroom, and bunk beds. Next down are the Mini Apartments, which sleep four and have kitchenettes and en suite bathrooms. The smaller family rooms also sleep four, and the smallest rooms are the doubles. Double and family rooms come in two versions, either a "Premier," with en suite bathrooms, or a "Standard," with shared bathrooms, but the difference in price is only $10. The quietest rooms are the Premier rooms overlooking a lane at the back of the hotel. Furnishings throughout are functional, and there are no TVs. The shops and restaurants of Chinatown are at the doorstep, and Darling Harbour is within easy walking distance. *37 Ultimo Rd., Haymarket, tel. 02/281–5555. 105 rooms, 30 with bath. Facilities: restaurant, roof lounge. MC, V.*

The Arts and Nightlife

The Arts

The most comprehensive listing of upcoming events is in the "Metro" section of the *Sydney Morning Herald* published on Friday; on other days, browse through the entertainment section of the same paper. Tickets for almost all stage presentations can be purchased through **Ticketek** agencies. In the city this agency is located in the Grace Bros. department store on the corner of Market and George streets. For credit-card bookings (AE, DC, MC, V), call the **Ticketek Phone Box Office** (tel. 02/266–4800). The **Halftix Booth** sells available tickets for each night's performances at half price on a cash-only basis. The booth is located in Martin Place near Macquarie Street and opens at noon. For recorded information on current stage and screen attractions, call 02/1–1681.

The **Sydney Opera House** is actually a showcase for all the performing arts: It has five theaters, only one of which is devoted to opera. In addition to the Australian Opera Company, the Opera House is the home of the Australian Ballet and the SydneyDance Company. The complex also includes two drama theaters and the 2,700-seat Concert Hall, where the Sydney Symphony Orchestra and the Australian Chamber Orchestra perform regularly. *Bennelong Point, tel. 02/250–7777. Box office open Mon.–Sat. 9–8:30, Sun. 9–4. Credit-card bookings, tel. 02/250–7777. AE, DC, MC, V.*

Dance **Aboriginal Islander Dance Theatre.** This troupe presents both traditional and modern interpretations of Aboriginal dances. Performances are characterized by wit and inventiveness. *153 Bridge Rd., Glebe, tel. 02/660–2851. AE, MC, V.*

Theater **Belvoir Street Theatre.** The specialty of this theater, situated a brief 10-minute walk from Central Station, is innovative and challenging political and social drama. *25 Belvoir St., Surry Hills, tel. 02/699–3444. AE, MC, V.*
Her Majesty's Theatre. Located near Central Station, this theater is a showcase for musical hits imported from Broadway and the West End. *Quay St., Haymarket, tel. 02/212–3411. AE, DC, MC, V.*
Stables Theatre. Dedicated to experimental works, this small theater occasionally shines with brilliant displays of young, local talent. *10 Nimrod St., Kings Cross, tel. 02/361–3817. No credit cards.*
Theatre Royal. This big mid-city theater is a regular venue for imported productions. *MLC Centre, King St., tel. 02/231–6111. AE, DC, MC, V.*
The Wharf Theatre. Located on a redeveloped wharf in the shadow of the Harbour Bridge, this is the home of the Sydney Theatre Company, one of the most original and highly regarded companies in Australia. For large-scale productions, the Sydney Theatre Company usually performs in the Opera House. *Pier 4, Hickson Rd., Millers Point, tel. 02/250–1700. AE, DC, MC, V.*

Nightlife

"Satan made Sydney," wrote Mark Twain, quoting a citizen of the city, and Satan was certainly the principal architect behind **Kings Cross,** Sydney's nightlife district. Indeed, The Cross is synonymous with sin! The temptations are varied and openly displayed, and although the area is reasonably safe, it is no place for the fainthearted. Strictly speaking, Kings Cross refers to the intersection of Victoria Street and Darlinghurst Road, although the name "The Cross" applies to a much wider area. Essentially, it is a quarter-mile stretch of bars, burlesque shows, cafés, video shows, and massage parlors. The area does not come to life much before 10 PM, and the action runs hot for most of the night (especially Friday and Saturday).

Sydneysiders in search of late-night action are more likely to head for Oxford Street, between Hyde Park and Taylor Square, where the choice ranges from pubs to the hottest discos in town. Oxford Street is also the nighttime focus for Sydney's large gay population.

The entertainment section published daily in the *Sydney Morning Herald* is the most informative guide to current attractions in the city's clubs and pubs. For inside information on the club scene—who's been seen where and what they were wearing—pick up a free copy of *3-D World*, available at just about any Oxford Street café.

Comedy Clubs   **Comedy Store.** This smartly renovated pub about 5 kilometers (3 miles) from the city is Sydney's leading comedy venue. *Cnr. Crystal St. and Parramatta Rd., Petersham, tel. 02/564–3900. Admission: $12–$15. Open Tues.–Sat.*

Gay Bars   **Albury Hotel.** The first and still one of the most popular of Sydney's gay pubs, it's especially popular with under-35s. *6 Oxford St., Paddington, tel. 02/361–6555. Open midday–1 AM.*

Club 77. This is the major lesbian club in the city area. *77 William St., East Sydney, tel. 02/361–4981. Admission: $5. Open Fri. and Sat., 8 PM–3 AM.*

Midnight Shift. This gay nightclub is renowned for its dance floor and laser light show. *85 Oxford St., Darlinghurst, tel. 02/360–4319. Admission: $8. Open Tues.–Sun. 8 PM–3 AM.*

Jazz Clubs   **The Basement.** Close to the waterfront at Circular Quay, this subterranean club is a regular venue for top Australian and overseas jazz musicians. Dinner is available, but plan to eat elsewhere if you want to eat well. *29 Reiby Pl., Circular Quay, tel. 02/251–2797. Admission: $4–$10. Open nightly 8 PM–1 AM.*

Real Ale Tavern. This mid-city club is one of the hottest jazz venues in town, with a regular lineup of top musicians. The atmosphere is casual and friendly, and meals are available until approximately 11:30 PM. *66 King St., Sydney, tel. 02/262–3277. Admission: $7–$15. Open Mon.–Tues. noon–9, Wed.–Thurs. noon–midnight, Fri.–Sat. noon–2 AM.*

Round Midnight. Located just off the main drag in Kings Cross, this stylish, sophisticated nightclub offers its older clientele cool jazz and cocktails. Meals are available until midnight. *2 Roslyn St., Kings Cross, tel. 02/356–4045. Admission: $10. Open nightly 9 PM–3 AM.*

Nightclubs   **Bobby McGees.** Set in a spectacular waterfront location at Darling Harbour, this fantasy nightclub includes a restaurant, cocktail lounge, and disco. Competitions and talent shows feature prominently in the action, and the waiters and waitresses are likely to break into a song or a dance routine at any moment. The clientele is mostly between 25 and 35, but the club appeals to anyone in the mood for a party. *South Pavilion, Festival Marketplace, Darling Harbour, tel. 02/281–3944. Admission: $10 Fri.–Sat. Admission charge is waived for diners. Open Mon.–Sat. noon–2 AM, Sun. noon–midnight.*

The Cauldron. This disco near Kings Cross is the place where Sydney's young, well-heeled sophisticates gather. Despite the name, the club is spacious and airy, except on weekends when it is jammed to the rafters. *207 Darlinghurst Rd., Darlinghurst, tel. 02/331–1523. Admission: $10 Fri. and Sat. after 9 PM. Open weekdays 7 PM–3 AM, weekends 8 PM–3 AM.*

The Craig Brewery. This large and popular pub has three bars, a brewery, and an open-air restaurant during the day, which becomes a nightclub after dark. The pub sports a lively disco from Thursday to Saturday, and a band on Sunday afternoon. *Festival Marketplace, Darling Harbour, tel. 02/281–3922. Admission: $5–$10.*

Open Mon.–Wed. 10 AM–midnight, Thurs.–Sat. 10 AM–3 AM, Sun. noon–midnight.

The Freezer. This is Sydney's hottest dance club—loud, crowded, and hyper-hip. If you look like you might have a mortgage, you probably won't even make it past the first doorman. *11 Oxford St., Paddington, tel. 02/332–2568. Admission: $10–$15. Open Tues.–Sun. 9 PM–5 AM.*

Harbourside Brasserie. With the lights of the Harbour Bridge twinkling in the background, this nightclub is a comfortable place to dine while listening to music in chic surroundings. The entertainment varies from rock to dance acts, but the club is best known as a contemporary jazz venue. A wide range of food, from light snacks to steaks with all the trimmings, is available until midnight. *Pier 1, Millers Point, tel. 02/252–3000. Admission: $5–$20. Open Tues.–Sun. 7 PM–3 AM.*

Juliana's. Located in the Hilton Hotel, this is a dimly lit, sophisticated nightclub for those who like to dress up and dance. The entertainment usually begins with a floor show followed by a disco. Prices are high and patrons are mostly over 25. *Hilton International Sydney, 259 Pitt St., tel. 02/266–0610. Admission: $5–$15. Open Tues.–Sat. 9 PM–3 AM.*

Kinselas. A nightclub inside a former funeral parlor might sound bizarre, but this one, located on a busy corner just off Oxford Street, attracts a large and avant-garde crowd. Stairs from the café/bar on the ground floor lead to a disco/cabaret on the floor above. *Bourke and Campbell Sts., Taylor Sq., tel. 02/331–6200. Admission (to disco/cabaret): $5 Thurs., $7 Fri., $8 Sat., free Sun.–Wed. Open Mon.–Sat. 5 PM–3 AM, Sun. 5 PM–midnight.*

Rogues. This Oxford Street club, always in the front line of Sydney's hottest and hippest, is still the place to see and be seen for the city's smart eastern suburbs set. "Members only" restrictions apply on some nights. *16 Oxford St., Darlinghurst, tel. 02/332–1718. Admission: $5–$10. Open nightly 9 PM–5 AM.*

Pubs with Music

Mercantile Hotel. Situated in the shadow of the Harbour Bridge, this hotel is Irish and very proud of it. Rising above the clamor, you can hear fiddles, drums, pipes, and lilting accents lifted in song, seven nights a week. *25 George St., The Rocks, tel. 02/247–3570. Mon.–Sat. 10 AM–midnight, Sun. noon–10 PM.*

Rose, Shamrock and Thistle. Popularly known as "The Three Weeds," this friendly, boisterous pub 4.8 kilometers (3 miles) from the city center is one of the best places to hear music in a traditional Aussie hotel. *193 Evans St., Rozelle, tel. 02/555–7755. Admission: $3–$8. Open daily 11 AM–11 PM, music 8–11 PM.*

Theater Restaurants

The Argyle Tavern. This is a regular stop for the tourist buses on the night tour of Sydney. The show begins at 7:30 with a rendition of traditional Australian songs and bush ballads and continues during the robust dinner of seafood and roast rib of beef. This is followed by the one-hour Jolly Swagman Show, an alphabet soup of Australiana featuring convicts, bushrangers, a didgeridoo performance, and a sheep-shearing demonstration. *12 Argyle St., The Rocks, tel. 02/ 247–7782. Reservations required. Cost: $59.50.*

3 New South Wales

*By Michael
Gebicki*

For many visitors Sydney *is* New South Wales, and they look to the other, less-populated states for the kind of wilderness experiences for which Australia is famous. While there is no substitute for Queensland's Great Barrier Reef or the Northern Territory's Kakadu National Park, anyone with limited time in Australia would be wise to concentrate on New South Wales. The state provides a taste of most of the natural wonders that Australia has to offer— from desert outback to subtropical rain forests and snow-covered mountains—all within easy range of the country's largest, most glamorous city.

New South Wales was named by Captain James Cook during his voyage of discovery in 1770, because the area's low, rounded hills reminded him of southern Wales. It was the first state to be settled by the British, whose plan to establish a penal colony at Botany Bay in 1788 was scrapped in favor of a site a short distance to the north— Sydney Cove. Successive waves of convicts helped swell the state's population, but the discovery in 1850 of gold at Bathurst on the western edge of the Great Dividing Range sparked a population explosion. In addition to the gold, the state's economic might was further strengthened by the discovery of huge coal seams in the Hunter Valley, as well as the development of a thriving wool and timber industry.

Today, with 5.5 million people, New South Wales is Australia's most populous state. While this may seem crowded by Australian standards, it's worth remembering that New South Wales is larger than every U.S. state except Alaska. The state can be divided into four main regions: In the east is a coastal plain, which varies in width from less than a mile to almost a hundred miles; this plain is bordered to the west by a chain of low mountains known as the Great Dividing Range; on the western slopes of this range is a belt of pastures and farmlands, and farther west still are the western plains, an arid, sparsely populated region that occupies about two-thirds of the state.

Above all, however, New South Wales has beaches. From Point Danger in the north to Cape Howe in the south, the state's 1,600-kilometer (1,000-mile) coastline is an almost continuous line of bleached blond sand, arranged in golden crescents that lie cradled by rocky headlands. No other state can match New South Wales's beaches, and (with the exception of Queensland) no other state offers so many luxury beach resorts. For the traveler who wants to do more than soak up the sunshine, however, the state offers plenty of possibilities, including bushwalking in the Blue Mountains, scuba diving off the north coast, wine tours of the Hunter Valley, trail riding or skiing in the Snowy Mountains, and white-water rafting on the spectacular Dorrigo Plateau.

The Blue Mountains

Sydneysiders have been doubly blessed by nature. Not only do they have a magnificent coastline right at their front door, but less than 80 kilometers (50 miles) to the west is one of the most spectacular wilderness parks in Australia—the Blue Mountains. Rising to a height of more than 1,300 meters (3,500 feet), these richly forested hills are superb examples of the continent's rugged beauty. Crisp mountain air, gardens that burn with autumn color, vast sandstone chasms where waterfalls shatter on the rocks, and little towns of timber and stone are just part of a broad repertoire of delights. The mountains' distinctive blue coloring is caused by the evaporation of

New South Wales

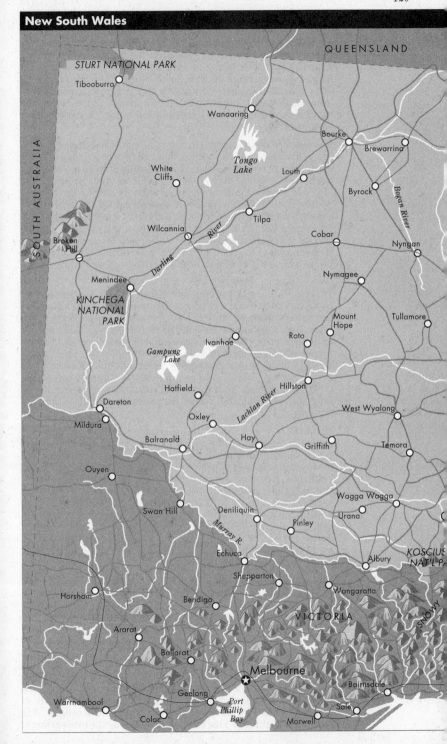

QUEENSLAND

STURT NATIONAL PARK

Tibooburra

Wanaaring

Bourke

Brewarrina

Tongo Lake

Louth

Byrock

Bogan River

White Cliffs

SOUTH AUSTRALIA

Wilcannia

Tilpa

Cobar

Nyngan

River

Broken Hill

Darling

Menindee

Nymagee

KINCHEGA NATIONAL PARK

Mount Hope

Tullamore

Gampung Lake

Ivanhoe

Roto

Hatfield

Hillston

Lachlan River

West Wyalong

Dareton

Oxley

Mildura

Balranald

Hay

Griffith

Temora

Ouyen

Wagga Wagga

Swan Hill

Deniliquin

Urana

Murray R.

Finley

Echuca

Albury

KOSCIUS NAT'L PA

Horsham

Shepparton

Wangaratta

Bendigo

VICTORIA

SNOWY

Ararat

Ballarat

Melbourne

Bairnsdale

Warrnambool

Geelong

Port Phillip Bay

Sale

Colac

Morwell

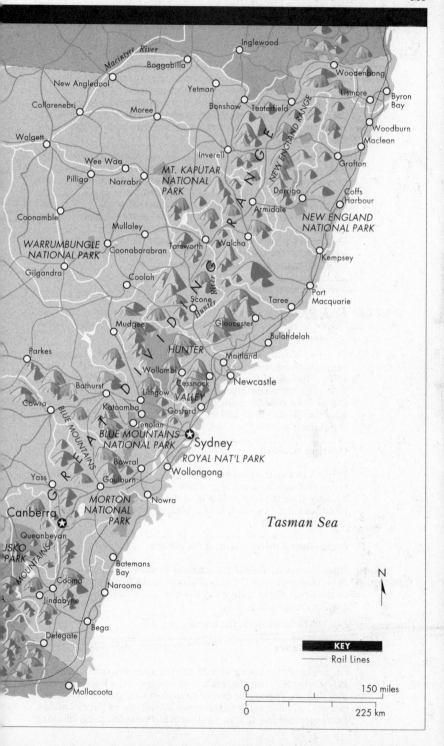

Inglewood

Macintyre River

Boggabilla

New Angledool

Yetman

Woodenbong

Lismore

Byron
Bay

Collarenebri

Moree

Bonshaw

Tenterfield

NEW ENGLAND RANGE

Woodburn

Maclean

Walgett

Inverell

Grafton

Wee Waa

MT. KAPUTAR
NATIONAL
PARK

Dorrigo

Coffs
Harbour

Pilliga

Narrabri

Armidale

NEW ENGLAND
NATIONAL PARK

Coonamble

Mullaley

Tamworth

Walcha

WARRUMBUNGLE
NATIONAL PARK

Coonabarabran

Kempsey

Gilgandra

Coolah

Hunter River

Port
Macquarie

Mudgee

Scone

Taree

Hunter

Gloucester

Parkes

HUNTER

Bulahdelah

Maitland

Bathurst

Wollombi

Lithgow

Cessnock

VALLEY

Newcastle

Cowra

Katoomba

Gosford

Jenolan

BLUE MOUNTAINS
NATIONAL PARK

Sydney

Yass

Bowral

ROYAL NAT'L PARK

Wollongong

Goulburn

Nowra

Canberra

MORTON
NATIONAL
PARK

Tasman Sea

Queanbeyan

USKO
PARK

Cooma

Batemans
Bay

N

MOUNTAINS

Narooma

Jindabyne

Bega

Delegate

Mallacoota

KEY
Rail Lines

0   150 miles

0   225 km

GREAT DIVIDING RANGE

BLUE MOUNTAINS

oil from the dense eucalyptus forests. This oil disperses the light in the blue colors of the spectrum, a phenomenon known as Rayleigh scattering.

For a quarter of a century after European settlement, these mountains marked the limits of westward expansion. Early attempts to find a route across ended at sheer cliff faces or impassable chasms. For the convicts, many of whom believed China lay on the far side, the mountains offered the tantalizing possibility of escape. But not until 1813 did explorers finally forge a crossing by hugging the mountain ridges, and it is this route that the Great Western Highway follows today.

When the railway line from Sydney was completed at the end of the 19th century, the mountains suddenly became fashionable, and guest houses and hotels flourished. Wealthy Sydney businessmen built grand weekend homes here, cultivating cool-climate gardens that are one of the highlights of the mountains today. Mountain walking was a popular activity at the time, and the splendid network of trails that crisscross the hills was created during this period. Combined with the dramatic natural beauty of the area, the history and charm of the mountain villages make the Blue Mountains an attraction that no visitor should overlook.

Arriving and Departing

By Car Leave Sydney via Parramatta Road and the F4 Freeway, and then follow the signs to Katoomba. The 100-kilometer (62-mile) journey to Katoomba takes about 90 minutes.

By Train The Blue Mountains are served by Sydney's network of commuter trains, with frequent service to and from the city between 5 AM and 11 PM. The round-trip fare between Sydney's Central Station and Katoomba, the main station in the Blue Mountains, is $17.20 for adults and $8.60 for children under 16. If you begin traveling after 9 AM, the adult fare falls to $10.60, and the children's to $5.30. For information on train schedules, telephone 13–1500.

Getting Around

Public buses operate between the various towns of the Blue Mountains, although the areas of greatest scenic beauty are located some distance from the towns. If you want to see the best that the Blue Mountains have to offer, hire a vehicle of your own (*see* Getting Around in Chapter 2).

Important Addresses and Numbers

Tourist Information Blue Mountains Tourist Information Centres are located at Echo Point (Katoomba, tel. 047/82–0756) and at the foot of the mountains on the Great Western Highway (Glenbrook, tel. 047/39–6266). Both centers are open daily 9–5.

Emergencies Dial 000 for **ambulance, fire brigade,** or **police.**

Guided Tours

On weekends beginning at 9:30 AM, the **Blue Mountains Explorer Bus** meets every morning train from Sydney at the Katoomba Railway Station. The double-decker bus makes 17 stops on its 50-minute circuit, including many of the major attractions of the mountains. Passengers are free to leave the tour at any point and join a following bus. Tickets cost $15 for adults, $7.50 for school-age children, and $37 for a family with up to three children, and are available from the Blue Mountains Tourist Information Centres (*see above*), from the Fantastic Aussie Tours office (tel. 047/82–1866) at the top of the steps in Katoomba Station, or from the bus driver.

On weekdays, a combination train/bus tour leaves Central Station in Sydney for Katoomba Station, where a **Blue Mountains Sightseeing Coach** takes passengers on a three-hour tour. The entire trip takes a little more than seven hours. *City Rail, tel. 13–1500. Tickets: $39 adults, $19.50 children under 16. Trains leave Central at 8:22, 9:02, 10:02, and 11:02.*

Australian Pacific Tours (tel. 02/252–2988) operates daily bus tours to the Blue Mountains (cost: $56 adults, $46 children under 15) and to Jenolan Caves (cost: $64 adults, $52 children under 15). The company also offers daily departures for a two-day Jenolan Caves/Blue Mountains tour, which includes accommodations at Jenolan Caves Guest House (cost: $197 adults, $177 children). Buses depart from the Overseas Shipping Terminal, on the Harbour Bridge side of Circular Quay. Free hotel pickup is available upon request.

Outland Expeditions (tel. 02/746–8025) operates one-day rappelling (cost: $59), canyon descent (cost: $90), and rock climbing (cost: $80) trips to the Blue Mountains, tailor-made for the part-time adventurer. No previous experience is necessary. Trips depart Sydney at about 7 AM and transport is available from any city hotel (cost: $10).

Exploring the Blue Mountains

Numbers in the margin correspond to points of interest on the Blue Mountains map.

It is possible to take in the major attractions of the mountains in a day trip from Sydney, but an overnight stop along the way gives visitors a far better impression of the area. This trip follows the Great Western Highway, starting 15 kilometers (9 miles) after the highway begins its ascent of the mountains.

Just outside the town of Springwood, a sign pointing to the right indicates the way to the **Norman Lindsay Gallery.** Lindsay is best known for his paintings, but he also built model boats, sculpted, and wrote poetry and children's books, of which *The Magic Pudding* has become an Australian classic. Some of his most famous paintings depict voluptuous nudes, and many of them were inspired by Greek and Roman mythology. This house, where Lindsay lived in the latter part of his life, contains a representative selection of his work. *"Marylands," Chapman Parade, Faulconbridge, tel. 047/51–1067. Admission: $5 adults, $2.50 students, $1 children under 12. Open Fri.–Sun. and public holidays 11–5.*

Return to the Great Western Highway and continue toward Katoomba. About 23 kilometers (14 miles) farther, a sign to the left points toward **Yester Grange.** Built largely from New Zealand kauri pine, this elegant Victorian house has been painstakingly restored and filled with period antiques. The balcony at the front of the house overlooks lush green lawns, which contrast with the rugged backdrop of the Jamison Valley. Wentworth Falls, the best known of the many mountain waterfalls, is only about 400 meters (440 yards) from the house, but the trail is not marked. (An alternative, signposted trail is described below.) *Yester Rd., Wentworth Falls, tel. 047/57–1110. Admission: $5 adults, $2.50 students, $1 children 5–12. Open*

The Blue Mountains

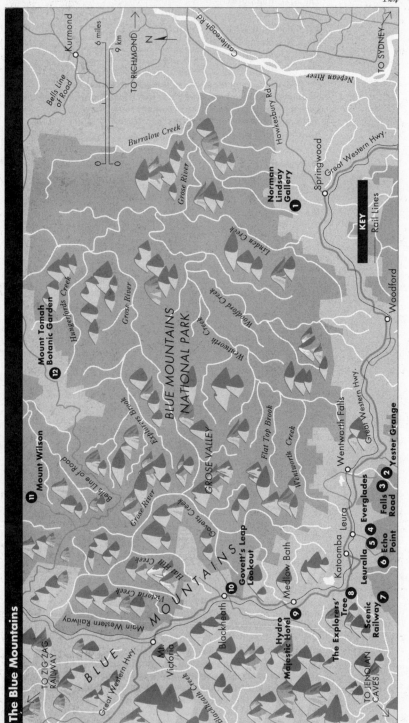

TO RICHMOND →

Kurmond

Bells Line of Road

6 miles

9 km

N

Burralow Creek

Grose River

Norman Lindsay Gallery **1**

Springwood

Great Western Hwy.

Hawkesbury Rd.

Castlereagh Rd.

Nepean River

TO SYDNEY →

KEY
— Rail Lines

Linden Creek

Woodford

Mount Tomah Botanic Garden **12**

Mount Wilson **11**

Hungerfords Creek

Grose River

Explorers Brook

Grose River

BLUE MOUNTAINS NATIONAL PARK

Woodford Creek

Wentworth Creek

Wentworth Falls

Great Western Hwy.

Yester Grange **2**

Falls Road **3**

Everglades **4**

Leura

Leuralla **5**

Echo Point **6**

GROSE VALLEY

Grose Valley

Flat Top Brook

Bells Line of Road

Govetts Creek

Victoria Creek

Govett's Leap Lookout

Medlow Bath

Hydro Majestic Hotel **9**

Blackheath

M O U N T A I N S

10

Katoomba

The Explorers' Tree **8**

Scenic Railway **7**

TO JENOLAN CAVES

Rd Hill Creek

Main Western Railway

Mt. Victoria

Blackheath Creek

Great Western Hwy.

B L U E

TO ZIG ZAG RAILWAY →

weekdays 10–4, weekends 10–5. Closed Mon.–Tues. except during school holidays.

Two kilometers (1 mile) farther along the highway, turn left onto **❸ Falls Road.** At the end of this road follow the gravel drive to the left, which leads to a parking area and a lookout with magnificent views across the valleys. As you face these valleys, the walking tracks to your left lead down to Wentworth Falls, although the trip is recommended only for those in good condition. On the far side of the falls, steps cut in the sheer cliff lead to one of the finest walking trails in the mountains, the National Pass. This trail doubles back beneath the falls and follows a narrow cliff ledge to the delightful Valley of the Waters. From this point another trail leads up past a succession of cascades to the Conservation Hut. The round-trip hike demands plenty of stamina, sturdy shoes, and at least three hours of your time.

Back on the highway, drive another 2 kilometers (1 mile) and turn left onto Scott Avenue, just before the railway bridge. A little farther along turn left onto Gladstone Road, then right onto Fitzroy **❹** Street, and follow the signs to **"Everglades."** The views from these gardens, which feature a blend of native bushland and exotic flora, are magnificent. *37 Everglades Ave., Leura, tel. 047/84–1938. Admission: $3 adults, children under 18 free. Open daily 9–5.*

Return to Scott Avenue and turn left, and then left again at The Mall. This is the beginning of **Leura,** one of the prettiest of all the mountain towns—even the shopping area has been classified by the National Trust. Turn left at the lower end of The Mall, and on the **❺** next corner is **Leuralla,** a mansion that once belonged to Dr. H. V. Evatt, a former president of the General Assembly of the United Nations and later the leader of the Australian Labor Party. This historic house contains a collection of 19th-century Australian art, as well as a small museum dedicated to Dr. Evatt. The tearoom inside the house is open on weekends. *Olympian Parade and Balmoral Rd., Leura, tel. 047/84–1169. Admission: $5 adults, $2 school-age children. Open Wed.–Sun. 10–5, daily during school holidays.*

Return up the hill and take the first turn on your left, Olympian Parade. This is the beginning of the Cliff Drive, a dazzling, 20-kilometer (12-mile) route that skirts the rim of the Jamison Valley, often only yards from the cliff edge.

❻ One of the highlights of the Cliff Drive is **Echo Point,** which overlooks the soaring sandstone pillars known as The Three Sisters. The name comes from an Aboriginal legend, which relates how three sisters were turned to stone by their witch-doctor father to save them from the clutches of a mythical monster. This formation also illustrates the geological character of the Blue Mountains. The whole area was once a seabed that lifted over a long period and subsequently eroded, leaving behind formations of sedimentary rock like The Three Sisters. From Echo Point you can clearly see the horizontal sandstone bedding in the rock. If you have powerful lungs, you can find out why it's called Echo Point. The formation is floodlit at night.

Time Out From Echo Point take the first turn on the left onto Lilianfels Avenue and then turn right onto Katoomba Street, which leads to the town center and **The Paragon Café** (65 Katoomba St., Katoomba, tel. 047/82–2928; open daily 9–5). This woodpaneled restaurant, with its chandelier, gleaming cappuccino machine, and bas-relief figures above the booths, recalls the 1930s, when the Blue Mountains were in their heyday. The menu is a traditional blend of roast meats, stews, pies, and puddings; afternoon teas—hot scones with whipped cream, jam, and coffee or tea—are delicious.

❼ Scenic Railway Turn right when you return to the Cliff Drive and watch for the **Scenic Railway** on the left. This railway was built into the cliff face during the 1880s to haul coal and shale from the mines in the valley. When the supply of shale was exhausted, the railway was abandoned until the 1930s, when the Katoomba Colliery began using the shale carts to give tourists the ride of their life on the steep incline. Today the carriages are far more comfortable, but the ride down to the foot of the cliffs is no less exciting. Just a few steps from the railway is the **Scenic Skyway,** a cable car that carries passengers for a short ride across the gorge, with a 300-meter (1,000-foot) drop below. (The railway is more spectacular.) *Cliff Dr., Katoomba, tel. 047/82–2699. Tickets for each ride: $3.80 adults, $1.80 children under 14. Open daily 9–5.*

❽ Continue along the Cliff Drive, which becomes Narrow Neck Road and rejoins the Great Western Highway. Turn left onto the highway, and 1 kilometer (.6 mile) farther along on the left is **The Explorers' Tree.** George Blaxland, William Charles Wentworth, and William Lawson, who pioneered the route across these mountains, carved their initials into the trunk of this tree, although all trace of this historic event has been erased by the elements.

❾ Four kilometers (2½ miles) farther on the left is the **Hydro Majestic Hotel** (Great Western Hwy., Medlow Bath, tel. 047/88–1002). Originally a European-style spa, this sprawling art deco building was a fashionable hotel in the 1930s and especially popular with honeymoon couples. Since that time the "Hydro" has fallen on hard times but, in spite of unsympathetic restoration work, it has great character, and the view from the lounge room across the Megalong Valley is outstanding. The ballroom to the left of the main entrance is worth a look, too. During World War II the U.S. Army used the hotel as a hospital for soldiers wounded in the Pacific.

❿ Continue along the highway to the town of **Blackheath** at the summit of the mountains, and turn right onto Govett's Leap Road. **Govett's Leap Lookout** offers striking views of the Grose Valley and Bridal Veil Falls to the right. Govett, a surveyor who mapped this region extensively in the 1830s, estimated the perpendicular drop near the falls to be 194 meters (528 feet). The nearby **Blue Mountains Heritage Centre** (tel. 047/87–8877, open daily 9–4), operated by the National Parks and Wildlife Service, has information on camping and hiking in the national park.

⓫ Continue to Mount Victoria along the highway, and turn right at the Victoria and Albert Guest House onto Bell's Line of Road. After 19 kilometers (12 miles), a road to the left—known as the Five Mile Road—snakes along a sandstone ridge to **Mount Wilson,** an enchanting village built more than a century ago by wealthy families seeking a retreat from the summer heat of Sydney. Avenues of elms, beeches, and plane trees give the town a distinctly European flavor. Mt. Wilson is at its prettiest during spring and autumn, and many of the gardens are open for inspection. At the far end of the town is a cool, shady woodland—the Cathedral of Ferns.

⓬ Retrace your steps back to Bell's Line of Road, turn left, and after about 20 kilometers (12 miles) turn into **Mount Tomah Botanic Garden.** An offshoot of Sydney's Royal Botanic Gardens, Mount Tomah provides a spectacular setting for many temperate-climate native plant species. The gardens were destroyed by bushfires that devastated the environs of Sydney in January 1994, but their rapid regeneration provides a vivid illustration of the essential role fire plays in the propagation of many Australian plants. *Bell's Line of Road, tel. 045/67–2154. Admission: $5 per car. Open daily 10–5.*

Continue along Bell's Line of Road, which leads through apple orchards to the town of Richmond. Sydney is a 90-minute drive from Richmond.

What to See and Do with Children

Megalong Valley Farm. Situated in a deep mountain valley, this working sheep and cattle property is also a demonstration farm, with displays of farm animals and pioneer farm skills. Events begin at 10:30 and include a cattle show, a Clydesdale horse show, tractor rides, horse jumping, and a sheep-shearing display. To reach the farm, turn left off the Great Western Highway at Blackheath, cross the railway line, and follow the signs to Megalong Valley. The farm is 1½ kilometers (1 mile) past the tearooms on the gravel road. *Megalong Valley, tel. 047/87–9165. Admission: $8.50 adults, $5 children 3–16, $24 family. Open daily 10–5.*

Off the Beaten Track

Jenolan Caves. The first European to set eyes on this labyrinth of underground rivers and vast limestone chasms filled with stalactites was James McKeown, an escaped convict who preyed on the stagecoaches traveling across the mountains and used the caves as a hideout. A search party eventually followed his horse's tracks and captured McKeown, whose secret caves were suddenly famous. Three caves near the surface can be explored without a guide, but to see the very best formations, you must take a guided tour. Three tours are available, graded according to difficulty, but even the easiest entails some 300 steps. For the robust the Lucas Cave tour is recommended. Each tour lasts from 1½ to 2 hours; tours depart every 15 minutes on weekends and about every 30 minutes on weekdays. The caves are located 48 kilometers (30 miles) south of the Blackheath-Lithgow section of the Great Western Highway along a narrow, twisting road. Drive carefully. *Jenolan 2790, tel. 063/59–3311. Admission: River, Jubilee, and Cerberus Caves is $10 adults, $5 children under 15; Lucas Cave is $15 per person. Open daily 8:30–5:30.*

Zig Zag Railway. Dramatic views and the huff-and-puff of a vintage steam engine make this cliff-hugging, 13-kilometer (8-mile) train ride a thriller. Built in 1869, this was the main line across the Blue Mountains until 1910. The track is laid on the cliffs in a giant "Z," and the train climbs the steep incline by chugging backward and then forward along alternating sections of the track—hence the name. The railway is located 10 kilometers (6 miles) on the Sydney side of Lithgow. *Bells Line of Road, tel. 063/51–4826. Admission: $9 adults, $4.50 children 5–15. Trains depart weekends at 10:30, 12:15, 2, 3:30; weekdays only during school holidays at 11, 1, and 3.*

Shopping

The Heritage Centre is a former convent that has been restored as a showcase for the Blue Mountains artists and artisans. Specialty shops inside the sprawling building include potters, weavers, and a hatter, as well as silversmiths and glassblowers. The complex also includes a bistro (open 10–4) and The Original Penny Arcade—a museum of antique fairground equipment. *227 Great Western Hwy., Katoomba, tel. 047/82–1044. Open daily 9–5.*

Participant Sports

The Blue Mountains Adventure Company. (190 Katoomba St., Katoomba, 2780, tel. 047/82–1271) offers courses in rappelling, rock climbing, canyon descent, and mountain biking, most of them on weekends and all from one to five days. One-day courses are timed to coincide with the arrival of the early morning train from Sydney, and all are suitable for novice adventurers. Costs range from $65 for a one-day mountain bike ride to $395 for five days of rock climbing.

Dining

The Blue Mountains are popular as a weekend retreat for well-heeled Sydneysiders, and the area boasts a number of fine restaurants as a result. Several cozy tearooms in the mountains are perfect for light lunches or afternoon teas.

Highly recommended restaurants are indicated by a star ★.

Category	Cost*
$$$$	over $50
$$$	$35–$50
$$	$20–$35
$	under $20

per person, excluding drinks

$$$$ **Cleopatra.** This diminutive, atmospheric guest house serves excep-
★ tional French country fare. Flavors are rich and robust, and the servings will satisfy the largest appetites. The fixed-price menu is limited to a choice of two or three dishes for each course. The food changes from week to week, but a typical summer menu might include a starter of sweetbreads with puff pastry and wild mushrooms and a main course of roasted guinea fowl with figs. Both the food and the restaurant's setting in an old farmhouse filled with antiques present a memorable meal. *4 Cleopatra St., Blackheath, tel. 047/87–8456. Reservations required. Dress: casual. MC, V. BYOB. Dinner Thurs.–Sun., lunch Sun.*

$$ **Cafe Bon Ton.** Situated at the lower end of Leura Mall, this bright,
★ elegant café is a good choice either for coffee and cake or for a three-course dinner. The food, like the decor, is essentially Italian, and the accent is on simplicity—veal scaloppine with sage and lemon; pasta with pine nuts, spinach, and ricotta; or a selection of crisp, well-stuffed baguettes. In winter a log fire burns in the grate, and on warm summer days the shady garden at the front is ideal for lunch. The café serves one of the best cups of coffee in the mountains. *192 The Mall, Leura, tel. 047/82–4377. Reservations not required. Dress: casual but neat. AE, DC, MC, V. BYOB. No dinner Mon.–Wed.*

$$ **La Sala.** This Italian-inspired restaurant in the heart of Leura has a bright, lively ambience that makes it one of the most attractive and atmospheric dining experiences in the mountains. The menu changes frequently, but patrons can expect simple, robust, northern Italian dishes. The restaurant is partly owned by local resident and well-known actor Reg Livermore, who often puts in an appearance. *128 The Mall, Leura, tel. 047/84–1623. Reservations advised. Dress: casual. MC, V. Closed Tues.*

$ **Bay Tree Tea Shop.** This cozy café is at its best on chilly afternoons when a fire is burning in the grate and the scones are served piping hot from the kitchen. The menu includes salads, ploughman's lunch, and open sandwiches. Almost everything is made on the premises— the bread, the cakes, and even the jam that comes with the cream tea. *26 Station St., Mt. Victoria, tel. 047/87–1275. No reservations. Dress: casual. No credit cards. Open Fri.–Tues. 10:30–5. Closed mid-Dec.–Jan. 1.*

$ **The Post House.** Housed in the old post office, this delightful restau-
★ rant offers a range of healthy, wholesome open sandwiches and salads. The homemade cakes—which might include strawberry shortcake, walnut-and-coffee gâteau, and a chocolate mud cake— are highly recommended. This is a favorite spot for enjoying scones with jam and cream after a walk through the town. *The Avenue, Mt. Wilson, tel. 047/56–2000. No reservations. Dress: casual. AE, MC, V. BYOB. Closed weekdays. No dinner.*

Lodging

The accommodations scene in the Blue Mountains is dominated by a few large resort hotels and by many small, traditional guest houses. Most accommodations are found in the upper reaches of the mountains, between Leura and Mt. Victoria. On weekends, prices are about 20% higher.

Highly recommended lodgings are indicated by a star ★.

Category	Cost*
$$$$	over $250
$$$	$150–$250
$$	$100–$150
$	under $100

*All prices are for a standard double room.

$$$$ **Cleopatra.** Tucked away in a leafy mountain village, this charmingly
★ restored farmhouse is stylishly decorated with huge baskets of wild-flowers, botanical prints, and fine antiques. The finest accommodations are in the apartment, which has its own private sitting room and a bedroom upstairs. Of the rooms without an en suite bathroom, the powder blue room upstairs at the front of the house is recommended. Below the house is an informal garden planted with Japanese maples, arbutus trees, rhododendrons, and a wisteria-covered pergola. The restaurant (*see above*) serves first-class provincial French food. The enormous popularity of this guest house makes it advisable to book well in advance. *4 Cleopatra St., Blackheath 2785, tel. 047/87–8456, fax 047/87–6092. 5 rooms, 3 with bath. Facilities: tennis court. Tariff includes meals. MC, V. Open Thurs.–Mon.*

$$$$ **Lilianfels.** Incorporating a historic mansion in its design, this chic hotel marries the manners and patrician airs of a traditional country hotel with five-star accommodations. Located in a separate wing from the original stone house, guest rooms are spacious and plushly decorated in warm-tone fabrics and colors. To fully savor the magnificent panoramas, book one of the slightly more expensive rooms with a valley view. The fine dining room, Darleys, serves exception-

al French provincial food with a modern accent. Game dishes often appear on the winter menu. *Lilianfels Ave., Leura, 2780, tel. 047/ 80–1200. 86 rooms with bath. Facilities: heated indoor pool, gym, tennis, 2 restaurants, bar. AE, DC, MC, V.*

$$$ **Echoes.** Perched precipitously on the edge of the Jamison Valley, this striking hotel combines the traditional warmth and comfort of a Blue Mountains guest house with such modern conveniences as a spa, a sauna, and an excellent restaurant. "Wentworth," the room on the corner of the top floor, is particularly recommended for postcard views on two sides. The hotel is close to the Three Sisters and the network of trails that lead down into the Jamison Valley. *3 Lilianfels Ave., Katoomba, tel. 047/82–1966, fax 047/82–3707. 12 rooms with bath. Facilities: spa, sauna, bar, restaurant. Includes breakfast and dinner. Children by arrangement. AE, MC, V.*

$$$ **Fairmont Resort.** This hotel has the facilities and style of an international resort, as well as a dramatic cliff-top location. Rooms are luxuriously equipped and decorated in blue-gray with honey-color wood furnishings. The valley rooms have the better view. Guests have access to the adjoining Leura Golf Course, the finest in the mountains. *1 Sublime Point Rd., Leura 2780, tel. 047/82–5222, fax 047/84–1685. 210 rooms with bath. Facilities: heated indoor and outdoor pools, golf course, squash, tennis, gym, sauna, spa, 2 restaurants, bar. AE, DC, MC, V.*

$$ **Little Company Guest House.** Built at the turn of the century, this sprawling, single-story guest house has a solid, imposing character as befits its status as a former convent. The house is surrounded by a tall hedge and flower-filled gardens and separated from the tennis court by an avenue of ancient conifers. Bedrooms are modest in size, but each has its own en suite bathroom, and the living rooms are inviting and well equipped with comfortable chairs, magazines, and board games. A full-size croquet lawn is at the back of the house, and the shops in Leura are located within walking distance. The guest house also operates six four-bedroom houses in the same area that are ideal for families or small groups. Bookings are heavy on weekends. *2 Eastview Ave., Leura 2781, tel. 047/82–4023, fax 047/82– 5361. 13 rooms with bath. Facilities: heated outdoor pool, lawn croquet, tennis court, lawn bowls, putting green. Includes breakfast and dinner. AE, DC, MC, V.*

$$ **Jemby Rinjah Lodge.** Set in bushland on the edge of the Blue Moun-
★ tains National Park, this is the perfect retreat for escapists in search of a wilderness experience. Each of the self-contained timber cabins consists of a large lounge/dining room, kitchen, and two bedrooms that sleep up to six. Furnishings are natural wood, and a large picture window in each cottage opens onto a small deck. Couples should make a special effort to book one of the one-bedroom "tree houses," cottages on stilts that put guests on the same level as the rosellas and kookaburras that abound in the trees. Several less expensive lodges without kitchens have recently been added; however, these do not offer the same level of privacy as the cabins. The lodge is situated close to the walking trails leading down into the Grose Valley. *336 Evans Head Rd., Blackheath 2785, tel. 047/87–7622, fax 047/87–6230. 15 lodge rooms share 6 baths, 8 cabins with bath. MC, V.*

$$ **Mountain Heritage Country House Retreat.** Set on a ridge close to the center of Katoomba, this rambling hotel has been entirely refurbished to offer a high standard of comfort at a reasonable price. The hotel is furnished throughout in a warm-toned, country-house style that makes extensive use of Australian motifs. *Apex and Lovel Sts., Katoomba, 2780, tel. 047/82–2155, fax 047/82–5323. 40 rooms* *with bath. Facilities: outdoor pool, restaurant, bar. AE, DC, MC, V.*

Nightlife

Nightlife in the Blue Mountains is confined to pubs, frequented by locals, and to hotel bars. If you don't mind a carpet that has been marinated in several years' worth of slopped beer, the pubs are fine; otherwise, stick to the hotels. The bars at Leura's **Fairmont Resort** and **Lilianfels** are warm and welcoming, especially on a winter evening when fires blaze in the grate. The clublike bar upstairs in **Echoes** is frightfully refined and rather hushed, but the armchairs are deep and seductively comfortable. Seekers of atmosphere will be drawn to the bar of the **Hydro Majestic** in Medlow Bath, which takes on a slightly Hitchcockian mood after dark. Arrive at dusk for a drink on the terrace while the sun is still illuminating the valley below.

The Hunter Valley

The meandering waterway that gives this valley its name is one of the most extensive river systems in the state. The Hunter Valley covers an area of almost 25,000 square kilometers (9,650 square miles), stretching from the town of Gosford north of Sydney to Taree, 175 kilometers (110 miles) farther north along the coast, and almost 300 kilometers (186 miles) inland. From its source on the rugged slopes of the Mount Royal Range, the river flows through rich grazing country and past the horse stud farms around Scone, home of some of Australia's wealthiest farming families. In the Lower Hunter region the river crosses the vast coal deposits of the Greta seam. Coal mining, both open-cut and underground, is an important industry for the Hunter Valley, and the mines in this area provide the fuel for the steel mills of Newcastle, the state's second-largest city, which is situated at the mouth of the Hunter River.

To almost everyone in Sydney, however, the Hunter Valley does not conjure up visions of coal mines or cows, but of *wine*. The Hunter is the largest wine-growing area in the state, with nearly 50 wineries and a solid reputation for producing high-quality vintages. Many of these wines have found a market overseas, and visiting wine lovers might recognize such Hunter Valley labels as Rosemount or Lindemans.

In recent years the area has become a favorite weekend destination for Sydneysiders. In addition to wine tasting, the Hunter Valley offers historic towns, bushland walks, and several excellent restaurants.

Arriving and Departing

By Bus Batterham's Bus Services (tel. 008/04–3339) makes the 2½-hour journey from Circular Quay West in Sydney to Cessnock daily. The round-trip fare is $36 for adults, $26 for students, and $18 for children under 15.

By Car Leave Sydney by the Harbour Bridge and follow the Pacific Highway toward Hornsby and Newcastle. Just before Hornsby this road joins the F3 Sydney–Newcastle Freeway. Take the exit from the freeway that is signposted "Hunter Valley Vineyards via Cessnock." From Cessnock, the route to the vineyards is clearly marked. Allow 2½ hours for the 200-kilometer (125-mile) journey from Sydney.

By Plane **Yanda Airlines** (tel. 065/72–3100) operates two flights daily between Sydney and Cessnock. The round-trip fare is $160 for adults and $80 for children under 15. In Sydney the flights depart from the Ansett terminal at Sydney Airport.

Getting Around

By Car Anyone planning to spend several days exploring the area will need a car. Contact **Budget** (Mobil Service Station, Wollombi Rd., Cessnock, tel. 049/90–6166).

Important Addresses and Numbers

Tourist Information Cessnock Tourist Information Centre. *Wollombi and Mount View Rds., Cessnock 2325, tel. 049/90–4477. Open daily 9–5.*

Emergencies Dial 000 if you need the **fire department, police,** or an **ambulance.**

Guided Tours

Orientation Tours **AAT King's** (tel. 02/252–2788) operates a one-day bus tour of the Hunter Valley and the Central Coast from Sydney on Thursday and weekends. Tours depart from the Overseas Shipping Terminal, on the Harbour Bridge side of Circular Quay. Free hotel pickup is available on request. Including lunch, the cost is $77 for adults, $52 for children under 15. Without lunch, the cost is $59.50 for adults, $46 for children. For the two-day tour, the cost is $199 for adults, $167 for children.

Horse-Carriage Tours **Somerset Carriages** (tel. 049/98–7591) offers a horse-drawn carriage tour along the back roads of the vineyards, culminating in a grand lakeside picnic. The tour costs about $100 per person.

Limousine Tours **Top Hat Tours** of Cessnock (tel. 049/90–1699) offers chauffeur-driven limousine tours of the vineyards for up to four passengers. The cost is $40 per hour for a minimum of four hours.

Exploring the Hunter Valley

If possible, avoid the Hunter Valley during the weekend when the crowds arrive from Sydney and Newcastle. During the week, you'll find quiet roads, empty picnic grounds, spare tables in the restaurants—and less expensive accommodations. This tour begins at Cessnock, the first major Hunter Valley town along the route from Sydney.

Cessnock is better known as the gateway to the Lower Hunter Valley than for any particular attraction in the town itself. Between 1890 and 1960 this was an important coal-mining area, but when coal production began to decline in the 1950s, the mines gradually gave way to vines.

Any tour of the area's vineyards should begin at the **Cessnock Tourist Information Centre,** at Wollombi and Mount View roads. The office can also provide maps of the vineyards, brochures, and copies of *Wine Hunter* magazine, which has vineyard news and tasting notes.

Drive away from Wollombi Road along Mount View Road. When you come to the T-junction, turn right onto Ingles Road and then take the second turn on the left onto Oakey Creek Road. This road leads to the lower slopes of Mt. Bright, one of the loveliest parts of the Lower Hunter region. About 2 kilometers (1¼ miles) farther along on the left is **Drayton's Bellvue Winery.** Wine making is a Drayton family tradition dating back to the middle of the 19th century, when Joseph Drayton first cleared these slopes and planted vines. Today, the chardonnay, semillon, and shiraz made by this winery are some of the most consistent award winners in the area. *Oakey Creek Rd., Pokolbin, tel. 049/98–7513. Open weekdays 8–5, Sat. 9–5, Sun. 10–5.*

Continue along Oakey Creek Road past the intersection of McDonalds Road. From the foot of the hill, where a farmhouse is slowly collapsing into a green hollow, this road winds up the side of a valley to a series of meadows separated by post-and-rail fences. In the evening the drive is particularly memorable, but the view from the top is well worth the detour at any time of day.

Return to the bottom of the hill and turn left onto McDonalds Road. One kilometer (.6 miles) along on the left is **Lindemans Winery,** one of the largest and most prestigious wine makers in the country. In addition to its Hunter Valley vineyards, the company also owns properties in South Australia, and a wide range of outstanding wines from these vineyards can be sampled in the tasting room. The winery also has two fine picnic areas—one near the antique wine-making equipment beside the parking lot and the other next to the willow trees around the dam. This second area also has a playground. *McDonalds Rd., Pokolbin, tel. 049/98–7684. Open weekdays 8:30–4:30, weekends 10–4:30.*

From Lindemans continue 3 kilometers (2 miles) along McDonalds Road to a driveway on the right leading to **Verona Vineyard and the Small Winemakers Centre.** As its name suggests, this is the showcase for the small boutique wineries, some of which are scattered a long way off the beaten track. Wines available for tasting include those from Hordern's Wybong, Simon Whitlam, and Verona itself—all prestigious small wineries. The center also sells home-baked pecan pies, made from nuts grown at Verona. *McDonalds Rd., Pokolbin, tel. 049/98–7668. Open daily 10–5.*

Return to McDonalds Road and turn left onto Broke Road. About 200 meters (220 yards) on the left is the **Hungerford Hill Wine Village.** This complex of low stone and timber buildings is the center of the Pokolbin wine-growing district. It includes motels, an antiques shop, a crafts gallery, restaurants, and The Cellars—the underground tasting rooms of the Hungerford Hill Winery. At the lower end of the complex is a large, shady picnic area with barbecues and an adventure playground.

Leave the wine village and turn right onto Broke Road. At the end of this road, turn right onto Allandale Road back toward Cessnock.

Thirty kilometers (19 miles) northeast of Cessnock is the historic town of **Maitland,** which boasts a number of colonial buildings. The history of the town is best absorbed by strolling along High Street, the winding main street that has been classified by the National Trust as a conservation area. Leading off this thoroughfare is Church Street, with its handsome two-story Georgian homes. The first of two identical buildings is Brough House, which contains the **Maitland City Art Gallery.** *Church St., tel. 049/32–7101. Open Thurs.–Fri. 1–4, Sat. 1:30–5, Sun. 10:30–5.*

Its adjoining twin is **Grossman House,** a National Trust property with a fine collection of colonial antiques. *Church St., tel. 049/33–*

6452. Admission: $2 adults, $1 students and children under 16. Open Sun. 1:30–4:30.

From Maitland follow the New England Highway toward Newcastle, turning left at the Melbourne Street traffic lights. A scenic 5-kilometer (3-mile) country drive runs along Morpeth Road to **Morpeth,** a riverside village. Due to the town's comparative isolation, its quaint shopfronts, wharves, and even the hitching posts have survived from the time when this was an important trading station for the Hunter River Steam Navigation Company. Today the town is a backwater of the best possible kind—a place for browsing through crafts shops or just sitting under a tree by the riverbank.

What to See and Do with Children

Rusa Park Deer Stud. Deer from all over the world mingle with wallabies, kangaroos, pheasants, goats, monkeys, and rabbits in this 20-acre bushland park. Barbecue and picnic facilities are provided. The park is located about 5 kilometers (3 miles) north of Cessnock on the Branxton Road. *Lomas La., Nulkaba, tel. 049/90–1217. Admission: $5 adults, $3 children 4–14. Open daily 10–5.*

Off the Beaten Track

Thirty kilometers (19 miles) southwest of Cessnock along the Wollombi Road is **Wollombi,** where nothing seems to have changed since the days when the Cobb & Co. stagecoaches rumbled through town. Founded in 1820, the town was the overnight stop for the coaches on the second day of the journey from Sydney along the convict-built Great Northern Road—at that time the only route north. The local hotel, the Wollombi Tavern, serves its own exotic brew, which goes by the name of Dr. Jurd's Jungle Juice.

Shopping

Part of a complex of stone buildings, **Peppers Creek Antique and Wine Company** sells jewelry, bric-a-brac, and rustic antique furniture. *Broke and Ekerts Rds., Pokolbin, tel. 049/98–7532. Open Wed.–Sun. 10–5.*

Participant Sports

Ballooning Drifting across the valley while the vines are still wet with dew is an unforgettable way to see the Hunter Valley. **Balloon Aloft** (tel. 049/38–1955) offers flights of about one hour and serves a champagne breakfast upon your return. Flights cost $185 for adults, $130 for children under 12.

Golf The Hunter Valley is home to several good courses. Of particular note are **Cessnock Golf Club** (Lindsay St., Cessnock, tel. 040/90–1876), **Maitland Golf Club** (Sinclair St., East Maitland, tel. 049/33–7512), and **Mudgee Golf Club** (Robertson St., Mudgee, tel. 063/72–1811). All three courses welcome visitors during the week; greens fees are $10–$20.

Dining

Highly recommended restaurants are indicated by a star ★.

Category	Cost*
$$$$	over $40
$$$	$30–$40
$$	$20–$30
$	under $20

per person, excluding drinks

$$$$ **Casuarina.** Surrounded by the vines of the Casuarina Estate at the foot of the Brokenback Range, this secluded, voguish, country restaurant provides an undeniably elegant night out. Many of the menu's appetizers blend local ingredients with piquant Asian sauces. Innovative main courses include the house specialty—a selection of meats flambéed at your table, accompanied by spectacular bursts of flame. Servings are generous, but patrons should leave room for the raspberry soufflé, the flambéed strawberries, or the baked blueberry cheesecake. *Hermitage Rd., Pokolbin, tel. 049/98–7888. Reservations advised. Dress: casual. AE, DC, MC, V. Lunch Sun., dinner daily.*

$$$$ **Old George and Dragon.** In an old coaching inn about 30 kilometers
★ (19 miles) northeast of Cessnock, this is one of the finest country restaurants in the state. Among the first courses are warm oysters and raspberries in puff pastry and a croutade of king prawns and leeks. Main courses include Tasmanian salmon with wild mushroom pâté in a champagne sauce, roast squab with a red wine sauce, and duck with oranges and Grand Marnier. Desserts are rich and exotic, and the wine list features a selection of about 250 wines. The atmosphere evokes the privileged air of an English country house—antique oak furnishings, Victorian watercolors in gilt frames, a blazing fire on winter evenings, vases brimming with fresh flowers. Accommodations are available in another part of the inn; guest rooms, all with private bath, are decorated in a style similar to the restaurant. Room 3 is particularly recommended. *48 Melbourne St., East Maitland, tel. 049/33–7272. Reservations required. Dress: casual but neat. AE, DC, MC, V. Closed Sun., Mon., no lunch Sat., no dinner Tues.*

$$$$ **Robert's at Pepper Tree.** Built around a century-old pioneer's hut and
★ surrounded by grapevines in one of the prettiest parts of the lower Hunter, this restaurant is the brainchild of Robbie Molines, who established a solid reputation as chef at the Pokolbin Cellar. The menu has been heavily influenced by regional French and Italian cooking. First courses include chargrilled quails and a seafood salad of octopus, tuna, prawns, and mussels. Among the main courses are osso bucco and braised rabbit in Dijon mustard. The decor is Ponderosa chic—a high-ceiling ranch house with chunky beams, bare timber floors, a big stone fireplace, and wagon wheels on the wall. *Hall's Rd., Pokolbin, tel. 049/98–7539. Reservations advised. Dress: casual but neat. AE, DC, MC, V.*

$ **Café Max.** Built above the tasting room of the Small Winemakers Centre, this café specializes in light, wholesome meals that are salt free and use organically grown vegetables and herbs. The menu features a selection of salads, vegetable soups, Thai fritters with homemade lime and mango chutney, vegetable flans, and cakes. Diners can purchase their wine at the Small Winemakers Centre on the floor below the café. *Verona Vineyard, McDonalds Rd., Pokolbin, tel. 049/98–7668. Dress: casual. AE, DC, MC, V. BYOB. No dinner Sun.–Thurs.*

Lodging

Most of the hotels in the Hunter Valley are concentrated in the Cessnock/Pokolbin region, which is also the center of the wine-growing industry. Prices are considerably higher on weekends.

Highly recommended lodgings are indicated by a star ★ .

Category	Cost*
$$$$	over $200
$$$	$150–$200
$$	$100–$150
$	under $100

All prices are for a standard double room between Monday and Thursday nights.

$$$$
★ **Belltrees Country House.** Located on a working sheep and cattle property about an hour's drive north of the lower Hunter wineries, this outstanding rural retreat offers its guests a taste of the finer side of Australian country life. Guests are welcome to watch the station hands at work with the livestock. The property has its own schoolhouse, store, and church; the house is surrounded by extensive gardens and vibrant bird life. The large, comfortable guest rooms are located in a modern building about a 10-minute walk from the homestead. Guests should bring their own wine to dinner at the house. *Gundy Rd., Scone 2337, tel. 065/45–1668, fax 065/45–2633. 7 rooms with bath. Facilities: outdoor pool, tennis. Tariff includes breakfast and dinner. MC, V.*

$$$$ **The Convent, Pepper Tree.** The most luxurious accommodations in the Hunter Valley, this imposing two-story timber building, once a convent, was transported 600 kilometers (375 miles) from its original home in western New South Wales. Rooms are cozy, spacious, and elegantly furnished with antiques, and each has doors that open to the wide verandas. The house is surrounded by the vineyards of the Robson Estate. The nearby Robert's at Pepper Tree enhances the experience with fabulous French and Italian-inspired dishes. *Halls Rd., Pokolbin, 2321, tel. 049/98–7764, fax 047/98–7323. 17 rooms with bath. Facilities: tennis, spa, restaurant, winery. AE, DC, MC, V.*

$$$ **Casuarina Country Inn.** Set amid a sea of grapevines in the shadow of the Broken Back Range, this lodging offers a dash of opulence with a difference. The palatial split-level guest rooms are furnished according to particular themes: The pièce de résistance is the Bordello suite, which features a four-poster bed topped with a mirrored canopy. Those with less exotic tastes might feel more at home in the Victorian, Colonial, or Asian suites. The highly regarded Casuarina Restaurant (*see above*) is located close to the inn. *Hermitage Rd., Pokolbin 2320, tel. 049/98–7888, fax 049/98–7692. 8 rooms with bath. Facilities: outdoor pool, sauna, tennis court, restaurant. Minimum 2-night booking on weekends. AE, MC, V.*

$$$ **Peppers Guest House.** In a grove of wild peppercorn trees you will find a cluster of houses built as reproductions of classic Australian homesteads—long, low buildings with corrugated iron roofs sur-

rounded by flagstone verandas. The country atmosphere continues in the luxurious guest rooms, decorated with scrubbed pine furnishings and floral print fabrics. The hotel has a devoted following who cherish its relaxed country manners and the restaurant's excellent cusine. Weekends are often booked well in advance. *Ekerts Rd., Pokolbin 2321, tel. 049/98–7596, fax 049/98–7739. 45 rooms with bath. Facilities: heated indoor pool, spa, sauna, gym, tennis court, restaurant, bar. AE, DC, MC, V.*

$$ **Wollombi House.** Situated in a delightful river valley near a historic
★ town about 30 kilometers (19 miles) southwest of the main wine-growing area, this charming house is a country classic. The rooms are furnished in 19th-century country style, and they are crowded with fresh flowers from the garden. The better of the rooms is the Blue Room at the end of the house. Dinner is optional, but guests should try owner/chef Evelyn Bloom's country cooking at least once. *Old Northern Rd., Wollombi 2325, tel. 049/98–3316. 2 rooms without bath. Tariff includes breakfast. No credit cards.*

$ **Glen Ayr Cottages.** Tucked away in bushland, these trim, colonial-style timber cottages have fully equipped kitchens, family-size space, and marvelous views from the verandas. The cottages are built on a ridge with vineyards on one side and eucalyptus forest on the other. The furnishings are simple but comfortable and neither televisions, radios, nor telephones are allowed to compete with the birds. Three of the cottages will sleep four comfortably, and both the Morrison and the two-story Ferguson sleep eight. *De Beyers Rd., Pokolbin, tel. 049/98–7784. 5 cottages with bath. MC.*

$ **Vineyard Hill Motel.** This hotel sits on a rise in a secluded part of the
★ Hunter Valley with views across the vineyards to the Pokolbin State Forest. Its smart, modern one- and twobedroom lodgings are an exceptional value. Each pastel-color suite has its own high-ceiling lounge area and a first-class kitchen equipped with such refinements as a coffee infuser and a choice of microwave or convection oven. French doors open onto a private deck. The reception area offers a wide selection of prepared dishes ready for the oven, as well as meats, salads, pâtés, and cheeses. The best views are from Rooms 4 through 8. *Lovedale Rd., Pokolbin 2320, tel. 049/90–4166. 8 rooms with bath. Facilities: outdoor pool, spa. Minimum 2-night stay on weekends. AE, DC, MC, V.*

Nightlife

Perhaps because so much alcohol is consumed in the daylight hours, nightlife in the wine-growing region of the lower Hunter tends to be subdued. If there is life after dark in the area, chances are you'll find it in the bars attached to the various hotels. The bars at **Peppers** and **Casuarina** are a good bet for sophisticated company and polished surroundings. The pub in **Wollombi** scores high marks for friendliness and local color. And, believe it or not, there is not a single example around of what one would call a wine bar!

The North Coast

Stretching almost 600 kilometers (375 miles) from Taree in the south to the Queensland border, the North Coast exhibits a parade of natural and man-made wonders that make this one of the most glorious and seductive stretches of terrain in the country. Along the coast is an almost continuous line of beaches, and to the west is the Great Dividing Range—a succession of rolling green pasturelands, mossy rain forests, towns dotted by red-roof houses, and waterfalls that tumble in a glistening arc from the escarpment.

The journey along the coast leads through a series of rich agricultural districts, beginning with the grazing country in the south, then into plantations of bananas, sugarcane, mangoes, avocados, and macadamia nuts. The North Coast is also a major vacation playground, studded with resort towns that offer a modest dose of sophistication.

Arriving and Departing

By Bus **Greyhound** (tel. 13–1238), **Bus Australia** (tel. 13–2323), and **Pioneer** (tel. 13–2030) operate frequent service between Sydney and Brisbane, with stops at all major North Coast towns.

By Plane From Sydney, **Ansett Express** (tel. 13–1300) operates daily services to Coffs Harbour, Ballina, and Coolangatta. **Qantas** (tel. 13–1313) also flies into Coolangatta.

Getting Around

By Car The main route along the 600-kilometer (372-mile) North Coast is the Pacific Highway. A car is essential for exploring the various attractions leading off the highway. Car-rental agencies are represented in several North Coast towns: **Avis** (Byron Bay, tel. 066/21–9022; Coffs Harbour, tel. 066/51–3600), **Budget** (Coffs Harbour, tel. 066/83–5144), **Hertz** (Byron Bay, tel. 066/85–6522; Coffs Harbour, 066/51–1899; Port Macquarie, 065/83–6599).

Important Addresses and Numbers

Tourist Information **Byron Bay Visitor Information Centre.** *Jonson St., tel. 066/85–8050. Open daily 9–5.*

Coffs Harbour and District Tourism Association. *City Centre Mall, Castle St. 2450, tel. 066/52–8824. Open daily 9–5.*

Port Macquarie Tourist Information Centre. *Horton St., Port Macquarie 2444, tel. 065/82–1293. Open weekdays 8:30–5, weekends 9–5.*

Tweed Tourist Association. *Pacific Hwy. and Alma St., Murwillumbah 2484, tel. 066/72–1340. Open daily 9–5.*

Emergencies Dial 000 if you require the **fire brigade, police,** or an **ambulance.**

Guided Tours

Mountain Trails 4WD Tours (tel. 066/58–3333) offers half- and full-day tours of the rain forests, waterfalls, and historic attractions of the Great Dividing Range to the west of Coffs Harbour in a seven-seat Toyota Safari. The half-day tour costs $40 for adults, $25 for children 2–14. The full-day tour is $70 for adults and $40 for children and includes lunch.

Exploring the North Coast

Numbers in the margin correspond to points of interest on the North Coast map.

The thread that knits the North Coast together is the Pacific Highway. Crowded, slow, and deadly dull, this highway rarely affords glimpses of the Pacific Ocean. If you take the time to explore along some of the side roads, however, the rewards will more than compensate for the tedium of the journey. It is feasible to drive the entire 600-kilometer (372-mile) length of the North Coast in a single day, but allow at least two—or, better still, a week—to sample properly some of the attractions.

The first major town along the North Coast is Taree, situated 337 kilometers (210 miles) from Sydney and the commercial center of the Manning River district. Apart from a few fine beaches in the area, however, there is little to delay the visitor before **Port Macquarie,** 83 kilometers (50 miles) farther north. Set at the mouth of the Hastings River, this port was founded as a convict settlement in 1821. The town was chosen for its isolation to serve as an open jail for prisoners convicted of second offenses in New South Wales. By about 1830 the pace of settlement was so brisk that the town was no longer isolated, and its usefulness as a jail had ended. Today's Port Macquarie has few reminders of its convict past and is flourishing as a vacation area.

Housed in a historic two-story shop near the Hastings River is the eclectic **Hastings District Historical Museum,** which includes relics from the town's convict days, period costumes, memorabilia from both world wars, farm implements, and antique clocks and watches. This wide-ranging collection represents the town's social history in a manner that is at once entertaining and enlightening. *22 Clarence St., tel. 065/83–1108. Admission: $3 adults, 50¢ children 5–15. Open Mon.–Sat. 9:30–4:30, Sun. 1–4:30.*

In the same area is **St. Thomas Church,** the country's third-oldest church, which was built by convicts using local cedar and stone blocks cemented together with powdered seashells. *Hay and William Sts. Open weekdays 9–4, closed noon–2.*

An alternative to the Pacific Highway from Port Macquarie is the rough gravel road that runs north beside a single, vast, and mostly deserted beach to **Crescent Head**—a beach renowned in the surfing world. To reach this road take the vehicular ferry across the Hastings River from the end of Settlement Road. At Crescent Head, 30 kilometers (19 miles) to the north, the road turns inland to rejoin the Pacific Highway at Kempsey.

Just south of the Macleay River Bridge in Kempsey, a road marked "South West Rocks" leads east to **Trial Bay Gaol.** Built in the 1880s by convicts, this jail occupies a dramatic position on the cliffs above the sea. The purpose of the jail was to teach prisoners useful skills, but the project proved too expensive and was abandoned in 1902. During World War I, the prison became an internment camp for about 500 Germans. *Arakoon, Kempsey, tel. 065/66–6168. Admission: $2.50 adults, $1 children under 16. Open daily 9–5.*

One hundred kilometers (62 miles) north, just before the Pacific Highway crosses the Bellinger River, is the turnoff for the road to **Bellingen.** Set in a river valley, Bellingen is one of the prettiest towns along the coast, and the detour will probably come as a welcome relief after the Pacific Highway. Many of the town's buildings have been classified by the National Trust.

Time Out   One of these buildings is **The Boiling Billy** (Church St., tel. 066/55–1947), which serves light meals at a very modest price.

If you have an hour to spare, cross the Bellinger River here and turn left onto the road to **Gleniffer.** This spectacular, rambling, 17-kilo-

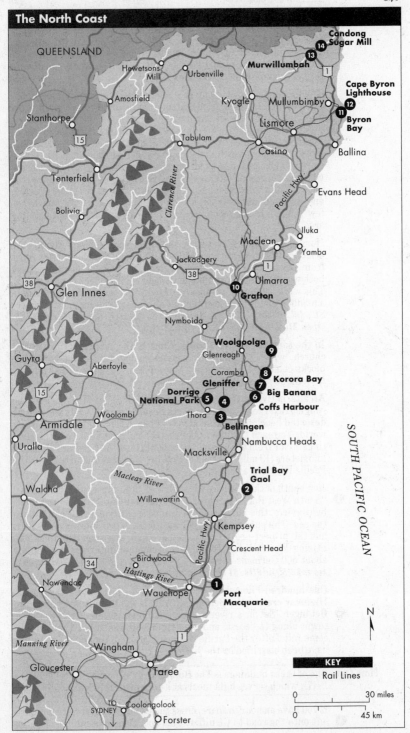

The North Coast

meter (11-mile) journey leads through farmlands and wooded valleys and across Never Never Creek to—believe it or not—the Promised Land! Several swimming holes and picnic areas are located along this road.

From Bellingen the main Dorrigo Road follows the river until Thora, where it climbs more than 305 meters (1,000 feet) up the heavily wooded escarpment to the Dorrigo Plateau. At the top is **Dorrigo National Park,** a small but outstanding subtropical rain forest included on the World Heritage List. Signposts along the main road indicate the walking trails. The Satinbird Stroll is a short rainforest walk, while the 6.4-kilometer (4-mile) Cedar Falls Walk leads to the most spectacular of the park's many waterfalls. Beyond Dorrigo township, a gravel road completes the loop to the town of Coramba, just 16 kilometers (10 miles) northwest of Coffs Harbour.

Coffs Harbour's major industry is obvious well before you reach the town. This is the state's "banana republic," and the surrounding hillsides are covered with long, neat rows of banana palms. Set at the foot of steep green hills, the town also has great beaches and a mild climate—an idyllic combination that has made it one of the most popular vacation spots along the coast. Coffs is a convenient halfway point in the 1,000-kilometer (620-mile) journey between Sydney and Brisbane.

The town has a lively and attractive harbor in the shelter of Muttonbird Island, and the stroll out to the island is delightful in the evening. To get there follow the signs to the Coffs Harbour Jetty and park near the fish cooperative. A wide path leads out along the breakwater to the island and up the side of the island. The trail is steep, but the views from the top are worth the effort. The island is named after the muttonbirds that nest here between September and April, spending their days at sea and returning to their burrows in the evening. In late April, the birds begin their annual migration to New Zealand, the Philippines, and past Japan to the Aleutian Islands between eastern Siberia and Alaska.

Time Out On High Street near the harbor is an area known as The Strip—a row of a dozen restaurants that offer a wide choice of cuisines. If you're in the mood for Italian, try **Avanti** (368 High St., tel. 066/52–4818), a popular local restaurant.

On the northern side of the town is the **Big Banana**—the symbol of Coffs Harbour. This monumental piece of kitsch is part of the **Horticultural World** complex, which offers a fascinating look at the past, present, and future of horticulture. After a preliminary video, a shuttle takes visitors on a 2.2-kilometer (1½-mile) elevated train ride across plantations containing an incredible variety of tropical fruits. Modern horticultural techniques, such as hydroponics, are illustrated during the entertaining tour, and the ride concludes with a look at futuristic horticulture on Earth from a space station. At the end of the tour, you can wander down the hill to the Farmer's Market to purchase some of the 1,000 varieties of tropical fruits grown at the complex. *Pacific Hwy., Coffs Harbour, tel. 066/52–4355. Shuttle cost: $10 adults, $6 children under 14. Open daily 9–3.*

Three kilometers (2 miles) north of the Big Banana, the Old Pacific Highway leaves the main road and loops through the banana plantations toward the sea. Turn off this road onto Korora Bay Drive, which will take you to **Korora Bay**—a small crescent of sand cradled between rocky headlands and one of the finest beaches in the area. About 10 kilometers (6 miles) farther north, a wide, shallow lagoon formed by Moonee Creek offers safe, sheltered bathing for children. Note that beaches between Korora Bay and Moonee, about 6 kilometers (3½ miles) farther north, are often unsafe for swimming.

9 Twenty-six kilometers (16 miles) north of Coff's Harbour is **Woolgoolga**—"Woopi" to the locals—known for its large Sikh population, whose ancestors came from India to Australia at the end of the 19th century. The Guru Nanak Sikh Temple is the town's main attraction, and visitors can request entrance at the Temple View Restaurant opposite.

10 **Grafton** is the center of the Clarence Valley, a rich agricultural district with a number of sugarcane farms. The highway bypasses the town, but it's worth detouring to see some of the notable Victorian buildings on Fitzroy, Victoria, and Prince streets. Grafton is famous for its jacaranda trees, which erupt in a mass of purple flowers in the spring. In the last week of October, when the trees are at their finest, the town holds its Jacaranda Festival. The festivities include arts and crafts shows, novelty races, children's rides, and a parade.

North of Grafton the Pacific Highway enters sugarcane country, where the tiny sugarcane trains and the thick, drifting smoke from burning cane fields are constant features.

11 As you near **Byron Bay,** it's worth recalling the words of novelist Craig McGregor, who lived there for five years. In *Real Lies*, a compilation of short stories, he wrote of approaching the town "past the dense green banana plantations and dairy farms and Bangalow palms, the ridge falling away rapidly to the right, and suddenly there it is; Byron Bay—an enormous, limitless, crescent-shaped sweep of sea water, fringed with white sand, culminating in a high rocky cape."

Byron Bay is the easternmost point of the continent and one of the reasons why Australia is sometimes called "The Lucky Country." Fabulous beaches, awesome whales, storms that leave rainbows in glistening arches across the mountains behind the town, and a sunny, relaxed style are just some of the reasons Byron Bay casts a spell over practically everyone who visits. For many years Byron Bay was a mecca for surfers lured by the abundant sunshine, the perfect waves on Watego Beach, and tolerant locals who allowed them to sleep on the sand. These days, Byron Bay has been discovered by a more upscale clientele, but fortunately the beachfront has—as yet—been spared from high-rise resorts. The town is at its liveliest on the first Sunday of each month, when Butler Street becomes a country market.

12 Byron Bay is dominated by the **Cape Byron Lighthouse,** the most powerful beacon on the Australian coastline. The headland above the parking lot near the lighthouse is a launching point for hanggliders, who soar for hours on the warm thermal currents. This is also a favorite place for whale-watching between June and September, when migrating humpback whales often come close inshore. *Lighthouse Rd., tel. 066/85–8565. Grounds open daily 8–4:30.*

Several superb beaches lie in the vicinity of Byron Bay. Situated in front of the town, Main Beach offers safe swimming, while Clarks Beach, closer to the cape, has better surf. The most famous surfing beach, however, is Watego, the only north-facing beach in the state. To the south of the lighthouse, Tallow Beach extends for 7 kilometers (4 miles) to a rocky stretch of coastline around Broken Head, which features a number of small sandy coves. Beyond Broken Head is Seven Mile Beach. Clothes are optional at many of these beaches.

⓭ Fifty kilometers (31 miles) farther north is **Murwillumbah,** a pleasant, rambling town situated amid the sugarcane plantations on the banks of the Tweed River—and the last town of any size before the Queensland border.

⓮ The **Condong Sugar Mill** some 5 kilometers (3 miles) north of town offers a hot, noisy tour of the mill during crushing time. The tour begins with a video, followed by a hands-on tour of the mill during which visitors are invited to scale ladders and dip their fingers into the vats to sample sugar in its various forms. *Pacific Hwy., tel. 066/72–2244. Admission: $3.50 adults, $2 children. Tour operates July–Oct., weekdays 9–3.*

What to See and Do with Children

Pet Porpoise Pool. Near the port in Coffs Harbour, this giant aquarium includes sharks, colorful reef fish, turtles, and dolphins. A 90-minute sea circus show can be viewed at 10:30 or 2:15. Children can help feed the dolphins. *Orlando St., Coffs Harbour, tel. 066/52–2164. Admission: $9.50 adults, $7 students, $4.50 children 3–15. Open daily 9–4:30.*

George's Gold Mine. Perched on a ridge high above the Orara Valley, this 250-acre cattle property still uses the slab huts and mustering yards built in the region's pioneering days. Owner George Robb is one of the legendary old-timers of the area, and his tour of his gold mine is a vivid account of the personalities and events from the days when "gold fever" gripped these hills. In addition to the mine and its historic steam-driven equipment, the property has its own rain forest, mountain springs, stands of red cedars, and a barbecue/picnic area. The property is located about 30 kilometers (19 miles) from Coffs Harbour along the Coramba Road, which runs northwest from the town. The last tour of the property departs at about 3 PM. *Dorrigo Rd., Lowanna, tel. 066/54–5355. Admission: $7.50 adults, $3 children 5–16, $20 family. Open Wed.–Sun. 10–5, daily during school holidays.*

Timbertown. This busy theme park re-creates life and work in a typical pioneer town of the late 1800s. Puffing bullock teams haul giant logs to a steam-powered sawmill, shingles and rails are split with axes, and the blacksmith's forge rings with the sound of a hammer on horseshoes. Visitors can wander through fully furnished homes, the church, and the school, and can tour the 100-acre site on horse-drawn drays or a steam train. *Oxley Hwy., Wauchope, tel. 065/85–2322. Admission: $12.50 adults, $6 children 5–16, $35 family. Open daily 9–5.*

Off the Beaten Track

The Golden Dog. Located in the tiny village of Glenreagh, this is a fine example of a bush pub. Its sense of theater extends to sheep-shearing contests in the main bar, by no means staged solely for the benefit of tourists. The best time to visit is during the midday Sunday barbecue, when jazz, bush, or folk bands perform in the beer garden. The pub is located about 35 kilometers (22 miles) northwest of Coffs Harbour. *Coramba Rd., Glenreagh, tel. 066/49–2162.*

Shopping

Lake Russell Gallery. Hidden by gum trees just off the Pacific Highway, this gallery houses a first-rate collection of contemporary

Australian craftwork. The leatherwork, ceramics, paintings, and woodwork come mostly from the North Coast, and the emphasis is on function as well as form. Prices are comparatively low. The gallery is located 16 kilometers (10 miles) north of Coffs Harbour. *Smiths Rd. and Pacific Hwy., tel. 066/56–1092. Open Mon.–Sat. 9–5.*

Shaw's Woodcraft Gallery. Located in the historic riverside village of Tumbulgum, this shop specializes in handcrafted furniture made from local timbers such as hoop pine, camphor laurel, teak, and cedar. The shop is located 10 kilometers (6 miles) north of Mullumbimby. *1 Ferry Rd., Tumbulgum, tel. 066/76–6270. Open weekdays 8–5.*

Participant Sports

Scuba Diving The warm seas around Coffs Harbour mark the southernmost limit of coral formations, making this particular part of the coast a favorite with scuba divers. **Solitary Island Diver Services** (396 High St., Coffs Harbour, tel. 066/52–2422) offers equipment and diving tours, as well as complete tuition for novice scuba divers. Most of the open-water instruction takes place on the Solitary Islands, home to moray eels, manta rays, turtles, and gray nurse sharks.

In Byron Bay, the **Byron Bay Dive Centre** (9 Lawson St., tel. 066/85–7149) offers snorkeling trips, scuba-gear rentals, and courses. The best local diving is at Julian Rocks, some 3 kilometers (2 miles) offshore, where the confluence of warm and cold currents supports a profusion of marine life.

White-Water **Wildwater Adventures** (Lot 4, Butler's Rd., Bonville, tel. 066/53– Rafting 4469) offers one-, two-, and four-day rafting trips down the Nymboida River. This is one of the finest white-water rivers in the state: Between shooting the rapids, the rafts travel through quiet rain forests and steep-sided gorges. The river is also relatively warm for most of the year. Trips begin from Bonville, 14 kilometers (9 miles) south of Coffs Harbour on the Pacific Highway.

Dining

Both excellent seafood and exotic fruits are plentiful on the North Coast. Nevertheless, gourmet experiences are rare here apart from such major resort centers as Coffs Harbour and Port Macquarie. Byron Bay has a wide selection of inexpensive vegetarian, Thai, and Indian restaurants.

Price categories for restaurants are the same as in the Hunter Valley Dining section, *above.* Highly recommended restaurants are indicated by a star ★.

$$$$ **Fig Tree Restaurant.** Set in a 100-year-old farmhouse with distant views of Byron Bay and the ocean, this restaurant offers inventive, cosmopolitan cooking in magnificently forested surroundings. First courses might include seared kangaroo fillets with snow peas and cashew nuts or coconut-coated shellfish tails with a lemongrass butter sauce. Main dishes on the summer menu might be lamb loin with pesto crust and a béarnaise sauce, or jewfish cooked in a banana leaf with vanilla bean. The restaurant is located 5 kilometers (3 miles) inland from Byron Bay. Ask for a table on the veranda. *4 Sunrise La., Ewingsdale, tel. 066/84–7273. Reservations required. Dress: casual but neat. AE, DC, MC, V. BYOB. Closed Sun.–Wed.*

$$ **Café D.O.C.** This smart, breezy café makes good use of a wide range

of locally made salamis and hams to produce robust and imaginative Italian-influenced food. Pasta dishes, which can be as simple as a spinach linguine teamed with fresh tomato, herbs, and parmesan, are a specialty. During winter, owner/chef Lisa Middleton creates dinners based on the cooking of individual Italian provinces. *Shop 7, Middleton St., Byron Bay, tel. 066/85–5252. Dress: casual. MC, V. No dinner.*

$$ **Seafood Mamas.** The specialty of this popular hilltop restaurant is Italian seafood dishes with finger-lickin' sauces. A favorite is *scaloppine del mare*—veal stuffed with seafood served with lemon butter sauce. Tables on the eastern side of the restaurant overlook the ocean. The restaurant is located 7 kilometers (4 miles) north of Coffs Harbour. *Pacific Hwy., Korora, tel. 066/53–6733. Reservations advised. Dress: casual but neat. AE, DC, MC, V. Lunch weekdays, dinner daily.*

$ **Beach Café.** A Byron Bay legend, this outdoor café is a perfect place
★ to sit in the morning sun and watch the waves. Breakfasts are wholesome and imaginative, and the fresh juices and tropical fruits alone are worth the 10-minute stroll along the beach from town. *Clarks Beach, Byron Bay, tel. 066/85–7598. Dress: casual. No credit cards. Open 7:30 AM–3 PM.*

$ **Carriageway Café.** Part of a magnificently restored emporium, this modish, brasserie-style café has a wide selection of light, healthful meals. The menu includes rolls, soups, salads, pasta dishes, cakes, and fresh fruit juices, as well as one of the best cups of coffee on the North Coast. *77 Hyde St., Bellingen, tel. 066/55–1672. Dress: casual. AE, MC, V. Open Mon.–Sat. 8 AM–8:30 PM, Sun. 9–6.*

Lodging

The main resort center along this coast is Coffs Harbour, which features several large complexes as well as a number of motels. It is currently the fastest-growing vacation town on the coast, but the sheer number of fine beaches in the area means that a quiet strip of sand is never far away—even in peak season.

Price categories for hotels are the same as in the Hunter Valley Lodging section, *above.* Highly recommended lodgings are indicated by a star ★.

$$$ **Aanuka Beach Resort.** Clustered in cabanas amid banana palms and
★ avocado trees, each of the cedar suites at this glamorous oceanfront resort has its own lounge, kitchen facilities, laundry, and spa bath set in a glass-ceiling bathroom. The landscaping is exotic and imaginative—the pool, for example, is immersed in a miniature rain forest. Suite 33 is the height of decadence, equipped with black leather couches, a glossy black Jacuzzi in the shape of a giant clamshell, and a king-size bed that twists and tilts every possible way. The beach is about 100 meters from the resort. *Firman Dr., Diggers Beach. Mailing address: Box 266, Coffs Harbour 2540, tel. 066/52–7555, fax 066/52–7053. 48 rooms with bath. Facilities: outdoor pool, spa, sauna, tennis, gym, 2 bars, 2 restaurants. AE, DC, MC, V.*

$$$ **On the Bay.** Overlooking Byron Bay's Main Beach, this large, modern guest house offers an exceptional standard of comfort, style, and facilities. Local fabrics and furniture have been used extensively in the house, and all guest rooms have ocean views and access to sundecks. The Penthouse offers extra space and luxury at a slightly higher price. Children are not accommodated. *44 Lawson St., Byron Bay, 2481, tel. 066/85–5125, fax 066/85–5198. 5 rooms with bath. Facilities: outdoor pool. Tariff includes breakfast. MC, V.*

$$$ **Pelican Travelodge Beach Resort.** This terraced, Mediterranean-style complex is one of the most striking resorts on the North Coast. Rooms are decorated in pastel blues and salmons, with cane chairs and glass tables. Each guest room also has a private balcony that faces either the sea or the mountains to the west. Facilities are stylish and well designed, including a huge saltwater swimming pool resembling a tropical lagoon. Children have their own playroom, a video arcade, fish ponds, and an outdoor junior gym. *Pacific Hwy., Coffs Harbour 2450, tel. 066/53–7000, fax 066/53–7066. 114 rooms with bath. Facilities: heated outdoor pool, spa, sauna, tennis, restaurant, 2 bars. AE, DC, MC, V.*

$$$ **Sakura Farm.** Genzan Kosaka, the owner, is a Zen Buddhist priest, and a stay at his farm is a unique experience in Japanese culture. Guests share a three-bedroom house—simple, neat, and Western in style—located just inland from the north coast town of Mullumbimby. The chance to sample authentic Japanese cooking is a big attraction, but chef Seiko Kosaka will also prepare Western meals if asked. Other options include shiatsu massage and instruction in Buddhist meditation techniques. To benefit fully from the experience, guests should plan to stay for at least two nights. *Lot 5, Left Bank Rd., Mullumbimby 2482, tel. 066/84–1724. 1 cottage. Tariff includes all meals. No credit cards.*

$$$ **Taylors.** Buried in a jungle of strangler figs and camphor laurels in
★ the hills behind Byron Bay, this luxurious guest house brings a dash of sophisticated living to the natural charm of the North Coast. Guest rooms are large and sumptuously furnished with antiques. Breakfasts are excellent, relying heavily on the fresh fruits and eggs from the 15-acre property. Guests are discouraged from bringing children. *McGettigans La., Ewingsdale 2481, tel. 066/84–7436, fax 066/84–7526. 5 rooms with bath. Facilities: heated outdoor pool. Tariff includes breakfast. DC, MC, V.*

$$ **Clarendon Farm.** If you're looking for self-catering accommodations with rustic surroundings, easy access to the beach, and a reasonable price, these modern timber cottages would be a good choice. The cottages are set low down in a valley surrounded by timbered hills, a 20-minute drive from the town of Taree. Each is spotlessly kept and equipped with a kitchen, laundry, two bedrooms, and a loft room. A recent addition is The Chapel, a sandstone cottage with such luxuries as a spa pool and antique furnishings. The range of activities on the 1,000-acre beef cattle property includes fishing, swimming, bushwalking, and wildlife watching. There are 30 horses on the property, and riders of all standards are welcome. The nearest surf beach is a 15-minute drive. The cottages should be booked at least a month in advance. A two-night minimum stay is required. *Coates Rd., Failford via Taree 2430, tel. 065/54–3162, fax 065/54–3242. 4 cottages with bath. MC, V.*

$ **Koompartoo.** Set on a hillside overlooking the riverside town of Bellingen, these self-contained cottages are superb examples of local craftsmanship, particularly in the extensive use of timbers from the surrounding forests. Each has a complete kitchen and family room, and they come at a bargain price. A small guest room is available closer to the main house. Dinner is available by arrangement. *Rawson and Dudley Sts., Bellingen 2454, tel. 066/55–2326. 2 cottages with bath, 1 room with bath. Facilities: spa. No credit cards.*

$ **The Wheel Resort.** In a secluded bushland setting adjacent to the beach, this delightful resort has facilities especially tailored to wheelchair users. Wide pathways afford easy access to the 6½-acre surroundings, the accommodations have been modified for safety and convenience, and the pool has a gently sloping ramp. The self-contained timber cabins, available with either one or two bedrooms, feature cork-tile floors, cool cream and natural wood colors, plain wood furniture with cotton cushions, and exposed rafters. The resort is located 2½ kilometers (1½ miles) south of Byron Bay. *39–51 Broken Head Rd., tel. 066/85–6139. 6 cabins with bath. Facilities: heated outdoor pool, adjoining restaurant, bar. V.*

Nightlife

The Arts Factory. Also known as The Piggery due to its former function, this Byron Bay venue has a regular Friday night disco and occasional performances by some of Australia's top rock bands. *Skinners Shoot Rd., Byron Bay, tel. 066/85–7276. Admission: $6–$10. Open Wed.–Sun. 6 PM–1 AM.*

The Snowy Mountains

Straddling the border between New South Wales and Victoria, this section of the Great Dividing Range contains the continent's highest peaks. The entire region is part of the Kosciusko National Park, a 6,734-square-kilometer (2,600-square-mile) portion of the state that includes glacial lakes, alpine meadows, snow gum forests, and Mt. Kosciusko itself—the highest peak in Australia. This is also the state's winter playground: All the ski resorts in New South Wales are located within the boundaries of the park. The area has recently been developed as a summer retreat for adventure sports, such as hiking, mountain biking, horseback riding, and kayaking.

Arriving and Departing

By Bus **Pioneer** (tel. 13–2030) offers daily service between Sydney and the Snowy Mountains via Canberra. The bus stops at Cooma, Berridale, Jindabyne, the Ski Tube Terminal, and Thredbo.

By Car Take Parramatta Road from Sydney to the juncture with the Hume Highway at Ashfield, about 8 kilometers (5 miles) from the city center. Follow the highway just south of Goulburn and then turn onto the Federal Highway to Canberra. The Monaro Highway runs south from Canberra to Cooma. The 400-kilometer (250-mile) journey takes at least five hours.

By Plane **Eastern Airlines Australia** (tel. 13–1313) operates daily flights between Sydney and Cooma.

Getting Around

During the winter, shuttle buses connect the regional towns with the ski fields. At other times of the year, the only practical way to explore the area is by rental car (*see* Getting Around in Chapter 2) or on a guided tour.

Important Addresses and Numbers

Tourist Information **Cooma Visitors' Information Centre.** *119 Sharpe St., tel. 064/52–1108. Open weekdays 8:30–5, weekends 9–noon.*

The Snow Centre provides brochures, information, and accommodations bookings for all New South Wales ski resorts. *33 Berry St., N. Sydney, tel. 02/957–1422.*

Snowy River Information Centre. *Shop 1, Petamin Plaza, Jindabyne, tel. 064/56–2444. Open summer daily 8–5; winter and school holidays, weekdays 8–4, weekends 6–6.*

Guided Tours

Murrays (tel. 062/95–3611) operates a two-day tour of the Snowy Mountains from Canberra that includes overnight accommodations at the Thredbo Alpine Hotel. Tours depart daily at 6:15 PM from the Jolimont Tourist Centre (Alinga St. and Northbourne Ave.).

Exploring the Snowy Mountains

This tour takes you on a loop through the middle of Kosciusko National Park, starting and ending at Cooma. The total distance is approximately 455 kilometers (280 miles) excluding sightseeing side trips. Travelers should plan to spend at least two days on this tour, with an overnight stop at either Jindabyne or Thredbo. During the winter, the tour may be impossible due to road closings. Before setting out, check with the Kosciusko National Park Visitors' Centre (tel. 064/56–2102) at Sawpit Creek.

Cooma is the gateway to the Snowy Mountains and also the headquarters of the Snowy Mountains Hydroelectric Authority, which administers the region's vast irrigation and power-generating scheme. Completed in 1972, this project is one of the engineering marvels of the modern world. The scheme's lakes, tunnels, pipelines, and power stations generate almost 4 million kilowatts of electricity, which is distributed to Victoria, South Australia, and New South Wales. The Snowy Mountains Hydroelectric Authority's information center offers a 35-minute video explaining the workings of this huge and complicated project. *Monaro Hwy., Cooma N, tel. 064/53–2004. Open weekdays 8–4.*

From Cooma, the Monaro Highway runs south to the lakeside town of **Jindabyne,** an all-season mountain resort. During the summer, the town offers a range of invigorating outdoor activities including canoeing, waterskiing, kayaking, bushwalking, and fishing. During the winter it becomes the major base for budget skiers, with a wide choice of inexpensive chalets and apartments.

From Jindabyne, Kosciusko Road leads to the **National Park Headquarters and Information Centre** (Sawpit Creek, tel. 064/56–2102). The fee for admission to the park is $12 per vehicle per day. Snow chains, which can be rented from gas stations in Cooma and Jindabyne, must be carried beyond this point between June 1 and October 10.

This road continues to the ski resorts of **Smiggin Holes** and **Perisher Valley.** These adjoining resorts can really be considered a single ski area—the largest in Australia—offering skiers a wide choice of runs and more than 30 ski lifts. Lift tickets, which cost about $50 for one day or $200 for five days, give skiers access to both ski areas, and shuttle buses run regularly between the two resorts.

In the other direction from Jindabyne, Alpine Way runs south to the **Bullocks Flat Skitube Terminal,** an underground/overground shuttle train that transports skiers to the terminals at Perisher and Mt. Blue Cow. From the Blue Cow terminal, skiers can schuss down the mountainside to a choice of four high-speed quad chair lifts and a double chair. Blue Cow has a good choice of beginner- and intermediate-level ski runs, but no accommodations are available at the resort.

Another 18 kilometers (11 miles) along Alpine Way is **Thredbo Village.** Nestled in a valley at the foot of Mt. Crackenback, this resort has a European flavor that is unique on the Australian snowfields.

Thredbo also has the longest downhill runs in the country, the only Australian giant slalom course approved for World Cup events, and the most extensive snow-making system of any skiing area in the country. The slopes at this resort are more heavily forested and the runs generally more challenging than those at Perisher or Smiggin. Lift tickets cost about $45 per day or $190 for five days.

Convenient access to Mt. Kosciusko, the tallest peak in Australia, is provided by the **Crackenback chair lift,** which operates year-round from Thredbo Village. From the upper chair-lift terminal at 1,965 meters, the journey to the 2,228-meter (7,310-foot) summit is a relatively easy 3-kilometer (2-mile) walk, but hikers should be prepared for unpredictable and sometimes severe weather. During November and December the ranges are covered with native alpine wildflowers.

Beyond Thredbo, Alpine Way turns south and then west as it skirts the flanks of Mt. Kosciusko. This 40-kilometer (25-mile) gravel section of the highway, often impassable in winter but reasonably good at other times, leads through heavily forested country with good views to the south. Twenty kilometers (12 miles) past Dead Horse Gap on the left is the turnoff to **Tom Groggin,** the highest point of the Murray River accessible by road. Australia's longest river travels west for another 2,500 kilometers (1,560 miles) before it meets the sea south of Adelaide.

Next along the highway is **Khancoban,** once a dormitory town for workers on the Snowy Mountains Hydroelectric Scheme and now a favorite with anglers who try their luck in the lake created by the damming of the Swampy Plain River. To the north, the Khancoban–Kiandra Road leads to Cabramurra, the highest town in Australia, before rejoining the Snowy Mountains Highway, which leads back to Cooma. Halfway between Kiandra and Cooma is Adaminaby, the town closest to Lake Eucumbene, the main storage dam for the Snowy Mountains Scheme. The lake holds eight times as much water as Sydney Harbour. The total distance from Khancoban to Cooma is 226 kilometers (140 miles).

What to See and Do with Children

Set in rugged high country, the 15-acre **Thredbo Valley Trout Springs** includes trout ponds, waterfalls, and deer that can be hand-fed. *Alpine Way, Jindabyne 2627, tel. 064/56–2142. Admission: $4.50 adults, $2 children 3–15. Open daily 10–5.*

Shopping

Paddy Pallin (Kosciusko Rd., Jindabyne, tel. 064/56–2922) is a clothing and equipment specialist for the outdoor adventurer. In addition to retail sales, the shop also rents out everything needed for a week in the wilderness, from Gore-Tex jackets to mountain bikes and cross-country ski gear.

Participant Sports

Adventure Sports **Paddy Pallin** (Kosciusko Rd., Jindabyne, tel. 064/56–2922) offers a wide range of activities for the outdoor adventurer, including bushwalking, mountain biking, white-water rafting, and horseback riding. An outstanding choice of cross-country ski programs is also available, from introductory weekends to snow-camping trips.

Sydney-based **Wilderness Expeditions** (73 Walker St., N. Sydney, tel. 02/956–8099) offers a variety of cycling, rafting, and bush-walking tours in the area.

Fishing **Eucumbene Trout Safari** (Adaminaby, tel. 064/54–2338) offers lodge-based or camping fishing trips to Lake Eucumbene in the Snowy Mountains.

Mike Spry's Fly Fisherman's Clinic (Khancoban, tel. 060/76–0406) conducts fly-fishing courses for both novices and advanced anglers in the southern Snowy Mountains region.

Skiing Downhill skis and equipment can be hired from **Paddy Pallin** (Kosciusko Rd., Jindabyne, tel. 064/56–2922), **Fleets** (ski-lift terminal, Thredbo Village, tel. 064/57–6383), or **Lakeside Ski Hire** (BP Service Station, Kosciusko Rd., Jindabyne, tel. 064/56–2127).

Dining

Price categories for restaurants are the same as in the Hunter Valley Dining section, *above*. Highly recommended restaurants are indicated by a star ★.

$$$$ **Bernti's.** In the heart of Thredbo Village, this mountain inn has an à la carte restaurant and a less expensive bistro. The combination of dark wood, soft lantern lighting, and antique prints gives the restaurant an Old World flavor. The booth-style bistro is bright and glittery, with a mustard-color decor. Both serve largely the same international dishes, including local trout and a variety of pastas. The wine list has a number of bottles from small boutique wineries. In fine weather, the best tables are outside on the terrace. *Mowamba Pl., Thredbo, tel. 064/57–6332. Reservations advised. Dress: casual. AE, DC, MC, V. Bistro open daily for lunch and dinner, restaurant open daily for dinner.*

$$$ **Toad Hall.** The exterior of this restaurant looks as if it belongs in the Austrian Alps, but the interior is typical of Australian high country—plenty of rough stone and raw timber, with a blazing fire. The house specialty is the "Kitzbühel Platter"—a heated marble slab on which customers cook their own meals. The venison and trout come from the local farm, and lunch guests are welcome to catch their own trout. The extensive wine list features a selection of Australia's finest wines at a moderate price. The restaurant is located about halfway between Jindabyne and Thredbo. *Alpine Way, Jindabyne, tel. 064/56–2142. Reservations advised. Dress: casual. AE, DC, MC, V. Lunch and dinner daily.*

$$ **Balcony Bistro.** Huge steaks and seafood are the house specials at this very popular restaurant—on busy winter weekends customers have to wait in line to grill their selections. Warmed by an open fire and a large charcoal grill, the bistro is small, dark, and intimate. On a balcony above the dining area is a bar with some tables on the outside deck overlooking Lake Jindabyne. *Top floor, Petamin Plaza, Jindabyne, tel. 064/56–2144. No reservations. Dress: casual. AE, DC. Open nightly June–Oct.; Nov.–May, Wed.–Sun.*

$ **Brumby Bar.** Only the lighting is subdued in this brash and brassy bistro, which is as popular for its live entertainment as it is for its food. The menu consists of grilled steaks, chicken, beef Stroganoff, and panfried trout. Patrons help themselves from the salad bar. *Alpine Gables, Kalkite St. and Kosciusko Rd., Jindabyne, tel. 064/56–2526. No reservations. Dress: casual. MC. Lunch and dinner daily.*

Lodging

Winter accommodations in the Snowy Mountains are expensive. Between early July and September hotel prices are generally 50% higher than at any other time of the year—and higher still on weekends. It is much cheaper to stay near the snowfields than on them. Jindabyne has a wide choice of apartments that charge about half the cost of on-snow accommodations of a similar standard.

Highly recommended lodgings are indicated by a star ★.

Category	Cost*
$$$$	over $250
$$$	$150–$250
$$	$100–$150
$	under $100

All prices are for a standard double room during peak winter season.

$$$$ **Perisher Valley Hotel.** The most luxurious accommodations on the snowfields, these exclusive granite and timber split-level suites feature floor-to-ceiling glass walls and drapes that can be closed from a switch by the bed. The guests-only dining room, decorated with cartoons by the famous Australian artist Norman Lindsay, is renowned for its breakfasts—fresh strawberries, smoked salmon omelets, and fresh croissants. The food and the service at all meals are outstanding. *Mt. Kosciusko Rd., Perisher 2630, tel. 064/57–5030, fax 064/57–5485. 21 rooms with bath. Facilities: spa, sauna, restaurant, bar. Tariff includes breakfast and dinner. AE, DC, MC, V. Closed Oct.–May.*

$$$ **Bernti's Mountain Inn.** This small inn has a cozy, personal style that has won it a large and devoted clientele. The spacious rooms are decorated in cream and pastel tones and most have king-size beds. Family suites with small kitchens are also available. The à la carte restaurant and bistro are two of the most popular spots in the village. *Mowamba Pl., Thredbo 2627, tel. 064/57–6332, fax 064/57–6348. 27 rooms with bath. Facilities: spa, sauna, 2 restaurants. AE, DC, MC, V.*

$$$ **Lake Crackenback Village Resort.** Poised on the banks of a lake that mirrors the surrounding peaks of the Crackenback Range, these luxury, two-story apartments offer family-size accommodations, although the après-ski scene at the hotel is almost nonexistent. The apartments in this all-seasons resort come in several configurations, from one bedroom plus loft (which can sleep up to four) to three bedrooms. Each one has a modern kitchen, a laundry with drying racks, underfloor heating as well as an open fireplace, and such thoughtful extras as garage parking and lockable ski racks outside the rooms. The apartments are serviced daily. Between February and the beginning of June, the room rates are heavily discounted. *Alpine Way, Thredbo Valley, 2627, tel. 064/56–2960, fax 064/56–1008. 47 rooms with bath. Facilities: golf range, 3 tennis courts, heated indoor pool, gym, sauna, restaurant, bar. AE, DC, MC, V.*

$$$ **New Valley Inn.** Situated at the base of the main chair lift in Perisher, this hotel offers comfortable accommodations at a reasonable price. Rooms in the new four-story wing are larger, and most have private balconies. Pastel colors and contemporary wood furniture predominate. *Perisher Valley Rd., Perisher 2630, tel. 064/57–5291,*

fax 064/57–5064. 47 rooms with bath. Facilities: restaurant, 2 bars, AE, MC, V.

$$ Alpine Gables. Situated in the village of Jindabyne, this hotel offers split-level suites, each with cooking facilities, a lounge, and a separate bedroom upstairs. The modern decor makes extensive use of wood and glass, and warm earth tones predominate. Suites can accommodate up to six people. *Kalkite St. and Kosciusko Rd., Jindabyne 2627, tel. 064/56–2555, fax 064/56–2815. 42 rooms with bath. Facilities: spa, sauna, restaurant, bar. AE, DC, MC, V.*

$$ Reynella. Set in rugged timber country near the highest point in
★ Australia, this sheep and cattle property offers guests a chance to saddle up, don a Drizabone riding cape, and head off into *The Man from Snowy River* country. The ranch's specialty is horseback riding, and a wide range of riding safaris is available. Novice riders of all ages are welcome. In winter the property becomes a cross-country skiing base, with lessons available from qualified instructors. Guests are accommodated in basic but comfortable alpine-style chalets. The property is off the Snowy Mountains Highway, just south of Adaminaby. *Main Rd., Adaminaby 2630, tel. 064/54–2386, fax 064/54–2530. 20 rooms with shared baths. Facilities: tennis, fishing, horseback riding. Tariff includes all meals. MC, V.*

$$ The Station Resort. With room for 1,500 guests, this sprawling complex is by far the largest resort in the Snowy Mountains. Popular with the under-30 crowd, the hotel offers relatively inexpensive lodging and a modest level of comfort. The simple, functional guest rooms can sleep either four or six. A daily shuttle service connects the hotel with the Skitube terminal and Thredbo. *Dalgety Rd., Jindabyne 2627, tel. 064/56–2895, fax 064/56–2544. 250 rooms with bath. Facilities: ski rental, dining room, bar, disco. Tariff includes breakfast and dinner. AE, DC, MC, V.*

$$ Thredbo Alpine Hotel. Within easy reach of the ski lifts at Thredbo, the rooms at this hotel are spacious and comfortable, decorated in warm autumn colors, and furnished with contemporary wood and glass. The hotel has a good choice of restaurants and après-ski facilities. *Village Center. Mailing address: Box 80, Thredbo 2627, tel. 064/57–6333, fax 064/57–6142. 64 rooms with bath. Facilities: heated outdoor pool, spa, sauna, 3 restaurants, bar. Tariff includes breakfast. AE, DC, MC, V.*

$ Eagles Range. The two cedar lodges on this 300-acre sheep property
★ offer perhaps the best combination of comfort and value in the mountains. For families or small groups, self-catering accommodations are available in a three-bedroom lodge. Other guests are housed on a full-board basis in a four-bedroom, two-story chalet. Both lodges are simple and rustic, with pine walls, exposed wood rafters, beanbag furniture, and great views of the surrounding ranges. The larger lodge has an open fireplace set in a stone wall, and the smaller one has a wood-burning stove. Weekend rates are more than double the weeknight tariff. The property is located about 12 kilometers (7½ miles) from Jindabyne. *Dalgety Rd., nr. Jindabyne. Mailing address: Box 298, Jindabyne 2627, tel. 064/56–2728. 4 rooms, one 3-bedroom lodge. Facilities: horseback riding, mountain bikes. Meals available. MC.*

Nightlife

Après-ski action in the Snowys is focused on the hotels in **Thredbo, Perisher/Smiggins,** and the subalpine town of **Jindabyne.** Most hotel bars have live music in the evenings during the ski season, ranging from solo-piano to jazz to rock bands. Thredbo tends toward the cosmopolitan end of the scale, while Jindabyne makes up with energy what it lacks in sophistication. In Perisher, the **New Valley Inn** has rock bands every night, while the high society of the après-ski set can be found in the cocktail bar of the **Perisher Valley Hotel**—suitably dressed for the occasion. At the center of Thredbo village, the **Thredbo Alpine Hotel** has a popular nightclub and a choice of three bars. In Jindabyne, the disco inside the **Station Resort** usually rocks on until at least 1 AM, and the **Jindabyne Hotel** has a long-standing reputation for its party atmosphere.

National Parks

Less than an hour from Sydney are parks and reserves filled with kangaroos, koalas, and other native fauna. For sheer beauty, the Blue Mountains and the Snowy Mountains—two of New South Wales's major parks—are hard to match (*see above*). And for those with time, a visit to the state's western parks—Kinchega, Mungo, and Sturt—can be immensely rewarding, particularly after the rainy season (July through September), when thousands of migrating birds can be observed. In total, the state boasts some 66 national parks and more than 170 nature reserves.

Royal National Park

Established in 1879, Royal has the distinction of being the first national park in Australia and the second in the world, after Yosemite. It bears some of the mistakes of a first-time endeavor, such as paved pathways and a now-defunct artillery range, but the park staff have made an admirable attempt to keep the original vegetation intact and replant native species. Originally set aside as a combination botanical and zoological garden for city dwellers, the park remains a popular destination for Sydneysiders on long weekends and holidays. Surprisingly few tourists visit Royal, however; those who do are guaranteed great bird-watching—more than 200 species of birds have been recorded—and some fine swimming holes. Many areas were severely burned in the bushfires of January 1994; luckily, however, fire is an integral part of the Australian ecosystem. Some native plant species rely on fire to crack open their seed pods, and apart from the rain forests, the park is expected to recover rapidly.

Several walking tracks traverse the park, most of which require little or no hiking experience. The Lady Carrington Walk, a 9½-kilometer (6-mile) trek, is a self-guided tour that crosses 15 creeks and passes several historic sites. Other tracks take hikers along the coast past beautiful wildflower displays and through patches of rain forest. Visitors can canoe the Hacking River upstream from the Audley Causeway. Canoes and boats can be rented at the Audley boat shed on the Hacking River. The park charges a $7.50 per vehicle entrance fee.

Arriving and Departing Royal National Park is 36 kilometers (22 miles) south of Sydney via Prince's Highway to Farnell Avenue (south of Loftus) or McKell Avenue at Waterfall. The Illawarra/Cronulla train line stops at Loftus, Engadine, Heathcote, Waterfall, and Otford stations, where most of the park's walking tracks begin.

Lodging Although most visitors stay for only a day, campsites are available. Camping facilities at Bonnie Vale Camping Area generally require reservations and deposits at the Park District Office in Audley, especially during school vacations and long weekends. Camping fees are $10 per night for two people and $2 for each additional person over five years of age. Hot showers, toilets, and laundry facilities are available at the eastern end of Bonnie Vale, 500 meters (1,650 feet) from the campsite. Bush camping is currently not allowed, to help speed the recovery of vegetation damaged by the bushfires. Groceries can be purchased in Bundeena, 2 kilometers (1 mile) from the camping area.

Information For more information contact **Royal National Park** (Box 44, Sutherland 2232, tel. 02/542–0648 or 02/542–0666).

Ku-Ring-Gai Chase National Park

Originally inhabited by the Guringai Aboriginal tribe from which it gets its name, the park is the site of many ancient Aboriginal rock engravings and paintings. The creation of the park in the 1890s also ensured the survival of large stands of turpentine, blackbutt, red cedar, and Sydney blue gum, as well as small pockets of rain forest in moist gullies. The many trails that traverse the park are a delight, designed for easy-to-moderate hikes. The 30-minute Discovery Trail, which is negotiable in a wheelchair, offers an excellent introduction to the region's flora and fauna. Signposts along the trail point out various species of trees and plants along the way, and visitors are almost guaranteed a glimpse of several bird species including sulphur-crested cockatoos, honey eaters, and rainbow lorikeets. Guided by a tape recording, walkers on the popular Senses Track are meant to travel sightless in order to experience the vegetation with their other senses.

Arriving and Departing The park is located only 24 kilometers (15 miles) north of Sydney. Take the Pacific Highway to Bobbin Head at Pymble or Mt. Colah, or the Mona Vale Road to the turnoff at Terry Hills for West Head. Trains leave from Central Station in Sydney to Mt. Colah, Mt. Ku-Ring-Gai, Berowra, and Cowan stations.

Lodging Camping in the park is allowed at The Basin in Pittwater. Sites must be booked in advance (tel. 02/974–4036 between 9:30 and 10:30 AM). Rates are $15 per night for two people during peak periods and $10 in the off-season. Each additional person is $2; children under 5 are free. Supplies can be purchased in Palm Beach.

Information For more information, contact the **National Parks and Wildlife Service** (Bobbin Head, Turramurra 2074, tel. 02/457–9322 or 02/451–3479) or the **Visitors' Centre** (tel. 02/457–9853).

4 Canberra

By Michael
Gebicki

Australians have strong opinions on many subjects, but as you travel around the country, you will hear few more strongly expressed than on the subject of the nation's capital. Its detractors use many pejorative metaphors to describe it: "Monumentsville," "a city without a soul," "the bush capital," "the city with the gray flannel mind," and "a great waste of prime sheep country." Those in favor refer to Canberra as "the garden city of the Commonwealth" or "the front window of the nation," and those who live there will give you the unanswerable proclamation that "to know Canberra is to love it."

The need for a national capital arose only in 1901, when the states were joined into a federation. An area of about 2,330 square kilometers (900 square miles) of undulating, sheep-grazing country in southeastern New South Wales was set aside and designated the Australian Capital Territory (A.C.T.). The inland site was chosen partly for reasons of national security and partly to end the bickering between Sydney and Melbourne, both of which claimed to be the country's legitimate capital. The name "Canberry"—an Aboriginal word meaning "meeting place" that had been previously applied to this area—was changed to "Canberra" for the new city. Like everything else about the city, the name was controversial and debate has raged ever since over whether the accent should be on the first or the second syllable. ("*Can*bra" is more common than "Can*ber*ra" these days.)

From the very beginning, this was to be a totally planned city. An international competition to design the new capital was won by Walter Burley Griffin, a Chicago architect and associate of Frank Lloyd Wright. Griffin arrived in Canberra in 1913 to supervise construction, but progress was slowed by two world wars and the Great Depression. By 1947 Canberra was little more than a country town with only 15,000 inhabitants.

Development escalated during the 1950s, however, and the city today has a population of more than 250,000—making it the largest inland city in Australia. Griffin's original plan has largely been fulfilled in the wide, tree-lined avenues and spacious parklands of present-day Canberra. The major public buildings are arranged on low knolls on either side of Lake Burley Griffin, the focus of the city. Satellite communities—using the same radial design of crescents and cul-de-sacs employed in Canberra, but with a shopping center at their nucleus—have been created to house the city's growing population.

The overall impression is one of spaciousness, calm, trees, and an almost unnatural order. There are no advertising billboards, no strident colors, and very few buildings more than a dozen stories high. Canberra is virtually a one-company town. About 65% of its workforce is employed in the government, giving the city a peculiar homogeneity. Canberra is also a showcase of national talent. Its galleries, libraries, sports academies, and technical institutions are the high temples of mainstream Australian culture, yet the city itself is paradoxically unlike anywhere else in Australia. Canberra is the product of a brave attempt to create an urban utopia, and whether it has failed or succeeded has fueled many a pub debate.

One fact that cannot be disputed is Canberra's magnificent setting. The surrounding mountain ranges and river valleys, combined with a climate that offers crisp springs and autumns, give the city a wide range of healthy outdoor pursuits that can be rewardingly sampled by the visitor.

Essential Information

Arriving and Departing by Plane

Airport and Airlines **Canberra Airport** is located 7 kilometers (4½ miles) east of the city center. The airport is served by **Ansett Australia** (tel. 13–1300) and **Qantas** (tel. 13–1313). Avis, Budget, Hertz, and Thrifty have car rental desks inside the terminal.

Between the Airport and City **ACT Minibuses** (mobile tel. 018/62–5719) operates a shuttle service between the airport and any Canberra address. Pick-up points are located outside both Ansett and Australian airlines terminals, and the minibus meets most incoming flights. The cost is $4.50 for one passenger, $7 for two.

Taxis are available from the rank at the front of the terminal. The fare between the airport and the city is about $13.

Arriving and Departing by Bus, Car, and Train

By Bus The main terminal for intercity coaches is the **Jolimont Tourist Centre** (65–67 Northbourne Ave.), although Greyhound and Pioneer are based at the **Canberra Rex Hotel** (150 Northbourne Ave.). Canberra is served by the following coach lines: **Greyhound** (tel. 13–1328), **Murrays** (tel. 06/295–3611), and **Pioneer** (tel. 13–2030).

By Car From Sydney, take the Hume Highway to just south of Goulburn and then turn south onto the Federal Highway to reach Canberra. Allow about 3½ hours for the 300-kilometer (190-mile) journey. From Melbourne, follow the Hume Highway to Yass and turn right beyond the town onto the Barton Highway. The 655-kilometer (410-mile) trip takes at least eight hours.

By Train **The Canberra Railway Station** (tel. 06/239–0111) is located on Wentworth Avenue, Kingston, about 5 kilometers (3 miles) southeast of the center city. Trains make the 4½-hour trip between Canberra and Sydney twice daily. A daily coach/rail service operates on the 10-hour run between Canberra and Melbourne. Passengers must travel between Canberra and Yass Junction by bus, a distance of 60 kilometers (38 miles).

Getting Around

By Bus Canberra's only public transportation system is the **ACTION bus network.** Buses operate weekdays between 6:30 AM and 11:30 PM, Saturday between 7 AM and 11:30 PM, and Sunday between 8 AM and 7 PM. Buses charge a flat fare of $1.80 for adults and 90¢ for children 5–15. Anyone who plans to travel extensively on buses should purchase a Daytripper ticket ($4.80 adults, $2.40 children 5–15), which gives passengers unlimited travel on the entire bus network after 9 AM. This ticket also allows travel on the "900 series" ACTION tourist buses. These buses depart from the Jolimont Tourist Centre on weekdays and visit most of the major attractions in the city and its surroundings, such as the Telecom Tower, Parliament House, the embassies, and Cockington Green. Tickets, maps, and timetables are available from the tourist bureau and from the **Bus Information Centre** (East Row and Alinga St., Civic, tel. 06/251–6566).

By Rental Car National car rental operators with agencies in Canberra include **Avis** (8 Lonsdale St., Braddon, tel. 06/249–6088 or toll-free 008/22–5533), **Budget** (29 Lonsdale St., Braddon, tel. 06/248–9788), **Hertz** (5

Lonsdale St., Braddon, tel. 06/257–4877, or toll-free 008/33–3377), and **Thrifty** (29 Lonsdale St., Braddon, tel. 06/247–7422). A local operator that offers discount car rentals is **Rumbles** (Kembla and Wollongong Sts., Fyshwick, tel. 06/280–7444).

By Taxi Taxis can be summoned by phone or hired from ranks, but they cannot be flagged down in the street. Contact **Aerial Taxis** (tel. 06/285–9222).

Important Addresses and Numbers

Tourist Information For travelers entering Canberra by road, the most useful source of information is the **Visitor Information Centre** (220 Northbourne Ave., tel. 06/205–0044), located on the northern approach to the city and open daily 8:30–5. For other travelers, the tourist information booth located inside the **Jolimont Tourist Centre** (65–67 Northbourne Ave., tel. 06/207–6004) is open Mon.–Sat. 9–5, Sun. 9–1:30.

Embassies and High Commissions **British High Commission** (Commonwealth Ave., Yarralumla, tel. 06/270–6666; open weekdays 9–noon and 2–4).

Canadian High Commission (Commonwealth Ave., Yarralumla, tel. 06/273–3844; open weekdays 8:30–12:30 and 1:30–4:30).

New Zealand High Commission (Commonwealth Ave., Yarralumla, tel. 06/273–3611; open weekdays 8:45–5).

U.S. Embassy (21 Moonah Place, Yarralumla, tel. 06/270–5000; open weekdays 8:30–12:30).

Emergencies For **fire, police,** or **ambulance** services, dial 000.

Woden Valley Hospital (Yamba Dr., Garran, tel. 06/244–2222) has a casualty ward that is open 24 hours.

Travel Agencies **American Express Travel** (Gallery Level, Centrepoint, City Walk and Petrie Plaza, tel. 06/247–2333).

Thomas Cook (Canberra Centre, Bunda St., tel. 06/257–2222).

Guided Tours

Orientation Tours **Monarch Tours** (tel. 06/257–7638) operates a number of imaginative full- and half-day bus tours with commentary by guides who introduce visitors to the architecture, history, and wildlife of Canberra and its environs. Tours depart from the Jolimont Tourist Centre (*see above*).

Murrays Canberra Explorer (tel. 06/295–3611) offers an economical introduction to Canberra. In its 25-kilometer (15½-mile) circuit of the city, the red Explorer bus stops at most of the major sights, including Parliament House, the National Gallery, the embassies, and the Australian War Memorial. Passengers are free to leave the bus at any of the 21 stops and board any following Explorer bus. Tours leave from the Jolimont Tourist Centre (*see above*) every hour from 10:15 AM to 4:15 PM. *Tickets: $15 adults, $8 children 4–14.*

Boat Tours **Canberra Cruises** (tel. 06/295–3544) offers 1½-hour guided cruises that travel the length of Lake Burley Griffin, departing daily at 10:30 and 12:30. A dinner cruise operates Wednesday through Saturday at 6 and 8, although services may be canceled due to insufficient demand. All cruises depart from the Acton Ferry Terminal on the north side of the lake, beside the Commonwealth Avenue Bridge. *Tickets: day cruise $10 adults, $5 children 4–14; dinner cruise $20 per person. Dinner cruise price includes main course.*

Exploring Canberra

Numbers in the margin correspond to points of interest on the Canberra map.

Canberra's major public buildings can be seen in one fairly long day tour, while the capital's parks and gardens, brimming with remarkable flora and fauna, can easily lure you to spend another day wandering through these quiet oases. Most of the public buildings are located within the Parliamentary Triangle formed by the lake on the north side and two long avenues, Commonwealth and Kings, which radiate out from Capital Hill, the political and geographical centerpiece of the city. The triangle itself can be explored comfortably on foot, but a car is necessary to visit some of the other sights on the tour.

❶ The best place to begin any tour of the national capital is from the city's tallest landmark—the 180-meter (600-foot) **Telecom Tower** on Black Mountain. Three viewing platforms give breathtaking views of the entire city as well as the mountain ranges to the south. The tower provides a communications link between Canberra and the rest of the country, and serves as a broadcasting station for radio and television networks. Its massive scale and futuristic style caused a public outcry when it was built more than a decade ago, but the focus of architectural debate has since shifted to the buildings within the Parliamentary Triangle. *Black Mountain, Canberra, tel. 06/248–1911. Admission: $3 adults, $1 children 4–16. Open daily 9 AM–10 PM.*

❷ Return to the base of the mountain and turn right into Clunies Ross Street. Then turn left onto Parkes Way, which leads along the edge of the lake to the **National Film and Sound Archive.** Australia's movie industry was booming in the early years of this century, but ultimately it could not compete with the sophistication and volume of imported films. Concern that film stock and sound recordings of national importance would be lost prompted the construction of this edifice to preserve Australia's movie and musical heritage. The archive contains an impressive display of Australian movie making skills, including a short film that was shot on Melbourne Cup Day in 1896—the oldest in the collection. On the video monitors in the exhibition room, visitors can watch a representative selection of the archive's diverse collection, including newsreels, TV advertisements, and highlights from feature films. *McCoy Circuit, Acton, tel. 06/267–1711. Open daily 9:30–4.*

As you leave the archive, notice the copper-dome building across the street. This is the **Australian Academy of Science,** which is sometimes referred to as the "Martian Embassy" due to its shape. It is not open to the public.

❸ Back on Parkes Way, drive underneath the Commonwealth Avenue overpass and then turn left onto the ramp that leads into the southbound lane of this avenue. The next turn on the left leads to the **National Capital Planning Exhibition.** Photographs, models, and audiovisual displays inside the lakeside pavilion illustrate the past, present, and future development of the national capital. However, these exhibits can hardly compete with the sweeping views from the pavilion's terrace of the Parliamentary Triangle across the lake: The National Library on the right and the National Gallery on the left form the base of the Parliamentary Triangle, which rises toward its apex at Parliament House. The terrace is a great spot from which to photograph these buildings, especially when the **Captain Cook Me-**

Australian-American
Memorial, **11**

Australian National
Gallery, **8**

Australian War
Memorial, **13**

Carillon, **10**

High Court of
Australia, **7**

National Capital
Planning Exhibition, **3**

National Film and
Sound Archive, **2**

National Library of
Australia, **4**

National Science and
Technology Centre, **5**

Old Parliament
House, **6**

Parliament House, **9**

St. John the Baptist
Church and
Schoolhouse, **12**

Telecom Tower, **1**

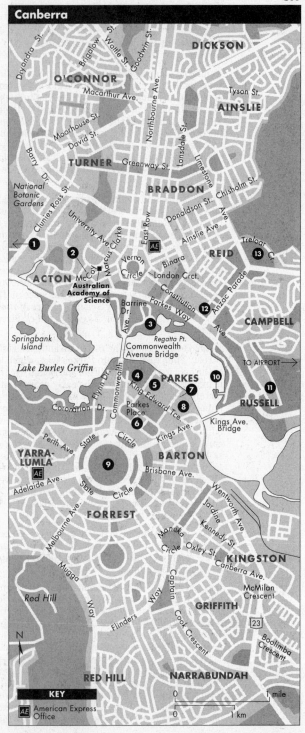

Canberra

morial Jet is sending a plume of water from the lake into the skies. On calm days, the waterspout reaches a height of 165 meters (450 feet)—one of the world's highest fountains. The cafeteria on the terrace serves only light snacks, but if the sun is shining, sit down at a table, relax, and enjoy the scenery. *Regatta Point, tel. 06/271-2888. Open daily 9-5.*

4 Cross the Commonwealth Avenue Bridge and take the first exit on the left, which leads to King Edward Terrace and the **National Library of Australia.** Based loosely on the design of the Parthenon in Athens, this treasury of knowledge contains more than 4 million books and 500,000 aerial photographs, maps, drawings, films, and recordings of oral history. Changing exhibitions from the library's various collections are displayed in the foyer and in the mezzanine gallery. Guided one-hour tours of the library leave the foyer at 2:15 on weekdays. *Parkes Pl., tel. 06/262-1111. Open Mon.-Thurs. 9-9, Fri.-Sat. 9-4:45, Sun. 1:30-4:30.*

5 Directly opposite the library is the **National Science and Technology Centre,** one of the newest buildings in Canberra. Built around a central "drum," this complex combines entertainment and education in about 150 hands-on exhibits. High-tech computer gadgetry is used along with pendulums and feathers to illustrate principles of mathematics, physics, and human perception. This stimulating environment is addictive—it's difficult to spend less than a couple of hours inside. *Parkes Pl., tel. 06/270-2800. Admission: $6 adults, $3 children 4-16. Open daily 10-5.*

6 With your back to the science center, cross the lawns beside the lake. On your right is a long white building—the **Old Parliament House.** Built in 1927, it was meant to serve only as a temporary seat of government, but it was more than 60 years before its successor was finally completed on the hill behind it. Now that the politicians have moved out, the building is open for public inspection. Guided tours, which depart from the foyer at 30-minute intervals, take visitors through the legislative chambers, the party rooms, and the suites that once belonged to the prime minister and the president of the Senate. While you're in the area, take a stroll through the Senate Rose Gardens. *King George Terr., tel. 06/273-4715. Admission: $2 adults, $1 children under 15, $5 family (2 adults, 2 children). Open daily 9-4.*

7 The next building along the lakeshore is the **High Court of Australia.** As its name implies, this gleaming concrete and glass structure is the ultimate court of law in the Australian judicial system. The court, which consists of seven justices, convenes only to determine constitutional matters or major principles of law. Inside the main entrance of the building, the public hall contains a number of wall murals depicting various constitutional and geographic themes. Each of the three courtrooms over which the justices preside has a public gallery, and when the court is in session, anyone may apply for admission at the information desk inside the building. *Parkes Pl., tel. 06/270-6811. Open daily 9:45-4:30.*

8 The last building before the bridge is the **Australian National Gallery,** containing a sprinkling of works by the masters, including Rodin, Picasso, Pollock, and Warhol. Its real strength, however, lies in its Australian artwork. The gallery houses the most comprehensive exhibition of Australian art in the country, with superlative collections of Aboriginal art as well as paintings by such famous native sons as Arthur Streeton, Sir Sidney Nolan, Tom Roberts, and Arthur Boyd. There is an excellent bookshop with an extensive selection of Australian art postcards, as well as a licensed restaurant. Guided tours begin from the foyer at 11 and 2. An additional charge sometimes applies to special-interest exhibitions. *Parkes Pl., tel. 06/271–2502. Admission: $3 adults, children under 15 free. Open daily 10–5.*

Return to Commonwealth Avenue and head south, taking the far right lane, until you turn onto the signposted ramp that leads to ❾ **Parliament House.** Much of this building is covered by a domed glass roof that follows the contours of Capital Hill. From a distance, the most striking feature of the billion-dollar building is its 75-meter (250-foot) flagpole—the tallest stainless-steel structure in the world. Although it might look only as big as a postage stamp, the Australian flag that flies night and day from the top is actually the size of a double-decker bus.

The design for the new Parliament House was chosen in an international contest that attracted more than 300 entries. The contest was won by the New York firm of Mitchell, Guirgola & Thorp, whose winning design merged structural elegance with the natural environment. Work commenced in 1980, and the building was completed for the Australian Bicentennial in 1988.

The Parliament building is approached across a vast courtyard featuring a central mosaic entitled *Meeting Place*, designed by Aboriginal artist Nelson Tjakamarra. Native timbers have been used almost exclusively throughout the building, and the work of some of Australia's finest contemporary artists hangs on the walls.

Parliament generally sits on weekdays between mid-February and late June, and again from mid-August to late December. Both chambers have public galleries, but debate in the House of Representatives—where the prime minister sits—is livelier and more newsworthy than in the Senate. The best time to be present is Question Time at 2 PM, when the government and the opposition are most likely to be at each other's throats. To secure a ticket for a parliamentary session, contact the sergeant-at-arms' office (tel. 06/277–4890). Book a week in advance, if possible. *Capital Hill, tel. 06/277–7111. Open daily 9–5.*

From Parliament House return to Commonwealth Avenue, heading back toward the lake. On the left you will see the **British High Commission.** Many such missions were established when Canberra was little more than a small country town, and it was only with great reluctance that many ambassadors and their staffs were persuaded to transfer from the temporary capital in Melbourne. Today, almost 70 nations are represented in the national capital, and on three Sundays in January, June, and October, a number open their doors for public inspection. For more details, contact the **Canberra Visitor Centre** (tel. 06/205–0044). Turn left just past the British High Commission onto Coronation Drive, past the unmistakable **Chinese Embassy,** left again at Flynn Drive, and then right onto State Circle. On your right is a handsome white neoclassical building, the **South African Embassy.** The next diplomatic mission is the Williamsburg-style **U.S. Embassy,** followed by the **Indian High Commission** and the **Embassy of the Philippines.**

Continue around State Circle in a counterclockwise direction and turn right onto Kings Avenue. As you cross Kings Avenue Bridge, notice the tall, elegant columns on the island to your left. These are ❿ the bell towers of the **Carillon,** a gift from the British government to mark Canberra's 50th anniversary. Carillon recitals can be heard on

Sunday afternoon between 2:45 and 3:30, and on Wednesday between 12:45 and 1:30.

At the far end of Kings Avenue is Russell Hill, where most of the defense departments are located. The slender monument directly ⑪ ahead with the eagle at its summit is the **Australian-American Memorial,** unveiled in 1954 to commemorate the role of American forces in the defense of Australia during World War II.

Return to the traffic circle and turn right onto Parkes Way and then right at the next traffic circle onto Anzac Parade. Turn left at the first set of traffic lights onto Constitution Avenue and right into the ⑫ parking lot of **St. John the Baptist Church and Schoolhouse,** the oldest surviving buildings in the Canberra district. When they were constructed in the 1840s, this land was part of a 4,000-acre property that belonged to Robert Campbell, a well-known Sydney merchant. The homestead, Duntroon, remained in the Campbell family until it was purchased by the government as a site for the military academy. The schoolhouse has now become a small museum with relics from the early history of the district. *Constitution Ave., Reid, tel. 06/ 247-4203. Museum open Wed. 10–noon, weekends 10–4. Church open daily 9:30–5.*

Continue along Anzac Parade. The name of this broad avenue comes from the initials of the Australian and New Zealand Army Corps, formed during World War I. The avenue is flanked by eight memorials commemorating the army, navy, and air force, as well as some of the campaigns in which Australian troops have fought.

⑬ At the top of this avenue is the **Australian War Memorial,** a monument to the troops who have served the nation in wartime, as well as a superb museum of military weaponry and memorabilia. Built roughly in the shape of a Byzantine church, this is the most popular tourist attraction in the national capital. Exhibits cover the period from the Sudan campaign of the late 19th century to the Vietnam War. The displays include a Lancaster bomber, a Spitfire, tanks, landing barges, the giant German Amiens Gun, and sections of two of the Japanese midget submarines that infiltrated Sydney Harbour during World War II. The memorial is the focus of the Anzac Day ceremony in Canberra, held on April 25. *Anzac Parade, Campbell, tel. 06/243-4211. Open daily 9–4:45.*

Canberra for Free

National Botanic Gardens. Australian plants and trees have evolved in complete isolation from the rest of the world, and these delightful gardens on the lower slopes of Black Mountain display some of the continent's unique flora. The rain forest, rockery, and the eucalyptus lawn—which contains more than 600 species of eucalyptus trees—are the main attractions of this 125-acre site. *Clunies Ross St., Black Mountain, tel. 06/250-9450. Open daily 9–5.*

Royal Australian Mint. If you really want to know how to make money, this is the place to visit. The Observation Gallery inside the mint has a series of windows where visitors can watch Australian coins being minted, from the time the blanks are brought up from the basement storage level to the furnaces where the blanks are softened, and finally to the presses where the coins are stamped. The foyer has a display of rare coins, and silver and gold commemorative coins are on sale. *Dennison St., Deakin, tel. 06/202-6999. Open weekdays 9–4, weekends 10–3; no coin production noon–12:40 PM.*

What to See and Do with Children

Rehwinkel's Animal Park. Set in 50 acres of natural bushland, this open zoo has almost 100 species of birds and other animals, with an emphasis on native fauna. Such animals as wombats, emus, kangaroos, and koalas roam freely around the park, while the dingoes are kept inside large enclosures. The park is located 24 kilometers (15 miles) northeast of Canberra, on the eastern side of the Federal Highway. *Macks Reef Rd., tel. 06/230–3328. Admission: $7.50 adults, $3.75 children 4–14. Open daily 10–5.*

Cockington Green. Thatched houses, castles, canals, and a football pitch have been reproduced in small scale to create a slice of England on this 5-acre site. The Parsons Nose Restaurant serves such suitably British dishes as steak and kidney pie and roast beef with Yorkshire pudding. The park is located about 11 kilometers (7 miles) north of the city center, off the Barton Highway. *Gold Creek Rd., Gungahlin, tel. 06/230–2273. Admission: $6.95 adults, $3.50 children 4–14. Open daily 9:30–4:30.*

Off the Beaten Track

Australian Institute of Sport. Established in 1980 to improve the performance of Australia's elite athletes, this 150-acre site north of the city includes athletic fields, a swimming center, an indoor sports stadium, and a sports medicine center. Guided tours depart from the AIS shop daily at 2 PM (cost: $2 per adult, $1 per school-age child), but at other times visitors can find their own way around with the help of a map, available from the shop for $1. *Leverrier Crescent, Bruce, tel. 06/252–1111.*

Shopping

Gininderra Village, a historic location on the northern outskirts of the city, has a number of rustic crafts shops that sell unusual souvenirs. Items on display include hand-painted clothing, pottery, handmade soaps, silverwork, woodwork, and a wide variety of wool and sheepskin products. Some of these items are made by craftworkers on the premises. The village is located 11 kilometers (7 miles) north of the city. *Barton Hwy., Gininderra, tel. 06/230–2695. Open daily 10–5.*

Cuppacumbalong Craft Centre, a pioneering homestead near the Murrumbidgee River, has now become a crafts gallery for potters, weavers, painters, and woodworkers, many of whom have their studios in the outbuildings. The quality of the work is universally high and there is an opportunity to meet and talk with the craftworkers. The center is located about 34 kilometers (21 miles) south of Canberra, off the Monaro Highway. The restaurant in the homestead serves healthy country food. *Nass Rd., Tharwa, tel. 06/237–5116. Open Wed.–Sun. 11–5.*

Sports and the Outdoors

Ballooning **Balloon Aloft** (tel. 06/285–1540) offers a choice of half-hour weekday flights or slightly longer flights on the weekend. Passengers can expect to drift across the lake, the city center, and the buildings in the Parliamentary Triangle. The balloon leaves at dawn and on weekends it concludes with a champagne breakfast on the ground. On weekdays, the cost is $130 per person, on weekends $185.

Bicycling Canberra has almost 160 kilometers (100 miles) of cycle paths, and the city's relatively flat terrain and dry, mild climate make it a perfect place to explore on two wheels. One of the most popular cycle paths is the 40-kilometer (25-mile) circuit around Lake Burley Griffin. **Mr. Spokes Bike Hire** (Barrine Dr., Acton Park, tel. 06/257–1188) has a wide range of bikes as well as tandems, baby seats, and backpacks. An adult bike is $6 per hour, $21 per day, plus $1 per day for helmet rental.

Boating Rowboats, paddleboats, Windsurfers, and catamarans can be hired on Lake Burley Griffin from **Dobel Boat Hire** (Barrine Dr., Acton, tel. 06/249–6861).

Golf On the lower slopes of Red Hill, the **Federal Golf Course** is regarded as the most challenging of the city's courses. Nonmembers are welcome on most weekdays, but they should contact the club professional in advance. *Red Hill Lookout Rd., tel. 06/281–1888. Cost: $40 for 18 holes.*

An undulating course on the edge of the lake, **Royal Canberra** is the city's premier golf club—due not only to the course itself but also to its membership list, which includes leading politicians from both sides of the government. The club welcomes nonmembers who can show evidence of membership in another golf club. Open days are generally Monday, Thursday, and Friday, but call first. *Westbourne Woods, Yarralumla, tel. 06/282–2655. Cost: $85 for 18 holes.*

Jogging A favorite jogging track is the circuit formed by the lake and its two bridges.

Tennis The **National Sports Club** offers play on synthetic grass courts. *Mouat St., Lyneham, tel. 06/247–0929. Cost: $8 per hr during daylight, $14 per hr under lights. Open daily 8:30 AM–10 PM.*

Dining

By Betty Forrest

Highly recommended restaurants are indicated by a star ★.

Revised by Michael Gebicki

Category	Cost*
$$$$	over $40
$$$	$25–$40
$$	$15–$25
$	under $15

per person, excluding drinks and service

Australian **Charcoal Restaurant.** Practically unchanged since it opened for
$$$ business 32 years ago, this restaurant still serves the capital's best beef. Politicians and businesspeople flock here for lunch—it sometimes seems more like a gentlemen's club than a restaurant. Wooden panels and wine racks line the walls, and at night soft lights and maroon upholstery provide a romantic glow. The superb King Island steaks vary from a ½-pound sirloin to a monster 2-pounder. A limited range of fish and poultry dishes is also available. The wine list has close to 100 red wines. *61 London Circuit, tel. 06/248–8015. Reservations advised. Dress: casual but neat. AE, DC, MC, V. No lunch Sat., closed Sun. and holidays.*

$$$ **The Republic.** Canberra's newest brasserie follows a formula that has been tried and tested in Australia's dining capitals, and the re-

Dining
Barocca Cafe, **4**
Café Lella, **21**
Charcoal Restaurant, **6**
Fringe Benefits, **3**
Gus' Coffee Lounge, **8**
Jean Pierre Le Carousel, **16**
The Oak Room, **13**
The Republic, **10**
Roberto's Trattoria, **17**
Tang Dynasty, **20**
Tosolini's, **7**
Vivaldi, **5**

Lodging
Argyle Executive Apartments, **11**
Avalanche Homestead, **23**
Brindabella Station, **14**
Capital Parkroyal, **9**
Country Comfort Inn, **1**
Down Town Speros Motel, **2**
Hyatt Hotel Canberra, **13**
Manuka Park Apartments, **18**
Olims Canberra, **12**
Pavilion Hotel, **15**
Regency Motor Inn, **22**
Telopea Park Motel, **19**

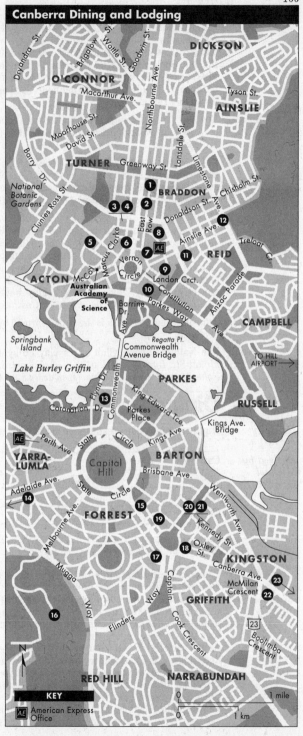

Canberra Dining and Lodging

sult has won the hearts and minds of the
Mediterranean with Asian influences a
tralian bush tucker evident in dishes s
tempura, venison medallions with lilli
and fillet of kangaroo on a papaya salad
num water jugs to the glass panels or
Sydney style to capital-city dining. *20*
Reservations not required. Dress: cas
No lunch Sat., closed Sun.

$$$ **Vivaldi.** Tony Wood's popular restaurant now has a lighter, less ex-
★ pensive lunch menu as an alternative to the à la carte dinner menu.
Imagination is still a high priority, with dishes such as a salad of rare
roast beef with papaya, mango, and date chutney; fillet of veal in
pastry with a wild mushroom and red wine sauce; and Cajun black-
ened baby snapper with cucumber, lime, and yogurt sauce. Dessert
could be macadamia nut parfait with warm, caramelized figs. The
courtyard is especially recommended on sunny days. *University*
Ave., Acton, tel. 06/257–2718. Reservations advised. Dress: casual
but neat. AE, DC, MC, V. No lunch Sat. Closed Sun. and first 2 wks
in Jan.

$$ **Barocca Cafe.** This smart, attractive café is a good choice if you want
dining with a dash of style and a reasonable price at the heart of the
city. The menu, which borrows heavily from Mediterranean cooking, lists bruschetta, Caesar salad, various pasta dishes, and several
chargrilled dishes. The dark wooden furnishings, aquamarine color
scheme, and art deco motifs show a sophistication rarely seen outside the most expensive dining rooms in Canberra. The lunchtime
clientele is largely upwardly mobile public servants. *60 Marcus*
Clarke St., City, tel. 06/248–0253. Reservations accepted. Dress: ca-
sual. AE, MC. BYOB. No lunch Sat., closed Sun.

Chinese **Tang Dynasty.** In Canberra, it's hard to beat the northern Chinese
$$$ and Szechuan specialties at Tang Dynasty, an upscale restaurant ex-
otically decorated with Tang dynasty reproductions and a grand pi-
ano. The popular first course of mermaid's tresses—shredded
Chinese broccoli deep-fried with sugar—is a must. Also consider
the Peking shredded beef, marinated and deep-fried with a touch of
garlic, chili, coriander, and vinegar, or the deboned chicken,
panfried and served with a Peking sauce. *27 Kennedy St., Kingston,*
tel. 06/295–3202. Reservations advised. Dress: neat but casual. AE,
DC, MC, V. No lunch Sun.

French **Jean Pierre Le Carousel.** Superb views from this restaurant take in
$$$$ the new Parliament House and all of Canberra. Owner Jean Pierre
Serex changes the menu seasonally, but he regularly features such
typical French appetizers as snails, frogs' legs, and warm salad of
quail. The fillet of kangaroo with pink peppercorn and black and red
currant sauce is terrific, as are many other entrée options including
seafood, lobster, game, and poultry. *Red Hill Lookout, Red Hill,*
tel. 06/273–1808. Reservations advised. Dress: casual but neat. AE,
DC, MC, V. No lunch Sat. Closed Sun.

$$$$ **The Oak Room.** Located in the Hyatt Hotel, this is Canberra's most
★ elegant restaurant and a must for a glamorous occasion. In the two
formal dining rooms, the privileged atmosphere is complemented by
spacious, formal surroundings and pale lighting. The food is as im-
peccable as the decor, and the result is a grand and cultured atmos-
phere. Dishes include fresh seafood; medallions of venison, beef, and
veal; and such delicacies as mousseline of lobster enveloped in spin-
ach and champagne beurre blanc. The presentation and service are
first-class. *Hyatt Hotel, Commonwealth Ave., Yarralumla, tel. 06/*

270–1234. Reservations required. Jacket required. AE, DC, MC, V.
No lunch Sat. Closed Sun.

ional **Fringe Benefits.** This class act has more polish than the brasserie tag
$$$$ suggests. The fishy, Mediterranean menu fashionably faces East:
★ Thai-style beef salad; seared tuna with a steamed ginger beer, soy,
and wasabi sauce; and chargrilled octopus with chili, basil, lemon,
and olive oil are recommended main courses. Delicious desserts include a quenelle of dark chocolate mousse with crème anglais or
orange tartlette served with white chocolate mousse glazed with
marinated orange slices. Service is polished and professional. *54*
Marcus Clarke St., tel. 06/247–4042. Reservations advised. Dress:
casual but neat. AE, DC, MC, V. No lunch weekends.

$ **Gus' Coffee Lounge.** During the early '70s, the owner of this café in-
curred the wrath of the city planning authorities when he placed tables outside on the sidewalk, and a coffee and slice of cheesecake at
Gus' was a gesture of wild defiance in staid, stolid Canberra. Now
there are at least half a dozen outdoor cafés nearby, but Gus' has
hardly changed, from the Stephane Grappelli music that competes
with the traffic noise to the eclectic range of magazines inside the
café and the powerful cappuccino. The menu is somewhere between
New York and Vienna, with such offerings as bagels, croissants,
waffles, and frankfurters with sauerkraut. *Bunda St. and Garema*
Pl., tel. 06/248–8118. No reservations. Dress: casual. No credit
cards.

$ **Tosolini's.** A current favorite with Canberra's café society, this bus-
tling, Italian-accented brasserie has a choice of indoor or sidewalk
table eating and a bright, energetic atmosphere that makes it
perfect for lunch, especially on a sunny day. The menu lists fresh
fruit juices, fruit shakes, focaccias, baguettes, and a small selection of main meals that usually includes pasta dishes. The coffee
is particularly good, and the cakes have an enthusiastic sweet-
toothed following. *East Row and London Circuit, tel. 06/247–*
4317. No reservations. Dress: casual. AE, DC, MC, V. No dinner
Sun.

Italian **Roberto's Trattoria.** Set on a corner in a leafy south-side shopping
$$$ center, this restaurant has fast become a favorite for its robust Ital-
ian provincial cooking and friendly atmosphere. The menu offers a
wide choice of pasta dishes with various sauces, available either as a
starter or a main course. These are fairly reliable; however, other
dishes that demand more expertise from the kitchen are often disap-
pointing. *Franklin and Furneaux Sts., Manuka, tel. 06/239–7424.*
Reservations advised on weekends. Dress: casual but neat. AE, DC,
MC, V. BYOB. No lunch Sat.

$ **Café Lella.** This cheerful little indoor/outdoor café is popular with
the locals, but unless you're in the area, neither the food nor the sur-
roundings would justify a special excursion. The menu offers Ital-
ian-style salads, pasta dishes, cakes, *granita* (flavored syrup over
crushed ice), and homemade gelato. Smoking is not permitted.
Jardine St., Green Sq., Kingston, tel. 06/239–6383. No reserva-
tions. Dress: casual. No credit cards. BYOB. No dinner Sat.–Wed.
Closed Mon.

Lodging

Most hotels in the city have sprung up since the 1960s, and few offer more than modern, utilitarian facilities. Exceptions are the country homesteads tucked away in the surrounding mountain ranges. These expansive country dwellings give visitors a chance to experience life on working sheep and cattle farms, often in magnificently rugged surroundings, without sacrificing creature comforts. In some cases, however, these properties are too remote from Canberra to serve as a practical base for exploring the national capital.

Highly recommended lodgings are indicated by a star ★.

Category	Cost*
$$$$	over $250
$$$	$150–$250
$$	$80–$150
$	under $80

All prices are for a standard double room.

$$$$ **Avalanche Homestead.** Set on a hillside above the thickly forested valleys of the Tinderry Mountains, this large, modern homestead offers its guests a luxurious taste of the "real" Australia. Rooms are spacious and comfortable, individually furnished with French antiques and plenty of wood; one of the rooms has a water bed. Dinners are splendid banquets, served in the house's vast Baronial Hall. Daily activities for guests include cattle mustering, sheep shearing, trout fishing, and bushwalking. The property is bordered by an 80,000-acre nature reserve, and kangaroos, wombats, foxes, and dingoes are frequently seen in the area. The homestead is located 45 kilometers (28 miles) south of Canberra. *Burra. Mailing address: Box 544, Queanbeyan 2620, tel. 06/236–3245, fax 06/236–3302. 7 rooms, 6 with shower, 1 with bath. Facilities: heated outdoor pool. Tariff includes all meals. AE, DC, MC.*

$$$$ **Brindabella Station.** Overlooking the Goodradigbee River in the rugged Brindabella Ranges, this classic turn-of-the-century Australian homestead combines the traditional lifestyle of a farm holiday with the added attraction of historic pioneer surroundings. Guest numbers are normally limited to a maximum of two couples at a time. Activities on the property include trout fishing, bushwalking, swimming, cycling, canoeing, and watching the abundant wildlife in the area. Guests are also welcome to join in the daily activities of the sheep and cattle property. As an alternative to the accommodations inside the house with all meals provided, guests may choose the inexpensive two-bedroom cottage next to the house. It's rustic but comfortable, and it has its own kitchen facilities. The house is located 60 kilometers (38 miles) west of Canberra. *Brindabella Valley, tel. 06/236–2121. 5 rooms share 2 baths. Nonsmoking guests only. Tariff includes all meals. No credit cards.*

$$$ **Capital Parkroyal.** In a prime location between the city center and the National Convention Centre, this modern, atrium-style hotel offers good facilities and a moderate level of luxury. Decorated in cream and honey tones, guest rooms are large, comfortable, and well equipped. Public areas have a cool, contemporary style, with plenty of chrome and glass accented by giant potted plants and fresh flowers. *1 Binara St., 2601, tel. 06/247–8999, fax 06/257–4903. 293*

rooms with bath. Facilities: outdoor pool, spa, gym, 2 restaurants, 2 bars. AE, DC, MC, V.

$$$ **Hyatt Hotel Canberra.** This elegant hotel is the finest in the national
★ capital. Re-created from the old Canberra Hotel, the unique blend of colonial and art deco styles has been effectively retained. Rooms are large, with luxurious furnishings. Warm peach and earth colors predominate, and the big black-and-cream marble bathrooms will appeal to anyone who enjoys a good soak in the tub. The hotel is within easy walking distance of the Parliamentary Triangle. *Commonwealth Ave., Yarralumla 2601, tel. 06/270–1234. 249 rooms with bath. Facilities: indoor heated pool, spa, sauna, gym, tennis court, 3 restaurants, 2 bars. AE, DC, MC, V.*

$$$ **Pavilion Hotel.** As one of Canberra's most luxurious hotels, this lodging attracts a large business clientele. The atrium features a striking ceiling composed of immense fabric sails. Rooms are large and well maintained, and although they include a number of thoughtful extras such as irons and ironing boards, their character is bland, like that of the rest of the hotel. The staff has been pared and many services—such as porters, concierge, and bedding turn-down—are missing. The hotel is located close to Parliament House, and in the evening its bar is always a stimulating source of political gossip from the parliamentary staff and members of the press who drop in regularly. *Canberra Ave., Forrest 2603, tel. 06/295–3144, fax 06/295–3325. 186 rooms with bath. Facilities: heated indoor pool, spa, sauna, gym, restaurant, bar. AE, DC, MC, V.*

$$ **Argyle Executive Apartments.** Located within a five-minute walk of
★ the city center, these smart, stylish two- and three-bedroom apartments offer good value for a family or small group. Each unit has a spacious living area, a separate kitchen with a microwave oven and dishwasher, and a laundry. Set amid gardens, each has either a balcony or a private courtyard. Apartments are serviced daily. The standby rate—available for on-the-spot bookings—is significantly less than the standard rate. *Currong and Boolee Sts., Reid 2601, tel. 06/275–0800, fax 06/275–0888. 24 apartments with bath. AE, DC, MC, V.*

$$ **Country Comfort Inn.** The rooms and facilities in this recently renovated inn rival those in some of Canberra's more expensive hotels. However, the proprietor dispensed with high-gloss packaging in the public areas and keeps room rates at comparative bargain rates. The dark timber furnishings, piano, and open fire create a cozy, clublike atmosphere in the reception area, while the olive and cinnamon color scheme and gum-leaf motif in the rooms give them a very Australian feel. Unfortunately, the hotel overlooks one of the city's major arteries, so light sleepers should request a poolside room at the back of the hotel. *102 Northbourne Ave., Braddon 2601, tel. 06/249–1411, fax 06/249–6878. 77 rooms with bath. Facilities: heated outdoor pool, bar, restaurant. AE, DC, MC, V.*

$$ **Manuka Park Apartments.** Although each of the comfortable one- and two-bedroom apartments in this low-rise building has cooking facilities, a living room, a laundry, and a separate bedroom, the cost is just slightly more than that for a standard motel room. The fully carpeted, open-plan rooms have a clean, contemporary feel, with cream couches and a black dining table and chairs. Located in a leafy suburb within easy walking distance of the restaurants, boutiques, and antiques shops of the Manuka shopping district, the apartments are serviced daily, and each has a private balcony or courtyard. *Manuka Circle and Oxley St., Manuka 2603, tel. 06/285–1175, fax 06/295–7750. 39 apartments with bath. Facilities: heated outdoor pool. AE, DC, MC, V.*

$$ Olims Canberra. Built around a landscaped courtyard, this former pub has been expanded to offer a choice of accommodations, from double rooms to split-level suites with kitchens to two- and three-bedroom suites. Furnishings and decor are contemporary in style, with laminated, pinelike wood finishes, fabrics and carpets tinged with red ocher, and beige walls. The tariffs are reduced between Friday and Sunday nights. The hotel is about 1 kilometer (½ mile) east of the city center, close to the Australian War Memorial. *Ainslie and Limestone Aves., Braddon 2601, tel. 06/248–5511, fax 06/247–0864. 125 rooms with bath. Facilities: 2 restaurants, bar. AE, DC, MC, V.*

$$ Telopea Park Motel. This motel lies in a tranquil location bordered by parklands in a leafy southern suburb; its rooms are small but a reasonable value. All of them were completely refurbished in 1991–92. Larger family rooms with kitchenettes are also available. *16 New South Wales Crescent, Forrest 2603, tel. 06/295–3722, fax 06/239–6373. 45 rooms with bath. Facilities: bar, restaurant, indoor pool, spa, sauna. AE, MC, V.*

$ Down Town Speros Motel. Even though rooms in this motel have a standard, functional design and the facilities are limited, both the price and the proximity to the city center make this a good choice for the budget traveler. The hotel is spotlessly clean. *82 Northbourne Ave., Braddon 2601, tel. 06/249–1388, fax 06/247–2523. 65 rooms with bath. Facilities: restaurant. AE, DC, MC, V.*

$ Regency Motor Inn. Situated close to the railway station and the tourist attractions on the south side of the lake, these motel rooms are reasonable value if you are looking for nothing more than a bed for the night. In addition to the double rooms, two-bedroom suites with cooking facilities ideal for families are also available. *47 McMillan Crescent, Griffith 2603, tel. 06/295–2700, fax 06/295–0827. 60 rooms with bath. Facilities: outdoor pool, playground, restaurant, bar. AE, DC, MC, V.*

The Arts and Nightlife

The Arts

The center for the performing arts is the **Canberra Theatre Centre** (Civic Sq., London Circuit, tel. 06/257–1077), which is composed of two theaters used by the local opera company, theatrical troupe, and symphony orchestra. Performances by major national musical and artistic companies such as the Australian Ballet are frequently held here. For a listing of current events, check the entertainment pages of the *Canberra Times.*

Nightlife

Canberra after dark has a reputation for drudgery. Actually, the city isn't quite as dull as the rest of Australia thinks, nor as lively as the citizens of Canberra would like to believe. There is no nightclub district—clubs are scattered throughout the city center and suburban shopping centers. Except on weekends, few places offer live music. The Thursday edition of the *Canberra Times* has a "What's On" section.

Bobby McGee's Conglomeration. The party atmosphere at this bright, popular restaurant/nightclub/disco appeals to a varied clientele. In the restaurant, you can be seated by Cinderella, offered cocktails by a matador, and waited on by a Roman centurion. In the

'50s-style disco, the music ranges from "Heartbreak Hotel" to this week's Top 40. Service is slick and professional, and it would be hard not to have a good time. *Lakeside Hotel, London Circuit, tel. 06/ 257–7999. Admission: $5 Sat. after 8 PM. Open weekdays 5 PM–3 AM, Sat. 6 PM–4 AM.*

Casino Canberra. Canberra's nightlife received a major boost when this modern casino opened in the National Convention Centre at the end of 1992. An attempt has been made to create a European-style facility by leaving out slot machines in favor of such more sociable games as roulette, blackjack, baccarat, and keno. *31 Constitution Ave., tel. 06/257–7074. Open weekdays 10 AM–4 AM, continuously Fri. 10 AM–Mon. 4 AM.*

Dorettes Bistro. This dark, smoky hangout is popular with the jazz crowd. Live bands play from 9 PM, and there's poetry every other Sunday afternoon. *Garema Pl., tel. 06/247–4946. Admission: $5 Fri.– Sat. Open Mon.–Sat. 5 PM–midnight, Sun. 4–7.*

Pandora's at Night. The disco on the upper level of this two-story entertainment center is one of the liveliest in the city, especially on Saturday night, when it attracts a large crowd of under-25s. *Mort and Alinga Sts., City, tel. 06/248–7405. Admission: $5 Fri.–Sat. Open Thurs.–Sat. 9:30 PM–5 AM.*

The Private Bin. One of Canberra's longest-running night spots, this large, loud club incorporates a bar, beer garden, and disco on three levels. The clientele is mostly under 25, but the Waffles Piano Bar attracts an older, more sophisticated group of patrons. The comedy nights, held every Wednesday from about 8 PM, are recommended. *50 Northbourne Ave., tel. 06/247–3030. Open Mon.–Sat. noon– approx. 2 AM, Sun. 8 PM–1 AM.*

Elsewhere in the A.C.T.

Lanyon. On the plain beside the Murrumbidgee River, this classic homestead from pioneering days has been magnificently restored. When it was built in 1859, the house was the centerpiece of a self-contained community, and many of the outbuildings and workshops have been preserved. The nearby Nolan Gallery displays a selection of the well-known Ned Kelly paintings by the famous Australian artist Sir Sidney Nolan. The property is located 30 kilometers (19 miles) south of Canberra off the Monaro Highway. *Tharwa Dr., Tharwa, tel. 06/237–5136. Admission: homestead, $2.50 adults, $1.30 children, $6.30 family (2 adults with unlimited children); homestead and gallery, $3.70 adults, $1.80 children, $9.20 family. Open Tues.–Sun. 10–4. Closed Mon.*

Tidbinbilla Nature Reserve. Set in eucalyptus forests in the mountain ranges 40 kilometers (25 miles) southwest of Canberra, this 12,000-acre reserve has large walk-through enclosures where you can observe kangaroos and koalas in their native environment. The walking trails offer a choice of rocky mountaintops, open grassland, or gullies thick with tree ferns. The reserve also has some unusual rock formations, including Hanging Rock—a granite outcrop used as a shelter by the Aboriginal inhabitants of the area. Between April and September, bird-watchers should plan to visit the reserve during the 2 PM feeding time, when many colorful species can be seen and photographed at close quarters. *Mountain Creek Rd., Tidbinbilla, tel. 06/237–5120. Open daily 9–6, 9–9 in summer.*

Tidbinbilla Space Tracking Station. Managed and operated by the Australian Space Office, this is one of the long-distance arms of the U.S. National Aeronautics and Space Administration (NASA). The function of the three giant antennae at this site is to relay commands and data between NASA and space vehicles or orbiting satellites. The first pictures of men walking on the moon were transmitted to this tracking station. The tracking station, located 40 kilometers (25 miles) southwest of Canberra, is not open to the public, but the visitors' information center houses models and audiovisual displays. *Paddy's River Rd., tel. 06/249–0811. Open daily 9–5.*

5 Melbourne and Victoria

By Walter Glaser and Michael Gebicki

Updated by Michael Gebicki

Separated from New South Wales by the mighty Murray River and backed by a coastline of rugged beauty, Victoria boasts within its small borders a terrain as varied as any in Australia. Visitors expecting big sky and vast desert horizons will be disappointed, however, for Victoria is a settled land of lush farms, vineyards, forests, and mountain peaks. Victoria is younger than its rival, New South Wales, but you would never know it. Visitors here will gain a sense of history and continuity often missing in other Australian states where humanity's grasp on the land seems temporary and precarious. Even the smallest rural community in Victoria seems to boast a museum.

If, like its dowager namesake, Victoria is a little stuffy and old-fashioned, then the state capital of Melbourne is positively Old World. This city of 3 million people is also Australia's cultural, financial, and intellectual capital—and Melburnians won't let you forget it. For all the talk of Australia's egalitarian society, Melbourne society displays an almost European obsession with class. The city is the site of the nation's most prestigious schools and universities, and nowhere is it more important to have attended the right one. And, in a country whose convict ancestors are the frequent butt of jokes, Melburnians pride themselves on the fact that unlike Sydney, their city was founded by free men and women who came to Victoria during the gold rush.

This difference between the two cities is just one element in a fierce rivalry that has waged unabated since Melbourne threatened to upstage Sydney as the major city during the 19th-century gold rush. Today, Melbourne is undoubtedly the nation's second city, but it has yet to come to terms with that position. The Victorian Arts Centre, for example, is the city's rather utilitarian response to the slickness of the Sydney Opera House. The difference between the two, Melburnians will point out, is that the Victorian Arts Centre actually gets used. If Melbourne is a slightly stuffy English governess, then Sydney is a bawdy California adolescent in a swimsuit!

Billy Graham gave Sydneysiders additional ammunition when he called Melbourne "one of the most moral cities in the world." But if Melburnians appear staid and stolid, it's only because they're saving themselves for the weekend sporting events. The city is sports mad, and Mr. Graham would have wished to reconsider his remarks if he had ever witnessed the glorious, freewheeling Melbourne Cup. On the first Tuesday of each November, Melburnians head out to Flemington Racetrack for the horse race that brings the entire nation to a grinding halt. Gaily dressed in all manner of outrageous costume, from tutus to tiaras, blue-collar workers and society dames converge here to sip champagne, picnic, and cheer on their favorite ponies before making the rounds of the Cup parties.

Perhaps the mania that accompanies almost all Melbourne sporting events is a holdover from the raucous excitement that blossomed in the city during the days of the gold rush. When gold was discovered in 1851, Victoria was overrun with fortune seekers. Before long, the towns of Bendigo, Castlemaine, and Ballarat were whirlwinds of activity, as miners poured in from around the country and the world to try their luck in the goldfields. These were wild times, and the diggers who rolled into nearby Melbourne to blow off steam were a colorful bunch. The lucky ones had plenty of money to spend, and spend they did—Melbourne grew by leaps and bounds, and many of the gracious, refurbished buildings that line Melbourne's streets today are products of that boom time. Melbourne's population quadrupled in the 10 years following the rush, as many of those who came to seek their fortunes in Victoria settled around what was rapidly becoming a bona fide capital city.

In recent years, Melbourne has seen another rush of immigrants, lured by the same dreams of success as their gold-hungry predecessors. Today, Melbourne is an ethnic melting pot swirling with dozens of nationalities, helping to recast this Victorian city in a more cosmopolitan light.

Melbourne

When she came to Melbourne in 1956 to make the film *On the Beach*, Ava Gardner is supposed to have said that the city *would* be a great place to make a movie about the end of the world. These days, Melburnians remember that remark with humor rather than rancor, which shows just how far this city of 3 million has come.

Unlike Sydney, Melbourne charms rather than dazzles. Sydney is marginally bigger—and bolder and brassier by far—but while Sydney has neither elegance nor calm, Melbourne has both. It is a city of parks, gardens, boulevards, and outdoor cafés—a city made for strolling, looking, and lingering. In a recent survey conducted by the Washington, D.C.–based Population Crisis Committee, Melbourne was named the most livable city in the world.

Melburnians may tell you—with some justification—that their city is the cultural capital of Australia, and yet its most recurring symbol is not the Victorian Arts Centre but its municipal trams. Solid, dependable, going about their business with a minimum of fuss, the trams are an essential part of Melbourne. A definitive Melbourne experience is to climb aboard a tram and proceed silently and smoothly up the "Paris end" of Collins Street.

Melbourne is built on a coastal plain at the top of the giant horseshoe of Port Phillip Bay. The city center is an orderly grid of streets laid out on the north bank of the Yarra River. Here stand the State Parliament building, the banks, the multinational corporations, and the splendid Victorian buildings that sprang up in the wake of the gold rush. This is the heart of Melbourne, and you can explore it at a leisurely pace in a couple of days. If you have longer, take an afternoon stroll along the Esplanade at St. Kilda, rub shoulders with the locals in the Victoria markets, nip into the Windsor for afternoon tea, hire a canoe at Studley Park to paddle along one of the prettiest stretches of the Yarra River—and you will discover Melbourne's soul as well as its heart.

Arriving and Departing by Plane

Airports and Airlines   **Melbourne Airport** is located 22 kilometers (14 miles) northwest of the central business district and can be reached easily from Melbourne on the Tullamarine Freeway. The international terminal is located in the center of the airport complex; domestic terminals are found on either side.

International airlines flying into Melbourne include **Air New Zealand, American, Ansett Australia, British Airways, Continental, Qantas,** and **United.** The local carriers currently serving Melbourne are **Ansett Australia/Kendell** (tel. 13–1300) and **Qantas** (tel. 13–1313).

Between the Airport and Center City	**Skybus** (tel. 03/335–3066) is a private bus service that operates between the airport terminals and the city, but for three or more people traveling together, a taxi to the city is a better value. En route from the airport, the bus makes a loop through the city before terminating at Spencer Street station. *Departures approximately every 30 min weekdays 6 AM–7:30 PM, weekends 6 AM–7 PM. Cost: $9 adults, $4.50 children under 15.*

Taxis are widely available. The cost of a taxi into town is approximately $29. **Limousines** to the city cost about $50. Some of the larger companies include **Astra** (tel. 03/819–7979), **Embassy** (tel. 03/326–6033), and **Hughes** (tel. 03/427–0533).

Arriving and Departing by Train, Bus, and Car

By Train **Spencer Street Railway Station** is located at Spencer and Little Collins streets. Public transportation is accessible from here, but travelers with cumbersome luggage may want to hire one of the many taxis waiting outside the station.

By Bus **Greyhound** (tel. 13–1238) and **Pioneer Express** (tel. 13–2030) link the city with all Australian capital cities and with major towns and cities throughout Victoria. The terminal for both is on the corner of Swanston and Franklin streets.

By Car The major route into Melbourne is the Hume Highway, which runs northeast to Canberra and Sydney. The Princes Highway follows the coast to Sydney in one direction and Adelaide in the other. The Western Highway runs northwest to Ballarat, and the Calder Highway travels north to Bendigo.

Getting Around

By Public Transportation The city's public transport system includes buses, trains, and trams (streetcars), and it is the extensive tram network that many visitors will find the most useful. Melbourne has one of the world's largest network of trams, with 365 kilometers (227 miles) of track in the inner city and suburbs, and for the visitor the system is a delight—fast, convenient, and dazzlingly cheap. The city's public transport system is operated by Metropolitan Transit (tel. 13–1638), which divides Melbourne into three zones. Zone 1 is the urban core, and most visitors will spend most of their time within that zone. The basic ticket is the one-zone ticket, which can be purchased from the tram conductor for $2.10 and is valid for travel within that zone on any tram, bus, or train for a period of two hours after purchase. For most visitors, the most useful ticket is the Zone 1 day ticket, which costs $3.80 and is available on board any tram. Children under 14 travel at half the adult fare. For anyone intending to make extensive use of Melbourne's public transport system, a route map is available for $2 from the Met Shop at 103 Elizabeth Street. Trams run until midnight and can be hailed wherever you see a red, black, and white tram-stop sign.

By Taxi Taxis are metered, and empty taxis can be hailed on the street and at taxi stands, or they can be ordered by phone. Some of the major taxi companies include **Silver Top** (tel. 03/345–3455), **Regal Combined** (tel. 03/810–0222), **Northern Suburban** (tel. 03/480–2222), **Embassy** (tel. 03/320–0320), and **Black Cabs** (tel. 03/567–3333).

By Car Two unusual road rules apply in Melbourne because of the tram traffic on the city's major roads. Trams should be passed on the *left*, and when a tram stops, the cars behind it also must stop, unless there is a railed safety zone for tram passengers.

At various intersections within the city, drivers wishing to turn *right* must stay in the *left* lane as they enter the intersection, then wait for the traffic signals to change before proceeding with the turn. The rule is intended to prevent traffic from impeding tram service. For complete directions, look for the black and white traffic signs suspended overhead as you enter each intersection where this rule applies. All other right-hand turns are made from the center. It is far easier to understand this rule by seeing it in action rather than reading about it.

The **Royal Automobile Club of Victoria** (230 Collins St., tel. 03/650–1522) is the major source of information on all aspects of road travel in Victoria. Offices in Melbourne are open weekdays 9–5; at other times or for other locations, call 03/795–5511.

By Rental Car **Avis** (tel. 008/22–5533), **Budget** (tel. 13–2727), and **Hertz** (tel. 03/698–2555) all have offices at Melbourne Airport as well as downtown. If you hire from a major car-rental company, expect to pay between $75 and $90 per day for an automatic sedan and about $65 per day for a compact standard model. If you do not need the latest model and can return the car to the pick-up point, the smaller local rental agencies offer vehicles for as little as $35 per day including insurance. Some of these smaller agencies are **Cheapa** (tel. 03/878–9882), **Delta** (tel. 13–3582), and **Dollar** (tel. 03/662–1188).

Important Addresses and Numbers

Tourist Information The main tourist information center is the **Royal Automobile Club of Victoria** (*see above*), which can also assist with accommodations and transport bookings.

Tourist information booths are located on the Collins Street side of City Square and in Bourke Street Mall, near the corner of Swanston Street.

For telephone inquiries, call **Statewide Tourist Information Service** (tel. 03/726–7777) weekdays 8–8, weekends 8–noon.

For a recorded listing of current events in Melbourne, call the **Information Line** (tel. 03/0055–34360).

Emergencies Dial 000 for **police, fire,** or **ambulance** services.

Alfred Hospital (Commercial Rd., Prahran, tel. 03/276–2000).

Royal Dental Hospital (cnr. Elizabeth St. and Flemington Rd., tel. 03/341–0222).

Royal Women's Hospital (132 Grattan St., Carlton, tel. 03/344–2000).

St. Vincent's Hospital (Victoria Parade, Fitzroy, tel. 03/288–2211).

Leonard Long Pharmacy (Williams Rd. and High St., Prahran, tel. 03/510–3977) is open 9 AM–midnight.

Guided Tours

Orientation Tours **Gray Line** offers several guided tours of Melbourne and its surroundings by coach and boat. The Melbourne Experience is a basic three-hour tour that visits the main attractions in the city center as well as some of the surrounding parks. The tour departs daily at 9 AM from 101 Bourke Street, near the Southern Cross Plaza. *181 Flin-*

ders St., Melbourne, tel. 03/654–7700. Fare: $33 adults, $16.50 children under 14.

The **Australian Pacific** City Explorer Tour is a do-it-yourself tour of the city aboard a bus that makes a circuit of the city's major attractions, including the zoo and the parks to the east. The tour ticket is valid for one complete circuit, and ticket holders can leave the double-decker bus at any of the eight stops along the route and board any following City Explorer bus. The tour begins at Flinders Street Station. Buses leave hourly beginning at 10 AM. The last bus is at 4 PM. *181 Flinders St., tel. 03/650–1511. Fare: $15 adults, $8 children under 14, $32 family (2 adults, 2 children).*

Special-Interest Tours
Sports Tours

Koala Golf Tours (tel. 03/598–2574) specializes in golf tours around the city. The tour cost, which includes golf clubs and shoes if necessary, varies from $90 to $200 per person, depending on the greens fees at the course.

Yarra River Cruises

The modern, glass-enclosed boats of the **Melbourne River Tours** fleet take 90-minute cruises daily from Berth 1, Princes Walk, either west through the commercial heart of the city or east through the parks and gardens. The boat departs from Princes Walk, on the opposite side of Princes Bridge from Flinders Street Station. *Melbourne River Tours, Vault 1, Princes Walk, tel. 03/629–7233 or 03/650–2055. Fare: $11 adults, $5.50 children under 15. Cruises: every hr 10 AM–4 PM (east); every hr 10:30 AM–4:30 PM (west).*

Bay Cruises

The *Wattle* is a restored steam tug that makes weekend cruises on Port Phillip Bay. The highlight of the one-hour voyage is a visit to a seal colony. The boat operates from Melbourne between mid-October and the end of June, except for the summer holidays, when cruises depart from Rye on the Mornington Peninsula. *Station Pier, Port Melbourne, tel. 03/328–2739. Cost: $8 adults, $5 senior citizens and children. Boat departs weekends 11, 12:30, 2, 3:30.*

Walking Tours

Melbourne Heritage Walks and Tours (tel. 03/827–1085) is a 90-minute stroll that takes its cues from the city's architecture to portray a fascinating picture of the social and political history of Melbourne. Tour guide Maxine Wood is lively and entertaining, and her contacts allow her entry to such seldom-seen places as the backstage chambers of Parliament House and the mayoral quarters at the Town Hall. The tour costs $20 per person, or $35 per hour for a private tour.

Orientation

The heart of Melbourne is an orderly grid of wide streets bordered by the Yarra River to the south and a string of parks to the east. The western half of the city is Melbourne's business district, and there is little reason for the tourist to stray into this world of suits and office towers. Most visitors will find that they spend the greater part of their time in the eastern half of the city. Tour 1 is a walking tour that explores the museums, churches, and grand municipal buildings at the center of the city. Tour 2 is a leisurely stroll through the city's fashionable shopping precinct to the parks and gardens to the east of the city center. Neither tour is demanding and both could be combined in a single day. For visitors with more time, the tribal villages of Melbourne such as St. Kilda and Fitzroy (*see* Other Places of Interest, *below*) are recommended.

Tour 1: City Center

Numbers in the margin correspond to points of interest on the Downtown Melbourne map.

❶ This tour begins at **Flinders Street Station,** a grand Edwardian building and the hub of Melbourne's suburban rail network. The clocks on the front of the building are a favorite meeting place for Melburnians.

❷ Cross Flinders Street to **St. Paul's Cathedral,** the headquarters of Melbourne's Anglican faith. Begun in 1877 and completed in 1892, the church is regarded as one of the most important works of William Butterfield, a leader of the Gothic Revival style in England. The interior is highly decorative, right down to the patterned floor tiles. The English organ is particularly noteworthy. *Flinders and Swanston Sts., tel. 03/650–3791. Open 7 AM–7 PM.*

Leave the church and continue along Flinders Street, passing the **statue of Matthew Flinders,** the Royal Navy lieutenant who is remembered as the first to circumnavigate the Australian coastline, in 1801–03.

❸ At the northern end of the cathedral is **City Square,** where Melbourne comes to eat lunch, listen to bands, and assemble for protest marches. Architecturally, this charmless square is regarded as a disaster, and a major redevelopment is planned for the site.

Turn left into Collins Street. On the right side of the road in this block is the **Royal Automobile Club of Victoria** (*see* Getting Around
❹ by Car, *above*). Turn right into the **Block Arcade,** Melbourne's most elegant 19th-century shopping arcade, which was restored in 1988 when a hundred years of grime was scraped back to reveal the magnificent mosaic floor. The arcade was built during the 1880s, when the city was flushed with the prosperity of the gold rushes, a period that is recalled as "Marvelous Melbourne."

Turn right between Hunt Leather and the Weiss clothing shop to leave the arcade. Cross Little Collins Street and bear slightly to the
❺ right to enter the **Royal Arcade.** Built in 1869, the arcade is the oldest shopping arcade in the city. Despite alterations, it retains an airy graceful elegance that is notably lacking in more modern shopping centers. Walk about 30 paces into the arcade, turn around, and look up to see the statues of Gog and Magog, the mythical monsters that toll the hour on either side of **Gaunt's Clock.** At the end of this arcade is a wrought-iron portico from the same period, one of the few remaining examples of the verandas that once populated the city
❻ center. This portico leads to the **Bourke Street Mall,** once the busiest east–west thoroughfare in the city and now a pedestrian zone (but watch out for the trams that still speed through). Two of the city's biggest department stores are located here, **Myer** (no. 314) and **David Jones** (no. 310). An essential part of growing up in Melbourne is being taken to Myer's at Christmas to see the window displays.

Leave the mall via Elizabeth Street, passing the front of the 1889 **General Post Office.** At the next major intersection is the Roman
❼ Catholic **Church of St. Francis,** constructed in 1845, when the city was barely a decade old. The simple, frugal design is in stark contrast to the Gothic exuberance of St. Paul's, built 40 years later. That difference is largely due to the prosperity bestowed on the city by the intervening gold rush.

Walk along Lonsdale Street to the corner of Swanston Street and turn left. A block up on the right, set on a rise behind lawns, heroic

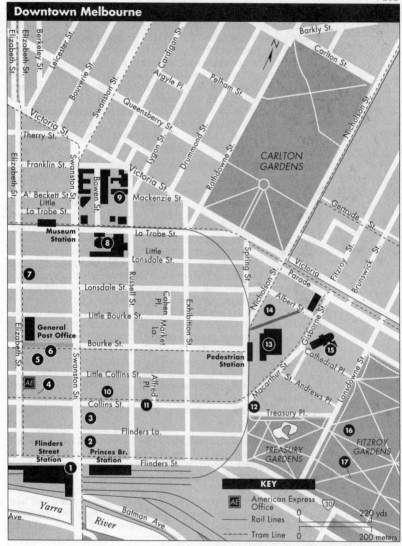

Downtown Melbourne

KEY

AE American Express Office

— Rail Lines

--- Tram Line

0 — 220 yds
0 — 200 meters

Athenaeum Theatre and Library, **10**
Block Arcade, **4**
Bourke Street Mall, **6**
Church of St. Francis, **7**
City Square, **3**
Cook's Cottage, **17**
Fitzroy Gardens, **16**
Flinders Street Station, **1**
Old Melbourne Gaol, **9**
Old Treasury Building, **12**
Paris End, **11**
Parliament Gardens, **14**
Royal Arcade, **5**
St. Patrick's, **15**
St. Paul's Cathedral, **2**
State Houses of Parliament, **13**
State Library and Museum of Victoria, **8**

8 statuary, and a classical portico is the **State Library and Museum of Victoria.** The handsome 1853 building was constructed during the financial boom that followed the Victorian gold rush. The collection of manuscripts in the century-old State Library is one of the finest in Australia. The library houses more than 1.5 million volumes and a vast number of maps, prints, and paintings. A highlight of the library's holdings is the records of the Burke and Wills Expedition. Visitors are welcome to walk inside the library to inspect the 35-meter (115-foot) dome of the Reading Room, the largest reinforced concrete dome in the world when it was built in 1913. A reader's ticket, granted free of charge to those pursuing genuine research, is necessary to obtain access to the library's books.

The Museum of Victoria houses the state's collections of natural history, science, and technology, including dioramas of Australian animals in their natural habitats, a collection of dinosaur specimens, a children's museum, a planetarium, and a display of Aboriginal artifacts. One of its most famous exhibits is the stuffed carcass of Phar Lap, a legend of the Australian track. The New Zealand–bred racehorse won 37 races of 51 starts in the 1930s. His death, which occurred under suspicious circumstances while he was competing in the United States, is still remembered with bitterness by some members of the racing fraternity. Another highlight of the collection is a suit of armor that was made for Ned Kelly, the most famous of all the bushrangers (outlaws) and subject of a famous series of paintings by Sir Sydney Nolan. The armor, made from plow blades, is crude but effective, as shown by the pockmarks made by police bullets. Kelly, whose gang murdered three policemen in the highlands of northern Victoria, was eventually captured after a shootout with the police at Glenrowan. The claim that Kelly was driven to a life of crime by police harassment is not supported by the facts, but he remains a folk hero. *328 Swanston St., tel. 03/669–9888. Museum admission: $5 adults, $2.50 children 5–16, $15 family. Library open Mon. 1–9, Tues. 10–6, Wed. 10–9, Thurs.–Sun 10–6. Museum open daily 10–5.*

Leave the museum and turn right into La Trobe Street, then left into Russell Street, past the ornate sandstone facade of the **Melbourne Magistrate's Court.** A short distance farther along Russell **9** Street is the **Old Melbourne Gaol,** now a museum run by the Victorian branch of the National Trust. The jail has three tiers of cells with catwalks around the upper levels. Its most famous inmate was Ned Kelly, who was hanged here in 1880. His death mask and one of the four suits of armor used by his gang are displayed in a ground-floor cell. *Russell St., tel. 03/663–7228. Admission: $6 adults, $3 children under 16, $15 family. Open daily 9:30–4:30.*

Time Out On the sunny side of Elizabeth Street opposite Victoria Market (*see* Shopping, *below*), **Cafe Swe-Dish** is a European-style café that serves a wide choice of dishes with a Scandinavian flavor, from herring to cold smorgasbord platters loaded with meat and cheese. For smaller appetites, the coffee and cakes are good value. *510 Elizabeth St., tel. 03/663–1910. Open daily 8–3.*

Tour 2: Paris End, Parliament, and Gardens

Begin at **City Square** and follow Collins Street as it rises to the east. On the right side at the top of the square is a **statue of Robert Burke and William Wills,** whose expedition was the first to cross Australia from south to north, in 1860–1861. In bronze as in life, their fate is to wander, and this statue has already been relocated several times.

⑩ Opposite the statue is the **Athenaeum Theatre and Library.** The present building, which includes an art gallery as well as a theater and library, was built in 1886. These days, the Athenaeum is used mainly for live theatrical performances, yet it is also remembered as the venue for the first talking picture show ever screened in Australia. If you can't get to a performance, take a peek inside between 8:30 and 5 on weekdays, and 8:30–noon on Saturday. *180 Collins St., tel. 03/650–3100.*

The area beyond the cream and red Romanesque-style facade of St.
⑪ Michael's Uniting Church is known as the **Paris End** of Collins Street, a name coined by Melburnians to identify the chic elegance of its fashion shops, as well as the highfalutin airs that apply here. The most famous of the shops is **Georges,** a name synonymous with old-fashioned service and outstanding quality. *162 Collins St., tel. 03/283–5555. Open Mon.–Thurs. 9–5:30, Fri. 9–9, Sat. 9–4.*

Another is **Le Louvre,** a favorite with Melbourne's high society and a study in minimalist window dressing—no need for haute couture to trumpet its wares. *74 Collins St., tel. 03/650–1300. Open weekdays 9–5:30, Sat. 9–12:30.*

At the end of Collins Street is the neoclassical brick and bluestone
⑫ facade of the **Old Treasury Building,** built in 1857 as a repository for the gold that was pouring into Melbourne from the gold mines in Ballarat and Bendigo. The gold was held in subterranean vaults protected by iron bars and foot-thick walls. The architect, J. J. Clark, designed this building when he was only 19. The building is not open to the public. *Treasury Pl. and Spring St.*

Turn left into Spring Street, walking past the genteel **Windsor Hotel** (*see* Off the Beaten Track and Lodging, *below*). A little farther
⑬ along on the right are the **State Houses of Parliament.** Begun in 1856, this building was used as the National Parliament from the time of federation in 1900 until 1927, when the first Parliament House was completed in Canberra. Today, this commanding building houses the Victorian Parliament. When Parliament is in session, visitors are welcome to watch the political process at work from the public gallery. At other times the Upper and Lower House chambers are open to the public. The Upper House, in particular, the Legislative Chamber, is a study in Victorian opulence. To view these chambers, simply ask at the reception desk inside the front door. Parliament usually sits on Tuesday afternoon and all day Wednesday and Thursday between March and July and again between August and November. The view down Bourke Street from the front steps is particularly spectacular at night. *Spring St., tel. 03/651–8911. Admission free. Open weekdays 9–4. Guided tours at 10, 11, 2, 3, and 3:45 when Parliament is not in session.*

Time Out **Pellegrini's Espresso Bar and Restaurant** (66 Bourke St., tel. 03/662–1885) serves industrial-strength coffee and bargain-priced cakes, sandwiches, and pasta dishes. At lunchtime, the narrow bar draws a mixed crowd of students, shoppers, and business executives, but the restaurant at the back is usually less crowded. For a slightly more formal meal, try the **Windsor Grill** in the Windsor Hotel (103 Spring St., tel. 03/653–0653). Both are just a stone's throw from Parliament House.

Walk down the front steps of the Parliament building and turn right
into Spring Street, then right again to walk through the **Parliament
Gardens.** Across Spring Street is the handsome yellow facade of the
Princess Theatre, which dates from 1886. The ornate, wedding-cake-
style theater was refurbished almost solely from the proceeds of a
single production, *Phantom of the Opera,* a blockbuster success for
the theater and an economic bonus for the city of Melbourne. At the
far end of the gardens is **St. Peter's,** which was built in 1846, making
it one of Melbourne's oldest buildings. It was on the steps of this
church that Melbourne was proclaimed a city in 1848.

Across the other side of Gisborne Street rises the grand bulk of **St.
Patrick's,** Melbourne's Roman Catholic cathedral. Construction on
the building began in 1858 and was not completed until 1940. This is
another example of the Gothic Revival style, yet it lacks the exuber-
ant decoration of St. Paul's, Melbourne's Anglican cathedral. Ireland supplied Australia with many of its early immigrants,
especially during the Irish potato famine in the middle of the 19th
century, and the church is closely associated with Irish Catholicism
in Australia. A statue of the Irish patriot Daniel O'Connell stands in
the courtyard. *Cathedral Pl., tel. 03/667–0377. Open weekdays
6:30–6, weekends 7:15 AM–7:30 PM.*

From the cathedral, follow Cathedral Place to its end and cross to
the 65-acre **Fitzroy Gardens,** turning slightly to the right to follow
the **Avenue of Elms** as it curves down the hill. This majestic stand of
130-year-old trees is one of the few in the world that has not been
devastated by Dutch elm disease.

Continue past the stone bridge on the left to **Cook's Cottage.** This
modest stone cottage, the property of the Pacific navigator Captain
James Cook, was transported stone by stone from Great Ayton in
Yorkshire and reerected here in 1934. It is believed that Cook lived
in the cottage between his voyages. The interior is simple and
sparsely furnished—suitable preparation for a man who would
spend much of his life in cramped quarters aboard small ships.
*Fitzroy Gardens, near Landsowne St. and Wellington Parade. Ad-
mission: $2.50 adults, $1.20 children under 14. Open daily 9–5, 9–
5:30 in summer.*

Melbourne for Free

The **parks and gardens** in and around Melbourne are among the most
impressive features of the capital of the Garden State. More than
one-quarter of the inner city has been set aside as recreational
space. The profusion of trees, plants, and flowers creates an atmosphere of rural tranquility within this thriving city.

The **Royal Botanic Gardens,** next to King's Domain Gardens, are a
fine example of landscaped gardens. The present design and layout
was the brainchild of W. R. Guilfoyle, curator and director of the
gardens from 1873 to 1910. Within its 100 acres are 12,000 species of
native and imported plants and trees, sweeping lawns, and ornamental lakes populated with ducks and swans that love to be fed.
The oldest section of the gardens is Tennyson lawn, where there are
four English elm trees more than 120 years old. A fern gully built
around an old billabong (pond) contains American swamp cypress,
the tallest tree in the gardens. You can discover the gardens on your
own or by joining the free guided walks that leave at 10 AM and 11 AM
daily from the Plant Craft Cottage. The main entrance to the gardens
is on Birdwood Avenue, near Dallas Brooks Drive. *Tel. 03/650–9424.
Admission free. Open Mon.–Sat. 7AM–sunset, summer; 7:30 AM–*

sunset, winter; Sun. and holidays, 8:30 AM–sunset, summer; 9 AM–sunset, winter. Friends of the Garden Shop, tel. 03/820–1125. Open daily 10–4:30. Tropical Plants Glasshouse, tel. 03/650–9424. Open daily 10–4. Plant Craft Cottage, tel. 03/650–3235. Open weekdays 10–3.

King's Domain Gardens include Queen Victoria Gardens, Alexandra Gardens, the Shrine of Remembrance, Pioneer Women's Garden, and the Sidney Myer Music Bowl. The floral clock in Queen Victoria Gardens talks and tells time, providing a brief recorded history of the gardens in and around Melbourne. It is situated opposite the Victorian Arts Centre on St. Kilda Road in one of the Domain's many informal gardens.

Carlton Gardens. The 40 acres of tree-lined paths, artificial lakes, and flower beds in this English-style 19th-century park form a backdrop for the Exhibition Buildings that were erected in 1880 and are still used for trade shows. The gardens are bounded by Victoria Parade and Nicholson, Carlton, and Rathdowne streets.

What to See and Do with Children

For thrills and excitement try **Luna Park,** an amusement park modeled after New York's Coney Island. The main attraction here is the Big Dipper. *Lower Esplanade, St. Kilda, tel. 03/534–0654. Major rides cost $3 for adults, $2 for children under 12. Free admission to park. Open Fri. 7:30 PM–11:15 PM, Sat. 1:30 PM–5:30 PM and 7:30 PM–11:15 PM, Sun. 1:30 PM–5:30 PM.*

Recognized as one of the finest zoos in the world, the **Melbourne Zoological Gardens** have recently undergone some major changes. The grounds have been transformed into gardens, and most of the animal enclosures have been renovated into "open-environment settings." Animals of particular interest are those unique to Australia, such as the koala, kangaroo, wombat, emu, and echidna. There are also a lion park, a reptile house, a butterfly pavilion, and, in a simulated African rain forest, the only group of gorillas in the country. The zoo is 4 kilometers (2½ miles) north of Melbourne city center. *Elliot Ave., Parkville, tel. 03/285–9300. Admission: $11 adults, $5.50 children 4–14. Open daily 9–5.*

The Children's Museum at the Museum of Victoria features hands-on exhibits explaining the workings of the human body. The museum is geared to children from 5 to 12 years of age. *328 Swanston St., tel. 03/669–9888. Open weekdays noon–5, weekends 10–5. Closed Christmas week.*

Other Places of Interest

The **Victorian Arts Centre** encompasses the Melbourne Concert Hall, Arts Complex, Performing Arts Museum, and National Gallery. While it lacks the architectural grandeur of Sydney's Opera House, the Arts Centre, on the south bank of the Yarra, is Melbourne's most important cultural landmark and the venue for performances by the Australian Ballet, Victorian Opera, and Melbourne Symphony Orchestra. The **Performing Arts Museum** houses lively, imaginative exhibitions that are often particularly appealing to children. One-hour tours of the complex leave from the Smorgon Family Plaza, level five of the theater building, which is located beneath the spire. Tours depart at noon and 2:30 on weekdays. A 90-minute backstage tour of the Concert Hall begins at 12:15 and 2:15 on Sunday. *100 St. Kilda Rd., tel. 03/684–8198. Performing Arts*

Museum: Admission: $5 adults, $3.50 children under 15. Open weekdays 11–5, weekends noon–5. General tours: $8 adults, $6 students, $15 family. Backstage tours (no children): $10 adults.

The **National Gallery of Victoria,** a massive bluestone and concrete edifice surrounded by a moat, was opened in 1968. Among the highlights are the stained-glass ceiling in the Great Hall (best seen by lying on the floor!), the collection of ancient Greek vases, Picasso's *Weeping Woman,* a series of Albrecht Dürer engravings, a number of Old Master paintings, William Blake watercolors, and works from the Australian school. *180 St. Kilda Rd., tel. 03/685–0203. Admission: $6 adults, $3 children, $12 family. Open daily 10–5, but on Monday several galleries are closed to the public. Closed Good Friday, Anzac Day (April 25), Dec. 25.*

Como House, a splendid white Victorian mansion overlooking the Yarra, is the finest example of an early colonial house in Melbourne. The main part of the mansion was built around 1855, although the kitchen wing dates back to the 1840s. The gardens that slope down toward the Yarra River are a tribute to the landscaping skill of Baron von Mueller, who was also responsible for the layout of the city's Royal Botanic Gardens. *16 Como Ave., South Yarra, tel. 03/827–2500. Admission: $7 adults, $3.50 children under 15, $16.50 family. Open daily 10–5. Closed Good Friday, Dec. 25.*

Rippon Lea is a sprawling polychrome brick mansion built in the Romanesque style. Begun in the late 1860s, the house was added to progressively until it had swollen into a 33-room mansion by the time it was completed in 1887. The gardens were inspired by the romantic Victorian concepts of landscape gardening that were fashionable in England at the time. Notable features include the grotto, the lookout tower that overlooks the lake, the fernery, and the humpback bridges. *192 Hotham St., Elsternwick, tel. 03/523–9150. Admission: $7 adults, $3.50 children under 15, $16.50 family. Open daily 10–5. Closed Good Friday, Dec. 25.*

Fitzroy, the suburb to the north of the city center, is Melbourne's bohemian quarter. What was once a drab, deprived working-class part of the city has come up in the world, and the area is now prized by upwardly mobile white-collar workers looking for affordable housing within easy reach of city jobs. Fitzroy's main street is **Brunswick Street.** There are no inspiring monuments or grand municipal buildings to be seen here, but if you're looking for an Afghan camel bag, a secondhand bookstore, or just a café where you can sit over a plate of *tapas* and watch Melbourne go by, Fitzroy is the place. **Roar Studios** (no. 115) and **The Women's Gallery** (no. 375) specialize in the work of up-and-coming Australian artists. **Port Jackson Press** (no. 397) publishes and sells prints by Australian artists. The **Brunswick Street Bookstore** (no. 305) has a good range of modern Australian literature. Along with Lygon Street in nearby Carlton, this is also one of Melbourne's favorite eat streets. **Soldini's** (63 Brunswick St., tel. 03/417–3785) specializes in northern Italian cuisine. **Nawab's** (312 Brunswick St., tel. 03/419–0861) is a Delhi-style Indian restaurant with a good reputation. **The Baretti Café** (323 Brunswick St., tel. 03/419–4296), one of café society's favorite haunts, is renowned for its pasta and risotto dishes. **The Fitz** (347 Brunswick St., tel. 03/417–5794) and **The Gypsy Bar** (334 Brunswick St., tel. 03/419–0548) are popular Italian cafés. While you're in the area, don't miss the entrance gates on the **Fitzroy Nursery,** designed by Michael Leunig, Melbourne's favorite cartoonist, whose whimsical decorations can also be seen on some of the city's trams.

The **Polly Woodside Maritime Park** encompasses both the *Polly Woodside,* a commercial square-rigged sailing ship, and a museum devoted to maritime history, with displays that cover the voyages of Captain James Cook, the First Fleet, sailors' crafts, and Victorian shipwrecks. *Normanby Rd. and Phayer St., S. Melbourne, tel. 03/699–9760. Admission: $7 adults, $4 children, $15 family (2 adults and 4 children). Open weekdays 10–4, weekends 10–5.*

St. Kilda is to Melbourne what Bondi is to Sydney, and what St. Kilda lacks in surf, it more than makes up for in the culinary department. This cosmopolitan bayside suburb 6 kilometers (4 miles) south of the city center is at its best on Sunday afternoon, when half of Melbourne comes here to promenade, eat ice cream, and watch the world go by. The St. Kilda experience begins at the pier—a fine place to stroll and watch the sailing boats. On Sunday, **The Esplanade,** which parallels the beach, is the scene of a lively and entertaining market crowded with arts and crafts stalls, which form a backdrop for performances by buskers and street-theater troupes. To the south The Esplanade curves around the Luna Park amusement area to Acland Street. This is St. Kilda's restaurant row—an alphabet soup of restaurants and cuisines, including Chinese, Lebanese, Italian, French, and Jewish. St. Kilda is the center for Melbourne's Jewish population, and the best known Jewish restaurant is **Scheherezade,** (99 Acland St., tel. 03/534–2722), which was opened in 1958 by Polish émigrés Masha and Avram Zeliznikow. Those with an eye for fashion prefer **Café di Stasio** (31 Fitzroy St., tel. 03/525–3999), a small Italian café with personality and a gutsy menu. By night, St. Kilda becomes Melbourne's red-light district, although it pales by comparison with Sydney's Kings Cross. To reach St. Kilda from the city, take Tram 10, 12, 15, or 16.

Off the Beaten Track

The **Windsor Hotel** is one of Melbourne's proudest institutions and at its best every afternoon between three and five o'clock, when the ritual of afternoon tea is reenacted in the lounge. Far more than a genteel graze, afternoon tea at The Windsor is an integral part of the Melbourne experience—a lesson in the city's manners and mores in what is probably the grandest hotel in the country. While you're in the hotel, take a peek at the Grand Dining Room just off the lobby, a Belle Époque extravaganza with a gilded ceiling set with seven glass cupolas through which streams tinted sunlight. *103 Spring St., Melbourne 3000, tel. 03/653–0653. Cost: weekdays $22 per person, weekends $25.*

Pubs are not generally known for their artwork, but if you climb the steps above **Young and Jackson's Hotel,** you will find *Chloe,* a painting that has scandalized and/or titillated Melburnians for many decades. The larger-than-life nude, painted by George Lefebvre in Paris in 1875, has hung on the walls of Young and Jackson's Hotel for most of this century. In a more prudish era, *Chloe* was a great drawing card for the pub, although nowadays the magazine covers on the newsstand outside are far more provocative. *Chloe's Bistro, Young and Jackson's Hotel, Swanston and Flinders Sts., tel. 03/650–3884.*

Shopping

From the haute couture of upper Collins Street's Paris End to the shops of suburban Toorak Village, Melbourne has firmly established itself as the fashion capital of Australia. Australian designer labels are available on High Street in Armadale, on Toorak Road and

Chapel Street in South Yarra, and on Carlton's Lygon Street. High-quality vintage clothing abounds on Greville Street in Prahran. Most shops are open Monday through Thursday, 9–5:30, Friday until 9, and Saturday until 5.

Department Stores
Daimaru (211 LaTrobe St., Melbourne, tel. 03/660–6666), a multilevel department store that is part of the 200-store Melbourne Central shopping complex, brings a new level of sophistication and the world's smartest fashions to the heart of the city.

David Jones (310 Bourke St., Melbourne, tel. 03/669–8200) is one of the city's prestige department stores, located on the Bourke Street Mall.

Georges (162 Collins St., Melbourne, tel. 03/283–5555) is Melbourne's oldest, most exclusive department store.

Myer Melbourne (314 Bourke St., Melbourne, tel. 03/66–111) is a vast department store with a long-standing reputation for quality merchandise.

Jewelry
Altmann and Cherny (120 Exhibition St., tel. 03/650–9685) is a leading jeweler that specializes in opals and offers tax-free prices to overseas tourists.

Makers Mark Gallery (85 Collins St., tel. 03/654–8488) showcases the work of some of the country's finest jewelers.

Markets
There are bargains galore at Victoria Market, but you don't have to be a shopper to enjoy this sprawling, spirited bazaar. Built on the site of the city's first graveyard, the century-old market is the city's main produce outlet, and it seems that most of inner-city Melbourne comes here to buy its strawberries, fresh flowers, and imported cheeses. On Sunday, jeans, T-shirts, bric-a-brac, and secondhand goods are the order of the day. *Elizabeth and Victoria Sts., Melbourne, tel. 03/658–9600. Open Tues. and Thurs. 6 AM–2 PM, Fri. 6–6, Sat. 6–1, Sun. 9–4.*

Meat Market Craft Centre. New life has been breathed into the city's former meat market, and the imposing Victorian building now houses a vast collection of work by leading jewelers, woodworkers, printers, and ceramic artists. *42 Courtney St., N. Melbourne, tel. 03/329–9966. Open Tues.–Sun. 10–5.*

Prahran Market. Located in one of Melbourne's most stylish suburbs, this market sells nothing but food—a fantastic, mouth-watering array imported from all over the world. *177 Commercial Rd., Prahran, tel. 03/522–3302. Open Tues. and Thurs. 7:30–5, Fri. 6–6, Sat. 7–1.*

Shopping Centers and Malls
Australia on Collins (260 Collins St., tel. 03/650–4355) is the latest downtown shopping center entrant, with one of its floors devoted to gifts and housewares. Aero Design and Made in Japan sell particularly striking designs.

High Street between the suburbs of Prahran and Armadale is where you are most likely to find the best collection of antiques shops in Australia.

The Jam Factory (500 Chapel St., South Yarra, tel. 03/826–0537) comprises a complex of historic bluestone buildings that house fashion, food, and gift shops, as well as a branch of Georges department store.

Melbourne Central (300 Lonsdale St., tel. 03/665–0000), a dizzying complex whose biggest tenant is Daimaru department store, is huge enough to enclose a 100-year-old shot tower (used to make bullets) in its atrium.

Southgate (4 Southbank Promenade, S. Melbourne, tel. 03/686–1000), directly opposite Flinders Street Station on the other bank of the Yarra, shelters the usual combination of shops and eateries. The spectacular riverside location, a short walk across Princes Bridge and from the Victorian Arts Centre, makes it an excellent choice for lunch; there's lots of outdoor seating next to the Southbank promenade.

Sportsgirl Centre (254 Collins St., Melbourne) sells some of Melbourne's most popular young women's clothing labels, with the emphasis on leisurewear. Food as well as fashion features in the four-level shopping mall.

Toorak Road (South Yarra) is where Melbourne's elite shop. Come here to find some of the ritziest boutiques in Melbourne, as well as art galleries and several fine restaurants.

Shopping Tours The true shopping enthusiast might want to take advantage of **Shopping Spree Tours** (tel. 03/543–5855), which offers lunch and escorted shopping tours to some of Melbourne's best manufacturers and importers. Tours depart weekdays at 9:15, weekends at 8. The cost is $38 per person.

Souvenirs You can shop for Australian-made goods at the **Australiana General Store** (1227 High St., Armadale, tel. 03/822–2324), **Aussieland Souvenirs and Sheepskin Products** (257 Elizabeth St., Melbourne, tel. 03/670–2329), and **Aboriginal Handcrafts** (125–133 Swanston St., 9th floor, Melbourne, tel. 03/650–4717). You might also try the **National Trust Gift Shop** (38 Jackson St., Toorak, tel. 03/827–9385).

Participant Sports

Many Melburnians can't muster as much enthusiasm for jogging as they can for a tin of Victoria Bitter, but participant sports nevertheless play a large role in the life of the city. Nowhere is this better evidenced than in the profusion of parks, fields, and sports grounds that freckle the Melbourne landscape. Visitors should have little difficulty finding somewhere to play their favorite sports.

Bicycling It is estimated that Melbourne and the surrounding area contain more than 100 kilometers (60 miles) of bike paths, including scenic routes along the Yarra River and around Port Phillip Bay. Bikes can be rented at one of the mobile rental shops in trailers alongside the bike paths, or at **Hire A Bike** (tel. 03/801–2156) on the Yarra Bank beside Princes Bridge, opposite the Victorian Arts Center. *Cost for 1 hr: $6 adults, $4 children; 4 hrs: $16 adults, $10 children. Open daily 11–5.*

Canoeing At the **Studley Park Boathouse,** canoes, kayaks, and rowboats are available for hire on this peaceful, delightful stretch of the Lower Yarra River, about 7 kilometers (4 miles) east of the city center. *Studley Park, Kew, tel. 03/853–8707. Cost: from $11 per hr for 1 person in a kayak to $24 per hr for 5 people in a rowboat. Open weekdays 9:30–6, weekends 9:30–7:30.*

Golf Melbourne has the largest number of championship golf courses in Australia, and some of the private courses, such as Metropolitan, Royal Melbourne, and Kingston-Heath, are world-class. A sampling of area courses includes **Albert Park Golf Course** (Queens Rd., Melbourne, tel. 03/510–5588), **Brighton Golf Links** (Dendy St., Brighton, tel. 03/592–1388), **Ivanhoe Public Golf Course** (Vasey St., E.

Ivanhoe, tel. 03/499–7001), **Sandringham Golf Links** (Cheltenham Rd., Cheltenham, tel. 03/598–3590), and **Yarra Bend Golf Course** (Yarra Bend Park Rd., Fairfield, tel. 03/481–3729).

Horseback Riding The Cheltenham Riding School (158 Byng Ave., Cheltenham, tel. 03/551–2552), runs one-hour trail rides on weekends and holidays for $18 per hour.

Jogging Some of the more popular jogging courses are the 4-kilometer (2.5-mile) **Tan,** beginning at Anderson Street and Alexandra Avenue and looping around the perimeter of the Royal Botanic Gardens; the 5-kilometer (3.1-mile) **Albert Park Lake Run** in Albert Park; and the **Bay Run,** an 18-kilometer (11-mile) round-trip run along Port Phillip Bay, starting at Kerford Road and Beaconsfield Parade in Albert Park and continuing on to Bay Street in Brighton.

Tennis Visitors who wish to play tennis during their visit should do so on weekdays, since most courts are booked solid at night and on weekends. Public tennis courts for hire in and around the city include **Camberwell Tennis Centre** (Bulleen and Thompson Rds., Bulleen, tel. 03/850–4500) with 16 outdoor Supergrass courts, **East Melbourne Tennis Centre** (Powlett Reserve, Albert St., E. Melbourne, tel. 03/417–6511) with four outdoor courts, and **Collingwood Indoor Tennis Centre** (100 Wellington St., Collingwood, tel. 03/419–8911) with five indoor synthetic grass courts.

Spectator Sports

Like Australians in general, Melburnians are sports mad. The Melbourne Cup horse race in November brings the entire city to a standstill. The same is true of Australian-Rules football, the nation's number one spectator sport, which has its stronghold in Melbourne. The season begins in March and reaches its climax at the Grand Final, held in September, when crowds of 100,000 are commonplace.

Australian-Rules Football The two most important venues for national league games are the **Melbourne Cricket Ground** (Brunton Ave., Yarra Park, tel. 03/654–5511) and **A.F.L. Park** (Wellington Rd., Mulgrave, tel. 03/654–1244). *Tickets available through BASS (tel. 03/11–566, inquiries; 03/11–522, credit-card bookings) or at playing field.*

Cricket From October through March, all big international and interstate cricket matches in Victoria are played at the **Melbourne Cricket Ground** (*see* Australian-Rules Football, *above*). The stadium has lights for night games and can accommodate 120,000 people. Tickets are sold at the gate and through BASS (*see above*).

Horse Racing Melbourne is the only city in the world to declare a public holiday for a horse race—the **Melbourne Cup**—held on the first Tuesday in November every year since 1861. In addition to a horse race, the Cup is also a fashion parade, and most of Melbourne society turns out in full regalia to watch, while the rest of the country comes to a standstill, with schools, shops, offices, and factories tuning in to the action. Melbourne has four top-class race tracks. **Flemington Race Course** (Epsom Rd., Flemington, tel. 03/376–4100), just 3 kilometers (1.9 miles) outside the city, is Australia's premier race course and home of the Melbourne Cup. **Moonee Valley** (McPherson St., Moonee Ponds, tel. 03/370–2633) is 6 kilometers (3.7 miles) from Melbourne and features the Cox Plate race in October. **Caulfield Race Course** (Station St., Caulfield, tel. 03/572–1111), 10 kilometers (6.2 miles) from the city, features the Blue Diamond in March and the Caulfield Cup in October. Finally, **Sandown Race Course** (Racecourse Dr.,

Springvale, tel. 03/572–1111), 25 kilometers (16 miles) from the city, features the Sandown Cup in November.

Soccer This sport is played almost year-round in **Olympic Park** (Ovals 1 and 2, Swan St., Melbourne, tel. 03/429–6288).

Tennis The **Australian Open** (tel. 03/655–1234), held in January, is one of four Grand Slam events in the world and is held at Flinders Park in Melbourne.

Dining

By Terry Durack

National food critic for Australian Gourmet Traveller magazine and restaurant critic for the Melbourne Age, Terry Durack is also the author of A Taste of Melbourne, Hot Food Cool Jazz, and Yum.

Victoria is the shopping basket of Australia; its fertile landscape keeps the country's larders stocked with wonderful farmhouse cheeses, luscious stone fruits, farmed pigeons, milk-fed lamb, and yabbies (a local crustacean). Proximity to such bounty has plunged Melburnians into a passionate relationship with good food, a love that is reflected in their home kitchens, busy cafés, and serious restaurants.

As if the great groceries weren't enough, Melbourne also boasts an incredible array of cooking techniques and ethnic fare. There is hardly a nation whose cuisine isn't represented on one of Melbourne's famous food streets. The Chinese restaurants on Little Bourke Street are the equal of anything in Hong Kong; Victoria Street, Richmond, does a convincing imitation of Vietnam; Lygon Street in Carlton could be Rome; and a little piece of the Mediterranean has popped up on Fitzroy Street, St. Kilda. A single block of Brunswick Street in Fitzroy offers a choice between Turkish, Indian, Spanish, Thai, Italian, and modern bistro cooking.

Reservations are generally advised, and while most restaurants are now licensed to sell alcohol, the few that aren't usually allow you to bring your own. Wine lists range from the encyclopedic to the small and selective; many feature Australian wines, which have an unequaled freshness and fruit flavor. Lunch is served between noon and 2:30, and dinner—usually a single seating—is between 7 and 10:30. A 10% tip is customary, and there may be a corkage fee in BYOB restaurants; there is neither sales tax nor a service charge.

Highly recommended restaurants are indicated by a star ★.

Category	Cost*
$$$$	over $60
$$$	$45–$60
$$	$30–$45
$	under $30

per person, excluding drinks and tip

Australian **Stephanie's.** Food writer, gifted cookery teacher, champion of local
$$$$ produce, and probably the most awarded chef in Australia, Stephanie Alexander is a modern pioneer of the Australian kitchen. Her seasonal menus mirror the land, sea, and sky and read like roll calls of Australia's freshest and most exciting ingredients. In her fairy-tale mansion of a restaurant, you can dress to the nines, sip Kir Royales, and marvel at her roasted Western Australian marrons (freshwater crustaceans), her soufflé of local goat's cheese, and her wilderness honey cheesecake. *405 Tooronga Rd., East Hawthorn,*

Downtown Melbourne Dining and Lodging

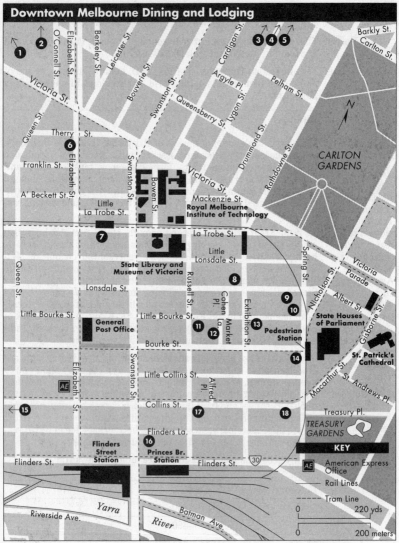

Dining

Akita, **1**
Baretti Café, **20**
Blakes, **29**
Browns, **43**
Café di Stasio, **35**
Caffe e Cucina, **41**
Café Provincial, **19**
Chinois, **40**
Chinta Ria R&B, **4**

Continenal Cafe, **44**
Dog's Bar, **32**
Flower Drum, **12**
France-Soir, **39**
The George Café, **33**
Isthmus of Kra, **30**
Jacques Reymond, **44**
Marchetti's Latin, **9**
Milan, **28**
Paul Bocuse
Restaurant, **7**

Purple Sands, **27**
Rhubarbs, **23**
The River Seafood
Grill, **29**
Shark Fin House, **11**
Stephanie's, **37**
Tho Tho, **24**
Tolarno Bar and
Bistro, **34**
Toofey's, **5**
Vlado's, **26**

Lodging

The Adelphi, **16**
Bryson Hotel, **13**
City Park Motel, **31**
Gordon Place, **10**
Grand Hyatt, **17**
Hotel Como, **38**
Le Meridien
Melbourne, **15**
Lygon-Carlton
Motel, **3**
Magnolia Court
Boutique Hotel, **21**
Melbourne Hilton on
the Park, **22**

Metropolitan Melbourne Dining and Lodging

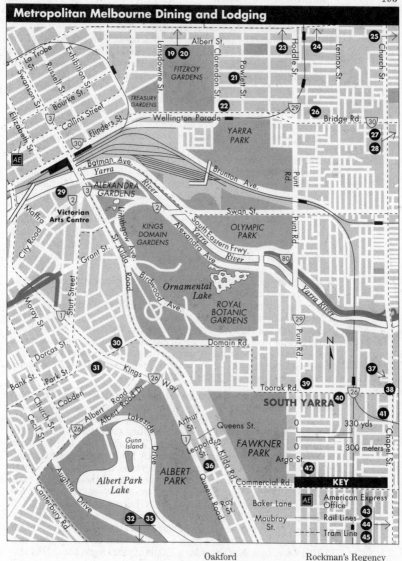

Oakford
Apartments, **42**
Oakford the
Fairways, **36**
Old Melbourne
Hotel, **2**
Pathfinder Motel, **25**
The Regent, **18**

Rockman's Regency
Hotel, **8**
Windsor Hotel, **14**
YWCA Motel, **6**

tel. 03/822–8944. Reservations required. Jacket and tie advised. AE, DC, MC, V. No lunch Sun.; closed Mon.

$$ **Blakes.** Since the Southgate complex opened on the banks of the Yarra a couple of years ago, it has redefined the way Melbourne spends its leisure time. Concurrently, the dozen or so restaurants in Southgate have redefined the way Melbourne eats. Blakes is the most polished of these eateries; indoor/outdoor seating areas, a wood-burning pizza oven, and serious wines by the glass offer a very '90s style. The salmon niçoise salad, Mediterranean-style lamb burger, and pear pizza are all recommended. *Ground Level, Southgate Complex, South Melbourne, tel. 03/699–4100. Reservations advised. Dress: casual. AE, DC, MC, V. No dinner Sun.*

$$ ★ **Rhubarbs.** From the street, Rhubarbs looks like just another tastefully tricked-out inner-suburban bistro—the real action is going on out back in the huge leafy courtyard. While away a sunny lunchtime under the glass atrium with motorized sun blinds, and enjoy chef Ian Curley's inventive, colorful food. His goat's cheese-and-potato terrine is already a Melbourne legend, and both his black pudding with ox cheek and his old-fashioned lemon and rhubarb tart pack quite a flavor punch. *243–245 Gertrude St., Fitzroy, tel. 03/416–3977. Reservations advised. Dress: casual. AE, DC, MC, V. No lunch Sat.; no dinner Sun.*

$ **Café Provincial.** Brunswick Street's favorite occupation is eating. In the space of just a few blocks, you'll find restaurants and cafés representing virtually every one of Australia's many different ethnic groups, in every price bracket and at every comfort level. This born-again pub with its deliberately deconstructivist decor, sunny Mediterranean food, and always-roaring wood-fired pizza oven is one of the street's real gems. Servings are big, bills are small, and quality is tops. *299 Brunswick St., Fitzroy, tel. 03/417–2228. No reservations. Dress: casual. AE, DC, MC, V.*

Bistros

$$ **France-Soir.** Suddenly, you're not just south of the Yarra River anymore; you're on the left bank of the Seine, lost in a world of paper tablecloths, long black aprons, Kronenbourg beer, and muscadet wine. Patrons sit elbow to elbow, smelling each other's food and listening to each other's conversations. The onion soup is the genuine article, the oysters are shucked strictly to order, the *pommes frites* are *fantastique*, and the andouillette raises the humble sausage to dizzy heights. Do leave room for the state-of-the-art apple *tarte Tatin*. *11 Toorak Rd., South Yarra, tel. 03/866–8569. Reservations advised. Dress: casual. AE, MC, V. BYOB and licensed.*

$$ **Tolarno Bar and Bistro.** For nearly 30 years, Tolarno has been dishing out good, honest bistro cooking in an atmosphere you could cut with a butter knife. Although a popular local television chef, Iain Hewitson, took over the place a couple of years back, the quirky murals, hideaway bar, and mock-colonial tables and chairs are still here. These days the food is more Provençal than Parisian. Those with a taste for Mediterranean cuisine really can't do better than the two-course lunch special: At less than $20 a head—including a trip to the vast antipasto table—it's one of this town's great bargains. *42 Fitzroy St., St. Kilda, tel. 03/525–5477. Reservations advised. Dress: casual. AE, DC, MC, V. No lunch Sat.*

$ **The George Café.** This once-neglected Victorian corner pub has blossomed into one of Melbourne's buzziest watering holes. Pick up some antipasto and crusty, grilled *casalinga* bread with prosciutto from the bar, or wander into the back café, where the stoves are shared by a French master pâtissier and a young, English-born chef trained by London legend Pierre Koffman. During the day you'll mingle with locals sipping coffee and nibbling on apricot tarts or custard slices; at night, the heavy-duty crowd drops in for light-as-air pork rillettes; a creamy, blue-eye cod *brandade* (smooth fish chowder); and the comforting duck confit. *8–10 Grey St., St. Kilda, tel. 03/525–3699. No reservations. Dress: casual. AE, MC, V. Open daily for breakfast.*

Café **Continental Café.** This is what café life in Melbourne is all about. In
$ the morning, night-lubbers draped artistically over their Peroni beers rub shoulders with the few remaining Melbourne yuppies, who dig into muesli and croissants. At lunchtime, the local rock stars and radio DJs—safe behind their Ray-Bans—show up to scarf salads, focaccia sandwiches, and mineral water. Then, at night, the cooler-than-cool drift in for pasta and red wine before disappearing upstairs to catch the live music. If you're not too distracted by the free-floating attitude, remember to order a coffee, which many say is the best in town. *132a Greville St., Prahran, tel. 03/510–2788. No reservations. Dress: casual. AE, MC, V.*

Chinese **Flower Drum.** Nobody takes the principles of fine Cantonese cook-
$$$ ing quite so seriously as the Flower Drum's owner, Gilbert Lau, the
★ undisputed Last Emperor of Chinatown. When renowned Hong Kong food critic Willy Mark last visited Melbourne, he breathlessly commented that even were it in Hong Kong, the Flower Drum would still rate among the very best. The restrained elegance of the decor and the intelligence of the wine list put many French restaurants to shame, and the service is breathtakingly meticulous. Simply ask your waiter what's good, and you may well wind up with an incredible feast: crisp-skinned Peking duck served with a second course of minced duck wrapped in lettuce, a perfectly steamed Murray cod, huge Pacific oysters daubed with black bean sauce, and fiery *dan dan* noodles. *17 Market La., tel. 03/662–3655. Reservations required. Jacket advised. AE, DC, MC, V. No lunch Sun.*

$ **Purple Sands.** Although the far-flung suburb of Doncaster is a good half-hour's drive from the city, the ride is well worth it. The local Chinese community flocks to this spacious, well-appointed restaurant to enjoy some of the very best dim sum in the country. The Hong Kong chef's dinner specialties are also notable: Try Macau sauce with four seasons' vegetables, pork ribs in prawn paste, or the double-boiled soup with quail and ginseng, described by one waiter as "a real wrinkle buster." We think he means it's good for the complexion. *862 Doncaster Rd., Doncaster East, tel. 03/848–8323. Reservations required. Dress: casual. AE, DC, MC, V. BYOB and licensed.*

$ **Shark Fin House.** Right in the middle of Melbourne's colorful Chinatown is this bustling, three-story restaurant with a style that's pure Hong Kong—expect gleaming elevators, a bank of TV monitors, and tanks full of live fish, crabs, and lobsters. At lunchtime, the place hums with the clang, clang, clang of dim sum trolleys. At night, all eyes turn hungrily toward those tanks when they're not gazing in disbelief at the groaning platters of suckling pig, roast meats, or clams and steamed abalone. *131 Little Bourke St., tel. 03/663–1555. Reservations advised. Dress: casual. AE, DC, MC, V. Open for dim sum daily 11:30–4:30.*

French **Browns.** Much like a fine wine, this formal, elegant, drawing room of
$$$$ a restaurant has only improved with age. Greg Brown, who trained under England's famous Roux brothers, has a seductive cooking style that relies on the freshest ingredients and impeccable technique. Every meal is an event, thanks to a masterful wine list, precision-engineered service, and specialties such as delicate tomato and tarragon "tea," silky smooth prawn ravioli, guinea fowl with lemon

vinaigrette, and a wine-based daube of milk-fed lamb. *1111 High St., Armadale, tel. 03/822-3188. Reservations advised. Jacket and tie advised. AE, DC, MC, V. No lunch Sat.; closed Sun.*

$$$$ **Jacques Reymond.** Fine dining is alive and well at this glamorous Victorian mansion, which boasts open fireplaces, soft candlelight, and a secret garden. The wine list—with its comprehensive Burgundy selection—is the stuff an enophile's dreams are made of, and the service is intelligent, intuitive, and informed. Asian influences and the finest Australian produce have tempered this Burgundian chef's natural tendencies, producing classics such as guinea fowl marinated in yogurt, barramundi fillet with ginger and lime cream, and a mille-feuille (layered puff-pastry) with King Island crab in a sauce of lemongrass, fish sauce, basil, and coconut milk. *78 Williams Rd., Windsor, tel. 03/525-2178. Reservations required. Jacket and tie advised. AE, DC, MC, V. No lunch Sat.; closed Sun.–Mon.*

$$$$ **Paul Bocuse Restaurant.** This lavish temple of French eating is lo-
★   cated smack-dab in the middle of the Japanese-owned Daimaru department store. Don't let the escalator ride put you off: Inside you'll find all the fuss and finery of a Parisian three-star restaurant, including black-tie service that's knowledgeable and attentive. From up on the wall, Paul Bocuse's benignly smiling image looks down. Many of the master's classic creations are available here, but diners in the know choose chef Philippe Mouchel's own stellar creations— perfect braised squab, shimmering oyster terrine, or sublime marinated salmon garnished with grilled salmon skin. *Level 4, Daimaru Dept. Store, 211 La Trobe St., tel. 03/660-6600. Reservations required. Jacket and tie advised. AE, DC, MC, V. Closed Sun.–Mon.*

Indian **Milan.** In too many of Melbourne's Indian restaurants the food has
$ an uncanny knack of tasting the same no matter what you order. Chef Prakash Satya, however, has a distinctive, almost delicate touch that distinguishes his cooking from the pack. "Milan" is an Indian word for "meeting place," and in recent years more and more Indian-food-loving locals have been meeting over Satya's plump spinach-and-onion *pakoras* (fritters), whole tandoori fish, or lamb marinated in rum and Kashmiri spices. *44 Cotham Rd., Kew, tel. 03/ 853-5379. Reservations advised. Dress: casual. AE, DC, MC, V. BYOB. Closed Mon.*

International **Chinois.** At this shimmering glamour-puss of a restaurant in the
$$$ modish inner suburb of South Yarra, East and West don't just meet,
★   they have a passionate affair. The chic decor—etched glass, blonde-wood floors, walls hung with ancient Chinese silk gowns—sets the scene for fashionable and fabulous eating. Don't miss the *char siu* rack of lamb, the wok-charred Atlantic salmon, and the roasted Chinois duck with scallion crepes. *176 Toorak Rd., South Yarra, tel. 03/826-3388. Reservations required. Jacket advised. AE, DC, MC, V.*

Italian **Marchetti's Latin.** The Latin has been a clubby and comfortable Mel-
$$$ bourne institution since it first opened its doors in 1919, but since Bill Marchetti took the restaurant over in 1984, it has achieved near cult status. Singer Robert Palmer called the Latin the best restaurant he had ever eaten in, and Frank Sinatra, Elton John, and Bruce Springsteen all gave it thumbs-up. Even mere mortals love the tortellini filled with Queensland mud crab, the sensational pumpkin-filled ravioli, and the scaloppine Latino. *55 Lonsdale St., tel. 03/ 662-1985. Reservations advised. Dress: casual but neat. AE, DC, MC, V. No lunch Sat.; closed Sun.*

$$ **Baretti Café.** With its aged, mock damp walls, discreet strip lighting, dark wood floors, and long, modish bar, Baretti projects the

serious air of a northern Italian ba
waistcoats and long aprons drift abo
tras in a big-budget movie, and paf
they were in their own living room. T
sics but has some unexpected twis
sardines sautéed in olive oil and ov
rella crumble, or slices of hearty
laid on a crisped risotto cake. *328*
419–4296. Reservations advised. D
Open daily for breakfast.

$$ **Café Di Stasio.** This café treads that very fine line between
★ nered elegance and sheer decadence. A sleek marble bar and mod-
ishly ravaged walls contribute to the sense that you've stepped into
a scene from *La Dolce Vita*. Luckily, Café Di Stasio is as much a
monument to chef Valerio Nucci's heavenly cooking as to Italian
style. The crispy roasted duck has achieved local fame, the
chargrilled baby squid is a sheer delight, and Nucci's pasta is as al
dente as it comes. If the *orecchiette* pasta with turnip tops is on the
menu, order that above all else. *31 Fitzroy St., St. Kilda, tel. 03/525–
3999. Reservations required. Dress: casual but neat. AE, DC, MC,
V.*

$ **Caffe e Cucina.** The critics have raved so much about this drop-dead
★ fashionable hole-in-the-wall that soon it will be hard to get into
Chapel Street, let alone the restaurant. Still, if you're lucky enough
to score a table, make the most of it: Order the melt-in-the-mouth
gnocchi, the peppery arugula salad, and a glass of Victorian pinot
noir. The coffee here is also great, and the *tiramisu* cake is even bet-
ter looking than the crowd. *581 Chapel St., South Yarra, tel. 03/
827–4139. Reservations required for upstairs dining room; no res-
ervations downstairs. Dress: casual. AE, DC, MC, V. Open daily
for breakfast.*

$ **Dog's Bar.** On most nights, you'll find down-at-heel fashion design-
ers, grantless film directors, and yet-to-be-discovered pop stars
warming themselves by the fire and tucking into hearty soups and
steaming bowls of penne Genovese. In the summer, the action
switches to the pavement tables, where everyone who's anyone sips
icy glasses of local Victorian chardonnays, picks at antipasto plat-
ters, and watches the world go by. *54 Acland St., St. Kilda, tel. 03/
525–3599. No reservations. Dress: casual. AE, MC, V.*

Japanese **Akita.** Melbourne has plenty of Japanese restaurants with breath-
$$ takingly beautiful decor, dazzling private tatami rooms, and a glitzy
★ clientele. This isn't one of them. Here the fancy footwork is confined
to the menu. The handwritten specials list could serve as a seasonal
calendar. In the summer, it's awash with clams in butter and sake or
vinegared crabs, while winter brings braised root vegetables and
savory egg custards. There's no better Japanese restaurant in the
city. *Cnr. of Courtney and Blackwood Sts., North Melbourne, tel.
03/326–5766. Reservations advised. Dress: casual. AE, DC, MC, V.
Closed Sun.*

Malaysian **Chinta Ria R&B.** Simon Goh, owner of Melbourne's three Chinta Ria
$ restaurants, has combined his passion for cool jazz with his love of
hot food. This is his biggest and funkiest restaurant ever, but the
spicy Malaysian dishes and the prices are as down-to-earth as ever.
Chinta Ria means "love and happiness" in Malay, and after you tuck
away some *char kuey teow* noodles to the mellow strains of a haunting sax, you'll be very happy indeed. *118 Elgin St., Carlton, tel. 03/
349–2599. Reservations advised. Dress: casual. AE, DC, MC, V.*

The River Seafood Grill. This place is yet another reason to check out the Southgate complex on the banks of the Yarra. At first glance, the huge room looks like a funky reception hall with polished stone floors, rough-hewn wooden tables, and a vaguely nautical theme. Racing sails hang from the ceiling, and the chef stares out from his kitchen through an open hatch, like a captain on the bridge. The seafood, however, is cooked with a gentle and innovative hand: The Neanderthal-looking, deep-fried whole coral perch—draped with coriander, capsicum, and cucumber batons in a Thai dressing—is a definite talking point, as is the egg noodle stir-fry with crabs, clams, and mussels. *Mid-Level West, Southgate, South Melbourne, tel. 03/ 690–4699. Reservations advised. Dress: casual. AE, DC, MC, V.*

$$ **Toofey's.** Michael Bacash's Middle Eastern background and Italian training merge to produce a refreshing Mediterranean approach to Australian seafood. The restaurant has the good looks of a trendy bistro and the good sense to serve only what's best at the fish markets that day. It's here that you'll find Melbourne's definitive spaghetti marinara, as well as wonderful Provençal-style mussels and whole grilled fish. *162 Elgin St., Carlton, tel. 03/347–9838. Reservations advised. Dress: casual. AE, DC, MC, V. BYOB and licensed. No lunch Sat.–Sun.; closed Mon.*

Steakhouse **Vlado's.** Vlado Gregurek snaps on a fresh pair of pristine white
$$$ gloves every time he picks up a new cut of beef and inspects it as tenderly as if it were a newborn baby. If you love a good steak, you'll love Vlado. His restaurant is amazingly single-minded: Pictures of grazing cattle hang on the walls above the businesspeople grazing on the set menus of liver, sausage, and perfectly grilled meat. To be honest, the salads are so-so, the mustards and horseradish are uninspired, and the strawberry pancake desserts are undistinguished—but oh, those steaks! *61 Bridge Rd., Richmond, tel. 03/428–5833. Reservations required. Jacket advised. AE, DC, MC, V. BYOB and licensed. No lunch Sat.; closed Sun.*

Thai **Isthmus of Kra.** Named after a constricted waistline of land that
$$ links Thailand with the Malay Peninsula, this restaurant looks like one of those very chic New York art galleries specializing in rare Asian artifacts; the real art, however, lies in a menu that blends Thai favorites with Malaysian Nonya specialties. The *pandan* chicken and *tom yam goong* (hot and sour prawn soup) are excellent, and don't on any account miss the monsoon oysters served in a special clay pot. *50 Park St., South Melbourne, tel. 03/690–3688. Reservations advised. Dress: casual but neat. AE, DC, MC, V. BYOB and licensed. No lunch Sat.; closed Sun.*

Vietnamese **Tho Tho.** Victoria Street, the heart of the local Vietnamese commu-
$ nity, has become one of Melbourne's most colorful, exciting, and exhilarating areas, full of good food and wonderful smells. With its walnut-veneer bar, madcap designer chairs, and stylish stucco walls, Tho Tho is a far cry from the formica-tabled noodle cafés that dominate the street. There's nothing fancy about the prices, though: Around $5 will buy you a gigantic bowl of *pho* noodle soup for lunch, and the sugarcane prawns, crisp spring rolls, and fresh rice paper rolls are equally reasonable and delicious. *66 Victoria St., Richmond, tel. 03/428–5900. Reservations not required. Dress: casual. MC, V.*

Lodging

Visitors who arrive without prebooked accommodations can usually find a selection of hotel rooms through the Royal Automobile Club of

Victoria (RACV) office (*see* By Car in Getting Around, *above*). The RACV often has good deals because it functions as a clearinghouse for hotels' discounted, suplus rooms.

The numerous bed-and-breakfasts in and around Melbourne are excellent alternatives to hotel or motel accommodations. Those interested in staying with host families at bed-and-breakfasts should request a detailed list of Australian accommodations from **Bed & Breakfast Australia** (Box 408, Gordon, N.S.W. 2072, tel. 02/498–5344).

Highly recommended lodgings are indicated by a star ★.

Category	Cost*
$$$$	over $220
$$$	$150–$220
$$	$100–$150
$	under $100

*All prices are for a standard double room.

$$$$ **Grand Hyatt.** Melbourne's number one hotel for glitz, glamour, and
★ top-notch service is located at the "Paris End" of Collins Street. Its clientele consists largely of business travelers and upscale tourists. Soft tones infuse the decor throughout, and the luxurious lobby is decorated with quantities of roseate marble and oak paneling. A separate atrium includes two floors of elegant shops and a vast international food court that supplements the hotel's dining rooms. The top floors offer attractive views, and all rooms are graced with marble bathrooms, king-size beds, and small sitting areas. The four Regency Club floors have their own check-in facility and lounge, and provide complimentary Continental breakfasts and refreshments throughout the day. *123 Collins St., tel. 03/657–1234, fax 03/650–3491. 559 rooms with bath. Facilities: business center, banquet rooms, 2 restaurants, bars, nightclub, shops, food court. AE, DC, MC, V.*

$$$$ **Hotel Como.** Located close to the restaurants and shops of South
★ Yarra, one of Melbourne's most prestigious suburbs, this luxury hotel attracts a large corporate clientele. The lobby is dominated by an impressive tapestry depicting Como's history, and gray marble and chrome are prominent throughout the smart art deco interior. The hotel is built in a horseshoe shape around a park, and some suites on the third and sixth floors have access to private Japanese gardens. Rooms are appointed with king-size beds, VCRs, Jacuzzis, wall safes, coffee machines, toasters, alarm clocks, hair dryers, bathrobes, and individual climate controls. Some suites feature fully equipped kitchenettes. This establishment enjoys a reputation for outstanding service. Guests receive complimentary evening drinks and valet parking. *630 Chapel St., S. Yarra, tel. 03/824–0400, fax 03/824–1263. 107 suites with bath. Facilities: indoor pool under retractable roof, health club, saunas, lounge. AE, DC, MC, V.*

$$$$ **Le Meridien Melbourne.** Behind an ornate Victorian neo-Gothic facade midway between the shopping and business districts, Le Meridien Melbourne feels like a small, intimate hotel despite its size. The interior was completely refurbished in 1993 and decorated in a lemon color scheme that brings a fresher, lighter character to what was once a rather somber establishment. The hotel has a strong corporate following, and the two atrium bars are popular after-work watering holes for local executives. The room rate is discounted between Friday and Sunday nights. *495 Collins St., tel 03/ 620–9111, fax 03/614–1219. 232 rooms with bath. Facilities: 2 restaurants, 2 bars, heated indoor pool, spa, sauna. AE, DC, MC, V.*

$$$$ **Melbourne Hilton on the Park.** One of the oldest of Melbourne's five-star elite, this imposing hotel offers a high standard of comfort and facilities even though rooms are often available at a significant discount. Built in 1974, the hotel has been recently redecorated in a warm, contemporary style. The city is a 15-minute walk away across Treasury Gardens. *192 Wellington Parade, E. Melbourne, tel. 03/ 419–3311, fax 03/419–5630. 406 rooms with bath. Facilities: heated outdoor pool, health club, sauna, executive floors, business center. AE, DC, MC, V.*

$$$$ **The Regent.** The hotel, the eastern half of this twin-towered Collins
★ Place complex, was designed by the world-famous architect I. M. Pei. The glossy hotel combines excellent facilities, glamour, and a prime location. Guest rooms, which begin on the 35th floor of the 50-story building, are built around a mirror-walled central atrium, and views are exceptional. Decorated with pastel Missoni fabrics, the rooms are large, luxurious, and comprehensively equipped. *25 Collins St., tel. 03/653–0000 or toll-free 008/33–1123, fax 03/650–4261. 363 rooms with bath. Facilities: 24-hr room service, business center, health facility, restaurants, shopping complex. AE, DC, MC, V.*

$$$$ **Rockman's Regency Hotel.** The personal attention given guests at this luxury hotel in the center of the theater district has earned it a loyal following, especially among show people and executive travelers. First-floor garden rooms have exterior terraces with outdoor dining facilities. All rooms are spacious and modern, with a separate dressing room, two vanity tables, and a full range of toiletries. Fresh fruit is provided in all rooms, along with a complimentary VCR movie library and daily newspapers. The hotel also includes Iain Hewitson's Memories of the Mediterranean—one of Melbourne's most talked-about restaurants. *Exhibition and Lonsdale Sts., tel. 03/662–3900, fax 03/663–4297. 184 rooms with bath. Facilities: heated indoor pool, Jacuzzis, solarium, spa, exercise room, complimentary parking, restaurant, café, bar, business center. AE, DC, MC, V.*

$$$$ **Windsor Hotel.** The aristocrat of Melbourne hotels, the century-old
★ Windsor combines the character and patrician dimensions of the Victorian era with the modern blessings of first-rate food and comfortable beds. Guest rooms are plushly decorated with Laura Ashley-style wall coverings and rosewood furnishings; the marble bathrooms are, however, modest in size compared with those in modern hotel rooms in the same price bracket. Standard rooms are rather small but the two-room Executive Suites are good value. For anyone who can afford a $600-per-day hotel room, the Victorian suites are vast and opulent. The hotel occupies a commanding position opposite the Victorian Parliament House and is close to theaters, parks, and some of Melbourne's finest shops. No one should miss a meal in the Grand Dining Room, where the sparkle of the crystal, fine porcelain, and full silver service almost matches that of the stained-glass ceiling domes and gaseliers. Here, a breakfast of coffee and toast feels like a banquet. *103 Spring St., tel. 03/653– 0653, fax 03/650–3233. 190 rooms with bath, including 34 suites. Facilities: 2 restaurants, 2 bars, business center. AE, DC, MC, V.*

$$$ **The Adelphi.** One of the latest arrivals on Melbourne's accommodation scene, The Adelphi is a boutique hotel that breaks new ground with its uncompromising design. The functionalist look makes extensive use of bare plywood and matte-finish metal surfaces, and while the clean, cool aesthetics might be a little brittle for some tastes, anyone tired of the predictable sameness of the L-shaped hotel room will welcome a different look. The location—a one-minute walk from City Square—is about as central as you can possibly get. The best rooms are those at the front, whose numbers end in "01." The Adelphi's pièce de résistance is the 25-meter-long lap pool on the top floor, which has a glass bottom that juts out from the edge of the building, so that bathers literally swim into space. The view from the bar on the same floor, framed by the Gothic Revival spires of St. Paul's, is heavenly. *187 Flinders La., tel. 03/650–2709, fax 03/654–7870. 34 rooms with bath. Facilities: 2 restaurants, 3 bars, outdoor heated pool. AE, DC, MC, V.*

$$$ **Bryson Hotel.** With an excellent location between the theater district and Chinatown, the Bryson is a popular choice for vacationers as well as cost-conscious corporate travelers. This four-star highrise hotel, built in the 1970s, was refurbished at the end of 1990. The cozy lobby is decorated with traditional wood paneling, parquet floors, and a neutral color scheme. Guest rooms, which are also done in neutral tones, are large and stylishly furnished and equipped with hair dryers, irons and ironing boards, and coffee machines. *186 Exhibition St., tel. 03/662–0511, fax 03/663–6988. 363 rooms with bath, 67 suites. Facilities: heated outdoor pool, sauna, restaurant, 2 bars, nightclub, complimentary garage parking. AE, DC, MC, V.*

$$$ **Gordon Place.** Located in a historic (1883) building, this is one of the
★ most interesting and comfortable apartment hotels in the city. Just a stone's throw from the Parliament Building, this hotel is surrounded by excellent restaurants and theaters and is frequented by corporate executives. The price is nonetheless a good value for vacationers seeking a city-center base. Apartments are light, modern, and comfortable, and they feature washing machines, dryers, and dishwashers. Breakfast is served on the covered terrace. The studios and one- and two-bedroom apartments face a vine-covered courtyard that features a 60-foot saltwater pool and a century-old palm tree. *24 Little Bourke St., tel. 03/663–2888, fax 03/639–1537. 59 apartments with bath. Facilities: heated outdoor pool, spa, sauna, restaurant. AE, DC, MC, V.*

$$$ **Old Melbourne Hotel.** A few minutes from the central business district by car or tram, this hotel mimics New Orleans architecture, with wrought-iron balconies and a cobblestone central courtyard. There is a small reception area instead of a traditional lobby, and the comfortable, spacious Victorian-style guest rooms, which are decorated with warm colors, feature brass beds. *5–17 Flemington Rd., tel. 03/329–9344 or toll-free 008/37–3005, fax 03/328–4870. 225 rooms with bath. Facilities: pool, restaurant. AE, DC, MC, V.*

$$ **City Park Motel.** Located close to the parks on the south side of the city, this ultramodern four-story motel is a favorite with interstate businesspeople. The lobby, accented in red and black, is open and spacious. Rooms have coffee machines and small refrigerators, and those in the front of this redbrick building have balconies. The executive/honeymoon suite has a spa and sauna. There are relatively few amenities, but this is the ideal motel for travelers on limited budgets. The city is about 1.5 kilometers (1 mile) away, and frequent tram service is available on St. Kilda Road, just a two-minute walk from the hotel. *308 Kings Way, tel. 03/699–9811, fax 03/699–9224. 40 rooms with bath, 6 suites. Facilities: spa and sauna, restaurant, bar, laundry, parking garage. AE, DC, MC, V.*

$$ **Oakford Apartments.** These all-suite town houses at various locations in the elegant suburb of South Yarra cater to visitors who prefer private apartments to hotel rooms. The studios and two- or three-bedroom apartments are light, modern, and comfortable, and all have washing machines, dryers, dishwashers, and Jacuzzis. *23 Argo St., S. Yarra, tel. 03/820–8544, fax 03/820–8517; 631 Punt*

Rd., S. Yarra, tel. 03/820–0853, fax 03/820–8517; 19 Kensington Rd., S. Yarra, tel. 03/820–8544, fax 03/820–8517; 26 Davis Ave., S. Yarra, tel. 03/820–8544, fax 03/820–88517. 20 apartments per property. Facilities: pool, tennis court, barbecue. AE, DC, MC, V.

\$\$ Oakford the Fairways. Opposite the Albert Park Lake and golf course and just 2 kilometers (1.2 miles) south of the central business district, this is another favorite with those who prefer apartment dwelling. The 1930s-style property consists of luxurious one- and two-bedroom apartments surrounded by private lawns and manicured flower beds. Avoid the east wing, because it faces Queens Road, a busy street with heavy traffic. The St. Kilda Road tram provides easy access to the city. *32 Queens Rd., tel. 03/820–8544, fax 03/820–8517. 48 apartments. Facilities: heated outdoor pool, tennis court, business center, complimentary parking. AE, DC, MC, V.*

\$ Lygon-Carlton Motel. In the heart of Melbourne's "Little Italy" and just a short tram ride from the center of the city, this motel is close to some of the city's best ethnic restaurants—the perfect place for the budget-conscious traveler who appreciates a colorful, lively neighborhood. The effects of the last renovation in 1989 have largely disappeared and rooms are in need of repainting, but the price and location ensure that the motel is usually full. Some deluxe rooms have kitchenettes, at only \$11 more than the standard rooms. *220 Lygon St., tel. 03/663–6633, fax 03/663–7297. 66 rooms with bath. Facilities: restaurant, laundry. AE, DC, MC, V.*

\$ Magnolia Court Boutique Hotel. Set in a prestigious historic suburb, this small, friendly hotel combines tranquility with accessibility. Rooms and furnishings are simple and spotless. Standard rooms are modest in size, but the Honeymoon Suite and the Cottage offer more space and comfort at a moderately higher cost. A family room with a kitchen and room for six is also available. The hotel is separated from the city by Fitzroy Gardens, about a 12-minute walk from Spring Street. *101 Powlett St., E. Melbourne, tel. 03/419–4222, fax 03/416–0841. 25 rooms with bath. Facilities: spa, café. AE, DC, MC, V.*

\$ Pathfinder Motel. Built in the early '60s in a quiet residential area, this relaxed, comfortable motel is on a direct tram line to the city, 7 kilometers (4 miles) away. The conservative reception area and lobby, furnished with antiques, face a courtyard with a small waterfall and fish pond. Guest rooms are done in cream-colored brick, with polished wood furniture and floral fabrics. *Burke and Cotham Rds., Kew, tel. 03/817–4551, fax 03/817–5680. 24 rooms with bath, including an apartment with kitchenette. Facilities: pool, restaurant, room service, barbecue, laundry. AE, DC, MC, V.*

\$ YWCA Motel. Built in 1975 to cater to the budget traveler, this motel provides clean, comfortable, no-frills accommodations. It is located within walking distance of the city center and is just half a block from the airline terminals. Rooms are simply furnished, and each has its own bathroom. There is a central television lounge in the building, along with a gym and pool. *489 Elizabeth St., tel. 03/329–5188, fax 03/328–2931. 56 rooms with shower. Facilities: pool, health club, saunas, cafeteria-style restaurant. No credit cards.*

The Arts

For a complete listing of performing arts events, galleries, and film, consult the Entertainment Guide Supplement in the Friday edition of the *Melbourne Age*. *Melbourne Events*, available from all tourism outlets, is a comprehensive monthly guide to what's happening.

Dance   Occupying the 2,000-seat State Theatre at the Arts Centre, **The Australian Ballet** provides five programs annually and frequently hosts visiting celebrity dancers from around the world. For information, telephone BASS (03/11–566, inquiries; or 03/11–500, credit card bookings).

Music   Contemporary music fans will want to find out who is playing at the major musical venues in the city: **Melbourne Concert Hall** (Arts Centre, 100 St. Kilda Rd., tel. 03/617–8211) and **Melbourne Sports and Entertainment Centre** (Swan St., Melbourne, tel. 03/429–6288).

Open-air concerts held during the summer (December–March) can be seen at the **Sidney Myer Music Bowl** (Kings Domain, Melbourne). Call BASS (tel. 03/11–566 or 03/11–500) for information. **Fantastic Entertainment in Public Places** (tel. 03/663–8395) is a varied entertainment program, held indoors in winter and outdoors from October to April.

The **Melbourne Symphony Orchestra** performs virtually year-round in the 2,600-seat Melbourne Concert Hall located in the Arts Centre (100 St. Kilda Rd., tel. 03/684–8198).

Opera   The **Victorian State Opera** and the **Australian Opera** both conduct regular seasons, often with performances by worldrenowned stars. The length and time of the seasons vary (best to call when you arrive), but all performances take place in Melbourne Concert Hall (100 St. Kilda Rd., tel. 03/684–8198). Further inquiries can be directed to BASS (tel. 03/11–566 or 03/11–500).

Theater   The **Half-Tix** ticket booth in the Bourke Street Mall sells tickets to a wide range of theater attractions at half price on the day of the performance. *Tel. 03/650–9420. Open Mon. 10–2, Tues.–Thurs. 11–6, Fri. 11–6:30, Sat. 10–2.*

Inside a former church hall, the **Antill Theatre Company** (199 Napier St., South Melbourne, tel. 03/699–3253) specializes in radical versions of French classics as well as modern, little-known works and an occasional reworked Australian play.

Set in a historic bluestone building, the **Comedy Café** (177 Brunswick St., Fitzroy, tel. 03/419–2869) is a casual, longrunning comedy venue that is a proving ground for many of Australia's most popular comedians.

The Last Laugh (64 Smith St., Collingwood, tel. 03/419–8600), is a theater-restaurant where comedy artists who have graduated to television frequently return to sharpen their act before a critical and very vocal audience.

The **Melbourne Theatre Company** (MTC) (tel. 03/654–4000), Melbourne's first and most successful theater company, has two seasons yearly, during which classical, international, and Australian works are performed. The company can be seen at the Russell Street Theatre (19 Russell St.) and the Playhouse, in the Theatres Building of the Arts Centre.

The city's second-largest company, the **Malthouse Theatre Company** (113 Sturt St., South Melbourne, tel. 03/685–5111) stages about 10 primary new or contemporary productions a year. The theater, the Malthouse, is a flexible space designed for a range of drama, dance, and circus companies.

The equivalent of Off Broadway in the United States, the **Universal Theatre** (UT) (13 Victoria St., Fitzroy, tel. 03/419–3777) is home to daring, avant-garde productions. The UT is an atmospheric, moody, oddly shaped theater that seats 300 on three sides of its stage. A smaller theater is located on the floor above.

Historic city theaters offering stage dramas and musical comedies include the **Princess Theatre** (163 Spring St., tel. 03/662–2911), **Her Majesty's Theatre** (219 Exhibition St., tel. 03/663–3211), and the **Comedy Theatre** (240 Exhibition St., tel. 03/662–2222).

New theaters offering innovative, intimate, and contemporary productions include **La Mama** (205 Faraday St., Carlton, tel. 03/347–6142) and **Theatreworks** (14 Acland St., St Kilda, tel. 03/534–4879).

Nightlife

Jazz Jazz is well represented in Melbourne in such establishments as **Bell's Hotel** (Moray and Coventry Sts., S. Melbourne, tel. 03/690–4511), **Bridge Hotel** (642 Bridge Rd., Richmond, tel. 03/428–3851), **Ruby Reds** (11 Drury La., tel. 03/662–1544), and **The Limerick Arms Hotel** (364 Clarendon St., South Melbourne, tel. 03/690–2626), probably the best known jazz venue in the whole country. Also there is a **Not Just Jazz After Dark** program held Friday and Saturday night at 11 PM in the foyer of the **Studio Theatre** at the Arts Centre (100 St. Kilda Rd., tel. 03/684–8198). Despite the name, jazz is the only music you are likely to hear. **Downstairs at Eric's** (Darling St. and Toorak Rd., Toorak, tel. 03/820–3804) is a sophisticated restaurant with live jazz most evenings. Some of these clubs include music and meals; some have cover charges.

Dancing **Chasers.** One of the city's most enduring night spots, this is a good bet for anyone from 20 to 35. Dress tends toward the Lycra-biker-shorts and running-shoes look, and the music varies from night to night—Wednesday is heavy metal, Friday is funk. *386 Chapel St, Prahran, tel. 03/827–6615. Admission: $5–$11. Open Wed.–Sun. 9 PM–7 AM.*

The Grainstore Tavern. This former grain warehouse incorporates bars, a video dance club, and an intimate cocktail lounge—a package that attracts the city's groovers and shakers. *46 King St., tel. 03/614–3570. Admission: $5–$8. Open Mon.–Sat. 6 PM–2 AM.*

Metro. This multilevel, high-tech nightclub has eight bars, a glass-enclosed café, and three dance floors, where the action ranges from fast to furious. Metro is one of the hottest clubs in town with Melbourne's twenty-somethings. *20–30 Bourke St., tel. 03/663–4288. Admission: Wed.–Thurs. $7, Fri.–Sat. $12. Open Wed.–Sat. 9 PM–5 AM.*

Bars Many of the more popular bars for early evening drinks are in the major hotels. Among them are the **Regent** (25 Collins St., tel. 03/653–0000), the **Hyatt on Collins** (123 Collins St., tel. 03/657–1234), the **Windsor** (103 Spring St., tel. 03/653–0653), the **Hilton on the Park,** (192 Wellington Parade, tel. 03/419–3311), **Le Meridien Melbourne** (495 Collins St., tel. 03/620–9111), and **Rockman's Regency** (Exhibition and Lonsdale Sts., tel. 03/662–3900). Live music is often featured, and rock, folk, and country bands move around from hotel to hotel. Bars that are not located in major hotels tend to be more casual. Some of the more popular bars are **Café Tapas** (36 Johnston St., Fitzroy, tel. 03/417–7417), **The George Hotel** (Fitzroy and Grey Sts., St. Kilda, tel. 03/525–5599), **Cha Cha's** (20 Chapel St., Windsor, tel. 03/525–1077), and **Pinchos** (11–13 Spring St., Fitzroy, tel. 03/419–5504).

Excursions from Melbourne

There are several areas in the vicinity of Melbourne that are ideal for
a day trip. To the east of the city are the Dandenong Ranges, where
a narrow, winding road will take you on a scenic journey through
rain forests and flower-filled towns of timber houses. South of Melbourne, the Bellarine Peninsula to the west and the Mornington
Peninsula to the east form a horseshoe around Port Phillip Bay. Of
the two, the Mornington Peninsula has more attractions to offer the
visitor (*see below*). To the southeast is Phillip Island, home of koalas,
seals, and thousands of fairy penguins that waddle out of the sea and
back to their burrows in the evening—this procession is the state's
number one tourist attraction.

Important Addresses and Numbers

Tourism
Information
Royal Automobile Club of Victoria Travel Centre (230 Collins St., tel.
03/650–1522).

Port Phillip
Phillip Island Information Centre (Phillip Island Tourist Rd.,
Newhaven, tel. 059/56–7447).

Emergencies
Dial 000 for **fire, police,** or **ambulance** services.

Guided Tours

Day trips from Melbourne are offered by local tour operators, including **Australian Pacific Tours** (tel. 03/650–1511), **Gray Line** (tel.
03/654–7700), and **AAT Kings** (tel. 03/650–1244)—all three of which
depart from 101 Bourke Street.

The Dandenongs

The Dandenong Ranges are where Melbourne comes for a breath of
fresh air, especially in the summer months, when these cool, moist
hills provide a welcome relief from the heat of the city. The Dandenongs are located about an hour's drive southeast of Melbourne.
Take Swanston Street south from the city and opposite Flinders
Street Station, turn left to join the South Eastern Freeway. Turn
left onto Toorak Road and continue as it becomes Burwood Road, following the signs to Ferntree Gully. At Ferntree Gully, continue to
Belgrave, where the road enters **Sherbrooke Forest,** a remnant of
the woodlands that once covered these ranges. At the turn of the
century, the government carved four narrow-gauge railway tracks
through these forests to assist the pioneers. The sole survivor from
this era is *Puffing Billy,* a gleaming little steam engine that hauls
passenger wagons from Belgrave to Emerald Lake, and an appropriate way to take in the picture-book scenery of forests and trestle
bridges. The 13-kilometer (8-mile) trip takes almost one hour each
way. *Old Monbulk Rd., Belgrave, tel. 03/754–6800. Tickets: $14
adults, $8.50 children 4–14, $43 family. Trains depart Mon.–Sat.
10:30, 2:30, more frequently on Sun. and school holidays.*

Leave Belgrave and continue toward Monbulk. Here the road
changes character dramatically as it loops through towering forests
of mountain ash and giant tree ferns. If you stop and listen for a minute, you will probably hear the tinkling calls of bellbirds and perhaps the cry of a whipbird, a piercing, drawn-out note that ends
with a sharp. Another bird common to this area is the flightless lyre-
bird, an accomplished mimic that has even been known to imitate the
distant sound of a chainsaw. At Kallista, turn left along the road to

Melbourne Environs

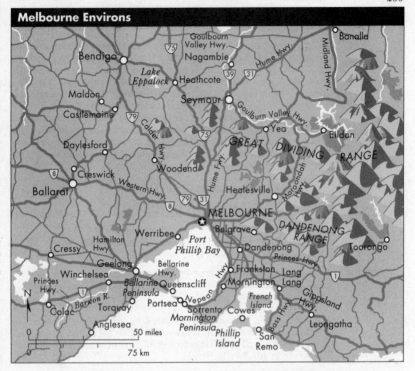

Sassafrass. On the right is the **George Tindale Memorial Garden,** 6 acres of azaleas, camellias, and hydrangeas that spill down the hillside. *Sherbrooke Rd., Sherbrooke, tel. 03/755–2051. Admission: $3 adults, free for children under 15. Open Mon.–Sat. 10–4.*

A short distance farther along this road is another famous garden, the **Alfred Nicholas Memorial Garden,** named after its founder, who made a fortune selling aspirin. The sprawling art deco mansion of the Nicholas family, which can be seen through the trees at the top of the hill, was a luxurious hotel until 1992, when it was forced to close for lack of business. The garden is particularly notable for its fuchsias and rhododendrons. Don't miss the waterfall and the ornamental lake, which is at its best when the surrounding trees are wearing their autumn colors. *Sherbrooke Rd., Sassafrass, tel. 03/750–1226. Admission: $3 adults, children under 15 free. Open daily noon–5.*

Continue along Sherbrooke Road, turn right at the intersection, and then left at the village of Sassafrass onto the Mountain Highway. This will return you to Burwood Road.

Mornington Peninsula

The Mornington Peninsula is the boot-shaped landform that encloses the eastern half of Port Phillip Bay, and visitors who set aside a sunny day for a drive down the peninsula will be treated to a glimpse of life in one of Melbourne's favorite weekend holiday retreats. Mornington has long been a favorite with moneyed Melburnians, and the tip of the peninsular boot is shod with Gatsbyesque weekenders and a scattering of stylish restaurants. If you are visiting the peninsula during the summer, be sure to pack your swimsuit and take advantage of the area's wonderful beaches.

To reach the Mornington Peninsula, take St. Kilda Road south from the city and follow the signs to Frankston via the Nepean Highway. Past Frankston there are a number of beaches hidden beyond the secondary roads that line the right side of the highway. You will find **Pelican Point** and the **Davey's Bay Yacht Club** if you turn right on Old Mornington Road, follow it to the end of Marathon Drive, and turn right again onto Davey's Bay Road. Pelican Point and Davey's Bay are well-kept secrets of the locals, who come here to swim and to picnic.

Back on the Nepean Highway, continue south, and on the corner of Conway Street on the left you will find one of Melbourne's most popular galleries, the **Omell Manyung Gallery,** featuring the work of up-and-coming Australian artists. *1408 Nepean Hwy., Mt. Eliza, tel. 03/787–2953. Admission free. Open Thurs.–Mon. 10:30–5.*

Continue on Mt. Eliza Way to Canadian Bay Road, turn right, and follow this to the **Canadian Bay Reserve,** another well-kept secret. Here you'll find a boat club and beach with excellent picnic facilities. Take Canadian Bay Road back toward the Nepean Highway, but turn right on Main Street past the Mornington Country Golf Club. At the end of Main Street you'll come across Schnapper Drive and Schnapper Point, home to the Mornington Jetty, boat ramps, and a beach and nature reserve.

One block southeast of Schnapper Drive is Vancouver Street, where you will find the **Mornington Peninsula Arts Centre,** one of Victoria's 16 regional galleries. Names to look for among its outstanding collection of works by Australian artists include Fred Williams, Sam Fullbrook, William Dobell, Sir Russell Drysdale, and John Passmore. *4 Vancouver St., Mornington, tel. 059/75–4395. Admission: $2 adults, $1 children 5–16. Open weekdays 10–4:30, weekends noon–4:30. Closed Dec. 25, Jan. 1.*

Pick up the Esplanade at Schnapper Drive and head southwest to **Mt. Martha Beach,** a great place to go swimming, and then proceed to Dromana Bay. At this point the Esplanade becomes Marine Drive. Continue on to McCulloch Street and turn left, then turn right onto Arthur's Seat Road. Here you'll find **Arthur's Seat Park,** where a ride on the chair lift will provide a sweeping view of the surrounding countryside. *Arthur's Seat Rd., Mornington Peninsula Fwy., tel. 059/87–2565. Chair lift tickets: $5.20 adults, $3.50 children 4–13. Open weekdays 11–4:30, Sat. 11–6 (later in summer), Sun. 11–6. Closed weekdays May–Sept.*

Return to McCulloch Street and take it to the Nepean Highway. Proceed southwest to Coburn Street and make a left, then turn right onto Burrell Street and left onto Charles Street. Built in 1844, the **McRae Homestead** on Charles Street was one of the first homes built in this area and is listed as a historic monument by the National Trust. The original furniture is on display, and guides give half-hour tours of the property. Even when the house is closed, the caretaker will often open the gate and show visitors around. *8 Charles St., McRae, tel. 059/81–2866. Admission: $3 adults, $2 children 6–18, $6.50 family. Open Apr.–Nov., weekends and holidays noon–4:30, Dec.–Mar., daily noon–4:30.*

Continue south along the Nepean Highway. The low, scrubby tree that grows prolifically along the shoreline is tea-tree, which appeared only in the 19th century, when the original vegetation of banksias and she-oaks was burned as fuel in the limestone kilns that supplied Melbourne with much of its building mortar. A species of melaleuca, tea-tree was actually used as a substitute for tea in the early days of the colony.

As you drive down the coast, notice that the timber beach huts that first appeared near Dromana have suddenly increased in number, especially around Rye. These are bathing boxes—privately leased beach huts that are one of the peculiarities of Victorian life. At some beaches they form an almost continuous line along the shore, identical—in size, in shape, in distance apart, in the little balconies that jut out above the sea—in every way, in fact, except in color. A peek inside says volumes about their owners. Some are like aquatic sports stores, complete with fishing tackle, Windsurfers, water skis, ropes, masks and flippers, and even dinghies lashed to the ceiling.

Continue south to Sorrento, one of the prettiest of the bayside beaches, with its lawns backed by shady trees, its trim white gazebo, and the fish-and-chips shop out over the water that leads to a tumbledown jetty—a picturesque roost for the pelicans. Sorrento developed as a fashionable resort more than a century ago when George Coppin formed a company named the Sorrento Ocean Amphitheatre Company, which built tramways through the town and linked it with Melbourne by paddle steamers. More recently, Sorrento has become the arts and crafts end of the peninsula, and the stretch of highway between Sorrento and Blairgowrie has no fewer than eight galleries.

At Sorrento, make a right onto St. Aubin's Way for a visit to the **Sorrento Marine Aquarium.** Aside from the extremely popular seal exhibits, visitors will find more than 200 species of fish on display. *St. Aubin's Way, Sorrento, tel. 059/84–4478. Admission: $5 adults, $2.50 children 5–12. Open daily 10–5; seal feeding at 3.*

At the end of the Nepean Highway, turn left onto Back Beach Road and make a right to **London Bridge,** a natural bridge formed by the ocean. Contrary to popular belief, this particular London Bridge is still standing. From London Bridge, the sole of the Mornington Peninsula boot runs in a straight line for 28 kilometers (17 miles), forming a long, narrow coastal park that ends at Cape Schanck. The sea can be violent along this coastline, and swimming is advisable only where the beach is patrolled by lifeguards. It was at Cheviot Beach, just west of London Bridge, that Harold Holt, the Australian prime minister, drowned in 1967.

Phillip Island

The greatest attraction here, and one of the most popular natural attractions in Australia, is the nightly commute of the fairy penguins, which waddle out of the sea and cross Summerland Beach to reach their burrows in the nearby sand dunes. A coach tour is the best way to visit Phillip Island (*see* Guided Tours, *above*). The coaches are well run and cover the island's main attractions. And because the penguins are viewed at dusk, it also means that visitors can rest on the long and dreary drive back to Melbourne.

Unlike the large and stately emperor penguins of the Antarctic, the tiny fairy penguins rarely grow much bigger than a large duck. During the day the fairy penguins feed in the sea, and each evening they return to their burrows in the sand dunes. This trip across the beach at Phillip Island has become the most popular tourist attraction in Victoria, but it's hardly a back-to-nature experience. The fairy penguins emerge from the surf onto the floodlit beach, while a commentator in a tower describes over a public address system their progress. Spectators, who watch from concrete bleachers, may number several thousand on a busy night. For many visitors, the most memorable part of the experience is the sight of the fluffy young penguins, who stand outside their burrows waiting for their parents to return with food. Camera flashbulbs may not be used to film the penguins, which effectively prevents still photography. For anyone interested in seeing the animals in a less touristy setting, fairy penguins are common to most of the southern Victorian coastline, and the locals in most coastal towns will point out places where they can be seen. Visitors should be prepared for wet and windy conditions at any time of the year. *Summerland Beach, tel. 059/56–8300 or 059/56–8691. Admission: $7 adults, $3 children 4–14, $20 family.*

Dining

For price categories, *see* the Melbourne Dining section, *above.*

The Dandenongs **Cotswold House.** One of the gastronomic gems of country Victoria, this rustic charmer combines epicurean food with a dazzling hillside setting. The dining room overlooks trees and gardens that are illuminated at night, and dishes include a sweet corn soufflé with a blue swimmer crab sauce, and Moroccan spiced-almond-and-pigeon pie. On weekdays, the lunch menu is simpler and less expensive. *Black Hill Rd., Menzies Creek, tel. 03/754–7884. Reservations advised. Dress: casual but neat. AE, DC, MC, V. No dinner Tues. and Wed. Closed Mon. $$$$*

Olinda Chalet. Located in a gracious old country home surrounded by gardens, fountains, and pools, this terrace restaurant offers splendid views and fine international cuisine. The blackboard menu, which changes daily, might offer pork fillet with a mustard and capsicum sauce, or peppered loin of lamb baked with tomato and basil. The banana soufflé is a popular dessert. *543 Mt. Dandenong Tourist Rd., Olinda, tel. 03/751–1844. Reservations advised. Dress: casual but neat. AE, DC, MC, V. No dinner Sun. Closed Mon. and Tues. $$$*

Mornington Peninsula **★** **Delgany.** This glamorous country-house restaurant is one of the finest in Australia, and new chef Juliana Landrivon has maintained its high reputation for creative, innovative French food. The glass-fronted outer dining room overlooks lovely gardens, while the inner dining area is centered on a large, open fire. The classic, elegant decor is enhanced by fresh flowers and pastel linens. Examples from the intriguing menu are a parfait of sliced quail and chicken livers, poached quail eggs and peeled marinated grapes, and lamb fillet on sweet potato puree with caramelized Japanese radish. The wine list is still outstanding. A less expensive bistro is planned for the former stables, scheduled for late 1994. *Nepean Hwy., Portsea, tel. 059/84–4000. Reservations advised. Dress: casual but neat. AE, DC, MC, V. $$$$*

Licciardo's. This noisy, bustling trattoria relies on the quality of its food, not its decor nor its casual service, to keep the crowds coming. It is located in a storefront, and its daily specials are listed on large blackboards on the walls. Dishes served here include tuna risotto with a spicy tomato sauce, barbecued mussels with herb bread, and rabbit fillets on a bed of noodles with basil. The seafood salads are highly recommended and the pasta dishes and antipasto are generally excellent. The exquisite chocolate soufflé is often available even when it does not appear on the menu. *84 Mt. Eliza Way, Mt. Eliza, tel. 03/787–7710. MC, V. No lunch Mon., Tues., and Sat. $$*

Poff's. Set on a hillside with views across a vineyard to the valley below, this modern restaurant has rapidly acquired a solid reputation. The menu is small and dishes are characteristically described with an austerity that downplays their caliber. Main courses might include ocean trout, lamb kebabs, roast duckling, and steak Diane—all simple and all delightful. Russian dishes, such as meat dumplings in a broth flavored with soya sauce, garlic, and chili and topped with sour cream, are a specialty. The crème caramel is sublime. *Red Hill Rd., Red Hill, tel. 053/89–2566. Reservations advised. Dress: casual but neat. AE, MC, V. Closed Mon.–Thurs. $$*

The West Coast Region

Arguably the country's most dramatic, spectacular coastal drive is Victoria's Great Ocean Road, heading west from Melbourne along rugged, windswept beaches. The road, built during the Great Depression atop majestic cliffs, occasionally dips down to sea level. Here, in championship surfing country, some of the finest waves in the world pound mile after mile of uninhabited golden sandy beaches. As you explore this coastline, don't miss Bell's Beach, site of the Easter Surfing Classic, one of the premier events of the surfing world. But be careful! Only the most competent swimmers should swim here, and then only at a lifeguard-patrolled beach with other swimmers. The fierce undertow along this coastline can be deadly.

Although this region is actually on the southeast coast of the Australian mainland, it lies to the west of Melbourne and to Melburnians is therefore "the West Coast." From Melbourne, travelers should allow two days for the West Coast journey.

Arriving and Departing

By Car Take the Princes Highway south from Melbourne to Geelong. From here, take the Torquay Road south to Torquay, where you will connect with the Great Ocean Road.

Guided Tours

AAT Kings (tel. 03/650–1244) has a choice of one- or two-night tours of the Great Ocean Road from Melbourne. The one-day tour costs $74 for adults, $69 for children under 14. A choice of accommodations is available on the two-day tour, and the price varies from $170 to $235 for adults, $150 to $215 for children.

The Wayward Bus (tel. 008/88–2823) is a minibus that takes three days to make a meandering journey from Melbourne to Adelaide via the Great Ocean Road, Mount Gambier, and the Coorong, with overnight stops at Port Fairy and Beachport. Aimed primarily at backpackers, the tour is enjoyable, informative, inexpensive, and highly recommended. Passengers can leave the bus at either overnight stop and catch the following bus. The tours depart Melbourne on Wednesday and Saturday, more frequently in summer. The cost is $125 per person, including picnic lunches but excluding accommodations.

Important Addresses and Numbers

Tourist Information **Geelong Tourist Information Centre.** *Moorabool St., Geelong, tel. 052/22–2900. Open daily 9–5.*

Port Fairy Tourist Information Centre. *Bank St., Port Fairy, tel. 055/68–2682. Open weekdays 10–4, weekends 10–12:30, 1:30–4.*

Warrnambool Tourist Information Centre, *600 Raglan Parade, tel. 055/64–7837. Open weekdays 9–5, weekends 10–4.*

Emergencies Dial 000 for **fire, police,** or **ambulance** services.

Exploring the West Coast

Follow the Princes Highway south from Melbourne to pick up the Geelong Road (Hwy. 1) for 75 kilometers (44 miles). When you reach Geelong, Victoria's second-largest town and a major industrial center, follow the signs through town and continue south on the Torquay Road for 23 kilometers (13 miles) to **Torquay.** Torquay is Australia's premier surfing and windsurfing resort. Bell's Beach is famous for its Easter surfing contests and its October international windsurfing competitions.

The towns and hamlets along the Great Ocean Road are in such spectacular visual surroundings that no tourist attractions have been, or are likely to be, built. None could compete with what nature has already provided.

The Great Ocean Road begins at Eastern View, 10 kilometers (6 miles) east of Lorne. Just before the road enters Lorne, it crosses the Erskine River. From the campsite near the bridge, an 8-kilometer (5-mile) track winds up the **Erskine River valley.** This lush, green haven of eucalyptuses, tree ferns, waterfalls, and rustic bridges is delightful; just remember to bring mosquito repellent and keep an eye out for leeches if you're barelegged. The track passes The Sanctuary, a rock amphitheater where early pioneers gathered for religious services. If the destination sounds appealing but the walk doesn't, Erskine Road, which exits Lorne to the north, passes close to the falls.

Lorne, a little town approximately 50 kilometers (30 miles) past Torquay at the edge of the Otway Range, is the site of both a wild celebration every New Year's Eve and the popular Pier-to-Pub Swim held shortly thereafter. Some people make their reservations a year in advance for these New Year's events. It's also a favorite surfing, sailing, and sunbathing spot, with a pretty park beside the beach, and the site of the Great Otway Classic, a footrace held annually on the second weekend in June.

After historic **Apollo Bay,** which is 45 kilometers (28 miles) past Lorne, the road turns inland through **Otway National Park** (Otway-Beach Forest Information Centre, tel. 052/35–9303). It is part of the Otway Ranges, and the rain forest here gets rainfall about 200 days a year. In this natural, primitive environment, ferns and shrubs define the color green. A striking feature of this forest is the mountain ash trees, among the tallest in the world. Some of the roads are not paved, and the going can be bumpy and slow.

The Great Ocean Road then swings out to the coast near Glenaire before heading inland again and running beside Melba Gully State Park. (To reach the park, take a left turn at Crowes; the park lies between Lavers Hill and Wangerrip.) The road then doubles back to the coastal town of Wattle Hill, where a dead-end side road will lead you to the coast at Moonlight Head, Otway National Park. The coastal formation was named by Matthew Flinders, the first person to circumnavigate Australia, who saw the headland during a fierce storm when the moon broke through the clouds for a second. The

Victoria

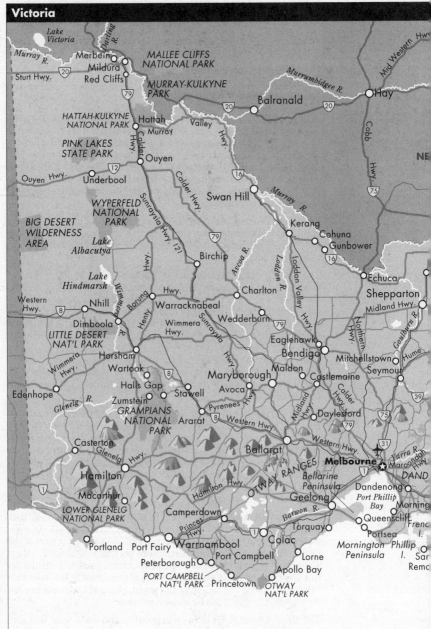

Lake Victoria

Murray R.

Sturt Hwy.

Merbein
Mildura
Red Cliffs

MALLEE CLIFFS
NATIONAL PARK

Darling R.

Murrumbidgee R.

Mid Western Hwy

Hay

MURRAY-KULKYNE
PARK

Balranald

NE

HATTAH-KULKYNE
NATIONAL PARK

Hattah

Murray

Valley

Calder Hwy.

Cobb Hwy.

PINK LAKES
STATE PARK

Ouyen

Swan Hill

Murray R.

Ouyen Hwy.

Underbool

Kerang

Cohuna
Gunbower

WYPERFELD
NATIONAL
PARK

Sunraysia Hwy. 12

Calder Hwy.

Avoca R.

Loddon R.

Loddon Valley Hwy.

Echuca

BIG DESERT
WILDERNESS
AREA

Lake
Albacutya

Birchip

Shepparton

Lake
Hindmarsh

Charlton

Midland Hwy.

Goulburn R.

Western
Hwy.

Nhill

Hwy.

Warracknabeal

Wedderburn

Eaglehawk

Hume

Dimboola

Wimmera R.

Borung Hwy.

Henty Hwy.

Wimmera
Hwy.

Sunraysia Hwy.

Bendigo

Mitchellstown

Northern Hwy.

LITTLE DESERT
NAT'L PARK

Horsham

Maldon

Castlemaine

Seymour

Wimmera Hwy.

Wartook

Maryborough

Avoca

Calder Hwy.

Edenhope

Halls Gap

Stawell

Pyrenees Hwy.

Daylesford

Glenelg R.

Zumstein

GRAMPIANS
NATIONAL
PARK

Ararat

Western Hwy.

Midland Hwy.

Casterton

Glenelg Hwy.

Ballarat

Western Hwy.

Melbourne

Yarra R.

Maroondah Hwy.

DAND

Hamilton

OTWAY RANGES

Bellarine
Peninsula

Dandenong

Hamilton Hwy.

Port Phillip
Bay

Morning

Macarthur

Geelong

LOWER GLENELG
NATIONAL PARK

Camperdown

Princes Hwy.

Barwon R.

Queenscliff

Frenc
I.

Portland

Port Fairy

Warrnambool

Colac

Torquay

Portsea

Mornington
Peninsula

Phillip
I.

Sar
Remo

Peterborough

Port Campbell

Lorne

PORT CAMPBELL
NAT'L PARK

Princetown

Apollo Bay

OTWAY
NAT'L PARK

Bass Strait

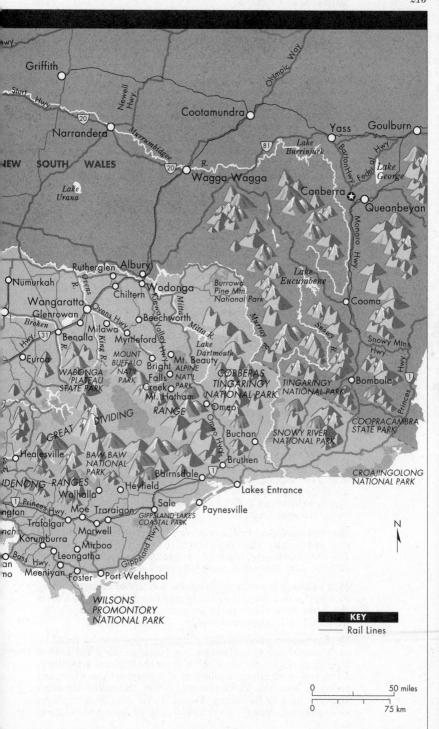

KEY
— Rail Lines

N

| 0 | | | 50 miles |
| 0 | | | 75 km |

cliffs below are some of the highest in the country, and several ships have foundered here. The main Great Ocean Road heads inland again slightly, coming back to the coast at Princetown. This is the beginning of **Port Campbell National Park,** the most dazzling section of the drive. For the next 32 kilometers (20 miles), the Great Ocean Road snakes along the cliff tops for a heart-stopping, roller-coaster ride. Along this coast the sheer limestone cliffs have been gnawed by the ferocious Southern Ocean, which has left tall pillars of more resilient rock standing 50–100 meters (165–330 feet) out to sea. There are several scenic lookouts along this coast, and each one seems more spectacular than the last. The most famous is the **Twelve Apostles,** as much a symbol for Victoria as the Sydney Opera House is for New South Wales. Despite the name, however, only eight rock stacks are visible—the rest have been claimed by the waves. (*See* Victoria's National Parks, *below.*) Equally dramatic are the formations at the **Bay of Martyrs** and the **Bay of Islands Coastal Reserve.** Both are less crowded with tour buses than the Twelve Apostles, and at the Bay of Islands you can watch the progress of new rock stacks taking shape.

Warrnambool, about 66 kilometers (41 miles) west of Port Campbell National Park, is the first major town after Geelong. This wool and dairy farm center is a friendly city of robust, hardy people who live off the land and the sea. A highlight in Warrnambool is **Flagstaff Hill Maritime Village,** a re-created 19th-century village built around a fort that was constructed in 1887, during one of the Russian scares that intermittently terrified the colony. In the village you can visit an 1853 lighthouse that is still in use today, wander through an old fort built in 1887, or board the *Reginald M*, a trading ship from the South Australian Gulf. *Merri and Banyan Sts., tel. 055/64–7841. Admission: $9.50 adults, $4.50 children 4–15, $26 family. Open daily 9–5. Closed Good Friday, Dec. 25.*

The **Wunta Fiesta,** held here in February, includes whale-boat races, a ball, a seafood and wine carnival, and children's activities.

Twenty-nine kilometers (18 miles) farther west is **Port Fairy,** the second-oldest town in Victoria. Originally a whaling station, the town, with sturdy old bluestone buildings set near the banks of the River Moyne, still thrives as the base for a fishing fleet. Founded during the whaling heyday in the 19th century, Port Fairy was once one of the largest ports in Victoria. More than 50 of the cottages and bluestone buildings in Port Fairy have been classified as landmarks by the National Trust.

The **Historical Society Museum** contains relics from the whaling days and from the many ships that have foundered along this coast. *The Old Courthouse, Gipps St., no tel. Admission: $2 adults, $1 children 5–16. Open Wed., weekends, and public holidays 2–5.*

Mott's Cottage is a restored limestone and timber cottage built by Sam Mott, a member of the whaling crew that discovered the town in the cutter *Fairy*. Light meals are available inside. *5 Sackville St., tel. 03/654–4711. Open weekdays 10–noon, weekends 2–4.*

Head inland from here through rolling gum-tree country for 82 kilometers (50 miles) to **Hamilton.** In Hamilton, stop and browse through the highly respected collection at the **Regional Art Gallery,** which houses an extensive collection of pottery, antique silver, and porcelain from the Mediterranean, before taking the Hamilton Highway back to Melbourne. *Brown St., tel. 055/73–0460. Donations accepted. Open Tues.–Fri. 10–5., Sat. 10–noon and 2–5, Sun. 2–5.*

What to See and Do with Children

Collect your **Kid's Country Treasure Hunt Guide** kit at the Warrnambool Tourist Information Centre (600 Raglan Parade, tel. 055/64–7837). Children who answer the questions on the "treasure map" (designed to introduce them to Warrnambool and its surroundings) get a free badge, book, or decal from the Information Centre.

Lake Pertobe Adventure Playground is a children's paradise set on 86 acres. Facilities include lakes with children's powerboats, paddleboats, kayaks, canoes, pleasure boats, and junior sailing craft; a playground; barbecue facilities; horse trails; and walking tracks. *Pertobe Rd., Warrnambool, tel. 055/64–7800. Admission free. Open daily.*

Off the Beaten Track

A pleasant side trip from Warrnambool is **Hopkins Falls,** 13 kilometers (8 miles) northeast of town. After parking your car, you can inspect the waterfalls on foot or hire a horse. Ponies are available at **St. Mary's Pony Farm** (Wangoom, tel. 055/67–1184).

In the sheltered bay at **Logan's Beach** near Warrnambool, **Southern Right whales** come very close to the shore each winter to give birth to their calves. They take up residence here for a considerable stretch of time and are easily observed from the shore. They are known as Right whales because they were once hunted extensively along this coast and, therefore, were "right" for killing. The Warrnambool Tourist Information Centre (tel. 055/64–7837) can advise you of their presence and direct you to the best observation points.

A half-hour drive northwest of Warrnambool is **Tower Hill State Game Reserve,** an extinct volcano abounding with flora and fauna. *Box 60, Koroit, tel. 055/65–9202. Admission free. Open daily 8–5. Closed Good Friday, Dec. 25.*

Within the reserve you will find a **Natural History Centre,** which provides extensive background information on this site. *Admission free. Open daily 9:30–12:30 and 1:30–4:30. Closed Good Friday, Dec. 25.*

Shopping

For crafts and homegrown produce, visit the **Warrnambool Town and Country Crafts Community Market** (Swan Reserve, Raglan Parade), which is held on the second Saturday morning of each month. The Warrnambool **Saturday Market** is held on the first Saturday of each month at the Safeway car park.

Participant Sports

Fishing Warrnambool and the surrounding district offer great fishing, including river and surf fishing. A 28-day fishing license costs $10 and is required for fishing the rivers and streams of Victoria. Contact **Warrnambool Shooters and Anglers Shop** (Liebig St., Warrnambool, tel. 055/62–3502) for further information.

Golf The **Warrnambool Golf Course** (tel. 055/62–2108) is a first-class 18-hole course located off Younger Street. Club tournaments are held at Easter and in September. Greens fees are $15, buggy hire is $8, and clubs are $12.

Spectator Sports

Car Racing The **Grand Annual Sprintcar Classic** (tel. 055/62–8229) is held at Premier Speedway in Allansford, east of Warrnambool, during the Australia Day long weekend in late January.

Cycling The **Melbourne to Warrnambool Road Race** is a cycling classic held annually on the second Saturday in October. The race starts at 7:15 AM at Port Melbourne and finishes at Raglan Parade in Warrnambool at approximately 2:30 PM.

Dining and Lodging

For price categories, *see* Melbourne Dining and Lodging.

Darlington **Yellangip Country House.** Tucked away in secluded grazing country
Dining and in western Victoria, this vast turn-of-the-century homestead offers
Lodging outstanding atmosphere, a dash of luxury, and fine country cooking. The house was totally restored in 1990 and invested with modern comforts. Guest rooms are plushly decorated with antiques and chintz fabrics, and scented with big bunches of wildflowers. The master bedroom, which overlooks the front garden, is recommended. The house is located off the Hamilton Highway, two hours' drive from Melbourne and midway between Port Campbell and The Grampians national parks. Dinner is available by arrangement; the cooking draws its inspiration from northern Italy. *Pura Pura Rd., Darlington, tel. 055/97–9203, fax 055/97–9276. 5 rooms with bath. Facilities: tennis court, dinner available. Breakfast included. MC, V. $$*

Hamilton **Stirring Pot.** Located in a converted hillside mansion, this combina-
Dining tion restaurant/art gallery is decorated in turn-of-the-century style. The international cuisine concentrates on huge, juicy steaks, beef with hot pepper sauce, rack of lamb, and local seafood. A two-course meal is available at a very reasonable price. As an alternative to the four cozy dining rooms inside the house, guests can dine in the garden on warm evenings. *212 Coleraine Rd., tel. 055/72–2535. Dress: casual. AE, DC, MC, V. BYOB. No lunch. Closed Sun. and Mon. $$*

Lorne **Kosta's.** Lively, bright, informal, and noisy, especially during the
Dining peak season, this gaily decorated taverna has a wine bar and specializes in Greek food and international dishes, such as Moroccan lamb casserole, a wonderful homemade *tsatsiki* (a yogurt, cucumber, and garlic appetizer), and chargrilled lamb. Fresh local specialties, including charcoal-grilled fish and lobster, are also offered. *48 Mountjoy Parade, tel. 052/89–1883. Dress: casual but neat. MC, V. Open daily Christmas–Easter. $$*

Lodging **Erskine House.** Set in a 12-acre garden, the house was built in 1868 and fully restored in 1930. This charming, spotless guest house, done in a 1930s style, is perfect for those who want a relaxed, art deco hotel without phones, televisions, or radios. Rates include breakfast. *Mountjoy Parade, tel. 052/89–1205. 72 rooms with bath, 25 suites. Facilities: 8 tennis courts, putting green. AE, DC, MC, V. $*

Port Fairy **Dublin House Inn.** This solid stone building was built in 1855 and is
Dining furnished in period style. Chef Wendy Ryan concentrates on the freshest local produce, creating dishes that incorporate everything from seafood to free-range chicken, duckling, and local beef. Especially recommended are the lobster, crab chowder, and (in the winter) game pie. Next door, Ryan's daughter runs a gourmet food shop

for those who prefer to pick up the ingredients for a picnic. The 32-seat dining room is open weekends only, but extra nights are added in the summer. *57 Bank St., tel. 055/68–1822. Dress: casual but neat. MC, V. BYOB. No lunch. Dinner Fri., Sat. $$*

Portofino. This Italian eatery is one of the few restaurants in Port Fairy that's open for Sunday dinner. The two small dining rooms are decorated with white balloon curtains, classic metal-and-cane Breuer chairs, a fireplace, and photographs of Italy. It's a two-person operation, with John Hayes in command of the kitchen while his wife, Amanda, serves the guests with warmth and humor. The food may be the most authentic, but one has to admire Portofino's pluck in presenting an ambitious menu in an area not known for its gourmet cuisine. The pastas tend toward the lusty; try the *saltati*, a Bolognese-style meat sauce with bacon, onion, carrots, tomatoes, and white wine. Main courses include osso bucco, salmon lasagna, and fresh grilled fish such as herring. For dessert, look for the chocolate and date torte with fresh cream. *Bank St., tel. 055/68–1047. Reservations advised on weekends and in summer. Dress: casual. MC, V. BYOB. Wed.–Sun. dinner only. $$*

Lodging **Seacombe House Motor Inn.** Dormer windows and skylights create a bright, airy atmosphere in this brick double-story motel. Rooms are larger than you'll find at an average motel, and they sport custom-made, colonial-style furniture. The cottage rooms have kitchen facilities, and some rooms have whirlpool tubs. *22 Sackville St., tel. 055/68–1082. 21 rooms with bath. Facilities: sundeck, laundry, car wash. AE, DC, MC, V. $*

Warrnambool **Mahogany Ship.** Decorated loosely on a nautical theme, this restau-
Dining rant above the Flagstaff Hill Maritime Village has splendid views of the harbor at Lady Bay and the ocean beyond. Local crayfish are a specialty; steak and poultry dishes are also available. Children are specially catered to by a separate menu, which includes a traditional Australian favorite: fish and chips. The tavern next door serves a basic selection of less expensive meals. *Flagstaff Hill Maritime Village, Merri St., tel. 055/61–1833. Dress: casual. AE, DC, MC, V. No lunch Sat. Closed Mon. $$*

Lodging **Central Court Motel.** On the Princes Highway opposite the Tourist Information Centre, this neat, contemporary twostory motel is just a 10-minute walk from the main shopping center. *581 Raglan Parade, Princes Hwy., tel. 055/62–8555. 38 rooms with bath including 2 suites. Facilities: pool, restaurant, live music Sat. night, laundry, car wash, baby-sitting. AE, DC, MC, V. Restaurant closed Sun. $*

Mid City Motor Inn. This modern, two-story motel, located on the Princes Highway, is set in a neatly manicured garden only minutes away from the town center. Dinner dances are held here on Saturday night. *525 Raglan Parade, tel. 055/62–3866. 62 rooms with bath including 2 suites. Facilities: pool and heated spa-pool, restaurant, bar, car wash, fax, 24-hr room service, baby-sitting, barbecue. AE, DC, MC, V. $*

Woolsthorpe **Quamby Homestead.** Located just 15 minutes north of Warrnam-
Dining and bool, this magnificently restored century-old homestead is fur-
Lodging nished with Australian antiques and is an ideal base from which to
★ explore the whole Warrnambool area. Guests are accommodated in modern rooms with en suite facilities in the former staff quarters, which are set apart from the homestead and surrounded by an English-style garden where native birdcalls compete with the shrieks of peacocks. The dining room, located in the homestead, serves fine country meals. Meals are available to nonresident guests on week-

ends. Children under 12 are not accommodated. *Caramut Rd., tel. 055/69–2395. 7 rooms with bath. Tariff includes breakfast and dinner. MC, V. BYOB. $$*

Gold Country

Victoria was changed forever in the mid-1850s by the discovery of gold in the center of the state. Some of the largest, richest goldfields in the world were unearthed, and immigrants from every corner of the world poured into Victoria to seek their fortunes as "diggers"—a name that has become synonymous with Australians ever since. Few miners became wealthy from their search, however—the real money was made by those supplying goods and services to the thousands who had succumbed to gold fever.

Gold towns that sprang up like mushrooms to accommodate these fortune seekers prospered until the gold rush receded, then became ghost towns or turned to agriculture to survive. Today, Victoria's gold is again being mined in limited quantities, but these historic old towns remain interesting relics of Australia's past.

Getting Around

By Car To reach Bendigo, take the Calder Highway northwest from Melbourne; for Ballarat, take the Western Highway. A round-trip tour touching on both of these towns as well as several other points of interest in the goldfields should take three or four days.

By Train Good rail service to Ballarat or Bendigo is available. For time-tables and rates, contact **V-Line** (tel. 03/619–3333) or the **Royal Automobile Club of Victoria** (230 Collins St., Melbourne, tel. 03/650–1522).

Guided Tours Operators who cover this area include **Gray Line** (tel. 03/654–7700), **Australian Pacific Tours** (tel. 03/650–1511), and **AAT Kings** (tel. 03/650–1244); all three depart from 101 Bourke Street in Melbourne.

Important Addresses and Numbers

Tourist Information **Ballarat Tourist Information Centre.** *39 Sturt St., Ballarat, tel. 053/32–2694. Open weekdays 9–5, weekends 10–4.*

Bendigo Tourist Information Centre. *Charing Cross, Bendigo, tel. 054/41–5244. Open daily 9–5.*

Daylesford Tourist Information Centre. *49 Vincent St., Daylesford, tel. 053/48–1399. Open daily 10–4.*

Emergencies Dial 000 for **fire, police,** or **ambulance** services.

Exploring the Gold Country

From Melbourne, take Flemington Road, which leaves the city to the northwest, and follow the signs for 106 kilometers (66 miles) to **Ballarat.** Allow 1½ hours for the drive from central Melbourne. In the local Aboriginal language, the name means "resting place," since a plentiful supply of food was to be found around Lake Wendouree, to the north of the present township. The town flourished when gold was discovered here in 1851. This was not Australia's first major gold strike. That honor belongs to Bathurst, in western New South Wales, but Victoria in 1851 *was* El Dorado; 90% of the gold mined in Australia during the boom years of the 19th century came from Victoria. The biggest finds were at Bendigo and

Ballarat, and the Ballarat diggings proved to be among the richest alluvial goldfields in the world. In 1854, Ballarat was the scene of the battle of the Eureka Stockade, a skirmish that took place between the miners and the authorities, primarily over the extortionate gold license fees that the miners were forced to pay. More than 20 men died in the battle, the only time that Australians have taken up arms in open rebellion against their government.

As you approach Ballarat, a sign points left toward **Montrose Cottage and Eureka Museum.** Built in 1856 by a Scottish miner, Montrose Cottage was the first bluestone house in Ballarat. Inside you can see furniture and handwork of the period. Adjoining the cottage is a museum building with an impressive display of artifacts from Ballarat's gold-mining days. The collection of irons and the Chinese water pump are particularly notable. The tours conducted by Laurel Johnson, the owner of the museum, are lively and informative. *111 Eureka St., tel. 053/32–2554. Admission: $4.50 adults, $2 children 4–16, $11 family. Open daily 9:30–5.*

Time Out Next door to Montrose Cottage is **Priscilla's Cottage,** which makes the most of its history with lace tablecloths and a cozy, cloistered atmosphere. The menu offers a choice of light meals, such as ploughman's lunch, Devonshire tea, soups, and salads. Prices are inexpensive. *109 Eureka St., tel. 053/31–5705. Open daily 10–5. Closed Mon. May–Oct.*

Continue to the bottom of Eureka Street, turn left at the roundabout into Main Road, and follow the sign to **Sovereign Hill Historical Park.** Built on the site of the Sovereign Hill Quartz Mining Company's mines, this is an authentic recreation of life, work, and play on the gold diggings at Ballarat following the discovery of gold here in 1851. On the lowest part of the site are the tent camp and the diggings, which were built in the first months of the gold rush, when the gold was panned from creeks or dug from the earth with picks and shovels. On Main Street, running uphill from the diggings, are the shops, workshops, and public buildings that existed on the site between 1854 and 1861. Notice the New York Hotel and the T. Murphy California Tentmaker shop, a reminder that many of the miners came from the United States. At the top of the hill is the third stage of Sovereign Hill—the mine and the pithead equipment. When the surface gold gave out, the miners were forced to dig along the ancient watercourses that lay deep underground, and this was where the real treasure lay. It was in such a mine on the Ballarat goldfields that the Welcome Nugget was discovered in 1858 by a group of Cornish miners. At today's prices, it would be worth just over a million dollars. Near the entrance to the complex is the **Voyage to Discovery,** an indoor museum designed to give visitors an overview of society and the world at large at the time of the gold rush. The museum is excellent, with imaginative dioramas and computer terminals that encourage the visitor to become an active participant in the process of discovery. *Sovereign Hill Park, Bradshaw St., tel. 053/31–1944. Admission: $15.50 adults, $8 children 5–15, $42.50 family. Open daily 9:30–5. Closed Dec. 25.*

Across Bradshaw Street from the historical park is the **Gold Museum,** which displays an extensive collection of nuggets from the Ballarat diggings as well as some examples of the finished product in the form of gold jewelry. *Bradshaw St., tel. 053/31–1944. Admission: $4.20 adults, $2.10 children 5–15. Open Sun.–Fri. 10–5:30, Sat. 12:30–5:20.*

Between October and May, Sovereign Hill is the backdrop for **Blood on the Southern Cross,** a 90-minute sound-and-light spectacular that focuses on the Eureka uprising. The story is told with passion and dramatic technical effects, although the sheer wealth of historical detail clouds the story line. The climax of the show is the battle of the Eureka Stockade. Be prepared for chilly nights, even in midsummer. Numbers are limited and advance bookings are recommended. *Admission: $17 adults, $8 children 5–15, $44 family. Show held daily except Sun.*

Leave Sovereign Hill and take Main Road to Ballarat, drive a short distance along the broad main street, Sturt Street, and turn right into **Lydiard Street.** The prosperity of the gold rush left the city well endowed with handsome buildings, and this short stretch has a number of notable examples. One of these historic buildings is now the **Ballarat Fine Arts Gallery,** which contains paintings by several famous Australian painters, including Russell Drysdale, Sidney Nolan, and Fred Williams. Its most impressive exhibit is the tattered remains of the original Southern Cross flag that was flown defiantly by the rebels at the Eureka Stockade. Many Australians advocate the adoption of the Southern Cross in preference to the present Australian flag, which features the Union Jack, regarded by them as an anachronistic symbol of the country's links with Great Britain. *40 Lydiard St., tel. 053/31–5622. Admission free. Open Tues.–Fri. 10:30–4:30, weekends 12:30–4:30.*

Continue through Ballarat along the Western Highway, and on the outskirts of town turn right into Pleasant Street. Turn left to follow the shore of Lake Wendouree, a curving drive along Ballarat's dress circle. To the left, identifiable by its flower gardens and classical statuary, is the **Botanic Gardens.** At the rear of the gardens, the Begonia House is the focus of events during the town's Begonia Festival, held annually in February or March. Another notable feature of the gardens is the Avenue of the Prime Ministers: busts of every Australian leader since federation. *Wendouree Parade. No phone. Admission free. Open 24 hrs. daily.*

From Ballarat, follow the Midland Highway north for 45 kilometers (28 miles) to **Daylesford** and take the short detour 3 kilometers (2 miles) on Hepburn Springs Road to **Hepburn Springs.** Nestled in the slopes of the Great Dividing Range, these twin towns form the spa capital of Australia. The water table here is naturally aerated with carbon dioxide and rich in soluble mineral salts, and the area's concentration of natural springs was first noted during the gold rush. A spa was established at Hepburn Springs, in 1875, at the time when spa resorts were fashionable in Europe. After a long period of decline, this spa has been revived in the health-conscious '90s (*see below*).

Perched on a hillside overlooking Daylesford is **The Convent Gallery,** a former nunnery that has been restored to its full Victorian splendor and now displays contemporary Australian pottery, glassware, jewelry, sculpture, and prints, all for sale. At the front of the gallery is Bad Habits, a sunny café that serves light lunches and snacks. *Daly St., tel. 053/48–3211. Gallery and café open daily 10–6.*

The main attraction in Hepburn Springs is the **Hepburn Springs Mineral Spa,** which was completely redeveloped in 1991. This bright, modern complex now offers a variety of mineral baths and treatments, including communal spa pools, private aerospa baths, massages, saunas, and float tanks. *Main Rd., Mineral Springs Reserve, tel. 053/48–2034. Admission: relaxation pool $7, aerospa* *bath $15, float tank $35, sauna $5, spa couch $5. Open weekdays 10–8, weekends 9–8.*

Above the spa, a path winds through the **Mineral Springs Reserve** past a series of mineral springs, each with a slightly different chemical composition—and a significantly different taste. Any empty bottles you have can be filled free of charge with the mineral water of your choice.

Continue north along the Midland Highway 38 kilometers (23 miles) to **Castlemaine.** This is another gold-mining town, yet the gold here was mostly found on the surface. Castlemaine lacked the deeper reef gold, which was where the real riches lay, and the town never reached the prosperous heights of Ballarat or Bendigo, as is evidenced by its comparatively modest public buildings. The single exception is the **Castlemaine Market,** built in 1862 to resemble an ancient Roman basilica. The statue on top of the building is Ceres, Roman goddess of the harvest. Today, the building houses a museum with local artifacts and audiovisual displays. *Mostyn St., tel. 054/72–2679. Admission: $3 adults, $2 children 5–16. Open daily 1 PM–5 PM.*

Drive through Castlemaine, turning right at Hunter Street to **Buda.** This historic house is a tribute to the diversity of talents drawn to the gold rush in the middle of the past century. Built in 1861, the house was purchased two years later by Ernest Liviny, a Hungarian jeweler who established a business on the Castlemaine goldfields. It was the last of his six daughters, Hilda, who left the house and its entire contents to the state when she died in 1981. The house is essentially simple, yet it exhibits an Eastern European love of culture. The 20th-century woodcuts in the hall are especially fine, and the work of several important artists is displayed. Look for the prints by Margaret Preston, whose prints of Australian native flowers completed in the 1920s show a strong, stylized sense of design. The house contains a number of Leviny's own designs for his jewelry, as well as the photographs, paintings, sculptures, and embroidery created by his industrious and talented daughters. The gardens are delightful, with a fresh discovery at every turn. *42 Hunter St., tel. 054/ 72–1032. Admission: $5 adults, $2 children 4–15, $12 family. Open daily 9:30–5.*

Drive back through Castlemaine and head west on Maryborough Road (Hwy. 122). Follow the signs to **Maldon.** Relative isolation has preserved this former gold-mining town almost intact, and today the entire main street is a magnificent example of vernacular goldfields architecture. (Look for the bullnose roofing over the verandas, a feature now back in architectural vogue.) Maldon's charm has become a marketable commodity, and the town is now busy with tourists— and thick with tea shops and antiques sellers. Its atmosphere is best absorbed in a short stroll along the main street.

Three kilometers (1.2 miles) south of Maldon is **Carman's Tunnel,** a gold mine that has remained unaltered since it closed in 1884. The mine, which can only be seen on a candlelight tour, offers fascinating insight into the ingenious techniques used by the early gold miners. The 570-meter (1,870-foot) tunnel is dry, clean, and spacious, and the tour is suitable for all ages. *Parkin's Reef Rd., tel. 054/75–2453. Admission: $2 adults, 50¢ children. Tours depart weekends and school holidays at 2 PM.*

Return to the Midland Highway and continue to **Bendigo.** In tandem with Ballarat, this is a city that was spawned by the gold rush. Gold was discovered here in 1851, and the boom lasted well into the 1880s;

the city's magnificent public buildings bear witness to the richness of its mines. Today Bendigo is a bustling, enterprising small city and not particularly relaxing, unlike many other goldfields towns, but its architecture is noteworthy. Most of Bendigo's distinguished buildings are arranged on either side of **The Mall** in the city center. These include the **Shamrock Hotel,** the **General Post Office,** and the **Law Courts,** all majestic and florid examples of late Victorian architecture.

At the fountain in the middle of The Mall, turn up **View Street** to see several handsome Victorian buildings on the right, although the unity of the streetscape has been marred by unsympathetic additions, among them the **Bendigo Art Gallery.** Despite its unprepossessing exterior, the gallery houses a notable collection of contemporary Australian paintings, including the work of Jeffrey Smart, Lloyd Rees, and Clifton Pugh. The latter once owned a remote outback pub famous for its walls daubed with the artist's pornographic cartoons! The gallery also houses some significant 19th-century French Realist and Impressionist works, bequeathed by a local surgeon. *42 View St., tel. 054/43–4991. Admission free. Open weekdays 10–5, weekends 2–5.*

The best introduction to the city is the tour aboard the **Vintage Talking Tram,** which includes a taped commentary on the town's history. The tram departs on its 8-kilometer (5-mile) circuit on the half-hour at one-hour intervals between 9:30 and 4:30. You can get off and on at any stop. The tram originates at the **Central Deborah Gold-Mine,** another of the city's main attractions. The 500-meter (1,667-foot) mine shaft yielded almost a ton of gold before it closed in 1954. Today visitors can experience life underground on a guided tour of the mine. An elevator takes visitors 61 meters (200 feet) below ground level. *Violet St., tel. 054/43–8322. Mine admission: $11 adults, $5.50 children 5–15. Tram tour: $6 adults, $3 children 5–15. Mine open daily 9:30–5. Closed Dec. 25.*

Along its route the tram stops at the **Joss House** (Temple of Worship), built by Chinese miners on the outskirts of the city. No longer used for sacred purposes, the temple is now a museum dedicated to the history of the Chinese miners, once a conspicuous presence on the Victorian goldfields. In the 1850s and '60s, at the height of the boom, about a quarter of the miners were Chinese. These men were usually dispatched from villages on the Chinese mainland, and they were expected to work hard and return as quickly as possible to their villages with their fortunes intact. Very few Chinese women ever accompanied the men, and apart from their graveyards and temples, there is little evidence of any Chinese presence in the goldfields. The Chinese were scrupulously law-abiding, ingenious, and hard-working—qualities that did not always endear them to the other miners—and anti-Chinese riots were common among the miners. In some areas, an Office of the Chinese Protector was established to safeguard their interests. *Finn St., Emu Point, tel. 054/42–1685. Admission: $2 adults, $1 children 5–14, $5 family. Open daily 10–5. Closed Dec. 25.*

To return to Melbourne from Bendigo, take the Midland Highway back to Bendigo, then follow the Calder Highway. Allow 2½ hours for the 160-kilometer (100-mile) journey.

What to See and Do with Children

Ballarat Wildlife and Reptile Park. This bushland park has native Australian wildlife from a wide range of habitats. Animals include saltwater crocodiles, snakes, lizards, wombats, echidnas, and kangaroos. A koala tour takes place daily at 11. The latest attraction is a giant African land tortoise. The park also has a café, and barbecue and picnic areas. *Fussel and York Sts., Ballarat E., tel. 053/33–5933. Admission: $8 adults, $4 children 4–14. Open daily 9–5:30. Closed Dec. 25.*

Castlemaine & Maldon Railway. This 45-minute loop aboard a historic steam train winds through forests of eucalyptus and wattle that are especially spectacular in spring. *Maldon Station, tel. 054/75–2966. Rides: $7 adults, $4 children, $20 family. Departs Maldon Station Sun. (and weekends during school holidays) 1, 2, 3, 4.*

Golda's World of Dolls. This private collection of about 2,000 dolls from around the world is enough to bring a gleam into any child's eyes. *148 Eureka St., tel. 053/31–4880. Admission: $3 adults, 50¢ children under 14. Open Sat.–Thurs. 1–5. Closed Fri.*

Shopping

Bendigo Mohair Farm (Maryborough Rd., Lockwood, tel. 054/35–3341) is a working Angora goat stud farm. The showroom displays handknit sweaters, mohair rugs, scarves, hats, ties, and toys for purchase. The farm also has barbecue and picnic facilities. The **Gold Museum** (tel. 053/31–1944) and **Sovereign Hill** (tel. 053/31–1944) in Ballarat have extensive souvenir shops. **Maldon** has a host of charming boutiques and antiques shops.

Participant Sports

Golf **Ballarat Golf Club** (Sturt St., W. Ballarat, tel. 053/34–1023). Green fees are $14, and visitors should ring the pro shop (tel. 053/34–1573) for bookings. Clubs are available for hire.
Bendigo Golf Club (Golf Links Rd., Epsom, tel. 054/48–4206). Green fees are $15; clubs and carts cost $10 per round.

Tennis **Bendigo Indoor Grass Tennis.** The five artificial grass courts are open daily. *Edwards Rd., Bendigo, tel. 054/42–2411. Rates: $12 per hr 9 AM–4 PM, $18 per hr 5 PM–midnight. Open approx. 9 AM–midnight.*

Dining and Lodging

Ballarat **Alibis.** Inside a historic bluestone building, this restaurant com-
Dining bines an elegant setting with a menu that takes its culinary cues
★ from a worldwide list of fashionable cuisines. Selections from the menu include prawns coated with garlic and coriander; ravioli filled with minced chicken, basil, and leeks; and Middle Eastern–style rack of lamb served in yogurt. *10 Camp St., Ballarat, tel. 053/31–6680. Reservations advised. Dress: casual but neat. MC, V. No lunch. Closed Sun. and Mon. $$$*
Dyer's Steak Stable. Set in a former hotel stable, this restaurant relies on a simple formula of robust food, fine wines, and a welcoming atmosphere. Game dishes and a range of steaks with various sauces are the house specialties. *Little Bridge St., Ballarat, tel. 053/31–2850. Reservations advised. Dress: casual. AE, DC, MC, V. No lunch Sat. Closed Sun. $$*
Porter's. This onetime corner pub has been renovated and decorated in art deco style to offer informal dining with a touch of class at a very reasonable price. The changing menu draws from a variety of culinary styles to provide something for every appetite, at any time

of the day. From Thursday to Saturday evenings the restaurant has live entertainment, usually a vocalist with piano accompaniment. Service is friendly and professional, and the wine list is a showcase of the best of central Victoria. *Mair and Peel Sts., Ballarat, tel. 053/ 31–4320. Reservations advised. Dress: casual but neat. AE, DC, MC, V. No lunch Sat., Mon. Closed Sun. $$*

Lodging **Ballarat Terrace.** This imposing, century-old Victorian terrace
★ house offers outstanding character and comfort at a reasonable price. The house has been magnificently restored, and the antique furnishings are accented with big bunches of fresh flowers, a pervasive scent of roses, and open fires in winter. The best of the three upstairs guest rooms is at the front, with a wide balcony that overlooks the street. Smoking is not allowed inside the house, nor are children under 13. *229 Lydiard St., N. Ballarat, tel. 053/33–2216. 3 rooms with bath. Tariff includes full breakfast. MC. $$*

Ravenswood. Tucked away behind a garden brimming with peach trees, pussy willows, fuchsias, and climbing roses, this three-bedroom timber cottage is ideal for anyone looking for family-size accommodation with kitchen facilities. The house, which was completely renovated in 1993, has been decorated with contemporary furniture, carpeting, and chintz fabrics to a high standard of comfort. The cottage is a little less than 1½ kilometers (1 mile) from the center of Ballarat. *404 Havelock St. (Private Box 1360, Ballarat Mail Centre, 3354), tel. 053/32–8296, fax 053/31–3358. 1 cottage with bath. Tariff includes breakfast supplies. No credit cards. $–$$*

Bendigo **Maxine's.** This sophisticated restaurant enjoys a long-standing rep-
Dining utation as Bendigo's finest. You'll dine in a room with pale pink
★ walls, soft lighting, and white table linen. The French-Italian menu relies on unfussy cooking, focusing on the rich flavors that come fresh from the surrounding farms and fields. *15 Bath La., Bendigo, tel. 054/42–2466. Reservations required. Dress: casual but neat. AE, DC, MC, V. No lunch Sat. Closed Sun., Mon., and first 2 wks of Jan. $$$*

Metropolitan. In a classic Australian country pub with wide verandas and distinctive stained-glass windows, this restaurant offers a choice of all-day dining in the brasserie, against a background of unobtrusive rock music, or in the more refined atmosphere of the Grillroom. Both offer an identical menu that features pasta dishes, sandwiches, salads, steaks, and seafood. Children have their own special menu. *244 Hargreaves St., Bendigo, tel. 054/43–4916. No reservations. Dress: casual. AE, DC, MC, V. Closed Dec. 25. $$*

The Shamrock Hotel. The formal dining room decor is almost as impressive as the ornate wedding-cake facade of this turn-of-the-century hotel (*see* Lodging, *below*). The menu makes good use of local ingredients in dishes such as roast venison with black currant sauce, and trout served with a butter and almond sauce. The grill room serves simple meals in less splendid surroundings. *Pall Mall and Williamson Sts., Bendigo, tel. 054/43–0333. Reservations advised. Dress: casual but neat. AE, DC, MC, V. $$*

Lodging **Nanga Gnulle.** On a hillside on the outskirts of Bendigo, Rob and Peg Green have created a haven in mud brick and timber, surrounded by a garden that does justice to their name. Pronounced "nanga nully," the name means small stream in the local Aboriginal language. The atmosphere is extremely relaxing and friendly, the decor warm, with lots of wood furniture and details and natural fabrics. The larger of the two rooms is on the lower part of the contemporary split-level house. The gardens won first prize in the Bendigo gardening competition in 1990 and 1992. Smoking and children under 16 are not allowed inside. *40 Harley St., tel. 054/43–7891, fax 054/43–3397. 2 rooms with bath. Includes breakfast. MC, V. $$*

The Shamrock Hotel. This landmark Victorian hotel at the city center offers a choice of accommodation, from simple, traditional pub rooms without en suite facilities to large suites. If you're looking for luxury, ask for the Amy Castles Suite, which comes at a very reasonable price. The rooms are spacious and well maintained, but the furnishings are dowdy and strictly functional. The central location and the character of the hotel itself are the real drawing cards. The formal dining room is recommended (*see* Dining, *above*). *Pall Mall and Williamson Sts., tel. 054/43–0333. 24 rooms, most with bath. Facilities: 2 restaurants, 3 bars. AE, DC, MC, V. $$*

Daylesford
Dining
★

Lake House Restaurant. Consistently rated one of the outstanding restaurants of central Victoria, this rambling lakeside pavilion brings a touch of glamour to spa country. Summer main courses on the seasonal menu might include panfried tuna steak in a pepper crust with grilled peppers, and a selection of imaginative Asian-accented and vegetarian dishes. Presentation is stylish and innovative. The tables out on the deck are especially recommended for lunch on a warm day. The wine list features some of the finest vintages of the surrounding vineyards. *King St., Daylesford, tel. 053/48–3329. Reservations required. Dress: casual but neat. AE, MC, V. $$$*

Lodging

Holcombe Homestead. This is country living at its aristocratic best: a century-old farmhouse that is one of the architectural glories of rural Victoria, complete with kangaroos, kookaburras, and an on-site trout stream. The house has been furnished in keeping with its Victorian character, and to preserve its architectural integrity, guests share one bathroom. Guests who arrive midweek often have the entire house to themselves. Guests can arrange to cook their own meals, and the owners, who live in a neighboring house, will prepare box lunches and dinner on request. The house is 15 kilometers (9 miles) from Daylesford. *Holcombe Rd. (RMB 3638, Glenyon, 3461), tel. 053/48–7514. 3 rooms share 1 bath. Facilities: mountain bikes, tennis court, fishing. Tariff includes full breakfast. No credit cards. $$*

Lake House. These smart, white-timber guest rooms have a breezy, contemporary feel that follows the style formula set by the much-lauded Lake House Restaurant (*see* Dining, *above*), at the foot of the hill. Rooms at the front open to a terrace that has a better view but slightly less privacy. Those at the back are screened from neighboring rooms by rose-entwined trellises. Children are not accommodated on weekends. *King St., Daylesford, tel. 053/48–3329, fax 054/ 48–3995. 11 rooms with bath. Facilities: outdoor pool, restaurant, bar. Tariff includes breakfast. AE, MC, V. $$*

Hepburn
Springs
Lodging

Dudley House. On the main street of this spa town, it's hard to miss this timber Federation classic—similar to the Queen Anne style in England and the United States—in cream and maroon behind a neat hedge with a picket gate. The house was painstakingly restored in 1991 and, with its antique furnishings and cozy atmosphere, offers a high standard of comfort and a dash of romance. The white room at the front and the blue room at the rear are the ones to ask for. The town's spa baths are within walking distance. Neither smoking nor children under 16 are allowed inside the house; dinners are available by arrangement. *101 Main St., tel. 053/48–3033. 4 rooms, 1 with bath, 3 with shower. Tariff includes breakfast. No credit cards. $$*

Northeast Wineries and the Murray River

Victoria, Tasmania, New South Wales, and Western Australia all were planted with vines during the 1830s, laying the foundations for an industry that has today earned an impressive international reputation. One of the earliest sponsors of Victorian viticulture was Charles LaTrobe, the first Victorian governor. LaTrobe had lived at Neuchâtel in Switzerland and had married the daughter of the Swiss Counsellor of State. As a result of his contacts, several Swiss wine makers emigrated to Australia and developed some of the earliest Victorian vineyards in the Yarra Valley, east of Melbourne.

Digging for gold was a thirsty business, and the gold rushes—which were centered in Victoria—acted as a powerful stimulus for the wine-growing industry. By 1890, well over half the total Australian production of wine came from Victoria, but a strain of tiny plant lice, phylloxera, had already arrived from Europe and was to devastate the Victorian vineyards. In the absence of wine, Australians turned to beer, and not until the 1960s did wine regain national prominence as a drink for the masses. Although most wine specialists predict that Victoria will never again recover its preeminence in the Australian viticultural industry, high-quality grapes are grown in several parts of the state, each with its own distinct specialty. The area is best known for its muscat, tokay, and port. The Rutherglen region in the northeast produces the finest fortified wines in the country, and anyone who enjoys the after-dinner "stickies" is in for a treat when touring this area.

All the wineries in this region have tasting rooms where visitors are welcome to sample the wares before they buy. However, each winery produces several wines, and even a mouthful of the whole range will leave the palate confused and jaded. Before you begin, indicate your general preference to the sales staff and allow them to guide you.

To the southeast of Rutherglen is the town of Beechworth, a fine example of a goldfields town. In addition to its historical credentials, Beechworth also has a choice of guest houses that offer atmospheric accommodations.

The Rutherglen wineries also lie close to the Murray River, the largest and most important river in the country. (Although the Murray River Valley Highway parallels the course of the river, it is only by making a detour that you will actually glimpse the brown river, lined with river red gums.) From its birthplace on the slopes of the Great Dividing Range in southern New South Wales, the Murray unwinds for 2,574 kilometers (1,609 miles) in a southwesterly direction before it empties into Lake Alexandrina, south of Adelaide. On the driest inhabited continent on earth, this river assumes particular importance, and the irrigation schemes that tap the river water have transformed its thirsty surroundings into a garden of grapevines and citrus fruits.

Once prone to flooding and droughts, the river has been laddered with dams that control the floodwaters and create reservoirs for irrigation. The lakes created in the process have become sanctuaries for native birds. Before the coming of the railways, the Murray also provided an artery for the inland cargoes of wool and wheat, and the old wharves in ports such as Echuca bear witness to the bustling and colorful era of the riverboats.

A tour of the Rutherglen wineries and the Beechworth area makes a convenient break for visitors making the trip between Sydney and Melbourne via the Hume Freeway (Rte. 31). The area can be easily toured in a single day. A second day could be spent driving along the Murray to Echuca, which is only 192 kilometers (119 miles) from Melbourne. West of Echuca the attractions are separated by long stretches of open country, and this part of the tour is recommended only for those travelers who are heading for Adelaide.

Getting Around

By Car The only efficient way to explore the wine country and Murray River region is by car. Beechworth and Rutherglen are located on opposite sides of the Hume Freeway, the main Sydney–Melbourne artery. Allow four hours for the journey from Melbourne, twice that from Sydney. Echuca is a three-hour drive from Melbourne, reached most directly by the Northern Highway (Hwy. 75).

Guided Tours

The **Gray Line** (tel. 03/654–7700) operates one-day tours of Echuca departing Melbourne daily at 8:50 AM. Including lunch, the cost is $83 for adults, $41.50 for children 4–14.

Important Addresses and Numbers

Tourist **Beechworth Tourist Information Centre.** *Ford and Camp Sts., tel.*
Information *057/28–1374. Open daily 9:30–5:30.*

Echuca Tourist Information Centre. *Leslie St. and Murray Esplanade, tel. 054/82–4525. Open weekdays 9–5, weekends 10–4.*

Mildura Tourist Information Centre. *Langtree Mall, tel. 050/23–3619. Open weekdays 9–12:30, 1–4, weekends 10–4.*

Rutherglen Tourist Information Centre. *Walkabout Cellars, 84 Main St., tel. 060/32–9784. Open daily 9–6.*

Swan Hill Regional Information Office. *306 Campbell St., Swan Hill, tel. 050/32–3645.*

Emergencies Dial 000 for **fire, police,** or **ambulance** services.

Exploring the Northeast Wineries and the Murray River

Leave Melbourne and head north along the Hume Freeway (Hwy. 31) to Wangaratta, 239 kilometers (148 miles) away. When you reach Wangaratta, turn east to Beechworth. From Sydney, the turnoff to Beechworth is located at Wodonga, on the Victoria side of the Murray River.

One of the prettiest towns in Victoria, **Beechworth** flourished in the gold rush of the mid-19th century. When the gold ran out, Beechworth was left with all the apparatus of prosperity—fine Victorian banks, imposing public buildings, breweries, parks, prisons, and hotels wrapped in wrought iron—but with scarcely two nuggets to rub together. However, poverty preserved the town from such modern amenities as aluminum window frames, and nowadays, in an age with a taste for nostalgia, many historic treasures that might have been destroyed in the name of progress have been restored and brought back to life. A stroll along the main street, Ford Street, is the best way to absorb the character of the town. You pass several notable buildings—among them **Tanswell's Commercial Hotel** and the **government buildings** (foremost among them is the jail)—antiques shops, and the sequoia trees in the **Town Hall Gardens.** Much of Beechworth's architecture is made of the honeycolored granite that surrounds the town. This is also Kelly country. Australia's favorite outlaw, Ned Kelly, once rode these hills, and Beechworth's most conspicuous public building is the handsome sandstone jail where Kelly was held before he was taken to Melbourne to be tried and hanged.

One street back from Ford Street is the **Burke Museum,** housed in the Beechworth Library. The museum takes its name from Robert Burke, who with William Wills became the first white explorers to cross Australia from south to north, in 1861. Burke was superintendent of police in Beechworth between 1856 and 1859. The section of the museum that is dedicated to Burke is quite small and includes only a few mementos. Far more fascinating are the exhibits that relate to the exploits and trial of Ned Kelly, which include letters, photographs, and memorabilia that give fascinating insight into the man and his misdeeds. Following the shooting of the police at Stringybark Creek, Kelly and his gang were seen in the hills 3 miles from Beechworth. The man who set out to report their whereabouts had to pass six pubs along the way, and he arrived at Beechworth so drunk that the police refused to believe his story and locked him up. A day later, the man sobered up, and the police realized their mistake and mounted a raid, but too late. The museum also displays a reconstructed streetscape of Beechworth in the 1880s. *Loch St., tel. 057/28–1420. Admission: $3.50 adults, $2 children under 14, $8 family. Open daily 10:30–3:30, during school holidays 10–4:30.*

On the other side of Ford Street, located in a corrugated-iron building that was once a stable, is the **Carriage Museum.** Displays range from simple farm carts to Cobb & Co. stagecoaches to buggies, some of which were modeled on U.S. designs. *Railway Ave. Admission: $1.50 adults, $1 children 5–15. Open daily 10–noon, 1–4; Feb., July, and Aug., 1–4 only.*

Leave Beechworth and take the road north to **Chiltern.** Originally known as Black Dog Creek, Chiltern is another gold rush town that fell into a coma when the gold ran out. The main street of this tiny village is an almost perfectly preserved example of a 19th-century rural Australian streetscape, a fact not unnoticed by contemporary filmmakers. Notable buildings include the **Athenaeum Library and Museum,** the **Pharmacy,** the **Federal Standard Office,** and the **Star Hotel,** which has in its courtyard the largest grapevine in the country, with a girth of almost 2 meters (6 feet) around its base.

On a slight rise at the edge of town is **Lake View House,** the childhood home of Henry Handel Richardson, a noted 19thcentury novelist whose best-known works are *The Getting of Wisdom* and *The Fortunes of Richard Mahony.* Despite the name, Richardson was a woman—Ethel Florence. In her novel *Ultima Thule,* one of Richardson's characters reflects on Chiltern, which Richardson fictionalized as Barambogie: "[O]f all the dead-and-alive holes she had ever been in, this was the deadest." Among the memorabilia from her life on display in the house is the ouija board Richardson used for her seances. *Victoria St., tel. 057/26–1416. Admission: $2 adults, $1 children 4–15, $5 family. Open weekends and school holidays 10–noon, 1–4.*

Leave Chiltern and head toward Rutherglen, 18 kilometers (11 miles) away. Drive north to the Murray Valley Highway (Hwy. 16), then west to **Rutherglen.** The town itself has little to delay the traveler, but the surrounding red loam soil signifies the beginning of the Rutherglen wine-growing district, the source of Australia's finest fortified wines. If the term conjures up visions of sticky, cloying ports, you're in for a surprise. "Like Narcissus drowning in his own reflection, one can lose oneself in the aroma of a great old muscat," wrote James Halliday in his authoritative *Australian Wine Compendium.*

Two kilometers (1 mile) to the northwest of Rutherglen, on the road to Corowa, is **Chambers Rosewood Winery,** established in 1882 and one of the heavyweight producers of fortified wines. The muscats produced by wine maker Bill Chambers are legendary, with blending stocks that go back more than a century; no visitor should miss the chance to sample them. *Off Corowa Rd., Rutherglen, tel. 060/ 32-9641. Open Mon.–Sat. 9–5, Sun. 10–5.*

Return to the Murray Valley Highway and drive the short distance to **Campbell's Rutherglen Winery.** Despite the slick image suggested by the winery, Campbell's is a family business that dates back for over 120 years. Ask for the Campbell Family Vintage Reserve wines, which are available only at the cellar door, and you can wander freely through the winery, glass in hand, on a self-guided tour. Campbell's Merchant Prince Brown Muscat, Second Edition, is highly regarded by connoisseurs. *Murray Valley Hwy., tel. 060/32– 9458. Open Mon.–Sat. 9–5, Sun. 10–5.*

Continue along the highway to **Buller's Calliope Vineyard.** Another long-established winery, Buller's was recently modernized, and many of its vintage stocks of muscat and fine sherry were released through the cellar door. Also on the winery's grounds is Buller Bird Park. *Three Chains Rd. and Murray Valley Hwy., tel. 060/32–9660. Open Mon.–Sat. 9–5, Sun. 10–5.*

Head north along Three Chains Road and follow the signs to **Pfeiffer Wines.** Along with a soil, climate, and heritage that favors exceptional fortified wines, the area lays claim to some fine varietal wines; the Pfeiffer chardonnay is an outstanding example. At this small, rustic winery, you can dine as well as wine on picnic baskets stuffed with crusty bread, pâté, cheese, fresh fruit, wine, and smoked salmon and sold by the winery, but be sure to order one in advance. Wine maker Chris Pfeiffer has set up tables on the old wooden bridge that spans Sunday Creek, just down from the winery. Phone ahead to book a table on the bridge. *Distillery Rd., Wahgunyah, tel. 060/33–2805. Open Mon.–Sat. 9–5, Sun. 11–4.*

Continue driving north on Three Chains Road, following the signs to **All Saints Vineyards & Cellars.** This castellated winery has been in business since 1864, and although it was taken over by another wine maker from northeast Victoria, Brown Brothers, in 1991, the All Saints traditions and the label remain. Particularly noteworthy is the Lyrebird Liqueur Muscat, a complex wine full of rich berry flavors followed by a clean, dry finish. *All Saints Rd., Wahgunyah, tel. 060/33–1922. Open daily 10–4:30.*

Return to the Murray Valley Highway and continue 194 kilometers (120 miles) to **Echuca.** The trip takes about three hours. The name is derived from a local Aboriginal word meaning meeting of the waters, a reference to the town's setting at the confluence of the Murray, Campaspe, and Goulburn rivers. In colonial times, these rivers were a natural artery for the products of the interior. When the railway from Melbourne reached Echuca in 1864, the town became a junction at which the cargoes of wool and wheat that came down on barges from far up the Darling River in western New South Wales were transferred to railroad cars. During the second half of the 19th century, Echuca was Australia's largest inland port. The river trade languished when the railway network extended into the interior, but reminders of Echuca's colorful heyday remain in the restored riverboats, barges, historic hotels, and the Red Gum Works, the town's sawmill, now a working museum. Echuca's importance was recognized in the 1960s, when the National Trust declared the port a historic area. Nowadays, Echuca is a busy town of almost 10,000, but the historic attractions are concentrated in a small area along the river.

A tour of the historic precincts of Echuca begins in the **Star Hotel,** where visitors can purchase a passport that gives admission to the hotel, the Bridge Hotel, and the Historic Wharf area. The Star Hotel displays a collection of machinery and equipment associated with the riverboat trade. *Murray Esplanade, tel. 054/82–4248. Admission (includes Historic Wharf and Bridge Hotel): $5.50 adults, $3 children 5–17, $16 family (2 adults, 3 children). Open daily 9:15–5.*

Across the road, in the **Historic Wharf,** is the heavy-duty side of the business, including a warehouse, old railroad tracks, and the riverboats themselves. Unlike the riverboats of the Mississippi or the Danube, the small, squat, utilitarian workhorses of the Murray are no beauties. Among the vessels docked at the wharf, all original, is the PS *Adelaide,* Australia's oldest operating paddle steamer. The *Adelaide* cannot be boarded, but it occasionally gets stoked up, with the attendant puff-puffs, chug-chugs, and toot-toots. For steam buffs, the mill engine, once used to power a local sawmill, is a sighing, hissing treat.

The **Bridge Hotel** (*see* Dining and Lodging, *below*) was built by Henry Hopwood, the father of Echuca, who had the foresight to establish a punt and later build a bridge at this commercially strategic point on the river. The hotel is rather sparsely furnished, however, and it takes great imagination to re-create what must have been a roistering, rollicking pub frequented by rivermen, railway workers, and drovers. *45 Murray Esplanade. Admission (includes Star and Bridge hotels and Historic Wharf): $5.50 adults, $3 children 5–17, $16 family (2 adults, 3 children). Open daily 9:15–5.*

Next door to the Historic Wharf is the **Red Gum Works.** Timber from the giant river red gums that flourish along the Murray was once a major industry in Echuca, and visitors are welcome to watch the wood turners, whose work is for sale in the gallery next door. *Murray Esplanade, tel. 054/80–6407. Admission free. Open daily 9–5.*

Directly opposite the wharf is **Sharp's Movie House and Penny Arcade,** a nostalgic journey back to the days of the penny arcades. Have your fortune told, test your strength, dexterity, and lovability, and watch a peepshow that was once banned in Australia. There are 34 machines here, the largest collection of operating penny arcade machines in the country. The movie house shows edited highlights of Australian movies that date back to 1896. In 1992, the museum won an Australian Tourism Award; a visit is highly recommended. *Bond Store, Murray Esplanade, tel. 054/82–2361. Admission $7 adults, $4 children 4–16, $22 family. Open daily 9–5. Closed Dec. 25.*

The **Echuca Coachhouse and Carriage Collection** houses 35 horse-drawn carriages collected from around the world. On weekends and during school holidays, carriages are available for rides at the front of the museum. *57 Murray Esplanade, tel. 054/82–5244. Admission: $4 adults, $2 children 4–12, $10 family. Open 9:30–4.*

Life-size wax effigies of U.S. presidents may be the last thing you would expect to find in Echuca, but the **World in Wax Museum** features Washington, Lincoln, and Kennedy—along with Fidel Castro, Lawrence of Arabia, Queen Elizabeth II, and Australian celebrities and native sons. *630 High St., tel. 054/82–3630. Admission: $5 adults, $2.50 children under 15, $13 family. Open daily 9–dusk.*

Riverboat trips along the Murray are especially relaxing if you've been following a hectic touring schedule. Several riverboats make short, one-hour excursions along the river, including the **PS Pevensey** and the **PS Canberra.** River traffic is limited to a few speed boats, small fishing skiffs, and an occasional kayak. The banks are thickly forested with river red gums, the spectacular eucalypts with the smooth white trunk, which require as much as half a ton of water per day. Pevensey: *Tickets at Star Hotel, Murray Esplanade, tel. 054/82–4248. Tickets: $9 adults, $4.50 children 5–17. Departs 10:15, 11:30, 1:45, 3.* Canberra: *Tickets at Bond Store, Murray Esplanade, tel. 054/82–2711. Tickets: $8 adults, $4 children 5–16. Departs 10, 11:30, 12:45, 2, 3.*

From Echuca, head west along the Murray Valley Highway for 97 kilometers (60 miles) to the town of **Swan Hill.** Named in 1836 by the explorer Major Thomas Mitchell for the swans that kept him awake, Swan Hill is a prosperous town surrounded by rich citrus groves and vineyards. The 12-acre **Swan Hill Pioneer Settlement** is the town's main attraction, providing an evocative look at life in a 19th-century Victorian river port. Among the features to be inspected are replicas of pioneer homes, stores, machinery, and the landlocked paddle wheeler *The Gem,* once the largest cargo-passenger boat on the Murray. Today it houses a restaurant, art gallery, and souvenir shop. At night, the settlement becomes the backdrop for a sound-and-light show, which uses state-of-the-art lighting effects to bring the history of Swan Hill vividly to life. *Horseshoe Bend, Swan Hill, tel. 050/32–1093. Admission: $9 adults, $5 children 5–16, $28 family. Open daily 1:30–5. Sound-and-light show: $6 adults, $3 children, $18 family. Show begins about 1 hr after sunset.*

Across the bridge from Swan Hill Post Office on the New South Wales side of the river is the 1866 **Murray Downs Homestead,** a 20-room mansion with displays of cottage crafts, oil paintings, and antiques. The property includes extensive gardens as well as an animal park harboring deer, kangaroos, and ostriches. *Moulamein Rd., tel. 050/32–1225. Admission: $6.90 adults, $3.50 children 5–15, $19.80 family. Open Tues.–Sun. 9–4:30.*

Reputedly Australia's largest private repository of military uniforms, flags, firearms, photographs, and documents, the **Swan Hill Military Museum** has a collection that dates from the Crimean to the Vietnam wars. The admission price includes target shooting with laser pistols and the chance to have your photograph taken wearing a historic military uniform. *400 Campbell St., tel. 050/32–4382. Admission: $8 adults, $4 children under 14, $24 family. Open Mon.–Sat. 9–5, Sun. 9–noon.*

From Swan Hill, follow the Murray Valley Highway northwest for 251 kilometers (155 miles) to **Mildura.** Much of the country along the way has been heavily irrigated—the only green you see in this rust-colored semidesert is that of the citrus crops and vineyards—but in some cases the land has been ruined by excess salinity, one of the side effects of irrigation. Experiments are under way to plant salt-tolerant native trees in affected areas. After passing Hattah-Kulkyne National Park, turn right onto the Calder Highway (Hwy. 79) and proceed north through Red Cliffs to Mildura.

Boasting more hours of sunshine per year than Queensland's Gold Coast, Mildura is known for dried fruit, wine, citrus, and avocados, as well as for its hydroponic vegetable-growing industry. Mildura was developed in 1885 by two Canadians, George and William Chaffey, who were persuaded to emigrate by the Victorian premier, Alfred Deakin. The Chaffey brothers were world pioneers in irrigation. The irrigated vineyards of the Riverland region are enormously productive, and provide Australians with much of their inexpensive cask wines—although rarely does a premium table wine bear a Riverland label.

The sights worth taking in in Mildura center on the town's river history and wine making. At the **Pioneer Cottage,** visitors can get a good idea of what life was like in the days when Mildura was the frontier of European settlement. *3 Hunter St., tel. 050/23–3742. Admission: $2.50 adults, 50¢ children 5–18. Open daily 10–4.*

It's worth a peek into the **Workingman's Club** (tel. 050/23–0531) on Deakin Avenue just to see the bar: At 91 meters (300 feet), it's one of the world's longest. All of Mildura turns out to drink at its 27 taps.

On the banks of the Murray River, the **Golden River Zoo** has an extensive collection of native and exotic birds in walk-through aviaries, as well as daily shows featuring pumas, dingoes, and monkeys. Camel rides and train rides along the river are available during school holidays. *Flora Ave., tel. 050/23–5540. Admission: $7.50 adults, $3.75 children 4–16, $20.50 family (2 adults, 2 children). Open daily 9–5.*

The Murray River paddle steamers based in Mildura are one of the city's major attractions. The **PS *Avoca*** is one of the oldest paddle steamers still operating on the river. Built in 1877, this steamer has been immaculately restored and now carries more than 200 passengers on a variety of daytime sightseeing cruises that include lunch and live entertainment; the evening dinner cruises also feature bands or shows. The Thursday dinner cruise is designed for families. *Mildura Wharf, tel. 050/21–1166. Lunch cruise: $23 adults, $10 children under 16; dinner cruise: $32–$35 adults, $9–$24 children. Lunch cruise departs Tues.–Sun. noon; dinner cruise departs Wed., Sat. 7:30, Thurs. 7.*

To the south of Mildura is **Lindeman's Karadoc Winery,** one of the largest and most sophisticated in the state. To reach it, take Highway 79, turning left on Hakea Street. Drive another 10 kilometers (6 miles). This winery produces much of Lindeman's bulk wines, which end up as "Château Cardboard" on Australian tables, but the entire range of Lindeman's wines can be sampled here. *Karadoc Rd., Karadoc, tel. 050/24–0357. Open weekdays 9–5, weekends 10–4:30.*

To reach another substantial operation, **Mildara Blass Winery,** drive west to Merbein on the Sturt Highway; at the Birdwood/Merbein turnoff, turn right and proceed to Merbein. Mildara Blass produces a range of wines with such prestige labels as Wolf Blass, Krondorf, Yellowglen, and Balgownie, all of which can be sampled. Mildara Blass also manufactures brandy; you can take a guided tour of the facilities where the liquor ages in oak casks. *Wentworth Rd., Merbein, tel. 050/25–2303. Open weekdays 9–5, Sat. 11–4, Sun. noon–4. Guided tour: $2 adults, free for children under 15. Tour weekdays 11, 2, 3:30.*

To return to Melbourne, take the Calder Highway (Hwy. 79). South of Ouyen, turn left to continue along Highway 79 to Melbourne.

What to See and Do with Children

Aquacoaster is a big complex of pools that includes an enormous water slide. *18 Orange Ave., Mildura, tel. 050/23–3663. Admission: $8 per hr adults, $7 per hr children. Open weekdays 2:30–6, weekends 1:30–6:30, school holidays 10–12:30 and 1:30–6:30.*

Shopping

Buckland Gallery sells a range of Australian crafts and souvenirs that are far superior to the average, including soft toys, hats, woolen and leather wear, edible Australiana, turned-wood candlesticks, lamp bases, and dolls, pottery, and children's wear. *Ford and Church Sts., Beechworth, tel. 057/28–1432. Open daily 9–5:30.*

Njernda Aboriginal Culture Centre sells Aboriginal artifacts made by the local Yorta Yorta and Wemba Wemba peoples. *Old Court House, Law Pl., Echuca, tel. 054/82–3904. Open daily 9–5.*

Participant Sports

Ballooning   **Balloon Flights Victoria** (tel. 057/98–5417, fax 057/98–5457) pilots hot-air balloon flights over farmland in the shadow of the Strathbogie Ranges in northeastern Victoria. A one-hour dawn flight costs $165 per person, including a champagne breakfast upon touchdown. The flights, generally available between March and November, depart from a farm at Longwood near Euroa, on the Hume Highway, 90-minutes' drive from Melbourne.

Canoeing and Kayaking   **Echuca Boat and Canoe Hire** (Victoria Park Boat Ramp, tel. 054/80–6208) offers one-person kayaks, canoes, and motorboats for river cruises. Combination camping/canoeing trips are also available. A kayak or canoe costs $12 for one hour, $40 for eight hours. The hours are 8–6 daily.

Fishing   No license is required to fish the Murray River on the Victorian side. Rods and bait are available from **Echuca Boat and Canoe Hire** (*see* Canoeing and Kayaking, *above*). Fishing is also popular on Lake Kangaroo, Lake Charm, and 37 other lakes within an hour's drive of Swan Hill.

Golf   **Rich River Golf Club** (west of Moama, across the Murray River from Echuca on the New South Wales side, tel. 054/82–2444), a superb 36-hole championship course, charges $15 green fees and $12 for the hire of clubs and a cart.

Spectator Sports

The **Southern 80 Water-Ski Race,** held during the first weekend in February, is best viewed from the Echuca Boat Ramp. The race consists of high-power boats that pull two skiers apiece for 80 kilometers (50 miles) around the twist and turns of the Murray River.

Dining and Lodging

For price categories, *see* Melbourne Dining and Lodging, *above*.

Beechworth   **The Bank Restaurant.** This restaurant has a refined, dignified ambi-
Dining   ence befitting its former status as a bank, although the paper nap-

kins strike a discordant note among the starched tablecloths and Rococo Revival balloon-back chairs. The food is proficiently prepared and presented with style, but the menu rarely strays into adventurous territory. Main courses include Scotch fillet with french fries and salad, and noisette of lamb with lemon rind, herbs, garlic, and a honey sauce. A selection of inexpensive pasta dishes is available Monday to Wednesday nights. Thursday to Saturday is reserved for more formal, à la carte dining, and a family-style carvery is available Sunday. *86 Ford St., Beechworth, tel. 057/28–2223. Reservations advised. Dress: casual but neat. AE, DC, MC, V. No lunch. $$*

Lodging **Kinross.** Just a two-minute walk from the center of Beechworth, this
★ former manse has been completely renovated to offer atmospheric accommodation with a good helping of creature comforts. Rooms are decorated with chintz fabrics and furnished with heavy, dark-wood antiques. Sink into one of the big armchairs or plush sofas and enjoy the fireplace. Each room has one, as well as electric blankets and eiderdowns on the beds. Room No. 2, at the front of the house, is the largest. The four-course dinners that are prepared by Anne Fanning and served by her husband, Steve, will be a highlight of your stay here. Children are accommodated by prior arrangement. *34 Loch St., tel. 057/28–2351. 5 rooms with bath. Tariff includes breakfast. AE, MC, V. $$*

Country Rose. In a quiet back street about a kilometer (½ mile) from the center of Beechworth, this converted garage adjoining a family home is large and extremely good value for anyone looking for comfort, privacy, and tranquility. The decor is rather frilly, with plenty of pink and an antique iron bedstead, and there's a fully equipped kitchen. The house is surrounded by a commercial rose garden, and guests are welcome to wander through. *Malakoff St., tel. 057/28–1107. 1 room with bath. Tariff includes breakfast. No credit cards. $*

Rose Cottage. Tucked away behind a pretty cottage garden close to the center of town, this small timber guest house oozes country charm. The guest rooms are comfortable, with French doors that open onto the garden. It's easy to see why "a trip down memory lane" is a popular sentiment in the guest book. The house is filled with antiques and crowded with lace doilies, Tiffany-style stained-glass lamps, and knickknacks—which might be a bit overpowering for some. Children are accommodated by arrangement. At these bargain prices, the rooms are often booked in advance. *42 Camp St., tel. 057/28–1069. 4 rooms with bath. Tariff includes breakfast. DC, MC, V. $*

Echuca **Bridge Hotel Restaurant.** Set on the ground floor of a historic hotel,
Dining this popular riverside restaurant offers generous country meals that make the most of regional produce. Dishes that feature local yabbies (crayfish) and beef are particularly recommended. The restaurant occupies three rooms that were redecorated in 1992 in Victorian style and furnished with period antiques. Adjoining the restaurant is a bistro that serves simpler, less expensive fare. Choices on the menu include fish tempura with garlic mayonnaise, and chicken and Italian sausage cassoulet. When the sun shines, request a table in the garden. *1 Hopwood Pl., tel. 054/82–2247. Reservations advised. Dress: casual but neat. AE, DC, MC, V. No lunch Mon.–Fri. except during school holidays. $$*

Lodging **Random House.** Framed by an arch of Moreton Bay figs on the banks
★ of the Campaspe River 26 kilometers (16 miles) south of Echuca, this is one of the grand old homesteads of rural Victoria. The rambling house, with its long verandas and enormous grounds, is furnished

eclectically with walnut cabinets, Balinese paintings, cameo collections, military prints, and porcelain figurines. Rooms are effusively decorated with late-19th-century antiques, and each overlooks the garden. The installation of en suite bathrooms has meant that some space has been sacrificed, but even the smallest is adequate for two. Dinners, available on request, are stage-managed with enormous pomp and ceremony by owners Len Keeper and Doug Hall. *22 Bridge St., Rochester, tel. 054/84–1792, fax 054/84–1024. 4 rooms with bath. Tariff includes breakfast. MC. $$$*

The River Gallery Inn. Opened in mid-1992, this hotel in a renovated 19th-century building consists of large suites, offering a high standard of comfort at a reasonable price. Each room is decorated and furnished according to a different theme, such as the pretty French provincial room, the opulent Victorian suite, or the mock-rustic early Australia suite. The rooms are located above an art and craft gallery. Although four rooms overlook the street, none is affected by street noise. Two rooms have whirlpool baths; the larger rooms can sleep four. *578 High St., tel. 054/80–6902. 6 rooms with bath. Tariff includes breakfast. AE, MC, V. $$*

Mildura
Dining

Rendezvous. Housed inside a converted 1930s coffee lounge, this stylish restaurant has been run by the same family for more than 40 years. The menu is a medley that ranges from traditional Anglo-Saxon fare to exotic international dishes. Local yabbies with fresh asparagus atop champagne sabayon is a winning starter. Main courses include steak, lobster, Thai-style fish dishes, and Indian curries. The bistro/wine bar next door is an inexpensive alternative to the restaurant. *34 Langtree Ave., tel. 050/23–1571. Reservations advised. Dress: casual. AE, DC, MC, V. No lunch Sat., Tues. Closed Sun., Mon. $$*

Lodging

Chaffey International Motor Inn. Rooms and facilities at this modern, centrally located motel are well above average for country Victoria—and certainly better than any other motel in town. From Friday to Sunday the room rate drops by more than $20. *244 Deakin Ave., tel. 050/23–5833, fax 050/21–1972. 32 rooms with bath. Facilities: outdoor pool, spa, restaurant, bar. AE, DC, MC, V. $*

Mildura Country Club Resort. This modern motel has spacious grounds, a large swimming pool, pleasantly decorated rooms, and a resortlike atmosphere, but what really sets it apart is the surrounding golf course. All rooms open to the 18-hole course. *12th Street Extension, tel. 050/23–3966, fax 050/21–1751. 40 rooms with bath. Facilities: outdoor pool, gym, bar, restaurant. AE, DC, MC, V. $*

Rutherglen
Dining

Mrs. Mouse's Teahouse. Decorated from top to toe with toy mice, this quaint country teahouse sells traditional scones and tea by day and wholesome country meals at night. The food relies on local produce, including the delicious berries and stone fruits of the Warby Ranges. Main courses include chicken breast with a quince cream sauce, and Thai-style fish with chili. Next door in the former pantry is a gourmet food shop that sells homemade preserves. *12 Foord St., Wahgunyah, tel. 060/33–1102. No reservations. Dress: casual. MC, V. No dinner Sun.–Wed. $*

Swan Hill
Dining

The Gem Restaurant. This restaurant is located on board the vintage paddle steamer PS *Gem*, which is moored high and dry at the town's Pioneer Settlement. The menu continues to offer some unusual Australian bush tucker—including witchetty grubs and kangaroo tail soup—but its real strengths are the excellent local yabbies, Murray cod, beef, and lamb dishes. The dining room, with its candlelit elegance of brass and redwood, brings an air of gauzy romance to the evening. *Pioneer Settlement, tel. 050/32–2463. Reservations advised. Dress: casual but neat. AE, DC, MC, V. No lunch. $$*

Lodging **Lady Augusta Motor Inn.** Completed in 1991, this two-story motel a short stroll from the town center surrounds a tree-lined courtyard and offers a choice of moderately large double rooms, two-bedroom suites, or spa suites. All are well maintained. *375 Campbell St., tel. 050/32–9677, fax 050/32–9573. 24 rooms with bath. Facilities: heated outdoor pool, bar, restaurant. AE, DC, MC, V. $*
Swan Hill Resort Motor Inn. Rooms at this large motel complex are spacious and moderately luxurious. The big swimming pool and sports facilities are a big plus for any weary traveler. *405 Campbell St., tel. 050/32–2726, fax 050/32–9109. 61 rooms with bath. Facilities: outdoor and heated indoor pools, spa, gym, squash court, bar, restaurant. AE, DC, MC, V. $*

Festivals

The main event on the northeastern wineries' festival calendar is the **Rutherglen Wine Festival,** held over the three days of the Labor Day weekend in March. The festival is a celebration of food, wine, and music, in particular jazz, folk, and country. The events are held at all the surrounding wineries, as well as in the town itself. For more information contact the Rutherglen Tourist Information Centre (tel. 060/32–9784).

Victoria's National Parks

Victoria has a number of outstanding national parks, which encompass everything from breathtaking coastal scenery to alpine hiking trails. They are easily reached via well-maintained roads and highways and are usually not far from major cities.

The parks discussed below, four of Victoria's most popular, offer the visitor a range of activities in different corners of the state. Consult preceding sections for points of interest in areas around the parks that can be incorporated into your visit.

Port Campbell National Park

Stretching some 30 kilometers (19 miles) along the southern Victoria coastline, Port Campbell National Park is the site of some of the most famous geological formations in Australia. Vantage points along the Great Ocean Road allow visitors to witness one of the finest examples of the ocean's power as the roaring waves continuously pound the coastline.

The level of the sea was much higher 25 million years ago, and as the water receded, towering sediments of sand, mud, limestone, and seashells were left standing to face the waves. The ocean is continuously carving these massive towers into strange shapes, even as the towers slowly fall victim to the sea.

The best time to visit the park is between January and April, when you can also witness events on nearby Muttonbird Island. Toward nightfall, hundreds of hawks and kites circle the island in search of hungry baby shearwaters emerging impatiently from their protective burrows. But the predators beat a hasty retreat at the sight of thousands of adult shearwaters, which approach as the last light fades from the sky, encircling the island with food for their chicks.

People do not visit Port Campbell to bushwalk, but those who wish to explore the area should pick up the self-guided Discovery Walk at the Visitors Centre. The walk begins near Port Campbell Beach and takes about 1½ hours to complete. It is safe to swim only at this beach—the pounding surf and undertow are treacherous at other nearby beaches. Swimmers should opt instead for the few isolated pools found in sheltered coves along the coastline.

Arriving and Departing Port Campbell is 250 kilometers (155 miles) southwest of Melbourne via Geelong. The area is accessible by car along the Great Ocean Road between Princetown and Peterborough.

Lodging Both the visitors center and the campground are located in Port Campbell. Campsites at the Port Campbell Recreation Reserve with hot water and showers cost $10 per day for a site without electricity, $12 for a site with power. Advance bookings suggested (tel. 055/98–6369).

Tourist Information Contact the **Port Campbell National Park** (Tregea St., Port Campbell, VIC 3269, tel. 055/98–6382).

Grampians (Gariwerd) National Park

The Grampians combine stunning mountain scenery, abundant native wildlife, and a variety of invigorating outdoor activities. Close to the western border of Victoria, this 412,000-acre region of sharp sandstone peaks has been lifted from the bed of an ancient sea, sculpted by eons of wind and rain, and carpeted with a fantastic array of wildflowers. There are more than 900 species of wildflowers in the park—and 200 species of birds and 35 species of native mammals.

"Gariwerd" is the Aboriginal name for this area. The abundant food supply made these ranges a natural refuge for Aboriginal tribes, and more than a hundred caves have been found daubed with their paintings, although they rarely approach the complex iconography and artistry of the Arnhem Land or Western Desert Aboriginal people.

Anyone with limited time can get a taste of the area's incredible scenery on a driving tour of the park. The circuit of the Wonderland Range from Halls Gap should not be missed, and the 15-kilometer (8-mile) drive from Halls Gap to Zumstein via the Mount Victory Road is highly recommended. The drive between Halls Gap and Dunkeld, at the southern entrance to the park, is similarly spectacular.

The park has more than 160 kilometers (100 miles) of walking trails, from short, easy tracks to challenging overnight expeditions through rugged terrain. For anything more than a short stroll, water and warm, waterproof clothing are a must. Some of the best short walks are the 2½-hour climb to the summit of Mt. William, the 2½-hour hike to the Pinnacle from the Wonderland Turntable (which leads past fantastic rock formations to a magnificent view), and the two-hour walk to MacKenzie Falls from Zumstein. In recent years, the Grampians National Park have become popular with rock climbers, who focus their activities on Mt. Arapiles.

The gateway to the Grampians is Halls Gap, a small, busy town where koalas can sometimes be found snoozing in the trees and kangaroos graze on the outskirts in the evening. The best time to visit the park is between October and December, when the wildflowers are in bloom, the weather is mild, and the summer crowds have yet to arrive.

Arriving and Departing Halls Gap is reached via Ballarat and Ararat on the Western Highway (Hwy. 8). The town is 260 kilometers (160 miles) northwest of Melbourne. Australian Pacific Tours (tel. 03/650–1511) operates a one-day tour of the Grampians, departing Melbourne at 9 AM on Thursday and Sunday (Cost: $67 adult, $61 children under 14).

Lodging The main base for the national park is Halls Gap, which offers a choice of motels, guest houses, host farms, and caravan parks. Several camping options are also available within the national park. The best equipped of the 16 designated camping areas is the Zumstein Recreation Area, which has showers, fireplaces, and even a swimming pool. The camping fee is $6 for up to six people. Bush camping is permitted outside designated areas, except in the Wonderland Range and in the watershed of Lake Wartook; however, bush campers must pitch their tent at least 1 kilometer (½ mile) from any designated camping area. For anyone looking for an atmospheric alternative to motel accommodation, the **Glenisla Homestead** (just off the Hamilton-Horsham Rd., via Cavendish, tel. 053/80–1532), an 1842 homestead on the western side of the national park, is highly recommended.

Tourist Information Contact **Grampians National Park Visitor Centre** (Dunkeld Rd., Halls Gap, VIC 3381, tel. 053/56–4381).

Alpine National Park

This park, formerly Bogong National Park, encompasses the Victorian Alps, the highest peaks in the state. Its many outdoor activities include excellent walking trails among the peaks, horseback riding, sailing, fishing (license required), and mountaineering.

The land around here is rich in history. *Bogong* is an Aboriginal word for "Big Moth," and it was to Mt. Bogong that the Aborigines came each year after the winter thaw in search of bogong moths, considered a delicacy. The Aborigines were eventually displaced by cattlemen who brought their cattle here to graze.

Today stately snow gums grace the hills throughout the year, complemented by a budding array of alpine wildflowers in bloom from October through March. There are half- and fullday trails scattered throughout the scenic area for bushwalkers, including the popular Bogong High Plains Circuit, a tough trail ascending Mount Bogong. Hikers could easily spend a week or more on the trails that crisscross this park. During winter months, the area is completely covered in snow, and bushwalkers are replaced by cross-country skiers, especially at Falls Creek and Mount Hotham.

Arriving and Departing Located 323 kilometers (200 miles) northeast of Melbourne, the park is reached by taking the Princes Highway east through Sale and Bairnsdale. Pick up the Omeo Highway north from here to Omeo, and then head west to Cobungra and Mt. Hotham. Bus and train service operates from Albury on the New South Wales border in the north. During ski season, buses depart from Mt. Beauty for Falls Creek and Mt. Hotham, and depart from Melbourne for Falls Creek.

Lodging Old cattlemen's huts are scattered throughout the park and may be used by hikers free of charge. These, however, are often occupied and shelter should not be assumed. Bush camping is permitted throughout the park, and there is a basic campground located at

Raspberry Hill. Commercial camping, caravan parks, hotels, and motels are located in the major towns around the park, including Mount Beauty, Harrietville, Anglers Rest, Glen Valley, and Tawonga. Ski resorts are open at Falls Creek and Mt. Hotham during the winter.

Tourist Information Contact **Alpine National Park** (Box 180, Mount Beauty, VIC 3699, tel. 057/57–2693).

Wilson's Promontory National Park

This granite peninsula, once connected to both the Australian mainland and Tasmania, is Victoria's southernmost point.

Visitors will find the park well endowed with wildlife. More than 180 species of birds have been sighted here, and Corner Inlet, along Five Mile Beach, is a seabird sanctuary. Near the visitor center at Tidal River, tame marsupials may be sighted, including kangaroos, wombats, and koalas.

There are more than 20 well-marked trails here, some meandering past pristine beaches and secluded coves excellent for swimming, others more strenuous. One tough but popular trail is the 9½-kilometer (6-mile) Sealer's Cove Walk, which traverses the slopes of Mt. Wilson Range before descending through Sealer's Swamp to the tranquil Sealer's Cove. The Lilly Pilly Gully nature walk, a 5-kilometer (3-mile) trip, gives a good introduction to the park's plant and animal life with the aid of informative signs posted along the way.

Arriving and Departing Wilson's Prom, 231 kilometers (143 miles) from Melbourne, can be reached via the Princes Highway to Dandenong, and then the South Gippsland Highway south to Meeniyan or Foster. There is no public transportation to the park.

Lodging With 500 campsites, the well-known Tidal River campground is easily among Australia's largest. Reservations at this popular spot during peak summer and holiday periods are hard to come by and should be made in advance. During the peak season (December through February and holiday weekends) sites cost $11 per night for up to three persons, $2.20 for each additional person. Off-season rates are $5.50 per night per person, $2.20 per night for each additional person. Stiff cancellation fees apply.

Heated apartments and lodges accommodating from two to six people are also available at Tidal River. During the peak season (September–April), these can be reserved only on a weekly basis. In the off-peak season, the minimum booking period is from Friday night to Sunday night. During peak season, the tariff is about $12 per person per night in a six-person lodge, and $20 per person per night in a two-person lodge. In the off-peak season, the nightly rate is about $5 less per person. Lodges and apartments may be reserved up to 12 months in advance through the **Royal Automobile Club of Victoria Travel Centre** (230 Collins St., Melbourne 3000, tel. 03/650–1522).

Single-room motor huts contain two double bunk beds, a hot plate, heaters, and running cold water. Blankets and linen are not provided. Toilets and showers are available at the campground. The trailers cost $30 each and can be booked through the **Tidal River park office** (tel. 056/80–8538).

Tourist Information Contact **Wilson's Promontory National Park** (Tidal River via Foster, VIC 3960, tel. 056/80–8538).

6 Tasmania

By Sharon Cohen

Updated by David McGonigel

No larger than Scotland, and with a population of less than half a million, the island of Tasmania is an unspoiled reminder of a simpler, slower lifestyle. It has been called the England of the south, and there is much truth in that description. Like England, Tasmania is a richly cloaked land of mists and rain, where an evening chill is not uncommon even in summer. The English tradition of a Christmas roast may seem incongruous during a steamy Sydney summer, but such rites are natural amid Tasmania's lush quilt of lowland farms and villages. Even the towns look English, with their profusion of Georgian cottages and buildings, the preservation of which is a testament to Tasmanians' attachment to their past.

There are parts of that past that many may wish to forget. Tasmania was first settled by Aborigines who walked here some 23,000 years ago, before it became an island. Europeans discovered it in 1642, when Abel Tasman arrived at its southwest coast, but not until 1798 was Tasmania (then called Van Diemen's Land) thought to be an island. Much of the island's subsequent history is violent. The entire population of full-blooded Aborigines was wiped out, and the establishment in 1830 of a penal settlement at Port Arthur for the colony's worst offenders ushered in a new age of cruelty.

The last convict was shipped to Port Arthur more than 140 years ago, and, today, walking through the lovely park at Port Arthur or the personable streets of Hobart, one finds it difficult to picture Tasmania as a land of desperation and death. That is the great dichotomy of this island, however, for in many ways Tasmania is still a wild, untamed land. It is one of the most mountainous islands in the world. Parts of the west and southwest coasts have never been explored, with access barred by impenetrable rain forests. Of all the states, Tasmania has set aside the greatest percentage of its land as national parks. Visitors planning a trip to these parks in the mountains of Tasmania should be prepared for sudden climatic changes—a snowstorm in summer is not unusual—for more than any other state, Tasmania is greatly affected by Antarctica.

Hobart

Sitting astride the Derwent River and backed by the forested slopes of Mount Wellington, Hobart may rival Sydney as Australia's most beautiful state capital. Founded as a penal settlement in 1803, Hobart is the second-oldest city in Australia after Sydney—but it seems like the oldest. Many of the colonial brick and sandstone buildings built by convicts have been restored and now set the tone for this small city of 185,000.

As in Sydney, life here revolves around the harbor. The Derwent is one of the deepest harbors in the world, and its broad estuary makes it a sporting paradise. It was the Derwent that attracted the original settlers, and they quickly capitalized on this natural treasure. The city became a base for the whaling fleet that operated off the coast, and many of the converted warehouses that line the wharf today were once used to store Hobart's other major exports—fruit, wool, and corn.

The city comes alive between Christmas and the New Year during the annual Sydney-to-Hobart yacht race. The race dominates conversations among Hobart's citizens, who descend on Constitution Dock to view the brightly colored yachts. Otherwise, Hobart is a quiet town whose nightlife is largely confined to the action at the Wrest Point Casino in Sandy Bay.

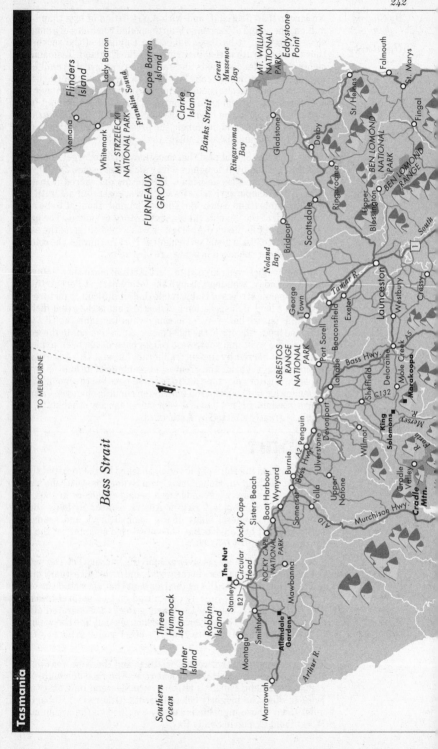

Tasmania

Bass Strait

Southern Ocean

TO MELBOURNE

Three Hummock Island

Hunter Island

Robbins Island

Flinders Island

Memana
Whitemark
MT. STRZELECKI NATIONAL PARK

Lady Barron

Franklin Sound

Cape Barren Island

FURNEAUX GROUP

Clarke Island

Banks Strait

Great Mussenoe Bay

MT. WILLIAM NATIONAL PARK

Eddystone Point

Marrawah

Montagu
Smithton
Allendale Gardens
Mawbanna
Arthur R.

Stanley
The Nut
Circular Head
ROCKY CAPE NATIONAL PARK
Rocky Cape
Sisters Beach
Boat Harbour
Wynyard
Somerset
Burnie
Penguin
Ulverstone
Yolla
Upper Natone
Wilmot

B21

A10

Bass Hwy.

A2

Devonport
Latrobe
Sheffield
Deloraine
Mole Creek
Marakoopa
King Solomons

Murchison Hwy.

Cradle Valley
Cradle Mtn.

Port Sorell
Beaconsfield
Exeter

George Town

Noland Bay

Tamar R.

ASBESTOS RANGE NATIONAL PARK

Bridport
Scottsdale

Ringarooma Bay

Gladstone
Derby
Ringarooma
Upper Blessington

BEN LOMOND NATIONAL PARK

BEN LOMOND RANGE

St. Helens

Falmouth
St. Marys
Fingal

Launceston
Westbury
Crossy

A5

Mersey R.

S132

South

1

South

Mersey R.

C132

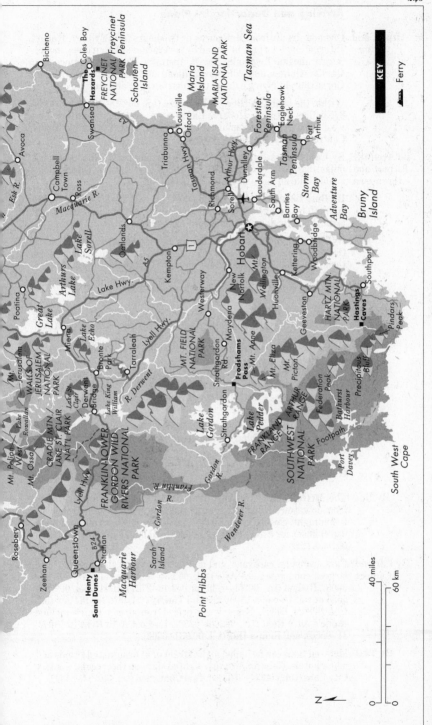

Arriving and Departing by Plane

Airport and Airlines One hour by air from Melbourne or two hours from Sydney, Hobart International Airport is served by several domestic airlines, including **Airlines of Tasmania, Ansett Australia, Eastwest Airlines,** and **Qantas. Qantas** and **Air New Zealand** offer a joint service from Christchurch, New Zealand, to Hobart every Saturday.

Within the island, **Airlines of Tasmania** (tel. 002/48–5030 or 003/91–8755) flies between Hobart, Launceston, and the northwest and west coasts. Tickets can also be booked through **Tasmanian Travel Centres** in cities around the island.

Between the Airport and Downtown **By Car: Hobart International Airport** is located 22 kilometers (14 miles) east of Hobart. The trip along the Eastern Outlet Road should take no more than 20 minutes by car.

By Bus: Tasmanian Redline Coaches (tel. 002/31–3233 or 008/006–006) offers a regular shuttle service for $6 per person between the airport and its downtown depot at 199 Collins Street.

By Taxi: For small groups, taxis are an economical way to travel to the city. Metered taxis are available at the taxi stand in front of the terminal. The fare to downtown Hobart is approximately $25.

Arriving and Departing by Bus and Car

By Bus **Tasmanian Redline Coaches** (*see above*) offers daily service to towns and cities across the state. Buses meet the ferry from Victoria that comes into Devonport. Called "Super Tassie Passes," a 15-day ticket for unlimited travel around Tasmania costs $139; a 20-day pass costs $155. **Hobart Coaches** (4 Liverpool St., tel. 002/34–4077) provides a similar range of intrastate services (including Port Arthur and the east coast). For $140 you can purchase a Wilderness and Highway Pass that gives 14 days' unlimited travel to the main cities and wilderness areas.

By Car Unlike mainland Australia, any location on Tasmania is within easy driving distance. Hobart is less than three hours from Launceston by car along Highway 1.

Getting Around

By Bus The **Metropolitan Transport Trust** (MTT) operates a bus system from downtown Hobart to the surrounding suburbs daily from 6 AM to midnight. Special "Day Rover" tickets for $2.60 permit unlimited use of buses for a day. *Inquiries at Metroshop, 18 Elizabeth St., tel. 002/33–4222.*

By Car and Camper Cars, campers, caravans, and minibuses are available for hire. The largest companies are **Avis** (tel. 002/34–4222 or toll-free 008/03–0008), **Budget** (tel. 002/34–5222 or 002/13–2727), **Hertz** (tel. 002/34–5555 or toll-free 008/13–6039), and **Thrifty** (tel. 002/34–1341 or toll-free 008/22–6434). Some lower-priced rental companies include **Annie's Auto Rent** (tel. 002/28–0252), **Lo-Cost Auto Rent** (tel. 002/31–0550), and **Rent-a-Bug** (tel. 002/31–0300).

By Taxi Metered taxis can be hailed in the street or at designated stands and major hotels. Cabs for hire have lighted signs on their roofs. Contact **City Cabs** (tel. 002/34–3633) or **Taxi Combined** (tel. 002/34–8444).

Important Addresses and Numbers

Tourist Information   The **Visitors' Information Centre** (20 Davey St., tel. 002/30–8394) is open weekdays 8:30–5:30, weekends and holidays 9–noon.

Emergencies   For emergencies requiring an **ambulance,** the **police,** or **fire brigade,** dial 000.

St. Helen's Private Hospital (186 Macquarie St., tel. 002/21–6444) and the **Royal Hobart Hospital** (48 Liverpool St., tel. 002/38–8308) provide emergency medical service.

Guided Tours

Orientation Tours   Walking tours led by the **National Trust** provide an excellent overview of Battery Point, including visits to mansions and 19th-century homes. Tours leave the wishing well (near the post office in Franklin Square) at Battery Point every Saturday at 9:30 AM. *Cost (includes morning tea): $5 adults, $2.50 children, $9 family.*

The **National Trust** also conducts daily tours (hourly 10–2) of the old penitentiary, courthouse, and chapel on Campbell Street. *National Trust, 6 Brisbane St., tel. 002/23–5200.*

Transderwent operates four daily cruises of Derwent Harbour aboard the MV *Emmalisa,* an old-fashioned ferry. Cruises (1¼ hours) include an excellent commentary on Hobart and its environs, and the lunchtime cruise includes a hot meal. *Franklin Wharf Ferry Pier, tel. 002/23–5893. Tickets: $10 adults, $5 children; lunch cruise $15 adults, $7.50 children, $35 family.*

Air Tours   **Par Avion Tours** (tel. 002/48–5390) offers some of the most exciting ways to see Hobart and its surroundings. One trip features a flight to Melaleuca Inlet, on the west coast, and a boat trip with **Wilderness Tours** around Bathurst Harbour, with stops for bushwalking. The cost is all-inclusive, and lunch and afternoon tea are provided.

Bicycle Tours   **Brake Out Cycling Tours** (tel. 002/78–2966) leads tours from Mt. Wellington, Mt. Nelson, and other neighboring scenic areas. All equipment is provided, and cyclists are accompanied by a guide and support vehicle. Lunch and morning and afternoon teas are included on most tours.

Exploring Hobart

Numbers in the margin correspond to points of interest on the Downtown Hobart map.

Any tour of Hobart should begin at the waterfront, where the city began and most of the historic sandstone buildings still stand. The area is uncrowded in comparison with the city center, and the fresh air that blows across the Derwent River creates a pleasant environment for a morning walk.

❶ **Constitution Dock** is a colorful marina where yachts competing in the annual Sydney-to-Hobart race moor during the first week of January. The buildings fronting the dock are century-old reminders of Hobart's trading history.

❷ The **Tasmanian Museum and Art Gallery,** across Davey Street from Constitution Dock, has a collection of exhibits on Tasmania's history. It is the best place in Hobart to learn about Tasmania's Aborigines and the island's unique wildlife. *40 Macquarie St., tel. 002/35–*

Arthur's Circus, **8**

Brooke Street Pier, **3**

Cat and Fiddle Arcade, **9**

Constitution Dock, **1**

Maritime Museum of Tasmania, **6**

Narryna Van Diemen's Land Memorial Folk Museum, **7**

Parliament House, **4**

Penitentiary Chapel and Criminal Courts, **10**

Salamanca Place, **5**

Tasmanian Museum and Art Gallery, **2**

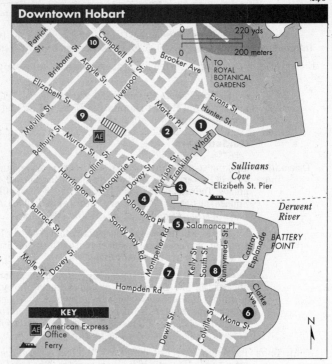

Downtown Hobart

0777. *Admission free. Open daily 10–5; closed Dec. 25, Good Friday, and Anzac Day (April 25).*

❸ ❹ Walk south along the docks past the **Brooke Street Pier,** the departure point for harbor cruises, to **Parliament House.** Built by convicts in 1840 as a customs house, it did not acquire its present function until 1856. Contact the Clerk of the House (tel. 002/33–2374) if you want to watch a session of parliament from the viewing gallery. The grounds of Parliament House are maintained by the Royal Botanic Gardens.

❺ Turn left onto **Salamanca Place** to reach Hobart's most famous historic district—Battery Point. Old whaling ships used to dock at Salamanca Place; today many of the warehouses once used by the whalers have been converted into excellent crafts shops, art galleries, and restaurants. On Saturday it is the site of a boisterous morning market offering a wide assortment of Tasmanian arts and crafts, as well as old records, books, and antiques. Keep an eye open for items made from Tasmanian timber.

Now walk south along Castray Esplanade; turn left onto Clarke Av-
❻ enue and then right onto Secheron Road. The **Maritime Museum of Tasmania,** located in Secheron House, is a fine example of Georgian architecture. Built in 1831, the museum houses one of the finest maritime collections in Australia, including figureheads, whaling implements, models, and photographs dating back to 1804. *21 Secheron Rd., tel. 002/23–5082. Admission: $2 adults, children free. Open weekdays and Sun. 1–4:30, Sat. 10–4:30.*

Take Secheron Road to Mona Street and turn right. Follow **Mona**
❼ Street onto Hampden Road, which leads to the **Narryna Van**

Diemen's Land Memorial Folk Museum. The museum features exhibits depicting the life of the Tasmanian pioneers. *103 Hampden Rd., tel. 002/34–2791. Admission: $4 adults, $1 children. Open weekdays 10–5, weekends 2–5.*

You could spend hours exploring Hampden Road, with its fascinating array of antiques shops, charming cottages, and other historic buildings. Head back toward Castray Esplanade, but this time turn **8** left onto Runnymede Street. **Arthur's Circus** is an enchanting collection of tiny houses and cottages set in a circle around a village green. Built in the 1840s and 1850s, most of these houses have been beautifully restored.

Proceed west on Salamanca Place, turning right on Davey Street and then left onto Elizabeth Street. Beyond the Elizabeth Mall is **9** the **Cat and Fiddle Arcade,** with a giant clock reenacting the nursery rhyme every hour—kitschy, but entertaining.

Walk up Bathurst Street and turn left on Campbell Street to visit **10** the **penitentiary chapel** and **criminal courts,** which were built and used during the early convict days. *Brisbane and Campbell Sts., tel. 002/31–0911. Admission: $5 adults, $2.50 children. Tours daily 10–2.*

What to See and Do with Children

At the **Kidzonly Restaurant** in the Sheraton Hobart Hotel (*see* Lodging, *below*), you can enjoy your meal while your children enjoy theirs at their own supervised table. The kids are weighed before the meal, which costs 40¢ per kilogram of kid up to a maximum of $9.50. *For reservations, tel. 002/35–4535.*

Both children and adults will love **Tudor Court** in lower Sandy Bay, a meticulously detailed replica of an English Tudor village. *827 Sandy Bay Rd., tel. 002/25–1194. Admission: $3 adults, $1 children. Open daily 9–5:30.*

The **Cadbury-Schweppes chocolate factory** is a 12-kilometer (7½-mile) drive north on the Lyell Highway. Very few children (or adults!) will be able to resist a tour of the best chocolate and cocoa factory in Australia. *Claremont. Book well in advance through the Visitors' Information Centre (tel. 002/30–8394). Admission $8 adults, $4 children, $20 family. Tours weekdays 9, 9:30, and 10:30.*

Off the Beaten Track

The **Royal Tasmanian Botanical Gardens** spread across the largest area of open land in Hobart. Part of the Queens Domain, the gardens are rarely crowded and are a welcome relief from the city. True to the best in the English horticultural tradition, the gardens are well kept, spacious, and filled with both native and imported plants. One section has been specially designed for wheelchairs. The Japanese Garden is dominated by a miniature Mt. Fuji. Children love the flowered clock. A museum and education center is open daily noon–4. *Adjacent to Government House at the Tasman Bridge, tel. 002/34–6299. Open daily 8–4:45.*

Only a 25-minute drive from Hobart, **Richmond** is one of the oldest communities in Australia. It features the nation's best-preserved convict jail, the oldest Roman Catholic church (St. John's), and the oldest standing bridge (built by convicts in 1823). Many visitors come to Richmond for the homemade ice creams and sweets sold in the village's charming little shops. *26 km (16 mi) northeast of Hobart via Eastern Outlet Rd.*

Shopping

Tasmania is noted for its arts and crafts, which make use of local timbers—huon pine, sassafrass, myrtle—and are crafted into such items as letter racks and salad bowls. Stores worth a visit include **Aspect Design** (79 Salamanca Pl., tel. 002/23–2642), **Handmark Gallery** (77 Salamanca Pl., tel. 002/23–7895), the **National Trust Gift Shop** (Galleria, 33 Salamanca Pl., tel. 002/23–7371), and **Sullivan's Cove** (47 Salamanca Pl., tel. 002/23–7262).

Participant Sports

Bicycling Bicycles can be rented from **Peregrine Adventures** (28 Criterion St., tel. 002/31–0977).

Bushwalking A variety of walking tracks are within easy reach of Hobart, including several routes around Mt. Wellington.

Fishing Tasmania is one of the best places in the world for trout fishing: Lakes and streams are well stocked, and the season runs from August through May. Licensed trout-fishing trips can be arranged through the **Visitors' Information Centre** (*see* Important Addresses and Numbers, *above*).

Skiing The Tasmanian snowfields are only an hour's drive from Hobart, so visitors can stay in town and be on the slopes early the next day. The main skiing ground is at Mt. Field, 81 kilometers (50 miles) northwest of Hobart. Contact the Visitors' Information Centre (*see* Important Addresses and Numbers, *above*) for information on conditions, accommodations, and equipment rental.

Swimming The **Hobart Olympic Pool** (tel. 002/34–4232) on Domain Road and **Clarence Swimming Centre** (tel. 002/44–2294) on Riawena Road, Montagu Bay are both open to visitors. River and ocean beaches are within easy reach of Hobart.

Spectator Sports

Cricket, rugby, soccer, and Australian-rules football are all played in Hobart. Cricket matches can be seen in the summer (November–March) at the **Bellerive Oval** (tel. 002/44–7099) in the Queens Domain. Rugby and football matches are played on Saturday afternoon in winter at **North Hobart Sports Ground** (tel. 002/34–3203). Tickets can be purchased at the gates.

Dining

Highly recommended restaurants are indicated by a star ★.

Category	Cost*
$$$$	over $40
$$$	$25–$40
$$	$10–$25
$	under $10

per person, excluding drinks and service

$$$$ **Alexander's Restaurant.** At this restaurant in Lenna of Hobart (*see*
★ Lodging, *below*), locals join hotel guests in savoring some of the finest cuisine in Tasmania. The setting is very fussy—more like a 19th-
century bordello than a restaurant—but the French/provincial
Australian fare is prepared with flair and the service is exemplary.
You can start your meal with, say, pigeon consommé; quail filled
with duck liver and grapes and served with a port and orange sauce;
or a beef and vegetable terrine in aspic atop finely diced tomato. For
a main course there are such beautifully presented dishes as crayfish quenelles with grilled prawns in puff pasty with crayfish sauce,
and smoked Tasmanian salmon over wild fennel with a green herb
sauce. A sweet finale might be toffee-coated strawberries with
Grand Marnier ice cream or cherries poached in spiced wine with
sabayon and cardamon ice cream. *Lenna of Hobart, 20 Runnymede
St., Battery Point, tel. 002/23–2911. Reservations required. Jacket
required. AE, DC, MC, V.*

$$$$ **Dear Friends.** One of the most elegant restaurants in Tasmania, this
★ converted flour mill by the wharf is famous for its nouvelle cuisine—
each meal is a carefully arranged piece of artwork. Tables are widely
spaced among Old World furniture and antique bric-a-brac. Game
dishes, such as roasted venison, are a specialty, as are Atlantic salmon and lamb cutlets. *8 Brook St., tel. 002/23–2646. Reservations required. Jacket required. AE, DC, MC, V. Closed Sun.*

$$$$ **Sullivan's Grill.** The chef at this chargrill restaurant has been rated
the best in Tasmania. The decor is simple, relying on subtle greens
and pastels. The menu features the best of Tasmanian produce in
season, especially crayfish and beef. *Sheraton Hobart Hotel, 1
Davey St., tel. 002/35–4546. Reservations required. Jacket required. AE, DC, MC, V. Closed Sun.*

$$$$ **Wrest Point Revolving Restaurant.** Breathtaking views of the city
easily justify a visit to this revolving restaurant atop one of Hobart's
tallest buildings. Luckily, the food is equally rewarding. Tables are
widely spaced around a huge mirrored central column, and all have
views. Specialties include the City Lights dinner—a three-course
meal based on seasonal produce—and prawns flambéed at the table
with a great deal of pomp. As an appetizer, try the smoked Tasmanian Atlantic salmon. *Wrest Point Hotel, 410 Sandy Bay Rd., tel. 002/
25–0112. Reservations required. Jacket required. AE, DC, MC, V.*

$$$ **Drunken Admiral.** The atmosphere here is noisy and raucous. The
walls and every other available space are hung with seafaring para-
phernalia. With all this naval kitsch, you would expect the food to be
of secondary importance, but it's not. Each dish is well prepared and
nautically named. Try the Sydney-to-Hobart seafood platter, a com-
bination of hot and cold delicacies, or Castaway Tom Sawyer's sea-
food cauldron, filled with a delicious combination of seasonal fish and
shellfish. *17–19 Hunter St., Old Hobart Town, tel. 002/34–1903.
Reservations required. Dress: casual but neat. AE, MC, V.*

$$$ **Mures Upper Deck Restaurant.** Situated on the upper floor of the
★ Mures Fish House complex on the wharf, the Upper Deck gives din-
ers superb views of the waterfront. The interior, made of Tasmanian
woods tends to amplify diners' chatter. Huge wooden, stuffed fishes
were suspended from the ceiling to combat the noise, and the restaurant is now famous for these flying undersea creatures. Try the superb flathead, the house version of a local fish, trevalla—panfried
with smoked trout pâté and brie—or the seafood tagliatelle, a mixture of fish, shellfish, bacon, mushrooms, onions, and cream served
over pasta. Downstairs, **Mures Lower Deck** (tel. 002/31–2121) is a
less expensive alternative: Patrons are served by number and take
their food out by the dock or to outside tables. *Victoria Dock, tel.*

002/31–1999. Weekend reservations advised. Dress: casual but neat. AE, DC, MC, V. No credit cards downstairs.

$$$ Sakura Restaurant. Patrons eat on a cushioned floor at low tables at this traditional Japanese restaurant decorated with beautiful Japanese prints and delicate screens. One-pan cooking is the specialty here, with meals prepared at the table. The fish, vegetable, and prawn tempuras are all excellent, as are the *yakitori* (grilled chicken fillets) and the *sunomono* (scallops, seaweed, cucumber, jellyfish, and oysters served raw with vinegar). *85 Salamanca Pl., Battery Point, tel. 002/23–4773. Reservations advised. Dress: casual but neat. AE, DC, MC, V. Closed Sun.*

$$$ Sisco's Restaurant. This is one of the best Spanish and Mediterrane-
★ an restaurants in Australia, as is reflected by the crowds that flock here on Friday and Saturday night. The decor is distinctly Spanish, with soft lighting, stucco walls, Spanish tiles, strolling guitar players, and heavy wood tables. The restaurant is renowned for its air-dried ham, homemade pork sausages, stuffed squid, and river trout. *121 Macquarie St., tel. 002/23–2059. Reservations advised. Dress: casual but neat. AE, DC, MC, V. Closed Sun.*

$$ The Aegean Restaurant. Don't go to this lively Greek restaurant looking for romance. This is the place to bring a large group—the larger the better—for a meal interspersed with belly dancing, plate throwing, and traditional Greek dancing. During lulls, enjoy moussaka, vegetarian platters, marinated chicken livers, or grilled chicken. *121 Collins St., tel. 002/31–1000. Reservations advised. Dress: casual but neat. AE, DC, MC, V. BYOB (wine only). Closed Sun.–Mon.*

$$ Ali Akbar. A roaring fire and Lebanese music welcome diners to this
★ traditional restaurant in northern Hobart. White tablecloths and fresh flowers add to the appealing atmosphere. Here you'll find some great modern interpretations of traditional dishes—and superb use of local produce. Typical Lebanese dishes include *maqlubat-al-qarnabeet* (a mixture of cauliflower, pine kernels, and spiced rice) and *sambousek* (yeast pastry filled with feta cheese, egg, and parsley). After 9 PM you can order the banquet plate, a combination of various hot and cold dishes. *321 Elizabeth St., tel. 002/31–1770. Reservations required. Dress: casual. AE, DC, MC, V. BYOB. Closed Mon.*

$$ Riviera Ristorante. On the wharf across the street from the Sheraton Hobart, this simply decorated restaurant is always busy and noisy. Diners can expect to stand in line for tables packed together on the restaurant's bare floor. The wait is worthwhile. All the food, including the pasta, is fresh. There are 15 choices of pizza and 16 different sauces to accompany four types of pasta. Try the pasta *tricolore*—three types of pasta served with three sauces. *15 Hunter St., Sullivans Cove, tel. 002/34–3230. No reservations. Dress: casual. AE, MC, V.*

Lodging

For travelers looking for more than just a hotel, **Homehost Tasmania** (Box 780, Sandy Bay, tel. 002/24–1612, fax 002/24–0472) arranges for visitors to stay as guests in Tasmanian homes, many of which are farms, cottages, and Federation-style houses. Prices are generally inexpensive to moderate, and breakfast is included. Dinners can be arranged. Bookings may also be made through any Tasmanian Travel Centre (*see* Important Addresses and Numbers, *above*).

Highly recommended lodgings are indicated by a star ★.

Category	Cost*
$$$$	over $150
$$$	$100–$150
$$	$60–$100
$	under $60

All prices are for a standard double room.

Hotels and Motels
$$$$

Salamanca Inn. Located close to the Salamanca Place market, these elegant self-contained units are built from Tasmanian timber and incorporate the latest energy-saving devices. The inn was built in 1988, but its architectural design blends in well with this historic district. Queen-size sofa beds, modern kitchens, and free laundry facilities make these apartments perfect for families. Ask for a room on the sunny western side, but don't expect great views in this three-story building. All apartments are serviced. *10 Gladstone St., 7000, tel. 002/23–3300 or toll-free 008/03–0944; fax 002/23–7167; telex 58388. 60 rooms with bath. Facilities: rooftop pool and spa, whirlpool, restaurant, game room. AE, DC, MC, V.*

$$$$
★

Sheraton Hobart Hotel. Across the street from the old wharf and some of the best restaurants in Hobart, this monolith seems a bit out of place amid Hobart's quaint colonialism. What it lacks in period charm, however, it more than makes up for in luxury, from the snappy, professional service to the marble floors and the complimentary cheese, wine, and fruit in the afternoon. All rooms feature a large wood desk, and thick white bathrobes are provided for guests' use. No detail, it seems, has been forgotten—music is even piped into the bathrooms! Some of the rooms overlook the harbor. *1 Davey St., 7000 (mailing address: Box 1601, 7001), tel. 002/35–4535 or toll-free 008/22–2229; fax 002/23–8175; telex AA58037. 234 rooms with bath. Facilities: health club with sauna, massage, beauty salon, children's game room (summer and holidays only), restaurants, 24-hr room service features a champagne brunch. AE, DC, MC, V.*

$$$$

Wrest Point Hotel and Casino. Built in 1940, this 17-floor luxury hotel earned its renown in 1973, when it opened the first legalized gambling casino in Australia. Guests have the choice of the more expensive tower or the moderately priced motor inn. All tower rooms were completely renovated at the end of 1989, with new furniture and peach-tone fabrics. The carpeted ceiling ensures complete quiet and privacy. The higher floors offer enjoyable views of either Mt. Wellington or the Derwent River. Regine's Videoteque and the nightclub are major entertainment spots in Hobart. *410 Sandy Bay Rd., Sandy Bay 7005, tel. 002/25–0112 or toll-free 008/03–0611; fax 002/25–2424; telex AA58115. Tower: 197 rooms with bath. Motor Inn: 81 rooms with bath. Facilities: indoor pool, health and beauty center, tennis court, massage, 9-hole minigolf course, playground, restaurants, 24-hr room service. AE, DC, MC, V.*

$$$
★

Islington Elegant Private Hotel. A converted 1845 mansion, this guest house exudes elegance from the moment you enter its spacious entrance hall with its high ceiling and black and white tiles. Rooms are decorated in a cozy colonial style with Laura Ashley curtains and matching bedspreads. Although it's only minutes from the city center, the hotel seems comfortably isolated, with a lush garden, an outdoor pool, and a stunning view of Mt. Wellington. Ask for a room with garden access. Personal service is stressed, and guests who are staying for an extended period are picked up from the airport and may even be driven into the city. A complimentary Continental breakfast is served in a sunny conservatory. *321 Davey St., 7000, tel.*

002/23–3900, fax 002/34–9053. 8 suites with bath. Facilities: pool, tennis court nearby. DC, MC, V.

$$$ **Lenna of Hobart.** This 19th-century hotel, just a short stroll from
★ Battery Point and Salamanca Place, is an eclectic mix of Old World charm and Australian colonial furnishings. Soft lights glow through stained-glass walkways lined with Greek statues and old urns in this 1874 Italianate mansion. Rooms are furnished with flower-uphol-stered wicker chairs, canopy beds, and antique-style telephones. Alexander's Restaurant offers some of the best cooking in the state (*see* Dining, *above*). *20 Runnymede St., 7000, tel. 002/23–2911 or toll-free 008/03–0633; fax 002/24–0112. 50 rooms with bath. Facili-ties: restaurant. AE, DC, MC, V.*

$$ **Westside Hotel.** From the large easy chairs in the reception area to rooms furnished with old-fashioned desks, mirrors, and candles, this elegant hotel in the center of the city is the epitome of good taste. Four executive suites, decorated in various styles from mod-ern to Japanese, feature Jacuzzis, and two double rooms are specifi-cally designed for disabled guests. *156 Bathurst St., 7000, tel. 002/ 34–6255; fax 002/34–7884; telex AA58228. 139 rooms with bath. Fa-cilities: restaurant, in-house movie channel, 24-hr room service. AE, DC, MC, V.*

Cottages and **Barton Cottage.** Built in 1837, this cottage in Battery Point main-
Guest Houses tains its colonial grace while offering modern conveniences. Rooms
$$ with such names as the Footman, Pantrymaid, and Chambermaid
★ are simply decorated with antiques, and all have private facilities. *72 Hampden Rd., 7000, tel. 002/24–1606, fax 002/24–1724. 6 rooms with bath. No credit cards.*

$$ **Colville Cottage.** From the moment you pass through the white pick-et fence and into the garden surrounding this cottage, you can't help but feel relaxed. The interior is nothing fancy, but the hardwood floors, fireplaces, fresh flowers, and bay windows create a warm, cozy atmosphere. Afternoon tea is served outside on the veranda. *32 Mona St., 7000, tel. 002/23–6968, fax 002/24–0500. 6 rooms with bath. Price includes breakfast. MC, V.*

$$ **Cromwell Cottage.** Built in the 1880s, this simple guest house is re-markable for its colorful rooms. Visitors have the choice of an all-red, an all-yellow (the sunniest), or an all-blue room. Otherwise, ask for the garden room with its large brass bed and ornate chandeliers. Some of the rooms have a view of the Derwent River. *6 Cromwell St., 7000, tel. 002/23–6734. 5 rooms with bath. Price includes break-fast. V.*

$$ **Warwick Cottages.** Annie's Room and Pandora's Box are identical cottages built by convicts in 1854 and now filled with an assortment of colonial bric-a-brac that lends them their individual charm. Pan-dora's Box, for example, features an antique meat grinder and old-style carriage lanterns. A winding staircase in each cottage leads to a double bed upstairs, while the ground floor has two single beds. *119–121 Warwick St., Old Hobart Town, tel. 002/54–1264, fax 002/ 54–1527. 2 units with bath. Facilities: fully equipped kitchens. V.*

The Arts

This Week in Tasmania, available at most hotels, is a comprehensive guide to current performances and rock and jazz concerts.

Concerts The **ABC Odeon** (167 Liverpool St., tel. 002/35–3634) hosts major concerts of the Tasmanian Symphony Orchestra and organizes youth concerts. The ABC and the Conservatorium of Music stage regular lunchtime concerts in the **State Library Auditorium** on Mur-ray Street.

Theater Plays are performed at the **Theatre Royal** (29 Campbell St., tel. 002/34–6266), an architectural gem that dates back to 1834. Look carefully at the magnificent dome, which features hand-painted portraits of famous composers. Other performances can be seen at the **Playhouse Theatre** (106 Bathurst St., tel. 002/34–1536).

Nightlife

Hobart's nightlife is very tame. Consult the Friday or Saturday editions of the local newspaper, *The Mercury*, for the latest in evening entertainment.

Located in the Wrest Point Hotel, the **Wrest Point Casino** offers blackjack, American roulette, minibaccarat, keno, minidice, craps, federal wheel, federal poker and stud poker, and two-up. Maximum stakes are $500 (a special suite on the ground floor caters to high rollers). The Wrest Point also offers late-night comedy and cabaret. **Regines Night Club** is open late for dancing (from 9 PM onward). *410 Sandy Bay Rd., Sandy Bay 7005, tel. 002/25–0112 or toll-free 008/03–0611. Open Mon.–Thurs. 1 PM–3 AM, Fri. and Sat. 1 PM–4 AM, Sun. noon–3 AM.*

Out at the **Carlysle Hotel** (232 Main Rd., Derwent Park, tel. 002/72–0299) every Friday and Saturday night there's the popular "Sixties in the Suburbs" night hosted by the local radio station DJ. If you'd prefer something more sedate, try the piano bar at the **Sheraton**, where there's someone on hand tickling the ivories Monday–Saturday 5:30–8:30; a vocal duo comes on at 9 PM. For the serious bop-till-you-drop set, try **Traveller's Rest** (394 Sandy Bay Rd., tel. 002/25–1181), **Round Midnight** (39 Salamanca Pl., tel. 002/23–2491), and **Stoppy's Waterfront Tavern** (21 Salamanca Pl., tel. 002/23–3799).

Oenophiles will want to try Tasmanian wines, some of which are exceptional. Look for the Pipers Brook, Heemskerk, Freycinet, and Moorilla Estate labels. For sampling in convivial surroundings, try **Nickelby's Wine Bar** (217 Sandy Bay Rd., tel. 002/23–6030).

Excursion to Port Arthur

When Governor Arthur was looking for a site to dump his worst convict offenders in 1830, the Tasman Peninsula was a natural choice. Joined to the rest of Tasmania only by the narrow Eaglehawk Neck, the peninsula was easy to isolate and guard. And so Port Arthur was born, a penal colony whose name became a byword for vicious cruelty and horror. Between 1830 and 1877, nearly 13,000 convicts served sentences in Britain's equivalent of Devil's Island, and nearly 2,000 of them died here. Few men escaped—dogs were used to patrol the narrow causeway, and sharks were reputed to infest the waters. Reminders of those dark days remain in some of the names—Dauntless Point, Stinking Point, Isle of the Dead. But today this once foreboding peninsula has become Tasmania's major tourist attraction, filled with beautiful scenery and historic attractions that recapture Australia's difficult beginnings. Although many visitors come here on a day trip from Hobart, consider at least an overnight stay. There is more than enough to do here to occupy a few days, and besides, watching the afternoon shadows lengthen over the ruins creates a mood much more in keeping with the settlement's doleful past. Walking through the grounds of the former penal settlement at dawn is magical, especially when taking in the view from the knoll behind the church.

Getting Around

By Car The trip to the Tasman Peninsula from Hobart takes just 1½ hours via the Lyell Highway across Eaglehawk Neck and the Arthur Highway.

Guided Tours

The **Port Arthur Penal Settlement** conducts a variety of daily tours around Port Arthur. Nightly ghost tours (9:30 PM) lead visitors in search of unexplained apparitions. *Information Office, tel. 002/50–2539. Admission: Ghost Tour: $6 adults, $3 children.*

Adventure Tours **Tasman Peninsula Detours** (Port Arthur Settlement, tel. 002/50–3355) gives daily four-wheel-drive tours of rain forests, beaches, and the convict ruins. The all-day tour includes morning and afternoon tea, as well as a barbecue lunch with wine.

Bus Tours The **Visitors' Information Centre** (20 Davey St., tel. 002/30–8394) organizes day trips from Hobart to Port Arthur by bus.

Remarkable Tours (tel. 002/50–2359, or book through the Visitors' Information Centre) offers minibus tours from the Port Arthur Penal Settlement to such nearby scenic sites as Remarkable Cave and observation points along the coast.

Self-Guided Tours The **Port Arthur Penal Settlement** offers an audiocassette tour that gives visitors a running commentary on the sites at the settlement. *Information Office, tel. 002/50–2363. Cost: $3 per person, $4 per couple, $7 family.*

Exploring Port Arthur

The grounds on which the **Port Arthur Penal Settlement** once stood now comprise one of the nicest parks in Tasmania—but be prepared to do a lot of walking among the widely scattered attractions. Standing by scenic Carnarvon Bay, it is hard to imagine the bloodshed and misery that existed here. But when you walk into the solitary confinement cells or the main penitentiary, you can't help but have an unsettled feeling. Most of the original buildings were damaged by bush fires in 1877 shortly after the settlement was abandoned, but you can still see the beautiful church, the round guard house, the commandant's residence, the model prison, the hospital, and the government cottages. The old **lunatic asylum** is now an excellent museum featuring a scale model of the Port Arthur settlement, a video history, and a collection of tools, leg irons, and chains. Besides a walking tour of the grounds and entrance at the museum, admission also includes a cruise to and tour of the **Isle of the Dead,** which sits in the middle of the bay. It is estimated that 1,769 convicts and 180 free people are buried here, mostly in communal pits. No headstones were used to mark the sites—the bodies were simply bundled in sailcloth, thrown in a hole, and sprinkled with quicklime. *Admission (valid for multiple entries over 24-hr period): $12 adults, $5 children, $30 family.*

About 1½ kilometers (1 mile) from Port Arthur is the **Bush Mill and Narrow Gauge Railway,** a great place to learn about a miller's life at the turn of the century. Highlights are the replica steam-powered bush sawmill, with a working steam engine, and a narrow-gauge steam railway that was once used to transport timber. Visitors can go for a ride. *Arthur Hwy., tel. 002/50–2221. Admission: $12 adults, $6 children, $32 family. Open daily 9–5.*

At **Taranna,** 11 kilometers (7 miles) north of Port Arthur, you'll find **Tasmanian Devil Park,** a wildlife refuge for injured animals of many species. It's probably the best place in the state to see Tasmanian devils (a burrowing carnivorous marsupial about the size of a dog), as well as quolls, boobooks, masked owls, eagles, and other native fauna. The park is unusual in that it conducts "night owl" tours that give you a great chance to observe these mainly nocturnal animals when they are at their most active. *Tel. 002/50–3203. Admission: $7 adults, $3.50 children. Open daily 8:30–7:30 peak season, 9:30–4:30 off-season.*

Dining and Lodging

Tracks. This small colonial-style restaurant at the Bush Mill specializes in salads and delicious home-baked scones. Other treats include a vegetable stockpot and a marinated Scotch fillet called bushman's steak. Try the apple crumble and ice cream for dessert. *Port Arthur, tel. 002/50–2221. No reservations. Dress: casual. AE, DC, MC, V. $$*

★ **Port Arthur Motor Inn.** Situated on a ridge behind the old church, this motel overlooks the entire historic Penal Settlement site. The comfortable but somewhat old-fashioned guest rooms sport 1960s decor, with small bathrooms. Although none of the accommodations have good views, you can dine on the freshest crayfish imaginable at the Commandant's Table, the hotel's main restaurant, while watching the sun set over the prison ruins. Other dishes include squid marinated in sweet chutney, honey, and garlic and then grilled; venison, wallaby, and rabbit sausages; and Port Authur porterhouse steak wrapped in a horseradish pancake. By the time you're tucking into desserts such as the golden sponge pudding in hot orange and caramel sauce, the floodlights are casting a benign glow over the grounds. *Tasman Hwy., Port Arthur 7182, tel. 002/50–2101 or toll-free 008/03–0747, fax 002/50–2417. 35 rooms with bath. Facilities: 2 restaurants, bar. AE, DC, MC, V. $$–$$$*

Launceston

Nestled in a fertile agricultural basin where the South Esk and North Esk rivers join to form the Tamar, the city of Launceston is the commercial center of Tasmania's northern region. Its abundance of unusual shops and markets is concentrated downtown, as opposed to the situation in Hobart, where the best shopping is found in the historic center, away from the commercial district. Launceston is far from bustling, and little stands out as remarkable. Nevertheless, it's a pleasant town filled with parks, turn-of-the-century homes, historic mansions, and private gardens. Perhaps its most compelling asset is the magnificent scenery on which it verges. Rolling farmland and rich loam reminiscent of English landscapes are powerfully accentuated by the South Esk River, which meanders through towering cliffs and gorges to its confluence with the Tamar River in the city itself.

Arriving and Departing

By Plane   The Launceston airport is served by several domestic airlines including **Airlines of Tasmania, Ansett Australia,** and **Qantas.**

By Bus **Hobart Coaches** (tel. 003/34–3600) and **Tasmanian Redline Coaches** (112 George St., tel. 003/31–9177) serve Launceston from Devonport, Burnie, and Hobart.

By Car Highway 1 connects Launceston with Hobart 2½ hours to the south, and with Devonport 1½ hours to the northwest.

Getting Around

By Car Cars, campers, caravans, and minibuses are available for hire at several agencies in Launceston: **Avis** (tel. 003/91–8314 or toll-free 008/22–5533), **Autorent Hertz** (tel. 003/31–2099), **Budget** (tel. 003/34–0099), and **Thrifty** (tel. 003/91–8105).

By Bike Bicycles can be rented from **Rent-a-Cycle** (36 Thistle St., tel. 003/44–9779).

By Taxi **Central Cabs** (tel. 003/31–3555) and **Taxi Combined** (tel. 003/31–5555) can be hailed in the street or booked by phone.

Important Addresses and Numbers

Tourist The **Tasmanian Information and Sales Centre** office is in Launces-
Information ton. *St. John and Paterson Sts., tel. 003/36–3111. Open weekdays 8:45–5, weekends and holidays 9–noon.*

Emergencies Three hospitals provide emergency medical services: **Launceston General** (Charles St., tel. 003/32–7111), **St. Luke's Hospital** (24 Lyttleton, tel. 003/31–3255), and **St. Vincent's Hospital** (5 Frederick St., tel. 003/31–4444).

For emergencies requiring an **ambulance,** the **police,** or the **fire brigade,** dial 000.

Guided Tours

Orientation A **City Sights** tour of Launceston may be booked through the Tasma-
Tours nian Information and Sales Centre. *St. John and Paterson Sts., tel. 003/31–3233. Tickets: $23 adults, $17 children. Tours Thurs. at 9:30 AM.*

Launceston Historic Walks conducts a leisurely stroll through the historic heart of the city. *Tel. 003/31–3679. Tickets: $10. Walks leave from outside the Tasmanian Information and Sales Centre* (see above), *weekdays 9:45 AM.*

Adventure **Tasmanian Wilderness Travel** (tel. 003/34–4442) leads day tours to
Tours Cradle Mountain and the Tamar Valley.

Exploring the Launceston Area

Aside from its parks and gardens, Launceston has few sights of interest to most visitors, but the sumptuous countryside in and around the city should not be missed. Begin at **Cataract Gorge,** which is almost in the heart of the city and can be reached by car via Paterson Street across the Kings Bridge. The South Esk River flows through the gorge on its way toward the Tamar River, and it is one of the most spectacular sights in Australia. A 1-mile path leads along the face of the towering cliffs to the Cliff Grounds Reserve, where picnic tables, a pool, and a restaurant are located. The park itself looks like a natural botanic garden, with ornate gazebos; peacocks strut on the open lawns. Take the chair lift in the first basin, which costs $3 for adults and $2 for children, for a thrilling aerial view of the gorge. At just over 1,000 feet, it is the longest single chair-lift span in the world. Several self-guided nature trails wind through the park as well. *Open daily 9–4:30.*

Take Trevallyn Road out of the gorge to Forest Road, bear left onto Cherry Road and then south at Reatta Road, following the signs to **Trevallyn Dam.** The dam, on the western outskirts of Launceston, is located in a stunning wildlife preserve. Boating down the South Esk River is common here, but for a unique adventure, try **cable hang gliding**—a 650-foot flight from the edge of a 60-foot cliff. Strapped into a harness and hooked onto a cable, you can experience the thrill of hang gliding with none of the risks. An 85-year-old woman has taken the ride, as has the owner's dog! *Trevallyn Dam Quarry, tel. 003/30–1567. Tickets: $7 per person. Open Dec.–Apr., daily 10–7; May–Nov., weekends and holidays 10–7.*

Launceston for Free

The **Queen Victoria Museum,** opened in 1891 in honor of Queen Victoria's Golden Jubilee, combines items of Tasmanian historical interest with natural history. The museum features a large collection of stuffed birds and animals (including the now-extinct thylacine, or Tasmanian wolf), as well as a Chinese Joss House and a display of coins. *Wellington and Paterson Sts. Open Mon.–Sat. 10–5, Sun. 2–5.*

What to See and Do with Children

The **Penny Royal World and Gunpowder Mill** is the closest thing to a large amusement park in Tasmania, and families can easily spend an entire day here. Rides in sailboats, barges, and trams are included in the ticket price, as are the exhibits in the various buildings. Inspect the foundry, the museum, and the historic gunpowder mills, where cannons are periodically fired. The admission price also includes a ride on the paddle steamer MV *Lady Stelfox*, which cruises up the Cataract Gorge and into the River Tamar. *Paterson St., tel. 003/31–6699. Admission: $15.50 adults, $8 children. Open daily 9–4:30.*

Off the Beaten Track

Right across the North Esk River at the intersection of the Tasman Highway are the **Waverly Woollen Mills,** which are still powered by a waterwheel. Opened in 1874, they pride themselves on using only the finest Tasmanian wool. A store on the premises sells products made in the mills. The building also incorporates the **National Automobile Museum of Tasmania.** *Waverly Rd., tel. 003/39–1106. Mills admission: $3 adults, $2 children; auto museum admission: $4 adults, $2 children. Both open weekdays 9–5. Closed Dec. 25.*

Shopping

The shopping in Launceston is excellent, with most of the shops centrally located on George Street and in nearby Yorktown Mall.

Some of the better arts and crafts shops include the **National Trust Old Umbrella Shop** (60 George St., tel. 003/31–9248), the **Design Centre of Tasmania** (Brisbane and Tamar Sts., tel. 003/31–5506), **Emma's Arts** (78 George St., tel. 003/31–5630), and **Gallery Two at Ritchie's Mill Arts Centre** (2 Bridge Rd., tel. 003/31–2339). **The**

Sheep's Back (53 George St., tel. 003/31–2539) sells woolen products exclusively.

Spectator Sports

Details about upcoming sporting events, including cricket and Australian-rules football, can be found in the *Examiner* newspaper on Friday.

Dining

Price categories are the same as in the Hobart Dining section, *above*.

$$$$ ★ **Fee and Me.** This new restaurant in a gracious Georgian-style mansion dating from 1838 is located on the edge of the Launceston city area. Chef Mark Lunnon's award-winning cuisine is Australian/Mediterranean with Asian overtones. His imaginative dishes include oysters in a coconut and chili sauce over vermicelli; crayfish baked with a whipped butter of saffron, lime, and crayfish flavors; and roast duckling with a green Chartreuse glaze and *rösti* potatoes. For dessert, try the citrus concoction of lemon potted cream, orange and mint sorbet, brandied orange segments, lemon glazed shortbread, and lemon ice-cream wedges. The wine list has a good representation of Tasmanian wines. *190 Charles St., tel. 003/31–3195. Reservations advised. Jacket and tie suggested. AE, MC, V. Closed Sun.*

$$$$ **The Terrace.** Situated in the Launceston Country Club Casino, this spacious restaurant was designed with the privacy of its diners in mind. Tables are separated by low walls, and each has its own silver champagne bucket. Specialties include smoked duck breast, local scallops, and Atlantic salmon. Steaks are served panfried or au poivre. Special fixed-priced dinners include tickets to the evening's cabaret show. *Launceston Country Club Casino, Country Club Ave., Prospect Vale 7250, tel. 003/44–8855. Reservations advised. Jacket and tie required. AE, DC, MC, V. Closed Sun. and Mon.*

$$$ **Shrimps.** For the best selection of seafood in Launceston, this is the place to go. Set in a brick building erected by convicts in 1824, the restaurant was preceded by a sweetshop and then a private residence. The tables are small and widely spaced, and the menu is chalked on a large blackboard. Nightly specials include oysters, trevalla, whitebait, mussels, and abalone served fresh from the restaurant's tank. *72 George St., tel. 003/34–0584. Reservations advised. Dress: casual but neat. AE, DC, MC, V. Closed Sun.*

$$$ **Victoria's Tassie Fare Restaurant.** Located in historic Albert Hall right in the middle of City Park, this is one of the few restaurants in Launceston to feature only Tasmanian produce on its menu. The casual garden furniture that is used at lunch is replaced at night with tables adorned with white tablecloths and silver table settings. Evening specialties include beef and seafood roasts and Tasmanian scallops. A few pasta and vegetarian dishes are featured on the extensive menu. *Cimitiere and Tamar Sts., tel. 003/31–7433. Reservations advised. Dress: casual but neat. AE, DC, MC, V. 10% surcharge Sun. and holidays.*

$$ ★ **Posh Nosh.** This noisy, busy deli serves some of the best and cheapest food in Launceston. Everything is served fresh or made on the premises. A delightful place for lunch, its specialties include a King Island platter of brie and smoked beef, and a gourmet ploughman's lunch of sea trout. A diverse range of soups is offered, including creole chicken and sweet corn, and potato and leek. *127 St. John St., tel.*

003/31–9180. No reservations. Dress: casual. No credit cards. BYOB. Open 7:30–5:30. Closed weekends.

$ **Ripples.** Part of Ritchie's Mill Arts Centre and directly across from the Penny Royal World, this tiny tearoom is a pleasant lunch or afternoon stopover. It serves the best pancakes and crêpes in town and offers good coffee. *Paterson St., tel. 003/31–4153. No reservations. Dress: casual. No credit cards. Breakfast and lunch only.*

Lodging

Price categories are the same as in the Hobart Lodging section, *above.*

$$$$ **Launceston Country Club Casino.** This luxury club and casino located on the outskirts of Launceston has recently been renovated and modernized. The gold and dark tones have been replaced by softer pastels of gray, blue, and pink. The curved driveway to the club is lined with flowers, and the gardens are beautifully manicured. The golf course, one of the best in Australia, attracts visitors from all over the area. The club offers gambling, dancing, and cabaret shows at night. *Country Club Ave., Prospect Vale 7250, tel. 003/44–8855 or toll-free 008/03–0211, fax 003/43–1880, telex 58600. 104 rooms with bath. Facilities: golf course, indoor pool, sauna/spa, tennis, horseback riding, squash, fitness track, massage, 24-hr room service, trout fishing nearby, casino, disco, barbecue facilities. AE, DC, MC, V.*

$$$ **Launceston International Travelodge.** This six-story building in the heart of Launceston was designed with elegance in mind. However, when empty, the soaring marble foyer can appear quite daunting. The guest rooms are much more comfortable, decorated in pastels with lightly colored furniture. The lower floors can be noisy from all the street activity, so ask for a room on a higher floor—but don't expect a view. One of the hotel entrances leads directly into the Yorktown Mall, a major shopping area in Launceston. *29 Cameron St., 7250, tel. 003/34–3434 or toll-free 008/03–0123, fax 003/31–7347. 165 rooms with bath. Facilities: 3 restaurants, 24-hr room service. AE, DC, MC, V.*

$$ **Alice's Place.** Constructed from the remains of three buildings erected in the 1840s, this delightful cottage is best known for its whimsical touches. The drawers of the antique furniture might contain old-fashioned gloves, eyeglasses, or books; an old turtle shell and a deer's head hang on the wall; and Victorian costumes, an old Victrola, and a four-poster canopy bed lend colonial charm. Modern conveniences are cleverly tucked away among the period furnishings—take a bath in the huge old tub, and then dry your hair with the electric dryer. *17 York St., 7250, tel. 003/34–2231, fax 003/34–2696. 1 unit with bath (sleeps 4 on 2 floors). Facilities: fully equipped kitchen. No credit cards.*

$$ **Launceston Holiday Village Resort.** A stone's throw from the Launceston Country Club Casino, this moderately priced complex consists of holiday units with fully equipped kitchens. Perfect for families, each wood and brick-lined unit features unobtrusive furnishings with simple bedding, matching curtains, and large picture windows. Guests can play golf on the country club's course and use its other facilities as well. *10 Casino Rise, 7250, tel. 003/43–1744, fax 003/44–9943. 55 units with bath. Facilities: pool, nearby gym, tennis court, game room, restaurant. AE, DC, MC, V.*

$$ **The Old Bakery Inn.** Guests in this colonial complex can choose from
★ three areas: a converted stable, the former baker's cottage, or the old bakery. The loft above the stables is also available. All rooms are

decorated in colonial style, with antique furniture and lace curtains. One room in the old bakery was actually the oven—its walls are 2 feet thick. *York and Margaret Sts., 7250, tel. 003/31–7900, fax 003/ 31–7756. 26 rooms with bath. Facilities: restaurant. AE, MC, V.*

$$ **Prince Albert Inn.** This inn, which first opened in 1855, shines like a
★ gem in the lackluster downtown area that surrounds it. After passing through the Italianate facade, you'll enter a Victorian time warp, complete with wall-to-wall portraits of British royalty in the plush dining room. Recent renovations of the seven guest rooms have not broken the spell—lace curtains, velvet drapery, and fluffy comforters continue to provide the requisite atmosphere—they've just maximized the comfort. This establishment is exclusively for nonsmokers. *Cnr. Tamar and William Sts., tel. 003/31–1931. 7 rooms with bath. Price includes Continental breakfast. MC, V.*

The Arts

Concerts **Silverdome** (Prospect St., tel. 003/44–9988) holds regular concerts—everything from classical to heavy metal.

Theater The **Princess Theatre** (Brisbane St., tel. 003/37–1270 or 003/26–3384) features local and imported stage productions.

Nightlife

Casino The **Launceston Country Club Casino** features blackjack, American roulette, minibaccarat, keno, minidice, federal and stud poker, federal wheel, and two-up. *Country Club Ave., Prospect Vale 7250, tel. 003/44–8855. Open Mon.–Thurs. 1 PM–3 AM, Fri. and Sat. 1 PM–4 AM, Sun. noon–3 AM.*

Disco Late-night dancing is available at the Launceston Country Club Casino (tel. 003/44–8855). There is no cover charge at **Regine's Discoteque.** *Open Wed.–Thurs. 9 PM–4 AM, Fri.–Sat. 10 PM–5 AM, Sun. 9 PM–4 AM.*

The Northwest Coast

The Northwest Coast of Tasmania is one of the most exciting and least known areas of this region. Most of the local inhabitants are farmers, anglers, or lumberjacks—they're a hardy bunch but also some of the friendliest folk in Tasmania. The rugged coastline here has long been the solitary haunt of abalone hunters, and the area's lush grazing land produces some of Australia's best beef and cheese. Tasmanian farmers are the only legal growers of opium poppies (for medicinal purposes) in the Southern Hemisphere, and some of the fields in the northwest are covered with their flowers.

Arriving and Departing

By Bus **Tasmanian Redline Coaches** has offices in Devonport (9 Edward St., tel. 004/24–5100), Burnie (117 Wilson St., tel. 004/31–3233), Smithton (19 Smith St., tel. 004/52–1262), and Queenstown (Orr St., tel. 004/71–1011). **Hobart Coaches** (tel. 002/34–4077) has offices in Devonport (9 Best St., tel. 004/24–6599) and Burnie (54 Cattley St., tel. 004/31–1971).

By Ferry The *Spirit of Tasmania* makes the 14-hour trip from Melbourne to Devonport three times a week. The ferry carries 1,278 passengers and up to 490 cars. Cabin rates range from $85 to $265 each way; ferrying a car costs between $90 and $150. Facilities include children's playrooms, gift shops, and several restaurants and bars. Advance bookings are essential. *Box 323, Port Melbourne, VIC 3207, or Box 168, E. Devonport, TAS 7310, tel. 03/645–2766, 004/27–9751, or toll-free 008/03–0344; fax 03/646–7450.*

By Plane Devonport and Wynyard are served by several domestic airlines, including **Airlines of Tasmania** and **Kendell Airlines.**

Wilderness Air (tel. 004/71–7280) flies seaplanes from Strahan Wharf over Frenchman's Cap, the Franklin and Gordon rivers, Lake Pedder, and Hells Gates. It's a great way to see the area's peaks, lakes, coast, and rivers.

Important Addresses and Numbers

Tourist **Tourism Tasmania** has travel centers in Devonport (18 Rooke St.,
Information tel. 004/21–6226) and Burnie (48 Cattley St., tel. 004/34–6111). Offices are open weekdays 9–5, Saturday and holidays 9–noon.

Guided Tours

Air Tours **Devonport Aviation** conducts scenic flights and departs from both Cradle Valley and Devonport. Flights take visitors over the valley and across to Barn Bluff, Mt. Ossa, the Acropolis, Lake St. Clair, Mt. Olympus, and other sights in the area. Doors on the planes are removable for photography. Travelers have the choice of 30- to 90-minute flights. *Cradle Valley, tel. 004/92–1132; Devonport, tel. 004/27–9777.*

Getting Around

By Bicycle Bicycles are available for rental in Devonport at **Hire a Bike** (51 Raymond Ave., tel. 004/24–3889).

By Car Many of the roads in the northwest are twisty and, in some of the more remote areas, unpaved. A very few may even require four-wheel-drive vehicles. However, two-wheel drive is sufficient for most touring. Be prepared for sudden weather changes—this is one of the colder parts of Tasmania, and snow in the summertime is not uncommon.

Cars, campers, and minibuses are available for rent in Devonport, Burnie, and Wynyard. The numbers of the following companies are for their offices in Devonport: **Autorent Hertz** (tel. 004/24–1013), **Avis** (tel. 004/27–9797), **Budget** (tel. 004/24–7088), **Thrifty** (tel. 004/27–9119).

Exploring the Northwest Coast

Devonport is a sleepy town that's more used to serving the local farmers than tourists. Stop at the **Tiagarra Aboriginal Cultural and Art Centre** to see remnants of Tasmania's Aboriginal past, including more than 250 images of rock engravings. *Mersey Bluff, tel. 004/24–8250. Admission: $2.50 adults, $1 children. Open daily 9–4:30.*

Head west on the Bass Highway toward Burnie. If you have time, stop in at **Penguin**—a charming little town that has little penguin statues on its sidewalks acting as litter baskets. It's everything you'd imagine a small town to be—the milk bar is larger than the nearest pub. From Penguin the road leads through the Table Cape region to Wynyard, passing through rich farm country and gentle, rolling hills.

Continue west on the Bass Highway past Wynyard to **Boat Harbour.** This secluded area, popular with summer vacationers, rarely gets cold even in winter.

Beyond Boat Harbour near Sisters Beach is the 10-acre **Birdland Native Gardens,** where visitors can see native Tasmanian birds flying in open aviaries. The picnic ground here is a fine spot for lunches and afternoon barbecues. *Wattle Ave., tel. 004/45–1270. Admission: $2.50 adults, 50¢ children. Open daily 9–5.*

Just after Wiltshire, turn right off the Bass Highway onto Route B21 toward Stanley and **Circular Head.** The famous **"Nut"**— Tasmania's version of Ayers Rock—is located here. Perched at the northernmost point of mainland Tasmania, the Nut, a sheer volcanic plug, some 12½ million years old, is almost totally surrounded by the sea. Visitors can either take the chair lift to the summit ($3.50 one way, $5.50 round-trip) or walk. From the top, walking trails lead in all directions—but hikers should be wary of snakes. *Contact Nut Chairlifts (Box 43, Stanley 7331, tel. 004/58–1286) for information.*

Stanley, the town at the foot of the Nut, is one of the prettiest villages in Tasmania and a must for anyone traveling in the northwest. It is filled with unique shops, friendly tearooms, and many historic cottages and inns.

Backtrack from Stanley and continue west along the Bass Highway toward **Smithton.** Although Smithton itself has few tourist attractions, it's an ideal base from which to tour the rugged Northwest Coast.

Visit the **Allendale Gardens,** which are situated south of Smithton on Route B22. These private gardens were cultivated as a hobby and now rival the Royal Botanic Gardens in Hobart. Around each corner is a surprise—a grouping of native Tasmanian ferns or a new thicket of shrubs and flowers. Forest walks of 10–25 minutes' duration take you past trees more than 500 years old. The gardens are filled with more birds than you're likely to see in other areas of Tasmania. *Eurebia, Edith Creek 7330, tel. 004/56–4216. Admission: $5 adults, $2.50 children. Open Sept.–May, daily 9–6.*

Backtrack to Somerset and head south on the Murchison Highway. A three-hour drive along this highway and Route B24 takes you to the little village of Strahan, and the scenery along the way is rugged and spectacular. A network of rivers and streams provides natural irrigation for the rich red soil, in which crops of potatoes and opium are grown. Past Rosebery, the land becomes hilly and increasingly barren as the route winds down to Strahan.

Detour toward the coast to visit the sleepy little historic town of **Zeehan.** During the past century, silver-lode discoveries transformed Zeehan into one of the state's largest towns—it had 26 hotels—but some 25 years later the deposits started to run out, and Zeehan went the way of many failed mining towns. A drive along Main Street takes you past the transient grandeur of the Grand Hotel and the Gaiety Theatre; both buildings now belong to the **West Coast Pioneers' Memorial Museum** and stand empty, awaiting renovation. The museum itself, in the historic old School of Mines Building, has an excellent mineral collection among its attractions. *Main St., tel. 004/71–6225. Admission free (donations accepted). Open daily, Apr.–Oct. 8:30–5, Nov.–Mar. 8:30–6.*

The direct road from here to Strahan is sandy track that is generally in fair condition, though the loose surface can be a challenge. It passes the vast **Henty Sand Dunes,** worth climbing for the desertscape they present. If you feel dubious about the road, cut back to the main highway, which will also get you to **Strahan,** a lovely, lazy fishing port with one of the deepest harbors in the world and a population of under 500. It used to be a major port for mining companies, and its waters are still brown from the effect of ore mixing with tannin from the surrounding vegetation. Cruises along the Gordon River to the ravishingly beautiful World Heritage site in the Wild Rivers National Park constitute the main tourist activity here. **Gordon River Cruises** operates three half-day cruises daily (9–1:30) that travel 24 kilometers (15 miles) up Macquarie Harbour and the Gordon River. An informative commentary accompanies the trip past historic Sarah Island (one of the most notorious penal settlements in Australia) and stands of tea tree, melaleuca, sassafrass, and huon pine. Passengers may get off at Heritage Landing and take a half-hour walk through the vegetation. *Box 40, Strahan 7468, tel. 004/ 71–7187. Rates: $40 adults, $20 children. Reservations required.*

World Heritage Cruises conducts daily cruises from mid-August until June aboard the MV *Heritage Wanderer*, which departs Strahan Wharf at 9 AM and returns at 4 PM. Meals and drinks are available on board. The boat goes at a leisurely pace, stopping at Sarah Island, Heritage Landing, and the Saphia Ocean Trout Farm on Macquarie Harbour. *Box 93, Strahan 7468, tel. 004/71–7174, fax 004/71–7431. Rates: $32 adults, $15 children.*

West Coast Yacht Charters operates daily twilight sailings on Macquarie Harbour ($40) that include a dinner of the famed local crayfish. The company also operates a two-day sailing excursion ($270 adults, $135 children) and a morning fishing trip ($30, including gear, bait, and morning tea). *The Esplanade, Strahan 7468, tel. 004/ 71–7422.*

Shopping

Devonport For a large selection of Australian colonial, English, and country cottage furniture and antiques, go to **Thomsons of Devonport** (13 Formby Rd., tel. 004/24–8360).

Boat Harbour Housed in a building made of convict brick, the **Shannondoah Cottage Handcrafts and Tea Rooms** (Bass Hwy., tel. 004/45–1141) offer a wide array of Tasmanian crafts at reasonable prices.

Stanley The **Plough Inn** (Church St., tel. 004/58–1226) has an adequate collection of handicrafts and antiques, but **Touchwood Quality Crafts** (Church St., tel. 004/58–1348) offers one of the finest selections of Tasmanian crafts in the state.

Dining

Price categories are the same as in the Hobart Dining section, *above.*

Smithton **Grey's Fine Dining.** Located in the Tall Timbers resort, this spacious
★ restaurant has high ceilings, wood walls, and rafters made from Tasmanian timber—even the menu is wood. Specialties include rock crayfish, chicken breasts, a rabbit hot pot, and Atlantic salmon. Try the crêpes suzette for dessert. *Scotchtown Rd., tel. 004/52–2755. Reservations required. Dress: casual but neat. AE, DC, MC, V. $$$*

Strahan **Franklin Manor.** Located in a restored building, this restaurant is known for its refined and comfortable ambience. The à la carte menu includes lobster, oysters, pot-roasted quail, and sea trout. *The Es-*

planade, tel. 004/71–7311. Reservations advised. Dress: casual but neat. MC, V. $$$

Lodging

Price categories are the same as in the Hobart Lodging section, *above.*

Smithton
★
Tall Timbers. This lodge is one of the classiest establishments in the entire northwest region. Built completely of Tasmanian wood, the hotel consists of two buildings: the annex, where the rooms are located, and the main house, which includes a cozy bar and two restaurants—one for formal dining and the other a huge bistro. The rooms are simply decorated and equipped with the latest energy-saving devices. The staff is young, energetic, and friendly. *Box 304, 7330, tel. 004/52–2755 or toll-free 008/03–0300, fax 004/52–2742. 32 units with bath. AE, DC, MC, V. $$*

Stanley
Touchwood Cottage. Built in 1836, this is one of Stanley's oldest homes and is furnished accordingly with plenty of period antiques. The product of an architect's whimsy (or incompetence), the cottage is known for its doorways of different sizes and oddly shaped living room. It is ideally located near the Nut and the popular Touchwood crafts shop, where guests are entitled to a discount. *33 Church St., 7331, tel. 004/58–1348. 3 rooms without bath. MC, V. $*

Strahan
★
Franklin Manor. When this newly renovated establishment, once a private home, opened its doors in 1990, it immediately became *the* place to stay in Strahan. Set in gardens near the harbor, it has been tastefully restored with Old World features such as open fires and a relaxing lounge, yet also includes TV, telephone, and heated towel rails. *The Esplanade, Strahan, 7468, tel. 004/71–7311. 13 rooms with shower. Facilities: video, tea-making, minibar. MC, V. $$*

Strahan Inn. The most popular hotel in Strahan (it's only 1,800 feet from the Gordon River cruise dock), this inn comprises a main building and an annex behind. Ask for rooms in the main building overlooking the harbor—rooms in the annex have limited views and are noisier. Colonial furniture and beds with quilt coverings create a welcoming ambience. *Jolly St., 7468, tel. 004/71–7160. 50 rooms with shower only, 11 with spa bath. Facilities: restaurant, room service at mealtimes only. AE, DC, MC, V. $$*

Ulverston
★
The Lighthouse Hotel. This unexpected delight in the small coastal town is a very contemporary looking, salmon-pink building with an enclosed garden atrium. Guest rooms have a predominantly blue color scheme and are furnished smartly with blond-wood pieces. The standard of the international cuisine at the resident bistro is very high. *33 Victoria St. (corner Reiby St.), Ulverstone 7315, tel. 004/25–1197, fax 004/25–5973. 28 rooms with bath. Facilities: restaurant, sauna/spa, gym, barbecue facilities. AE, MC, V. $$*

National Parks

Tasmania is a bushwalker's state, and many of its parks remain largely undeveloped. However, hikers should be prepared to be wet and cold—at any time of year. Winters are particularly bitter, and it is inadvisable to plan hikes then. During summer hikes, it isn't unusual to be sweating in the noonday sun, braving a brief snowstorm two hours later, and ending the day drenched from pouring rain.

There is an entry fee payable that covers all Tasmanian national parks. The scale ranges from $5 for one day to $20 for 14 days or $40 for a month. Children under 18 enter free.

Southwest National Park

The largest park in Tasmania, Southwest encompasses the entire southwestern portion of the state. One of the few areas of Australia with virgin land unaffected by human tampering, the park boasts trees topping 300 feet in its dense, temperate rain forest. Indeed, its five mountain ranges and more than 50 lakes were unknown to all but the most avid bushwalkers until the park gained notoriety in 1974 with the drowning of Lake Pedder: To boost the power of the nearby hydroelectric dam, the lake was flooded, and it now lies under a lake 25 times the size of the orginal one.

The road into the park passes through a rain forest and offers views of rock formations dating back more than 500 million years. During the summer months, the road is lined with beehives brought here by keepers taking advantage of the blossoms of the leatherwood tree.

Southwest is a park for the hardiest of travelers. Only one trail—the Western Arthurs Transverse—is well marked, and it is a seven-day trek. Parts of it require short ascents, best made with ropes, up steep gullies and cliff faces. The hike should not be attempted by anyone who minds being wet and cold, because the park is often hit with violent storms, snow, and rainfall even during the summer months. Do not embark on walks in the park without registering (and logging out) with the Tasmanian Police in Hobart. Admission is $2 per car.

Arriving and Departing

By Plane Two companies provide air service into the park at Cox Bight and Melaleuca: **Par Avion** (tel. 002/48–5390) and **TASAIR** (tel. 002/48–5088).

By Car Southwest is located 174 kilometers (108 miles) from Hobart and may be reached by car from the north via Strathgordon Road, passing through Maydena to Frodshams Pass, where a left turn leads to Scott's Peak Road and the park.

By Bus A regularly scheduled minibus is available from **Tasmanian Wilderness Transport and Tours** (tel. 003/34–4442 or 008/03–0505) in Hobart on Tuesday, Thursday, and weekends from December to March. The cost is $35 one way or $65 round-trip.

Lodging Free campsites are available at Lake Pedder, Scott's Peak Dam, and Edgar Dam. Gas, food, and accommodations are available in Strathgordon.

Information Contact the **Department of Parks, Wildlife, and Heritage** (Box 41, Westerway 7140, tel. 002/88–1283).

Mount Field National Park

Mount Field was the first national park created in Tasmania and still ranks first in popularity among Tasmanians and visitors alike. The park's easily navigable trails, picnic areas, and well-maintained campsites are ideal for family outings. Many popular animals—including Bennett's and rufous wallabies as well as Tasmanian devils—may be spotted toward dusk.

The park offers the most popular ski area in southern Tasmania. Located on Mt. Mawson, it has challenging trails for cross-country skiers. For walkers, however, summer is the best time to visit. The most popular trail is the **Russell Falls Nature Walk.** This 1-kilometer (.6-mile) path is paved part of the way and suitable for wheelchairs. Numbered pegs inform walkers about the vegetation along the route; the path leads bushwalkers from eucalyptus forest into temperate rain forest and ends at the Russell Falls. Along the way, the trail passes the tallest hardwood trees in the world—a variety of eucalyptus known as mountain ash (or locally as swamp gum), some of which tower at more than 100 meters (325 feet).

Arriving and Departing   The park is located 80 kilometers (50 miles) northwest of Hobart. From Hobart, drive north on the Lyell Highway and then west on Maydena Road. Scheduled buses leave Hobart for the park Monday through Friday, except public holidays.

Lodging   A campground and a caravan park, equipped with toilets, hot water, showers, and laundry facilities, are located near the entrance to Mount Field. Firewood is provided free of charge. Fees are $10 for a campsite, $12 for a powered site for two. Minimal grocery supplies may be purchased at the kiosk near the caravan park. Free wilderness huts are situated on certain trails throughout the park. Check with the ranger about their specific locations.

Information   Contact the park (Box 41, Westerway 7140, tel. 002/88–1149).

Cradle Mountain/Lake St. Clair National Park

Cradle Mountain/Lake St. Clair National Park contains the most spectacular alpine scenery in Tasmania and the best mountain trails in Australia. The park, which is popular with hikers of all levels of ability, encompasses several high peaks, including the highest in Tasmania, Mt. Ossa (more than 1,617 meters/5,300 feet). The Cradle Mountain section of the park lies in the north, where the Waldheim Chalet, built by the park's founder, Gustav Weindorfer, stands guard over the valley below.

The southern section of the park, Lake St. Clair, is popular not only for boat trips but also for the trails that circumnavigate the lake. Trout fishing is permitted with a license, and boat trips can be arranged from Cynthia Bay.

It is impossible to visit the park without hearing of the **Overland Track.** The most famous trail in Australia, the track traverses 85 kilometers (53 miles) from the northern to the southern boundary of the park. Traveled by more than 200 people a week, the trail has several basic accommodation huts along the route that are available on a first-come, first-served basis. Because space in the huts is limited, hikers are advised to bring their own tents. For those who wish to do the walk in comfort—and are prepared to pay for the privilege— there are also relatively well equipped (and heated) private huts operated by Cradle Mountain Huts, a commercial concern. *See* Chapter 16, Adventure Vacations, for details.

The toughest part of the Overland is in the northern section of the park where most hikers begin—a moderately steep climb of Cradle Mountain must be made on the first day. The climbing is not nearly as difficult to bear as the weather, however; even in summer, frequent storms are guaranteed to douse hikers. The trail, which takes between 5 and 10 days to traverse, passes over and around many of the mountains and lakes in the park as well as through temperate rain forests.

For those who are less adventurous or have less time, the park contains many rewarding shorter trails.

Arriving and Departing

By Car **Cradle Mountain** is located 85 kilometers (53 miles) south of Devonport. It can be reached by car via Claude Road from Sheffield or via Wilmot. Both lead 30 kilometers (19 miles) along Route C132 to Cradle Valley. The last 10 kilometers (6 miles) are unpaved.

Lake St. Clair is 173 kilometers (107 miles) from Hobart and can be reached via the Lyell Highway or from Launceston via Deloraine or Poatina.

By Bus **Invicta Coaches** (tel. 008/03–0505) operates buses to Cradle Mountain from Devonport. **Mountain Stage Line** (tel. 003/34–0442) operates a bus service to Cradle Mountain and Cynthia Bay from Launceston. **Tasmanian Redline Coaches** (tel. 002/34–4577) operates buses daily (except Sunday) from Hobart and Queenstown to Derwent Bridge, near the entrance to the park.

Lodging Caravan, car, and bus campgrounds are located 2 kilometers (1.3 miles) north of the park boundary and provide showers, toilets, laundry facilities, and enclosed cooking shelters with electric barbecues. Usage is free. Tent sites cost $10 per night for two persons. Bunkhouse accommodations are $15 per person per night. Advance booking is essential (tel. 004/92–1395).

Four-, six-, and eight-bed huts in Cradle Valley must be booked in advance. Rates average about $15 per person per night. Huts may be rented at Cynthia Bay as well.

★ **Cradle Mountain Lodge.** The property that really established the whole genre of wilderness lodges in Australia, this is the most comfortable place to stay at Cradle Mountain. The accommodations are not luxurious, but they're homey. The high-ceilinged guest rooms, two per cabin, each have their own kitchenette and are decorated with a green and burgundy fabric. The surroundings are what count here, and they are magnificent. There are many walking trails that begin at the lodge door. After a good meal in the dining room, you can walk outside to see a gathering of Tasmania's wildlife come to dine on the lodge's leftovers. *Box 153, Sheffield 7306, tel. 004/92–1303, fax 004/92–1309. 77 rooms with bath. Facilities: restaurant, kitchenettes, store, conducted walks (summer only), gold-panning, canoeing, rappelling. MC, V. $$$*

Information Contact **Cradle Mountain National Park** (Box 20, Sheffield 7306, tel. 004/92–1133) or **Lake St. Clair National Park** (Derwent Bridge 7465, tel. 002/89–1172).

7 Queensland

By Walter
Glaser

Updated by
David
McGonigal

Queensland is a state of enormous geographic and social disparities. As its license plates proclaim, Queensland is the "Sunshine State," Australia's equivalent of Florida—a laid-back land of beaches and sun, where many Australians head for their vacations. Queensland has actively pursued the tourist industry, and today areas such as the Gold Coast in the south have exploded into mini-Miamis, complete with high-rise buildings, casinos, and beachfront amusements.

At the same time, Queenslanders see themselves as upholding traditional Australian values that have been lost in the other states—values championed by conservative Sir Joh Bjelke-Petersen, whose 20-year span as premier ended in 1989 with an election-day rout by Labor candidate Wayne Goss. Until revelations of large-scale corruption surfaced within his adminstration, Bjelke-Petersen's muzzling of public dissent and censorship of films and magazines found wide support with Queenslanders, who are often criticized by other Australians as provincial, old-fashioned, and even racist. Airline timetables for flights along the east coast become chaotic when the other states change to daylight savings time—a newfangled notion that Queenslanders staunchly reject. Residents in Australia's southern cities quip that when you visit Queensland, "you should turn your watch back an hour and your mind back 20 years." Yet a bizarre law that forbids bartenders to serve "sexual perverts" exists side-by-side with the lifestyle of the Gold Coast, a mecca for scantily clad hedonists.

Whatever the vagaries of Queensland's politics, its people are noteworthy for their friendliness and hospitality. Typical of lands blessed with hot weather and plenty of sunshine, the pace is a little slower and life takes on a different perspective. In Queensland, life is lived barefoot and in shorts.

Queensland, however, cannot be viewed as a single, homogeneous entity. The sheer size of the state defies homogeneity. Queensland occupies 1,727,999 square kilometers (667,000 square miles) and stretches from the subtropical Gold Coast to the wild and steamy rain forests of the far north. Only in recent years has the Cape York Peninsula at the northern tip been fully explored, and crocodiles still claim a victim once in a while. Across the dividing range, away from sugar and banana plantations of the coast, Queensland looks as arid and dust-blown as any other part of Australia's interior. Few paved roads cross this semidesert, and as in the Red Centre, communication with remote farms is mostly by radio and air. Not surprisingly, most of Queensland's 2.5 million inhabitants reside on the coast, where the living is easier.

In the south, bordering New South Wales, is the Gold Coast—an Australionized version of Miami Beach or Waikiki. The Sunshine Coast, north of Brisbane, is somewhat quieter and less touristy, with long, deserted beaches and beautiful rain forests. The major attraction for Australians and foreign tourists alike, however, is the Great Barrier Reef. Stretching from Brisbane as far north as New Guinea, this ecological masterpiece is home to thousands of different species. (For more information about the Great Barrier Reef, see Chapter 8.) Dive boats and guided tours leave from towns and cities up and down the Queensland coast, giving tourists firsthand views of this living colossus. With such an abundance of marine life, it's not surprising that Queensland is a fishing mecca. Cairns and Lizard Island in the far north are renowned for their big-game fishing—black marlin weighing more than half a ton are not uncommon.

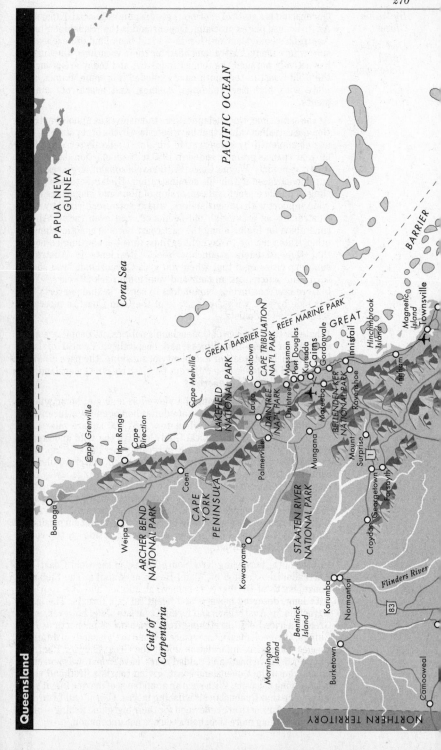

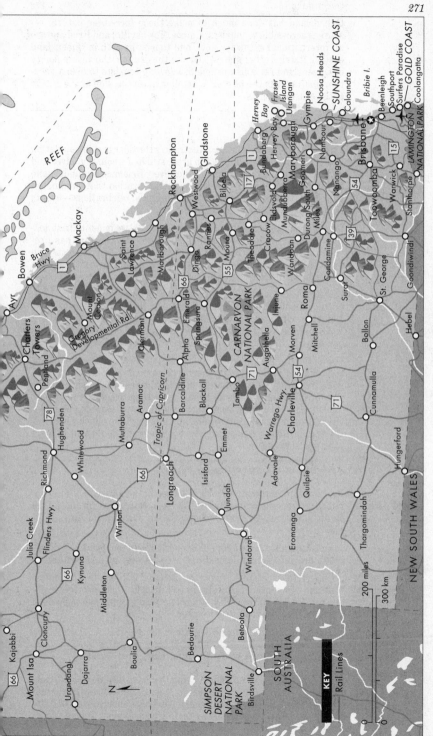

Queensland has done much to make these incredible natural resources accessible to tourists. Cairns, Townsville, and Brisbane are all international gateways now, and tourist growth in Queensland easily outstrips other states. Despite the growth, the vast majority of Queensland remains unspoiled, allowing tourists to plan a vacation that takes in the best of Australian nature as well as the glitter of the coastal resorts.

Brisbane

Until the mid-1970s this city, Australia's third largest in population and one of the world's largest in area, still had a country flavor and attitude. In the last decade or so, however, Brisbane has undergone an impressive spurt of growth and modernization that culminated with Expo '88 and the Australian bicentennial celebrations—events that helped put the city on the world map.

Strangely enough, it is the city's proximity to two major tourist destinations, the Gold Coast and the Sunshine Coast, that has prevented Brisbane from becoming a major tourist attraction in its own right. Almost invariably, visitors to Queensland travel either north or southeast of the city for their vacations.

Brisbane was founded as a penal colony for prisoners who had committed a crime after their arrival in Australia. The waterway across which the city sprawls was discovered by two escaped convicts in 1823, and the penal settlement was established on its banks the following year, 32 kilometers (20 miles) from Moreton Bay.

Few of the city's historic buildings have survived the wrecker's ball, and today's Brisbane is very much a product of recent development. Far surpassing the architecture in Brisbane are its open spaces: It is a beautifully landscaped city brimming with jacarandas, tulip trees, flame trees, oleanders, frangipani, and the ever-stunning bougainvillea. In summer the city broils, and although the climate is pleasant at other times of the year, there is never any doubt that this is a subtropical region.

Arriving and Departing by Plane

Airport and Airlines **Brisbane International Airport** is served by a multitude of international airlines including **British Airways, Singapore Airlines, Thai Airways, Qantas, Air New Zealand, Cathay Pacific,** and **Air Caledonia.**

Ansett Australia (tel. 07/854–2828 or 13–1300), and **Qantas** (tel. 13–1313), provide regular domestic service between all major cities.

Between the Airport and Center City Brisbane International Airport is located 9 kilometers (6 miles) from the city center. **Coach Trans** (tel. 07/236–1000) provides daily bus service to and from city hotels every 30 minutes between 6 AM and 8 PM. The fare is $6.50 per person.

Taxis to downtown Brisbane cost approximately $20.

Arriving and Departing by Bus, Car, and Train

By Bus Long-distance bus companies serving Brisbane include **Coach Trans** (Brisbane Transit Centre, Roma St., tel. 07/236–1000), **Greyhound Pioneer Australia** (Brisbane Transit Centre, Roma St., tel. 07/840–9350 or 13–2030), and **McCafferty's** (Brisbane Transit Centre, Roma St., tel. 07/236–3033).

By Car Brisbane is located 1,002 kilometers (622 miles) from Sydney along Highway 1. An inland route from Sydney follows Highway 1 to Newcastle and then heads inland on Highway 15.

By Train **Railways of Australia** offers nightly service between Sydney and Brisbane (14 hours). The *Sunlander* and the luxurious *Queenslander* trains make a total of four runs a week between Brisbane and Cairns in the north. Other long-distance passenger trains are the *Capricornian* between Brisbane and Rockhampton (three times a week), the *Inlander* between Townsville and Mt. Isa (twice a week), and the *Midlander* between Rockhampton and Winton (twice a week). Trains depart from the Roma Street Station. For details contact the **Railways Information Centre** (305 Edward St., tel. 07/235–2222) or the **City Booking Office** (tel. 13–2232—no prefix).

Getting Around

By Bus Brisbane has an excellent public transportation system. Buses depart from the **Brisbane Transit Centre,** Roma St. (tel. 07/236–1000), and all bus stops are clearly marked. The **Public Transport Information Centre** (69 Ann St., tel. 07/225–4444) provides details of routes, schedules, and fares.

By Car All major car-rental agencies have offices in Brisbane, including **Avis** (tel. 07/221–2900), **Thrifty** (tel. 07/252–5994), **Hertz** (tel. 07/221–6166 or toll free 008/33–3377), and **Budget** (tel. 13–2727). Four-wheel-drive vehicles are available.

By Taxi Taxis are metered and relatively inexpensive. They are available at designated taxi stands outside hotels, downtown, and at the railway station, although it is usually best to phone for one. The best taxi companies in Brisbane are **Yellow Cabs** (tel. 07/391–0191) and **Black and White Taxis** (tel. 07/238–1000).

Important Addresses and Numbers

Tourist Information The **Queensland Travel Centre** (corner Edward and Adelaide Sts., GPO Box 9958, 4001, tel. 07/221–6111) is an outstanding source for information about Brisbane and other parts of Queensland. For information on Brisbane only, visit a branch of the **Brisbane Visitors and Convention Bureau** (Box 12260, Elizabeth St., 4002, tel. 07/221–8411) at the airport (tel. 07/860–4688), Queens Street Mall (tel. 07/229–5918), or Brisbane City Hall (Adelaide St.). Also recommended is **"Out and About in Brisbane,"** a free pocket guide (available at most hotels) that lists events, services, and attractions in the city.

Emergencies **Royal Brisbane Hospital** (tel. 07/253–8111).

For emergencies requiring the **police, fire department,** or an **ambulance,** dial 000.

Guided Tours

Orientation Tours **Australian Pacific Tours** (3rd Level, Brisbane Transit Centre, Roma St., tel. 07/236–3355) offers an excellent range of half- or full-day tours of Brisbane, as well as trips to the Gold Coast, Noosa Heads, and the Sunshine Coast.

The Brisbane City Council operates **City Sight tours** by open tram-style buses, which make half-hourly circuits of city landmarks and other points of interest. Passengers can get on or off at any of 20 stops. *Brisbane City Council, 69 Ann St., tel. 07/225–4444. Tickets: $10 adults, $8 senior citizens, $8 children. Tours Wed.–Mon. 9–4.*

The **Kookaburra Queen Paddle Wheeler** offers morning or afternoon tea and buffet or à la carte lunch and dinner cruises along the Brisbane River; they often feature live entertainment. *The Eagle Street Pier, Creek and Eagle Sts., tel. 07/221–1300. Tickets: $10–$50 per person.*

Exploring Brisbane

Numbers in the margin correspond to points of interest on the Brisbane map.

Brisbane inner-city landmarks—a combination of Victorian, Edwardian, and slick high-tech architecture—are best explored on ❶ foot. Start at **St. John's Anglican Cathedral** near the corner of Wharf and Ann streets. Built in 1901 of porphyry, the cathedral is a fine example of Gothic-style architecture. Like so many other grand edifices in Australia, however, the building was never completed—the western end remains unfinished. The cathedral offers interesting brass-rubbing workshops on Wednesday and Friday from 10 to 1, or by arrangement.

Inside the cathedral grounds is the **Deanery**, which predates the construction of the cathedral by almost 50 years. The proclamation declaring Queensland separate from New South Wales was read from the building's east balcony on June 6, 1859. The building served as Government House for Queensland for three years after the declaration. Unfortunately, the interior isn't open to the public.

Walk southeast along Wharf Street, across Queen Street, down Ea- ❷ gle Street, and southwest on Elizabeth Street to **St. Stephen's Church,** which adjoins St. Stephen's Catholic Cathedral on Elizabeth Street. Opened in May 1850, this is Brisbane's oldest house of worship and a particularly fine example of neo-Gothic architecture. St. Stephen's Church is no longer open to the public.

❸ One block northwest of the church is the **National Bank Building,** constructed in 1885 and thought to be one of the country's best Italian Renaissance–style structures. Aside from the majestic entrance hall with its ornate ceilings and eye-catching dome, the most interesting features are the front doors, which were crafted from a single cedar log. *308 Queen St., tel. 07/234–5222. Admission free. Open weekdays 9–4.*

❹ Continue southwest along Queen Street for one block to **MacArthur Chambers,** the World War II headquarters of General Douglas MacArthur. As commander-in-chief of the Allied Forces fighting in the Pacific, MacArthur came to Australia from the Philippines, leaving the Japanese in control there but vowing, "I shall return." This is now an office building. *Queen and Edward Sts.*

Head northwest along Edward Street and turn right onto Adelaide ❺ Street. On the left is **Anzac Square and the Shrine of Remembrance,** a memorial erected in 1930 to commemorate Australian soldiers who died in World War I. Walking paths through the square stretch across green lawns, directing all eyes toward the shrine, which is constructed of Queensland sandstone, and its eternally burning flame within. Equally spine-tingling is the **Shrine of Memories,** a crypt below the flame, which stores soil samples labeled "forever Australian" that were collected from battlefields on which Australian soldiers perished. *Adelaide St. Admission free. Open weekdays 11–3.*

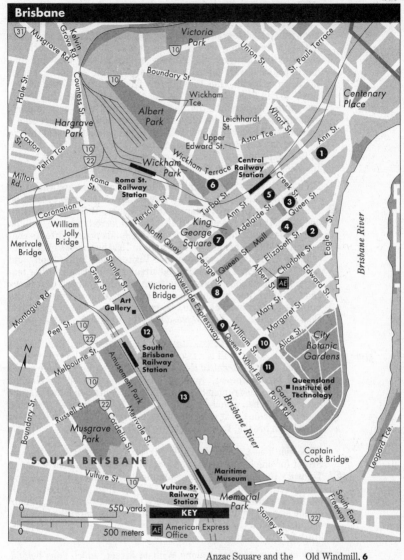

Brisbane

Anzac Square and the Shrine of Remembrance, **5**
Brisbane City Hall, **7**
MacArthur Chambers, **4**
The Mansions, **10**
National Bank Building, **3**
Old Commissariat Store, **9**

Old Windmill, **6**
Parliament House, **11**
Queensland Cultural Centre, **12**
St. John's Anglican Cathedral, **1**
St. Stephen's Church, **2**
South Bank Parklands, **13**
Treasury Building, **8**

KEY

AE American Express Office

0   550 yards
0   500 meters

Return to Edward Street and head northwest to Wickham Terrace.
6 Turn left and follow the street as it curves to the **Old Windmill,** also
known as the Observatory. Built by convicts in 1828, it is the oldest
of the few remaining convict buildings in Brisbane. The poorly designed windmill never worked very well; whenever the wind died
down, convicts were forced to power a treadmill to crush grain for
the colony's bread, thus tagging this landmark the "Tower of Torture." When fire erupted across the city in 1864, scorching almost
everything in its path, the windmill survived with only minimal
damage. Stripped of its blades, the tower now looks more like a
lighthouse. The large copper ball on top of the building used to drop
at 1 PM every day so people could set their watches accurately. As early
as 1930, experimental television broadcasts were beamed from here to
Ipswich, 33 kilometers (20 miles) away. *Wickham Terr.*

Back on Edward Street, walk two blocks southeast and then turn
right onto Adelaide Street. Past David Jones department store and
7 abutting King George Square is the Italianate **Brisbane City Hall,**
one of Australia's largest city halls. Once referred to as the "million
pound town hall" because of the massive funds poured into its construction, this community center built in 1930 has been a major con-
tributor to Brisbane's civic pride. Visitors and locals "ooh" and
"aah" at the grand pipe organ and circular concert hall. Other features include an observation platform affording superb city views
and a ground floor museum and art gallery. You can tour both the
building and its huge clock tower, home to Australia's largest civic
clock. *Adelaide St., tel. 07/225-4404. Admission free. Open weekdays 8-5.*

Time Out The **Queen Street Mall** is a two-block pedestrian boulevard stretching from George Street to Edward Street. It features a wide selection of places to eat, ranging from take-out food to elegant
restaurants. Also remember that the **David Jones** department store
(on the mall) has a well-stocked food hall, where you can assemble
your own picnic to eat in nearby King George Square with locals on
their lunch breaks. Public toilets are available.

Walk southwest along Adelaide Street and turn left on George
Street for one block, where you won't miss the prominently placed
8 **Treasury Building** and its surrounding bronze figurative statuary.
Constructed of sandstone between 1885 and 1928, this massive Italian Renaissance Revival edifice, which is closed to the public, stands
on the site of the officers' quarters and military barracks from the
original penal settlement. Plans are now afoot to return it to its mon-
etary function—albeit as a casino, not a treasury.

Now continue southeast along William Street, which runs behind
9 the Treasury Building, to the **Old Commissariat Store** on the next
block. Constructed by convicts in 1829, this was the first stone
building in Brisbane and has previously served as a customs house,
storehouse, and immigrants' shelter. Currently the headquarters of
the Royal Historical Society of Queensland, it is built on the spot
where Brisbane's original timber wharf was located. *115 William
St., tel. 07/221-4198. Admission: $1 adults, 50¢ senior citizens, 30¢
children. Open Tues.-Fri. 11-2, Sun. 11-4.*

Continue southeast along William Street before turning left onto
10 Margaret Street and then right onto George Street. **The Mansions,**
constructed in 1890, were originally six fashionable town houses.
Recently restored, these splendid Victorian terrace houses with elegant wrought-iron lace are now home to the National Trust gift

shop, restaurants, bookshops, and professional offices. *40 George St., tel. 07/221–1887. Open weekdays 10–4.*

Directly across Alice Street and set among tropical palms is **①** **Parliament House,** a splendid example of French Renaissance architecture, which earned its colonial designer a meager 200-guinea salary. Opened in 1868, this handsome building, with its imposing stone facade and roof made of Mt. Isa copper, has recently been restored to its original glory and a new legislative annex added. The interior is filled with polished timber, brass, and frosted and engraved glass. If State Parliament is sitting, you can observe the action from the visitors gallery. *George and Alice Sts., tel. 07/226–7111. Free group tours on sitting days, 10:30 and 2:30, and on nonsitting days at 10:30, 11:15, noon, 1:45, 2:30, and 3:15.*

Wander through the City Botanic Gardens adjacent to Parliament House, and then return along George Street to Queen Street and walk over Victoria Bridge. Across the Brisbane River, the glitzy **②** **Queensland Cultural Centre** extends for a block on either side of Melbourne Street. This sleek complex incorporates the Queensland Art Gallery, the Queensland Museum, the State Library, the Performing Arts Complex, and a host of restaurants, cafés, and shops. On weekdays at noon there are free tours of the Performing Arts Complex, the site of the 2,000-seat Concert Hall and Cremorne Theatre, where backstage peeks are often included. *Stanley St. Queensland Art Gallery: tel. 07/840–7303. Admission free. Open daily 10–5, Wed. 10–8. Queensland Museum: tel. 07/840–7601. Admission free. Open daily 9–5, Wed. 9–8. State Library: tel. 07/840–7785. Admission free. Open Mon.–Thurs. 10–8, Fri.–Sun. 10–5. Performing Arts Complex: tel. 07/840–7482 or toll-free 008/77–7699.*

In 1992 the Brisbane World Expo '88 site, located just south of the **③** Cultural Centre along the river, reopened as **South Bank Parklands,** one of the most appealing urban parks in Australia. In it you can experience various ecosystems: The Gondwana Rainforest Sanctuary re-creates a Queensland rain forest (complete with a 12-meter/40-foot-high waterfall), and Our World Environment takes you from a hot, dry desert to the frozen Antarctic—you can even find out what it's like to get caught in a fishing driftnet. Aside from many shops and restaurants, the 16-hectare complex encompasses a live-butterfly house, an artificial beach beside a swimming lagoon, a Nepalese-style carved-wood pagoda, and cycling paths, and provides excellent views of the city center. A tiny ferry called *South Ship* plies the waterways of the park; one complete ride takes 25 minutes. *Tel. 07/867–2000; entertainment information: 07/867–2020. Admission free. Open daily 5 AM–midnight. Gondwana Rainforest Sanctuary: Admission: $8 adults, $7 senior citizens, $5.50 children. Open daily 10–5:30. Our World Environment: Admission: $6 adults, $5 children and senior citizens. Open daily 10–5. Butterfly House: Admission: $6 adults, $3 children, $4.50 senior citizens. Open daily 10–4. South Ship: Day pass: $5 adults, $3 children.*

What to See and Do with Children

Lone Pine Koala Sanctuary is probably Queensland's most famous fauna park. Founded in 1927, it claims to be the oldest animal sanctuary in the world. The real attraction for most visitors is the koalas, although there are also emus, wombats, and kangaroos. Some of the animals can be petted, and for a small extra charge visitors can have a quick cuddle and their photo snapped with a trained koala. *Jesmond Rd., Fig Tree Pocket, tel. 07/222–7278. Admission: $10* *adults, $7 senior citizens, $6 children 12–17. Open daily 8:45–5. Closed Dec. 25.*

Cruise boats travel to the Lone Pine Koala Sanctuary from North Quay next to the Victoria Bridge. *Mirimar Cruises, tel. 07/221–0300. Tickets: $15 adults, $8 children 3–13, $13 senior citizens. Cruises daily.*

Australian Woolshed presents a real slice of Australiana that is fascinating for both children and adults. In a one-hour stage show, the performers are eight rams from the major sheep breeds found in Australia. This is not a circus, however, but an opportunity to gain insight into the dramatically different appearances—and personalities—of sheep. There is also a koala sanctuary; for a fee of $6.50, you can be photographed holding a koala. Barbecue lunches are available, and there is an extensive craft shop. Australian Woolshed can be reached by train to Ferny Grove Station or by taxi (about a $14 ride). *148 Samford Rd., Ferny Hills, tel. 07/351–5366. Tickets: $9 adults, $4 children. Shows daily 11, 2.*

Off the Beaten Track

Watch kernels pop and puff at the **Popcorn Factory,** Australia's largest popcorn manufacturer. Overhead walkways allow you to view the entire process; then you can select your favorite at the on-site confectionary shop. *358 Nudgee Rd., Hendra, tel. 07/268–4877. Admission free. Open weekdays 8–6.*

Shopping

Malls   The **Queen Street Mall,** which includes the **Wintergarden Complex,** is considered the best downtown shopping area, with numerous buskers, flower stalls, and a generally festive atmosphere. **Myer Centre** (Queen, Elizabeth, and Albert Sts.) houses the national department store of the same name, as well as boutiques, specialty shops, delis, restaurants, cinemas, and an upstairs amusement park. Other worthwhile shopping areas are **Rowes Arcade** (235 Edward St.), a renovated 1920s ballroom and banquet hall; **Post Office Square** (280 Queen St.), a modern complex adjacent to Rowes Arcade; **The Pavilion** (Queen and Albert Sts.), with two levels of exclusive shops; the **T&G Arcade** (141 Queen St.), a less-hurried area of speciality shops and restaurants; **Savoire Faire** (20 Park Rd., Milton), an upscale shopping area 10 minutes from the business district; and **Chopstix** (249 Brunswick St., Fortitude Valley), a collection of 20 Asian shops and restaurants in the heart of Chinatown.

Department   The famous **David Jones** and **Myer** department stores are located
Stores   downtown on Queen Street.

Markets   The Riverside Centre (123 Eagle St.) is home to the **Cat's Tango Riverside Markets,** an upscale arts and crafts market, which is open Sunday 8–4.

Paddy's Market (Florence and Commercial Rds., New Farm) features everything from fresh fruits and vegetables to secondhand bric-a-brac and is open daily 9–4.

Specialty   **Queensland Aboriginal Creations** (135 George St., tel. 07/224–5730)
Stores   specializes in genuine Aboriginal hunting and returning boomer-
Aboriginal   angs, woomeras, spears, didgeridoos, bark paintings, pottery, and
Crafts   carvings.

Antiques **Cordelia Street Antique and Art Centre** (Cordelia and Glenelg Sts., tel. 07/844–8514), housed inside an old church, offers an interesting range of antiques and jewelry.

Brisbane Antique Market (791 Sandgate Rd., Clayfield, tel. 07/262–1444), near the airport, showcases more than 40 dealers' antiques, collectibles, and jewelry under one roof.

Australian **Baa Baa Black Sheep** (Brisbane Arcade, Queen St. Mall, tel. 07/221–
Products 0484) features high-quality pure Australian wool sweaters and other knitwear. Overseas shipping is available.

Craftsman's Collections (Broadway on the Mall, 133 Adelaide St., tel. 07/229–0541) stocks a large selection of arts and crafts hand-made by Australian artisans.

Greg Grant Country Clothing (Myer Centre, Queen St., tel. 07/221–4233) specializes in Driza-bone oilskin coats, Akubra and leather hats, whips, R. M. Williams boots, and moleskins.

Opals **Quilpie Opals** (Lennons Hotel, 68 Queen St. Mall, tel. 07/221–7369) offers a large selection of Queensland boulder opals as well as a selection of high-grade opals, available as individual stones or already set.

Souvenirs **The National Trust Gift Shop** (The Mansions, 40 George St., tel. 07/221–1887) specializes in quality Australian-made handicrafts, plus postcards, books, and novelty items.

Participant Sports

The sporting clubs and associations listed below welcome overseas visitors and waive membership requirements when possible. You must telephone ahead, however, to make arrangements.

Golf To play a round of golf at one of the city's premier courses contact **Indooroopilly Golf Club** (Meiers Rd., Indooroopilly, tel. 07/870–3728) or **Royal Queensland Golf Club** (Curtin Ave., Eagle Farm, tel. 07/268–1127).

Fishing Advice about fishing trips and local regulations can be obtained from the **Moreton Bay Game Fishing Club** (31 Goodwin St., Bulimba, tel. 07/399–1533).

Tennis For information about playing at Brisbane's municipal or private courts or for details of upcoming tournaments, contact **Queensland Lawn Tennis Association** (316 Milton Rd., Milton, tel. 07/369–5325).

Walking The National Trust puts out an informative Historic Walks brochure that is available from the Queensland Government Travel Centre (corner Edward and Adelaide Sts., tel. 07/221–6111) and some hotels.

Spectator Sports

Cricket **Queensland Cricketers Club** (Vulture St., E. Brisbane, tel. 07/391–6533) provides playing schedules and ticket information for the nation's favorite sport.

Rugby Rugby League, a professional game that is a variation of rugby, is played in winter at **Lang Park** (Castlemaine St., Milton, tel. 07/223–0444). Rugby Union, a game more familiar to Americans, is played at **Ballymore** (Clyde Rd., Herston, tel. 07/356–7222).

Dining

By Jacki Passmore

Jacki Passmore is the author of cookbooks published worldwide and the food writer for the Courier Mail *and* Sunday Mail, *Brisbane's leading newspapers.*

Brisbane's restaurants offer superb dining in a relaxed atmosphere. Menus are influenced by the Mediterranean-Asian flavors that are the basis of Australia's new cuisine, by Queensland's excellent seafood, and by native meats such as kangaroo and crocodile. Outdoor seating areas, which capitalize on the almost year-round warm weather, are common. Neat, casual attire usually suffices, but a jacket and tie are recommended for those dining in the finer hotel restaurants. You may have to bring your own alcoholic beverages (BYOB), which can often be purchased from hotel bottle shops. Most restaurants have smoking restrictions.

Highly recommended restaurants are indicated by a star ★.

Category	Cost*
$$$$	over $50
$$$	$40–$50
$$	$30–$40
$	under $30

*per person, excluding drinks and service

Asian
$$ **Michael's Oriental Restaurant.** The 20-minute trek out to this lilac-hued restaurant is easily justified by a snappy mix of Malay, Chinese, and Thai dishes and the likelihood of dining with local celebs. After you taste the wisps of crisp honey-dipped beef, the steamed whole coral trout with garlic and chilies, or the tongue-teasing *lembu rendang* curry, you may even want to stay late for a karaoke session. *Sunnybank Plaza Shopping Centre, Mains Rd., Sunnybank, tel. 07/344–2888. Reservations required weekends. Dress: casual but neat. AE, DC, MC, V. No lunch weekends.*

$$ **Oriental Bangkok.** Only a pleasant 20-minute walk from the central business district, this Thai restaurant serves meals as good as any in Bangkok. Begin with a sour hot soup or a creamy chicken soup with Thai ginger, then try a selection of curries and salads. The seafood salad is a sensation of complementary citrus flavors and fresh prawns, and the roast duck curry and the whole coral trout Thai style are unforgettable entrées. The staff recommends a slightly sweet and fruity wine of the gewürztraminer style to complement the hot and spicy curries. *454 Upper Edward St., tel. 07/832–6010. Reservations advised. Dress: casual but neat. AE, DC, MC, V. No lunch Sat.; closed Sun.*

$ **Vung Tao Seafood Restaurant.** Large tanks of live fish, crabs, and lobsters provide the raw material for some of the best seafood in Brisbane, but it's the dim sum—called *yum cha* in Australia—that draws huge crowds to this Chinatown restaurant. This traditional Cantonese brunch cuisine is both inexpensive and a great deal of fun. Trolleys heavily laden with dozens of different little buns, dumplings, meatballs, and assorted crisply fried seafood nibbles are continually wheeled about the restaurant; diners pick their favorites as they roll by. Try the plump shrimp dumplings, shark-fin dumplings, and combination dumplings of peanuts and vegetables in semitransparent rice dough. *149 Wickham St., Fortitude Valley (Chinatown), tel. 07/252–9810. Reservations required weekends. Dress: casual. AE, DC, MC, V.*

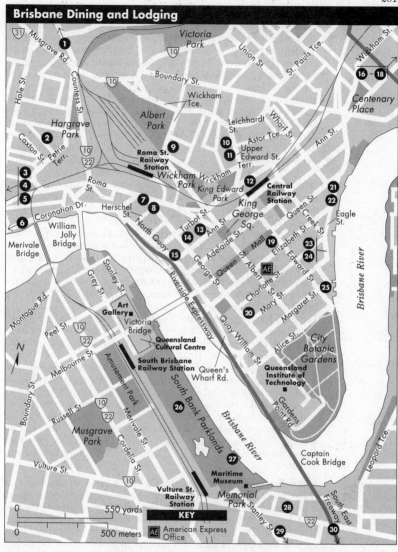

Brisbane Dining and Lodging

Dining

About Face, **1**

Daniel's Steakhouse, **2**

Fiasco's, **14, 29**

Il Centro, **23**

Le Bronx BYO Restaurant, **17**

Mediterraneao, **2**

Michael's Oriental Restaurant, **30**

Michael's Riverside, **22**

Ned Kelly's Bushtucker Restaurant, **27**

Oriental Bangkok , **11**

Oxley's on the River, **6**

Park Road Brasserie, **3**

Peperina's Restaurant and Tapas Bar, **4**

Pier 9 Oyster Bar and Seafood Grill, **24**

Restaurant Baguette, **16**

Siggi's at the Port Office, **25**

Sirocco Mediterranean Cafe, **26**

Tables of Toowong, **5**

Victoria's, **19**

Vung Tao Seafood Restaurant, **18**

Lodging

All Seasons Abbey, **8**

Annie's Shandon Inn, **10**

Beaufort Heritage, **25**

Bellevue Hotel, **20**

Brisbane City Travelodge, **7**

Brisbane Hilton, **19**

Gateway Hotel Brisbane, **15**

Gazebo Hotel, **9**

Hillcrest Central Apartments, **28**

Mayfair Crest International Hotel, **13**

Sheraton, **12**

Australian
$$$$
★

Victoria's. This elegant hotel restaurant offers one of Brisbane's finest dining experiences: There's an award-winning team in the kitchen, a wine list to compete with the best in the country, comfortable furnishings at large, well-spaced tables, and impeccable yet friendly service. The modern Australian cuisine combines classic cooking techniques with seasonal produce and Asian and Mediterranean ingredients. Look for the smoked and sugar-cured Tasmanian salmon and the outstanding rare roasted pigeon stuffed with tasso ham and served with glazed pears and kumquats. *Brisbane Hilton, Queen Street Mall, Brisbane, tel. 07/231–3131. Reservations required. Jacket and tie advised. AE, DC, MC, V. No lunch Sat.; closed Sun.*

$$$
★

About Face. Andrew Mirosh, one of Brisbane's finest young chefs, went out on his own in 1992 and opened this brilliantly innovative restaurant in a former tavern dating from 1878. The Pacific Rim menu, which melds Asian, French, and even Australian influences, changes weekly. For appetizers, consider the duckling wontons flavored with coriander, or the sautéed squid with chili on basil risotto; star entrées include a seared milk-fed veal liver on sweet potato puree with avocado, and a chargrilled fillet of kangaroo with orange and Grand Marnier *jus.* Leave room for one of the sensational desserts. The restaurant is a 10-minute drive from the city center. *252 Kelvin Grove Rd., Kelvin Grove, tel. 07/356–8605. Reservations necessary (reserve 1 wk ahead for weekdays, 1 month ahead for weekends). Dress: casual but neat. AE, DC, MC, V. BYOB. No lunch Mon.–Thurs. and Sat.; closed Sun.*

$$$
★

Tables of Toowong. Chef Russell Armstrong's irrepressible culinary imagination—coupled with bold use of Asian spices, French technique, and fine local produce—place him on the cutting edge of modern Australian cuisine. Hope that his confit of duck over lightly curried lentils or his grilled lamb fillet with Eastern-spiced sabayon (a wine custard sauce) are on the menu. Even his desserts are like an edible fireworks display, a spectacular explosion of color and flavor. All this bounty resides in a tastefully converted, Queenslander-style wooden house in a quiet suburb about 15 minutes from the city center. Bring along a top Australian wine to round out the meal. *85 Miskin St., Toowong, tel. 07/371–4558. Reservations required. Dress: casual. AE, DC, MC, V. BYOB. Lunch Fri. only; closed Sun. and Mon.*

Australian
Rustic
$$

Ned Kelly's Bushtucker Restaurant. Besides the landscaped ecosystems, South Bank Parklands includes a host of eateries on the riverfront boardwalk directly across from the city center. Among them is Ned Kelly's, Brisbane's only authentic bushtucker restaurant and steakhouse. The outback-theme, wood and corrugated-iron building sets the stage for a menu of Australian game meats—kangaroo, crocodile, buffalo, and emu—which are chargrilled as steaks or kebabs. Bushmen's meals such as steak-and-kidney pie, barbecued Moreton Bay bugs (a type of lobster), and dumplings in golden syrup supplement the huge, sizzling slabs. Adventuresome macadamia-nut enthusiasts will appreciate the flavor of witchetty grubs, a kind of moth larvae, made into ice cream or pan-grilled at the table for dessert. *Boardwalk, South Bank Parklands, South Brisbane, tel. 07/846–1880. Reservations accepted. Dress: casual. AE, DC, MC, V.*

Brasserie
$

Fiasco's. The dining and bar area of the decrepit Morrison Hotel was imaginatively refurbished by a Queensland restaurateur and is now one of the hippest spots in town. The menu owes its focus to a wood-fire pizza oven, which turns out thin-crusted pies topped with Cajun chicken, smoked salmon, or Thai marinated meats, as well as rolled focaccia with fillings as cross-cultural as the clientele. This original Fiasco's is still on the south side; a second, larger branch recently opened at North Quay and Turbot Street just a few minutes from downtown. *640 Stanley St., South Brisbane, tel. 07/391–1413. Reservations required. Dress: casual. AE, DC, MC, V. Closed Sun. and early Jan.*

$ **Park Road Brasserie.** There's a Louisiana-born chef in the kitchen of this bright and lively brasserie in Park Road, one of the city's bubbliest entertainment areas. Attention-grabbing decor is matched by equally bold Cajun food. Start your meal with fresh focaccia or corn bread baked in terra-cotta, some snappy jalapeño fritters, or barbecued andouille. The powerfully flavored blackened meats and seafood are tasty if you like your entrées hot; if you want to stay cool, head outdoors and enjoy the passing parade over American pork ribs, bowls of pasta, cappuccino, or decadent white chocolate and coconut cream pie. Nonsmokers have the box seats at the front of the house indoors. *Savoir Faire Mall, 16 Park Rd., Milton, tel. 07/367–0144. Reservations advised weekends. Dress: casual. AE, DC, MC, V.*

French **Le Bronx BYO Restaurant.** The cooking style at this elegant bistro, a
$$ consistent award winner, has swung toward the Mediterranean
★ since David Speck took over the kitchen in 1994. This exciting young chef may surprise you with his composition and ingredients. Bring some excellent wine, and look for innovative combinations such as grilled tuna on balsamic tomato sauce or blackened kangaroo salad with rocket and cress peanut vinaigrette. Desserts are equally sensational; try the citrus sauternes cake with chocolate marmalade ice cream. *722 Brunswick St., New Frome, tel. 07/358–2088. Reservations required. Dress: casual but neat. AE, DC, MC, V. BYOB. Closed Sun. and Mon.*

International **Michael's Riverside.** Sleek decor, a location in the financial district,
$$$$ and a sweeping view of the Brisbane River make this restaurant a favorite of businessmen and ladies-who-lunch. An unusual touch is the trolley of fresh, beautifully arranged seafood that's wheeled to your table along with the menu so you can pick what you're going to eat. Try a collage of Queensland seafood or the mud crab claws steamed with black beans, ginger, and shallots. No worries about BYOB here: Michael's has perhaps the best wine cellar in town. The adjoining café, Marco's, offers inexpensive dining in the Mediterranean-Italian tradition. *Riverside Centre, 123 Eagle St., Brisbane, tel. 07/832–5522. Reservations required. Jacket and tie advised (Marco's more casual). AE, DC, MC, V. No lunch Sat.; closed Sun.*

$$$$ **Siggi's at the Port Office.** Socialites rub shoulders with visiting celebrities and high-powered businesspeople at this award-winning restaurant in the luxurious Beaufort Heritage Hotel. As befits the restaurant's setting, the service is impeccable and the decor of the adjoining dining and bar areas is warm, welcoming, and supremely comfortable. The compact, French-inspired menu changes frequently and is supplemented on Wednesday and Thursday evenings with a tasting menu that lets you sample many small courses. Look for the creamy cappuccino of lobster—a frothy soup served in a demitasse—and roasted Rannoch quail, served on sautéed Asian greens with a spicy shiitake mushroom *jus*. Desserts are just as devilishly rich. *Edward and Margaret Sts., tel. 07/221–4555. Reservations required. Jacket and tie advised. AE, DC, MC, V. No lunch; closed Sun. and Mon.*

$$ **Oxley's on the River.** A five-minute taxi ride from the city center takes you to the only restaurant in Brisbane that's built right on the

river. By day the dining room is sun filled and has a bird's-eye view of the river traffic; by night, light from the city and the moon dimple the water and lend an intimate, romantic ambience. Traditional Oxley's chargrilled New York–cut sirloin, Queensland barramundi or mud crab, and fillets of coral trout stuffed with a ragout of seafood are all rightly famed. *330 Coronation Dr., Milton, tel. 07/368–1866. Reservations advised Fri. and Sat. Dress: casual but neat. AE, DC, MC, V.*

Italian
$$
★

Il Centro. No expense has been spared in creating this handsome Eagle Street Pier eatery with gleaming wood floors, terra-cotta and dark blue tiles, and enormous windows that take advantage of the river view. Wondrous aromas spill out of an open kitchen into the stylish, buzzy dining room—while perusing the menu of modern Italian-influenced cuisine, you may need to put in an urgent order for an individual pizza. Enticing *primi piatti* include peppered, rare tuna with kalamata olive vinaigrette, and a warm autumn salad of forest mushrooms, asparagus, fennel, and the endive known as witlof. While sand-crab lasagna has become a signature dish for chef Gillian Hirst, don't ignore the veal kidneys with balsamic vinegar and polenta or the lamb loin with caramelized garlic, both of which explode with flavor. *Eagle Street Pier, Waterfront Pl., tel. 07/221– 6090. Reservations advised on weekends. Dress: casual but neat. AE, DC, MC, V. No lunch Sat.*

Mediterranean
$$$$
★

Restaurant Baguette. Located in a fashionable suburb that's something of a dining mecca, Baguette has been a star on the Brisbane culinary scene for almost two decades. This success is due to an enterprising wine list, professional service in the French tradition, and a menu of updated French classics. The upscale dining room, which doubles as an art gallery, overlooks an orchid-filled tropical garden. The lush surroundings enhance the rich Asian and Mediterranean undertones of such dishes as chargrilled quail on a bed of citrus-flavored couscous. Renditions of duck are equally superb; try the breast of Thirlmere farm duck dressed with warm mustard seed salad and Tassie gold potatoes. In 1993 a semialfresco bistro was attached to the front of the main dining room; this casual, less pricey spot serves such delectables as Marseilles-style seafood soup with a nose-teasing saffron broth. *150 Racecourse Rd., Ascot, tel. 07/268– 6168. Reservations required. Dress: casual but neat. AE, DC, MC, V.*

$$
★

Peperina's Restaurant and Tapas Bar. Jose and Ali Fernandes run the only genuine tapas bar in town. This charming, Spanish-style restaurant with terra-cotta flagstones and white stucco walls is a short taxi ride from the city heart. The glass-enclosed courtyard is a favorite among lunching businesspeople, and nonsmokers appreciate the three casually elegant dining rooms. On balmy nights the best tables are outdoors under the peperina trees. Order a bottle of La Rioja and savor rosemary-seared baby lamb cutlets, grilled Spanish sausage, or barbecued sardines with lemon and garlic while seated under the stars. *140 Sylvan Rd., Toowong, tel. 07/870–9981. Reservations advised weekends. Dress: casual but neat. AE, DC, MC, V. No smoking indoors. No lunch Sat.; closed Sun. and early Jan.*

$$

Sirocco Mediterranean Cafe. No kitsch Mediterraneanism has gone unused in the decor of this South Bank Parklands eatery, from custom-glazed tiles and stencil-decorated chairs to faux-stucco walls and an open charcoal grill pit. Nonetheless, yuppies vie to be seen in the more nautical outdoor area noshing on slivers of pita dipped into *melitzanosaláta* (eggplant dip). Heartier options include souvlaki, marinated baby octopus, and *tsigano kleftiko* (a huge homemade sausage stuffed with spicy meats, nuts, and orange zest). *South Bank Parklands, S. Brisbane, tel. 07/846–1803. Reservations advised. Dress: casual. AE, DC, MC, V.*

$ **Mediterraneao.** This bright addition to the Brisbane restaurant scene has a breezy ambience. The sunny yellow walls are hung with evocative paintings, and a fleet of aluminum and wood-veneer furniture sits in the cobbled courtyard to the rear. In fine weather, the retractable roof opens the courtyard to the sky. Start with a generous Caesar salad or oysters served chilled in shot glasses with tequila and lime juice. A traditional, wood-fired, brick-and-stucco oven churns out wafer-crisp pizzas with exotic toppings. The compact, moderately priced wine list highlights good Australian and Italian wines. *25 Caxton St., Petric Terr., tel. 07/368–1933. Dress: casual. Reservations advised for courtyard on summer weekends. AE, DC, MC, V.*

Seafood **Pier 9 Oyster Bar and Seafood Grill.** The city's brightest and best-
$$–$$$ looking seafood place prepares a host of fish dishes, from fish-and-
★ chips to lobsters, in considerable style. The dining room's big glass walls admit plenty of sunshine and provide an outstanding view of the river. The menu changes frequently to reflect the availability of seafood. Only the best of the catch from the Northern Territory to Tasmania is served here, with several types of fresh oysters delivered daily and shucked to order. Marinated seviche and tartare of gravlax are made on the premises. Blackened barramundi is a particular favorite among Brisbane diners. There is a sizable list of Australian wines, with four or five always available by the glass. *Eagle Street Pier, Waterfront Pl., tel. 07/229–2194. Reservations advised. Dress: casual but neat. AE, DC, MC, V.*

Steakhouses **Daniel's Steakhouse.** These steaks are very big, very tasty, and rea-
$$ sonably priced, considering the top quality. Only folks with large appetites need to order appetizers, but if you haven't eaten for a couple of days, you might like to try the oysters, pâté, avocado, smoked Tasmanian trout, marinated barbecued prawns, or prawns deep-fried with mango sauce as a prelude to your steak. The dining room, decorated with Aboriginal art, has a fine view of the river. *145 Eagle St., tel. 07/832–3444. Reservations required. Dress: casual but neat. AE, DC, MC, V. Closed weekends.*

Lodging

Highly recommended lodgings are indicated by a star ★.

Category	Cost*
$$$$	over $200
$$$	$100–$200
$$	$60–$100
$	under $60

All prices are for a standard double room.

$$$$ **Beaufort Heritage.** Located on the riverfront next to the City
★ Botanic Gardens, this is one of Brisbane's newest hotels. Its soaring lobby, with artworks, flower arrangements, and an expanse of natural woods, is warm and inviting, and is already a popular gathering spot. Guest rooms, at least the equals of those on the Sheraton Towers floors, are decorated in neo-classical style in muted pastel

yellows and beiges, and come equipped with VCR, CD player, television in the bathroom, and the services of a butler (one for each of the 21 floors). Every room has clear views over the river. The staff's attention to detail is already legendary; if you require a fax machine in your room, your fax number will be the same on subsequent visits. The hotel's signature restaurant, Siggi's (*see* Dining, *above*), features one of Queensland's best wine cellars. *Cnr. Edward and Margaret Sts., tel. 07/221–1999 or 008/77–3700, fax 07/221–6895 or 008/ 77–3900. 232 rooms with bath, 20 suites. Facilities: 3 restaurants, 3 bars, heated pool, spa, sauna, gym. AE, DC, MC, V.*

$$$$ **Brisbane Hilton.** Designed by award-winning Australian architect Harry Seidler, the 25-story building features an eye-catching curved design and the largest atrium in the Southern Hemisphere. All rooms open onto the atrium and are spacious, well-appointed, and feature small sitting areas. The Queen Street Mall is located just a block away, and the Wintergarden shopping center is housed on the first three floors of the hotel. *190 Elizabeth St., 4000, tel. 07/ 231–3131, fax 07/231–3199. 322 rooms with bath. Facilities: outdoor heated pool, tennis court, Nautilus health club, 3 restaurants, 5 bars, disco/supper club. AE, DC, MC, V.*

$$$$ **Sheraton.** Despite its position directly above the city's main com-
★ muter station, this high-rise hotel is a quiet and extremely pleasant place to stay. The mezzanine lobby features a travertine marble floor, complemented by plenty of brass and natural timber, and there is a spectacular skylight atrium. Floors 27 through 29 constitute the pricier Sheraton Towers, where service and comfort are extended to include personalized registration, use of the exclusive Towers Club lounge on the 27th floor, and full use of the facilities on the lower floors. Decorated in soft pastels, the rooms in both sections of the hotel are spacious and elegant, with marble bathrooms and small sitting areas. *249 Turbot St., 4000, tel. 07/835–3535, fax 07/835–4960. 392 rooms with bath, 26 suites. Facilities: 3 restaurants, 5 lounges, shops, beauty salon. AE, DC, MC, V.*

$$$ **All Seasons Abbey.** Located opposite the Transit Centre, this 16-floor hotel is a five-minute walk from the city center. The lobby, which overlooks a tropical garden, makes extensive use of black marble, leather sofas, and original works by leading Aboriginal artists. The "Club Premiere" section of the hotel is designed for business-people, and secretarial services are provided upon request. With its interconnecting suites, the "Superior" section of the hotel is popular with families. The suites themselves are cool and inviting, decorated in soft creams enlivened by ivory and blue tapestries. *160 Roma St., 4000, tel. 07/236–1444 or toll-free 008/77–7911, fax 07/ 236–1134. 88 suites. Facilities: heated pool, sauna, Jacuzzi, exercise area, coffee lounge. AE, DC, MC, V.*

$$$ **Brisbane City Travelodge.** Located in the Brisbane Transit Centre and just a short walk from the business district, this 18-story hotel caters to businesspeople. The hotel's dark-glass exterior is rather lackluster, but the use of wicker in the lounge area gives the lobby a distinctive Queensland flavor. The hotel's Verandah Café is open and airy; the Drawing Room Restaurant is formal and elegant; and the Jazz 'n' Blues Club is a casual and locally popular lounge for drinks and live music. Furnished in shades of beige and blue, the guest rooms are unusually large and comfortable, and all feature air-conditioning and color TVs. Standard double rooms have queen-size beds; king studios have king-size beds. *Roma and Hershel Sts., 4000, tel. 07/238–2222, fax 07/238–2288. 191 rooms with bath. Facilities: 2 licensed restaurants, 3 bars, sauna, 2 whirlpools, sun deck, laundry. AE, DC, MC, V.*

$$$ **Gazebo Hotel.** Set on the crest of Spring Hill, this terraced hotel of-

fers magnificent views of the city from all rooms. The area around the hotel is quiet, although the city center is within easy walking distance. Nearby Albert Park has a jogging track, and the Victoria Park Golf Course is just 1 kilometer (½ mile) north. The hotel foyer is distinctly modern, with high ceilings, soft peach carpets, gray leather sofas, and glass tables. Rooms are air-conditioned and decorated in peaches and grays, with cane headboards, writing desks, and private balconies. Each room overlooks the city through a floor-to-ceiling glass wall. *345 Wickham Terr., 4000, tel. 07/831–6177, fax 07/832–5919. 180 rooms with bath. Facilities: pool, restaurant, bistro, sidewalk café. AE, DC, MC, V.*

$$$ **Mayfair Crest International Hotel.** Located opposite City Hall in the
★ center of town, this hotel consists of two white-brick towers. The hotel's ground level, with alfresco cafés and tropical palms, has an informal Queensland atmosphere. The lobby, however, is from another time and place altogether, with hanging medieval tapestries, paintings, bronze statues, and a huge chandelier as its centerpiece. Guest rooms are furnished in pastel tones, with modern furniture and queen-size beds. All rooms feature minibars, refrigerators, and in-house movies. *Ann and Roma Sts., 4000, tel. 07/229–9111 or toll-free 008/77–7123, fax 07/229–9618. 406 rooms with bath, 36 suites. Facilities: 2 outdoor pools, saunas, restaurant, 6 bars. AE, DC, MC, V.*

$$ **Bellevue Hotel.** The rooms in this modern, multistory hotel are rather plain, but the location in the heart of Brisbane is hard to beat. Despite their lack of character, rooms have a large number of amenities, including air-conditioning, color TVs, refrigerators, and tea/coffee makers. *103 George St., 4000, tel. 07/221–6044, fax 07/221–7474. 100 rooms with bath. Facilities: pool, restaurant, coffee shop, laundry. AE, DC, MC, V.*

$$ **Gateway Hotel Brisbane.** Set in a modern brick building overlooking the Brisbane River and the Queensland Cultural Centre, this 13-story hotel is just a five-minute walk from the city center. The lobby is bright and airy, with comfortable sofas, mirrored walls, and lush greenery. Rooms are air-conditioned and pleasantly furnished in soft grays, blues, and peaches. Each room features a small sitting area decorated with modern cane furniture, as well as a refrigerator and minibar. *85–87 N. Quay, 4000, tel. 07/236–3300, fax 07/236–1035. 175 rooms with bath. Facilities: pool, whirlpool, sauna, 2 restaurants, 2 bars, coffee shop, laundry. AE, DC, MC, V.*

$$ **Hillcrest Central Apartments.** This nine-story cream building has magnificent river and city views from its location close to the Performing Arts Complex, Art Gallery, and Museum. The lobby is light and delicate, decorated in green with hints of pink and peach. Apartments have modern Italian decor in pale shades of yellow and blue-gray, with sliding glass doors leading onto private balconies. Each apartment is air-conditioned and features a fully equipped kitchen and color TV. Large family units with two bedrooms are available, as well as studios and one-bedroom apartments that can sleep as many as six people. *311 Vulture St., S. Brisbane, 4000, tel. 07/846–3000 or toll-free 008/07–7777, fax 07/846–3578. 32 two-bedroom apartments with bath and kitchen, 24 one-bedroom apartments with bath and kitchen, 8 studios with bath and kitchen, 16 rooms with bath. Facilities: pool, sauna, whirlpool, restaurant, tennis court, game room, laundry. AE, DC, MC, V.*

$ **Annie's Shandon Inn.** A five-minute walk from the railway station,
★ this small, modern, no-frills motel features pleasant rooms decorated with Laura Ashley wallpaper and linen. Tour buses conve-

niently stop outside. *405 Upper Edward St., 4000, tel. 07/831–8684, fax 07/831–3073. 19 rooms, 5 with bath. AE, MC, V.*

The Arts and Nightlife

The Arts Concerts, ballet, opera, theater, jazz, and other events are listed in the Saturday edition of the *Courier Mail* newspaper.

The **Performing Arts Complex** and **Art Gallery,** the city's cultural heart, host both international and Australian entertainers and performing troupes, as well as a good range of permanent and visiting art exhibitions. A listing of events is available at the **Cultural Centre** (Stanley St., tel. 07/840–7200) and most of the better hotels.

Nightlife **Friday's** caters to a sophisticated clientele in the thirty-something age group. Overlooking the Brisbane River, the club has three bars, three restaurants, and a nightclub with live music on Friday, Saturday, and Sunday nights. *123 Eagle St., tel. 07/832–2122. Admission: $4–$7. Open daily 11 AM–4 AM.*

Transformers draws a younger and more hip crowd than Friday's. Housed in an old electricity station, the club has four bars and a two-floor disco—with airplane wings and other props hanging from the ceiling, as well as pieces of old transformers and generators. *127 Charlotte St., tel. 07/221–5555. Admission: $6. Open Thurs.–Sat. 8 PM–5 AM.*

The **Breakfast Creek Hotel** is a classic old Australian pub that has hardly changed during the last century. Popular with bluecollar workers, the bar serves pub food and steaks. There is a restaurant in the garden outside. *2 Kingsford-Smith Dr., Breakfast Creek, tel. 07/262–5988. Open daily 10–10.*

The Gold Coast

For many years, this was the fastest growing playground in Australia. As a result, skyscraper condominiums jostle for waterfront positions, often casting giant shadows onto the beaches, and the streets are lined with souvenir shops, fast-food stalls, and restaurants. The area can be garish, glitzy, and even crass—but it is never, *never* dull. Don't come here if you want to get away from it all, because life on the Gold Coast is a nonstop party.

Located an hour south of Brisbane, the Gold Coast officially comprises the 32 kilometers (20 miles) from Southport to Coolangatta, but has sprawled almost as far inland as Nerang. Without doubt the most developed tourist destination in Australia, its popularity is ensured by 300 days of sunshine a year, and an average temperature of 75°F (24°C). Christmas and June through August are peak seasons.

Arriving and Departing

By Bus Long-distance buses traveling between Sydney and Brisbane stop at Coolangatta and Surfers Paradise. **Coach Trans** (tel. 07/236–1000), **Greyhound** (tel. 07/236–3033), and **McCafferty's Pioneer Australia** (tel. 07/840–9350) all offer service to the Gold Coast from the Roma Street Transit Centre in Brisbane. **Greyhound Pioneer Australia** (6 Beach Rd., Surfers Paradise, tel. 13–2030) runs an express coach from the Gold Coast to Brisbane International Airport and Coolangatta Airport, as well as day trips that cover southeast Queensland with daily connections to Sydney and Melbourne.

By Car The Gold Coast is located 65 kilometers (40 miles) south of Brisbane. Take the Pacific Highway (Highway 1) south to the Gold Coast Highway, which runs through the towns of Southport, Surfers Paradise, and Coolangatta. From Brisbane International Airport take the Toll Road over the Gateway Bridge to avoid having to drive through Brisbane, and then follow the signs to the Gold Coast.

By Plane **Qantas** (tel. 13–1313) and **Ansett Australia** (tel. 13–1300) offer regular flights from Brisbane, Sydney, Melbourne, and Cairns to **Coolangatta Airport.**

Getting Around

By Bus The **Surfside Tweed Bus Link** (tel. 075/36–7666) runs an excellent bus service every 15 minutes between Gold Coast attractions, along the strip between Tweeds Head and Southport.

By Car All major car-rental agencies have offices in Brisbane and at the airport. On the Gold Coast itself, cars can be rented from **Avis** (Surfers Paradise, tel. 075/39–9388; airport, tel. 075/36–3511), **Budget** (Gold Coast Hwy., tel. 075/38–1344; airport, tel. 075/36–5377), **Hertz** (Gold Coast Hwy., tel. 075/38–5366; airport, tel. 075/36–6133), and **Thrifty** (Gold Coast Hwy., tel. 075/38–6511; airport, tel. 075/36–6955). Four-wheel-drive vehicles are available.

Important Addresses and Numbers

Tourist Information **Gold Coast Information Centres** (Beach House Plaza, Marine Parade, Coolangatta, tel. 075/36–7765; Cavill Mall Kiosk, Surfers Paradise, tel. 075/38–4419).

Gold Coast Tourism (Level 2, 64 Ferny Ave., Surfers Paradise 4217, tel. 075/92–2699).

Emergencies For emergencies requiring the **police, fire brigade,** or an **ambulance,** dial 000.

Emergency medical aid is available at **Gold Coast Hospital** (tel. 075/71–8211) and **Tweeds Head Hospital** (tel. 075/36–1133).

Guided Tours

Terranova Coach Tours (85 Anne St., Southport, tel. 075/32–0574) and **Coachtrans** (52 Davenport St., Southport, tel. 075/38–8344) operate a variety of day tours of the Gold Coast.

Exploring the Gold Coast

Dreamworld, 40 minutes outside Brisbane and 20 minutes from Surfers Paradise along the Pacific Highway, is one of the most enchanting theme parks outside the Disney empire. Children and adults alike will enjoy its paddle-steamer rides, barbershop quartets, magnificent gardens, excellent dining facilities, and six-story Imax Theatre. It also has a very strong Australian orientation, with one of the best koala enclosures in the country. *Dreamworld Pkwy., Coomera, tel. 075/73–3300 or toll-free 008/07–3300. Admission: $32 adults, $20 children and senior citizens; 2-day passes available. Open daily 10–5. Closed Dec. 25.*

A few minutes' drive south on the Pacific Highway will bring you to **Warner Bros. Movie World.** One of the most popular tourist attractions in Australia, this enormous complex is the only movie theme park outside the United States. Although Movie World is not as technically impressive or hands-on as its American counterparts, watching a movie studio at work, learning how special effects *Lethal-Weapon* style and stunts in the *Police Academy* movies are executed, and riding on Batman Adventure are still a lot of fun. *Pacific Hwy., Oxenford, tel. 075/73–3891 or 075/73–3999. Admission: $32 adults, $21 children 4–14. Open daily 10–5:30. Closed Dec. 25.*

Between Dreamworld and Warner Bros. Movie World, past Coomera on the Pacific Highway, take the turnoff to Hope Island/Sanctuary Cove on the left-hand side. Home to a five-star Hyatt Regency hotel, **Sanctuary Cove** (tel. 075/30–8400) is a huge resort complex with two golf courses, an outstanding marina, and a shopping center filled with boutiques, restaurants, a cinema, a health club, and even a small brewery.

Back on the highway, continue south to where the Gold Coast and Pacific highways fork. Stay in the left lane and follow the Gold Coast Highway for 10 minutes to Southport. Once in Southport, look for the turnoff on the left to **The Spit,** a natural peninsula that contains some of Southport's best attractions.

The foremost attraction here is **Seaworld,** Australia's largest marine park. Six daily shows feature whales, dolphins, sea lions, and waterskiing. Seaworld also has a large number of rides, including a monorail, a corkscrew roller coaster, and some exceptional water slides. All rides except helicopter and parasailing flights are included in the ticket price. *The Spit, Main Beach, tel. 075/88–2222. Admission: $32 adults, $21 children and senior citizens. Open daily 10–5. Closed Dec. 25.*

Time Out   **Fisherman's Wharf** (tel. 075/32–7944), a complex of shops and restaurants next to Seaworld, has marvelous views across the water and is a great place to stop for a drink or a snack. Kids will enjoy a workout on the playground, and an on-site swimming pool is available for everyone to cool off in.

Within walking distance of Seaworld is the **Marina Mirage** (Seaworld Dr., Broadwater Spit, Southport, tel. 075/91–0898), undoubtedly the Gold Coast's most elegant shopping center, complete with designer-name boutiques and restaurants.

Drive south on the Gold Coast Highway for five minutes into **Surfers Paradise.** Park wherever you can, but preferably as close to Cavill Avenue as possible. This is the heart of Surfers Paradise, a tawdry collection of high rises overlooking the beach, where bodies bake in the sand under signs warning of the risks of skin cancer.

Nearby is **Ripley's Believe It or Not Museum,** with displays that will appeal to anyone whose thirst for the bizarre is not satisfied by the crowds in Surfers Paradise. *Raptis Plaza, Cavill Mall, Surfers Paradise, tel. 075/92–0040. Admission: $9.50 adults, $5 children, $26 family. Open daily 9 AM–11 PM.*

Continuing south on the highway, you will spot the pyramid-shape **Jupiter's Casino** looming on the right. For those who want to try their hand at everything from blackjack to roulette, baccarat, and two-up, this establishment is on a par with anything in Las Vegas or Reno. *Gold Coast Hwy., Broadbeach, tel. 075/92–1133. Admission free. Dress: casual (but no thongs or T-shirts). Open daily 24 hrs.*

From the casino the Gold Coast Highway wends its way past Mermaid Beach, Miami, and on to Burleigh Heads. Just before you reach Burleigh Heads, turn right onto West Burleigh Road to reach

Fleay's Fauna Centre. Presented to the National Parks and Wildlife Association by wildlife naturalist David Fleay, the park features wetlands and rain forests in their natural states and 4 kilometers (2½ miles) of magnificent bushwalks. Visitors can see koalas, swamp wallabies, brolgas, ibises, platypuses, swans, and crocodiles. *W. Burleigh Rd., Burleigh Heads, tel. 075/76–2411 or 075/76–2767. Admission: $7.50 adults, $5 senior citizens, $3.50 children, $20 family. Open daily 9–5.*

Farther south along the Gold Coast Highway past Palm Beach is the community of Currumbin and the **Currumbin Sanctuary.** What started off as a bird park many years ago is now a 50-acre National Trust Reserve that boasts huge flocks of Australian lorikeets, as well as other exotic birds, fairy penguins, kangaroos, and koalas. Aim to be there between 8 AM and 10 AM or 4 PM and 5 PM, when the lorikeets arrive to be fed. The park's lovely grounds are ideal for picnics, and there are also cafeterias. *Off Gold Coast Hwy. at 28 Tomewin St., Currumbin, tel. 075/34–1266. Admission: $12.50 adults, $6.50 children and senior citizens. Open daily 8–5. Closed Dec. 25.*

What to See and Do with Children

Children's Adventure Playground at Currumbin Sanctuary has slides, rope ladders, climbing poles, and futuristic racing cars on tracks. *28 Tomewin St., Currumbin, tel. 075/34–1266. Sanctuary admission: $12.50 adults, $6.50 children and senior citizens. Open daily 8–5. Closed Dec. 25.*

One of the best amusement parks in Queensland, **Wet 'n' Wild** is the home of Matilda, the giant kangaroo mascot of the 1982 Brisbane Commonwealth Games. The ideal place to take children, the park has magnificent water slides as well as a wave pool where meter-high surf breaks over bathers. *Pacific Hwy., Oxenford, tel. 075/73–2277. Admission: $15 adults, $11.50 children, senior citizens free. Open Sept.–Apr., daily 10–5. Closed Dec. 25 and Apr. 2.*

Shopping

The most elegant shopping center on the Gold Coast is the **Marina Mirage** (74 Seaworld Dr., Broadwater Spit, Southport, tel. 075/77–0088). Here you'll find some of the world's best designer boutiques, including Gucci, Lowe, Louis Vuitton, and Hermès, as well as fine antiques, beach and leisure wear, perfume, and an excellent duty-free store. **The Galleria Shopping Centre** (Holiday City, Gold Coast Hwy., Surfers Paradise, tel. 075/92–1100) houses 47 boutiques and specialty stores, as well as a medical center and pharmacy. Thirty-minute fashion parades are held three times daily. **Raptis Plaza** (between Cavill Mall and The Esplanade, Surfers Paradise, tel. 075/92–2133) is another center filled with enticing boutiques. **The Paradise Centre** (Hanlan St., Surfers Paradise, tel. 075/92–0155) features 120 shops and restaurants, as well as an extensive amusement arcade.

Participant Sports

Boating Yachts and cabin cruisers can be rented from **Popeye Marine and Boat Hire** (Mariner's Cove, 212 Seaworld Dr., Main Beach, tel. 075/91–2553).

Fishing Fishing trips can be arranged at **Sanctuary Cove** (Manor Circle, Hope Island, tel. 075/30–1234). Fishing tackle can be rented from

Redback Rentals Shop (3B RSL Centre, 9 Beach Rd., Surfers Paradise, tel. 075/92–1655).

Golf The **Carrara Golf Centre** (Alabaster Dr., Carrara, tel. 075/94–4400) has an 18-hole golf course open from 6 AM daily, and a floodlit driving range that is open until 9 PM. Club rentals, lessons, and golf carts are available.

Dining and Lodging

Price categories for restaurants and hotels are the same as in the Brisbane Dining and Lodging sections, *above*. Highly recommended restaurants and lodgings are indicated by a star ★.

Broadbeach **Hotel Conrad and Jupiters Casino.** Shaped like a horseshoe, this ul-
Lodging tramodern luxury hotel offers every amenity. The atmosphere from the hotel's bustling casino overflows into the large, noisy lobby and attractive coffee lounge, with its tented ceiling, potted plants, and cane chairs. The rooms boast magnificent views. *Broadbeach Island, Gold Coast Hwy., 4218, tel. 075/92–1133, fax 075/92–8219. 622 rooms with bath. Facilities: casino, pool, coffee shop, restaurants. AE, DC, MC, V. $$$*

Coolangatta **Oskar's on the Beach.** One of the few restaurants overlooking
Dining Coolangatta Beach, this establishment serves food worthy of the
★ many awards it has won. Try the warm seafood salad with pink peppercorn dressing, the rack of lamb, or the splendid green prawns dipped in coconut and macadamia nuts and fried in beer batter. The wine selection is excellent, too. *Marine Parade, tel. 075/36–4621. Reservations advised. Dress: casual but neat. AE, DC, MC, V. $$–$$$*

Elanora **Isle of Palms.** Ideal for those who want to get away from the mad-
Lodging ding crowd, this complex of luxury town houses is located a short
★ distance outside Elanora on a man-made island. The resort features private beaches, a heated rock lagoon, and a swimming pool with an outdoor whirlpool. Guests can fish from the jetties or windsurf on the quiet waters of the lake. Most of the town houses have views of the waterfront, although some look onto courtyard gardens instead. Spacious, airy, and gracefully furnished in pastel motifs, all town houses are equipped with full kitchens and laundry facilities. *Coolgardie St., Elanora, 4221, tel. 075/98–1733, fax 075/98–1653. 174 suites. Facilities: 2 outdoor pools, 2 tennis courts, whirlpools, restaurant. AE, DC, MC, V. $$*

Mermaid **Sailfish Point Resort.** Located just a short drive from the Pacific Fair
Beach Shopping Centre and Surfers Paradise, this resort complex offers a
Lodging selection of two- and three-bedroom town houses. Guests can choose between luxury waterfront town houses or garden-court villas, all decorated in pastel colors with comfortable, modern furnishings. The resort offers a full-size tennis court, a heated pool and whirlpool, and a large barbecue area set among landscaped gardens. *300 Cottlesloe Dr., 4218, tel. 075/72–0677, fax 075/72–9501. 98 suites with bath. Facilities: heated pool, whirlpool, tennis court. AE, DC, MC, V. $*

Southport **The Great Wall.** Situated at the Marina Mirage with wonderful views
Dining across the Broadwater, this establishment is the most authentic
★ Chinese restaurant in Queensland—for good reason. Master chefs and hosts were brought from the Sheraton Hotel in Chengdu, China, to re-create traditional Szechuan dishes. However, they have now diversified into cuisine from Korea, Indonesia, Japan, and Thailand. The Peking duck and shark-fin soup are highly recommended. The

atmosphere is quiet, and the red and black decor is elegant without being glitzy. Dining here is a memorable experience. *Lobby Level, Marina Mirage, Seaworld Dr., Broadwater Spit, tel. 075/91–0898. Reservations advised. Dress: casual but neat. AE, DC, MC, V. Open for dinner Thurs.–Mon. $$$*

Grumpy's Wharf Restaurant. The atmosphere is as commendable as the food at Ron D'Albora's superb seafood restaurant, which sports a nautical decor and overlooks the moored boats at the wharf. The seafood is inspired and is widely regarded as the best on the coast. You will have a hard time choosing between the mixed seafood platters and the seafood risotto. Don't expect to dine and dash, however, because the service here tends to be slow. *66–70 Seaworld Dr., The Spit, tel. 075/32–2900. Reservations advised. Dress: casual but neat. AE, DC, MC, V. $–$$*

Lodging **Sheraton Mirage.** A low-rise building nestled amid lovely gardens
★ and fronting a secluded beach, this top-flight resort has a distinctly Australian look. Rooms are tastefully furnished in soft pastel colors and overlook the Pacific Ocean, lush gardens, or vast saltwater lagoons. A suspension bridge over the road links the resort with the elegant Marina Mirage shopping and restaurant center, although guests would be wise to sample the excellent fare at the resort's own restaurants first. The weekly poolside barbecue should not be missed. *Seaworld Dr., The Spit, Broadwater, 4217, tel. 075/91–1488, fax 075/91–2299. 323 rooms with bath, 40 suites. Facilities: pool, restaurants, coffee shop. AE, DC, MC, V. $$$$*

Surfers **Danny's.** The late Danny Zoli established this very popular restau-
Paradise rant on the waterfront in Surfers Paradise. In a spacious and elegant
Dining room overlooking the river, guests are seated in comfortable booths
★ while a trio plays Continental and Latin American music. The restaurant serves memorable international and Italian dishes such as *capeletti*, small hats of pasta filled with ricotta cheese, cream, and mushrooms; or baby veal panfried in white wine, lemon, and rosemary. It continues to serve the pasta that that well-fed tenor Luciano Pavarotti says is his favorite: spinach spaghetti with Moreton Bay bugs (a type of lobster). For dessert, have Mamma's gelato—the homemade Italian ice cream that is a house specialty. *Tiki Village, Riverfront, Cavill Ave., tel. 075/38–2818. Reservations advised. Dress: casual. AE, DC, MC, V. Dinner daily except Dec. 25 and Jan. 1. $$$*

Pellegrini Restaurant. Serving creative Italian cuisine, this restaurant has a dining room decorated in charcoal and apricot tones and graced with a cathedral ceiling; it exudes a sense of airiness and space. The house prides itself on its seafood dishes. Other favorites are the homemade pasta and the veal. *3120 Gold Coast Hwy., tel. 075/38–7257. Reservations advised. Dress: casual but neat. AE, DC, MC, V. No lunch; closed Dec. 25–26, Good Friday. $$*

★ **Shogun.** Incongruously set in the middle of a light industrial area, this little Japanese restaurant, which opened in 1984, receives consistent ratings as the best Japanese restaurant on the Gold Coast. Guests walk through a classic Japanese garden to the Oriental dining room, where they are served such traditional delicacies as *shishamon* (grilled marinated fish filled with roe), tempura, yakitori, and *chawan mushi* (steamed egg soup with small pieces of fish and prawns). *90 Bundall Rd., tel. 075/38–2872. Reservations advised. Dress: casual but neat. AE, DC, MC, V. No lunch; closed Mon. $$*

Lodging **Beachpoint Apartments.** Opposite the beach and within strolling distance of the center of Surfers Paradise, all one- and two-bedroom apartments in this 17-story complex have ocean views. The accommodations are large, and those with two bedrooms also have two bathrooms. Some apartments are air-conditioned, while others only have ceiling fans. All have laundry facilities and fully equipped kitchens (some with dishwashers). *Staghorn Ave. and The Esplanade, 4217, tel. 075/38–4355, fax 075/92–2881. 142 apartments with bath. Facilities: 2 pools, wading pool, saunas, tennis courts, babysitting. AE, DC, MC, V. $$$*

★ **Marriott Surfers Paradise Resort.** Unlike many of its Gold Coast peers, this grand hotel has a distinctive style. There's an extensive use of sandstone and polished natural wood, and the lobby, which features giant columns and a grand circular staircase, is cooled by a colorful Indian punkah. The guest rooms, all large and decorated in gentle hues of beige, light plum, and moss green, have VCRs, walk-in closets, marble bathrooms, and safes. The hotel is close to both the Nerang River and the beach, and all rooms have balconies and ocean views. It's a five-minute walk to the ocean, but the hotel has its own beach on a saltwater lagoon that is deep enough for scuba lessons and is well stocked with brilliantly colored marine fish. The freshwater outdoor pool, surrounded by gardens, is heated in the winter. There are dive and watersports shops on the premises, and boardsailing equipment, water skis, and catamarans can be rented for use on the river. *158 Ferny Ave., 4217, tel. 075/92–9800, fax 075/92–9888. 330 rooms with bath, 13 suites. Facilities: 2 restaurants, 3 bars, saltwater swimming lagoon, outdoor pool (heated in winter), spa, sauna, steam room, gym, 2 tennis courts, childcare center, shops. AE, DC, MC, V. $$$*

ANA Hotel Gold Coast. Operated by a Japanese group, this 22-story hotel is one of the best-managed establishments in Surfers Paradise. A minute's walk from the beach and Cavill Avenue, this hotel is perfect for those who like to be in the center of the action. Rooms feature a soft pastel decor with blond-wood furniture, minibars, air-conditioning, and balconies with views over central Surfers Paradise. The service is impeccable. *22 View Ave., 4217, tel. 075/79–1000, fax 075/70–1260. 403 rooms with bath, 17 suites. Facilities: heated outdoor pool, 2 tennis courts, gym, sauna, whirlpool, 3 restaurants, 3 bars, shopping center. AE, DC, MC, V. $$*

★ **Paros on the Beach.** Set on the beach amid lovely landscaped gardens, this Mediterranean-style six-story complex features two-bedroom apartments, each with a balcony and fully equipped kitchen. Bedrooms have ceiling fans and *en suite* bathrooms. *26 Old Burleigh Rd., 4217, tel. 075/92–0780 or toll-free 008/07–9050, fax 075/92–1421. 26 apartments with bath. Facilities: pool, whirlpool, tennis court, laundry. MC, V. $$*

Nightlife

New night spots are springing up in Surfers Paradise all the time. Some of the long-running favorites are **Melba's** (46 Cavill Ave., tel. 075/38–7411), **Penthouse** (Cavill and Orchid Aves., tel. 075/38–1388), and **Benson's** (22 Orchid Ave., tel. 075/38–7600).

For the most elegant disco on the Gold Coast, head for the Sheraton Mirage and its **Rolls** nightclub. The decor is built around a glorious vintage Rolls-Royce that is fitted with a small table so that you can enjoy your snacks and drinks in ultimate luxury. This is the place to come for champagne, cocktails, light suppers, and live music. *Sheraton Mirage, Seaworld Dr., Broadwater Spit, Southport, tel. 075/91–1488. Open Tues.–Sat. 8 PM–early morning.*

The Sunshine Coast

One hour north of Brisbane by car to its southernmost point, the Sunshine Coast is a 60-kilometer (36-mile) stretch of white-sand beaches, inlets, lakes, and mountains. Except for a few touristy eyesores, the Sunshine Coast, which stretches from the Glass House Mountains in the south to Rainbow Beach in the north, and as far inland as Kenilworth, 40 kilometers (25 miles) to the west, has avoided the high-rise glitz of its southern cousin, the Gold Coast. Visitors here will find a quieter, more relaxing pace, with abundant national parks, secluded coves, and magnificent rain forests spilling down to the ocean.

The Sunshine Coast is for people who want to be physically active—the swimming and surfing are superb, and the sports facilities every bit as good as those along the Gold Coast.

Arriving and Departing

By Bus   **Coach Trans** (tel. 07/236–1000) offers daily bus service from Brisbane Airport and the Roma Street Transit Centre in Brisbane to Caloundra, Mooloolaba, Maroochydore, Noosa, and Tewantin.

By Plane   **Ansett Australia** (tel. 074/43–4579), **Ansett Express** (tel. 074/43–4579), and **Qantas** (tel. 13–1313) operate direct flights from Sydney and Melbourne to Maroochydore Airport. It is almost as convenient to fly into Brisbane, which is only an hour's drive away.

By Train   Trains leave regularly from **Central Station** (Ann St., tel. 07/235–2222) in Brisbane to Nambour in the heart of the Sunshine Coast. However, once in Nambour you will need a car, so it makes more sense to drive from Brisbane.

Getting Around

By Car   The Sunshine Coast is an hour's drive north of Brisbane along the Bruce Highway (Hwy. 1) to the Glass House Mountains, two hours' drive to Noosa, the heart of the area. All major car-rental companies have offices in Brisbane (*see* Getting Around in the Brisbane section, *above*). The following international companies have local offices: **Avis** (Maroochydore and airport, tel. 074/43–5055), **Budget** (Maroochydore, tel. 074/43–6555), **Hertz** (Noosa, tel. 074/49–2033; airport, tel. 074/43–6422), and **Thrifty** (Maroochydore and airport, tel. 074/43–1733). To repeat, a car is a necessity on the Sunshine Coast.

Important Addresses and Numbers

Tourist Information   **Sunshine Coast Information Centre** (6th Ave., Maroochydore, tel. 074/79–1566). Open weekdays 8:30–5, weekends 10–4.

Caloundra City Tourist Information Centre (7 Caloundra Rd., Caloundra, tel. 074/91–0202).

Noosa Heads Tourist Information Centre (Hastings St., Noosa Heads, tel. 074/47–4988).

Emergencies   In emergencies requiring the **police, fire department,** or an **ambulance,** dial 000.

Emergency medical help is also available at **Caloundra District Hospital** (tel. 074/91–1888), **Nambour General Hospital** (tel. 074/41–

9600), **Selangor Private Hospital** (Nambour, tel. 074/41–2311), and **Noosa District Hospital** (tel. 074/47–6022).

Guided Tours

Orientation Tours

Tropical Coast Tours (Box 360, Noosa Heads 4567, tel. 074/49–0822) operates regular tours to tourist attractions around the Sunshine Coast, Brisbane, and the Gold Coast.

Adventure Sunshine Coast (69 Alfriston Dr., Buderim, tel. 074/44–8824) offers one-day treks from Noosa Heads and Caloundra that take you to rain forests, the mountains, Barrier Reef islands, and tourist attractions in Brisbane, the Sunshine Coast, and the Gold Coast. You'll see everything from pineapple plantations to isolated beaches to casinos with nonstop action.

Balloon Tours

Balloon Aloft (tel. 074/41–5020) offers flights over the Sunshine Coast for approximately $200 an hour, including the traditional champagne celebration.

Boat Cruises

Cooloola Cruises (Gympie Terr., Noosaville, tel. 074/49–7884) offers a variety of cruises through the Everglades and the Noosa River and Lakes. The Cooloola Safari is the most comprehensive and adventurous tour, combining a boat cruise with a four-wheel-drive trip to Coloured Sands, Cherry Venture, and the rain forest.

Everglades Water Bus Co. (Harbour Town Marina, Tewantin, tel. 074/47–1838) conducts combined boat/four-wheel-drive tours from Harbour Town Jetty in Tewantin to the Everglades, Cooloola National Park, Cherry Venture, Bubbling Springs, and Coloured Sands. Another boat tour takes passengers to the Jetty Restaurant in Boreen Point.

Exploring the Sunshine Coast

Numbers in the margin correspond to points of interest on the Sunshine Coast map.

The Bruce Highway runs north from Brisbane through flat eucalyptus country and past large stands of pine. Shortly after the Caboolture turnoff, 44 kilometers (27 miles) north of Brisbane, is a region that was once home to a large Aboriginal population, but is now a prosperous dairy center. Here also is the turnoff to Bribie Island, located 25 kilometers (15 miles) to the east, which offers magnificent beaches, some with glass-calm waters and others with rolling Pacific surf.

1 Half an hour outside Brisbane, the **Glasshouse Mountains** appear on the far left. The old main road used to run right past these 10 dramatic outcrops, more than 20 million years old, that look like gigantic inverted ice-cream cones. Today, the highway hugs the coast, but the old road is still open and is now a scenic route. The mountains are a favorite destination for rock climbers as well as experienced hangglider pilots.

Just north of Palmview, on the left side of the Bruce Highway, is a large, red-roof parody of a classic Australian pub. A veteran car is perched precariously on the roof, and the whole building appears on **2** the verge of collapse. This is the **Ettamogah Pub,** whose name and design are based on the famous pub featured for decades in the work of Australian cartoonist Ken Maynard. The place is within an amusement area called Aussie World but is run as a real pub, serving a large variety of Australian beers. It has an upstairs bistro, a beer

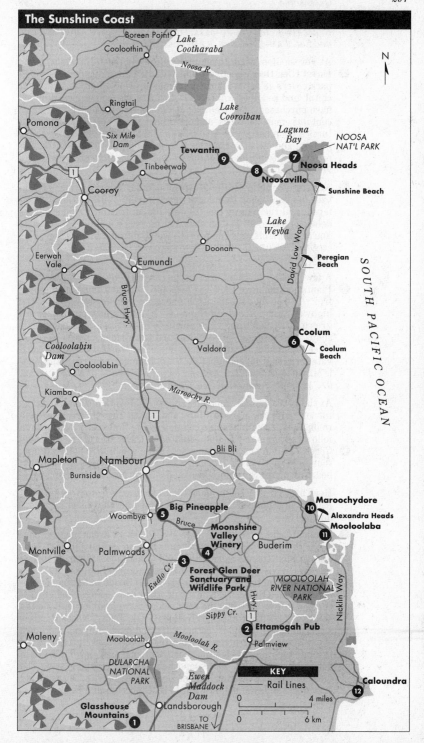

The Sunshine Coast

Boreen Point
Cooloothin
Lake Cootharaba
Noosa R.

Ringtail
Lake Cooroiban

Pomona
Six Mile Dam
Laguna Bay
NOOSA NAT'L PARK

Tewantin **9**
8 Noosaville
7 Noosa Heads
Sunshine Beach

Tinbeerwah
Cooroy

Eerwah Vale
Eumundi
Doonan
Lake Weyba

Peregian Beach
David Low Way

Cooloolabin Dam
Cooloolabin
Valdora
SOUTH PACIFIC OCEAN

Kiamba
Maroochy R.
Coolum **6**
Coolum Beach

Mapleton
Burnside
Bli Bli

Nambour
Maroochydore
10
Alexandra Heads
Mooloolaba
11

Montville
Palmwoods
Woombye **5** **Big Pineapple**
Bruce
Moonshine Valley Winery
4
Buderim

3
Forest Glen Deer Sanctuary and Wildlife Park
Endlo Cr.
MOOLOOLAH RIVER NATIONAL PARK
Nicklin Way

Maleny
Mooloolah
Mooloolah R.
Sippy Cr.
2 Ettamogah Pub
Palmview

DULARCHA NATIONAL PARK
Ewen Maddock Dam

KEY
Rail Lines
0   4 miles
0   6 km

Glasshouse Mountains
1
Landsborough
TO BRISBANE

Caloundra
12

Bruce Hwy

garden, and a bar, and the adjacent complex houses a range of shops. *Bruce Hwy., tel. 074/94–5444. Open Mon.–Thurs. 9 AM–10 PM, Fri. and Sat. 9 AM–2 AM, Sun. 9 AM–midnight.*

At Forest Glen, some 15 minutes before you reach Nambour, is the
❸ **Forest Glen Deer Sanctuary and Wildlife Park.** This drive-through park covers 48 acres of forest and pastureland where rusa, fallow, chital, and red deer will come right up to the car, especially if you have purchased a 50¢ feed bag at the hunting lodge. The park also contains emus, peacocks, and other bird-life. A nocturnal house features a wide variety of Australian night animals, such as possums, gliders, and owls. *Bruce Hwy., Forest Glen, tel. 074/45–1274. Admission: $10 adults, $5 children and senior citizens. Open daily 9–5. Closed Dec. 25.*

❹ Another attraction is the **Moonshine Valley Winery,** which specializes in wines made from locally grown fruit. Wine tastings are offered, and the winery has its own Italian trattoria, which serves delicious pasta, as well as excellent barbecue and picnic facilities. You can work off your lunch on the walking trails. *Bruce Hwy., Forest Glen, tel. 074/45–1198. Admission free. Open daily 10–5. Closed Good Friday, Dec. 25.*

A few minutes farther north on the Bruce Highway is the Sunshine
❺ Plantation, home of the **Big Pineapple.** You can't miss this piece of fruit: The 50-foot super-kitsch fiberglass monster towers over the highway, and visitors can climb inside to learn how pineapples are grown. The plantation, a complete tourist complex with souvenir shops, restaurants, flume rides, and train rides, is also the best place to see how macadamia nuts and other tropical fruits are cultivated. If that's not enough, take the Nutmobile for a trip to the Magic Macadamia Nut. *Bruce Hwy., 6 km (4 mi) south of Nambour, tel. 074/42–1333. Admission free. Open daily 9–5.*

At the north end of Nambour, opposite a Toyota dealership, is the turnoff to Bli Bli, Maroochydore, and Noosa. Take this road through rolling sugar and pineapple country to the first traffic circle, then follow the signs to Coolum. Situated at the center of the Sunshine
❻ Coast, **Coolum** makes an ideal base from which to explore the surrounding countryside. Coolum also has what is probably the finest beach along the Sunshine Coast and offers a placid, easygoing pace.

Head north from Coolum along the David Low Way to Noosa Heads. Along the route are many quiet, deserted beaches ideal for swimming.

❼ **Noosa Heads** is one of the most stylish resort areas in Australia. While the country's new money tends to head for the glitter of Surfers Paradise (*see* Exploring the Gold Coast, *above*), the old money retreats to Noosa. Set beside the calm waters of Laguna Bay at the northern tip of the Sunshine Coast, Noosa Heads consisted of nothing more than a few shacks just a dozen or so years ago. Surfers discovered it first, lured by the spectacular waves that curl around the sheltering headland of Noosa National Park. Today, Noosa Heads is a charming mix of sophistication, surf, and sand. Elegant boutiques and restaurants lure you in from the streets. Lovely trails wind through the rain forest of the nearby national park, leading down to beautiful coves with white-sand beaches and crashing surf. The views along the trail from Laguna Lookout to the top of the headland encompass miles of magnificent beaches, ocean, and thick vegetation.

Noosa Heads is just one of three towns that make up the community of Noosa. Three kilometers (2 miles) inland along the Noosa River is **⑧ Noosaville,** a small town dotted with small hotels and apartment complexes. Noosaville is the access point for trips to the **Teewah Coloured Sands,** an area that features multicolored sands that were created by natural chemicals in the soil. Dating back to the Ice Age, some of the 72 different hues of sand form cliffs rising up to 200 meters (600 feet).

⑨ The third Noosa community, **Tewantin,** is located 6 kilometers (4 miles) up the river and features the **House of Bottles and Bottle Museum,** one big "bottle building" constructed from 35,000 bottles of different sizes and shapes. More than 5,000 other bottle-art exhibits are featured. *19 Myles St., Tewantin, tel. 074/47–1277. Admission: $3 adults, $2 senior citizens, 50¢ children. Open daily 9–5. Closed Dec. 25.*

The Sunshine Coast has an obsession with monstrously proportioned kitsch, and Tewantin is right on the cutting edge. Not content with its big bottle, the town also features the **Big Shell.** This tacky attraction has displays of all types of art incorporating the coast's famous colored sands, as well as seashells, coral, and other marine items. *Gympie and Hay Sts., Tewantin, tel. 074/47–1268. Admission free. Open daily 9–5.*

Return to David Low Way and drive the 27 kilometers (17 miles) **⑩** south to **Maroochydore.** Located at the mouth of the Maroochy River, this town has been a popular beach resort for several years and suffers its fair share of high-rise towers. Nevertheless, the beach here offers excellent surfing and swimming.

For the best surfing in the area, however, head for the beach at **Alexandra Heads,** 5 kilometers (3 miles) south. From here, follow the **⑪** coast road south for about 10 minutes to **Mooloolaba**—the port for the local prawning and fishing fleets as well as deep-sea charter boats.

Mooloolaba's most notable attraction is **Underwater World,** which features a walk-through aquarium. Visitors walk through a clear acrylic underwater tunnel to stare face-to-face at giant sharks, stingrays, and other local marine species. The marine complex, one of the very best in Australia, incorporates shark feeding, the Oceanarium, Ocean Discover Centre, and Theatre of the Sea. Allow extra time for this attraction. *Parkyn Parade, Mooloolaba, tel. 074/44–2255 or 074/44–8088. Admission: $14.50 adults, $7.50 children, $9 students and senior citizens, $39 families. Open daily 9–5:30.*

Finally, drive 15 minutes farther south along the coast to **⑫ Caloundra.** It's not just excellent beaches that make Caloundra so popular: The town is an ideal family destination, free of the glitz and glamour of some of the more touristy Queensland resorts. Retirees have been moving here for some time now, and it is also popular with Brisbanites, many of whom have weekend houses or apartments here.

From Caloundra head west for 11 kilometers (7 miles) to the Bruce Highway; turn south to return to Brisbane.

What to See and Do with Children

Children love the **Bli Bli Castle,** a surprisingly realistic replica of a Norman castle at Bli Bli. It features everything necessary for a rousing game of make-believe, including dungeons and a torture chamber. *David Low Way, Bli Bli, tel. 074/48–5373. Admission: $6 adults, $3.50 children, $5 senior citizens. Open daily 9–4:30.*

Off the Beaten Track

The **Tramstop** in Beerwah, 5 kilometers (3 miles) south of the Glasshouse Mountains township, features miniature trams, a cable car, and double-decker buses that offer rides through the meadow and the forest. *Beerwah via the Glasshouse Mountain Tourist Dr. from Caboolture, tel. 074/94–1555. Admission: $3.50 adults, $2 children. Open daily 10–5, weekends only Feb.–June.*

Next door is the **Queensland Reptile and Fauna Park** with a collection of Australian animals including pythons, taipans, adders, kangaroos, crocodiles, emus, and wallabies. Guided tours are offered twice daily. *Beerwah via the Glasshouse Mountain Tourist Dr. from Caboolture, tel. 074/94–1134. Admission: $10 adults, $5 children, $8 senior citizens. Open daily 8–4 in summer, 7:30–4:30 in winter.*

Shopping

Shopping Centers The best shopping centers on the Sunshine Coast are **Bay Village** (Hastings St., Noosa Heads), with chic boutiques and basic beach shops, and the **Wharf Shopping Centre** (Parkyn Parade, Mooloolaba), a re-creation of a 19th-century fishing village.

Markets One of the best open street markets on the Sunshine Coast is held on Saturday from 6:30 AM to noon on **Memorial Drive in Eumundi** (tel. 074/46–8476), where you'll find wares by local craftspeople and lots of local color.

Specialty Stores
Arts and Crafts Few high-quality arts and crafts stores are to be found along the coastal strip of the Sunshine Coast. Those visitors interested in buying some of Queensland's local crafts work should head inland to the little villages in the Blackhall range. The **Lasting Impressions Gallery** (6 Elizabeth St., Kenilworth, tel. 074/46–0422) offers a collection of fine arts and crafts by Australian artisans. (Kenilworth lies southwest of Mapleton.)

Participant Sports

Boating Sailboats can be rented at **Boreen Point** (tel. 074/85–3213) on the western side of Lake Cootharaba. Motorboats can be rented by the day or half day from **Queensland Marine Service** (Lauries Marina, Orana St., Mooloolaba, tel. 074/44–1499).

Fishing Deep-sea fishing charters can be arranged through **Mooloolaba Deep Sea Charters** (The Wharf, Mooloolaba, tel. 074/44–6077). Rods and reels can be bought at **Fisherman's World** (Fisherman's Wharf, Maroochydore, tel. 074/47–2714).

Golf The **Headland Golf Course** (Golf Links Rd., Buderim, tel. 074/44–5800) accepts visiting players.

Tennis Courts and coaching are available at **Alinga Tennis Centre** (121 Sugar Rd., Maroochydore, tel. 074/43–4584).

Water Sports **Sea Wind Charters and Holiday Tours** (10 Cooloosa St., Sunshine Beach, tel. 074/47–3042) rents a variety of yachts and jet skis. The company also offers a half-day cruise ($65 adults, children half price) during which the captain teaches sailing fundamentals, and snorkeling and surf ski rides are possible. The company also organizes scuba-diving lessons, daily boat dives, and equipment rental.

Dining and Lodging

Price categories for restaurants and hotels are the same as in the Brisbane Dining and Lodging sections, *above*. Highly recommended restaurants and lodgings are indicated by a star ★.

Boreen Point
Dining
★

The Jetty Licensed Restaurant. Located upriver from Noosa Heads on the edge of Lake Cootharaba, this restaurant can be reached either by car or by boat. Simple fare, with an emphasis on seafood and local produce, is served on a glassed-in veranda overlooking the lake. The menu changes continually, but typical dishes include grilled barramundi, Moreton Bay bugs (a type of lobster), or grilled prawns. This restaurant is a favorite with locals. *Boreen Parade, Boreen Point, tel. 074/85-3167. Reservations advised. Dress: casual but neat. MC, V. Open for lunch Wed.–Sun., dinner Fri.–Sat. $$*

Coolum Beach
Lodging
★

Hyatt Regency Resort. Spread out at the foot of Mount Coolum, this may be the best health spa and resort in Australia. The spa has everything a fitness fanatic could want—several pools, aerobics rooms, a supervised gym, squash, hot Jacuzzis, cold plunge baths, and massage facilities. In addition, the resort features a championship 18-hole golf course designed by Robert Trent Jones, Jr., lighted tennis courts, a beach club, and a mile of ocean surf. The accommodations consist of a series of villas, each containing two to six apartments. Set amid gardens overlooking the tennis courts or the golf course, the villas are grouped in clusters around their own swimming pools and club houses, where complimentary Continental breakfasts and predinner champagne are served. One- and two-bedroom apartments, decorated in soft pastel colors with comfortable, modern furniture and marble bathrooms, are available. Boutiques, a deli, a wine shop, and sidewalk restaurants with umbrella-shaded tables are arranged around a village square within the complex. The only drawback to the resort is that there is a lot of walking involved to get from one facility to the other in the 150-hectare (370-acre) complex. *Warran Rd., Coolum Beach, 4573, tel. 074/46–1234, fax 074/46–2957. 330 apartments with bath. Facilities: 8 restaurants, shops, golf, 9 tennis courts, 8 pools, Jacuzzis, gym, disco. AE, DC, MC, V. $$$*

Maroochydore
Dining

BC's Tex Mex. Considering how few Mexicans live in Australia, it's surprising how popular Mexican food has become. BC's is particularly popular with a younger set attracted by the fiery-hot dishes and low prices. Lit as much by the glare of the McDonald's golden arches next door as by its own lights, the decor is, to put it mildly, unpretentious. The place is noisy, too, with long tables that seat 40 people comfortably. The food is the main attraction here, however. Try the guacamole dip made from the outstanding avocados grown in this region of Queensland, or piquant enchiladas with refried beans and Mexican Corona beer. *23 Aerodrome Rd., tel. 074/43–5155. Reservations advised. Dress: casual. AE, MC, V. No lunch. $*

Lodging

Camargue. Spectacularly located on the beachfront within 100 yards of the local surf club, this modern, three-story block of luxury apartments is within easy walking distance of restaurants and shops. Apartments are spacious, each with two bedrooms, two bathrooms (one off the main bedroom), a lounge, a laundry, and a fully equipped kitchen. They are furnished differently, but they all overlook tropical gardens. A minimum stay of one week may be required during peak season. *52 Alexandra Parade, Maroochydore, 4558, tel. 074/43–6656, fax 074/43–6656. 24 apartments with bath and shower. Facilities: outdoor heated pool, sauna, whirlpool, laundry. MC, V. $$*

Noosa Heads
Dining
★

Touché. Located on a second-floor balcony, this restaurant serves an eclectic menu of light, innovative dishes. Its owners have created a version of Queensland cuisine that blends European and Thai flavors with exotic local fruits and vegetables. Starters range from panfried lamb's brains and brioche with a tangy plum and ginger chutney, to a carpaccio of Atlantic salmon. Main dishes include chargrilled fillet of beef with mustard butter and fried mushrooms and onion rings, and a warm salad of Moreton Bay bugs with fresh mango, burnt honey, and lime vinaigrette. The restaurant, which seats 60 people inside and 40 outside, used to have an unrelentingly chic decor that has been considerably softened as the cuisine has been sharpened. *Hastings St., tel. 074/47–2222. Reservations advised. Dress: casual but neat. AE, DC, MC, V. Closed Christmas night, Good Friday, and New Year's lunch. $$–$$$*

★ **Pavillions.** This restaurant on the ground floor of the Netyana Noosa resort features first-class service and international cuisine. Try such dishes as stir-fried lamb with garlic, chili, and mint in lettuce leaves, or fresh king prawns and oysters with peaches and a chili mint dressing. Other classic dishes include peppered duck breast with piquant raspberry sauce, and medallions of beef, lobster, and veal with a trio of sauces. For dessert, don't miss the profiteroles. A wide selection of Australian and French wines is available. *75 Hastings St., tel. 074/47–4848. Reservations required. Dress: casual but neat. AE, DC, MC, V. $$*

Lodging
★

Sheraton Noosa Resort. This six-story, horseshoe-shape complex faces fashionable Hastings Street on one side and the river on the other. The center of the horseshoe is planted with attractive gardens. Whoever picked the building's annoying pink, blue, and green color scheme, however, was having a bad day. Fortunately, the color scheme does not extend to the guest rooms. Indeed, it would be hard to find fault with the air-conditioned rooms, each of which features a balcony, Jacuzzi, microwave oven, refrigerator, minibar, and tea/coffee maker. *Hastings St., 4567, tel. 074/49–4888, fax 074/49–2230. 169 rooms with bath. Facilities: outdoor pool, health club, saunas, game room. AE, DC, MC, V. $$$$*

Netyana Noosa. Popular with middle- and upper-management Australians, this low-rise complex of one- and two-bedroom suites is on the beach. There is one staff member for every two visitors, and guests are pampered with such touches as soft bathrobes, English toiletries, and hair dryers in the rooms. All suites feature verandas large enough for elegant room-service dining. The Presidential suite has a private terrace with an outdoor Jacuzzi, and a magnificent dining room in which the resort chef will serve specially prepared dinners on request. *75 Hastings St., 4567, tel. 074/47–4722, fax 074/47–3914. 48 suites with bath. Facilities: 2 pools (1 heated), sauna, gym, restaurant, bar, laundry. AE, DC, MC, V. $$$*

Little Cove Court. Despite its position just minutes from the cosmopolitan shops and restaurants of Noosa's Hastings Street, this two-story glass complex belongs in another world altogether. Set on a hillside near a cascading waterfall, its comfortable two-bedroom apartments overlook tropical vegetation and the sea. Each air-conditioned apartment features a balcony with barbecue, whirlpool bath, color TV, fully equipped kitchen, and laundry. The apartments are serviced weekly. *Park Rd., 4567, tel. 074/47–5977. 12 apartments with bath. Facilities: heated pool, sauna. AE, DC, MC, V. $$*

**Peregian
Beach
Dining
★** **Peregian Park Homestead.** Located 5 kilometers (3 miles) from Peregian Beach along an unpaved road, this restaurant is not one you are likely to stumble onto. The trip is worth any amount of getting lost, however, for this is a real find—a traditional old Queensland home with log fires in winter, and a wide veranda overlooking a lake for summertime dining. The fixed menu consists of canapés, soup, an appetizer, a main course, dessert, and coffee. Considering the prices, the cuisine is surprisingly sophisticated, featuring such dishes as prawn and reef fish quenelles with lobster sauce, or fillet of pork stuffed with apple and dates. Remember to bring your own wine, because the restaurant is unlicensed. *Woodland Dr., tel. 074/ 48-1628. Reservations advised. Dress: casual. MC, V. BYOB. Open dinner Fri. and Sat., lunch Sun.* $$

Nightlife

Discos **Tropo's** features live entertainment and dancing. *Mooloolaba Hotel, The Esplanade, Mooloolaba, tel. 074/44-1700. Open Wed.–Sat. 8 PM–3 AM, Sun. 9 PM–3 AM.*
Illusions Niteclub (71 The Esplanade, Mooloolaba, tel. 074/44-1048) serves full meals and features a nightclub open daily, and until 3 AM on weekends.

Fraser Island

Situated some 200 kilometers (125 miles) north of Brisbane, Fraser Island is both the largest of Queensland's islands and the most unusual. Instead of coral reefs and coconut palms, it has wildflower-dotted meadows, freshwater lakes, a teeming and exotic bird population, dense stands of rain forest trees, towering sand dunes, and sculpted, multicolored sand cliffs along its east coast—a lineup that has won the island a place on UNESCO's World Heritage list. The surf fishing is legendary, and humpback whales and their calves can be seen wintering in Hervey Bay between May and September.

Arriving and Departing

Hervey Bay is both the expanse of water between Fraser Island and the Queensland coast and also the generic name given to a conglomeration of four nearby coastal towns—Urangan, Pialba, Scarness, and Torquay—that have grown into a single settlement. This township is the jumping-off point for most excursions to Fraser Island. Travelers should be aware, however, that maps and road signs usually refer to the individual town names, not Hervey Bay.

By Bus **McCafferty's Coaches** (tel. 07/236–3033) and **Pioneer** (tel. 07/840–9350) operate bus service between Brisbane and Hervey Bay, where the bus terminal is near the Fraser Island ferry dock.

By Car While the southernmost tip of Fraser Island is 200 kilometers (125 miles) north of Brisbane, the best access to the island is from the Hervey Bay area, 290 kilometers (180 miles) away. Take the Bruce Highway to Maryborough, then follow the signs to Urangan.

By Plane **Sunstate Airlines** (tel. 13–1313) has several flights daily between Brisbane and Hervey Bay Airport.

By Ferry **Vehicle ferries** operate to Fraser Island from Urangan, Mary River Heads (12 kilometers/7 miles south of Urangan), and Inskip Point (opposite the island's southern tip). Round-trip fare is about $35 per vehicle, plus $5 for each passenger older than 14. Four-wheel-drive rentals may be cheaper on the mainland, but once you factor in the ferry ticket, it's still less expensive to get your rental on Fraser Island proper.

The *Kingfisher I* is a passenger catamaran that operates between Urangan and North White Cliffs, near Kingfisher Bay Resort. *Tel. 071/25–5155. Fare: $18 adults, $9 children 4–14. Departs daily 8:30, 11, and 4, plus Fri. 7:30 PM and Sat. 6:30 PM.*

Getting Around

By Car Four-wheel-drive vehicles can be hired from the **Kingfisher Bay Resort** (tel. 071/20–3333) for $130 per day. The **Happy Valley Resort** (tel. 071/27–9144) rents four-wheelers for the same price, but it's difficult to get there unless you're already four-wheel equipped.

Despite the island's free-range feeling, the rules of the road still apply: Wear seat belts, drive on the left, obey the speed limit—and remember that the island has a serious accident rate of about one per week. Watch out for the creek crossings and keep an eye on the tide. Tide tables are available from ranger stations or from any shop on the island. It is generally advised to keep your vehicle off the beach for three hours before high tide and four hours after.

Important Addresses and Numbers

Fraser Coast Tour Booking Office and Whale Watch Centre is a good source of information, maps, and brochures. The center will also help you with tour and accommodations bookings. *Buccaneer Ave., Urangan, tel. 071/25–3287. Open daily 9–5.*

Hervey Bay Tourist Office. *Shop 4, 46 Main St., Pialba, tel. 071/24–2448. Open weekdays 9–4:30.*

Guided Tours

Orientation Tours **Fraser Island Discovery Tours** operates three-day safaris to Fraser Island from Brisbane. A maximum of 14 passengers tour the island by four-wheel-drive vehicle and spend two nights at the Cathedral Beach campground. *Tel. 07/821–1694. Prices: $295 adults, $250 children under 16.*

Whale-Watching Tours **Air Fraser Island** operates 45-minute whale-watching flights across Hervey Bay between July and October. *Tel. 071/24–3549. Price: $100 per person.*

Tasman Venture II, a 52-foot catamaran, makes whale-watching cruises on Hervey Bay. Weather permitting, the vessel departs daily between August and October at 8 AM and 1 PM. *Tel. 071/24–3222. Prices: $50 adults, $18 children under 15.*

Exploring Fraser Island

Once you've seen Fraser Island's 140-kilometer (90-mile) east coast—nearly one continuous beach—it will come as no surprise that this is the world's largest sand island. However, the drab images usually summoned by the word "sand" do not apply to the striking landscape of Fraser's coast. Colors stray from the typical beige to deep rust and sugar white, while shapes range from sensuous drifts to huge dunes.

Major highlights of a drive north along the east coast include the rusting hulk of the *Maheno,* which lies half-buried in the sand, a roost for seagulls and a prime hunting ground for fishermen when the tailor are running. North of the wreck are the **Pinnacles**—also known as the Cathedrals—a stetch of dramatic, deep red cliffs.

Just past the Cathedral Beach Resort is the southern border of the **Great Sandy National Park** (tel. 071/27–9177), which covers the top third of the island. The park's beaches around Indian Head are known for their shell middens—basically, attractive garbage heaps that were left behind after Aboriginal feasting. The head's name is another kind of relic: Captain James Cook saw Aborigines standing on the headland as he sailed past, and he therefore named the area after inhabitants he believed to be "Indians." Farther north, past Waddy Point, is one of Fraser Island's most magnificat variations on sand: Wind and time have created enormous dunes, which are constantly swept clean of footprints by a breeze that blows off Hervey Bay.

Fraser's east coast also marks the intersection of two serious Australian passions: an addiction to the beach and a love affair with the motor vehicle. Unrestricted vehicle access means that Fraser's east coast has become a giant sandbox for four-wheelers. If you prefer your wilderness sans enthusiastic dune-buggying, head for the unspoiled interior of the island. This quiet, green garden boasts paperbark swamps, giant satinay and brush box forests, wildflower heaths, and 40 freshwater lakes—including the spectacularly clear **Lake McKenzie,** which is ringed by a beach of incandescent whiteness.

The island's excellent network of walking trails converges at **Central Station,** a former logging camp at the center of the island. Services here are limited to a map board, a parking lot, and a campground. It's a promising place for dingo spotting, however. Comparative isolation has meant that Fraser Island's dingoes are the most purebred on the east coast of Australia; to ensure the future of the breed, domestic dogs are not permitted. The dingoes here are unfazed by human contact, but they are still wild animals: Don't feed them, and keep a close eye on children.

Two noteworthy walking tracks lead from the station: A boardwalk heads south to **Wanggoolba Creek,** a favorite spot of photographers; this little stream snakes through a green palm forest, trickling over a bed of white sand between clumps of the rare angiopteris fern. A slightly longer trail leads north to **Pile Valley,** where a stand of giant satinay trees can be seen. This timber is so dense and durable that it was shipped to Egypt to be used as pilings for the Suez Canal.

Dining and Lodging

Apart from Kingfisher Bay Resort (*see below*), accommodation on Fraser Island is limited to campsites and the bungalows along the island's eastern beaches. Camping is permitted only in designated areas. Price categories are the same as in the Brisbane Dining and Lodging sections, *above*.

$$$ **Kingfisher Bay Resort.** Since this resort opened in mid-1992, the island has had accommodations to match the superstar attractions bequeathed by mother nature. Wrapped around a bay on the island's west coast, the resort is a stylish, high-tech marriage of glass, stainless steel, dark timber, and corrugated iron; although the two-story structures are by no means inconspicuous, the developers have succeeded in attractively integrating the resort with its environment. Highly recommended are the Ocean View rooms, which are just

slightly more expensive than those that overlook the access roads and forests at the rear. The expansive glass-and-timber pavilion at the center of the complex has a fine dining room with some unexpected wildlife such as buffalo and emu on the menu. The resort also offers a full range of island tours, from short, ranger-guided strolls to whale-watching trips on Hervey Bay. Four-wheel-drive vehicles are available for hire. *Booking address: GPO Box 1122, Brisbane 4001, tel. 07/221–1811, fax 07/221–3270. 150 rooms with bath. Facilities: 2 restaurants, bar, 2 pools, spa. AE, DC, MC, V.*

$$ **Happy Valley Resort.** This is the pick of the accommodations on the east coast. While Happy Valley might not quite live up to its "resort" tag, its one- and two-bedroom bungalows were completely rebuilt in 1992 and are now big and breezy, with polished timber floors and bamboo furnishings. The on-site restaurant has a pleasant atmosphere, but the food is nothing to write home about. A small store sells groceries and fishing supplies, as well as gas and diesel. *Tel. 071/27–9144, fax 071/27–9131. 8 rooms with shower. Facilities: restaurant, bar, store. AE, MC, V.*

$ **Queensland National Parks and Wildlife Service.** This agency operates campsites with hot showers and toilets at Dundabara and Waddy Point; some wood is also supplied. Permits for the **Cathedral Beach Camping Park,** a privately managed site that's one of the best on the island, are also available from either of the parks service offices. *Hervey Bay City Council, 10 Bideford St., Torquay, tel. 071/ 25–1855; open weekdays 9–5. Rainbow Beach Rd., Rainbow Beach, tel. 074/86–3160; open daily 8:30–5:30.*

Cairns

Cairns is the capital of the region known as the Far North. The city is closer to Papua New Guinea than it is to most of Australia, and its sense of isolation has only just begun to lessen with its recent role as an international gateway. Nevertheless, it still feels like a sleepy tropical town. Many of the older homes are built on stilts to catch the ocean breezes, and overhead fans are ubiquitous. The city itself is totally flat, surrounded by rain forests and macadamia, sugarcane, and pineapple plantations. The Coral Sea forms the town's eastern boundary, and to the west are the slopes of the dividing range leading up to the Atherton Tableland.

If you're a serious angler, you have reached your mecca. Scores of charter boats leave here in pursuit of black marlin, tuna, and reef fish. Other cruise boats take visitors to the islands and coral of the Great Barrier Reef. In many respects, Cairns is nothing more than a dormitory or staging post—high-rise hotels, motels, and cheap hostels abound, but most people use the town only as a base for exploring the surrounding ocean and rain forests.

Arriving and Departing

By Bus   **Greyhound Pioneer Australia** (tel. 070/51–2411 or 13–2030), **Sunliner** (tel. 070/51–6399) and **McCafferty's** (tel. 070/51–5899), operate daily express buses from major southern cities.

By Car   The 1,712-kilometer (1,063-mile) route from Brisbane to Cairns runs along the Bruce Highway (Route 1), which later becomes the Captain Cook Highway. Although the entire route is now paved, there are many tortuous sections that make driving difficult. Throughout its length, the road rarely touches the coast—so, unless you crave endless fields of sugarcane, it's not even picturesque. Consider instead flying to Cairns and renting a car.

By Plane Direct flights to **Cairns International Airport** from the United States are available aboard **Qantas. Ansett Australia** (tel. 13–1300), and **Qantas** (tel. 13–1313) provide regular service from Brisbane, and nonstop flights from Melbourne and Sydney.

By Train The *Sunlander* and *Queenslander* trains make the 32-hour journey between Brisbane and Cairns. The *Sunlander* runs three times a week to Cairns, the *Queenslander* once a week. The *Queenslander* has recently been refurbished to the level of most luxury cruise ships, making the journey equal in comfort to that of the world's great deluxe trains. Trains arrive at the station on McLeod Street (tel. 070/51–1111).

Getting Around

By Car Cars can be rented from **Avis** (tel. 070/51–5911), **Budget** (tel. 070/51–9222), **Hertz** (tel. 070/51–6399), and **Thrifty** (tel. 070/51–8099). Four-wheel-drive vehicles are available.

By Taxi **Black and White Taxis** (tel. 070/51–5333).

Important Addresses and Numbers

Tourist Information **Far North Queensland Promotion Bureau** (Port Authority Bldg., corner Hartley and Grafton Sts., tel. 070/51–3588).

Cairns Convention and Visitors Bureau (Shields St., tel. 070/51–3766).

Emergencies **Cairns Base Hospital** (tel. 070/50–6333).

For emergencies requiring the **police, fire department,** or an **ambulance,** dial 000.

Guided Tours

Orientation Tours **Red Explorer Bus Lines** offers hourly tours of the city accompanied by commentary. Passengers can disembark at any point along the tour and board a later bus. *85 Lake St., tel. 070/55–1240. Tickets: $20 adults, $10 children. Hourly tours Mon.–Sat. 9–4.*

Great Barrier Reef Tours For information about cruises to the Great Barrier Reef, *see* Chapter 8. While you're still in Cairns, however, attend one of the informative and entertaining lectures presented by **Reef Teach** at the City Library. Six nights a week, a marine biologist uses slides and samples of coral—not to mention his sterling fish imitations—to inform prospective divers about the Great Barrier Reef's evolution and the unique inhabitants of this delicate marine ecosystem. *Cairns City Library, 117–125 Lake St; Reef Teach office, 300 Draper St., tel. 070/51–6882. Admission: $10. Lectures Mon.–Sat. 6:15–8:30.*

Nature Tours **Daintree Wildlife Safari** (tel. 070/98–6125 or toll-free 008/07–9102) and **Daintree Rainforest River Trains** (tel. 070/90–7676 or toll-free 008/17–9090) run full-day, half-day, and self-drive tours through mangrove swamps and thick rain forest to see native orchids, birds, crocodiles, and butterfly farms. *Prices range from $12 to $85.*

Tropic Wings Tours offers a variety of trips in the Cairns area, including tours to Atherton Tablelands, waterfalls, Kuranda, Port Douglas, Daintree Rain Forest, the Outback, and the Gulf of Carpentaria. *278 Hartley St., tel. 070/35–3555.*

Train Tours The **Kuranda Scenic Railway** from Cairns to Kuranda is a trip that ranks as one of the great rail journeys of the world. Kuranda is the gateway to the Atherton Tableland, an elevated area of rich volcanic soil that is one of Australia's finest beef-, dairy-, and vegetable-producing areas. Between this tableland and the narrow coastal strip is a rugged dividing range filled with waterfalls, lakes, caves, and gorges. The train makes the 1½-hour ascent through the rain forest via the Barron River Gorge and 15 hand-carved tunnels. The train has two classes: Commentary Class and Royale Class (where champagne is served). There are several departures daily, and a wide range of tours are available, from full-day rain-forest safaris to simple round-trip train and bus rides. For departure times and bookings, contact Cairns Station (McLeod St., Cairns 4870, tel. 070/52–6250). The one-way fare for Commentary Class is $20 for adults, $29 round-trip; $10 for children, $14.50 round-trip. Royale Class (book through Kuranda Connection, tel. 070/55–2222) costs $30 for adults one way, $20 for children; the round-trip fare is double.

Exploring Cairns

The center of town is **City Place,** a quaint pedestrian mall where you can watch the passing parade. Some of the town's few authentic pubs, as well as the major shopping area, are located around the square.

The **Cairns Museum** is situated next to City Place on Shields Street. The museum houses a collection of artifacts and photographs of Cairns's history, including a fascinating exhibit on the life of the Aborigines in the rain forests. *Lake and Shields Sts., tel. 070/51–5582. Admission: $2 adults, 50¢ children. Open Mon.–Sat. 10–3.*

Walk down Shields Street to the **Esplanade** and the waterfront, the focal point of life in Cairns. Fronting Trinity Bay, the Esplanade is the site of many of the town's best stores and hotels. It is also where many of the backpackers who throng to Cairns like to gather, giving it a lively, slightly bohemian feel. Unfortunately, Trinity Bay is shallow and rather unappealing—hundreds of yards of ugly mangrove flats are uncovered at low tide. Over the past few years, some of the waterfront has been filled in and Pier Market Place, a shopping/hotel complex, was constructed. Walk south along the Esplanade to where it turns into Wharf Street. Cairns traces its beginnings in 1876 to this small area, which was the port for the gold and tin mined inland. The area later became known as the Barbary Coast because of the criminal element that lurked here. Today, it's once again a thriving port. Wander onto **Marlin Jetty** where the charter fishing boats are moored. Big-game fishing is a major industry, and fish weighing more than 1,000 pounds are sometimes caught in the waters off the reef. South of Marlin Jetty are the docks for the catamarans that conduct tours of the islands and marine life of the Great Barrier Reef (for more information about these tours, *see* Chapter 8).

What to See and Do with Children

Cairns Sugarworld, 14 kilometers (9 miles) south of Cairns, is a tourist park with an old sugar mill, rain forest, and tropical orchards of such fruit as papaya, jackfruit, and durian. Also featured are water slides, a barbecue area, a children's farm, and a park with kangaroos and other Australian animals. *Hambledon Mill Rd., Edmonton, tel. 070/55–5477. Admission: $10 adults, $8 children. Open weekends 10–5.*

Off the Beaten Track

The **Tjapukai Dance Theatre** in Kuranda is home to an a[...]
ning Aboriginal dance group with a wonderful sense of hun[...]
perform two shows daily on the life and times of Aborigina[...]
21 Main St., near Kuranda Railway Sta., tel. 070/93–7544. T[...]
$16 adults, $8 children. Shows daily at 11 and 1:30.

Much further afield are the **Undara Lava Tubes,** a fascinating geo[...]
ical oddity in the Outback. These hollow basalt tubes created b[...]
volcanic outpouring 190,000 years ago are attracting an ever-i[...]
creasing number of visitors despite being 400 kilometers (248 miles)
from Cairns, on the western side of the ranges. There are several
places where it is possible to walk into the tubes. Leaving the ferns,
vines, and wallabies at the entrance behind, one steps onto the
smooth and dry tunnel floor. Above, horseshoe bats twitter and flit-
ter in the crannies. Patterns etched in the ceiling by water seepage
create an incongruous cathedral effect. Day tours to Undara from
Cairns-ceiling are operated by **Australian Pacific Tours** (Orchid Plaza, Lake St., tel. 070/51–9299) and depart Tuesday, Thursday, and
Saturday at 8 AM, returning at 7 PM. The cost of the tour is $92. There
are accommodations at **Lava Lodge** (tel. 070/97–1411, fax 070/97–
1450).

Shopping

Malls   **Palm Court** (34–42 Lake St.) is a modern complex featuring such
stores as Le Classique Duty Free, Boutique Lacoste, Carla Zampat-
ti, and Mario Ferri. Located on the waterfront, **Trinity Wharf**
(Wharf St., tel. 070/31–1519) has everything from designer clothes
and souvenirs to resort wear, hairdressers, and restaurants. Shoppers can request complimentary transportation from their hotels.
On the Esplanade, **Pier Market Place** (Pierpoint Rd., tel. 070/51–
7244) houses international chains such as the Gap and Country
Road, and the offices of yacht brokers and tour operators. Many of
the cafés, bars, and restaurants open onto verandas on the water
side. **Orchid Plaza** (between Lake and Abbot Sts., tel. 070/51–7788)
has 14 fashion shops, several cafés, record stores, and a post office.

Markets   Held on Saturday and Sunday mornings, **Rusty's Bazaar** (Grafton
and Sheridan Sts.) is the best street market in Cairns. Everything
from homegrown fruit and vegetables to second-hand items and antiques is on sale.

Specialty   An excellent place to buy authentic Aboriginal handicrafts and art is
Stores   **Outback Images** (Central Court Hotel, Lake and Spence Sts., tel.
070/31–2167).

The well-respected **Original Dreamtime Gallery of Alice Springs** (7/8
Palm Court, Lake St., tel. 070/51–3222) has a branch in Cairns sell-
ing top-quality artworks created by the Aborigines of the Northern
Territory.

Gallery Primitive (26 Abbott St., tel. 070/31–1641) has native crafts
of Papua New Guinea on display.

Pier Gallery (The Pier Marketplace, tel. 070/51–6533) features
paintings by leading local artists.

Australian Craftworks (Shop 20, Village La., Lake St., tel. 070/51–
0725) has one of the finest collections of local crafts.

nt Sports

beaches of its own, and the majority of visitors head
to swim and snorkel. Situated just north of the
wever, are **Palm Cove, Trinity Beach, Clifton Beach,**
Beach, Yorkey's Knob, Holloway's Beach, and **Machan's**
. Do not swim in these waters from October to May, though,
en extremely dangerous box jellyfish known as "stingers" are
found in the water along the coast. Some beaches have small netted
areas, but it is advisable to stick to hotel pools. Stingers are not
found around the Great Barrier Reef or any offshore islands.

Diving A large number of diving schools in Cairns offer everything from be-
ginner's lessons to equipment rentals and expeditions for experienced divers. Contact **Deep Sea Divers Den** (319 Draper St., tel. 070/
31–2223), **Don Cowrie's Down-Under Dive** (27 Shields St., tel. 070/
31–1588), **Pro Dive** (Marlin Parade, tel. 070/31–5255), **Quicksilver**
Diving Services (Marina Mirage, Port Douglas, tel. 070/99–5050),
and **Sunlover Dive** (Trinity Wharf, tel. 070/31–1055).

White-Water R&R Whitewater (74 Abbot St., tel. 070/51–7777) offers very excit-
Rafting ing one- and two-day white-water expeditions that are suitable only
for the physically fit.

Dining

Price categories for restaurants are the same as in the Brisbane
Dining section, *above.* Highly recommended restaurants are indicated by a star ★.

$$$ **The Captain's Table.** Situated on the waterfront in the Radisson Pla-
za Hotel, this restaurant has an exceptionally professional staff. The
decor is gracious and elegant, and tables are laid with silver cutlery.
The cuisine is French with tropical influences, but make sure you
save room for dessert—the dessert tray has to be seen to be be-
lieved. Try the mouth-watering chocolate mousse cake. *Radisson*
Plaza Hotel at the Pier, Pier Point Rd., tel. 070/31–1411. Reserva-
tions recommended. Dress: casual but neat. AE, DC, MC, V. No
lunch; closed Sun.

$$ **Breeze's Restaurant.** Ceiling-to-floor windows overlooking Trinity
★ Inlet and the distant mountains set the mood in this attractive res-
taurant in the Cairns Hilton. The decor is bright with tropical
greenery, white tablecloths, candles, and silver tableware. Diners
can feast on everything from quick sandwiches to full-course dinners. The specialty, however, is seafood, and a spectacular seafood
buffet is offered on Friday and Saturday nights. *Cairns Hilton In-*
ternational, Wharf St., tel. 070/52–6786. Reservations recom-
mended. Dress: casual but neat. AE, DC, MC, V.

$$ **Verandahs.** Located upstairs directly adjacent to the city mall, this
★ elegant restaurant is a culinary highlight in Cairns. The dining room
is spacious and comfortable, with a tropical ambience created by the
extensive use of large plants, veranda railings, potted palms, and
white-cane furniture. Floor-to-ceiling windows overlook the city
mall, and a cozy cocktail bar is located next to the main dining room.
The cuisine emphasizes seafood, but a variety of Asian-influenced
dishes are also available. Daily specials are posted on a blackboard
and often include bouillabaisse (a simmering crock pot of spicy
Queensland seafood), a warm salad of shovel-nosed lobster (known
as Moreton Bay bugs) and selected prawns with garlic, or Japanese
sushi and chicken yakitori. *10B Shields St., tel. 070/51–0011. Reser-*

vations advised. Dress: casual but neat. AE, DC, MC, V. Closed Sat. lunch, Sun.

$ **Roma Roulette.** Popular with locals and visitors alike, this restaurant has an easygoing, informal atmosphere, and smiling chef Antonio often personally advises customers on what to order. Two of the restaurant's favorites are *pasta tricolore* (three differentcolored pastas and sauces) and *scaloppine al vino bianco* (veal with white wine). The seafood is also recommended. *48A Aplin St., tel. 070/51–1076. Reservations advised. Dress: casual. AE, DC, V. BYOB.*

Lodging

Price categories for hotels are the same as in the Brisbane Lodging section, *above*. Highly recommended lodgings are indicated by a star ★.

$$$$ **Hilton International Cairns.** Popular with Americans, this water-
★ front hotel curves along the shoreline and offers wonderful sea views. The seven-story hotel is near the business district and the famous game-fishing club. The lobby, which looks out past lush gardens to the ocean, is distinctly tropical, with ceramic floor tiles and a glass-dome atrium filled with rain-forest palms and ferns. A rooftop garden hangs down along the external walkways, and rooms on the lowest level open onto a palm forest on the lobby's roof. Decorated in pinks and blue-greens with touches of brown, the rooms feature natural wood furniture, color TVs, and air-conditioning. All rooms have private balconies. *Wharf St., 4870, tel. 070/521599, fax 070/52–1370. 264 rooms with bath and shower. Facilities: outdoor pool, Jacuzzi, sauna, laundry service. AE, DC, MC, V.*

$$$$ **Radisson Plaza at the Pier.** The conservative, low-rise design of this popular hotel is typical of northern Queensland, with a nautical theme as befits its location on the waterfront overlooking Trinity Bay and Marlin Marina—the main terminal for cruises to the Barrier Reef. The hotel also adjoins Pier Market Place with its 90 shops, food court, and restaurants. The lobby's atrium features a tropical theme so spectacular (or horrific—it depends how you regard fake indoor rain forests) that it's a tourist attraction in its own right. All rooms are spacious, with air-conditioning, ceiling fans, color TVs, tea/coffee makers, and minibars. Rooms designed for disabled guests are also available. *Pier Point Rd., 4870, tel. 070/31–1411, fax 070/31–3226. 223 rooms with bath. Facilities: pool, 2 restaurants, Jacuzzi, business center, laundry. AE, DC, MC, V.*

$$$ **Holiday Inn.** This seven-story hotel is built in a unique figure-eight shape overlooking Trinity Bay and the Coral Sea. Decorated with a marble floor, luxurious rugs, and cane sofas, the glass-walled lobby features a landscaped tropical atrium and views over the hotel gardens. The guest rooms are large, decorated in soft aqua hues with cane chairs and wood tables. The hotel is centrally located, within walking distance of shops, restaurants, and the business district. *Esplanade and Florence St., 4870, tel. 070/31–3757, fax 070/31–4130. 259 rooms with bath. Facilities: restaurant, 3 bars, laundry service, 2 laundries, room service. AE, DC, MC, V.*

$$$ **Pacific International.** Facing the waterfront and the marina, this 11-
★ story hotel has a soaring three-story lobby—with palms, a marble floor, rattan furniture, and two spectacular brass chandeliers—that provides an awesome entrance. Guest rooms are furnished with cane and rattan chairs, soft pastels, tropical plants, and Gauguin-style prints. All are air-conditioned, with private balconies, color TVs,

and tea/coffee makers. Rooms for disabled guests are available. *Esplanade and Spence St., 4870, tel. 070/51–7888 or toll-free 008/07–9001, fax 070/51–0210. 176 rooms with bath. Facilities: restaurant, coffee shop, bistro, 4 bars, hairdresser. AE, DC, MC, V.*

$$ **Cairns Aquarius.** Located five minutes from the heart of Cairns, this cream-color hotel–apartment building is set right on the waterfront Esplanade. Large glass windows and wide-open balconies offer spectacular views over the Coral Sea. The lobby features creamy marble, mirrors galore, a colorful tropical mural, and a tropical garden leading off the reception area. All guest rooms are furnished differently; two-bedroom apartments with two bathrooms are available; and rooms are serviced weekly. A barbecue area is located in the landscaped gardens on the mezzanine level. *107 Esplanade, 4870, tel. 070/51–8444, fax 070/31–1448. 35 apartments with shower. Minimum booking periods apply. Facilities: 2 pools, sauna, whirlpool, ½-size tennis court, photocopying and fax service. AE, DC, MC, V.*

$$ **Cairns Colonial Club Resort.** Set in 8 acres of lush tropical gardens, this two-story, colonial-style complex won the Beautiful Garden Award for the Cairns area for several years in a row. The resort is built around two saltwater swimming pools, and the public areas and rooms are simply furnished with cane furniture, ceiling fans, and vivid tropical cushions. Rooms are equipped with refrigerators, color TVs, air-conditioning, and tea/coffee makers. Apartments with cooking facilities are also available. Two of the rooms offer special facilities for the handicapped. A free shuttle bus makes the 7-kilometer (4-mile) run to the city center hourly, and courtesy airport transfers are also provided. *18–26 Cannon St., Manunda, 4870, tel. 070/53–5111, fax 070/53–7072. 264 rooms with bath, 82 one-bedroom units with bath. Facilities: 2 outdoor pools, 2 restaurants, 3 bars, limited room service. AE, DC, MC, V.*

$ **Hides of Cairns.** Located within a heartbeat of the city center, this three-story circa-1890 structure, with its breezy verandas, is a superb example of colonial Outback architecture. An adjoining motel section features modern rooms with tropical decor, air-conditioning, color TVs, radios, and refrigerators. Rates include full or Continental breakfast. *Lake and Shields Sts., 4870, tel. 070/51–1266, fax 070/31–2276. 72 rooms, most with private bath and shower. Facilities: pool, Jacuzzi, restaurant, 5 bars, tour office. AE, DC, MC, V.*

Nightlife

Reno Club International (Palm Court Shopping Centre, 34–42 Lake St., tel. 070/52–1480) is a smart, two-level disco.

The Nest (82 McLeod St., tel. 070/51–8181) is a snappy spot to meet and mingle with the locals in their party mood.

The Pier Tavern (The Pier Marketplace, the Esplanade, tel. 070/31–4677), overlooking the waterfront, is a more sophisticated, upmarket (and touristy) watering hole.

North from Cairns

The Captain Cook Highway runs from Cairns to Mossman, a relatively civilized stretch known mostly for the chic resort town of Port Douglas. Past the Daintree River, however, wildlife parks and sunny coastal villages fade into one of the most sensationally wild corners of the continent. If you came to Australia in search of high-octane sun, empty beaches and coral cays, steamy jungles filled with exotic bird noises and rioting vegetation, and a languid, beachcomber lifestyle, then the coast from Daintree to Cooktown should appeal.

The southern half of this coastline lies within Cape Tribulation National Park, part of the Greater Daintree Wilderness Area, a region named to UNESCO's World Heritage list because of its unique ecology. If you want to get a peek at the natural splendor of the area, then there's no need to go past Cape Tribulation. However, the Bloomfield Track does continue on to Cooktown, a destination that will tack two days onto your itinerary. This wild, rugged country breeds some notoriously maverick personalities and can add a whole other dimension to the Far North Queensland experience.

It is not advisable to tackle the wilderness of the Far North alone. By its very nature, the national park requires an expert interpreter because, to untrained eyes, the rain forest can look like nothing more than giant roots underfoot and palm trees overhead. Therefore, it's recommended that visitors take a guided tour; many tour operators offer day trips across the Daintree River from either Cairns or Port Douglas. Better still, stay a couple of days at Cape Tribulation, leaving your footprints on empty beaches, snorkeling off the coral reefs, and drifting off to sleep while the jungle croaks, drips, and squeaks around you.

Prime time for visiting the area is between May and September, when the daily maximum temperature averages around 26°C (80°F) and the water is comfortably warm. During the wet season, which lasts from about December to March, you can expect monsoonal conditions. Toxic box jellyfish make the coastline unsafe for swimming during the wet period, but this problem is confined to mainland beaches, not coral reefs.

Arriving and Departing

By Bus **Coral Coaches** (tel. 070/31–7577) operates a bus service between Cairns, Port Douglas, and Cape Tribulation. The bus departs Cairns daily at 8 AM and 3 PM. The cost is $25 each way, $12.50 for children 4–14.

KCT Connections (tel. 070/31–2990) operates package tours that include bus transport from Cairns and overnight dormitory accommodations at either the Jungle Lodge or Crocodylus Village (*see* Dining and Lodging, *below*). Cost of a one-night stay is $69; two nights is $79. For children under 15, the cost is approximately half the adult fare.

Strikies Safaris (tel. 070/99–5599) operates an air-conditioned bus service between Cairns and Cooktown along the inland route. The bus departs Cairns at 6 AM on Monday, Wednesday, and Friday. On the return journey, the bus departs Cooktown on the same days at about 2 PM. The round-trip costs $69 for adults, $40 for children 4–14.

By Car To head north by car from Cairns, head down Florence Street from the Esplanade for four blocks and then turn right onto Sheridan Street, which is the beginning of northbound Highway 1. Highway 1 leads past the airport and forks 12 kilometers (7 miles) north of Cairns; take the right fork for Cook Highway, which goes as far as Mossman. From Mossman, the turnoff for the Daintree River crossing is 29 kilometers (17 miles) north on the Daintree-Mossman Road. Except for four-wheel-drive vehicles, rental cars are not permitted on the narrow, twisting road north of the Daintree River. **Avis** (tel. 070/51–5911) has four-wheel-drive Toyota Landcruisers for rent from Cairns; the cost is $135 per day for the first 100 kilometers (62 miles) plus 25¢ for each additional kilometer.

By Plane **Hinterland Aviation** (tel. 070/35–9323) links Cairns with Cow Bay— the airport for Cape Tribulation—and the Bloomfield River. The flight to Cow Bay costs $60 per person each way; children under 3 not occupying a seat fly free. To Bloomfield, the cost is $75. Both airfields are isolated dirt strips, and passengers must arrange onward transport to their destination. The coastal views, however, are spectacular.

Getting Around

The **Coral Coaches** bus (tel. 070/31–7577) travels between the Daintree Ferry crossing and Cape Tribulation twice daily in each direction.

Important Addresses and Numbers

Tourist Information **Cooktown Travel.** *Charlotte St., Cooktown, tel. 070/69–5377. Open weekdays 9–12:30 and 1:30–5, Sat. 9–noon.*

Emergencies **Mossman Police** (tel. 070/98–1200).

Port Douglas Police (tel. 070/99–5220).

In the event of a medical emergency, contact the **Mossman District Hospital** (tel. 070/98–1211).

Be advised that doctors, ambulances, firefighters, and police are scarce to nonexistent between the Daintree River and Cooktown.

Guided Tours

Orientation Tours **Australian Wilderness Safari** operates a one-day wildlife and wilderness trip into Cape Tribulation National Park—as well as tours of the Daintree Rain Forest—aboard air-conditioned four-wheel-drive vehicles. Passenger pickup is available from Cairns, Port Douglas, and occasionally Palm Cove and Mossman. All tours are led by naturalists and include use of binoculars and reference books. Morning tea or lunch is included. This is one of the longest-established rain forest tours and one of the best. *Tel. 070/98–1766. Prices: from Cairns, $115 adults, $57 children 4–14; from Port Douglas, $105 adults, $52.50 children.*

Native Guide Safari Tours is operated by Hazel Douglas, an Aboriginal woman whose knowledge and passion for her ancestral homeland—which extends from Mossman to Cooktown—sets this one-day tour apart. After departing from Port Douglas at 7:30 AM, you'll sample some of the edible flora of the Daintree region, learn how the Aboriginal people exploited the rain forest ecosystem, and hear legends that have been passed down over thousands of years. *Tel. 070/99–*

5327. *Prices: $80 adults, $60 children under 15, including lunch plus morning and afternoon teas.*

Strikies Safaris operates a two-day, four-wheel-drive safari along the coast from Cairns to Cooktown. The bus departs Cairns on Wednesday, Friday, and Sunday. *Tel. 070/99–5599. Prices: $199 adults, $169 children 4–14, excluding accommodations.*

Boat Tours **Big River Cruises** operates a sunset tour, which includes a cruise along the Daintree River, a forest walk, and a barbecue. Generally, this is the most profitable time of day for wildlife viewing. *Tel. 070/90–7515. Prices: $55 adults, $25 children 4–14.*

The *Crocodile Express* is a flat-bottom boat, which cruises the Daintree River on crocodile-spotting excursions. The boat departs from the Daintree River crossing at 10:30 and 1:30 daily for a two-hour cruise. Cruises also depart at frequent intervals throughout the day from the Daintree Eco Centre, 3 kilometers (2 miles) upstream of the village of Daintree. *Tel. 070/98–6120. Prices: $22 adults, $10 children under 15.*

Walking Tour **Paul Mason** is an entertaining local who offers guided walking tours of the rain forest around Cape Tribulation. A choice of walks is available, including two-hour strolls, half-day walks, and night walks. Prices start at $15.50 for adults, $8 for children 4–14. Tours can be booked through the store at Cape Tribulation; it doesn't have a phone so you have to just drop by and see what's available.

Reef Tour *Taipan Lady,* a sailing catamaran, makes daily trips out to Mackay Cay or Undine Reef from the beach at Cape Tribulation. The waters around both atolls are a far cry from the graveyards that surround many of the atolls south of the Daintree; you can expect to see a wealth of marine life, including giant clams, pristine coral, and, occasionally, sea turtles. Would-be divers can take a $50 resort dive—a brief introduction to scuba diving with an instructor, who will fit you out with a wetsuit, flotation jacket, and air tank, and then descend with you to a depth of about 10 meters (33 feet) for a dive that lasts around 30 minutes. *Tel. 070/98–0086. Prices: $69 adults, $49 children 4–14, including lunch and gear.*

Exploring North from Cairns

Numbers in the margin correspond to points of interest on the North Queensland Coast map.

1 A 20-minute drive from Cairns brings you to the turnoff for **Palm Cove,** one of the jewels of Queensland and an ideal base for exploring the far north. Palm Cove is an oasis of quietude that those in the know seek out for its magnificent trees, calm waters, and excellent restaurants. The loudest noises you are likely to hear are the singing of birds and the lapping of the Pacific Ocean on the beach.

2 Right on the highway near Palm Cove is **Wild World,** a 10-acre park with a wide variety of Australian wildlife, including kangaroos, 150 crocodiles and other reptiles, pelicans, and cassowaries. Most distinguished among its residents is Sarge, a crocodile that the park claims is more than 100 years old and the largest female in captivity. At 700 kilograms (1,540 pounds) and more than 5 meters (17 feet) in length, Sarge won't leave many unconvinced. The park also features a snake show, a snake-handling demonstration, trained cockatoos that perform twice daily, and a giant North Queensland cane-toad race. *Captain Cook Hwy., Palm Cove, tel. 070/55–3669. Admission: $14 adults, $7 children. Open daily 9–5. Closed Dec. 25.*

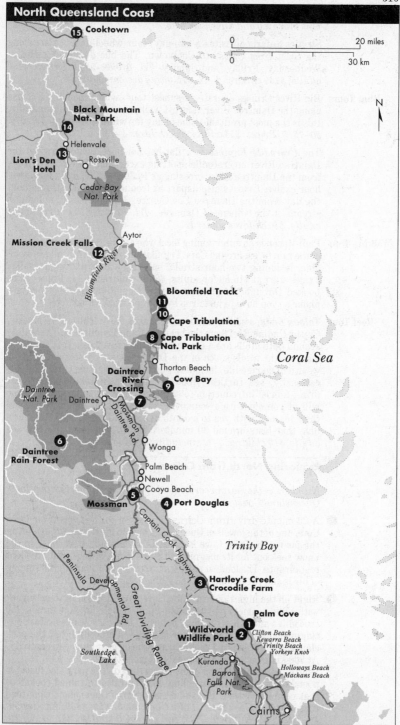

North Queensland Coast

0   20 miles

0   30 km

N

15 Cooktown

**Black Mountain
Nat. Park**

14

○ Helenvale

13

**Lion's Den
Hotel**

○ Rossville

*Cedar Bay
Nat. Park*

Mission Creek Falls   ○ Aytor

Bloomfield River

12

Bloomfield Track

11

10

Cape Tribulation

8 **Cape Tribulation
Nat. Park**

Coral Sea

○ Thorton Beach

**Daintree
River
Crossing**

Cow Bay

9

*Daintree
Nat. Park*

○ Daintree

7

*Mossman
Daintree Rd.*

**Daintree
Rain Forest**

6

○ Wonga

○ Palm Beach

○ Newell

○ Cooya Beach

Mossman

5

4 **Port Douglas**

Captain Cook Highway

Trinity Bay

Peninsula Developmental Rd.

Great Dividing Range

3 **Hartley's Creek
Crocodile Farm**

Palm Cove

1

2

Clifton Beach

Kewarra Beach

Trinity Beach

Yorkeys Knob

**Wildworld
Wildlife Park**

*Southedge
Lake*

○ Kuranda

*Barron
Falls Nat.
Park*

Holloways Beach

Machans Beach

Cairns ○

Next door to Wild World is the **Outback Opal Mine,** where those interested in this unique Australian gemstone can glimpse huge specimens and opalized seashells and fossils. The owners, who were once opal miners at Coober Pedy, show how an opal is formed, and then how it is cut and polished. *Cook Hwy., Palm Cove, tel. 070/55–3492. Admission free. Open daily 9–5.*

❸ Also on the main Cook Highway is **Hartley's Creek Crocodile Farm,** highlighted by Charlie, a 1,000-kilogram (2,200-pound) male crocodile that makes Sarge look positively svelte. In a rain-forest setting, visitors can also see dingoes, birds, snakes, and the rare cassowary, which is found only in New Guinea and parts of Australia. The bird has a large, bony casque with which it defends itself. *Cook Hwy., 40 km (24 mi) north of Cairns, tel. 070/55–3576. Admission: $10 adults, $5 children. Open daily 8–5; snake shows at 2; crocodile shows at 3.*

Continuing north, the Cook Highway passes glorious headlands that look almost too good to be true. Every winding turn in the road unfolds more lush, emerald-green tropical vegetation on one side and miles of pristine beach on the other. The road soon widens, flanked by palm trees that were planted during World War II for ❹ palm oil and then transferred to form the avenue leading to **Port Douglas.** Within 10 minutes you are in Port Douglas itself. Ten years ago this was a sleepy little fishing village, but today it's one of the "in" destinations in Australia. Known as "The Port" to locals, the town has an indefinable mystique. Enough of the old Queensland colonial buildings remain to give it an authentic feel, despite the growing presence of modern resorts and hotels. A major activity here is taking a high-speed cruise to the outer reef (*see* Guided Tours in Chapter 8).

❺ Continue on to **Mossman,** a sugar town with a population of less than 2,000. Five kilometers (3 miles) out of town are the beautiful water- ❻ falls and river at Mossman Gorge. The **Daintree Rain Forest,** now a national park, is 35 kilometers (22 miles) farther along the road. New species of fauna and flora are still being discovered here, and the rain forest vegetation is as impressive as anything found in the Amazon Basin. It is wise to explore this area in a four-wheel-drive vehicle with a guide. Some of the tracks through the rain forest are unpaved and muddy, and it is often necessary to ford streams. Consider taking one of the guided tours of the area, or at least enjoy a ride on a riverboat (*see* Guided Tours, *above*).

North of Mossman, the Mossman-Daintree Road winds through ❼ sugarcane plantations and towering green hills to the **Daintree River crossing.** The Daintree is a relatively short river, yet it's fed by heavy monsoonal rains that make it wide, glossy, and brown—and a favorite inland haunt for saltwater crocodiles. The relationship between the area's reptile and human inhabitants is not always harmonious: During a 1985 New Year's Eve party, a local resident was snatched from the bank of the river, and her enraged companions took their revenge on every crocodile they could find. To dramatize the resulting decline in the crocodile population, local tour operator Brian Strike swam across the river at the ferry crossing—with nary a nibble. While the waters right at the ferry may have been thinned, during most times of the year you won't have to travel far to spot a croc. *Cost: $5 per vehicle. Ferry crossings every 20 min 6 AM–midnight.*

❽ On the north bank, a sign announces the beginning of **Cape Tribulation National Park** (*also see* National Parks, *below*). This ecological wonderland is a remnant of the forests in which flowering plants first appeared on earth—an evolutionary leap that utilized insects in the pollination process and provided an energy-rich food supply for the early marsupials that were replacing the dinosaurs. Experts can readily identify species of angiosperms, the most primitive flowering plant on the planet, many of which are found nowhere else but in this area. If you were searching for the most ancient roots of humankind, sooner or later you would find yourself here, in this very forest. Thankfully, the gravel road beyond the ferry crossing was recently upgraded and paved; the increasing tour traffic had been kicking up dust, which was not beneficial to the forest's rare flora.

9 About 10 kilometers (6 miles) beyond the river, Buchanans Creek Road turns toward the sea and **Cow Bay.** The sweep of sand at Cow Bay is fairly typical of the beaches north of the Daintree, with the advantage that the fig trees at the back of the beach offer welcome shade.

10 North of Cow Bay, the road plays a game of hide-and-seek with the sea, climbing high over the Noah Range before reaching **Cape Tribulation,** where a tiny settlement is set dramatically at the base of Mount Sorrow. The cape was named by Captain James Cook, who was understandably peeved after a nearby reef inflicted a gaping wound in the side of his ship, HMS *Endeavour,* forcing him to seek refuge at the present-day site of Cooktown.

The Cape Tribulation settlement is the activities and accommodations base for the national park, although it's easy to shoot through without realizing that you've arrived. You'll find a shop, a couple of lodges, and that's about it. The cape's natural credentials are impeccable, however: Nowhere else on the Australian coastline do coral reef and rain forest exist in such proximity, and this happy coincidence and the area's barefoot manners make it special. Until recently, the only tourists who came this way were backpackers who holed up in lodges here for a few dollars a night, and tourism in the area still has a casual, back-to-nature flavor. For example, all of the regional tours—including rain forest walks, reef trips, horseback riding, and fishing—can be booked through the village shop. If you'd rather loaf on the beach, the one nearest to town is about a five-minute walk along a boardwalk that cuts through a mangrove swamp; the beach to the north of Cape Tribulation is more scenic, however.

11 Just beyond the cape, the **Bloomfield Track** takes up the journey north. The track is less than 30 kilometers (19 miles) long but it still generates powerful passions. The decision in the early '80s to carve a road through the Daintree wilderness provoked one of the most bitter conservation battles of recent memory. The road went through, but the ruckus was instrumental in securing a World Heritage listing for the Daintree, thereby effectively shutting out logging operations. At Cape Tribulation a sign warns that the track is open only to four-wheel-drive vehicles, and although no one will stop you from driving through in a conventional vehicle, the rough passage over the Cowie Range essentially closes the road to all but the most rugged of vehicles.

The Bloomfield River is subject to tides at the ford, and vehicles must wait until the level has dropped sufficiently to allow safe crossing. Extreme care is needed because the submerged causeway can be difficult to follow, and it is fairly common for vehicles to topple off. At the Aboriginal settlement of Wujal Wujal on the north bank **12** of the river, make the short detour inland to **Mission Creek Falls,** where the river is safe for swimming. There's another great swimming spot 20 minutes' drive north of the Bloomfield River: Pull over to the left where a sign identifies the Cedar Bay National Park and walk down the steep gully to a creek; at the bottom of a small cascade is one of the most perfect swimming holes you're ever likely to find.

After a long, slow wander through the national park, the road leaves the rain forest and enters an open woodland. On the border between the two is the **Lion's Den Hotel,** a pub whose corrugated-iron walls and tree-stump chairs ooze un-self-conscious character. The walls are covered in graffiti, from the simple KILROY WAS HERE variety to the totally scandalous, and for the price of a donation to the Royal Flying Doctor Service, you can add your own wit to the collection. It's easy to pass a pleasant afternoon here just observing who and what wanders in the door.

At the junction of northern road—you'll see it called the Bicentennial National Trail on some maps—and the Mulligan Highway, the jumbled piles of rock beside the road identify **Black Mountain National Park.** The distinctive coloration of these granite boulders is caused by a black algae. Climbing the rocks is difficult and dangerous, and the formations are best appreciated from the roadside.

The highway continues another 28 kilometers (17 miles) to **Cooktown,** the last major settlement on the east coast of the continent. A frontier town on the edge of a difficult wilderness, its wide main street consists mainly of two-story pubs with four-wheelers parked out front. Despite the temporary air, Cooktown has a long and impressive history. It was here in 1770 that Captain James Cook beached the *Endeavour* to repair her hull. Any tour of Cooktown should begin at the waterfront, where a statue of Captain Cook gazes out to sea, overlooking the spot where he landed.

A hundred years after Cook's landfall, a town was established when gold was discovered on the Palmer River. Cooktown mushroomed and quickly became the largest settlement in Queensland after Brisbane, but like many mining boomtowns, life was hard and often violent. Chinese miners flooded into the goldfields and anti-Chinese sentiment flared into race riots, echoing the events that had occurred at every other goldfield in the country. Further conflict arose between miners and local Aborigines, who resented what they saw as a territorial invasion and the rape of the region's natural resources; place names such as Battle Camp and Hell's Gate testify to the pattern of ambush and revenge.

Although Cooktown is now a sleepy shadow of those dangerous days—when it had 64 pubs on a main street 3 kilometers (2 miles) long—a significant slice of history has been preserved at the **James Cook Historical Museum,** formerly a convent of the Sisters of Mercy. The museum houses relics of the gold-mining era, Chinese settlers, both World Wars, Aboriginal artifacts, canoes, and a notable collection of seashells—not to mention artifacts relating to the intriguing story of Mrs. Watson, who escaped from a party of hostile Aborigines on Lizard Island with her son and a Chinese servant in a huge cooking pot, only to perish of thirst on another island. The museum also contains mementos of Cook's voyage, including the anchor and one of the cannons that were jettisoned when the *Endeavour* ran aground. *Helen St., tel. 070/69–5386. Admission: $4 adults, $1 children. Open daily 10–4.*

From Cooktown, the northern tip of the Australian mainland is still some 800 kilometers (500 miles) distant via the road that runs along the middle of Cape York.

Shopping

Port Douglas Unquestionably the best and most elegant shopping complex in northern Queensland, the **Marina Mirage** (Wharf St., tel. 070/99–5775) contains 40 fashion and specialty shops for souvenirs, jewelry, accessories, resort wear, and designer clothing.

Dining and Lodging

Towns on the Cairns-to-Mossman leg of the coast have some excellent dining and lodging options. Restaurants and accommodations between the Daintree River crossing and Cooktown, however, are of a rougher breed: Basic lodges outnumber luxury resorts, and most dining is both on-site and unremarkable: other than ambience, there's no reason to prefer the restaurants of more expensive hotels to those of backpacker lodges. One exception is the Bloomfield Wilderness Lodge, which serves better-than-average food—but only to its guests.

Price categories are the same as in the Brisbane section, *above*. Highly recommended establishments are indicated by a star ★.

Bloomfield River **Bloomfield Wilderness Lodge.** This lodge sits in rugged surroundings near the mouth of the Bloomfield River and consists of a dozen smart, timber bungalows, each of which has a balcony at the front, lots of open latticework, and a ceiling fan. Activities include guided walks, fishing, beachcombing along the small but deserted beaches, and croc-spotting cruises on the Bloomfield River. The most convenient access is by plane from Cairns. *Box 966, Cairns 4870, tel. 070/ 35–9166, fax 070/35–9180. 22 rooms with bath. Facilities: pool, restaurant, bar. Tariff includes all meals. AE, DC, MC, V. $$$$*

Cape Tribulation **Coconut Beach Rainforest Resort.** The pick of the accommodations at Cape Tribulation sits swathed in a jungle of fan palms, staghorn ferns, giant melaleucas, and strangler figs, about 2 kilometers (1 mile) south of the cape itself. The centerpiece of the resort is the Long House, a striking, pole-frame building that overlooks the main swimming pool. Stay in individual chalets built in 1994 or in less-expensive, older-style rooms, which are clustered in blocks of three. The resort makes much of its eco-awareness, so the rooms are fan-cooled rather than air-conditioned. The beach is only a two-minute walk away, or you can take advantage of an elevated walkway set into the nearby rain forest canopy, the habitat of most local birds. *Box 6903, Cairns 4870, tel. 070/98–0033, fax 070/98–0047. 67 rooms with shower. Facilities: restaurant, bar, pool, mountain bikes. AE, DC, MC, V. $$$–$$$$*

Jungle Lodge. The number one choice for backpackers, this lively lodge has a choice of motel rooms, dormitory bunks, or shared accommodations with cooking facilities and bathrooms. The lodge also boasts the only thing resembling nightlife at the cape. At press time, a separate lodge with luxurious rooms and facilities was under construction just below the Jungle Lodge. The new lodge, Ferntrees, will offer split-level suites and large villas, a pool, restaurant, and bar, all tucked away among the trees. These will be the first air-conditioned rooms north of the Daintree. *PMB 31 Cape Tribulation, tel. 070/98–0086, fax 070/98–0099. Jungle Lodge: 10 dormitory huts, 6 shared rooms, 8 motel rooms. Ferntrees: 10 split-level suites, 20 villas. Facilities: restaurant, bar, pool. AE, DC, MC, V. $*

Cooktown **Sovereign Hotel.** This attractive, colonial-style hotel in the heart of town is the best in Cooktown. Guest rooms overlook tropical gardens at the rear of the building, a two-story timber-and-brick affair with verandas across the front. Decor in the rooms is based on soothing pastels, and every room is equipped with a shower. *Charlotte St., tel. 070/69–5400. 18 rooms with shower. Facilities: restaurant, bar, pool. AE, MC, V. $$*

Cow Bay **Crocodylus Village.** Set in a rain forest clearing about 3 kilometers (2 miles) from Cow Bay, the Village is highly recommended for budget-conscious or other adventurous travelers. Guests are accommodated in large, fixed-site tents, which are raised from the ground and enclosed by a waterproof material and insectproof mesh. Some tents are set up as dormitories with bunk beds; others are private rooms with showers. Both styles are basic, but the entire village is neat and well maintained and offers an excellent activities program. Restaurant prices are low, and the atmosphere is friendly and relaxed. The village is enormously popular, so guests must book ahead, especially during the peak season between June and August. *Lot 8, Buchanans Creek Rd., Cow Bay 4873, tel. 070/98–9166, fax 070/98–9131. 10 dormitory tents, 2 private tents. Facilities: restaurant, bar, pool. MC, V. $*

Mossman **Silky Oaks Lodge and Restaurant.** Situated on a hillside surrounded
★ by National Park land, this hotel is reminiscent of the best African safari lodges. Air-conditioned cabins on stilts overlook either the rain forest and the river below or a natural rock swimming pool. The colonial-style cabins are lined with wood and feature exceptionally comfortable beds with matching Laura Ashley bedspreads and curtains. Views from the verandas are stunning. Dining in the open-sided timber restaurant is nothing short of idyllic. Dishes range from the classical to the nouvelle, including such items as Kessler pork in filo pastry, fillet of lamb wrapped in spinach, and Australian buffalo with crayfish and béarnaise sauce. The seafood platter for two features three varieties of local fish, each cooked a different way. The restaurant has an excellent selection of Australian wines. Breakfast is also served. The lodge, which also has a bar and a lounge, is the starting point for four-wheel-drive trips into otherwise inaccessible National Park rain forest. *Finlayvale Rd., Mossman Gorge, 4873, tel. 070/98–1666, fax 070/98–1983. 35 rooms with bath and shower. Facilities: 2 pools, tennis, bar, library. Reservations suggested. Dress: casual. AE, DC, MC, V. Lodge $$$$, restaurant $$*

Palm Cove **Corals.** This airy, colonial-style restaurant in the Reef House hotel
Dining features high ceilings, wood shutters, and ceiling fans. Some tables overlook a pool that is floodlit at night. The cuisine prepared by the Austrian chef is a mélange of French and Australian, with an emphasis on seafood. Try the sea rolls Carpentaria, which is a selection of seafood in Chinese pastry with a spicy peanut sauce, or the blackened barramundi. *Williams Esplanade, tel. 070/55–3633. Reservations advised. Dress: casual but neat. AE, DC, MC, V. $$*

Lodging **Jewel of the Reef.** This four-story complex of vacation apartments opens directly onto a large white-sand beach. The complex's white colonial-style design is enhanced by magnificent landscaping with pools, barbecues, and plenty of sunny areas in which to relax. Each suite has a large, private veranda, a comfortable sitting and dining area, two bathrooms, and two or three bedrooms with king-size beds. The furnishings are all custom-designed in a cheery, modern style. Kitchens have granite-top counters, and there is a separate laundry room. *1 Veivers Rd., 4879, tel. 070/55–3000 or toll-free 008/ 07–9052, fax 070/55–3090. 70 apartments with bath, 6 with*

Jacuzzis. Facilities: 3 pools, spa, tennis court, game room. AE, DC, MC, V. $$$

Ramada Great Barrier Reef Resort. Built around a free-form swimming pool that is shaded by giant melaleucas and palm trees, this very pretty, low-rise resort is an escapist's delight. Guests can enjoy all the amenities of a deluxe resort, including private balconies, at a more reasonable rate. *Corner Vievers Rd. and Williams Esplanade, Box 122, Palm Cove, 4879, tel. 070/55–3999, fax 070/55–3902. 175 rooms with bath, 4 suites. Facilities: pool, spa, playground, tennis court, child care, restaurant, bar, laundry. AE, DC, MC, V. $$$*

★ **Reef House.** Set amid lovely gardens, this charming hotel seems more like a private club. The main building was constructed in 1885 by a retired politician, and a new wing was added in 1986. The lobby, which features a huge mural of the Queensland rain forest, is decorated with a superb collection of New Guinea Sepik River handicrafts. The comfortable rooms have a turn-of-the-century atmosphere characterized by mosquito netting, white walls, and pastel furnishings. All rooms have bars and refrigerators. *Williams Esplanade, 4879, tel. 070/55–3633, fax 070/55–3305. 41 rooms with bath and shower, 5 suites. Facilities: 3 pools, laundry. AE, DC, MC, V. $$$*

Port Douglas
Dining

Macrossans. This modern, glass-walled restaurant in the Sheraton Mirage (*see* Lodging, *below*) is a study in opulence. High-quality antiques, floor-length white tablecloths, and elegant silver settings complement the fine cuisine. French dishes, with an accent on fresh seafood and local produce, are lightened to suit the tropics. The food is beautifully presented, usually with a garnish of exotic fruit. Try the Mossman prawns if they are available, and save some room for dessert—the chocolate-laden black-and-white terrine is the chef's speciality. *Sheraton Mirage Resort, tel. 070/98–5888. Reservations advised. Dress: casual but elegant. AE, DC, MC, V. No lunch. $$$$*

★ **Nautilus Restaurant.** Patrons here sit outside under a canopy of magnificent tropical palms in a lush garden setting. The cuisine is fresh and original with an emphasis on seafood. The Nautilus is famous for its mud crabs cooked to order. Try the wonton mille-feuille of marinated barramundi, or leeks and capsicum with coconut and lemon dressing, or Thai chicken curry with steamed rice. For dessert, you can't go wrong ordering poached peach with passion-fruit sabayon. *17 Murphy St., tel. 070/99–5330. Reservations required. Dress: casual but neat. AE, DC, MC, V. No lunch. $$$*

★ **Sassi Island Point Restaurant.** Master chef Tony Sassi made a name for himself in Melbourne before moving here to run this charming, open-air restaurant set in a lovely garden. The view of the rain forest, the cane fields, and the distant mountains may be the best of any restaurant in Australia. Instead of being a mere sideshow to the view, however, the Italian-based food rises to the challenge. Try such mouth-watering delicacies as panfried baby calamari, mussels poached in white wine with herbs, chili prawns, ravioli stuffed with fresh ricotta cheese and tomato sauce, and *zuppa di pesce* (Italian fish stew). *2 Island Point Rd., tel. 070/99–5323. Reservations advised. Dress: casual but neat. AE, DC, MC, V. Closed Mon. $$*

Lodging
★

Sheraton Mirage. This is unquestionably the far north's best resort in the most deluxe bracket—and it's priced accordingly. Those who enjoy glitz, polished marble, and lagoon-size pools will find them all here. The lobby is large, with marble floors and pillars centered around an atrium filled with exotic foliage. The elegant guest rooms are decorated with cane furniture upholstered in subtle greens and pinks, and tropical-print bedspreads. Rooms overlook the hotel gardens, the golf course, or the beautiful lagoons that surround the resort. Butlers are available 24 hours a day to assist with everything from replenishing ice buckets to arranging special candlelight dinners in the room. Guests are free to use the gym and tennis courts at the neighboring Mirage Club. *Port Douglas Rd., 4871, tel. 070/99–5888, fax 070/99–5398. 298 rooms with bath and shower, 4 suites with Jacuzzi. Facilities: pool, gym, tennis, restaurant, coffee shop, 3 bars, laundry service. AE, DC, MC, V. $$$$*

National Parks

Queensland has one of the most extensive and organized park systems in Australia, an accomplishment all the more remarkable because much of the parkland consists of marine areas and tiny islands. Driving up its eastern coast it seems as if there is a park every few miles, although no major parks exist in the state's arid center. Many of the islands off the coast are national parks and are easily accessible by boat.

Access to the Cape York Peninsula used to be granted to only a lucky (or crazy) few, but new roads now make it relatively easy to travel in a four-wheel-drive vehicle from Cairns right to the tip of the Cape.

Carnarvon National Park

Despite its remote location 700 kilometers (437 miles) northwest of Brisbane, Carnarvon is one of the most popular parks in central Queensland. Its 21 kilometers (13 miles) of walking tracks are suitable for the whole family, with only a few side tracks that involve difficult ascents. Even on hot days, the park's shady gorges are cool and refreshing.

Carnarvon is famous for its ancient Aboriginal paintings, particularly those in the Art Gallery and Cathedral Cave. Both galleries span more than 50 meters (165 feet) of sheer sandstone walls covered with red ochre stencils of ancient Aboriginal artifacts, weapons, and hands. An extensive boardwalk system with informational plaques allows visitors easy access to the fragile paintings.

Several popular walking trails wend through the park, most of them branching off the main trail, which begins near the campground. The 18.6-kilometer (11.5-mile) round-trip trail to Cathedral Cave leapfrogs back and forth across the Carnarvon Creek via well-placed, round boulders. Except for the stream crossings, the trail is flat and well marked. Side trips off the main trail lead to the popular Moss Garden, a collection of sandstone walls blanketed in green moss, and the Amphitheatre, an enclosed gorge accessible via a 30-foot steel ladder. Take water with you when hiking, because it is not advisable to drink creek water. Carnarvon is best visited during the dry season, April through October, when most roads to the park are passable.

Arriving and Departing A four-wheel-drive vehicle is recommended for travel to Carnarvon, especially right after the wet season (January–late April) when many roads may still be flooded. Two-wheel-drive vehicles are adequate during the height of dry season. From Brisbane, take the Warego Highway 486 kilometers (302 miles) west to Roma, then 271 kilometers (168 miles) north toward Injune and Carnarvon. The final 70 kilometers (44 miles) is rather rough. Be sure to bring food for at least two extra days in case of road flooding.

Lodging One main campground (tel. 079/84–4505) is located at Carnarvon at the end of the only road into the park. Fees are $7.50 per night for up to six people, and facilities include cold-water showers, and toilets. Cabin and safari tent accommodations are available at the **Carnarvon Gorge Oasis Lodge** (tel. 079/84–4503), where rates are $150 per person, including full board and activities. The lodge has a general store that sells food staples as well as fuel, gas, and ice.

Information Contact **Carnarvon National Park** (via Rolleston 4702, tel. 079/84–4505).

Lamington National Park

A visit to the Gold Coast wouldn't be complete without a short journey to nearby Lamington National Park. However, it can induce culture shock: The natural grandeur of the rain forests contrasts dramatically with the man-made excesses of the coastal strip. The valleys and peaks of Lamington are home to two types of dense rain forest: the warm tropical rain forest common in Queensland, and remnants of the cooler subtropical rain forest that blanketed Australia when it was still part of Gondwanaland some 50 million years ago.

This is the most northerly point in Australia where the Antarctic beech grows, although it is found only at higher elevations. The park is also a bird-watcher's delight, with more than 200 species identified, including 14 parrot, 16 honeyeater, and five owl species. Flashy crimson rosellas are particularly noticeable—the park is home to thousands of these birds, which are not shy about eating out of people's hands. Campers shouldn't be surprised to see brushtail and ringtail possums lurking around the campground at night.

Only two roads lead into the park, one ending at Binna Burra in the northeast, and the other at Green Mountains Lodge (O'Reilly's Mountain Resort) in the south. Several trails wind through the park from these two privately run facilities. The Border Track is a 42.8-kilometer (26.5-mile) round-trip walking trail that connects the two lodges and takes two days to complete. Other trails branch off this track and lead to some of the more than 500 waterfalls in the park. The Senses Track at Binna Burra is a short loop of either 400 meters (1,300 feet) or 700 meters (2,300 feet). Designed for the blind, the trail features guiding ropes and informational signs along the trail in Braille. For those who cannot read Braille, a tape-recorded commentary is also available. Both resorts offer short introductory walks through the rain forest.

Rain is likely to fall at any time of the year, but April through October is usually the driest period. The park is 850 meters (2,805 feet) above sea level, so the evenings are generally cool.

Arriving and Departing Access to O'Reilly's Mountain Resort from Brisbane is via Route 13 through Tamborine and Canungra. The road is twisting and steep, and too narrow for RVs—four-wheel-drive vehicles are recommended. To reach Binna Burra, drive south on Route 13 and turn off at Beaudesert to Nerang and the park. Buses leave Brisbane for O'Reilly's Sunday through Friday at 9:30 AM (Allstate Scenic Tours, Transit Centre, Roma St., Brisbane 4000, tel. 07/285–1777); round-trip tickets are $32.

Lodging **O'Reilly's Rain Forest** (Green Mountains, via Canungra 4275, tel. 075/44–0644) charges $270 per night for two persons, and **Binna Burra Mountain Lodge** (Binna Burra, via Nerang 4211, tel. 075/33–3622) charges $130–$145 per person. Rates at both facilities include all meals and activities. Binna Burra also has a campground that charges $12 per night for two people. Gasoline and supplies can be bought in Canungra.

Information Contact the **Green Mountains** (via Canungra 4275, tel. 075/44–0634), **Binna Burra** (via Nerang 4211, tel. 075/33–3584), or **Queensland** (Southern Regional Centre, Box 42, Kenmore 4069, tel. 07/202–7000) National Parks and Wildlife Service.

Bellenden Ker National Park

Located only 50 kilometers (31 miles) south of Cairns, Bellenden Ker National Park is nestled in the heart of the Atherton Tableland, one of the most densely vegetated areas in Australia. Rain forest dominates Bellenden Ker, from lowland tropical rain forest to the stunted growth on Mt. Bartle Frere, the highest point in Queensland. The largest area of upland rain forest remaining in Australia is to be found here.

Encompassing both the eastern and western slopes of the Bellenden Ker range, the park is largely undeveloped. It still shows the effects of a major cyclone that hit in 1986, which destroyed much of the vegetation. A profusion of vines has replaced many of the lost trees, temporarily depriving them of a chance to regenerate.

The park's major trails are geared toward experienced bushwalkers, but a short 800-meter (2,640-foot) paved trail leads from the parking area to Josephine Falls, a fine place to swim. Picnic facilities and toilets are located there as well. For the more adventurous, a 30-kilometer (18.6-mile) return trail leads from the parking area to the summit of Mt. Bartle Frere. The two-day hike has some rough patches along the way, including steep climbs and rock scrambling, but it is well worth the effort for the spectacular view of the surrounding rain forests—unless the mountain is shrouded in fog.

Avoid the gympie tree: Its large, round leaves are covered with sharp barbs that can inflict a painful sting.

Arriving and Departing The park can be reached by driving south from Cairns along the Bruce Highway via Babinda.

Lodging Bush camping is allowed with ranger permission throughout the park, except at Josephine Falls. Permits cost $2 per night per site for as many as six people. Supplies can be bought in Babinda.

Information Contact **Bellenden Ker National Park** (Box 93, Mirriwinni 4871, tel. 070/67–6304).

Cape Tribulation National Park

In many ways, Cape Tribulation is a microcosm of Queensland's diverse climates and terrains. Along this undeveloped coastal strip, rain forest, mangroves, coral, and sea all come together, and the combination is fascinating. Menacing saltwater crocodiles lurk in Cape Tribulation's larger streams, and swimming in the ocean from October through April is dangerous because of a preponderance of marine stingers.

The beach is usually empty, except for the tiny soldier crabs that move about by the hundreds and scatter when approached. Hikers exploring the mangroves are likely to see an incredible assortment of small creatures that depend on the trees for survival. Most evident are mudskippers and mangrove crabs, but keen observers may spot green-backed herons crouched among the mangrove roots.

The best time to see the rain forest is in the dry season, May through September. Walking along the dry creek beds is the best way to explore the forest.

Arriving and Reaching Cape Tribulation is half the adventure. Located about 100
Departing kilometers (62 miles) north of Cairns, the park is accessible via the Captain Cook Highway to Mossman. It is necessary to take a car ferry across the Daintree River.

Several tour companies in Cairns offer day trips to the rain forest in four-wheel-drive buses and vans.

Lodging Camping is permitted at **Noah's Beach** for $6 per night. Privately run campgrounds and small resorts can be found along the Daintree Road at Myall Creek and Cape Tribulation. Free public campsites are available at Thornton's Beach.

Information Contact the **Queensland National Parks and Wildlife Service** (Far North Region, Box 2066, Cairns 4870, tel. 070/53–4310, or Cape Tribulation, tel. 070/98–0052).

8 The Great Barrier Reef

By Walter Glaser

Updated by David McGonigal

More than 2,000 kilometers (1,200 miles) long and as much as 80 kilometers (50 miles) wide, the Great Barrier Reef runs parallel to the Queensland coast from the Sunshine Coast in the south as far north as Papua New Guinea. It is the world's largest living organism, composed of billions of coral polyps whose structures are home to myriad plants and animals. The Great Barrier Reef is the richest marine resource in the world—and offers the most remarkable diving and snorkeling anywhere. Today, much of the reef has been incorporated into the Great Barrier Reef Marine Park and is protected by strict laws governing its preservation. Nevertheless, the reef is attracting more and more visitors, to whom a host of island resorts now cater. Although the islands on which these resorts are built are billed as Great Barrier islands, most are not on the reef at all but close to shore. Hamilton, for instance, is more than 70 kilometers (43 miles) from the reef. Although these islands are not built on the coral of the reef, they do have fringing coral that grows in the islands' sheltered coves and can be every bit as fascinating as the main reef.

Essential Information

Important Addresses and Numbers

Tourist Information **Queensland Tourist and Travel Corporation** (Government Travel Centre, Adelaide and Edward Sts., Brisbane, tel. 07/221–6111).

Emergencies Emergencies are handled by the front desk of the resort on each island. Each resort can summon aerial ambulances or doctors. Hamilton Island has its own doctor and dentist.

Arriving and Departing

Regular boat and air service are available to most of the Great Barrier Reef resorts. But because all of the following destinations are islands, they require extra travel time, sometimes as much as a day. Plan on scheduling the last leg of your trip for the early morning, when most charters and launches depart. In some cases, travel is limited to certain days of the week—you will need to coordinate international and domestic flights as well as helicopters and launches. In many cases, it is necessary to stay overnight at a nearby mainland city before reaching your final destination. For information about reaching the various islands, *see* Arriving and Departing under the individual island headings.

Getting Around

By Chartered Boat In recent years, sailing around the Great Barrier Reef islands in your own boat has become very popular, and there are a number of charter companies that rent out yachts and cabin cruisers.

For uncrewed charters, contact **Australian Bareboat Charters** (Box 357, Airlie Beach, Queensland 4802, tel. 079/46–9381 or toll-free 008/07–5000), **Cumberland Charter Yachts** (Box 49, Abel Point Marina, Airlie Beach, Queensland 4802, tel. 079/46–7500), **Queensland Yacht Charters** (Box 293, Airlie Beach, Queensland 4802, tel. 079/46–7400 or toll-free 008/07–5013), and **Whitsunday Rent a Yacht** (PMB 25, Mackay, Queensland 4741, tel. 079/46–9232 or toll-free 008/07–5111).

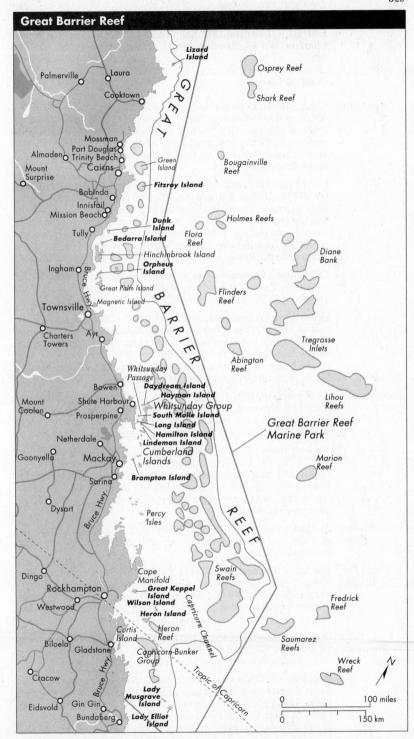

Great Barrier Reef

Palmerville
Laura
Cooktown
Lizard Island
Osprey Reef
Shark Reef

GREAT

Mossman
Port Douglas
Almaden
Trinity Beach
Cairns
Green Island
Bougainville Reef
Mount Surprise
Babinda
Fitzroy Island
Innisfail
Mission Beach
Tully
Dunk Island
Holmes Reefs
Bedarra Island
Flora Reef
Diane Bank
Hinchinbrook Island
Orpheus Island
Ingham
Great Palm Island
Flinders Reef
Magnetic Island
Townsville
Charters Towers
Ayr

BARRIER

Tregrosse Inlets
Abington Reef
Whitsunday Passage
Bowen
Daydream Island
Hayman Island
Lihou Reefs
Shute Harbour
Mount Coolon
Whitsunday Group
Prosperpine
South Molle Island
Long Island
Hamilton Island
Netherdale
Lindeman Island
Great Barrier Reef Marine Park
Goonyella
Mackay
Cumberland Islands
Marion Reef
Sarina
Brampton Island
Dysart

REEF

Percy Isles
Dingo
Cape Manifold
Swain Reefs
Rockhampton
Great Keppel Island
Wilson Island
Westwood
Heron Island
Fredrick Reef
Curtis Island
Heron Reef
Biloela
Gladstone
Capricorn-Bunker Group
Saumarez Reefs
Cracow
Wreck Reef
Lady Musgrave Island
Eidsvold
Gin Gin
Tropic of Capricorn
Bundaberg
Lady Elliot Island

Bruce Hwy.
Capricorn Channel

0   100 miles
0   150 km

Crewed charters are available from **MV Achilles** (Box 98, Port Douglas, Queensland 4871, tel. 070/99–5189) and **Hamilton Island Charters** (Box 65, Hamilton Island, Queensland 4803, tel. 079/46–9900).

Guided Tours

From Cairns **Great Adventures** (Wharf St., tel. 070/51–5644 or toll-free 008/079–080) operates fast catamaran service daily to Green and Fitzroy islands, Michaelmas Cay, Norman Reef, and Moore Reef (where helicopter overflights are available). Some trips include barbecue luncheon and coral viewing from an underwater observatory and a semisubmersible.

Coral Princess (Breakwater Marina, Townsville, Queensland 4810, tel. 077/21–1673 or toll-free 008/079–545) conducts a four-day trip from Cairns to Townsville or round-trip aboard a mini-cruise ship that carries 54 passengers in great comfort. There are plenty of stops for snorkeling, fishing, and exploring Dunk and Orpheus islands. The crew includes marine biologists who lecture on board and on excursions. Diving gear can be rented, and lessons are available.

Quicksilver Connections (tel. 070/99–5500) operates tours to the Reef from Cairns, Palm Cove, and Port Douglas (*see* From Port Douglas, *below*, for more information).

Ocean Spirit Cruises (143 Lake St., tel. 070/31–2920) offers a full-day tour aboard the *Ocean Spirit*, the largest sailing vessel of its type in the world, and two other boats. A daily trip to Michaelmas Cay includes four hours at the Great Barrier Reef, coral viewing in a semisubmersible, swimming and snorkeling, and a fresh seafood lunch. Introductory diving lessons are available.

From Mackay **Air Pioneer** (tel. 079/57–6661) offers a daily flight by amphibious aircraft to a lagoon at Bushy Island, a coral atoll 96 kilometers (60 miles) northeast of Mackay. The three-hour tour includes coral viewing from a glass-bottom boat, snorkeling, and a reef walk.

Roylen Cruises (Box 169, Mackay 4740, tel. 079/55–3066 or toll-free 008/075–032; in the United States, 800/551–2012) operates daily cruises to Brampton Island from Mackay, proceeding on to Credlin Reef on Monday, Wednesday, and Friday. Trips include coral viewing at the underwater observatory; snorkeling and scuba diving gear are available for hire.

From Mission The **Quick Cat** (tel. 070/68–7289) catamaran offers tours to Dunk Is-
Beach land and then continues on to the Great Barrier Reef for snorkeling and coral viewing.

From Port **Quicksilver Connections** (Marina Mirage, Port Douglas, tel. 070/99–
Douglas 5500) offers a wide variety of one-day excursions to the Great Barrier Reef aboard the MV *Quicksilver*, a high-speed catamaran. Guests can also board the *Quicksilver Sub*, a semisubmersible that provides superb underwater views through its keel windows.

From **Coral Princess** (Breakwater Marina, Townsville, Queensland 4810,
Townsville tel. 077/21–1673 or toll-free 008/079–545) operates cruises to Cairns (*see* From Cairns, *above*, for more information).

Pure Pleasure Cruises (tel. 077/21–3555) offers day cruises from the Great Barrier Reef Wonderland wharf to the company's pontoon at Kelso Reef, on the outer edge of the Great Barrier Reef. The trip takes 2½ hours by high-speed catamaran. Once out there, you have a choice of fishing, snorkeling, diving, or viewing the reef through the floor of a glass-bottom boat. Morning and afternoon tea and a buffet lunch are included in the cost ($110 adults, $55 children). The boat departs daily (except Monday and Friday) at 9 AM.

Camping

Brochures and guides to the Queensland coast often leave the impression that you have the choice of staying either on the mainland or at an island resort, but for the adventurous there is a third option: On many uninhabited islands lying within national parks, you are allowed to camp, as long as you have permission from the National Parks and Wildlife Service. For details or to find out which regional office looks after a particular island, contact the service's head office in Brisbane (Dept. of Environment and Heritage, Box 155, Brisbane Albert St., Queensland 4002, tel. 07/227–8185). The myriad islands of the Whitsunday Group are especially popular with young campers. For more information, contact the Whitsunday Information Centre of the Department of Environment and Heritage, 3 kilometers (1.8 miles) from Airlie Beach toward Shute Harbour (Conway Ranger Station, Box 332, Airlie Beach, Queensland 4802, tel. 079/46–7022, fax 079/46–7023).

Dining and Lodging

Visitors cannot pick and choose between different hotels on a Great Barrier Reef island, but they can and should choose an island based on their individual taste and budget. Many islands cater to those wanting peace and tranquillity, whereas others attract a crowd wishing for just the opposite. Read each description carefully to avoid planning a vacation at the wrong place. An island generally has only one resort, although the resort may offer a variety of accommodations. In choosing where to go, guests are best advised to consider the resort and the island as a single entity.

With some exceptions, most sports activities are normally included in the base rate. Trips to the Great Barrier Reef, fishing charters, and sports requiring fuel usually cost extra, however.

Similarly, at many resorts all meals are included in the price and are served in the dining room, although outdoor barbecues and seafood buffets are also commonplace. Some of the resorts now offer more than one choice of restaurant, as well as a premium restaurant for which guests must pay extra.

With the exception of Lady Elliot, all the island resorts listed may be booked through **SO-PAC Travel Marketing Inc.,** the official U.S. representative of many of the resorts as well as tour and charter boat companies (1448 15th St., Suite 105, Santa Monica, CA 90404, tel. 800/551–2012).

Highly recommended restaurants and lodgings are indicated by a star ★.

Dining	Category	Cost*
	$$$$	over $50
	$$$	$40–$50
	$$	$30–$40
	$	under $30

per person, excluding drinks and service

Lodging

Category	Cost*
$$$$	over $300
$$$	$200–$300
$$	$100–$200
$	under $100

*All prices are for a standard double room.

The Islands

Lady Elliot Island

Within easy reach of Brisbane, Lady Elliot is a 100-acre coral cay on the southern tip of the Great Barrier Reef. Fringed on all sides by the reef and graced with a white coral beach, this oval isle is diving heaven. Its clear, calm waters afford superb views of schools of mantas, turtles, morays, wobbegong sharks, and millions of tropical fish. Wildlife easily outnumbers the 160 guests on this vacation spot for those wanting to get away from it all. Even the top-level lodgings pale in comparison to those on other islands. And Lady Elliot is one of the few islands in the area where camping (modified) is part of the resort's offering. There are no televisions, there's only one guest telephone, and social activities revolve around diving, reef-walking, and the island's lively bar and restaurant. Between October and April, Lady Elliot also becomes a busy breeding ground for birds and sea turtles.

Arriving and Departing
By Plane

Lady Elliot is the only coral cay with its own airstrip. Small aircraft make the 80-kilometer (50-mile) flight northeast from Hervey Bay and Bundaberg, a coastal town 320 kilometers (200 miles) north of Brisbane. Bundaberg and Brisbane are connected by daily flights. A round-trip fare of $100 for the 30-minute flight from Bundaberg to Lady Elliot via Whitaker Air is built into the first night's tariff at the island resort. There are strict limitations on luggage—only 10 kilos (22 lbs) per person. Be sure to confirm your transfer flight to the island with the resort. You cannot arrive on the island by boat.

Day Trips

Day trips from Bundaberg may be arranged through the resort. They include the flight, lunch, a glass-bottom boat ride ($10), a reef walk (if tides are appropriate), and snorkeling gear. The cost is $105 per person from Bundaberg or $109 from Hervey Bay (tel. 071/52-2322 or toll-free 008/07–2200).

Participant Sports

Scuba diving lessons can be arranged through Lady Elliot's excellent dive school for $395 per person. Visitors coming for this five-day program must plan to stay from Sunday to Saturday and bring a medical report and two passport photos. Certified divers can rent diving equipment at the resort's dive shop. In addition, the resort offers reef walks, glass-bottom boat rides ($10 per adult, $6 per child), and island walks.

Dining and Lodging

Lady Elliot Island Resort. Don't go to Lady Elliot if you're looking for luxury. Guests here stay in simple waterfront cabins that are sparsely furnished with plastic chairs, polished wood floors, and pine furniture. Cabins are serviced twice weekly. Campers stay in permanent oceanfront safari tents and share facilities. Dinner and breakfast are included in the basic price and served in the dining room; they tend to be simple (with an emphasis on grilled dishes, salads, and seafood) and served buffet style. Dress is casual. *Mail-*

ing address: Box 206, Torquay, Queensland 4655, tel. 071/51–6077 or toll free 008/07–2200. 24 rooms with shower, 14 tents, 10 lodge rooms. Facilities: pool, dining room, bar, laundry, shop. AE, DC, MC, V. $–$$

Lady Musgrave and Wilson Islands

Both of these uninhabited coral cays lie at the southern end of the Great Barrier Reef Marine Park. Lady Musgrave Island, which measures only about 500 yards across, is 40 kilometers (25 miles) to the north of Lady Elliot Island. You reach it on the catamaran MV *Lady Musgrave*, which departs from Port Bundaberg, 20 minutes northeast of Bundaberg, each Tuesday, Thursday, Saturday, and Sunday at 8:30 AM, returning at 5:45 PM. The trip takes 2½ hours in each direction and costs $90. *1 Quay St., Bundaberg, tel. 071/52–9011 or toll-free 008/07–2110.*

Lady Musgrave can accommodate up to 50 campers at one time (*see* Camping, *above*)—but the total infrastructure consists of two toilets. Compressors are allowed (and the boat will carry over your supplies, including water), so it's a popular destination for divers, and yacht crews also drop in to take advantage of its favorable anchorage. When day trippers, yachties, and campers all converge, Lady Musgrave can feel like a traffic island. But it offers some of the best diving and snorkeling in Queensland. And in quiet times campers have a chance to come to terms with the infinite variety of life surrounding a tiny speck of land in the Pacific.

Wilson Island, on the other hand, is never crowded. In fact the maximum population of this tiny coral cay is 16 people housed in eight permanent tents. It's an attractive adjunct of the Heron Island Resort 10 kilometers (6 miles) to the south, through which it is accessed, and like Heron it's controlled by P&O Resorts (*see* Heron Island, *below*). You are accompanied by a Heron Island staffer, who acts as guide, cook, boat crew, and general factotum for anyone staying on the island. The tents are basic, but there is an open shelter under which meals are served—and a solar-powered hot-water shower! During January and February, Wilson Island becomes the breeding ground for roseate terns and may be closed to visitors.

Heron Island

Most resort islands lie inshore sheltered by the distant reef, but this most famous of the Queensland islands is actually part of the reef. Located 70 kilometers (43 miles) northeast of Gladstone, Heron Island is great if you want to learn about indigenous life on a coral island, but it will disappoint visitors looking for a wide range of activities and entertainment.

Heron covers only 40 acres and houses a maximum of 250 people in the Heron Island Resort, the island's only accommodation. Thousands of green turtles and a large number of loggerhead turtles make their home there, and the island becomes a vast breeding ground during October and November. Staff from the resort escort guests out to watch the turtles come ashore, make their nests, and lay their eggs. In February and March you can watch the last eggs being laid and the first hatchlings emerge. Between July and October (September is best), humpback whales pass here on their journey from the Antarctic.

Heron Island is also a breeding ground for thousands of birds, including noddy terns, reef herons (hence the island's name), and silver gulls. Guests should be aware that they will never be far from the sound or smell of birds.

The waters are spectacular, teeming with fish and coral, and ideal for snorkeling. The area around the channel leading to the resort is particularly good. Farther out toward the reef the ocean becomes more agitated, with a consequent loss of visibility. The water is clearest during June and July and cloudiest during the rainy season from January through March.

Arriving and Departing
By Helicopter Lloyd's Helicopter Service (tel. 079/78–1177) offers a 20-minute helicopter flight to Heron Island from Gladstone, a town on the Queensland coast, for $354 round-trip (children half price).

By Boat The *Reef Adventurer* (tel. 07/268–8224), a high-speed catamaran, operates a two-hour service to Heron Island from Gladstone for $130 round-trip (children half price). The trip can be rough and some visitors have problems with gas fumes and seasickness.

Participant Sports Snorkeling and diving lessons are offered by the dive shop. Open-water diving courses are available for about $300–$350, but it is essential that you bring a medical certificate and passport photos. The resort also offers a range of excursions for experienced divers: One-tank boat dives cost about $35, and three-day packages are available for $168.

Nondivers who want to explore the reef's underwater world can board a semisubmersible sub that offers tours from Heron Island twice daily, or go on one of the guided reef walks.

In addition, Heron is equipped with a large pool, table tennis, tennis courts, and a game room. Beach fishing and spearfishing are prohibited.

Dining and Lodging **The Heron Island Resort.** Set among palm trees and connected by sand paths, the accommodations here range from simple cabins with shared bathrooms to large, comfortable suites. With their private balconies, cane furniture, and pastel decor, the modern suites are worth the extra expense. All rooms in the resort feature ceiling fans, radios, refrigerators, and tea/coffee makers, but there are no telephones or TVs in the guest rooms. In December 1992, a grand extension of the main building was completed; it houses an airy bar and a coffee shop whose seaward side is made primarily of glass. These are the best spots to wind down after a day outdoors—organized entertainment here is sparse, although the resort does screen excellent movies about the reef and diving. Meals are included in the resort's basic rate, but food isn't going to lure you away from the reef. The restaurant serves the usual island cuisine, with an emphasis on salads, barbecued seafood, and steaks. Breakfast and lunch are served buffet style. Dress is resort casual. *P&O Resorts, Level 10, 160 Sussex St., Sydney, NSW 2000, tel. 02/250–0700 or toll-free 13–2469; in the U.S., 408/685–8902 or 800/225–9849. 83 rooms plus some cheaper bunk rooms. Facilities: pool, tennis courts, bar, restaurant, laundry. AE, DC, MC, V. $$$–$$$$*

Great Keppel Island

Over the years the Great Keppel Island Resort, owned by Qantas, has garnered a reputation similar to Fort Lauderdale's at spring break. The crowds are smaller, but the emphasis is squarely on fun, with plenty of action in the bars and disco. Guests tend to be young singles, although the resort does draw its fair share of young families. Like its sister resort at Dunk Island (*see below*), the Great

Keppel Resort has a following that returns year after year. Situated only 13 kilometers (8 miles) off the coast and 48 kilometers (30 miles) northeast of Rockhampton, Great Keppel was originally a sheep station, and the old homestead remains on the hill overlooking the island. It's large—8 kilometers (5 miles) wide and 11 kilometers (7 miles) long—and there are several private residences in addition to the resort. Unfortunately, Great Keppel is also located 40 kilometers (25 miles) from the Great Barrier Reef, which makes any trip out there a lengthy journey. However, it's blessed with its own natural advantages, including 17 stunning beaches and a wide array of walks and trails. The irregular shape of the island is conducive to excellent coral growth in the many sheltered coves. An underwater observatory at nearby Middle Island allows visitors to watch the marine life without getting wet. A confiscated Taiwanese fishing boat has been sunk alongside the Underwater Observatory to provide shelter to myriad tropical fish.

Arriving and Departing
By Plane

Great Keppel Island is owned by **Qantas** (tel. toll-free 13–1313—no prefix), which offers connecting flights from Rockhampton for $72 one way.

By Boat

Reefseeker Cruises (tel. 079/33–6744) operates two vessels to the island from Rosslyn Harbour near Rockhampton and Yeppoon. It also operates a round-trip coach pickup between Rockhampton hotels and Rosslyn Harbour ($10 adults, $5 children). The *Spirit of Keppel* departs at 9:15, 11, and 3:30 and costs $12 each way. The larger *Reefseeker II* departs at 9 and returns at 5. On Tuesday and Thursday it goes to Barten Island, and on Saturday it continues beyond Great Keppel Island on a day cruise to the outer reef. The outer reef trip includes lunch, morning and afternoon tea, and snorkeling gear for $106 adults, $53 children. On other days the *Reefseeker II* circumnavigates Great Keppel Island, with a stop for snorkeling and lunch. (Lunch is not included in the cost of this cruise, but can be purchased on the island.) The cost, including snorkeling gear, is $32. A tour of the underwater observatory costs $10. The rates for children are: cruise $17, observatory $5.

Participant Sports

Great Keppel Island offers almost every conceivable sport. Included in the basic tariff are snorkeling, fishing, sailing, windsurfing, tennis, squash, golf, archery, basketball, baseball, volleyball, and badminton. Guests must pay an extra fee for any activity that requires fuel, including island cruises, Barrier Reef cruises, motorboating, and parasailing. Horseback rides along the beach, tandem skydiving, and scuba-diving lessons are also available.

Dining and Lodging

Great Keppel Island Resort. Situated amid beautifully manicured gardens adjacent to the airstrip and extending up the hills, this resort, which recently underwent an extensive building and renovation program, consists of bungalows and two-story buildings. Rooms are modern and comfortable, decorated in cheery pinks and greens, with natural timber and spacious balconies. All rooms feature refrigerators, ceiling fans, televisions, telephones, and tea/coffee makers. The Oceanview Villas are air-conditioned and have wonderful views, but are some distance from the beach. Set in a large, open room overlooking the beach and the bay, the Admiral Keppel restaurant serves meals without any frills. Dishes tend to be a mélange of Continental and island cuisines, and the menu changes daily according to the availability of fresh ingredients. Barbecues and buffets predominate, although there are occasional theme dinners. Dress is resort casual. *CMB, Great Keppel Island, Rockhampton, Queensland 4702, tel. 079/39–5044; in United States, 800/922–5122. 192 rooms with shower. Facilities: 3 outdoor* *pools, 3 tennis courts, 2 squash courts, 4 bars, disco, 6-hole golf course. AE, DC, MC, V. $$–$$$*

Brampton Island

Part of the Cumberland Islands near the southern entrance to the Whitsunday Passage, 195-acre Brampton Island is one of the prettiest in the area. Seven coral and white sandy beaches ring the island, while the hilly interior boasts rain forests populated by kangaroos, colorful rainbow lorikeets, and butterflies. Most of the island is designated national park, but not the Brampton Island Resort at Sandy Point. The resort has a loyal clientele that returns annually, attracted by a vacation style far less structured than on other resort isles. Live entertainment is offered every evening, as are a variety of theme nights, dancing, and floor shows. The biggest attraction, however, is the water—especially the snorkeling over the reef between Brampton and adjoining Carlisle islands.

Arriving and Departing
By Plane
Brampton Island is owned and operated by Qantas (tel. 13–1313), which offers flights to Brampton via the coastal town of Mackay ($70 one-way). From Mackay, passengers make the 35-kilometer (22-mile) flight to Brampton aboard a Twin Otter light aircraft.

By Boat **Roylen Cruises** (tel. 079/55–3066) offers daily service from Mackay to Brampton Island on the *Spirit of Roylen* for $40 per adult and $20 per child round-trip. Boats leave on Tuesday, Thursday, Saturday, and Sunday at 9 AM.

Guided Tours Brampton Island is 50 kilometers (31 miles) from the Great Barrier Reef. Guests can travel to the reef aboard one of the cruises offered by the resort or take a cruise through the Whitsunday Islands. A 45-minute aerial tour of the outer reef is also available.

Participant Sports Brampton Island offers a huge array of activities, including free tennis courts, a six-hole golf course, archery, table tennis, beach volleyball, water trikes, snorkeling, sailing, and windsurfing. For an extra charge, the resort also offers water tobogganing, water-skiing, and fishing trips.

Dining and Lodging **Brampton Island Resort.** Popular with overseas visitors in the 30–50 age group, this resort offers comfort and quiet at reasonable prices. Rooms are in large, Polynesian-style buildings, many of which directly face the beach. High ceilings and verandas give the rooms an airy atmosphere, enhanced by rattan furniture, ceiling fans, and a soft gray and pink decor. Some of the rooms are as high as 10 feet off the ground, allowing the ocean breezes to waft underneath. Telephones, televisions, radios, refrigerators, tea/coffee makers, and air-conditioning are standard. The restaurant at Brampton Island offers a buffet breakfast, smorgasbord lunch, and à la carte dinner emphasizing local seafoods. Meal packages can be purchased for $60 for breakfast, lunch, and dinner, or $42 for breakfast and dinner only. An "Island Night" is held on Saturday, during which the chefs prepare a huge seafood dinner. The chefs will also prepare any fish caught by guests. The dining room is part of the entertainment complex that overlooks the main beach, with its magnificent views of the Whitsunday Passage. You can also arrange room-service dinners, beach picnics, or barbecues. Dress is resort casual. *Brampton Island, via Mackay, Queensland 4740, tel. 079/51–4499; in the U.S., 800/922–5122. 108 rooms with shower. Facilities: golf, 2 pools, boutique, gift shop, 2 bars, disco, laundry. AE, DC, MC, V. $$$–$$$$*

Lindeman Island

Located 40 kilometers (25 miles) northeast of Mackay at the southern entrance to the Whitsunday Passage, Lindeman Island is one of the largest islands (2,000 acres) of the Whitsunday Group. More than half of the island is national park, with 20 kilometers (12 miles) of walking trails that wind through the tropical growth. The bird-watching is excellent here, and the blue tiger butterflies that can be seen in Butterfly Valley may be even more impressive than the birds. It's worth climbing some of the island's hills just for the views. Seven sandy beaches as well as superb snorkeling around the fringing reefs are added attractions.

The Lindeman Island Resort was purchased by Club Med, which rebuilt the resort, then reopened it in 1992, having doubled its guest capacity.

Arriving and Departing
By Boat
Boats depart regularly from Shute Harbour, a small port 36 kilometers (22 miles) east of Proserpine and the major coastal access point for all the resorts in the Whitsunday region. The trip takes about an hour and costs $20 one way. There are also direct half-hour water taxi transfers from Hamilton Island airport that cost $39 one way.

What to See and Do with Children
The Club Med Village operates a Mini-Club for children ages four to seven and a Kids' Club for those 8–12. (Under-twos are not accepted at the village.) Swimming, tennis, and archery are among the planned events, and there are also hikes into the national park and boat trips around the island.

Participant Sports
Lindeman has one of the most picturesque nine-hole golf courses anywhere. The resort also offers free use of its six lighted tennis courts, paddle skis, snorkeling equipment, catamarans, and Windsurfers. Archery, cricket, volleyball, basketball, football, badminton, hiking, aquagym, and aerobics are all included in the basic price. Resort and refresher scuba diving courses are provided for a fee, and there are diving excursions to the outer reef by air (30 minutes each way) and boat (two hours each way).

Dining and Lodging
Club Med Village Resort. Opened in late 1992, this is one of Queensland's newest resorts. All rooms on the three floors overlook the sea (each has a balcony or patio), and all border the beach and pool. The resort, on the southern end of the large island, incorporates palm trees and rain forests in its grounds. Away from the main village are the golf clubhouse, sports center, disco, and restaurant. Entertainment includes traditional Club Med staff theater. All rooms are air-conditioned, with ceiling fan, private bath, TV, telephone, and minibar. *Club Med, Lindeman Island via Mackay, Queensland 4741, tel. 079/46-9333. 224 rooms with shower (some with bath as well). Facilities: 2 pools, restaurant, 4 bars, boutique, laundry. AE, DC, MC, V. $$$$*

Long Island

This aptly named, narrow mainland island lies just off the coast south of Shute Harbour. Although it's 40 kilometers (26 miles) long, it's a mere 200 meters (655 feet) wide at the Palm Bay resort. It has large areas of thick, undisturbed rain forest (through which there are walking trails) protected as national parkland. Over the years the island has seen several styles of resort; the most dramatic conclusion to any of them came when the original Palm Bay, which opened in 1933, was leveled by a cyclone in 1970. Today there are two very different resorts here.

Arriving and Departing
Access to Long Island is by **Whitsunday All Over and Water Taxi** (tel. 079/46–9499) from either Shute Harbour or Hamilton Island. Departures from Shute Harbour are at 7:15, 9:15, 4, and 5:15, and the 15-minute trip costs $20 return. A water taxi meets each flight into Hamilton Island, and the 30- to 45-minute transfer to either resort costs $37 one way for adults and $18.50 round-trip for children.

Dining and Lodging
Club Crocodile Long Island. The emphasis at this resort, which is a sister property to one in Airlie Beach, is on the outdoors (especially water sports). The constant stream of guests flies into the Hamilton Island airport and takes the transfer boat to the resort. It's very comfortable and geared for families (child care is available). It's not the place for a quiet holiday communing with nature. *PMB 26, Mackay, Queensland 4070, tel. 079/46–9400. 140 units with shower. Facilities: pool, spa, sauna, water sports, air-conditioning or fans, refrigerator, cooking facilities, TV, phones, gym, tennis, barbecue. AE, DC, MC, V. $$*

Palm Bay. Much smaller than Club Crocodile (*see above*), it's also much quieter. The six Polynesian-style bungalows and eight cabins stand scattered along a sandy beach leading to a quiet lagoon. Guests have the choice of taking an accommodation package that includes meals in the restaurant (definitely more home-style than haute), or paying a room-only rate and buying supplies at the resort's Island Trader store (which has reasonable prices and a fair selection—though if you crave something particular, you'd better bring it along). All activities except motorized ones are included in the tariff: canoeing, paddle skiing, catamaran sailing, and windsurfing. *Palm Bay Hideaway, PMB 28, Mackay, Queensland 4740, tel. 079/46–9233 or toll-free 008/33–4009. 14 units with shower. Facilities: pool, spa, water sports, fans, refrigerator, cooking facilities, barbecue. MC, V. $$*

Hamilton Island

Part of the Whitsunday chain, Hamilton Island is the site of the largest hotel in Australia and most controversial Queensland island resort. In building the resort, Australian entrepreneur Keith Williams paid scant attention to conservationists, dynamiting the top off one of Hamilton's hills to make a helipad, building a seawall to prevent the tides from draining the swimming area, dredging a boat marina, erecting a high-rise apartment tower, and then removing the side of a hill to accommodate a runway for the Whitsundays' major airport. The result is a lot of development and a concrete infrastructure quite unlike any other resort in Australia. (Development has now slowed: In 1992 receivers were appointed for this resort.) Still, the place has the greatest range of activities and amenities of any Queensland island. In addition to an extensive sports complex and Barrier Reef excursions, there are six different types of accommodations, eight restaurants, a full range of shops and boutiques, a pool with trained dolphins, a 200-acre fauna park, and even a motorcycle museum. The nightlife ranges from Durty Nellie's Nightclub, which swings into the wee hours six nights a week, to the 24-hour Pink Pizza Parlour.

Hamilton Island is divided into two distinct areas: the resort—a combination of high-rise and cottage accommodations that overlook Catseye Beach—and the boat harbor—flanked by restaurants, shops, an ice cream parlor, a fish-and-chips take-out, and the best bakery in the Whitsundays.

Arriving and Departing
By Plane Hamilton is the only Queensland island with an airport large enough to accommodate commercial jets. **Ansett Australia** (tel. 13–1344—no prefix) operates direct flights to the island from Sydney (2 hours), Melbourne (2¾ hours), and Cairns and Brisbane (1½ hours). Boat transfers to all other Whitsunday resort islands can be made from the wharf adjoining the airport.

By Boat Fantasy Cruises' catamaran *2000* makes the 35-minute journey from Shute Harbour twice daily. *Tel. 079/46–5111. Round-trip tickets: $35 adults, $17.50 children.*

Guided Tours **Helijet Whitsunday** flies guests from Hamilton Island, Shute Harbour, or any of the Whitsunday Islands to the Hardy Reef Lagoon on the outer barrier reef. *Tel. 079/46–8249. Tickets: $310. Tour lasts approx. 3 hrs.*

Fantasy Cruises offers Great Barrier Reef trips daily. Cruises depart Hamilton Harbour at 9:45 AM for the 75-kilometer (46-mile) trip to the company's own pontoon on magnificent Hardy Reef Lagoon. For 2½ hours, passengers can swim or snorkel around the reef, or ride in a glass-bottom boat or submarine. A buffet lunch is included. *Activity Desk, tel. 079/46–8535. Cost $100 adults, $50 children under 15.*

On Tuesday, Thursday, and Sunday, the catamaran *1000* also offers **cruises to Whitehaven Beach,** a 6.5-kilometer (4-mile) stretch of glistening white silica sand that has to be seen to be believed. The cruise leaves the harbor at 9 AM and 1:30 PM for the 30-minute trip to the beach, returning to Hamilton about 3½ hours later. *Cost: $30 adults, $15 children under 15.*

A large number of vessels at Hamilton Island are available for charter and group trips. Call for information (Charter Base, tel. 079/46–8226).

What to See and Do with Children The **Hamilton Island Kids Club** caters to children eight years old and younger. Activities include trips to the fauna park, beach Olympics, and visits to the harbor. *Tel. 079/46–9999, ext. 8546. Cost: $25 full day, $17 half day, $115 weekly.*

Shopping The island has a waterfront shopping area that features a host of restaurants, a bakery, a butcher, a general store, a fast photo service, a bank, an art gallery, a pharmacy, and a post office. Several stores selling men's and women's clothing are located off the lobby in the main complex.

Participant Sports Unlike most of the other Barrier Reef resorts, Hamilton Island charges a fee (a steep one) for almost all offered activities. Nevertheless, the resort's sports complex is one of its greatest strengths, with a fully equipped gym, aerobics classes, and squash and tennis courts. All activities can be booked through the resort's Island Activity Desk (tel. 079/46–8535). The island has one of the largest freshwater swimming pools in the Pacific area, and five smaller pools—some of which feature Jacuzzis—are scattered throughout the resort. The resort recently added an 18-hole mini golf course, a golf driving range, tandem sky diving, rappelling, skeet and rifle range shooting, and archery to its long list of activities.

Fishing The island's game-fishing boat, *Sea Baby II,* skippered by Captain Paul Whelan, takes guests in search of the marlin, sailfish, Spanish mackerel, and tuna that thrive in the waters of the Whitsundays. Charters for six people can be arranged through Hamilton Island's Activity Desk. *Cost: $1,020 full day, $690 half day.*

Scuba Diving For those who have not dived before, Hamilton offers an introductory scuba course, including pool instruction, equipment rental, and a dive with a qualified diver. For those who are already qualified, all equipment can be rented and a variety of diving trips arranged.

Tennis The resort has six floodlit tennis courts. Social nights, held twice a week, feature a tennis tournament involving guests and the resort pros, followed by cold drinks and steak sandwiches from the barbecue.

Water Sports Jet skis can be hired, as can catamarans, paddle skis, and Windsurfers. Waterskiing, parasailing, and snorkeling are also easily arranged, and instruction is available. All of the above can be booked through the resort's Activity Desk (tel. 079/46–8535).

Dining The Hamilton Island Resort does not include meals in the tariff.

Dolphin Room Restaurant. Situated in the very center of the main Catseye Beach, this à la carte restaurant uses high timber ceilings and sliding wood and glass partitions to create an airy, tropical atmosphere. The menus, printed in Japanese and English, offer such standards as oysters Kilpatrick (lightly grilled with bacon and Worcestershire sauce), seafood tempura, fillet of pork cordon blue (stuffed with cheese and ham and lightly fried), and coral trout meunière, as well as a selection of salads. *Main resort complex, tel. 079/ 46–9999. Reservations advised. Jacket required. AE, DC, MC, V. Open for breakfast daily, dinner Mon.–Sat. $$$*

Outrigger Restaurant. Large glass panels with louvered windows give this elegant restaurant an unobstructed view of Catseye Beach. High timber ceilings and plenty of tile and wood set the scene for predominantly French cuisine with an emphasis on seafood. Try such innovative dishes as *coquillage en feuillette,* a puff-pastry boat filled with oysters, scallops, and lobster on a julienne of leeks set on a champagne and green peppercorn sauce, or *langouste grille aux petites légumes et sauce Robert,* grilled lobster with vegetables and Dijon mustard sauce. *Main resort complex, tel. 079/46–9999, ext. 8582. Reservations advised. Dress: casual but neat. AE, DC, MC, V. No lunch. Closed Mon. $$$*

Romeo's Italian Restaurant. With polished wood floors and a balcony overlooking the harbor, this gracious restaurant offers a tranquil dining experience. Apprenticed in Venice, chef and owner Romeo Rigo is always creating new and exciting dishes, such as *pollo Zeeland* (chicken breasts sautéed with mushrooms) or *fettuccine della casa,* made with homemade pork, veal, and garlic sausages, and cooked in tomato and cream. *Front St., Harbourside, tel. 079/46–9999. Reservations advised. Dress: casual but neat. AE, DC, MC, V. Closed Tues. $$$*

Lodging Overlooking Catseye Beach, **Hamilton Island Resort** offers the widest selection of accommodations of any Queensland island resort. Guests have a choice of seven types of lodging, ranging from high-rise towers to privately owned homes. All accommodations have air-conditioning, ceiling fan, color TV, refrigerator, minibar, and tea/coffee maker. Unlike many other resorts in the region, the tariff covers only accommodations, not meals or activities.

Situated in a four-story brick building at the end of the main resort pool, the **Allamanda Lodge** offers views over the main resort complex and Catseye Beach. Rooms feature king-size beds and private balconies, and have tile floors, beige wallpaper, and furniture in earthy hues. *60 rooms with shower. $$$$*

Rooms in the **Bougainvillea Lodge,** a two-story complex overlooking Hamilton's freshwater pool and Catseye Beach, have tile floors, wicker furniture, and sliding doors onto private balconies. Decorated in earth tones, each room contains two queen-size beds. The complex also contains a number of rooms specially designed for the disabled. *60 rooms with shower. $$$*

With their steeply sloping roofs and small balconies, **The Bures** resemble Polynesian huts. Each of these small, individual units contains a king-size bed, a small bar, and a furnished patio. *51 units, 31 with bath, 20 with shower only. $$$*

In August 1990 the newest complex on the island, the high-rise **Hamilton Towers,** was completed. Papered in off-white and beige with fawn tiles and blond wood furniture, rooms are enlivened by bedspreads with cool, tropical patterns and dark green curtains. All rooms feature queen- or king-size beds and balconies with ocean views. The towers house a bar, a restaurant, and a lobby shop. *350 rooms, 18 suites, 18 junior suites. $$$*

Illalangi, a privately owned home in the super-luxury class, is rented by the resort on the owner's behalf. It is a four-bedroom, three-bathroom house with a formal dining area, a breakfast room, and an ultramodern kitchen and laundry. A landscaped pool and a sauna are located within the grounds. Guests are attended by a butler and have use of a six-seater minibus. A chef and a maid can be hired. *$$$$*

Looking out over the Coral Sea toward Whitsunday Island, the twin 14-story **Whitsunday Towers** feature a variety of self-contained suites and apartments. One-bedroom suites come complete with fully equipped kitchens, balconies, and dining and sitting areas. Although there is only one bedroom, these suites can accommodate up to five people by utilizing the two sofa beds. The larger, two-bedroom apartments feature a main bedroom with a king-size bed and bathroom, and a second bedroom with two single beds and a connecting bathroom. These apartments, decorated with cool cane furniture and tile floors, also have washing machines. *168 suites with bath, 41 apartments with 2 baths. $$$$*

Yacht Harbour Towers is a white high-rise overlooking the marina. Six owners rent out their four-bedroom apartments during their absence. Although all are furnished differently, each is 3,500 square feet and comes complete with marble floors, a balcony, four bathrooms, a fully equipped kitchen, and a laundry room. The $1,800-per-day tariff includes the use of a personal golf cart. *6 apartments with 4 baths each. $$$$*

Guests in all the resort's lodges and towers have access to a host of services and amenities, including a beauty salon, professional masseuse, nightclub, piano bar with live entertainment, art gallery, and doctor and dentist. *Hamilton Island Resort, PMB, Post Office, Hamilton Island, Queensland 4803, tel. 079/46–9999 or toll-free 008/07–5110; in the U.S., 800/366–1300. AE, DC, MC, V.*

South Molle Island

South Molle is a relatively large island (1,040 acres) not far from Shute Harbour. Although now a national park with a single resort, the island has had many other roles. Aborigines used to come here to collect the basalt used in their axes. Much later it became the first of the Whitsundays to be used for grazing—hence its extensive grassy tracts. The most exceptional area is the very attractive Bauer Bay at the northern end—the site of the resort. Sheltered between two headlands, the bay often remains calm when wind is ripping the rest of the Whitsundays.

Arriving and Access is by **Whitsunday All Over and Water Taxi** (tel. 079/46–9499)
Departing from Hamilton Island (*see above*) or by the island's own boats from
Shute Harbour. The latter depart Shute Harbour at 9, 1, and 5. The
30-minute trip costs $30 for adults round-trip, $15 for children. A
water taxi meets each flight into Hamilton Island; the 30-minute
transfer costs $37 one-way for adults, $18.50 for children.

Dining and **South Molle Island Resort.** From the water it doesn't look very large;
Lodging it's only when you explore the complex that you realize there are
over 200 guest rooms, which can accommodate 500 visitors. The resort, operated by Ansett Australia, nestles in a bay at the northern
end of the island, with a long jetty reaching out into deep water beyond the fringing reef. The standard of facilities and fittings is high,
and their appeal spreads across the board, from young couples to
families and retirees. There is full child-care service and a nine-hole
golf course. Every room has a balcony. Several standards of accommodation are available but all have air-conditioning, telephones,
TVs, and refrigerators. All meals in the dining room and most activities are included in the tariff; as at most other resorts, only sports
requiring fuel cost extra. Apart from the regular dining room, the
Island Restaurant and Bar, the resort has a signature restaurant
known simply as the **A La Carte,** which costs extra. South Molle is
understated in promoting itself, but it's one of the most pleasant resorts in the Whitsundays. *South Molle Island, via Shute Harbour,
Queensland 4741, tel. 079/46–9433. 202 units with shower. Facilities: 9-hole golf course, 2 floodlit tennis courts, squash court, half-
Olympic-size pool, gym, spa, sauna, full range of beach equipment,
laundry. AE, DC, MC, V. $$$*

Daydream Island

Only a 20-minute boat ride from Shute Harbour, every part of this
little island in the heart of the Whitsundays is incorporated into the
resort. Yet somehow it manages to keep the original feel of a tropical
paradise—much of the rain forest is intact and there are lush gar-
dens everywhere. The island is divided, with 303 guest accommoda-
tions at the northern end and a day-visitor center in the south. The
resort reopened in December 1990 after a $100-million redevelop-
ment project that completely revamped and modernized all the
rooms and facilities. The nightly entertainment, reasonable cost,
and wide range of activities keep guests returning year after year.

Arriving and Although most people arrive by boat from Hamilton Airport, an al-
Departing ternative is to fly to Proserpine via **Ansett Australia** (tel. 13–1344—
By Plane no prefix) or **Qantas** (13–1313) and then catch a bus to Shute Har-
bour with **Sampsons Bus Line** (tel. 079/45–2377; cost: $13) and a boat
from Shute Harbour (*see below*).

By Boat **Whitsunday All Over and Water Taxi** (tel. 079/46–9499) runs regular-
ly scheduled launches to Daydream from Shute Harbour ($20 round-
trip). The company also offers transit from Hamilton Island (*see
Hamilton Island, above,* for airlines details) for $74 round-trip (half
that for children).

Participant Most sports (except those requiring fuel) are free to guests. The
Sports most popular are tennis, badminton, volleyball, windsurfing, para-
sailing, fishing, snorkeling, and waterskiing. Two-hour scuba div-
ing lessons are conducted upon request, for $60 per day. Much of the
daily resort activity takes place at the centrally located swimming
pool and bar.

Day Trips This is one of the few islands where day visits are not merely allowed but actively encouraged. Day visitors are not permitted to use the resort facilities but have their own visitor center. This miniresort has a pool, cash bar, and late-night disco and offers water sports for a fee. In addition, there are many boutiques and shops.

From Daydream, visitors can take most of the excursions to the outer reef that are available from Shute Harbour.

Dining and Lodging Besides the difference in price and size, the three types of accommodations offered are all well-appointed by Barrier Reef island standards. The Garden rooms do not offer views of the ocean, but they make up for this with their pool and tropical garden views. The larger Daydreamer and Sunlover suites view the Whitsunday Passage, and the two superluxurious, multilevel suites sit right on the beach. All rooms contain modern, light-color furnishings with ceiling fan and air-conditioning. Rooms have private balcony, tea/coffee maker, refrigerator, radio, television, and telephone. Food is not included in the basic price of the resort; guests can choose between the Waterfall Café Restaurant and the more elegant Sunlover Restaurant, where seafood is the specialty. *Daydream Island, PMB 22, Mackay, Queensland 4740, tel. 079/48–8488 or toll-free 008/07–5040. 301 suites. Facilities: pool, 2 tennis courts, fully equipped exercise room, sauna, 2 spas, in-house movies, boutique, game room. $$*

Hayman Island

Quite simply, Hayman Island is one of the best resorts in the world. Situated in the northern approaches to the Whitsunday Passage, the resort caters to people for whom luxury rather than price is the foremost concern. The architecture of the hotel is breathtaking, with reflecting pools, sandstone walkways, manicured tropical gardens, and sparkling waterfalls. The atmosphere is closer to an expensive club than a resort.

The swimming pools at Hayman are delights. One wing of the hotel has a huge seawater lagoon with walkways leading over the top to a central island that, in turn, encircles a large, pentagon-shape freshwater pool. Deck chairs are arranged under the shelter of palms and umbrellas. The hotel's other wing features another freshwater pool partly surrounded by tropical gardens, and a vast fish pond across which white swans glide.

Hayman Island itself is a 900-acre crescent with a series of hills along its spine. The area around the resort is rather arid, but there are beautiful walking trails through the rain forest on the other side of the island. The view of the Whitsunday Passage from the ridge of the hills is unbeatable. The main beach is right in front of the hotel, but more secluded beaches, as well as fringing coral, can be reached by boat or on foot.

Hayman has its own marina with a sheltered anchorage for the island's diving and cruise boats, charter vessels, and yachts. The resort also offers a disco. Several boutiques selling fashions, perfume, cosmetics, and jewelry are located in the hotel's shopping arcade, and there is an organized children's activity center.

Arriving and Departing Hayman does not have an airstrip of its own. Instead, guests take **Ansett Australia** (tel. 13–1344—no prefix) to Hamilton Island, where they board one of Hayman's two luxury motor yachts: *Sun Goddess* or *Sun Paradise*. Champagne is served during the 45-minute trip to Hayman Island. On arrival at the wharf, guests are driven to the resort about 1 kilometer (.6 mile) away.

Guided Tours The 25-knot catamaran *Capricorn* (tel. 079/46–6900) offers **Great Barrier Reef excursions** on Monday, Wednesday, and Saturday from 10 AM to 4 PM. The $90-per-person charge includes snorkeling, coral viewing in the semisubmersible *Coral Sub*, a video presentation on the Great Barrier Reef, and a buffet lunch. There is a dive master on board, and the ship operates a cash bar.

The $310 **Reef Discovery Helicopter Tour** (tel. 079/46–8249) includes an aerial sweep of the Great Barrier Reef, snorkeling (equipment supplied), and coral viewing from the resort's submarine. Tours are offered daily.

Passengers on the **Reef Bird** (book through reception) fly over the Great Barrier Reef aboard a float plane that leaves from Hayman Island. After a 2½-hour aerial tour, the plane lands in the sheltered waters of Hardy Reef Lagoon, where passengers board a semisubmersible boat for a tour of the reef. More adventurous passengers can snorkel or reef walk. Snorkeling gear is available. The cost of the tour is $190 for adults, $95 for children.

Participant Sports Many of the activities offered on Hayman Island cost extra. In addition to its spectacular pools, the resort features floodlit tennis courts, billiards tables, badminton, and a variety of bushwalks through the island's national park. A health center offers a fully equipped gym, aerobics classes, and a beauty center. It also has a new activities center with squash courts, plus an 18-hole putting green and driving range.

Adjacent to the marina, the resort's water-sports center features its own training tank for diving lessons. A dive shop sells everything from snorkels to complete wet suits and sports clothing. The marina organizes parasailing, waterskiing, sailing, boating, windsurfing, and snorkeling. Fishing trips, as well as trips out to the reef for scuba diving and coral viewing, can be arranged through the hotel's Recreation Information Centre at ext. 758.

Dining The base rate at the Hayman Island Resort does not include meals other than the buffet breakfast. Guests sign for their meals and the charges are added to the hotel bill. Reservations are recommended for all restaurants and can be booked through the resort's operator.

La Fontaine. With its Waterford chandeliers and Louis XVI decor, this elegant French restaurant is the resort's culinary showpiece. The cuisine rivals the finest restaurants on the mainland and features such innovative dishes as *suprême de volaille et langouste en crème d'Algues* (supreme of chicken filled with lobster in a cream sauce) and *noisettes d'agneau rôties à la compote d'échalote* (roast medallions of lamb with a compote of shallots and a red capsicum coulis). Dinner is usually accompanied by live music. Private rooms are available. *No lunch. Jacket required. $$$$*

The Oriental Seafood Restaurant. This authentically Asian restaurant overlooks one of the most realistic Japanese gardens in Australia. Black lacquer chairs, shoji screens, and superb Japanese artifacts such as Buddhist statues give this outstanding restaurant a comfortably exotic ambience. Try the *hoi man poo* (Thai-style mussels in black bean sauce), shark's-fin soup, or jellyfish vinaigrette. *Dress: resort casual. No lunch. $$$$*

The Beach Pavilion. Popular with guests coming directly from the beach or the pool for lunch, this restaurant serves snacks, hamburgers, steaks, and a variety of other dishes in a pleasantly informal atmosphere. *Dress: casual. $$*

The Coffee House. Serving dishes that range from simple sandwiches and cakes baked in the hotel's kitchens to full meals, this coffee shop offers a choice between air-conditioned comfort indoors and breezy, sunlit outdoor tables. *Dress: casual. $$*

La Trattoria. With its red-and-white check tablecloths and furnishings, this classic provincial Italian restaurant could easily be in Sorrento or Portofino. Seated either inside or outdoors, diners can choose from an extensive list of pastas and traditional Italian dishes. The prices are very reasonable. *Dress: resort casual. $$*

Planters. This Australian restaurant uses rattan furniture, ceiling fans, and hibiscus artwork to create a relaxed local mood. Diners can feast on seafood or such specialties as kangaroo, emu, and buffalo. *Dress: resort casual. No lunch. $$*

Lodging **Hayman Island Resort.** This resort was refurbished in 1987 at a cost of $200 million, and it seems that money *can* buy almost everything. Asian artifacts, European tapestries, Persian rugs, and exquisite objets d'art enliven the lobby, restaurants, and rooms, which almost echo from the amount of marble adorning the walls and floor. Guests can choose from a number of different types of rooms, although all feature air-conditioning, TV, ceiling fan, minibar, personal safe, refrigerator, and tea/coffee maker. Set in tropical gardens next to the pool and lagoon areas, the Palm Court and Palm Garden rooms have their own terraces (Palm Garden terraces are larger), while guests in the Beachfront Rooms can walk from their terraces straight onto the coral-sand beach. All rooms have spectacular views of the distant islands. For utter luxury, nothing could top the 11 Penthouse Suites, each of which is decorated in a different style ranging from Californian to Moroccan, French to Australian. *Hayman Island, Queensland 4801, tel. 079/46–9100. Airline/accommodations packages available through Ansett Australia (Hayman Sales and Marketing, tel. 03/623–2323 or toll-free 008/33–5855; in the U.S., tel. 800/366–1300). 214 rooms, including 11 penthouses. AE, DC, MC, V. $$$$*

Orpheus Island

Volcanic in origin, this narrow island—11 kilometers (6 miles) long and 1 kilometer (.6 mile) wide—uncoils like a snake in the waters between Halifax Bay and the Barrier Reef. More than half the island is national park, fringed by unspoiled sandy beaches and superb coral. Wild goats—descendants of goats placed here early in the century as provisions for shipwrecked sailors—roam the hilly interior, and large numbers of birds thrive in the island's subtropical vegetation.

Situated on the west coast of the island with a distant view of the Queensland coast, the Orpheus Island Resort is a luxury accommodation emphasizing privacy and relaxation. The resort appeals to affluent businesspeople as well as celebrities. Day-trippers are not allowed, and the resort accommodates no more than 74 guests at one time. The hotel does not accept children under 15.

The resort itself is a cross between a South Seas island and an elegant Italian hotel. Set right on the beach, it boasts elegant terracotta floors, Persian rugs, and comfortable rattan furniture. Although a full array of activities and water sports is offered, many of the guests seem content to laze about, waiting for the next culinary offering—an area in which Orpheus distinguishes itself. On request, the kitchen will also prepare gourmet picnic hampers. No nightclubs, discos, TV, or organized activities are provided, although the staff will lead cross-island hikes if requested.

Arriving and Departing Orpheus Island is situated 24 kilometers (15 miles) offshore opposite Ingham, and about 80 kilometers (50 miles) northeast of Townsville. **Nautilus Aviation** (tel. 077/25–6056) offers 25-minute flights from Townsville to Orpheus aboard its seaplanes for $260 per person round-trip. The flight from Cairns costs $400 per person round-trip.

Guided Tours The coral around Orpheus is among the best in the entire area, and cruises to the outer reef can be arranged through the resort. Whereas most of the islands are more than 50 kilometers (31 miles) from the reef, Orpheus is situated just 15 kilometers (9 miles) away.

Participant Sports Most activities are included in the price. The resort has two freshwater swimming pools, a Jacuzzi, a tennis court, and a host of walking trails that wind through the large national park.

The snorkeling and diving from the island's beaches are spectacular, although at low tide, guests must travel by boat to the float anchored in the middle of the bay. In addition, the resort features waterskiing, windsurfing, sailing, canoeing, boating, and rides in a glass-bottom boat. Fishing charters can also be arranged.

Dining and Lodging **Orpheus Island Resort.** Facing the beach and shaded by swaying coconut palms, guest rooms are decorated in warm colors with terra-cotta tiling, wicker furniture, and a rear wall of patterned wood. Guests can choose between terrace suites, grouped four to a building, studio units in five groups of three, or two freestanding bungalows, which feature a queen-size bed, sitting area, and round whirlpool bath. All beachfront rooms feature radio, minibar, ceiling fan, air-conditioning, and tea/coffee maker. Six luxury Mediterranean-style villas, on the hill behind the resort, can be rented for $470 per person per night and are absolutely stunning.

All meals are included in the price, and the cuisine at Orpheus is truly superior. Some of the finest chefs in Australia are on hand to create dishes that emphasize seafood from the nearby Barrier Reef, although the kitchen, given enough time, will also accommodate special orders. Much of the cuisine reflects both European and tropical Queensland influences, and guests can choose from such dishes as deviled king prawns, sautéed scallops with ginger and broccoli, and broiled barramundi with capers, beets, and ginger. The restaurant also presents a magnificent selection of salads and a splendid bar. Even the buffet breakfasts are sumptuous affairs. Since the resort houses a maximum of 74 guests, dinners tend to be friendly, intimate occasions. Potted plants, large palms, and blond wicker and wood give the open-sided dining room a distinctly tropical feel. Dress is casual but neat. *Orpheus Island, PMB 15 Townsville Mail Centre, Queensland 4810, tel. 077/77–7377 or toll-free 008/ 07–7167. 8 rooms with bath, 23 with shower only. AE, DC, MC, V. $$$$*

Dunk Island

Situated 5 kilometers (3 miles) off the coast of Queensland's tropical north, Dunk Island is, at 3,000 acres, the largest of the Family Group islands. The island—which provided the setting for E. J. Banfield's 1908 escapist classic *Confessions of a Beachcomber*—is divided by a hilly spine that runs its entire length. The eastern side is mostly national park, with dense rain forest and secluded beaches accessible only by boat. Beautiful paths have been tunneled through the rain forest, along which walkers may see the large blue Ulysses butterfly, whose wingspan can reach 6 inches. The Dunk Island Resort is on the western side of the island overlooking the mainland. Operated by Qantas, it's particularly popular with middle-income Australians and families. The resort's prize-winning gardens are some of the best maintained in Australia, and the cascading series of swimming pools is a delight. The atmosphere is informal—guests are not required to change for dinner—and light entertainment is offered every night in the main lounge.

Arriving and Departing
By Plane
Dunk Island has its own grass landing strip. **Sunstate Airlines** (tel. 070/860–4577) serves the island daily from Cairns and Townsville. The one-way fare is $110 from Cairns and $100 from Townsville.

By Boat
The catamaran **MV *Quick Cat*** (tel. 070/68–7289) departs Clump Point Jetty in Mission Beach daily at 10:15 for the 15-minute ride to Dunk Island and returns from Dunk Island at 4:30 PM. Round-trip fare is $18; children travel half price.

Guided Tours
MV *Quick Cat,* a large passenger catamaran, offers daily trips to the reef 35 kilometers (22 miles) away, leaving Dunk Island at 10:30 and returning at 4. *Tel. 070/68–7289. Tickets: $86 adults, $52.50 children.*

Participant Sports
In addition to Barrier Reef cruises and fishing charters, the resort offers a full range of water sports, including snorkeling, sailing, windsurfing, waterskiing, tandem skydiving, and parasailing. Freshwater swimming is available in huge cascading pools.

Dunk Island also features a six-hole golf course, skeet shooting, horseback riding, archery, two squash courts, and three tennis courts. The resort tariff includes all sports except horseback riding, skeet shooting, and those activities requiring fuel.

Guests can wander throughout the island along prepared trails with the help of a map provided by the resort. All walks are graded according to difficulty. Some of the harder ones—particularly to the top of Mount Koo-ta-loo—pay off the extra effort with beautiful views.

Dining and Lodging
Dunk Island Resort. Set among coconut palms, flowering hibiscus, and frangipani, the resort overlooks the waters of Brammo Bay. Guests have a choice of three types of accommodation; the more expensive beachfront units offer the best value and the most privacy. These spacious rooms feature latticed balconies, cool tile floors, modern wicker furniture, and a pink and cream decor. Housed in two-story buildings, the less expensive Banfield units also have balconies overlooking either the beach or the resort gardens, and double family rooms are available for couples with children. The Cabana suites do not have beach views but are located instead among tropical gardens. High ceilings and large glass sliding doors create a sense of airiness, augmented by a simple decor that relies on light colors, woven mats, and basic tiling. However, in this very wet climate, some of the garden accommodations can still feel too damp. All rooms have television (with in-house movies), radio, telephone, air-conditioning, ceiling fan, refrigerator, and tea/coffee maker. Rooms are serviced daily.

If guests choose the full-board package (an extra $65 per day), meals—but not cold drinks—are included in the price with the exception of the Rainforest Brasserie, the resort's signature à la carte restaurant. The Rainforest Brasserie is *the* romantic restaurant on Dunk Island. Amid a riot of tropical plants, guests sit in comfortable cream-colored chairs at tables set with pink napery and elegant silverware. Terra-cotta tiles and a stunning view of the resort's swimming pools add to the restaurant's elegance. The Beachcomber Restaurant is the resort's main dining spot, and all meals here are included in the full-board rate. Overlooking lovely gardens and a shoreline lit by gas flares at night, this open-air restaurant has a South Seas atmosphere enhanced by wood beams, cane furniture, and plentiful potted plants. Dress at both spots is casual but neat. *Dunk Island, Queensland, PMB 28, via Townsville 4810, tel. 070/68–8199; in the U.S., 800/922–5122. 74 beachfront units, 36 garden cabanas, 38 Banfield units. Facilities: 2 pools, spa, tennis, squash, golf, sailing, games room, laundry. AE, DC, MC, V. $$$–$$$$*

Bedarra Island

Within the 247 acres of this tiny island lie natural springs, a dense rain forest, and eight separate beaches. The island, located just 5 kilometers (3 miles) off the northern Queensland coast, is also the site of two of the Barrier Reef's smallest and finest resorts: The Bedarra Hideaway and the Bedarra Bay are situated on opposite ends of the island, connected by a trail that winds through the interior rain forest. Owned by Qantas, these two resorts are popular with affluent executives who want a complete escape. They are the only Great Barrier Reef resorts with open bars, and the liquor (especially the champagne) flows freely. The two resorts combined accommodate only 64 people; guests stay in their own freestanding architect-designed villas hidden amid thick vegetation. A stone's throw away are golden sandy beaches with fringing coral less than 20 meters (65 feet) from the shore. This is not a place to look for organized activity. Privacy and quiet are what Bedarra is all about: There are no discos or nightclubs, and guests are discouraged from bringing children.

Arriving and Departing Bedarra Island is just a few minutes by boat from Dunk Island. All guests travel first to Dunk (*see* Dunk Island, Arriving and Departing, *above*) and then transfer to a small boat for the 20-minute complimentary ride to Bedarra.

Guided Tours Guests wishing to visit the Barrier Reef must travel to Dunk Island, from which all reef excursions and tours depart.

Participant Sports Snorkeling around the island is good, although the water can get cloudy. In addition, guests can windsurf, sail, fish, or boat. Both resorts also have swimming pools and floodlit tennis courts. Fishing charters can be organized.

Lodging ★ **Bedarra Hideaway and Bedarra Bay.** These two resorts take the title as the most expensive in Queensland. They attract wealthy travelers seeking a discreet retreat; the high cost buys a quiet holiday of absolute luxury. Elevated on stilts, the duplex villas at both resorts blend into the island's dense vegetation. Polished wood floors, ceiling fans, and exposed beams set the tone for bright, airy suites that bear little resemblance to standard hotel rooms. Each air-conditioned villa has its own balcony with a view of the ocean, queen-size bed, refrigerator, television, telephone, and minibar. Bedarra Hideaway had been closed for renovations, but reopened in late 1994.

All meals and liquor are included in the price. Each resort is limited to 32 guests, which translates into superb cuisine without a hint of the institutional food sometimes found at larger resorts. Despite the full à la carte menu, guests are urged to request whatever dishes they want. The emphasis is on fresh seafood and tropical fruit, including such dishes as freshly made pasta with skewered lobster, prawns, and chicken. Breakfast includes splendid thick muesli and such morning delicacies as eggs Benedict. The restaurant at the Bedarra Hideaway is modern, with glossy beams, black and red decor, and sharp architectural angles. The restaurant at Bedarra Bay is airier, set in a round timber building with tile floors and plenty of natural wood. At both, the bar is wide open and well stocked. Dress is casual but neat. *Bedarra Island, PMB 20, Townsville 8810, tel. 070/68–8233 (Bedarra Bay); in the U.S., 800/922–5122. 16 villas with bath at each resort. AE, DC, MC, V. $$$$*

Fitzroy Island

Fitzroy Island is just a 50-minute boat trip from the bustling tourist center of Cairns. (The boat departs daily at 8:30 and 10:30 AM from Great Adventures, Wharf Street, Cairns, tel. 070/51–0455; round-trip cost: $21 adults, $10.50 children.) Yet it has remained distinctly low-key. It is a rugged, heavily forested national park with the main island walk (a two-hour loop) taking you past one of the last staffed lighthouses in Australia and onto a lookout almost 900 feet above the surrounding waters. Fitzroy Island Resort is a casual affair of only eight units, each with two bedrooms furnished in natural woods and bright prints. The island also has camping facilities and bunkhouse accommodation for backpackers.

The resort opened only in 1981, and the island is still better-known as a popular day excursion from Cairns (*see* Guided Tours at the beginning of this chapter). It has a good fringing reef, which is excellent for snorkeling and diving. Overall, Fitzroy is a good option for visitors to Cairns seeking an island experience but unable to pay the rates at Lizard Island. *Fitzroy Island, Box 2120, Cairns, Queensland 4870, tel. 070/51–9588. 8 units with shower. Facilities: TV, radio, minibar, fans; pool, laundry, shop, dive shop, recreation room, water sports. AE, DC, MC, V. $$$*

Lizard Island

The farthest north of any of the Barrier Reef resorts, Lizard Island Lodge is small, secluded, and very upmarket. Only 64 guests can be accommodated at any one time. Don't come looking for 24-hour action, discos, or organized activities: This is a place to relax and unwind, safely protected from business pressures and prying eyes. As on Qantas's other luxury hideaway, Bedarra Island, the standards are high—and so are the prices.

The island itself is large and quite different from the other Barrier Reef islands: Composed mostly of granite, it displays a remarkable diversity of vegetation and terrain, and grassy hills give way to rocky slabs interspersed with valleys of rain forest. The whole island is a national park ringed by miles of white-sand beaches, and it may have the best examples of fringing coral of any of the resort islands. Excellent walking tracks lead to key lookouts with spectacular views of the coast. The highest point, Cooks Look (360 meters/ 1,180 feet), is the historic spot from which, in August 1770, Captain James Cook of the *Endeavour* finally spied a passage through the reef that had held him captive for a thousand miles. (Lizards, for which he named the island, often bask on the lodge's front lawn.)

Diving and snorkeling in the crystal-clear waters off Lizard Island are a dream. Twenty kilometers (12 miles) from Lizard is the Cod Hole, rated by divers among the best sites in the world. Here you will find giant potato cod that swim up to be fed and petted—an awesome experience, considering these fish weigh more than 250 pounds and are over 6 feet long! In the latter part of the year, when the black marlin are running, Lizard Island becomes the focal point for big-game anglers from around the world.

Arriving and Departing Lizard Island has its own small airstrip served by **Sunstate Airlines** (tel. 070/860–4577). Daily flights from Cairns to Lizard cost $286 round-trip.

Guided Tours The resort offers cruises to the outer reef, which lies just 16 kilometers (10 miles) away, as well as tours aboard a glass-bottom boat. The reefs around the island, however, feature some of the best marine life and coral anywhere.

Participant Sports Lizard Island Lodge has an outdoor pool, a tennis court, catamarans, outboard dinghies, and Windsurfers. Fishing gear and archery supplies are also available. There is superb snorkeling around the island's fringing coral.

Game Fishing Lizard Island is one of the main centers for big-game fishing in Australia. The 1991, 1992, and 1993 seasons were exceptional, with several world records set each year. The fishing is best between August and December, and marlins weighing more than 1,200 pounds are no rarity here. A day's big-game fishing (minimum of four people), including use of tackle, costs $230 per person (possibly the best fishing value in Australia). During the marlin season between September and December, an entire heavy-tackle boat can be rented for $1,400 per day. Inner reef and night fishing are also available.

Scuba Diving The resort will arrange supervised scuba diving trips to both the inner and outer reef, as well as local dives and night dives. Introductory courses are available, as are refresher courses. A full-certification scuba course lasting four or five days is available for $650 and includes all equipment and local dives.

Dining and Lodging **Lizard Island Lodge.** The 32 self-contained rooms in this resort are large and comfortable, decorated in pastel grays, beiges, and coral pinks. Each has its own veranda and modern blond-wood furniture. Two suites, separate from the other units, feature a separate living room and are situated closer to the beach. All rooms have king- or queen-size beds, telephones, refrigerators, minibars, and air-conditioning. The entire resort received a substantial face-lift in 1992.

The cost of meals (but not drinks) is included in the base rate. A change of management has meant that the quality of the cooking, always high, has been elevated to new heights. The resort has a spacious dining room with a modern tropical decor accented by cane-backed chairs and ceiling fans. Large glass windows, partly louvered to admit the ocean breeze, offer diners splendid views across the gardens and palms to the water. There is also dining on the veranda. Seafood from the reef provides the foundation for the restaurant's nouvelle cuisine. Although the menu changes daily, diners can expect such dishes as New Zealand mussels poached in white wine and served with a light cream and garlic sauce, fresh coral trout panfried and served with a passion-fruit sauce, or tournedos of Northern Territory buffalo on a bed of mushrooms accompanied by a tomato sauce. Vegetarian dishes are also available. The menu is complemented by an excellent wine list. Upon request, the chef will prepare picnic hampers complete with a bottle of chilled wine. Dress is resort casual. *Lizard Island Lodge, PMB 40, Cairns, Queensland 4870, tel. 070/60–3999; in the U.S., 800/922–5122. 32 rooms with bath and shower. Facilities: laundry, bar, pool, tennis, shop. AE, DC, MC, V. $$$$*

9 Adelaide and South Australia

*By Michael
Gebicki*

Often called "the City of Churches" or "the Festival City"—a reference to the biennial Festival of Arts—Adelaide is easy to explore, thanks to William Light, the first surveyor-general of the colony. In 1836, on a flat saucer of land between the Mount Lofty Ranges and the sea, Light laid out the city center—one square mile divided into a grid of broad streets running from north to south and east to west, and surrounded by parks. He put a large square at the center and other squares in each quarter of the city.

Today Light's plan is recognized as a work that was far ahead of its time. Largely due to his foresight, this city of a million people moves at a leisurely pace, free of the usual urban woes of traffic jams and concrete canyons. Yet Adelaide's poised, well-mannered face hides a paradox, for on the very doorstep of this genteel city lies the harshest, driest state in the most arid of the Earth's populated continents.

Almost 99% of South Australia's population lives in the fertile south around Adelaide, leaving the northern half of the state virtually unchanged since the first settlers arrived in Australia. Here heat and desolate desert terrain have thwarted all but the most determined efforts to conquer the land. Indeed, "conquer" is too strong a word for what is often little better than subsistence. For instance, in Coober Pedy, an opal mining town in the far north, residents live underground to avoid temperatures that top 120°F.

To the north of Adelaide are the Flinders Ranges, scorched hills that hold Aboriginal cave paintings and fossil remains from when the area was an ancient seabed. Beyond that is Lake Eyre, a great salt lake that in 1989 filled with water for only the third time in recorded history. To the west is the Nullarbor Plain, a mind-numbing expanse of flat, treeless desert that stretches into Western Australia.

In comparison, Adelaide is a veritable Eden, but everywhere through the city are reminders of the harsh desiccated land on which it verges. Notice that the poles that support the electric wires are made from steel and cement rather than wood, because timber is precious. Toward the end of the summer months it is quite common to find trees in the city parks crowded with brilliantly colored parrots, which have fled to these oases from the desert. For many residents, the most urgent concern is not rising crime or property taxes but bush fires. The city is still haunted by the memory of the Ash Wednesday bush fires that devastated the Adelaide Hills at the end of the long, hot summer of 1983, casting a pall of smoke over the city that blotted out the sun. Yet nature has bestowed its bounty on South Australia, too, as anyone will discover who takes a walk among the seals on Kangaroo Island, or a drive through the rolling orchards of the Adelaide Hills. And then there is the Barossa Valley with its patchwork vineyards, and the Murray River with its towering cliffs and lakes.

South Australia is, ironically, well equipped for the good life. The state produces most of the country's wines, and the sea ensures a plentiful supply of lobster and tuna. Cottages and guest houses tucked away in the countryside around Adelaide are among the most charming and relaxing in the country. Although South Australia does not have attractions on the scale of Sydney Harbour or the Great Barrier Reef, and it draws far fewer visitors than the eastern states, those who take the time to visit this multifaceted location will discover one of Australia's best-kept secrets.

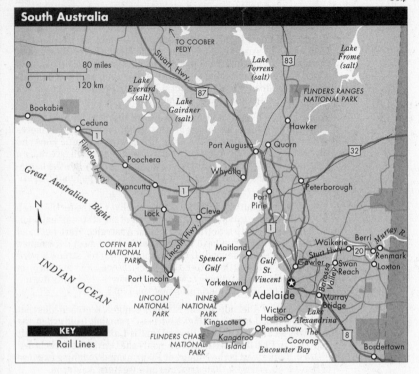

KEY

—— Rail Lines

Adelaide

Arriving and Departing by Plane

Adelaide Airport is located 6 kilometers (3.7 miles) west of the city center. The international and domestic terminals are about ¼ mile apart.

International airlines serving Adelaide are **British Airways** (tel. 08/238–2138), **Singapore Airlines** (tel. 13–1011), **Japan Air Lines** (tel. 08/212–2555), and **Qantas** (tel. 08/237–8541).

Domestic airlines flying into Adelaide include **Ansett Australia** (tel. 13–1300), **Air Kangaroo Island** (tel. 08/234–4177), **Augusta Airways** (tel. 08/234–3000), **Kendell** (tel. 08/231–9567), and **Qantas** (tel. 13–1313).

Between the Airport and Center City

By Bus The **Transit Bus** (tel. 08/381–5311) costs $4 for adults, $1.50 for children and links the airport terminals with the city hotels and the rail and bus stations. On weekdays, the bus leaves the terminals at 30-minute intervals between 7:30 AM and 1:30 PM and 4:30 PM and 9 PM. Between 1:30 and 4:30, the bus departs at one-hour intervals. On weekends, the bus departs every hour between 7:30 AM and 8:30 PM.

By Taxi Taxis are available from the ranks outside the terminal buildings. The fare to the city is about $13.

Arriving and Departing by Train and Bus

By Train   The station for interstate and country trains is the **Keswick Rail Terminal,** just to the west of the city center. The *Overlander* makes daily 12-hour runs between Melbourne and Adelaide; the *Ghan* makes the 20-hour journey to Alice Springs weekly from November to April, and at least twice weekly from May to October (*see* Alice Springs, Arriving and Departing by Car, Train, and Bus in Chapter 10); the *Indian Pacific* links Adelaide with Perth (37½ hours) and Sydney (28 hours) twice a week. The terminal has a small café and snack bar, and taxis are available from the rank outside (tel. 08/217–4111).

By Bus   The **Central Bus Station** (tel. 08/233–2733), near the city center at 101 Franklin Street, is the terminal for all intercity bus companies: **Bus Australia** (tel. 08/212–7999), **Greyhound** (tel. 08/233–2777), **Pioneer** (tel. 08/233–2700), **Premier** (tel. 08/233–2744), and **Stateliner** (tel. 08/233–2755). The terminal is open 6 AM to 10 PM.

Getting Around

By Bus and   The public transportation network is divided into three zones, and
Train   fares are calculated according to the number of zones traveled. The area within a 5-kilometer (3-mile) radius of the city center is Zone 1. Between 9 AM and 3 PM on weekdays, the fare for any bus journey within Zone 1 is $1.60 for adults, 80¢ for children 4–14; at other times the fare is $2.60 for adults, 90¢ for children 4–14. Anyone who expects to travel frequently can economize with a **Multitrip Ticket** ($14.60 for adults, $5.10 for children 4–14), which gives 10 rides throughout the three bus zones. Another economical way to travel is with the **Daytrip Ticket,** which allows unlimited bus, train, and tram travel throughout Adelaide and most of its surroundings after 9 AM. It costs $4 for adults and $1.70 for children 4–14. Tickets are available from most railway stations and from the STA City Information Centre. Approximately a 10% surcharge is added to tickets purchased on board a bus, train, or tram.

The free **Bee Line Bus** (no. 99B) makes 10 express stops in downtown Adelaide, including Hindley Street, Victoria Square, and Rundle Mall. The bus operates Monday–Thursday 8 AM–6 PM, Friday 8 AM–9 PM, and Saturday 8 AM–12:15 PM.

Travelers who expect to make extensive use of Adelaide's public buses should purchase a copy of the Public Transport map for 30¢, also available from the **STA Information Centre.** *Currie and King William Sts., tel. 08/210–1000. Open weekdays 9–5, Sat. 9–noon.*

By Taxi   Taxis can be hailed on the street, booked by phone, or collected from a rank. It is often difficult to find a cruising taxi beyond the central business district. Some taxis will accept credit cards. **Suburban Taxi Service** (tel. 08/211–8888) offers a reliable booking service.

By Tram   One of the city's last surviving trams runs between Victoria Square at the heart of the city and the lively beachside suburb of Glenelg. The fare is $2.70 for adults, $1 for children 4–14.

By Bicycle   Adelaide's parks, flat terrain, and wide, uncluttered streets make it a perfect city for two-wheel exploring. **Bike Moves** (10 Canterbury Terr., Black Forest, tel. 08/293–2922) has mountain bikes for daily or weekly rental. The price is $20 per day, $65 per week, and all come supplied with a helmet, water bottle, and city map.

Important Addresses and Numbers

Tourist
Information

The **South Australian Government Travel Centre** provides brochures and maps, and makes travel and accommodation bookings throughout the state. *1 King William St., tel. 08/212–1505. Open weekdays 9–5, weekends 9–2.*

The **State Information Centre** has travel books and brochures on South Australia and an especially good range of hiking and cycling maps. *25 Grenfell St., tel. 08/226–0000. Open Fri.–Wed. 9–4:30, Thurs. 9–5.*

What's on in Adelaide (tel. 08/11–699) is a recorded information service that covers current events and attractions in both the city and the Adelaide Hills.

Travel
Agencies

American Express Travel is located at 13 Grenfell Street (tel. 08/212–7099). **Thomas Cook** is located at 45 Grenfell Street (tel. 08/212–3354).

Emergencies

For assistance from **fire, police,** or **ambulance** services, dial 000.

Royal Adelaide Hospital (North Terr. and Frome Rd., tel. 08/223–0230) provides 24-hour medical services.

Guided Tours

Orientation
Tours

The *Adelaide Explorer* is a replica tram that takes passengers on a two-hour tour of the highlights of the city and Glenelg, Adelaide's seaside suburb. Passengers may leave the vehicle at any of the attractions along the way and join a following tour. *18 King William St., tel. 08/212–1505. Cost: $18 adults, $12 children under 16, $45 family (2 adults, 2 children). Daily tours at 9:15, 10:45, 12:20, 1:25, 2:55, 3:55.*

Every Wednesday and Saturday, **Festival Mini Tours** operates a half-day city tour of North Terrace, the Festival Centre, and Windy Point, which has a view of the city from its scenic lookout. *18 King William St., tel. 08/374–1270. Tickets: $28 adults, $20 children under 14. Tours depart at 1:15.*

Exploring Adelaide

Numbers in the margin correspond to points of interest on the Adelaide map.

❶ The central section of Adelaide, bordered by parks on all sides, is easily explored on foot. Start in **Victoria Square** at the very heart of Adelaide. The fountain in the square uses the Torrens, Onkaparinga, and Murray rivers as its theme. The square itself is surrounded by some excellent examples of Adelaide's colonial buildings constructed from local stone, although many have been replaced by office blocks. One of the few grand survivors is the three-story stone **Torrens Building** on the east side of the square. On your left as you head north on King William Street, you will see the **General Post Of-**

❷
❸ **fice,** which was constructed in 1867. Directly opposite is the **Old Treasury Building Museum.** The exploration and survey of South Australia is a story of quiet heroism, and the museum is dedicated largely to the memory of explorers who feature prominently in the state's history, such as Charles Sturt of Murray and Darling rivers fame, and Edward Eyre, who in 1840–1841 walked the desert from Adelaide to Perth. Included in the display of gleaming brass surveying equipment is Light's theodolite, which was used in

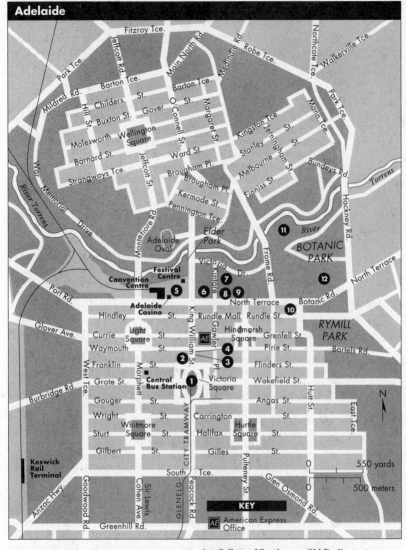

Art Gallery of South Australia, **9**
Ayers House, **10**
Botanic Gardens, **12**
General Post Office, **2**
Migration and Settlement Museum, **7**
Old Treasury Building Museum, **3**

Old Parliament House, **5**
South African War Memorial, **6**
South Australian Museum, **8**
Town Hall, **4**
Victoria Square, **1**
Zoological Gardens, **11**

the planning of Adelaide. *Flinders and King William Sts., tel. 08/ 226–4130. Admission free. Open weekdays 10–4.*

❹ The next building along King William Street is the imposing **Town Hall,** built in 1863 in 16th-century Renaissance style. Continue up King William Street, a wide avenue flanked by banks and insurance companies, until you reach North Terrace. Many of the city's prime attractions are clustered along this road.

Across North Terrace on the corner is the formidable Greco-Roman **❺** facade of the present Parliament House, and to the left is **Old Parliament House,** where South Australia's constitutional history began in 1843. The building was restored in 1980 and now houses a display of computer terminals that illustrate the state's electoral and legislative systems, as well as changing exhibitions on social and political themes. With its antique furnishings and high ceiling, the former library on the ground floor, now known as the Kingston Room, best captures a sense of the building's history. *North Terr., tel. 08/207– 1077. Admission: $4 adults, $2.50 children under 16, $10 family. Open weekdays 10–5, weekends noon–5.*

Cross King William Street to the bronze statue of the mounted **❻** trooper—the **South African War Memorial.** This statue was unveiled in 1904 to commemorate the volunteers of the South Australian Bushmen's Corps who fought with the British in the Boer War. Through the gates behind the statue you can catch a glimpse of **Government House,** the official residence of the state governor, completed in 1878.

Walk up Kintore Avenue, past the white marble facade of the **City of ❼ Adelaide Lending Library,** and turn right to enter the **Migration and Settlement Museum,** which chronicles the origins, hopes, and fates of some of the millions of migrants who have settled in Australia over the past two centuries. The museum is starkly realistic, and the bleak welcome that awaited many migrants as recently as the 1970s is graphically illustrated in the reconstructed quarters of a migrant hostel. The museum is housed in the historic buildings of the Destitute Asylum, which is where many migrants found themselves when the realities of Australian life failed to match their expectations. For anyone interested in the evolution of Australian society, this is a fascinating and rewarding museum. *82 Kintore Ave., tel. 08/223–8748. Admission free. Open weekdays 10–5, weekends 1–5.*

Return to North Terrace, walk past the **Royal Society of Arts** and the City of Adelaide Lending Library and turn left at the wide, grassy **❽** courtyard to the **South Australian Museum.** This museum houses an extensive collection of Melanesian artifacts; don't be put off by the dusty, rather jumbled and old-fashioned displays—the objects deserve careful inspection. Unfortunately, the museum lacks the space to display more than a fraction of its outstanding Aboriginal anthropological collection. *North Terr., tel. 08/223–8911. Admission free. Open daily 10–5.*

❾ Next along North Terrace is the neoclassical facade of the **Art Gallery of South Australia.** Although the gallery is not large, many famous Australian painters are represented in its collection, including Tom Roberts, Margaret Preston, Clifford Possum Tjapaltjarri, Russell Drysdale, and Sidney Nolan. *North Terr., tel. 08/223–7200. Open daily 10–5.*

Leave the Art Gallery, proceed along North Terrace and cross to **❿** **Ayers House.** Between 1855 and 1897, this sprawling colonial structure was the home of Sir Henry Ayers, the premier of the state and the man for whom Ayers Rock was named. Ayers made his fortune from the copper mines at Burra, which enabled him to build this 41-room mansion. Since 1970 the house has been the headquarters of the National Trust of South Australia, caretaker of the state's historic buildings. Most of the rooms have been restored with period furnishings, although few of the pieces actually belonged to the Ayers family. The admission price includes a one-hour tour. Two restaurants are located inside Ayers House: the elegant, café-style Conservatory and the opulent Henry Ayers Restaurant. Both are operated independently. *288 North Terr., tel. 08/223–1655. Admission: $4 adults, $2 children under 18. Open Tues.–Fri. 10–4, weekends 2–4.*

⑪ Cross North Terrace and walk up Frome Road, the shady avenue that leads to the **Zoological Gardens.** Adelaide's zoo is small, but the landscaping and the lack of crowds make this a pleasant place to see Australian fauna. An aviary of Australian birds recently opened. *Frome Rd., tel. 08/267–3255. Admission: $8 adults, $4 children 4–14. Open daily 9:30–5.*

From the zoo you can return to the city either by the footpath that follows the river Torrens through a pretty park or aboard one of the "Popeye" launches. The boats travel between the front gate of the zoo and Elder Park, in front of the **Festival Centre** (*see* The Arts, *below*), the setting for most of the mainstream events of the Adelaide Festival. *Cost: $2 adults, $1 children under 16. Boats depart weekdays hourly 11:25–3:25, weekends every 20 min 11–5.*

⑫ Otherwise, return to the entrance of the zoo, turn left and cross the broad lawns of Botanic Park to the **Botanic Gardens.** These magnificent formal gardens include roses, giant water lilies, an avenue of Moreton Bay figs, an Italianate garden, acres of green lawns, and duck ponds. The latest addition to the gardens is the Bicentennial Conservatory, an enormous glass dome that provides a high-humidity, high-temperature environment for rain-forest species. Guided tours leave from the Simpson Kiosk in the center of the gardens Tuesday and Friday at 10:30. The **Botanic Gardens Restaurant** (*see* Dining, *below*) at the center of the grounds has one of the prettiest views of any city restaurant, and good food to go with it. *North Terr., tel. 08/228–2311. Gardens open weekdays 7–sunset, weekends 9–sunset.*

Adelaide for Free

During the warmer months you can relax on the grassy lawns along the riverbank while jazz, folk, and orchestral ensembles perform on the rotunda in front of the Festival Centre. *Elder Park. Sun. 4–6.*

What to See and Do with Children

Magic Mountain is a beachside amusement park in Glenelg that features video games, a huge water slide, and assorted amusement park rides. A tram runs from Victoria Square to Glenelg. The fare is $2.70 adults, $1 children 4–14. *Colley Reserve, Glenelg, tel. 08/294–8199. Open late Sept.–Easter, daily 9:30 AM–10 PM; Easter–late Sept., Mon.–Thurs. 11–5, Fri.–Sun. 11–10 (closing hours may vary according to the weather).*

Off the Beaten Track

The **"pie floater,"** a meat pie submerged in pea soup, is South Australia's contribution to the culinary arts. Many locals insist that you have not really been to Adelaide unless you've tasted this dish, and the traditional place to try one is from the pie cart usually found in the vicinity of the Adelaide Casino between 6 PM and 1 AM. Another nocturnal stand can be found on Grote Street just off Victoria Square.

The **South Australian Maritime Museum,** located inside a restored stone warehouse, brings maritime history vividly to life with ships' figureheads, relics from shipwrecks, intricate scale models, slot machines from a beachside amusement park, and a full-size sailing coaster. In addition to the main display in the warehouse, the museum also includes a lighthouse, a collection of historic sailing vessels, and a steam tug tied up at the wharf nearby. *117 Lipson St., Port Adelaide, tel. 08/240–0200. Admission: $7 adults, $3 children 6–16, $17 family. Open Tues.–Sun. 10–5, daily during school holidays.*

Steam buffs will delight in the historic collection of locomotive engines and rolling stock at the **Port Dock Station,** located in the former Port Adelaide railway yard. The finest of its kind in Australia, the collection includes enormous "Mountain"-class engines, the small engines that were used to pull suburban trains, and the historic "Tea and Sugar"—once the lifeline for the railway camps scattered across the deserts of South and Western Australia. *Lipson St., Port Adelaide, tel. 08/341–1690. Admission: $6 adults, $2.50 children under 16, $15 family. Open Sun.–Fri. 10–5, Sat. noon–5.*

Shopping

Malls   Adelaide's main shopping area is **Rundle Mall** (Rundle St. between King Williams and Pulteney streets), a pedestrian plaza lined with boutiques and department stores. Shops in this area are open Monday–Thursday 9–5:30, Friday 9–9, Saturday 9–12:30. For information on specific shops in this area, visit the Rundle Mall Information Centre (open weekdays 9–5, weekends 10–1) in the booth near the corner of King William Street.

Markets   The **Central Market** is the largest produce market in the Southern Hemisphere. The stalls in this sprawling complex also sell T-shirts, records, and electrical goods. *Victoria Sq. Open Tues.–Thurs. 7 AM–6 PM, Fri. 7 AM–10 PM, Sat. 7 AM–1 PM. Closed Sun.*

Jewelry and Gems   South Australia is the world's largest source of opals. Excellent selections of opals and other gems can be found at **Opal Field Gems** (3rd Floor, 29 King William St., tel. 08/212–5300) and **The Opal Mine** (30 Gawler Pl., tel. 08/223–4023). For high-quality antique jewelry try the **Adelaide Exchange** (10 Stephens Pl., behind David Jones department store, tel. 08/212–2496) and **Megaw & Hogg Antiques** (26 Leigh St., off Hindley St., tel. 08/231–3071).

Participant Sports

Golf   Situated close to the city, the **City of Adelaide Golf Links** offer two short 18-hole courses and a full championship course. Clubs and carts may be hired from the Pro Shop. *War Memorial Dr., N. Adelaide, tel. 08/231–2359. Greens fees: $10.*

Jogging   The parks to the north of the city offer excellent routes for jogging, especially along the track beside the river Torrens.

Tennis Located just across the Torrens from the city, the **Memorial Drive Tennis Courts** offer a choice of hard or grass courts. *War Memorial Dr., N. Adelaide, tel. 08/231–4371. Hard court: $12 per hr to 5 PM, $16 to 10 PM; grass court: $16 per hr to 5 PM only, $24 per hr on weekends. Open weekdays 9 AM–10 PM, Sun. 9–5; closed to public Sat.*

Spectator Sports

Cricket The main venue for interstate and international competition is the **Adelaide Oval** (War Memorial Dr. and King William St., tel. 08/231–3759).

Football Australian-Rules football is the most popular winter sport in South Australia. Games are generally played on Saturday either at **Football Park** (Turner Dr., West Lakes, tel. 08/268–2088) or the Adelaide Oval.

Beaches

Adelaide's coastline from North Haven to Brighton is practically one long beach—a distance of about 25 kilometers (15 miles). There is no surf, but the beach is clean. The most popular beaches are those to the west of the city, including **Henley Beach** and **West Beach.** Farther south, **Glenelg** has a carnival atmosphere that makes it a favorite with families.

Dining

By Jacquie van Santen

Highly recommended restaurants are indicated by a star ★.

Revised by Michael Gebicki

Category	Cost*
$$$$	over $40
$$$	$30–$40
$$	$20–$30
$	under $20

*per person, excluding drinks and service

Australian
$$$
★
Chloe's. Dining in the grand manner, a modern French menu, and the all-seeing eyes of owner and maiître d' Nick Papazahariakis are the ingredients that define this glamorous and polished yet unpretentious restaurant. The dining room appointments—Georgian chairs, crystal decanters, Lalique chandeliers, and gleaming silver—give any meal a sense of occasion, but the prices are surprisingly modest. The panfried duck breast with game wonton and the fresh date tart with lemon glaze are signature dishes on a menu that draws its inspiration from European and Eastern cuisines. The 20,000-bottle cellar—a must-see for patrons—showcases Australia's best labels, plus some top-notch French favorites. *36 College Rd., Kent Town, tel. 08/363–1001. Reservations advised. Jacket required. AE, DC, MC, V. No lunch Sat.; closed Sun.*

$$$ **The Grange Restaurant and Brasserie.** The best in-house restaurant of any hotel in town, the Hilton's upbeat brasserie has a casual, contemporary flair and a menu that's right for any time of day. Mediterranean and Asian cooking styles fuse on a menu that lists Atlantic salmon with braised witloof and bok choy, and milk-fed veal loin on stir-fried vegetables with a green curry sauce. *Hilton Internation-*

al Adelaide, 233 Victoria Sq., tel. 08/217–0711. Reservations advised. Dress: casual but neat. AE, DC, MC, V. No dinner Sun.

$$$ **Magic Flute.** This elegant, long-established restaurant, which also
★ houses a less expensive café, features white linen napery, peach-color walls, an enclosed courtyard, and lots of greenery. The menu lists roasted milk-fed lamb with mushroom ragout, in addition to peppered venison fillet with *rosti* potatoes and a black-currant sauce. In the café, look to the specials board rather than the à la carte menu for inspiration. Desserts, particularly the crème brûlée, are always special. *109 Melbourne St., N. Adelaide, tel. 08/267–3172. Reservations required. Jacket required. AE, DC, MC, V. No lunch Sat. Closed Sun.*

$$$ **Nediz tu.** The starchy white interior punctuated by dramatic floral
★ arrangements conveys a note of sanctity, and all who come must be prepared to worship at one of Australia's altars of gastronomy. The kitchen is under the direction of award-winning chefs Le Tu Thai and Kate Sparrow, who combine the rigor of Sino-Vietnamese cooking with the classical flavors of France. Every dish shows innovation, yet this epicurean experience comes at a very reasonable price. Appetizers might include chili squid with whitebait, and goat cheese coquettes with avocado mousse and eggplant. Among the entrées are such dishes as lobster mille-feuille with champagne butter, and roast squab with parsley ravioli in a truffle-scented sauce. Desserts like the celebrated passion-fruit tart, as well as hot kumquat soufflé and vanilla-bean ice cream round out this exotic menu. Smoking is not permitted until after 10:30 PM. *170 Hutt St., tel. 08/223–2618. Reservations required. Dress: casual but neat. MC, V. Dinner only. Closed Sun. and Mon.*

$$ **Boltz Café.** With semi-industrial decor—dull blue-green paint, exposed ducts, metal and vinyl chairs—medium-volume rock music, and a midnight closing time, this café targets the young and vibrant. The menu lists a choice of salads, pizzas, focaccias, and a few surefire crowd pleasers such as fish and chips, chicken curry, and pork ribs. Live entertainment is a feature on some nights, when a cover charge of $12–$15 per person may apply. The coffee is great. *286 Rundle St., tel. 08/232–5234. No reservations. Dress: casual. AE, MC, V. No dinner Sun.*

$$ **Botanic Gardens Restaurant.** This delightful restaurant sits in the heart of the idyllic Adelaide Botanic Gardens. It serves modern Australian cuisine with an Asian influence, along with some of the finest vintages from South Australia's smaller wineries. Beef dishes are a particular specialty. The flowery decor is dominated by peaches and creams, and large windows provide expansive views of the gardens. In addition to the daily lunch, a traditional afternoon tea of scones, jam, and cream is served. *North Terr., tel. 08/223–3526. Reservations required. Dress: casual. AE, DC, MC, V. Lunch only. Closed Dec. 25.*

$$ **Red Ochre Grill.** Restaurateur and chef Andrew Fielke is on a crusade to the gastronomic outback; he wants nothing more than to shift bush tucker from the campfire to the starched white tablecloth. Examples of his success include yabby tails with tomato and lemon myrtle jelly, and yam gnocchi flavored with sun-dried tomatoes, Warrigal olives, and parmesan; swanky items from the barbie include grilled emu steak, tomato and eggplant galette with a bush-tomato glaze, and lamb medallions with artichokes, sage, and Illawarra plums. A glossary of outback food terms—with helpful descriptions—is included with the menu. An adjoining café offers a less extensive version of the menu. *129 Gouger St., tel. 08/212–7266. Reservations advised. Dress: casual. AE, DC, MC, V. Restaurant closed Sun.; no lunch Sat.; café open daily.*

Continental
$$$$
★

Blake's. The fine-dining restaurant of the Hyatt Regency Adelaide Hotel (*see* Lodging, *below*), this sophisticated spot would be perfect for a big night out. Rough timber and small, cozy spaces create a relaxed, intimate atmosphere. Highlights of the main-course menu are the blackened fish with vegetable couscous and lemongrass butter sauce and the braised duck on lentils with a ginger sauce, while a tandoor oven permits such novelties as a clay-roasted fillet of lamb with tomato and bean salsa and roasted quail breasts on snow-pea sprouts with oyster mushrooms. The impressive wine list features past winners of the Hyatt's own awards for the best South Australian wines, which have included some of the finest winemakers in the country. *Hyatt Regency Hotel, North Terr., tel. 08/231–1234. Reservations required. Jacket required. AE, DC, MC, V. No lunch; closed Sun.*

$$$
★

Mezes. Artistry and flamboyance are reserved for the food rather than the decor at this superb restaurant. Owner and chef Lew Kathreptis brings a new dimension to the peasant cooking of the Mediterranean. The daily menu is limited to five appetizers and five entrées; these imaginative and superbly presented dishes include such gutsy combinations as a "sandwich" of beef carpaccio with anchoyade (anchovy purée) and roasted garlic; oxtail flavored with thyme, cumin, and orange; and a sublime asparagus-and-egg-yolk ravioli with parmesan and olive oil. *287 Rundle St., tel. 08/223–7384. Reservations advised. Dress: casual but neat. AE, DC, MC, V. No lunch Sat.–Thurs.; closed Mon.*

$$

Jolley's Boathouse. Blue canvas deck chairs and white-painted timber create a relaxed, nautical air, befitting the restaurant's position overlooking the river Torrens. The menu emphasizes grilled delicacies such as goat cheese with chargrilled witloof, chicken with tomato and pesto, and braised lamb shanks with leeks, mushroom, and cumin. The restaurant is very popular for Sunday lunch, and it's fabulously romantic on a warm evening. *Jolley's La., tel. 08/223–2891. Reservations advised. Dress: casual. AE, DC, MC, V. No dinner Sun.–Tues.*

$$

Ruby's Café. Sunday brunch is an institution at this chrome and vinyl 1950s-style café. The menu offers dishes such as lemon-scented chicken, kangaroo fillet with fresh egg noodles, and ham, potato, and pea soup. Traditional puddings—banana, vanilla, toffee—are prominent. *255B Rundle St., tel. 08/224–0365. Reservations advised. Dress: casual. MC, V. BYOB. Open for dinner daily, lunch and dinner Sun.*

$$
★

The Universal. This high-gloss, split-level bar/café with giant mirrors and exposed wine racks along one wall remains a favorite of Adelaide's café society. Main meals include chargrilled quail and radicchio, grilled goat-cheese salad, and duck dishes—but grazing is the name of the game here. The bar plate—an antipasto platter that usually features such exotic treats as witloof with balsamic dressing and kangaroo pastrami—is a meal for two. Don't miss the grape cake. You can choose from a wide and interesting selection of wines by the glass. *285 Rundle St., tel. 08/232–5000. Dinner reservations advised. Dress: casual. AE, DC, MC, V. Closed Sun.*

French
$$

La Guillotine. This pleasantly rustic restaurant is a long-standing favorite with those who appreciate traditional French cooking. Tables on the balcony overlook Gouger Street, Adelaide's bustling market center, and tables are also available in the courtyard garden. Highlights include *moules marinières* (mussels steamed in white wine), onion soup, and rabbit in Dijon mustard sauce. The profiterole cake is a signature dessert. *125 Gouger St., tel. 08/212–*

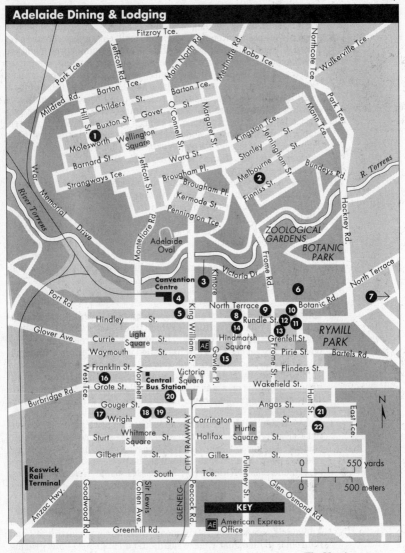

Adelaide Dining & Lodging

Dining

Amalfi Pizzeria
Ristorante, **9**

Blake's, **4**

Boltz Cafe, **10**

Botanic Gardens
Restaurant, **6**

Chloe's, **7**

The Grange
Restaurant and
Brasserie, **20**

Jasmin, **14**

Jolley's Boathouse, **3**

La Guilloutine, **19**

Magic Flute, **2**

Mezes, **12**

Mona Lisa's Bistro, **21**

Nediz Tu, **22**

Red Ochre Grill, **18**

Ruby's Cafe, **13**

The Universal, **11**

Lodging

Adelaide's Bed and
Breakfast, **16**

Directors Studios and
Suites, **17**

The Earl of
Zetland, **15**

Hilton
International, **20**

Hyatt Regency
Adelaide, **4**

The Mansions, **8**

North Adelaide
Heritage
Apartments, **1**

Terrace
Inter-Continental, **5**

2536. Reservations required. Dress: casual but neat. AE, DC, MC, V. No lunch Sat.–Tues. Closed Sun. and Christmas week.

Indian **Jasmin.** Traditional Indian prints and artifacts give an authentic am-
$$ bience to this celebrated restaurant. Jasmin specializes in Punjabi
cooking and offers more than 200 wines from some of Australia's
smaller vineyards. Tandoor-style fish and chicken are recom-
mended, as is the vegetable curry. *31 Hindmarsh Sq., tel. 08/223–
7837. Reservations advised. Dress: casual but neat. AE, DC, MC,
V. No lunch Sat. Closed Sun., Mon., and holidays.*

International **Mona Lisa's Bistro.** One of Adelaide's more adventurous restau-
$$$ rants, the Mona Lisa offers a refreshing change of pace for jaded pal-
ates. You can choose from a number of imaginative combinations,
such as spiced lamb shanks with tomato, garlic, and black-eyed
beans; chicken with quince and potato khoresh; and Kurdish goat
curry. The decor is smart and modern with a touch of rusticity—
stone walls, brick floor, bare wooden tables set with starched white
napery and sparkling wine glasses. *160 Hutt St., tel. 08/223–3733.
Reservations advised. Dress: casual but neat. AE, DC, MC, V.*

Italian **Amalfi Pizzeria Ristorante.** Along with the low prices, bustle, no-
$$ frills atmosphere, and menu of Italian favorites, this mid-city bistro
serves up a few surprises. The flavors here speak of sunlight: The
specials board might list linguine with fresh blue swimmer crab,
chicken breast stuffed with cheese and wrapped in prosciutto, or
barbecued, chili-infused squid with chargrilled vegetables. Be-
sides, the pasta dishes are big and the pizzas are some of the best in
town. *29 Frome St., tel. 08/223–1948. No reservations. Dress: casu-
al. AE, DC, MC. No lunch Sat. and Mon.; closed Sun.*

Lodging

Adelaide's accommodations are bargains compared with those in
any other Australian capital city, but even so, travelers might con-
sider staying outside the city in the Adelaide Hills. The hills offer
the best of both worlds: easy access to the sophisticated pleasures of
the city, as well as to the vineyards, orchards, and rustic villages
that are tucked away in this idyllic, rolling landscape. Within a 32-
kilometer (20-mile) radius of the city there is a wide choice of guest
houses, small hotels, and country cottages. For more information,
see The Adelaide Hills, *below.*

Highly recommended lodgings are indicated by a star ★.

Category	Cost*
$$$$	over $175
$$$	$100–$175
$$	$60–$100
$	under $60

*All prices are for a standard double room.

$$$$ **Hilton International.** Overlooking Victoria Square in the heart of
the city, this hotel has extensive facilities and a highly professional
staff. Guest rooms are large, comfortable, and well maintained, and
have a warm, bright look. The rooms on the corners of the building
are slightly larger than the standard rooms. The best view facing
the Adelaide Hills is from the rooms on the eastern side of the hotel
above the 10th floor. *233 Victoria Sq., 5000, tel. 08/217–0711, fax 08/*

231–0158. Mailing address: Box 1871, 5001. 387 rooms with bath. Facilities: heated outdoor pool, spa, tennis court, gym, 24-hr room service, 3 restaurants, 2 bars, nightclub, AE, DC, MC, V.

$$$$ Hyatt Regency Adelaide. Adelaide's premier hotel, this statuesque
★ atrium-style building offers a luxurious blend of facilities, location, service, and comfort. The hotel's octagonal towers create unusual room shapes, which are a welcome change from the uniformity of most hotel accommodations. The best view is from the riverside rooms above the eighth floor. The four Regency Club floors offer extra facilities, including separate concierge service as well as complimentary Continental breakfast and evening aperitifs and hors d'oeuvres. The hotel also includes a first-rate international restaurant, Blake's (*see* Dining, *above*), as well as one of the finest Japanese restaurants in Adelaide. *North Terr., 5000, tel. 08/231–1234, fax 08/231–1120. 369 rooms with bath. Facilities: heated outdoor pool, spa, sauna, gym, 24-hr room service, 3 restaurants, nightclub. AE, DC, MC, V.*

$$$ Terrace Inter-Continental. Set in a prime location on North Terrace, this hotel has excellent facilities and the best range of restaurants of any city hotel. Reopened at the end of 1989 after extensive remodeling, the rooms and decor reflect a cool, contemporary style. The ones on the northern side of the hotel above the 10th floor overlook Government House and the parks that border the Torrens River. The hotel's fine dining room, the Crystal Room, has an excellent reputation. *150 North Terr., 5000, tel. 08/217–7552, fax 08/231–7572. 334 rooms with bath. Facilities: heated outdoor pool, spa, sauna, gym, 24-hr room service, 4 restaurants, bar, nightclub. AE, DC, MC, V.*

$$ Adelaide's Bed and Breakfast. An intimate alternative to the big hotels, this stone guest house evokes its Victorian ancestry with bold colors and big brass beds. For a small surcharge, guests can have the ground floor bedroom, which is equipped with its own bathroom. Of the four bedrooms on the upper floor, those at the front are larger but more affected by traffic noise during the daytime. The house is a 10-minute walk from the city center and about ¾ kilometer from the main attractions in North Terrace. *239 Franklin St., 5000, tel. 08/231–3124, fax 08/212–7974. 5 rooms, 1 with private bath. Includes Continental breakfast. Facilities: restaurant, courtyard garden. AE, DC, MC, V.*

$$ Directors Studios and Suites. The rooms in this smart, modern hotel
★ rival those in many of the city's luxury hotels. The absence of expansive public areas, however, means the room rate is about half that of the others. The functional but stylish layout features corridors enclosed by a glass roof and miniature tropical gardens. The studio apartments that were added in mid-1991 include kitchenettes and baths as well as showers, which easily justify their marginally higher price. Of these, numbers 301 and 302 are more spacious and have city views. The hotel is equipped with business and secretarial facilities for the traveling executives who form a large part of its clientele. Adjoining the hotel is a pub with a dining room open for all meals. *259 Gouger St., 5000, tel. 08/231–3572, fax 08/231–5989. 66 rooms and apartments with bath. AE, DC, MC, V.*

$$ The Mansions. If you are looking for self-catering accommodations that combine a central location with good value, look no further. These studio and one-bedroom serviced apartments are spacious, comfortable, and equipped with complete kitchen facilities, although the furnishings and decor are totally lacking in personality. For those who intend to do their own cooking, the slightly higher cost of a one-bedroom apartment is worth it. The hotel has no dining facilities, but the restaurant district of Hindley Street is within easy walking distance, and Rundle Mall, the main shopping area, is less than 50 yards from the front door. *21 Pulteney St., 5000, tel. 08/232–0033, fax 08/223–4559. 52 apartments. Facilities: spa, sauna. AE, MC, V.*

$ The Earl of Zetland. Set above a pub in a busy mid-city location, the rooms and furnishings in the Earl are comfortable and slightly old-fashioned, but so is the price. Perhaps its greatest attraction is its four bars, one of which offers a range of 275 malt whiskeys—a choice unrivaled in the Southern Hemisphere. *Gawler Pl. and Flinders St., 5000, tel. 08/223–5500, fax 08/223–5243. 30 rooms with bath. Facilities: 4 bars. AE, DC, MC, V.*

$ North Adelaide Heritage Apartments. Tucked away in several historic villas in a leafy corner of the city, these apartments offer character, a dash of luxury, and a bargain-basement price tag. The creation of antique dealers Rodney and Regina Twiss, the apartments vary in size and furnishings, but each has a bathroom, sitting room, kitchen, and from one to three bedrooms, and each is lavishly furnished with antiques and decorated in an opulent, late-Victorian style. The city is about 2 kilometers (1 mile) away, and no villa is more than a 10-minute walk from a bus stop. A two-night minimum stay is required. Breakfast is available at a minimal charge. *Office at 109 Glen Osmond Rd., Eastwood, 5061, tel. 08/272–1355, fax 08/272–6261. 6 apartments with bath, 2 cottages with bath. MC, V.*

The Arts

For a listing of performances and exhibitions, see the entertainment pages of *The Advertiser.* Tickets for concerts and plays can be purchased from **Bass** ticket agencies, which are located at the Festival Centre, Myer Center Point, Hindley Street, Rundle Street, and Her Majesty's Theatre. For credit card bookings, call **Bass Dial 'n' Charge.** *Tel. 08/213–4777. Mon.–Sat. 9–6. AE, DC, MC, V.*

The Adelaide Festival Centre is the city's major venue for the performing arts. The **State Opera,** the **South Australian Theatre Company,** and the **Adelaide Symphony Orchestra** perform here regularly. On the lighter side, the center also hosts champagne brunches on Sunday morning in the bistro (tel. 08/216–8744), and outdoor rock-and-roll, jazz, and country music concerts in the amphitheater. The complex includes a restaurant (tel. 08/216–8720) and the **Fezbah,** a piano bar featuring some of Adelaide's finest cabaret acts on Friday night. *King William Rd., tel. 08/213–4788. Box office open Mon.–Sat. 9:30–8:30.*

The biggest arts festival in the country, the three-week **Adelaide Festival,** which takes place in March in even-numbered years only, is a cultural smorgasbord of outdoor opera, classical music, jazz, art exhibitions, comedy, and cabaret presented by some of the world's top artists. In past years, performers have included Dublin's Abbey Theatre, Kiri Te Kanawa, Placido Domingo, Billy Connolly, Muddy Waters, and writer Salman Rushdie. The festival also encompasses events as diverse as Writers' Week and a food fair, when a city street is taken over by food stalls devoted to gourmet grazing. For information on festival events, contact the South Australian Government Travel Centre (*see* Important Addresses and Numbers, *above*).

Nightlife

Adelaide's nightlife is concentrated on **Hindley Street** close to King William Street. The pubs and discos along this street are a magnet for the city's young "ragers," but there are also many restaurants and outdoor cafés where the clientele is older and quieter. Sophisticated revelers will usually be found in the nightclubs in the city's top hotels. Cover charges vary according to the night and the time of evening. A listing of nightlife for the coming week can be found in *The Guide*, a pullout section of the Thursday edition of *The Advertiser*. The daily edition lists attractions for that day.

Casino   Compared to Las Vegas the action inside the **Adelaide Casino** is sedate, but this stately sandstone building is undoubtedly one of Adelaide's main draws. All the major casino games are played here, as well as a highly animated Australian game, two-up, in which players bet against the house on the fall of two coins. The casino complex includes five bars and a restaurant. *North Terr., tel. 08/212–2811. Open Mon.–Thurs. 11 AM– 4 AM; continuously from 11 AM Fri.–4 AM Mon.*

Nightclubs   **Margaux's on the Square** is a plush, elegant nightclub and a regular haunt for the city's sophisticates. *Hilton Hotel, Queens Sq., tel. 08/ 217–0711. Admission: $5–$15. Open Thurs.–Sat. 9 PM–3 AM.*

The **Cargo Club** attracts a stylish clientele with live funk, jazz, and soul music. *213 Hindley St., tel. 08/231–2327. Open Tues.–Sat. 10 PM–dawn.*

Dark, stylish, and intimate, **Mystics** attracts the sleek, over-25 crowd with disco and live music. *Terrace Hotel, North Terr., tel. 08/ 217–7552. Open Fri. and Sat. 8 PM–3 AM.*

Performances by some of Adelaide's top jazz and cabaret acts have made **Fezbah** one of the city's favorite late-night spots. *Adelaide Festival Centre, tel. 08/213–4788. Admission: $10. Open Fri. 10 PM–4 AM.*

The most upbeat disco on Hindley Street, **Lipstick Cocktail Club/ Pineapple Club Disco** is a throbbing complex of mirrors and lights. Patrons have a choice of live bands in the Lipstick Cocktail Club (only open Fri. and Sat. 8 PM–5 AM), or disco music in the Pineapple Club. Both are slick and well run, and only the well-groomed are allowed inside. *100 Hindley St., tel. 08/231–3023. Admission: up to $10. Open Sun.–Tues. 10:30 PM–3 AM, Wed. and Thurs. 9:30 PM– 5 AM, Fri. and Sat. 8:30 PM–5 AM.*

The Adelaide Hills

With their green slopes, wooded valleys, and gardens brimming with flowers, the Adelaide Hills are a pastoral oasis in this desert state. Indeed, the combination of orchards, vineyards, avenues of tall conifers, and towns of rough-hewn stone give this region a distinctly European feel and make the hills one of the best reasons to visit Adelaide. Furthermore, during the steamy summer months these hills, barely 15 kilometers (10 miles) from the heart of Adelaide, are consistently cooler than the city.

Getting Around   The best way to explore the area is by car. The hills are covered by Adelaide's public bus network, but traveling by bus does not give you the freedom to explore the country lanes and villages that are an essential part of the hills experience.

Tourist Information   **Adelaide Hills Tourist Information Centre.** *64 Main St., Hahndorf, tel. 08/388–1185. Open daily 10–4.*

Guided Tours   **Adelaide Sightseeing** (tel. 08/231–4144) offers a half-day coach tour of the Adelaide Hills and historic Hahndorf village (Tues., Thurs., and Fri. 1:30–5:30; cost: $25 adults, $17 children under 16). The tour departs from the Central Bus Station at 101 Franklin Street.

Exploring the Adelaide Hills

Payneham Road heads northeast from Adelaide, and about 8 kilometers (5 miles) from the city a right turn onto Gorge Road takes you to **Torrens Gorge.** This captivating drive leads through a succession of orchards, vineyards, shady valleys, and historic towns, with the river flashing through the trees. Highlights include the **Chain of Ponds** and the towns of **Birdwood** and **Mt. Pleasant.**

Leave Torrens Gorge at Birdwood and travel south to Mt. Torrens. Then follow the signs to **Mt. Lofty.** This 2,300-foot peak offers spectacular views across the entire city of Adelaide. Much of the surrounding area was devastated during the Ash Wednesday bush fires of 1983; behind the television antennas just below the summit, you can see the skeletal remains of some historic mansions.

From the summit of Mt. Lofty, head south to the town of Stirling and follow the signs to Aldgate. Turn right at the far end of the town onto Strathalbyn Road; about 6½ kilometers (4 miles) farther on, turn right again onto Stock Road. **Warrawong Sanctuary** is 1½ kilometers (1 mile) along on the right. There are no koalas to cuddle at this wildlife sanctuary, but this is one of the few chances you will have to see kangaroos, wallabies, bandicoots, and platypuses in their native habitat. With introduced species such as cats, foxes, and rabbits excluded, native species have flourished on this 35-acre property of rain forest, gurgling streams, and black-water ponds—without being fed or molested by humans. Visitors are guided around the property on walks at various times of day, and because most of the animals are nocturnal, the evening walk is the most productive for wildlife watching. *Williams Rd., Mylor, tel. 370–9422. Cost: dawn and evening walks $12, noon and 2 PM walks $6. Open daily for guided walks only; reservations required.*

Return to Aldgate and follow the signs to Bridgewater. It would be difficult to miss the handsome 130-year-old **stone flour mill** with its churning waterwheel that stands at the entrance to the town. These days the mill houses the first-class Granary Restaurant (*see* Dining, *below*) and serves as the shopfront for Petaluma Wines, one of the finest labels in the state. The prestigious Croser champagne is matured on the lower level of the building, and visitors may tour the cellars by appointment. *Mt. Barker Rd., Bridgewater, tel. 08/339–3422. Open for wine tasting daily 11–5.*

Leave Bridgewater and follow the signs to **Hahndorf,** a picture-perfect little village that might have sprung to life from the cover of a chocolate box. Founded 150 years ago by German settlers, Hahndorf consists of a single shady main street lined with stone and timber shops and cottages. Most of the shops have become arts-and-crafts galleries and antiques shops, although German traditions survive in the cake shops and butcher's shop. The village is extremely crowded on Sunday.

The **Hahndorf Academy** contains several works by Sir Hans Heysen, a famous Australian landscape painter who lived in this area at the turn of the century. *68 Main St., tel. 08/388–7250. Admission: $2.50, children under 12 free. Open daily 10:15–5.*

Dining

Price categories for restaurants are the same as in the Adelaide Dining section, *above*. Highly recommended restaurants are indicated by a star ★.

$$$$ **Hardy's.** The formal dining room inside Mount Lofty House is one of the highlights of this elegant country-house hotel. While it reflects the opulence of the restaurant, the international menu is also stylishly modern; try the panfried emu on a macadamia nut brioche with cranberry glaze, or the beetroot chips, hollandaise, and wild rice pilaf. The wine list is a selection of South Australia's finest. *74 Summit Rd., Crafers, tel. 08/339-6777. Reservations required. Dress: dinner, jacket required; lunch, casual but neat. AE, DC, MC, V.*

$$$ **Uraidla Aristologist.** Food is taken very seriously indeed at this
★ small, rustic country restaurant that evokes the flavors and scents of rural Tuscany. Typical selections from the changing, fixed-price menu are an anchovy dip with fresh vegetables, osso bucco with tomatoes, pumpkin pasta, fried zucchini flowers, and oxtail with peeled grapes. Many of the vegetables and herbs come from the gardens that surround the pretty two-story restaurant. Allow several hours for the experience of dining here. *Greenhill and Basket Range Rds., Uraidla, tel. 08/390-1995. Reservations required. Dress: casual but neat. MC, V. Closed Mon.–Thurs., no lunch Fri.*

$$ **Granary Restaurant.** More commonly known as Bridgewater Mill,
★ this stylish restaurant inside a converted flour mill is one of the best in the state. The contemporary Australian menu is small and limited to lunch, but the food is as fresh, original, and well presented as the surroundings. Imaginative use is made of local produce in such dishes as goat cheese baked with eggplant and roasted capsicum and the miniature oyster pie served with mushrooms and chervil cream. In the summer, book ahead to get a table on the deck beside the waterwheel. If you're feeling wealthy, ask to see the special wine list. *Mt. Barker Rd., Bridgewater, tel. 08/339-3422. Reservations advised. Dress: casual but neat. AE, DC, MC, V. Lunch only.*

$ **Aldgate Pump.** This friendly country pub has a huge menu that ranges from a hearty moussaka to Thai curries and salad dishes. The bistro overlooks a shady beer garden, while the restaurant is slightly more formal—and more expensive. *1 Strathalbyn Rd., Aldgate, tel. 08/339-2015. No reservations. Dress: casual. AE, DC, MC, V.*

Lodging

The Adelaide Hills are served by the city's bus network, and travelers with a vehicle of their own will find that even the most remote accommodation is only a 40-minute drive from the city center.

Price categories are the same as in the Adelaide Lodging section, *above*. Highly recommended lodgings are indicated by a ★.

$$$$ **Mount Lofty Country House.** This is country living at its finest. The
★ sophisticated pleasures of gourmet dining and first-rate service at this refined country house are set against a backdrop of rolling hills and crisp mountain air. The house sits in a commanding position just below the summit of Mt. Lofty, overlooking the patchwork of vineyards, farms, and bushland in the Piccadilly Valley. The house itself is surrounded by informal gardens and shaded by giant sequoias. Guest rooms are large, luxuriously furnished, and abundantly supplied with fresh flowers. *74 Summit Rd., Crafers 5152, tel. 08/339-6777, fax 08/339-5656. 30 rooms with bath. Facilities: heated outdoor pool, restaurant, bar. AE, DC, MC, V.*

$$$$ **Thorngrove Country House.** A visit to this gothic fantasy house will take you on a memorable journey through another century and another country. Vaulted arches, carved heraldic beasts, stained-glass windows, ornate plaster ceilings, heavy woodwork, and a wealth of quasimedieval details have transformed this house into a baronial castle. Beneath the fantasy is a very comfortable and well-run establishment, with no lack of modern amenities. At one side of the house is The Keep, a less-expensive area with three levels, and although whirlpool tubs and other opulent touches are in place, the medieval theme isn't so aggressive here. *2 Glenside La., Stirling 5152, tel. 08/339–6748, fax 08/370–9950. 4 rooms with bath. Includes full breakfast. AE, MC, V.*

$$ **Apple Tree Cottage and Gum Tree Cottage.** This is your chance to es-
★ cape to your own country cottage in idyllic surroundings. Set in rolling countryside on a cattle stud near the historic village of Hahndorf, both cottages come complete with antique furnishings, open log fires, well-equipped kitchens, and air-conditioning. Apple Tree Cottage is a two-story Georgian farmhouse surrounded by gardens close to an orchard. Guests can go rowing to the large dam next to the house, or stretch out in a hammock slung underneath a walnut tree. Gum Tree Cottage was built only a few years ago, but the stonework, red gum beams, and post-and-rail fence suggest a pioneer's house of the last century. Adelaide is about 40 minutes away by car. *Mailing address: Box 100, Oakbank 5243, tel. 08/388–4193. 2 cottages. Includes supplies for full breakfast. No credit cards.*

$$ **Chippings.** Guests in this family home are treated more as friends than customers. Private facilities include a lounge and a pine-paneled bathroom, but the family portraits and memorabilia in these rooms might prove a little too intimate for some tastes. The house is almost submerged beneath giant conifers, and parrots and kookaburras are frequent visitors. *32 Ludgate Hill Rd., Aldgate 5154, tel. 08/339–1008. 1 room with bath. Includes full breakfast. No credit cards.*

Kangaroo Island

Kangaroo Island, Australia's third largest island, is barely 16 kilometers (10 miles) from the Australian mainland, yet the distance between the two is not so much in miles as in years. Kangaroo Island belongs to another age—a folksy, friendly, less sophisticated time when cars were left unlocked and drivers waved at one another as they passed.

The interior of the island is stark and barren for the most part, but the coastline is sculpted into a series of bays and inlets teeming with bird and marine life. For the overseas visitor, the island's wildlife is probably its greatest attraction. In a single day, you can stroll along a beach crowded with sea lions, and watch koalas, kangaroos, pelicans, sea eagles, and fairy penguins in their native environment.

Kangaroo Island has a turbulent history. At the beginning of the 19th century, the island was a haven for escaped convicts and sailors who had deserted their whaling ships—some of them from North American ports. These castaways preyed on the coastal Aborigines and made a living from trading sealskin. Eventually their raids became too bold and the colonial government sent an armed expedition to the island in 1827. Most of the renegades were dragged away to Sydney in chains, and Kangaroo Island was left with a population of less than a dozen.

Despite its abundant natural wonders, there are many who treasure Kangaroo Island for what it lacks. There are no resorts and virtually no nightlife, and its only luxuries are those of salty sea breezes, sparkling clear water, and solitude.

Arriving and Departing

By Plane **Air Kangaroo Island** (tel. 08/234–4177) operates daily flights between Adelaide and the towns of Kingscote, American River, and Pardana. The one-way adult fare is $56 to $64 depending on the destination, and $28 to $32 for children 3–14. **Kendell Airlines** (tel. 08/231–9567) flies daily between Adelaide and Kingscote, the island's main airport. The one-way fare is $72 for adults, $36 for children 3–14.

By Ferry The **M.V.** *Philanderer III* and **M.V.** *Island Navigator* (tel. 13–1301) are roll-on/roll-off vehicle and passenger ferries that make the one-hour crossing between Cape Jervis on the mainland and Penneshaw. There are three sailings per day between March and December, and up to eight per day in the summer months. These ferries are by far the most popular means of transport between the island and the mainland, and reservations are advisable during the summer vacation period. The one-way crossing costs $58 per vehicle, $27.50 for adults, and $15 for children under 15. The **M.V.** *Island Seaway* (tel. 08/47–5577), another vehicle and passenger ferry, makes the seven-hour journey between Port Adelaide and Kingscote. The fare is $61 per vehicle, $25 for adults, and $13 for children under 15. The ferry departs Adelaide Monday at 11 AM and, during summer holidays, also Wednesday at 1:30 PM.

Getting Around

Apart from a bus service that connects Kingscote, American River, and Penneshaw, there is no public transport on the island. The main attractions are widely scattered and the most practical way to see them is either on a guided tour or by car.

By Rental Car **Budget Rent-a-Car** (76 Dauncey St., Kingscote 5223, tel. 0848/2–3133).

Important Addresses and Numbers

Tourist Information **Kangaroo Island Tourist Information Centre,** *27 Dauncey St., Kingscote, tel. 0848/2–2381. Open weekdays 9–5.*

Guided Tours

Adventure Charters of Kangaroo Island (Kingscote 5223, tel. 0848/3–3204) offers a standard one-day tour of the island as well as trips for sea fishing, cliff climbing, kayaking, and diving among the island's seals.

Australian Odysseys (Box 494, Penneshaw 5222, tel. 0848/3–1294) operates four-wheel-drive tours, canoe tours, nocturnal tours, camel trekking, and horseback riding.

The Island Travel Center (27 Gresham St., Adelaide, tel. 08/212–4550) is an Adelaide travel agent specializing in tours and transport to Kangaroo Island as well as accommodations there.

Kangaroo Island Searoad (Box 570, Penneshaw 5222, tel. 008/08–8836 or 0848/3–1122) operates a one-day coach tour of the island in conjunction with the ferry service from Cape Jervis.

Kendell Airlines (*see* Arriving and Departing By Plane, *above*) also packages its air services in conjunction with the tours offered by various travel operators on the island. Choices include a standard one-day island bus tour or a four-wheel-drive tour with the emphasis on adventure. However, visitors are also able to construct individual itineraries.

Exploring Kangaroo Island

The towns and most of the accommodations are located in the eastern third of Kangaroo Island. The main attractions are situated on the southern coast, so it's advisable to tour the island in a clockwise direction—leaving the beaches of the north coast for later in the day. The major sights can be covered in a single day, but if you want to explore more of the island, allow three days at least. Except in the main towns, gas stations and shops are scarce. Before embarking, travelers should have a full tank of gas and a picnic lunch. Many of the roads are loose gravel and great care should be taken when driving.

The major attractions are located within national parks, for which an entry fee is charged. At the start of your journey, it is advisable to purchase an **Island Pass** available from any national parks ranger station or from the Environment and Natural Resources office (27 Dauncey St., Kingscole, tel. 0848/2–2381). The pass covers all national park entry fees, vehicle fees, ranger guided tours, and camping fees for 14 nights, and is valid from July 1 to June 30 of the following year. The cost of the Island Pass is $15 for adults, $40 per family.

Kingscote is where the ferries from Port Adelaide arrive. The largest town on Kangaroo Island, Kingscote has a more substantial character than its sister towns Penneshaw and American River. Reeves Point, at the northern end of the town, marks the beginning of South Australia's colonial history. It was here that settlers landed in 1836 and established the first official town in the new colony, but you will have to use your imagination at Reeves Point. Little trace remains of the original settlement, which was abandoned barely three years after it began due to poor soil and a lack of fresh water. The town comes alive in mid-February for a weekend of horse races.

Leave Kingscote by the Playford Highway, following the signs to Seal Bay, which is situated 60 kilometers (37 miles) to the southwest.

Seal Bay Conservation Park is one of the most accessible sea lion colonies anywhere, and the sight of these animals lazing on the beach, suckling their young, and body surfing in the waves is the highlight of any trip to Kangaroo Island. The Australian sea lions, which recover here from their long and strenuous fishing trips, allow humans to approach within about 15 feet. The colony numbers approximately 500 and about a hundred sea lions can usually be found on the beach, except on stormy days when they take shelter in the sand dunes. Visitors can visit the beach only in a tour party led by a park ranger, but apart from the busy summer holiday period you are usually allowed to wander the beach freely (albeit while still under the watchful eye of the ranger). The slope leading from the ranger station to the beach is moderately steep, and there are steps at the bottom. *Seal Bay, tel. 0848/2–8233. Admission: $4 adults, $2.50 children and students, $10.50 family. Daily tours depart Dec.–Jan., every 15 min between 9 AM and 7 PM; Feb.–Nov., every 45 min between 9 AM and 4:30 PM.*

From Seal Bay Road, turn left onto the South Coast Highway and 7 kilometers (4½ miles) farther, just before a one-lane bridge, turn left onto the rough track that leads to **Little Sahara.** Towering white sand dunes cover several square miles here and a short walk is hard to resist—but you must go a long way before you catch a glimpse of the sea.

Drive about 6½ kilometers (4 miles) farther west on the South Coast Highway and take a left at the signpost pointing to the little harbor of **Vivonne Bay.** Little is to be seen here besides a jetty, a few crayfish boats, and a beach that disappears into the distance, but if you continue to **Point Ellen,** the views of the bay and the Vivonne Bay Conservation Park are superb.

Twenty kilometers (12½ miles) west of Vivonne Bay, a left turn leads to a narrow, winding road that ends at **Hanson Bay,** a perfect little sandy cove. The gentle slope of the beach and the rocky headlands on either side provide safe swimming. On the far side of the headland to the east are several secluded beaches, although these are more exposed and the riptides make swimming dangerous. Sea salmon can be caught from these beaches.

The entire western part of the island is taken up by the Flinders Chase National Park (*see* National Parks, *below*) with its spectacular scenery and walking trails. From the park head north on the West End Highway. At the end of this road turn right onto the Playford Highway, and then 8 kilometers (5 miles) farther on, turn left at the North Coast Road. This winding road leads through rolling pastures to Kangaroo Island's finest beaches.

Surrounded by high, rolling pastures, **Snellings Beach** is a broad sandy beach and one of the best on the island. The swimming is safe, although there are no facilities. Continue east on North Coast Road to return to Kingscote.

What to See and Do with Children

Throughout January, rangers from the **Environment and Natural Resources Service** run an extensive program of events designed to introduce children to the natural and historic attractions of the island. Events include lighthouse tours, tidal-pool walks, and evenings on the beach to watch the fairy penguins waddle ashore. *Government Office Bldg., 27 Dauncey St., Kingscote, tel. 0848/2–2381.*

Participant Sports

Fishing The beaches, bays, and rivers of the island offer excellent fishing. Crayfish can be caught from the rocks, sea salmon and mullet from the beaches, and the rivers promise good bream fishing. The island's deep-sea fishing fleet holds several world records for tuna. No permit is required, although restrictions apply over the size and quantity of fish that can be kept. Boats and fishing tackle can be rented from **The Tacklebox Boat Hire** (American River Wharf, tel. 0848/3–3150).

Dining

Kangaroo Island has very little to offer in the way of restauran
The pubs and a few small cafés in the main towns serve light lunche
but visitors must either cook their own dinners or eat in their mote.
dining room.

Lodging

Accommodations on the island fall into two categories: motels and
self-catering farm cottages. The cottages are usually set in remote
locations, and guests should have their own vehicle and food supplies. For a family or a small group intending to spend several days
on the island, the cottages offer comfortable accommodations at a
low price. Towels and sheets are not normally supplied, although
these can often be provided if necessary.

Category	Cost*
$$$$	over $95
$$$	$75–$95
$$	$60–$75
$	under $60

All prices are for a standard double room.

$$$$ **The Settlement.** Set in hilly grazing country above one of the finest
beaches on the island, these two adjacent cottages are perfect for a
total getaway holiday. Of the two, the stone Settlers Cottage is the
more modern and better equipped. Each cottage sleeps up to six.
Middle River, N. Coast Rd. via Kingscote 5223, tel. 0848/3–6237.
Includes breakfast. Dinners available on request. No credit cards.

$$$ **Sorrento Resort.** Overlooking a beach that is home to a colony of
fairy penguins, this hotel offers a choice of motel rooms or one-,
two-, or three-bedroom units, each with its own cooking facilities.
Village rooms are less expensive and are not serviced daily, but they
have a garden setting that is preferable to the neat, clean, but rather
charmless motel rooms. *North Terr., Penneshaw. Mailing address:*
Box 352, Penneshaw 5222, tel. 0848/3–1028, fax 0848/3–1024. 27
rooms and apartments with bath. Facilities: heated outdoor pool, ½-
size tennis court, spa, sauna, restaurant, bar. AE, DC, MC, V.

$$ **Hanson Bay Cabins.** These neat, self-contained log cabins are set in
coastal heath land near Flinders Chase National Park, one of the
most isolated spots on the island. Fifty yards away is a pristine
white-sand beach that offers safe swimming for children. *Hanson*
Bay. Mailing address: 10 McKenna St., Kensington Park 5068, tel.
08/333–0646. 6 cabins. No credit cards.

$$ **Wanderers Rest.** The size, furnishings, and stylish decor of these mo-
tel rooms make this establishment one of the best bargains on the
island. *Bayview Rd., American River. Mailing address: Box 34,*
American River 5221, tel. 0848/3–3140, fax 0848/3–3282. 8 rooms
with bath. Facilities: outdoor pool, spa, restaurant/bar. Includes
Continental breakfast. AE, DC, MC, V.

$ **Barbaree Cottage.** Despite its unimpressive exterior, this cottage is
cozy and comfortable and provides self-catering accommodations
for up to six people. Located about 5 kilometers (3 miles) from
American River, it is pleasantly close to the main farmhouse on an
exposed promontory above a lagoon where black swans and pelicans
come to fish. *Pelican Lagoon, near American River. Mailing ad-*

dress: Australian Odysseys, Box 778, Penneshaw 5222, tel. 0848/3–3190. No credit cards.

The Barossa Valley

Less than an hour's drive northeast of Adelaide is the Barossa Valley, Australia's most famous wine-producing area. The 30 wineries located in this wide, shallow valley produce a huge array of wines, from aromatic Rhine Rieslings that sell for $6 a bottle, to Seppelts Para Port that sells for $1,500, to Penfold's Grange Hermitage—Australia's most celebrated wine.

What sets the Barossa apart is not so much the quality of its wines as its cultural roots. The area was settled by Silesian immigrants who came from Germany or Poland to escape religious persecution. These conservative, hardworking farmers brought traditions that can still be seen in the solid bluestone architecture; the tall, slender spires of the Lutheran churches; and the Black Forest cake that has taken the place of Devonshire tea. These traditions give the Barossa a character and identity that is found in no other wine-growing area of Australia. While it would be a shame to go to the Barossa and *not* taste the wines, its scenery, history, architecture, and distinctive cuisine can be appreciated by anyone.

Getting Around

The main towns in the Barossa are linked by local bus services, but the wineries are often located well away from the towns, and the only practical way to visit them is either by car or on a guided tour. From the center of Adelaide, head north on King William Road. About 1 kilometer (.6 miles) past the Torrens River Bridge, take the right fork onto the Main North Road. After 6 kilometers (3.75 miles) this road forks to the right—follow the signs to the Sturt Highway and the town of Gawler. At Gawler, leave the highway and follow the signs to Lyndoch on the southern border of the Barossa. The 50-kilometer (31-mile) journey should take about an hour.

Guided Tours

Festival Mini Tours (tel. 08/374–1270) operates a full-day tour, daily except Wednesday and Saturday, of the Barossa from Adelaide for $43 for adults and $33 for children under 15. The price includes lunch. Tours depart at 9:30 from 18 King William Street.

Barossa Valley Tours (tel. 085/62–1524) operates a six-hour coach tour of the wineries and churches of the Barossa for $30 for adults and $12 for children under 15, with pick up in Lyndoch, Tanunda, Angaston, and Nuriootpa. The price includes lunch.

Important Addresses and Numbers

Tourist Information   **The Barossa Wine and Tourism Association,** *68 Murray St., Nuriootpa 5355, tel. 085/63–0600. Open weekdays 9–5, weekends 10–4.*

Exploring the Barossa Valley

Numbers in the margin correspond with points of interest on the Barossa Valley map.

The Barossa lives, thinks, and breathes wine, and any tour of the area will usher you into the mysterious world of wine tasting. The jargon in which this activity/rite is enveloped might seem obscure and intimidating at first, but the only requirements are an appreciation of the amazing variety of wines that come from the grape and a willingness to learn.

Every winery in the Barossa operates sale rooms, which will usually have between 6 and 12 wines available for tasting. Generally, the procedure is to begin with a light, aromatic white, such as a Riesling, move on through the heavier whites, and then repeat the process with red wines. Sweet and fortified wines should be left until last. You are not expected to sample the entire range; to do so would overpower your taste buds. It's far better to give the tasting-room staff some idea of your personal preference and let them suggest the wines.

This driving tour will take the better part of a day to complete. Three of the four wineries included in the tour are relatively small producers whose labels are rarely seen on the liquor-store shelves. In these wineries you also stand a fair chance of buying your wine directly from the vintner, which makes uncorking the bottles an even more rewarding experience.

The tour begins at the town of Lyndoch, which marks the southern border of the Barossa vineyards. Follow the road that runs through the vineyards toward Tanunda. About 2 kilometers (1¼ miles) past **①** the big Orlando winery, turn left at the sign pointing to **Grant Burge** winery. This is the label of one of the most successful of the young, independent winegrowers of the Barossa. Grant Burge produces mainly white wines, and the Semillon and Rhine Riesling in particular are highly regarded by wine judges. The style of this wine maker is reflected in the tasting room, which uses the traditional bluestone architecture of the Barossa to striking effect. *Jacobs Creek, tel. 085/63-3700. Open daily 10-5.*

Leave the winery, turn left at the gate and 1.3 kilometers (.8 mile) farther on, turn left and stop outside the large green shed on your **②** left. This is the **Keg Factory**, where traditional methods are still used to make oak casks for the Barossa wineries. Visitors can watch coopers working the American and French oak staves inside the iron hoops. The small port kegs make a wonderful souvenir of the Barossa, but the waiting list is several months long. *St. Halletts Rd., Tanunda, tel. 085/63-3012. Open Mon.-Sat. 8-5.*

Go back up the hill and across the intersection, past the painted figures standing on the wine cask marked with the word "Krondorf." Watch for the barn with a corrugated iron roof covered with thatch on the left—a reminder of the Barossa's European heritage. Cross **③** the railway line and on the left is the low stone building of **Rockford,** another small wine maker. The tasting room at Burge's winery is modern and stylized, while Rockford's is a small, dark stone barn. Rockford's specialty is heavy, rich wines made from some of the oldest vines in the Barossa. These vines bear small quantities of fruit with an intense flavor and often survive only in areas as small as a single acre, which makes them uneconomical for anyone but a small-scale, dedicated winery like Rockford's to handle. A range of notable wines have appeared under the Rockford label, and nobody should miss the opportunity to taste the cabernet sauvignon and the Basket Press Shiraz, an outstanding example of this most traditional of Australian varieties. *Krondorf Rd., Tanunda, tel. 085/63-2720. Open daily 11-5:30.*

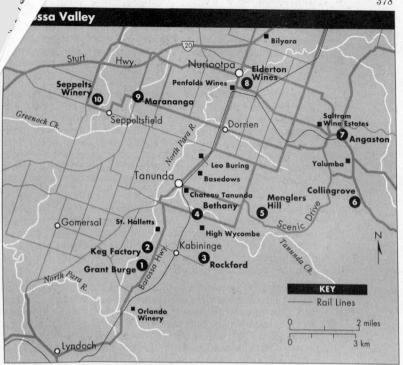

Return to the Barossa Highway, turn right, and go 2.2 kilometers (1.3 miles) before making another right onto Bethany Road. The village of **Bethany** was the original German settlement in the Barossa. The settlers who established the town in 1842 divided the land exactly as they did in their Silesian homeland—with the farmhouses side by side at the front of long, narrow strips of land that run down to Bethany Creek. Today Bethany is a sleepy hollow, eclipsed in size and importance by the nearby towns. Its one shop, the Bethany Art and Craft Gallery, is set in a garden brimming with flowers.

Continue through Bethany and follow the signs to **Menglers Hill**. The parking lot near the summit overlooks the patchwork of vineyards in the valley below. Like so much of South Australia, the Barossa suffers from a shortage of rain; during the summer months, the landscape is scorched brown. Only the vineyards—most of which are irrigated—stand out as bright green rectangles.

Keep going up the hill and 6 kilometers (3¾ miles) farther on turn right at the sign pointing to Angaston. After 1 kilometer (.6 miles) turn right onto Hurns Road, and after another 1.3 kilometers (.8 mile), turn right again. Take this road 3.3 kilometers (2 miles) before turning right into the driveway of **Collingrove**. Until 1975, this patrician country house was the ancestral home of the Angas family, the descendants of George Fife Angas, one of the founders of South Australia. The family carved a pastoral empire from the colony, and at the height of their fortunes controlled 14½ million acres from this house. Today the house is administered by the National Trust, and visitors can inspect the Angas family portraits and memorabilia, including Dresden china, a hand-painted Louis XV cabinet, and Chippendale chairs. The veranda at the front of the house overlooks formal gardens. *Eden Valley Rd., Angaston, tel. 085/64-2061. Admission: $3 adults, $1 children under 15. Open weekdays 1-4:30, weekends 11-4:30. Closed Fri. July-Sept.*

7 Leave the house and proceed to the town of **Angaston.** This part of the Barossa was settled largely by immigrants from the British Isles, and the town's architecture differs noticeably from the low stone buildings of the German towns.

From Angaston, follow the road to Nuriootpa. At the end of this road turn right onto the Barossa Highway and, 100 yards later, **8** right again into the parking lot of **Elderton Wines.** This is another of the small "boutique" wineries of the area, and its elegant wines have rapidly garnered an enviable reputation. Elderton's strength is its red wines, most notably its Pinot noir, although the Chablis Exclusive and Rhine Riesling are both excellent. Every Tuesday and Thursday, Elderton conducts a 20-minute tour of its vineyard starting from its tasting rooms. *Murray St. and New Rd., Nuriootpa, tel. 085/62-1058. Open weekdays 9-5, weekends 10-5.*

Return the way you came, following the Barossa Highway for 2 kilometers (1¼ miles) to the turnoff for Seppeltsfield. This road will **9** take you through the vineyards to the hamlet of **Marananga,** one of the prettiest corners of the Barossa. The original name for this area was *Gnadenfrei,* which means "Freed by the Grace of God"—a reference to the religious persecution the German settlers suffered under the Prussian kings before they emigrated to Australia. Marananga, the Aboriginal name, was adopted in 1918, when a wave of anti-German sentiment spurred many name changes in the closing days of World War I. The barn at the lower end of the parking lot is one of the most photogenic in the Barossa.

Marananga marks the beginning of a 3-kilometer (1.8-mile) avenue of date palms planted during the Depression as a work-creation scheme devised by the Seppelts, the wine-making family. Look for the Doric temple on the hillside to the right—it's the Seppelt family **10** mausoleum. The palm trees end at **Seppelts Winery,** one of the most magnificent in the Barossa. Joseph Seppelt was a Silesian farmer who arrived in Australia in 1849 and purchased land in the Barossa. Under the control of his son, Benno, the wine-making business flourished, and today the winery and its splendid grounds are a tribute to the family's industry and enthusiasm. Fortified wines are a Seppelts specialty: This is the only winery in the world that has vintage ports for every year as far back as 1878. Seppelts operates an excellent tour of the winery, which takes visitors from the crushing area to the fermentation tanks and the maturation cellars, where the fortified wines are stored and the air is filled with rich, spicy aromas. The 45-minute tour also includes an inspection of the Seppelts carriage museum, which houses some of the finest horse-drawn vehicles in the country. *Seppeltsfield, tel. 085/62-8028. Open weekdays 8:30-5, Sat. 10:30-4:30, Sun. 11-4. Tours: weekdays 11, 1, 2, 3; weekends 11:30, 1:30, 2:30. Admission: $2 adults, children under 18 free.*

The tour ends at Seppeltsfield. If you leave the winery and turn right at the gate, a left turn onto Highway 20 will take you to Adelaide in less than an hour.

Shopping

Bethany Art and Craft Gallery is housed in the Old Police Station and Courthouse, an 1855 building with stone walls 6 meters (20 feet) thick. What was once the prisoners' exercise yard—now covered with a translucent roofing—is used to exhibit the work of some of the finest artisans in Australia. *12 Washington St., Angaston, tel. 085/64-3344. Open daily 10-5.*

Pooters Old Wares, situated in a charming corrugated-iron building, houses a fascinating treasury of handmade furniture and farm implements—much of it unearthed from the cellars of the local German community. *Seppeltsfield Rd., Marananga, tel. 085/62-2538. Open Tues.-Thurs. and weekends 11-5. Closed Mon., Fri.*

Dining

Highly recommended restaurants are indicated by a star ★.

Category	Cost*
$$$$	over $35
$$$	$30–$35
$$	$25–$30
$	under $25

*per person, excluding drinks and service

$$$$ **The Vintners.** This relaxed, sophisticated restaurant combines the
★ techniques of French and Asian cooking with the finest local produce. Local trout, lamb, kangaroo, and homemade sausages—with seasonings that hail from Paris to Penang—appear on a menu that appeals to conservative as well as creative tastes. Try the Tuscan scalded cream with caramel sauce for dessert. The fabulous wine list comes with enthusiastic and eloquent advice from front-of-house manager Doug Coats. *Nuriootpa Rd., Angaston, tel. 085/64-2488. Reservations advised. Dress: casual but neat. AE, DC, MC, V. No dinner Tues.-Thurs. Closed Mon.*

$$$ **Lanzerac.** The earthy flavors of French and Italian provincial cooking are rekindled in this former barn, which has rapidly become a local favorite. Typical dishes are carpaccio of Atlantic salmon, eye fillets of venison with pasta, and wok-fried pigeon. *Menge Rd., Tanunda, tel. 085/63-0499. Reservations advised. Dress: casual but neat. MC, V. No dinner Mon.-Tues.*

$$ **1918 Bistro and Grill.** Housed in a restored villa, this pretty, rusticated restaurant makes exemplary use of the distinctive regional produce of the Barossa Valley, which ranges from olive oil to almonds to sausages. Dishes might include a leek risotto with lemon parsley and parmesan or a chargrilled snapper with leek, mint, and pea vinaigrette. The restaurant is partly owned by Robert O'Callaghan of Rockford's Winery, so, as you might expect, the wine list is outstanding. *94 Murray St., Tanunda, tel. 085/63-0405. Dinner reservations advised. Dress: casual. AE, DC, MC, V.*

$ **Barossa Picnic Baskets.** These baskets come stuffed with all the pâté, cheeses, salads, and fruit needed for a perfect lunch outdoors. Three feasts are available, including a vegetarian basket, and each comes with a bottle of wine and a map directing you to selected picnic spots. *Gnadenfrei Estate, Marananga, tel. 085/62-2522.*
list is outstanding. *94 Murray St., Tanunda, tel. 085/63-0405. Dinner reservations advised. Dress: casual. AE, DC, MC, V.*

Lodging

For anyone looking for more than just a place to sleep, the guest rooms found in some of the stately homes and farm cottages offer a more intimate look at the Barossa and its people.

Highly recommended lodgings are indicated by a star ★.

Category	Cost*
$$$$	over $150
$$$	$125–$150
$$	$85–$125
$	under $85

All prices are for a standard double room.

$$$$ ★ The Lodge. This rambling, aristocratic bluestone homestead was built in 1903 for one of the 13 children of Joseph Seppelt, the founder of the showpiece winery across the road. The house has a library, a wine cellar, a formal dining room, and a sitting room furnished with big, comfortable sofas. At the front are a semiformal English-style garden of roses; lawns; an orchard planted with plum, peach, pear, almond, and apple trees; and a woodland of native trees. Located off a lounge room at the rear of the house, the four guest bedrooms are large, luxuriously equipped, and furnished in period style. Meals make good use of local produce—smoked salmon from the Adelaide Hills, meats from the German butcher down the road, and local olives. The communal dinners vary from a formal banquet one night to a barbecue the next. Children are not accepted. *RSD 120, Seppeltsfield via Nuriootpa, 5355, tel. 085/62–8277, fax 085/62–8344. 4 rooms with bath. Facilities: pool, tennis court. MC, V. Closed Tues.–Wed. except by arrangement.*

$$$ The Hermitage of Marananga. Located on a quiet back road, this hilltop inn features large, modern guest rooms furnished with a sense of style that sets them apart from the standard motel room. *Seppeltsfield and Stonewell Rds., Marananga, tel. 085/62–2722, fax 085/62–3133. Mailing address: Box 330, Tanunda 5352. 10 rooms with bath. Facilities: spa, heated outdoor pool, restaurant. Tariff includes full breakfast. AE, DC, MC, V.*

$$$ ★ Lawley Farm. Built around a courtyard shaded by peppercorn trees, these charming stone cottages have been created from barns that date from the pioneering days of the Barossa. They are surrounded by vineyards and orchards in the shadow of the Barossa Range, their rustic character enhanced by antique furnishings and a family of peacocks that rules the grounds. Recommended are the sunny Bethany Suite and the large Jabobs Suite, which has a separate lounge. *Krondorf Rd., Tanunda, tel. and fax 085/63–2141. Mailing address: Box 103, Tanunda 5352. 7 suites with bath. Facilities: spa. Tariff includes full breakfast. MC, V.*

$$ ★ Miners Cottage. It would be hard to imagine a more romantic hideaway than this peaceful, perfumed country charmer. Set among giant gum trees above a billabong, the small, century-old stone cottage consists of a slate-floor kitchen sitting room, a bedroom, and a bath. The decor is delightful—bouquets of dried wildflowers, lace, rustic antiques, tiny windows, thick stone walls, and a veranda at the back that overlooks the swimming pool in the garden below. The cottage is situated on a 66-acre farm in rolling country with a number of fine walks close by. The nearest restaurants are a 10-

minute drive away, but dinner is available by arrangement. *Box 28, Cockatoo Valley 5351, tel. 085/24–6213, fax 085/24–6650. Facilities: outdoor pool. Tariff includes Continental breakfast. MC, V.*

\$\$ **Collingrove.** This stately country house, situated on undulant graz-
★ ing land, was built more than a century ago by the Angas family, one of South Australia's pioneering dynasties. Guests stay in the former servants' quarters at the back of the house, where large, comfortable rooms are furnished in a rustic style with antique iron bedsteads, cane chairs, and pine wardrobes. The house operates under the auspices of the National Trust and is open to the public during the day, but guests may inspect the house during closed hours and use the former library as a lounge room. Dinner is available by arrangement. *Eden Valley Rd., Angaston 5353, tel. and fax 085/64–2061. 4 rooms share 3 baths. Facilities: spa. Tariff includes full breakfast. AE, DC, MC, V.*

\$\$ **Warrenda Cottage and the Dairy.** Situated on grazing property in the hills that rim the Barossa Valley, Warrenda is a perfect choice if you need family-size space in rustic surroundings. The three-bedroom, century-old house is stylishly furnished with red-gum tables and pine dressers, which are complemented by white-sponged walls and country scenes out the window. There are mosquito nets and linen sheets on the beds and a huge, old-fashioned bathroom with its own fireplace. Breakfasts include home-cured bacon plus preserves made from fruit grown on the property. The Dairy is a romantic one-bedroom cottage prettily decorated in a Mediterranean style and furnished with 18th-century antiques. *Box 391, Lyndoch, 5351, tel. and fax 085/24–4507. Tariff includes full breakfast. MC, V.*

\$ **Blickinstal.** These motel-style units are set on a farm on the lower slopes of the Barossa Ranges. The name means "look into the valley," which perfectly describes the view across the almond trees and vineyards. Guest rooms have a contemporary, functional design, and each has kitchen facilities. *Rifle Range Rd., Tanunda, tel. 085/63–2716. Mailing address: Box 17, Tanunda 5352. 4 rooms with bath. Tariff includes full breakfast. MC, V.*

The Murray River

The "Mighty Murray" is not only the longest river in Australia but also one of the longest in the world. From its source in the Snowy Mountains of New South Wales, it travels about 2,415 kilometers (1,500 miles) before it enters the ocean southeast of Adelaide. As pioneers settled the interior, the river became a major artery for their cargoes of wool and livestock. During the second half of the 19th century, the river reverberated with the churning wheels of paddle steamers and the shrieks of their whistles. This colorful period ended when the railways connected the continent at the turn of the century, destroying the monopoly of the river barges. Today the river is a sporting paradise for water-skiers, boaters, and anglers.

The Murray's role as an industrial waterway may be over, but it remains a vital part of the economy and life of South Australia. It provides the water for the vast irrigation schemes that have turned the desert into a fruit bowl—as well as supplying Adelaide with its domestic water. The Riverland region is one of the country's largest producers of citrus fruits and supplies more than 40% of the nation's wine (though the quality can't compare with the wines of the Barossa).

The journey along the broad brown river is still an adventure, and the history of the little towns bordering its banks merits some study. More rewarding, however, is the area's natural beauty. Couched within high ochre cliffs, the Murray is home to red river gums, still lagoons, and abundant bird life.

Arriving and Departing

By Bus **Stateliner Coaches** (111 Franklin St., Adelaide, tel. 08/233–2755) operates a daily service between Adelaide and the towns of Berri and Renmark. The one-way fare from Adelaide to Renmark/Berri is $24.50 for adults, $12.25 for children under 16. The trip to Berri takes 3½ hours; to Renmark, 4 hours.

By Car Leave Adelaide by the Main North Road and follow the signs to the Sturt Highway and the town of Gawler. This highway continues east to Renmark. Allow 3½ hours for the 295-kilometer (185-mile) trip to Renmark.

Getting Around

The only way to see the river properly is to spend a few days on a boat. Although the Sturt Highway crosses the river several times between Waikerie and Renmark, and smaller roads link the more isolated towns along the river, the most impressive sections of the Murray can only be seen from the water. Cruise vacations on the river are available aboard one of the large riverboats or in a rented houseboat. Houseboats sleep between 4 and 10 people, and range in quality from the most basic to luxurious. During the peak summer holiday season, a deluxe eight-berth houseboat costs about $1,200 per week, and a four-berther goes for $650. Outside the peak season, prices drop by as much as 20%. Water and power for lights and cooking are carried on board. No previous boating experience is necessary—the only requirement is a driver's license.

Liba-Liba has a fleet of 30 houseboats for rent and is based in both Renmark and Wentworth, at the junction of the Murray and Darling rivers in southwestern New South Wales, which is useful if you want to sail one-way only. *Jane Eliza Landing, Renmark. Mailing address: Box 1, Renmark 5341, tel. 085/86–6734.*

Swan Houseboats are among the most comfortable, well-equipped, and luxurious accommodations on the river. *Murray River, near Sturt Hwy., Berri. Mailing address: Box 345, Berri 5343, tel. toll-free 008/08–3183.*

Important Addresses and Numbers

Tourist Information **Berri Tourist Information Centre** (24 Vaughan Terr., Berri, tel. 085/82–1655) is open weekdays 9–5. **Renmark Tourist Centre** (Murray Ave., Renmark, tel. 085/86–6703) is open weekdays 9–5, Saturday 9–4, and Sunday 10–4.

Guided Tours

PS *Murray Princess* is a copy of a Mississippi River paddle wheeler that makes six-day cruises from Renmark. All cabins are air-conditioned and include en suite bathrooms. Passengers have access to a spa and sauna. For reservations, contact Murray River Cruises (Captain Sturt Marine, Goolwa 5214, tel. toll-free 008/88–8524).

Proud Mary takes passengers on five-day cruises upstream from Murray Bridge, which is only a 45-minute drive from Adelaide. Passengers travel in comfortable, air-conditioned cabins. The cost is about $875 per person on a twin-share basis. For reservations, contact Proud Australia Cruises (33 Pirie St., Adelaide 5000, tel. 08/ 231–9472).

Exploring the Murray River

This boat tour starts at the town of Renmark, a center for the paddle steamers and houseboats of the Murray. Heading upstream from Renmark toward Wentworth in Victoria, the river is at its tranquil best, gliding between tall cliffs and spilling out across broad lakes filled with bird life. No towns lie along this section of the river, so if you want peace and quiet, this is the way to go. Downstream from Renmark the river is more populated, although it is only during peak summer periods that the Murray becomes even remotely crowded. This tour follows the river downstream to Murray Bridge, which is just 60 kilometers (37 miles) from Adelaide.

Sitting on a bend in the river lined with willow trees, **Renmark** is a busy town and one of the most important on the Murray—a center for the fruit industry, the mainstay of the Riverland region. The industry began here in 1887, when the Canadian Chaffey brothers were granted 250,000 acres to test their irrigation scheme. One of the original wood-burning water pumps they devised can still be seen on Renmark Avenue.

Today **Olivewood,** the original homestead of Charles Chaffey, has been restored and opened to visitors by the National Trust. *21st St., Renmark, tel. 085/86–6175. Admission: $2.50 adults, $1 students, 50¢ children under 16. Open Thurs.–Mon. 10–4, Tues. 2–4.*

Fifty-two kilometers (28 miles) downstream is **Berri,** once a refueling station for the river steamers and today the economic heart of the Riverland. The **Riverland Display Centre** has an exhibition of classic cars and motorcycles. *Sturt Hwy., tel. 085/82– 2325. Admission: $2 adults, $5 family. Open daily 10–4.*

For anyone who wants to see what the Riverland is all about, the **Berrivale Orchards** showroom has a 15-minute video on various stages of the fruit-growing process. *Sturt Hwy., tel. 085/82–1455. Open weekdays 8:30–4:30, Sat. 9–noon.*

Surrounded by orchards and the vineyards of the Penfold's winery, **Loxton** is 43 kilometers (23 miles) downstream from Berri. This hard-working town is one of the most attractive on the river, highlighted by its **Historical Village,** where many of the town's 19th-century buildings have been reconstructed beside the river. The town is at its liveliest on Wednesday evening, when the paddle wheeler *Murray Princess* berths for the night. Loxton also has a large shopping area. *East Terr., Loxton, tel. 085/84–7194. Admission: $4 adults, $2 children 5–15, $11 family. Open weekdays 10–4, weekends 10–5.*

More than 120 kilometers (65 miles) farther down the river is **Waikerie.** The teeming bird life in this part of the river gave the town its name—an Aboriginal word meaning "many wings." Surrounded by irrigated citrus orchards and vineyards overlooking the river gums and cliffs on the far bank, the town is also a center for gliding. If you've never tried this exhilarating sport, the **Waikerie Gliding Club** offers joy flights—a great way to see the river and the rich farmland along its banks. *Sturt Hwy., Box 320, Waikerie 5330, tel. 085/41–2644. Cost: $45 for 20-min flight.*

Downstream on the northern bank near Lock 2 is a large field filled with unearthed fossils. Forty-eight kilometers (26 miles) farther down the river is **Morgan.** When you round the bend in the river and catch a glimpse of this sleepy little backwater, it seems unbelievable that this was once the state's second busiest port. In its heyday at the end of the last century, freight from the upper reaches of the Murray was unloaded here and sent by train to Port Adelaide. The demise of the river steamers put an end to its prosperity; fortunately, the towering wharves, railway station, and the shops and hotels along Railway Terrace have been preserved largely in their original state.

Eighteen kilometers (11 miles) downstream from the town is **Murbko,** known for its natural beauty, and **Blanchetown,** the site of the lowest of Murray's 11 locks. The town is within easy driving distance of Adelaide via the Sturt Highway, and as a result, the water here is often buzzing with ski boats.

Another chapter in the colorful history of the river begins at **Swan Reach,** 33 kilometers (18 miles) farther downstream. This quiet town overlooks some of the prettiest scenery on the Murray. Below the town, the river makes a huge curve—known as the Big Bend—before flowing on to **Mannum.** The Murray River paddle steamers had their origins here when the first riverboat, the *Mary Ann*, was launched in 1853. The town has a number of reminders of its past, including the paddle steamer *Marion*, now a floating museum. *William Randell's Wharf. Admission: $2 adults, $1 children under 16. Open daily 10–4.*

Murray Bridge marks the end of this tour. It is the largest town on the river, and its proximity to Adelaide makes it a popular spot for fishing, waterskiing, and picnics—crowds are heavy on weekends. If you happen to be there on a Sunday at 2:30, don't miss the town's most unusual attraction: Mary the Blacksmith, who wields a 12-pound hammer to work the iron on her anvil. *41 Doyle Rd., tel. 085/ 32–5526. Admission: $3.50 adults, $2 children.*

National Parks

Much of South Australia is desert, so the national parks tend to be concentrated in a strip near its eastern border and the Murray River. Travelers should always carry water in this dry state, and campers are usually not permitted to burn wood.

Summers are exceedingly hot and dry in South Australia, and winters can be very cold. The best time to visit any park in South Australia is in spring and autumn.

Cleland Conservation Park

Just a half-hour drive from Adelaide, Cleland Conservation Park is one of the most unusual in Australia. Although it offers only a few bushwalking trails, its main attraction is its Native Wildlife Park in the center of the park. Developed in the 1960s, the zone is divided into five separate environments through which animals roam freely. This is one of the few places where you are guaranteed to see wombats, emus, and many species of kangaroo. The swampy billabongs harbor waterfowl rarely seen elsewhere, and enclosures protect endangered species, such as yellow-footed rock wallabies and Cape Barren geese.

Two major walking tracks are open to visitors wishing to explore the terrain outside the Wildlife Zone. The track leading from Wildlife Park to Waterfall Gully takes two hours to walk round-trip, while the track from Wildlife Park to the summit of Mt. Lofty takes one hour round-trip. Both are steep climbs offering panoramic views of neighboring Adelaide. Also popular are guided night walks led by rangers. *Admission: $6.50 adults, $4 children 3–15, $16 family (2 adults, 2 children). Open daily 9:30–5. Closed Dec. 25. and fire-ban days.*

Arriving and Departing Access to the park from Adelaide is possible via the Greenhill Road, turning right at Summit Road, or via the Southeastern Freeway, turning left through Crafers to Summit Road. No regular bus service runs from Adelaide, but many tour companies operate daily tours. Contact **Adelaide Sightseeing** (tel. 08/231–4144) or the **Central Bus Station** (tel. 08/233–2733) for details.

Lodging Camping is not permitted in the park, but there is a self-catering youth hostel nearby. Bookings may be made through the **Youth Hostel Association of South Australia** (38 Sturt St., Adelaide 5000, tel. 08/231–5583).

Information For more information contact the park (Box 245, Stirling 5152, tel. 08/339–2444).

Flinders Chase National Park

Some of the most beautiful coastal scenery in Australia may be found on the western end of Kangaroo Island at Flinders Chase National Park. The rest of the island has been subjected to heavy agricultural and grazing activity, but the park has maintained much of its original vegetation since it was declared a national treasure in 1919. A trip to the national park, located just 200 kilometers (120 miles) from Adelaide, can easily be combined with a visit to the other parts of Kangaroo Island (*see* Kangaroo Island, *above*). *Admission: $6.50 per vehicle.*

The seas crashing onto the southern coast of Australia are merciless, and the effects may be seen in the oddly shaped rock sculptures off the coast of Kangaroo Island. At Cape du Couedic, on the island's southwestern shore, for instance, the limestone promontory has been carved from underneath, producing what is now known as **Admiral's Arch.**

About 4 kilometers (2½ miles) east along the coast are the **Remarkable Rocks**—huge boulders balanced precariously on the promontory of Kirkpatrick Point.

Starting in the 1920s, animals from the mainland were introduced to the island. Today a large population of koalas and Cape Barren geese live in the park. Much of the wildlife is so tame that a barricade had to be constructed at the Rocky River Campground to keep humans in and kangaroos and geese out.

Flinders Chase has several walking trails, ranging from 3 to 7 kilometers (2 to 4 miles) in length, which take anywhere from one to three hours to complete. The trails meander along the rivers to the coast, passing mallee scrub and sugar gum forests. The 3-kilometer (1.8-mile) Rocky River Walking Trail leads to a powerful waterfall before ending on a quiet sandy beach. Self-guided walks can be taken along the river valleys and beach.

The organized campground and visitor center is at **Rocky River,** where many koalas can usually be found.

Arriving and Departing For information about reaching the park and getting around, *see* Kangaroo Island, *above.* The park, located on the western end of the island, is bordered by both the Playford and West End highways.

Lodging Camping is allowed only at designated sites for $2 per tent site at Rocky River and at bush campground, plus $2 for each adult and $1 for each child. Less rustic accommodations can be found at several cottages and lodges. The **Old Homestead and Mays Cottage,** built by the Mays family for their family and their mailman, can be rented on a nightly basis. The Homestead (which sleeps six) rents for $40 a night; the cottage (which sleeps four) rents for $22.50 a night. At **Cape du Couedic,** 20 kilometers (12½ miles) from the Rocky River Headquarters, there are two cottages, Karatta and Parndana, which each sleep six and cost $45 per night total. **Flinders Lodge at Cape Borda** sleeps six and rents for $60 a night, while the **Borda Hut** sleeps four and rents for $27.50 a night. Visitors at the majority of these accommodations are required to bring their own bedding and supplies.

Information For information and accommodation bookings, contact the **Environment and Natural Resources Service** (27 Dauncey St., Kingscote, tel. 0848/2–2381).

Flinders Ranges National Park

Extending from the northern end of Gulf St. Vincent, the Flinders Ranges consist of a chain of desert mountains—and one of the most impressive outback parks in the country. These dry, craggy mountain peaks, once the bed of an ancient sea, have been cracked, folded, and sculpted by millions of years of rain and sun. This furrowed landscape of deep valleys is covered with casuarinas and cypress pines, which slope into creeks lined with river red gums. The area is fascinating for geologists, but all those who revel in wild, raw scenery and exotic plant and animal life will find the park richly rewarding.

The scenic epicenter of the Flinders is **Wilpena Pound,** an 80-square-kilometer (207-square-mile) bowl ringed by red hills that curve gently upward, only to then fall away in sheer cliffs, forming a rim. The only entrance to the Pound is a narrow cleft through which the Wilpena Creek sometimes trickles.

With its many steep trails, Flinders Ranges is a bushwalking mecca, although the park has few amenities. Water in this region is scarce and should be carried at all times. The best time for walking in the area is during the relatively cool months between April and October. This is also the wettest time of year, so hikers should be prepared for rain. Between September and late October, the wildflowers that bring a flush of color to the hillsides are an additional draw.

The most spectacular of the park's walking trails leads to the summit of St. Mary's Peak (1,170 meters/3,840 feet)—the highest point in the Pound's rim and the second-tallest peak in South Australia. The more scenic of the two routes to the summit is the outside trail; give yourself a full day to get up and back. The final ascent is difficult, but the views from the top—including the distant white glitter of the salt flats on Lake Frome—make the climb worthwhile.

Arriving and Departing The park is 460 kilometers (285 miles) north of Adelaide via the Princes Highway to Port Augusta, and then east toward Quorn and Hawker. A four-wheel-drive vehicle is highly recommended for traveling on the many gravel roads in the area. **Buses** leave the Central Bus Terminal in Adelaide on Thursday and Friday, returning to Adelaide on Thursday and Sunday.

Lodging Between April and October, nightly motel rates (including Continental breakfast) at the **Wilpena Pound Holiday Resort** (tel. 086/48–0004) are $82 for a double room and $76 for a single. During the warmer summer months, the room rate falls by about $12. The campground at Wilpena is operated by the motel. Campsites are $9 per night for two people, and $2 for each additional person. The resort operates a general store and gas pumps.

The **Cooinda Campsite** is the only bush campsite within the Pound, although camping with a permit is allowed throughout the rest of the park. A small rock hole about 850 meters (2,790 feet) from Cooinda is usually filled with fresh water. Otherwise, water must be carried into the campsite.

Information For more information, contact the park (tel. 086/48–0048) or the **National Parks and Wildlife Service** (55 Grenfell St., Adelaide 5000, tel. 08/207–2000).

10 The Red Centre

By David McGonigal

An Australian travel writer, David McGonigal is the author of several books, including Wilderness Australia *and* Australian Geographic Book of the Kimberley.

The Northern Territory is vast, undeveloped—and different. The Australian government doesn't know quite what to make of it—it has yet to be made a state—or its inhabitants, who enjoy a reputation as drinkers (in Australia no less!) and eccentrics. One thing is perfectly clear, however: The Northern Territory suffers from climatic schizophrenia. The northern half, often referred to as the Top End, is a land of cyclones, monsoons, and tropical vegetation. The southern half—the Red Centre—is the exact opposite. From the air, visitors can get the impression that the landscape has a veneer of green vegetation. Once on the ground, however, one sees that the greenery turns out to be nothing more than a few tufts of spinifex and some hardy desert plants. The rest is a rich red—the rocks, the dust, even the Aboriginal art. Only where water (irrigation) is available has the Red Centre turned lush green, offering a dramatic counterpoint to the all-pervading ochre tones.

This is the famous Australian Outback—an inhospitable land that stretches for hundreds of miles. The temperature in summer can top 110°F, and winter nights can cause the thermometer to plunge below freezing. This great emptiness in the heart of the continent has its own stark appeal, and its two special features lure many visitors. One is Ayers Rock, an enormous red monolith that rises like a sentinel from the featureless plains; the other is Alice Springs, a settlement of some 27,000 that is commonly referred to as the Alice. Other impressive sights, like the western MacDonnell Ranges and Kings Canyon, had been known for years, but until recently were largely inaccessible to visitors. Because their pioneer atmosphere has not yet dissipated in air-conditioned comfort, these areas are in some ways even more rewarding to explore.

Alice Springs

Alice Springs has always been thought of as a desert shantytown, but a few hours of wandering through the modern air-conditioned shops that line Todd Mall reveal a normal Australian town in an extraordinary setting. The Todd is the river that flows intermittently through the center of Alice Springs. More often than not, it is simply a sandy indentation straggling between gum trees. It is in this dried-up creek bed that the residents of Alice Springs hold their annual Henley-on-Todd regatta, a rendition of the more famous regatta that takes place in England. Some differences exist between the two events other than their distant locations: For starters, beer is the only liquid likely to flow down the Todd, so race entrants must pick up their boats and run the course! Not surprisingly, it is a slapstick, raucous event.

Life in the Alice wasn't always such a party. The first European settlement in the area, the Old Telegraph Station, was established in 1872. The service town for the cattle and mining industries was established in present-day Alice Springs in 1888. Originally called Stuart in honor of explorer John Stuart, the settlement changed its name to Alice Springs in 1933, when the telegraph repeater station was moved into town from its original site by the permanent springs. The springs had been named Alice in honor of the wife of Charles Todd, superintendent of telegraphs.

Today Alice Springs functions largely as a tourist town and supply base for the U.S. secret-communications station at Pine Gap, 26 kilometers (16 miles) to the southwest. The headlong rush to modernize over the past 20 years has erased most of the pioneering spirit that marked the Alice's early history. Wander a couple of miles out-

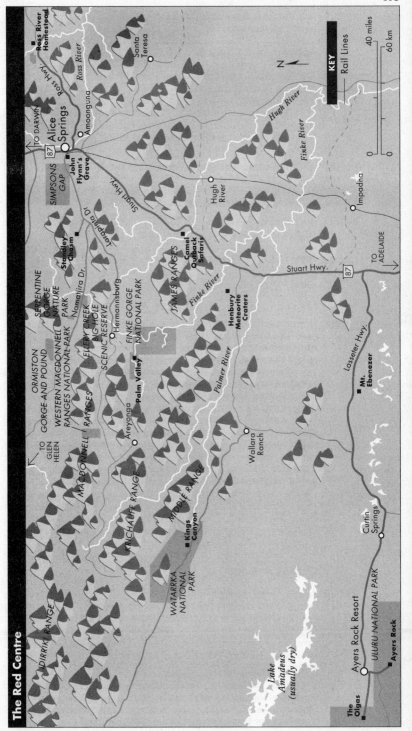

The Red Centre

KEY
Rail Lines

40 miles
60 km

Ross River Homestead

Santa Teresa

Ross River

Ross Hwy.

Amoonguna

TO DARWIN

Alice Springs

87

John Flynn's Grave

Hugh River

Finke River

SIMPSONS GAP

Stuart Hwy.

Standley Chasm

Larapinta Dr.

Hugh River

Impadna

SERPENTINE GORGE NATURE PARK

ORMISTON GORGE AND POUND

WESTERN MACDONNELL RANGES NATIONAL PARK

Namatjira Dr.

ELLERY CREEK BIG HOLE SCENIC RESERVE

Hermannsburg

FINKE GORGE NATIONAL PARK

JAMES RANGES

Camel Outback Safaris

Finke River

TO ADELAIDE

Stuart Hwy.

87

TO GLEN HELEN

MACDONNELL RANGES

Palm Valley

Areyonga

Henbury Meteorite Craters

Lasseter Hwy.

Mt. Ebenezer

Palmer River

KRICHAUFF RANGE

MIDDLE RANGE

Wallara Ranch

Kings Canyon

WATARRKA NATIONAL PARK

Curtin Springs

TJIDIRRIKE RANGE

The Olgas

Lake Amadeus (usually dry)

Ayers Rock Resort

ULURU NATIONAL PARK

Ayers Rock

N

side the town, however, and you are still face-to-face with one of the planet's final frontiers.

Arriving and Departing by Plane

Airport and Airlines **Alice Springs Airport** is 15 kilometers (9⅓ miles) southeast of the center of town. The bright and cool passenger terminal is a welcome relief for anyone who sweated through the shedlike structure it replaced. It is currently served by **Ansett Australia** (tel. 13–1300) and **Qantas** (tel. 13–1313). The flight from either Sydney or Melbourne takes 2¾ hours; from Brisbane, three hours; from Adelaide, two hours.

Between the Airport and Town Center
By Bus **Alice Springs Airport Shuttle Service** (113 Todd St., tel. 089/53–0310) has a shuttle bus that meets every flight. The ride to your hotel costs $15 round-trip. On request, the bus will also pick you up at your hotel and take you to the airport.

By Taxi **Alice Springs Taxis** (tel. 089/52–1877) maintains a taxi rank at the airport. The fare to most parts of town is about $16.

Arriving and Departing by Car, Train, and Bus

By Car There is only one road into Alice Springs, running north–south: the Stuart Highway, commonly called the Track. The town center lies east of the highway. The drive from Adelaide takes about 24 hours.

By Train It's impossible to miss your stop at Alice Springs—it's the end of the line. The ***Ghan*** (Australian National Railways, tel. 008/88–8480), named after the Afghan camel-train drivers who traveled the route before the railway, provides one of the world's classic rail journeys. It's comfortable and well run (though the food does tend toward standard fare). The train leaves Adelaide at 2 PM each Thursday, arriving in Alice Springs at 10 AM Friday. The return train leaves Alice Springs at 2 PM Friday, arriving in Adelaide at 11 AM Saturday. Between April and December there are an additional departure from Adelaide each Monday and an additional departure from Alice Springs each Tuesday. Departure and arrival times are the same as those of the regular service. (A third train is added during school holidays; contact Australian National Railways for the 1995 schedule). Alice Springs's railway station is 2½ kilometers (1½ miles) west of Todd Mall.

By Bus Interstate buses operated by **Greyhound** (tel. 089/53–1022) arrive and depart from outside **Melanka Lodge** (94 Todd St.). The **AAT Kings** office doubles as its terminal (74 Todd St., tel. 089/52–5266). The **McCafferty's Buses** (tel. 089/52–3952) office and terminal are located at 91 Gregory Terrace.

Getting Around

By Car Several rental-car companies have offices in Alice Springs: **Avis** (tel. 089/52–4366), **Budget** (tel. 089/52–4133), **Hertz** (tel. 089/52–2644), **Territory Rent-a-Car** (tel. 089/52–9999), and **Thrifty** (tel. 089/52–6555). When traveling off the few paved roads, drivers should be sure to carry survival rations, water, and spares. Rental cars cannot be driven out of the Northern Territory except by special arrangement.

By Bus The ***Alice Wanderer*** (tel. 089/55–0099) completes an hourly circuit (with commentary) of most tourist attractions in and around Alice Springs between 9 and 5 daily. Passengers can leave and rejoin the bus whenever they like for a flat fee of $15 per day.

Important Addresses and Numbers

Tourist Information The **Central Australian Tourism Industry Association** dispenses information, advice, and maps. *Cnr. Gregory Terr. and Hartley St., tel. 089/52–5199. Open weekdays 9–6, weekends and holidays 10–3.*

Emergencies Dial 000 for **police, fire,** or **ambulance** service. The number for **Alice Springs Hospital** is 089/50–2211.

Doctors 76 Todd St. (all hours, tel. 089/52–1088).

1 Traeger Ave. (tel. 089/52–3842).

Dentists **Department of Health Dental Clinic** (tel. 089/52–4766).

Road Assistance **Road Conditions Information** (tel. 089/52–3833) gives drivers the latest information about conditions on the many unpaved roads in the area. In the event of a breakdown, contact the **Automobile Association of N.T.** (58 Sargent St., tel. 089/52–1087; 105 Gregory Terr., tel. 089/53–1322).

Pharmacies **Alice Springs Pharmacy.** *Shop 19, Hartley St., tel. 089/52–1554. Open weekdays 8:30–5:45, Sat. 9–1, Sun. 10–1.*

Plaza Amcal Chemist. *Ford Plaza, Todd Mall, tel. 089/53–0089. Open daily 8:30–8.*

Guided Tours

Orientation Tours Several companies offer half-day tours of Alice Springs. All tours include visits to the Royal Flying Doctor Service Base, the School of the Air, the Old Telegraph Station, and the Anzac Hill scenic lookout.

AAT Kings's three-hour tour offers free hotel pickup and also visits Panorama Guth, an unusual circular art gallery. *74 Todd St., tel. 089/52–5266. Cost: $35 adults, $32 senior citizens with pension cards or equivalent, $25 children under 15. Tours leave at 2 PM.*

Tailormade Tours & Outback Limousines offers a three-hour minibus tour that covers the same sights as AAT Kings's tour. The company will also provide a chauffeur-driven, air-conditioned car (maximum four passengers) for city sightseeing at $45 per hour. *23 Gosse St., tel. 089/52–1731. Cost: $33 adults, $32 senior citizens with pension cards or equivalent, $25 children under 15. Daily tours at 2 PM. Min. of 4 required for Sun. tours.*

Special-Interest Tours **AAT Kings** also conducts a half-day Aboriginal Dreamtime tour to a bush site outside town, where local Aborigines explain their way of life, show how to find bush foods, and demonstrate how their weapons (including boomerangs) are made and used. Courtesy hotel pickup is provided. *74 Todd St., tel. 089/52–5266. Cost: $59 adults, $54 senior citizens with pension cards or equivalent, $36 children under 15. Tour can be combined with town tour at a reduced rate. Tours depart 8 AM.*

Exploring Alice Springs

Numbers in the margin correspond to points of interest on the Alice Springs map.

❶ Just north of the downtown area is **Anzac Hill,** which has an excellent view of Alice Springs and the surrounding area. It's an ideal place from which to begin a walking tour. To reach the top, head up Lions Walk, which starts opposite the Catholic church on Wills Ter-

Anzac Hill, **1**

Adelaide
House, **4**

Alice Springs
Telegraph
Station
Historical
Reserve, **11**

Old Court
House, **5**

Old Hartley
Street School, **8**

Panorama
Guth, **9**

The Residency, **6**

Royal Flying
Doctor Service
Base, **10**

School of the
Air, **12**

Spencer and
Gillen Gallery, **3**

Strehlow
Research
Centre, **13**

Stuart Town
Gaol, **7**

Todd Mall, **2**

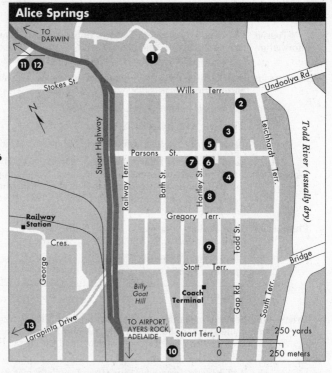

2 race downtown. Coming back down, turn left on Wills Terrace and go one block until you reach the top end of **Todd Mall.** This pedestrian area, one block west of the Todd River, is the heart of Alice Springs, crammed with cafés, galleries, banks, and tourist shops.

3 On the western side of the mall between Wills Terrace and Parsons Street you will encounter the Ford Plaza Building, which contains the **Spencer and Gillen Gallery** of art and natural history from central Australia. Its collection of animal and mineral specimens is interesting, and the range of high-quality central Australia Aboriginal artwork on display provides a good introduction to their sand-painting style. *Todd Mall, tel. 089/52–5378. Admission: $2 adults, children free. Open weekdays 9–5, weekends 10–5.*

4 On the same side of the mall, across Parsons Street, is **Adelaide House,** which was the first Alice Springs Hospital. Designed by the Reverend John Flynn and run by the Australian Inland Mission (which Flynn established) from 1926 to 1939, the hospital used an ingenious system of air tunnels and wet burlap bags to cool the rooms. Today it's a museum devoted to the mission and pioneering days in Alice Springs. It would be difficult to overstate the contribution of John Flynn to the settlement of inland Australia. The stone hut at the rear of Adelaide House was the site of the first field radio transmission in 1926, which made viable John Flynn's concept of a flying doctor. Today the Royal Flying Doctor Service maintains its "mantle of safety" over Australia's remote settlements. *Todd Mall, tel. 089/52–1856. Admission: $2.50 adults, $2 senior citizens with pension cards or equivalent and students, $1 children. Open weekdays 10–4, weekends 10–noon. Closed Dec.–Feb.*

⑤ One block west along Parsons Street is the **Old Court House.** With its wide, simple roof lines, it's a typical example of the Pioneering style of architecture. The building is still the Crown Law Department, so it can be viewed only from the outside. Across Parsons Street, the
⑥ building on the corner with the high white picket fence is **The Residency.** Built in 1927 for John Cawood, the first government resident to be appointed to central Australia, it is now a museum with displays depicting the social and economic history of the area. *Parsons and Hartley Sts., tel. 089/52–1001. Admission free (donations welcome). Open weekdays 9–4, weekends 10–4.*

Across Hartley Street and on the same side of Parsons Street is the
⑦ **Stuart Town Gaol.** Built in 1908, it is the oldest surviving building in Alice Springs—and it looks it! With almost no air coming through the tiny barred windows, imprisonment here on a long, hot summer day was punishment indeed. *Parsons St. Admission: $1. Open Sat. 9:30–11:30.*

Next, backtrack to Hartley Street and turn right. On the opposite side of the street, halfway down the block (past the Post Office), is
⑧ the **Old Hartley Street School.** There is little here that recalls the old blackboards and lift-top integrated desks and benches in use in the year 1929, when Miss Pearl Burton was installed in the building as the first teacher. *Hartley St., tel. 089/52–5199. Admission free. Open weekdays 9–5, weekends/holidays 10–4.*

Continue along Hartley Street across Gregory Terrace until you
⑨ reach the **Panorama Guth,** an unusual crenellated building. Artist Henk Guth found canvases too restrictive for his vision of central Australia, so he created a panoramic circular painting: It has a circumference of 200 feet and stands 20 feet high. *65 Hartley St., tel. 089/52–2013. Admission: $2.50 adults, $1 children. Open Mon.–Sat. 9–5, Sun. 2–5.*

Head down Hartley Street and turn right on Stuart Terrace. On the
⑩ opposite side of the street is the **Royal Flying Doctor Service (RFDS) Base.** Directed from this radio base, doctors use aircraft to make house calls on settlements and homes hundreds of miles apart. There are a display of historical material, an audiovisual show, and tours every half hour during the midyear tourist season. Like the School of the Air, the RFDS is still a vital part of life in the Outback. *Stuart Terr., tel. 089/52–1129. Admission: $3 adults, $2 students, $1 children. Open Mon.–Sat. 9–4, Sun. 1–4.*

To explore the first white settlement in this area, drive 3 kilometers (1.9 miles) north along Stuart Highway, then take the turnoff on the
⑪ right to **Alice Springs Telegraph Station Historical Reserve.** The track continues for 2 kilometers (1.2 miles), crossing a rocky ridge before dropping down to the original Alice Springs. The telegraph station buildings have been restored and are now evocative reminders of the Red Centre as it existed at the turn of the century. Within the buildings are exhibits of life at the station as well as a display of early photographs chronicling its history from 1872. There are pleasant picnic areas on the grassy banks of the river. *Tel. 089/52–1013. Admission: $2.50 adults, $1.20 children. Open May–Sept., daily 8–7; Oct.–Apr., daily 8 AM–9 PM.*

Returning to town from the telegraph station, take the second street to the right off Stuart Highway (Head Street) to visit the
⑫ **School of the Air.** Operating in many remote areas of Australia, this facility offers an ingenious way of teaching students separated by hundreds of miles: Basically, the children take their classes by correspondence course, supplemented by lessons over the Royal Flying

Doctor radio network. Observing the teacher-student relationship via radio is fascinating. *Head St., tel. 089/52–2122. Admission free (donations accepted). Open during school term, weekdays 8–noon.*

⑬ Head south on Stuart Highway and take a right onto Larapinta Drive. Drive about 1 kilometer (.6 mile) and you'll come upon a distinctive multiroof building with a huge curved rammed earth wall on the left side of the road. The $3-million **Strehlow Research Centre,** which opened in 1992, commemorates the work of Theodor Strehlow (b. 1908), an anthropologist who grew up with and later spent many years studying the Aranda people, central Australia Aborigines who have traditionally lived on the land extending north to central Mt. Stuart and south beyond the South Australia border. The center's collection, which consists chiefly of "men's-only" ceremonial artifacts, cannot be displayed because of its contemporary religious significance. Still, the exhibits open to the public give rare insight into the beliefs of the Aranda people, their homelands, and their special association with Dr. Strehlow, who became their *ingkata,* or ceremonial chief. *Larapinta Dr., tel. 089/51–8000. Admission: $4 adults, $2.50 children, $10 families. Open daily 10–5.*

Off the Beaten Track

Ten kilometers (6 miles) south of Alice Springs on Stuart Highway is the turnoff to the MacDonnell Siding, where the now-restored *Old Ghan* train is located. Named after the Afghans who led camel trains on the route from Adelaide, the *Ghan* began passenger service on August 6, 1929. Over the next 51 years the *Ghan* provided a vital, if erratic, link with the south. In times of flood it could take up to three months to complete the journey. A new train began service in 1980 (*see* Arriving and Departing, *above*). On Friday evenings you can take a trip on the *Ghan* down the track to a bush setting for a two-course, camp-oven roast dinner. The train departs at 6 and returns at 10:30. The cost is $49 for adults, $25 for children; transfers are an additional $10 per person. For reservations call 089/55–5047. *MacDonnell Siding, S. Stuart Hwy., tel. 089/52–5047. Open 9–5. Admission: $3 adults, $2 senior citizens with pension cards or equivalent, $1.50 children under 15.*

Shopping

Apart from the ubiquitous souvenir shops, whose T-shirt designs have reached the level of an art form, the main focus of shopping in Alice Springs is Aboriginal art and artifacts. Central Australian Aboriginal art is characterized by intricate patterns of dots, commonly called "sand paintings" because they were originally drawn on sand as ceremonial devices. Prices for oil paintings on canvas range from less than a hundred dollars to several thousand, but the prices are considerably lower here than elsewhere in Australia. Two of the better galleries are the **Aboriginal Art Gallery** (88 Todd St., tel. 089/52–3408) and the **Original Dreamtime Art Gallery** (63 Todd Mall, opposite Flynn Church, tel. 089/52–8861). The latter is particularly impressive for the number of important Aboriginal artists it represents.

Sports and the Outdoors

Ballooning At dawn on most mornings, hot-air balloons can be seen in the sky around Alice Springs. **Outback Ballooning** (18 The Links, Desert Springs, Alice Springs, tel. 089/52–8723) will pick you up from your hotel about one hour before dawn and return you between 9 AM and 10 AM. The $110 fee covers 30 minutes of flying time and a champagne and chicken breakfast.

Golf **Alice Springs Golf Club** (Cromwell Dr., tel. 089/52–5440) welcomes visitors.

Tennis The public tennis courts in **Traeger Park** (entrance on Traeger Ave.) can be rented from the caretaker at the courts. The **Vista** and **Melia** hotels have tennis courts for guests' use (*see* Lodging, *below*).

Dining

Although restaurants in Alice Springs are unlikely to surprise visitors with innovative cuisine, they do feature some foods rarely seen on menus outside Australia, including crocodile, kangaroo, and camel. Highly recommended restaurants are indicated by a star ★.

Category	Cost*
$$$$	over $40
$$$	$30–$40
$$	$20–$30
$	under $20

* *per person, excluding drinks*

$$$ **The Overlander Steakhouse.** When local residents take out-of-town
★ guests to a restaurant, this is often the one they choose. The atmosphere is clearly Outback, with an abundance of old saddles, lamps, equipment, and artifacts from local cattle stations, plus live entertainment every night in the form of Australian folk songs. Overall, the Overlander is that rarity: a folkloric experience that preserves a satisfactory standard of cooking and presentation. It has a full range of Northern Territory specialties, including an appetizer of vol-au-vent filled with crocodile that lets the unusual chicken-fish flavor of this white meat come through. For nonresidents, the inevitable main course is the mixed grill of buffalo, kangaroo, camel, and barramundi. *72 Hartley St., tel. 089/52–2159. Reservations accepted. Dress: casual. AE, DC, MC, V.*

$$$ **Rossini's.** This restaurant in the Diplomat Hotel is another local favorite for special occasions. The excellent food—French-Australian, not Italian—is served in a formal setting with lace tablecloths, silver service, and crystal. Considering the location, it's a surprise to find that one of the restaurant's specialities is oysters, but the oysters Caspan (poached in champagne, folded into a béarnaise sauce and topped with caviar) are worth the trip to the heart of Australia. *Corner Hartley St. and Gregory Terr., tel. 089/52–8977. Reservations advised. Dress: casual but neat. AE, DC, MC, V. No lunch.*

$$ **El Patio.** This relaxing bistro, located in the Melia Alice Springs Hotel, is enhanced by a serene view of the hotel lawns, bounded by the impressive MacDonnell Range. The menu is varied, from mushroom stroganoff sautéed with onion and bell peppers and served in yogurt and paprika sauce, to dry Indonesian beef curry or panfried barramundi. There are also a buffet lunch and, on Sunday, a champagne brunch. *Melia Alice Springs Hotel, Barrett Dr., tel. 089/52–8000. Reservations accepted. Dress: casual. AE, DC, MC, V.*

$$ **Kings.** A large, bright restaurant in Lasseters Casino, Kings serves dishes from Mexico, Indonesia, and China. Try the whole baby barramundi with mushrooms, bacon, and bell peppers cooked with white wine, or, for a lighter fare, sample from the large salad bar. *Lasseters Casino, 93 Barrett Dr., tel. 089/52–5066. Dress: casual but neat. AE, DC, MC, V. No lunch.*

$$ **Puccini's.** This is Alice Spring's best ethnic restaurant. Dark wood
★ paneling, subdued lighting, and friendly service are complemented by first-rate Italian cuisine that, in the middle of the Outback, is nothing short of a revelation. For starters at this bistro/brasserie, try the carpaccio with pine nuts or fettuccine Calabrese, tossed in hot chili, spices, tomatoes, and black pepper. The barramundi baked in lemon, garlic, and vermouth is very good; so, too, is the tournedos *funghi*—medallions of grain-fed beef with brandy and mushrooms. *Corner Todd Mall and Parsons St., tel. 089/53–0935. Reservations advised (esp. weekends). Dress: casual but neat. AE, DC, MC, V. Closed Sun.*

$ **Oriental Gourmet.** The best Chinese food in the Red Centre is found in this restaurant, which looks a lot like an Australian house from the outside and like every Chinese restaurant in the world inside. There are no surprises on the menu—honey prawns, beef with black bean sauce, duck with lemon sauce, and the like—but all the dishes are fresh, simple, and soundly prepared. *80 Hartley St., tel. 089/53–0888. Reservations accepted. Dress: casual. AE, MC, V. No lunch.*

Lodging

The tourism boom of the 1980s resulted in the rapid growth of accommodations in Alice Springs. Several of the newer and better hotels are located out of walking distance from the downtown area. Highly recommended properties are indicated by a star ★.

Category	Cost*
$$$$	over $170
$$$	$120–$170
$$	$70–$120
$	under $70

*All prices are for a standard double room, excluding the NT Tourism Marketing Levy of 2.5%.

Hotels and **Melia Alice Springs Hotel.** With its pastel hues and landscaped
Motels lawns, this hotel is by far the best in Alice Springs. Situated 1½ ki-
$$$$ lometers (1 mile) from town, it's a long walk or a $4 cab ride. The
★ rooms are softly appointed with bleached wood and enhanced by views overlooking the pool and the low, barren mountains behind the hotel. The Melia also offers an eclectic menu at El Patio (*see* Dining, *above*). *Barrett Dr., NT 0870, tel. 089/52–8000, fax 089/52–3822. 250 rooms with bath, including 7 suites. Facilities: lighted tennis courts, health club, sauna, outdoor pool, restaurant, bars with entertainment, nightly barbecue, shops. AE, DC, MC, V.*

$$$ **Alice Springs Pacific Resort.** Completely renovated and expanded in 1987, this hotel is on the east bank of the Todd River, 1 kilometer (.6 mile) from the main downtown area. The spacious and airy restaurant and reception areas are graced with high ceilings and are filled with potted palms. Many of the rooms open directly onto a large lawn; all are plainly furnished in cane with green carpeting. *34 Stott Terr., NT 0870, tel. 089/52–6699, fax 089/53–0995. 107 rooms with* *bath. Facilities: outdoor pool, game room, bars, restaurants, laundry. AE, DC, MC, V.*

$$ ★ **Desert Rose Inn.** This motel provides the best value for families staying in Alice Springs. Budget rooms are cramped and standard rooms are unexceptional, but the deluxe family rooms (built in 1988) are spacious and well furnished. Exposed brick walls set the tone for the deluxe rooms, which contain a double bed, two single beds, a balcony, and a kitchenette with a sink, microwave, and breakfast table. *15–17 Railway Terr., NT 0870, tel. 089/52–1411 or toll-free 008/89–6116, fax 089/52–3232. 73 rooms (most with bath or shower), including 27 budget, 9 standard, and 37 deluxe units. Facilities: outdoor pool, laundry, restaurant. DC, MC, V.*

$$ ★ **The Diplomat.** The location of this hotel is ideal, especially if you don't have a car. It's only 100 meters (300 feet) from the town center, but far enough away to be quiet in the evening. All 71 rooms, which are carpeted and decorated with dark bedspreads and drapes, are air-conditioned and have televisions. Avoid the ground-floor rooms if you want privacy—their full glass doors open onto the central car park/pool area. The rooms are comfortable and the staff friendly. *Cnr. Gregory Terr. and Hartley St., tel. 089/52–8977 or toll-free 008/80–4885, fax 089/53–0225. 71 rooms with bath. Facilities: pool, laundry, restaurant. AE, DC, MC, V.*

$$ **Ross River Homestead Resort.** Situated among rugged ranges next to the river after which it is named, this resort lies 85 kilometers (53 miles) east of Alice Springs. Accommodations are basic wood cabins, each with its own bathroom. A bar and a restaurant are on the premises, and the resort features horse and camel riding. It's a place to experience the remote Outback in relative comfort, and with plenty to keep you occupied. *Ross River Rd., NT 0870, tel. 089/56–9711, fax 089/56–9823. 30 cabins with bath. Facilities: outdoor pool, bar, restaurant. MC, V.*

$$ **Territory Motor Inn.** The main advantage of this hotel is its central downtown location. The disadvantage is that rooms facing Todd Mall and Leichhardt Terrace can be noisy, and rooms facing the central courtyard can be claustrophobic. The ones on the first and second floors are much cooler than those higher up. The pool area and the cobbled courtyard with its old horse carriage are attractive. *Leichhardt Terr., NT 0870, tel. 089/52–2066, fax 089/52–7829. 109 rooms with shower (70 with hip bath also), 1 suite. Facilities: outdoor pool, laundry, bar, restaurant. AE, DC, MC, V.*

$$ **Vista Alice Springs.** Built in 1987, the Vista is bounded by the mountain range that forms the southern periphery of the town. The downtown area is 2½ kilometers (1½ miles) away, but there's a courtesy transport. Apart from the pool/barbecue area at the back of the hotel, there are few public areas. The rooms have bare brick walls, comfortable modern furnishings, and molded fiberglass bathrooms. *Stephens Rd., NT 0870, tel. 089/52–6100, fax 089/52–6234. 140 rooms with bath, including 5 for the disabled. Facilities: outdoor pool, tennis court, bicycles for rent, bar, restaurant, laundry, gift shop. AE, DC, MC, V.*

$ **Melanka Lodge.** Just south of the main shopping area, this lodge offers a range of accommodations, including dormitories and double rooms for backpackers, standard rooms, and 30 deluxe rooms with private bathrooms. *94 Todd St., NT 0870, tel. 089/52–2233, fax 089/52–3819. 112 rooms, 49 with shower. Facilities: 2 pools, restaurant, bar, recreation room, barbecue, laundry. AE, DC, MC, V.*

$ **Outback Motor Lodge.** This motel offers simple, clean accommodations. The only public areas are the lawn around a small pool and the office. There is no dining room, but all rooms have kitchen facilities.

Guests are provided with a breakfast "to go," which they can cook in the privacy of their rooms. *South Terr., NT 0870, tel. 089/52–3888, fax 089/53–2166. 42 rooms with shower. Facilities: outdoor pool, laundry, barbecue. AE, DC, MC, V.*

$ **YHA Hostel.** Available only to members of the Youth Hostels Association, this facility is right in the center of town and features 15 dormitories with a total of 64 beds, plus one twin room. *Corner Leichhardt Terr. and Parsons St., NT 0870, tel. 089/52–8855, fax 089/52–4144. 15 dormitories and 1 double. Facilities: pool, communal kitchen, recreation room, laundry. No credit cards.*

Caravan Parks **Heavitree Gap Caravan Park.** Located where Stuart Highway inter-
$ sects Heavitree Gap on the south side of Alice Springs, this large park lies 4 kilometers (2½ miles) from downtown. It has ample shady sites and barbecue areas. *Ross Hwy., NT 0870, tel. 089/52–2370, fax 089/52–9394. 400 sites, including 100 powered. Facilities: pool, town water, hot showers, laundry, minimart and hotel adjacent. MC, V.*

$ **MacDonnell Range Tourist Park.** Tucked behind the ranges 5 kilom-
★ eters (3 miles) south of town, this is an extensive and well-planned park. There is little shade, however. *Palm Pl. off Ross Hwy., tel. 089/52–6111, fax 089/52–5236. 230 sites, including 150 powered (68 with private amenities). Facilities: 2 pools, children's pool, town water, hot showers, baths, laundry, minimart, playground. MC, V.*

Nightlife

At central Australia's only winery, **Chateau Hornsby** (Petrick Rd., off Stuart Hwy., tel. 089/55–5133), bush balladeer Ted Egan alternates with a bush band to entertain during the busy season; call ahead to see who's performing.

Lasseters Casino (Barrett Dr., tel. 089/52–5066) operates all night with the full range of games: blackjack, roulette, slot machines, keno, and the Australian game of two-up.

Excursion to the MacDonnell Ranges

The MacDonnell Ranges west of Alice Springs are broken by a series of chasms and gorges, many of which can be visited in a single day, depending on your stamina. To reach them, drive out of town on Larapinta Drive, the western continuation of Stott Terrace.

John Flynn's Grave is 7 kilometers (4½ miles) from town on the left-hand side of the highway. Situated on a rise with the stark ranges behind, the setting is memorable. The grave is unmistakable, too: a rock cairn with a large round stone (one of the Devil's Marbles from near Tennant Creek) on top.

Simpsons Gap National Park, located 24 kilometers (15 miles) west of Alice Springs and then a farther 6 kilometers (3.7 miles) along a side road, isn't dramatic, but it has the gorge closest to town. Stark white ghost gums, red rocks, and the purple-hazed mountains give visitors a taste of the scenery to be seen farther into the ranges. The gap itself can be crowded, but it's only 200 yards from the car park. *Tel. 089/55–0310. Admission free. Open 8–8.*

Standley Chasm, 48 kilometers (30 miles) from Alice Springs and an additional 9 kilometers (5½ miles) along a side road, is one of the most impressive canyons. At midday, when the sun is directly overhead, the canyon (which is only 10 yards wide) glows red from the reflected light. The walk from the car park takes about 20 minutes and is rocky toward the end. There is a kiosk at the park entrance. *Tel. 089/56-7440. Admission: $2.50 per person. Open 8:30-4:30.*

Beyond here, the distances grow. Six kilometers (3.7 miles) after the Standley Chasm Road, take Namatjira Drive to **Ellery Creek Big Hole Scenic Reserve,** believed to have the coolest swimming hole in the Red Centre. **Serpentine Gorge,** 106 kilometers (66 miles) from town and 4 kilometers (2½ miles) along a rough track, requires a swim through the gorge to see it all. **Ormiston Gorge and Pound National Park,** 135 kilometers (84 miles) from town, is one of the few really breathtaking sights of the ranges. Unfortunately, it can be crowded at times. There are several walks in the park. **Glen Helen Gorge National Park,** 140 kilometers (87 miles) from town, has a gorge that is much larger than any of the others. Accommodations are available at **Glen Helen Lodge** (tel. 089/56-7489).

Another alternative is to continue on Larapinta Drive from Standley Chasm toward **Hermannsburg,** 132 kilometers (82 miles) from Alice Springs. Hermannsburg has tearooms, a supermarket, and a service station. The buildings of the early Lutheran Mission have been restored. *Admission free. Open Tues.-Sun.*

You need a four-wheel-drive vehicle to proceed the 21 kilometers (13 miles) beyond Hermannsburg to **Palm Valley** in **Finke Gorge National Park.** The valley is a remnant of a time when Australia had a moister climate and supported palm trees over large areas. The trees here are the unique *Livistonia mariae* (a type of cabbage palm) which have survived as a species for over 10,000 years. Palm Valley is like a slice of the tropical north dropped into the middle of the Red Centre.

South to Ayers Rock

Ayers Rock is 441 kilometers (273 miles) from Alice Springs, down the Stuart Highway and along Lasseter Highway. The drive takes about five hours nonstop, but there are some interesting sights along the way, particularly if you're prepared to make a few detours. **Camel Outback Safaris** (tel. 089/56-0925), located 93 kilometers (58 miles) south of Alice Springs, is owned by a local legend, Noel Fullerton, who raises and trains his own camels for tourist expeditions. Camel rides are available 7:30-5. The duration of the rides varies from one hour to 14 days. For rides of half a day (which include a light lunch) or longer, be sure to book in advance, if only the evening before.

Another 39 kilometers (24 miles) south is the exit to Kings Canyon. The **Henbury Meteorite Craters,** a collection of 12 craters between 6 and 600 feet across, are located 13 kilometers (8 miles) down this road. These craters were probably formed by a meteorite shower about 5,000 years ago. One of them is 60 feet deep.

Kings Canyon, 200 kilometers (124 miles) west of Stuart Highway in Watarrka (formerly Kings Canyon) National Park, is one of the finest sights in Central Australia. Sheltered within the sheer cliff walls of the canyon is a world of ferns and rock pools, permanent springs, and woodlands. Several walking tracks wind through the gorge and along the ridge tops. The main path is the 6-kilometer- (3.7-mile-) long Canyon Walk, which starts with a fairly steep climb to the top of the escarpment but leads to a delightful water hole in the so-called Garden of Eden around the middle of the four-hour walk. The local Aboriginal communities join in offering a series of exceptional tours, including a 2½-hour walk (cost $25) that takes you to rock paintings and areas of cultural significance and trail rides costing from $45 for two hours to $150 for a full day. You can make reservations through the **Frontier Kings Canyon Lodge** (tel. 089/56–7442). The park is now acessible by car on the Mereenie Track from Glen Helen. However, an Aboriginal Land Entry Permit is required to make this loop around the western MacDonnell Ranges: the permit can be obtained free of charge from the **Central Australian Tourism Association** (tel. 089/50–2211) in Alice Springs.

Dining and Lodging
$$$$

Kings Canyon Frontier Lodge. Only 7 kilometers (4 miles) from the canyon, this recently built accommodation is the only place to stay within Watarrka National Park. All rooms are air-conditioned, with satellite TV, refrigerators, and direct-dial phones. There are souvenir and provision shops. **Carmichael's ($$)** is the premier restaurant, with seating for 250 and a feature wall of Aboriginal art that provides a counterpoint to the sweeping desert views through the large windows. For travelers on a budget, there are two- and four-bed backpacker rooms as well as a large amply serviced campground adjoining. *Ernest Giles Rd., Wattarka National Park. Mailing address: PMB 136, Alice Springs, NT 0871, tel. 089/56–7442, fax 089/ 56–7410. 68 rooms with showers; 24 backpacker rooms ($). Facilities: pool, laundry, shops, in-house movies, 2 restaurants, 2 bars, barbecues. AE, DC, MC, V.*

Ayers Rock and the Olgas

It's not difficult to see why the Aborigines attach spiritual significance to Ayers Rock. Rising more than 1,100 feet from the flatness of the surrounding plain, it is one of the world's largest monoliths. More impressive than its size, however, is its color—a glowing red that changes constantly throughout the day. The Olgas are a series of 36 gigantic rock domes that lie 63 kilometers (39 miles) away, hiding a maze of fascinating gorges and crevasses. The aforementioned names are used for familiarity only—out at the site, you'll find the Aboriginal names Ulura and Kata Tjuta used for Ayers Rock and the Olgas, respectively.

The Olgas and Ayers Rock have very different compositions: The Olgas are composed of conglomerate, and the rock is a type of sandstone called arkose. For a long time it was thought that they sit upon the sandy terrain like pebbles. That isn't true: Both formations are the tips of tilted rock strata that extend into the earth for thousands of meters; perhaps two-thirds of each formation extends below the surface. During a period of intense geological activity over 300 million years ago the strata were tilted—the arkose by nearly 90 degrees and the conglomerate only about 15 degrees. The rock surrounding the formations had been fractured and thus quickly eroded away, leaving the present structures standing as separate entities about 40 million years ago.

Ayers Rock and the Olgas both lie within Uluru National Park, which is protected as a World Heritage Site. All the tourist facilities are just outside the national park at the Ayers Rock Resort. A visit here will be remembered for a lifetime.

Arriving and Departing by Plane

Airport and Airlines

Connellan Airport is 6 kilometers (3.7 miles) north of the resort complex. It is served by **Ansett Australia** (089/56–2168 or 13–1300) and **Qantas** (tel. 089/56–2255 or 089/13–1313). **Kendall Airlines** (tel. 08/234–0056) operates a weekly service from Adelaide.

Between the AAT Kings (tel. 089/56–2171) operates a shuttle bus that meets ev-
Airport and ery flight.
Yulara
The cost of a taxi from the airport to the resort is $5 per person with
Sunworth Taxi Service (tel. 089/56–2152).

Arriving and Departing by Bus and Car

By Bus Bus companies traveling to Ayers Rock Resort from Alice Springs
include **AAT Kings** (tel. 089/52–1700), **Bus Australia** (tel. 089/53–
1022), **Australian Pacific** (tel. 089/52–6922), and **Greyhound** (tel. 089/
52–8700).

By Car It is 441 kilometers (273 miles) from Alice Springs to Ayers Rock Resort; the trip takes about five hours (*see* South to Ayers Rock,
above). The road is paved and in very good condition.

Getting Around

By Bus **AAT Kings** (tel. 089/56–2171) offers a range of daily tours.

By Car From the resort it's about 20 kilometers (12 miles) to Ayers Rock or
53 kilometers (33 miles) to the Olgas. The road to the Olgas is a recently tarred highway. Routes between the hotels and the sights are
clearly marked, and because prices are competitive with the bus
tours—especially for larger parties—renting a car may be your
most thrifty and convenient option. There are several rental car
companies at the resort: **Avis** (tel. 089/56–2266), **Territory Rent-a-
Car** (tel. 089/56–2030), and **Hertz** (tel. 089/56–2244). For a
chauffeur-driven limousine, contact **V.I.P. Chauffeur Cars** (tel. 089/
56–2283).

By Taxi **Sunworth Taxi Service** (tel. 089/56–1700) can whisk you from the resorts to the sights for much less than the cost of a guided bus tour.
Plus, you can go at your own convenience.

Important Addresses and Numbers

Tourist The **Visitors Centre** is located near the Desert Gardens Hotel on
Information Yulara Drive. *Tel. 089/56–2240. Open 8 AM–9 PM.*

The **ranger station** of Uluru National Park is located on Lasseter
Highway near the entrance to the park. *Tel. 089/56–2299. Open daily 8–5.*

Emergencies Dial 000 for **ambulance, fire brigade, or police.**

Ambulance (tel. 089/56–2286).

Police (tel. 089/56–2166).

Medical Clinic. *Flying Doctor Base (near police station). Open
weekdays 9–noon and 2–5, weekends 10–11. Emergencies (24 hrs),
tel. 089/56–2286.*

Guided Tours

Special- Several free slide shows about local wildlife and flora are given at the
Interest Tours Auditorium, near the resort's Visitors Centre.

The **Liru Walk** is led by Aboriginal rangers who show you the land
from their special perspective. The walk starts from the ranger station. *Tel. 089/56–2299. Admission free. Tues., Thurs., Sat. 8:30 AM
(summer) or 9:30 AM (winter).*

Uluru Experience (tel. 008/80–3174), which specializes in small group tours at Ayers Rock, employs several trained geologists, biologists, and other scientists with extensive local knowledge as guides. Tours, which should be booked at least a day ahead, include a 10-kilometer (6-mile) walk around the base of Ayers Rock. The Uluru Walk gives fascinating insight into the significance of the area to the Aboriginal people. The walk, which includes breakfast, departs daily at 5 AM (6 AM in winter), and costs $52 for adults, $40 for children. An all-day four-wheel-drive excursion to Kings Canyon departs daily at 5 AM and costs $160 per person. A tour of the remarkable flat-topped Mt. Conner, which continues on to the Curtin Springs cattle station for a champagne dinner, costs $99 for adults, $83 for children.

Perhaps the most fascinating tour offered at Ayers Rock, and also led by Uluru Experience, is the 2½-hour Aboriginal Desert Culture Tour, an examination of the bush foods and medicines of the Aborigines, frequently led by Aboriginal staff. Daily departures are at 8:30 AM and cost $40 for adults, $29 for children.

Central Australia has some of the clearest and cleanest air in the world—perfect for stargazing. A small observatory with a good telescope has been set up within the grounds of the resort for just that purpose. Viewing times vary with the seasons; the sessions last for about an hour, and can be booked through Uluru Experience. The cost is $15 for adults, $8 for children, and $40 for a family.

Flightseeing Tours An ideal view of the Olgas and the rock is from the air. A variety of light-plane tours are offered (with courtesy pickup from your hotel included), from half-hour flights over Ayers Rock and the Olgas for $55 per person to $120 per person for 110-minute flights that also fly over Kings Canyon. Contact **Skyport** (tel. 089/56–2093) or **RockAyer** (tel. 089/56–2345).

Helicopter flights are more expensive: $55 per person for 15 minutes over Ayers Rock or $70 for 20 minutes over the Olgas. A flight over both sights costs $120 per seat. The local operators are Skyport and RockAyer (*see above*).

Motorcycle Tour The normally fine climate of the desert makes **Uluru Motorcycle Tours** enjoyable (and popular) and provides the chance for some very different vacation photographs. Guides communicate with their passengers via helmet intercoms. Prices range from $65 for a 1½-hour trip to view sunrise over the Rock to $120 for a three-hour tour to the Olgas; picnic lunches are also available. *Tel. 089/56–2019 or 008/80–2728.*

Exploring Ayers Rock and the Olgas

Orientation Allow about 20 minutes to drive to Ayers Rock from the resort. The drive to the Olgas will take at least 45 minutes. The park entrance fee of $10 is valid for a week. The sunset-viewing area is 13 kilometers (8 miles) from the resort on the way to Ayers Rock.

Ayers Rock There is no ranger station at the entrance to the park, just a tollgate. The station, which houses informative displays that cover, among other subjects, the return of Ayers Rock to Aboriginal ownership in the 1980s, is located on the right side of the road just before you reach the rock. Comprehensive explanatory material is available at the station, as are descriptions of local plant and animal life for sale. There is a good paved road right around Ayers Rock, and the perspective changes greatly as you drive the circuit. Alternatively, you can walk the 10 kilometers (6.2 miles) around the rock in about four hours with time to explore the several deep crevices along the way. Be aware that some places are Aboriginal sacred sites and cannot be entered. These are clearly signposted. There is some Aboriginal art to be found in caves at the base of the rock. These are neither as extensive or impressive as those in Kakadu National Park (*see* Chapter 11).

Only one trail leads to the top of the rock. From the base the climb is about 1.6 kilometers (1 mile), and the round-trip walk takes about two hours. Be careful: The ascent is very steep, and climbers have fallen to their deaths and had heart attacks; even experienced hikers should use the safety chain on the steep initial incline. Don't attempt the climb if you aren't in good condition. You'll also need to be well prepared with hiking boots that have a good grip, a hat, sunscreen, and drinking water. Once you are on top of the rock, the trail is much easier. Visitors can sign a guest book at the summit. In the summer the climb is prohibited during the middle of the day.

The other popular way of experiencing Ayers Rock is far less taxing but no less intense: watching the sun set against it from one of the two sunset-viewing areas. As the last rays of the sun strike, the rock seems lit from within: It positively glows. Just as quickly, the light is extinguished, and the color changes to a somber mauve and finally to black. The resort offers cocktail service to the sunset-viewing points—discuss your order with the receptionist upon check-in. The cost is $28 adults, $15 children, for a 1½-hour excursion that includes transportation, alcoholic and soft drinks, and canapés. Viewing of the reverse process at dawn is usually far less crowded.

The Olgas In many ways, the Olgas are more satisfying to explore than Ayers Rock. The rock is one immense block, so you feel as if you're always on the outside looking in. But you can really come to grips with the Olgas. As their Aboriginal name of *Kata Tjuta* (the many-headed one) suggests, they're a jumble of huge rocks containing numerous hidden gorges and chasms. There are three main walks. The first is from the car park into **Olga Gorge,** the deepest valley between the rocks. This is a 2-kilometer (1-mile) walk, and the round-trip journey takes about one hour. From the parking lot farther along, the walk to **Kata Tjuta Lookout** is about a 1.5-kilometer (1-mile) journey round-trip and takes about an hour. More rewarding but also more difficult is a walk that continues through the major cleft between the Olgas known (for reasons you can probably guess) as the **Valley of the Winds.** Experienced walkers can complete this 7-kilometer (4-mile) walk in about four hours. All visitors should remember to carry at least a quart of water for each hour of walking and avoid walking during the hottest part of the day.

What to See and Do with Children

The resort's hotels have joined to form a free Kids Only Club for 5–12 year olds that operates daily 8–noon and 6–10 during peak holiday seasons. Activities include sports, excursions to the rock, and finding bush tucker. Bookings should be made the evening before through reception at your hotel. The **Child Care Centre** will look after children between the ages of three months and eight years. *Next to the Community Hall, tel. 089/56–2097 or 089/56–2060. Open weekdays 8–5:30.*

Shopping

Until recently, Ayers Rock Resort could not claim to inspire shoppers. It had a news agency, a very reasonably priced supermarket (open 8 AM–9 PM), and a couple of souvenir shops. Then the **Mulgara Gallery** (tel. 089/56–2200) opened in the foyer of the Sails in the Desert Hotel. It specializes in high-quality Australian arts and crafts, including Aboriginal works and stunning opal jewelry. A lack of competition ensures that the art is likely to cost more here than in Alice Springs. At press time there are plans to open several new stores at the resort. These will include a delicatessen, a drugstore, a patisserie, and a coffee shop. Already each of the hotels has an Ayers Rock Logo Shop selling Australian-made fashion garments and leather goods.

The ranger station (tel. 089/56–2299) at Ayers Rock houses the **Ininti Store** (tel. 089/56–2558), which sells a range of souvenirs (including refrigerator magnets that declare "I climbed Ayers Rock" and "I didn't climb Ayers Rock"—take your choice), and the adjoining **Maruku Arts and Crafts Centre** (tel. 089/56–2214), which sells Aboriginal paintings and handicrafts.

Dining and Lodging

This is a planned resort. Travelers can choose from five types of accommodation, priced on a descending scale from the luxurious rooms of the Sails in the Desert to the campsites of the Ayers Rock Campground. All reservations can be made through a central reservation service, Southern Pacific Hotels' Travelex (toll-free tel. 008/222–446) or directly through the resort's new central reservations service (tel. 089/56–2747).

The choice of dining is limited to hotel restaurants and the cheaper **Yulara Tavern** (tel. 089/56–2377), which serves breakfast, lunch, and dinner at its indoor Bistro, and steaks and barramundi outside at night at its Courtyard Barbecue. Guests who eat outside their hotel can have the meals billed to their room. A brasserie-style café with terrace seating and a great view of the rock is being planned for the building currently occupied by the resort's administrative offices. Not to be missed is the "Sounds of Silence" Dinner in the Desert, where you dine under the open sky, surrounded by the vastness of central Australia.

Highly recommended lodgings are indicated by a star ★.

Category	Cost*
$$$$	over $220
$$$	$170–$220
$$	$100–$170
$	under $100

All prices are for a standard double room, excluding the NT Tourism Marketing Levy of 2.5%.

Hotels and Motels
$$$$
★

Sails in the Desert. With its designer shade sails (for protection from the sun), manicured lawns, fine Aboriginal artwork, and wide range of facilities, this three-story hotel is clearly the best address at the resort. Open-air stairways and passages contribute to the overall sense of space and light. Rooms are decorated in cool pastels and feature balconies overlooking the central lawns and gardens. A viewing tower offers good views to Ayers Rock in the distance. The foyer has a good collection of (expensive) works by Aboriginal and other Australian artists. You'll normally find resident artists working here. The Sails in the Desert also features the best restaurant, the Kunia Room ($$$), which serves such local specialties as barramundi, buffalo, and kangaroo. The Desert Rose ($$) serves buffet-style breakfast, lunch, and dinner, with a comprehensive array of international dishes. The Rock Pool ($$) is open for lunch and dinner in the warmer months, featuring fresh seafood flown in daily—here in the middle of the desert you can select from dishes such as shark in crisp champagne batter, chargrilled moonfish, and grilled barramundi fillet. *Yulara Dr., NT 0872, tel. 089/56–2200, fax 089/56–2018 or 089/56–2298. 230 rooms with bath, including 4 suites. Facilities: pool, tennis courts, barbecue, bars, 3 restaurants. AE, DC, MC, V.*

$$$ **Desert Gardens.** This two-story hotel is much smaller than Sails in the Desert, but in terms of service and quality it's almost on a par. Like Sails in the Desert, it is built around a lawn, pool, and extensive gardens that feature, as the hotel's name suggests, the spectacular native flora. The modern rooms are small but comfortable, and recently renovated. The hotel is located near the Visitors Centre and the Shopping Square. Its best restaurant is the White Gums ($$$), which is open for breakfast and dinner. Diners will discover central Australian dishes such as light salads incorporating local fruits, nuts, and berries, as well as cooking with a clear Mediterranean influence. Another option is the Terrace Restaurant ($), which serves lunch and dinner. The emphasis here is on fresh, healthy, affordable meals enjoyed in a relaxed atmosphere. *Yulara Dr., NT 0872, tel. 089/56–2100, fax 089/56–2156. 100 rooms with bath. Facilities: pool, half-court tennis, 2 restaurants, bar, barbecue, laundry. AE, DC, MC, V.*

$$ **Emu Walk Apartments.** These one- and two-bedroom apartments were completely renovated in 1993 and now have fully equipped kitchens (right down to the champagne glasses), refurbished living rooms, and daily maid service. Each unit has a sofa bed, so one-bedrooms sleep four, while the balconied two-bedrooms can accommodate six or eight. There's no restaurant on-site, but guests are welcome to dine in any of the resort's eateries. A minimum stay of three nights is required. *Yulara Dr., NT 0872, tel. 089/56–2100, fax 089/56–2156. 24 apartments with bath. Facilities: use of nearby pool, air-conditioning, TVs, VCRs. AE, DC, MC, V.*

$$ **Outback Pioneer Hotel and Lodge.** Although the theme here is the
★ Outback of the 1860s, complete with rustic decor and evening activities such as bush games, you won't be roughing it at this simple, comfortable motel-style accommodation. The major drawback here is location—the hotel is situated on the other side of the resort from the other hotels and the Shopping Square. It is, however, served by a shuttle bus that runs to the other properties every 15 minutes. The Bough House ($$), open daily for breakfast, lunch, and dinner, features rack of lamb, wild beef ribs, emu, and other hearty central Australian dishes as well as lighter food. The Pioneer Self-Cook Barbecue ($) is open nightly: As the name suggests, you buy a cut of meat and cook it yourself. There is also a kiosk open daily from morning till night where you can buy light meals, snacks, and soft drinks; there's also a fully equipped kitchen for those who want to cook their own meals. *Yulara Dr., NT 0872, tel. 089/56–2170, fax 089/56–2320. 125 rooms with bath, 2 dormitories, 28 cabins. Facilities: restaurant, barbecue, laundry. MC, V.*

$$ **Spinifex Lodge.** Originally used to house the resort staff, most of the rooms in this establishment each have two single beds or two bunk

beds and most of the amenities you would expect in a good hotel, plus kitchenettes and daily maid service. Bathrooms are shared. *Yulara Dr., NT 0872, tel. 089/56–2131, fax 089/56–2163. 68 rooms with kitchenette, no bath. Facilities: use of nearby pool, barbecues, laundry, breakfast packs available. AE, DC, MC, V.*

Caravan Parks
$

Ayers Rock Campground. This large campground has 240 sites for campers, 500 tent sites, and 10 air-conditioned cabins. It has recently been remodeled: New features include rolling green lawns, refrigerators, tables and chairs, and an Outback-style barbecue shelter where you can even do split roasts. It is the only site for private camping in the area. *Yulara Dr., NT 0872, tel. 089/56–2055, fax 089/56–2260. Facilities: pool, barbecue, general store/tour desk, laundry, hot showers, refrigerator. MC, V.*

11 Darwin, the Top End, and the Kimberley

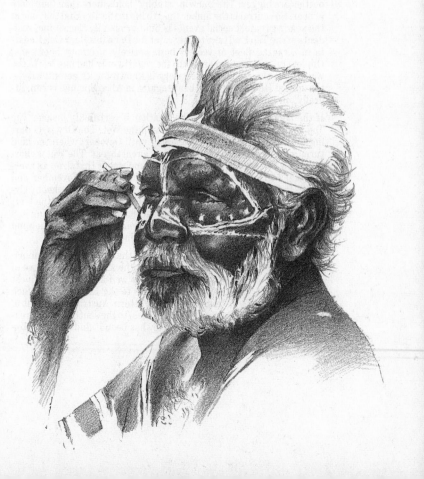

By David McGonigal

Updated by Chips Mackinolty

Comprising the upper half of the Northern Territory, the Top End is the essence of rugged tropical Australia. The movie *Crocodile Dundee*, about a bush-smart Australian, was loosely based on life in the Top End, and for all the devil-may-care bravado of the film, the Top End does indeed seem larger than life. This is, after all, a land where streams and rivers are marked with signs warning of crocodiles, where tropical downpours close roads for months on end, and where a major geological formation the size of Delaware went undetected in the neighboring Kimberley region until 1983.

Perhaps the most notable aspect of life in the Top End is its isolation. The entire Northern Territory, including Alice Springs and all the land south of it, is home to a mere 120,000 people—70,000 of whom live in Darwin. Residents of the Top End are keenly aware of their geographic—and political—isolation, and have maintained a frontier attitude of independence that has changed little in more than a century. The Northern Territory has yet to be made a state, and its residents regard the machinations of Canberra and the southern states with equal amounts of suspicion and scorn.

Perhaps as a result of their isolation, the citizens of the Top End drink more beer than anyone else in the world. On average, each resident of Darwin drinks 230 liters (60 gallons) of beer a year—the equivalent of 650 American bottles. Up here, however, even the beer bottles are bigger: The Darwin "stubby" holds more than four pints of beer. So central is the amber fluid to life in the Top End that one of the year's greatest social events is built around it. Each June, residents of the Top End take to the water for Darwin's Beer Can Regatta in a ragtag fleet of vessels built entirely of empty beer cans. Obviously, whoever dreamed up the regatta only had one oar in the water, but the Northern Territory is known for its eccentricity—the annual Henley-on-Todd boat regatta in Alice Springs is run, literally, on a dry riverbed.

If the people are eccentric, the weather is certifiably insane. The Top End has two seasons—the Dry and the Wet. The Dry lasts during the Australian winter, from May until October, when the land turns a dry brown and bush fires pose a real threat. The Wet is characterized by terrible heat and tropical monsoons that drop an average of 1,500 millimeters (5 feet) of rain between November and April. It was during the Wet in 1974 that Darwin was leveled by Cyclone Tracy, which packed winds of 220 kph (136 mph). In the Wet, roads wash away and dry riverbeds become impassable roaring torrents. Under such circumstances, common sense rather than blind enthusiasm should guide your choice of itinerary.

Across the border in Western Australia is the Kimberley, a combination of empty desert ranges and tropics the size of Japan. Some of Australia's most fantastic landscapes, as well as some of its finest national parks, are located here. Access to the Kimberley is much easier from Darwin than from the Western Australian capital of Perth, some 3,000 kilometers (1,900 miles) to the south. For this reason, information about the Kimberley has been included in this Top End chapter.

Darwin

Darwin knows all about the winds of change. On Christmas Day in 1974, Cyclone Tracy leveled the city, killing 66 people and destroying nearly 60% of its buildings. But the city has reemerged as a thriving port and administrative center. Little remains of the old Darwin, and the downtown area is now a collection of modern office blocks and public buildings. The city's appeal lies in its people and a way of life that's an alluring mixture of Outback openness and cosmopolitan multiculturalism. A large population of Asians and Aborigines makes Darwin the most racially diverse of Australian cities.

Isolated by thousands of miles of harsh desert, Darwin is closer to Indonesia and Southeast Asia than it is to any Australian city, and it tends to look as much north as it does south. Change has always come from the north, it seems, whether from Cyclone Tracy or the Japanese. Back in 1942 the threat of a Japanese invasion was very real, and Darwin became a major Allied military base. Over the course of the war, Japanese aircraft launched 64 bombing attacks on the city, killing 243 people.

It was with a view to preempting two other powers—the French and the Dutch—that the British had originally sought to establish a settlement in the Top End. Beginning in 1824, numerous attempts were made to gain a solid foothold on this inhospitable coast. After several failures, Darwin was founded in 1869 on a small peninsula enfolded by forests, swamplands, and the sea. Today Darwin is an ideal base from which to explore those same swamps and forests, as well as the wonders of Kakadu, Katherine Gorge, and the mighty Kimberley region.

Arriving and Departing By Plane

Airports and Airlines
Darwin's International Airport is serviced from overseas by **Ansett Australia, Garuda, Merpati, Malaysia, Qantas, Royal Brunei,** and **Singapore Airlines.** Domestic carriers flying into Darwin are **Qantas Australian** and **Ansett Australia.**

Between the Airport and Downtown
By Bus: Tour North (tel. 089/41–1656) offers regular bus transportation between the airport and the downtown area. The cost is $5 per person.

By Car: The airport is 12 kilometers (8 miles) northeast of the city. After leaving the terminal, turn left onto McMillans Road and left again onto Bagot Road. Continue until you cross the overpass that merges into the Stuart Highway, which later becomes Daly Street. Turn left onto Smith Street to reach the Smith Street Mall in the heart of the city.

By Taxi: Taxis are available from the taxi rank at the airport. The journey downtown costs about $12.

Arriving and Departing by Bus and Car

By Bus
Greyhound Pioneer (tel. 089/81–8700) operates intercity bus service to the **Darwin Transit Centre** (69 Mitchell St., tel. 089/81–3833) in the middle of town.

By Car
The Stuart Highway is Darwin's land connection with the rest of Australia, and anyone arriving by car will enter the city on this road. Darwin is 1,706 kilometers (1,058 miles) by road from Alice Springs and 4,095 kilometers (2,539 miles) from Sydney.

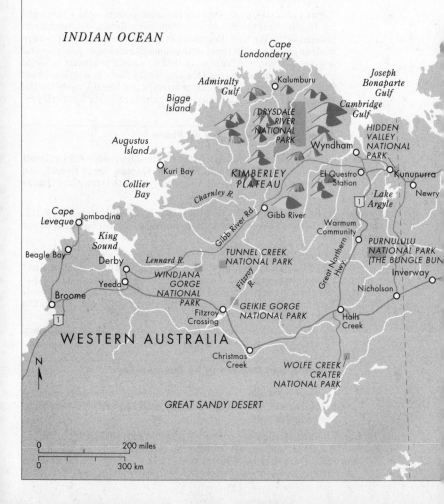

INDONESIA

Timor Sea

INDIAN OCEAN

Cape
Londonderry

*Joseph
Bonaparte
Gulf*

*Admiralty
Gulf*   Kalumburu

*Bigge
Island*

*Cambridge
Gulf*

DRYSDALE
RIVER
NATIONAL
PARK

HIDDEN
VALLEY
NATIONAL
PARK

*Augustus
Island*

KIMBERLEY
PLATEAU

Wyndham

*Collier
Bay*   Kuri Bay

El Questro
Station

Kununurra

Newry

Charnley R.

Lake
Argyle

Cape
Leveque   Lombadina

Gibb River

*King
Sound*

Warmum
Community

PURNULULU
NATIONAL PARK
[THE BUNGLE BUN

Beagle Bay

Derby

Lennard R.

TUNNEL CREEK
NATIONAL PARK

Inverway

Yeeda

WINDJANA
GORGE
NATIONAL
PARK

Fitzroy R.

Nicholson

Broome

GEIKIE GORGE
NATIONAL PARK

Fitzroy
Crossing

Halls
Creek

WESTERN AUSTRALIA

N

Christmas
Creek

WOLFE CREEK
CRATER
NATIONAL PARK

GREAT SANDY DESERT

0   200 miles

0   300 km

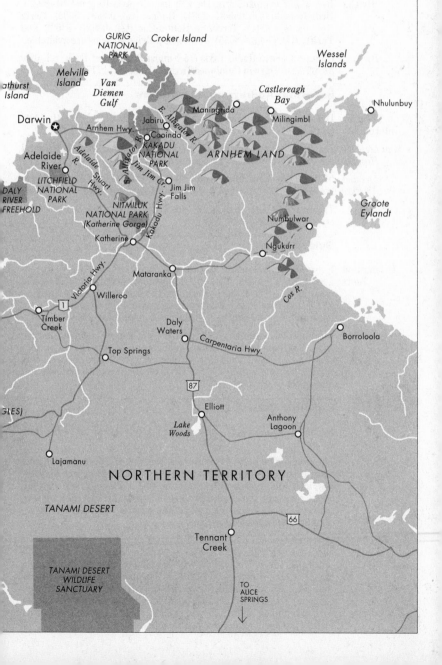

Arafura Sea

GURIG NATIONAL PARK

Croker Island

Wessel Islands

Melville Island

Van Diemen Gulf

Castlereagh Bay

Nhulunbuy

athurst Island

Darwin ✪

Arnhem Hwy

E. Alligator R.

Jabiru

Maningrida

Milingimbl

Adelaide River

Adelaide R.

Cooinda

KAKADU NATIONAL PARK

ARNHEM LAND

LITCHFIELD NATIONAL PARK

Stuart Hwy.

Alligator R.

Jim Jim Cr.

Groote Eylandt

DALY RIVER FREEHOLD

Jim Jim Falls

NITMILUK NATIONAL PARK (Katherine Gorge)

Numbulwar

Katherine

Kakadu Hwy.

Ngukurr

Victoria Hwy.

Mataranka

Cox R.

Willeroo

GLES)

Timber Creek

1

Daly Waters

Carpentaria Hwy.

Borroloola

Top Springs

87

Lajamanu

Elliott

Lake Woods

Anthony Lagoon

NORTHERN TERRITORY

TANAMI DESERT

66

TANAMI DESERT WILDLIFE SANCTUARY

Tennant Creek

TO ALICE SPRINGS
↓

Getting Around

By Bus The bus network in Darwin links the city with its far-flung suburbs. The main bus terminal (Buslink, tel. 089/47–0577) for city buses is on Harry Chan Avenue, near the Bennett Street end of Smith Street Mall.

By Car Rental car companies in Darwin include **Avis** (tel. 089/81–9922), **Brits-Rentals** (tel. 089/81–2081), **Budget** (tel. 089/81–9800), **Hertz** (tel. 089/41–0944), **Territory Rent-a-Car** (tel. 089/81–8400), and **Thrifty** (tel. 089/81–8555). Four-wheel-drive vehicles are available.

By Taxi Contact **Darwin Radio Taxis** (15 Finniss St., Stuart Park, tel. 089/81–8777) or **Darwin Combined Taxis** (tel. 089/41–1777).

Important Addresses and Numbers

Tourist **Darwin Region Tourism Association.** *33 The Mall, tel. 089/81–4300.*
Information *Open May–Oct., weekdays 8:30–6, Sat. 9–2, Sun. 10–4.*

Emergencies Dial 000 for **police, fire,** or **ambulance** service. **Royal Darwin Hospital**
Hospital (tel. 089/22–8888) has a 24-hour emergency room.

Doctors and **Night & Day Medical & Dental Surgery.** *Casuarina Shopping Cen-*
Dentists *tre, tel. 089/27–1899. Open Mon.–Sat. 8 AM–9 PM, Sun. 9–9.*

Trower Road A/H Medical Service. *Trower Rd., tel. 089/27–6905. Open daily 8 AM–10 PM.*

Guided Tours

Orientation Every day but Sunday, **Darwin Day Tours** (tel. 089/81–8696) con-
Tours ducts half-day tours ($27) of the downtown historic buildings, the main harbor, the Botanic Gardens, the Museum of Arts and Sciences, the East Point Military Reserve, and the Fannie Bay Gaol Museum. Fish-feeding at Aquascene is sometimes included.

Boat Tours Daytime and sunset cruises around one of the most beautiful and unspoiled harbors in the world are available on **Darwin Harbor Tours's** *Darwin Duchess.* There's a licensed bar on board. *Stokes Hill Wharf, tel. 089/78–5094. Cost: $18–$20. Cruises 2 PM and 5:30 PM, May–Sept.*

Exploring Darwin

Numbers in the margin correspond to points of interest on the Darwin map.

The orientation point for visitors is The Mall at Smith Street. Normally crowded with locals in shorts and T-shirts, groups of Aborigines, and well-dressed office workers, this is a place where cowboy meets croissant. The downtown grid of streets around the mall is at the very tip of a peninsula; most of the suburbs and outlying attractions are out beyond the airport.

There are several buildings dating back to the early settlement of northern Australia in downtown Darwin. From The Mall head southwest down Knuckey Street across Mitchell Street. On the right, at the intersection with the Esplanade, is **Lyons Cottage.** Built in 1925 for executives of the British-Australian Telegraph Company (B.A.T.), this stone building is now a historical museum with exhibits on life in Darwin, the Macassans, the Chinese, pearl diving, the early explorers, and the operation of the telegraph. *74*

Aquascene, **15**

Australian Pearling
Exhibition, **11**

Browns Mart, **13**

Christ Church
Cathedral, **12**

Darwin Aviation
Museum, **21**

Darwin's Botanic
Gardens, **16**

East Point
Reserve, **19**

Fannie Bay Gaol, **18**

Government House, **5**

Hotel Darwin, **3**

Indo Pacific
Marine, **10**

Lyons Cottage, **1**

Military Museum, **20**

Museum of Arts and
Sciences, **17**

Old Admiralty
House, **2**

Old Police Station and
Court House, **6**

Overland Telegraph
Memorial, **4**

Stokes Hill Wharf, **9**

Survivor's Lookout, **7**

Victoria Hotel, **14**

WWII Fuel Storage
Tunnels, **8**

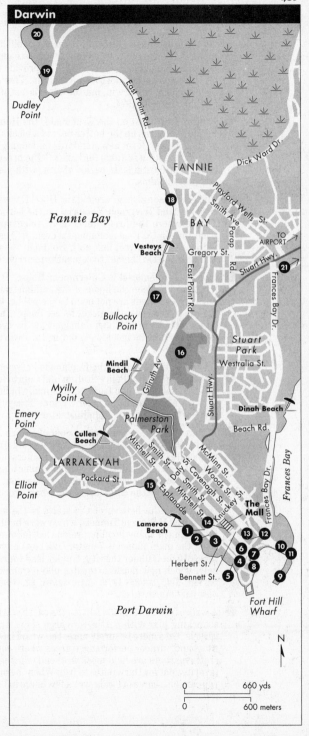

Esplanade, tel. 089/41–0607. Admission free. Open daily 9:30–3:30.

On the other side of Knuckey Street is an old house elevated on columns—a design well suited to Darwin's steamy climate. This is the **2** **Old Admiralty House,** build in 1937 to provide lodging for the naval officer commanding northern Australia. This style of building was once common in Darwin, but the home is one of only a few to survive Cyclone Tracy in 1974.

3 Farther southeast on the Esplanade, the **Hotel Darwin** (*see* Lodging, *below*) takes up the better part of a block. When this hotel first opened in 1883, it set new standards for lodging in Darwin, including "accommodation suitable for ladies." The present building, erected in 1936, still retains its period charm, with plenty of wicker, cane, and potted palms.

The Esplanade zigzags around the Hotel Darwin to a cairn known as **4** the **Overland Telegraph Memorial** on the harbor side of the street. This is where the first international telegraph cable came ashore from Java in 1871—a monumental event in Australia's history, providing the first direct link with England. Before that, information and orders from "home" took months to arrive by ship.

5 Facing the memorial is **Government House,** Darwin's oldest building. This has been the home of the administrator for the area since 1870. The grounds are not open to the public, but most of the building can be seen over the picket fence. Despite being bombed by Japanese aircraft in 1942 and damaged by the cyclones of 1897, 1937, and 1974, it looks much as it did in 1879 when it was finally completed.

On the opposite side of the Esplanade between Mitchell and Smith **6** streets are the **Old Police Station and Court House,** with their long veranda and old stone facades. Originally built in 1884, both buildings were reconstructed after Cyclone Tracy to serve as offices for the Northern Territory administrator.

7 Across the road is **Survivor's Lookout,** which overlooks the site of World War II's first Japanese bombing raid on Australia and commemorates those who died, including sailors of the USS *Peary*. The shaded viewing platform holds a panoramic illustrated map describing the events of that fateful day. The lookout is also the gateway, via stairs down the cliff face, to the wharf precinct.

Directly at the bottom of the stairs is the entrance to Darwin's **8** **World War II Storage Tunnels,** which were built to store and protect fuel from the many bombing raids that followed. Carved into solid rock, the main tunnel is 7 meters (22 feet) high and extends 65 meters (210 feet) under the city. Guides lead tours of the dimly lit tunnels, which now house extensive photographic records of the war period. *Tel. 089/85–4779. Admission: $3. Tour leaves daily at 20 min past the hr, 10–2.*

9 A walk of 400 meters (435 feet) to the east leads to **Stokes Hill Wharf,** a working pier with berths for cargo ships, trawlers, and defense vessels. On a more leisurely note, the wharf has a number of restaurants and outdoor performance areas where concerts and arts-and-crafts markets are held most weekends during the Dry. It's also a favorite spot for Darwinites to fish: When the mackerel are running, you can join scores of locals over a few beers in late-night fishing parties.

⑩ If you'd rather ogle fish than eat them, visit the wharf's **Indo Pacific Marine.** Housed in a huge, glass-side tank is the only self-contained coral-reef ecosystem in the Southern Hemisphere. Among the exotic corals are reef fish and other marine life. *Stokes Hill Wharf, tel. 089/81–1294. Admission: $8.50 adults, $7 senior citizens, $3 children 5–15, $20 family. Open daily June–Sept. 9–6, Oct.–May 10–5.*

⑪ Next door is the **Australian Pearling Exhibition,** which displays 100 years' worth of history on the hunt for pearls in Australia's northern waters. Exhibits cover everything from pearl farming to pearl jewelry settings. *Stokes Hill Wharf, tel. 089/41–2177. Open daily 10–6. Admission $5 adults, $3 children 5–15.*

⑫ Returning up the cliff to Smith Street, you'll find **Christ Church Cathedral.** This Anglican church was largely destroyed by Cyclone Tracy, but the remains of the original 1902 structure have been incorporated into the new building. A little farther along Smith Street **⑬** on the same side of the road is **Browns Mart.** Erected in 1885, this building, which has seen duty as an emporium and a mining exchange, is now a theater.

Time Out Across Bennett Street on the left-hand side is the **Victoria Hotel,** **⑭** known as the "Vic." A Darwin institution since its construction in 1894, it has been damaged by every cyclone and rebuilt afterwards—most recently in 1978. A drink on the balcony is a good way to conclude the walking part of the tour.

Scattered along a line from downtown to the end of East Point, about 8 kilometers (5 miles) away, are a few sites that every visitor should **⑮** see. At **Aquascene,** on the northwestern end of the Esplanade, visitors have the chance to hand-feed thousands of fish. Starting with a few mullet over 30 years ago, fish have been coming here to be hand-fed. At high tide, people wade into the water with buckets of bread to feed the schools of batfish, bream, catfish, milkfish, and mullet that now come inshore in a feeding frenzy. *Doctors Gully, Esplanade, tel. 089/81–7837. Cost: $3.50 adults, $2 children over 3. Opening hours depend on tides.*

⑯ Take Woods Street north to Gardens Road and **Darwin's Botanic Gardens** (Gardens Rd., tel. 089/89–5535), an ideal spot in which to escape the tropical heat. Originally started in 1879, the gardens were largely destroyed by Cyclone Tracy. They have now been replanted with large collections of figs and palms (400 species), as well as a wetland flora area, a rain forest, and a waterfall. The greenhouse displays ferns and orchids.

⑰ Just to the north is the **Museum of Arts and Sciences,** most notable for its Gallery of Aboriginal Man, including an exceptional collection of bark paintings. The displays of Aboriginal art and culture provide an excellent insight into the lives of the most ancient inhabitants of the Top End. Other exhibits deal with natural science, Pacific Island cultures, and fine arts. The stuffed remains of Sweetheart, a 5.1-meter (17-foot) crocodile taken from a Top End water hole, are also on display. *Conacher St., Bullocky Point, Fannie Bay, tel. 089/82–4211. Admission free. Open weekdays 9–5, weekends 10–5.*

⑱ Located a short distance north along East Point Road, **Fannie Bay Gaol** served as a prison from 1883 to 1979. It is now a museum where visitors can observe the former prison's living conditions as well as the gallows where the last execution in the Northern Territory was performed in 1952. The most fascinating part of the museum, however, is the exhibits about Cyclone Tracy, which devastated Darwin on

Christmas Day 1974. *E. Point Rd., Fannie Bay, tel. 089/41–0341. Admission free. Open daily 10–5.*

⑲ East Point Road leads past the beaches of Fannie Bay onto the headland occupied by the **East Point Reserve.** This is a pleasant expanse of small beaches, cliffs, lawns, and forest, where wallabies can be seen grazing at dawn and dusk.

⑳ The **Military Museum** at East Point has an interesting collection of artillery and vehicles. *E. Point Rd., tel. 089/81–9702. Admission: $5 adults, $4 senior citizens, $3 children under 12, $12 family. Open daily 9:30–5.*

South of the airport, 8 kilometers (5 miles) down Stuart Highway, is
㉑ the impressive **Darwin Aviation Museum.** Displays trace the history of flight in the Northern Territory, which, because of its isolation and sparse population, played an important role in the expansion of aviation in Australia. Planes on exhibition here include a massive B-52 bomber on permanent loan from the United States—one of only very few not on U.S. soil—as well as a Japanese Zero shot down on the first day of bombing raids in 1942. *557 Stuart Hwy., Winnellie, tel. 089/47–2145. Admission: $6, $5 military personnel, $4 senior citizens, $15 family. Open daily 8:30–5.*

What to See and Do with Children

The Crocodile Farm. More than just a tourist park, this farm supplies much of the crocodile meat you'll find on menus around the Territory. It is also a research station studying both fresh- and saltwater crocodiles. The best time to visit is during the daily feeding and tour at 2 PM, when the generally lethargic crocodiles become active in the presence of food. A second feeding time is held later in the afternoon on Monday, Wednesday, Saturday, and Sunday. *40 km (25 mi) south on Stuart Hwy., tel. 089/88–1450. Admission: $8.50 adults, $6 senior citizens, $3 children 5–15. Open daily 9–5. Tours daily at 11.*

Territory Wildlife Park. In addition to water buffalo, dingoes, and water birds, this large park features an underwater viewing area from which to observe freshwater fish, and a nocturnal house kept dark for viewing animals that are active only at night. Visitors ride around the 960-acre park on a motor-train. Allow at least two hours to tour the park. *Berry Springs, turnoff 46 km (29 mi) down Stuart Hwy., tel. 089/88–6000. Admission: $10 adults; $5 senior citizens, students, and children; $25 family. Open daily 8:30–4.*

Off the Beaten Track

Built as a water supply for the ill-fated rice-growing project of Humpty Doo in the late 1950s, **Fogg Dam** has remained untouched by commercialism in its remote location 67 kilometers (42 miles) east of Darwin. The project failed largely because the birds of the region regarded the rice crop as a rather tasty smorgasbord. The birds have remained, and they provide an unforgettable sight at sunrise and sunset during the Dry. Exercise care driving through this swampland, however, and wear clothes that you don't mind getting dirty. No toilet facilities are available. From Darwin, take the Stuart Highway to the Arnhem Highway. After 24 kilometers (15 miles) turn left and continue for another 7 kilometers (4.3 miles); then turn right and drive for 1 kilometer (.6 mile) to the dam.

Northeast of Darwin on the Cobourg Peninsula is an international resort accessible only by a one-hour light-plane flight. **Seven Spirit Bay** may well be the most remote resort on earth. The Cobourg Peninsula has miles of pristine bays and beaches, colonial ruins, and exotic wildlife. The resort spreads over several hectares in Gurig National Park and consists of groups of individual hexagonal huts linked to the main complex by winding paths. Each hut contains a single spacious room and each has its own fenced outdoor bathroom. The main building is drab outside, but the polished timbers, high ceilings, and bright coverings inside draw the visitor's eye to the glass doors leading to the deck and pool and the ocean beyond. There is a resident naturalist, and excursions include photographic tours, bushwalks to tented camps, sailing excursions, and mountain-bike rides. The dining room serves some of the Territory's best meals. Seafood comes from the surrounding waters, herbs are from the gardens, and the light, modern Australian dishes incorporate some traditional bush foods as well as Indonesian and Malaysian influences. All meals are included in the tariff. *Reservations: Seven Spirit Wilderness Pty. Ltd., Box 4721, Darwin, NT 0801, tel. 089/79–0277, fax 089/79–0284. 24 rooms with bath. Facilities: outdoor pool, shop, bar. $$$$*

Shopping

Markets For Darwin locals, markets have become as much a form of popular entertainment as they are a shopping venue. Up to a fifth of the city's population may show up for the movable feast that is the **Mindil Beach Sunset Markets** (Mindil Beach, tel. 089/81–3454), an extravaganza that takes place every Wednesday evening during the Dry (April–October). After the hard work of snacking at hundreds of food stalls, shopping at artisans' booths, and watching singers, dancers, and musicians, Darwinites unpack tables, chairs, and bottles of wine and then watch the sun plunge into the harbor.

Other markets for food, secondhand, and crafts stands include the **Big Flea Market** (Rapid Creek Shopping Centre, Trower Rd., Rapid Creek, tel. 089/85–5806, Sun. 8–2), which specializes in Asian-influenced produce and cuisine; the **Parap Market** (Parap Sq., Parap, Sat. 8–2); the **Palmerston Night Market** (Frances Mall, tel. 089/32–1322, Fri. 5:30 PM–9:30 PM); the **Smith Street Mall Markets** (Fri.–Wed. 6 PM–late); and the **Banyan Junction Market** (Transit Centre, Mitchell St., nightly from 7 PM).

Aboriginal Art As in Alice Springs, the best buys in Darwin are Aboriginal paintings and artifacts. A visit to the Museum of Arts and Sciences (*see* Exploring Darwin, *above*) will give you a good idea of the highest standards attainable. The extensive Aboriginal art collection on public display at the **Supreme Court** (State Sq., Mitchell St.) is complemented by a spectacular floor mosaic of an Aboriginal desert "dot" painting. The best commercial galleries in Darwin are the **Raintree Aboriginal Art Gallery** (Shop 1, 14 Knuckey St., tel. 089/81–2732), **Shades of Ochre** (178 The Esplanade, tel. 089/81–3252), and **Framed** (55 Stuart Hwy., tel. 089/81–2994).

Sports and the Outdoors

Bicycling Darwin is fairly flat, so cycling is a good way to get around—except during the Wet, when you are liable to get soaked. Bicycles can be hired from **U-Rent** (51 Mitchell St., tel. 089/41–1280).

Fishing The best-known fish of the Top End, barramundi, which grows to up to 50 kilograms (110 pounds), is an excellent fighting fish and tastes great on the barbecue afterwards. Fishing safaris can be arranged through **Big Barra** (tel. 089/32–1473) and **NT Barra Fishing Trips** (tel. 089/45–1841). For ocean game-fishing contact **NT Coastal Fishing Charters** (tel. 089/81–9879).

Golf The only 18-hole course in Darwin is **Darwin Golf Club** (Links Rd., Marrara, tel. 089/27–1015). The **Gardens Park Golf Links** (Botanic Gardens, tel. 089/81–6365) and **Palmerston Golf Club** (Dwyer Crescent, Palmerston, tel. 089/32–1324 or 089/32–2681) are nine-hole courses. Clubs can be rented at all three.

Health and Fitness Clubs Several hotels have their own gyms (*see* Lodging, *below*). The most central commercial gym is **Darwin Gym** (78 Esplanade, tel. 089/41–0020).

Jogging The waterfront park parallel to the Esplanade is a good area for jogging within the city. For a longer run, the beachfront parks along the shores of Fannie Bay to East Point provide generally flat terrain and a great view.

Tennis Several hotels have tennis courts (*see* Lodging, *below*), and there are four courts at the **Darwin Tennis Centre** (Gilruth Ave., The Gardens, tel. 089/85–2844).

Water Sports Marine stingers and other hazards restrict water activities around Darwin. The beaches of Fannie Bay and Nightcliff are popular, however, especially on weekends. For diving, contact **Fannie Bay Dive Centre** (Shop 2/9 Fannie Bay Pl., tel. 089/81–3049) or **Sand Pebbles Dive Shop** (De Latour St., Coconut Grove, tel. 089/85–1906). To rent sailboats, contact **Darwin Sailing Club** (tel. 089/81–1700).

Dining

The menus in Darwin seem to indicate that there is little the average Territorian won't eat—buffalo, crocodile, camel, and kangaroo are all frequently featured. Barramundi is one of the tastiest fish in the world. Buffalo can be tough, but a tender piece is like a gamey piece of beef. Opinion is divided about crocodile—it, too, can be tough, but (like every reptile, it seems) a good piece tastes like chicken.

Highly recommended restaurants are indicated by a star ★.

Category	Cost*
$$$$	over $45
$$$	$35–$45
$$	$25–$35
$	under $25

per person, excluding drinks and service

$$$$ **Siggi's.** With a classic French menu that changes every few weeks,
★ Siggi's may be the finest restaurant in Darwin. In a faintly Asian setting, guests enjoy privacy in large, softly lit cubicles separated by glass panels. The seasonal menu features such dishes as barramundi with prawns, panfried buffalo fillet with blackberry sauce, and a ragout of chicken with leek and mango in a martini sauce. *Beaufort Hotel, Esplanade, tel. 089/82–9911 or toll-free 008/89–1119. Reservations strongly advised. Dress: casual but neat. AE, DC, MC, V. No lunch. Closed Sun. and Mon.*

$$ Christo's on the Wharf. Part of the Wharf Precinct, Christo's features Darwin's most unusual setting. Situated at the end of a commercial wharf in a renovated corrugated-iron storage shed, this large restaurant is dominated by a traditional Macassarese fishing prau seized by Australian customs in 1990. Open to sea breezes, it is an ideal place to escape from the Darwin heat without being confined by air-conditioning. The food is good, with an emphasis on seafood. Greek dips such as *taramasalata* can be followed by chili bugs, lightly cooked calamari, or garlic prawns, a specialty of the house. *Stokes Hill Wharf, tel. 089/81–8658. Reservations accepted. Dress: casual but neat. AE, DC, MC, V. Lunch Tues.–Fri. noon–3, dinner Tues.–Sun. from 6:30.*

$$ ★ Hanuman Thai and Nonya Restaurant. Established in 1992, the Hanuman has set new standards for dining in Darwin and has been rated one of the best restaurants in Australia. Dark furniture and deep peacock blue walls with touches of gold do not detract from the fine food or a wine list that includes the best from every grape-growing region in Australia. By drawing on Thai and Nonya (Malaysian) culinary traditions, Hanuman's chefs turn locally produced herbs, vegetables, and seafood into a wide range of innovative dishes. Of special note are the Hanuman oysters, lightly cooked in a spicy coriander-and-lemongrass sauce; the barramundi baked with ginger flower; the *tom yum* soups; and any of the many curries. *28 Mitchell St., tel. 089/41–3500. Dinner reservations strongly advised. Dress: casual but neat. AE, DC, MC, V. Lunch weekdays noon–2:30, dinner nightly from 6:30.*

$$ La Vela. The Australian obsession with buildings constructed of corrugated iron has spread to restaurants, yielding perhaps doubtful architectural results at La Vela. However, this is made up for by the food, with its emphasis on country-style Italian cuisine. All pastas are made on the premises and are incorporated into deliciously fresh and well-crafted dishes. La Vela's best results are marinara pastas, which make good use of local produce, and vegetarian lasagna. *Cnr. Vimy La. and Gregory St., Parap, tel. 089/81–6844. Reservations accepted. Dress: casual but neat. AE, DC, MC, V. Lunch Tues.–Fri. 11:30–2; dinner Mon. 6–10, Tues.–Thurs. 6–11, Fri.–Sat. 6–midnight.*

$$ ★ Lindsay Street Cafe. Lush tropical gardens surround this old-style, elevated Darwin house. The bottom-level café serves some of Darwin's more exotic cuisine, with the emphasis on adapting Asian and European food to tropical climes. Perhaps the best time to visit Lindsay Street is for the long, relaxed Sunday brunches—for which reservations are essential. The menu is regularly updated, but some perennial customer favorites include the rice pancakes with pawpaw salad, shallots, and oyster mushrooms and the grilled escalopes of kangaroo with lemongrass-and-red-wine sauce, cracked coriander, and sweet pickled mango slices. *2 Lindsay St., tel. 089/81–8631. Reservations accepted. Dress: casual but neat. MC, V. Lunch Tues.–Fri. 11:30–2:30, dinner Tues.–Sat. 6:30–10, Sun. brunch 10–3.*

$ Kafe Neon. Nestled in the corner of an old storage shed in the Wharf Precinct, Kafe Neon reflects the best and least expensive aspects of Darwin's casual lifestyle. The al fresco dining area, just yards from the magnificent harbor, is a particularly relaxing spot to try some of the eatery's special Greek salads or a cup of excellent coffee. The *mezethes*, a combination of olives, anchovies, feta cheese, artichoke hearts, and pickled octopus, is particularly good. *Stokes Hill Wharf, tel. 089/41–0266. No reservations. Dress: casual. No credit cards.*

$ Roma Bar. The decorative theme of the Roma Bar seems only accidentally Italian and the clientele is similarly eclectic: Office workers, lawyers, and magistrates from the surrounding business district mingle with artists, entertainers, and students. Visitors enjoy the good coffee and somewhat rowdy hubbub of business-suited and barefoot Darwinites in their natural habitat. The food is good, too—fresh tossed green salads, pasta, and focaccia stand out. *30 Cavenagh St., tel. 089/81–6729. No reservations. Dress: casual. No credit cards. Open weekdays 7–5, weekends 8–2.*

Lodging

Highly recommended hotels are indicated by a star ★.

Category	Cost*
$$$$	over $160
$$$	$100–$160
$$	$60–$100
$	under $60

*All prices are for a standard double room, excluding the NT Tourism Marketing Levy of 2.5%.

$$$$ **Beaufort Hotel.** With its colorful, round exterior, this is the most
★   striking and unusual hotel in Darwin, as well as the most expensive. Built in 1986 and completely refurbished in 1994, the hotel has five floors of guest rooms around a central foyer. The rooms are decorated in subtle greens and pinks with plenty of natural wood and have panoramic views over the city or harbor. *Esplanade 0800, tel. 089/82–9911 or toll-free 008/89–1119, fax 089/81–5332. 196 rooms with bath, including 32 suites. Facilities: outdoor pool, 2 saunas, gym, shops, restaurants, bars, laundry. AE, DC, MC, V.*

$$$$ **Melia Darwin Hotel.** Central to the business district, this 12-story hotel is the highest in Darwin. Built in 1986, the rooms offer a pleasant mixture of art deco–style lamps and cool pastel furnishings. With its raised piano bar and elegant armchairs, the high-ceiling lobby can seem rather formal if you have arrived straight from a fishing trip or the mud pools of Kakadu. Equally posh is the hotel's gourmet restaurant, Flinders. *32 Mitchell St., 0800, tel. 089/82–0000 or toll-free 1800/89–1101, fax 089/81–1765. 233 rooms with bath, including 12 suites. Facilities: outdoor pool, gym, shops, restaurants, bars. AE, DC, MC, V.*

$$$ **Atrium.** This vies with the Beaufort as Darwin's prettiest hotel.
★   Served by glass elevators, the hotel's seven floors open onto a central vine-hung atrium. And in the foyer, set around a tiny artificial stream amid palm trees and ferns, are the hotel's bars and restaurants. Guest rooms are attractive and airy, decorated in pastel blues, and each has its own kitchenette. *Peel St. and Esplanade, 0800, tel. 089/41–0755, fax 089/81–9025. 140 rooms with bath, including 4 suites. Facilities: outdoor pool, restaurants, bars, barbecue, laundry. AE, DC, MC, V.*

$$$ **Darwin Travelodge.** Built in 1974, this 10-story hotel offered the best accommodations in Darwin until a rash of new hotels and resorts went up in the mid-1980s. Nevertheless, the views of the city or Fannie Bay from rooms on floors 6–10 are still the best in town. The lobby is decorated in pale green with white cane chairs. The green color scheme is continued in the rooms, giving them a cool feel; each room has its own small bar. *122 Esplanade, 0800, tel. 089/81–5388, fax 089/81–5701. 182 rooms with bath, including 2 suites. Facilities: outdoor pool, restaurant, bar, barbecue, laundry. AE, DC, MC, V.*

$$$ Diamond Beach Hotel Casino. Shaped like pyramids with square tops, this casino and the smaller adjoining hotel are two of the most distinctive structures in the city. This three-story hotel is *the* luxury resort in Darwin: It offers the city's only beachfront accommodations amid lush lawns and gardens. The lobby is small and uninspired, but the pleasant rooms have an elegant bamboo theme. *Gilruth Ave., Mindil Beach 0800, tel. 089/46–2666, fax 089/81–9186. 97 rooms with bath, including 18 suites. Facilities: outdoor pool, sauna, gym, tennis courts, restaurant, bars, casino. AE, DC, MC, V.*

$$ Hotel Darwin. Once the grande dame of Darwin, this two-story colonial hotel has faded a great deal. The Green Room—the bar where much of the city's business has been discussed over the years—is still a pleasant indoor/outdoor area next to the pool. The rooms belong to an earlier era and their carpets are worn, but they have a pleasant view over the garden or pool. Despite its slightly run-down look, the hotel maintains some of its colonial character, including ample wicker and cane. *10 Herbert St., 0800, tel. 089/81–9211, fax 089/81–9575. 63 rooms with shower, 7 with bath, 1 suite. Facilities: pool, restaurant, bars, laundry. AE, DC, MC, V.*

$$ Top End Best Western. Overlooking a central garden and pool, this
★ two-story hotel has a country ambience that belies its position only a few minutes' walk from The Mall at Smith Street. The rooms have cane furnishings, carved wood headboards, and a maroon color scheme. All ground-floor rooms open onto the central lawn and pool, while those upstairs have private balconies. *Mitchell and Daly Sts., 0800, tel. 089/81–6511, fax 089/41–1253. 40 rooms without bath. Facilities: outdoor pool, bars, restaurant, laundry. AE, DC, MC, V.*

$ Darwin Transit Centre. Spread over six blocks and two floors, the Darwin Transit was originally a workers' residential complex and is now the largest hotel in town. The large white rooms are simple and neat, with basic furnishings and washbasins. Some have air-conditioning, although most are cooled only by fan. *69 Mitchell St., 0800, tel. 089/81–3995, fax 089/81–6674. 200 rooms without bath. Facilities: outdoor pool, sauna, gym, game room, laundry, cooking facilities. AE, MC, V.*

$ Larrakeyah Lodge. One of several inexpensive hotels and hostels grouped around the central bus station, this lodge is both the most expensive and the nicest. None of the rooms on the two floors has a shower or toilet, but each has a washbasin. All rooms are air-conditioned, but otherwise the furnishings are spartan. The property is operated jointly by the YMCA and the YWCA. *50 Mitchell St., 0800, tel. 089/81–2933, fax 089/81–1908. 56 rooms without bath. Facilities: outdoor pool, barbecue, laundry. MC, V.*

$ YHA Hostel. This hostel provides the cheapest accommodations in town for members of the Youth Hostel Association only. Painted green, the rooms consist of beds with bare mattresses, old wood wardrobes, and stainless-steel sinks. Light comes from louvered windows and fluorescent bulbs. *69A Mitchell St., 0800, tel. 089/81–3995, fax 089/81–7222. 182 beds in 90 rooms without bath. Facilities: laundry, cooking facilities. AE, MC, V.*

The Arts and Nightlife

Theaters/ The **Performing Arts Centre** (93 Mitchell St., tel. 089/81–1222), next
Concerts door to the Beaufort Hotel, has a large theater that regularly stages concerts, dance, and drama. Check the *Northern Territory News* or the *Sunday Territorian* for current shows, or call the center.

Bars and Lounges	Visit the **Top End Best Western** (Daly and Mitchell Sts., tel. 089/81–6511) and sample the beer brewed on the premises. Other notable night spots include **Big Country Saloon** (21 Cavenagh St., tel. 089/41–1811) and **Squire's Tavern** (3E Edmund St., tel. 089/81–9761).
Casino	**Diamond Beach Hotel Casino** (Gilruth Ave., tel. 089/46–2666) is Darwin's most popular source of evening entertainment.

The Kimberley

The Kimberley is one of Australia's last frontiers. The first European explorers ventured into the heart of the region in 1879, and it remains sparsely populated. Only about 20,000 people live in an area of 350,000 square kilometers (135,000 square miles), filled with desert ranges, cattle stations, rivers, tropical forests, and towering cliffs. Several of the country's most spectacular national parks are here, including Bungle Bungle—a vast area of bizarrely shaped and colored rock formations that became widely known to white Australians only in 1983. Facilities in this remote region are few, but for visitors seeking the genuine bush experience, the Kimberley represents the opportunity of a lifetime.

Arriving and Departing

By Bus	**Greyhound Pioneer** (tel. 089/81–8700) operates bus services between Darwin and Broome.
By Car	The distance from Darwin to Kununurra and the beginning of the Kimberley is 900 kilometers (560 miles). From Darwin to Broome on the far side of the Kimberley is 2,000 kilometers (1,240 miles). The route runs from Darwin to Katherine along the Stuart Highway, and then along the Victoria Highway to Kununurra. The road is paved all the way but quite narrow in parts—especially so, it may seem, when a road train (an extremely long truck) is coming the other way—so drive with care. Fuel and supplies can be bought at the small settlements along the way.
By Plane	**Ansett** (tel. 13–1300) flies from Darwin to Kununurra, Derby, and Broome.

Guided Tours

General Tours	**Amesz Tours** (Box 1060, Midlands, WA 6056, tel. 09/250–2577 or toll-free 008/99–9204, fax 09/250–2634) operates a 12-day bus safari from Broome to Darwin that travels right across the Kimberley and the Top End to Kakadu. Amesz also offers a 12-day tour in a four-wheel-drive bus that covers the region in more detail with a smaller group.
	AAT King's (95 Coonawappa Rd., Winnellie, NT 0820, tel. 089/47–1207) conducts tours throughout the Kimberley.
Aerial Tours	**Belray Diamond Tours** (Box 561, Kununurra 6743, tel. 091/68–1014) offers an interesting air tour from Kununurra to the Argyle Diamond Mine—the world's largest diamond mine, producing about 6½ tons of diamonds a year!

Important Addresses and Numbers

Tourist Information	**Western Australian Tourism Commission** (16 St. Georges Terr., Perth 6000, tel. 09/220–1700, toll free 1800/99–3333, fax 09/220–1702).

Katherine Visitors Information Centre (Lindsay St. and Stuart Hwy., Katherine, tel. 089/72–2650).

Broome Tourist Bureau (Great Northern Hwy., Box 352, Broome 6725, tel. 091/92–2222, fax 091/92–2063).

Derby Tourist Bureau (2 Clarendon St., Derby 6728, tel. 091/91–1426, fax 091/91–1609).

Kununurra Tourist Bureau (Coolibah Dr., Kununurra 6743, tel. 091/68–1177, fax 091/68–2598).

Emergencies   For emergency assistance, go to the casualty section of the local hospitals or call the **Royal Flying Doctor Service** (Derby, tel. 091/91–1211).

Broome District Hospital (Anne St., 091/92–1401).

Derby Regional Hospital (Loch St., tel. 091/93–3333).

Kununurra District Hospital (Coolibah Dr., tel. 091/68–1522).

Exploring the Kimberley

This tour begins in **Kununurra,** 376 kilometers (233 miles) west of Katherine, across the border in Western Australia. With a population of 2,000, the town is the eastern gateway to the Kimberley. Developed in the 1960s for the nearby Lake Argyle and Ord River irrigation scheme, it is a modern planned township with little of inherent interest. Nearby, however, is **Hidden Valley National Park,** which contains good examples of the strange banded sandstone towers and cliffs typical of the Kimberley.

Beyond Kununurra the Victoria Highway intersects with the Great Northern Highway. Turn right to reach **Wyndham,** a small port on Cambridge Gulf about 100 kilometers (62 miles) from Kununurra. This historic town, established in 1886 to service the Halls Creek goldfields, looks as if nothing much has happened there in the century since. The wharf at Wyndham is the best location in the Kimberley for spotting saltwater crocodiles as they bask on the mud flats below.

Drive back south down the Great Northern Highway for about 200 kilometers (124 miles) to the turnoff for **Purnululu National Park** (*see* National Parks, *below*), a bizarre area of red-and-black-striped sandstone domes and towers that ranks among Australia's most beautiful sights. The park is at the end of a very tough 80-kilometer (50-mile) track that is suitable only for four-wheel-drive vehicles.

Continue south to **Old Halls Creek,** the site of the short-lived Kimberley gold rush in 1885. Set on the edge of the Great Sandy Desert, the town has been a crumbling shell since its citizens decided in 1948 to move 14 kilometers (9 miles) away to the site of the present Halls Creek, which offers a better water supply. The old town is a fascinating place to explore, however, and small gold nuggets are still found in the surrounding gullies. Halls Creek is the closest town to the **Wolfe Creek Meteorite Crater,** the world's second largest. The crater is 1 kilometer (½ mile) wide, and its shape has been well preserved in the dry desert air.

The main attraction of Fitzroy Crossing, 291 kilometers (180 miles) beyond Halls Creek, is **Geikie Gorge** (*see* National Parks, *below*), cutting through one of the best preserved fossil coral reefs in the world.

On the back road, between Fitzroy Crossing and the coastal town of Derby, are two other geological oddities. **Tunnel Creek,** 110 kilometers (69 miles) from Fitzroy Crossing, was created when a stream cut an underground course through a fault line in a formation of limestone. You can follow the tunnel's path on foot along the stream for 750 meters (½ mile), with the only natural light coming from those areas where the tunnel roof has collapsed. Flying foxes and other types of bats inhabit the tunnel. **Windjana Gorge,** 145 kilometers (90 miles) from Fitzroy Crossing, boasts cliffs nearly 100 meters (325 feet) high, which were carved out by the flooding of the Lennard River. During the Wet, the Lennard is a roaring torrent, but it dwindles to just a few still pools during the Dry.

With its port, **Derby** has long been the main administrative and economic center of the western Kimberley, as well as a convenient base from which to explore the nearby gorges. The town is famous for its giant boab trees—kin to Africa's baobab trees—which have enormously fat trunks. The hollow trunk of one of these trees was reputedly used as a prison at one time. Known as the Prison Tree, this boab has a circumference of 14 meters (45 feet) and is located 7 kilometers (4 miles) south of town.

Located 216 kilometers (134 miles) southwest of Derby, **Broome** is the holiday capital of the Kimberley. It's the only town in the region with sandy beaches, so it has seen the growth of several resorts, a crocodile farm, and a large, if sparsely populated, zoo. Until the recent tourist boom, Broome had depended on pearling for its livelihood. Early in the century, 300 to 400 sailing boats employing 3,000 men provided most of the world's mother-of-pearl shell. Many of the pearlers were Japanese, Malays, and Filipinos, and the town is still multiracial today. Each August during the famous Shinju Matsuri (Pearl Festival), the town remembers the good old days. All but a few of the traditional old wood luggers have disappeared, and Broome now cultivates most of its pearls at nearby Kuri Bay. The town itself has retained a faint air of its boisterous shantytown days, with wood sidewalks and a charming Chinatown.

Although there are no scheduled boat cruises, there are several boat charter operations in Broome and Derby for single-day or extended fishing expeditions. The myriad empty islands and deserted beaches off the coast, and the 11-meter (35-foot) tides that surge through here creating waterfalls and whirlpools in the narrows, make the Kimberley coast an adventurer's delight. Broome marks the end of the Kimberley. From here it's another 2,213 kilometers (1,372 miles) south to Perth.

Off the Beaten Track

Gibb River Road, the cattle-carrying route through the heart of the Kimberley, provides an alternative to the Great Northern Highway between Wyndham and Kununurra. The unpaved 700-kilometer (434-mile) road runs through a remote area, and the trip should be done only in a four-wheel-drive vehicle and with a great deal of caution.

Should you decide to head this way, consider stopping for some R&R at **El Questro Cattle Station and Wilderness Park,** a working ranch in some of the most rugged country in Australia. Besides providing an opportunity to see outback station life, El Questro has a full complement of such recreational activities as fishing, swimming, and horse, camel, and helicopter rides. On individually tailored walking and four-wheel-drive tours through the bush, guests can bird-watch or see ancient spirit figures depicted in the unique *wandjina* style of Kimberley Aboriginal rock painting—one of the world's most striking forms of religious art. The turnoff for El Questro is 28 kilometers (17 miles) down the Gibb River Road as you head west from Kununurra. Various accommodations are available on the station (*see* Lodging, *below*). *Box 909, Banksia St., Kununurra, WA 6743, tel. 091/69–1777, fax 091/69–1383.*

Shopping

Aboriginal Art Prices for Aboriginal art in the Kimberley are generally well below those in Darwin or Alice Springs. In Broome, **Kimberley Kreations** (Carnarvon St., tel. 091/92–2260) specializes in Kimberley arts and crafts, and **Kreations Gallery** (60 Hammersley St., tel. 091/93–5811) regularly holds exhibitions by local artists, including Aborigines. **Waringarri** (Speargrass Rd., Kununurra, tel. 091/68–2212) has an even larger selection in a more spacious gallery.

Jewelry The number of jewelry stores in Broome is completely out of proportion to the size of the town. **Paspaley Pearling** (2 Short St., Chinatown, tel. 091/92–2203) specializes in high-quality, very expensive pearls and jewelry. The same is true of **Linneys** (Dampier Terr., tel. 091/92–2430), the **Pearl Emporium** (Dampier Terr., tel. 091/92–1531), and **Broome Pearls** (Dampier Terr., tel. 091/92–1295.

Dining

Highly recommended restaurants are indicated by a star ★.

Category	Cost*
$$$$	over $45
$$$	$30–$45
$$	$20–$30
$	under $20

per person, excluding drinks and service

Broome **Club Restaurant.** In keeping with the standards of the Cable Beach Club, where it is located (*see* Lodging, *below*) this restaurant is Broome's premier dining establishment. The sophisticated decor features dark wood beams and plenty of antiques. The menu changes every few days, and the chef prides himself on using no frozen ingredients. If available, try the zucchini stuffed with chicken mousse or the fried prawns with coconut. Other innovative dishes include pigeon with garlic and marsala, and a crayfish salad with a champagne vinaigrette. *Cable Beach Club, Cable Beach Rd., tel. 091/92–2505 or toll-free 800/09–5508, fax 091/92–2249. Reservations required. Dress: casual but neat. AE, DC, MC, V. $$$$*

★ **Weld St. Bistro.** This sparkling bistro at the Continental Hotel gets its brightness from red-and-white slate tiles and tables and its view of palms and the hotel pool through the plate-glass windows. The menu changes daily, but the cuisine is Continental with an emphasis on seafood. *Continental Hotel, Weld St., tel. 091/92–1002. Reservations accepted. Dress: casual. AE, DC, MC, V. $$*

Kununurra **The George Room in Gulliver's Tavern.** Lots of dark jarrah timber gives the George Room an old English atmosphere in keeping with its name. While the tavern alongside offers simple counter meals, the George aims for greater things. Although the food is good, the service can be erratic. The cuisine is Continental, with a strong emphasis on northern Australian specialties: beef and barramundi. Beef à la Ord is locally fattened grilled beef served with fresh mushrooms and onions. The favorite fish dish is barramundi brushed with butter and wine, coated in bread crumbs, and then topped with cheese and grilled. *196 Cottontree Ave., tel. 091/68–1435. Reservations advised. Dress: casual but neat. AE, DC, MC, V. No lunch. Closed Sun. $$$*

★ **Chopsticks Chinese Restaurant.** This restaurant is the most pleasant dining surprise in the Kimberley: Australian country-town Chinese cooking is generally mediocre or worse, but the food here is uniformly excellent. All tables are outdoors, either along the covered veranda or in the courtyard, with pleasant views over gardens illuminated by colored lights. The emphasis is on China's spicier dishes and various Szechuan specialties. Try the honey chili king prawns, or the excellent chili mussels served on a cast-iron frying dish with vegetables. The lightly battered barramundi served with lemon or any of a variety of sauces is memorable. *Country Club Private Hotel, 76 Coolibah Dr., tel. 091/68–1024. Reservations advised. Dress: casual but neat. AE, DC, MC, V. Open daily. $$*

Lodging

Price categories are the same as in the Darwin Lodging section, *above.* Highly recommended hotels are indicated by a star ★.

Broome   **Cable Beach Club.** Located a few minutes out of town opposite the
  ★   broad, beautiful Cable Beach—the only sandy beach near any Kimberley town—this resort is the area's most luxurious accommodation. Built in 1988, the club has 84 bungalows spread through tropical gardens, as well as 174 studio rooms and three suites. The decor is colonial with a hint of Asia, and the extensive resort facilities include two pools and 12 tennis courts. There's also a fine restaurant, the Club Restaurant (*see* Dining, *above*). *Cable Beach Rd. (Box 1544), 6725, tel. 091/92–0400 or toll-free 008/09–5508, fax 091/ 92–2249. 261 rooms with bath, including 3 suites. Facilities: pool, 12 tennis courts, restaurant, laundry. AE, DC, MC, V. $$$$*

Mangrove Hotel. Situated on a rise overlooking Roebuck Bay, this highly regarded hotel has the best location of any accommodation in Broome. All the spacious, pastel-color rooms have private balconies, many of which overlook the bay. The pool is set in a large, palm-shaded area of lawn. *Carnarvon St., Box 84, 6725, tel. 091/ 92–1303 or toll-free 008/09–4818, fax 091/93–5169. 60 rooms with bath, 2 suites. Facilities: pool, restaurant, barbecue. AE, DC, MC, V. $$$*

Gibb River   **El Questro Cattle Station.** Accommodations on the huge station (*also*
Road   *see* Off the Beaten Track, *above*) run the gamut from luxury to barebones: Staying at the Homestead can be very expensive—$540 per person per night, with a two-night minimum—but its location at the top of a cliff face above the Chamberlain River rates as one of the most spectacular in Australia, and the price includes all drinks and food, room service, laundry, most activities, and transportation to and from Kununurra. Nearby are the considerably less expensive Bungalows ($60 per person) and the campground ($7.50 per person), which is a great deal—the 30 secluded sites are right on the river and barbecue and bathroom facilities are available. At the Emma Gorge Resort, which lies in a different section of the station, family cabins sleeping four are available for $136. *Box 909, Banksia St., Kununurra, WA 6743. Homestead/Bungalow/campground tel. 091/*

61–4318, fax 091/61–4360; Emma Gorge Resort tel. and fax 091/61–4388. $–$$$$

Halls Creek **Kimberley Hotel.** If you arrive by aircraft, you'll practically bump
★ into the Kimberley Hotel—it's located right at the end of the run-
way! Fortunately for the hotel's guests, the airstrip is used irregu-
larly and only by light planes, so noise isn't a problem. With its
lawns, airy rooms, and swimming pool, the hotel is something of an
oasis in this dusty town on the edge of the desert. Originally a simple
Outback pub with a few rooms, it was completely renovated in 1987
and is now a surprisingly pleasant place to rest. Staying in one of the
old, cheaper rooms would be a false economy—the newer ones, with
their pine furnishings, tile floors, and peach decor, are among the
best in the region. The high-ceilinged restaurant, which overlooks
the lawns and pool, has an excellent wine list and serves some of the
best meals in town. *Roberta Ave. (Box 244), 6770, tel. 091/68–6101,
fax 091/68–6071. 44 rooms with shower. Facilities: pool, restaurant,
spa, barbecue. AE, DC, MC, V. $$*

Kununurra **Kimberley Court.** Separated from Kununurra's shopping center by a
★ wide park, this small hotel has a relaxed atmosphere that makes it
almost impossible not to meet fellow guests. Every room opens onto
a cool veranda, and the central courtyard is filled with tropical
plants, a pond, and a small aviary. The swimming pool installed in
1993 is a nice place to relax at the end of a hot day. The Kimberley
Court may not be the place for a high-powered holiday, but this hotel
succeeds where the vast majority fail—it feels like a home away
from home. *Erythrina St. (Box 384), 6743, tel. 091/68–1411, fax
091/68–1055. 21 rooms with shower. Tariff includes light breakfast.
Facilities: barbecue, cooking facilities, laundry. MC, V. $$*

Raintree Lodge Youth Hostel. With just six rooms and 26 beds in
each of them, this hostel is neither spacious nor plush. For only $10
per night, however, it offers the cheapest accommodations in the
Kimberley for members of the Australian Youth Hostels Association
or affiliated organizations. Situated within the grounds of the Unit-
ing Church, the hostel is very close to the shops and service facilities
of Kununurra. *Uniting Church, Coolibah Dr. (Box 3), 6743, tel. 091/
68–1372, fax 091/68–1330. 6 rooms without bath. Facilities: kitchen.
No credit cards. $*

Travellers. This outfit provides low-cost, quality accommodations in
shared, twin, or single rooms from $10 per night. Budget-priced sa-
faris also operate out of here—including trips to the Bungle Bungle
Range. *Nutwood Crescent (Box 492), 6743, tel. 091/68–1711, fax
091/68–1253. 46 beds, shared baths. Facilities: pool, kitchen. MC, V.
$*

National Parks

Kakadu National Park

Kakadu National Park is a jewel in the array of Top End parks, and
many visitors come to the Top End just to experience this tropical
wilderness. Located 256 kilometers (159 miles) from Darwin, the
park covers 20,000 square kilometers (7,720 square miles) and pro-
tects a large system of unspoiled rivers and creeks, as well as a rich
Aboriginal heritage that extends back to the earliest days of human-
kind. The park's superb gathering of Aboriginal art may be
Kakadu's highlight.

Two major types of Aboriginal artwork are found here. The Mimi style is the oldest—it is believed to be up to 20,000 years old—and uses red-ochre stick figures to depict hunting scenes and other pictures of Aboriginal life. Aborigines believe that Mimi spirits created these images. The more recent artwork, known as X-ray painting, dates back less than 9,000 years and depicts freshwater animals— especially fish, turtles, and geese—from the newly created floodplains, complete with heart, spinal cord, lungs, and intestines.

Most of the park is owned and managed by Aboriginal communities, and visitor access is restricted to certain areas. The entrance fee is $15 per person; children under 16 are admitted free. Most of the region is virtually inaccessible during the Wet, so it is strongly advisable to visit the park between May and September. As the dry season progresses, water holes (called billabongs) become increasingly important to the more than 280 species of birds that inhabit the park: Huge flocks can be found at Yellow Water, South Alligator River, and Magela Creek.

The **Kakadu National Park Visitors Information Centre** (tel. 089/38–1100) opened mid-1994. State-of-the-art audiovisual displays, as well as more traditional exhibits, offer an introduction to the park's several ecosystems and to its bird population, the world's most diverse. The park's Aboriginal owners contribute to the flora and fauna information and provide some insight into their culture's traditional hunting practices, land management techniques, and use of raw materials. An Aboriginal Cultural Centre is in the planning stages.

From the Park Headquarters, drive 19 kilometers (12 miles) down the Kakadu Highway to the left-hand turnoff to **Nourlangie Rock.** A parking area 12 kilometers (7 miles) down this paved road is accessible year-round. Like the main Kakadu escarpment, Nourlangie Rock is a remnant of an ancient plateau that is slowly eroding away, leaving sheer cliffs rising high above the floodplains. The main attraction here is the **Anbangbang Gallery,** an excellent frieze of Aboriginal rock paintings near the main parking lot.

Ubirr, 44 kilometers (27 miles) north of the Park Headquarters along a paved road, has an even more impressive array of Aboriginal paintings scattered through six shelters in the rock. The main gallery contains a 15-meter (49-foot) frieze of X-ray paintings depicting animals, birds, and fish. A 1-kilometer (½-mile) path around the rock leads to all the galleries.

The best way to gain a true appreciation of the natural beauty of Kakadu is to visit the waterfalls running off the escarpment. Some 39 kilometers (24 miles) south of the Park Headquarters along the Kakadu Highway, a track leads off to the left toward Jim Jim and Twin falls. This unpaved road is suitable only for four-wheel-drive vehicles and is closed in the Wet. Even in good conditions, the 60-kilometer (37-mile) ride to Jim Jim takes about two hours; the Twin Falls car park is 10 kilometers (6 miles) farther on. From the parking area at **Jim Jim Falls,** visitors must walk 1 kilometer (½ mile) over boulders to reach the falls and the plunge pool it has created at the base of the escarpment. On the right-hand side before the main pool is a beautiful sandy beach shelving to a pleasant, shallow swimming area. After May, the water flow over the falls may cease but the pools remain well worth visiting.

Twin Falls is more difficult to reach, but the trip is rewarding. After a short walk from the parking lot, you must swim along a small creek for a few hundred meters to reach the falls—many visitors use inflatable air beds as rafts to float their lunch and towels in. As you approach, the ravine opens up dramatically to reveal a beautiful sandy beach scattered with palm trees, as well as the crystal waters of the falls spilling onto the end of the beach. If you are feeling energetic, swim across the large pool to a track leading up to the top of the falls. On top, the river has worn the rocks smooth, creating fantastic stone sculptures.

The paved section of the Kakadu Highway ends near Yellow Water. In the Dry you can continue down the road to Pine Creek, a worthwhile shortcut if you are heading from Kakadu to Katherine (or vice versa).

Arriving and Departing Access from Darwin is via the Arnhem Highway east to Jabiru. Although four-wheel-drive vehicles are not necessary to travel to the park, they are required for many of the unsealed roads within, including the track to Jim Jim Falls.

Guided Tours
General Tours Park rangers offer free walks and tours at popular locations throughout the Dry. **Billy Can Tours** (Box 4407, Darwin, NT 0801, tel. 089/41–0065 or toll-free 800/81–4702, fax 089/81–7222) provides a range of two- and three-day tours in Kakadu, including special wet-season tours and tours that combine excursions to Kakadu with Litchfield and Nitmiluk (Katherine Gorge) Parks (*see below*).

Wildquest (Box 62, Howard Springs, NT 0835, tel. 089/41–0704 or toll-free 800/89–1190, fax 089/83–1585) offers a similar range of tours, with an emphasis on natural history and photographic four-wheel-drive safaris to Kakadu, Litchfield, and Nitmiluk.

Aerial Tours **Air North Ltd.** (tel. 089/81–7188 or 089/81–7477) operates aerial tours from Darwin, and **Kakadu Air Services** (tel. 089/79–2731, 089/79–2411, or toll-free 008/08–9113) flies out of Jabiru.

Boat Tours The **Gagudju Cooinda Hotel** arranges boat tours of Yellow Water, the major water hole during the Dry, where innumerable birds and crocodiles gather. *Tel. 089/79–0111. Cost: $22.50. Tours daily at 6:45, 9, 4:30.*

Lodging The best of the area's three hotels is the unusual **Gagudju Crocodile Hotel** (Flinders St., Jabiru, tel. 089/79–2800; $$$), which is shaped like a crocodile. The reception is through the mouth, the swimming pool is in the open courtyard in the middle, and the gardener's shed is at the end of the tail. Only 2.5 kilometers (1½ miles) before the Arnhem Highway crosses the South Alligator River is **Frontier Kakadu Village** (tel. 089/79–0166; $$$), a 129-room hotel that has a pool, water slide, spa, barbecue, and laundry. Near Yellow Water is the **Gagudju Cooinda** (tel. 089/79–0145; $$), a 48-room facility with its own pool and barbecue. Campgrounds at Merl, Muirella Park, Mardukal, and Gunlom have toilets, showers, and water. A fee of $7 per tent per night is charged. There are privately operated camping grounds available at Frontier Kakadu Village and the Gagudju Cooinda.

Information For more information, contact the **Darwin Region Tourism Association** (33 The Mall, Darwin, NT 5744, tel. 089/81–4300) or the park itself (Box 71, Jabiru, NT 5796, tel. 089/79–9101).

Litchfield National Park

Litchfield, one of the Northern Territory's newest parks, is also one of the most accessible from Darwin. Convenience hasn't spoiled the park's beauty, however: Almost all of the park's 1,430 square kilometers (515 square miles) are covered by an untouched wilderness of monsoonal rain forests, rivers, and escarpment—cliffs formed by erosion. The highlights of this dramatic landscape are four separate spectacular waterfalls supplied year-round by natural springs from aquifers deep under the plateau.

Lovely trails lead to **Florence, Tjaynera,** and **Wangi Falls,** all of which have secluded plunge pools at their base. **Tolmer Falls** looks out over a natural rock arch and is within a short walk of the parking lot. Near Tolmer Falls—although accessible only by four-wheel-drive vehicles—is a series of large, freestanding sandstone pillars known as the **Lost City.** The living landscape is no less unusual: Look for groves of extremely slow-growing **cycad palms,** an ancient plant species that is unique to the area; some of the larger specimens here are thought to be hundreds of years old.

Magnetic Termite Mounds, which have an eerie resemblance to eroding grave markers, dot the black-soil plains of the northern part of the park. To avoid being crisped by the hot tropical sun, termites have learned to orient their mounds so that they face north–south, leaving only a thin edge exposed to direct light.

Arriving and Departing
Litchfield is an easy 124 kilometers (76 miles) from Darwin. Take the Stuart Highway 86 kilometers (53 miles) south to the turnoff for the town of **Batchelor,** and continue on the Batchelor Road to the park's northern border. Most parts of the park are accessible by conventional vehicles; four-wheel-drive vehicles are advised after the rains and are necessary to enter the park from Adelaide River or Berry Springs.

Guided Tours
Both **Billy Can Tours** and **Wildquest** provide a number of tours to Litchfield (*see* Guided Tours in Kakadu, *above*).

Lodging
If you want to stay in Litchfield, you'll have to camp; sites are available at Florence Falls, Wangi Falls, Buley Rockhole, and Sandy Creek. These **campgrounds** are basic—Buley has no shower facilities and Sandy Creek is accessible only by four-wheel-drive vehicles—but the price can't be beat: You'll never pay more than $5 per person per night. Contact the Conservation Commission (*see below*) for more information. In Batchelor, you'll find a number of caravan parks as well as the moderately priced **Rum Jungle Motor Inn** (220 Rum Jungle Rd., Batchelor NT 0845, tel. 089/76–0123, fax 089/76–0230).

Information
For more information contact the **Conservation Commission of the Northern Territory** (Box 45, Batchelor, NT 0845, tel. 089/76–0282).

Purnululu (Bungle Bungle) National Park

Covering nearly 3,200 square kilometers (1,200 square miles) in the southeast corner of the Kimberley, the great beehivelike domes called the **Bungle Bungles** were "discovered" in 1983, proving that much is still unknown about this incredibly vast continent. The local Kidja Aboriginal tribe knew about these scenic wonders long ago, however, and called the area Purnululu.

The Bungle Bungles' orange silica and black lichen–striped mounds bubble up on the landscape. Climbing is not permitted, because the sandstone encrusted beneath the thin layer of lichen and silica is fragile and would quickly erode without protection. Walking tracks consist of rocky, dry creek beds. One popular walk leads hikers along the **Piccaninny Creek** to **Piccaninny Gorge,** passing through gorges with towering 100-meter (328-foot) cliffs to which slender fan palms cling.

The Bungle Bungles are best seen from April through October and are closed from January through March. The park charges an entrance fee of $11 for adults and $1 for children. Anyone who has the time and a sense of adventure should spend a few days at Purnululu National Park. Facilities are primitive (*see* Lodging, *below*), but the setting and experience are incomparable.

Arriving and The Bungle Bungles are located 300 kilometers (186 miles) south of
Departing Kununurra along the Great Northern Highway. A rough unpaved road, negotiable only in a four-wheel-drive vehicle, leads to the park from the turnoff at Warmum Community. The ride takes about 2½ hours. The ideal way to see the park is to arrive by air. There is an airstrip at Purnululu National Park suitable for light aircraft, but access is restricted by the authorities. Recently several operators have been given permission to fly clients from Kununurra, Broome, and Halls Creek to the airstrip, where they are collected by guides with four-wheel-drive vehicles. The most popular of these fly/drive tours includes one night of camping in the park. The two companies operating these trips are **East Kimberly and Safari Trek Tours** (Box 537, Kununurra, WA 6743, tel. 091/68–2213) and **Halls Creek and Bungle Bungle Tours** (Box 58, Hall Creek, WA 6770, tel. 091/68–6217).

Guided Tours This is the quickest way to take in these amazing formations. **Alliga-**
Aerial Tours **tor Airways** (Box 10, Kununurra, WA 6743, tel. 091/68–1575) operates both fixed-wing float planes from Lake Kununurra and land-based flights from the airstrip. **Slingair Tours** (tel. 091/69–1300) conducts two-hour flights over the Bungle Bungles for $140 for adults, $70 for children under 12. A more expensive alternative is to take a helicopter flight with **Slingsby Helicopters** (tel. 091/68–1811).

Four-Wheel- **East Kimberley and Safari Trek Tours** (*see above*) conducts tours
Drive Tours from Kununurra into the Bungle Bungle massif. Based to the south in Halls Creek, **Halls Creek and Bungle Bungle Tours** (*see above*) also offers a range of tours to the park.

Lodging Camping is permitted only at two designated campgrounds at Purnululu National Park. None of the campsites has facilities—both the Bellbyrn Creek and Walardi campgrounds have simple pit toilets—and fresh drinking water is available only at the Belburn Creek. The nearest accommodations are in Kununurra (*see* The Kimberley, *above*), and most visitors fly in from there.

Information For more information contact the **Department of Conservation and Land Management,** State Government Offices (Box 942, Kununurra, WA 6743, tel. 091/68–0200).

Geikie Gorge National Park

Geikie Gorge is part of a 350-million-year-old reef system formed from fossilized layers of algae—evolutionary precursors of coral reefs—when this area was still part of the Indian Ocean. The limestone walls you see now were cut and shaped by the mighty Fitzroy River. During the Wet, the normally placid river roars through the region, threatening to uproot the red river gums that line its banks. The walls of the gorge are stained red from iron oxide, except where they have been leached to their original white by the floods, which have washed as high as 16 meters (52 feet) from the bottom of the gorge.

When the Indian Ocean receded, it left a number of stranded sea creatures, which managed to adapt to their new conditions. Geikie is one of the few places in the world where freshwater barramundi, mussels, stingrays, and prawns are found. The park is also home to the freshwater archerfish, which can spit water as far as a yard to knock insects out of the air. Aborigines call this place Kangu, meaning "big fishing hole."

Both sides of the gorge are wildlife sanctuaries that are off-limits to visitors, except for a small area on the western bank at the end of a 2-kilometer (1-mile) trail. The only way to see the gorge is aboard one of the two daily boat tours led by park rangers, at 9 and 3. The 1½-hour flat-bottom boat trip costs $12 for adults and $2 for children. The rangers are extremely knowledgeable and helpful in pointing out the vegetation, strange limestone formations, and the many freshwater crocodiles along the way. Tourists get to see only a part of the noisy fruit bat colony—estimated at 600,000—that inhabits the region.

Arriving and Departing From Broome, drive 380 kilometers (236 miles) east along the Great Northern Highway to Fitzroy Crossing, then 16 kilometers (10 miles) north on a paved side road to the park. Since 1989 camping has not been permitted at the gorge, so you must stay in Fitzroy Crossing.

Information For more information contact the **National Park Ranger** (c/o Post Office, Fitzroy Crossing, WA 6765, tel. 091/91–5121).

Nitmiluk (Katherine Gorge) National Park

One of the Territory's most famous parks, Nitmiluk—named after a *cicada* dreaming site at the mouth of the first gorge—is now owned by the local Jawoyn Aboriginal tribe and leased back to the Conservation Commission. Katherine Gorge, the park's European name, is derived from the area's most striking feature: The power of the Katherine River in flood during the Wet has created an enormous system of gorges—13 in all—connected by the river. Rapids separate the gorges, much to the delight of experienced canoeists, and there really is no better way to see the gorges than by boat. Regularly scheduled flat-bottom tour boats take visitors on all-day safaris to the fifth gorge, a trip that requires hiking to circumnavigate each rapid.

For the more adventurous traveler, Katherine Gorge National Park offers some of the best bushwalking trails in the Top End. Ten well-marked walking tracks, ranging from one hour to five days, lead hikers on trails parallel to the Katherine River and north toward Edith Falls at the edge of the park. Some of the longer overnight walks lead past Aboriginal paintings and through swamps, heathlands, and small patches of rain forest. Hikers just out for the day may want to carry rafts with them so they can float downstream back to the campground. Canoes can be rented from **Kookaburra Canoe Hire** (tel. 089/72–3604) at the Gorge boat ramp for about $8 an hour or $25–$45 a day. Fishing is permitted at Katherine, but check with the ranger about license and size requirements. The best time to visit is during the Dry, from May through early November.

Arriving and Departing **Greyhound Pioneer** (tel. 089/81–8700) operates bus services between Darwin and Alice Springs with a stop at Katherine.

Located 343 kilometers (213 miles) southeast of Darwin, the park can be reached by car by traveling south along the Stuart Highway to Katherine and then east on a paved road.

Ansett (tel. 13–1300) takes bookings for weekday flights to Katherine on local commuter airlines.

Guided Tours   **Travel North** (tel. 089/72–1044) offers tours ranging from two hours ($28.50) to nine hours ($63) up the Katherine River aboard a flat-bottom boat. The fit and adventurous may wish to consider the dry-season-only **Manyallaluk Four-Day Trekking Adventure** (tel. 089/75–4727, fax 089/75–4724). Led by Aboriginal guides, this 30-kilometer (19-mile) trek starts from Eva Valley Station, east of the park across the top of the Katherine River escarpment, and travels by boat down the gorge system to the entrance of Nitmiluk National Park.

Lodging   The campground and most other facilities at Katherine Gorge are privately owned. Campsites located near the Katherine River cost $8 a person per night. Bush camping along the river past the second set of rapids is allowed with the ranger's permission.

Information   For more information contact the **Northern Territory Conservation Commission** (Box 344, Katherine 5780, tel. 089/72–1886 or 089/72–1222).

12 Perth and Western Australia

By Lorraine Ironside

Lorraine Ironside is a Perth-based travel writer whose work appears regularly in Western Australia's Sunday Times *and in other Australian publications such as the* Herald-Sun *in* Sydney, *Adelaide's* Advertiser, *the* Sun-Herald *in* Melbourne, *and the national* Weekend Australian.

When the English buccaneer William Dampier landed on the west coast of Australia in 1688, he described its inhabitants as "the miserablest people in the world." Today, such a description is apt to raise smiles from Western Australians, who consider themselves the luckiest people in "the lucky country." Just as Texans tend to draw their character and self-assurance from the immensity of their land, so, too, do Western Australians. Like Texans, they have an outspoken, opinionated style and a sense of identity that occasionally finds expression in secessionist talk. They will also be the first to tell you that Western Australia is four times the size of Texas.

The place is *huge*—it occupies 1 million square miles, fully one-third of the continent. There are sheep stations here that are the size of Kentucky. The population, however, is little more than 1.5 million.

Despite the paucity of citizens, Western Australia and its capital, Perth, display a dynamism that is often lacking elsewhere in Australia. Some of the country's richest entrepreneurs come from Western Australia. Perhaps their grandiose achievements are reflections of an identity rooted in geographic immensity. More likely, it is a dynamism born of self-reliance. Perched on the edge of the continent more than 2,800 kilometers (1,750 miles) from the nearest capital, Perth is one of the most isolated cities in the world. It is too far from Melbourne and Sydney to ride on the coattails of their success. Indeed, Perth is much closer to Indonesia than to any of these places, but in the case of Southeast Asia, cultural distance is just as effective a barrier. Such social isolation would ordinarily doom a community to life as a backwater, and for most of its existence that is what Perth has been. Although the gold rush of the 1890s brought a boom to the city, it did little to change Perth's insularity. The discovery of vast mineral deposits in the 1970s, however, gave Perth an economic and social impetus that shows no sign of diminishing. Today Perth is a young and vibrant town, the destination for a generation of youthful settlers from the eastern states and abroad, lured by the city's economic energy and carefree lifestyle. About half the population is under 24 years of age and a third of it is teenage!

The city is blessed with fantastic beaches, a beautiful river, and a Mediterranean-like climate that averages eight hours of sunshine a day. Within easy reach are lush farmland, vineyards, hillsides covered in wildflowers, and a spectacular coastline. For the 1 million citizens of Perth, life indeed is lucky.

It is to the north and the east that the city must look for its wealth, however, out in the fly-blown desert that constitutes the majority of Western Australia. In the 1890s it was the goldfields verging on the treeless wastes of the Nullarbor Plain; today it is the Pilbara, the richest source of iron ore in the world. Here, huge machines capable of lifting 5 tons at a time gouge 24,000 tons of rock out of the earth each day. The air conditioner is the most precious possession in the Pilbara, where the temperature frequently hits 120°F. The pay is high, but there is little for the employees in the small, company-operated towns to buy. No one thinks twice about driving 1,000 miles round-trip for a long weekend.

For many, work on Western Australia's strip mines or natural gas wells is a necessary hardship that they endure before scuttling back to the easy living in Perth. The basic tenet of Western Australian life remains the same, however: To make money, *you have to dig!*

Note: The Kimberley region in Western Australia's tropical north is closer geographically and in character to the Northern Territory city of Darwin than it is to Perth. For this reason, information about

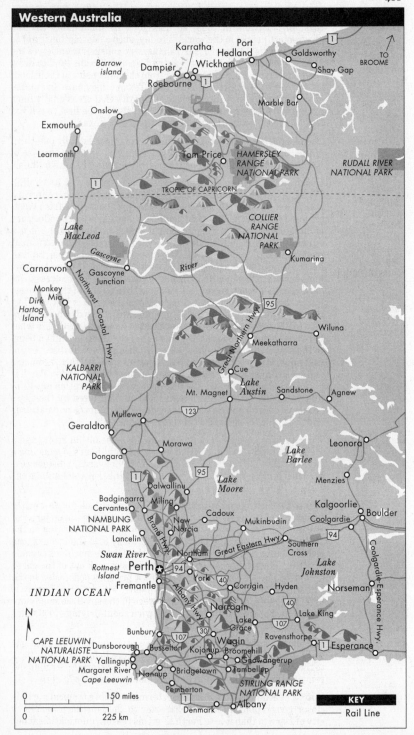

Western Australia

TO BROOME

Barrow Island

Karratha
Port Hedland
Goldsworthy
Shay Gap
Dampier
Wickham
Roebourne

Marble Bar

Onslow

Exmouth

Learmonth

Tom Price
HAMERSLEY RANGE NATIONAL PARK
RUDALL RIVER NATIONAL PARK

TROPIC OF CAPRICORN

Lake MacLeod

COLLIER RANGE NATIONAL PARK

Gascoyne

Carnarvon
Gascoyne Junction
River
Kumarina

Monkey Mia
Dirk Hartog Island

Northwest Coastal Hwy.

Wiluna
Meekatharra
Great Northern Hwy

KALBARRI NATIONAL PARK

Cue
Lake Austin
Mt. Magnet
Sandstone
Agnew

Geraldton
Mullewa
Morawa

Dongara

Lake Barlee

Leonora

Menzies

Dalwallinu

Kalgoorlie
Coolgardie
Boulder

Badgingarra
Cervantes
NAMBUNG NATIONAL PARK
Lancelin

Miling
Lake Moore

New Norcia
Cadoux
Mukinbudin

Swan River
Perth
Rottnest Island
Fremantle

Brand Hwy.

Northam
York

Great Eastern Hwy
Southern Cross

Lake Johnston

Coolgardie-Esperance Hwy.

INDIAN OCEAN

N

Corrigin
Hyden

Norseman

Narrogin

Lake Grace
Lake King

CAPE LEEUWIN NATURALISTE NATIONAL PARK

Bunbury
Dunsborough
Busselton
Yallingup
Margaret River
Cape Leeuwin
Nannup

Kojanup
Wagin
Broomehill
Gnowangerup
Tambellup

Ravensthorpe

Esperance

Bridgetown

Pemberton

STIRLING RANGE NATIONAL PARK

Denmark
Albany

0 _____ 150 miles
0 _____ 225 km

KEY
—— Rail Line

Broome and the Kimberley is included in Chapter 11, Darwin, the Top End, and the Kimberley.

Perth

Orbiting Earth in 1962, John Glenn was surprised to see a beacon of light shining up from the black void of a Western Australian night. That beacon was Perth, whose residents had turned on every light in the city as a greeting, prompting Glenn to dub it the "City of Lights." In many ways Perth remains Australia's city of lights, for just as its citizens reached out to the future then, so do they now. Nowhere else on the continent is there such a sense of energy or optimism about what lies ahead. Buoyed by its mineral wealth and foreign investment, the city is growing by leaps and bounds. New high-rise buildings dot the skyline, and an influx of immigrants has given the city a healthy diversity.

Despite the expansion, Perth has maintained its relaxed pace of living—probably attributable to its sunny climate and its location astride the Swan River, just 16 kilometers (10 miles) from the port of Fremantle. The city's residents live for the water: Half of Perth is always heading for their boats, the old joke goes, while the other half is already on them! And who can blame them? Some of the finest beaches, sailing, and fishing in the world are on the city's doorstep. It's no accident that the 1983 America's Cup was won by a contender from Perth.

For all its modernity, Perth is not a driver's town. Traveling around downtown is easiest on foot. The city's main thoroughfare is St. George's Terrace, an elegant street along which many of Perth's most intriguing sights are located. Perhaps the highlight of the city is King's Park, a 1,000-acre garden atop Mount Eliza affording a panoramic view of Perth.

Arriving and Departing by Plane

Airports and Airlines Located 16 kilometers (10 miles) from the city center, Perth International Airport opened in 1987. It's the international gateway to Australia for visitors from Europe, Africa, and Southeast Asia traveling on **Ansett Australia, Qantas, British Airways, Malaysian Airlines, Thai Airways International, Singapore Airlines, Air New Zealand,** and **Japan Airlines,** among others.

Perth's former international airport now serves as the domestic terminal. Situated 11 kilometers (7 miles) from the city, it is served by **Ansett Australia** and **Qantas. Ansett WA** and **Skywest** connect Perth with other towns within the state.

Taxis between the airports and the city cost approximately $25. Shuttle buses offer regular service to the major hotels and city center and cost approximately $7.

Arriving and Departing by Train, Bus, and Car

By Train Crossing the Nullarbor Desert from the eastern states on **Westrail** (East Perth Terminal, West Parade, tel. 09/326–2244) is one of the great rail journeys of the world. The *Indian Pacific* makes three-day runs from Sydney on Monday, Thursday, and Saturday; and the *Trans-Australia* makes two-day runs from Adelaide on Wednesday and Saturday.

By Bus **Greyhound Pioneer Australia** (Upper Level, Bus Station, Wellington St., tel. 09/481–7066) travels to Perth from capital cities around the country.

By Car The Eyre Highway crosses the continent from Port Augusta in South Australia to Western Australia's transportation gateway, Norseman. From there, take the Coolgardie–Esperance Highway north to Coolgardie, and the Great Eastern Highway on to Perth. Driving to Perth—2,560 kilometers (1,600 miles) from Adelaide and 4,000 kilometers (2,500 miles) from Sydney—is an arduous journey, which should be undertaken only with a car in top condition. Carrying a supply of spares and drinking water is essential. Service stations and motels are situated at regular intervals along the route.

Getting Around

By Taxi Cab fare between 6 AM and 6 PM weekdays is an initial $2.10 plus 83¢ every kilometer. From 6 PM to 6 AM the rate rises to $3.10 plus 83¢ per kilometer. Try **Swan Taxis** (tel. 09/444–4444) or **Black and White** (tel. 09/333–3333).

By Bus The Perth central business district and suburban areas are well connected by the **Transperth** bus line (tel. 13–2213). Tickets are valid for two hours and can be used on Transperth trains and ferries. The main terminal is at the Perth Central Bus Station on Mounts Bay Road, and buses run daily between 6 AM and 11:30 PM, with reduced service on weekends and holidays. Rides within the city center are free. Free **City Clipper** buses circle the city center, running approximately every 10 minutes on weekdays from 7 AM to 6 PM, Saturday 9 AM to 11:30 AM. Routes and timetables are available from Transperth.

By Train **Fastrack** trains operate from Perth to Fremantle, Midland, Armadale, Joondalup, and stations en route weekdays from 5:40 AM to 11:30 PM, with reduced service on weekends and public holidays. Suburban and Bunbury trains depart from the city station on Wellington Street.

By Ferry **Transperth** ferries make daily runs from 6:45 AM to 7:15 PM between Barrack Street Jetty in Perth to Mends Street, across the Swan River in South Perth.

By Car All major rental car companies, including **Hertz** (tel. 09/321–7777) and **Avis** (tel. 09/325–7677), have depots at both the international and domestic airports.

By Bicycle Perth's climate and its network of excellent trails make cycling a safe and enjoyable way to discover this city. Bicycles can be hired for about $15 a day from **About Bike Hire** on the western side of the causeway (tel. 09/221–2665). Free brochures detailing a wide variety of trails, including stops at historical spots, are available from the **Ministry for Sport and Recreation** (tel. 09/387–9700).

Important Addresses and Numbers

Tourist Information **Western Australian Tourist Centre.** *Cnr. Forrest Pl. and Wellington St., tel. 09/483–1111. Open weekdays 8:30–5:30, Sat. 9–1.*

Emergencies Dial 000 for **police, fire,** or **ambulance** emergency assistance. Otherwise, dial 09/222–1111 for police.

Hospital The emergency rooms are open all night at the **Royal Perth Hospital** (Wellington St., tel. 09/224–2244) and **Sir Charles Gairdner Hospital** (Verdun St., Nedlands, tel. 09/398–3333).

Dental   The **Perth Dental Hospital** (196 Goderich St., tel. 09/220–5777) runs an emergency service daily from 2 to 5.

Guided Tours

Orientation Tours   **Australian Pacific** (tel. 09/221–4000), **Great Western Tours** (tel. 09/421–1411), and **Feature Tours** (tel. 09/479–4131) run day tours of Perth and its major attractions. Most include visits to major sights outside the city as well, including Atlantis Marine Park and Underwater World in Fremantle, and the best beaches.

Special-Interest Tours
Flowers   Springtime in Western Australia (August–November) is synonymous with wildflowers, as 8,000 species blanket an area that stretches 644 kilometers (400 miles) north and 403 kilometers (250 miles) south of Perth. Tours of these areas are popular, and early reservations are essential with **Westrail** (tel. 09/326–2159), **Feature Tours** (*see above*) or **Great Western Tours** (*see above*).

Whale Watching   From late October to late November, **Boat Torque** (tel. 09/221–5844) conducts whale-watching tours off the coast following the migratory route of humpback whales.

Wine   **Boat Torque** (*see above*) runs regular river tours to some of the best-known Swan Valley wineries.

Walking Tours   **Guntrip's Walking Tours** (tel. 09/293–1132) offers a two-hour historical walking tour of the city daily from 5 PM to 7 PM.

King's Park (tel. 09/321–4801) is the heart of Perth's bushland, and a walking tour through the area provides an excellent orientation for visitors. Free walking tours are available from April through October.

Boat Tours   **Captain Cook Cruises** (tel. 09/325–3341) offers five different cruises on the Swan River from Perth to the Indian Ocean at Fremantle.

Exploring Perth

Numbers in the margin correspond to points of interest on the Perth map.

Home to almost a million people, Perth is a surprisingly compact city best explored on foot. Though the city was carefully planned and its streets follow a grid system, Perth has managed to avoid the sterile orderliness of Canberra. Its public buildings, however, are not nearly as grand as those in Melbourne, which is not surprising considering that Perth was a poor country cousin until the gold rush at the turn of the century and the more recent minerals boom of the 1970s. Today it's a pleasant, easily negotiated blend of old and new. Begin your tour in the major downtown area, on the north bank of the Swan River.

Perth's major business thoroughfare is **St. George's Terrace;** the city center is located along this street as well as on parallel Hay and Murray streets to the north. Our tour will begin on Forrest Place at the
❶ **Post Office,** a handsome, colonnaded sandstone building facing
❷ **Citiplace,** a newish pedestrian mall. This square has rapidly become the stage for a wide variety of street theater and free outdoor jazz concerts.

❸ Head east along Murray Street, passing the new **Forrest Chase Shopping Plaza.** Near the corner at Irwin Street, three blocks away,
❹ is the **Old Fire Station,** one of Perth's fine limestone buildings. No longer operational, it houses a museum featuring a photographic

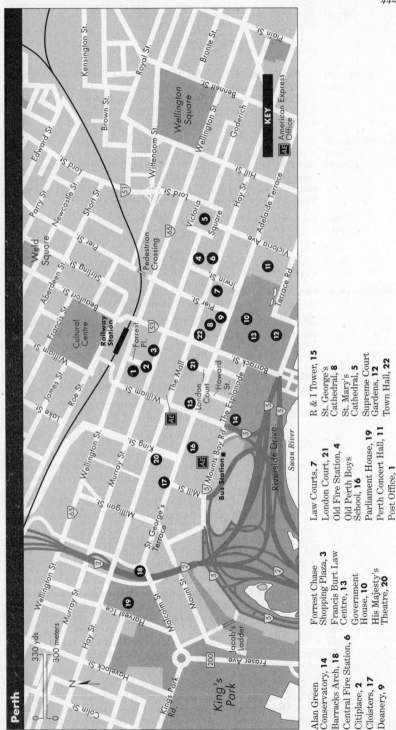

Perth

330 yds
300 meters

Alan Green
Conservatory, 14
Barracks Arch, 18
Central Fire Station, 6
Cittiplace, 2
Cloisters, 17
Deanery, 9

Forrest Chase
Shopping Plaza, 3
Francis Burt Law
Centre, 13
Government
House, 10
His Majesty's
Theatre, 20

Law Courts, 7
London Court, 21
Old Fire Station, 4
Old Perth Boys
School, 16
Parliament House, 19
Perth Concert Hall, 11
Post Office, 1

R & I Tower, 15
St. George's
Cathedral, 8
St. Mary's
Cathedral, 5
Supreme Court
Gardens, 12
Town Hall, 22

display documenting the history of the fire brigade from its beginnings, when it used horses and carts, to the present day, as well as a splendid display of old vehicles and equipment. *Murray and Irwin Sts., tel. 09/323–9300. Admission free. Open weekdays 10–4.*

Continue east on Murray Street to Victoria Square, one of Perth's most appealing plazas, which is dominated by **St. Mary's Cathedral.** Turn right onto Victoria Avenue for a block, then right again on Hay Street, passing two of Perth's newer buildings—the **Central Fire Station** (480 Hay St.) on your right and the **Law Courts** (30 St. George's Terr.), on your left. Turn left on Pier Street and head toward St. George's Terrace. On the corner, adjacent to **St. George's Cathedral,** is the **Deanery.** Built in the late 1850s as a residence for the first dean of Perth, the Deanery is one of the few remaining houses in Western Australia from this period, and is now used as offices for the Anglican Church.

Across St. George's Terrace is **Government House.** Built between 1859 and 1864, this is the official residence of the governor and home to members of the royal family during visits to Perth. It was constructed in a Gothic Revival style, with arches and turrets reminiscent of the Tower of London. Continue east on St. George's Terrace to the **Perth Concert Hall** and cut through its forecourt to Terrace Road. Head west to the **Supreme Court Gardens,** a favorite lunch spot for hundreds of office workers and home of some of the finest Moreton Bay fig trees in the state.

In the rear of the gardens is a band shell used for summer concerts, and at the western end is the charming Georgian **Francis Burt Law Centre.** Dating from 1836, the former Court House is the oldest public building in the city. It now houses the WA Law Museum and features an audiovisual presentation and memorabilia. *Supreme Court Gardens, tel. 09/325–4787. Admission free. Open Tues. and Thurs. 10–2.*

Continue west to the pyramid-shape **Alan Green Conservatory.** Dominating the neat Esplanade lawns, the conservatory houses a wide variety of rare and remarkable exotic plants in the carefully controlled environment of a glass pyramid. *William St. and the Esplanade, tel. 09/265–3153. Admission free. Open Mon.–Sat. 10–4, Sun. and holidays noon–4.*

Return to Howard Street and turn left onto St. George's Terrace, where you can stroll by many of Perth's most impressive new office buildings, including the notable **R & I Tower** (108 St. George's Terr.) on the corner of William Street. Built in 1988 as a joint venture between one of the state's largest banks and former millionaire Alan Bond, the R & I Tower wraps around the historic old Palace Hotel, now used as bank offices. The hotel has been faithfully restored and is a fine example of the ornate architecture that once dominated the city.

Continue along St. George's Terrace to King Street. Here you will see the **Old Perth Boys School,** built with convict labor in 1854 in Gothic style. It is now used as the gift shop for the National Trust in Western Australia. *139 St. George's Terr., tel. 09/321–2754. Open weekdays 9–5.*

As you continue along the terrace, you will pass the **Cloisters** (200 St. George's Terr.) on your right, an attractive brick building erected in 1858 to serve as the city's first boys' high school. At the top of the terrace is the city's oddest architectural curiosity, the **Barracks Arch,** which stands in front of **Parliament House.** This brick monument is all that remains of the headquarters of the Pensioner Forces, which was demolished in 1966. The Tudor-style edifice, built in the 1860s in Flemish bond brickwork, stands as a memorial to the state's earliest settlers.

Turn back toward the city center and make a left onto Milligan Street. Go right on Hay Street and continue east. At the corner of King Street is the opulent Edwardian exterior of **His Majesty's Theatre.** It is among Perth's most gracious buildings, and restoration has transformed it into a handsome home for the Western Australian Opera and Ballet companies. *825 Hay St., tel. 09/322–2929. Admission free. Open weekdays 10–4. Guides are available for conducted tours at any time.*

Continue to the Hay Street Mall, one of many city streets closed to traffic, where you will find **London Court,** an arcade running north to south between Hay Street and St. George's Terrace. Its mock-Tudor facade is considered less than attractive by most Western Australians, or "Sandgropers," as they are known, but it is a popular spot for photographers. Built in 1937 by gold-mining entrepreneur Claude de Bernales, it includes statues of Sir Walter Raleigh and Dick Whittington, the legendary lord mayor of London. Costumed mechanical medieval knights joust with one another when the clock strikes the quarter hour.

Continue along the Hay Street Mall to the **Town Hall** at the corner of Barrack Street. The hall was built in the style of an English Jacobean market by convicts.

Perth for Free

The **Museum of Western Australia** houses a splendid Natural History section, plus a comprehensive one on the history of the state and a vintage car display. Within the complex is the Old Gaol, built in 1856 and a fine example of colonial architecture. It served as Perth's prison until 1888 and was the site of numerous executions. *Beaufort St., tel. 09/328–4411. Open weekdays 10:30–5, weekends 1–5.*

The **Art Gallery of Western Australia** is part of the impressive **Perth Cultural Centre.** It displays works from around the world. *James St., tel. 09/328–7233. Open daily 10–5.*

Francis Burt Law Centre (*see* Exploring Perth, *above*).

Old Mill. Perth's first flour mill has been restored and contains relics of pioneer days. *Mill Point Rd., South Perth, no phone. Open Sun., Mon., Wed., Thurs. 1–5; Sat. 1–4.*

His Majesty's Theatre (*see* Exploring Perth, *above*).

Museum of Western Australia Sport houses an extensive historical collection of sporting memorabilia. *Superdrome, Stephenson Ave., Mt. Claremont, tel. 09/387–8542. Open daily 8–8.*

What to See and Do with Children

Adventureworld features a variety of entertainment for children including rides, native animals, and 50 acres of waterways and gardens. *179 Progress Dr., Bibra Lake, tel. 09/417–9666. Admission: $19.50 adults, $16 children. Open Oct.–Apr., daily 10–5.*

The **Museum of Childhood,** recognized internationally as a pioneer in the conservation of childhood heritage in Australia, is an enchanting hands-on journey for both children and their parents.

Among its most prized exhibits is an original alphabet manuscript written, illustrated, and bound by William Makepeace Thackeray in 1833. *Edith Cowan University Campus, Bay Rd., Claremont, tel. 09/383–0373. Admission: $2.50 adults, $1 children. Open weekdays 10–3, Sun. 2–5; closed Sat.*

It's a Small World is a wonderland for children and their parents, a museum of toys and miniatures from around the world, including doll's houses, train stations, and a formula 1 racing car just 2 meters (6½ feet) long. *12 Parliament Pl., Perth., tel. 09/322–2020. Admission: $5 adults, $3 children. Open Sun.–Fri. 10–5, Sat. 2–5.*

Underwater World takes visitors on a moving walkway through a submerged acrylic tunnel to view some 5,000 varieties of underwater life. *Hillary's Boat Harbour, West Coast Hwy., tel. 09/447–7500. Admission: $13.50 adults, $6.50 children. Open daily 9–5.*

Scitech Discovery Centre is a hands-on display of science and technology that entertains children of all ages while they learn. *City West, W. Perth, tel. 09/481–6295. Admission: $10 adults, $7 children. Open daily 10–5.*

Cohunu Wildlife Park gives visitors the chance to cuddle live koalas in daily sessions between 11 and 4. While there, also take time to view other native animals in their natural surroundings, ride a miniature railway, and wander through the largest aviary in the Southern Hemisphere. *Mills Rd., Gosnells, tel. 09/390–6090. Admission: $9 adults, $4.50 children. Open daily 10–5.*

Whiteman Park is an enormous recreation area providing barbecue facilities and picnic spots, cycle trails, vintage trains and electric trams, and historic wagons and tractors. The Arts and Crafts section of the park gives visitors the opportunity to see potters, blacksmiths, leatherworkers, toymakers, printers, and stained-glass artists at work. Natural wildlife includes kangaroos. *Lord St., Whiteman Park, 6056, tel. 09/249–2446. Admission: $3 per car. Open daily 9–6.*

Shopping

Most centrally located stores are open Monday–Saturday 8:30–5:30. **Citiplace,** flanked by the Post Office and the new **Forrest Chase** shopping complex, is the largest mall area. The major department stores, **Myer** (tel. 09/221–3444) and **Aherns** (tel. 09/323–0101), both open onto the Murray Street pedestrian mall.

Gems   Broome, in the far north of the state, has been regarded as the pearl capital of the world for decades. **Linneys** (37 Rokeby Rd., Subiaco, tel. 09/382–4077) has an excellent selection of Broome pearls and will set them in the design of your choice. Opals from South Australia's Coober Pedy are available at the **Opal Centre** (47 London Court, tel. 09/325–2486), and the famous pink diamonds from the Argyle diamond mines are incorporated in stunning pieces by **Charles Edward Jewellers** (Hay St. Mall, tel. 09/321–5111).

Souvenirs   Australian souvenirs and knickknacks are on sale at small shops throughout the city, although the most comprehensive range is to be found at **Purely Australian** (tel. 09/325–4328) in London Court, Hay Street Mall, and City Arcade. Authentic Aboriginal artifacts can be purchased from **Creative Native** (32 King St., tel. 09/322–3398). **Carillon Arcade** (Hay Street Mall), in the center of the city, offers two distinctively Australian stores, **Australia Presents** (tel. 09/321–6620), which features small characters and crafts made from gum nuts, among other souvenirs, and **R. M. Williams** (tel. 09/321–7786), which offers everything for the Australian sheepman, including moleskin trousers, hand-tooled leather boots, and Akubra hats. The **Contempo Gallery** (329 Murray St., tel. 09/322–2306) has a collection of bowls, goblets, and lamps crafted from Western Australia's native jarrah and blackboy wood. Out of town, in Subiaco, a former car dealer's workshop has been transformed into an Outback setting, which provides a backdrop for **Indigenart** (115 Hay St., Subiaco, tel. 09/381–1705), an art gallery cum Aboriginal cultural center, where visitors can view artworks and talk with the works' Aboriginal creators. Contemporary and traditional works are complemented by jewelry, fabrics, and clothing. It's a unique journey into the Aboriginal Dreamtime.

Participant Sports

Beaches
Perth's beaches are among its greatest attractions, and visitors should plan to make an excursion to the seaside during their stay. There are plenty of beaches from which to choose. Working north from Fremantle, **Leighton** is for wave jumpers and windsurfers; **Cottesloe** for young matrons and well-heeled stock exchange executives; **North Cottesloe** for dogs and topless bathers, and **Swanbourne** for those wearing even less. The teenage crowd favors **Scarborough**, while **City Beach**, just 11 kilometers (7 miles) outside Perth, is more sedate. **Trigg** is home to the surfboard crowd.

Bicycling
The vast network of trails in and around the city, particularly in King's Park, makes cycling a pleasure in Perth. Details on trails and free brochures are available from the **Ministry of Sport and Recreation** (tel. 09/387–9700).

Golf
Perth is home to numerous public golf courses, each offering clubs for hire. The 18-hole course at **Burswood Resort** (Great Eastern Hwy., Victoria Park, tel. 09/362–7576) is closest to the city. Call the **Western Australia Golf Association** (tel. 09/474–1005) for further details. **Golf Escort** (tel. 09/450–2046) is a unique service for golfers who wish to play on Perth's most exclusive courses, most of which are not normally open to the public. It includes limousine service, quality clubs, a motorized buggy, greens fees, and of course a golfing partner.

Jogging and Health Clubs
A number of jogging tracks lead along the Swan River and through King's Park, while health clubs with spas, saunas, and exercise equipment are available to guests at most luxury hotels.

Lords Health Club (588 Hay St., Subiaco, tel. 09/381–4777) features fitness equipment, aerobics, a heated indoor pool, sauna, spa, and indoor tennis and squash courts. *Admission: $10. Open weekdays 6 AM–9 PM, weekends 8–4.*

At **Lifesport** (Superdrome, Stephenson Ave., Mt. Claremont, tel. 09/387–2699) the fitness center is medically supervised, with aerobics, three Olympic-size heated pools, and an in-house physiotherapist, a dietician, and an exercise physiologist. *Admission: $8. Open Mon.–Wed. 6 AM–9 PM; Thurs., Fri. 6 AM–8 PM; Sat. and public holidays 8–4; Sun. 9–1.*

Swimming
Western Australia prides itself on beaches rivaling any in the world, but swimmers who prefer freshwater should try the pool at the **Superdrome** (Stephenson Ave., Mt. Claremont, tel. 09/441–8222).

Tennis
Tennis West (tel. 09/472–1195) can provide details on the variety of tennis courts available throughout the metropolitan area.

Water Sports Parasailing is available on the South Perth foreshore every weekend, weather and winds permitting. Rent through **Flying High Parasailing** (Narrows Bridge, tel. 09/446–1835). Those who want to enjoy the Swan River at a more leisurely pace can opt to hire a catamaran or a sailboard from **Mainsail Surfcat Hire** at the **Coode Street jetty.** *S. Perth, tel. 018/927–971. Open daily 9–7:30. Advance reservations essential on weekends.*

Spectator Sports

Australian-Rules Football This unique blend of soccer and Gaelic football is played every Saturday afternoon throughout the winter (March–September) at various locations around the metropolitan area. For details, contact the **Western Australia Football Commission (Inc.)** (tel. 09/ 381–5599).

Cricket The national game is played professionally during the summer at the **Western Australia Cricket Association** (WACA) grounds in Nelson Crescent, East Perth. For further information, contact the WACA (tel. 09/325–9800).

Dining

By Peter Forrestal

In addition to being the wine columnist of the West Australian, *Peter Forrestal is a freelance food and wine writer who contributes to magazines such as* Australian Gourmet Traveller.

Perth now claims more than 1,000 restaurants, but what's remarkable is the quality, not quantity, of the city's establishments. Dine al fresco at any of the booming new cafés and brasseries that emphasize simple but clever food and you'll experience more than the lovely weather: A culinary shake-up is going on, and several of Perth's chefs, including Gary Jones of San Lorenzo, Chris Taylor of Fraser's, and Marg Johnson, a food consultant to several local brasseries, are leading the way.

Although Perth's culinary history has long been shaped by such external influences as postwar European immigration and the more recent influx of Asian migrants, many believe that an indigenous West Coast cuisine is beginning to develop. Like much of the innovative cooking in Australia, this style fuses Asian, European, and native Australian herbs and spices with French technique to bring out the best in what is grown locally. In Western Australia's case, that means some of the country's finest seafood, as well as beef, lamb, and kangaroo.

Reservations are strongly recommended for Thursday, Friday, and Saturday nights, especially during the summer holidays (December–February). Lunch is usually served from noon to 3 and dinner from 7 to 10, though some establishments stay open until about midnight. Many restaurants in Perth are closed on either Sunday or Monday.

Highly recommended restaurants are indicated by a star ★ .

Category	Cost*
$$$$	over $60
$$$	$45–$60
$$	$25–$45
$	under $25

per person, excluding drinks and service

Asian **Choi's Inn.** Northbridge, Perth's restaurant district north of the
$$ railway line, is the home of one of the best Chinese spots in town.

448

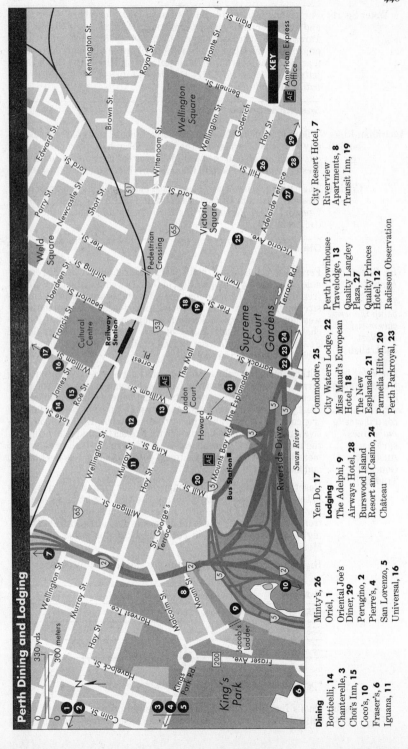

Perth Dining and Lodging

Dining
Botticelli, **14**
Chanterelle, **3**
Choi's Inn, **15**
Coco's, **10**
Fraser's, **6**
Iguana, **11**

Minty's, **26**
Oriel, **1**
Oriental Joe's
Diner, **29**
Perugino, **2**
Pierre's, **4**
San Lorenzo, **5**
Universal, **16**

Yen Do, **17**

Lodging
The Adelphi, **9**
Airways Hotel, **28**
Burswood Island
Resort and Casino, **24**
Château

Commodore, **25**
City Waters Lodge, **22**
Miss Maud's European
Hotel, **18**
The New
Esplanade, **21**
Parmelia Hilton, **20**
Perth Parkroyal, **23**

Perth Townhouse
Travelodge, **13**
Quality Langley
Plaza, **27**
Quality Princes
Hotel, **12**
Radisson Observation

City Resort Hotel, **7**
Riverview
Apartments, **8**
Transit Inn, **19**

KEY

AE American Express
Office

Large, airy dining rooms, decorated in a traditional style, create the backdrop for part-owner and chef Choi Wing Yuen's authentic Cantonese and hot Szechuan dishes. The house specialties are an excellent, three-course Peking duck and the very popular beggar's chicken; the restaurant requests that both of these dishes be ordered in advance, but they are almost always available on the spot. Service is friendly and accommodating; if you're not sure what to order or would like a special dish prepared, consult the manager, Soo Yong Lim. *68 Roe St., Chinatown, tel. 09/328–6350. Reservations advised. Dress: casual. AE, DC, MC, V. BYOB.*

$ Oriental Joe's Diner. There's a rather Disneyesque concept behind this classy, street-level eatery in the Hyatt Regency: An American merchant loses a fortune traveling the Orient before using his experience to establish a noodle house in Shanghai. The result is tasty Asian food at very reasonable prices. Wood, natural brick, terracotta, and teak antiques are used to reinforce the theme, and Thai, Indonesian, Malaysian, and Singaporean dishes are whipped up in the display kitchen. The filling soups are complemented by a delicious range of noodle dishes such as *kway teow* (noodles with bean sprouts, prawn, and chicken), or the *laksa* (rice noodles in a rich, spicy, coconut-milk soup with chicken, bean curd, and prawns). Also try the Thai green chicken curry and *nasi goreng* (Indonesian fried rice) with chicken and beef satay. *99 Adelaide Terr., tel. 09/225–1268. Weekend reservations advised. Dress: casual but neat. AE, DC, MC, V. No lunch Sat.; closed Sun.*

$ Yen Do. Although this popular restaurant specializes in Chinese cooking, it also serves Vietnamese, Indian, and Malaysian food. Situated on the outskirts of Northbridge, the Yen Do consists of a single large room with an open kitchen area in back. Although the decor is basic and the laminated tables are packed close together, there's plenty of natural light from the large, shopfront windows, everything is spotlessly clean, and the service is quick and efficient. Most important, the food is consistently good and cheap. In addition to daily specials, there are Chinese noodle dishes; half a dozen soups; appetizers such as spring rolls, satay, curry puffs, and samosas; and specialties such as mussels, Mongolian chicken, and, for lunch, curry laksa. *416 William St., Northbridge, tel. 09/227–8833. Weekend reservations required. Dress: casual. AE, DC, MC, V. BYOB.*

Australian
$$$
★
San Lorenzo. The success of this elegant restaurant near the Swan River can easily be attributed to the talent of chef and part-owner Gary Jones. Never-ending experimentation, a commitment to excellent local ingredients, and control of classical technique make Jones's cooking the most exciting in town. The restaurant, a 15-minute cab ride from the city, resembles a Mediterranean courtyard: stone paving, limestone walls, a sprawling grapevine that glows with tiny lights at night, and a wall fountain complete with pet eel create the mood. The menu hints at Jones's Yorkshire heritage—his signature dish is pork fricassee, with black pudding and mashed potatoes—but he's no slouch at contemporary combinations. Witness his twice-cooked Kervella goat's cheese soufflé or his great Moroccan fried chicken with couscous, spicy tomato sauce, eggplant tahini, chickpea chips, chorizo sausage, and preserved lemon. To top it all off, the service is always excellent and there is a very good wine list. *23 Victoria Ave., Claremont, tel. 09/384–0870. Weekend reservations required. Jacket suggested. AE, DC, MC, V. Licensed and BYOB premium wines. No lunch Sat.; closed Sun.–Mon.*

$$ Coco's. A great location on the river in South Perth, a trendy crowd, and fine food have made this one of the city's most popular upmarket restaurants. No one seems to mind that the comfortable furniture is crowded too close together or that the restaurant is often packed and noisy. After all, the floor-to-ceiling windows show off fabulous views of Perth Water and the city skyline, the food is consistently well-prepared, and the service is speedy and efficient. There are 15 items on the à la carte menu—many of which are available in either appetizer or main-course portions—as well as daily seafood, beef, and dessert specials. The beef, which is aged in the restaurant's own cool room, has a formidable reputation: Try the chargrilled Waroona rib eye with steamed new potatoes and a Madeira and mushroom *jus*. The seafood dishes are always fresh and simply yet imaginatively presented; dhufish, a local specialty, is particularly good. *Southshore Centre, 85 The Esplanade, South Perth, tel. 09/474–3030. Reservations required. Jacket advised. AE, DC, MC, V. Sun. breakfast 9–11.*

$$ **Fraser's.** This elegant, bilevel restaurant is another room with a view. Delicious meals come with vistas of the city and Swan River. When the weather is good—most of the time in Perth—the large outdoor area fills with happy diners. Under the direction of Chris Taylor, both an owner and the head chef, the food is super fresh, imaginatively presented, and full of flavor. The menu changes daily and heavily emphasizes local seafood. Recent standouts include red emperor chargrilled or panfried with lemon butter sauce, coral trout fillet with penne and a field-mushroom cream, and breast of chicken flavored with *harissa* (a spicy North African herb and pimento paste) and accompanied by chickpea puree, yogurt, cucumber, and mint salsa. *Fraser Ave. King's Park, tel. 09/481–7100. Reservations required. Dress: casual but neat. AE, DC, MC, V.*

Brasseries and Cafés
$$
Iguana. Near the center of Perth's business district is one of the best brasseries in town. The decor is modern, with bright primary colors, bold furnishings, and black iron balustrades; during the day, natural light floods the restaurant and sparkles off the two waterfalls that grace one wall. Movement through Iguana's four sections—a casual sit-down area with an à la carte menu, a self-service deli for the lunchtime trade, a mezzanine bar, and a liquor store—keeps the atmosphere bustling without being intrusive. A daily hot dish, focaccia, rolls, open sandwiches, salad platters, and quiche are available at the deli; the à la carte offerings change regularly and are often Asian influenced. Chargrilled scallops served with a mild Indian curry sauce, a gateau of *dahl* (lentil soup) and *poori* (puffed fried bread), and chicken breast teriyaki are all worth a try, as are more familiar pasta dishes and pizzas baked in a wood-fired oven. *Shafto La., 397 Murray St., 09/321–3258. Reservations advised. Dress: casual. AE, DC, MC, V. Closed Sun.; no dinner Mon.–Tues.*

$$ **Oriel.** Ten minutes from the city center lies the quintessential Perth brasserie: Both the dimly lit interior and the outdoor areas are crowded with tables and overflow with people and noise for most of the 24 hours the restaurant is open (breakfast is served 2 AM–11:30 AM). The food is uncomplicated, but imaginative and tasty; try the carpaccio of ocean trout with crunchy Chinese pastry, virgin olive oil, and roasted peppers, or the Provençal lamb burger with eggplant, tomato, greens, bacon, chargrilled onions, and béarnaise sauce. The coffee is always superb, as is the range of cakes, and the impressive wine list offers more than 20 wines by the glass. *483 Hay St., Subiaco, tel. 09/382–1886. No reservations. Dress: casual. AE, MC, V.*

$$ **Universal.** Renovations to Northbridge's best café have softened the decor, adding warmth and intimacy to the dining room while placing more emphasis on the bar area. You can expect regular changes in

the globally influenced menu, too, although chargrilled duck confit, fillet steak with béarnaise sauce, a Thai green curry, and Caesar salad are perennial favorites. A risotto, some pasta dishes, a fish of the day, and an antipasto bar plate also make frequent appearances. Good coffee, tasty cakes, and an extensive wine list—which always includes some rare bottles and about 20 reasonably priced wines by the glass—round out the offerings. *221 William St., Northbridge, tel. 09/227-6771. Reservations advised. Dress: casual but neat. AE, MC, V.*

French **Pierre's.** Owners Emily and Jean-Daniel Ichallalene have turned a
$$$ beautifully restored colonial mansion into Perth's grandest restaurant. The service is impeccable, the decor is opulent, the furniture is elegant, the lighting is soft, and even the tableware is of the highest quality. Chef Gweneal Lesle uses both imported luxuries—snails, foie gras, and Iranian caviar—and prime local produce like marron (a freshwater crustacean), pigeon, lamb, and venison in his rich renditions of traditional French dishes. Try the medallions of marron wrapped in lettuce and served on a shiraz wine-and-crustacean sauce or the boned roast pigeon with lentils, chorizo tart, and date puree. Lesle's bread and butter pudding is a subtle rendition of the homey original. Not surprisingly, the wine list is outstanding. *8 Outram St., West Perth, tel. 09/322-7648. Reservations required. Jacket required at dinner. AE, DC, MC, V. No lunch weekends.*

$$ **Chanterelle.** A Scottish couple, the Peastons, serve high-quality food without pretension at this popular BYOB restaurant in Subiaco, 10 minutes from downtown. Located in a converted house, the elegant dining area offers a happy blend of formality and friendliness. While Elaine Peaston manages the front of the house, classically trained Andrew holds down the kitchen. The menu offers some rich dishes from the traditional French repertoire, such as a trio of cream soups and some of the best savory and sweet soufflés in town, but also has lighter, more modern moments. The confit of duck and potato terrine with onion marmalade, the Atlantic salmon with cucumbers and English spinach, and the grilled emu fillet with sautéed beet and deep-fried celery are all noteworthy. *210 Rokeby Rd., Subiaco, tel. 09/381-4637. Reservations essential. Jacket advised at dinner. AE, DC, MC, V. BYOB. No lunch Sat.; closed Sun.–Mon.*

$$ **Minty's.** The new ownership team of chef Gilles Racape and maître d' Petra Mehl has reinvigorated this elegant restaurant across from the Perth Mint. The renovated building, formerly a residence, is notable for its French windows, intimate dining areas, and large bar, which dominates the entrance hall. The short menu, which changes every few weeks, is otherwise varied enough to satisfy all tastes. Asparagus in a pastry case with mousseline sauce, medallions of lamb with an herb crust, and whole roast pink snapper on a bed of artichokes, mushrooms, and broad beans are typical of Minty's fresh, flavorsome, and well-presented dishes. The wine list is comprehensive, reasonably priced, and includes a dozen wines by the glass. *309 Hay St., East Perth, tel. 09/325-5299. Reservations suggested. Jacket advised at dinner. AE, DC, MC, V. No lunch weekends; closed Mon.*

Italian **Botticelli.** This dark, comfortable restaurant in the heart of
$$ Northbridge serves traditional Italian food to a faithful clientele. Veal and lamb dishes are a specialty here, so you might try the chargrilled lamb chops, veal rib, or veal medallions panfried with hazelnuts and balsamic vinegar. If pasta is more your speed, there's the tasty spinach gnocchi with a three-cheese sauce and spaghetti with a chicken and pistachio sauce. The daily antipasto selection is

also a good bet. *147 James St., Northbridge, tel. 09/328–3422. Week-end reservations advised. Dress: casual but neat. AE, DC, MC, V. No lunch Sat.; closed Sun.*

$$ **Perugino.** A major renovation has enhanced the garden setting of
★ this Perth institution and made it an even more impressive venue for business lunches, romantic trysts, or formal dinners. Even before remodeling, Perugino had a deserved reputation as the city's best Italian restaurant, largely because of chef Giuseppe Pagliaricci's emphasis on fresh produce and imaginative yet simple approach to the cuisine of his native Umbria. Co-owner Enrico Carnevali con-tributes by supervising some of the most professional, knowledge-able, and good-humored service in town. Entrées to look for are the *scottadito* (baby goat chops grilled with olive oil and herbs) and the *coniglio* (farmed rabbit in a tomato sauce with garlic and chilies). The à la carte menu is supplemented with numerous seasonal spe-cials—usually several excellent risottos and pastas filled with such tasty combinations as spinach, ricotta, and chicken. *77 Outram St., West Perth., tel. 09/321–5420. Reservations required. AE, DC, MC, V. No lunch Sat.; closed Sun.*

Lodging

The large number of luxury hotels in Perth has proven to be a head-ache for some proprietors, who counted on the America's Cup to stay in Perth and keep the hotels filled with spectators. Without the cup, many luxury establishments have suffered low occupancy rates—a bonus for travelers who may now choose from a wide selec-tion of hotels with competitive prices.

Highly recommended lodgings are indicated by a star ★.

Category	Cost*
$$$$	over $125
$$$	$90–$125
$$	$50–$90
$	under $50

*All prices are for a standard double room.

$$$$ **Burswood Island Resort and Casino.** Although Burswood's architec-
★ tural merits may be questionable, this is nevertheless a true luxury resort, from the top of its 10-story glass atrium to the last blade of grass on its 18-hole golf course. The adjoining casino (the largest in the Southern Hemisphere) is open around the clock for roulette, blackjack, baccarat, keno, craps, and two-up, as is its cabaret. The rooms are as lush as the public spaces, each featuring a Japanese-style bathroom with sliding screen doors and a view of either the riv-er or the city. Suites have Jacuzzis. *Great Eastern Hwy., Victoria Park, 6100, tel. 09/362–7777, fax 09/470–2553. 410 rooms with bath, including 16 suites with Jacuzzi. Facilities: indoor and outdoor pools, health and fitness center, spa, saunas, solarium, 4 tennis courts, 18-hole golf course, restaurants, bars. AE, DC, MC, V.*

$$$$ **Parmelia Hilton.** The Parmelia has retained its individuality despite
★ its sale to the Hilton hotel chain. The antiques, which are liberally sprinkled throughout the property, have remained, so guests may gaze upon a Chinese silk tapestry or Mussolini's mirror as they await the elevator. Most rooms have been refurbished in a contemporary style, featuring blue carpets, cream walls, and rosewood reproduc-

tion Queen Anne furniture. Suites are luxuriously appointed with damask fabrics, original artwork, and antique furniture, and each enjoys river views, while other rooms overlook the hotel pool and cityscape. *Mill St., Perth, 6000, tel. 09/322–3622, fax 09/481–0857. 275 rooms with bath, including 53 suites. Facilities: pool, health club, sauna, restaurants, bars. AE, DC, MC, V.*

$$$$ **Perth Parkroyal.** Parkroyal Hotels are the signature properties of the Southern Pacific Hotel Corporation. Every room in the Perth Parkroyal has an outstanding view across Langley Park to the Swan River, and each one has a balcony. The hotel is decorated in cobalt and lemon, colors that reflect the river's moods. The 83 tower block rooms have showers, and the 16 cabana rooms come with king-size beds and baths. The bistrostyle Royal Palm restaurant is popular for lunch and has been nominated for several awards. On a given day it might serve up chargrilled buffalo or angel-hair noodles with goat cheese; the innovative menu changes every two weeks. *Terrace Rd., Perth, 6000 tel. 09/325–3811, fax 09/221–1564. 99 rooms with bath, 2 suites. Facilities: pool, spa, health club, restaurant, bar, guest laundry, room service. AE, DC, MC, V.*

$$$$ **Radisson Observation City Resort Hotel.** Watching the sun sink into
★ the Indian Ocean from this luxury beachside resort is one of Western Australia's great experiences, as is a meal in the hotel's fine restaurant, the Ocean Room. The peppermint, salmon, and blue color scheme is continued through the guest rooms, each of which has an ocean view. The elegant decor is highlighted by marble bathrooms and mirrored wardrobes. *The Esplanade, Scarborough, 6019, tel. 09/245–1000, fax 09/245–1345. 336 rooms with bath, 5 suites. Facilities: fitness center, sauna, spa, tennis courts, restaurants, bars. AE, DC, MC, V.*

$$$ **Château Commodore.** One of Perth's older hotels, the Château Commodore enjoys a reputation for quality and has garnered a loyal following. Rooms are spacious and are in the process of being redone in shades of blue, green, and pink, with white and blue carpets. Request a room with a view. *417 Hay St., 6000, tel. 09/325–0461, fax 09/221–2448. 133 rooms with bath. Facilities: pool, restaurant. AE, DC, MC, V.*

$$$ **Perth Townhouse Travelodge.** The location is hard to beat. Complete-
★ ly gutted and rebuilt, this hotel opened in early 1992, within a stone's throw of the central business district, major shopping areas, cinemas, and restaurants. Its spacious rooms are a relaxing pale peppermint with dark blue-green bedspreads. The bar and brasserie, with their warm terra-cotta tiling and wrought-iron furniture, have a Mediterranean feel. An added bonus is the only indoor heated hotel pool in Perth. *Hay St., Perth, 6000, tel. 09/321–9141, fax 09/481–2250. 83 rooms with bath, including 1 suite and 3 family rooms. Facilities: pool, spa, sauna, health club, restaurant, bar, guest laundry. AE, DC, MC, V.*

$$$ **Quality Langley Plaza.** Though the lobby and rooms here are barely big enough to swing a suitcase in, the panoramic views of the Swan River from the guest rooms can't be beat. The hotel is clean and comfortable, with a refurbished foyer, porte cochere, and buffet restaurant due by 1995. *221 Adelaide Terr., 6000, tel. 09/221–1200, fax 09/ 221–1669. 253 rooms with bath. Facilities: restaurant, bar, live entertainment. AE, DC, MC, V.*

$$$ **Transit Inn.** This quiet, unassuming, and attractive hotel is close to the central business district and entertainment quarter. Ruby's, an award-winning restaurant with an old-fashioned feel, is located adjacent to the hotel. The south side of the building features apricot-color furnishings, and some of the higher floors have fine views of

the Swan River; the cooler north side is bedecked with green, modern, light wood furniture. Most guests find the north side rooms more appealing. *37 Pier St., 6000, tel. and fax 09/325–7655. 120 rooms with bath. Facilities: pool, restaurant, bar. AE, DC, MC, V.*

$$ **Airways Hotel.** Tucked away behind the Sheraton, this pleasant establishment offers visitors the best of both worlds: a good location convenient to luxury facilities and a reasonable price tag. The light, airy rooms feature a pink and gray color scheme and modern furniture. *195 Adelaide Terr., 6000, tel. 09/323–7799, fax 09/221–1956. 156 rooms with bath. Facilities: restaurant, laundry. AE, DC, MC, V.*

$$ **Miss Maud's European Hotel.** Run by the same woman who pio-
★ neered smorgasbord in Western Australia, it's no surprise that this neat hotel has a Scandinavian air, from its pine furniture to the bright blue and gold color scheme in the rooms. Well positioned at the center of town, the hotel is adjacent to Miss Maud's restaurant and bakery. The famous smorgasbord of delicacies, which brings back customers again and again means a meal here is mandatory. *97 Murray St., 6000, tel. 09/325–3900, fax 09/221–3225. 51 rooms with bath. Facilities: restaurant, room service. AE, DC, MC, V.*

$$ **The New Esplanade.** Ideally situated on the Esplanade, this hotel enjoys the same million-dollar view of the Swan River for which flamboyant mining tycoons have forked over fortunes. An added bonus is the location—just a chopstick's toss from the Grand Palace, one of the best Chinese restaurants in town. The rooms are comfortable and are in the process of being redecorated in shades of green, gray, and blue, with contrasting teak woodwork. *18 The Esplanade, 6000, tel. 09/325–2000, fax 09/221–2190. 85 rooms with bath. Facilities: restaurant, bar. AE, DC, MC, V.*

$$ **Quality Princes Hotel.** Closer to the shopping and nightclub action than many central city hotels, the Princes is efficient and pleasant, a firm favorite with visiting U.S. military personnel. Rooms are compact but cheerful, decorated in pinks and blues and featuring light, modern furniture and VCRs. *34 Murray St., 6000, tel. 09/322–2844, fax 09/321–6314. 167 rooms. Facilities: restaurant, bar. AE, DC, MC, V.*

$ **The Adelphi.** One of the most delightful aspects of this property is its
★ location. While the main thoroughfare running alongside it can be noisy, the hotel sits at the bottom of King's Park bluff opposite the duck-filled lakes of the freeway parklands. An enormously popular self-catering facility, its neat and airy rooms are done in pinks and blues and filled with cane furniture. Rooms on the higher floors have views of the river. *130A Mounts Bay Rd., 6000, tel. 09/322–4666, fax 09/322–4580. 61 rooms with bath. Facilities: laundry. AE, DC, MC, V.*

$ **City Waters Lodge.** Though far removed from the excitement of downtown, these self-catering units are nonetheless quite pleasant. The guest rooms are bright and cheerful; some feature rather old, heavy furniture, others have pine lounges with pretty floral cushions. The lodge is only a short distance from the river, but only three units have views. Request Room 201, which has a separate sitting room. *118 Terrace Rd., 6000, tel. 09/325–1566, fax 09/479–1537. 70 rooms with bath. Facilities: room service, laundry. AE, MC, V.*

$ **Riverview Apartments.** Situated in one of the city's most prestigious residential areas, these serviced units are just a short stroll from both the city and King's Park. The rooms are clean and serviceable, if somewhat dated. *42 Mount St., 6000, tel. 09/321–8963, fax 09/322–5956. 50 rooms with bath. Facilities: cooking facilities. No credit cards.*

The Arts

The arts scene in Perth is as young and thriving as the city itself. The highly acclaimed annual **Festival of Perth,** which is held in February and March and attracts some of the world's finest names in music, dance, and theater, is showcased throughout the city. Further information is available from the Festival of Perth office (University of Western Australia, Mounts Bay Rd., Crawley, 6009, tel. 09/386–7977). Full details on all cultural events in Perth are contained in a comprehensive guide in every Thursday edition of *The West Australian.*

Theater **His Majesty's Theatre** (825 Hay St., tel. 09/322–2929) opened in 1904, was restored in 1980, and is loved by everyone who has stepped inside. It is the home of most theatrical productions in Perth. **The Playhouse** (Pier St., tel. 09/325–3344), the **Regal Theatre** (47 Hay St., Subiaco, tel. 09/381–5522), and the **Hole in the Wall** (180 Hamersley Rd., Subiaco, tel. 09/381–2403) also feature regular productions.

Ballet The **West Australian Ballet Company,** at His Majesty's Theatre (*see above*), runs four annual short seasons, in February, May, June, and October. Director Barry Moreland oversees a combination of traditional ballets such as *Don Quixote,* modern works by choreographers such as Balanchine, and contemporary ballets choreographed by Moreland himself.

Concerts Regular recitals by both Australian and international artists are conducted at the **Perth Concert Hall** (5 St. George's Terr., tel. 09/325–9944), a modern building overlooking the Swan River.

Opera Also at His Majesty's Theatre (*see above*), the **West Australian Opera Company** presents three seasons annually, in April, August, and November. The company's repertoire includes classical opera, Gilbert and Sullivan operettas, and the occasional musical.

Nightlife

Nightclubs Most luxury hotels in Perth offer upscale, sophisticated nightclubs appealing to the over-30 crowd. A Las Vegas–style cabaret, which showcases national and international artists, is presented at the **Burswood Island Resort** (tel. 09/362–7777). **Margeaux's** at the Parmelia Hilton (Mill St., tel. 09/322–3622), **Chicago's** at the Orchard (707 Wellington St., tel. 09/327–7000), and **Clouds** at the Sheraton (207 Adelaide Terr., tel. 09/325–0501) feature DJs who play Top-40 hits. Along more sedate lines, the **Piano Bar** at the Sheraton and the **Millstrasse** at the Parmelia Hilton provide piano music along with the drinks.

As for nonhotel clubs, the property that debuted in 1967 as Pinocchio's emerged from major renovations in December 1993 as **The Globe** (393 Murray St., tel. 09/321–4080), and its new, stylish mix of '50s, '60s, and '70s decor, plus live bands and DJs, draws a twentysomething crowd. **Exit** (187 Stirling St., tel. 09/227–8200), one of the most popular spots in the Northbridge area, draws the 18–25 age group with Top-40 hits. Midway between Perth and Fremantle is **Club Bay View** (20 St. Quentin's Ave., Claremont, tel. 09/385–1331), an upmarket cocktail bar–cum–nightclub, which caters to the well-heeled stockbroker set. In Fremantle proper, the nightclub crowd goes no farther than **Metropolis** (58 South Terr., tel. 09/336–1511), which claims the largest dance floor in the state. Its Federation-style, two-story facade belies an ultramodern interior, where nine bars, a café, and a pool room can hold up to 1,500 revelers.

Bars Until the Matilda Bay Brewing Company opened a few years ago, Perth bars were generally lacking in character and charm. The boutique brewing company has set a new standard for drinking establishments in Western Australia, and architect Michael Patroni has transformed a number of Perth's dilapidated bars into stylish, popular spots such as the **Brass Monkey Pub and Brasserie** (209 William St., Northbridge, tel. 09/227–9596), the **Queen's Tavern** (520 Beaufort St., Highgate, tel. 09/328–7267), the **Oriel Cafe and Brasserie** (483 Hay St., Subiaco, tel. 09/382–1886), and **The Vic** (226 Hay St., Subiaco, tel. 09/380–0868). **The Adelphi** (tel. 09/322–3622) in the Hilton is a swanky wine bar and coffee shop, where the waiters are energetic and the beer flows from brass pumps, while **The Astoria** (37 Bay View Terr., Claremont, tel. 09/384–1372) is the place to see and be seen, at any hour, for Perth's young socialites. It's the last word in California chic.

In Fremantle (*see below*), you can watch the beer being brewed while you slake your thirst. The **Sail and Anchor** (64 South Terr., tel. 09/335–8433) offers a historic hostelry and boutique beer, while the handsome sandstone surrounds of the **Norfolk** (47 South Terr., tel. 09/335–5405) provide a lovely garden from which patrons can watch the goings-on at the Fremantle Markets opposite.

Excursions to Fremantle and Rottnest

Fremantle and Rottnest Island, sunny retreats for the residents of Perth, make ideal day trips for visitors to the area. It's hard not to fall in love with the pretty port city of Fremantle, 19 kilometers (12 miles) southwest of Perth where the Swan River meets the Indian Ocean. And Rottnest Island's bleached beaches, rocky coves, and blue-green waters, just 19 kilometers (12 miles) off the coast, are an unbeatable combination for a day's escape from civilized Perth.

Arriving and Departing

Fremantle is well served by both train and bus. Trains depart approximately every 20 minutes from the **Perth Central Station** on Wellington Street, and bus information is available from **Transperth** (tel. 13–2213).

Boat Torque Cruises (tel. 09/221–5844) runs ferries to Rottnest Island from both Perth's Barrack Street Jetty and from Fremantle. Air service to the island is available on the **Rottnest Airbus** (tel. 09/478–1322).

Important Addresses and Numbers

Tourist Information **Fremantle Town Hall Information Centre** (High and Adelaide Sts., tel. 09/430–2346).

Rottnest Island Board (Thomson Bay, tel. 09/372–9727).

Emergencies **Rottnest Medical Centre,** Rottnest Hospital (tel. 09/372–9727). Dial 000 to request emergency assistance from an operator.

Guided Tours

Fremantle Trams (39A Malsbury St., Bicton, tel. 09/339–8719) provides a number of tours, including sightseeing trips along the harbor and a history trail. **Pride of the West Stagecoach** (Marine Terr., tel. 09/417–5523) offers tours around town in replica Cobb & Co. horse-drawn carriages.

The **Rottnest Island Board** (Thomson Bay, tel. 09/372–9727) runs a daily two-hour coach tour of the island's highlights, including convict-built cottages, World War II gun emplacements, and salt lakes.

Exploring Fremantle

Tour Fremantle on foot, strolling along the harbor, browsing through bookshops, and stopping for a cappuccino in one of the sidewalk cafés along the way. The town was primped, painted, and thoroughly spruced up for the America's Cup a few years back, and it has retained a salty, lighthearted air ever since. Start at the **Fremantle Railway Station** at Elder Place, opened to service the harbor in 1907. Head southwest along Phillimore Street for four blocks until you reach Cliff Street, and make a left. At High Street turn right, and ahead you will spot **Round House**, built originally as a jail in 1831, and today the state's oldest surviving building. *Information Centre, 10 Arthur Head Rd., tel. 09/430–2326. Admission free. Open daily 10–5.*

Return to High Street and head east for five blocks to the **Town Hall,** an elegant and gracious building opened in 1887 as part of Queen Victoria's Jubilee. Bear left onto Adelaide Street for a block and turn right onto Queen Street, passing **St. John's Anglican Church,** consecrated in 1881. A block farther turn right onto Henderson Street, where the **Warders' Quarters** are still used to house guards from the Fremantle prison. These pretty rows of attached houses have remained virtually unchanged since they were built by convict labor in 1851. Continue on Henderson to its junction with South Terrace. Here you will find the **Fremantle Markets,** where you can buy everything from potatoes to paintings, incense to sausages. *Tel. 09/335–2515. Open Fri. 9–9, Sat. 9–5, Sun. 11–5.*

Across Henderson Street is the **Sail and Anchor,** a historic hostelry that served as the center of operations during the America's Cup. You might like to stop in at the small brewery for a pint before continuing south on Essex Street toward the harbor.

Time Out The port's most ambitious project is **Lombardo's** (Fishing Boat Harbor, tel. 09/430–4343), on the pier at Mews Road. This complex offers bistros, outdoor cafés, restaurants, and food stalls with panoramic views of the harbor.

While you are wandering along the harbor, you can visit the **Fremantle Crocodile Park,** home to almost 200 salt- and freshwater crocodiles. Feeding is Tuesday–Sunday at 11:30 AM and 2 PM. *Mews Rd., tel. 09/430–5388. Admission: $8 adults, $4 children. Open daily 10–5.*

The **Fremantle Museum** traces the early days of Fremantle's settlement. *Ord and Finnerty Sts., tel. 09/430–7986. Open Mon.–Thurs. 10:30–5, Fri.–Sun. 1–5.*

The **WA Maritime Museum** offers a fascinating glimpse into the state's nautical past, with a reconstruction of the Dutch vessel *Bata-*

via and relics from the Dutch and colonial ships that came to grief on Western Australia's rocky coastline. A changing gallery of prints and photographs complements the exhibition. *1 Cliff St., tel. 09/ 431–8444. Open Mon.–Thurs. 10:30–5, Fri.–Sun. 1–5. No admission fee; donations appreciated.*

At the **Sails Museum,** in the B shed at Victoria Quay, boating enthusiasts will appreciate the extensive range of vessels on display, including the *Perie Endeavour*, the craft in which yachtsman Jon Sanders completed his solo circumnavigation of the globe. *Victoria Quay, tel. 09/430–4680. Open daily 10–4.*

Samson House is a historic house museum that hosts a fine collection of antique furniture and historic photographs. *Ellen and Ord Sts., no phone. Open Thurs. and Sun. 1–5.*

Fremantle Prison, a fine sandstone building constructed in 1855 with convict labor, was decommissioned in 1991 and opened as a tourist attraction the next year. Guided tours provide a fascinating glimpse of the state's oldest prison. *The Terrace, tel. 09/430–7177. Admission: $10 adults, $3 children (free if accompanied by 2 adults). Open daily 10–6.*

Rottnest Island

The most convenient way to get around Rottnest is by bicycle, because cars are not allowed on the island and bus service is infrequent. Bicycles can be rented from **Rottnest Bike Hire** (tel. 09/372–9722) in the main settlement at Thomson Bay. A bicycle tour of the island covers 26 kilometers (16 miles) and can be done in as little as three hours, though you really ought to set aside an entire day to enjoy the beautiful surroundings. It's impossible to get lost, because the one main road circles the island and will always bring you back to your starting point.

Heading south from Thomson Bay, between Government House and Herschell lakes, you'll encounter a **quokka colony.** Quokkas are small wallabies that are easily mistaken for rats. In fact, the island's name means "rat's nest" in Dutch. Well fed by visitors, the quokkas are quite tame.

Past the quokka colony you'll come upon **gun emplacements** from World War II, and as you continue south to **Bickley Bay,** you'll be able to spot the wreckage of those ships that met ill-fated ends on Rottnest's rocky coastline.

Follow the main road past Porpoise, Salmon, Strickland, and Wilson bays to **West End,** the westernmost point on the island and another graveyard for unfortunate vessels. If you've brought a fishing rod, now is the time to unpack it. As you head back to the Thomson Bay settlement, you'll pass a dozen rocky inlets and bays, the prettiest of which, **Parakeet Bay,** is situated at the northernmost tip of the island.

Back at the main settlement, visit the **Rottnest Museum** (09/372–9752), which provides an intriguing account of the island's convict history. You might also like to stop in at the **Rottnest Island Bakery** (tel. 09/292–5023), famous throughout the state for its mouthwatering breads.

Dining

Price categories for restaurants are the same as in the Perth Dining section, *above.*

Fremantle
$$$

Chunagon. This large Japanese restaurant has superb views of the Fremantle boat harbor on one side and the ocean on the other. You can choose from a range of *teppanyaki* (Japanese barbecue) menus—including the house special, grilled crayfish—or from the à la carte menu, which features tempura, teriyaki, and sashimi dishes as well as an extensive list of sushi. Ricepaper-screened tatami rooms host à la carte diners, and a special teppanyaki area allows guests to watch as their meal is barbecued with great theatricality. *46 Mews Rd., tel. 09/336–1000. Reservations advised. Dress: casual but neat. AE, DC, MC, V.*

$$

Surf Club. One of the most comfortable and relaxed beachfront restaurant complexes in the state overlooks Port Beach in North Fremantle. With a kiosk, an à la carte restaurant, and a café designed for families—there's a playground and plenty of shade under a large, tensile, fabric canopy—the Surf Club has something for everyone. The café and restaurant, only about 100 meters (300 feet) from the water, are protected by walls of glass, which let in the ocean views while shutting out the wind. The regular menu, which is supplemented by about 10 daily specials, emphasizes the excellent local seafood: Dhufish, red emperor, and mulloway are presented grilled, panfried, or cooked in batter. The superb Waroona sirloin or fillet and the chargrilled chicken in soy and honey are also worth trying. *Port Beach Rd., North Fremantle, tel. 09/430–6866. Reservations required. Dress: casual but neat. AE, DC, MC, V. Closed Mon.*

$$

Williams. An unprepossessing exterior masks one of the best seafood restaurants in town. Inside, one large room houses a comfortable bar area and elegantly decorated tables. On many dishes chef Greig Olsen attempts to emphasize natural flavors while offering complementary sauces for those who want them. The à la carte menu is quite small and includes nonseafood dishes; additional options are provided by about 20 specials that are changed regularly, often daily. These might include a trio of king prawn, Moreton Bay bugs (a type of lobster), and yabbies (a small, sweet, freshwater crayfish) chargrilled and served with a soy and honey glaze, fresh fillet of pink snapper panfried in Cajun spices, or local cobbler fillet either deep-fried in a light beer batter with a chili-plum dipping sauce or grilled with an herb and garlic butter. The wine list features many local specialties. *82 Stirling Hwy., North Fremantle, tel. 09/430–5233. Reservations required. Jacket advised. AE, DC, MC, V. No lunch Sat.; closed Sun.*

Rottnest
$$

Brolly's. The Rottnest Hotel (affectionately known as the Quokka Arms after the island's small marsupials) recently remodeled, so now its restaurant has one section for fine dining and one for more casual occasions. At the latter, patrons barbecue their own steaks or seafood before helping themselves to the salad bar, whereas the former has the more usual à la carte menu. *Rottnest Hotel, Thomson Bay, Rottnest, tel. 09/292–5011. Reservations required. Dress: casual. AE, MC, V.*

$$

Rottnest Island Lodge. The dining room at this hotel offers an à la carte menu that specializes in seafood. *Rottnest Island Lodge, Thomson Bay, Rottnest, tel. 09/292–5161. Reservations required. Dress: casual but neat. AE, DC, MC, V.*

The Southwest

It's not surprising that Western Australia's southwest region is the state's most popular destination. Fine vineyards, rugged coastal cliffs, rolling green fields, majestic forests, and a Mediterranean climate combine happily to make any trip there memorable.

Getting Around

By Plane   **Skywest** (tel. 09/334–2288) provides regular service to the southern coastal town of Albany.

By Car   A comprehensive network of highways makes exploring the southwest practical and easy. Take Highway 1 down the coast from Perth to Bunbury, switch to Route 10 through Busselton and Margaret River, and on to Bridgetown, where you rejoin Highway 1 south to Albany.

Guided Tours

Westrail (tel. 09/326–2159) runs regular tours of the southwest, with departures from the East Perth rail terminal.

Important Addresses and Numbers

Tourist   **The WA Tourism Commission** operates a comprehensive network of
Information   travel centers throughout the region. Its central office (corner of Forrest Pl. and Wellington St., Perth, tel. 09/483–1111) has an excellent library of free information for visitors.

Emergencies   Dial 000 for emergency assistance. Regional **hospitals** can be found in Bunbury (tel. 097/21–4911), Margaret River (tel. 097/57–2000), and Albany (098/41–2955).

Exploring the Southwest

Begin your tour in **Bunbury,** the major seaport and administrative center of the region. While here, visit the **King Cottage Museum,** a pretty family home built in 1880 using a Flemish bond-brick design. Today it is furnished with a valuable collection of pioneer artifacts from the area. *77 Forrest Ave., tel. 097/21–3929. Admission: $1.50 adults, 50¢ children. Open weekends.*

From Bunbury, follow Route 10 through the only natural **tuart forest** in the world. These magnificent trees have been standing on this land for 400 years. Continue on to **Busselton,** which was settled by the Bussell family in 1834 and is among the state's oldest towns. Its history, and that of the southwest dairy industry's early years, is recorded in the **Old Butter Factory.** *Peel Terr., Busselton, tel. 097/54–2166. Admission: $2 adults, 50¢ children. Open daily except Tues. 2–5.*

Follow the Bussell Highway to **Dunsborough,** another captivating seaside town, where the **Hutchings Antique Shop and Museum** (58 Gifford Rd., tel. 097/55–3098) features, among other curiosities, the largest private collection of mounted wildlife in the state. **Yallingup Caves,** a few miles north of the town, house massive stalagmites, stalactites, delicate straws, and shawl formations, and are a pleasant diversion outside the pretty town of Yallingup (*see* National Parks, *below*). *Caves Rd., Yallingup, tel. 097/55–2152. Admission: $6 adults, $2.50 children. Open daily 9:30–4:30.*

Caves Road continues along the coast into the Margaret River area. Some of Australia's finest wines are grown by numerous wineries here, most of which are open for tastings and sales. A brochure with details on the individual cellars is available from the **Augusta/Margaret River Tourist Bureau.** *Bussell Hwy., Margaret River, tel. 097/ 57–2911. Open daily 9–5.*

A few minutes' walk from the center of town in Margaret River is the **Old Settlement Craft Village,** which features a house, farm buildings, and machinery from the 1920s. This and other "group settlement" farms were built by English veterans of World War I, who were recruited by the Australian government to establish a dairy industry in the then-virgin bush of the southwest. Parcels of 160–180 acres were allocated to each family, but groups of families generally worked collectively to clear the land. The Old Settlement Craft Village traces this history, as well as the less utopian fallout that resulted from various plots, lies, and cover-ups engineered by the government to dupe innocent newcomers—none of whom knew anything about farming. This conspiracy-laden past has given way to a benign present: Now a blacksmith gives demonstrations five days a week, and high-quality craft items are available from the craft and souvenir shop. *Bussell Hwy., Margaret River, tel. 097/57–2775. Admission: $4 adults, $2 children. Open daily 10–5. Closed Fri. during school year.*

Continue south and east on Route 10 to **Pemberton,** known for the karri forests that feature some of the tallest trees in the world. A few miles outside this timber town, rejoin Highway 1 and continue along through the "Rainbow Coast's" rolling green countryside. Stop at **Denmark's** historic butter factory, now occupied by the **Denmark Winery, Craft and Gallery.** Michael and Alison Goundrey produce wines at Mt. Barker, north of Denmark, and sell them through the gallery. Sample the '93 Langton chardonnay or the '89 Windy Hill cabernet while you inspect the work of local craftspeople and watercolorist Alexander E. Hills. *11 North St., Denmark, tel. 098/ 48–2525. Open Mon.–Sat. 10–4:30, Sun. 11–4:30.*

Albany, the earliest settlement in Western Australia, lies east of Denmark on Highway 1. Founded in 1826, the site became a boomtown with the establishment of the whaling fleet in the 1840s. Centered in Albany's fine harbor, whaling claimed up to 850 sperm whales every season until the practice was stopped in 1978. The old whaling station has been converted to a museum. *Whaleworld, Cheynes Beach, tel. 098/44–4021. Admission: $5 adults, $2 children. 30-min tours every hr on the hr, 10–4. Open daily 9–5.*

Two other museums in Albany are worth a visit. **The Old Gaol** on Stirling Terrace was built in 1851 and served as the district jail from 1872 until it was closed in the 1930s. Restored by the Albany Historical Society in 1968, it now contains a collection of social and historical artifacts. *Stirling Terr., Albany, tel. 098/41–1401. Admission: $3.50 adults, $2 children. Open daily 10–4:15.*

The **Residency Museum,** one of the finest small museums in Australia, is a focal point for both the social and natural history of the Albany region. It's housed in the former offices of the Government Resident; the lovely sandstone building has sweeping views of the harbor. The saddlery adjoining the museum is also interesting. *Residency Rd., Albany, tel. 098/41–4844. Admission free. Open daily 10–5.*

The wattle and daub cottage built for the original government resident, Captain Sir Richard Spencer, can be seen at the **Old Farm,**

Strawberry Hill. The building was restored by the National Trust in 1964. You can enjoy Devonshire teas in the adjoining historic miner's cottage, which now houses a tearoom. *Middleton Rd., Albany, tel. 098/41–3735. Admission: $2.50 adults, $1.50 children. Open daily 10–5. Closed June.*

What to See and Do with Children

Adjacent to the Residency Museum is a faithful replica of the brig *Amity,* on which Albany's original settlers arrived. The replica was built in 1975 by local artisans using timber from the surrounding forest. Visitors who board the ship can climb below deck to speculate on how 45 men, plus livestock, fit into such a small craft. *Port Rd., Albany, tel. 098/41–6885. Admission: $1.50 adults, 50¢ children. Open daily 9–5.*

Dining

Price categories for restaurants are the same as in the Perth Dining section, *above.*

Albany
$$

Kooka's. This engaging colonial cottage is dominated by kookaburras of every description—on lampshades and trays, as salt cellars, teapots, and ornaments. There's even a live one in the garden at the rear. The food is wholesome country fare, prepared with flair and expertise by the English and Scottish chefs. Local produce is the order of the day, with rabbit, venison, kangaroo, and spanking fresh oysters and mussels featured strongly. Patrons have been known to travel from miles around for the chilli crab or fillet of beef in black currant and whiskey sauce. *204 Stirling Terr., tel. 098/41–5889. Reservations advised. Dress: casual. AE, DC, MC, V. BYOB. No lunch Sat.; closed Sun.–Mon.*

$$

Penny Post. Located in the historic old Post Office building, this upscale but casual restaurant has enormous character and serves the sort of food that wins awards again and again. The extensive menu, which offers both traditional and nouvelle cuisine, features chargrilled steaks and locally caught oysters, prawns, and crayfish. The pretty, colonial dining-room decor completes the experience. *33 Stirling Terr., tel. 098/41–1045. Reservations required weekends. Dress: casual but neat. AE, DC, MC, V.*

$

Earl of Spencer. Sitting high on a hill overlooking a harbor of spectacular proportions, this pub was constructed in the 1870s and became one of Albany's most popular meeting places. Renowned for its fine ale, it continues to exude character. Its recent restoration has earned it a fistful of awards, and you won't find a better vantage point from which to appreciate this handsome seaside town. Pasta and steaks are the specialties. *Earl and Spencer Sts., tel. 098/41–1322. Reservations advised. Dress: casual. AE, DC, MC, V.*

Bunbury
$$
★

Memories of the Bond Store. The century-old Customs Bond Store provides a handsome home for one of the state's finest country brasseries. The menu, which chef Joe Knierum changes regularly, centers on local venison, emu, crocodile, and kangaroo; Knierum also serves substantial soups, at least one Asian and one Cajun dish, and the standout Bond burgers with buffalo and wild mushrooms. The wine list is eclectic without being extensive, and a lovely outdoor area seats 40. *22 Victoria St., tel. 097/91–2922. Reservations advised. Dress: casual. AE, DC, MC, V.*

Busselton
$$
★
Newton House. The finest restaurant in the region is housed in a charming, whitewashed, 1851 colonial cottage with polished wooden floors and open fireplaces. Master chef Stephen Reagan, who has a string of culinary awards to back up his reputation, makes magic from regional produce whether he's putting together a simple Devonshire tea or stylish entrées of marron and asparagus or the excellent local beef. The menu changes regularly and is never less than exciting. *Bussell Hwy., Vasse, tel. 097/55–4485. Reservations advised. Dress: casual. MC, V. BYOB. No dinner Sun.–Wed.*

Margaret
River
$$$$
1885. This restaurant has a well-deserved reputation. The pretty Victorian dining room in this 100-year-old home is filled with antiques and candlelight. If the 200 labels in the wine cellar aren't reason enough to make the three-hour drive from Perth, then the excellent French food is. The menu is dictated by fresh market produce, and often includes dishes built around a game, pasta, or seafood theme. *Farrelly St., tel. 097/57–3177. Reservations required weekends. Dress: casual but neat. AE, DC, MC, V.*

$$$
★
Flutes Cafe. The incomparable setting here—over the dammed-up waters of the Willyabrup Brook and surrounded by the Brookland Valley Vineyard—is almost as delicious as the food. Dee and Malcolm Jones offer a menu with great style and flair: local yabbies (freshwater crayfish), hearty steak and red wine pies, and spicy curries. The scones, cakes, and muffins are delectable and thoroughly decadent. *Caves Rd., Willyabrup, tel. 097/55–6250. Reservations essential. Dress: casual but neat. AE, DC, MC, V.*

$$$
Merribrook Lodge. Set in the heart of a karri forest overlooking a lake populated with ducks, this lodge and restaurant complex (*see* Lodging, *below*) has earned many awards since its debut in 1986. The emphasis is on fresh food cooked with simplicity and flair. The menu features whatever was bought fresh in the markets or picked from Merribrook's vegetable garden that day. *Cowaramup Rd., tel. 097/55–5490. Reservations required. Dress: casual. AE, DC, MC, V. BYOB.*

Lodging

Much of the lodging available in the southwest is motel style or self-catering. **The WA Tourism Commission** can provide a comprehensive directory. Price categories for hotels are the same as in the Perth Lodging section, *above*.

Albany
$$$
★
The Esplanade Hotel. Albany's only five-star hotel opened in 1991, the culmination of a dream for the late Paul Terry, a millionaire descendant of Western Australia's pioneers, the Bussell family. This three-story Rainbow Coast beach resort is reminiscent of Albany's first Esplanade, a grand turn-of-the-century hotel. Each of its rooms opens onto the library lounge, which features leather couches and open fireplaces. The adjoining gallery provides a showcase for artworks and for a clutch of vintage cars. *Middleton Beach, Albany, 6330, tel. 098/42–1711, fax 098/42–1033. 40 rooms with bath, 8 suites. Facilities: pool, spa, sauna, tennis courts, health club, restaurant, bars. AE, DC, MC, V.*

Margaret
River
$$$$
Gilgara Homestead. This 1987 replica of an 1870 station homestead on 23 gently rolling acres provides a bucolic atmosphere for a maximum of 14 guests. The award-winning property has pretty, romantic rooms furnished with antiques and lace and scented with lavender, so it's no surprise that many honeymooners choose to stay here. Open fireplaces and a cozy lounge complete the picture. Sports enthusiasts can play aqua golf on the lake, although the owners have

yet to teach the ducks to retrieve stray balls. Rates include a full breakfast. *Caves and Carter Rds., 6285, tel. 097/57–3259. 6 rooms with bath. Facilities: dining room; tea, coffee, and cakes 24 hrs. No children. AE, MC, V. BYOB.*

$$$ **Cape Lodge.** Early morning calls come courtesy of a chorus of kooka-
★ burras, and evening is heralded by the caroling of magpies at this lovely Cape Dutch–style property in the heart of Margaret River. The decor has a Dutch-Indonesian theme with colonial furniture, captain's chairs, and rattan settees; each of the airy rooms is also festooned with plump proteas cultivated on the property. Guests can be found canoeing on the lake, napping in front of the gargantu-an, marble open fire, or snacking on a superlative Continental breakfast, which is included in the room rate. Dinner is not offered because Cape Lodge is surrounded by a clutch of fine restaurants, but owner Jo Johnson will provide picnic hampers and supper plat-ters or a room-service dinner from the Wildwood Brasserie next door. *Caves Rd., Yallingup, 6282, tel. and fax 097/55–6311. 11 rooms with bath, 4 with Jacuzzi. Facilities: TV, VCR, radio in all rooms; tea and coffee available 24 hrs. No children. AE, DC, MC, V. BYOB.*

$$ **1885 Inn.** An extension of a huge 100-year-old Victorian home, the suites in the modern wing blend well with the original house and fea-ture canopy beds, bay windows, and hand-carved marble-top wash-stands. Each unit opens onto a lovely garden filled with rhododendrons, waterfalls, and dovecotes. *Farrelly St., 6285, tel. 097/57–3177, fax 097/57–3076. 10 rooms. Facilities: restaurant (see Dining, above). AE, DC, MC, V.*

$$ **Merribrook Lodge.** This property in the heart of the Australian bush features nine cottages scattered around a lake that is ideal for canoe-ing, fishing, and swimming. Each cottage has a private bathroom and sleeps up to six people. The appealing main dining room serves some of the finest food to be found outside the capital (*see* Dining, *above*), and breakfast can be taken on the flower-filled terrace over-looking the lake. Rates include room, dinner, and breakfast. *Cowaramup Rd., 6285, tel. 097/55–5490, fax 097/55–5343. 9 rooms with shower only. Facilities: pool, sauna, restaurant, tea and coffee machines in rooms. AE, DC, MC, V. BYOB.*

Nannup **The Lodge.** Built in 1987 from century-old materials, The Lodge at
$$ Nannup has already garnered tourism awards. The charming coloni-al property, which features exposed beams and stone fireplaces, is set amid 10 timbered acres overlooking the Blackwood Valley 280 ki-lometers (175 miles) south of Perth, within easy reach of tennis, golf, and horseback riding. Rates include a full hot breakfast, and owners Bill and Tania Jones will indulge their guests with the din-ner of their choice. The accent is on fresh local produce, with organi-cally grown vegetables from the lodge garden. *Grange Rd., 6275, tel. 097/56–1276, fax 097/56–1394. 7 rooms, 1 with Jacuzzi, 4 with private bath, 2 with nonadjoining private bath. Facilities: pool, res-taurant. No smoking, no children. MC. BYOB.*

The Goldfields

Since the day Paddy Hannan stumbled over a gold nugget on the site of what is now Kalgoorlie, Western Australia's goldfields have ranked among the richest in the world. In their heyday, more than 100,000 men and women were scattered throughout the area, all hoping to make their fortunes. It's still an astonishingly productive area, though today the population of Kalgoorlie and Boulder has fallen to 30,000, and many other communities are now nothing more than ghost towns.

The goldfields remain special to Australians, however. Kalgoorlie retains the rough-and-ready atmosphere of a frontier town, with streets wide enough to accommodate the camel teams that were once a common sight here. Open-cut mines gouge the earth everywhere, and a nugget or two might still be found if you've the time, patience, and a reliable metal detector.

Arriving and Departing

By Plane Ansett WA (tel. 13–1300) operates a daily service to Kalgoorlie. The 531-kilometer (330-mile) journey takes an hour.

By Train *The Prospector* is an appropriate name for the train that runs a daily seven-hour service between Perth and Kalgoorlie. Fast, clean, and efficient, it departs from the East Perth Railway Terminal (tel. 09/326–2244).

By Bus **Greyhound Pioneer Australia** (tel. 09/481–7066) provides service to the goldfields.

Getting Around

The center of Kalgoorlie is compact enough to explore on foot. Hannan Street, named after the man who discovered gold here, is the main thoroughfare and contains the bulk of the hotels and tourist attractions. Taxis (tel. 090/21–2177) are available around the clock.

Important Addresses and Numbers

Tourist Information The **Kalgoorlie/Boulder Tourist Bureau** (250 Hannan St., tel. 090/21–1966) is open weekdays 8:30–5, Sat. 9:30–5, Sun. 9–12:30 and 1:30–5.

Emergencies Dial 000 for emergency assistance.

Kalgoorlie Regional Hospital (tel. 090/80–5888).

Guided Tours

All-inclusive package tours from Perth are available by plane, rail, and bus with each of the companies mentioned under Arriving and Departing, above.

Allan Young's **Goldrush Tours** (Palace Chambers, Maritana St., tel. 090/21–2954) runs an excellent series of tours on the goldfields' history and ghost towns, the profusion of wildflowers in the area, and the nearby ghost town of Coolgardie.

Boulder, located just south of Kalgoorlie, is home to the **Loop Line Railroad,** whose train the *Rattler* offers tours of the Golden Mile by rail. The train leaves from the Boulder Railway Station (Burt St., tel. 090/93–1157) Monday through Saturday at 10 AM, Sunday at 11:45, and holidays at 10 and 11:45.

Goldfields Air Services (tel. 090/93–2116) offers an air tour that gives visitors a bird's-eye view of the open-cut mining technique now used instead of more traditional shaft mining. By the turn of the century, a pit measuring 8 kilometers (5 miles) by 5 kilometers (3 miles) is expected to run adjacent to the town.

Exploring the Goldfields

Kalgoorlie's impressive **Post Office,** built from local pink stone, has dominated Hannan Street since it was constructed in 1899. Opposite the post office is the **York Hotel,** one of the few hotels in Kalgoorlie to remain untouched. Be sure to take a peek at its fine staircase and intricate cupola.

A block south, the **Kalgoorlie Town Hall,** built in 1908, features an excellent example of the stamped metal ceilings that once were a feature of the goldfields. The Victorian cast-iron seats in the balcony were imported from England at the turn of the century.

Outside sits **Paddy Hannan,** arguably the most photographed statue in the nation. This life-size bronze of the town's founder, holding a water bag that contains a drinking fountain, is a replica; the original, which was suffering the vagaries of wind, weather, and the occasional vandal, has been moved inside the Town Hall.

The **Museum of the Goldfields** is housed partly within the historic British Arms—once the narrowest pub in the Southern Hemisphere. This outstanding small museum paints a colorful portrait of life in this boisterous town. Climb to the top of the massive steeple rising over the main mine shaft for a panoramic view of both the city and the Mt. Charlotte Mine. The hands-on exhibits are a hit with children. *17 Hannan St., tel. 090/21–8533. Admission free, donations welcome. Open daily 10–4:30.*

Located 40 kilometers (25 miles) west of Kalgoorlie on the Great Eastern Highway, tiny **Coolgardie** is probably the best-maintained ghost town in Australia. A great deal of effort has gone into preserving this historic community, and there are some 150 historical markers placed around the town.

The Coolgardie Railway Station operated until 1971 and is' now home to the **Railway Station Museum**'s display on the history of rail transport. The museum also includes a display of photographs, books, and artifacts that together offer a gripping portrayal of a famous mining rescue that was once carried out in these goldfields. *Woodward St., tel. 090/26–6388. Admission free; donations appreciated. Open Sat.–Thurs. 8:30–4:30.*

One of the most unusual museums in Australia, **Ben Prior's Open Air Museum** features the machinery, boilers, and other equipment used to mine the region at the turn of the century, as well as a variety of other relics from Coolgardie's boom years. Items include large covered wagons, old cars, and statues of explorers. *Bayley St., no phone. Admission free. Open daily until dusk.*

The stark, weathered headstones in the **Coolgardie Cemetery,** off the Great Eastern Highway about half a mile east of town, recall stories of tragedy and the grim struggle for survival in a harsh, unrelenting environment. Many of the graves remain unmarked because the identities of their occupants were lost during the wild rush to the eastern goldfields. Look for the graves of several Afghan camel drivers at the rear of the cemetery.

Also on the Great Eastern Highway, 3.2 kilometers (2 miles) west of Coolgardie, is the **Coolgardie Camel Farm,** which offers a look at the animals that played a vital role in life in the goldfields. If the roads in town seem overly wide, you'll realize that such dimensions were necessary to accommodate those great beasts. A variety of camel rides are offered, including rides around the yard and one-hour, daylong, or overnight treks. Longer treks include the chance to hunt for gems and gold. *Great Eastern Hwy., tel. 090/26–6159. Admission: $2 adults, $1 children. Open daily 9–5.*

Dining

Price categories for restaurants are the same as in the Perth Dining section, *above*.

Kalgoorlie **Amalfi.** The flocked wallpaper may not suit everyone's taste, but ap-
$$$$ preciation for Amalfi's food must be universal. This Italian restaurant has been serving the best scaloppine in town for years. *409 Hannan St., tel. 090/21–3088. Reservations required weekends. Dress: casual but neat. AE, DC, MC, V.*

$$ **Basil's on Hannan.** This pretty café in the heart of town owes its Mediterranean feel to terra-cotta, wrought-iron, indoor-garden decor. The food is equally casual, with veal dishes and a wide range of pasta dishes as the specialties. The popular Sunday brunch offers something different for Kalgoorlie—namely focaccia, seafood fettuccine, and a renowned Caesar salad. *168 Hannan St., tel. 090/21–7832. Reservations advised. Dress: casual. AE, MC, V. BYOB. No dinner Sun.*

$ **Exchange Hotel.** The miners in Kalgoorlie favored slaking their thirst before filling their bellies, but here you can do both at once. Rather tacky, but a superb example of a rough-and-ready goldfields pub, the Exchange is replete with exquisite stained glass and pressed metal ceilings. The best counter meals (grills and salads) anywhere in the goldfields are served here. *Hannan and Maritana Sts., tel. 090/21–2833. Reservations advised. Dress: casual. No credit cards.*

Lodging

Price categories for hotels are the same as in the Perth Lodging section, *above*.

Kalgoorlie **Plaza Motel.** This modern hotel complex offers a quiet location on a
$$$ tree-lined street, just a stone's throw from busy Hannan Street. Its motel-style rooms are nicely furnished in grays and blues. *45 Egan St., tel. 090/21–4544, fax 090/91–2195. 100 rooms with bath. Facilities: pool, restaurant, 24-hr room service. AE, DC, MC, V.*

$$ **York Hotel.** The historic York has retained an authentic look, exemplified in its lovely stained-glass windows and pressed metal ceilings. Its staircase and dining room are a historian's dream. Rooms are small but functional, and the rates include breakfast. *259 Hannan St., tel. 090/21–2337. 16 rooms share 6 baths. Facilities: restaurant. AE, DC, MC, V.*

National Parks

Western Australia's national parks are not easy to reach from Perth, and visits generally require advance planning and long drives. The parks are some of the best in Australia, though, precisely because they are so remote and uncrowded. Those parks located in the far north of the state—including Geikie Gorge, the Kimberley, and Bungle Bungle—are most easily visited from Darwin in the Northern Territory; consequently, they've been included in the chapter on Darwin, the Top End, and the Kimberley (*see* Chapter 11).

Hamersley Range National Park

The huge rocks, crags, and gorges that make up the Hamersley Range are among the most ancient land surfaces in the world. Sediments deposited by an inland sea more than 2.5 billion years ago were forced up by movements in the earth's crust and slowly weathered by natural elements through succeeding centuries. Much of the 320-kilometer (200-mile) range is being mined for its rich iron deposits, but a small section is incorporated into the national park. With its towering cliffs, lush fern-filled gullies, and richly colored stone, this is one of the most beautiful parks in Australia.

The park's trails are rated as easy, moderate, and difficult; all require sturdy shoes, and you should carry plenty of drinking water. Gorges may be reached only on foot from parking areas. Dales Gorge is the most popular and easily accessible. The walk is a one-hour return trip from the parking area and ends at the only permanent waterfall in the park, Fortescue Falls. Ferns and mosses line the gorge walls, providing a stunning contrast with the arid landscape outside the park. This walk can be lengthened by hiking downstream to Circular Pool. Other gorges in the park are far more challenging and should be undertaken only by experienced hikers, who must brave freezing water, cling to rock ledges, and scramble over boulders through the Joffre, Knox, and Hancock gorges. Notify the ranger before hiking into any of these gorges.

Because summer temperatures often top 110°F, it's best to visit during the cooler months, from April through early November.

Arriving and Departing The park is most easily reached by driving 550 kilometers (342 miles) south from Broome, along the Great Northern Highway via Port Hedland. Turn off south from Port Hedland for 295 kilometers (183 miles) to the park.

Lodging Camping is permitted only in designated sites at Yampire Gorge, Circular Pool, Joffre Turnoff, and Weano. Campsites have no facilities except toilets, but gas barbecues are available for free. The burning of wood is prohibited.

Nightly fees are $5 for two adults, $3 for additional adults, $1 for children. Food and supplies may be purchased in Wittenoom, where hotel and motel accommodations can be arranged as well. Drinking water is available at Yampire and Joffre roads.

Information Contact the **Department of Conservation and Land Management** (Box 835, Karratha, WA 6714, tel. 091/86–8288).

Nambung National Park

Located on the Swan coastal plain, 245 kilometers (152 miles) north of Perth, Nambung National Park is best known for the Pinnacles Desert situated in the center of the park. These eerie limestone structures, which look like roughly carved tombstones, are fossilized roots of ancient coastal plants fused with sand. Over the years, wind and drifting sand have sculpted the exposed forms into shapes that loom as high as 15 feet or merely poke out of the sand three or four inches.

Visitors may walk among the pinnacles on a 500-meter (1,650-foot) walking trail from the parking area, or drive the Pinnacles Desert Loop (not suitable for large RVs or buses). For visitors with more time, the park offers beautiful beaches and coastal dunes where more than 100 bird species can be spotted. Fishing is permitted at

Hangover Bay and Kangaroo Point. The best time to visit the park is from August through October, when the heath is ablaze with wildflowers. Entrance fees are $3 per car or $2 per bus passenger.

Arriving and Departing From Perth, go north about 190 kilometers (120 miles) on the Brand Highway toward Badgingarra, then west toward Cervantes and south into the park.

Tours of the park can be arranged in Perth through the **Western Australian Tourist Commission** (772 Hay St., WA 6000, tel. 09/32–2999) or in Cervantes through the **Caravan Park** or the **service station** (tel. 096/52–7041).

Lodging Toilets are located near the Pinnacles, but no camping is permitted at the park. Accommodations are available in Cervantes at the **Cervantes Motel** (tel. 096/52–7145) or the **Cervantes Caravan Park** (tel. 096/52–7060).

Information Contact the **Department of Conservation and Land Management** (Box 62, Cervantes, WA 6511, tel. 096/52–7043).

Cape Leeuwin–Naturaliste National Park

Located on the southwest tip of the continent, this 150-kilometer (93-mile) stretch of coastline is one of Australia's most fascinating areas. The limestone-based Leeuwin-Naturaliste Ridge directly below the park contains more than 360 known caves, with evidence dating both human and animal habitation here to more than 40,000 years ago.

The coastal scenery changes drastically from north to south: rocks at some points, calm sandy beaches at others, all interspersed with heathlands, eucalyptus forests, and swamps. It would take days to explore all the intricacies of this park.

Four major caves between Margaret River and Augusta are easily accessible to visitors: Yallingup, Mammoth, Lake (where stalagmites and stalactites are reflected in the cave's pools of water), and Jewel. Bats live in the caves, as do primitive crustaceans and insects that have evolved in the dark to be sightless and colorless. Three caves—Bride's, Giant's, and Calgardup—which require flashlights, sturdy shoes, and protective clothing, are for the adventurous only. Spelunkers in Bride's Cave should have roping experience.

The view from the top of the lighthouse at Cape Leeuwin allows visitors to witness the meeting of two oceans, the Southern and the Indian. At some places, this alliance results in giant ocean swells that smash among the rocks. At others, small coves are blessed with calm waters ideal for swimming and fishing. Smith's Beach in Yallingup is a popular surfing hangout.

The Caves Road leads to several lookout points including the Boranup Lookout (a 600-meter/1,980-foot trail overlooking Hamelin Bay) and the Boranup Forest (where karri, one of the largest trees in the world, grows). North in Yallingup, a 1.5-kilometer (1-mile) trail leads from Cape Naturaliste to Canal Rocks, passing rugged cliffs, quiet bays, and curving beaches.

Arriving and Departing The park can be reached from Perth by heading south on the Old Coast Road (Route 1) for 265 kilometers (165 miles) to the northernmost section of the park. Entrance to the park is free.

Lodging Campgrounds with toilets, showers, and an information center are located north in Injidup. Campsites cost $5 for two adults, $3 for each additional adult, $1 for children.

Information Contact the district manager (Queen St., Busselton, WA 6280, tel. 097/52–1677).

Stirling Range National Park

During the height of the wildflower season (September and October), the Stirling Ranges rival any botanical park in the world. Rising from the flat countryside, the ranges fill the horizon with a kaleidoscope of color. The Stirlings are considered the only true mountain range in southwest Australia. They were formed by the uplifting and buckling of sediments laid down by a now dried-up ancient sea. More than 1,000 wildflower species have been identified, including 69 species of orchid. This profusion of flowers attracts equal numbers of insects, reptiles, and birds, as well as a host of nocturnal honey possums. Emus and kangaroos are frequent visitors as well.

The extensive road system makes travel from peak to peak easy. Treks may be made from designated parking areas. Do not be fooled by the apparently short distances—a 3-kilometer (2-mile) walk up 1,073-meter (3,541-foot) Bluff Knoll takes about three hours round-trip. The walks are rated easy to moderate, but the going is strictly uphill. Take plenty of water and wet-weather gear—the park's location on the south coast makes Stirling subject to sudden storms. Before attempting longer hikes, register your intended routes in the ranger's log book, and remember to log out upon return.

Arriving and Departing Located 400 kilometers (248 miles) southeast of Perth, the park can be reached by traveling along the Albany Highway to Kojonup, proceeding east via Broome Hill and Gnowangerup, and then veering south through Borden onto the Albany Road.

Lodging The only camping within the park is at **Moingup Springs,** which provides toilets, water, and barbecues. The burning of wood is prohibited. Fees are $5 a night for two adults, $3 for additional adults, $1 for children. The privately owned **Stirling Range Caravan Park** (Borden, WA 6333, tel. 098/27–9229) is just north of the park's boundary opposite Bluff Knoll on Chester Pass Road, where hot and cold showers, laundry facilities, swimming pool, powered and unpowered sites, chalets, and cabins are available. Campfires are permitted. Camping fees are $8 for two adults; other accommodation starts at $22 per night.

Information Contact the **Stirling Range National Park** (Amelup via Borden, WA 6338, tel. 098/27–9230).

Elsewhere in the State

Monkey Mia. This is the setting for one of the world's most extraordinary natural wonders, for nowhere else do wild dolphins interact so freely with human beings. In 1964 a woman from one of the makeshift fishing camps in the area hand-fed one of the dolphins that regularly followed the fishing boats home. Other dolphins followed that lead, and today, an extensive family of wild dolphins now come of their own accord to be fed. For many visitors, standing in the shallow waters of Shark Bay to hand-feed a dolphin is the experience of a lifetime. There are no set feeding times—the wild dolphins can show up at any hour of the day at the public beach, where they will be fed by park rangers. The rangers will share their food with visitors who want to get close. There is also a Dolphin Information Centre, which has videos and information on the dolphins. *Hwy. 1 north from Perth* *for 800 km (500 mi) to the Denham/Hamelin Rd., then follow well-posted signs. Tel. 099/48–1366. Information center open daily 7–6.*

New Norcia. In 1846 a small band of Benedictine monks arrived in Australia to establish a mission for Aborigines. They settled in New Norcia, 128 kilometers (80 miles) north of Perth, and eventually built boarding schools and orphanages. Today the brothers in the monastic community continue to live a simple life of prayer and work—their devotion and labor produce the best olive oil in the state, pressed from the fruit of century-old trees. The original schools have developed into a Catholic college attended by more than 200 students. Follow the New Norcia Heritage Trail to explore the monastery, church, old mill, hotel, and jail, in addition to the museum and art gallery, which house unique collections of European and Australian paintings. *From Perth, take the Great Northern Hwy. (Rte. 95) north for 128 km (80 mi) to New Norcia.*

Ningaloo Reef Marine Park. Some of Australia's most pristine coral reef runs 260 kilometers (156 miles) along the coast of the Exmouth Peninsula, 1,200 kilometers (720 miles) north of Perth. A happy conjunction of migratory routes and accessibility make it one of the best places on earth to see huge manta rays, giant whale sharks, and the annual coral spawning. Tour operators differ from year to year, but the **Western Australian Tourist Centre** (tel. 09/483–1111) keeps up with current information. A unique tour, inaugurated in early 1993, allows a handful of travelers to assist in the tagging of the giant loggerhead and hawksbill turtles that come ashore to nest in December and January. This hands-on opportunity, organized by officers of the Department of Conservation and Land Management, is offered nowhere else in the country. For more information, contact **Coate's Wildlife Tours** (tel. 09/447–6016, fax 09/246–1995). *Take the North West Coastal Hwy. north 1,034 km (620 mi) to the Minilya turnoff; Exmouth, the peninsula's largest town, is 219 km (132 mi) north.*

York. Founded in the 1830s, this town stands as an excellent example of historic restoration. It sits in the lovely Avon Valley, 128 kilometers (80 miles) east of Perth, and its restored main street, Avon Terrace, still evokes the days of the 1890s gold rush. The tiny town is easy to explore on foot and contains lovely local sandstone edifices. The **York Motor Museum** (Avon Terr., tel. 096/41–1288) is open daily and houses more than 150 classic and vintage cars, motorcycles, and even some horse-drawn vehicles. Motorcoach rides are available. If you are going to spend the night, you might consider the lovely colonial **Settler's House** (Avon Terr., tel. 096/41–1096), a romantic hostelry with four-poster beds. *From Perth, take Great Eastern Hwy. (Rte. 94) 98 km (59 mi) to Northam, then head south on the Great Southern Highway 35 km (21 mi); Westrail provides bus service.*

13 Auckland and the North

By Michael Gebicki

Auckland, with a population of more than 800,000, is the largest city in New Zealand and the country's major gateway. It's the only city in the nation large enough to have a traffic problem (though one most international cities would envy), and your first impressions will probably be of calm, cleanliness, and a fertility that extends into the heart of the city. The drive from the airport will take you past the tall cones of extinct volcanoes, where grass as green and smooth as a billiards table is cropped by four-footed lawnmowers known as sheep.

Chances are that along the way you'll pass knots of cyclists and joggers. Aucklanders, like all New Zealanders, are addicted to the outdoors. There are some 70,000 powerboats and sailing craft in the Greater Auckland area—about one for every four households. Within an hour's drive of the city center are 102 beaches. Yet the city has not been kind to its greatest asset, Waitemata Harbour—a Maori name meaning "Sea of Sparkling Waters." Where there should be harborfront parks edged with palm trees and gardens, there are dockyards and warehouses instead.

Auckland is not an easy city to explore: It sprawls across its isthmus, with the Pacific Ocean on one side and the Tasman Sea on the other. If you arrive at the end of a long flight and time is limited, the best introduction to the city is the commuter ferry that crosses the harbor to Devonport, where you can soak up the atmosphere in a leisurely stroll.

Beyond Auckland, the Bay of Islands, to the north, is an area that's both beautiful and—as the place where modern New Zealand came into being with the signing of the Treaty of Waitangi in 1840—historic. Finally, off in a different direction, we outline a drive around the rugged and exhilarating Coramandel Peninsula.

Auckland

Important Addresses and Numbers

Tourist Information

Auckland Visitor Information Centre. *Aotea Sq., Queen and Myers Sts., tel. 09/366–6888. Open weekdays 8:30–5:30, weekends 9–5.*

Published every Thursday, *Auckland Tourist Times* is a free newspaper with the latest information on tours, exhibitions, and shopping. The paper is available from hotels and from the Visitor Information Centre.

Consulates

U.S. Consulate. *General Assurance Bldg., Shortland and O'Connell Sts., tel. 09/303–2724. Open weekdays 8–4:30.*

British Consulate. *Fay Richwhite Bldg., 151 Queen St., tel. 09/303–2971. Open weekdays 9:30–12:20.*

Canadian Consulate. *Jetset Centre, 48 Emily Pl., tel. 09/309–8516. Open weekdays 8:30–4:30.*

Australian Consulate. *Union House, 32–38 Quay St., tel. 09/303–2429. Open weekdays 8:30–4:45.*

Emergencies

Dial 111 for **fire, police,** or **ambulance** services.

Hospital

Auckland Hospital. *Park Rd., Grafton, tel. 09/379–7440. Open daily 24 hrs.*

Doctors

Auckland Accident and Emergency Clinic. *122 Remuera Rd., tel. 09/524–5943 or 09/524–7906. Open daily 24 hrs.*

Dentists For emergency dental services, phone **St. John's Ambulance** and ask for the nearest dentist on duty. *Tel. 09/579–9099. Open daily 24 hrs.*

Where to Change Money The Bank of New Zealand branch inside the international terminal of Auckland International Airport is open for all arriving and departing flights. There are several currency-exchange agencies at the lower end of Queen Street, between Victoria and Customs streets, offering the same rate as the banks (weekdays 9–5, Sat. 9–1; closed Sun.). Foreign currency may also be exchanged daily 8–4 at the cashier's office above Celebrity Walk, at the Drake Street entrance of Victoria Park Market (tel. 09/309–6911). Automatic teller machines can be found throughout the city center. A 24-hour exchange machine outside the Downtown Airline Terminal on Quay Street will change notes of any major currency into New Zealand dollars, but the rate is significantly less than that offered by banks.

Late-night Pharmacy The Late-night Pharmacy. *60 Broadway, tel. 09/520–6634. Open weekdays 5:30 PM–7 AM, weekends 9 AM–7 AM.*

Travel Agencies American Express Travel Service. *101 Queen St., tel. 09/379–8243.*

Thomas Cook. *107 Queen St., tel. 09/379–3924.*

Arriving and Departing by Plane

Airport **Auckland International Airport** lies 21 kilometers (13 miles) southwest of the city center. The **Visitor Information Centre** inside the terminal provides free maps and brochures as well as a booking service for tours and accommodations (open 5 AM–2 AM). Avis, Budget, and Hertz have offices inside the international terminal. A free **Interterminal Bus** links the international and domestic terminals, with frequent departures in each direction 6 AM–10 PM. Alternatively, the walk between the two terminals takes about 10 minutes along the signposted walkway. Luggage for flights aboard the two major domestic airlines, Air New Zealand and Ansett New Zealand, can be checked in at the international terminal.

Airlines Major international carriers serving Auckland include **British Airways** (tel. 09/367–7500), **Canadian Airlines International** (tel. 09/309–0735), **Qantas Airways** (tel. 09/379–0306), and **United Airlines** (tel. 09/379–3800).

Domestic carriers with services to Auckland are **Air New Zealand** (tel. 09/379–3510), **Air Nelson** (tel. 09/379–3510), **Ansett New Zealand** (tel. 09/302–2146), and **Mount Cook Airlines** (tel. 09/309–5395).

Airport to City Center The journey between the airport and the city center takes about 30 minutes.

By Bus **Johnston's Shuttle Express** (tel. 09/256–0333) operates a minibus service between the airport and any address in the city center. The cost is $12 for a single traveler, $9 per person for two traveling together. The service meets all incoming flights.

The **Airbus** (tel. 09/275–9396) leaves the international terminal every 20 minutes between 6:20 AM and 8:20 PM. The fixed route between the airport and the Downtown Airline Terminal, on the corner of Quay Street and Albert Road, includes a stop at the railway station and, on request, at any bus stop, hotel, or motel along the way. Returning from the city, the bus leaves the Downtown Airline Terminal at 20-minute intervals between 6:20 AM and 9 PM. *Cost: $9 adults, $3 children 5–14.*

By Taxi The fare to the city is between $30 and $35.

By Limousine **Gateway Limousines and Tours** (tel. 09/528–9198) operates Ford LTD limousines between the airport and the city. The cost is approximately $60.

Arriving and Departing by Car, Train, and Bus

By Car By the standards of most cities, Auckland's traffic is light, parking space is inexpensive and readily available, and motorways pass close to the heart of the city. On the other hand, unless your accommodation is some distance from the city, there's no real advantage in having a car of your own.

By Train The terminal for all InterCity train services is **Auckland Central Railway Station** (tel. 09/358–4085) on Beach Road, about 1½ kilometers (1 mile) east of the city center. A booking office is located inside the Auckland Visitor Information Centre at Aotea Square, 299 Queen Street.

By Bus The terminal for **InterCity Coaches** (tel. 09/358–4085) is the Auckland Central Railway Station (*see above*). **Newmans Coaches** (tel. 09/309–9738) arrive and depart from the Downtown Airline Terminal, on the corner of Quay and Albert streets.

Getting Around

By Bus Auckland's public bus system, the **Yellow Bus Company,** operates Monday–Saturday 6 AM–11:30 PM, Sunday 9 AM–5 PM. The main terminal for public buses is the **Municipal Transport Station,** between Commerce Street and Britomart Place near the Central Post Office. The bus network is divided into zones; fares are calculated according the number of zones traveled. For travel within the inner city, the fare is 40¢ for adults, 20¢ for children 5–15. **BusAbout passes,** which allow unlimited travel on all buses after 9 AM daily, are available from bus drivers for $8 adults, $4 children. For timetables, bus routes, fares, and lost property, stop by the **Bus Place,** on the corner of Hobson and Victoria streets (weekdays 8:15–5), or call **Buz A Bus** (tel. 09/366–6400, Mon.–Sat. 7–7).

By Taxi Taxis can be hailed in the street but are more readily available from the cab ranks located throughout the city. Auckland taxis operate different tariffs depending on which company you use, but the fare and flag fall are listed on the driver's door. Most taxis will accept American Express, Diners, MasterCard, or Visa cards. **Alert Taxis** (tel. 09/309–2000), **Auckland Cooperative Taxi Service** (tel. 09/300–3000), and **Eastern Taxis** (tel. 09/527–7077) are reliable operators with radio-controlled fleets.

Guided Tours

Orientation The most economical introduction to Auckland is the **United Airlines Explorer Bus** (tel. 09/360–0033). The blue-and-silver double-decker bus travels in a circuit, stopping at six of the city's major attractions; passengers can leave at any stop and reboard any following Explorer bus. The buses depart from the Downtown Airline Terminal every hour between 11 and 4 daily; tickets are available from the driver. *Fares: $10 adults, $5 children 5–15.*

Scenic Tours (tel. 09/634–0189) operates a three-hour *City Highlights* guided bus tour, which takes in the main attractions in the city and Parnell and the view from the lookout on Mount Eden. Tours leave at 9:30 and 2, and tickets are $32 adults, $16 children 5–14, $5 children 2–4. The **Gray Line** (tel. 09/358–5868) operates a Morning

Highlights tour, which includes admission to Kelly Tarlton's Underwater World (*see* What to See and Do with Children, *below*). This tour departs daily from the Downtown Airline Terminal on Quay Street at 9 AM and costs $42 adults, $21 children 5–14.

Special-Interest The **Antipodean Explorer** (tel. 09/302–2400) offers a minibus tour of
Tours the wineries, coast, and native forests of the Waitakere Ranges west of Auckland, including a visit to a gannet colony. It costs $55 and departs daily at 9:30 AM from the Downtown Airline Terminal.

Boat Tours Various companies offer cruises of Waitemata Harbor; one of the best and least expensive is the **Devonport commuter ferry.** The ferry terminal is located on the harbor side of the Ferry Building on Quay Street, near the corner of Albert Street. Ferries depart Monday–Thursday 6:15 AM–11 PM, Friday and Saturday 6:15 AM–1 AM, and Sunday 7 AM–11 PM. *Round-trip tickets: $7 adults, $3.50 children 5–15.*

The **Pride of Auckland Company** (tel. 09/373–4557) operates lunch and dinner sailing cruises on the inner harbor, departing at 12:30 and 6 from the wharf opposite the Downtown Airline Terminal on the corner of Quay and Albert streets. *Tickets: $35 lunch, $75 dinner.*

Fullers Cruise Centre (tel. 09/377–1771) offers a variety of cruises of the harbor and to the islands of the Hauraki Gulf. The two-hour coffee cruise ($22 adults, $11 children 4–14) departs daily at 9:30, 11:30, 1:30, and 3:30. The Supercat cruise ($50 adults, $25 children) to Great Barrier Island, the most distant of the Hauraki Gulf Islands, is a popular day trip for Aucklanders. The cruise departs Tuesday, Thursday, and weekends at 9.

Exploring Auckland

Numbers in the margin correspond to points of interest on the Auckland map.

1 This walk begins at the **Civic Theatre** on the corner of Queen and Wellesley streets, one block down Queen Street from the Visitor Information Centre. This extravagant art nouveau movie theater was the talk of the town when it opened in 1929, but just nine months later the owner, Thomas O'Brien, went bust and fled, taking with him the week's revenues and an usherette. During World War II a cabaret show in the basement was popular with Allied servicemen in transit to the battlefields of the Pacific. One of the entertainers, Freda Stark, is said to have appeared regularly wearing nothing more than a coat of gold paint.

2 Walk up Wellesley Street toward the white building with the clock on top. This is the **Auckland City Art Gallery,** which houses the country's finest collection of contemporary art as well as paintings of New Zealand dating back to the time of Captain Cook. Watch for works by Frances Hodgkins, New Zealand's best-known artist. *Cnr. Kitchener St. and Wellesley St. E, tel. 09/379–2020. Admission free. Open 10–4:30.*

3 Turn into Kitchener Street, walk past the fountain, and climb the stone stairs on the right. At the top is **Albert Park,** 15 acres of formal gardens, fountains, and statue-studded lawns. The park is built on the site of a garrison that was intended to protect the settlement from the neighboring Maori tribes. There are still remnants of its stone walls (with rifle slits) behind the university buildings on the eastern side of the park.

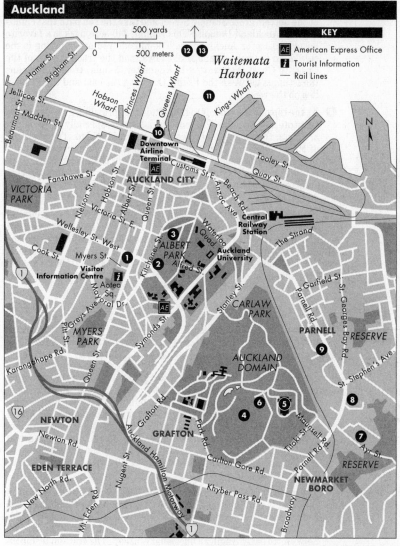

Auckland

KEY

AE American Express Office

ⓘ Tourist Information

— Rail Lines

Waitemata Harbour

0 — 500 yards

0 — 500 meters

Hamer St.

Brigham St.

Jellicoe St.

Beaumont St.

Madden St.

Hobson Wharf

Princes Wharf

Queens Wharf

Kings Wharf

Downtown Airline Terminal

Customs St. E.

Anzac Ave.

Beach Rd.

Tooley St.

Quay St.

AUCKLAND CITY

AE

Fanshawe St.

VICTORIA PARK

Nelson St.

Hobson St.

Albert St.

Victoria St. E.

Queen St.

Wellesley St. West

Cook St.

Myers St.

Visitor Information Centre

ⓘ

Aotea Sq.

Mayoral Dr.

Kitchener St.

ALBERT PARK

Waterloo Quad

Alfred St.

Auckland University

Central Railway Station

The Strand

Garfield St.

Parnell Rd.

St. Georges Bay Rd.

Stanley St.

CARLAW PARK

PARNELL

RESERVE

Greys Ave.

Pitt St.

MYERS PARK

Queen St.

Symonds St.

AE

Karangahape Rd.

AUCKLAND DOMAIN

St. Stephen's Ave.

NEWTON

Newton Rd.

Grafton Rd.

GRAFTON

Park Rd.

Carlton Gore Rd.

Maunsell Rd.

Thoki Rd.

Parnell Rd.

Ayr St.

RESERVE

EDEN TERRACE

New North Rd.

Mt. Eden Rd.

Nugent St.

Auckland Hamilton Motorway

Khyber Pass Rd.

Broadway

NEWMARKET BORO

Albert Park, **3**

Auckland City Art Gallery, **2**

Auckland Domain, **4**

Auckland Institute and Museum, **5**

Cathedral Church of St. Mary, **8**

Civic Theatre, **1**

Ewelme Cottage, **7**

Ferry Building, **10**

Mount Victoria, **13**

Parnell Village, **9**

Victoria Road, **12**

Waitemata Harbour, **11**

Wintergardens, **6**

Leave the park and cross onto Alfred Street. Continue downhill and at the bottom cross Stanley Street and take the red path that climbs

❹ into the **Auckland Domain.** This rolling, 340-acre park is a favorite leisure space for Aucklanders. The hillside you are climbing is the side of an extinct volcano, Pukekawa, and the track is part of the Coast to Coast Walkway, a 13-kilometer (8-mile) track that spans the isthmus between the Pacific Ocean on the east and the Tasman Sea on the west.

❺ At the top of the path, off to the left, is the sprawling gray **Auckland Institute and Museum.** The museum is known especially for its Maori artifacts, the largest and finest collection of its kind. The portraits of Maori chiefs by C. F. Goldie are splendid character studies of a fiercely martial people. Other collections in the museum are dedicated to natural history, geology, military history, and a reconstructed streetscape of early Auckland. *Auckland Domain, tel. 09/ 309–0443. Admission free. Open daily 10–5.*

Leave the museum by the front door, pausing for a fine view of Waitemata Harbour with Rangitoto Island to the right. Turn left and walk down toward the twin-domed buildings. These are the

❻ greenhouses of the Wintergardens, housing an exotic collection of tropical plants and palms. The wisteria-covered loggia surrounding the sunken courtyard is a shady spot for a rest on a warm day. *Auckland Domain. Admission free. Open daily 10–4.*

Return to the museum, walk past the entrance and on to the back of the building, and follow the road down the hill past the Parnell Lawn Tennis Club. Continue as this road becomes Maunsell Road, turn left into Parnell Road, and turn right at Ayr Street. Behind a white

❼ picket fence on the left is **Ewelme Cottage,** built by the Reverend Vicesimus Lush and inhabited by his descendants for more than a century. The house is constructed of kauri, a resilient timber highly prized by the Maoris for their war canoes. With the arrival of Europeans, kauri became the basic building material for the new settlement, and the kauri forests were rapidly depleted. All kauris are now protected by law, but only a few majestic examples of mature ones remain in the forests. Ewelme Cottage contains much of the original furniture and personal effects of the Lush family. *14 Ayr St., tel. 09/379–0202. Admission: $2.50 adults, 50¢ children 5– 15. Open daily 10:30–noon and 1–4:30.*

Return to Parnell Road and turn right. The splendid white church on

❽ the right is the Anglican **Cathedral Church of St. Mary,** built in 1886 and regarded as one of the world's finest examples of a Gothic wooden church. This is one of a number of churches built by Bishop Selwyn, an early Anglican missionary bishop. The craftsmanship inside the church is remarkable, but just as remarkable is the story of the church's relocation. St. Mary's originally stood on the other side of Parnell Road, but in 1982 the entire structure was jacked up, placed on a bed of steel girders, put on rollers, and hauled across to the other side. Photographs inside show the progress of the work. The church now forms part of the Cathedral of the Holy Trinity. *Parnell Rd. and St. Stephen's Ave. Open daily 8–6.*

Just below the intersection of St. Stephen's Avenue, the streetscape

❾ suddenly changes character. This is the beginning of **Parnell Village,** an avenue of pretty Victorian timber villas that have been transformed into antiques shops, designer boutiques, street cafés, and restaurants. Parnell Village is the creation of Les Harvey, who saw the potential of the quaint but run-down shops and houses and almost single-handedly snatched them from the jaws of the developers' bulldozers by buying them, renovating them, and leasing them out. Harvey's vision has paid handsome dividends, and today this village of trim pink-and-white timber facades is a delightful part of the city. At night its restaurants, pubs, and discos attract Auckland's smart set. Parnell is also one of the few places in Auckland where the shops are open Sunday.

Time Out   At the heart of Parnell Village, **Konditorei Boss** is a pleasant and inexpensive sidewalk café selling open sandwiches, soups, salads, and a wicked but irresistible collection of cakes. There is no table service; walk inside and make your selection from the counter. *305 Parnell Rd., Parnell, tel. 09/377–8953. Open daily 8–5.*

Find the United Airlines Explorer Bus stop, about 50 yards above Konditorei Boss, and take the next bus to the Downtown Airline Terminal ($1 adults, 50¢ children 5–15). Explorer buses depart this stop at 11:45 and then at one-hour intervals until 4:45.

⑩ At the terminal, cross Quay Street to the imposing **Ferry Building** and purchase a ferry ticket for Devonport ($7 adults, $3.50 children 5–15 round-trip). Ferries leave for Devonport weekdays on the hour between 10 and 3, and at half-hour intervals during the morning and evening commuter periods; on Saturday they leave every hour from 6:15 AM until 1 AM, on Sunday from 7 AM to 11 PM.

⑪ The 20-minute ride to Devonport across **Waitemata Harbour** provides one of the finest views of Auckland. The first harbor ferry service began with whaleboats in 1854. Later in the century the Devonport Steam Ferry Co. began operations, and ferries scuttled back and forth across the harbor until the Harbour Bridge opened in 1959. The bridge now carries the bulk of the commuter traffic, but the ferry still has a small, devoted clientele.

From the Devonport wharf, cross Marine Square and walk along **⑫ Victoria Road.** Devonport, the first settlement on the north side of the harbor, was originally known as Flagstaff, after the signal station on the summit of Mount Victoria. Later the area drew some of the city's wealthiest traders, who built their homes where they could watch their sailing ships arriving with cargoes from Europe. These days the village of Devonport has a relaxed, seaside atmosphere, despite its proximity to the city.

Walk away from the harbor along Victoria Road, past the shops and cafés that line this pleasant avenue. At the end of the street, bear **⑬** right into Kerr Street and turn left to climb **Mount Victoria.** Don't be put off by the name—this is more molehill than mountain. Long before the era of European settlement, this ancient volcano was the site of a Maori *pa*, a fortified village of the local Kawerau tribe. On the northern and eastern flanks of the hill you can still see traces of the terraces that palisades of sharpened stakes once protected.

Return to the ferry terminal via Victoria Road. On weekdays, ferries leave for the city every hour on the half hour between 9:30 and 2:30, and every half hour during the morning and evening commuter periods. On weekends, ferries leave Devonport at 6:30 AM, then every hour on the half hour until 9:30 PM. The last boat leaves Devonport at 11:30 PM Monday–Thursday, 12:30 AM on Friday and Saturday, and 10:30 PM on Sunday.

Auckland for Free

On weekdays during the spring and summer months, **Aotea Square** becomes the venue for a series of free outdoor performances by groups ranging from classical string quartets to jazz artists to Pacific Islander dance companies. The one-hour performances generally begin at 12:30. For recorded "what's on" information, phone the **Aotea Centre Hotline** (tel. 09/309–2678). *BNZ Foyer, Aotea Sq., Queen St. near Myers St.*

What to See and Do with Children

Hobson Wharf. New Zealand's rich seafaring heritage is celebrated at the National Maritime Museum, housed in a new marina complex on Auckland Harbour. Exhibits include Polynesian outrigger canoes, a brigantine, a scow, a steam crane ship, and examples of the sleek sailboats that can still be seen racing in the harbor. The museum also hosts workshops, where traditional boatbuilding, sailmaking, and rigging skills are kept alive. The pride of the museum is the *KZ1*, the 133-foot racing sloop built for the America's Cup challenge in 1988. *Eastern Viaduct, Quay St., tel. 09/358–3010. Admission: $9 adults, $4 children 5–17, $18 family. Open Oct.–Easter Mon.–Thurs. 10–6, Fri.–Sun. 10–9; Easter–Sept. daily 10–5.*

Kelly Tarlton's Underwater World and Antarctic Encounter. The creation of New Zealand's most celebrated undersea explorer and treasure hunter, this harborside marine park offers a fish-eye view of the sea without getting wet. The main attraction is a submerged transparent tunnel, 120 yards long, where a slow-moving walkway makes a circuit while moray eels and lobsters peer from rock caverns and sharks and stingrays glide overhead. The second part of the complex is Antarctic Encounter, opened in early 1994. Visitors enter through a replica of Scott's Hut at McMurdo Sound, then circle around a deep-freeze environment aboard a heated snow cat that winds through a penguin colony and an aquarium exhibiting marine life of the polar sea. The ride emerges at Scott Base 2000 for a glimpse of the next century's antarctic research and exploration. *Orakei Wharf, Tamaki Dr., tel. 09/528–0603. Admission: $16 adults, $8 children 4–11.*

Museum of Transport and Technology. This fascinating collection of aircraft, telephones, cameras, locomotives, steam engines, and farming equipment is a tribute to Kiwi ingenuity. One of the most intriguing exhibits is the remains of an aircraft built by Robert Pearse, who made a successful powered flight barely three months after the Wright brothers first took to the skies. The flight ended inauspiciously when his plane crashed into a hedge, but Pearse, considered a wild eccentric by his farming neighbors, is recognized today as a mechanical genius. *Great North Rd., Western Springs, tel. 09/846–0199. Admission: $8.50 adults, $4.50 children 5–15. Open weekdays 9–5, weekends 10–5.*

Off the Beaten Track

On Friday and Saturday after 7 PM, the regular Devonport ferry is replaced by the **MV *Kestrel,*** a turn-of-the-century ferry restored to its brassy splendor and fitted out with a bar and a jazz band ($7 adults, $3.50 children 5–15). For a night to remember, leave the ferry at Devonport, dine at the Torpedo Bay Bar and Brasserie above the ferry terminal, then take an evening stroll through the historic streets.

Shopping

Shopping Districts
Auckland's main shopping precinct for clothes, outdoor gear, duty-free goods, greenstone jewelry, and souvenirs is **Queen Street. Ponsonby,** about 1½ kilometers (1 mile) west of the city center, is known for its antiques shops and fashion boutiques.

Department Stores
Smith and Caughey Ltd. is Auckland's only department store. *253–261 Queen St., tel. 09/377–4770. Open Mon.–Thurs. 9–5, Fri. 9–9, Sat. 9–1.*

Street Markets
Victoria Park Market is Auckland's main bazaar—2½ acres of clothing, footwear, sportswear, furniture, souvenirs, and crafts at knockdown prices. It's housed in the city's former garbage incinerator. The International Foodhall has a range of inexpensive dishes from Thai to Texan. *Cnr. Victoria and Wellesley Sts., tel. 09/309–6911. Open Mon.–Sat. 9–7, Sun. 10–7.*

Specialty Stores
Books
Whitcoulls is a general bookshop with a good selection of New Zealand titles. *186 Queen St., tel. 09/377–8329. Open Mon.–Thurs. 9–5:30, Fri. 9–9, Sat. 9–noon.*

Clothes
Action Downunder is part of a nationwide chain of stores selling high-quality outdoor clothing for men and women. *75 Queen St., tel. 09/309–0241. Open Mon.–Thurs. 9–5:30, Fri. 9–9, Sat. 9–4, Sun. 11–5.*
Wool 'n' Trends has a high-quality selection of knitted woolen garments and woven hangings. *85 Victoria Rd., Devonport, tel. 09/445–2226. Open Oct.–Mar., daily 9–6, closed Sun. Apr.–Sept.*

Sports and Hiking
Kathmandu sells quality New Zealand–made clothing and equipment for the outdoor enthusiast. *350 Queen St., tel. 09/309–4615. Open Mon.–Thurs. 9–5:30, Fri. 9–9., Sat. 9–2, Sun. 10–2.*
Infomaps, published by the Department of Survey and Land Information, are essential equipment for wilderness walkers. The complete range is available from the department's office. *6th Floor, AA Centre, cnr. Albert and Victoria Sts., tel. 09/377–1899. Open weekdays 8–4.*

Souvenirs
He Kohinga specializes in high-quality Maori art, including carved greenstone and wooden bowls and flutes made from native totara. *259 Parnell Rd., tel. 09/366–4585. Open Mon.–Sat. 10–5:30, Sun. 11–4.*
Wild Places sells posters, T-shirts, books, and cards on the themes of whales, rain forests, and native birds. All proceeds go to conservation projects in New Zealand and the Pacific. *28 Lorne St., tel. 09/358–0795. Open Mon.–Thurs. 9–5:30, Fri. 9–9, Sat. 9–noon.*

Sports and the Outdoors

Biking
Auckland is a pleasant and relaxed city for two-wheeled exploring, especially around its waterfront. **Penny Farthing Cycle Shop** hires out mountain bikes for $25 per day or $140 per week. *Cnr. Symonds St. and Khyber Pass Rd., tel. 09/379–2524. Open Sept.–Apr., Mon.–Thurs. 8:30–5:30, Fri. 8:30–9, weekends 9:30–3; May–Aug., Mon.–Thurs. 8:30–5:30, Fri. 8:30–9, Sat. 9:30–3.*

Golf
Chamberlain Park Golf Course is an 18-hole public course in a parkland setting a five-minute drive from the city. Clubs and golf carts can be hired from the club shop. *Linwood Ave., Western Springs, tel. 09/846–6758.*

Titirangi Golf Course, a 15-minute drive south of the city, is one of the country's finest 18-hole courses. Nonmembers are welcome to play provided they contact the professional in advance and show evidence of membership at an overseas golf club. Clubs and golf carts can be hired; the greens fee is $50. *Links Rd., New Lynn, tel. 09/827–5749.*

Jogging Auckland's favorite running track is **Tamaki Drive,** a 10-kilometer (6-mile) route that heads east from the city along the southern shoreline of Waitemata Harbour and ends at St. Heliers Bay. Close to the city, the **Auckland Domain** (*see* Exploring Auckland, *above*) is popular with executive lunchtime joggers.

Tennis **Auckland Tennis Inc.** offers a choice of 12 hard courts, either indoors or outdoors, a half mile east of the city center. *48 Stanley St., tel. 09/373–3623. Cost: $18 per hr outdoors, $30 per hr indoors. Open 11–7.*

Swimming **The Tepid Baths,** located near the heart of Auckland, has a large indoor swimming pool, a spa pool, saunas, and a steam room. *102 Customs St. W, tel. 09/379–4794. Admission: $5.50 adults, $3 children under 15; swimming pool only, $3.50 adults, $1.50 children under 15. Open weekdays 6 AM–10 PM, weekends 7–7.*

Spectator Sports **Eden Park** is the city's major stadium for sporting events. For information on current events, *Auckland Alive* is a quarterly guide available from the Visitor Information Centre. Tickets can be booked through Bass New Zealand (tel. 09/307–5000).

Beaches

Auckland's beaches are commonly categorized by area—East, West, or North. The ones closest to the city are the east coast beaches along Tamaki Drive, which are well protected and safe for children. **Judge's Bay** and **Mission Bay** are particularly recommended for their settings. The best swimming is at high tide. The west coast beaches are popular in the summer, but the sea is often rough, and sudden rips and holes can trap the unwary. The most popular of these is **Piha,** some 40 kilometers (25 miles) from Auckland, which has pounding surf as well as a sheltered lagoon dominated by the reclining mass of Lion Rock. **Whatipu,** south of Piha, is a broad sweep of sand offering safe bathing behind the sand bar that guards Manukau Harbour; **Bethells,** to the north, is exposed and often subject to heavy surf. Across Waitemata Harbour from the city, a chain of magnificent beaches stretches north as far as the Whangaparaoa Peninsula, 40 kilometers (25 miles) from Auckland. In the Hauraki Gulf, the island of **Waiheke** is ringed by a number of splendid small beaches.

Dining

Highly recommended restaurants are indicated by a star ★.

Category	Cost*
$$$$	over $45
$$$	$35–$45
$$	$25–$35
$	under $25

*per person, excluding drinks, service, and general sales tax (12.5%)

$$$$ Varick's. Varick Neilsen's converted two-story terrace house is still the first choice for many Aucklanders looking for a warm atmosphere and innovative food. The fried spicy tuatara fritters with mushrooms, lemon oil, and balsamic vinegar and the eel fillets with caramelized onions, garlic, and a red-wine *jus* are two of the first-course choices on a varied and imaginative menu. Main courses include roast venison cutlets with grilled vegetables and risotto, and grilled beef tournedos with a sweet pepper and black bean sauce. Varick's attracts a sophisticated, dressy clientele. *70 Jervois Rd., Herne Bay, tel. 09/376–2049. Reservations advised. Jacket required. AE, DC, MC, V. No lunch Mon., Tues., Sat. Closed Sun.*

$$$ The Brasserie. Auckland's Regent hotel has replaced its fine dining room with a bright, breezy, less formal dining room that's right for all seasons. Wild rice and shrimp chowder, crayfish tempura with mustard-seed sauce and potato cake, barbecued salmon steak with red caviar, and grilled lamb loin with *rösti* potatoes (hash browns) and spinach are offered on a menu that is essentially Mediterranean, with a fashionable tilt toward the Orient. Service is regally Regent. *Albert St., tel. 03/309–8888. Reservations not required. Dress: casual. AE, DC, MC, V.*

$$$ The French Café. Prices have crept up to match the reputation of
★ this modestly elegant city-fringe restaurant, whose menu draws from a variety of Mediterranean cuisines. A first-course salad of bocconcini, olives, tomatoes, and basil, and a main course of sautéed breast of chicken stuffed with sheep-milk cheese and prosciutto are representative of the summer menu. The restaurant has a brasserie-style dining room looking out onto the street and a more formal restaurant at the rear. On warm evenings you can sit in the courtyard. *210B Symonds St., tel. 09/377–1911. Reservations advised. Jacket required. AE, DC, MC, V. Closed Sun.*

$$$ Harbourside Seafood Bar and Grill. Overlooking the water from the upper level of the restored ferry building, this vast, modish, seafood restaurant is the perfect choice for warm-weather dining. Some of the finest New Zealand fish and shellfish, including orange roughy, salmon, and snapper, appear on a menu with a fashionably Mediterranean accent. Lobster fresh from the tank is a house specialty and the reason the restaurant is a favorite with Japanese tourists. Non–fish eaters have their choice of venison, lamb, and poultry. On warm nights, book ahead and request a table outside on the deck. *Auckland Ferry Bldg., 99 Quay St., tel. 09/307–0486. Reservations advised. Dress: casual. AE, DC, MC, V.*

$$$ Saint's Waterfront Brasserie. On any warm weekend, this stylish brasserie, a 15-minute drive from the city, is the perfect place to enjoy the city of sails sunny side up. The extensive lunch menu is mostly derived from French and Italian cooking, and includes soups, salads, open sandwiches, pasta, fish, beef, lamb, and sweetbreads. The dinner menu is a more substantial variation on the same theme. The weekend brunch menu offers healthy combinations of fresh fruit plates with yogurt, bagels, croissants, fruit whips, and muesli. The gray carpet and white tablecloths under glass create a smart, clean atmosphere, accented by art deco motifs. Big concertina doors frame an impressive sea view dominated by the cone of Rangitoto. *425 Tamaki Dr., St. Heliers, tel. 09/575–5210. Reservations advised on weekends. Dress: casual but neat. AE, DC, MC, V.*

$$$ Vinnie's. The decor—white tablecloths, black chairs, and a gunmetal-gray carpet—borders on austere, but there is nothing restrained about the gutsy French-Italian provincial cooking at this shopfront restaurant in suburban Herne Bay. Carpaccio of salmon with vanilla and olive oil, figs wrapped in prosciutto and flavored with melted

Auckland Dining and Lodging

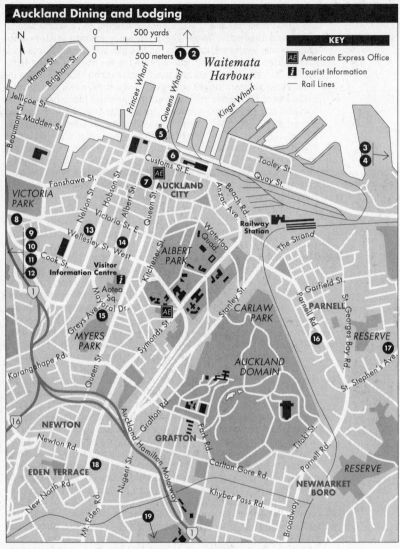

N

0   500 yards
0   500 meters

Waitemata Harbour

KEY

AE   American Express Office

i   Tourist Information

—   Rail Lines

Hamer St.

Brigham St.

Jellicoe St.

Beaumont St.

Madden St.

Princes Wharf

Queens Wharf

Kings Wharf

Tooley St.

Quay St.

Fanshawe St.

Customs St. E.

AE

AUCKLAND CITY

Beach Rd.

Anzac Ave.

Railway Station

The Strand

VICTORIA PARK

Nelson St.

Hobson St.

Albert St.

Queen St.

Victoria St. E.

Wellesley St. West

Cook St.

Visitor Information Centre

Kitchener St.

ALBERT PARK

Waterloo Quad

Stanley St.

CARLAW PARK

Garfield St.

Parnell Rd.

PARNELL

St. Georges Bay Rd.

RESERVE

Aotea Sq.

Mayoral Dr.

Greys Ave.

MYERS PARK

Queen St.

Symonds St.

AE

AUCKLAND DOMAIN

St. Stephen's Ave.

Karangahape Rd.

Auckland Hamilton Motorway

Grafton Rd.

NEWTON

Newton Rd.

EDEN TERRACE

New North Rd.

Nugent St.

Mt. Eden Rd.

GRAFTON

Park Rd.

Carlton Gore Rd.

Khyber Pass Rd.

Titoki St.

Parnell Rd.

RESERVE

NEWMARKET BORO

Broadway

Dining
The Brasserie, **7**
Cin Cin on Quay, **5**
Death by Chocolate, **12**
The French Café, **18**
Harbourside Seafood Bar and Grill, **5**
Iguacu, **16**

Rick's Café Americain, **8**
Saint's Waterfront Brasserie, **3**
Torpedo Bay Bar and Brasserie, **1**
Tuatara, **9**
Varick's, **10**
Vinnie's, **11**

Lodging
Albion Hotel, **13**
Ascott Parnell, **17**
Centra, **14**
Devonport Villa, **2**
Florida Motel, **4**
Hotel du Vin, **19**
Pan Pacific, **15**
Parkroyal, **6**
The Regent, **7**

mascarpone, lamb shanks cooked in red wine and rosemary with roasted garlic, and braised ox tongue with baby leeks are typical selections from a menu that also includes many imaginative game dishes. *166 Jervois Rd., Herne Bay, tel. 09/376–5597. Reservations advised. Dress: casual. AE, DC, MC, V. No lunch. Closed Sun.*

$$ **Cin Cin on Quay.** This busy, bold, waterfront oyster bar and
★ brasserie is an appealing combination to Auckland's 20-to-30-somethings, who come as much to let their hair down as for the menu. The food varies from pizzas made in the wood-fired oven to bar snacks such as sweet-potato fries with chili-spiced sour cream, to exotic main courses such as Thai-style seafood cooked in a clay pot. The aqua-and-amber decor and the music are anything but subtle. New Zealand wines are well represented on the extensive wine list, and a wide range of domestic and imported beers is available. The site right next to the Devonport ferry terminal is a bonus for anyone with time to kill before the next ferry. *Auckland Ferry Bldg., 99 Quay St., tel. 09/307–6966. Reservations advised. Dress: casual. AE, DC, MC, V.*

$$ **Iguacu.** At the leading edge of restaurant chic in Auckland, this restaurant is big, funky, and different. Flares blaze at the front, and dappled red ocher walls, enormous mirrors in Mexican metalwork frames, a big glass ceiling, and a pair of chandeliers made from copper tubing create a polished if culturally cacophonous atmosphere. The menu, like the decor, grazes the galaxy, with dishes such as Cajun-blackened kingfish with jambalaya rice, chicken curry with dahl and fried rice, teriyaki roast venison, and Polish sausage with sauerkraut; however it fails to leave an imprint with any distinctive cuisine of its own. *269 Parnell Rd., Parnell, tel. 09/309–4124. Reservations not required. Dress: casual. AE, DC, MC, V.*

$$ **Rick's Café Americain.** Owned by an American named Rick, this casual bistro in the Victoria Park Markets is aimed at a young market, but the chrome-and-neon decor, spirited service, reasonable prices, and subdued rock and funky jazz give it a wide appeal. Burgers, spare ribs, steaks, and pasta are staples on the menu, but there are several exotic surprises, such as tandoori lamb satay, wild mushroom ragout, and a vegetarian pie with spinach and feta cheese. Rick's is open daily for breakfast. In Parnell, **Rick's Blue Falcon** has an identical menu. *Victoria Park Market, tel. 09/309–9074. No reservations. Dress: casual. AE, DC, MC, V. Rick's Blue Falcon: 27 Falcon St., Parnell, tel. 09/309–0854.*

$$ **Torpedo Bay Bar and Brasserie.** Overlooking the harbor from the new Devonport ferry terminal, Auckland's breeziest restaurant has exceptional views. The two dozen dishes on the summer menu include pizzas, pasta, salads, and main courses such as baked salmon, chicken breast with scallops, panfried pork medallions, and baked venison. The art deco–inspired interior is pleasant but a long second to the deck; it's essential to book ahead to ensure an outside table. *Devonport Wharf, tel. 09/445–9770. Reservations advised. Dress: casual but neat. AE, DC, MC, V.*

$$ **Tuatara.** Although it takes its name from a local reptile, there is nothing sluggish about Auckland's hippest bistro. The menu is a capable but unambitious roundup of current crowd pleasers, with a choice of salads, focaccia, an antipasto plate, pasta, fish and shellfish, and main courses such as grilled chicken breast with sweet peppers, sun-dried tomatoes, and baby potatoes. Ambience is consciously understated: bare wooden floors, cream-color walls, chunky tables, a big wooden bar in the middle, medium-volume reggae music, and folding glass doors that allow the inevitably

crowded tables to spill out onto Ponsonby Road. *198 Ponsonby Rd., Ponsonby, tel. 09/360–0098. No reservations. Dress: casual but neat. AE, DC, MC, V.*

$ **Death by Chocolate.** This dessert-only restaurant is strictly for
★ chocoholics. Butterscotch pecan ice cream with fresh cream, chocolate flakes in a chocolate-covered waffle cone, chocolate scallop shells with melon and summer berries dusted with caster sugar, and ice cream studded with caramel balls and served with hot fudge sauce are typical of the gooey delights. *42 Jervois Rd., Ponsonby, tel. 09/360–2828. Reservations not required. Dress: casual but neat. AE, DC, MC, V. No lunch.*

Lodging

Highly recommended lodgings are indicated by a star ★.

Category	Cost*
$$$$	over $200
$$$	$125–$200
$$	$80–$125
$	under $80

*All prices are for a standard double room, excluding general sales tax (12.5%).

$$$$ **Hotel du Vin.** There can be no finer introduction to New Zealand
★ than to head south from the Auckland International Airport to this smart, luxurious hotel, set on the floor of a valley and surrounded by native forests and the grapevines of the de Redcliffe Estate. Standard rooms are palatial, and the rooms built in 1987 were upgraded in 1994, but request one of the newer rooms at the far end of the resort. The decor is crisp and modern, and the central restaurant and reception areas glow with honey-color wood and rough stone fireplaces. The restaurant has an excellent reputation, though prices are high. The hotel is 40 miles from Auckland, a 45-minute drive from both Auckland airport and the city via the motorway. *Lyons Rd., Mangatawhiri Valley, tel. 09/233–6314, fax 09/233–6215. 46 rooms with bath. Facilities: bar, restaurant, heated indoor pool, spa, gym, tennis courts, bicycles, winery. AE, DC, MC, V.*

$$$$ **Pan Pacific.** When this atrium-style hotel opened early in 1990, it became the most glamorous member of the city's five-star elite. Guest rooms are spacious and elegantly furnished, and the bathrooms are particularly well equipped. The best views are from the rooms that overlook the parklands and the harbor to the east. Polished granite and warm, earthy tones have been used liberally throughout the hotel. A favorite with business travelers, it is located close to the Aotea Centre and the business and shopping districts. *Mayoral Dr., tel. 09/366–3000, fax 09/366–0121. 286 rooms with bath. Facilities: 2 bars, 2 restaurants, 24-hr coffee shop, tennis court. AE, DC, MC, V.*

$$$$ **Parkroyal.** This was Auckland's premier hotel for almost two decades after it was built in the late '60s, but its age is difficult to ignore. The hotel is scrupulously maintained and constantly upgraded, but no amount of tender loving care can overcome the slightly cramped rooms and, by today's standards, limited natural lighting. On the positive side, it has a comforting clublike atmosphere, and its location at the lower end of Queen Street, close to the ferry terminal, is one of the best of any city hotel. *8 Customs St., tel.*

09/377–8920, fax 09/307–3739. 188 rooms with bath. Facilities: 4 bars, 2 restaurants. AE, DC, MC, V.

$$$$ ★ The Regent. This mid-city hotel brought a dash of style to Auckland when it opened in the mid-'80s, and despite some energetic competitors, its service, sophistication, and attention to detail keep it on top. Standard rooms are large and furnished extensively with natural fabrics and native timbers. The marble bathrooms are luxuriously appointed. Due to a refurbishment, to be substantially completed by early 1995, the rooms are decorated in a warmer style, with dark wood furnishings and patterned fabrics, creating an art deco flavor. The best rooms are on the harbor side—the higher the better. *Albert St., tel. 09/309–8888, fax 09/379–6445. 332 rooms with bath. Facilities: bar, 3 restaurants, heated outdoor pool. AE, DC, MC, V.*

$$$ Centra. Rooms at this city landmark are equal to those in just about any of Auckland's leading hotels, but cutting down on the facilities and the glossy public areas has made the price substantially lower. Rooms have a standard, functional layout, and each has its own iron and ironing board. Accommodation begins on the 16th floor, and every room has a view. The suites on the 28th floor have great views and bigger bathrooms for just a slightly higher price. The hotel, which opened in 1991, is aimed primarily at the business traveler. Service is keen and professional. *128 Albert St., tel. 09/302–1111, fax 09/302–3111. 252 rooms with bath. Facilities: bar, restaurant, gym. AE, DC, MC, V.*

$$ Ascott Parnell. Accommodations and facilities in this sprawling guest house are comfortable and functional, but space and character have been sacrificed to provide rooms with en suite facilities or private bathrooms at a reasonable price. The room with the attached sunroom at the back of the house is small but pleasant. The house stands on a leafy back street, within easy walking distance of the shops and nightlife of Parnell Village. Smoking is not permitted inside, and children 2–8 are not accommodated. *36 St. Stephens Ave., Parnell, tel. 09/309–9012, fax 09/309–3729. 9 rooms with bath. Tariff includes full breakfast. AE, MC, V.*

$$ ★ Devonport Villa. This guesthouse has just relocated to a new villa: the former Towers Bed & Breakfast. The new location is one block away from the old one—still two minutes' walk to Cheltenham Beach and a bit closer to Devonport Village—and still combines tranquil, historic surroundings and fresh sea air, with the city just a boat ride away. Rooms are individually decorated and have handmade quilts, queen-size beds with Edwardian-style headboards, lace curtains, and colonial furniture. Cheltenham Beach, which offers safe swimming, is a two-minute walk away. The house is a 10-minute walk from the ferry terminal, but the owner will pick up arriving guests. *46 Tainui Rd., Devonport, tel. 09/445–8397, fax 09/445–9766. 4 rooms with bath. Tariff includes full breakfast. Facilities: garden, guest lounge. AE, V.*

$$ Florida Motel. Located in a harborside suburb a 15-minute drive east of the city center (and close to a major bus route into the city), this motel offers exceptional value. Rooms come in three versions: studios or one- or two-bedroom units. The units have a lounge room separate from the bedroom, and the two-bedroom units are particularly good for families. All rooms have separate, fully equipped kitchens and a few extra touches of luxury, such as wall-mounted hair dryers, plunger-type coffee makers, and ironing boards with irons. The motel is immaculately maintained and extremely popular, and rooms must be booked several months in advance. *11*

Speight Rd., Kohimarama, tel. 09/521–4660, fax 09/521–4662. 8 rooms with bath. AE, DC, MC, V.

$ **Albion Hotel.** If you're looking for comfortable, modern accommodations in the heart of the city and outstanding value, look no further. The rooms are modest in size and offer no views, but all are neat and well kept. The best room in the house, the Hobson Suite, is equipped with a waterbed and Jacuzzi and costs only slightly more than the standard rooms. Despite the busy corner location, the area is quiet after 6 PM. However, rooms on the lower floor can be affected by noise from the pub on the ground floor, which is especially popular on Friday nights. The Aotea Centre and the shops of Queen Street are only two blocks away. *Cnr. Hobson and Wellesley Sts., tel. 09/379–4900, fax 09/379–4901. 20 rooms with bath. Facilities: pub, brasserie. AE, DC, MC, V.*

The Arts

For a current listing of plays, opera, dance, and musical events in Auckland, a brochure called ***Auckland Alive*** is available from the Visitor Information Centre and the Aotea Centre. For current films, check the entertainment pages of the daily newspapers. Auckland's main venue for music and the performing arts is the **Aotea Centre** (at Aotea Square, near the corner of Queen and Myers streets), which hosts performances of music and drama throughout the year. For general inquiries there is an Information Desk (tel. 09/307–5050) in the Owens Foyer, level 2 of the complex. For recorded information on current events at the Aotea Centre, phone 09/309–2678. For bookings, phone **Bass New Zealand** (tel. 09/307–5000). Bass is the central booking agency for all theater, music, and dance performances, as well as for major sporting events.

Theater **The Mercury Theatre,** the country's largest professional company, gives regular performances of the latest hits in its 700-seat auditorium. The theater has two bars and a café, open before and after all shows. *9 France St., Newton, tel. 09/303–3869. Shows Mon.–Sat.*

Music The **Auckland Philharmonia Orchestra** performs regularly at the Aotea Centre (*see above*). The **New Zealand Symphony Orchestra** performs at the Town Hall and at the Aotea Centre.

Opera Dame Kiri Te Kanawa often performs at the Aotea Centre on return visits to her homeland, but tickets are usually sold out months in advance.

Nightlife

After sunset, the liveliest area of the city is Parnell, which has several restaurants, bars, and nightclubs.

Bars and **Cactus Jacks** is a mid-city bar that would like to believe it's some-
Lounges where deep in the heart of Texas. If you're looking for a convivial bar with a Tex-Mex menu and an impressive lineup of tequilas, this is the place. *Finance Plaza, 96 Albert St., tel. 09/302–0942. Open Mon.–Sat. 11 AM–1 AM.*

The Civic Tavern, at the heart of the city center, looks unremarkable from street level, but inside it, the **London Bar** has a vast selection of beers, **Murphy's Irish Bar** has jazz bands every night from Wednesday to Saturday, and **Younger's Tartan Bar** is "Auckland's only Scottish bar," with an impressive choice of Scotch whiskey. *1 Wellesley St., tel. 09/373–3684. Open Mon.–Sat. 11 AM–midnight.*

The Loaded Hog, one of the newest arrivals on Auckland's entertainment scene, is a popular, casual brewery and bistro with a choice of indoor or outdoor dining and drinking. Part of the new Hobson's Wharf development, the tavern has a vaguely nautical feel to go with its harborside location. Jazz musicians perform most evenings. *104 Quay St., tel. 09/366–6491. Open approx. 11 AM–1 AM.*

The Safari Bar, on the top floor of the Exchange Hotel, is a lively and attractive place that attracts a young, well-heeled crowd, especially on Friday and Saturday nights. On the floor below, the **Long Room** is a more subdued cocktail bar. Drinks are expensive. *99 Parnell Rd., Parnell, tel. 373–2531. Open Mon.–Sat 11 AM–midnight. Closed Sun.*

The Shakespeare Tavern is an atmospheric and popular pub in the middle of the city. The Shakespeare makes and serves its own beers, which go by such colorful names as Willpower Stout and Falstaff's Real Ale. There are several bars inside and live rock or jazz most evenings. *Cnr. Albert and Wyndham Sts., tel. 09/373–5396. Open Mon.–Sat. 11–11.*

Nightclubs **Number 7** is a long-standing favorite with Auckland's sophisticates, and you'll have to dress up to get through the door. On most evenings the club offers live jazz as well as disco music. *7 Windsor St., Parnell, tel. 09/379–4341. Admission: $6–$10. Open Wed.–Sat. 9 PM–3 AM.*

Rick's Blue Falcon is Auckland's version of the Hard Rock Café: a voguish interior decorated with car parts, rainbow-colored cocktails, and a steak and burger menu. Here, as elsewhere, this well-tested recipe attracts a varied clientele. Prices are moderate. The Attic Bar has live jazz or restrained rock every night. *27 Falcon St., Parnell, tel. 09/309–0854. Open daily noon–midnight.*

Studebaker Diner and Bar is a cross between a 50s-style diner and a stage set for *Phantom of the Opera*. The loud bar, disco, and café appeal to Auckland's early-20s set. Theme nights vary from rock on Tuesday to psychedelic on Sunday. *3 Lower Albert St., tel. 09/377–1950. Open Sun.–Tues. 5 PM–midnight, Wed.–Thurs. 5 PM–2 AM, Fri.–Sat. 5 PM–3 AM.*

Discos **The New Testament,** popularly abbreviated to TNT, is still rocking and shaking on Auckland's nefarious "K Road," the nucleus of the city's sex trade. The cavernous, two-level complex is composed of the Mosaic Bar, the China Beach Bar, the Cinema Dance Club—all open to the public—and The Sanctuary—open to members only. Drinks are moderately priced. *340 Karangahape Rd., tel. 09/379–9320. Admission: $5. Open Wed.–Sun. 9 PM–5 AM.*

Northland and the Bay of Islands

Beyond Auckland, the North Island stretches a long arm into the South Pacific. This is Northland, an undulating region of farms, forests, and marvelous beaches. The main attraction here is the Bay of Islands, an island-studded seascape with a mild, subtropical climate, and one of the finest game-fishing waters in the country—witness its record catches of marlin and mako shark. Big-game fishing is expensive, but many small fishing boats will take you out for an evening of trawling for as little as $35.

It was on the Bay of Islands that the first European settlement was established, and here that New Zealand became a nation with the signing of the Treaty of Waitangi in 1840. The main town is Paihia, a strip of motels and restaurants along the waterfront. If you plan to spend more than a day in the area, the town of Russell, just a short ferry trip away, makes a more atmospheric and attractive base.

Important Addresses and Numbers

Tourist Information Bay of Islands Visitor Information Centre. *Maritime Reserve, Paihia, tel. 09/402-7426. Open Nov.–Mar., daily 7:30–7:30; Apr.– Oct., daily 8–5.*

Emergencies Dial 111 for **fire, police,** or **ambulance** services.

Arriving and Departing

By Car The main route from Auckland is Highway 1. Leave the city by the Harbour Bridge and follow the signs to Whangarei. Driving time for the 250-kilometer (150-mile) journey to Paihia is about four hours.

By Bus **Northliner Express** (tel. 09/307–5873), **InterCity** (tel. 09/358–4085), and **Newmans** (tel. 09/309–9738) operate several daily bus services between Auckland and Paihia.

Guided Tours

Orientation **Fuller's Northland** operates one-, two-, and three-day tours from Auckland to the Bay of Islands. Recommended is its Bay Explorer tour, which includes a tour of the historic Waitangi Treaty House, a trip to Cape Reinga, a swim with dolphins, a voyage around the bay aboard a schooner, and accommodations in Russell. *Bay of Islands Travel Centre, Shop 2, Downtown Shopping Centre, Customs St., Auckland, tel. 09/358-0259. Tickets: $435 adults, $220 children 4–14.*

Russell Mini Tours offers a one-hour guided tour of the historic sights of Russell. Tours depart from the Fullers office, opposite the wharf. *Box 70, Russell, tel. 09/403–7891. Tickets: $8 adults, $4 children 5–15. Tours at 11, 1, 2, 3:30.*

Boat Tours **Fullers Northland** (*see above*) operates several cruises in the Bay of Islands, departing from both Paihia and Russell. The most popular is the half-day catamaran cruise to Cape Brett, at the eastern extremity of the bay. The Cream Trip is a six-hour cruise that stops in at many of the bay islands. *Maritime Bldg., Paihia, tel. 09/402-7421. Tickets: Cape Brett, $47 adults, $24 children 4–14; Cream Trip, $49 adults, $24 children. Cape Brett Cruise departs Paihia daily 9 AM and 1:30 PM; Cream Trip departs Paihia 10 AM, daily Oct.– May; Mon., Wed., Thurs., Sat. 10 AM, June–Sept.*

Exploring Northland

This tour begins at Auckland, traveling north to the Bay of Islands via Highway 1 and returning along the western side of the peninsula. The return route, Highway 12, adds almost two hours to the driving time, but the tranquil landscape makes an attractive alternative to Highway 1, which is particularly busy during the December–January holiday period.

Numbers in the margin correspond to points of interest on the Northland and the Bay of Islands map.

North of Waitemata Harbour, Highway 1 quickly leaves the city and the suburbs behind and weaves into rolling green hills around the town of **Albany.** In December, the pohutukawa trees along the roadside celebrate the arrival of Christmas by erupting in a blaze of scarlet blossoms, and hence their other name—the New Zealand Christmas tree. To the Maoris, the flowers had another meaning: the beginning of the shellfish season. The spiky-leaved plants that grow in clumps by the roadside are the New Zealand flax. The fibers of this plant, the raw material for linen, were woven into clothing by the Maoris. The huge tree ferns—common throughout the forests of North Island, where they can grow as high as 10 meters (30 feet)—are known locally as "pungas."

At the town of **Warkworth,** 69 kilometers (43 miles) from Auckland, turn right into McKinney Road, right again into Thompson Road, and then follow the signs to the **Warkworth Museum.** The main attraction here is the two giant kauri trees in the car park. The larger one, the **McKinney Kauri,** measures almost 25 feet around its base, yet this 800-year-old colossus is a mere adolescent by kauri standards. Kauri trees, once prolific in this part of the North Island, were highly prized by Maori canoe builders, because a canoe capable of carrying a hundred warriors could be made from a single trunk. Unfortunately these same characteristics—strength, size, and durability—made kauri timber ideal for ships, furniture, and housing, and the kauri forests were rapidly depleted by the early European settlers. Today the trees are protected by law, and many infant kauris are again appearing in the forests of the North Island, although their growth rate is painfully slow. The museum contains a collection of Maori artifacts and farming and domestic implements from the pioneering days of the Warkworth district. *Tudor Collins Dr., tel. 09/425–7093. Admission: $2 adults, 50¢ children 5–15. Open Dec.–Feb., daily 9:30–4; Mar.–Nov., daily 10–3:30.*

When you get to the town of **Whangarei,** cross the river and look for a sign on your left to **Clapham's Clock Museum.** Just about every conceivable method of telling time is represented in this collection of more than 1,400 clocks, from primitive water clocks to ships' chronometers to ornate masterworks from Paris and Vienna. Some of the most intriguing specimens were made by the late Mr. Clapham himself, including a World War II air force clock that automatically changed the position of aircraft over a map. Ironically, the one thing you won't find here is the correct time. If all the bells, chimes, gongs, and cuckoos went off together the noise would be deafening, so all the clocks are set to different times. *Water St., Cafler Park, Whangarei, tel. 09/438–3993. Admission: $3.50 adults, $1.20 children 5–15. Open daily 10–4.*

Paihia, the main holiday base for the Bay of Islands, is an unremarkable stretch of motels at odds with the quiet beauty of the island-studded seascape and the rounded green hills that form a backdrop to the town, yet nearby Waitangi is one of the country's most important historic sites. It was near here that the Treaty of Waitangi, the founding document for modern New Zealand, was signed.

At the northern end of town, on the far side of the Waitangi River, a side road turns right toward the **Waitangi National Reserve.** Inside the visitor center, a 23-minute video, shown every hour on the hour, sketches the events that led to the Treaty of Waitangi. The center also houses a display of Maori artifacts and weapons, including a musket that belonged to Hone Heke Pokai, the first Maori chief to sign the treaty. After his initial display of enthusiasm for British rule, Hone Heke was quickly disillusioned, and less than five years later he attacked the British in their stronghold at Russell.

Northland and the Bay of Islands

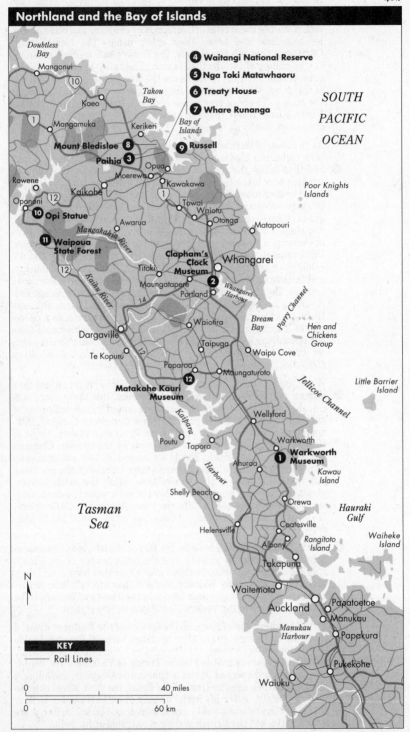

4 Waitangi National Reserve

5 Nga Toki Matawhaoru

6 Treaty House

7 Whare Runanga

SOUTH PACIFIC OCEAN

Doubtless Bay

Mangonui

(10)

Kaeo

Takou Bay

Mangamuka

(1)

Kerikeri

Bay of Islands

Mount Bledisloe 8   9 **Russell**

Paihia 3

Opua

Rawene

Moerewa

Kawakawa

(1)

Opononi

(12)

Opi Statue 10

Kaikohe

Towai

Waiotu

Otonga

Poor Knights Islands

Awarua

Matapouri

Waipoua State Forest 11

Mangakahia River

Clapham's Clock Museum

Titoki

Whangarei

(12)

Maungatapere

2

Portland

Whangarei Harbour

Kaihu River

14

Bream Bay

Parry Channel

Hen and Chickens Group

Waiotira

Dargaville

Taipuga

Waipu Cove

Te Kopuru

12

Paparoa

Jellicoe Channel

Little Barrier Island

12 Maungaturoto

Matakohe Kauri Museum

Kaipara Harbour

Wellsford

Poutu

Tapora

Warkworth

1 **Warkworth Museum**

Ahuroa

Kawau Island

Tasman Sea

Shelly Beach

Orewa

Coatesville

Hauraki Gulf

Helensville

Albany

Rangitoto Island

Waiheke Island

Takapuna

N

Waitemata

Auckland

Papatoetoe

Manukau

Manukau Harbour

Papakura

Pukekohe

Waiuku

KEY

— Rail Lines

0 ——— 40 miles

0 ——— 60 km

From the visitor center, follow the short track through the forest to
⑤ **Nga Toki Matawhaoru,** a Maori war canoe. This huge kauri canoe,
capable of carrying 150 warriors, is named after the vessel in which
Kupe, the Polynesian navigator, is said to have discovered New Zealand.

⑥ Follow the shoreline track and then cross the vast lawn to the **Treaty
House,** a five-minute stroll from the war canoe. There can have been
few more modest beginnings on the road to nationhood than this simple white timber cottage, which has a remarkable air of dignity despite its scale. The interior is fascinating, especially at the back,
where exposed walls give an insight into the difficulties that the early administrators faced—such as an acute shortage of bricks (since
an insufficient number had been shipped out from New South Wales)
with which to finish the walls.

The Treaty House was prefabricated in New South Wales for the
British Resident, James Busby, who arrived in New Zealand in
1832. Busby had been appointed to protect British commerce and
put an end to the brutalities of the whaling captains against the Maoris, but Busby lacked either the judicial authority or the force of
arms necessary to impose peace. On one occasion, unable to resolve a
dispute between Maori tribes, Busby was forced to shelter the
wounded of one side in his house. While tattooed head hunters
screamed war chants outside the windows, one of the warriors sheltered Busby's infant daughter, Sarah, in his cape.

The real significance of the Treaty House lies in the events that took
place here on February 6, 1840, the day that the **Treaty of Waitangi**
was signed by Maori chiefs and Captain William Hobson, represent-
ing the British crown. Under the treaty, the chiefs agreed to accept
the authority of the crown; in return, the British recognized the Maoris as the legitimate landowners and granted them all the rights
and privileges of British subjects. The treaty also confirmed the status of New Zealand as a British colony, forestalling French over-
tures in the area, and legitimized—at least according to European
law—the transfer of land from Maori to European hands. In recent
years the Maoris have used the treaty successfully to reclaim land
that, they maintain, was misappropriated by white settlers.

The Treaty House has not always received the care its significance
merits. When Lord Bledisloe bought the house and presented it to
the nation in 1932, it was being used as a shelter for sheep.

⑦ On the northern boundary of Waitangi National Reserve is **Whare
Runanga,** a Maori meeting house with an elaborately carved interi-
or. Inside, an audio show offers a brief outline of traditional Maori
society. *Waitangi Rd., Waitangi, tel. 09/402–7437. Admission: $5
adults, children under 15 free. Open daily 9–5.*

Three kilometers (2 miles) from the Treaty House, on the other side
of the Waitangi Golf Course, there is a small parking area on the
right of Waitangi Road. Stop here and take the short track, which
⑧ rises above a pine forest to the summit of **Mount Bledisloe** and a
splendid view across Paihia and the Bay of Islands. The handsome
ceramic marker at the top showing the distances to major world cities was made by Doulton in London and presented by Lord Bledisloe
in 1934 during his term as governor-general of New Zealand.

The second town in the Bay of Islands, at the tip of a peninsula oppo-
⑨ site Paihia, is **Russell.** You can drive, but the quickest and most convenient route is by ferry. Three passenger ferries make the crossing
between Paihia and Russell, with departures at least every 30 min-

utes in each direction from 7:30 AM to 11 PM. The one-way adult fare is $1, 50¢ for children 5–14. The car ferry is at Opua, about 5 kilometers (3 miles) south of Paihia. This ferry operates from 6:40 AM to 8:50 PM (9:50 PM Friday), with departures at approximately 20-minute intervals from either shore. The last ferry leaves from Russell at 8:50 (9:50 Friday), from Opua at 9 (10 Friday). The one-way fare is $6 for the car and driver plus $1 for each passenger.

Hard as it is to believe these days, sleepy little Russell was once dubbed the Hellhole of the Pacific. Early last century (when it was still known by its Maori name, Kororareka) it was a swashbuckling frontier town, a haven for sealers and for whalers who found one of the richest whaling grounds on earth along the east coast of New Zealand. The tales of debauchery were probably exaggerated, but the British administrators in New South Wales (as Australia was known at the time) were sufficiently concerned to dispatch a British Resident in 1832 to impose law and order. After the Treaty of Waitangi, Russell was the national capital, until in 1844 the Maori chief Hone Heke attacked the British garrison and most of the town burned to the ground. Hone Heke was finally defeated in 1846, but Russell never recovered its former prominence, and the seat of government was shifted first to Auckland, then to Wellington. Today Russell is a delightful town of timber houses and big trees that swoon low over the seafront, framing the yachts and the big-game fishing boats in the harbor. The atmosphere can best be absorbed in a stroll along the Strand, the path along the waterfront.

At the southern end of the Strand is **Pompallier House,** named after the first Catholic bishop of the South Pacific. Marist missionaries built the original structure out of rammed earth (mud mixed with dung or straw—a technique known as *pise* in their native France), since they lacked the funds to buy timber. For several years the priests and brothers operated a press here, printing Bibles in the Maori language. The original building forms the core of the elegant timber house that now stands on the site. *The Strand, Russell, tel. 09/403–7861. Admission: $5 adults, children under 15 free when accompanied by adults, $2 unaccompanied children. Open daily 9–5.*

Set back slightly from the waterfront some 50 yards to the north is the **Captain Cook Memorial Museum,** which houses a collection of Maori tools and weapons and some fine portraits. The pride of its display is a ⅕-scale replica of Captain Cook's ship, HMS *Endeavour,* which entered the bay in 1769. *York St., Russell, tel. 09/403–7701. Admission: $2 adults, 50¢ children 5–15. Open daily 10–5.*

A block farther back from the harbor is **Christ Church,** the oldest church in the country. One of the donors to its erection in 1835 was Charles Darwin, at that time a wealthy but unknown young man making his way around the globe on board HMS *Beagle.* Behind the white picket fence that borders the churchyard, the gravestones tell a fascinating and gruesome story of life in the early days of the colony. Several graves belong to sailors from HMS *Hazard* who were killed in this churchyard by Hone Heke's warriors in 1845. Another headstone marks the grave of a Nantucket sailor from the whaler *Mohawk.* As you walk around the church, look for the musket holes made when Hone Heke besieged the church. The interior is simple and charming; the embroidered cushions on the pews are examples of a folk-art tradition that is still very much alive. *Church and Robertson Sts., Russell. Open daily 8–5.*

To return to Auckland via the west coast road, turn south toward the town of Kawakawa, then right onto Highway 1, and after about 16 kilometers (10 miles), take Highway 12 left toward Kaikohe. This road winds into steep green hills before wandering down toward a broad sea inlet, Hokianga Harbour. In the town of **Opononi,** near the mouth of the harbor, a statue in front of the pub commemorates a

⑩ tame dolphin, **Opi,** that came to play with swimmers in the mid-1950s, putting the town on the national map for the first and only time in its history.

⑪ South of Opononi is the **Waipoua State Forest,** the largest remnant of the kauri forests that once covered this part of the country. A short path leads from the parking area through the forest to **Tane Mahuta,** "Lord of the Forest," standing nearly 173 feet high and measuring 43 feet around its base. The largest tree in New Zealand, it's said to be 1,200 years old.

⑫ The **Matakohe Kauri Museum** is one of the most intriguing museums in the country. Its vast collection of artifacts, tools, photographs, documents, and memorabilia tells the story of the pioneers who settled this part of the country in the second half of the 19th century—a story that is interwoven with the kauri forests. Here you'll find superb examples of kauri craftsmanship and furniture, a complete kauri house, and an early example of an American-built Caterpillar bulldozer, which was used to drag logs from the forest. One of the most fascinating displays is the room of kauri gum, the transparent lumps of resin that form when the sticky sap of the kauri tree hardens. This gum, which was used to make varnish, can be polished to a warm, lustrous finish that looks remarkably like amber—right down to the insects that are sometimes trapped and preserved inside. At one time collecting this gum was an important rural industry. Many of the gum diggers, as they were known, came from Dalmatia, part of present-day Croatia. *Matakohe, tel. 09/431-7417. Admission: $5 adults, $1.50 children 5–15. Open daily 9–5.*

Twenty kilometers (12½ miles) beyond the museum, Highway 12 joins Highway 1 for the final leg of the return journey to Auckland.

What to See and Do with Children

High and dry on the banks of the Waitangi River, the *Tui* is a historic kauri sailing vessel that was built to carry sugar to a refinery in Auckland. Below decks is an exhibition of artifacts recovered from shipwrecks by the famous New Zealand salvage diver Kelly Tarlton. In addition to the brass telescopes, sextants, and diving helmets that can be tried on for size, there is an exquisite collection of jewelry that belonged to Isidore Jonah Rothschild (of the famous banking family), which was lost when the SS *Tasmania* sank in 1897. Rothschild was on a sales trip to New Zealand at the time. *Waitangi Bridge, Paihia, tel. 09/402–7018. Admission: $4 adults, $2 children under 12. Open daily 10–5.*

Sports and the Outdoors

Boating **Marine Rentals** (tel. 09/402–8105), on the waterfront at Paihia, offers catamarans, jet skis, kayaks, and aqua bikes for hire. In the same location, **Charter Pier Paihia** (tel. 09/402–7127) has 16-foot powerboats suitable for fishing and diving for up to six people, available by the hour or the day. A catamaran operated by **Straycat Day Sailing Charters** (Doves Bay Rd., Kerikeri, tel. 09/407–7342) makes one-day sailing trips in the Bay of Islands from Russell and Paihia at $50 per person.

Diving The Bay of Islands offers some of the finest scuba diving in the country, particularly around Cape Brett, where the marine life includes moray eels, stingrays, and grouper. Water temperature at the surface varies from 62°F in July to 71°F in January. From September to November, underwater visibility is often affected by a plankton bloom. **Paihia Dive Hire and Charter** (Box 210, Paihia, tel. 09/402–7551) offers complete equipment hire and regular boat trips for accredited divers.

Fishing The Bay of Islands is one of the world's premier game-fishing grounds for marlin and several species of shark. Operators in the area include **Dudley Smith** (Box 203, Russell, tel. 09/403–7200), **Nighthawk** (tel. 09/407–8999), and **NZ Billfish Charters** (Box 416, Paihia, tel. 09/402–8380). A far less expensive alternative is to fish for snapper, kingfish, and John Dory in the inshore waters of the bay. Among several boat operators in Russell and Paihia who offer a half day of fishing, including bait and rods, for about $40 per person are **Skipper Jim** (tel. 09/402–7355) and **MV *Arline*** (tel. 09/402–8511).

Dining

During the January summer-vacation period, dinner reservations are essential at all restaurants in the area. Price categories are the same as in the Auckland Dining section, above. Highly recommended restaurants are indicated by a star ★.

$$$ **The Gables.** This trim little cottage restaurant on the waterfront at Russell is one of the more sophisticated in the Bay of Islands. First courses on the mostly seafood menu include terrine of smoked snapper and a warm salad of chicken livers. The panfried snapper fillets with balsamic vinegar and the char-grilled fillet of lamb with a ginger and honey sauce are recommended. The lunch menu is limited but less expensive. *The Strand, Russell, tel. 09/403–7618. Reservations advised. Dress: casual. AE, DC, MC, V. No lunch weekdays except during summer. Closed Mon.*

$$ **Bay of Islands Swordfish Club.** Overlooking Kororareka Bay in a pretty cream-and-white timber building, the restaurant of the Swordfish Club is dedicated to fish and fish people, from the decor to the menu to the conversation. First courses are a salad of mussels or fresh oysters; entrées include fresh scallops and asparagus with oyster sauce. Request a table at the window, and begin the evening with a drink in the friendly bar upstairs—where, in the summer holiday period, you may have to wait for a table anyway. Officially visitors must be signed in by a member of the club, but provided you look sober, neat, and capable of enthusing over marlin fishing, the barman will request a club member to countersign the visitor's book for you (after which it would be diplomatic to stand the member to a drink). *The Strand, Russell, tel. 09/403–7652. No reservations. Dress: casual. AE, MC, V. No lunch.*

$$ **Cafe Over the Bay.** This breezy, bistro-style restaurant has an unambitious menu with an Italian accent, but the fish is excellent. First courses include minestrone, seafood chowder, and sweet and sour fish. Main dishes are tortellini with a wine and cream sauce, and fish with a coconut and lime sauce. Most of the fish dishes are made with the delicate, white-fleshed orange roughy. *Waterfront, Paihia, tel. 09/402–8147. No reservations. Dress: casual but neat. DC, MC, V.*

$$ **The Quarterdeck.** The specialty of this seafront restaurant is fish al fresco—crayfish, lobster, flounder, scallops, and snapper, and chips and salads—and while the prices are rather steep for less than glam-

orous dining, the outdoor tables overlooking the lively harbor are a
pleasant spot on a warm evening. The Quarterdeck is popular with
families. *The Strand, Russell, tel. 09/403–7761. No reservations.
Dress: casual. AE, DC, MC, V. BYOB. No lunch weekdays except
summer.*

Lodging

Price categories for hotels are the same as in the Auckland Lodging
section, above. Highly recommended lodgings are indicated by a
star ★.

$$$$ **Kimberley Lodge.** The most luxurious accommodation in the Bay of
★ Islands, this splendid white timber mansion occupies a commanding
position overlooking Russell and Kororareka Bay. The house has
been designed with big windows and sunny verandas to take maximum advantage of its location. Below, terraced gardens fall away
down a steep hillside to the sea. The house is opulently furnished in
contemporary style, and the en suite bathrooms are equipped to
five-star standards. Only one bedroom at the rear of the house—
Pompallier—lacks impressive views. The best room in the house is
the Kimberley Suite, which costs more than the standard suites.
Dinner is available by arrangement. *Pitt St., Russell, tel. 09/403–
7090, fax 09/403–7239. 4 rooms with bath. Facilities: outdoor heated
pool. Tariff includes breakfast. No smoking indoors. AE, DC, MC,
V.*

$$ **Austria Motel.** The large, double-bed rooms at this motel are typical
of motel accommodations in the area—clean and moderately com-
fortable. Each has a kitchenette. The motel also offers a family unit
on the ground level of the two-story wing. The shops and waterfront
at Paihia are a two-minute walk away. *36 Selwyn Rd., Paihia,
tel. 09/402–7480. 7 rooms with bath. Facilities: spa. AE, DC, MC,
V.*

$$ **Duke of Marlborough Hotel.** This historic hotel is a favorite with the
yachting fraternity, for whom ready access to the harbor and the bar
downstairs are the most important considerations. Rooms are clean
and tidy enough, and all have en suite facilities, but they offer no
memorable character despite the hotel's long and colorful history.
The front rooms with harbor views are the most expensive but also
the ones most likely to be affected by noise from the spirited crowd
in the bar, especially on weekends. *The Waterfront, Russell, tel. 09/
403–7829, fax 09/403–7760. 29 rooms with bath. Facilities: restaurant, bar. DC, MC, V.*

$$ **Waitangi Resort Hotel.** The biggest hotel north of Auckland and a
favorite with coach tour groups, this complex sprawls along a penin-
sula within walking distance of the Treaty House. Standard rooms,
which are often booked by coach parties, show signs of long and
heavy use, but many "premium" rooms were renovated in 1991 and
offer more stylish accommodations. *Waitangi Rd., Paihia, tel. 09/
402–7411, fax 09/402–8200. 138 rooms with bath. Facilities: outdoor
pool, guest laundry, 3 restaurants, 2 bars. AE, DC, MC, V.*

$ **Russell Lodge.** Surrounded by quiet gardens two streets back from
the waterfront, this lodge—owned and operated by the Salvation
Army—offers neat, clean rooms in several configurations. It's an es-
pecially good value for budget travelers and families. The family
units have a separate bedroom with two single beds, and either a
double or a single bed in the main room. The largest room is Unit 15,
a two-bedroom flat with a kitchen, which will sleep six. Backpacker-
style accommodation is also available in rooms for four; towels and
sheets are not provided in these rooms but may be rented. All rooms

have en suite bathrooms, and five have kitchen facilities. *Chapel and Beresford Sts., Russell, tel. 09/403-7640, fax 09/403-7641. 24 rooms with bath. Facilities: outdoor pool, guest laundry. AE, MC, V.*

The Coromandel Peninsula

New Zealand has countless pockets of beauty that are not included in the standard tourist itineraries. One of the most accessible is the Coromandel Peninsula, which juts out like a hitchhiker's thumb east of Auckland. The center of the peninsula is dominated by a craggy spine of volcanic peaks that rise sharply to a height of almost 900 meters (3,000 feet). The west coast is sheltered, while on the unprotected east coast the Pacific Ocean has gnawed a succession of beaches and inlets separated by rearing headlands. From the town of Thames, the gateway to the region, Highway 25 combines with the 309 Road to circle the lower two-thirds of the peninsula—an exhilarating drive with the sea on one side and big forested peaks on the other. The journey will add a day (at the very least) to your New Zealand itinerary, but it would be hard to find a finer introduction to the country.

Important Addresses and Numbers

Tourist Information
Coromandel Visitor Information Centre. *Kapanga Rd., Coromandel, tel. 07/866-8958. Open weekdays 10-3.*

Thames Visitor Information Centre. *405 Queen St., Thames, tel. 07/868-7284. Open weekdays 9-5, weekends 10-3.*

Emergenices
Dial 111 for **fire, police,** or **ambulance** services.

Arriving and Departing

By Car
From Auckland, take the Southern Motorway, following the signs to Hamilton. Just past the end of the motorway, turn left onto Highway 2 and follow the signs to Thames. Allow two hours for the 118-kilometer (73-mile) journey.

By Bus
Murphy Buses (tel. 07/867-6829) link Whitianga, Thames, and Auckland daily. Bookings can be made through InterCity (tel. 09/358-4085).

Guided Tours

The **Coromandel Peninsula Pass** is a three-day tour that includes transport to and from Auckland, hiking through native forests, kayaking, and fishing. Meals and accommodations are not included. *Fredericks and Rings Rds., Coromandel, tel. 07/866-8468. Tickets: $110.*

Doug Johansen's full- and half-day tours are a fascinating—and often hilarious—look at a majestic part of the country that he has known and loved since birth. Glowworm caves, abandoned gold mines, flora and fauna, thermal springs, and odd bits of history and bush lore are all covered in the tour, which will provide some of the most evocative memories of your visit to New Zealand. But be warned: Doug Johansen is an incurable practical joker. *Box 76, Pauanui Beach, tel. 07/864-8859. Tickets: $75 full day, $45 half day.*

Green Beetle Tours operates from Auckland a three-day tour of the Coromandel Peninsula designed primarily for young travelers. The emphasis is on low-impact ecotourism; kayaking, hiking, swimming with dolphins, and a history tour are highlights of the trip. Meals and accommodations are not included. *Box 31-228, Auckland, tel. 09/358–5868. Tickets: $118.*

Exploring the Coromandel Peninsula

This tour begins at **Thames** and follows Highway 25 in a clockwise direction as it circles the peninsula. If you leave Auckland early in the morning, it's possible to do the trip in a single day.

Numbers in the margin correspond to points of interest on the Coromandel Peninsula map.

Leave Thames and head north along Highway 25, which snakes along the seafront at the foot of the Coromandel Ranges, with expansive views across the Firth of Thames. At the former gold-mining town of Tapu, a narrow road turns inland to follow the Tapu River upstream along a narrow gorge that becomes prettier with every turn. About 6 kilometers (4 miles) from the start of this road, a **1** sign on the right points to **Rapaura Falls Park,** a garden of native and exotic flowering species that has been sculpted from the wilderness. Paths wind through a riot of rhododendrons, lilies, azaleas, and orchids, while giant tree ferns and rata, remu, and kauri trees lock arms to form a green canopy overhead. The combination of delicacy and rugged grandeur has moved the hardworking gardener to philosophy, or at least to nuggets of wisdom painted on signs ("Keep your values in balance and you will always find happiness"). Be sure to take the 10-minute walk from the parking lot to the waterfall. *Admission: $5 adults, $1.50 children under 15. Open Sept.–May daily 10–5.*

2 Return to Highway 25 and continue toward **Coromandel.** In 1852 the town became the site of New Zealand's first gold strike when Charles Ring, a sawmiller, found gold-bearing quartz at Driving Creek, just north of town. The find was important for New Zealand, since the country's manpower had been severely depleted by the gold rushes in California and Australia. Ring hurried to Auckland to claim the reward that had been offered to anyone finding "payable" gold. The town's population soared, but the reef gold could be mined only by heavy and expensive machinery, and within a few months Coromandel resumed its former sleepy existence as a timber town—and Charles Ring was refused the reward.

From Coromandel, drive back along Highway 25 for about 4 kilometers (2½ miles) and turn inland where a sign points to "Whitianga—309 Road." If you haven't seen kauri trees yet, stop at Waiau Falls for the kauri grove, which is a 10-minute walk beyond the waterfall and swimming hole. At the end of the 309 Road turn right toward Tairua. This road skirts Mercury Bay, where Captain James Cook observed the transit of the planet Mercury in November 1769. Cook's landfall—the first by a European—is commemorated by a **3** plaque on the southern side of the bay at **Cook's Beach;** however, the beach itself is one of the less attractive in the area.

Turn left on the southern side of Mercury Bay where a sign points to **4** **Hahei.** At the entrance to the town, Pa Road turns to the right off Hahei Beach Road and, after 1½ kilometers (1 mile), ends at a small parking area at the Te Pare Historic Reserve. If you're feeling fit, follow the red arrow down the hill, and after about 50 yards take the right fork, which leads through a grove of giant pohutukawa trees, then through a gate and across a grassy, open hillside. The track is

The Coromandel Peninsula

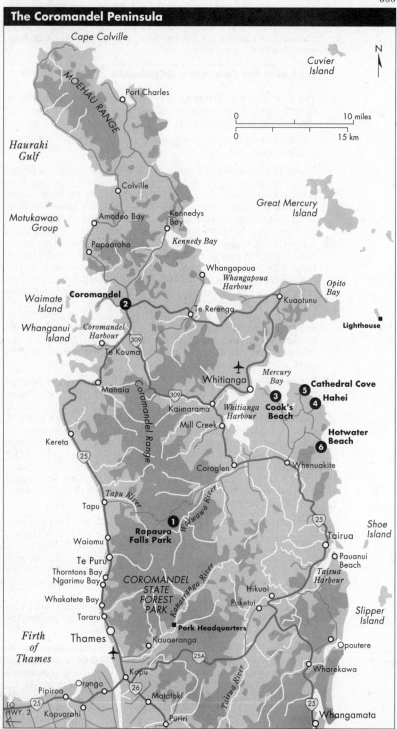

Cape Colville

*Cuvier
Island*

N

MOEHAU RANGE

Port Charles

0   10 miles

0   15 km

*Hauraki
Gulf*

Colville

*Great Mercury
Island*

*Motukawao
Group*

Amodeo Bay

Kennedys
Bay

Papaaroha

Kennedy Bay

Whangapoua

*Whangapoua
Harbour*

*Opito
Bay*

Coromandel
②

Te Rerenga

Kuaotunu

*Waimate
Island*

*Coromandel
Harbour*

309

■
Lighthouse

*Whanganui
Island*

Te Kouma

Whitianga

✈

*Mercury
Bay*

⑤ Cathedral Cove

Manaia

309

*Whitianga
Harbour*

**③
Cook's
Beach**

④ Hahei

Kaimarama

Mill Creek

**⑥ Hotwater
Beach**

Kereta

25

Coroglen

Whenuakite

Tapu River

Tapu

①

**Rapaura
Falls Park**

Waiwawa River

25

*Shoe
Island*

Tairua

Waiomu

Te Puru

Thorntons Bay

Ngarimu Bay

Whakatete Bay

Tararu

**COROMANDEL
STATE
FOREST
PARK**

Kauaeranga River

Pauanui
Beach

*Tairua
Harbour*

*Slipper
Island*

Hikuai

*Firth
of
Thames*

Thames

✈

■ **Park Headquarters**

Kauaeranga

Puketui

Opoutere

Kopu

26

Matatoki

25A

Tairua River

Wharekawa

Pipiroa

Orongo

TO
HWY. 2

25

Kopuarahi

Puriri

25

Whangamata

steep in places and becomes increasingly overgrown as you climb, but persist until you reach the summit, and then head toward the pohutukawas off to your right at the southern end of the headland. This is the site of an old Maori *pa*, a fortified hilltop, though no trace remains of the defensive terraces and wooden spikes that once ringed the hill. Another, much larger pa was located on the hilltop overlooking this site. If you happen to be there at high tide, the blowhole at the foot of the cliffs will add its booming bass note to the crash of the waves and the sighing of the wind in the grass.

❺ Return to Hahei Beach Road, turn right toward the sea, and then, just past the shops, turn left into Grange Road and follow the signs to **Cathedral Cove.** The road ends at a parking lot with dramatic coastal views. Cathedral Cove, a vast rock arch accessible at low tide, is a 45-minute walk each way.

❻ The popular **Hotwater Beach** lies a few kilometers to the south. To find the beach from Hahei, retrace your route toward the highway and watch for the signposts that point left. A thermal spring seeps beneath the beach, and by scooping a shallow hole in the sand you can create a pool of warm water; the deeper you dig, the hotter the water becomes. (The phenomenon occurs only at low to mid-tide.) For a swim without the spa treatment, follow Hahei Beach Road to its end at a well-protected cove, one of the finest along this coastline. The sands of this island-sheltered beach are tinted pink with crushed shells.

Time Out | **Calenso Orchard and Herb Garden,** on Highway 25 just south of the Hahei turnoff, is a relaxed cottage café set in a garden full of lavender. The menu lists fresh juices, vegetable soup, focaccia with ham, homemade chocolate fudge biscuits, and Devonshire teas—simple, wholesome fare that goes with the droning of the bees and the sound of the wind chimes. Prices are low. *Main Rd., Whenuakite, tel. 07/ 866–3275. Open daily 10–5.*

South of the coastal resort of Tairua, Highway 25 turns inland to skirt Tairua Harbour and then continues west across the spine of the peninsula to Thames—a short, dramatic journey between forested peaks. From Thames, the journey to Waitomo Caves or Rotorua takes about three hours.

What to See and Do with Children

Driving Creek Railway is one man's magnificent folly. Barry Brickell is a local potter who discovered that the clay on his land was perfect for his work. The problem was that the deposit lay in a remote area at the top of a steep slope; so he hacked a path through the forest and built his own miniature railroad. Visitors to his studio began asking if they could go along for the ride, and Brickell now takes passengers on a daily tour aboard his toy train. The route that the diesel-powered, narrow-gauge locomotive follows incorporates a cutting, a double-decker bridge, two tunnels, a spiral, and a switchback. The round-trip takes about 50 minutes. The "station" is located about 3 kilometers (2 miles) north of Coromandel township. *410 Kennedy's Bay Rd., Coromandel, tel. 07/866–8703. Tickets: $6 adults, $3 children 5–15. Departs Dec.–Mar., 10:30, 2, 5; Apr.–Oct., 2, 4; Nov., 2, 5.*

Sports and the Outdoors

Hiking **Coromandel State Forest Park** has more than 30 walking trails which offer anything from a 30-minute stroll to a three-day trek. The most accessible starting point is the delightful Kauaeranga Valley Road, where the Coromandel Forest Park Headquarters provides maps and information (tel. 07/868–6381; open weekdays 8–4). To reach the Kauaeranga Valley, head south from Thames and on the outskirts of the town turn left on Banks Street, then right on Parawai Road, which becomes Kauaeranga Valley Road.

Dining

The Coromandel Peninsula is not well endowed with restaurants. In most towns the choice is between coffee shops and pubs, which usually offer cooked meals such as steaks and fish-and-chips, and sometimes salads. An outstanding exception is the dining room at the **Puka Park Lodge** (*see* Lodging, *below*), which brings an international menu and a dash of glitter to this remote part of the world. *Reservations required. Jacket required. AE, DC, MC, V. No lunch. $$$$*

Lodging

Price categories for hotels are the same as in the Auckland Lodging section, *above*. Highly recommended lodgings are indicated by a star ★.

$$$$ **Puka Park Lodge.** This stylish lodge, which attracts a largely Euro-
★ pean clientele, lies immersed in native bushland on Pauanui Beach, at the seaward end of Tairua Harbour on the east coast of the peninsula. (The turnoff from Highway 25 is about 6 kilometers, or 4 miles, south of Tairua.) The timber chalets are smartly furnished with black cane tables and wooden Venetian blinds; the gauze mosquito nets draped over the beds are there for effect rather than practical reasons. Sliding glass doors lead to a balcony perched up among the treetops. The bathrooms are well equipped but small. The lodge offers a full range of activities for those who want to take advantage of the splendor of the surrounding beaches and forests. The tariff is comparatively low for accommodations of this standard. The food and service in the international restaurant are outstanding. *Private Bag, Pauanui Beach, tel. 07/864–8088, fax 07/864–8112. 32 rooms with bath. Facilities: heated outdoor pool, tennis court, bicycles, restaurant, bar. AE, DC, MC, V.*

$$ **Coromandel Colonial Cottages.** These six immaculate timber cot-
★ tages offer spacious and comfortable self-contained accommodations for about the same price as a standard motel room. Each has two bedrooms, a lounge room with convertible beds, a large, well-equipped kitchen, and a dining area. Arranged with military precision in two ranks, the cottages face each other across a tailored lawn surrounded by green hills on the northern outskirts of Coromandel. During vacation periods, they must be booked several months in advance. *Rings Rd., Coromandel, tel. 07/866–8857. 6 cottages. Facilities: spa, croquet lawn, minigolf, guest laundry. AE, DC, MC, V.*

$$ **Karamana.** Mary and Bill Hoyles's historic house provides homestay accommodations that are exceptional on the peninsula. The kauri house is simply constructed yet embellished with ornamental architraves and a delightful veranda. Guest rooms are furnished with high-quality antiques and are scented with potpourri. The location,

at the foot of steep, forested peaks, is majestic and serene; the view has been further enhanced by the Hoyles's gardening skills. Dinner is available by arrangement. *Whangapoua Rd., Coromandel, tel. and fax 07/866–7138. 3 rooms, 1 with en suite bath, 2 share 1 bath, 1 shower. Tariff includes breakfast. MC.*

14 Rotorua to Wellington

*By Michael
Gebicki*

The first part of this chapter covers the central area of the North Island, from the Waitomo Caves to the surroundings of Lake Taupo. In this area, focused on the town of Rotorua, nature has crafted a gallery of surreal wonders that includes limestone caverns, volcanic wastelands, steaming geysers, and hissing ponds. From the shores of Lake Taupo—the country's biggest lake and the geographic bull's-eye of the North Island—Mount Ruapehu, the island's tallest peak, is plainly visible. The mountain is the site of New Zealand's largest ski area and is the dominant feature of Tongariro National Park, a haunting landscape of craters, volcanoes, and lava flows that ran with molten rock as recently as 1988.

Southeast of Lake Taupo, on the shores of Hawke's Bay, lies the town of Napier, an unexpected oasis of Art Deco architecture. Napier is also the center of an excellent wine region. Our tour of the North Island ends at its southern tip, in the charming—if windy—city of Wellington, the nation's capital.

Rotorua, the Waitomo Caves, and Lake Taupo

It's one of the most extraordinary sights in the country. Everywhere you turn the earth bubbles, boils, spits, and oozes. Drainpipes steam, flowerbeds hiss, rings tarnish, cars corrode; the rotten-egg smell of hydrogen sulfide hangs in the air, and even the local golf course has its own mud-pool hot spots where a lost ball stays lost forever.

New Zealand's most famous tourist attraction, Rotorua, sits smack on top of the most violent segment of the Taupo Volcanic Zone, which runs in a broad belt from White Island in the Bay of Plenty to Tongariro National Park, south of Lake Taupo. While the spurting geysers and sulfur springs are perfectly good reasons to visit, there's a lot more to the area than hellfire and brimstone. Drive outside the city limits and you'll find yourself in magnificent, untamed country, where spring-fed streams sprint through native forests into lakes that are home to some of the biggest rainbow trout on earth. Not only are these trout large and abundant, but they seem to be genetically programmed for suicide: Anglers still regularly pull 10-pound rainbow trout from Lake Tarawera, and there are fishing guides who guarantee that no client will come home empty-handed.

Rotorua also has a well-established Maori community tracing its ancestry back to the great Polynesian migration of the 14th century. Maori culture is stamped indelibly on the town, although the majority of visitors will have their most intimate contact with that culture at a *hangi*—a traditional feast—followed by a Maori concert.

Important Addresses and Numbers

Tourist
Information

Tourism Rotorua Visitor Information Centre. In addition to an information office, this modern complex houses a café, a film-processing service, a map shop operated by the Department of Conservation, and a lost-luggage facility. *67 Fenton St., Rotorua, tel. 07/348–5179. Open daily 8–5:30*

Taupo Visitor Information Centre. *13 Tongariro St., Taupo, tel. 07/378–9000. Open daily 8:30–5.*

Waitomo Caves Visitor Information Centre. *Waitomo Museum of Caves, tel. 07/878–7640. Open daily 9–5:30.*

Emergencies   Dial 111 for **fire, police,** and **ambulance** services.

Arriving and Departing

By Plane   **Air New Zealand** (tel. 07/346–1001) and **Ansett New Zealand** (tel. 07/347–0146) have daily flights that link Rotorua with Auckland and Wellington, with further connections throughout New Zealand. **Mount Cook Airline** (tel. 0800/80–0737) schedules daily flights between Rotorua and Auckland, Wellington, Christchurch, and Queenstown. **Rotorua Airport** stands about 10 kilometers (6 miles) from the city center. Taxi fare to the city is $15.

By Car   From Auckland, take Highway 1 south, following the signs to Hamilton. From Hamilton, follow Highway 3. The Waitomo Caves are located 6 kilometers (4 miles) east of the highway. Driving time for the journey is about three hours.

By Bus   **InterCity** (tel. 09/358–4085) has four bus services daily between Auckland and Rotorua. InterCity also operates a daily service between Auckland and Waitomo Caves and between Waitomo Caves and Rotorua. **Newmans** (tel. 09/309–9738) operates twice daily on the Auckland–Rotorua route.

Guided Tours

Gray Line (tel. 09/377–0904) offers two-day tours of the Waitomo Caves and Rotorua from Auckland. The tour costs $359 for adults, $247 for children 5–15.

Mount Tarawera 4WD Tours offers a sensational half-day, four-wheel-drive trip to the edge of the Mount Tarawera crater. Departures are available at 8:30 AM or 1:30 PM. *Box 5157, Rotorua, tel. 07/357–4026. Cost: $52 adults, $26 children under 12, $135 family (2 adults, 2 children).*

The **Waimangu Round Trip** is probably the most complete and spectacular tour of Rotorua. The full-day tour includes an easy 5-kilometer (3-mile) hike through the Waimangu Thermal Valley to Lake Rotomahana, where a cruiser takes visitors past steaming cliffs to the narrow isthmus that divides the lake from Lake Tarawera. After crossing the lake on a second cruiser, the tour visits a village that was buried by a volcanic eruption and ends with a dip in the Polynesian Pools in Rotorua. Lunch is included. *Bookings at Rotorua Visitor Information Centre, or tel. 07/347–1199. Tickets: $125 adults, $65 children 5–14.*

Rotorua Sightseeing Shuttle is a bus service making a circuit of the city's 23 major attractions. Passengers may leave at any stop and catch any following bus. The first bus departs from Rotorua Visitor Centre at 8:15, and the service terminates at 5:10. *Visitor Information Centre, 67 Fenton St., Bookings at Rotorua tel. 07/348–5179. Tickets: $14 for half day, $20 for full day, half price for children 4–14.*

Tamaki Tours' Volcanic Wilderness Safari is a two-day trip that combines horse trekking in the Rainbow Mountain/Mount Tarawera area, rafting on the Rangitaki River, and an introduction to traditional Maori legends and lifestyle. The company is a Maori-owned and -operated venture. *Box 1492, Rotorua, tel. 07/346–2823. Cost: $320.*

Tarawera Helicopters (tel. 07/348–1223) offers a choice of scenic flights, from a short flight over the city and Whakarewarewa Thermal Reserve ($50 per person) to a longer flight over crater lakes and the Waimangu Valley, with a landing on top of Mount Tarawera ($325 per person).

Tour Magic (tel. 07/345–6080) has a choice of half- and full-day minibus tours of Rotorua's prime attractions, with pickup and drop-off at your accommodation. These tours are recommended for their personal, attentive style. Half-day tours cost $38–$54 per person.

The **MV** *Wairaka* (tel. 07/374–8338) is a vintage riverboat that cruises from Taupo to Huka Falls daily at 10 and 2. The two-hour cruise costs $18 for adults, $8 for children under 12. A barbecue cruise departs at 12:30 and costs $35 for adults, $15 for children.

The Waitomo Caves

This itinerary begins at Auckland and travels south through Hamilton to the Waitomo Caves, east to Rotorua, and finally south again to Lake Taupo. It's possible to complete the journey in three days, but for those who want to experience the vast range of activities in the area, four days is a practical minimum.

Numbers in the margin correspond to points of interest on the Central North Island map.

❶ The **Waitomo Caves** are an ancient seabed that was lifted and then spectacularly eroded into a surreal landscape of limestone formations and caves, many of them still unexplored. Only two caves are open to the public for guided tours: the Aranui and the Waitomo, or Glowworm Cave. The **Waitomo Cave** takes its name from the Maori words *wai* and *tomo*, water and cave, since the Waitomo River vanishes into the hillside here. Visitors are taken through by boat, and the highlight is the **Glowworm Grotto.** The glowworm is the larva of *Arachnocampa luminosa*, a member of the gnat family, which looks like a small daddy longlegs later when it emerges from its cocoon. The larva, measuring between one and two inches, lives on the roof of caves and snares its prey by dangling filaments of tiny, sticky beads; insects attracted to the light it emits through a chemical oxidation process get trapped in the deadly necklace. In one of nature's crueler ironies, it is often the adult *Arachnocampa luminosa* that is caught and eaten by the infant of the species. A single glowworm produces far less light than any firefly, but when massed in great numbers, the effect is electrifying. **Aranui Cave,** 2 kilometers (1¼ miles) beyond the Glowworm Cave, is a very different experience. Eons of dripping water have sculpted a delicate garden in pink and white limestone. The cave is named after a local Maori, Te Rutuku Aranui, who discovered the cave in 1910 when his dog disappeared inside in pursuit of a wild pig. Each cave tour lasts 45 minutes. The Glowworm Cave is high on the list of every coach tour, so try to avoid visiting between 11 and 2, when many tour groups arrive from Auckland. *Te Anga Rd., tel. 07/878–8227. Admission to Aranui Cave: $13.50 adults, $6.75 children under 12. Admission to both caves: $21 adults, $10.50 children under 12. Glowworm Cave tours: every hr on the hr 9–4, with late tours at 4:30 and 5:30 Nov.–Easter. Aranui Cave tours: 10, 11, 1, 2, 3.*

In the center of the caves village, the **Museum of Caves** provides an entertaining and informative look at the formation of the caves and the life cycle of the glowworm, with a number of interactive displays designed especially for children. *Waitomo Caves Village, tel. 07/*

Central North Island

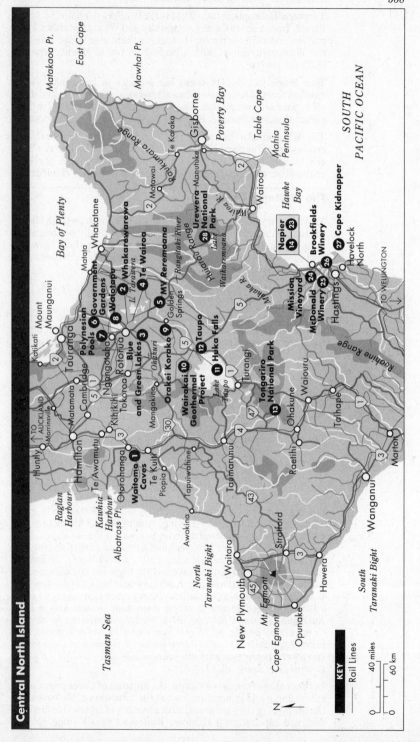

KEY
— Rail Lines

0 ——— 40 miles
0 ——— 60 km

N

Waitomo Caves **1**
Whakarewarewa **2**
Blue and Green Lakes **3**
Te Wairoa **4**
Mt. Reremoana **5**
Government Gardens **6**
Polynesian Pools **7**
Waiotapu **8**
Orakei Korako **9**
Wairakei Geothermal Project **10**
Huka Falls **11**
Taupo **12**
Tongariro National Park **13**
Napier **14** – **23**
McDonald Winery **24**
Mission Vineyard **25**
Brookfields Winery **26**
Cape Kidnapper **27**
Urewera National Park **28**

878–7640. Admission: $3 adults, children under 15 free. Open daily 9–5:30.

The **Waitomo Walkway** is a 5-kilometer (3-mile), 2½-hour walk that begins across the road from the Museum of Caves and follows the Waitomo River. The track, which passes through forests and impressive limestone outcrops, provides many visitors with their fondest memories of Waitomo. It is relatively easy and highly recommended, but there is no transport from the end of the walk back to Waitomo Caves Village. If you prefer an alternative to the complete walk, take Te Anga Road from the village, turn left onto Tumutumu Road, park at Ruakuri Reserve, and walk the short final section of the track through this delightful reserve.

From Waitomo Caves Village, return to Highway 3 and turn right to the town of Te Kuiti, where Highway 30 turns east to Rotorua. Driving time for the 150-kilometer (95-mile) journey is 2½ hours.

Rotorua and Lake Taupo

This driving tour begins at the Visitor Information Centre on Fenton Street and takes a day. (If you take the 11 AM cruise on Lake Tarawera, which is highly recommended, it will mean rearranging the tour to reach Tarawera Landing in time for the boat's departure.) From Rotorua, allow 25 minutes for the drive to Tarawera Landing. Limited picnic supplies are available from the café at the Buried Village, about 1½ kilometers (1 mile) before the landing.

2 From the front door of the Visitor Centre, turn right and follow Fenton Street for 3 kilometers (2 miles) to **Whakarewarewa**— a mouthful of a name that the locals reduce to "Whaka." (In Maori names, "wh" is pronounced as "f," and "Whaka" is therefore spoken as "Faka.") This is easily the most accessible and popular of Rotorua's thermal areas, and also the most varied, since it gives an insight into Maori culture. Visitors are free to wander at their own pace, but you'll gain far more from the experience if you take one of the guided tours, which leave at frequent intervals from the Arts and Crafts Institute, near the ticket office. The trails that wind through the complex pass sinister, steaming pools, spitting mud ponds, and smooth silica terraces that appear to be coated in melted candle wax. The highlight is **Pohutu** ("the big splash"), a geyser that sometimes shoots to a height of over 80 feet; however, its eruptions are erratic. At the top end of the complex is a reconstructed Maori village with houses, gates, and a *marai*, a meeting house. At the lower end is a modern Maori village, but its people still cook in the traditional manner by placing meat and vegetables in flax baskets and dunking them in the steaming pools at the back of the village. At the village entrance is a graveyard in which the graves are all above ground, since it's impossible to dig down into the earth. A one-hour Maori concert takes place daily at 12:15 in the Arts and Crafts Institute. *Hemo Rd., Rotorua, tel. 07/348–9047. Admission: $10 adults, $4 children 5–14, $26 family. Concert: $10 adults, $4 children, $26 family. Open daily Nov.–Easter 8–6; Easter–Oct. 8–5.*

3 Return to the city along Fenton Street and turn right into Amohau Street, which is easy to identify by the McDonalds on the left corner. After almost 3 kilometers (2 miles), turn right where a sign points to Tarawera and the **Blue and Green Lakes.** This road loops through forests and skirts the edge of the two lakes. The color contrast varies with the time of year and the weather conditions.

❹ Just past the lakes is **Te Wairoa,** the buried village. At the end of the 19th century this village was the starting point for expeditions to the pink and white terraces of Rotomahana, on the slopes of Mount Tarawera. These silica terraces were formed by the mineral-rich water from a geyser. As the water cascaded down the mountainside, it formed a series of baths, which became progressively cooler as they neared the lake. In the latter half of the last century these fabulous terraces were the country's major tourist attraction, but they were completely destroyed when Mount Tarawera erupted in 1886. The explosion, which was heard as far away as Auckland, killed 153 people and buried the village of Te Wairoa under a sea of mud and hot ash. The village has been excavated, and today a path makes a circuit of this fascinating and deceptively tranquil spot, complete with grazing deer. Of special interest is the *whare* (hut) of the *tohunga* (priest) Tuhoto Ariki, who predicted the destruction of the village. Eleven days before the eruption, two separate tourist parties saw a Maori war canoe emerge from the mists of Lake Tarawera and disappear again—a vision the tohunga interpreted as a sign of impending disaster. Four days after the eruption, the hundred-year-old tohunga was dug out of his buried whare still alive, only to die in the hospital a few days later. The path, after circling the village, dives down the hill alongside Te Wairoa Falls, then passes through a cave, crosses a bridge, and ascends the moist, fern-covered slope on the far side. The walk is a delight, although the lower section of the track is steep and slippery in places. *Tarawera Rd., tel. 07/362–8287. Admission: $8 adults, $2 children 6–15, $18 family. Open daily 9–4:30, summer 8:30–5:30.*

Four kilometers (2½ miles) beyond the village is Spencer Road, where a sign points to "Launch Cruises." This road leads to a parking lot on the shores of Lake Tarawera, where a restored lake cruiser, the **MV *Reremoana,*** makes regular scenic runs. Especially ❺ recommended is the two-hour cruise, which departs at 11 AM and stops for 30 minutes at the foot of Mount Tarawera, where passengers can picnic, swim, or walk across the isthmus to Lake Rotomahana. Forty-five-minute cruises depart from the landing at one-hour intervals from 1:30 to 4:30. *Tarawera Launch Cruises, tel. 07/362–8595. Tickets: $15 adults, $7.50 children under 15, $35 family.*

Return to Rotorua by the same route and turn right into Hinemaru Street, then right again through the gates of the **Government Gar-** ❻ **dens.** The Maoris call this area *Whangapiro,* "evil-smelling place"—a far more appropriate name for these bizarre gardens, where sulfur pits bubble and fume behind the manicured rose beds. The focus of interest here is the extraordinary neo-Tudor **Bath House.** Built as a spa at the turn of the century, this building is now Rotorua's Art and History Museum. One room on the ground floor is devoted to the eruption of Mount Tarawera, with a number of artifacts that were unearthed from the debris and a remarkable collection of photographs that show the terraces of Rotomahana before the eruption. *Arawa St., tel. 07/348–4199. Admission free. Open weekdays 10–4:30, weekends 1–4:30.*

Leave the gardens by the main gate, turn left into Hinemaru Street, and take the first left, Hinemoa Street. This road ends at the ❼ **Polynesian Pools.** A trip to Rotorua would hardly be complete without a dip in these soothing, naturally heated mineral baths. A wide choice of baths is available, from large communal pools to family pools to small, private baths for two. Massage and saunas are also available. *Hinemoa St., tel. 07/348–1328. Admission to family pool:*

$6.50 adults, $2 children 5–14; adult pool: $6.50; private pool (per half hr): $7.50 adults, $2 children 5–14. Open 6:30 AM–10 PM.

Leave Rotorua by Fenton Street, which becomes Highway 5, and follow the signs to Taupo. After 30 kilometers (19 miles), turn left where a sign points to **Waiotapu.** This is a complete thermal wonderland—a freakish, fantastic landscape of deep, sulfur-crusted pits, jade-color ponds, silica terraces, and a steaming lake edged with red algae and bubbling with tiny beads of carbon dioxide. The most spectacular feature is the **Lady Knox Geyser,** which erupts precisely at 10:15 daily—but not through some miracle of Mother Nature's. Five pounds of soap powder poured into the vent of the geyser causes the water to boil, and the vent is then blocked with rags until the pressure builds sufficiently for the geyser to explode. The phenomenon was discovered early this century. Wardens from a nearby prison farm would bring convicts to a pool here to wash their clothes. They found that when the water became soapy the pool would boil fiercely, and one of the wardens built a rock cairn to serve as a nozzle, concentrating the force of the boiling water and making the geyser rise even higher. *State Hwy. 5, tel. 07/366–6333. Admission: $8 adults, $3 children 5–15, $20 family. Open daily 8:30–5.*

Continue toward Taupo along Highway 5. At Mihi Bridge, just past Golden Springs, turn right along a road signposted "Orakei Korako." If by now you think you've seen enough bubbling mud pools and fuming craters to last a lifetime, this captivating thermal valley will change your mind. On the shores of Lake Ohakuri, a jet boat waits to take passengers across to **Orakei Korako,** where geyser-fed streams hiss and steam as they flow into the waters of the lake. One of the most impressive features of this area is the multicolored silica terrace, believed to be the largest in the world since the destruction of the terraces of Rotomahana. At the bottom of Aladdin's Cave, the vent of an ancient volcano, is a jade-green pool that was once used exclusively by Maori women as a beauty parlor, which is where the name Orakei Korako—"a place of adorning"—originated. *Tel. 07/378–3131. Admission: $10 adults, $4.50 children 5–15, $25 family. Open daily 8:30–4:30, winter 8:30–4.*

Return to Highway 5 and proceed toward Taupo. Just past the junction with Highway 1 you can see the **Wairakai Geothermal Project** in the distance, wreathed in swirling clouds of steam. The steam, tapped through underground shafts, drives generators that provide about 5% of New Zealand's electrical power. There are no guided tours of the plant, but the Geothermal Information Centre close to the highway has an informative display of the process by which steam is converted into electricity. *State Hwy. 1, tel. 07/374–8216. Admission free. Open daily 9–noon, 1–4.*

Beyond the power station, at the top of the next hill, a road turns left off the highway toward **Huka Falls,** where the Waikato River thunders through a narrow chasm and over a 35-foot rock ledge before it pours into Lake Taupo. The view from the footbridge is superb.

The town of **Taupo** is the services base for Lake Taupo, the largest lake in New Zealand. You can take your pick here from a wide range of water sports—sailing, cruising, waterskiing, swimming, but most of all, fishing: Taupo is the rainbow-trout capital of the universe. The average Taupo trout weighs in at around 4 pounds, and there is no closed season. For nonanglers, several sailing boats, modern catamarans, and vintage riverboats offer sightseeing cruises. From Taupo, the driving time back to Rotorua is about 90 minutes.

⑬ At the southern end of Lake Taupo is **Tongariro National Park,** the country's first, established on land donated by a Maori chief. The park is dominated by the peaks of three active volcanoes, one of which, Mount Ruapehu, is, at 2,752 meters (9,175 feet), the tallest mountain on the North Island. Ruapehu last erupted in 1988, spewing a shower of volcanic rocks. Tongariro's spectacular combination of dense rimu forests, crater lakes, barren lava fields, and bird life makes it the most impressive and popular of the North Island's national parks. It has many walking trails, from the 40-minute Ridge Track to the Mount Tongariro Traverse, which crosses the mountain from one side to the other and is one of the finest one-day walks in the country. The longest walk in the park is the six-day Round the Mountain track. The Whakapapa ski area, on the north side of Mount Ruapehu, is New Zealand's largest. On the southern side of the mountain is a second ski area, Turoa, which generally offers a longer ski season than Whakapapa's June to October.

Highway 1 skirts the eastern side of the park, but the easiest access is from Highway 47, on the western side. For more information, contact the Department of Conservation Field Centre at Whakapapa Village off Highway 47 (mailing address: Whakapapa Visitor Centre, Private Bag, Mount Ruapehu, tel. 07/892–3729). Accommodations in the village range from the **THC Tongariro Hotel** (Mount Ruapehu, tel. 07/892–3809; $$$$) to the cabins and campsites in the motor camp. The park has nine huts for hikers.

What to See and Do with Children

Agrodome. Most of this sprawling complex is dedicated to the four-footed woolly New Zealander. Shows daily at 9:15, 11, and 2:30 demonstrate the different breeds of sheep, shearing techniques, and sheepdogs at work. Children can participate by feeding lambs and milking a cow. In another part of the complex, **Trainworld,** scale-model trains rumble through a miniature slice of English countryside. The complex is part of a 320-acre farm, a 10-minute drive northwest of Rotorua. *Riverdale Park, Western Rd., Ngongotaha, tel. 07/357–4350. Admission to Agrodome: $9 adults, $4.50 children 5–15; Trainworld: $5 adults, $3 children. Open daily 9–4:30.*

Leisure World. This giant complex includes waterslides, three-wheeler dirt bikes, slot cars, a minigolf course, and video games. *Marguerita St., Rotorua, tel. 07/348–9674. Admission free. Rides cost $3–$6 per person. Open weekdays 10–5, weekends 10–6.*

Rainbow Springs. Situated some 5 kilometers (3 miles) from Rotorua, this leafy park is home to many species of New Zealand wildlife, including deer, kiwis and other native birds, wild pigs, and most of all, trout. The trout that congregate for feeding sessions at the Rainbow and Fairy Springs are the King Kongs of the trout world. On the other side of State Highway 5 is the second part of the complex, Rainbow Farm, which demonstrates New Zealand farming life. A show similar to the one at the Agrodome takes place daily at 10:30, 11:45, 1, and 2:30. *Fairy Springs Rd., tel. 07/347–9301. Admission (Rainbow Springs or Rainbow Farm): $9.70 adults, $3 children 5–15. Open daily 8–5.*

Off the Beaten Track

At the northern end of Rotorua, on the shores of the lake, stands **St. Faith's,** the Anglican church for the Maori village of Ohinemutu. Before the present Tudor-style church was built in 1910, one of the ministers was Seymour Spencer Mills, of Hartford, Connecticut, who preached to the Arawa people for 50 years. He is commemorated in a small window above the organ chancel, preaching to a group of Maoris as he holds his habitual umbrella. The interior of the church, which is richly decorated with carvings inset with mother-of-pearl, deserves attention at any time, but it's at its best during Sunday services, when the rich, melodic voices of the Maori choir rise in hymns. The service at 8 AM is in the Maori language; the 10 AM service is in both Maori and English. *Memorial Dr., Rotorua.*

Sports and the Outdoors

Fishing The lakes of the Rotorua/Taupo region are one of the few places where tales of the big one can be believed. If you want to keep the trout of a lifetime from becoming just another fishy story, it pays to have a boat with some expert advice on board. Expect to pay about $55 per hour for a fishing guide and a 20-foot cruiser that will take up to six passengers. The minimum charter period is two hours, and fishing gear and bait are included in the price. A one-day fishing license costs $11 per person and is available on board the boat. In Rotorua, fishing operators include **Clark Gregor** (tel. 07/347–1730), **Bryan Colman** (tel. 07/348–7766), and **Ray Dodunski** (tel. 07/349–2555). Highly recommended is *Clear Water Pride* (tel. 07/362–8590), a luxury 38-foot launch that operates fishing trips on Lake Tarawera. The cost for up to seven passengers is $80 per hour, including all gear and light refreshments. For 8 to 15, the cost is $120 per hour and a hostess is provided. In Taupo, contact **Richard Staines** (tel. 07/378–2736) or **Punch Wilson** (tel. 07/378–5596). At the other end of the scale, a luxury cruiser on Lake Taupo costs about $150 per hour; for more information, contact **Chris Jolly Boats** (Box 1020, Taupo, tel. 07/378–0623).

Rafting The center of the North Island has a number of rivers with grade-3 to grade-5 rapids that make excellent white-water rafting. For scenic beauty, the Rangitaki River is recommended. For experienced rafters who want a challenge, the Wairoa and the Mohaka rivers have exhilarating grade-5 rapids. The climax of a rafting trip on the Kaituna River is the drop over a 21-foot waterfall, probably the highest to be rafted by a commercial operator anywhere. In Taupo, contact **Rapid Descents** (tel. 07/377–0419); in Rotorua, **Rafting Kaituna** (tel. 07/348–0223). Transport, wet suits, and meals are provided. The price of a one-day trip is about $65 per person.

Black-Water Rafting This is an unusual way to see the caves, and a lot of fun. Participants must first prove themselves with a giant leap into the Huhunoa Stream; the next three hours are spent dressed in wet suits and equipped with cavers' helmets and inflated inner tubes, floating through underground caverns. While the combination of darkness and freezing water might sound like a refined form of torture, the trip is an exhilarating one that will live vividly in your memory long after the goose bumps have disappeared. The cost is $50 per person. Departure times vary, depending on daily demand. *Information and bookings: Black Water Rafting, Box 13, Waitomo Caves, tel. 07/878–7640.*

Dining

Rotorua offers a unique New Zealand dining experience: the *hangi*, or Maori feast. Traditionally, meat and vegetables placed in flax baskets were gently steamed in an earth oven lined with heated stones and wet leaves. Several of the larger hotels in Rotorua offer a hangi, and although the food is still cooked by steam, it's unlikely that it will be buried in the traditional earth oven. Lamb, pork, and seafood are usually available at the buffet-style meals, together with pumpkin and *kumara* (sweet potato), a staple of the Maori diet. Almost without exception, hangis in Rotorua are followed by a Maori concert, a performance of traditional songs and dances. The hangis at the **Sheraton** (tel. 07/348–7139) and the **Lake Plaza** (tel. 07/348–1174) enjoy long-standing reputations as two of the best in town. Expect to pay about $40 per person. **Tamaki Tours'** (tel. 07/346–2823) hangi is the only one that takes place at a Maori *marae*, or meeting house, on the shores of Lake Rotoiti.

Price categories for restaurants are the same as in the Auckland Dining section in Chapter 13.

$$$ Poppy's Villa Restaurant. This florid restaurant with its pink walls and scalloped, flower-patterned blinds is Rotorua's big-occasion restaurant, yet prices are relatively moderate. First courses on the modern, European-style menu include mussels poached in a spicy tomato and Parmesan sauce as well as sweetbreads in wine and tarragon sauce served with a walnut brioche. Baby rack of lamb with honey, mustard, and a rosemary glaze served in a red-berry sauce is a long-standing favorite main course. *4 Marguerita St., Rotorua, tel. 07/347–1700. Reservations advised. Dress: casual but neat. AE, DC, MC, V. No lunch.*

$$$ You and Me. Despite the restaurant's furry pink-and-black decor, the food at least pays lip service to modern trends with a fashionable eastern accent. The menu offers smoked salmon marinated in lime juice and served with avocado; fillet of lamb marinated in lemongrass and olive oil; and cervena venison with zucchini flowers stuffed with scallops and roasted garlic. Gourmet opinions regard this as the only restaurant in Rotorua that has achieved a notable culinary style. *31 Pukuatua St., Rotorua, tel. 07/347–6178. Reservations advised. Dress: casual but neat. AE, DC, MC, V. BYOB. No lunch. Closed Sun. and Mon.*

$$ Incas Cafe. This casual café caters to most tastes, with beef bourguignon, vegetable moussaka, spare ribs, steamed mussels, and coconut lamb curry, but despite the name, nothing south-of-the-border appears on the menu. The restaurant's 1 AM closing time draws the night owls. *Pukaki and Fenton Sts., Rotorua, tel. 07/348–3831. Reservations not required. Dress: casual. AE, DC, MC, V. No lunch.*

$$ Zanelli's Italian Cafe. Rotorua's favorite Italian restaurant offers a predictable range of dishes—spaghetti bolognese, lasagna, cannelloni, and fettuccine with various sauces—but the food is well flavored and the service is efficient. The decor—walls lined with split cane, a stone-tile floor, Formica tables—and the up-tempo Italian music create a slightly hectic atmosphere. *23 Amohia St., Rotorua, tel. 07/348–4908. Reservations not required. Dress: casual. DC, MC, V. No lunch. Closed Sun.*

$ International Cafe. Situated beneath the veranda of the Princes Gate Hotel, this outdoor café is the perfect place for warm-weather eating. The menu lists soups, focaccia, salads, bruschetta, grilled chicken, eggplant lasagna, and burgers. *1 Arawa St., Rotorua, tel. 07/348–1179. No reservations. Dress: casual. AE, DC, MC, V. No dinner.*

$ Orchid Gardens Cafe. If you are staying close to the city and want an alternative to hotel breakfasts, this is just the place. The café is located at the end of the Government Gardens, and diners are treated to a breakfast surrounded by palm trees and the sound of bird calls and trickling water. The breakfast menu lists fruit juices, cereals, toast, eggs, and bacon. Later in the day the menu expands to include soup, quiche, shrimp cocktail, and steaks. The café opens at 8 on weekdays, 7 on weekends. *Government Gardens, Hinemaru St., Rotorua, tel. 07/347-6182. No reservations. Dress: casual. MC, V. No dinner.*

Lodging

The accommodations scene in Rotorua is highly competitive. For most of the year there are many more hotel beds than visitors, and a number of hotels and motels offer significant discounts on their standard rates. The Tourism Rotorua Visitor Centre on Fenton Street acts as a clearinghouse for discount accommodations, and you can often save up to half the published rate of a particular hotel by booking through the center on arrival in Rotorua. The exception is school holidays, when accommodations should be booked in advance.

Price categories for hotels are the same as in the Auckland Lodging section in Chapter 13. Highly recommended lodgings are indicated by a star ★.

$$$$ **Huka Lodge.** Buried in parklike grounds at the edge of the frisky
★ Waikato River, this superb lodge is the standard by which New Zealand's other sporting lodges are judged. It is run in the European style, however, and the atmosphere of aristocratic privilege may be a little overwhelming for some tastes. The large, lavish guest rooms, decorated in muted grays and whites, are arranged in blocks of two or three. All have sliding glass doors that open to a view across lawns to the river. In the interest of tranquillity, guest rooms are not equipped with telephones, televisions, or radios. The five-course formal dinners are gourmet affairs served at a communal dining table. The wine list is a showcase of the very best New Zealand has to offer. Breakfasts include such luxuries as fresh croissants, brioches, and pastries. *Huka Falls Rd., Taupo (mailing address: Box 95, Taupo), tel. 07/378-5791, fax 07/378-0427. 17 rooms with bath. Facilities: tennis court, fishing, spa, bar, restaurant. Tariff includes breakfast and dinner. AE, DC, MC, V.*

$$$$ **Muriaroha Lodge.** Although it lacks trout streams and lake views, when it comes to style, facilities, food, and comfort, this handsome lodge on the outskirts of Rotorua evokes the finest traditions of the luxury sporting lodge—at a much reduced rate. Guest rooms are paired in bungalows, which are separate from the main building; to ensure privacy, the adjoining room is not assigned when one of the pair is occupied. The guest rooms, gardens, lounge, and dining room all have an English country house flavor. For the duration of their stay, guests are extended complimentary membership at the Arikikapaka Golf Course just across the road. *411 Old Taupo Rd., Rotorua, tel. 07/346-1220, fax 07/346-1338. 8 rooms with bath. Facilities: outdoor pool, bar, restaurant. AE, DC, MC, V.*

$$$$ **Sheraton Rotorua.** Close to the Whakarewarewa thermal area on the outskirts of town, this hotel offers the chain's usual high standard of comforts and amenities. Request a room on one of the top two floors overlooking the golf course. The hotel's nightly hangi is one of the best in town. *Fenton and Sala Sts., Rotorua, tel. 07/348-7139, fax 07/348-8378. 130 rooms with bath. Facilities: outdoor pool, spa, sauna, gym, tennis court, 2 restaurants, bar. AE, DC, MC, V.*

$$$$ **Solitaire Lodge.** It would be difficult to imagine a finer backdrop than the lakes, forests, and volcanoes that surround this plush retreat. Set high on a peninsula that juts out into Lake Tarawera, the

lodge has been designed as a sophisticated hideaway where a few guests at a time can enjoy the scenery in a relaxed, informal atmosphere. All the suites are luxuriously equipped, though the bathrooms in the junior suites are modest in size. The best room is the Tarawera Suite, which has panoramic views. The surrounding lakes and forests hold many possibilities for hiking, boating, and fishing. Lake Tarawera is well-known for its king-size rainbow trout, and the lodge has boats and fishing gear. Smoking is not permitted indoors. *Ronald Rd., Lake Tarawera, Rotorua, tel. 07/362–8208, fax 07/362–8445. 10 rooms with bath. Facilities: spa, bar, restaurant, sailing boats, motorboat, fishing. Tariff includes all meals. AE, DC, MC, V.*

$$ ★ **Cascades Motor Lodge.** Set on the shores of Lake Taupo, these attractive brick and timber rooms are large, comfortable, and furnished and decorated in a smart contemporary style. The two-story "luxury" apartments, which sleep up to seven, have a lounge room, bedroom, kitchen, and dining room on the ground floor in an open-plan design, glass doors leading to a large patio, and a second bedroom and bathroom on the upper floor. Studio rooms have only one bedroom. All rooms are equipped with a spa bath. Room 1 is closest to the lake and the small beach. *Lake Terr., Taupo, tel. 07/378–3774, fax 07/378–0372. 22 rooms with bath. Facilities: heated outdoor pool. AE, DC, MC, V.*

$$ **Cedar Lodge Motel.** These spacious modern units, about a half-mile from the city center, are good value, especially for families. All the double-story units have a kitchen and lounge room on the lower floor and a bedroom on the mezzanine floor above. All have at least one queen-size and one single bed, and some have a queen-size bed and three singles. Every unit has its own spa pool in the private courtyard at the back. The gray-flecked carpet, smoked-glass tables, and recessed lighting have a clean, contemporary flavor. Request a room at the back, away from Fenton Street. *296 Fenton St., Rotorua, tel. 07/349–0300, fax 07/349–1115. 15 rooms with shower. Facilities: guest laundry. AE, DC, MC, V.*

$$ **Princes Gate Hotel.** This ornate timber hotel occupies a prime position across the road from the Government Gardens. It was built in 1897 on the Coromandel Peninsula and brought here in 1917, and efforts have been made to re-create a turn-of-the-century flavor inside. The rooms are large and comfortable, although the old-fashioned carpets and furnishings look slightly dowdy. The motel rooms, located in a separate wing, have been renovated to make suites with kitchens; these make a better choice for families. *1 Arawa St., Rotorua, tel. 07/348–1179, fax 07/348–6215. 28 hotel rooms, 12 motel units. Facilities: spa pool, mineral baths, tennis court, 2 restaurants, bar. AE, DC, MC, V.*

$ **Eaton Hall.** This well-kept, friendly guest house has an outstanding location one street from the heart of Rotorua. Guest rooms are homey and comfortable and maintained to a standard well above that in most guest houses. Room 4, a twin-bedded room with its own shower, is available at no extra charge. *39 Hinemaru St., Rotorua, tel. 07/347–0366, fax 07/348–6287. 8 rooms share 2 baths. Facilities: spa. Tariff includes breakfast. AE, DC, MC, V.*

Napier and Hawke's Bay

New Zealand is a country that prides itself on natural wonders, but Napier is an exception: This city of 50,000, situated about two-thirds of the way down the east coast of the North Island, is best known for its architecture. After an earthquake devastated Napier in 1931, the citizens rebuilt it in the Art Deco style fashionable at the time. Today the city is an Art Deco treasure.

The mild climate and beaches of Hawke Bay make this a popular vacation area for New Zealanders. (*Hawke* Bay is the body of water; *Hawke's* Bay is the region.) Another attraction is wine: The region produces some of New Zealand's best.

Important Addresses and Numbers

Tourist Information
Napier Visitor Information Centre. *Marine Parade, Napier, tel. 06/835–4949. Open weekdays 8:30–5, weekends 9–5.*

Emergencies
Dial 111 for **fire, police,** and **ambulance** services.

Arriving and Departing

By Plane
Air New Zealand (tel. 06/835–3288) has several flights daily between Napier and Auckland, Wellington, and Christchurch.

By Car
The main route between Napier and the north is Highway 5. Driving time from Taupo is 2½ hours. Highway 2 is the main southern route. Driving time to Wellington is five hours.

By Bus
Newmans (tel. 09/309–9738) and **InterCity** (tel. 09/358–4085) both operate daily bus services between Napier and Auckland, Rotorua, and Wellington.

Guided Tours

Bay Tours features a four-hour tour of the various wineries in the area. It offers a chance to sample some of the boutique wines unavailable to independent travelers. *Napier Visitor Information Centre, tel. 06/843–6953. Tickets: $34 adults, first child and children under 10 free, other children $17. Sun.–Fri. 10:30, Sat. 1:15.*

The Art Deco Trust offers an excellent and informative guided walking tour of Napier. The 1-mile walk takes two hours. *Hawke's Bay Museum, 9 Herschell St., tel. 06/835–0022. Cost: $5 adults, children under 13 free. Tours Sun., Wed. 2 PM.*

Exploring Napier and Hawke's Bay

Numbers in the margin correspond to points of interest on the Napier map.

14 This tour begins with a short walk around the center of **Napier**, focusing on the city's Art Deco buildings. Art Deco, the style born at the 1925 International Exposition of Modern Decorative and Industrial Arts in Paris, can be recognized by its stylized decorative motifs, such as chevrons, zigzags, sunbursts, and deer or dancers silhouetted in mid-leap. In some cases, Napier's Art Deco heritage has been spoiled by the addition of garish advertising or unsympathetic alterations to shopfronts. The classic Art Deco features that remain are often found above ground-floor level, and the first part of this tour might well result in a stiff neck. The walk is followed by a brief wine-tasting tour. The visit to the gannet colony at the end of the tour is possible only between October and March.

Begin at the **Napier Visitor Information Centre** in Marine Parade. Walk north along Marine Parade with the sea on your right and turn left at the clocktower of the A & B Building. The first notable build-

⑮ ing is the **ASB Bank,** on the left. The Maori theme on the lintels above the main entrance is echoed in the ceiling inside the building.

Continue along Emerson Street and cross into the pedestrian mall.

⑯ The **Criterion Hotel** on the right is typical of the Spanish Mission style, whose popularity in the reconstructed Napier was due largely to its success in Santa Barbara, California, which had been devastated by its own earthquake just a few years before. Buildings along both sides of this mall number among Napier's finest examples of

⑰ Art Deco, including **Hannahs,** the **Bowman's Building, McGruers,** and the **Hawke's Bay Chambers.** Detour left into Dalton Street and look across the road to the balcony of the pink **Countrywide Bank Building,** one of Napier's Art Deco masterpieces.

Return to the intersection of Emerson Street and continue along Dalton Street to the next corner. Cross to the left side of the street

⑱ to view the decorative frieze on **Hildebrand's,** the building on the corner of Tennyson Street. Hildebrand was a German who migrated to New Zealand—thus the German flag at one end, the New Zealand at the other, and the wavy lines in the middle to symbolize the sea passage between the two countries.

Turn right into Tennyson Street; just past the next corner on the left

⑲ is the **Daily Telegraph Building,** an Art Deco classic. On the right at

⑳ the corner of Hastings Street is the **Market Reserve Building,** the first to rise from the rubble following the earthquake. Turn left into

㉑ Hastings Street. The facade of **Hartson's Bar,** on the left, has altered little since its previous incarnation as Hartson's Music Shop, which survived the quake.

Turn right into Browning Street; on the opposite corner is the

㉒ **Ministry of Works** building with its decorative lighthouse pillar at the front, still considered Art Deco despite its slightly forbidding appearance.

㉓ On the next corner, on the right, is the **Hawke's Bay Art Gallery and Museum.** Using newspaper reports, photographs, and audiovisuals, the museum re-creates the suffering caused by the earthquake. The museum also houses a unique display of artifacts of the Ngati Kahungunu people of the east coast. *65 Marine Pde., tel. 06/835–9668. Admission: adults $3, children under 14 free. Open daily 10–4:30.*

Numbers in the margin correspond to points of interest on the Central North Island map.

Leave Napier by Kennedy Road, which runs southwest from the city center toward Taradale. Just past Anderson Park, turn right into Avenue Road. At the end of this road on the other side of Church

㉔ Road is the entrance to the **Mission Vineyard,** the oldest in the country. The vineyard at Taradale was established by Catholic Marist brothers in the late 1850s, after an earlier vineyard farther to the north at Poverty Bay was abandoned. Legend has it that in 1852 one of the brothers made a barrel of sacramental wine and shipped it to Napier; the seamen broached the cargo, drank the wine, and filled

ASB Bank, **15**

Criterion
Hotel, **16**

Daily Telegraph
Building, **19**

Hannahs, **17**

Hartson's
Bar, **21**

Hawke's Bay
Art Gallery and
Museum, **23**

Hildebrand's, **18**

Market Reserve
Building, **20**

Ministry of
Works, **22**

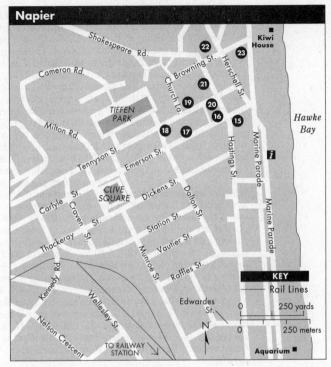

the empty cask with seawater. The pinot noir and semillon/
sauvignon blanc blend both deserve attention. *Church Rd.,
Taradale, tel. 06/844–2259. Open Mon.–Sat. 8–5, Sun. 1–4.*

Drive back to Church Road, turn right, and about ½ kilometer (¼
mile) farther is the **McDonald Winery.** This long-established vineyard benefited from an injection of capital and expertise when it became part of the Montana wine-making group in 1989. The Church
Road Chardonnay and Cabernet Sauvignon have excited oenophiles. The winery operates free tours on weekdays at 11 and 2,
weekends at 11, 1, 2, and 3. *200 Church Rd., Taradale, tel. 06/844–
2053. Open summer Mon.–Thurs. 9–5, Fri.–Sat. 10–6, Sun. 11–5;
Mar.–Nov., Mon.–Sat. 9–5, Sun. 11–4.*

Farther along Church Road, turn left at the intersection of
Puketapu Road; follow it as it changes its name to Meeanee Road,
and after about 6 kilometers (4 miles) turn right into Brookfields
Road and follow the signs to **Brookfields Winery.** This is one of the
most attractive wineries in the area, befitting its status as a premier
producer. The Reserve Chardonnay and the pinot gris are usually
outstanding, but the showpiece is the cabernet-merlot blend, characterized by intense fruit and assertive oak. *Brookfields Rd.,
Meeanee, tel. 06/834–4615. Open daily 9–5.*

Return toward Napier along Brookfields Road, and at the intersection with State Highway 2 turn right and then left, following the
signs to Te Awange and Clifton. The road follows the southern curve
of Hawke Bay and ends at **Cape Kidnapper.** Named by Captain
James Cook after local Maoris tried to kidnap the servant of Cook's
Tahitian interpreter, the cape is the site of a large **gannet colony.**

The gannet is a big white sea bird with black-tipped flight feathers, a golden crown, and wings that can reach a span of up to 6 feet. When the birds find a shoal of fish, they fold their wings and plunge straight into the sea at tremendous speed. Their migratory pattern ranges from western Australia to the Chatham Islands, about 800 kilometers (500 miles) east of Christchurch, but they generally nest only on remote islands. The gannet colony at Cape Kidnappers is believed to be the only mainland sanctuary in existence. Between October and March, about 15,000 gannets build their nests here, hatch their young, and prepare them for their long migratory flight. It is possible to walk to the sanctuary along the beach from Clifton, which is about 24 kilometers (15 miles) south of Napier, but the journey cannot be made at high tide. The 8-kilometer (5-mile) walk must begin no earlier than three hours after high tide; the return journey must begin no later than four hours before the next high tide. Tidal information is available at Clifton. A rest hut with refreshments is available near the colony. A far easier alternative is to ride aboard one of the **Garret Beach Adventures** (tel. 06/875–0898) tractor-trailers that are pulled along the beach starting from Charlton Road, Te Awanga, 21 kilometers (13 miles) south of Napier. The fare is $14 for adults, $11 for children 12–17, $9 for children under 12; the tractors depart two hours before low tide. The trip takes 4–4½ hours. If tides prevent the trip along the beach, the only other access is across private farmland. However, **Gannet Safaris** (tel. 06/875–0511) operates a four-wheel-drive bus to Cape Kidnappers from Summerlee Station, just past Te Awanga. A minimum of four is required for this tour, and the fare is $35 adults, $17 children 4–15. **Kidnappers Sea Escape** (tel. 06/875–0556) offers boat rides to view the gannet colony from the sea. The boats depart from Te Awanga; the fare is $45 per person.

28 Northeast of Napier is **Urewera National Park,** a vast, remote region of forests and lakes straddling the Huiarau Range. The park's outstanding feature is the glorious **Lake Waikaremoana** ("Sea of Rippling Waters"), a forest-girded lake with good swimming, boating, fishing, and walks. The lake is circled by a 50-kilometer (31-mile) walking track; the three- to four-day walk is popular and in the summer months the lakeside tramping huts are often heavily used. There are many other short walks nearby. The one-hour walk to Lake Waikareiti Track is especially recommended. For information, contact the Department of Conservation Field Centre at Aniwaniwa, on the eastern arm of Lake Waikaremoana (mailing address: Aniwaniwa, Private Bag, Wairoa, tel. 06/837–3803). The motor camp on the lakeshore has cabins, chalets, and motel units. In the summer months a launch operates sightseeing and fishing trips from the motor camp.

What to See and Do with Children

Kiwi House. New Zealand's national symbol is the star attraction at this nocturnal wildlife house. After the half-hour educational and environmental show at 1, visitors may handle the kiwis. *Marine Pde., Napier, tel. 06/835–7553. Admission: $3 adults, $1.50 children 5–15, $7.50 family. Open daily 11–3.*

Napier Aquarium. Sharks, rays, tropical fish, saltwater crocodiles, turtles, and piranha are displayed in this drum-shape building on the waterfront. *Marine Pde., Napier, tel. 06/835–7579. Admission: $6.50 adults, $3.25 children 5–15, $17 family. Open daily 9–5.*

Dining

Price categories for restaurants are the same as in the Auckland Dining section in Chapter 13. Highly recommended restaurants are indicated by a star ★.

$$$ **Bayswater on the Beach.** This bayside restaurant has a long-stand-
★ ing reputation as Napier's finest. Fillet of salmon with a scallop mousse, boned quails stuffed with a puree of zucchini and sweet peppers, and a warm salad of mussels filled with mozzarella are listed on a summer dinner menu that scores high marks for originality. The voguish, white interior has a faintly art deco flavor and big doors that open to a sparkling sea view. The moderately priced wine list offers some of the best that Hawke's Bay produces. In warm weather, request a table on the deck outside; otherwise, a table at the window. The restaurant can be hard to spot at night, but look for the chicken take-away, about 2 kilometers (1 mile) from the town center. *Hardinge Rd., Napier, tel. 06/835–8517. Reservations advised. Dress: casual. AE, DC, MC, V.*

$$$ **Bucks Great Wall Restaurant.** Housed in a landmark building on
★ Napier's Marine Parade, this opulent and sophisticated restaurant is a real treat for anyone who enjoys Cantonese cooking. The menu lists almost 100 dishes, from Peking duck to crayfish to sautéed prawns with crispy rice, and while it rarely ventures into unfamiliar territory, the food is delicious and beautifully presented. The earthen-pot dishes are particularly good. In addition to the à la carte menu, there are three fixed-price selections, from $30 to $40 per person. The gregarious owner imports her chefs and even installed a laundry on the premises when the local service sent back tablecloths that were not quite whiter than white. *Marine Pde. and Emerson St., Napier, tel. 06/835–0088. Reservations not required. Dress: casual. AE, DC, MC, V. No lunch weekends.*

$$ **Brookfields Winery Restaurant.** A simple, satisfying menu and an outdoor setting amid the vines make this prestige boutique winery a good choice for sunny-weather lunches. Salads, sandwiches on rye and sourdough bread, pasta, and homemade cakes are offered, as is wine by the glass. *Brookfields Rd., Meeanee, tel. 06/834–4615. No reservations. Dress: casual. AE, DC, MC, V. No dinner. No lunch Mon.–Thurs. except during Jan.*

$$ **Pierre sur le quai.** This sparse, smart, modern bistro is the backdrop
★ for Pierre Vuilleumier's robust French provincial cooking. Braised lamb shanks with a tomato and white wine sauce, baked eel in red wine with rice, and a seafood casserole with spring vegetables in a champagne sauce are examples from a menu that allows the flavors to speak for themselves and also offers outstanding value. Combined, the ambience, service, price, and uncluttered cooking should serve as an example to the rest of New Zealand. This waterfront restaurant may take some finding, but make the effort. *62 West Quay, Ahuriri, tel. 06/834–0189. Reservations advised. Dress: casual. MC.*

$$ **Vidal's Barrel Room Restaurant.** Set in a vineyard on the southern outskirts of Hastings, this restaurant has a relaxed country atmosphere that's perfect for family dining. The menu relies heavily on steaks, but there is usually a choice of grilled salmon, spare ribs, and pasta dishes, plus a changing blackboard menu. Old wine barrels, chunky furniture, and stained-glass windows give the restaurant an earthy appeal. In the winter there are open fires; in summer, a courtyard for open-air dining. If time allows, visit the wine shop and take a vineyard tour. *913 St. Aubyn St., East Hastings, tel. 06/*

876–8105. Reservations advised weekends. Dress: casual but neat.
DC, MC, V. Closed Sun.

Lodging

Price categories for hotels are the same as in the Auckland Lodging section in Chapter 13. Highly recommended lodgings are indicated by a star ★.

$$$ **Ormlie Lodge.** This ornate, sprawling timber house offers a taste of gracious country living at a reasonable price. Guest rooms, located on the upper level of the double-story house, are large, comfortable, and furnished with antiques. Room 4 has a Jacuzzi and French doors onto the balcony. To one side of the lodge is a group of four comfortable, modern timber chalets, an especially good value for a family. The hosts are warm and welcoming people who will happily point out golf courses or prime fishing spots in the area. The lodge is located in pastoral wine-growing country, about a 15-minute drive south of Napier. *Omarunui Rd., Waiohiki, Taradale, tel. 06/844–5774, fax 06/844–5499. 4 lodge rooms, 4 chalets. Facilities: restaurant, bar. AE, DC, MC, V.*

$$ **Edgewater Motor Lodge.** These motel rooms are about average in size, facilities, and character, but they offer a central location and sea views. Rooms on the upper level have balconies, and there are several room styles to suit couples or families. *359 Marine Pde., Napier, tel. 06/835–1140, fax 06/835–6600. 20 rooms with bath. Facilities: spa pool, outdoor pool, guest laundry. AE, DC, MC, V.*

$$ **Mon Logis Hôtel Privé.** The French owner of this seafront house has
★ modeled his accommodation on the *logis* of his homeland—a refined version of traditional bed-and-breakfast accommodations. Rooms are large and prettily decorated in a Continental style with eiderdowns and feather pillows. Although they lack the sea view, the two rooms at the back of the house are quieter: Buttes Chaumont has an en suite bathroom, while Paris's bathroom is located off the hall. But what most sets this place apart from the standard B&B is the food. In the morning guests have complimentary coffee and a basket of freshly baked French breads delivered to their rooms. Children are not accommodated. A four-course dinner at $45 per person, including wine, is available by arrangement. *415 Marine Pde., Napier, tel. 06/835–2125, fax 06/435–4196. 4 rooms with bath. Tariff includes breakfast. AE, DC, MC, V.*

Wellington

Most visitors find themselves in the capital more by necessity than by choice. Perched at the southern tip of the North Island, Wellington is the jumping-off point for the ferry south, and many travelers, in their rush to the South Island, pass through without a second glance. Yet those who delay their departure for even a single day will discover a sociable city of real charm, small enough to be easily explored on foot, yet large enough to cater to cultured tastes.

The city was named after the Duke of Wellington, the conqueror of Napoléon in his final defeat at Waterloo, and originally settled by English pioneers who purchased land from the New Zealand Company. Shortly after the Treaty of Waitangi was concluded in 1840, Auckland was chosen as the site for the new national capital, but the prosperous and influential gold miners of the South Island waged a campaign for a more central capital, and in 1865 the seat of government was shifted to Wellington.

This city of 354,000 sits in a glorious location on the western shores of Port Nicholson, squeezed against the sea by peaks that rear up to almost 900 meters (3,000 feet). Behind it, suburbs of quaint timber houses spill down precipitous slopes. "Windy Wellington" is a nickname that springs readily to the lips of every New Zealander. Frequently the streets are roped to help pedestrians avoid being bowled over. The cause of this bitter wind is the air currents funneled through the narrow neck of Cook Strait, the 18-kilometer (11-mile) channel between the two islands.

Important Addresses and Numbers

Tourist Information
Wellington Visitor Information Centre. *Civic Administration Bldg., Victoria and Wakefield Sts., tel. 04/801–4000. Open weekdays 8:30–6, weekends 9–5.*

Embassies and High Commissions
Australian High Commission. *72–78 Hobson St., Thorndon, tel. 04/473–6411. Open weekdays 8:45–12:15.*

British High Commission. *44 Hill St., tel. 04/472–6049. Open weekdays 9:30–noon and 2–3:30.*

Canadian High Commission. *61 Molesworth St., Thorndon, tel. 04/473–9577. Open weekdays 8:30–4:30.*

United States Embassy. *29 Fitzherbert Terr., Thorndon, tel. 04/472–2068. Open weekdays 10–noon and 2–4.*

Emergencies Dial 111 for **fire, police,** or **ambulance** services.

Hospital Wellington Hospital. *Riddiford St., Newtown, tel. 04/385–5999.*

Late Night Pharmacy
The After-Hours Pharmacy. *17 Adelaide Rd., Newtown, tel. 04/385–8810. Open weekdays 5 AM–11 PM, Sat. 9 AM–11 PM, Sun. 10–10.*

Travel Agencies
American Express Travel Service. *203 Lambton Quay, tel. 04/473–1221.*

Thomas Cook. *108 Lambton Quay, tel. 04/473–5167.*

Arriving and Departing

By Plane Wellington International Airport lies about 8 kilometers (5 miles) from the city. **Super Shuttle** (tel. 04/387–8787) operates a 10-seater bus between the airport and any address in the city ($8 for one person, $10 for two). The bus meets all incoming flights; tickets are available from the driver.

By Car The main access to the city is via the Wellington Urban Motorway, an extension of National Highway 1, which links the city center with all towns and cities to the north.

By Train The **Wellington Railway Station** (tel. 04/498–3000) is on Bunny Street, 1½ kilometers (½ mile) from the city center.

By Bus InterCity buses (tel. 04/495–2443) arrive and depart from Wellington Railway Station. The terminal for **Newmans** buses (tel. 04/499–3261) is the InterIslander Ferry Terminal, 3 kilometers (2 miles) from the city center.

By Ferry The **InterIsland Line** (tel. 04/498–3999) operates vehicle and passenger ferries between Wellington and Picton, at the northern tip of the South Island. The one-way adult fare is $38 during school holidays, $30 at other times. Children ages 4–14 pay half price. The fare for a medium-size sedan is $114 during school holidays, $92 at other times. The crossing takes about three hours and can be very rough.

There are at least two departures in each direction every day, and bookings should be made in advance, particularly during holiday periods. The ferry terminal is about 3 kilometers (2 miles) from the city. A free bus leaves Platform 9 at the Wellington Railway Station for the ferry terminal 35 minutes before sailings.

Getting Around

By Bus Wellington's public bus network is known as **Ridewell.** For trips around the inner city, the fare is $1 for adults and 50¢ for children 4–14. **Daytripper** tickets ($5), allowing unlimited travel for one adult and two children, are available from bus drivers after 9 AM. For maps and timetables, contact the information center (142–146 Wakefield St., tel. 04/801–7000).

By Bicycle If the sun is shining and the wind is still, a bicycle is an ideal way to explore the city and its surrounding bays. **Penny Farthing Cycles** (89 Courtenay Pl., tel. 04/385–2772) hires out mountain bikes for $25 per day or $140 per week, including helmet.

Guided Tours

Harbour Capital Bus Tours' Coastline Tour takes in attractions in the city center as well as along the Miramar Peninsula to the east. The 2¾-hour tour departs from the Visitor Information Centre at the corner of Victoria and Wakefield streets. *Tel. 04/499–1282. Tickets: $21 adults, $10 children under 15.*

Wally Hammond, a tour operator with a great anecdotal knowledge and a fund of stories about the city, offers a 2½-hour minibus tour of the city and Marine Drive. Tours depart from Travel World, Mercer and Victoria streets, at 10 and 2. Passengers can be picked up at their city hotels at no extra cost. *Tel. 04/472–0869. Tickets: $20 per person.*

The **Trust Bank Ferry,** a commuter service between the city and Days Bay, on the eastern side of Port Nicholson, is one of the best-value tours in the city. Weekdays the catamaran departs from Queens Wharf at 7:10, 8:20, noon, 2, 4:15, and 5:30; weekends, at 10:30, noon, 2, and 4:15. The trip takes about 25 minutes. *Queens Wharf, City, tel. 04/499–1273. Round-trip tickets: $12 adults, $6 children 3–15.*

Exploring Wellington

This walking tour of the city includes city views, formal gardens, literary history, some fine examples of 19th-century architecture, and the seat of government. Allow about three hours.

Numbers in the margin correspond to points of interest on the Wellington map.

❶ Begin at the **Kelburn Cable Car** terminus in Cable Car Lane off Lambton Quay, opposite Grey Street. The Swiss-built funicular railway makes a short but sharp climb to Kelburn Terminal, which offers views across parks and city buildings to Port Nicholson. Sit on the left side during the six-minute journey for the best scenery. *Cost: $1.50 adults, 70¢ children 4–15. Departures about every 10 min, weekdays 7 AM–10 PM, Sat. 9:20–6, Sun. 10:30–6.*

Leave the Kelburn Terminal and take the Northern Walkway, following the arrow that points to St. Mary Street. This path skirts the ❷ edge of the **Botanic Garden,** with city views on one side and the

Ascot Street, **5**

Botanic Garden, **2**

Cenotaph, **13**

Executive Office, **12**

John Seddon Memorial, **4**

Katherine Mansfield House, **8**

Kelburn Cable Car, **1**

Lady Norwood Rose Garden, **3**

Maritime Museum, **14**

National Library, **10**

No. 306 Tinakori Road, **6**

Old St. Paul's Cathedral, **9**

Parliament Buildings, **11**

Premier House, **7**

Southward Museum, **15**

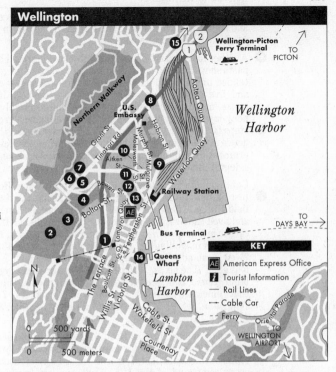

domes of the Dominion Observatory on the other. As you round the hilltop, you'll see an immense green hill with transmission towers on top; this is Tinakori Hill, known to the Maoris as Ahumairangi—"sloping down from the sky."

Continue along the path, which becomes quite steep as it plunges down toward the **Lady Norwood Rose Garden** and the **Begonia House.** There are more than 100 types of roses in the garden, which erupts in a blaze of color between November and the end of April.

Turn your back on the roses and walk to the right around the enclosed Anderson Park, following the sign to Bolton Street Memorial Park. At the end of this short road, make a detour to the monument on the right. The **John Seddon Memorial** is dedicated to the colorful and popular liberal politician who was prime minister from 1893 to 1906. Under Seddon's leadership, New Zealand became the first country to pay its citizens an old-age pension, and the first to give women the vote.

Close to the memorial a track zigzags down the hill beneath a stand of pohutukawa trees. At the bottom, cross Bowen Street, walk downhill, take the path to your left, and climb narrow **Ascot Street.** The tiny, doll-like cottages along this street were built in the 1870s, and this remains the finest example of a 19th-century streetscape in Wellington. At the top of the rise, stop for a breather on the bench that has been thoughtfully provided in the shady courtyard.

Turn right into **Tinakori Road.** The lack of suitable local stone combined with the collapse of most of Wellington's brick buildings in the earthquake of 1848 ensured that timber was used almost exclusively for building here in the second half of the 19th century. Most of the carpenters of the period had learned their skills as cabinetmakers and shipwrights in Europe, and the sturdy houses in this street are a tribute to their craftsmanship.

6 Another fact of early life in Wellington is illustrated by **No. 306,** the pasta shop. Pressed for level ground, the citizens of early Wellington tended to build tall, narrow houses. This example—one room wide and five stories high—took things to extremes. Just below the house, make a short detour to see the three superbly restored timber houses side by side in Upton Terrace. Behind a green fence a few **7** steps farther down Tinakori Road is **Premier House,** the official residence of the prime minister until 1935, when the new Labour government, caught up in the reforming zeal of socialism, turned it into a dental clinic.

Continue down a relatively drab part of Tinakori Road to No. 25, **8** just beyond the Hobson Street bridge. This is the **Katherine Mansfield House,** where the writer was born (as Kathleen Beauchamp) and lived the first five years of her life. Mansfield left to pursue her career in Europe when she was only 20, but many of her short stories are set in Wellington. A year before her death in 1923, she wrote, "New Zealand is in my very bones. What wouldn't I give to have a look at it!" The house, which has been restored as a typical Victorian family home, contains furnishings, photographs, videos, and tapes that elucidate Mansfield's life and times. *25 Tinakori Rd., Thorndon, tel. 04/473–7268. Admission: $4 adults, $1 children 4–15. Open Tues.–Sun. 10–4.*

Walk back along Tinakori Road to the Hobson Street overpass, and on the far side of the motorway turn right to walk through the elms of Katherine Mansfield Memorial Park. Turn left around the rather stern compound of the U.S. Embassy, and walk down Murphy **9** Street, which becomes Mulgrave Street, to **Old St. Paul's Cathedral.** Consecrated in 1866, the church is a splendid example of the English neo-Gothic style executed in wood. Even the trusses that support the roof transcend their mundane function with their splendid craftsmanship. The hexagonal oak pulpit was a gift from the widow of Prime Minister Richard Seddon, in memory of her husband. *Mulgrave St., Thorndon, tel. 04/473–6722. Open Mon.–Sat. 10–4:30, Sun. 1–4:30.*

Walk down Mulgrave Street and turn right at Archives House into **10** Aitken Street. The modern building on the right is the **National Library,** which houses the largest collection of books in the nation as well as the remarkable Alexander Turnbull Library. This latter collection, named after the noted bibliophile who founded it, contains a particularly impressive Pacific history section, which includes accounts of every important European voyage of discovery since Magellan. The art collection includes many sketches of New Zealand made by early visitors; these are displayed in changing exhibitions. *Molesworth and Aitken Sts., tel. 04/474–3000. Open weekdays 9–5, Sat. 9–1.*

Cross Molesworth Street and walk through the gate to the **11** **Parliament Buildings** on the far side. The green Gothic structure on the right is the General Assembly Library, a soaring, graceful building compared with the ponderous gray bulk of the Parliament House next door. The layout of the House of Representatives, where legislation is presented, debated, and either passed or rejected by majority vote, is a copy of the British Houses of Parliament at Westminster, right down to the Speaker's mace and the despatch boxes. Tours of the building explain the parliamentary process in detail.

Molesworth St., tel. 04/471–9999. Admission free. Tours depart weekdays at varying times.

⓬ It would be difficult to imagine a more complete contrast in architectural styles than the **Executive Office** building to the left of the Parliament House, known for obvious reasons as "the Beehive"—though the people of Wellington will often add that it produces nothing sweet. This building houses the offices of parliamentarians and their staffs.

⓭ Walk down the hill from the Beehive to the **Cenotaph,** the memorial to New Zealanders killed in battle. New Zealand has a proud and distinguished war record. "Few Americans appreciate the tremendous sacrifices made by New Zealanders in the last two world wars," James A. Michener wrote in *Return to Paradise.* "Among the allies, she had the highest percentage of men in arms—much higher than the United States—the greatest percentage overseas, and the largest percentage killed."

The wide street that curves away to the back of the bronze lions is **Lambton Quay.** As its name suggests, this was once Wellington's waterfront. All the land between your feet and the present-day shoreline has been reclaimed. From this point, the shops of the city center are within easy walking distance along Lambton Quay.

Other Places of Interest

⓮ **Maritime Museum.** Housed in the handsome Harbour Board Building, this museum has paintings, figureheads, various nautical apparatuses, and some fine scale models of ships, including the *Wahine,* which sank in Cook Strait in 1968 with the loss of 51 lives. However, most of the displays belong to the old-fashioned, glass-cabinet school of museum design. *Queens Wharf, tel. 04/472–8904. Admission: $2 adults, 50¢ children under 12. Open weekdays 9:30–4, weekends 1–4:30.*

⓯ **Southward Museum.** The largest collection of vintage and veteran cars in the Southern Hemisphere, this amazing collection of more that 250 vehicles includes Bugattis, a Hispano-Suiza, one of only 17 Davis three-wheelers ever made, a De Lorean, a gull-wing 1955 Mercedes 300SL, gangster Micky Cohen's armor-plated 1950 Cadillac, and another Cadillac once owned by Marlene Dietriech. The motorcycle collection, which has a number of early Harley-Davidsons and Indians, a Brough Superior, and a Vincent V-twin, is almost as impressive. The museum is located just off Highway 1, about a 45-minute drive north of Wellington. *Otaihanga Rd., Paraparaumu, tel. 04/297–1221. Admission: $4 adults, $1 children 5–14. Open daily 9–4:30.*

Dining

Courtenay Place is Wellington's restaurant row. Turkish, Indian, French, and Italian restaurants jostle for attention, along with several bar/brasseries that make this a favorite nightspot for the city's sophisticates.

Price categories for restaurants are the same as in the Auckland Dining section in Chapter 13. Highly recommended restaurants are indicated by a star ★.

$$$$ **Le Petit Lyon.** The anonymous brick wall at the front hides what ★ many regard as the finest epicurean restaurant in the country. Inside, classical French cuisine is presented with all the trimmings:

silver, crystal, plush surroundings, and solicitous service. The menu degustation, at $125 per person including wines, is recommended for those who want to totally indulge themselves. *8 Courtenay Pl., tel. 04/364–9402. Reservations required. Jacket and tie required. AE, DC, MC, V. No lunch Sat. Closed Sun.*

$$$ **Brasserie Flipp.** Highly fashionable with Wellington's sophisticates, ★ the innovative international menu makes this restaurant a good choice for lunch or dinner. Main courses include smoked pork kassler sausage with red cabbage, char-grilled baby octopus salad, and grilled lamb steak with a green pea puree. The decor is smart and stylish: polished timber floors, dazzling white napery, and subdued lighting. The wine list has a good selection of New Zealand wines, and a token bottle from just about everywhere else. *RSA Bldg., 103 Ghunzee St., Wellington, tel. 04/385–9493. No reservations. Dress: casual. AE, DC, MC, V.*

$$$ **Tinakori Bistro.** Set in a miniature Thorndon shopfront, this popular bistro has a modern, French-influenced menu and a long-standing reputation for reliability. Main courses include char-grilled scotch fillet with sour cream and horseradish dressing, and grilled venison medallions with a blackberry and port sauce. *328 Tinakori Rd., Thorndon, tel. 04/499–0567. Reservations advised. Dress: casual but neat. AE, MC, V. BYOB. No lunch weekends. Closed Sun.*

$$ **Bellissimo Trattoria Italiana.** This is simply great Italian food— ★ served with far more style and panache than the name "trattoria" might suggest. First courses include fish carpaccio with olive oil and calamari in a chili sauce. Among the mains might be panfried veal stuffed with vegetables or venison stew. All the pasta is made on the premises by the Neapolitan owner/chef. *Dukes Arcade, Manners St., tel. 04/499–1154. Reservations not required. Dress: casual. AE, DC, MC, V. No lunch weekends.*

$$ **Chevy's.** With a name like that and a flashing neon cowboy out front, the burgers, nachos, chicken wings, BLTs, and barbecue spareribs come as little surprise. The salads are crisp, the fries are crunchy, the service is prompt, the quasi-American decor is bright and attractive, and the restaurant stays open until at least 10:30. *97 Dixon St., Wellington, tel. 04/384–2724. No reservations. Dress: casual. AE, DC, MC, V. BYOB.*

$$ **Dockside.** Part of the redeveloped warehouse complex on the waterfront, this new, informal restaurant has a nautical theme, a reasonably priced menu, and a choice of casual dining in either the bar or the upstairs restaurant. *Moules marinières* (pasta with mussels in a tomato and chili sauce), *salad niçoise*, smoked chicken salad, and a salad of warm vegetables and cervena venison appear on a menu that is particularly strong on seafood. *Shed 3, Queens Wharf, Jervois Quay, tel. 04/499–9900. Reservations not required. Dress: casual. AE, DC, MC, V.*

$ **Dixon Street Gourmet Deli.** This city-center delicatessen stocks one ★ of the best ranges of gourmet treats in the country. There are homebaked breads and bagels, an international choice of meats, cheeses, pickles, and preserves, plus local smoked fish and oysters—everything you need for a superior picnic. *45–47 Dixon St., tel. 04/384–2436. No credit cards. Closed weekends.*

$ **Gourmet Lane.** These half-dozen cafés in the basement of the Bank of New Zealand Building offer a choice of light meals, from spring rolls to fish and chips to pies, pastries, and salads. Try to avoid the 12:30 crush, when the place is crowded with office workers. *1 Willis St. No credit cards. Lunch only. Closed weekends.*

$ **The Lido.** This popular, bustling corner café across from the tourist information center is a particularly good choice if you're looking for budget-priced breakfast or lunch. *Victoria and Wakefield Sts., tel. 04/499–6666. No reservations. Dress: casual but neat. No credit cards.*

Lodging

Lodging in Wellington is peculiarly polarized, with elegant and expensive hotels on one end, homestays on the other, and nothing in between. Price categories for hotels are the same as in the Auckland Lodging section in Chapter 13. Highly recommended lodgings are indicated by a star ★.

$$$$ **Parkroyal Wellington.** If you are looking for the luxury, facilities,
★ gloss, and glamour that only a big international hotel can deliver, this is the best in town—and possibly the best in the country. Opened in 1990, the bronze tower building has an art deco flavor in its public areas. Guest rooms are decorated in sea greens and blues with blond wood furnishings, and each has its own iron and ironing board. The bureau rooms, which have a desk and a queen-size bed instead of two doubles, are tailored especially for traveling executives. Request a room with ocean views. Service by the young staff is excellent throughout the hotel. The Parkroyal is located in the city center, within walking distance of shops, restaurants, and the central business district. The Panama Street Brasserie is a favorite breakfast spot for the city's power brokers. *Featherston and Grey Sts., Wellington, tel. 04/72–2722, fax 04/472–4724. 232 rooms with bath. Facilities: spa pool, sauna, gym, heated indoor pool, guest laundry, 2 bars, 2 restaurants. AE, DC, MC, V.*

$ **Halswell Lodge.** Rooms at this hotel on the edge of the city center are compact and functional, but each has en suite facilities and a reasonable standard of comfort. The surroundings offer a wide choice of restaurants. Rooms at the front are affected by street noise during the daytime. *21 Kent Terr., Wellington, tel. 04/385–0196, fax 04/385–0503. 19 rooms with bath. AE, DC, MC, V.*

$ **Homestay.** Located just a five-minute drive from the city center, this timber house offers comfort, style, and good value for those looking for homestay accommodations. The ground-level guest room is rather small and does not have an en suite bathroom, but the apartment on the floor below has a separate kitchen, bathroom, lounge, and room for four. Throughout, the owners (one is an Austrian, one a New Zealander) have decorated their house simply but stylishly with bunches of dried wildflowers, rustic wooden furniture, Oriental rugs, and polished timber floors. The house has marvelous views across timber houses and gardens that spill down to the harbor in the distance. *33 Mortimer Terr., tel. 04/385–3667. 1 room, 1 apartment with bath. Tariff includes breakfast. No credit cards.*

$ **Tinakori Lodge.** Situated in a historic suburb overlooking the city, this lodge offers atmospheric bed-and-breakfast accommodations in tranquil surroundings at a reasonable price. The rooms, which can sleep up to three, are simply furnished but comfortable. The city center is a 10-minute walk away, and there are several restaurants in the vicinity. The owners are extremely friendly and helpful. Children are accommodated by arrangement. *182 Tinakori Rd., Thorndon, tel. 04/473–3478, fax 04/472–5554. 10 rooms share 3 baths. Tariff includes breakfast. AE, DC, MC, V.*

The Arts and Nightlife

The Arts   Wellington is the home of the **New Zealand Ballet Company** and the **New Zealand Symphony Orchestra.** The main venue for the performing arts is the **Michael Fowler Centre** (Wakefield Street, tel. 04/472–3088).

The **Downstage Theatre** holds frequent performances of stage classics. *Hannah Playhouse, Courtenay Pl. and Cambridge Terr., tel. 04/384–9639.*

Nightlife   At the heart of the city, the **St. George Hotel** has several bars, live jazz music most nights of the week, and Legends of the George, a late-night restaurant. *Willis and Boulcott Sts., tel. 04/473–9139. Open 11 AM–midnight.*

The most vigorous sign of life after dark in Wellington is found in its bars. On the ground floor of the Parkroyal Hotel at the corner of Grey and Featherstone streets, the **Arizona Bar** (tel. 04/495–7867) is packed on Friday and Saturday nights, as is the nearby **Malthouse** at 47 Willis St. (tel. 04/499–4355). However, the main action is on Courtenay Place, where the bar scene operates at fever pitch on Friday and Saturday nights.

15 The South Island

By Michael Gebicki

The South Island is separated from the North Island by Cook Strait, an expanse of just 17 kilometers (11 miles); yet the difference is far greater than the distance suggests. Whether you first glimpse the South Island from the deck of the ferry as it noses into Marlborough Sounds or through the window of a plane bound for Christchurch, the immediate impression is that the landscape has turned feral: The green, mellow beauty of the North Island has given way to jagged snowcapped mountains and rivers that charge down from them and sprawl across vast shingle beds. The locals will tell you that you haven't seen rain until you've been drenched by a rainstorm on the west coast—one of the wettest places on earth.

The headline attractions are Queenstown, the adventure-sport capital of the country; Mount Cook and its glaciers; and the sounds of Fiordland National Park. Beyond the well-defined tourist routes, the island's beech forests, lakes, trout streams, mountain trails, and beaches form a paradise for hikers, anglers, and just about anyone who enjoys a dose of fresh air. Sperm whales, dolphins, penguins, seals, and royal albatrosses can be seen in the wild along the coastline. And Stewart Island, off the southern tip of South Island, is remote enough to satisfy even the most determined escapist.

Marlborough, Nelson, and the West Coast

These three regions, which form the northern and western coasts of the South Island, offer an immense variety of scenery, from the siren seascapes of Marlborough Sounds to the mellow river valleys of the north coast to the icy world of the glaciers and the Southern Alps, where 12,000-foot peaks rise within 32 kilometers (20 miles) of the shore.

After the well-ordered serenity of the North Island, the wild grandeur of the west coast will come as a surprise. This is Mother Nature with her hair down, flaying the coastline with huge seas and drenching rains and littering its beaches with bleached driftwood sculptures. It is a country that creates a special breed, and the rough-hewn and powerfully independent people—known to the rest of the country as "coasters"—occupy a special place in New Zealand folklore.

For visitors who ferry across from Wellington, Marlborough Sounds will provide the first taste of the South Island. Together with the city of Nelson and Abel Tasman National Park to the west, this is a sporting paradise, with a mild climate that allows a year-round array of adventure activities.

Important Addresses and Numbers

Tourist Information

Nelson Visitor Information Centre. *Trafalgar and Halifax Sts., tel. 03/548–2304. Open daily 9–5.*

Franz Josef Glacier Visitor Information Centre. *State Hwy. 6, Franz Josef, tel. 03/752–0796. Open daily 8–4:30.*

Greymouth Visitor Information Centre. *Regent Theatre Bldg., McKay and Herbert Sts., tel. 03/768–5101. Open weekdays 9–5.*

Emergencies

Dial 111 for **fire, police,** or **ambulance** services.

Arriving and Departing

By Plane **Air New Zealand** (tel. 03/546–9300) and **Ansett New Zealand** (tel. 04/471–1044) link Nelson with Christchurch, Queenstown, Dunedin, the west coast town of Hokitika, and all major cities on the North Island. **Nelson Airport** lies 10 kilometers (6 miles) west of the city. **Super Shuttle** (tel. 03/547–5782) operates buses that meet all incoming flights and charge $6 to the city for one passenger, $5 each for two. The taxi fare to the city center is about $12.

By Car From Nelson, Highway 6 runs southwest to the west coast, down the coast to the glaciers, then south to Queenstown and Invercargill. Highway 1 follows the east coast to Christchurch and Dunedin. Allow at least seven hours for the 458-kilometer (284-mile) journey from Nelson to Franz Josef.

By Bus From Nelson, **InterCity** buses travel the length of both the west and east coasts daily. For bookings from Nelson, tel. 03/548–1539; Greymouth, tel. 03/768–1435; Franz Josef, tel. 03/752–0780.

By Ferry The berth for the **InterIsland Ferries** from Wellington is at Picton, 145 kilometers (90 miles) east of Nelson. At the ferry terminal, buses are readily available for travel either east to Blenheim and Christchurch or west to Nelson.

By Train The west coast in general is poorly served by the rail network, but one glowing exception is the **TranzAlpine Express,** which ranks as one of the world's great rail journeys. This passenger train crosses the Southern Alps between Christchurch and Greymouth, winding through beech forests and mountains that are covered by snow for most of the year. The bridges and tunnels along this line, including the 8-kilometer (5-mile) Otira Tunnel, represent a prodigious feat of engineering. The train is modern and comfortable, with panoramic windows as well as dining and bar service. Smoking is not permitted on board. The train departs Christchurch daily at 9:15 AM and arrives in Greymouth at 1:25 PM; the return train departs Greymouth at 2:35 PM and arrives at Christchurch at 6:40 PM. The one-way fare is $66 adults, $33 children 4–14. For bookings, tel. 800/802–802.

Guided Tours

Abel Tasman National Park Enterprises operate launches that follow the majestic shoreline of the park. A popular option is to leave the boat at Bark Bay on the outward voyage, take a two-hour walk through the forests, and reboard the boat at Torrent Bay. The 6½-hour cruise departs daily from Kaiteriteri, a one-hour drive northwest of Nelson, at 9 AM. A bus connection from Nelson leaves the Visitor Information Centre at 7:35 AM. A cruise/flight option is also available. Passengers should buy a take-out lunch at Motueka—supplies on board are basic. *Old Cedarman House, Main Rd., Riwaka, tel. 03/528–7801. Cost: cruise (from Kaiteriteri), $42 adults, $14 children 4–14; cruise/flight (from Nelson): $112 adults, $97 children 4–14; bus (Nelson–Kaiteriteri round-trip), $17.*

The *Glenmore,* a small launch that makes a daylong trip ferrying mail and supplies around the reaches of Pelorus Sound, offers one of the best ways to discover this waterway and meet the people who live there. The boat departs from Havelock Tuesday to Thursday at 9:30 and returns about 5:30. On Fridays from mid-December to Easter, passengers can combine the cruise with a four-hour bushwalk along the Nydia Track. *Glenmore Cruises, 73 Main Rd., Havelock, tel. 03/574–2276. Tickets: $45 adults, $22.50 children 4–14.*

The **Helicopter Line** operates several scenic flights over the glaciers from the heliport at Franz Josef. The shortest is the 20-minute flight over the Franz Josef Glacier ($40 per person); the longest is the Mountain Scenic Spectacular, a one-hour flight that includes a landing on the head of the glacier and a circuit of Mount Cook and Mount Tasman ($130 per person). *Box 45, Franz Josef, tel. 02/883–1767.*

The **Scenic Mail Run** is a five-hour tour aboard the bus that delivers the mail and supplies to isolated farming communities around Cape Farewell, at the northern tip of the South Island. The tour includes lunch on a 2,500-acre grazing property. The eight-seater bus departs from the Collingwood Post office. *Collingwood Bus Services, P.O. Collingwood, tel. 03/524–8188. Tickets: $25 adults, $15 children under 12. Tour departs 9:30 weekdays.*

Exploring Marlborough, Nelson, and the West Coast

This driving tour begins at Picton, where the InterIslander Ferries berth, and travels west to Nelson and Motueka, then south on Highway 6 along the coast. The detour through Motueka adds almost two hours; anyone who intends to make the seven-hour drive from Nelson to the glaciers in a single day should ignore this section of the tour and leave Nelson by Highway 6 instead.

Numbers in the margin correspond to points of interest on the Marlborough, Nelson, and the West Coast map.

① Picton is the base for cruising holidays in the **Marlborough Sounds,** the labyrinth of waterways that was formed when the sea invaded a series of river valleys at the northern tip of the South Island. Backed by forested hills that at times rise almost vertically from the water, the Sounds are a wild, majestic place edged with tiny beaches and rocky coves and studded with islands where such native wildlife as gannets and the primitive tuatara have remained undisturbed by introduced species. These waterways are the country's second-favorite cruising waters, after the Bay of Islands, but in terms of isolation and rugged grandeur they are in a class of their own. Much of the area is a national park; it has changed little since the 1770s, when Captain James Cook called in on five separate occasions to repair his ships and stock up with fresh provisions. There are rudimentary roads on the long fingers of land jutting into the Sounds, but the most convenient access is by water. One of the best ways to discover the area is hitching a ride at Havelock aboard the launch *Glenmore*, which delivers mail and supplies to outlying settlements scattered around Pelorus Sound (*see* Guided Tours, *above*).

② From the InterIslander ferry terminal, turn right and follow the signs to **Queen Charlotte Drive.** This road rises spectacularly along the edge of the sound, then cuts across the base of the peninsula that separates Queen Charlotte Sound from Pelorus Sound. Beyond Havelock the road winds through forested river valleys before it rounds the eastern side of Tasman Bay and reaches Nelson.

③ Set on the broad curve of its bay with views of the Tasman Mountains on the far side, it would be hard to find a city and a climate better suited for year-round adventure than **Nelson.** To the east are the sheltered waters of Marlborough Sounds; to the west, the sandy crescents of the Abel Tasman National Park; and to the south, mellow river valleys and the peaks and glacial lakes of the Nelson Lakes National Park, a pristine wonderland for hikers, mountaineers, and cross-country skiers. Beyond those geographic splendors, Nelson

Marlborough, Nelson, and the West Coast

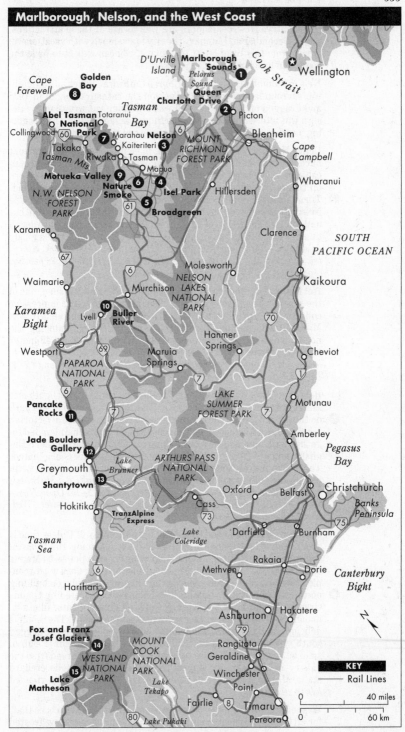

has a mild climate with more hours of sunlight than any other city in the country. New Zealanders are well aware of these attractions, and in December and January the city is swamped with vacationers. Apart from this brief burst of activity, you can expect to have the roads and beaches almost to yourself.

Nelson is dominated by **Christ Church Cathedral,** which sits on a hilltop surrounded by gardens. Work on the cathedral began in 1925 and dragged on for the next 40 years. During construction the design was altered to withstand earthquakes, and despite its promising location, it looks like a church designed by a committee.

Leave Nelson by **Rutherford Street,** named in honor of the eminent nuclear physicist Ernest Rutherford, who was born nearby and educated at school here. On the outskirts of the city, take the right fork off this road, Waimea Road, and continue as it becomes Main Road.

❹ Turn left into Marsden Road, where a sign points to **Isel Park.** The **Nelson Provincial Museum** in the grounds of the park has a small but outstanding collection of Maori carvings. The museum also has a number of artifacts relating to the "Maungatapu murders," a grisly goldfields killing committed near Nelson in 1866. *Isel Park, Stoke, tel. 03/547–9740. Admission: $2 adults, $1 children 5–15, $5 family. Open Tues.–Fri. 10–4, weekends 2–5.*

Isel House, near the museum, was built for Thomas Marsden, one of the region's prosperous pioneers. The Marsden family's impressive collection of porcelain and furniture is displayed inside. It was Marsden who laid out the magnificent gardens surrounding the house, which include a towering California redwood and a 42-meter (140-foot) Monterey pine. *Isel Park, tel. 03/547–9740. Admission to house: $2.50 adults, $1 children 5–15. House open weekends 2–4. Closed June–Aug.*

❺ Return to Main Road, turn right at the next set of traffic lights into Songer Street, turn right into Nayland Road, and stop at the park on the left. In the middle is **Broadgreen,** a fine example of a Victorian "cob" house. Cob houses, made from straw and horsehair bonded together with mud and clay, are commonly found in the southern English county of Devon, where many of Nelson's pioneers originated. The house is furnished as it might have been in the 1850s, with patchwork quilts and kauri furniture. *276 Nayland Rd., Stoke, tel. 03/546–0283. Admission: $2 adults, 50¢ children 5–15. Open Nov.–Apr., Tues.–Fri. 10:30–4:30, weekends 1:30–4:30; May–Oct., Wed. and weekends 2–4:30.*

❻ Return to Main Road and turn right onto Highway 6. Unless time is short, turn right again onto Highway 60, following the "coastal route" signs to Motueka. Turn right where a sign points to Mapua and continue to Mapua Port. This road ends at a tiny dock with a couple of ramshackle warehouses; in the blue corrugated iron building on the wharf is **Nature Smoke.** The business is operated by Dennis Crawford, who buys his fish right off the fishing boats, fillets it, marinates it according to a secret recipe, and smokes it. The result is delicious, and Crawford will happily offer samples. If you're headed south, you won't find a better lunch along the way than a slab of smoked snapper or albacore tuna with a loaf of crusty bread from the bakery in Motueka and apples from one of the roadside orchard stalls. *Mapua Wharf, tel. 03/540–2280. Open daily 9–5:30, extended hrs in summer.*

West of Mapua, Highway 60 loops around quiet little sea coves that, for all but the warmest months of the year, mirror the snow-frosted peaks on the far shore. The tall vines along the roadside are hops, used in the making of beer.

Beyond the town of Motueka, Highway 60 passes close to the fine swimming beach at Kaiteriteri, then turns inland to skirt the **Abel Tasman National Park,** the smallest of New Zealand's national parks. Its coastline is a succession of idyllic beaches backed by a rugged hinterland of beech forests, granite gorges, and waterfalls. The park has a number of walking trails, both from Totaranui at its northern end and Marahau in the south. The most popular is the two- to three-day **Coastal Track,** open year-round. Launches of the Abel Tasman National Park Enterprises (tel. 03/528–7801) will drop off and pick up hikers from several points along the track. A popular way to explore the coastline is by sea kayak (*see* Sports and the Outdoors, *below*). The park information center is at the Department of Conservation Field Centre (1 Commercial St., Takaka, tel. 03/525–9136). The main accommodations base for the national park is Motueka.

Highway 60 returns to the sea near the town of Takaka. The sweep of sand to the north is known, deservedly, as **Golden Bay,** but it once had a very different name. The Dutch navigator Abel Tasman anchored here briefly just a few days before Christmas 1642; his visit ended tragically when four of his crew were killed by Maoris. Bitterly disappointed, Tasman named the place Moordenaers, or Murderers' Bay, and sailed away without ever setting foot on New Zealand soil. For those who have time to explore, Golden Bay is a delight—a sunny 40-kilometer (25-mile) crescent of rocks and sand with a supremely relaxed crew of locals who firmly believe they live in paradise.

Time Out   Next door to the Motueka Museum, **Annabelles Café** serves snacks and light, inexpensive meals: scones, muffins, salads, sandwiches, and great espresso. The café offers a choice of indoor or outdoor tables. *140 High St., Motueka, tel. 03/528–8696. Open daily 11–3.*

At the entrance to Motueka, at the Rothmans Clock Tower, turn south onto Highway 61, following the sign to Murchison. The road snakes through **Motueka Valley** alongside the Motueka River, which is edged with poplars and yellow gorse, with the green valley walls pressing close alongside. If this river could talk, it would probably scream "Trout!" There are many deer farms in the area, easily identified by their high fences.

Fifty-seven kilometers (35 miles) beyond Motueka, Highway 61 joins Highway 6 for the journey south. Beyond Murchison, the road parallels the broad **Buller River** as it carves a deep gorge from the jagged mountain peaks. Nineteen kilometers (12 miles) south of Murchison, the **Newtown Hotel,** no longer licensed, teeters on the brink of the gorge, surrounded by a fantastic junkyard of obsolete farm machinery. The Buller once carried a fabulous cargo of gold, but you have to use your imagination to reconstruct the days when places such as Lyell, 34 kilometers (21 miles) beyond Murchison, were bustling mining towns. **Hawk's Crag,** where the highway passes beneath a rock overhang with the river wheeling alongside, is the scenic climax of the trip along the Buller. Before the town of Westport, turn left to continue along Highway 6.

After a journey through coastal scrub, Highway 6 meets the sea; shortly thereafter it arrives at a tiny collection of shops called **Punakaiki.** From the visitor center, an easy 10-minute walk leads to a fantastic maze of limestone rocks stacked high above the sea.

⓫ These are commonly known as the **Pancake Rocks,** and they are the outstanding feature of the surrounding **Paparoa National Park.** At high tide, the blowhole spouts a thundering geyser of spray. Mount Cook is sometimes visible to the south. *Paparoa National Park, tel. 03/731–1895.*

The town of Greymouth is aptly named—a dull, dispirited strip of motels and timber mills. Yet the **Jade Boulder Gallery** is a great place ⓬ to pick up a distinctive souvenir. The gallery exhibits the work of Ian Boustridge, one of the country's most accomplished sculptors of greenstone, the jade that was highly prized by the Maoris. Earrings start at about $35, and sculptures can cost anything up to $1,000. *1 Guiness St., Greymouth, tel. 03/768–0700. Open daily 8–5.*

⓭ On the southern outskirts of Greymouth, **Shantytown** is a lively re-enactment of a gold-mining town of the 1880s. Except for the church and the town hall, most of the buildings are replicas, but the gold diggings are authentic and fascinating. Displays include a water jet for blasting the gold-bearing quartz from the hillside, water sluices, and a stamper battery or crusher powered by a 30-foot water wheel. Visitors can pan for gold, and since the creek is salted with gold dust, there is a good chance of striking "color." *Rutherglen, Greymouth, tel. 03/762–6634. Admission: $7 adults, $4 children 5–15. Open daily 8:30–5.*

South of Greymouth the highway threads through farming country as it heads toward the Southern Alps and the glaciers of **Westland National Park.** The glaciers are formed by the massive rainfall of the west coast—up to 300 inches per annum—which descends as snow on the névé, or head, of the glacier. The snow is compressed into ice, which flows downhill under its own weight. There are more than 60 ⓮ glaciers in the park; the most famous and accessible are **Fox** and **Franz Josef,** the only glaciers on earth that grind through a rain forest. They lie about 24 kilometers (15 miles) apart. You can park a 15-minute walk away from the terminal face of Fox Glacier, and a 30-minute walk from the Franz Josef terminal. Both parking lots are terrorized by keas—mountain parrots—which specialize in destroying the rubber molding around car windows. (Keas are harmless to humans, and a coating of insect repellent around the window frames should safeguard your vehicle.)

Trails from the parking lots wind across the valley floor to the glacier faces, where a tormented vocabulary of squeaks, creaks, groans, and gurgles can be heard as the glacier creeps down the mountainside at an average rate of 5 feet per day. Care must be taken here, since rocks and chunks of ice frequently drop from the melting face. These being New Zealand glaciers, there is much to do besides admire them. You can fly over them and land on their névé, walk on them, even make a bloodcurdling and very cold white-water rafting trip down the Waiho River where it emerges from the base of Franz Josef (*see* Guided Tours, *above,* and Sports and the Outdoors, *below*). Flights should be made early in the morning, when the visibility is better. Fox Glacier is slightly larger and longer than Franz Josef, but you'll miss nothing important if you see only one. Both glaciers have separate townships, and if you are spending the night, Franz Josef is marginally preferable.

At the town of Fox Glacier, turn toward the sea where a sign points ⓯ to Gillespies Beach, then turn right toward **Lake Matheson** for one of the country's most famous views. A walking trail winds along the lakeshore, and the snowcapped peaks of Mount Cook and Mount Tasman are reflected in the water. Allow at least an hour for the complete walk to the "View of Views." The best time is early morning, before the mirrorlike reflections are fractured by the wind.

Beyond the glaciers Highway 6 continues along the south coast to Haast, where it turns inland to Wanaka and Queenstown. The driving time between Fox Glacier and Wanaka is six hours. The best accommodation along this road is the Lake Moeraki Wilderness Lodge, just north of Haast (*see* Lodging, *below*).

Sports and the Outdoors

Hiking **Abel Tasman Enterprises** operates two-, three-, and four-day guided treks along the southern half of the Abel Tasman Track. Travelers spend all nights in comfortable lodges; during the days they explore the coastline and forests of the national park. One day of the four-day trip is spent sea kayaking. Walkers carry only a light day pack, and all meals are provided. The guided walks, which have an "easy" grading, depart each Tuesday and Friday. *Old Cedarman House, Main Rd., Riwaka, tel. 03/528-7801. Cost: $250–$680 adults, $175–$500 children 8–14.*

Alpine Guides offers guided walks on Fox Glacier, the only way to safely experience the ethereal beauty of the ice caves, pinnacles, and crevasses on top of the glaciers. The three-hour walks travel about 2 kilometers (1 mile) up the glacier. The climb is quite strenuous and extremely slippery, despite the metal-pointed staves and spiked boots supplied to hikers. *Box 38, Fox Glacier, tel. 03/751-0825. Cost: $32. Tours depart daily at 9:30 and 2.*

Boating and Rafting **Abel Tasman Kayaks** has one- and two-person kayaks for hire at Marahau, at the southern end of Abel Tasman National Park, which gives paddlers ready access to beaches and campsites that are often inaccessible to hikers. The company does not rent to solo kayakers, and a minimum two-day rental is required. The cost is $90 for two days. Guided kayak tours cost $80 for one day, $260 for three days. *Marahau, RD2 Motueka, tel. 03/527-8022.*

The **Marlborough Sounds Adventure Company** offers one- and four-day guided kayak tours of the Sounds, as well as kayak rentals for experienced paddlers. The cost is $60 for a one-day guided tour, $450 for a four-day guided tour. A kayak rental costs $35 per day. *1 Russell St., Picton, tel. 03/573-6078.*

Nelson Raft Company has various trips along the Motueka and Buller Rivers, from $28 for two hours to $95 for a full day. Transport to and from Nelson is included. *Lodder La., RD 3, Motueka, tel. 03/546-6212.*

Cycling **Cycle Treks** offers several escorted cycle tours, from a two-day trip through mountains and lakes ($185) to a seven-day tour of Marlborough Sounds ($1379). Cyclists are supplied with 21-speed mountain bikes, group size is limited to 10, a backup van is provided, and trips begin and end at either Nelson or Picton. *Box 733, Nelson, tel. 03/547-9122.*

Dining

Apart from Nelson, gourmet highlights are rare in this area. Price categories for restaurants are the same as in the Auckland Dining section in Chapter 13. Highly recommended restaurants are indicated by a star ★.

$$ **Chez Eelco Coffee House.** The menu, with its array of steaks, burgers, seafood, and salads, may not try too hard, but it's impossible to ignore this cheerful sidewalk café at the foot of the cathedral on Nelson's main street. In warm weather, the outside tables are recommended; otherwise, try elsewhere. *296 Trafalgar St., Nelson, tel. 03/548–7595. No reservations. Dress: casual. No credit cards. BYOB.*

$$ **La Bonne Vie.** This attractive seafood restaurant is a favorite with
★ the locals for its lively atmosphere, brisk service, and a menu that pairs the excellent local seafood with delicate sauces. Main courses include salmon fillet with lime and coriander, and a baked flounder stuffed with cottage cheese and almonds. Outdoor seating is available in summer. Vegetarians and steak-eaters are also provided for. *75 Bridge St., Nelson, tel. 03/548–0270. Reservations advised. Dress: casual. AE, DC, MC, V. No lunch.*

$$ **Pomeroy's.** This smart, popular bistro brings a modern European selection and a touch of class to Nelson's dining scene. The menu offers croissants, focaccia, bagels, and more substantial fare such as lamb stuffed with sun-dried tomatoes and served with a spinach salad. *276 Trafalgar St., Nelson, tel. 03/548–7524. Reservations not required. Dress: casual. AE, DC, MC, V. BYOB. No dinner Mon.– Wed. Closed Sun.*

Lodging

Price categories for hotels are the same as in the Auckland Lodging section in Chapter 13. Highly recommended lodgings are indicated by a star ★.

$$$$ **Lake Brunner Sporting Lodge.** Set on the southern shore of Lake
★ Brunner a 40-minute drive southeast of Greymouth, this sprawling lodge offers excellent fishing, a variety of activities, and a high level of comfort at a price that is relatively low by the standards of New Zealand's elite lodges. Guest rooms are large and well equipped, with the emphasis on comfort rather than opulence. The best rooms are at the front of the house, overlooking the lake. The lodge is known for its "clear water stalking," since the brown trout can be easily seen in the clear waters of the surrounding rivers. Hunting, hiking, boating, mountain biking, and bird-watching are also available. Children are welcome, a rare concession at sporting lodges. *Mitchells, RD1, Kumara, Westland, tel. 03/738–0163, fax 03/738– 0163. 9 rooms with bath. Facilities: fishing, mountain bikes, nature tours, hunting. Tariff includes all meals. AE, DC, MC, V. Closed July–Sept.*

$$$$ **Motueka River Lodge.** A recent addition to New Zealand's list of exclusive fishing retreats, this lodge offers tranquillity, marvelous scenery, and a superb standard of comfort. Owned and operated by a former Auckland adman, the lodge is set on a hillside with views across a deer farm to the valley of the Motueka River. Inside, the rustic flavor of the house is accented with folk art collected around the world. Guest rooms are luxuriously equipped but do not have telephones or TVs. The lodge offers a range of activities—tramping, river rafting, golf, tennis—but its specialty is fishing, especially dry-fly fishing for brown trout in the wild river country, which can be reached only by helicopter. The activities are restricted outside the October–April fishing season. *Hwy. 61, Ngatimoti, Motueka, tel. 03/526–8668, fax 03/526–8668. 4 rooms with bath. Facilities: fishing, tennis court. Tariff includes all meals. AE, DC, MC, V.*

$$$ **California Guest House.** Set at the end of a garden brimming with
★ flowers, this country charmer is recommended for anyone looking

for a bed-and-breakfast with character. Guest rooms are moderately large and comfortable and furnished with antiques. The best rooms are the slightly more expensive Victorian Rose and Everett. Breakfasts include muffins, filter coffee, ham-and-sour-cream omelets, fresh fruit, and pancakes with strawberries and cream. Children are not accommodated. Smoking is not permitted indoors. *29 Collingwood St., Nelson, tel. 03/548–4173. 4 rooms with bath. Tariff includes breakfast. MC, V.*

$$$ **Cambria House.** Built for a sea captain, this 1860 house has been
★ sympathetically modernized to offer B&B accommodations with personality and a dash of luxury. The furnishings mix antiques and floral-print fabrics, and the rooms are very comfortable. Each has an en suite bathroom. The house is located in a quiet street within easy walking distance of the center of Nelson. Children are not accommodated. *7 Cambria St., Nelson, tel. 03/548–4681, fax 03/546–6649. 5 rooms with bath. Tariff includes breakfast. MC, V.*

$$$ **Doone Cottage.** This serene, homey farmstay is set in a pretty part of the Motueka River Valley, within easy reach of five trout streams and a 40-minute drive from Nelson. The hosts are a relaxed, hospitable couple who have lived in this valley for many years. Guest accommodations are comfortable and crowded with family memorabilia. Dinners are likely to feature organically grown vegetables, local meat, and fish fresh from the rivers. Children are not accommodated. *RD1, Motueka, tel. 03/526–8740. 2 rooms with bath. Tariff includes breakfast and dinner. V.*

$$$ **Lake Moeraki Wilderness Lodge.** While these simple motel suites
★ lack the luxurious frills of many other lodges, the natural splendor of the surroundings is the equal of any—and the price is a bargain. The lodge is located on Lake Moeraki, just north of the west coast town of Haast. There are penguins and seals along the beaches, a feisty river on the doorstep, canoes and kayaks for paddling the lake, and forest trails that echo with the sound of rushing streams and birdcalls. The lodge is owned and operated by Dr. Gerry McSweeney and his family. Dr. McSweeney, a leading voice in New Zealand's conservation movement, took over the lodge with the intention of demonstrating that tourism was an economic alternative to logging in the forests of South Westland. His knowledge of and feeling for the area contribute much to any visit. *Private Bag, Hokitika, tel. and fax 03/750–0881. 20 rooms with bath. Facilities: nature tours, canoes, fishing, restaurant, bar. AE, DC, MC, V.*

$$ **Ashley Motor Inn.** This motor inn has modern, comfortable rooms, though Greymouth and its surroundings, compared with other parts of the west coast, have little to justify an overnight stop. *70 Tasman St., Greymouth, tel. 03/768–5135. 60 rooms with bath. Facilities: indoor pool, spa, guest laundry, restaurant, bar. AE, DC, MC, V.*

$$ **Westland Motor Inn.** The largest motel in the glacier region, this complex at the center of Franz Josef village offers rooms a cut above the average in size and furnishings. Larger suites with upgraded facilities are also available, and the motor lodge has a choice of dining facilities. *State Hwy. 6, Franz Josef, tel. 02/883–1729. 100 rooms with bath. Facilities: 2 spa pools, guest laundry, restaurant, bar. AE, DC, MC, V.*

Christchurch
and Canterbury

The Canterbury region includes both the Canterbury Plains, the flattest land in the country, and the Southern Alps, the steepest. Its capital is New Zealand's third-largest city, Christchurch, which has a population approaching 300,000. Christchurch is the only South Island city with an international airport, and many travelers begin or end their New Zealand journeys here.

Christchurch is something of a paradox—a city under the grand delusion that it is somewhere in southern England. The drive from the airport into town takes you through pristine suburbs of houses lapped by seas of flowers and past playing fields where children flail at one another's legs with hockey sticks. The heart of this pancake-flat city is dominated by church spires; its streets are named Durham, Gloucester, and Hereford; and instead of the usual boulder-leaping New Zealand torrent there bubbles, between banks lined with willows and oaks, the serene River Avon, suitable only for punting. The city is compact and easy to explore, and most of its major sights can be seen on a half-day walking tour.

The big attraction in this region is Mount Cook National Park—a wonderland of snow and ice—but if you have an extra day, the sperm whales that spout off the coast at Kaikoura provide a memorable trip. For a rewarding half-day excursion through delectable country scenery and seascapes, journey out to Akaroa, a pretty little town on a big blue bay.

Important Addresses and Numbers

Tourist Information **Christchurch Visitor Information Centre.** *Worcester St. and Oxford Terr., Christchurch, tel. 03/379–9629. Open weekdays 8:30–5, weekends 8:30–4.*

Mount Cook Visitor Information Centre. *Mount Cook Village, tel. 03/435–1818. Open daily 8–5.*

Emergencies Dial 111 for **fire, police,** or **ambulance** services.

Arriving and Departing

By Plane **Ansett New Zealand** (tel. 03/371–1146) and **Air New Zealand** (tel. 03/379–5200) link Christchurch with cities on both the North and South islands. **Mount Cook Airline** (tel. 03/379–0690) flies from Christchurch to Queenstown and Mount Cook. **Christchurch Airport** is located 10 kilometers (6 miles) northwest of the city. **Avon City Shuttle** buses (tel. 03/379–9999) meet all incoming flights and charge $7 per passenger to city hotels. **CANRIDE** buses operate between the airport and Cathedral Square from 6 AM to 11 PM daily. The fare is $2.40 for adults, $1.20 for children 4–14. A **taxi** to the city costs about $15.

By Car Highway 1 links Christchurch with Kaikoura and Blenheim in the north and Dunedin in the south. Driving time for the 330-kilometer (205-mile) journey between Christchurch and Mount Cook Village is five hours; between Christchurch and Dunedin, 5½ hours.

By Bus **Mount Cook Landline** (tel. 03/343–8085) and **InterCity** (tel. 03/377–0951) operate daily bus services between Christchurch and Dunedin, Mount Cook, Nelson, and Queenstown.

Getting Around

The city of Christchurch is flat and compact, and the best way to explore it is on two legs. It's unlikely that visitors will have occasion to use the public bus system, which is just as well since the once efficient, city-owned system has recently been divided among several different companies and is now a mess. Timetables and maps are unobtainable. The only reliable way to find out whether a bus is going your way is to ask the drivers at the terminal in Cathedral Square. Another option is bicycle. **Trailblazers** hires out mountain bikes for $25 per day. *96 Worcester St., tel. 03/366–6033. Open weekdays 9–5:30, weekends 10–4.*

Guided Tours

Guided walking tours of the city depart daily at 10 and 2 from the red-and-black booth in Cathedral Square. The cost of the two-hour tour is $8 per person.

Punting on the Avon is perfectly suited to the languid motion of Christchurch. Punts with expert boatmen may be hired from the Worcester Street bridge, near the corner of Oxford Terrace, from 10 to 6 in summer and 10 to 4 the rest of the year. The price of a 20-minute trip is $8 per adult, $4 for children under 12.

The **Gray Line** (tel. 03/343–3874) operates a half-day Morning Sights tour ($25) and a full-day tour of Akaroa ($52), both daily at 9 AM. All tours leave from the Christchurch Visitor Information Centre. Children 5–14 pay half fare.

Exploring Christchurch

This is a gentle stroll from the Visitor Centre through the heart of the city. Aim to finish at 1 PM, in time to catch the Wizard in Cathedral Square.

Numbers in the margin correspond to points of interest on the Christchurch map.

❶ From the front door of the Visitor Centre, cross Worcester Street to the statue of **Captain Robert Falcon Scott** (1868–1912), "Scott of the Antarctic," who visited Christchurch during his two Antarctic expeditions. The statue was sculpted by his widow, Kathleen Lady Kennett, and inscribed with his last words, written as he and his party lay dying in a blizzard on their return journey from the South Pole.

❷ Follow the curve of the River Avon past the arched **Bridge of Remembrance.** The bridge was built in memory of the soldiers who crossed the river here from King Edward Barracks, just down Cashel Street, on their way to the battlefields of Europe during the First World War.

❸ A little farther along the riverbank is the white timber **St. Michael and All Saints Anglican Church.** Christchurch was founded in 1850 by the Canterbury Association, a group of leading British churchmen, politicians, and peers who envisioned a settlement that would serve as a model of industry and ideals, governed by the principles of the Anglican faith. The first settlers the Association sent out were known as the "Canterbury Pilgrims," and their churches were a focal point for the whole community. Built in 1872, St Michael's is an outstanding example. One of the bells in the wooden belfry came from England aboard one of the four ships that carried the Canter-

Antigua
Boatshed, **4**

Arts Centre, **8**

Botanic
Gardens, **5**

Bridge of
Remembrance, **2**

Canterbury
Museum, **6**

Captain Robert
Falcon Scott
Statue, **1**

Christchurch
Cathedral, **9**

Robert
McDougal Art
Gallery, **7**

St. Michael and
All Saints
Anglican
Church, **3**

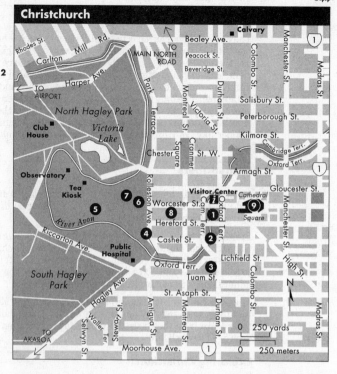

Christchurch

bury Pilgrims. *Oxford Terr. and Durham St. Open daily noon–2 PM.*

4 Follow the Avon upstream, cross to the far bank at the next bridge, and turn immediately left along the avenue of chestnuts and silver birches to the **Antigua Boatshed.** Built for the Christchurch Boating Club, this is the only boat shed that remains of the half dozen that once stood along the Avon. Canoes may be hired for short river trips. *Rolleston Ave., tel. 03/366–5885. Single canoes $5 per hr, double $10 per hr. Open daily 9:30–4:30.*

5 Walk along Rolleston Avenue and turn left at the first gate into the **Botanic Gardens,** a green jewel of woodland and rose gardens that might easily have been transplanted from the home counties of England. *Rolleston Ave., tel. 03/366–1701. Open daily dawn–dusk.*

6 At the northern end of the gardens is the **Canterbury Museum.** Of special interest here are the reconstruction of an early Christchurch streetscape and the display of Maori artifacts. The Hall of Antarctic Discovery charts the links between the city and the U.S. bases on the frozen continent from the days of Captain Scott; Christchurch is still used as a forward supply depot for U.S. Antarctic bases. *Rolleston Ave., tel. 03/366–8379. Admission by donation. Open daily 9:30–4:30.*

7 Behind the museum is the **Robert McDougal Art Gallery,** built in the 1930s by a prominent businessman. The gallery has works by 19th-century New Zealand artists and an international collection of painting and sculpture, including two Rodins. *Rolleston Ave., tel. 03/365–0915. Admission free. Open daily 10–4:30.*

8 From the museum, cross Rolleston Avenue into Worcester Street and turn right into the **Arts Centre.** These Gothic stone buildings once housed Canterbury University, whose most illustrious pupil was Ernest Rutherford (1871–1937). Just past the information desk inside is "Rutherford's Den," the modest stone chamber where the eminent physicist conducted experiments in what was at the time a new field, radioactivity. It was Rutherford who first succeeded in splitting the atom, a crucial step in the harnessing of atomic power. In 1908 Rutherford's work earned him the Nobel prize—not for physics but for chemistry. *Worcester St., tel. 03/366–0989. Open weekdays 8:30–5, weekends 10–4.*

Time out Housed in a mock-Tudor building, **Dux de Lux** is a popular cafeteria-style restaurant that bills itself as "gourmet vegetarian." The blackboard menu offers quiches, crepes, sandwiches, pies, fresh vegetable juices, and a range of crisp salads and breads. The courtyard is a great spot on a sunny day, especially with a beer from the brewery next door. *41 Hereford St., near Montreal St., tel. 03/366–6919. No credit cards. $*

Continue along Worcester Street and cross the river to **Cathedral Square.** The square is the city's focal point, functioning as a bus terminal and a venue for an arts and crafts market, food stalls, and street musicians, as well as a hangout for the city's unemployed **9** youth. **Christchurch Cathedral,** the city's dominating landmark, was begun in 1864, 14 years after the arrival of the Canterbury Pilgrims, but not consecrated until 1904. Carvings inside commemorate the work of the Anglican missionaries, including Tamihana Te Rauparaha, the son of a fierce and, for the settlers, troublesome Maori chief. Free guided tours begin daily at 11 and 2. For a view across the city to the Southern Alps, climb the 133 steps to the top of the bell tower. The cathedral is known for its boys choir, which can be heard singing evensong at 4:30 Friday, except during school holidays. *Cathedral Sq. Open daily 8:30 AM–9 PM. Admission to tower: $2 adults, $1 children 5–15.*

If it's close to 1 PM when you emerge from the cathedral, look for the bearded gentleman with long hair, who is easy to spot because of the crowd that instantly forms around him. This is **the Wizard,** who offers funny and irreverent dissertations on just about any controversial subject—especially religion, politics, sex, and women's issues. Originally a freelance soapbox orator, the Wizard (whose real name is Ian Channel) became so popular that he is now employed by the city council—one of his frequent targets. *1 PM, Cathedral Sq. No performances May–Oct.*

Shopping

Inside the Christchurch Arts Centre is the **Galleria,** a dozen shops and studios for artisans and craftworkers. The quality of the work, however, is not representative of the finest of New Zealand's craftsmanship. Most of the shops are open 10 to 4; some are closed weekends. Most do not take credit cards. *Worcester St., tel. 03/379–7573.*

Bivouac sells a complete range of outdoor gear and maps. *76 Cashel St., tel. 03/366–3197. Open weekdays 9–5:30, Sat. 10–1.*

Dining

Price categories for restaurants are the same as in the Auckland Dining section in Chapter 13. Highly recommended restaurants are indicated by a star ★.

$$$$ **Sign of the Takahe.** Set in a splendid baronial castle that overlooks the city and the Southern Alps from the heights of the Cashmere Hills, this mock gothic restaurant is well known for its game and lobster, the house specialty. The buffet lunch is a less expensive option, but it lacks the stiff white napery, silver service, and candlelit tables that make the dinners magic. The restaurant is a 20-minute drive from the city center. Dinners are heavily booked by Japanese tour groups, and other diners may face long delays. *Dyers Pass and Hackthorne Rds., Cashmere Hills, tel. 03/332–4052. Reservations required. Jacket and tie required at dinner. AE, DC, MC, V.*

$$ **Bardellis.** The name says it all—a bar, a deli, and an Italian accent. Stylish and medium loud, this bar/brasserie is where Christchurch's chic crowd comes for marinated octopus salads and Coronas straight from the bottle. The international menu, which changes frequently, is heavy on seafood, salads, pizza, and pasta. Typical dishes are fresh pasta with mussels in a tomato and chili sauce, and grilled chicken focaccia. Steaks and the standard New Zealand rack of lamb also make an appearance. This is a good choice for casual outdoor eating on a warm summer evening. *98 Cashel Mall, tel. 03/353–0001. Reservations advised for dinner. Dress: casual. AE, DC, MC, V.*

$$ **Espresso 124.** This smart, modern restaurant is a good bet for mid-
★ morning coffee or midnight snacks. Simplicity is the key on a menu that features char-grilled steaks, lamb, and seafood, and salads dressed with olive oil and balsamic vinegar. The restaurant has a high-energy atmosphere generated by the fashionable crowd that frequents it. The river and the heart of the city are both conveniently close. Next door to the restaurant is a lunch deli, which offers inexpensive sandwiches, focaccia, pasta, and savory pies, and a choice of indoor or outdoor dining. *124 Oxford Terr., tel. 03/365–0547. Reservations advised for dinner. Dress: casual but neat. AE, DC, MC, V.*

$$ **Lone Star Cafe.** Quarterback-size servings of steaks, chicken, ribs, burgers, and french fries are the specialty at this big, pleasant restaurant within a five-minute walk of the city center. *26 Manchester St., tel. 03/365–7086. No reservations. Dress: casual but neat. AE, DC, MC, V. BYOB. No lunch.*

Lodging

Price categories for hotels are the same as in the Auckland Lodging section in Chapter 13. Highly recommended lodgings are indicated by a star ★.

$$$$ **Parkroyal Christchurch.** This plush hotel, in a prime location over-
★ looking Victoria Square and the river, brings a touch of glamour to the city's accommodation scene. The rooms are large, luxurious, and styled in a powder-blue-and-cream color scheme. Be sure to request one overlooking Victoria Square. The hotel is especially well equipped with restaurants and bars. The Canterbury Tales dining room and the Japanese restaurant, Yamagen, are among the city's finest. *Kilmore and Durham Sts., tel. 03/365–7799, fax 03/365–0082. 297 rooms with bath. Facilities: gym, sauna, bicycles, 4 restaurants, 3 bars. AE, DC, MC, V.*

$$ Pacific Park. Rooms at this attractive peach-and-white complex on the northern fringe of the city are marginally better than at the average motel; all were refurbished during 1991–1992. Two-bedroom executive suites are available. Special rates apply on weekends and during winter. The motel is about 2 kilometers (1¼ miles) from the city center. *263 Bealey Ave., tel. 03/379–8660, fax 03/366–9973. 66 rooms with bath. Facilities: restaurant, bar. AE, DC, MC, V.*

$$ Riverview Lodge. This grand Edwardian manor overlooking the
★ Avon is the pick of the bed-and-breakfast accommodation in Christchurch. Completely restored in 1991, it offers superbly comfortable, historic accommodations and a cooked breakfast at about the same price as a motel room. The best room is the Turret Room, which has access to the front balcony. Children are accommodated by arrangement. The city center is a 15-minute walk along the river. *361 Cambridge Terr., tel. and fax 03/365–2860. 3 rooms with bath. Facilities: canoe, bicycles, golf clubs. Tariff includes breakfast. MC, V.*

$$ Turret House. This century-old lodge has comfortable, well-maintained rooms and a friendly atmosphere that makes it a standout among Christchurch's bed-and-breakfast accommodations. All the rooms are different, and prices vary accordingly. The largest, the Apartment, has a lounge room, a separate bedroom, and a kitchen, and could easily sleep four. For a couple, the medium-size rooms offer a good combination of space and value. Despite its location close to a major intersection, noise is not a problem. *435 Durham St., tel. 03/365–3900. 8 rooms with bath. Tariff includes breakfast. AE, DC, MC, V.*

Excursion to Akaroa

Allow at least a half day for this trip to the scenic Banks Peninsula.

Getting There The main route to Akaroa is Highway 75, which leaves the southwest corner of Christchurch as Lincoln Road. The 82-kilometer (50-mile) drive takes about 90 minutes. **Akaroa Tours** (tel. 03/379–9629) operates a shuttle service between the Christchurch Visitor Information Centre and Akaroa; buses depart Christchurch weekdays at 10:30 and 4, Saturday at noon, and Sunday at noon and 6:45; buses depart Akaroa weekdays at 8:20 and 2:20, weekends at 10:30 ($30 adults, $16 children 5–15 round-trip).

Exploring *Numbers in the margin correspond to points of interest on the Canterbury map.*

Dominated by tall volcanic peaks, the **Banks Peninsula**—the knobbly landform that juts into the Pacific Ocean south of Christchurch—has a wonderful coastline indented with small bays where sheep graze almost to the water's edge. Its main source of fame is
❶ the town of **Akaroa**, which was chosen as the site for a French colony in 1838. The first French settlers arrived in 1840 only to find that the British had already established sovereignty over New Zealand by the Treaty of Waitangi. Less than 10 years later, the French abandoned their attempt at colonization, but the settlers remained and gradually intermarried with the local English community. Apart from the street names and a few surnames, there is little sign of a French connection any more, but the village has a splendid setting, and on a sunny day it makes a marvelous trip from Christchurch.

The best way to get the feel of the town is to stroll along the waterfront from the lighthouse to Jubilee Park. The focus of historic interest is the **Akaroa Museum,** which has a display of Maori greenstone and embroidery and dolls dating from the days of the French settlement. The museum includes Langlois-Eteveneaux House, the two-

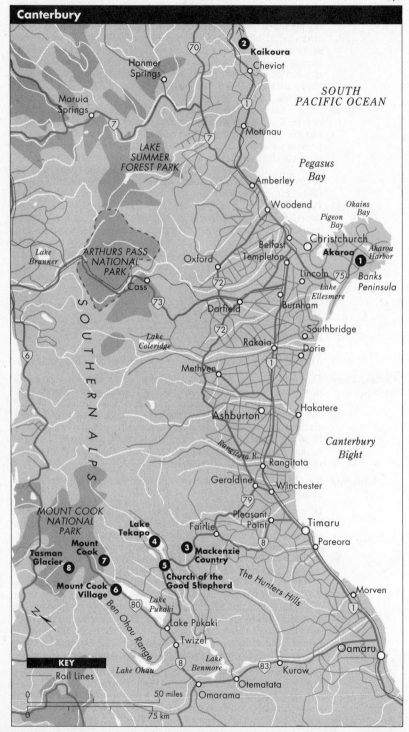

Canterbury

SOUTH
PACIFIC OCEAN

Hanmer
Springs

Maruia
Springs

Cheviot

2 **Kaikoura**

Motunau

Pegasus
Bay

*Okains
Bay*

*Pigeon
Bay*

Christchurch

*Lake
Brunner*

LAKE
SUMMER
FOREST PARK

ARTHURS PASS
NATIONAL
PARK

Cass

Amberley

Woodend

Belfast

Oxford

Templeton

Akaroa

*Akaroa
Harbor*

1

Lincoln

*Lake
Ellesmere*

Banks
Peninsula

Darfield

Burnham

S
O
U
T
H
E
R
N

A
L
P
S

*Lake
Coleridge*

Rakaia

Southbridge

Dorie

Methven

Ashburton

Hakatere

Canterbury
Bight

Rangitata R.

Rangitata

MOUNT COOK
NATIONAL
PARK

Geraldine

Winchester

**Lake
Tekapo**

4

Fairlie

Pleasant
Point

Timaru

**Mount
Cook**

7

3 **Mackenzie
Country**

Pareora

**Tasman
Glacier**

8

5

**Church of the
Good Shepherd**

The Hunters Hills

**Mount Cook
Village**

6

*Lake
Pukaki*

Lake Pukaki

Morven

Ben Ohau Range

Twizel

*Lake
Benmore*

Oamaru

KEY

Rail Lines

Lake Ohau

Kurow

Otematata

Omarama

50 miles

75 km

room cottage of an early French settler, which bears the imprint of his homeland in its architecture. *Rue Lavaud and Rue Balguerie, tel. 03/304–7614. Admission: $2.50 adults, 50¢ children 5–15. Open daily 10:30–4:30.*

The picture-book **Church of St. Patrick,** near the museum, was built in 1864 to replace two previous Catholic churches—the first destroyed by fire, the second by tempest. *Rue Pompallier. Open daily 8–5.*

Lodging **Glencarrig.** Buried in greenery on a hillside a three-minute walk
$$ from Akaroa, this charming lodge offers a high standard of B&B ac-
★ commodations at a reasonable price. Built in 1851, the house is filled with antiques and kilims, which complement its rustic character. The best of the three rooms is the Aylmer, which opens onto the veranda; however, Catherine's Room has an en suite bathroom at no extra charge. The rambling country garden, bordered by a stream with its own waterwheel, is a real delight. This is a nonsmoking house. *7 Percy St., Akaroa, tel. 03/304–7008. 1 room with bath, 2 rooms share 1 bath. Facilities: outdoor pool. Tariff includes breakfast. No credit cards.*

Excursion to Kaikoura

This excursion from Christchurch up the coast to Kaikoura requires a full day.

Getting There The 190-kilometer (120-mile) drive up Highway 1 takes 3½ hours. InterCity (tel. 03/72–8297) and Mount Cook Landline (tel. 03/79–0690) operate daily buses between Christchurch and Kaikoura.

Exploring The town of **Kaikoura** lies to the north of Christchurch. The name
❷ means "to eat crayfish" in Maori, and while the crayfish sold from roadside stalls are an excellent reason to go, an even better one is the sperm whales that can be seen off the coast in greater numbers than anywhere else on earth. The sperm whale, the largest toothed mammal, can reach a length of 60 feet and a weight of 70 tons. The reason for the whales' concentration in this area is the abundance of squid, their main food, in the deep trench just off the continental shelf, barely a kilometer off Kaikoura. Sperm whales are most likely to be seen between October and August. **Whale Watch Kaikoura Ltd.** (tel. 0800/65–5121) operates three-hour whale-spotting trips at varying times, depending on weather ($85 adults, $50 children 5–15). Even in calm weather, the sea often has a sizable swell.

Christchurch to Mount Cook

The 330-kilometer (205-mile) drive from Christchurch straight through to Mount Cook Village takes five hours.

The **Canterbury Plains,** which ring Christchurch, are the country's finest sheep pastures, as well as its largest area of flat land. But while this may be sheep heaven, the drive south along the plain is mundane by New Zealand standards—until you leave Highway 1 and head toward the Southern Alps.

At Rangitata, on the south bank of the wide Rangitata River, Highway 79 turns inland from Highway 1 and travels toward the distant mountains through the town of Geraldine to Fairlie, where Highway 8 takes up the journey. When the highway crosses Burkes Pass, the woodland is suddenly replaced by the high-country tussock grassland, which is dotted with lupines in the summer months. This is
❸ known as the **Mackenzie Country** after James ("Jock") Mackenzie,

one of the most intriguing and enigmatic figures in New Zealand history. Mackenzie was a Scot who may or may not have stolen the thousand sheep that were found with him in these secluded upland pastures in 1855. Arrested, tried, and convicted, he made several escapes from jail before he was granted a free pardon nine months after his trial—and disappeared from the pages of history. Regardless of his innocence or guilt, there can be no doubt that Mackenzie was a master bushman and herdsman.

Cradled by snowy mountain peaks, the long, narrow expanse of **❹ Lake Tekapo** is one of the most photographed sights in New Zealand. Its extraordinary milky-turquoise color comes from rockflour—rock ground by glacial action and held in a soupy suspension. ❺ On the eastern side of the lakeside power station is the tiny **Church of the Good Shepherd,** which strikes a dignified note of piety in these majestic surroundings. A nearby memorial commemorates the sheepdogs of the area. Before fences were erected around their runs, shepherds would tether dogs at strategic points to stop their sheep from straying.

At Lake Pukaki, Highway 80 turns north between the lake and the Ben Ohau Range, a scenic spectacular that reaches its climax when ❻ the road ends at **Mount Cook Village.** The village consists of a visitor center, a grocery store, and a couple of hotels, one of which, the Hermitage, is probably the most famous in the country (*see* Lodging, *below*). Surrounding the village is Mount Cook National Park. The park includes 22 peaks topping the 3,000-meter (10,000-foot) ❼ mark, the tallest of which is **Mount Cook**—at approximately 3,684 meters (12,283 feet), the highest peak between Papua New Guinea and the Andes. The mountain was dramatically first scaled in 1894 by three New Zealanders, Fyfe, Graham, and Clarke, just after it was announced that an English climber and an Italian mountain guide were about to attempt the summit. In a frantic surge of national pride, the New Zealand trio resolved to beat them to it, which they did on Christmas Day. Mount Cook is still considered a difficult ascent. In the summer of 1991 a chunk of it broke away, but fortunately there were no climbers in the path of the massive avalanches. High Peak, the summit of the mountain, is now about 20 meters (66 feet) lower, but a much more difficult ascent. Provided the sun is shining, the views are spectacular and the walks are inspiring. If the cloud ceiling is low, however, you may wonder why you came—and the mountain weather is notoriously changeable. Since a lengthy detour is required to reach Mount Cook Village, it is advisable to contact the Visitor Information Centre (tel. 03/435–1818) to check weather conditions.

Radiating from the visitor center is a network of trails offering walks of varying difficulty, from the 10-minute Bowen Track to the 5½-hour climb to the 1,445-meter (4,818-foot) summit of Mount Sebastapol. Particularly recommended is the walk along the Hooker Valley, a two- to four-hour round-trip. There are frequent ranger-guided walks from the visitor center, with informative talks on flora, fauna, and geology along the way.

The other main activity at Mount Cook is **flightseeing.** From the airfield at Mount Cook Village, helicopters and fixed-wing aircraft make spectacular scenic flights across the Southern Alps. One of the most exciting is the one-hour trip aboard the skiplanes that touch ❽ down on the **Tasman Glacier** after a dazzling scenic flight. The 10-minute stop on the glacier doesn't allow time for much more than a snapshot, but the sensation is tremendous. The moving tongue of ice beneath your feet—one of the largest glaciers outside the Himalayas—is 29 kilometers (18 miles) long and up to 600 meters (2,000 feet) thick in places. The intensity of light on the glacier can be dazzling, and sunglasses are a must. Generally, the best time for flights is early morning. During winter the planes drop skiers on the glacier at 3,000 meters (10,000 feet), and they ski down through 13 kilometers (8 miles) of powder snow and fantastic ice formations. With guides, this run is suitable even for intermediate skiers. Skiplane flights cost about $184 for adults, $138 for children under 12; helicopter flights range from $120 to $270. Ski-plane flights are operated by **Mount Cook Line** (tel. 03/435–1848), helicopters by the **Helicopter Line** (tel. 03/435–1801). **Alpine Guides Ltd.** (Box 20, Mount Cook, tel. 03/435–1834) can assist with guides for all treks and ski trips in the national park.

Dining

$$$ Panorama Room. It's the view rather than the food that dazzles at the dining room of the Hermitage Hotel (*see* Lodging, *below*). The service is efficient and the food well presented, but the meals are vastly more expensive than in the neighboring Alpine Restaurant. Choices from the menu include fillet of sole stuffed with spinach, crayfish thermidor, and hare with a juniper berry and wild mushroom sauce. *Mount Cook Village, tel. 03/435–1809. Reservations required. Jacket required. AE, DC, MC, V. No lunch. Closed Apr.–Sept.*

Lodging

Lodging at Mount Cook Village is controlled by a single company that operates the four hotels there. Although it is the most expensive of the four, only The Hermitage can be said to offer reasonable value.

$$$$ The Hermitage. Famed for its stupendous mountain views, this rambling hotel is the luxury option at Mount Cook Village. The guest rooms are gradually being remodeled and decorated with green plaid–upholstered wood furniture and brass accents to enhance the rustic-lodge atmosphere. Request one of these renovated rooms. *Mount Cook Village, tel. 03/435–1809, fax 03/435–1879. 104 rooms with bath. Facilities: sauna, 3 restaurants, bar. AE, DC, MC, V.*

$$$ Kimbell Colonial Cottages. These neat, self-contained cottages are located in the Mackenzie Country north of Fairlie, about midway between Christchurch and Mount Cook. Prettiest of the three is Laurel, a simple timber cottage in the midst of flower beds and sheep pastures. Furnishings in each are simple and appropriately rustic. The surroundings offer trout fishing and deer hunting, and the Kimbell pub is a great source of local color. *RD 17, Fairlie, South Canterbury, tel. 03/658–8170, fax 03/685–8179. 3 cottages with bath. Tariff includes breakfast. AE, MC, V.*

$$$ Mount Cook Travelodge. The views here are similar to those at the Hermitage, but the drop in the quality of rooms and facilities is far greater than the drop in price. *Mount Cook Village, tel. 03/627–1809, fax 03/435–1879. 55 rooms with bath. Facilities: restaurant. Tariff includes breakfast. AE, DC, MC, V. Closed early May–Oct. (actual dates vary).*

$$ Mount Cook Chalets. These metal-roof A-frames with cooking facilities are the budget option at Mount Cook Village, although in terms of comfort and facilities they are vastly overpriced. Each has two small bedrooms plus a fold-down couch and can sleep up to six.

Mount Cook Village, tel. 03/627–1809, fax 03/435–1879. 18 chalets.
AE, DC, MC, V.

Southland, Otago, and Stewart Island

These areas make up the lower third of the South Island. Most of Southland (to the west) is taken up by two giant national parks, Fiordland and Mount Aspiring. Fiordland, the name generally given to the southwest coast, is a majestic wilderness of rocks, ice, and beech forests, where glaciers have carved deep notches into the coast. The scenic climax of this area—and perhaps of the whole country—is Milford Sound. The cruise on the Sound is a must, but anyone who wants to experience Fiordland in all its raw grandeur should hike along one of the many trails in the area, among them the famous four-day Milford Track, "the finest walk in the world." The accommodation base and adventure center for the region is Queenstown.

To the southeast is the flatter area known as Otago. Its capital, Dunedin, is one of the unexpected treasures of New Zealand: a harbor city of steep streets and prim Victorian architecture, with a royal albatross colony on its doorstep. Invercargill, at the southern tip of this region, is essentially a farm service community that few travelers will find any reason to visit unless they are traveling on to Stewart Island, the southernmost of New Zealand's three main islands.

Queenstown to Milford Sound

Tourist Information **Queenstown Visitor Information Centre.** *Clocktower Centre, Shotover and Camp Sts., tel. 03/442–8238. Open daily 7–7.*

Emergencies Dial 111 for **fire, police,** and **ambulance** services.

Arriving and Departing

By Plane Queenstown is linked with Auckland, Christchurch, Rotorua, and Wellington by both **Ansett New Zealand** (tel. 03/442–6161) and **Mount Cook Airlines** (tel. 03/442–7650), which also flies several times daily to Mount Cook. **Queenstown Airport** is 9 kilometers (6 miles) east of town. The **Johnston's Shuttle Express** (tel. 03/442–3639) meets all incoming flights and charges $5 per person to hotels in town. The taxi fare is about $13.

By Car Highway 6 enters Queenstown from the west coast; driving time for the 350-kilometer (220-mile) journey from Franz Josef is eight hours. From Queenstown, Highway 6 continues south to Invercargill—a 190-kilometer (120-mile) distance that takes about three hours to drive. The fastest route from Queenstown to Dunedin is via Highway 6 to Cromwell, south on Highway 8 to Milton, then north along Highway 1, a distance of 280 kilometers (175 miles) that can be covered in five hours.

By Bus From Queenstown, both **Mount Cook Landline** (tel. 03/442–7650) and **InterCity** (tel. 03/442–8238) operate daily bus service to Christchurch, Mount Cook, and Dunedin. **InterCity** buses operate daily to Nelson via the west coast glaciers.

Guided Tours

Fiordland Travel has a wide choice of fly/drive tour options to Milford and Doubtful sounds from Queenstown. The cost of a one-day bus tour and cruise on Milford Sound is $132, $66 for children 4–14. *Steamer Wharf, Queenstown, tel. 03/442–7500.*

Milford Sound Adventure Tours offers a bus/cruise trip to Milford Sound from Te Anau ($85) that includes a cycling option. From the Homer Tunnel, passengers can leave the bus and coast 13 kilometers (8 miles) down to the Sound on mountain bikes. *Box 134, Te Anau, tel. 03/249–7227. Tour departs Te Anau 7:30 AM.*

The **T.S.S. *Earnslaw*** is a vintage lake steamer that has been restored to brassy, wood-paneled splendor and put to work cruising Lake Wakatipu from Queenstown. A lunch cruise, an afternoon cruise across the lake to a sheep station, and a dinner cruise are available from July to May. *Steamer Wharf, Queenstown, tel. 03/442–7500.*

The **Double Decker** (tel. 03/442–6067) is an original London bus that makes a 2½-hour circuit from Queenstown to Arrowtown and the bungee-jumping platform on the Karawau River. Tours ($25 adults, $10 children 5–15) depart Queenstown daily at 10 and 2 from the Mall and the Earnslaw wharf.

Exploring Queenstown and Fiordland National Park

Numbers in the margin correspond to points of interest on the Southland, Otago, and Stewart Island map.

Set on the edge of a glacial lake beneath the saw-toothed peaks of the Remarkables, **Queenstown** is the most popular tourist destination on the South Island. Once prized by the Maoris as a source of greenstone, the town boomed when gold was discovered in the Shotover, which quickly became famous as "the richest river in the world." Queenstown could easily have become a ghost town when the gold gave out—except for its location. With ready access to mountains, lakes, rivers, ski fields, and the glacier-carved coastline of Fiordland National Park, Queenstown has become the adventure capital of New Zealand. Its shop windows are crammed with skis, Gore-tex jackets, Asolo walking boots, and Marin mountain bikes. Along Shotover Street, the travel agents offer white-water rafting, jet boating, caving, trekking, heliskiing, parachuting, and bungee jumping.

Despite its marvelous location, Queenstown is basically a comfortable, cosmopolitan base camp. The best views of the town are from
❶ the **Queenstown Gardens**, on the peninsula that encloses Queenstown Bay, and from the heights of Bob's Peak, 435 meters above the
❷ lake. The **Skyline Gondola** whisks passengers to the top for a panoramic view of the town and the Remarkables on the far side of the lake. The summit terminal has a cafeteria, a carvery restaurant, and *Kiwi Magic*, a 25-minute aerial film tour of the country with stunning effects. *Brecon St., Queenstown, tel. 03/442–7540. Gondola: $20 adults, $3 children 4–15, $20 family. Open daily 10–10. Kiwi Magic screens every hr on the hr, 11–9. Admission: $6 adults, $3 children under 15.*

❸ Another gold-mining town, **Arrowtown,** lies 20 kilometers (13 miles) to the northeast. It had long been suspected that there was gold along the Arrow River, and when Edward Fox, an American, was seen selling large quantities of the precious metal in nearby Clyde,

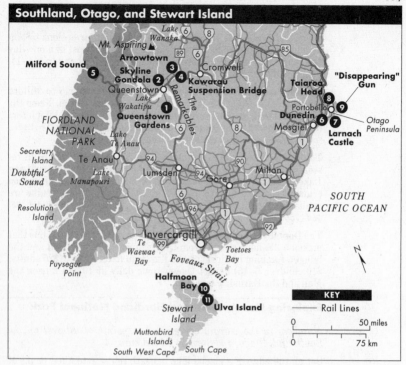

Southland, Otago, and Stewart Island

the hunt was on. Others attempted to follow the wily Fox back to his diggings, but kept giving his pursuers the slip, on one occasion even abandoning his tent and provisions in the middle of the night. Eventually a large party of prospectors stumbled on Fox and his team of 40 miners. The secret was out, miners rushed to stake their claims, and Arrowtown was born.

After the gold rush ended, the place was just another sleepy rural town until tourism created a new boom. Lodged at the foot of the steep Crown Range, this atmospheric little village of weathered-timber shop fronts and white stone churches shaded by ancient sycamores was simply too gorgeous to escape the attention of the tour buses. These days it has become a tourist trap, but a highly photogenic one, especially when autumn gilds the hillsides.

In a less visited part of the town is the former **Chinese settlement.** Chinese miners were common on the goldfields in the late 1860s, but local prejudice forced them to live in their own separate enclave. A number of their huts and Ah Lum's Store, one of the few Chinese goldfield buildings to survive intact, have been preserved. *Bush Creek, at the western end of town. Open daily 9–5.*

❹ On Highway 6 not far from Arrowtown is the **Kawarau Suspension Bridge,** where the bungee jumpers make their leaps—a spectacle well worth the short detour. As a promotional stunt, the AJ Hackett company (*see* Sports and the Outdoors, *below*) once offered a free jump to anyone who would jump nude, but there were so many takers that the scheme had to be abandoned.

From Queenstown, the road to Milford Sound passes through the town of Te Anau, then winds through deep, stony valleys where waterfalls cascade into mossy beech forests as it enters **Fiordland National Park.** Allow at least 2½ hours for the 119-kilometer (74-mile) journey from Te Anau to Milford Sound. Fiordland, the largest national park in New Zealand, takes its name from the deep sea inlets, or sounds, on its western flank. This is the most rugged part of the country. Parts of the park are so remote that they have never been explored, and visitor activities are mostly confined to a few of the sounds and the walking trails. The nearest services base is the town of Te Anau, which offers a choice of motel, hotel, or motor camp accommodation. For information, contact the Fiordland National Park Visitor Centre (Box 29, Te Anau, tel. 03/249–7921).

⑤ For most visitors, Fiordland's greatest attraction is **Milford Sound**—the sort of overpowering place where photographers run out of film. Hemmed in by walls of rock that rise, almost sheer, from the sea up to 4,000 feet, the 16-kilometer (10-mile) -long inlet was carved by a succession of glaciers as they gouged a track to the sea. Its dominant feature is the 5,560-foot pinnacle of Mitre Peak, which is capped with snow for all but the warmest months of the year. Opposite the peak, Bowen Falls tumbles 520 feet before exploding into the sea. Milford Sound is also spectacularly wet: The average annual rainfall is around 20 feet. An inch an hour for 12 hours straight isn't uncommon, and two days without rain is reckoned to be a drought. In addition to a raincoat you'll need insect repellent—the sound is renowned for its sandflies. From the road end, a number of cruise boats depart frequently, from about 11 AM to 3 PM, for trips around the sound; expect to pay about $40 for adults, $15 for children. During the summer holiday period it's essential to book ahead. *Fiordland Travel, Steamer Wharf, Queenstown, tel. 03/442–7500.*

Sports and the Outdoors

Bungee Jumping **AJ Hackett Bungy,** the pioneer in the sport, offers two jumps in the area. Kawarau Bridge is the original jump site, 23 kilometers (14 miles) from Queenstown on State Highway 6. Daredevils who graduate from the 143-foot plunge might like to test themselves on the 230-foot Skippers Canyon Bridge. The price is $89 for the Kawarau jump, $145 for Skippers Canyon. *Box 488, Queenstown, tel. 03/442–1177. Open winter, daily 8:30–5; summer, daily 9–7.*

Horse Trekking **Moonlight Stables** offers a choice of full- or half-day rides along the scenic Moonlight Trail, which follows the Shotover Gorge. No previous riding experience is necessary. Transport from Queenstown is provided. *Box 784, Queenstown, tel. 03/442–8892. $45 per person for ½-day trip.*

Jet Boat Rides The **Dart River Jet Boat Safari** is a 2½-hour journey 32 kilometers (20 miles) upstream into the ranges of the Mount Aspiring National Park. This rugged area is one of the most spectacular parts of the South Island, and the trip is highly recommended. Buses depart Queenstown daily at 8, 11, and 2 for the 45-minute ride to the boats. *Box 76, Queenstown, tel. 03/442–9992. Tickets: $99 adults, $55 children 5–16.*

The **Shotover Jet** is the most famous jet boat ride in the country (and one of the most exciting): a high-speed, heart-stopping adventure on which the boat pirouettes within inches of canyon walls. If you want to stay relatively dry, sit beside the driver. The boats are based at the Shotover Bridge, a 10-minute drive from Queenstown, and depart frequently between 8 AM and 7 PM from December to April, 9:30–4:30 the rest of the year. *Shotover River Canyon, Queenstown, tel. 03/442–8570. Tickets: $65 adults, $24 children under 15.*

Rafting **Kawarau Raft Expeditions** offers various half-, full-, and two-day white-water rafting trips in the Queenstown area. For intrepid rafters, the grade-4 to -5 rapids of the Shotover River provide an unforgettable journey, which ends with the rafts shooting through the 560-foot Oxenbridge Tunnel. *35 Shotover St., Queenstown, tel. 03/442–9792. Cost: $94 to $239 per person.*

Dining

Price categories for restaurants are the same as in the Auckland Dining section in Chapter 13.

$$ **Avanti.** This restaurant at the heart of Queenstown serves better-than-average Italian dishes at a far lower price than most in this resort area. Pastas and pizzas are prominent on the extensive menu, but so are more substantial meals such as venison goulash and several veal dishes. Servings are designed for appetites honed on the mountain slopes. *The Mall, Queenstown, tel. 03/442–8503. No reservations. Dress: casual. AE, DC, MC, V. BYOB.*

$$ **The Continental.** At the lake end of Queenstown Mall, this clublike bar/bistro is a notch up the smartness stakes from most of the town's restaurants. Among the main courses, you might choose the lamb cutlets with a sauce of thyme and mustard or the salmon with a cream, pepper, and dill sauce. The service is professional and friendly. *5 The Mall, Queenstown, tel. 03/442–8372. No reservations. Dress: casual. AE.*

$$ **The Cow.** The pizzas and pastas at this tiny, stone-wall restaurant are some of the best-value meals in town, but the place is immensely popular, so be prepared to wait for a table. A roaring fire provides a cozy atmosphere on chilly evenings, but patrons aren't encouraged to linger over dinner, and you may be asked to share your table. *Cow La., Queenstown, tel. 03/442–8588. No reservations. Dress: casual. MC, V. BYOB. No lunch.*

$ **Gourmet Express.** The food may not reach gourmet standards, but the service is certainly express. A popular breakfast spot, this casual diner at the front of a shopping arcade serves pancakes with maple syrup, eggs any way you want, and heart-starting coffee. A variety of inexpensive grills and burgers is available for lunch and dinner. *Bay Centre, Shotover St., Queenstown, tel. 03/442–9619. No reservations. Dress: casual. AE, DC, MC, V. BYOB.*

$ **Stonewall Cafe.** There is nothing remarkable about the sandwiches, salads, soups, and pasta at this center-of-town café, but the outdoor tables are a good choice for lunch on a sunny day. *The Mall, Queenstown, tel. 03/442–6429. No reservations. Dress: casual. AE, MC, V. Closed weekends.*

Lodging

Price categories for hotels are the same as in the Auckland Lodging section in Chapter 13. Highly recommended lodgings are indicated by a star ★.

$$$$ **Millbrook Resort.** A 20-minute drive from Queenstown, this glamor-
★ ous new resort offers luxurious, self-contained accommodation with special appeal for golfers. The resort is an elevated cluster of big, comfortable, two-story villas surrounded by an 18-hole golf course that was designed by New Zealand professional Bob Charles. The villas are decorated in country style: pine tables, textured walls, shuttered windows, and a cream-and-cornflower-blue color scheme. Each has a fully equipped kitchen, laundry facilities, a large

lounge/dining room, ski closet, and two bedrooms, each with an en suite bathroom, and the price is a bargain. *Malaghans Rd., Arrowtown, tel. 03/442–1563, fax 03/442–1145. 20 villas with bath. Facilities: golf course, tennis court, bar, restaurant. AE, DC, MC, V.*

$$$$ **Nugget Point.** Poised high above the Shotover River, this modern, ★ stylish retreat offers the finest accommodation in the Queenstown area. Rooms are cozy and luxuriously large, and each has a balcony, a kitchenette, and a bedroom separate from the lounge area. The lodge is a 10-minute drive from Queenstown on the road to Coronet Peak, one of the top ski areas in the country. *Arthurs Point Rd., Queenstown, tel. 03/442–7630, fax 03/442–7308. 35 rooms with bath. Facilities: heated pool, sauna, spa, squash, tennis, restaurant, bar. AE, DC, MC, V.*

$$$$ **Queenstown Parkroyal.** This modern resort complex sits in a prime position close to town. Guest rooms are large and luxuriously equipped, and about half overlook the steamer wharf. Request one on the top floor. *Beach St., Queenstown, tel. 03/442–7800, fax 03/442–8895. 139 rooms with bath. Facilities: heated pool, sauna, restaurant, bar. AE, DC, MC, V.*

$$$ **Hulbert House.** Set in tranquil gardens overlooking Queenstown and the lake, this century-old timber home offers a high standard of bed-and-breakfast lodging. Rooms are large and comfortably furnished with antiques. Request one with lake and mountain views. The city center is a five-minute walk away down a very steep hill. *68 Ballarat St., Queenstown, tel. 03/442–8767. 5 rooms with bath. Tariff includes breakfast. MC.*

$$ **Trelawn Place.** Perched on the brink of the Shotover Gorge 3 kilometers (1½ miles) from Queenstown, this stone and timber colonial-style house offers homey comforts and million-dollar views. The most popular of the three spacious guest rooms is the blue room, on the ground floor. For guests who want more privacy and the option of making their own meals, the two-bedroom cottage, which costs $20 more, is recommended. *Box 117, Queenstown, tel. 03/442–9160. 3 rooms with bath, 1 cottage with bath. Facilities: spa. Tariff includes breakfast. No credit cards.*

Dunedin and Otago

Tourist **Dunedin Visitor Information Centre.** *48 The Octagon, tel. 03/474–*
Information *3300. Open weekdays 8:30–5, weekends 9–5.*

Emergencies Dial 111 for **fire, police,** and **ambulance** services.

Arriving and Departing

By Plane Dunedin is linked with all other New Zealand cities by **Ansett New Zealand** (tel. 03/477–4146) and **Air New Zealand** (tel. 03/477–5769). **Dunedin Airport** lies 20 kilometers (13 miles) south of the city. **Johnston's Shuttle Express** (tel. 03/476–2519), a shuttle service between the airport and the city, meets all incoming flights and charges $10 per person. Taxi fare to the city is about $30.

By Car Driving time along the 280 kilometers (175 miles) between Queenstown and Dunedin (via Highway 6 and Highway 1) is five hours. The main route between Dunedin and Invercargill is Highway 1—a 3½-hour drive. A slower, scenic alternative is Highway 92 along the coast, which adds another 90 minutes to the journey.

By Bus Dunedin is served by **Mount Cook Landline** (tel. 03/474–0674) and **InterCity** buses (tel. 03/477–8860).

Guided Tours

Twilight Tours offer various minibus tours of Dunedin and its sur- roundings, including an afternoon tour that focuses on the alba- trosses, penguins, and seals of the Otago Peninsula. The penguin sanctuary is a privately operated venture, and this tour is the only way to see the rare yellow-eyed and little blue penguins. The tour price does not include admission to the albatross colony. *Box 963, Dunedin, tel. 03/474–3300. Cost: $48 adults, $40 children under 15. Tours depart daily at 1:45 from Dunedin Visitor Information Cen- tre.*

Exploring Dunedin

❻ Clinging to the walls of the natural amphitheater at the western end of Otago Harbour, the South Island's second-largest city, **Dunedin,** combines wildlife, inspiring seascapes, and a handsome Victorian townscape. Dunedin also has a large number of university students, who give the city a vitality far greater than its population of 120,000 might suggest.

Dunedin is the Gaelic name for Edinburgh, and the city's Scottish roots are obvious. It was founded in 1848 by settlers of the Free Church of Scotland, a breakaway group from the Presbyterian Church; today it has the only kilt shop in the country and the only whiskey distillery. A giant statue of Robert Burns presides over the heart of the city. The most compelling attraction for visitors is prob- ably the royal albatross colony at Taiaroa Head, the only place on earth where these majestic seabirds can be seen with relative ease. The city is noted for its rhododendrons, which are at their best in October.

This walking tour begins at the Visitor Information Centre in the **Octagon,** the city's navel. Dunedin prospered mightily during the gold rush of the 1860s. For a while it was the largest city in the coun- try, and the riches of the Otago goldfields are reflected in the bricks and mortar of Dunedin, most notably in the Italianate Municipal Chambers building.

Turn away from the figure of Burns, who sits in front of the cathe- dral "with his back to the kirk and his face to the pub," and walk down the hill along Stuart Street. On the corner of Dunbar Street you'll come to the late-Victorian **Law Courts.** Above the Stuart Street entrance stands the figure of Justice, scales in hand but with- out her customary blindfold (though the low helmet she wears prob- ably has the same effect).

On the far side of Anzac Avenue is the **Dunedin Railway Station,** a cathedral to the power of steam. The massive bluestone structure in the Flemish Renaissance style is lavishly decorated with heraldic beasts, coats of arms, nymphs, scrolls, a mosaic floor, and even stained-glass windows portraying steaming locomotives. This ex- travagant building earned its architect, George Troup, the nick- name "Gingerbread George" from the people of Dunedin, and a knighthood from the king. The station has far outlived the steam en- gine, and for all its magnificence it receives few trains these days. *Open daily 7–6.*

Walk away from the front of the station into High Street; on the corner of Cumberland Street stands the **Early Settlers Museum.** The museum preserves an impressive collection of artifacts, from the years when this was a whaling station to the days of the early Scottish settlers to the prosperous gold-rush era of the late-19th century. *220 Cumberland St., tel. 03/477–5052. Admission: $4 adults, children under 15 free. Open weekdays 10–5, weekends 1–5.*

Overlooking the museum is the spire of the **First Presbyterian Church,** perhaps the finest example of a Norman Gothic building the country. Turn into Burlington Street and walk to the left of the church, turn left into Moray Place, and cross the Octagon into George Street. Turn left into Pitt Street and left again at Royal Terrace to **Olveston.** This 35-room Jacobean-style mansion was built in 1904–1906 for David Theomin, a wealthy businessman and patron of the arts, who amassed a handsome collection of antiques and contemporary furnishings. The house and its furnishings are undoubtedly a treasure from an elegant age, but apart from some paintings collected by Theomin's daughter there is very little in it to suggest that it's in New Zealand. Even the oak staircase and balustrade were prefabricated in England. The one-hour guided tour is recommended. *42 Royal Terr., tel. 03/477–3320. Admission: $9 adults, $3 children 5–15. Open daily 9–5. Tours daily 9:30, 10:45, 12, 1:30, 2:45, 4.*

The Otago Peninsula

The main areas of interest on the claw-shaped peninsula that extends northeast from Dunedin are the albatross colony and Larnach Castle. On the return journey to Dunedin, the Highcliff Road, which turns inland at the village of Portobello, is a scenic alternative to the coastal Portobello Road.

7 Set high on a hilltop with commanding views from its battlements, **Larnach Castle** is the grand baronial fantasy of William Larnach, an Australian-born businessman and politician. The castle was a vast extravagance even in the free-spending atmosphere of the gold rush. Larnach imported an English craftsman to carve the ceilings, which took 12 years to complete, and the solid marble bath, the marble fireplaces, tiles, glass, and even much of the wood came from Europe. The mosaic in the foyer depicts Larnach's family crest and the modest name he gave to his stately pile: The Camp. Larnach rose to a prominent position in the New Zealand government of the late 1800s, but in 1898, beset by a series of financial disasters and possible marital problems, he committed suicide in Parliament House. (According to one romantic version, Larnach's third wife, whom he married at an advanced age, ran off with his eldest son; devastated, he shot himself.) A café in the castle ballroom serves Devonshire teas and light snacks. *Camp Rd., tel. 03/476–1302. Admission: $9.50 adults, $3.50 children 5–15. Open daily 9–5.*

8 **Taiaroa Head,** the eastern tip of the Otago Peninsula, is the site of a breeding colony of royal albatrosses. Among the largest birds in the world, with a wingspan of 11 feet, the albatrosses can take off only from steep slopes with the help of a strong breeze. Outside of Taiaroa Head and the Chatham Islands to the east, they are found only on windswept islands deep in southern latitudes, remote from human habitation. The colony is open for viewing from October through August, with the greatest number of birds present shortly after the young hatch around the end of January. Between March and September the parents leave the fledglings in their nests while they gather food for them. In September the young birds fly away, returning about eight years later to start their own breeding cycle. From the visitor center, groups follow a steep trail up to the Albatross Observatory, from which the birds may be seen through narrow windows. They are only rarely seen in flight. Access to the colony is strictly controlled, and visitors must book in advance. The tour takes about an hour. *Taiaroa Head, Dunedin, tel. 03/478–0499. Admission: $18 adults, $9 children 5–16. Open mid-Nov.–Aug., daily 10:30–4.*

❾ In the same area as the colony is the **"Disappearing" Gun,** a six-inch artillery piece installed during the Russian Scare of 1888. When fired, the recoil would propel the gun back into its pit, where it could be reloaded out of the line of enemy fire. The gun has been used in anger only once, when it was fired across the bow of a fishing boat that had failed to observe correct procedures before entering the harbor during World War II. *Admission: $8 adults, $4 children 5– 15. Combined albatross colony/gun admission: $18 adults, $9 children. Open 10:30–4.*

Dining

Price categories for restaurants are the same as in the Auckland Dining section in Chapter 13. Highly recommended restaurants are indicated by a star ★.

$$$$ **Bell Pepper Blues.** One of the country's most respected chefs, Michael Clydesdale, combines esoteric ingredients with recipes drawn from both the Pacific and the Mediterranean to produce food with flair. Blue cod comes baked in a parcel of rice paper, venison is roasted with an onion and orange bourbon *jus*, and steak tournedos come with wasabi and sesame seed butter. The setting, inside a converted pub, is casual and attractive. *474 Princes St., Dunedin, tel. 03/474–0973. Reservations advised. Dress: casual. AE, DC, MC, V. No lunch Mon., Tues., and Sat. Closed Sun.*

$$$$ **95 Filleul.** New owner Adrienne Molloy has breathed new life into one of Dunedin's long-standing favorites with an imaginative menu that makes the most of the local game and seafood. The modern, international menu includes grilled cervena venison with a tangy blueberry sauce, as well as lamb fillets with a kumera (sweet potato) and polenta timbale. *95 Filleul St., Dunedin, tel. 03/477–7233. Reservations advised. Dress: casual. AE, DC, MC, V. No lunch. Closed Sun.*

$$$
★ **Harbour Lights.** Poised on the shores of the Otago Peninsula overlooking the harbor, this restaurant is an exception to the rule that good food and good views don't usually coincide. Fish and game dishes are prominent on a menu that features such main courses as smoked South Island salmon with fresh herbs, wild boar shnitzel, and grilled grouper steak with a béarnaise sauce. The balcony is a favorite spot for summer dining. *494 Portobello Rd., MacAndrew Bay, tel. 03/476–1604. Reservations advised. Dress: casual but neat. AE, DC, MC, V. No lunch Mon. and Tues.*

$$ **Palms Cafe.** Vegetarians are especially well served at this casual, popular restaurant. The menu sometimes includes a casserole of olives, feta cheese, mushrooms, and tomatoes, and a Greek pastry roll filled with spinach and feta. Nonvegetarian mains may include lamb kebabs with peanut sauce, a whole sole with garlic sauce, and fillet of lamb with a green peppercorn glaze. The restaurant has a no-smoking policy. *84 Lower High St., Dunedin, tel. 03/477–6534. Res-*

ervations advised. Dress: casual but neat. AE, DC, MC, V. BYOB. No lunch.

Lodging

Price categories for hotels are the same as in the Auckland Lodging section in Chapter 13.

$$ Cargills Motor Inn. In a convenient location close to the city center, this motor inn offers superior motel-style rooms as well as two-bedroom family suites. Reduced rates apply Friday to Sunday nights. *670 George St., Dunedin, tel. 03/477-7983, fax 03/477-8098. 51 rooms with bath. Facilities: bar, restaurant. AE, DC, MC, V.*

$ Larnach Lodge. A modern timber building on the grounds of Larnach Castle, 19 kilometers (12 miles) from Dunedin, the lodge offers comfortable motel suites with marvelous views. Dinners are available in the castle by arrangement; otherwise the nearest restaurant is a 10-minute drive away. Budget rooms with shared facilities are available in the converted coach house. *Camp Rd., Otago Peninsula, Dunedin, tel. 03/476-1302. 27 rooms with bath. AE, DC, MC, V.*

$ Magnolia House. Overlooking the city of Dunedin in a prestige suburb, this gracious B&B offers atmospheric accommodations. The spacious guest rooms are furnished with antiques, and the house is surrounded by a pretty garden that includes native bushland. The house has a no-smoking policy. Dinners are available by arrangement, and children are welcome. *18 Grendon St., Maori Hill, Dunedin, tel. 03/467-5999. 3 rooms share 1 bathroom. Tariff includes breakfast. No credit cards.*

Stewart Island

Tourist Information Stewart Island Visitor Information Centre. *Halfmoon Bay, tel. 03/219-1218. Open weekdays 8-4:30.*

Emergencies Dial 111 for **fire, police,** and **ambulance** services.

Arriving and Departing

By Plane **Southern Air** (tel. 03/218-9129) operates several flights daily between Invercargill and Halfmoon Bay. The round-trip fare for the 20-minute flight is $118 for adults. One child under 14 is allowed to fly free of charge with each adult. For unaccompanied children under 14, the fare is $59. The free baggage allowance is 15 kilograms (33 pounds) per passenger.

By Boat **Stewart Island Marine** (tel. 03/212-7660) operates a ferry service between the island and the port of Bluff, the port for Invercargill. The one-way fare is $37 for adults, $18.50 for children under 15. Ferries depart Bluff on Monday, Wednesday, and Friday at 9:30 and 3:30 between May and November, daily at 9:30 and 5 during the rest of the year.

Guided Tours

For information on fishing trips, bird-watching trips to Ulva Island, and boat trips around Paterson Inlet, contact **Stewart Island Travel** (Box 26, Stewart Island, tel. 03/219-1269).

Exploring Stewart Island

The third and most southerly of New Zealand's main islands, Stewart Island is separated from the South Island by the 24-kilometer (15-mile) Foveaux Strait. Even by New Zealand standards, Stewart Island is remote, raw, and untouched. Electricity is a recent innovation, roads total about 20 kilometers (13 miles), and apart from the settlement of **Halfmoon Bay** on Paterson Inlet, the place is practically uninhabited. For most visitors, the attractions are its seclusion, its relaxed way of life, and—despite a once-busy sawmilling industry—its untouched quality.

The island, which covers some 1,700 square kilometers (650 square miles) and measures about 64 kilometers (40 miles) from north to south and about the same distance across at its widest point, forms a rough triangle, with a deep indentation, Paterson Inlet, on its eastern flank. On the coastline, sharp cliffs rise from a succession of sheltered bays and beaches; in the interior, forested hills rise gradually toward the western side of the island. Seals and penguins frequent the coast, and the island's prolific birdlife includes a number of species rarely seen in any other part of the country. One of the best spots for bird-watching is **Ulva Island,** a one-hour launch trip from Halfmoon Bay (*see* Guided Tours, *above*).

Outdoor Activities

Hiking　A network of walking trails has been established on the northern half of the island, leaving the south as a wilderness area. A popular trek is the **Northern Circuit,** a 10-day walk from Halfmoon Bay that circles the north coast and then cuts through the interior to return to its starting point. The island's climate is notoriously changeable, and walkers should be prepared for rain and mud. For information on walks, contact the **Department of Conservation** (Main Rd., Halfmoon Bay, tel. 03/219–1218).

Hunting　Another major activity for visitors to the island is hunting. Red deer and Virginia or whitetail deer were introduced earlier this century and may be hunted all year round. Hunting permits are available from the Department of Conservation office at Halfmoon Bay (*see* Hiking, *above*).

Dining and Lodging

Price categories are the same as in the Auckland Dining and Lodging sections in Chapter 13.

$$$$　**Stewart Island Lodge.** The most luxurious accommodation on the island offers comfortable, centrally heated suites with private baths. The focal points of life at the lodge are the guest lounge and the dining room, both of which offer expansive views across the bay. The owners have a game fishing launch and can arrange scenic tours of the island. Local seafood is a specialty on the dinner menu. *Halfmoon Bay, Nichol Rd., Stewart Island, tel. and fax 03/219–1085. Tariff includes all meals. 4 rooms with bath. AE, DC, MC, V.*

$　**Rakiura Motel.** Within easy walking distance of Halfmoon Bay, the Rakiura offers standard motel units that sleep up to six. *Horseshoe Bay Rd., Halfmoon Bay, tel. 03/219–1096. 5 rooms with bath. MC.*

16 Adventure Vacations

By David
McGonigal

Visitors miss an important element of Australia and New Zealand if they don't get away from the cities to explore "the bush" that is so deeply ingrained in the down-under character. Australians pride themselves on their ability to cope in the great outdoors even if, in many cases, this has never been tested beyond lighting the backyard barbecue. Nevertheless, the heroes of Australian history are those men who opened this vast, unforgiving land—men like Ludwig Leichhardt, who pioneered the 4,800-kilometer (3,000-mile) route between Brisbane and Port Essington (Darwin) in 1844, only to vanish without a trace during a transcontinental trek in 1848, or Robert O'Hara Burke, who died in 1861 after completing a north–south transcontinental trip with camels. Many of the adventure vacations offered today were journeys of exploration only a generation ago. Even now, the four-wheel-drive vehicle is a necessity, not a plaything, in the great heart of Australia. Indeed, there remains a raw element to Australia that makes it ideally suited to adventure vacations. You can still travel for hours or days in many areas without seeing another person or any sign of human habitation, and the climate and terrain are perfect for a wide range of activities. From the tropical jungles of the north to the deserts of the Red Centre to the snowfields of New South Wales and Victoria, one is constantly reminded of how old this country is. The mountains you walk or ride through have become rounded with age, and the animals and flora you encounter have long since disappeared from the rest of the planet.

Adventure vacations are commonly split into soft and hard adventures. A hard adventure requires a substantial degree of physical participation, although you usually don't have to be perfectly fit; in a few cases, prior experience is a prerequisite. In soft adventures the destination rather than the means of travel is often what makes it an adventure. With most companies, the adventure guides' knowledge of flora and fauna—and love of the bush—is matched by a level of competence that ensures your safety even in dangerous situations. The safety record of Australian adventure operators is very good. Visitors should be aware, however, that most adventure-tour operators require participants to sign waiver forms absolving the company of responsibility in the event of an accident or a problem. Australian courts normally uphold such waivers except in cases of significant negligence.

New Zealand is small in comparison, but it has much to offer the adventure traveler. The mountains in this green, clean land are made for hiking and climbing; the sparsely populated roads for bicycling; the rivers for rafting. The rugged coastline looks wonderful from the deck of a small vessel or, even closer to the water, a sea kayak. And this is the country that invented jet-boating. New Zealand is farther south than most of Australia, so its seasons are more marked—and you can't escape winter and summer (as you often can in Australia) by heading north for warmth or south to cool down.

Far more adventure-tour operators exist than can be listed in this chapter. Most are small and receive little publicity outside their local areas, so contact the relevant state tourist office if you have a specific area of interest. Here are the addresses of the major adventure-tour operators mentioned in the following pages:

Australia **Adventure Center** (1311 63rd St., #200, Emeryville, CA 94608, USA, tel. 510/654–1879); **Adventure Charters of Kangaroo Island** (Bayview Rd., American River, Kangaroo Island, SA 5221, tel. 0848/3–3204); **Blue Mountains Adventure Company** (Box 242, Katoomba, NSW 2780, tel. 047/82–1271); **Bluff & Beyond Trailrides** (Box 287, Mansfield, VIC 3722, tel. 057/75–2212 or 057/75–2954); **Bogong Horseback Adventures** (Box 230, Mt. Beauty, VIC 3699, tel. 057/57–2849); **Bogong Jack Adventures** (Box 221, Oxley, VIC 3678, tel. 057/27–3382); **Boolabinda** (Box 379, Glenn Innes, NSW 2370, tel. 067/32–1599); **Brake Out Cycling Tours** (Box 275, Sandy Bay, TAS 7005, tel. 002/78–2966); **Camel Outback Safaris** (PMB 74, via Alice Springs, NT 0871, tel. 089/56–0925); **Cradle Mountain Huts** (Box 1879, 22 Brisbane St., Launceston, TAS 7250, tel. 003/31–2006); **East Kimberley Tours** (Box 537, Kununurra, WA 6743, tel. 091/68–2213); **Equitrek Australia** (5 King Rd., Ingleside, NSW 2101, tel. 02/913–9408); **Frontier Camel Tours** (Box 2836, Alice Springs, NT 0871, tel. 089/53–0444 or book through Worldventure; *see below*); **Go Bush Safaris** (Box 71, Gladesville, NSW 2111, tel. 02/817–4660); **Intrepid Tours** (Box 31, Quorn, SA 5433, tel. 086/48–6277); **Lake Keepit Soaring Club** (Keepit Dam, NSW 2340, tel. 067/69–7640 or 067/69–7514); **Mountaincraft** (Box 582, Camberwell, VIC 3124, tel. 03/877–4177); **Mountain River Riders** (Box 95, Oberon, NSW 2787, tel. 063/36–1890); **Osprey Wildlife Expeditions** (27 Strathalbyn Rd., Aldgate, SA 5154, tel. 08/370–9337); **Packsaddlers** (Megalong Rd., Megalong Valley, NSW 2785, tel. 047/87–9150); **Paddy Pallin Jindabyne** (PMB 5, Jindabyne, NSW 2627, tel. 064/56–2922); **Peregrine Adventures** (258 Lonsdale St., Melbourne, VIC 3000, tel. 03/663–8611, or book through Adventure Center); **Port Macquarie Camel Safaris** (20 Kennedy Dr., Port Macquarie, NSW 2444, tel. 065/83–7650); **Reynella Rides/Kosciusko Trails** (Adaminaby, NSW 2630, tel. 064/54–2386 or 008/02–9909); **Southern Cross Gliding Club** (Box 132, Camden, NSW 2570, tel. 02/874–1854); **Tasmanian Expeditions** (59 Brisbane St., Launceston, TAS 7250, tel. 003/34–3477); **Tourism Commission of New South Wales** (2121 Ave. of the Stars #450, Los Angeles, CA 90067, USA, tel. 213/552–9566); **Waikerie Gliding Club** (Box 320, Waikerie, SA 5330, tel. 085/41–2644); **Walkabout Gourmet Adventures** (book through Mary Rossi Travel, 65 Berry St., suite 3, North Sydney, NSW 2060, tel. 02/957–4511); **White Water Connection** (Box 720, Turramurra 2070, tel. 02/905–9314); **Whitewater Rafting Professionals** (Box 133, Coffs Harbour 2450, tel. 066/514–066); **Wilderness Expeditions** (3rd Floor, 441 Kent St., Sydney, NSW 2000, tel. 02/264–3721); **Wild Escapes** (GPO Box 4799, Sydney, NSW 2001, tel. 02/247–2133); **World Expeditions** (3rd Floor, 441 Kent St., Sydney, NSW 2000, tel. 02/264–3366); **Worldventure** (Ste. 1, 860 Military Rd., Mosman, NSW 2088, tel. 02/960–1677).

New Zealand **Abel Tasman National Park Enterprises** (Old Cederman House, Main Rd., Riwaka, Motueka RD3, Nelson, tel. 03/528–7801); **Adventure Center** (1311 63rd St., #200, Emeryville, CA 94608, USA, tel. 510/654–1879); **Alpine Guides** (Box 20, Mt. Cook, tel. 03/435–1834); **Alpine Recreation Canterbury** (Box 75, Lake Tekapo, tel. 03/680–6736); **Danes Shotover Rafts** (Corner Shotover and Camp Sts., Queenstown, tel. 03/442–7318); **Hollyford Tourist and Travel Company** (Box 205, Waikaitipu, Central Otago, tel. 03/442–3760); **Karavan Adventure Treks** (117 Harris Crescent, Christchurch, tel. 03/352–2177); **Landsborough River Expeditions** (Box 410, Queenstown, tel. 03/442–3630); **New Zealand Pedaltours** (Box 37-575, Parnell, Auckland, tel. 09/302–0968); **New Zealand Travel Professionals** (Box 219, Auckland, tel. 09/377–0761); **Ocean River Adventure Company** (Main Rd., Marahau Beach, RD2, Motueka, tel. 03/527–8266); **The Rafting Company** (Box 2392, Rotorua, tel. 073/480–233); **Routeburn Walk Ltd.** (Box 568, Queenstown, tel. 03/442–8200); **Southern Heritage Expeditions** (Box 22, Waikari, North Canterbury, tel. 03/314–4393); **Te Anau Travelodge** (Box 185, Te Anau, tel. 03/249–7411); **Wilder-

ness Expeditions (3rd Floor, 441 Kent St., Sydney, NSW 2000, tel. 02/264–3721).

Bicycling

Bicycles may seem an impractical way to travel, but cycling is actually an excellent way to explore a small region, allowing you to cover more ground than on foot and observe far more than from the window of a car or bus. And while a bike may not be much fun in the fumes of city traffic, riding down quiet country lanes is a great way to relax and get fit at the same time. Cycling rates as a hard adventure because of the level of exercise.

New South Wales
Season: Year-round.
Locations: Blue Mountains, Snowy Mountains, Southern Highlands.
Cost: From $50 for one day to $650 for seven days.
Tour Operators: Blue Mountains Adventure Company, Wilderness Expeditions, Wild Escapes.

Wilderness Expeditions offers several bicycle tours, which include all meals, a support vehicle, guides, mountain bikes, group camping gear, and national park entry fees (where applicable). Its main cycling region is the Snowy Mountains. The same operator leads a weekend ride exploring the Southern Highlands, two hours southwest of Sydney, an area of large manor houses, spectacular formal gardens, and rolling farmland interspersed with patches of dense forest. The trip is most memorable when the spring flowers are in bloom. Blue Mountains Adventure Company offers several day rides on mountain bikes through these plunging walled valleys that border Sydney, actually ridges left from a collapsed plateau rather than mountains. The trips include a spectacular ride along Narrow Neck, which affords wonderful views into the gum-tree-carpeted Jamison Valley, and a ride through a glowworm tunnel. Wild Escapes has a four-day camping tour suitable for fit first-timers that traverses the Great Dividing Range. It takes in Wollemi National Park, an hour northwest of Sydney, which contains the largest unaltered forest in Australia, with tall eucalypts and pockets of rain forest; a network of bush trails takes riders far from other visitors.

Queensland
Season: April–October.
Location: Atherton Tablelands.
Cost: $260–$365 for two to three days.
Tour Operator: Peregrine Adventures.

Rising up behind the coastal town of Cairns, the Atherton Tablelands are a mixture of tropical rain forests and sleepy towns—an area to be savored rather than rushed through. The tablelands are reached on board a steam train that labors up the steep gradient from Cairns onto the escarpment. The tablelands themselves are relatively level and ideal for bicycles. Staying overnight in quaint old wooden pubs, swimming in cool highland ponds, exploring a huge curtain fig tree, and then heading off for a drink at the next pub are good ways to attain a Queensland frame of mind.

Tasmania
Season: November–March.
Location: North and east coasts.
Cost: From $25 for a half-day tour to $800 for eight days or $1,600 for two weeks, including camping equipment, support vehicle, bicycles, and all meals.
Tour Operators: Adventure Center, Brake Out Cycling Tours, Pere-

grine Adventures, Tasmanian Expeditions, Wilderness Expeditions.

Tasmania is small enough to make cycling a pleasant option. The classic tour is Tasmanian Expeditions' Cycle Tasmania, an eight-day trip from Launceston that leads through peaceful, pastoral lands down to the fishing villages of the east coast. The tour encompasses a wide range of terrains, from undulating hills to full-scale mountains, coastal plains, and dense temperate rain forests. Wilderness Expeditions and Tasmanian Expeditions have very similar 14-day tours, which include cycling, bushwalking, and rafting. Intended for beginners, the trip features some of the best adventures Tasmania has to offer: walking in the Cradle Mountain area and the Walls of Jerusalem National Park, cycling down the east coast, and rafting on the relatively peaceful Picton River. Brake Out specializes in Tasmanian cycling tours, offering everything from a series of half-day tours of Hobart to an eight-day ride along the scenic east coast.

New Zealand **Season:** October–March.
Locations: Both islands.
Cost: From $1,600 for eight days to $4,500 for 19 days, including accommodations, meals, and support vehicle. Bikes can be rented for about $15 a day.
Tour Operators: Adventure Center, New Zealand Pedaltours.

The combination of spectacular scenery and quiet roads is ideal for cycle holidays. Traditionally the South Island, with its central alpine spine, has been more popular, but Auckland is where most people arrive, and the North Island has enough curiosities—the hot mud pools of sulfurous Rotorua, the Waitaimo Caves, and the old gold-mining area of the Coromandel Peninsula—to fill each day. The average daily riding distance is about 60 kilometers (37 miles), and the support vehicle is large enough to accommodate all riders and bikes if circumstances so demand. The rides on the South Island extend from the ferry port of Picton to picturesque Queenstown, the center of a thriving adventure day-trip industry.

Bushwalking

The Australian bush is unique. The olive-green foliage of the eucalypti seems drab at first, but when you walk into a clearing carpeted with thick grass and surrounded by stately blue gums, its special appeal becomes apparent. The bush is a bright and noisy place, too—crimson- and harlequin-hued parrots screech from the canopy overhead, while kookaburras laugh hysterically from the treetops. Chances are good that you will cross paths with kangaroos, wallabies, goannas, and even echidnas (spiny anteaters). This is a land of a million oddities that is best appreciated on foot. New Zealand's terrain is very different and every bit as spectacular. A long bushwalk is intensely satisfying, but it doesn't have to be hard work. An easy ramble with a picnic lunch through the Blue Mountains of New South Wales can be every bit as rewarding as a challenging 20-kilometer (12½-mile) hike to a muddy camp in the Tasmanian wilderness. Depending on the type of walk, therefore, bushwalking can be a soft or hard adventure. Associated high-adrenaline hard adventures are abseiling (or rappelling) and canyoning—forms of vertical bushwalking well suited to some parts of Australia, notably the Blue Mountains of New South Wales.

New South **Season:** Year-round.
Wales **Location:** Throughout the coastal and mountain areas.

Costs: From about $80 per day, including packs, camping equipment, guide, and food.

Tour Operators: Blue Mountains Adventure Company, Paddy Pallin Jindabyne, Wild Escapes, Wilderness Expeditions.

The scope for casual bushwalking in New South Wales is extensive. The best one-day walks in the Blue Mountains originate in Blackheath and wind through Grand Canyon or Blue Gum Forest. The Snowy Mountains beyond Perisher also offer excellent walking, as do the national parks to the north—especially Barrington Tops, a mysterious place of narrow paths running through huge rain forests and past streams shaded by giant tree ferns and tall hardwoods. The same areas are ideal for longer treks, too. The advantage of joining an adventure tour is the experience and knowledge of the guides, who identify all the animals and plants encountered along the way and show you places of interest off the main trails. The camping equipment provided by tour operators on overnight walks is a welcome alternative to buying it in Australia (where prices for outdoor gear are high) or bringing it from home. Wilderness Expeditions operates four-day and one-week walking tours in the Snowy Mountains and weekend hikes (including rappelling) in the Bungonia Gorge south of Sydney. During the summer, Wilderness Expeditions and Wild Escapes conduct one-day guided walks in the Blue Mountains from Sydney for $80–$100 including lunch. The deeply eroded sandstone canyons of the Blue Mountains are perfect for abseiling down sheer vertical crags and through deep, clean canyons. There is intense competition between tour operators in this area, so a full day of canyoning in the spectacular Grand Canyon or the sublime Claustral Canyon costs less than $100 including lunch.

Tasmania   **Season:** November–May.

Location: Central highlands, west coast.

Cost: From about $100 per day, including camping equipment and meals, to $1,095 for the six-day Cradle Mountain Huts walk or $1,600 for a comprehensive 11-day gourmet tour of the island.

Tour Operators: Cradle Mountain Huts, Peregrine Adventures, Tasmanian Expeditions, Wilderness Expeditions, Worldventure.

Until recently, overnight walks in Tasmania were major expeditions suitable only for the highly experienced and very fit. Plenty of these treks are still available, including the South Coast Track trip operated by Tasmanian Expeditions. The trail includes some easy stretches along pristine, secluded beaches, as well as difficult legs through rugged coastal mountains. Hikers must fly into this remote area—it's the combination of difficult trails and extreme isolation that gives this walk spice.

A much easier walk is conducted in Freycinet Peninsula, which lies about 200 kilometers (120 miles) north of Port Arthur on the east coast. Much of it can only be explored on foot: The road ends at the pink granite domes of the Hazards, which form a rampart across the top of the peninsula. Those who take the time to venture beyond them will discover a world of pristine bush where wallabies loll, and white sand beaches fringing crystal clear water. One organized walk, led by Freycinet Experience, a branch of Cradle Mountain Huts, lasts five days, the average walk per day covering only 8 kilometers (5 miles). Participants stay in Tasmanian hardwood log huts furnished with scatter rugs and wood furniture and situated to take advantage of the best views.

The best-known walk in Tasmania, however, is the trail from Cradle Mountain to Lake St. Clair. It's such a popular walk that boardwalks have been placed along some sections to prevent the path from turning into a quagmire. The walk starts and finishes in dense forest but much of it runs along exposed highland ridges. The construction of the Cradle Mountain Huts a couple of years ago made this trail far more accessible. However, these huts are available only to hikers on one of Cradle Mountain Huts' escorted walks. Although basic, the huts provide a level of comfort unimaginable to anyone forced to camp in the mud of the area's mountain ranges. Each hut is well heated and carries extensive supplies; there are even warm showers. Other operators continue to conduct camping tours along the trail as well as elsewhere in Tasmania. The rapid weather changes typical of this area present an extra challenge, but the spectacular mountain scenery makes any discomfort that the cold or wet causes worthwhile.

Victoria **Season:** October–April.
Location: Grampians, Wilsons Promontory, Bogong High Plains.
Cost: From $35 for a day walk to $1,000 for 10 days.
Tour Operators: Adventure Center, Bogong Jack Adventures, Peregrine Adventures, Walkabout Gourmet Adventures, Wilderness Expeditions, Worldventure.

Victoria offers a range of bushwalking vacations to suit every taste. Bogong Jack Adventures leads challenging treks to the summit of the state's three highest peaks and other, less demanding, walks through forests of mountain ash and snow gums. Wilderness Expeditions has a trip consisting of five daily walks in the High Country; hikers spend each night at a lodge in Falls Creek. Walkabout Gourmet Adventures offers a more epicurean bushwalking experience, during which participants stay in a country lodge and the emphasis is on good food, wine, wildlife, and relaxation. These gourmet adventures are designed for healthy, active people, and the number of walkers in any group is kept under 10.

New Zealand **Season:** October–March for high-altitude walks, year-round for others.
Location: South Island.
Cost: From $425 for four days to $2,500 for 13 days. The climbing school costs $1,525 for seven days (including aircraft access, meals, accommodation, and transport).
Tour Operators: Abel Tasman National Park Enterprises, Adventure Center, Alpine Guides, Alpine Recreation Canterbury, Hollyford Tourist and Travel Company, Karavan Adventure Treks, New Zealand Travel Professionals, Routeburn Walk Ltd., Te Anau Travelodge, Wilderness Expeditions.

If it seems from the list above that every New Zealand company is involved in trekking, wait till you see the trails—particularly in the peak months of January and February; they can be crowded enough to detract from the nature experience. An advantage of a guided walk is that companies have their own tent camps or huts, with such luxuries as hot showers—and cooks. For the phobic, it's worth mentioning one very positive feature: New Zealand has no snakes or predatory animals.

The most famous New Zealand walk, the Milford Track—a four-day trek through Fiordland National Park—covers a wide variety of terrains, from forests to high passes, lakes, a glowworm grotto, and the spectacle of Milford Sound itself. There are other walks in the same area: the Greenstone Valley (three days) and the Routeburn Track (three days)—combined they form the Grand Traverse; and the Hollyford Valley (five days). For something different, the three-to six-day walks along the beaches of Queen Charlotte Sound and through forests in the Abel Tasman National Park (northwest South Island) are very popular, relatively easy, and well suited to family groups; your pack is carried for you, and you stay in lodges. Karavan Adventure Treks has a series of unusual walks throughout the South Island. One of the most appealing is a four-day trip in Nelson Lakes National Park, near the top of the island; for two nights your base is the Angelus Basin Hut, spectacularly located beside a beautiful mountain lake beneath towering crags. Another option is the Alpine Recreation Canterbury 13-day minibus tour of the South Island, with one-day walks along the way; it provides an extensive and scenic cross section, but it misses the magic of completing a long single walk.

For the very enthusiastic, Alpine Guides has a world-renowned seven-day course on the basics of mountain climbing, in the area of Mt. Cook, the highest point in the New Zealand Alps. There is also a 10-day technical course for experienced climbers. New Zealand is the home of Sir Edmund Hillary, who, with Tenzing Norgay, made the first ascent of Mt. Everest; clearly the country has a fine mountaineering tradition, and Alpine Guides is the nation's foremost training school.

Camel Treks

Riding a camel is rather like riding two horses strapped together at right angles. Surprisingly, though, sitting astride a wide, padded camel saddle is more comfortable than horseback riding, and the animals aren't nearly as aggressive as many people believe. In fact, they can be quite endearing, although they do have quite revolting personal habits. The night silence of your desert campsite will regularly be broken by the sound of camels regurgitating, followed by their dawn screams as they object to their roles as beasts of burden. Strange as it may seem, a camel trek is an extremely pleasant way to spend a week or two and beautifully recaptures the experience of desert travel as it was in the past. Australian camels come from Afghan stock (hence the name of the *Ghan* train, which follows the old desert route of the Afghan camel trains from Adelaide to Alice Springs), and many now roam wild in the Outback. Camel treks rate as soft adventure.

New South Wales **Season:** Year-round.
Location: Port Macquarie.
Cost: $160 for two days.
Tour Operator: Port Macquarie Camel Safaris.

Located on the north coast of New South Wales, 420 kilometers (260 miles) north of Sydney, Port Macquarie is a long way from any desert, but it does have an impressive array of expansive, long sandy beaches. Ron Keating set up his camel operation in 1990 and it has now won several tourism awards. The first day of the Gourmet Camel Safari Weekend takes you to a camp by a freshwater lagoon behind the dunes. All meals (which include local crayfish and oysters) and camping equipment are provided. On day two, participants can relax around the beach and camp until morning tea, then ride back to Port Macquarie in time for lunch.

Northern Territory **Season:** April–September (weekly departures), October–March (every two weeks).
Location: Alice Springs.
Cost: From $45 for a half-day ride to about $400 for three days or $430–$700 for a week.

Tour Operators: Adventure Center, Camel Outback Safaris, Wilderness Expeditions, Worldventure.

With his long white beard and enthusiastic riding style, Noel Fullerton is one of the Northern Territory's most colorful characters. He obtained his first camel in 1969, and his company now conducts camel rides of an hour or a day along with a series of camel safaris through the Red Centre from his farm outside Alice Springs (*see* Chapter 10, The Red Centre). Among the places these treks visit is Rainbow Valley, remote gorge country that includes the oldest watercourse in the world and an ancient stand of palms. Worldventure and Wilderness Expeditions represent Frontier Camel Tours, which is closer to Alice Springs. Its six-day safaris roam through the red dunes of the Simpson Desert to the bizarre 58-meter- (190-foot-) high sandstone monolith of Chambers Pillar.

South Australia
Season: Year-round.
Location: Kangaroo Island, Flinders Ranges, Simpson Desert.
Cost: From $70 for one day to $2,400 for 20 days.
Tour Operator: Worldventure.

The major camel-tour operator in South Australia, Rex Ellis has a fascination with the Outback that led him to make the only north–south boat crossing of normally dry Lake Eyre. From his camel farm on Kangaroo Island, he runs a series of one- to five-day camel safaris of that island's rugged and unusual geological formations. He also offers one- to seven-day tours in the Wilpena Pound area of the Flinders Ranges. For the more adventurous, he operates a series of camel expeditions over the winter months that strike deep into the desert, with no particular destination. The success of these trips relies on the spirit of adventure of the expedition members, to say nothing of the camels' unique ability to cope with arid conditions.

Canoeing and Sea Kayaking

Once they leave their mountain headwaters and enter the flatness of the plains, Australian rivers become placid streams. Unlike rafting, where much of the thrill comes from negotiating white water, commercial canoeing involves paddling down these gentle stretches of river. The enjoyment comes from the relaxing pace, the passing scenery, and the constant, comforting murmur of the river. Canoeing is soft adventure—and so is sea kayaking, its oceanic equivalent.

Queensland
Season: May–October.
Location: Coral Sea.
Cost: $790–$930 for seven days.
Tour Operators: Peregrine Adventures, Wilderness Expeditions.

Peregrine Adventures and Wilderness Expeditions lead trips in two-person sea kayaks through the tranquil waters around Hinchinbrook Island, one of the largest and most impressive islands off the Queensland coast. No previous experience is necessary, and the pace of the trip is leisurely, with plenty of time set aside for snorkeling, fishing, or lazing about on a beach. Participants explore rain forests and deserted beaches, and study dolphins and other sea life. During the trip, curious turtles and manta rays are likely to approach for a closer look. With its granite peaks and rugged aspect, Hinchinbrook Island is a wonderful place in its own right to explore.

New Zealand
Season: December–May.
Location: Abel Tasman National Park, South Island.

Cost: From $85 for one day to $370 for four days, including kayaks, tents, cooking and camping equipment, and park permits.
Tour Operator: Ocean River Adventure Company.

This tour along the sheltered waters of the Abel Tasman National Park provides a waterline view of a beautiful coastline. It allows you to explore otherwise inaccessible golden-sand beaches and remote islands and to meet fur seals on their home surf. When wind conditions permit, paddles give way to small sails, and the kayaks are propelled home by an onshore breeze.

Cross-Country Skiing

Unlike the jagged peaks of alpine regions elsewhere in the world, the Australian Alps have round summits, making them ideal for cross-country skiing. Although cross-country skiing doesn't offer the same adrenaline rush as downhill skiing, there are no expensive lift tickets to buy—your legs must do the work. While the crowds build up on the groomed slopes, cross-country skiers have a chance to get away from the hordes and experience the unforgettable sensation of skiing through forests of eucalyptus trees, with their spreading branches, pale leaves, and impressionistic bark patterns. Cross-country skiing is hard adventure, even though many tours are arranged so that skiers stay in lodges every night. The joy of leaving the first tracks across new snow and the pleasure afforded by the unique scenery of the snowfields is tempered by the remarkable fatigue that your arms and legs feel at the end of the day.

New South Wales
Season: July–September.
Location: Jindabyne.
Cost: From $32 for a half day of instruction to $600 for a five-day course or $700 for a seven-day tour.
Tour Operator: Paddy Pallin Jindabyne.

Some 450 kilometers (279 miles) south of Sydney, Jindabyne is a gateway to the Snowy Mountains. Paddy Pallin Jindabyne is an offshoot of Australia's most respected outdoor-equipment retail store. It offers a complete range of ski tours and cross-country instructional programs. Most of the courses are based out of a lodge, but there are also two- and five-day camping tours across the snow trails of the Main Range.

Victoria
Season: July–September.
Location: Mansfield, Mt. Beauty.
Cost: From about $270 for a weekend course to $700 for a five-day and $1,000 for an eight-day course or tour.
Tour Operators: Bluff & Beyond Trailrides, Bogong Jack Adventures, Peregrine Adventures.

Bluff & Beyond Trailrides operates weekend and five-day ski tours that depart midweek throughout the winter months. The treks, which go through the rural back country of the Victorian Alps far from the downhill ski areas, are segregated by ability and thus are suitable for everyone from novices to advanced skiers. Accommodations consist of old cattlemen's huts that are heated and located above the snow line. Bogong Jack Adventures offers a comprehensive program of lodge-based trips, camping expeditions, skiing instruction, and snow-craft courses. Groups are kept small (fewer than 15 people), and there are enough instructors to ensure that you learn quickly. Building snow caves and mastering the art of survival in the snow are excellent skills—even if Australia seems like a strange place to learn them. In reality, however, the open, gentle slopes of Australia are ideal for learning how to ski cross-country. The scenery of the Victorian Alps is dramatic, with the valley sides rising steeply to the high-country plains. A major advantage of skiing in Victoria is that the lodges where skiers stay are close to the snowfields. The lodges are located below the snowline and they are far from luxurious, but evenings by the fire and the inevitable camaraderie of the group make these stays most enjoyable.

New Zealand **Season:** June–September.
Location: Mt. Cook.
Cost: $1,550 for seven days, including guide fees, accommodations, food, transport, and aircraft access.
Tour Operator: Alpine Guides.

Mt. Cook and its attendant Murchison and Tasman glaciers offer wonderful ski touring, with terrains to suit all levels of skiers. The tour commences with a flight to the alpine hut that becomes your base; from here the group sets out each day for skiing and instruction.

Four-Wheel-Drive Tours

Australia is a vast land with a small population, so many Outback roads are merely clearings through the bush. Black soil that turns into skid pans after rain, the ubiquitous red dust of the center, and the continent's great sandy deserts make a four-wheel-drive vehicle a necessity for exploring the countryside. Outback motoring possesses a real element of adventure—on some roads it's standard practice to call in at the few homesteads along the way so they can initiate search procedures if you fail to turn up at the next farm down the track. At the same time, the laconic Aussies you meet along the way are a different breed from urban Australians, and time spent with them is often memorable. Despite the rugged nature of many of the bush tracks that pass for roads in Australia, four-wheel-drive tours are definitely soft adventure.

New South **Season:** Year-round.
Wales **Locations:** Blue Mountains, Broken Hill.
Cost: From $100 for one day or $360 for three days to $890 for eight days.
Tour Operator: Mountain River Riders.

Some parts of New South Wales are accessible only by four-wheel-drive vehicle. Although such Outback locations as Broken Hill can be reached on good roads, beyond there you leave civilization behind. And the Blue Mountains—only a short distance west of Sydney—provide some of the state's most challenging four-wheel-drive conditions, as well as a sense of great remoteness. Mountain River Riders, a specialist company based deep in a mountain valley, has a range of day tours to show the best of this spectacular area.

Northern **Season:** April–October.
Territory **Location:** Throughout the Northern Territory, but mainly in Kakadu National Park.
Cost: From about $800 for six days to $1,440 for 16 days.
Tour Operators: Adventure Center, Go Bush Safaris, Wilderness Expeditions, Worldventure.

While the number of tourists at Kakadu National Park has risen dramatically each year, some sites can still be reached only by four-wheel-drive vehicle, including Jim Jim Falls and Twin Falls—two of Australia's most scenic attractions. At both of these falls, the water plunges over the escarpment to the flood plains below. Below the picturesque falls are deep, cool pools and beautiful palm-shaded beaches. The **Darwin Regional Tourism Association** (31 Smith St. Mall, Darwin, NT 0800, tel. 089/81–4300) can provide more information about the numerous tour operators based in Darwin. Both Worldventure and the Adventure Center have comprehensive tours of this remarkable area. Wilderness Expeditions offers a combined four-wheel-drive/canoeing vacation, which takes in the highlights of Kakadu on land, then continues to the Daly River for a few days of tropical canoeing. Go Bush Safaris conducts a single 16-day four-wheel-drive tour that covers both Kakadu and Uluru national parks.

Queensland **Season:** May–November.
Location: North of Cairns.
Cost: From $1,300 for two-week return trip.
Tour Operators: Adventure Center, Peregrine Adventures, Wilderness Expeditions.

The most northerly point of the Australian mainland, Cape York is the destination sought by every four-wheel-drive enthusiast in Australia. After passing through the rain forest north of Port Douglas, the track travels through relatively dry vegetation the rest of the way. Several galleries of spectacular Aboriginal rock paintings are here, as are a historic telegraph station and the notorious Jardine River, whose shifting bottom made fording very tricky in the past. Until a few years ago, reaching the cape was a major achievement; now a ferry service across the Jardine makes it easier, but Cape York is still frontier territory—a land of mining camps, Aboriginal settlements, and enormous cattle stations. For all intents and purposes, civilization stops at Cooktown.

South **Season:** Year-round.
Australia **Location:** Kangaroo Island, Flinders Ranges.
Cost: From $670 for three days on Kangaroo Island or $500 for a four-day tour through the Outback.
Tour Operators: Adventure Charters of Kangaroo Island, Intrepid Tours.

Unless you have the time to walk, the rugged areas of South Australia are best explored by four-wheel-drive vehicle. Kangaroo Island boasts a huge variety of animals including kangaroos, koalas, fur seals, penguins, and sea lions, as well as such bizarre natural features as huge limestone arches and weather-worn rocks that resemble Henry Moore sculptures. Adventure Charters of Kangaroo Island operates a series of tours, the most comprehensive being a three-day/two-night package. Alternatively, heading north, the desert starts just north of Adelaide. The Flinders Ranges are a low finger of mountains stretching into the desert. Their most notable feature is Wilpena Pound, a huge natural amphitheater filled with small trees and grasses overlooking the barren plains below. Intrepid Tours offers a series of one-day and overnight tours throughout the region.

Western **Season:** May–November.
Australia **Location:** The Kimberley.
Cost: From $300 for three days to $600 for six days to $2,000 for a 16-day tour.
Tour Operators: East Kimberley Tours, Go Bush Safaris, Wilderness Expeditions.

Most of the four-wheel-drive adventures in Western Australia take place in the Kimberley region in the far north (*see* Chapter 11). The only practical time to visit the Kimberley is during the Dry (May–November) because roads are often flooded during the Wet. The

Kimberley boasts Australia's richest Aboriginal cultural heritage, which can be explored on the East Kimberley Tours three-day trip into the Bungle Bungles or its six-day tours along the remote Gibb River Road between Kununurra and Broome. Aboriginal rock art is also explored in Wilderness Expeditions's four-wheel-drive trip to the Bungle Bungles from Darwin through the recently opened Gregory National Park, whose 10,500 square miles of rugged ranges and gorges encompass rare flora and fauna, historic houses, and observation points offering superb views of Stokes Range. The trip also includes some canoeing. Go Bush Safaris covers similar territory on its 16-day round-trip tour from Darwin to Derby.

Gliding

Gliding is the safest, cheapest—and most thrilling—way to fly, and Australia's climate and terrain make the country possibly the best place on earth to do it. Every club welcomes visitors, and a member will take you for a short flight to see if you like it. The first flight in a glider is always memorable: Towed aloft behind a light plane (normally a superannuated crop duster), the glider is released from the tow rope in rising air and the silent flight begins. Heights of 12,000 feet (and flights of several hours) aren't unusual during the summer months. This is not an energetic sport—it's soft adventure at best—but what it lacks in activity it more than makes up for in excitement. Soaring just below the cloud base at high speed offers an unmatched sensation of pure flight. For more information about gliding in Australia, contact the **Gliding Federation of Australia** (130 Wirraway Rd., Essendon Airport, VIC 3041, tel. 03/379–7411).

New South Wales

Season: Mainly October–April.
Locations: Throughout the state but particularly at Camden and Lake Keepit (near Tamworth).
Cost: $50 for a half-hour flight, $500–$900 for basic training, $700–$1,500 to go solo.
Operators: Lake Keepit Soaring Club, Southern Cross Gliding Club.

Situated about 60 kilometers (37 miles) west of Sydney at Camden Aerodrome, **Southern Cross** is one of the largest gliding clubs in Australia. The club's proximity to Sydney ensures that it is very busy, particularly on weekends. The club's basic training course, which lasts five days, includes 10 instructional flights, probationary membership, a logbook, and an instruction manual. This won't get you flying solo, but you'll be well on your way.

Its laid-back approach to gliding, the abundance of cheap accommodations nearby, and the best scenery from the air of any club in Australia make **Lake Keepit** the most appealing club in New South Wales. Fifty kilometers (31 miles) west of Tamworth and 450 kilometers (279 miles) north of Sydney, the club is set amid lush pastoral land with densely timbered mountains in the distance. The five-day/six-night course includes a minimum of 32 flights, accommodations, and a three-month club membership. Many participants are flying solo by the end of the week.

South Australia

Season: Mainly October–April.
Location: Waikerie.
Cost: $35 for a 20-minute flight; $1,050 for a five-day course (including dormitory accommodations); $270 for a weekend course (including one night's accommodations).
Operator: Waikerie Gliding Club.

Waikerie, an attractive region along the Murray River, is filled with orchards and vineyards. The terrain is ideal for the creation of the thermal currents that keep a glider aloft, and the Waikerie Gliding Club inevitably becomes crowded on weekends.

Horseback Riding

Trail bikes and four-wheel-drive vehicles have slowly been replacing horses on Australian farms and stations over the past 20 years. On the plains and coastal lowlands the transformation is complete, but horses are still part of rural life in the highlands, and it is here that the best horseback adventures are to be found. On a horse trek you come closer to the life of the pioneer Australian bushmen than in any other adventure pursuit. Indeed, the majority of treks are led by Australians with close links to the traditions of bush life. Riding through alpine meadows and along mountain trails and sleeping under the stars is an excellent way to see the Australian bush. A typical horseback vacation lasts several days, and the food and equipment for each night's camp is brought in by packhorse or four-wheel-drive vehicle. Although a cook, a guide, and all specialist equipment are provided, participants are expected to help look after the horses. An Australian saddle is a cross between the high Western saddle and the almost flat English one. The horses are normally real workhorses, not riding hacks, and they are used to rough bush work. These trips are essentially soft adventures, for most of the work is done by the horses—it's just hard to convince your cramping leg muscles of this after a long day in the saddle.

New South Wales

Season: All year, but mainly November–April.
Locations: Blue Mountains, Snowy Mountains, New England Highlands.
Cost: From $50 to $80 for a day ride to $165 for a weekend and $940 for a week.
Tour Operators: Boolabinda, Equitrek Australia, Mountain River Riders, Packsaddlers, Paddy Pallin Jindabyne, Reynella, Wilderness Expeditions.

The Great Dividing Range, which extends right through New South Wales, has some excellent trails for horseback riding. Almost every country town has a riding school with horses for hire, but a few long rides are particularly outstanding. In the Snowy Mountains, a six-day summer ride from Reynella homestead through Kosciusko National Park covers terrain ranging from open plains to alpine forests. Riders camp out in some of the most beautiful valleys in the park—valleys not easily accessible except by horse. Two of the best stables in the Blue Mountains are Mountain River Riders and Packsaddlers in the Megalong Valley, which conduct regular one-, two-, and three-day rides through the rugged countryside to Cox's River. Leaving the farmlands behind and descending through the forest into the river valley, riders enter a part of the country that has changed little since European settlers first arrived in Australia. Although you're only a few hours due west of Sydney, eating a lunch from a saddlebag by the river while the horses graze nearby is a memorable bush experience. One of the most unusual rides in Australia is the "Pub Crawl on Horseback," a 140-kilometer (87-mile) ride through the New England Ranges, with nights spent at old bush pubs along the early stagecoach routes. Operated by Steve Langley from his property, Boolabinda, the tour emphasizes the bush experience, not drinking, because riding into a tiny village and booking into a historic pub is thrill enough. All the communities en route could fairly be described as one-horse towns—at least until your posse hits town.

Victoria **Season:** October–April.
Location: Victorian high plains.
Cost: $80–$150 per day.
Tour Operators: Bluff & Beyond Trailrides, Bogong Horseback Adventures, Peregrine Adventures.

An important part of the Australian rural mythology is an A. B. (Banjo) Patterson poem entitled *The Man from Snowy River*, based on the equestrian feats of riders in the Victorian high plains who round up stock and horses from seemingly inaccessible valleys. For those who wish to emulate the hero of that work, several operators offer rides of 3–10 days in the area. Part of the journey is spent above the treeline, where, as Banjo Patterson said, "the horses' hooves strike firelight from the flintstones every stride." Accommodation is either in tents or in the original bushmen's huts that dot the high country.

Rafting

The exhilaration of sweeping down into the foam-filled jaws of a rapid is always tinged with fear—white-water rafting is, after all, rather like being tossed into a washing machine. While this sort of excitement appeals to many people, the attraction of rafting in Australia and New Zealand encompasses much more. As you drift downriver during the lulls between the white water, it's wonderful to sit back and watch the wilderness unfold, whether it's stately river gums overhanging the stream, towering cliffs, or forests of eucalyptus on the surrounding slopes. Rafting means camping by the river at night, drinking billy tea brewed over the campfire, going to sleep with the sound of the stream in the background, or sighting an elusive platypus at dawn. The juxtaposition of action and serenity gives rafting an enduring appeal that leads most who try it to seek out more rivers with more challenges. Rivers here are smaller and trickier than the ones used for commercial rafting in North America, and rafts usually hold only four to six people. The rafting companies provide all rafting and camping equipment—you only need clothing that won't be damaged by water (cameras are carried in waterproof barrels), a sleeping bag (in some cases), and sunscreen. Rafting qualifies as a hard adventure.

New South Wales **Season:** September–May.
Locations: The Murray River in the southern part of the state, the Shoalhaven and Gwydir rivers in the center, and the Nymboida River in the north.
Cost: From $95 for a one-day Nymboida trip to about $230–$300 for a weekend. All camping and rafting equipment is supplied.
Tour Operators: Whitewater Connection, White Water Rafting Professionals, Wild Escapes.

The upper reaches of the Murray River are open for rafting between September and November, when the stream is fed by melting snow. The river is cold, but the rapids are challenging, and the Australian Alps appear in all their spring glory. The Gwydir River is fed by a large dam, and the scenery downriver is mainly pastoral, but the river has a series of challenging rapids. The Shoalhaven south of Sydney passes through some of the most impressive scenery in the coastal ranges. The Nymboida River flows through beautiful subtropical rain forest near Coffs Harbour and is the warmest river with white water in the state.

South Australia **Season:** July–October.
Location: Nullarbor Plains.
Cost: $1,095 for eight days.
Tour Operator: Osprey Wildlife Expeditions.

The Nullarbor Plain is a flat, treeless desert that stretches for nearly 1,000 miles through Western Australia and South Australia. Below its arid surface, however, lies the largest underground lake in the Southern Hemisphere. On one of the most unusual adventure trips in Australia, participants descend below ground to explore several huge caves, both on foot and by raft. Although only a few of the eight days are spent underground (none of the campsites are underground), they are the most memorable: Swimming in Weebubblie Cave is an unbelievably strange sensation; the water in another cave is so clear that you feel as if you are space-walking through liquid crystal; an 8-kilometer (5-mile) trail winds through another cavern. No previous caving experience is required, and participants are not required to squeeze through any tight spaces. The tour also includes a trip to vantage points along the coast overlooking the breeding grounds of the southern right whale, as well as a visit to an underground rock gallery of Aboriginal paintings in the Great Victoria Desert. Unlike most rafting trips, this is a soft adventure.

Tasmania **Season:** December–March.
Location: Franklin River, west coast.
Cost: Around $900 for five to seven days, $1,300–$1,500 for 11–12 days.
Tour Operators: Peregrine Adventures, Tasmanian Expeditions, World Expeditions.

The most exciting white-water rafting provides an instant adrenaline rush. Fortunately, most rivers provide plenty of quiet reaches where you can regain your breath and appreciate the scenery. Nowhere is this more true than on the Franklin River, which offers the most spectacular and rewarding rafting experience in Australia. Deep rocky chasms, grand forested valleys, beautiful sandy beaches, and miles of untouched wilderness make the Franklin something special. The river leads through a truly remote area of Tasmania—there are only a few places where you can join or leave the river. You have the choice of exploring either the lower or upper parts of the Franklin, or the entire navigable length. By far the most rewarding option is covering the entire river. The combination of isolation, beauty, difficult rapids, and strenuous portages ensures that rafters finish the trip with a real feeling of achievement. It's a difficult and challenging journey that should be tackled only by people who are reasonably fit and comfortable in the bush.

Victoria **Season:** September–January.
Location: Mitchell, Snowy, Mitta Mitta, and Thomson rivers.
Cost: From $235 for a weekend, $400–$500 for five to six days.
Tour Operators: Peregrine Adventures, World Expeditions.

The driving time from Melbourne to Victoria's rafting rivers is generally less than from Sydney to the main New South Wales rafting locations. Nevertheless, you need to budget at least a weekend for the trip and be prepared to camp out. The scenery ranges from the rugged Alps of the north to the pastoral areas of eastern Victoria. The Thomson River is close enough to Melbourne to allow for one- or two-day trips, and the Mitta Mitta River is invariably rafted as part of a two-day trip. The Mitchell River descent, however, can be extended to a five-day, moderately strenuous journey. The Snowy River offers spectacular rafting trips of one to six days through the Australian Alps. The Snowy River doesn't rely on the spring snow melt, so it can be rafted from August to February, but its rapids are gentler than those on the upper Murray River, which also descends through the Alps.

New Zealand   **Season:** Mainly October–May.
Location: North and South Islands.
Cost: From $70 for one day to $675 for three days (with helicopter set-down), including all equipment (wetsuits, helmets, footwear).
Tour Operators: Danes Shotover Rafts, Landsborough River Expeditions, The Rafting Company.

There are several rafting rivers on both islands of New Zealand. Near Rotorua, the Rangitaiki offers exciting grade-4 rapids and some good scenery. Nearby, the Kaituna River has the highest raftable waterfall in the world: a 7-meter (21-foot) free fall. On the South Island, the great majority of activity centers on Queenstown; the most popular spot here is the upper reaches of the Shotover beyond the tortuous Skippers Canyon. In winter the put-in site for the Shotover is accessible only by helicopter, and wet suits are essential year-round, as the water is very cold. Some of the rapids are grade 5—the highest before a river becomes unraftable.

To combine the thrill of white water with a wilderness experience, take a two-day trip down the Landsborough River, which rises in Mt. Cook National Park and flows past miles of virgin forest and into some very exciting rapids.

Sailing

Australia's immense coastline is dotted with myriad offshore islands, particularly off Queensland near the Great Barrier Reef. The tropical climate and the lure of these often uninhabited and undeveloped islands have made sailing extremely popular in Australia. It's also an excellent way to take in the varied coastline of New Zealand. While the image of beautiful people sipping gin slings and watching the sunsets in the tropics may be a little exaggerated, your role as a passenger on a commercial sailing vessel can hardly be described as strenuous. You are likely to participate in the sailing of the vessel more than you would on a regular cruise line, but for all intents and purposes this is a soft adventure in paradise.

Queensland   **Season:** Year-round.
Location: Whitsunday Islands.
Cost: $760 for one week.
Tour Operators: Adventure Center and World Expeditions arrange tours on the *Coral Trekker*.

The feel of a square-rigger ship under full sail instantly transports passengers back to the romantic days of the trading clippers. The *Coral Trekker* currently plies the waters of the Whitsunday Passage, which wends its way past coral-fringed tropical islands and is renowned for its consistent trade winds. The itinerary varies, but generally the ship sails from one island to the next, mooring at will. The vessel carries snorkeling gear and sailboards, free for passengers; it also has diving gear available for an extra fee to certified divers. On-board accommodations, included in the cost, are decidedly not luxurious, and thus the cruise appeals mainly to young adults.

New Zealand   **Season:** Year-round.
Location: South Island
Cost: From $1,240 for five days in the Doubtful Sound area to $2,000

for eight days in Fiordland National Park to $3,850–$10,350 for 11–18 days cruising the sub-Antarctic islands of Australia and New Zealand.

Tour Operators: New Zealand Travel Professionals, Southern Heritage Expeditions.

Southern Heritage Expeditions uses the eight-cabin, 65-foot MV *Affinity*, a diesel-powered New Zealand–built vessel, to take visitors to otherwise inaccessible parts of the coastline. From June to August it explores the deeply indented shores of Fiordland National Park. In September and October it heads for the top of the South Island and the warmer waters of Marlborough Sounds—a maze of waterways and islands of incredible beauty. Throughout the summer months (December–January), Southern Heritage Expeditions operates a 140-foot vessel, the MV *Pacific Ruby*, down to the sub-Antarctic islands of Australia and New Zealand. On these stark, rocky outcrops can be seen the ruins of early attempts at settlement and animals such as the royal albatross, Hookers sea lion, elephant seal, and penguins.

New Zealand Travel Professionals offers two cruises along the shores of the South Island aboard the 15-meter (50-foot) *Waverley*. Accommodations for eight passengers are on a twin-share basis. A five-day cruise goes around Doubtful Sound.

Index

Abel Tasman National Park, *533, 537, 539*
Aboriginal art and culture
Alice Springs, *396*
books on, *31*
Brisbane, *278*
Canberra, *161–162*
Darwin, *417, 419*
Hobart, *245–246*
Kimberley, *427*
New South Wales, *154*
Queensland, *308, 309*
Red Centre, *404–405*
Sydney, *91–92, 115*
Tasmania, *261*
Top End, *430*
Victoria, *233*
Aboriginal Islander Dance Theatre, *115*
Adelaide (riverboat), *230*
Adelaide, *353*
the arts, *367*
beaches, *361*
children, *359*
emergencies, *356*
festivals, *367*
guided tours, *356*
hotels, *365–367*
nightlife, *367–368*
restaurants, *361–365*
shopping, *360*
sightseeing, *356, 358–360*
sports, *360–361*
tourist information, *356*
transportation, *354–355*
travel agencies, *356*
Adelaide Hills, *368–371*
Adelaide House (museum), *394*
Admiralty House, *70–71*
Adventure vacations, *4–5, 564–566*
in Australia, *564–565*
bicycling, *566–567*
camel treks, *570–571*
canoeing, *571–572*

cross-country skiing, *572–573*
four-wheel-drive tours, *573–575*
gliding, *575–576*
hiking, *567–570*
horseback riding, *576–577*
in New Zealand, *565–566*
rafting, *577–579*
sailing, *579–580*
sea kayaking, *571–572*
Adventureworld, *444*
Agrodome, *512*
Akaroa, *547, 549*
Akaroa Museum, *547, 549*
Alan Green Conservatory, *443*
Albany, *461, 462, 463, 491*
Albert Park, *476*
Alexandra Heads, *299*
Alfred Nicholas Memorial Gardens, *206*
Alice Springs, *390, 392–402*
climate, *7*
emergencies, *393*
excursions, *400–402*
festivals, *9*
guided tours, *393*
hotels, *398–400*
nightlife, *400*
pharmacies, *393*
restaurants, *397–398*
shopping, *396*
sightseeing, *393–396*
sports, *396–397*
tourist information, *393*
transportation, *392*
Allendale Gardens, *262*
All Saints Vineyards & Cellars, *229*
Alpine National Park, *238–239*
American Express, *12, 13, 39*
Amity replica, *462*

Anbangbang Gallery, *430*
Angaston, *379*
Antigua Boatshed, *544*
Anzac Hill, *393–394*
Anzac Square, *274*
Apartment and Villa Rentals, *46*
Apollo Bay, *211*
Aquacoaster (water slide), *233*
Aquariums
New South Wales, *143*
North Island, *520*
Queensland, *299*
Sydney, *87*
Victoria, *208*
Aquascene, *417*
Aranui Cave, *507*
Argyle Cut, *76*
Argyle Steps, *76*
"Argyle Stores" (retail complex), *76*
Army Museum, *85*
Arrowtown, *553–554*
Art Deco, *517, 518*
Art galleries and museums
Adelaide, *358*
Alice Springs, *394, 396*
Auckland, *476*
Brisbane, *277, 288*
Canberra, *161–162, 172*
Darwin, *419*
Melbourne, *207*
New South Wales, *123, 133, 143–144*
Perth, *444*
South Australia, *369*
South Island, *538, 544*
Sydney, *71, 74, 75, 80, 81–82, 85, 88–89*
Tasmania, *245–246*
Victoria, *207, 214, 220, 220, 222, 233*
Art Gallery of New South Wales, *81–82*
Art Gallery of South Australia, *358*
Art Gallery of Western Australia, *444*

Arthur McElhone Reserve, *84*
Arthur's Circus, *247*
Arthur's Seat Park, *207*
the Arts. *See under cities and areas*
Arts Centre, *545*
ASB Bank, *518*
Athenacum Theatre and Library, *183*
Atherton Tableland, *306*
Auckland, *473*
arts, *488*
beaches, *482*
children, *480*
climate, *8*
consulates, *473*
emergencies, *473–474*
festivals, *10*
free attractions, *480*
guided tours, *475–476*
hotels, *486–488*
money, *474*
nightlife, *488–489*
pharmacy, *474*
restaurants, *479, 482–486*
shopping, *481*
sightseeing, *476–480*
sports, *481–482*
tourist information, *473*
transportation, *474–475*
travel agencies, *474*
Auckland City Art Gallery, *476*
Auckland Domain, *477*
Auckland Institute and Museum, *478*
Australian Academy of Science, *159*
Australian-American Memorial, *163*
Australian Ballet, *203*
Australian Capital Territory. *See also Canberra, 156, 172–173*
Australian Institute of Sport, *164*

Australian Maritime Museum, *88*

Australian Museum, *88*

Australian National Gallery, *161–162*

Australian Pearling Exhibition, *417*

Australian War Memorial, *163*

Australian Woolshed (stage show), *278*

Avoca (paddle steamer), *232*

Ayers House, *358–359*

Ayers Rock, *401, 402–408*

Baby-sitting services, *27*

Baby Supplies, *27*

Ball, Shirley, *75*

Ballarat, *218–219, 220, 223–224*

Ballarat Fine Arts Gallery, *220*

Ballarat Wildlife and Reptile Park, *222–223*

Ballooning

Alice Springs, *396–397*

Canberra, *164*

New South Wales, *134*

Queensland, *296*

Victoria, *233*

Balmoral Beach, *96*

Banks Peninsula, *547*

Barossa Valley, *376–382*

festivals, *9*

guided tours, *379*

hotels, *381–382*

restaurants, *380*

shopping, *379–380*

sightseeing, *376–379*

tourist information, *376*

transportation, *376*

Barracks Arch, *443–444*

Bath House, *510*

Battery Point, *246*

Bay of Islands, *10, 489–490*

Bay of Islands Coastal Reserve, *214*

Bay of Martyrs, *214*

Beaches, *43.* See also

Gold Coast; Sunshine Coast

Adelaide, *361*

Auckland, *482*

in Australia, *43*

Coromandel Peninsula, *499, 501*

Melbourne area, *207*

New South Wales, *139, 141–142*

in New Zealand, *52*

Perth, *446*

pollution information, *96*

Queensland, *299, 301, 310*

South Australia, *373–374*

Sydney, *94–99*

Victoria, *207, 208–209, 215*

Western Australia, *468, 469*

Beare Park, *84*

Bed-and-breakfasts, *46*

Bedarra Island, *348–349*

Beechworth, *227–228, 233–234*

Begonia House, *525*

Bellenden Ker National Park, *325*

Bellingen, *139*

Bell's Beach, *210*

Bendigo, *221–222, 224–225*

Bendigo Art Gallery, *222*

Ben Prior's Open Air Museum, *466*

Berri, *384*

Berrivale Orchards, *384*

Bethany, *378, 379–380*

Bethells beach, *482*

Bicycling,

Adelaide, *355*

adventure vacations, *566–567*

Auckland, *481*

in Australia, *41*

Canberra, *165*

Darwin, *419*

Melbourne, *189*

New South Wales, *149, 566*

New Zealand, *49, 567*

North Island, *524*

Perth, *440, 446*

Queensland, *566*

races, *216*

South Island, *539*

Tasmania, *245, 248, 256, 261, 566–567*

Victoria, *216*

Western Australia, *458*

Big Banana, *141*

Big Pineapple, *298*

Big Shell, *299*

Birdland Native Gardens, *262*

Blackheath, *126*

Black Mountain National Park, *319*

Blanchetown, *385*

Bli Bli Castle, *299–300*

Bligh, William, *71, 74*

Blood on the Southern Cross, *220*

Bloomfield River, *320*

Bloomfield Track, *318*

Blue Lake, *509*

Blue Mountains, *67–68, 119, 121*

children, *127*

emergencies, *122*

guided tours, *122–123*

hotels, *126, 129–131*

nightlife, *131*

restaurants, *125–126, 128–129*

shopping, *127–128*

sightseeing, *123, 125–127*

sports, *128*

tourist information, *122*

transportation, *122*

Blue Mountains Heritage Centre, *126*

Boat Harbour, *262, 263*

Boating and sailing,

adventure vacations, *579–580*

in Australia, *41*

Brisbane, *278*

Canberra, *158, 165*

Great Barrier Reef, *334, 335, 336, 337, 339, 344, 346, 347*

Hobart, *245*

Melbourne, *179*

New Zealand, *49, 579–580*

North Island, *490, 495*

Queensland, *291, 296, 300, 315, 579*

South Island, *539, 555, 561*

Bogong National Park, *238–239*

Bondi Beach, *43, 67, 86, 96–97*

Books on Australia, *31–32, 92*

Books on New Zealand, *32*

Boomerang (villa), *84*

Boreen Point, *301*

Botanic Gardens

Adelaide, *359*

Christchurch, *544*

Darwin, *417*

Lake Wendouree, *220*

South Islands, *544*

Wellington, *524–525*

Botany Bay Beach, *97*

Bourke Museum, *228*

Brampton Island, *336*

Bridge of Remembrance, *543*

Brisbane, *272*

the arts, *288*

children, *277–278*

City Hall, *276*

emergencies, *273*

festivals, *9*

guided tours, *273–274*

hotels, *285–288*

nightlife, *288*

restaurants, *276, 280–285*

shopping, *278–279*

sightseeing, *274–278*

sports, *279*

tourist information, *273*

transportation, *272–273*

British High Commission (Canberra), *162*

Broadbeach, *292*

Broadgreen house, *536*

Bronte Beach, *43, 97*

Brooke Street Pier (Hobart), *246*

Brookfields Winery, *519*

Broome, *426, 427, 428*
Buda, *221*
Buller River, *537*
Buller's Calliope
  Vineyard, *229*
Bunbury, *460, 462*
Bungan Beach, *98*
Bungle Bungle
  (domes), *432–433*
Bungy Jumping, *554,*
  555
Bush Mill and
  Narrow Guage
  Railway, *254*
Bush pubs, *143*
Bushwalking. *See*
  Hiking
Business hours
  Australia, *40*
  New Zealand, *48*
Busselton, *460, 463*
Bus travel
  Adelaide, *354, 355*
  advantages of, *37–38*
  Alice Springs, *392*
  Auckland, *475*
  Brisbane, *272, 273*
  bus passes, *24, 37–38*
  Canberra, *157*
  Coromandel
    Peninsula, *498*
  Darwin, *411, 414*
  the Kimberley, *424*
  Melbourne, *177*
  Napier, *517*
  New South Wales,
    131, 138, 147
  New Zealand, *47*
  North Island, *490,*
    517, 523, 524
  Perth, *440*
  Queensland, *288, 289,*
    295, 303, 306, 313
  Red Centre, *403*
  Rotorua, *506*
  South Australia, *383*
  South Island, *533,*
    542, 552, 558
  Sydney, *62, 63*
  Tasmania, *244, 254,*
    256, 260, 261, 265
  times and costs,
    36–37
  Western Australia,
    456, 465
Byron Bay, *142*

Cadbury-Schweppes
  chocolate factory,
  247

Cadman's Cottage, *74*
Cairns, *306–312*
  children, *308*
  climate, *8*
  emergencies, *307*
  festivals, *10*
  guided tours,
    307–308, 330
  hotels, *311–312*
  nightlife, *312*
  restaurants, *310–311*
  shopping, *309*
  sightseeing, *308–309*
  sports, *310*
  tourist information,
    307
  transportation,
    306–307
Cairns Museum, *308*
Cairns Sugarworld,
  308
Caloundra, *299*
Camcorders, *18*
Camel farms, *401,*
  466–467
Camel treks, *401,*
  570–571
Campbell's
  Storehouse, *74*
Campbell's Ruther-
  glen Winery, *229*
Camp Cove Beach, *96*
Camping, *41, 331,*
  408, 468, 469–470
Canadian Bay
  Reserve, *207*
Canberra (riverboat),
  231
Canberra, *156*
  the arts, *171*
  children, *164*
  embassies, *158, 162*
  emergencies, *158*
  guided tours, *158*
  hotels, *169–171*
  nightlife, *171–172*
  restaurants, *165–168*
  shopping, *164*
  sightseeing, *159,*
    161–164
  sports, *164–165*
  tourist information,
    158
  transportation,
    157–158
  travel agencies, *158*
Canberra Theatre
  Centre, *171*
Canoeing and rafting,
  41

adventure vacations,
  571–572, 577–579
  Melbourne, *189*
  New South Wales,
    144, 149, 577
  New Zealand,
    571–572, 579
  North Island, *513*
  Queensland, *310, 571*
  South Australia, *578*
  South Island, *539,*
    552
  Tasmania, *578*
  Top End, *434*
  Victoria, *233,*
    578–579
Canterbury, *10, 542*
Canterbury Museum,
  544
Canterbury Plains,
  549
Cape Byron
  Lighthouse, *142*
Cape Kidnapper, *519*
Cape
  Leeuwin-Naturaliste
  National Park,
  469–470
Cape Tribulation,
  318, 320
Cape Tribulation
  National Park, *314,*
  317–318, 325–326
Captain Cook
  Memorial Jet, *159,*
  161
Captain Cook
  Memorial Museum,
  494
Carillon (Canberra),
  162–163
Carlton Gardens, *185*
Carman's Tunnel, *221*
Carnarvon National
  Park, *323*
Car racing, *216*
Car rentals, *21–22*
  Alice Springs, *392*
  in Australia, *21*
  Canberra, *157–158*
  Darwin, *414*
  disabilities, travelers
    with, *28*
  Melbourne, *178*
  in New Zealand,
    21–22
  Perth, *440*
  South Australia, *372*
  Sydney, *65*
Carriage Museum,

228
Car travel, *38*
  Alice Springs, *392*
  Auckland, *475*
  Brisbane, *273*
  Canberra, *157*
  Coromandel
    Peninsula, *498*
  Darwin, *411, 414*
  the Kimberley, *424*
  Melbourne, *177–178*
  Napier, *517*
  New South Wales,
    122, 131–132, 138,
    147
  New Zealand, *47*
  North Island, *490,*
    517, 523
  Perth, *440*
  Queensland, *289, 295,*
    303, 304, 306, 307,
    314
  Red Centre, *403*
  Rotorua, *506*
  South Australia, *383*
  South Island, *533,*
    542, 552, 557
  Sydney, *63*
  Tasmania, *244, 254,*
    256, 261, 265
  Victoria, *210, 218,*
    227, 237, 238, 239
  Western Australia,
    460
Cash machines, *13*
Casinos
  Adelaide, *368*
  Alice Springs, *400*
  Canberra, *172*
  Darwin, *424*
  Queensland, *290*
  Tasmania, *253, 260*
Castlecrag, *70*
Castlemaine, *221*
Castlemaine &
  Maldon Railway, *223*
Castlemaine Market,
  221
Cat and Fiddle
  Arcade, *247*
Cataract Gorge,
  256–257
Cathedral Church of
  St. Mary, *478*
Cathedral Cove, *501*
Cathedral Square, *545*
Caverns
  Coromandel
    Peninsula, *498, 501*
  New South Wales,

Caverns *(continued)*
127
North Island, *513*
Rotorua, *507*
Western Australia,
469
Cemeteries, *466*
Cenotaph memorial,
527
Central Deborah
Gold-Mine, *222*
Cessnock, *132*
Chambers Rosewood
Winery, *229*
Children. *See under*
cities and areas
traveling with, *26–27*
Children's Adventure
Playground, *291*
Children's Museum,
185
Chiltern, *228*
Chinese settlement,
554
Chowder Bay, *70*
Christchurch, *542*
climate, *8*
emergencies, *542*
excursions, *547,*
549–552
guided tours, *543*
hotels, *546–547*
restaurants, *545, 546*
shopping, *545*
sightseeing, *543–545*
tourist information,
542–543
transportation, *542*
Christ Church, *494*
Christ Church
Cathedral (Darwin),
417
Christ Church
Cathedral (South
Island), *536*
Christchurch
Cathedral, *545*
Church of St.
Francis, *180*
Church of St. Patrick,
549
Church of the Good
Shepherd, *550*
Churches
Auckland, *478*
Brisbane, *274*
Canberra, *163*
Darwin, *417*
Melbourne, *180, 184*
New South Wales,

139
North Island, *494*
Perth, *443*
Rotorua, *512–513*
South Island, *536,*
543–544, 545, 549,
550, 559
Sydney, *76, 80, 81,*
89
Tasmania, *247*
Wellington, *526*
Western Australia,
457
Church of St.
Francis, *180*
Circular Head, *262*
Civic Theatre, *476*
Claphams Clock
Museum, *491*
Cleland Conservation
Park, *385–386*
Climate, *6–9*
Cloisters, *443*
Clovelly Beach, *97*
Cockington Green
(exhibit), *164*
Coffs Harbour, *138,*
141
Cohunu Wildlife
Park, *445*
Collaroy/Narrabeen
Beach, *98*
Colleges and
universities
Sydney, *78–79*
Collingrove (country
house), *378–379*
Colonial House
Museum, *75*
Colonial Secretary's
Office, *78*
Como (19th-century
house), *186*
Concerts
Canberra, *171*
Darwin, *423*
Melbourne, *203, 204*
Perth, *455*
Sydney, *86*
Tasmania, *252, 260*
Condong Sugar Mill,
143
Conservatorium
(Sydney), *78, 86*
Constitution Dock,
245
Consulates. *See*
Embassies
Contacts, *30–31*
Convent Gallery, *220*

Coogee Beach, *43, 97*
Cook's Beach, *499*
Cooktown, *319,*
320–321
Coolangatta, *292*
Coolgardie, *466–467*
Coolgardie Camel
Farm, *466–467*
Coolgardie Cemetery,
466
Coolum, *298, 301*
Cooma, *147, 148*
Coromandel
Peninsula, *498*
beaches, *499, 501*
children, *501*
emergencies, *498*
guided tours,
498–499
hotels, *502–503*
restaurants, *502*
sightseeing, *499, 501*
sports, *502*
tourist information,
498
transportation, *498*
Coromandel town,
499
Coromandel State
Forest Park, *502*
Cost of the trip
Australia, *14*
New Zealand, *14–15*
Cow Bay, *318, 321*
Cradle
Mountain/Lake St.
Clair National Park,
266–267
Crescent Head Beach,
139
Cricket
Adelaide, *361*
Brisbane, *279*
Hobart, *248*
Melbourne, *190*
Perth, *447*
Sydney, *94*
Tasmania, *248*
Crocodiles, *315, 317,*
418, 426, 457
Cronulla Beach, *97*
Cuisine of Australia,
43–45
Currency
Australia, *13*
Exchange services,
12–13
New Zealand, *13–14*
Currumbin
Sanctuary, *291*

Customs, *16–17*
Customs House
(Sydney), *77–78*

Daintree Rain Forest,
317
Daintree River, *317*
Dance
Canberra, *171*
Melbourne, *203, 204*
North Island, *530*
Perth, *455*
Sydney, *115*
the Dandenongs,
205–206, 209
Darling Harbor, *89*
Darlington, *216*
Darwin, *410, 411*
the arts, *423*
children, *418*
climate, *7*
emergencies, *414*
festivals, *9*
guided tours, *414*
hotels, *417, 422–423*
nightlife, *424*
restaurants, *420–422*
shopping, *419*
sightseeing, *414–419*
sports, *419–420*
tourist information,
414
transportation, *411,*
414
Darwin, Charles, *494*
Darwin Aviation
Museum, *418*
Darwin's Botanic
Gardens, *417*
Davey's Bay Yacht
Club, *207*
Daydream Island,
342–343
Daylesford, *220, 225*
Deanery (Brisbane),
274
Deanery (Perth), *443*
Dee Why/Long Reef
Beach, *98*
Denmark, *461*
Department stores,
90, 180, 188, 276,
278, 481
Derby, *426*
Devonport
(Tasmania), *261, 263*
Disabilities, hints for
travelers with, *27–29*
"Disappearing" Gun,
560

Disco, *260, 368, 489*
Dixson Gallery, *79*
Dolphins, *496*
Dorrigo National
  Park, *141*
Drayton's Bellvue
  Winery, *133*
Dreamworld, *289*
Dunedin
  emergencies, *557*
  guided tours, *558*
  hotels, *561*
  restaurants, *560–561*
  sightseeing, *558–559*
  tourist information,
    557
  transportation,
    557–558
Dunedin Railway
  Station, *558*
Dunk Island, *346–348*
Dunsborough, *460*
Duties, *16–17*
Duty-free shops, *91*

Early Settlers
  Museum, *559*
Earth Exchange, *88*
East Point Reserve,
  418
Echo Point, *125*
Echuca, *227,
  229–231, 234–235*
Echuca Coachhouse
  and Carriage
  Collection, *230–231*
Elanora, *292*
Elderton Wines
  (winery), *379*
Electricity, *11*
Elizabeth Bay House,
  84
Ellery Creek Big Hole
  Scenic Reserve, *401*
El Questro Cattle
  Station and
  Wilderness Park,
  426–427
Embassies, high
  commissions, and
  consulates
  Auckland, *473*
  Canberra, *158, 162*
  North Island, *523*
  Sydney, *65*
Emergencies
  Adelaide, *356*
  Alice Springs, *393*
  Auckland, *473–474*
  Blue Mountains, *122*

Brisbane, *273*
Cairns, *307*
Canberra, *158*
Coromandel
  Peninsula, *498*
Darwin, *414*
Gold Coast, *289*
Gold Country, *218*
Goldfields, *465*
Great Barrier Reef,
  328
Hobart, *245*
Hunter Valley, *132*
Kimberley, *425*
Launceston, *256*
Melbourne, *178*
Melbourne region,
  205
Mossman, *314*
Napier, *517*
Nelson, *532*
New South Wales,
  122, 132, 138
North Coast, *138*
North Island, *490,
  517, 523*
Northeast Wineries,
  227
Perth, *440*
Port Douglas, *314*
Queensland, *273, 289,
  295–296, 307, 314*
Red Centre, *393, 403*
Rotorua, *506*
Rottnest, *456*
South Island, *532,
  542, 552, 557, 561*
Sunshine Coast,
  295–296
Sydney, *65*
Tasmania, *245, 256*
Victoria, *211, 218,
  227*
Western Australia,
  456, 460, 465
Erskine River Valley,
  211
Esplanade
  Cairns, *308*
  Melbourne, *187*
Ettamogah Pub, *296,
  298*
Eumundi, *300*
Eureka Museum, *219*
Everglades (gardens),
  125
Ewelme Cottage, *478*
Executive Office
  (Wellington), *527*
Explorers' Tree, *126*

Fairy penguins,
  208–209
Fannie Bay Gaol,
  417–418
Farm Cove, *68*
Farms, *127*
Ferries
  Auckland, *476, 479,
    480*
  North Island,
    493–494, 523
  Perth, *440*
  Queensland, *303–304*
  South Australia, *372*
  South Island, *533*
  Sydney, *64*
  Tasmania, *244,
    260–261*
  Western Australia,
    456
Festivals and seasonal
  events, *9–10*
Film and cameras, *18*
Film Archive, *159*
Finke Gorge National
  Park, *401*
Fiordland National
  Park, *532, 555*
First Presbyterian
  Church, *559*
Fishing,
  in Australia, *41–42*
  Brisbane, *279*
  Darwin, *420*
  Great Barrier Reef,
    *335, 336, 339, 342,
    346, 347, 348, 350*
  New South Wales,
    150
  in New Zealand,
    49–50
  North Island, *496,
    513*
  Queensland, *291–292,
    300*
  South Australia, *374*
  Tasmania, *248*
  tours, *5*
  Victoria, *215, 233*
Fitzroy Gardens, *184*
Fitzroy Island, *349*
Flagstaff Hill
  Maritime Village,
  214
Flats, *53–54*
Flea markets, *91*
Fleays Fauna Centre,
  291
Flinders Chase
  National Park,

386–387
Flinders Ranges
  National Park,
  387–388
Flinders Street
  Station, *180*
Florence Falls, *432*
Fogg Dam, *418*
Football,
  Australian-Rules
  Adelaide, *361*
  Hobart, *248*
  Melbourne, *190*
  Perth, *447*
  Sydney, *94*
  Tasmania, *248*
Forest Glen Deer
  Sanctuary and
  Wildlife Park, *298*
Fort Denison, *70, 75*
Four-wheel-drive
  tours, *573–575*
Fox glacier, *538*
Francis Burt Law
  Centre, *443*
Fraser Island
  guided tours, *304*
  hotels, *305–306*
  restaurants, *305–306*
  sightseeing, *304–305*
  transportation,
    303–304
Franz Josef (glacier),
  538
Fremantle, *456–458,
  459*
Fremantle Crocodile
  Park, *457*
Fremantle Museum,
  457
Fremantle Prison, *458*
Fremantle Railway
  Station, *457*
Freshwater Beach, *98*

Gannet colony,
  519–520
Garden Island, *68*
Gardens
  Adelaide, *359*
  Auckland, *478*
  Canberra, *163*
  Melbourne, *184–185*
  Melbourne region,
    206
  New South Wales,
    125, 126–127
  North Island,
    524–525
  Perth, *443*

Gardens *(continued)*
Rotorua, *510*
Sydney, *77, 83*
Tasmania, *247, 262*
Victoria, *220*
Gariwerd (national park), *237–238*
Gasoline, *38*
Gaunt's Clock, *180*
Gay and lesbian travelers, hints for, *30*
Geikie Gorge National Park, *425, 433–434*
General Post Office, (Melbourne), *180*
George Tindale Memorial Gardens, *206*
Gibb River Road, *428–429*
Gininderra, *164*
Glacier, *538*
Glasshouse Mountains, *296*
Glenelg, *359, 361*
Glen Helen Gorge National Park, *401*
Gleniffer, *139, 141*
Gliding
adventure vacations, *575–576*
New South Wales, *575*
South Australia, *384–385, 575–576*
Glowworm caves, *498, 507*
Glowworm Grotto, *507*
Golda's World of Dolls, *223*
Gold Coast, *288*
beaches, *43*
children, *291*
emergencies, *289*
guided tours, *289*
hotels, *292–294*
nightlife, *294*
restaurants, *290, 292–293*
shopping, *291*
sightseeing, *289–291*
sports, *291–292*
tourist information, *289*
transportation, *288–289*
Gold Country (Victoria), *218*

children, *222–223*
emergencies, *218*
guided tours, *218*
hotels, *223–225*
restaurants, *219, 223–225*
shopping, *223*
sightseeing, *218–225*
sports, *223*
tourist information, *218*
transportation, *218*
Golden Bay, *537*
Golden Dog (bush pub), *143*
Golden River Zoo, *232*
Goldfields region (Western Australia), *464–467*
Gold mines
Coromandel Peninsula, *498*
New South Wales, *143*
South Island, *553–554*
Victoria, *221, 222*
Western Australia, *466*
Gold Museum, *219*
Golf
Adelaide, *360*
Alice Springs, *397*
Auckland, *481–482*
in Australia, *42*
Brampton Island, *336*
Brisbane, *279*
Canberra, *165*
Darwin, *420*
Dunk Island, *347*
Lindeman Island, *337*
Melbourne, *189–190*
New South Wales, *134*
in New Zealand, *50*
Perth, *446*
Queensland, *292, 300*
Sydney, *93*
tours, *5*
Victoria, *215, 223, 233*
Gordon River Cruises, *263*
Government Gardens, *510*
Government House (Adelaide), *358*
Government House (Darwin), *416*

Government House (Perth), *443*
Government Tourist Offices, *2*
Govett's Leap Lookout, *126*
Grafton, *142*
Grampians National Park, *237–238*
Grant Burge Winery, *377*
Great Barrier Reef, *328*
Bedarra Island, *348–349*
Brampton Island, *336*
camping, *331*
children, attractions for, *337, 339*
Daydream Island, *342–343*
Dunk Island, *346–348*
emergencies, *328*
Fitzroy Island, *349*
Great Keppel Island, *334–336*
guided tours, *307, 330–331, 336, 339, 344, 346, 347, 348, 350*
Hamilton Island, *338–341*
Hayman Island, *343–345*
Heron Island, *333–334*
hotels, *331–332*
Lady Elliot Island, *332–333*
Lady Musgrave Island, *333*
Lindeman Island, *337*
Lizard Island, *349–351*
Long Island, *337–338*
Orpheus Island, *345–346*
restaurants, *331*
shopping, *339*
South Molle Island, *341–342*
tourist information, *328*
transportation, *328, 330*
Wilson Island, *333*
Great Keppel Island, *334–336*
Green Lake, *509*
Great Sandy National

Park, *305*
Greenway, Francis, *77, 78, 80, 81*
Greymouth, *538*
Griffin, Walter Burley, *156*
Grossman House, *133–134*
Gumnut Tea Garden, *77*

Hahei, *499, 501*
Hahndorf, *369*
Hahndorf Academy, *369*
Halfmoon Bay, *562*
Halls Creek, *429*
Hamersley Range National Park, *468*
Hamilton, *214*
Hamilton Island, *338–341*
Hanson Bay, *374*
Harbour Bridge Pylon, *76*
Harry's Café de Wheels, *87*
Hartley Creek Crocodile Farm, *317*
Hastings District Historical Museum, *139*
Hawke's Bay, *505, 517*
Hawke's Bay Art Gallery and Museum, *518*
Hawk's Crag, *537*
Hayman Island, *343–345*
Health, *19*
Henbury Meteorite Craters, *401*
Henty Sand Dunes, *262–263*
Hepburn Springs, *220, 225*
Hepburn Springs Mineral Spa, *220–221*
Hermannsburg, *401*
Heron Island, *333–334*
Hero of Waterloo (pub), *75*
Hidden Valley National Park, *425*
High commissions. *See* Embassies

High Court of Australia, *161*

Hiking,
adventure vacations, *567–570*
in Australia, *42*
Brisbane, *279*
Coromandel Peninsula, *498, 502*
New South Wales, *149, 567–568*
New Zealand, *50–51, 569–570*
South Island, *539, 562*
Tasmania, *248, 568–569*
Victoria, *237, 569*

His Majesty's Theatre, *444*

Historical Society Museum (Port Fairy), *214*

Historical Village, *384*

Historic Wharf (Echuca), *230*

History House, *78*

History of Australia books on, *31–32*

History of New Zealand books on, *32*

Hobart, *241*
the arts, *252–253*
children, *247*
climate, *8*
emergencies, *245*
guided tours, *245*
hotels, *250–252*
nightlife, *253*
restaurants, *247, 248–250*
shopping, *248*
sightseeing, *245–248*
sports, *248*
tourist information, *245*
transportation, *244*

Hobson Wharf, *480*

Hogan, Paul, *74*

Holy Trinity Church, *76*

Home and farm stays, *45–46, 53*

Home exchanges, *46*

Hopkins Falls, *215*

Horseback riding
adventure vacations, *576–577*
Melbourne, *190*

New South Wales, *149, 576–577*
South Island, *555*
tours, *5*
Victoria, *577*

Horse racing, *190–191*

Horticultural World, *141*

Hospitals, historic, *77, 79*

Hotel Darwin, *416*

Hotels. *See also under cities and areas*
in Australia, *45–46*
children's accommodations, *27*
disabilities, accommodations for travelers with, *28*
in New Zealand, *53–54*
tipping, *40, 48*

Hotwater Beach, *501*

Houseboats, *383*

House of Bottles, *299*

Houses, historic
Adelaide, *356, 358–359*
Auckland, *478*
Darwin, *416*
Melbourne, *184, 186, 207*
New South Wales, *123, 125, 133–134*
North Island, *493, 494*
South Australia, *378–379*
South Island, *536*
Sydney, *74, 75, 84–85*
Tasmania, *246*
Victoria, *207, 214, 219, 221, 222, 228*
Wellington, *525, 526*
Western Australia, *457, 458, 461–462*

Huka Falls, *511*

Hungerford Hill Wine Village, *133*

Hunter Valley, *67, 131*
children, *134*
emergencies, *132*
guided tours, *132*
hotels, *136–137*
nightlife, *137*
restaurants, *135–136*
shopping, *134*
sightseeing, *132–134*
sports, *134*

tourist information, *132*
transportation, *131–132*

Hunting, *51–52, 562*

Hutchings Antique Shop and Museum, *460*

Hyde Park Barracks, *80*

Hydro Majestic Hotel, *126*

Il Porcellino (statue), *80*

Indo Pacific Marine (ecosystem), *417*

Insurance, *19–21*

Isel Park, *536*

Isel House, *536*

Isle of the Dead, *254*

It's a Small World (museum), *445*

Jade Boulder Gallery, *538*

Jails
Alice Springs, *395*
Darwin, *417–418*
Melbourne, *182*
New South Wales, *139*
Tasmania, *247, 254*
Western Australia, *458, 461*

James Cook Memorial Museum, *319*

Jenolan Caves, *127*

Jim Jim Falls, *430*

Jindabyne, *148*

Jogging
Adelaide, *360*
Auckland, *482*
Canberra, *165*
Darwin, *420*
Melbourne, *190*
Perth, *446*
Sydney, *93*

John Flynn's Grave, *400*

John Seddon memorial, *525*

Joss House, *222*

Judge's Bay beach, *482*

Juniper Hall, *86*

Jupiter's Casino, *290*

Kaikoura, *549*

Kakadu National

Park, *429–431*

Kalgoorlie, *466, 467*

Kangaroo Island, *371–376*
beaches, *374*
children, *374*
guided tours, *372–373*
hotels, *375–376*
restaurants, *375*
sightseeing, *373–374*
sports, *374*
tourist information, *372*
transportaiton, *372*

Karri forests, *461*

Katherine Gorge National Park, *434–435*

Katherine Mansfield House, *526*

Katoomba, *122*

Kauaeranga Valley, *502*

Kauri trees, *491*

Kawarau Suspension Bridge, *554*

Keg Factory, *377*

Kelburn Cable Car, *524*

Kelly, Michael, *81*

Kelly Tarlton's Underwater World and Antarctic Encounter, *480*

Kestrel, *480*

Khancoban, *149*

the Kimberley, *410, 424*
emergencies, *425*
guided tours, *424*
hotels, *428–429*
restaurants, *427–428*
shopping, *427*
sightseeing, *425–427*
tourist information, *424–425*
transportation, *424*

King Cottage Museum, *460*

Kings Canyon, *401–402*

Kingscote, *373*

Kings Cross, *83–86*

King's Domain Gardens, *185*

Kiwi House, *520*

Koala Park Sanctuary (Sydney), *86*

Korora Bay, *141–142*

Kosciusko National Park, *147*

Kununurra, *424, 425, 427–428, 429*

Kuranda Scenic Railway, *307–308*

Ku-Ring-Gai Chase National Park, *154*

Lady Elliot Island, *332–333*

Lady Jane Beach, *43, 96*

Lady Knox Geyser, *511*

Lady Musgrave Island, *333*

Lady Norwood Rose Garden, *525*

Lake Matheson, *538–539*

Lake McKenzie, *305*

Lake Pertobe Adventure Playground, *215*

Lake Rotomahana, *506*

Lake Tarawera, *505, 506, 509*

Lake Taupo, *505, 511–512*

Lake Tekapo, *550*

Lake Waikaremoana, *520*

Lake Wendouree, *220*

Lambton Quay, *527*

Lamington National Park, *324–325*

Lands Department building, *78*

Language, *18–19*

Lanyon (homestead), *172*

Laptops, *18*

Larnach Castle, *559*

Launceston, *255*

the arts, *260*

children, *257*

emergencies, *256*

guided tours, *256*

hotels, *259–260*

nightlife, *260*

restaurants, *258–259*

shopping, *257–258*

sightseeing, *256–257*

sports, *258*

tourist information, *256*

transportation, *255–256*

Law Courts, *558*

Leisure World, *512*

Leura, *125*

Leuralla, *125*

Libraries

Adelaide, *358*

Canberra, *161*

Melbourne, *182, 183*

North Island, *526*

Sydney, *79*

Victoria, *228*

Light Horse Monument, *79*

Lighthouses

New South Wales, *142*

Victoria, *214*

Lindeman Island, *337*

Lindeman's Karadoc Winery (Murray region), *232*

Lindemans Winery (Hunter Valley), *133*

Litchfield National Park, *431–432*

Little Sahara (coastal area), *374*

Lizard Island, *349–351*

Locomotive engines, *360*

Logan's Beach, *215*

London Bridge (natural bridge), *208*

London Court, *444*

Lone Pine Koala Sanctuary, *277–278*

Long Island, *337–338*

Loop Line Railroad, *465*

"Lord of the Forest", *495*

Lorne, *211, 216*

Lost City, *432*

Loxton, *384*

Luggage, *11–12*

airline rules, *11–12*

insurance, *20*

Luna Park, *185*

Lyons Cottage, *414*

MacArthur Chambers, *274*

MacDonnell Ranges, *400–401*

Mackay, *330*

Mackenzie Country, *549–550*

Macleay, Alexander, *84*

Macquarie, Lachlan, *77, 78, 80–81*

Macquarie's Chair, *83*

Magic Mountain (amusement park), *359*

Magistrate's Court, *182*

Magnetic Termite Mounds, *432*

Mail

in Australia, *39*

in New Zealand, *48*

Maitland, *133*

Maitland City Art Gallery, *133*

Maldon, *221*

Manly Beach, *43, 98*

Mannum, *385*

The Mansions, *276–277*

Maoris, *473, 491, 493, 494, 505, 507, 509, 510, 512–513*

Marananga, *379*

Marble Bar, *87*

Margaret River (town), *460, 463–464*

Marina Mirage, *290*

Maritime Museum (Wellington), *527*

Maritime Museum of Tasmania, *246*

Marlborough

emergencies, *532*

guided tours, *533–534*

hotels, *540–541*

restaurants, *537, 539–540*

sightseeing, *534–539*

sports, *539*

tourist information, *532*

transportation, *533*

Marlborough Sounds, *534*

Maroochydore, *299, 301*

Maroubra Beach, *43, 97*

Masterton, *10*

Matakohe Kauri Museum, *495*

McDonald Winery, *519*

McRae Homestead, *207*

Megalong Valley Farm, *127*

Melbourne, *175–176*

the arts, *202–204*

Bourke Street Mall, *180*

children, *185*

climate, *8*

downtown area, *180–182*

emergencies, *178*

excursions, *205–210*

festivals, *9–10*

free attractions, *184–185*

guided tours, *178–179*

hotels, *187, 198–200*

nightlife, *204*

public transportation, *177*

restaurants, *182, 183, 186, 187, 191–198*

Royal Arcade, *180*

shopping, *180, 183, 186, 187–189*

sightseeing, *179–187*

sports, *189–191*

tourist information, *178, 205*

transportation, *176–178*

walking tours, *179*

Melbourne region, *205*

beaches, *207–209*

emergencies, *205*

guided tours, *205*

restaurants, *209–210*

sightseeing, *205–209*

tourist information, *205*

Melbourne Magistrate's Court, *182*

Melbourne Zoological Gardens, *185*

Menglers Hill, *378*

Mermaid Beach, *292*

Meteorite craters

Red Centre, *401*

Top End, *425*

Migration and Settlement Museum, *358*

Mildara Blass Winery, *232*

Mildura, *227, 231–232, 235*

Milford Sound, *555*

Military Museum (Darwin), *418*

Military Museum (Swan Hill), *231*

Mineral Springs
  Reserve, *221*
Mint Museum, *80*
Mission Bay beach,
  482
Mission Beach, *330*
Mission Creek Falls,
  318
Mission Vineyard,
  518–519
Mrs. Macquarie's
  Point, *83*
Monasteries, *471*
Money, *12–14, 474*
Monkey Mia, *470–471*
Montrose Cottage,
  219
Mooloolaba, *299*
Moonshine Valley
  Winery, *298*
Moran, Patrick, *81*
Morgan, *385*
Mornington
  Peninsula, *206–208,
  209–210*
Mornington Peninsula
  Arts Centre, *207*
Morpeth, *134*
Mort, Thomas, *78*
Mossman, *313, 314,
  317, 321*
Motels, *53*
Mott's Cottage, *214*
Motueka Valley, *537*
Mount Bledisloe, *493*
Mount Cook, *532,
  550*
Mount Cook National
  Park, *542, 550*
Mount Cook Village,
  550
Mount Field National
  Park, *265–266*
Mt. Kosciusko, *36, 149*
Mt. Lofty, *369*
Mt. Martha Beach,
  207
Mount Ruapehu, *505,
  512*
Mount Tarawera, *506,
  510*
Mount Tomah
  Botanic Garden,
  126–127
Mount Victoria
  (Auckland), *479*
Mount Wilson (town),
  126
Movies
Canberra, *159*

Echuca, *230*
Murbko, *385*
Murray Bridge
  (town), *385*
Murray Downs
  Homestead, *231*
Murray region
  (Victoria), *226–227.*
  See Northeast
  Wineries region
  (Victoria).
Murray River (New
  South Wales), *149*
Murray River region
  (South Australia),
  382–385
Murwillumbah, *143*
Museum of Arts and
  Sciences (Darwin),
  417
Museum of
  Childhood, *444–445*
Museum of Caves,
  507, 509
Museum of
  Contemporary Art
  (Sydney), *71, 88–89*
Museum of the
  Goldfields, *466*
Museum of Transport
  and Technology, *480*
Museum of Victoria,
  182
Museum of Western
  Australia, *444*
Museum of Western
  Australia Sport, *444*
Museums. *See also*
  Art galleries and
  museums; Wax
  museums
Adelaide, *356, 358,
  360*
Alice Springs, *394,
  395*
Auckland, *478, 480*
Brisbane, *277*
Canberra, *159*
Darwin, *414, 416,
  417, 418*
Launceston, *257*
Melbourne, *182,
  185–186*
New South Wales,
  139
North Island, *491,
  494, 495, 507, 509,
  518, 527*
Perth, *441, 443,
  444–445*

Queensland, *290, 299,
  308, 319*
Rotorua, *510*
South Australia, *379*
South Island, *536,
  544, 547, 549, 559*
Sydney, *71, 74, 75,
  80, 85, 88–89*
Tasmania, *245–247,
  257, 262*
Victoria, *214, 219,
  223, 228, 231*
Western Australia,
  *457–458, 460, 461,
  466*
Muttonbird Island,
  141

Nambung National
  Park, *468–469*
Nannup, *464*
Napier, *505, 517*
children, *520*
emergencies, *517*
guided tours, *517*
hotels, *522*
restaurants, *521–522*
sightseeing, *517–520*
tourist information,
  517
transportation, *517*
Napier Aquarium, *520*
Narryna Van
  Diemen's Land
  Memorial Folk
  Museum, *246–247*
National Automobile
  Museum of
  Tasmania, *257*
National Bank
  Building, *274*
National Botanic
  Gardens, *163*
National Capital
  Planning Exhibition,
  159, 161
National Film and
  Sound Archive, *159*
National Gallery of
  Victoria, *186*
National Library of
  Australia, *161*
National Library
  (New Zealand), *526*
National Science and
  Technology Centre,
  161
Nature reserves
Brisbane, *277*
Canberra area, *172*

Darwin, *418*
North Island, *491*
Queensland, *291, 298*
South Australia, *369,
  373–374*
Tasmania, *257*
Victoria, *205, 207,
  215*
Nelson, *532, 534, 536*
Nelson Lakes
  National Park, *534*
Nelson Provincial
  Museum, *536*
New Norcia, *471*
Newport Beach, *98*
New South Wales,
  119. See also Sydney
adventure vacations,
  *566, 567–568, 570,
  572, 573, 575,
  576–577*
Blue Mountains
  region, *119, 122–131*
Hunter Valley,
  131–137
north coast, *137–147*
parks, national, *141,
  148, 153–154*
Snowy Mountains,
  147–153
New South Wales
  north coast, *137–138*
beaches, *139, 141–142*
children, *143*
emergencies, *138*
guided tours, *138*
hotels, *145–147*
nightlife, *147*
restaurants, *139,
  144–145*
shopping, *143–144*
sightseeing, *138–139,
  141–143*
sports, *144*
tourist information,
  138
transportation, *138*
Nga Toki
  Matawhaoru, *493*
Nielsen Park, *96*
Nightlife. *See under
  cities and areas*
Ningaloo Reef Maine
  Park, *471*
Nitmiluk (Katherine
  Gorge) National
  Park, *434–435*
Nolan Gallery, *172*
Noosa Heads,
  298–299, 302

Noosaville, *299*
Norman Lindsay
 Gallery, *123*
Northeast Wineries
 region (Victoria),
 226–227
children, *233*
emergencies, *227*
guided tours, *227*
hotels, *233–236*
restaurants, *233–236*
sightseeing, *227–233*
sports, *233*
tourist information,
 227
transportation, *227*
Northern Territory.
 See Red Centre; Top
 End
North Island, *473*,
 489–490
beaches, *52*
children, *495*
emergencies, *490*
guided tours, *490*
hotels, *497–498*
restaurants, *496–497*
sightseeing, *490–495*
sports, *495–496*
tourist information,
 490
transportation, *490*
Nourlangie Rock, *430*
Nude beaches, *43*
"Nut" (rock
 formation), *262*

the Observatory
 (Brisbane), *276*
the Observatory
 (Sydney), *75*
Observatory Hill
 (Sydney), *75*
Old Admiralty House,
 416
Old Butter Factory,
 460
Old Commissariat
 Store, *276*
Old Court House
 (Alice Springs), *395*
Older travelers, hints
 for, *29–30*
Old Farm, Strawberry
 Hill, *461–462*
Old Fire Station
 (Perth), *441, 443*
Old Gaol (Albany),
 461
Old Ghan train, *396*

Old Hartley Street
 School, *395*
Old Halls Creek, *425*
Old Melbourne Gaol,
 182
Old Mill (Perth), *444*
Old Parliament House
 (Adelaide), *358*
Old Parliament House
 (Canberra), *161*
Old Perth Boys
 School, *443*
Old Police Station
 and Court House
 (Darwin), *416*
Old St. Paul's
 Cathedral, *526*
Old Settlement Craft
 Village, *461*
Old Treasury
 Building (Adelaide),
 356, 358
Old Treasury
 Building
 (Melbourne), *183*
Old Windmill, *276*
the Olgas (rock
 formation), *402–408*
"Olivewood"
 (homestead), *384*
Olveston, *559*
Omell Manyung
 Gallery, *207*
Opal mines, *317*
Opal shops, *92–93*,
 279
Opera
Auckland, *488*
Melbourne, *203*
Perth, *455*
Sydney, *82–83, 115*
Opononi, *495*
Orakei Korako, *511*
Orchards, *384*
Ormiston Gorge and
 Pound National
 Park, *401*
Orpheus Island,
 345–346
Otago Peninsula, *552*,
 557–561
Otway National Park,
 211
Outback Opal Mine,
 317
Overland Track, *266*
Overland Telegraph
 Memorial, *414*

Package deals, *5–6*

Packing, *11–12*
Paddy Hannan statue,
 466
Paihia, *489–490, 491*,
 496, 497
Palace Gates, *78*
Palace Hotel, *443*
Palm Beach, *98–99*
Palm Cove, *315*,
 321–322
Palm Valley, *401*
Pancake rocks, *538*
Panorama Guth (art
 gallery), *395*
Paparoa National
 Park, *538*
Parakeet Bay, *458*
Parks, national
New South Wales,
 141, 148, 153–154
North Island, *505*,
 512, 520
Queensland, *305*,
 317–318, 319,
 323–326
Red Centre, *400–401*,
 403–404
South Australia,
 373–374, 385–388
South Island, *533*,
 537, 538, 542, 550,
 555
Tasmania, *264–267*
Top End, *425*,
 429–435
Victoria, *236–239*
Western Australia,
 467–470
Parliament Buildings
 (Wellington),
 526–527
Parliament House
 (Brisbane), *277*
Parliament House
 (Canberra), *162*
Parliament House
 (Hobart), *246*
Parliament House
 (Perth), *443*
Parnell Village,
 478–479
Passports, *15–16*
Pearls, *426*
Pelican Point, *207*
Pemberton, *461*
Penguin (town), *261*
Penguins, *208–209*
Penny Royal World
 and Gunpowder Mill,
 257

Peregian Beach, *303*
Performing Arts
 Museum, *185–186*
Perisher Valley
 (resort), *148*
Perth, *437, 439*
the arts, *455*
beaches, *43, 446*
children, *444–445*
emergencies, *440*
guided tours, *441*
hotels, *452–454*
nightlife, *455–456*
restaurants, *447–452*
shopping, *445–446*
sightseeing, *441–445*
sports, *446–447*
tourist information,
 440
transportation, *439–440*
Perth Cultural
 Centre, *444*
Pet Porpoise Pool, *143*
Pevensey (riverboat),
 231
Pfeiffer Wines
 (winery), *229*
Phillip, Arthur, *61*
Phillip Island, *208–209*
Photographers, tips
 for, *18*
Piccaninny Creek,
 432–433
Piha beach, *482*
Pile Valley, *305*
Pinnacles, *305*
Pioneer Cottage
 (Mildura), *232*
Plane travel
Adelaide, *354*
airlines and airports,
 32–33
airlines, Australia,
 36–37
airlines, domestic,
 36–37
airlines, New
 Zealand, *47*
Alice Springs, *392*
Auckland, *474*
Brisbane, *272*
Canberra, *157*
children, *26*
cutting costs, *33–34*,
 35
Darwin, *411*
disabilities, travelers
 with, *28*
distances and flying
 times, *33*

Plane travel
(continued)
enjoying the flight,
34–35
flight-cancellation
insurance, 20
Great Barrier Reef,
332, 335, 336, 339,
342, 346, 347, 350
the Kimberley, 424
luggage, 11–12, 20
Melbourne, 176–177
Napier, 517
New South Wales,
132, 138, 147
from North America,
32–35
North Island, 517,
523
Perth, 439
Queensland, 272, 289,
295, 303, 307
Red Centre, 392, 402
Rotorua, 506
smoking, 35, 37, 47
South Australia, 372
South Island, 533,
542, 552, 557, 561
Sydney, 62
Tasmania, 244, 255,
261, 265
from United
Kingdom, 35
Western Australia,
456, 460, 465
Pohutu geyser, 509
Point Piper, 69
**Polly Woodside
Maritime Park,** 187
Polynesian Pools,
510–511
Pompallier House,
494
Popcorn Factory, 278
Port Arthur, 253–255
**Port Arthur Penal
Settlement,** 254
**Port Campbell
National Park,** 214,
236
Port Dock Station,
360
Port Douglas, 313,
317
emergencies, 314
guided tours, 314,
330
hotels, 322–323
restaurants, 322
shopping, 320

sightseeing, 317
Port Fairy, 214,
216–217
Port Macquarie, 139
Powerhouse Museum,
89
Premier House, 526
***Puffing Billy* steam
train,** 205
**Purnululu National
Park,** 425, 432–433

Quarantine Station,
70
Queensland, 269, 272.
See also Brisbane
adventure vacations,
566, 571, 574, 579
Cairns, 306–312
Fraser Island,
303–306
Gold Coast, 288–294
north from Cairns,
313–323
parks, national, 305,
317–318, 319,
323–326
Sunshine Coast,
294–303
**Queensland Cultural
Centre,** 277
**Queensland Reptile
and Fauna Park,** 300
Queenstown, 532
climate, 8
emergencies, 552
guided tours, 552
hotels, 556–567
restaurants, 556
sightseeing, 552–555
sports, 555–556
tourist information,
552
transportation, 552
Queenstown Gardens,
553
**Queen Charlotte
Drive,** 534
**Queen Victoria
Museum,** 257
Quokkas, 458

Rafting. *See*
Canoeing and
rafting
Rail passes, 23–24
Railroads
Coromandel
Peninsula, 501
New South Wales,

126, 127
New Zealand, 512
Queensland, 295,
307–308
Red Centre, 396
Tasmania, 254
Victoria, 205, 223
Western Australia,
465
**Railway Station
Museum,** 466
Rainbow Springs, 512
Rain forest tours,
138, 315
**Raintree Aboriginal
Art Gallery,** 419
R & I Tower, 443
Rapaura Falls, 499
Red Centre, 390. *See
also* Alice Springs;
Ayers Rock; the
Olgas
MacDonnell Ranges,
400–401
parks, national,
400–401, 403–404
Red Gum Works, 230
Regional Art Gallery
(Hamilton), 214
**Rehwinkel's Animal
Park,** 164
Renmark, 384
The Residency (Alice
Springs), 395
Residency Museum
(Albany), 461
Restaurants. *See also
under cities and
areas*
in Australia, 43–45
children, 26–27
in New Zealand, 53
tipping, 40, 48
Richmond, Tasmania,
247–248
**Ripley's Believe It or
Not Museum,** 290
Rippon Lea (stately
home), 186
Riverboat rides
Rotorua, 507
South Australia,
383–384
Victoria, 231, 232
**Riverland Display
Centre,** 384
**Robert McDougall
Art Gallery,** 544
Rockford Winery, 377
Rose Bay, 69

Rotorua, 505
children, 512
emergencies, 506
guided tours,
506–507
hotels, 515–516
restaurants, 513–515
sightseeing, 507–513
sports, 513
tourist information,
505
transportation, 506
Rottnest Island, 456,
458, 459
Rottnest Museum, 458
Round House, 457
**Royal Australasian
College of
Physicians,** 78–79
**Royal Australian
Mint,** 163
**Royal Botanic
Gardens**
(Melbourne),
184–185
**Royal Botanic
Gardens** (Sydney),
83, 86
**Royal Flying Doctor
Service,** 395
Royal Hotel, 85
Royal National Park,
153–154
**Royal Tasmanian
Botanical Gardens,**
247
Rugby
Brisbane, 279
Hobart, 248
Sydney, 94
Rusa Park Deer Stud,
134
Russell, 490, 493–494,
495, 496, 497
**Russell Falls Nature
Walk,** 266
Rutherglen, 227, 229,
235, 236

Sailing. *See* Boating
and sailing
Sails Museum, 458
St. Faith's, 512–513
**St. George's
Cathedral,** 443
St. James Church
(Sydney), 80, 81
**St. John's Anglican
Cathedral**
(Brisbane), 274

St. John's Anglican Church (Fremantle), *457*

St. John the Baptist Church and Schoolhouse, *163*

St. Kilda, *187*

St. Mary's Cathedral (Perth), *443*

St. Mary's Cathedral (Sydney), *81*

St. Mary's Pony Farm, *215*

St. Michael and All Saints Anglican Church, *543–544*

St. Patrick's Cathedral (Melbourne), *184*

St. Paul's Cathedral, *180*

St. Peter's Church (Melbourne), *184*

St. Stephen's Church, *274*

St. Thomas Church, *139*

Salamanca Place, *246*

Samson House, *458*

Sanctuary Cove, *290*

Scenic Railway, *126*

Schoolhouses, *395–396, 443*

School of the Air, *395–396*

Scitech Discovery Centre, *445*

Scott, Robert Falcon (statue), *543*

Scuba diving. *See Water sports*

Sea Kayaking, *571–572*

Seal Bay Conservation Park, *373–374*

Seaworld, *290*

Self-catering apartments, *45*

Seppelts Winery, *379*

Serpentine Gorge, *401*

Seven Spirit Bay, *419*

Shantytown, *538*

Sharp's Movie House and Penny Arcade, *230*

Shelly Beach, *97–98*

Sherbrooke Forest, *205*

Ship travel
  Great Barrier Reef, *328, 330–331, 334, 335, 336, 337, 339, 342, 344, 346, 347, 348, 350*
  Sydney, *63*

Shopping. *See also under cities and areas*
  business hours, *40, 48*
  department stores, *90, 180, 188*
  duty-free shops, *91*
  flea markets, *91*
  tips on, *40, 48–49*

Shrine of Memories, *274*

Shrine of Remembrance (Brisbane), *274*

Sikh Temple, *142*

Simpsons Gap National Park, *400*

Skiing,
  adventure vacations, *572–573*
  in Australia, *42*
  New South Wales, *149, 150, 572*
  New Zealand, *52, 573*
  Tasmania, *248*
  Victoria, *238, 572–573*

Skyline Gondola, *553*

Small Winemakers Centre, *133*

Smiggin Holes (resort), *148*

Smithton, *262, 263, 264*

Snellings Beach, *374*

Snorkeling. *See Water sports*

Snowy Mountains, *147–153*
  children, *149*
  guided tours, *148*
  hotels, *151–152*
  nightlife, *152–153*
  restaurants, *150*
  shopping, *149*
  sightseeing, *148–149*
  sports, *149–150*
  tourist information, *147*
  transportation, *147*

Soccer
  Hobart, *248*
  Melbourne, *191*

Sorrento Beach, *208*

Sorrento Marine Aquarium, *208*

Southern Alps, *542*

South African Embassy, *162*

South African War Memorial, *358*

South Australia, *353.* *See also* Adelaide
  Adelaide Hills, *368–371*
  adventure vacations, *571, 574, 575–576, 578*
  Barossa Valley, *376–382*
  Kangaroo Island, *371–376*
  Murray River area, *382–385*
  parks, national, *385–388*

South Australian Maritime Museum, *360*

South Australian Museum, *358*

South Bank Parklands (urban park), *277*

South Island, *532*
  Christchurch and Canterbury, *542–552*
  emergencies, *532, 542, 552, 557, 561*
  excursions, *547, 549–552*
  festivals, *10*
  guided tours, *533–534, 543, 553, 558, 561*
  hotels, *540–541, 546–547, 549, 556–557, 561, 562*
  Marlborough, Nelson, and the West Coast, *532–541*
  restaurants, *537, 539–540, 545, 546, 556, 560–561, 562*
  shopping, *545*
  sightseeing, *534–539, 543–545, 553–555, 558–560, 562*
  Southland, Otago, and Steward Island, *552–562*
  sports, *539, 555–556, 562*

tourist information, *532, 542, 552, 557, 561*

transportation, *533, 542–543, 552, 557–558, 561*

Southland, *552*

South Molle Island, *341–342*

Southport, *292–293*

Southward Museum, *527*

Southwest National Park, *265*

Sovereign Hill Historical Park, *219, 223*

Space stations, *172–173*

Speakers' Corner, *86*

Spencer and Gillen Gallery, *394*

Spit, *290*

Sporting Lodges, *54*

Sports. *See also specific sports; under cities and areas*
  Australia, *41–43*
  New Zealand, *49–52*

Springwood, *123*

Standley Chasm, *400–401*

Stanley, *262, 263, 264*

State Houses of Parliament (Melbourne), *183–184*

State Library
  Melbourne, *182*
  Sydney, *79*

State Parliament House (Sydney), *79*

Stewart Island, *532*
  emergencies, *561*
  guided tours, *561*
  hotels, *562*
  restaurants, *562*
  sightseeing, *562*
  sports, *562*
  tourist information, *561*
  transportation, *561*

Stirling Range National Park, *470*

Stokes Hill Wharf, *416*

Stone flour mill, *369*

Strahan, *263–264*

Strehlow Research Centre, *396*

Stuart Town Gaol, *395*

Student and youth travel, *24–25*

discount cards, *25*

hostels, *25*

travel agencies, *25*

Sugar mills, *143*

Sunshine Coast, *295*

children, *299–300*

emergencies, *295–296*

guided tours, *296*

hotels, *301–303*

nightlife, *303*

restaurants, *301–303*

shopping, *300*

sightseeing, *296, 298–300*

sports, *300*

tourist information, *295*

transportation, *295*

Supreme Court Gardens, *443*

Surfers Paradise, *290, 293–294*

Surfing. *See* Water sports

Survivor's Lookout, *416*

Swan Hill, *227, 231, 235–236*

Swan Hill Military Museum, *231*

Swan Hill Pioneer Settlement, *231*

Swan Reach, *385*

Swanbourne (beach), *43*

Sydney, *61–62*

Argyle Place, *76*

Arthur McElhone Reserve (park), *84*

the arts, *86, 87, 114–115*

Atherden Street, *74*

beaches, *43, 94–99*

boat tours, *66*

bus tours, *66*

buses, *62, 63, 64*

children, attractions for, *86–87*

Circular Quay, *74*

climate, *7*

consulates, *65*

Darling Harbour, *89*

emergencies, *65*

ferry system, *64*

festivals, *9*

free attractions, *86*

guided tours, *66*

history of, *61–62*

hotels, *110–114*

Kings Cross area, *83–86, 115*

limousines, *62, 64*

Macquarie Place, *78*

Macquarie Street, *77–82*

Macquarie's Point, *83*

monorail, *64*

nightlife, *115–117*

Nurses Walk, *77*

Observatory Hill, *75*

Paddington area, *83–86*

restaurants, *76, 77, 80, 86, 87, 99–110*

The Rocks area, *71, 74–77*

Shadforth Street, *85*

shopping, *76, 90–93*

sightseeing, *67–90*

sports, *93–94*

Suez Canal (street), *77*

Sydney Harbour, *68–71*

tank stream, *71*

taxis, *62, 64*

tourist information, *65*

transportation in, *63–65*

travel agencies, *65*

walking tours, *67*

Sydney Aquarium, *86–87*

Sydney Cove, *68*

Sydney Harbour Bridge, *74, 93*

Sydney Hospital, *79*

Sydney Opera House, *82–83, 115*

Sydney Tower, *89–90*

Taiaroa Head, *559–560*

Tamarama Beach, *97*

Tane Mahuta (tree), *495*

Taranna, *255*

Taronga Park Zoo, *87*

Tasman, Abel, *79*

Tasman Glacier, *550–551*

Tasmania, *241. See also* Hobart; Launceston

adventure vacations, *566–567, 568–569, 578*

northwest coast, *260–264*

parks, national, *264–267*

Port Arthur, *253–255*

Tasmania northwest coast, *260*

guided tours, *261*

hotels, *264*

restaurants, *263–264*

shopping, *263*

sightseeing, *261–263*

tourist information, *261*

transportation, *260–261*

Tasmanian Devil Park, *255*

Tasmanian Museum and Art Gallery, *245–246*

Taupo, *505, 511–512*

Taupo Volcanic Zone, *505*

Taxes, *14*

Taxi travel

Adelaide, *354, 355*

Alice Springs, *392*

Auckland, *475*

Canberra, *158*

Darwin, *414*

disabilities, travelers with, *28*

Hobart, *244*

Melbourne, *177*

Red Centre, *403*

Sydney, *62*

Teewah Coloured Sands, *299*

Telecom Tower, *159*

Telegraph Station Historical Reserve, *395*

Telephones

Australia, *38–39*

New Zealand, *48*

Tennis, *42*

Adelaide, *361*

Alice Springs, *397*

Auckland, *482*

Brisbane, *279*

Canberra, *165*

Darwin, *420*

Great Barrier Reef, *334, 335, 336, 337, 339, 340, 342, 344, 346, 347, 348*

Hamilton Island, *340*

Melbourne, *190, 191*

Perth, *446*

professional, *191*

Sunshine Coast, *300*

Sydney, *93–94*

tour, *5*

Victoria, *223*

Territory Wildlife Park, *418*

Te Wairoa, *510*

Tewantin, *299*

Thames, *498*

Theater

Auckland, *476, 488*

Canberra, *171*

Darwin, *423*

Melbourne, *183, 184, 203–204*

North Island, *530*

Perth, *444, 455*

Sydney, *115, 117*

Tasmania, *253, 260*

Thredbo Valley Trout Springs, *149*

Thredbo Village, *148–149*

Three Sisters (sandstone pillars), *125*

Tiagarra Aboriginal Cultural and Art Centre, *261*

Tidbinbilla Nature Reserve, *172*

Tidbinbilla Space Tracking Station, *172–173*

Timbertown (theme park), *143*

Tinakori Road, *525–526*

Tipping

Australia, *40*

New Zealand, *48*

Tjapukai Dance Theatre, *309*

Tjaynera Falls, *432*

Tolmer Falls, *432*

Tom Groggin, *149*

Tongariro National Park, *505, 512*

Top End, *410. See also* Darwin; the Kimberley

adventure vacations, *570–571, 573–574*

parks, national, *425, 429–435*

Torquay, *211*

Torrens Gorge, *369*

Tour groups, *3–5*

Tourist cabins, *53–54*

Tourist information, *2. See also under cities and areas*

Tower Hill State Game Reserve, *215*

Townsville, *330–331*

Train travel. *See also Railroads*

Adelaide, *355*

Alice Springs, *392*

Auckland, *475*

Brisbane, *273*

Canberra, *157*

disabilities, travelers with, *28*

information and reservations, *37*

interstate trains, *37*

Melbourne, *177*

New South Wales, *122*

New Zealand, *47*

North Island, *523*

Perth, *439*

Queensland, *273, 295, 307*

rail passes, *23–24*

South Island, *533*

Sydney, *62–63, 64*

Victoria, *218*

Western Australia, *456, 465*

Tramstop, *300*

Tram travel, *355*

Traveler's checks, *12*

Treasury Building (Brisbane), *276*

Treasury Building (Sydney), *78*

Treaty House, *493*

Treaty of Waitangi, *10, 489, 491, 493*

Trevallyn Dam, *257*

Trial Bay Gaol, *139*

Tuart forest, *460*

Tudor Court, *247*

Tunnel Creek, *426*

Twelve Apostles, *214*

Twin Falls, *430–431*

Ubirr Rock, *430*

Uluru National Park, *402*

Ulva Island, *562*

Ulverston, *264*

Undarra Lava Tubes, *309*

Underwater World (Mooloolaba), *299*

Underwater World (Perth), *445*

U.S. Government travel briefings, *2–3*

Urewera National Park, *520*

Utzon, Joern, *82–83*

Valley of the Winds, *405*

Vaucluse, *69*

Verona Vineyard, *133*

Victoria, *175. See also Melbourne*

adventure vacations, *569, 571–573, 577, 578–579*

Gold Country, *218–225*

Melbourne environs, *205–210*

Murray River, *226–236*

Northeast Wineries, *226–236*

parks, national, *214, 236–238*

west coast region, *210–218*

Victoria Barracks, *84–85*

Victorian Arts Centre, *185*

Victoria Hotel, *417*

Victoria Square (Adelaide), *356*

Victoria west coast, *210*

children, *215*

emergencies, *211*

guided tours, *210*

hotels, *216–218*

restaurants, *216–218*

shopping, *215*

sightseeing, *211, 214–215*

sports, *215–216*

tourist information, *210–211*

transportation, *210*

Videotape, *18*

Vintage Talking Tram, *222*

Visas, *15–16*

Vivonne Bay, *374*

Volcanos, *510, 512*

Voyage to Discovery museum, *219*

Waiheke, *482*

Waikerie, *384–385*

Waimangu Thermal Valley, *506*

Waiotapu, *511*

Waipoua State Forest, *495*

Wairaka, *507*

Wairakai Geothermal Project, *511*

Waitangi, *10*

Waitangi National Reserve, *491*

Waitemata Harbour, *479*

Waitomo Caves, *505, 507, 509*

Waitomo Caves Village, *507, 509*

Wanggoolba Creek, *305*

Wangi Falls, *432*

Warders' Quarters, *457*

Warkworth, *491*

Warkworth Museum, *491*

Warner Bros. Movie World, *289–290*

Warrawong Sanctuary, *369*

Warriewood Beach, *98*

Warrnambool, *214, 215, 217*

Waterfalls

New South Wales, *125*

New Zealand, *511*

Top End, *430, 432*

Victoria, *211, 215*

Water-skiing. *See Water sports*

Water sports, *42–43. See also Boating and sailing; Canoeing and rafting; Fishing*

Auckland, *482*

Coromandel Peninsula, *498–499*

Darwin, *420*

Great Barrier Reef, *332, 334, 335, 336, 337, 339–340, 342, 344, 346, 347, 348, 350*

New South Wales, *144*

Perth, *447*

Queensland, *300, 310*

scuba tours, *5, 496*

surfing competitions, *94*

Sydney, *94*

Tasmania, *248*

waterski races, *233*

Watson's Bay, *69–70*

Waverly Woollen Mills, *257*

Wax museums, *231*

WA Maritime Museum, *457–458*

Weather information, *6–9*

Wellington, *505, 522–523*

arts, *530*

embassies, *523*

emergencies, *523*

festival, *10*

guided tours, *524*

hotels, *529*

nightlife, *530*

restaurants, *527–529*

sightseeing, *524–527*

tourist information, *523*

transportation, *523–524*

travel agencies, *523*

Wentworth Falls, *125*

West Coast, *532*

West Coast Pioneers' Memorial Museum, *262*

West Coast Yacht Charters, *263*

Western Australia, *437, 439. See also Perth*

adventure vacations, *574–575*

children, *462*

emergencies, *456, 460, 465*

Fremantle and Rottnest Island, *456–459*

Goldfields region, *464–467*

guided tours, *457, 460, 465*

hotels, *463–464, 467, 468, 469, 470*

parks, national, *467–470*

restaurants, *457, 459, 462–463, 467*

sightseeing, *457, 460–462, 466–467*

the Southwest,

Western Australia
(continued)
460–464
tourist information,
456, 460, 465, 468,
469, 470
transportation, *456,*
460, 465, 468, 469,
470
Western Union, *13*
Westland National
Park, *538*
Westpac Banking
Museum, *74*
Wet 'n' Wild
(amusement park),
291
Whakarewarewa, *509*
Whale watching, *142,*
215, 304, 441, 549
Whangarei, *491*
Whare Runanga, *493*
Whatipu beach, *482*
Whiteman Park, *445*

Whitsunday Islands.
See Great Barrier
Reef
Wildlife tours, *5*
Wild World (wildlife
park), *315*
Wilson Island, *333*
Wilson's Promontory
National Park, *239*
Windjana Gorge, *426*
Windmills, *276*
Windsurfing. *See*
Water sports
Wine Country, *See*
also Northeast
Wineries region
(Victoria)
Wineries
Napier, *519*
New South Wales,
132–133
North Island, *519*
Queensland, *298*
South Australia, *377,*

379, 384
tours of, *5, 441*
Victoria, *226–227,*
229, 232
Western Australia,
461
Wines, *44–45*
Wintergardens, *478*
Wolfe Creek Meteorite
Crater, *425*
Wollombi, *134*
Woolgoolga, *142*
Woolsthorpe, *217–218*
Workingman's Club,
232
World Heritage
Cruises, *263*
World in Wax
Museum, *231*
World War II Storage
Tunnels, *416*
Writers in the Park
(readings), *87*
Wunta Fiesta, *214*

Wyndham, *425*

Yallingup Caves, *460*
Yester Grange
(house), *123, 125*
York, *471*
York Motor Museum,
471
Youth hostels, *25*

Zeehan, *262*
Zig Zag Railway, *127*
Zoological Gardens
(Adelaide), *359*
Zoos
Adelaide, *359*
Canberra, *164*
Melbourne, *185*
Queensland, *277–278*
Sydney, *87*
Victoria, *232*

Personal Itinerary

Departure *Date*

Time

Transportation

Arrival *Date* *Time*

Departure *Date* *Time*

Transportation

Accommodations

Arrival *Date* *Time*

Departure *Date* *Time*

Transportation

Accommodations

Arrival *Date* *Time*

Departure *Date* *Time*

Transportation

Accommodations

Personal Itinerary

Arrival *Date*   *Time*

Departure *Date*   *Time*

Transportation

Accommodations

Arrival *Date*   *Time*

Departure *Date*   *Time*

Transportation

Accommodations

Arrival *Date*   *Time*

Departure *Date*   *Time*

Transportation

Accommodations

Arrival *Date*   *Time*

Departure *Date*   *Time*

Transportation

Accommodations

Personal Itinerary

Arrival *Date*   *Time*

Departure *Date*   *Time*

Transportation

Accommodations

Arrival *Date*   *Time*

Departure *Date*   *Time*

Transportation

Accommodations

Arrival *Date*   *Time*

Departure *Date*   *Time*

Transportation

Accommodations

Arrival *Date*   *Time*

Departure *Date*   *Time*

Transportation

Accommodations

Personal Itinerary

Arrival *Date*   *Time*

Departure *Date*   *Time*

Transportation

Accommodations

Arrival *Date*   *Time*

Departure *Date*   *Time*

Transportation

Accommodations

Arrival *Date*   *Time*

Departure *Date*   *Time*

Transportation

Accommodations

Arrival *Date*   *Time*

Departure *Date*   *Time*

Transportation

Accommodations

Personal Itinerary

Arrival *Date* *Time*

Departure *Date* *Time*

Transportation

Accommodations

Arrival *Date* *Time*

Departure *Date* *Time*

Transportation

Accommodations

Arrival *Date* *Time*

Departure *Date* *Time*

Transportation

Accommodations

Arrival *Date* *Time*

Departure *Date* *Time*

Transportation

Accommodations

Personal Itinerary

Arrival *Date*   *Time*

Departure *Date*   *Time*

Transportation

Accommodations

Arrival *Date*   *Time*

Departure *Date*   *Time*

Transportation

Accommodations

Arrival *Date*   *Time*

Departure *Date*   *Time*

Transportation

Accommodations

Arrival *Date*   *Time*

Departure *Date*   *Time*

Transportation

Accommodations

Personal Itinerary

Arrival	*Date*	*Time*
Departure	*Date*	*Time*
Transportation		
Accommodations		

Arrival	*Date*	*Time*
Departure	*Date*	*Time*
Transportation		
Accommodations		

Arrival	*Date*	*Time*
Departure	*Date*	*Time*
Transportation		
Accommodations		

Arrival	*Date*	*Time*
Departure	*Date*	*Time*
Transportation		
Accommodations		

Addresses

Name	*Name*
Address	*Address*
Telephone	*Telephone*
Name	*Name*
Address	*Address*
Telephone	*Telephone*
Name	*Name*
Address	*Address*
Telephone	*Telephone*
Name	*Name*
Address	*Address*
Telephone	*Telephone*
Name	*Name*
Address	*Address*
Telephone	*Telephone*
Name	*Name*
Address	*Address*
Telephone	*Telephone*
Name	*Name*
Address	*Address*
Telephone	*Telephone*
Name	*Name*
Address	*Address*
Telephone	*Telephone*

Addresses

Name	*Name*
Address	*Address*
Telephone	*Telephone*
Name	*Name*
Address	*Address*
Telephone	*Telephone*
Name	*Name*
Address	*Address*
Telephone	*Telephone*
Name	*Name*
Address	*Address*
Telephone	*Telephone*
Name	*Name*
Address	*Address*
Telephone	*Telephone*
Name	*Name*
Address	*Address*
Telephone	*Telephone*
Name	*Name*
Address	*Address*
Telephone	*Telephone*
Name	*Name*
Address	*Address*
Telephone	*Telephone*

Addresses

Name	*Name*
Address	*Address*
Telephone	*Telephone*
Name	*Name*
Address	*Address*
Telephone	*Telephone*
Name	*Name*
Address	*Address*
Telephone	*Telephone*
Name	*Name*
Address	*Address*
Telephone	*Telephone*
Name	*Name*
Address	*Address*
Telephone	*Telephone*
Name	*Name*
Address	*Address*
Telephone	*Telephone*
Name	*Name*
Address	*Address*
Telephone	*Telephone*
Name	*Name*
Address	*Address*
Telephone	*Telephone*

Addresses

Name	*Name*
Address	*Address*
Telephone	*Telephone*
Name	*Name*
Address	*Address*
Telephone	*Telephone*
Name	*Name*
Address	*Address*
Telephone	*Telephone*
Name	*Name*
Address	*Address*
Telephone	*Telephone*
Name	*Name*
Address	*Address*
Telephone	*Telephone*
Name	*Name*
Address	*Address*
Telephone	*Telephone*
Name	*Name*
Address	*Address*
Telephone	*Telephone*
Name	*Name*
Address	*Address*
Telephone	*Telephone*

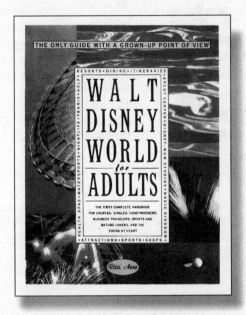

Fodor's Travel Guides

Available at bookstores everywhere, or call 1–800–533–6478, 24 hours a day.

U.S. Guides

Alaska

Arizona

Boston

California

Cape Cod, Martha's Vineyard, Nantucket

The Carolinas & the Georgia Coast

Chicago

Colorado

Florida

Hawaii

Las Vegas, Reno, Tahoe

Los Angeles

Maine, Vermont, New Hampshire

Maui

Miami & the Keys

New England

New Orleans

New York City

Pacific North Coast

Philadelphia & the Pennsylvania Dutch Country

The Rockies

San Diego

San Francisco

Santa Fe, Taos, Albuquerque

Seattle & Vancouver

The South

The U.S. & British Virgin Islands

USA

The Upper Great Lakes Region

Virginia & Maryland

Waikiki

Walt Disney World and the Orlando Area

Washington, D.C.

Foreign Guides

Acapulco, Ixtapa, Zihuatanejo

Australia & New Zealand

Austria

The Bahamas

Baja & Mexico's Pacific Coast Resorts

Barbados

Berlin

Bermuda

Brittany & Normandy

Budapest

Canada

Cancún, Cozumel, Yucatán Peninsula

Caribbean

China

Costa Rica, Belize, Guatemala

The Czech Republic & Slovakia

Eastern Europe

Egypt

Euro Disney

Europe

Florence, Tuscany & Umbria

France

Germany

Great Britain

Greece

Hong Kong

India

Ireland

Israel

Italy

Japan

Kenya & Tanzania

Korea

London

Madrid & Barcelona

Mexico

Montréal & Québec City

Morocco

Moscow & St. Petersburg

The Netherlands, Belgium & Luxembourg

New Zealand

Norway

Nova Scotia, Prince Edward Island & New Brunswick

Paris

Portugal

Provence & the Riviera

Rome

Russia & the Baltic Countries

Scandinavia

Scotland

Singapore

South America

Southeast Asia

Spain

Sweden

Switzerland

Thailand

Tokyo

Toronto

Turkey

Vienna & the Danube Valley

Special Series

Fodor's Affordables

Caribbean

Europe

Florida

France

Germany

Great Britain

Italy

London

Paris

Fodor's Bed & Breakfast and Country Inns Guides

America's Best B&Bs

California

Canada's Great Country Inns

Cottages, B&Bs and Country Inns of England and Wales

Mid-Atlantic Region

New England

The Pacific Northwest

The South

The Southwest

The Upper Great Lakes Region

The Berkeley Guides

California

Central America

Eastern Europe

Europe

France

Germany & Austria

Great Britain & Ireland

Italy

London

Mexico

Pacific Northwest & Alaska

Paris

San Francisco

Fodor's Exploring Guides

Australia

Boston & New England

Britain

California

The Caribbean

Florence & Tuscany

Florida

France

Germany

Ireland

Italy

London

Mexico

New York City

Paris

Prague

Rome

Scotland

Singapore & Malaysia

Spain

Thailand

Turkey

Fodor's Flashmaps

Boston

New York

Washington, D.C.

Fodor's Pocket Guides

Acapulco

Bahamas

Barbados

Jamaica

London

New York City

Paris

Puerto Rico

San Francisco

Washington, D.C.

Fodor's Sports

Cycling

Golf Digest's Best Places to Play

Hiking

The Insider's Guide to the Best Canadian Skiing

Running

Sailing

Skiing in the USA & Canada

USA Today's Complete Four Sports Stadium Guide

Fodor's Three-In-Ones (guidebook, language cassette, and phrase book)

France

Germany

Italy

Mexico

Spain

Fodor's Special-Interest Guides

Complete Guide to America's National Parks

Condé Nast Traveler Caribbean Resort and Cruise Ship Finder

Cruises and Ports of Call

Euro Disney

France by Train

Halliday's New England Food Explorer

Healthy Escapes

Italy by Train

London Companion

Shadow Traffic's New York Shortcuts and Traffic Tips

Sunday in New York

Sunday in San Francisco

Touring Europe

Touring USA: Eastern Edition

Walt Disney World and the Orlando Area

Walt Disney World for Adults

Fodor's Vacation Planners

Great American Learning Vacations

Great American Sports & Adventure Vacations

Great American Vacations

Great American Vacations for Travelers with Disabilities

National Parks and Seashores of the East

National Parks of the West

The Wall Street Journal Guides to Business Travel

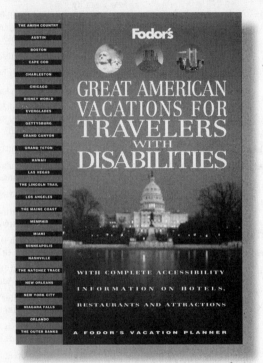

AT LAST

YOUR OWN PERSONALIZED LIST
OF WHAT'S GOING ON IN THE
CITIES YOU'RE VISITING.

KEYED TO THE DAYS WHEN
YOU'LL BE THERE, CUSTOMIZED
FOR YOUR INTERESTS,
AND SENT TO YOU BEFORE YOU
LEAVE HOME.

GET THE INSIDER'S
PERSPECTIVE. . .

UP-TO-THE-MINUTE
ACCURATE
EASY TO ORDER
DELIVERED WHEN YOU NEED IT

Now there is a revolutionary way to get customized, time-sensitive travel information just before your trip.

Now you can obtain detailed information about what's going on in each city you'll be visiting <u>before</u> you leave home—up-to-the-minute, objective information about the events and activities that interest you most.

Your Itinerary: Customized reports available for 160 destinations

Travel Updates contain the kind of time-sensitive insider information you can get only from local contacts – or from city magazines and newspapers once you arrive. But now you can have the same information before you leave for your trip.

The choice is yours: current art exhibits, theater, music festivals and special concerts, sporting events, antiques and flower shows, shopping, fitness, and more.

The information comes from hundreds of correspondents and thousands of sources worldwide. Updated continuously, it's like having your own personal concierge or friend in the city.

You specify the cities and when you'll be there. We'll do the rest — personalizing the information for you the way no guidebook can.

It's the perfect extension to your Fodor's guide and the best way to make the most of your valuable travel time.

Use Order Form on back or call 1-800-799-9609

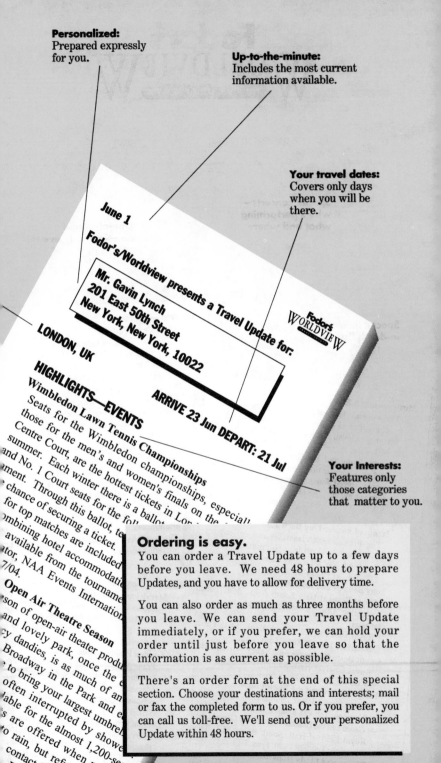

Personalized:
Prepared expressly for you.

Up-to-the-minute:
Includes the most current information available.

Your travel dates:
Covers only days when you will be there.

June 1

Fodor's/Worldview presents a Travel Update for:

Mr. Gavin Lynch
201 East 50th Street
New York, New York, 10022

Fodor's
WORLDVIEW

LONDON, UK

ARRIVE 23 Jun DEPART: 21 Jul

Your Interests:
Features only those categories that matter to you.

HIGHLIGHTS—EVENTS

Wimbledon Lawn Tennis Championships

Seats for the Wimbledon championships, especiall
those for the men's and women's finals on the
Centre Court, are the hottest tickets in Lon
summer. Each winter there is a ballot
and No. 1 Court seats for the foll
ament. Through this ballot, te
chance of securing a ticket.
for top matches are included
ombining hotel accommodati
available from the tournam
ator, NAA Events Internation
7/04.

Open Air Theatre Season

son of open-air theater produ
and lovely park, once the
y dandies, is as much of an
Broadway in the Park and e
to bring your largest umbre
often interrupted by showe
able for the almost 1,200-seat
s are offered when perfor-
to rain, but refunds are not
contact Sheila Benj
Regent's Par
Rege

Ordering is easy.

You can order a Travel Update up to a few days before you leave. We need 48 hours to prepare Updates, and you have to allow for delivery time.

You can also order as much as three months before you leave. We can send your Travel Update immediately, or if you prefer, we can hold your order until just before you leave so that the information is as current as possible.

There's an order form at the end of this special section. Choose your destinations and interests; mail or fax the completed form to us. Or if you prefer, you can call us toll-free. We'll send out your personalized Update within 48 hours.

**Special concerts—
who's performing
what and where**

**One-of-a-kind,
one-time-only events**

**Special interest,
in-depth listings**

Children — Events

Angel Canal Festival
The festivities include a children's funfair, entertainers, a boat rally and displays on the water. Regent's Canal. Islington. N1. Tube: Angel. Tel: 267 9100. 11:30am-5:30pm. 7/04.

Blackheath Summer Kite Festival
Stunt kite displays with parachuting teddy bears and trade stands. Free admission. SE3. BR: Blackheath. 10am. 6/27.

Megabugs
Children will delight in this infestation of giant robotic insects, including a praying mantis 60 times life size. Mon-Sat 10am-6pm; Sun 11am-6pm. Admission 4.50 pounds. Natural History Museum, Cromwell Road. SW7. Tube: South Kensington. Tel: 938 9123. Ends 10/01.

Childminders
This establishment employs only women, providing nurses and qualified nannies to

Music — Jazz & Blues

Tito Puente's Golden Men of Latin Jazz
The father of mambo and Cuban rumba king comes to town. Royal Festival Hall. South Bank. SE1. Tube: Waterloo. Tel: 928 8800. 8pm. 7/15.

Georgie Fame and The New York Band
Riding a popular tide with his latest album, the smoky-voiced Fame and his keyboard are on a tour yet again. The Grand. Clapham Junction. SW11. BR: Clapham Junction. Tel: 738 9000. 7:30pm. 7/07.

Jacques Loussier Play Bach Trio
The French jazz classicist and colleagues. Kenwood Lakeside. Hampstead Lane. Kenwood. NW3. Tube: Golders Green, then bus 210. Tel: 413 1443. 7pm. 7/10.

Tony Bennett and Ronnie Scott
Royal Festival Hall. South Bank. SE1. Tube: Waterloo. Tel: 928 8800. 8pm. 7/11.

Santana
Royal Festival Hall. South Bank. SE1. Tube: Waterloo. Tel: 928 8800. 8pm. 7/12.

Count Basie Orchestra and Nancy Wilson Trio
Royal Festival Hall. South Bank. SE1. Tube: Waterloo. Tel: 928 8800. 8pm. 7/14.

King Pleasure and the Biscuit Boys
Royal Festival Hall. South Bank. SE1. Tube: Waterloo. Tel: 928 8800. 6:30 and 9pm. 7/16.

Al Green and the London Community Gospel Choir
Royal Festival Hall. South Bank. SE1. Tube: Waterloo. Tel: 928 8800. 8pm. 7/13.

BB King and Linda Hopkins
Mother of the blues and successor to Bessie Smith, Hopkins meets up with "Blues Boy" — Festival Hall. South Bank. SE

Music — Classical

Marylebone Sinfonia
Kenneth Gowen conducts music by Puccini and Rossini. Queen Elizabeth Hall. South Bank. SE1. Tube: Waterloo. Tel: 928 8 7:45pm. 7/16.

London Philharmonic
Franz Welser-Moest and George Benjamin conduct selections by Alexander Goehr, Messiaen, and some of Benjamin's own positions. Queen Elizabeth Hall. South B SE1. Tube: Waterloo. Tel: 928 8800. 8pm

London Pro Arte Orchestra and Forest C
Murray Stewart conducts selection Rossini, Haydn and Jonathan Willcocks. Queen Elizabeth Hall. South Bank. Tube: Waterloo. Tel: 928 8800. 7:45pm.

Kensington Symphony Orchestra
Russell Keable conducts Dvorak's D

Here's what you get . . .

Detailed information about what's going on — precisely when you'll be there.

Reviews by local critics

Show openings during your visit

Handy pocket-size booklet

Exhibitions & Shows—Antique & Flower

Westminster Antiques Fair

Over 50 stands with pre-1830 furniture and other Victorian and earlier items. Thu-Fri 11am-8pm; Sat-Sun 11am-6pm. Admission 4 pounds, children free. Old Royal Horticultural Hall. Vincent Square. SW1. Tel: 0444/48 25 14. 6-24 thru 6/27.

Royal Horticultural Society Flower Show

The show includes displays of carnations, summer fruit and vegetables. Tue 11am-7pm; Wed 10am-5pm. Admission Tue 4 pounds, Wed 2 pounds. Royal Horticultural Halls. Greycoat Street and Vincent Square. SW1. Tube: Victoria. 7/20 thru 7/21.

mpton Court Palace International Flower Show
Major international garden and flower show taking place in conjunction with

Theater — Musical

Sunset Boulevard

In June, the four Andrew Lloyd Webber musicals which dominated London's stages in the 1980s (Cats, Starlight Express, Phantom of the Opera and Aspects of Love) are joined by the composer's latest work, a show rumored to have his best music to date. The 1950 Billy Wilder film about a helpless young writer who is drawn into the world of a possessive, aging silent screen star offers rich opportunities for Webber's evolving style. Soaring, aching melodies, lush technical effects and psychological thrills are all expected. Patti Lupone stars. Mon-Sat at 8pm; matinee Thu-Sat at 3pm. In-person sales only at the box office; credit card bookings, Tel: 344 0055. Admission 15-32.50 pounds. Adelphi Theatre. The Strand. WC2. Tube: Charing Cross. Tel: 836 7611. Starts: 6/21.

Leonardo A Portrait of Love

A new musical about the great Renaissance artist and inventor comes in for a London pre-
tested by a brief run at Oxford's Old
The work explores

Spectator Sports — Other Sports

Greyhound Racing: Wembley Stadium

This dog track offers good views of greyhound racing held on Mon, Wed and Fri. No credit cards. Stadium Way. Wembley. HA9. Tube: Wembley Park. Tel: 902 8833.

Benson & Hedges Cricket Cup Final

Lord's Cricket Ground. St. John's Wood Road. NW8. Tube: St. John's Wood. Tel: 289 1611. 11am. 7/10.

Business-Fax & Overnight Mail

Post Office, Trafalgar Square Branch

Offers a network of fax services, the Intelpost system, throughout the country and abroad. Mon-Sat 8am-8pm, Sun 9am-5pm. William IV Street. WC2. Tube: Ch

Fodor's WORLDVIEW
TRAVEL UPDATE

London, England
Arriving: June 23
Departing: July 21

Interest Categories

For your personalized Travel Update, choose the categories you're most interested in from this list. Every Travel Update automatically provides you with *Event Highlights* - the best of what's happening during the dates of your trip.

1.	**Business Services**	Fax & Overnight Mail, Computer Rentals, Photocopying, Protocol, Secretarial, Messenger, Translation Services

Dining

2.	**All Day Dining**	Breakfast & Brunch, Cafes & Tea Rooms, Late-Night Dining
3.	**Local Cuisine**	In Every Price Range—from Budget Restaurants to the Special Splurge
4.	**European Cuisine**	Continental, French, Italian
5.	**Asian Cuisine**	Chinese, Far Eastern, Japanese, Other
6.	**Americas Cuisine**	American, Mexican & Latin
7.	**Nightlife**	Bars, Dance Clubs, Casinos, Comedy Clubs, Ethnic, Pubs & Beer Halls
8.	**Entertainment**	Theater—Comedy, Drama, English Language, Musicals, Dance, Ticket Agencies
9.	**Music**	Country/Western/Folk, Classical, Traditional & Ethnic, Opera, Jazz & Blues, Pop, Rock
10.	**Children's Activities**	Events, Attractions
11.	**Tours**	Local Tours, Day Trips, Overnight Excursions, Cruises
12.	**Exhibitions, Festivals & Shows**	Antiques & Flower, History & Cultural, Art Exhibitions, Fairs & Craft Shows, Music & Art Festivals
13.	**Shopping**	Districts & Malls, Markets, Regional Specialities
14.	**Fitness**	Bicycling, Health Clubs, Hiking, Jogging
15.	**Recreational Sports**	Boating/Sailing, Fishing, Golf, Ice Skating, Skiing, Snorkeling/Scuba, Swimming, Tennis & Racquet
16.	**Spectator Sports**	Auto Racing, Baseball, Basketball, Boating & Sailing, Football, Golf, Horse Racing, Ice Hockey, Rugby, Soccer, Tennis, Track & Field, Other Sports

Please note that interest category content will vary by season, destination, and length of stay.

Destinations

The Fodor's/Worldview Travel Update covers more than 160 destinations worldwide. Choose the destinations that match your itinerary from this list. (Choose bulleted destinations only.)

Europe
- Amsterdam
- Athens
- Barcelona
- Berlin
- Brussels
- Budapest
- Copenhagen
- Dublin
- Edinburgh
- Florence
- Frankfurt
- French Riviera
- Geneva
- Glasgow
- Istanbul
- Lausanne
- Lisbon
- London
- Madrid
- Milan
- Moscow
- Munich
- Oslo
- Paris
- Prague
- Provence
- Rome
- Salzburg
* Seville
- St. Petersburg
- Stockholm
- Venice
- Vienna
- Zurich

United States (Mainland)
- Albuquerque
- Atlanta
- Atlantic City
- Baltimore
- Boston
* Branson, MO
* Charleston, SC
- Chicago
- Cincinnati
- Cleveland
- Dallas/Ft. Worth
- Denver
- Detroit
- Houston
* Indianapolis
- Kansas City
- Las Vegas
- Los Angeles
- Memphis

- Miami
- Milwaukee
- Minneapolis/ St. Paul
* Nashville
- New Orleans
- New York City
- Orlando
- Palm Springs
- Philadelphia
- Phoenix
- Pittsburgh
- Portland
* Reno/ Lake Tahoe
- St. Louis
- Salt Lake City
- San Antonio
- San Diego
- San Francisco
* Santa Fe
- Seattle
- Tampa
- Washington, DC

Alaska
- Alaskan Destinations

Hawaii
- Honolulu
- Island of Hawaii
- Kauai
- Maui

Canada
- Quebec City
- Montreal
- Ottawa
- Toronto
- Vancouver

Bahamas
- Abaco
- Eleuthera/ Harbour Island
- Exuma
- Freeport
- Nassau & Paradise Island

Bermuda
- Bermuda Countryside
- Hamilton

British Leeward Islands
- Anguilla

- Antigua & Barbuda
- St. Kitts & Nevis

British Virgin Islands
- Tortola & Virgin Gorda

British Windward Islands
- Barbados
- Dominica
- Grenada
- St. Lucia
- St. Vincent
- Trinidad & Tobago

Cayman Islands
- The Caymans

Dominican Republic
- Santo Domingo

Dutch Leeward Islands
- Aruba
- Bonaire
- Curacao

Dutch Windward Island
- St. Maarten/ St. Martin

French West Indies
- Guadeloupe
- Martinique
- St. Barthelemy

Jamaica
- Kingston
- Montego Bay
- Negril
- Ocho Rios

Puerto Rico
- Ponce
- San Juan

Turks & Caicos
- Grand Turk/ Providenciales

U.S. Virgin Islands
- St. Croix
- St. John
- St. Thomas

Mexico
- Acapulco
- Cancun & Isla Mujeres
- Cozumel
- Guadalajara
- Ixtapa & Zihuatanejo
- Los Cabos
- Mazatlan
- Mexico City
- Monterrey
- Oaxaca
- Puerto Vallarta

South/Central America
* Buenos Aires
* Caracas
* Rio de Janeiro
* San Jose, Costa Rica
* Sao Paulo

Middle East
* Jerusalem

Australia & New Zealand
- Auckland
- Melbourne
* South Island
- Sydney

China
- Beijing
- Guangzhou
- Shanghai

Japan
- Kyoto
- Nagoya
- Osaka
- Tokyo
- Yokohama

Pacific Rim/Other
* Bali
- Bangkok
- Hong Kong & Macau
- Manila
- Seoul
- Singapore
- Taipei

* Destinations available by 1/1/95

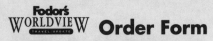 **Order Form**

THIS TRAVEL UPDATE IS FOR (Please print):

Name

Address

| City | State | Country | ZIP |

Tel # (   )   -   Fax # (   )   -

Title of this Fodor's guide:

Store and location where guide was purchased:

INDICATE YOUR DESTINATIONS/DATES: You can order up to three (3) destinations from the previous page. Fill in your arrival and departure dates for each destination. **Your Travel Update itinerary (all destinations selected) cannot exceed 30 days from beginning to end.**

		Month Day	Month Day
(Sample) LONDON	From:	6 / 21	To: 6 / 30
1	From:	/	To: /
2	From:	/	To: /
3	From:	/	To: /

CHOOSE YOUR INTERESTS: Select up to eight (8) categories from the list of interest categories shown on the previous page and circle the numbers below:

1   2   3   4   5   6   7   8   9   10   11   12   13   14   15   16

CHOOSE WHEN YOU WANT YOUR TRAVEL UPDATE DELIVERED (Check one):

❑ Please send my Travel Update immediately.
❑ Please hold my order until a few weeks before my trip to include the most up-to-date information.
   Completed orders will be sent within 48 hours. Allow 7-10 days for U.S. mail delivery.

ADD UP YOUR ORDER HERE. *SPECIAL OFFER FOR FODOR'S PURCHASERS ONLY!*

	Suggested Retail Price	Your Price	This Order
First destination ordered	$ 9.95	$ 7.95	$ 7.95
Second destination (if applicable)	$ 6.95	$ 4.95	+
Third destination (if applicable)	$ 6.95	$ 4.95	+

DELIVERY CHARGE (Check one and enter amount below)

	Within U.S. & Canada	Outside U.S. & Canada
First Class Mail	❑ $2.50	❑ $5.00
FAX	❑ $5.00	❑ $10.00
Priority Delivery	❑ $15.00	❑ $27.00

ENTER DELIVERY CHARGE FROM ABOVE: +

TOTAL: $

METHOD OF PAYMENT IN U.S. FUNDS ONLY (Check one):

❑ AmEx   ❑ MC   ❑ Visa   ❑ Discover   ❑ Personal Check (U. S. & Canada only)
❑ Money Order/ International Money Order
   Make check or money order payable to: Fodor's Worldview Travel Update

Credit Card —/—/—/—/—/—/—/—/—/—/—/—/—/—/—/ **Expiration Date:___/___**

Authorized Signature

SEND THIS COMPLETED FORM WITH PAYMENT TO:
Fodor's Worldview Travel Update, 114 Sansome Street, Suite 700, San Francisco, CA 94104

OR CALL OR FAX US 24-HOURS A DAY
Telephone **1-800-799-9609** • Fax **1-800-799-9619** (From within the U.S. & Canada)
(Outside the U.S. & Canada: Telephone 415-616-9988 • Fax 415-616-9989)

(Please have this guide in front of you when you call so we can verify purchase.)
Code: FTG   Offer valid until 12/31/95.